BLACK ATHENA

The Afroasiatic Roots of Classical Civilization

Volume II:
The Archaeological and Documentary Evidence

MARTIN BERNAL

BLACK ATHENA

Black Athena

The Afroasiatic Roots
of Classical Civilization

VOLUME II
The Archaeological and Documentary
Evidence

Martin Bernal

Rutgers University Press
New Brunswick, New Jersey

Second paperback printing, November 1991

First published in the United States of America by
Rutgers University Press, 1991
First published in Great Britain by Free Association Books, 1991

Copyright © 1991 by Martin Bernal
Typeset by G&S Typesetters, Austin, Texas
Printed and bound by Malloy Lithographing, Ann Arbor, Michigan
Manufactured in the United States of America

Library of Congress Cataloging-in-Publication Data
(Revised for volume 2)

Bernal, Martin
    Black Athena.

    Includes bibliographies and indexes.
    Contents: v. 1. The fabrication of ancient Greece,
1785–1985 — v. 2. The archaeological and documentary
evidence.
        1. Greece—Civlization—Egyptian influences.
    2. Greece—Civilization—Phoenician influences.
    3. Greece—Civilization—To 146 B.C.   I. Afroasiatic
roots of classical civilization.   II. Title.
    DF78.B398   1987   949.5   87-16408
    ISBN 0-8135-1583-1
    ISBN 0-8135-1584-X (pbk.)

To the memory of V. Gordon Childe
as a champion of modified diffusionism

Contents

PREFACE AND
ACKNOWLEDGEMENTS

THE PUBLICATION OF Volume I of *Black Athena* transformed my life. Before then, I was working in isolation or, to be accurate, with a few close friends and colleagues, with whom I had many fruitful discussions and correspondences. Nevertheless, my ideas were essentially figments of my imagination, remaining in my head as private possessions. With the appearance of the book they took on a social substance. I was both delighted and disconcerted to hear other people discuss and dispute them; they have become public property over which I have little control or even influence. This is, of course, quite proper, because the ways in which ideas are received are much more important than their author's original and often convoluted intentions.

Thanks to Robert Young and all at Free Association Books, *Black Athena* got off to a remarkably successful start. I had expected a low key and generally hostile response, but within days of its publication in March 1987, the book had received a double-page feature in the *Guardian*. Soon after that, came the start of a string of reviews, which were either friendly or mixed. For the first two years, there were none of the outright denunciations or frontal attacks on my competence to write such a work that I had expected. The mixed reviews usually accepted the historiographical portion of my work, but suspended judgement on the archaeological aspects and expressed scepticism about my linguistic claims.

These reviews attracted the interest of a number of American university presses and some who had previously rejected the manuscript now wanted to reopen the issue. Once again, however, the professional reviewers turned the project down, although in much friendlier and more respectful terms than before. Kenneth Arnold, the director of Rutgers University Press, decided – with the enthusiastic backing of Leslie Mitchner, the humanities editor – to use his right to publish three books a year without going through the normal professional reviewing process in order to accept *Black Athena* unconditionally. This bypassing of the usual channels in both England and the US answers the criticism made by at least one reviewer that the appearance of my book itself disproves my claim that the normal operation of university presses restricts the range of ideas that can be published. Anyhow, I now have two editors, Robert Young and Kenneth Arnold, to thank for sticking out their necks by publishing my books. Free Association Books did, however, receive generous financial backing from the Hull Fund which lends publishers money to help with the publication of books written by members of Cornell faculty.

There were interesting similarities and differences in the reception of the book in Britain and in the United States. The most striking difference was political. In Britain, the reaction fell into very neat categories. There was one hostile review in the Trotskyist *Socialist Worker* – I do not know whether this reflected merely the views of the individual critic or the Eurocentrism of Trotskyism as a whole. In general, however, the left and liberals liked the book, but from the *Independent* rightwards it was ignored.

The pattern was more complicated in the US. From the start, *Black Athena* was welcomed by the left, but, interestingly, it received scrupulously fair treatment in a feature in *Insight Magazine,* a journal whose editors see it 'as a right-wing version of *Time*'! The gap in US response was from the liberal establishment; although *Black Athena* has become increasingly newsworthy, it has not been reviewed or discussed in *Time* or *Newsweek* and for a long time it was completely ignored by the *New York Times*.

The similarities between the British and American responses, however, outweigh the differences. In both countries there was an immediate and positive response from the Black and other non-European communities. Intellectuals from these communities have reviewed the book favourably and have actively promoted its sale and given me many chances to express my ideas at meetings and in interviews with the media.

There has also been a remarkable degree of interest by visual artists and designers and many of the most perceptive reviews of *Black Athena* have been published in journals concerned with the arts. I think this comes in part from the general radicalism and refusal to accept orthodoxies among those concerned with the arts, but even more because *Black Athena* provided a historical framework which explained the close relationships between Egyptian and Greek art they had long sensed.

Even more to my surprise, I found that in both countries there was a significant number of ancient historians and classicists who were sympathetic to my views and had in fact begun to articulate similar ones. Although delightful, this discovery revealed a major flaw in my sociology of knowledge. Despite my friendship with the distinguished classicist Fred Ahl, who has given me an immense amount of help and encouragement for many years, I had retained a hopelessly over-simplified image of classics as a monolithic discipline. Taking classics as a single adversary, I believed that it could be overcome only by out-flanking it, that is, by convincing the cultivated lay public, especially scholars in other disciplines. I was wrong in both respects. In fact, classicists know better than anyone what the Greeks and Romans wrote about their distant past and that, whatever the truth of the matter, I was thinking along the same lines as the people they were studying. Furthermore, there had already been unpublished rumblings of resistance to the Aryan Model and its positivist historiography, of which I was unaware. For these and other reasons, a significant number of classicists have been more ready to accept my arguments than the lay public, who knew little or nothing about the field.

The most startling example of this openness among professionals came from Molly Myerewitz Levine, a classicist who has taught at Bar Ilan University in Israel and now teaches at Howard, one of the leading black universities in the United States. She read *Black Athena* and was sensitive to her students' interest in it. Although she generally liked the book, she felt unsure of the extent she could trust or use it for teaching. Therefore, she organized a panel to discuss it, which she proposed to the American Philological Society for a meeting at their annual conference.

When she asked me whether I would be willing to attend such a session, I agreed readily, though I was convinced that the proposal would never be accepted or, if, by some extraordinary chance it were, it would be marginalized by being put in a back room at an obscure hour. I was completely wrong. In the event, the session was named as the 'Presidential Panel' and was held in a ballroom at prime time.

I found the criticisms and the meeting as a whole fascinating, but the thing that impressed me most was the patience of the audience sitting for three straight hours in a hot room. I have no idea whether anyone was converted to my ideas. On the other hand, there was no doubt that there was intense interest in the issues being discussed. This was also reflected by the fact that three professional journals asked to publish the proceedings and they have now appeared in a special issue of *Arethusa*, the liveliest classical journal.[1]

After the meeting had been announced but before it took place, I happened to meet the historian and philosopher of science Thomas Kuhn. His reaction was that the meeting was being held far too soon and that disciplines did not usually respond so quickly to fundamental challenges. My first response was to say that we were all living in a 'post-Kuhnian age' in which the possibility of fundamental or 'paradigmatic' shifts was now seen in all disciplines. My second answer, at another level, was to point out that the classicists might dismember me to their satisfaction. Kuhn's reply to this was that what actually happened at the meeting 'was totally uninteresting'. What was important was the legitimacy given by the holding of the meeting.

There is no doubt that he was right. Since January 1989 when the meeting was held, while the ideas that I put forward are far from being accepted by classicists as 'the orthodoxy', they are now widely considered to be a respectable variant of it. This is not to say that there is no opposition; there has always been, but up until the summer of 1989 it was almost entirely *sotto voce*. The passionate depths of this hostility can be seen from the response of one Indo-European linguist who compares my work – in private conversation – to that of the 'revisionists' who deny that the Holocaust ever took place. The comparison is fascinating on at least two counts. Firstly, as an emotional response to my case for setting the Aryan Model and the Holocaust in the same general movement and, secondly, as an example of the way in which the members of a discipline can believe that their reconstructions of distant linguistic relationships have the same veracity as a massive and massively attested historical event that took place within living memory. This, however, like attacks on my competence, is the subject of dinner-party conversations and not of public utterances or published articles.

Since the summer of 1989 some resistance has come out into the open and there have been a number of fierce public attacks on the book, provoked partly by the meeting at the American Philological Association and partly by the uses being made of the book by American Blacks, both of which made it clear that the ideas in *Black Athena* were not simply going to fade away into decent obscurity.

Two journals of the far right, the *New Criterion* and the *National Review,* have launched an attack on my politics. In the first, the reviewer, who had clearly read and thought about *Black Athena,* admitted that it might contain some interesting arguments. However, he maintained that these were vitiated by the essential evil of the project. He saw this as inspired by the Marxism of my father – a crystalographer and historian of science, who was a well-known Communist. Although the reviewer somewhat contradicted his case by his accurate perception that Marxism was perfectly compatible with the Aryan Model and that there have been many distinguished Marxist classicists working within it.

I think there is something in his argument, in that I have been heavily influenced by my father. However, this has been more by the general features of his thought, his broadness of historical vision and sympathy for the underdog, than by the specifics of his Marxism.

The attack in the *National Review* was far less interesting and informed. It initially claimed such absurd irrelevancies as that I was black and that Herodotos had written that the Greeks were blond. But a letter published soon after from an ex-student of mine accused me of being a 'pasty-faced' English Maoist. Nevertheless, I was pleasantly surprised that my letter in response to this was printed in full.

Conservative classicists, whose academic attitudes have no necessary correlation with political conservatism, have taken the tack I had initially expected. They often say or at least imply that I am an incompetent 'crackpot'. This charge, which might well have been shattering to the book's academic reputation in 1987 or 1988, has come far too late.

This is because, if we are to use institutional or social criteria to judge who is or is not a 'crank' or 'crackpot' – as I think we must, if we are to avoid complete subjectivity – I can no longer qualify for the epithets. It stretches the meanings of the terms 'cranky' or 'cracked' to breaking-point if they are applied to ideas that have had special sessions devoted to them in the annual conferences of the leading American professional organizations of the two most relevant disciplines, classics and Egyptology, and their author has been asked to address an international congress of archaeometry. There have also been two special numbers of professional journals on *Black Athena*.

My other mistaken prediction was that the cultivated lay public in Britain and America would rally to my cause. This is because, by and large, they know nothing about *Black Athena*. As I mentioned above, readers of the *Independent, The Times,* the *Sunday Times* and the *Times*

Literary Supplement have seen no mention of it. In the US there has been no review of the book in the *New York Times*. This omission is so important and interesting that it is worth considering in some detail. It is difficult for me to reconstruct the whole story. However, as I understand it, when *Black Athena* first came to the book review committee in 1988, it was refused peremptorily. Later that year, Henry Louis (Skip) Gates, the most influential Black academic in the United States, asked me to compile a dossier of reviews and news items, which he kindly forwarded to the paper with his strong endorsement. Nothing happened. At the end of the year a Black correspondent on the *New York Times*, seeing me on the New York television talk show 'Like It Is', checked back for his paper's review of *Black Athena* and, not finding it, asked me to send a copy for review. Nothing happened, even though, when someone from Rutgers University Press asked about it, she was assured that it was just about to come out. In the autumn of 1989, after the publication of the *Arethusa* special issue on the APA meeting, Rutgers tried again. This time the *New York Times* agreed to plan a feature article on the book and the response to it. This seemed to me the best thing to do as it would not oblige a reviewer to take a stand on the book one way or the other. I was interviewed at some length and a photographer was sent up to take pictures of me in my academic habitat. At this point, I was telephoned by another *Times* correspondent, who was working on a feature on Black claims that Egypt was Black. She too interviewed me for over an hour and her article appeared. As *Black Athena* is only peripherally concerned with this issue, it rightly did not feature largely in the piece, but the tone was hostile and dismissive, clearly aimed at discouraging readers from looking at the book. After that there has been no trace of the feature article.

What are the forces blocking any discussion of the ideas behind the book in this crucial newspaper? I suspect that it was the following sequence: initially the work was thought to be absurd; then, when it was believed to be worth refuting, there was difficulty in finding experts who were willing or able to do this. As time went on, it became increasingly embarrassing to admit the slowness of their response. Finally a new factor entered, the fear that, even if they were able to do an effective hatchet job on *Black Athena*, there would be a barrage of angry letters from my Black supporters. Underlying this sequence, I suspect that there is a fundamental discomfort with the ideas that a respectable academic discipline could have racist roots and that racism has permeated liberal thought as well as that of obvious bigots.

The lack of a review in the *New York Times* means that *Black Athena* has not reached the liberal, cultivated white public in America that is so dependent on the *Times*. Information about the book has been spreading by word of mouth from its two centres, academia and the Black community. This means that its sales pattern in the US has been very unusual. Instead of rising to a peak and falling off, sales have risen steadily for over two years.

It is now simply too late to crush the ideas I have been proposing. They have become an established academic discourse. As Nixon's henchman John Haldemann put it so well after the Watergate revelations, 'you can't put toothpaste back in the tube'. *Black Athena* has also reinforced many long-standing beliefs in the American Black community. Some of my classicist friends have asked me whether I am not disturbed by the uses made of *Black Athena* by Black racists. My answer to this is that I am disturbed because I hate racism of any kind. I would prefer to be in my position than theirs, however, as I am infinitely less concerned by black racism than I am by white racism, and white racists, directly or indirectly, make constant use of orthodox views of the classical world and the Aryan Model. In any event, regardless of the politics of the situation, the reason why I am devoting the second half of my life to this project is not simply as an attack on white racism but because I believe the Revised Ancient Model to be a less inaccurate representation of the history with which it is concerned and I know that untangling its ramifications is fascinating.

I should like to thank again everyone I acknowledged in the preface to Volume 1. This includes the Government Department at Cornell, which has not merely tolerated my irregular activities but has encouraged and rewarded them. Once again, I should like to express my especial gratitude to Frederick Ahl, Gregory Blue, Saul Levin and David Owen, to whose number I should like to add Eric Cline, Susan Hollis, Edward Meltzer, Gary Rendsburg, Anthony Snodgrass and James Weinstein, all of whom have provided me with much important information and have shown enormous patience in answering my importunate questions.

Another group of women and men, who have encouraged me enormously and have aided the project as whole over the past three years, to whom I should like to express my deep gratitude, are Anouar Abdel Malik, Meg Alexiou, Tariq Ali, Ahmed Ben Bella, Geoffrey Chester, Eleni Cubitt, Basil Davidson, Margaret Drabble, Grégoire Dunant, Skip Gates, Angela Gilliam, Richard Gott, Shomarka Keita, Molly Myerewitz Levine, Listervelt Middleton, Jonathan Miller, John Najemi, Gil Noble, John Peradotto, Jamil Ragep, John Ray, Nancy Ramage,

Edward Said, Robert Stieglitz, Michael Vickers, Raymond Westbrook and Jack Winkler.

I should also like to thank a number of other people who have been especially helpful in the writing of this volume. These include Michael Baillie, George Bass, Patricia Bikai, John Coleman, D. O. Edzard, Lucy Goodison, Peter Huber, Bernard Knapp, Peter Kuniholm, A. Lambropoulou, Connie Lambrou-Phillipson, Ernest McClain, Sarah Morris, Scott Noegel, Kevin Pang, Andrew Ramage, Barry Strauss, Cornelius Vermeule, Emily Vermeule and Anita Yannai.

I want to thank Bob Young, Ann Scott and all those who were working at Free Association Books during the winter of 1986/1987 for their extraordinary efforts and the splendid and attractive volume they produced. This time, I should like to thank the women and men working there now. I am especially grateful to my editor Selina O'Grady for the tireless work she has put into rescuing my disorganized text as well as to Dr. Leofranc Holford-Strevens and Adaya Henis, the proofreader, and Jane Dieckmann, the indexer, all of whom have saved me from some of what remain a multitude of errors. Naturally, I want to take full responsibility for the many mistakes of fact and interpretation that remain.

As well as thanking my publishers in England, I should also like to express my gratitude to those in America, particularly Leslie Mitchner, Marilyn Campbell and Ken Arnold, who have consistently given me encouragement, support and good advice. I am also very grateful to Jenny Jardine for the splendid maps she has drawn on the basis of my very rough sketches and even vaguer directions.

As before, I cannot imagine having completed this volume without the love and support of my family, my wife Leslie and my children Sophie, William, Paul, Adam and Patrick, my son in-law Mark and my mother Margaret. They have kept and will always keep me in touch with a reality, without which all scholarly achievement is meaningless.

Transcription
and Phonetics

THE ORTHOGRAPHY USED in Egyptian words is the standard
one accepted by modern Egyptologists, the only exception
being the ꜣ used to represent the 'vulture or double 'aleph',
which is often printed as two commas on top of each other.

Whatever the exact sound of the ꜣ in Old Egyptian it was transcribed into Semitic scripts as r, l, or even n. This consonantal value
was retained at least until the 2nd Intermediate Period in the 17th
century BC. In Late Egyptian it appears to have become an 'aleph and
later, like the Southern English r, it merely modified adjacent vowels.
The ꜣ is the first sign of the alphabetical order used by Egyptologists,
and I shall continue with other letters with obscure or difficult sound
values.

The Egyptian i̯ corresponds to both the Semitic 'aleph and yōd.
'Aleph is found in many languages, and nearly all Afroasiatic ones. It
is a glottal stop before vowels, as in the Cockney 'bo'le' or 'bu'e'
('bottle' and 'butter').

The Egyptian 'ayin, which also occurs in most Semitic languages, is
a voiced or spoken 'aleph. The Egyptian form seems to have been associated with the 'back' vowels o and u.

In early Egyptian the sign w, written as a quail chick, may have had
purely consonantal value. In Late Egyptian, the form of the language
which had the most impact on Greek, it seems to have been frequently
pronounced as a vowel, either o or u.

The Egyptian sign written as r was more usually transcribed as l in

Semitic and Greek. In later Egyptian it seems, as with the ꜣ, to have weakened into becoming merely a modifier of vowels.

The Egyptian and Semitic letters Romanized as ḥ appear to have been pronounced as an emphatic h.

The Egyptian and Semitic ḫ represents a sound similar to the ch in 'loch'. In later times it became thoroughly confused with the letter š.

The Egyptian letter ẖ appears to have represented the sound ḫy. It too became confused with š.

The letter written here as s was transcribed as either s or z.

š was pronounced as sh or skh. In later times it became very confused with ḫ and ẖ.

ḳ represents an emphatic k. Inconsistently, I have followed the common practice of Semitists and have employed q to represent the same sound in Semitic.

The letter t was probably originally pronounced as tʸ. However, even in Middle Egyptian it was being confused with t.

Similarly, the ḏ was frequently alternated with d.

EGYPTIAN NAMES

Egyptian divine names are vocalized according to the commonest Greek transcription – for example, Amon for ʾlmn.

Royal names generally follow Gardiner's (1961) version of the Greek names for well-known pharaohs, for instance, Ramessēs.

COPTIC

Most of the letters in the Coptic alphabet come from Greek and the same transcriptions are used. Six extra letters derived from Demotic are transcribed as follows:

͏		
ш š	ϣ ẖ	ϫ d
ϧ f	ϩ h	ϭ ǧ

SEMITIC

The Semitic consonants are transcribed relatively conventionally. Several of the complications have been mentioned above in connection with Egyptian. Apart from these, one encounters the following:

In Canaanite the sound ḫ merged with ḥ. Transcriptions here sometimes reflect the etymological ḫ rather than the later ḥ. ṭ is an emphatic t.

The Arabic sound usually transcribed as th is written here as tʸ. The same is true of the dh/dʸ.

The letter found in Ugaritic which corresponds to the Arabic *ghain* is transcribed ġ.

The Semitic emphatic k is written q, rather than ḳ as in Egyptian. The Semitic letter *tsade*, almost certainly pronounced ts, is written ṣ. In Hebrew from the 1st millennium BC the letter *shin* is written as š. Elsewhere, however, it is transcribed simply as s, not as š, because I question the antiquity and the range of the latter pronunciation (Bernal, 1988). This, however, causes confusion with Samekh, which is also transcribed as s. Sin is transcribed as ś.

Neither *dagesh* nor *begadkephat* is indicated in the transcription. This is for reasons of simplicity as well as doubts about their range and occurrence in Antiquity.

VOCALIZATION

The Masoretic vocalization of the Bible, completed in the 9th and 10th centuries AD but reflecting much older pronunciation, is transcribed as follows:

Name of sign	Plain	with י y	with ו w	with ה h
Pataḥ	בַ ba	–	–	– –
Qåmeṣ	בָ bå	בָּי bâ	–	בָּה båh
Ḥîreq	בִ bi	בִּי bî	–	– –
Ṣērê	בֵ bē	בֵּי bê	–	בֵּה bēh
Sᵉgōl	בֶ be	בֶּי bê̦	–	בֶּה beh
Ḥōlem	בֹ bō	– –	בּוֹ bô	בֹּה bōh
Qibûṣ	בֻ bu	– –	בּוּ bû	– –

The reduced vowels are rendered:

בְּ bᵉ   חֲ ḥă   חֱ ḥĕ   חֳ ḥŏ.

Accentuation and cantillation are not normally marked.

GREEK

The transcription of the consonants is orthodox.

υ is transcribed as y.

The long vowels η and ω are written as ē and ō, and where it is significant the long α is rendered ā.

Accentuation is not normally marked.

GREEK NAMES

It is impossible to be consistent in transliterating these, because certain names are so well known that they have to be given in their Latin forms – Thucydides or Plato – as opposed to the Greek Thoukydidēs or Platōn. On the other hand, it would be absurd to make Latin forms for little-known people or places. Thus the commoner names are given in their Latin forms and the rest simply transliterated from Greek. I have tried wherever possible to follow Peter Levi's translation of Pausanias, where the balance is to my taste well struck. This, however, means that many long vowels are not marked in the transcription of names.

CHRONOLOGICAL TABLES

Chart 1 **Egyptian chronologies**

Dynasty	Breasted	Meyer	CAH	Helck	Mellaart	Bernal
1st	3400	3315±100	3100	2955	3400	3400
2nd			2900	2780	3200	3200
3rd	2980	2895±100	2730	2635	2950	3000
4th	2900	2840±100	2613	2570	2850	2920
5th	2750	2680±100	2494	2450	2725	2800
6th	2625	2540±100	2345	2290	2570	2630
7th	2475	—	2181	2155	2388	2470
8th	2475	—	—	—	2388	2470
9th	2445	2360±100	2160	—	—	2440
10th	—	—	2130	—	—	—
11th	2160	2160	2133	2134	2287	2140
12th	2000	2000/1997	1991	1991	2155	1979
13th	1788	1778	1786	?	1946	1801
14th	—	—	—	—	—	—
15th	—	—	1674	1655	1791	1750
16th	—	—	1684	—	—	—
17th	—	—	—	—	—	—
18th	1580	1580/75	1567	1552	1567	1567
19th	1315	1320	1320	1306	1320	1320
20th	1200	1200	1200	1196/86	1200	1200

Sources: Breasted (1906, I, pp. 40–5); Meyer (1907b, pp. 68 and 178); *Cambridge Ancient History* (charts at the end of vols I.2B, II.1 and II.2); Helck (1971, chart; 1979, pp. 146–8); Mellaart (1979, pp. 9 and 19).

Chart 2 **Mesopotamian and Syrian chronologies**

	Lagash Umma Kish	Akkad	Assur	Mari	Ebla
2600					
2550			Tudia	Eblul-li	Igris-Kalam Irkab-Damu
2500				Iku-Šar	Ar-Ennum Ebrium
2450	Eannatum			Šuru-Damu	Ibbiš–Šipiš–
2400	Lugalzaggizi	Sargon (2380–2325)			
2350					
2300		Naram-Sin (2300–2238)			
2250					
2200		Šu-Durul (2214–2199)			

Long Chronology	Babylon	Assur	Mari
2000		Erišum I (1997–71)	
1950		Ikunum Šarum-kin Puzzur-Aššur II Naram-Sin	
1900		Erišum II	
1850	Hammurabi (1848–1806)	Šamši-Adad (1869–36)	
			Zimri-Lim (1831–18)
1800	Šamšuiluna (1805–1767)		
	Kassites		
1750			
1700	Ammisaduqa (1701–1683) Šamšuiditana (1681–51) Hittite Conquest followed by Kassite rule		
1600			
1250		Tukulti-Ninurta I (1244–1208)	
	conquers Babylon 1235.		

Middle Chronology Cambridge Ancient History	Babylon	Assur	Mari
1900		Erišum I (1906–1867)	
1850		Ikunum Šarum-kin Puzzur-Aššur II Naram-Sin Erišum II	
1800		Šamši-Adad (1813–1781)	Iakhtun-Lim
	Hammurabi (1792–50)		
			Zimri-Lim (1775–62)
1750	Šamšuiluna (1749–12)		
Kassites			
1700			
1650	Ammisaduqa (1646–26)		
	Šamšuiditana (1625–1595)		
1600	Hittite Conquest followed by Kassite rule		
1250		Tukulti-Ninurta I (1244–1208)	
	conquers Babylon 1235.		

Short or Low Chronology	Babylon	Assur	Mari
1900		Erišum I (1885–4?)	
1850		Ikunum Šarum-kin Puzzur-Aššur II Naram-Sin	
1800		Erišum II	Iakhtun-Lim
		Šamši-Adad (1749–16)	
1750	Hammurabi (1728–1684)		
			Zimri-Lim (1711–1698)
1700	Šamšuiluna (1675–47)		
	Kassites		
1650			
1600	Ammisaduqa (1581–63) Šamšuiditana (1561–31) Hittite Conquest followed by Kassite rule		
1600			
1250		Tukulti-Ninurta I (1244–1208)	
	conquers Babylon 1235.		

Chart 3 **Aegean chronology**

Ceramic Period	CAH	K & M	Bet.	Bernal 1	Bernal 2
EMI	3000?				3300
EMII	2500?				3000
EMIII	2200				2400
MMIA	1900				2050
MMIB		2000			1950
MMII	1800				1820
MMIII	1700	1775–50		1730	1730
LMIA	1600	1675–50		1650	1675
LHI	1550				
LMIB/LHIIA	1500	1600–1575	1610	1550	1600
LMII	1450	1500–1475	1550	1450	1520
LHIIB	1430	1550			1520
LHIIIA1	1400		1490		1470
LMIIIA	1380		1490		1470
LMIIIA2/ LHIIIA2			1430–10		1420
LMIIIB/ LHIIIB	1275	1375–50	1365		1370
LMIIIC/ LHIIIC	1180		1200		1220

CAH = *Cambridge Ancient History*, 3rd edition.

K & M = Kemp and Merrillees (1980) *Minoan Pottery in Second Millennium Egypt.*

Bet. = Betancourt (1989) 'High chronology and low chronology: Thera archaeological evidence.'

Bernal 1 = *Black Athena*, Volume 1.

Bernal 2 = *Black Athena*, Volume 2.

BLACK ATHENA

INTRODUCTION

V OLUME 1 OF THIS series was concerned with two views of the origins of Ancient Greece. In the first of these, which I called the Ancient Model, it was maintained that Greece had originally been inhabited by Pelasgian and other primitive tribes. These had been civilized by Egyptian and Phoenician settlers who had ruled many parts of the country during the 'heroic age'. According to the second view, the Aryan Model, Greek civilization was the result of cultural mixture following a conquest from the north by Indo-European–speaking Greeks of the earlier 'Pre-Hellenic' peoples. In Volume 1 I tried to trace the processes by which the Ancient Model current in 5th-century Greece survived until the end of the 18th century and was overthrown in the early 19th century to be replaced by the Aryan Model in the 1840s.

The introduction to Volume 1 contained an outline of the project as a whole. In this I announced my belief that the Aryan Model should be superseded by what I call the Revised Ancient Model. This model accepts, on the one hand, that Egyptians and Phoenicians settled in and had a massive influence on Ancient Greece. On the other hand, it takes into account the undoubted fact that Greek is fundamentally an Indo-European language. It also makes various chronological adjustments suggested by recent archaeology. At the end of Volume 1, I wrote that the

> conception in sin, or even error [of the Aryan Model] does not necessarily invalidate it. Darwinism, which was created at very much

the same time and for many of the same 'disreputable' motives, has
remained a very useful heuristic scheme. One could perfectly well
argue that Niebuhr, Müller, Curtius and the others were 'sleep-
walking' in the sense in which Arthur Koestler used the term – to
describe useful 'scientific' discoveries made for extraneous reasons
and purposes which are not accepted in later times. All that I claim
for this volume is that it has provided a case to be answered. That is,
if the dubious origin of the Aryan Model does not make it false, it
does call into question its inherent superiority over the Ancient
Model.[1]

In the many reviews of the first volume, there has been some scepticism about the utility or 'truth' of the Revised Ancient Model I propose. On the other hand, there has been a general acceptance of my
historiographical scheme and of my contention that most of the men
who established the Aryan Model were – to put it bluntly – racists and
anti-Semites. There has also been a recognition that these attitudes
could have affected their writing of history. I take this reception as a
licence to continue my project.

The form of the continuation of the project has changed fundamentally. Many critics of the first volume wrote or hinted that I would
have great difficulty in producing convincing work in the way I had
set it out in the introduction. They were quite right. In the event, I
have had to alter my project in three important respects. In the first
place, where I had originally planned to cover the evidence from archaeology and Bronze Age documents in two chapters, I have now
found it necessary to devote a whole volume to these two sources of
information.

Secondly, my intention to keep the different kinds of evidence
neatly apart has broken down completely as I have found it impossible
to indicate the significance of one type without reference to others.
For instance, I claim that the establishment of palaces in Crete in the
21st century BC was heavily influenced by the contemporary restoration of central power in Egypt at the beginning of the Middle Kingdom. I believe that this argument can be made convincingly only if
one links it to the contemporary introduction of a bull cult to Crete
and the latter's Egyptian precedents and parallels. Similarly, in examining the significance of the Mit Rahina inscription, I have felt obliged
to look quite extensively at Classical and Hellenistic sources and at the
archaeological evidence. Thus, I abandoned the attempt to apply disciplinary rigour to the material in favour of 'thick description' involving many different types of information simultaneously.

This leads to the third and most important change to my original plan. I have given up the mask of impartiality between the two models. Given my commitment to the Revised Ancient Model, I had always known that this would be difficult. In the event, I have found it impossible. Now, instead of judging their competitive heuristic utility in a 'neutral' way, I shall try to show how much more completely and convincingly the Revised Ancient Model can describe and explain the development and nature of Ancient Greek civilization than can the Aryan Model.

INTRINSIC REASONS FOR PREFERRING THE REVISED ANCIENT MODEL TO THE ARYAN ONE

In a fascinating, though to my mind fundamentally misleading, article, published in 1972, the classicist R. A. McNeal argued that the 'prehistoric' Aegean could be approached in four ways: '(1) archaeological artifacts, (2) language, (3) skeletal material, if he wants to use it, and (4) Greek myth and legend.'[2] Apart from minor objections such as the fact that archaeologists today are extremely interested in buildings, settlement patterns and traces of agricultural and industrial activity, which are not restricted to artifacts, and that the fact that the extraordinarily ambiguous skeletal evidence can easily be subsumed under archaeology, the chief problem with this scheme is its omission of contemporary documents. The Aegean Bronze Age was not as 'prehistoric' as McNeal supposes. There are many references to the Aegean in Egyptian, Levantine and Mesopotamian texts and what is more, there are the tablets written in the Aegean syllabaries Linears A and B. Therefore, I think documentary information is of primary importance. It was for this reason that I had originally intended to begin this volume with a chapter on 'Contemporary Documents'. However, because archaeology can reach back to the Neolithic and the Early Bronze Age, from which there is virtually no documentary evidence on the Aegean, I have altered the scheme so that in this volume the documentary evidence on contacts between the Near East and the Aegean comes only in the tenth chapter.

McNeal argues forcefully against any attempts to synthesize evidence from his four categories of archaeology, language, physical anthropology and legend, claiming sensibly that one can never be certain of correlations between them and, less convincingly, that scholars should not poach in their neighbours' fields because they cannot hope to understand the others' professional mysteries. My objections to the last argument should be evident to readers of the first volume.

Furthermore, I cannot accept his requirement of certainty. I have based my case in this whole project on the principle of competitive plausibility rather than certainty, simply because the latter is impossible to achieve in these areas. Thus, I believe that the most one can do is to achieve plausibility and this is best done by combining evidence from all sources, even while aware of the dangers involved. In this volume, therefore, although I attempt to distinguish the different approaches, I am not distressed when I fail to keep them apart.

Before examining the value of the Revised Ancient Model in the light of the different sources of evidence, I should like to consider its relative inherent plausibility in the face of the Aryan Model. The Ancient Model has the advantage of having existed nearer the period concerned. It could be argued that there is a gap of twelve hundred years between the 5th century, when the Ancient Model is first attested, and the 18th century BC, when I believe there to have been Near Eastern settlements in Greece, which is more than the time that separates us from Charlemagne, and also that this temporal divide between Mycenaean and Classical Greece is not qualitatively shorter than the thirty-five hundred years between us and the hypothetical settlements by Phoenicians and Egyptians.

There are several good reasons for denying this contention. Firstly, as Ruth Edwards has shown in her book *Kadmos the Phoenician: A Study in Greek Legends and the Mycenaean Age,* there is a mass of literary and artistic circumstantial evidence suggesting that the Ancient Model existed in Archaic (776–500 BC) and even Geometric times (950–776 BC). This shortens the historical gap by some centuries.[3] Furthermore, evidence from Linear B tablets, reinforced by an increasing amount of information from archaeology, has confirmed that, in religion at least, there was considerable continuity from Mycenaean to Classical Greece.[4]

I have argued elsewhere that the West Semitic alphabet was introduced into the Aegean before 1400 BC and, in any event, recent epigraphical discoveries and interpretations make it extremely unlikely that the Greek alphabet was borrowed or adapted after the 11th century.[5] Even if the introduction were as late as the 9th century, the survival of the Cypriot syllabary – until recently – without attestation for more than five centuries, and apparently that of Linear A in Eastern Crete for over a thousand years, makes it extremely unlikely that all knowledge of Linear B disappeared immediately with the collapse of Mycenaean palatial society in the 12th century.[6] Thus, there is every reason to suppose that some documents survived from the Late Bronze into the Early Iron Age. On the other hand, while there is no doubt that there was considerable cultural regression between the 12th and the 8th centuries and that during this period much factual information was lost and much myth, legend and folktale accreted, nevertheless, it is certain that the Linear scripts and the alphabet overlapped in time, probably for several centuries. It is now impossible to maintain that the Greek Bronze and Iron Ages were separated from each other by impermeable centuries of illiteracy.

For instance, the second book of the *Iliad* contains an extensive descriptive list of Mycenaean cities, many of which appear to have disappeared by the time Homer wrote in the 9th century. Thus, it would seem very likely to have been based on Bronze Age written material. Furthermore, as well as possessing written and oral traditions, Classical and Hellenistic writers were able to visit some well-preserved Mycenaean ruins and we know that some sort of archaeology was carried out.[7]

On the other side of the Mediterranean, substantial records from the Bronze Age were available in the Classical period to Egyptian priests as well as to Phoenicians and Mesopotamians. In Hellenistic times some of these ancient texts were translated into Greek or summarized by priests and scholars like the Egyptian Manetho, the Phoenician Philo of Byblos and Berossos from Mesopotamia.[8] These and other sources were available to Greek writers, Hekataios of Abdera, Menander of Ephesos and others. Well before this, in the 6th century, Pherekydes of Syros is supposed to have based his work on Egyptian and Chaldaean works.[9]

By contrast, Herodotos, Diodoros Sikeliotes and other ancient writers had garbled views of Egyptian history that were, in many respects, inferior to those of modern Egyptologists with their access to original sources.[10] However, the discovery of the Mit Rahina inscription – describing previously unknown extensive expeditions and voyages to Syria and beyond in the 12th Dynasty – shows us that we should not let the undoubted triumphs of Egyptology lead us to overestimate the completeness of modern knowledge. In this case, it is striking to note that Herodotos, as well as other Greek writers, seem to have referred to these activities in their descriptions of the conquests of Sesōstris (see Chapters V and VI below). Thus, it is quite possible that Greeks knew things about Egypt's relations with the Aegean that are unknown to modern scholars.

On a more general level, it is important to note that Egyptologists rely on the Egyptian tradition transmitted by Manetho for many points and still use the traditional dynastic framework as he transmitted it. They also refer frequently to Herodotos, Plutarch and Diodoros whose direct contact gave them a 'feel' for ancient Egypt that can never be equalled by modern scholars.

The relative superiority of modern Egyptologists over the Classical and Hellenistic Greeks is not paralleled with the Levant. The tablets from Ugarit have provided a fascinating and detailed picture of a major Syrian port for over a century in the Late Bronze Age as well as important, if scrappy, evidence on West Semitic religion and myth. The cuneiform letters found at Amarna give us an idea of the political situation in coastal Syria and Palestine for some decades in the 14th century. However, in the Southern Levant the predominant writing material was papyrus and the Phoenician cities were particularly lavish in their use of it. As the Jewish politician and historian Josephus put it in the 1st century AD,

> Of the care bestowed by the Egyptians and Babylonians on their chronicles from the remotest ages . . . among the nations in touch with the Greeks, *it was the Phoenicians who made the largest use of writing* both for the ordinary affairs of life and for the commemoration of public events; of this I think I need say nothing, as the facts are universally admitted.[11]

Furthermore, despite the many destructions of Phoenician cities in the 1st millennium, some documents appear to have survived right up to Hellenistic and even Roman times. As Josephus wrote,

> For many years past the people of Tyre have kept public records, compiled and very carefully preserved by the state, of the memorable events in their internal history and in their relations with foreign nations. . . . Many of the letters which they [Hiram and Solomon in the 10th century] exchanged are preserved to this day.[12]

None of these documents survived into modern times and the only substantial piece of Canaanite literature we possess today is the Old Testament. This has extraordinary historical value but it is largely concerned with Israel, an inland state with very little contact with the Mediterranean, let alone the Aegean. With so very few texts and an extremely ambiguous and scrappy archaeological record, modern scholars' knowledge of the Levantine coast in the Late Bronze Age is minute in comparison to that of Classical and Hellenistic times.

In the Aegean itself, Linear B tablets have provided invaluable linguistic evidence and given important information on the Late Mycenaean palatial economy. They have also dropped some tantalizing hints on the religion of Late Bronze Age Greece. They do not contain, however, any mythological or historical texts.

During the past century there has been more systematic digging in Greece than ever before and much significant evidence has been unearthed. Consecutive ceramic stratigraphies have been established for the Middle and Late Bronze Age. However, the absolute dating has been uncertain and for one of the periods with which we are most concerned, the border between the Middle and Late Bronze Age, has until recently been particularly obscure, and the synchronisms or dating parallels with the Middle East have been fiercely debated.[13] There has also been a tendency to distrust carbon 14 and the other independent methods of dating where they do not fit preconceived chronologies; see, for example, the following statement made by the distinguished archaeologist Paul Åström:

> I should like to emphasize that carbon 14 dates are useless for exact dating of the Aegean Bronze Age. This may be demonstrated by an example. The average corrected carbon 14 dates for a short-lived group of seven samples from the time of the destruction of Thera or a little earlier in 1688 ± 57 B.C. The results are obviously quite ridiculous, as there is a general agreement on other grounds that the eruption occurred some time in the first half of the fifteenth century.[14]

In this case, so many other independent measures have confirmed the high dates that Åström considered 'ridiculous' and – as I shall show in Chapter VII – many scholars are now beating a retreat.[15] The point I am trying to make here is that the orthodoxy of the Aryan Model was established long before the new scientific techniques had been applied to Aegean archaeology and the reaction to their results has generally been to squeeze them into the model rather than to adjust or discard it. This aspect of the competition between the two models must thus be judged not on all the information available to their adherents *after* they were established but on the state of knowledge in the periods in which they were formed. In the case of the Aryan Model, this was the middle of the 19th century. For instance, at that time there was no archaeological knowledge of chronology whatsoever. This was not established until the 1880s when Flinders Petrie was able to date Minoan and Mycenaean pottery found in Egypt.[16]

Today, even if the pottery is beginning to be dated accurately and it is possible to discover where it was made, it will never be able to tell us the languages spoken by its makers and users, nor can it prove or rule out any invasion or population movement, unless this involved a complete cultural break, and these are fortunately very rare. Thus archaeology, on its own, cannot answer the questions in which we are interested: the type, extent and duration of Egyptian and Phoenician influences on the Aegean during the Bronze Age.

Much of the assessment of the Classical and Hellenistic Greeks' knowledge of the Bronze Age depends on the extent of the cultural break after the 13th century BC. In Egypt, as the Egyptian priests were alleged to have told Solon in the first half of the 6th century, there was none.[17] It is clear that, although there was some political instability and economic decline in Egypt for the next few centuries, there was virtually no disruption of cultural continuity or knowledge of the past. The invasions of the Near East by the Sea Peoples in the 13th and 12th centuries – described in the Appendix to Volume 1 – did cause a break on the Levantine coast, which appears to have led to the replacement of the predominantly monarchical, though thoroughly commercial, cities of the Bronze Age by cities of a new type, dominated by a temple not a palace, and the inauguration of what we may usefully call 'Slave Society'.[18] Despite these fundamental social changes, however, the cities revived decades not centuries after their destructions with strong continuities in their material culture. We even know from the 11th-century Egyptian traveller Wen Amon that, at least in the key city of Byblos, official records had been kept for over a century.[19]

In Anatolia, the disturbances destroyed the Hittite Empire forever but, as the Hittite specialist James Macqueen has written, 'We cannot now postulate four hundred years of chaos and an almost complete return to nomadic life.'[20] Many of the Empire's traditions survived well into the Iron Age. Greece was no exception, as I have argued above; the break was not as drastic as it has commonly been portrayed. All in all, while the break was catastrophic locally, in the East Mediterranean as a whole, the so-called Dark Ages did not make a clean break from the past.

'Dark Ages' have, in fact, been given a bad name by the quite exceptional cultural collapse between the 5th and 8th centuries AD. Although Byzantium survived this crisis, it had to be radically reformed to do so. Islam, while it too preserved some Egypto-Greek-Babylonian institutions, science and philosophy, did create a completely new beginning. In Western Europe, the Frankish Empire was nothing like the Roman one it claimed to succeed. All in all, the Bronze Age civilizations of the Middle East had been weakened by the Hellenistic and Roman conquests but they survived until the Gothic and Arab invasions and the triumphs of Christianity and Islam.[21]

The destruction of civilization accompanying the rise of monotheism included the loss of the great written languages of the early civilization: Sumerian, Akkadian and Egyptian. Hence the drastic cultural break between AD 500 and AD 800 makes the disturbances of the 12th century BC look trivial. Consequently, while the proponents of the Ancient Model lived when the traditions of the Bronze Age had faded, they were still in the ancient world. By contrast, the champions of the Aryan Model have lived many centuries after a true *coupure*.

In general, then, it is clear that, as well as having a 'feel' for the topic from their common culture, the writers working in the Ancient Model had more information about the Bronze Age than do supporters of the Aryan one. However, proponents of the Aryan Model base their claim to superiority less on the amount of information available to them than on the contention that they, unlike the 'credulous' Classical and Hellenistic writers, have a 'critical approach' and a scientific viewpoint which more than compensate for any lack of information.

The term *Altertumswissenschaft*, used in German for the new study, has a less restrictive sense than its English translation 'science of antiquity'. Nevertheless, the sense of being 'scientific', even in the broad meaning of the word, indicates the feelings of excitement and confidence in the early 19th century which enabled scholars to disregard all their 'baroque' predecessors. To be precise, this claim to be 'scientific' was first made in the 1790s under the influence of Kantian terminology and before the technological breakthroughs of steam and electricity in the 1810s and 1820s. Nevertheless, just as railways, steamships and telegraphs surpassed all previous means of transport and communication, the philologists and ancient historians of the 19th century were convinced that their scientific and 'critical' historical approach or 'method' put them on a categorically higher plane than all their predecessors.

For the new scholars, the Ancient Model was a delusion. Just as 'scientific' historians had to discount all Greek references to centaurs, sirens and other mythical creatures that offended against the laws of natural history, the Ancients' view of Greece as having been civilized by Egyptians and Phoenicians had to be removed because it offended against the laws of 'racial science'. It should be emphasized that, for many of these scholars, this was the supreme science which subsumed all the rest, and the so-called 'ethnic principle of history' was widely seen as the new historians' prime contribution to historiography.[22]

The Aryanists' claim to objectivity does not seem convincing in the light of the relationships between classical scholarship and political ideology discussed in some detail in Volume 1.[23] To put it simply, while 19th-century scholars might be more reliable than Classical writers on zoology or physics, on the issue of Near Eastern influences on Greece, most of the founders of the Aryan Model were much less 'objective' than the ancient Greeks. The latter were torn between the wish to be attached to the ancient civilizations and the desire not to be culturally inferior to the Egyptians and Phoenicians, who were still very much around and were generally disliked. In sharp contrast to this – with very few exceptions – 19th-century classicists were pushed in a single direction to affirm the persistence of 'racial' characteristics and the essential superiority of Europeans.

As mentioned above, the fact that the Aryan Model arose and was sustained, at least partially, by Eurocentrism and racism does not in itself make it false or heuristically useless. People who detest Malthusianism can still find Darwin's theories, which were explicitly based on it, extremely useful. Even more directly relevant to our topic is the hypothesis of an Aryan conquest of North India. The undoubted fact that racialist 19th-century Indologists revelled in the hypothesis does not make it untrue. Recent criticism from radical scholars has failed to make it redundant.[24] It should also be noted that in India, unlike Greece, there was a strong ancient tradition of a northern conquest and a survival of pre-Aryan languages more or less where one would expect to find them. I shall argue in Chapter VIII of this volume that the Victorian and early 20th-century historians were probably right when they saw the Hyksos invasion of Egypt as involving some peoples from Northern Syria, possibly including speakers of Indo-Iranian or even Indo-Aryan. Thus, there are cases where an 'Aryan Model' would seem appropriate. Why should this not be true in the case of Greece? Might it not be that the racist creators of the Aryan Model were 'sleep-walking', to use Koestler's term; that is to say, they could have established a successful and fruitful model for extraneous reasons in very much the same way as their contemporary Darwin.

The fact is, however, that the Aryan Model has not been heuristically successful, at least since the 1880s when the Indo-European aspects of Greek language and culture had been largely worked out. Thus, its triumph over the Ancient Model cannot be taken as an indication of its superiority. There is, in fact, a striking contrast between the long-term fruitfulness of Darwinism for the understanding of natural history and the blatant inadequacies of the Aryan Model for explaining either the origin or the nature of Ancient Greek civilization. Whether or not readers agree with my analyses or etymologies, no one can deny that a huge range of Ancient Greek culture is still mysterious. Thus, as well as the intrinsic reasons for preferring the views of the Ancient Greeks about their own history, there is the massive inadequacy of the Aryan Model and, as I hope to show in this and the following volumes, the far greater explanatory power of the Revised Ancient Model.

SOME THEORETICAL CONSIDERATIONS

Let us return to the shift from the Ancient to the Aryan Model, looking at it in a more abstract way. Although Kuhn's schema were designed for the history of physical sciences, I am convinced that they also have heuristic utility for studying revolutionary change in the humanities. I am also less hesitant than I was in Volume 1 to view the Ancient and Aryan 'models' as paradigms or disciplinary matrices. The Aryan Model fits Kuhn's requirement that a 'disciplinary matrix' be '"disciplinary" because it is the common possession of the practitioners of a professional discipline; "matrix" because it is composed of ordered elements of various sorts, each requiring futher specification.'[25] At times Kuhn argues, as the sociologist Barry Barnes puts it, that with a 'paradigm' or 'disciplinary matrix':

> it is never possible . . . to produce any context-independent 'rational justification' for preferring the new to the old, any indefeasible proof of 'advance' or 'progress'. Concepts, theories and procedures are changed; problems are changed; criteria of judgement are changed. . . . Nothing provides the essential stable anchorage for comparative evaluation. Revolutions separate incommensurable forms of scientific life.[26]

This is a statement in theoretical terms of the reasons behind my change of project from that of a detached 'neutral' assessment of the heuristic utility of the two models into a demonstration of what can be done working within the new model or paradigm. Kuhn also argues, in terms that are remarkably reminiscent of the Marxist dialectic, of the shift from one mode of production to the next that:

> scientists will be reluctant to embrace it [the new paradigm] unless convinced that two all-important conditions are being met. First, the new candidate must seem to resolve some outstanding and generally recognized problem that can be met in no other way. Second, the new paradigm must promise to preserve a relatively large part of the concrete problem-solving ability that has accrued to science through its predecessors.[27]

This seems in many ways similar to the 'surplus explanatory value' that Lacatoš insisted on, in his critique of what seemed to him the arbitrariness of Kuhn's paradigmatic shifts.[28]

The great anomaly that brought down the Ancient Model was the contradiction between its tenet that Greece had been civilized by

Egyptians and Phoenicians and the *Weltanschauung* of the 19th century, in which races were seen as primary determinants of history and their hierarchical descent white > brown > black was axiomatic. The 'Model of Autochthonous Origin', which was made explicit by Colin Renfrew only in the 1970s but was implied by K. O. Müller and George Grote between 1820 and 1840, transcended this problem.[29] However, this gave no advantage for the study of the internal dynamics of early Greek history which, in fact, Grote abandoned entirely.[30]

The Aryan Model has been able to do more than this, it has provided what Kuhn calls an 'exemplar' in the relating of Greek to the Indo-European languages. However, the new model has not fulfilled Kuhn's second requirement that 'the new paradigm must promise to preserve a relatively large part of the concrete problem-solving ability that has accrued to science through its predecessors.' Quite the contrary, the men who destroyed the Ancient Model and those who established the Aryan one swept the board clean and began *de novo*. Why then do 19th-century ancient historians not fit into Kuhn's pattern? The answer would seem to be in what they perceived to be the enormity of the anomaly in the Ancient Model, which made any other model – or no model at all – preferable. The only internal reason for the Aryan Model's success was its power to explain the Indo-European basis of the Greek language. Thus, there was an exchange between this undoubted advantage and the need to deny the Greek tradition on the one hand and the many traces of Near Eastern culture in Greece seen by earlier scholars on the other. In short, the fact that the Ancient Model was replaced by the Aryan one does not in itself give the latter any superiority.

A SUMMARY OF THE ARGUMENT

At this point, I should like to outline the contents of this book, in order to give readers some threads to guide them through the labyrinth of facts and opinions they are about to enter. As I mentioned above, this volume concentrates on two sources of information about Bronze Age Greece and its relations to the rest of the Eastern Mediterranean: archaeology and contemporary documents. Other sources – language, toponyms, mythology and religion – are also discussed here but they will be the focus of Volumes 3 and 4.

Chapter I is about Crete before 2100 BC. This island, placed in the midst of the three continents, Africa, Europe and Asia, has often been considered as one of the most important 'bridges' between them.

There is a brief survey of the New Stone Age or Neolithic period in Crete, from the introduction of agriculture and pottery there from Anatolia before 6000 BC, and the influences from Egypt and Libya and the Levant as well as from the Cyclades and Mainland Greece to the north that are evident from the archaeological remains from this long period.

During the Neolithic period, Crete was relatively unimportant as the most prosperous regions around the Aegean were the large wheat-growing plains of Northern Greece. With the beginning of the Bronze Age some time before 3000 BC, these tended to fall back and the coasts and islands of the Southern Aegean became richer and more developed. There is some discussion about the causes of this geographical switch. Some scholars argue that it was the introduction of new 'Mediterranean' crops from the East, notably grapes and olives, but others question the date of their arrival and prefer to emphasize improvements in shipping and increase of trade. In either or both cases the shift from north to south would seem to indicate more contact with the Near East.

New scientific techniques which can pinpoint the local origin of pottery and metal objects containing traces of lead have confirmed the theories of the 'Modified Diffusionists' of the early 20th century and go against those of the extreme isolationist revisionists led by Colin Renfrew, a professor of archaeology at Cambridge. It is now clear that the period at the end of the 4th millennium and the beginning of the 3rd was one of wide-ranging trade stretching from the Middle East as far west as Spain and Hungary and as far east as Afghanistan. In this larger sphere, the notion that contacts around the East Mediterranean were limited or restricted has become absurd.

In Chapter I, which is focused on Crete, there is some discussion of the arrival on the island at this time of new metallurgy and a new style of pottery, together with other cultural features that would seem to have their origins in the Levant. The beginning of the Early Bronze Age would seem to be the most probable time for a West Semitic language to have entered Crete to become an important if not the dominant language there until the rise of Greek on the island in the second half of the 2nd millennium BC. At the same time it is clear that Cretan religion of the Early Minoan Period was heavily influenced from Egypt, and Egyptian objects and artistic motifs as well as Levantine ones have been found in the island from the 3rd millennium.

There is also some discussion of the work on this period by the feminist archaeologist Lucy Goodison. Goodison has attacked the notion that Cretans had a chthonic or earthly mother goddess. She has demonstrated that the iconography indicates rather that the sun was seen as female. There are interesting ideological reasons why the 19th- and 20th-century scholars should prefer the image of the earth mother as a suitable object for worship among non-Aryans. From the beginning of the 19th century, linguists saw the Aryans as a masculine, spiritual people worshipping the sky and those they conquered as essentially female and concerned with the earth and matter. In Egypt, while the sun was masculine, the sky was female and the earth tended to be male. Lucy Goodison rightly sees the religion she reconstructs as specifically Cretan. Nevertheless, she points out striking parallels with Egyptian religion, such as the notion of the sun sailing across the sky in a boat and the representation of two mourning ladies, who seem to resemble the Egyptian goddesses Isis and Nephthys, who lamented the death of Osiris.

All in all, it seems clear that there were regional variations of culture within Crete and that all of these contained local elements continuing from the Neolithic. However, they also show heavy influences from neighbouring cultures; from the Cyclades to the north and Anatolia to the northeast but even more from Egypt to the south and the Levant to the southeast. This cautious, common-sense view would have been perfectly acceptable until the 1960s, long after the emergence of the extreme Aryan Model. Until then, acceptance of 'Oriental' influences on Pre-Hellenic culture posed little threat to the Aryan Model. The non–Indo-European–speaking yet Caucasian and somehow European Pre-Hellenes acted as a filter purifying the African and Semitic influences on Greek culture. Thus, for instance, the distinguished and progressive archaeologist and archaeological theoretician Gordon Childe argued for 'Modified Diffusion' and the crucial influences on early Europe from the Near East, although as a young man he was an outspoken champion of Aryan superiority.

Since 1972, the dominant figure in interpreting the Aegean in the 3rd millennium BC has been the Cambridge archaeologist Colin Renfrew. Renfrew has followed the trend in archaeological and religious studies of Greek civilization which increasingly saw the origins of Greek culture not in that of the Aryans who allegedly swept in from the north but in the indigenous peoples of the Aegean. Renfrew, in fact, argues for the Model of Autochthonous Origin, claiming that Indo-European speech arrived with agriculture not only in Greece but in Europe as a whole. According to his scheme, the massive Levantine and Egyptian influence seen in 3rd-millennium Crete by earlier scholars would have had an unmitigated impact on Greek civi-

lization. Therefore, it was necessary for him that Greece should have
a pure childhood without eastern influences. As he put it,

> Throughout the southern Aegean, for a thousand years, striking
> changes were taking place in every field. . . . These developments
> owed very little to Oriental inspiration. Yet it was at this time that
> the basic features of the subsequent Minoan-Mycenaean civilisation
> were being determined.[31]

Having used the term 'Extreme Aryanist' to describe scholars who denied all Egyptian and Phoenician influences on the Greeks, it is difficult to find a term appropriate for those who go beyond this to deny
all Middle Eastern influences on the Pre-Hellenes, while at the same
time seeing the first Europeans as Neolithic farmers rather than
bronze-using, chariot-riding Aryans. I think 'Ultra-Europeanist' is the
least unsatisfactory.

Chapters II and III are largely concerned with Boiotia. The province of Boiotia in Central Greece is a plain surrounded by mountains.
Flowing into the plain are a number of rivers, which tend to form into
shallow swampy lakes, the largest and most famous of which was Lake
Kopais. These are frequently blocked from the sea, but at some time
in the Bronze Age channels were dug and tunnels excavated linking
caves to give outlets to the sea and drain the lakes. The drainage and
irrigation techniques were extremely intricate and sophisticated and,
when they broke down at the end of the Bronze Age, they were not
replaced until the 19th century AD despite a number of determined
attempts.

The sophistication of these dikes and tunnels was at a level only
achieved in the Mediterranean basin at that time in Egypt. This, together with the existence of an extremely ancient stepped artificial
mound that its latest excavator believed to be an imitation of an Egyptian pyramid, raises the possibility of Egyptian influence if not colonization in Early Bronze Age Boiotia.

Chapter II begins with a survey of the connections seen by Classical
and Hellenistic writers between Boiotia and Egypt. These were partly
the result of the capitals of both being called 'Thebes' and even more
the similarities between the Nile banks and Delta and the marshy
shores of Lake Kopais in Boiotia. Most of the chapter, however, is
concerned with mythical and cultic parallels between Boiotia and
Egypt. In particular, there is the importance of the cult of Athena on
the southern shore of Kopais, which I believe can be traced to the cult
of Athena's Egyptian counterpart Nēit as an organizer of water. One

Egyptian myth portrays Nēit as a cow swimming in the Delta to settle at the spot that later became her sacred city Sais. This is strikingly similar to the Greek myth of Kadmos, the founder of Thebes, following a cow until she lay down at the site of his future city.

Kadmos sacrificed the cow there and established a cult of Athena, with the mysterious *epiclesis* or title of Onga or Onka. The ancient writer Pausanias had no explanation for this name but, while others thought it Egyptian, he thought it Phoenician. The name Onka almost certainly comes from the name of the Egyptian Goddess, ʿnḳt, known to Greeks in the Hellenistic period as Anukis. Anukis was the goddess of the Nile cataracts and the islands set among its various strands. It is therefore fascinating to find that the Greek Thebes was built on the edge of an escarpment over which three streams tumbled. The other mythical name parallel to the name Onka, Onkaios in Arkadia in the Peloponnese, was associated with the reach of the fast-flowing river Ladōn, where it broke up to form islands. It is also clear that there was punning involved with the Semitic root ʿnq, meaning 'necklace', as the foundation myths of Thebes, especially those around Kadmos' queen Harmonia, are laced with references to necklaces and other strings.

There is also some consideration of another mythical lady closely associated with the Greek Thebes, Alkmēnē, who was seduced by Zeus and, as a result, gave birth to Herakles. A long section of Chapter II is devoted to looking at the many Mesopotamian, West Semitic and Egyptian strands that went to make up the greatest Greek and specifically Theban hero. These precedents are largely slippery divinities from all three cultures but they also include Egyptian pharaohs, particularly those of the Middle Kingdom, whose conquests and possible impact on Greece will be discussed in later chapters.

This raises two more general issues. The first of these is the possibility that what is generally seen as the peculiarly Greek concept of the semi-divine hero – who was always royal – had its origin in the Egyptian man-god or divine pharaoh. The second is that there may be some substance to the ideas of the Greek writer Euhemeros, who was a contemporary of the extraordinary conquests of Alexander the Great and the foundation of the Hellenistic godlike monarchies. Euhemeros argued that the conception of the gods came from exceptional men. In modern times the word 'euhemerism' has been used – and I am guilty of this myself – in exactly the opposite sense, to describe the transforming of mythological beings into historical characters. There is no doubt, in fact, that both processes occur relatively frequently and it is likely in this case that the Middle Kingdom pharaohs were an important component in the formation of Herakles.

Taken as a whole, Chapter II demonstrates detailed and intricate mythological parallels between Boiotia and the Near East, most of which date back to the Bronze Age and some of which would seem to come from the 3rd millennium. This is essentially to provide a background from which to assess the conflicting claims of modern archaeologists of Boiotia discussed in Chapter III. As mentioned above, there are two main material indications of possible Egyptian influence in the Bronze Age. Firstly, there is the tomb or 'pyramid' of Amphion and Zethos. It is certain that it is huge and man-made, and that it had a quite extraordinary sanctity throughout Classical and Hellenistic times and that Amphion and Zēthos were considered as founders of Thebes. There has been controversy since Classical times as to whether they were the *first* founders of Thebes, that is, whether they came before the much better known Kadmos. The older tradition, that of Homer, claimed that this was so and Pherekydes, who was thought to have used Phoenician sources, added that their city was later destroyed and that Kadmos refounded Thebes on its ruined site.

There is also little doubt that the mound dates back to the ceramic period Early Helladic II, that is between 3000 and 2400 BC, the period of the Egyptian Old Kingdom. Theodore Spyropoulos, who excavated it, believes that the sophisticated step construction resembles that of the earlier Egyptian pyramids. The tomb at the top of the mound was looted and, while Spyropoulos believes them to have come from Egypt, it is difficult to pinpoint the origins of the very few remains recovered there. Given the mythological background referred to above and the fact that we know Egyptians to have been making pyramids at this period, it would seem reasonable to suppose that there was at least Egyptian influence if not Egyptian presence involved in the massive construction work required for the erection of the monument.

Recent excavations have shown a high level of prosperity and urbanization in Boiotia in EHII. More striking still are the so-called *Rundbauten* or 'round buildings' of this period found near Orchomenos on the northern shore of Lake Kopais. The most plausible explanation of these constructions is to see them as granaries. The doyen of Greek archaeology until his death in the late 1970s, Spyridon Marinatos, showed that these granaries closely resembled ones found in Egypt and clearly illustrated in Egyptian tomb paintings. Therefore, he argued, they showed Egyptian influence at this very early period.

The existence of such granaries would also indicate large grain surpluses in their districts. Such surpluses could possibly have come naturally from the shores of Lake Kopais or the banks of the river Kēphissos
that flows into it. It would seem much more plausible, however, to
suppose that they were the result of artificial drainage and irrigation.

The idea that the earliest dikes and polders of the Kopais basin date
back to EHII is not new. The German engineer and archaeologist
Lauffer, who devoted his scholarly life to the hydraulic works, believed them to come from this period. His modern successors have
been more cautious, merely maintaining that the earliest works are
pre-Mycenaean. Spyropoulos, however, maintains that he has found
EHII pottery on a dike, thus confirming Lauffer's position. Thus,
there is a convergence of evidence from the 'pyramid', the dikes, the
Rundbauten and the general prosperity of the period to indicate that
there were massive construction works in Boiotia in the middle of the
3rd millennium BC. Furthermore, it is not merely the 'pyramid' and
the *Rundbauten* that indicate that these works were connected to
Egypt. By this time, there had been sophisticated drainage and irrigation in Mesopotamia for many millenniums. Nevertheless, Egypt was
far closer and engaged in massive hydraulic works throughout the
Old Kingdom. Thus, it would seem that Egypt was the most likely
source of the expertise necessary to tackle the complicated problems
involved in controlling the Kopais.

Boiotia was not the only region of Greece to have been drained and
irrigated in the Bronze Age. There are several similar dikes and dams
in the mountainous region of Arkadia at the centre of the Peloponnese. These have not been dated but archaeologists and engineers
who have surveyed them believe that the similarities indicate that they
were constructed at the same time as those in Boiotia. Even more remarkable is a huge dam near Tiryns in the Argive plain. This is on an
even grander scale than the Boiotian and Arkadian dams and no parallels have been drawn between it and them.

The possibility that the Tiryns dam too may have been begun in the
Early Bronze Age is increased by the find of an EHII *Rundbau* at
Tiryns of such gigantic proportions that it would seem to have been
capable of storing the whole production of the Argive plain. This indicates not only great prosperity but also strong centralized political
or at least economic control of a type not envisaged by Renfrew in his
model of small-scale farming at this period. This scale of organization
is also suggested by the discovery at Lerna of a substantial building of
the period known as the 'House of Tiles'. Whether this was a small

palace or the centre of a council, it confirms the picture suggested by the *Rundbau* of a sophisticated centralized administration.

Chapter III also gives particular consideration to the toponyms of floods and irrigation. The name Pheneos or Pēneios is a common river or lake name, which occurs throughout Greece and in particular in both Thessaly to the north of Boiotia and Arkadia. It has no Indo-European etymology and would seem most likely to come from the Egyptian P3 Nw(y) (the flood). In both of these cases there are strong indications that earthquakes could cause blockages leading to floods and strong ancient traditions associating them with floods and heroic irrigation.

One of the most frequent river names in Greece is Kēphis(s)os. I believe that this comes from the Egyptian toponym Ḳbḥ(w), which appears commonly in Egypt for streams, rivers and other bodies of water. It is clearly linked to the Egyptian roots *ḳbb* (cool) and *ḳbḥ* (purify). Ḳbb was one of the names of the two caverns near Elephantine on the First Cataract from where the Nile was supposed to spring and there seems to have been a general association of the name Ḳbḥ(w) with cool pure water springing from the ground. Many if not most of the Greek Kēphisoi came or went underground and were used for ritual purification. Ḳbḥ(w) was also used as a place name for marshy ponds and lakes with aquatic birds. This would seem an appropriate etymology for Lake Kaphyai in Arkadia as well as Kopais itself, into which flowed a river called Kēphisos.

Both Boiotia and Arkadia have cities called Orchomenos sited close to Bronze Age dikes and channels. The toponym clearly dates back to the Bronze Age as it is found on Linear B tablets. An Indo-European etymology for this has been proposed from a root meaning 'close', reconstructed from a Lithuanian verb *veržiu* (enclose). However, there would seem to be a more plausible etymology from the Canaanite root *ʿrk*. Its basic meaning is to 'arrange in order' or 'set in rows' or, in the military sense, 'draw up a battle line'. This would seem to be the origin of the rich cluster of Greek words beginning *arch-*, which have no Indo-European etymologies meaning 'go first' or 'command' in a military sense. It would seem likely then that *orcho-* and *ercho-* as well as *arch-* were loans from Semitic *ʿrk*. This would seem to strengthen the hypothesis that Orchomenos, and Erchomenos, means 'regulated' or 'enclosed place' and refers to the nearby dikes and channels. Despite its ultimate Semitic origin, the final *-menos* would seem to be the Greek passive participle, which would make the toponym itself Greek. It may be, however, that there was what linguists interestingly call 'contamination' from the Semitic *mayîm* (waters). 'Regulated waters' would fit the context exactly.

These possible etymologies are to be seen in the context of the actual ancient irrigation works, the probability that the skills needed for them must have come primarily from Egypt, and secondly from the Levant, and traditions associating emigrants from Egypt with early irrigation. The great difficulty, however, is to distinguish the period within the Bronze Age in which the names arrived. While it seems clear that the waterworks themselves were begun in the 3rd millennium, they were still being developed in the 2nd and it may be that the vocabulary arrived only in the later period. This would seem virtually certain, in fact, if one dates the arrival of Indo-European speech to Greece to the end of EHII or to the beginning of the Middle Bronze Age. It is possible, however, that some of the cults and traditions, particularly those concerning the irrigating Nēit/Athena and her battles with Seth/Poseidon, the force of the wilderness, do go back to the earlier period.

There are, interestingly, frequent references in Greek tradition to double foundations. One explanation to this may simply be the common theological and mythological practice of doubling to make more mysterious, as with gods with two births, two mothers, two fathers, and so on. Or it may be a Lévi-Straussian mythological structural requirement. In this case it would seem likely that the doubling has a historical basis and it is possible that Greeks of the Iron Age were dimly aware that there had not been only one dark age, that of the Fall of Mycenae and the Return of the Heraklids in the decades after the Trojan War, but there had also been earlier ones: that around Deukalion's Flood, which we would put around 1600 BC, and the still earlier one, which, among other things, had destroyed the Thebes of Amphion and Zethos.

There is no doubt that the society and economy of Greece in the ceramic period EHII were extremely prosperous and sophisticated and that many of their surviving features look very Egyptian, and further that Egyptian influence on Greece at this time would not be surprising as it was the height of the Old Kingdom. While no clearly Egyptian objects of this period have been found in Boiotia or Arkadia, a small number of significant Old Kingdom Egyptian objects have been found elsewhere in the Aegean and not merely in Crete. All in all, I argue in Chapter III that there is a good circumstantial case to be made for significant Egyptian, and to a lesser extent Levantine, influence on Mainland Greece as well as the Aegean in the 3rd millennium BC.

Towards the end of the 3rd millennium, developments in Crete took a very different form from those on the Greek mainland. Before that, the prosperity and the scale of economic operations in the north seem if anything to have been greater than those in Crete. Furthermore, although more Old Kingdom Egyptian and early and mid-3rd millennium Levantine objects have been found on the island, as argued above there seems to have been equally great contact between the Central and Northern Aegean and the Middle East. The difference arose after the end of the Greek ceramic period EHII and the Cretan EMII in the 24th century. In Greece, there were destructions, after which urbanization and density of settlement declined. In Crete, by contrast, there was the development of what has been called the Proto-Palatial Period, which led on to the great Cretan palaces, which appear to have first been built in the last century of the 3rd millennium.

There has been considerable debate on the causes of the Cretan development from the cultivated but largely unurbanized Crete of the Early Minoan period to the palatial society made up of reasonably large and bureaucratically run states. While they admit that the shift was of critical significance, Renfrew and the Ultra-Europeanists, not surprisingly, argue that it was essentially indigenous. Modified Diffusionists, including the founder of Cretan archaeology Sir Arthur Evans and his most brilliant pupil J.D.S. Pendlebury, on the other hand, noted both the significant number of Levantine and Egyptian objects found in EMIII strata and the fact that the changes in metallurgical technology and in the design of stone and pottery jars reflect Levantine and Egyptian influences respectively. They have also noted the essential similarity of the architecture of the Cretan palaces and the palatial systems that were run from them to those of the Middle East – which preceded them by many centuries. Thus, they have tended to associate this transformation with Eastern influences.

Interestingly, a number of the younger Cambridge archaeologists are arriving at a similar conclusion by a very different route. Taught by Ultra-Europeanists, they have been struck by the difficulties in fitting the archaeological evidence into the smooth evolutionary model assumed by Evans and to some extent by Renfrew. Thus, they now use the language of the critics of Darwinian evolution and talk of *punctuated equilibria*. They also note that the Proto-Palatial Period was marked by a sharp increase of evidence of communications with the Near East. Even so, they, like the older generation of Modified Diffusionists, are very vague as to how and why these developments should have taken place.

The explanation would seem to come from the strong likelihood that the first Cretan palaces were built when Egypt was ruled by the 11th Dynasty. This dynasty, founded by Black Upper Egyptians from the Theban nome, restored the unity of Egypt, establishing what was later known as the Middle Kingdom. There is no doubt that under this dynasty Egyptian military power grew and there were expeditions into the Levant. We also know from lead isotope analysis that 11th-Dynasty Egypt was importing silver mined from the mines of Laurion in Attica, south of Athens. This and the finds of Egyptian objects of the period in Crete suggests the possibility that the establishment of the Cretan palaces was in some way the result of the contemporary re-establishment of Egyptian power. Nevertheless, the connection still appears tenuous on archaeological grounds alone.

There is, however, another source of evidence. One of the most striking features of Cretan palatial society was its bull cult. Evidence for this appears from the remains of the Cretan palaces as well as from the Greek traditions of Minos' labyrinth and the Minotaur. Although there are some plains on the island suitable for cattle, its most striking feature is its mountains, which make it essentially country for goats or wild goats, *agrimi*. Thus, geographically it is no surprise that there is no evidence of a bull cult until the very end of the Early Minoan Period. This absence compounds the difficulty of accepting the most frequently suggested origin for the Cretan bull cult of the 2nd millennium BC, which is the powerful bull cult in the Çatal Hüyük Neolithic culture of the 7th millennium BC. It is probably true that Crete, like Mainland Greece, received much or most of its agricultural techniques from this Anatolian civilization and I have frequently argued against the 'argument from silence'. Nevertheless, a gap of attestation of a bull cult in either Anatolia or the Aegean for four thousand years does present some difficulties. The plausibility of the hypothesis shrinks to nothing as there is another possible place of origin almost equally close geographically and at exactly the same time in the 21st century BC, namely Egypt in the 11th Dynasty.

Bulls as powerful and beautiful animals have been the objects of religious veneration in many different cultures. In Egypt bulls and bulls' horns have been of great cultic significance since Predynastic times. From the beginning of pharaonic times there had been a number of bull cults, the most famous of which was that of the Apis bull, founded by the first ruler and great lawgiver of the 1st Dynasty, known later to the Greeks as Mēnēs or Min, near Memphis or Mn nfr. It is striking that the legendary lawgiver and ruler of Crete, Minos, was also closely associated with the bull cult and the *Mino*taur. The last was represented very much in the tradition of Egyptian portraiture of gods with a bull's head and a human body.

There were also other important Egyptian bull cults. At Heliopolis, just northeast of the modern Cairo, there was the cult of Mnevis, whose Egyptian name was written with the hieroglyphic sign ⊔ (winding wall). According to Greek tradition, Minos' architect Daidalos built the Cretan labyrinth on an Egyptian model and the first extant Greek mention of a 'labyrinth' did not refer to the building in Knossos but the massive funerary temple of the 12th-Dynasty pharaoh Amenemḥe III at the mouth of the Fayyum Lake. I believe that the name Labyrinthos probably came from another name of the pharaoh, N mȝꜥ.t Rꜥ, which was rendered by Greeks in Hellenistic times in many ways, including Labarēs and Labaris.[32]

There is, then, a remarkable triple parallel. In Egypt there were bull cults associated with the name Mn, which was also the title of the founding pharaoh/lawgiver and a bull associated with a 'winding wall'. All of these date back to the Old Kingdom, that is, before the foundation of the Cretan palaces. In Crete, there was a bull cult associated with a King Minos and a labyrinth. The parallels become even more intricate as traditions reported that King Minos was not always a dignified lawgiver but was sometimes a lecherous satyr. This resembles yet another Egyptian figure, the god Min, distinguished iconographically by his enormous phallus and in later times seen as the original of the Greek god Pan, the patron of the satyrs. It would also seem that the god Min was at times confused or syncretized with the founder Min/Mēnēs.

Another Egyptian cult linked to bulls was that of Mnṯw, an important god of war and conquest especially of the north, who rose to national prominence as the patron of the pharaohs of the 11th Dynasty named Menthotpe, 'Mnṯw is content', after him. Thus, the Cretan bull cult appears to have arisen in the 21st century BC at precisely the same time as the 11th Dynasty reunited Egypt and spread its influence abroad, while promoting a bull cult. It may even be that the name of Mnṯw in the form *Rdi Mnṯw, 'Mnṯw gives' or 'whom Mnṯw has given', is preserved in the legendary King Rhadamanthys, the brother of King Minos who was a king, conqueror and judge in his own right. In New Kingdom Egypt, Min, founder of the 1st Dynasty, and Menthotpe, founder of the Middle Kingdom, were sometimes worshipped together, which would neatly parallel the relationships between Minos and Rhadamanthys in Greek tradition. As there appears to have been some fusing of god and pharaoh, between Min/Mēnēs and Min and

Mntw and Menthotpe in Egypt, it would seem plausible to suggest that the Cretan Minos and Rhadamanthys drew from both the divine and the royal sources.

There are a number of ways in which to explain this pattern of coincidence. The first of these is simply to put it down to chance. This would seem unlikely because of the parallel's elaboration and density.

The second explanation is to attribute it to Classical and Hellenistic concoctions between Egyptian and Greek priests. This is virtually impossible because the names of Minos and Rhadamanthys appear in Hesiod and Homer and their writings make it clear that most of the legends concerning them already existed in the 10th or 9th centuries. Thus, any concoction of parallels would have had to have taken place earlier, perhaps in the 'Dark Ages'. This would seem very unlikely because of the nature of contacts between Egypt and Greece and the disorganized state of Greek religion at that time. If the concoction were any earlier, the most probable period would have been in the 15th and 14th centuries, when there was contact around the East Mediterranean and religion was flourishing in both regions. In fact, it may well be that the Greek legends were shaped at this time. As archaeology shows that the Cretan bull cult began precisely when the cult of Mntw was at its most flourishing, however, there would seem every reason to suppose that the basic parallels date back to then.

Another reason for placing this coincidence at the end of the 3rd millennium is that around 2000 BC the Egyptian national cult changed from the bull Mntw to the ram Amon. Thus, while it is true that Mntw remained an important member of the Egyptian pantheon, especially associated with northern conquests, and Amon as the ram Zan or Zeus became extremely important in Cretan religion, Crete preserved the centrality of the bull cult after Egypt had abandoned it. This would seem to fit a general cultural pattern in which peripheral regions preserve aspects of culture abandoned at the centre, in the way for instance Buddhism survives in Sri Lanka, Southeast Asia and Nepal and Tibet but not in its country of origin, India. The same is true of Christianity, which survived in Europe and East Africa but not as the majority religion in Syro-Palestine and Egypt where it was created.

The near certainty that the Cretan bull cult was introduced from Egypt and the architectural and social similarities between the Cretan and Near Eastern palaces, as well as a number of other cultic and iconographic parallels, make it clear that the cultural 'leap' from Pre-Palatial to Proto-Palatial Crete was the result of at least indirect stimulus from the contemporary Middle East and that this was connected to the reassertion of Egyptian primacy in that region. I also believe that the traditions of Rhadamanthys and archaeological evidence suggest the possibility of some Egyptian suzerainty in the Southern Aegean in the 21st century.

Chapter V and Chapter VI are concerned with the 'conquests' of the 12th-Dynasty pharaoh Senwosre I or, as the Greeks knew him, Sesōstris. Herodotos and later Greek writers wrote at some length and in considerable detail about his conquests, achieved in campaigns that took him and his army across Asia, Scythia – the South Russian Steppe – to the Caucasus. Writers after Alexander the Great's conquests, which had reached India, argued that Sesōstris had gone equally far. All of these reports have been discounted since the 18th century by modern scholars, most of whom were for a long time unwilling to identify Senwosre with Sesōstris. They have tended to argue that the reports were clearly Egyptian attempts to find a national hero whose conquests could surpass those of their Persian rulers after Cyrus the Great and their Macedonian ones after Alexander, and hence the exaggerations of Diodoros Sikeliotes in the Hellenistic period. The modern scholars' incredulity was also heavily affected by their difficulties in accepting that a civilized African army could have made significant conquests not merely in Southwest Asia but also in Europe. Such a scheme flew in the teeth of systematic late 19th- and early 20th-century racism.

Until the middle of this century, it was generally agreed, on the basis of inscriptional evidence and archaeology, that there had been an Egyptian 'Empire' or at least a zone of influence in Syro-Palestine during the 12th Dynasty. Since then, however, scepticism had reached such a point that some scholars were doubting its existence. Without a base in the Levant, the conquests of Senwosre/Sesōstris were completely out of the question.

Defenders of the 12th-Dynasty 'Empire' in Syro-Palestine have been supported by the discovery and preliminary reading of a large inscription from Memphis or the modern village of Mit Rahina, describing many major expeditions led by Senwosre I and his successor Amenemḥe II, by both land and sea. Some of these went to Nubia and Kush further south in Africa but more went north into Asia, to Sinai Lebanon but also to Stt, a country still further to the north, which in later times was equated with the Greek 'Asia'. A number of cities – with names unknown from other Egyptian sources – were destroyed. The expeditions sent back considerable booty to Egypt, most notably prisoners and metals, particularly lead and silver.

Georges Posener, a senior scholar who devoted a lifetime to the study of Middle Kingdom Egypt and especially its relations with

Southwest Asia, immediately saw the inscription as powerful evidence
to back his strongly held belief in Middle Kingdom suzerainty over
Syro-Palestine. He was supported in this by the Israeli archaeologist
Raphael Giveon.

Equally predictably, the American Egyptologist and champion of
the Lebanese William Ward, who had opposed ideas of a '12th-Dy-
nasty Empire', claimed that the inscription was much later, belonging
to the 19th Dynasty, and therefore could not be used as evidence as it
was inscribed seven hundred years after the supposed events. However, Wolfgang Helck, probably the most distinguished living German Egyptologist, who had previously opposed the idea of extensive
Middle Kingdom activities in Southwest Asia, has been convinced by
Posener's use of the evidence from the inscription, which he too accepts as coming from the 12th Dynasty. He has also argued that the
expeditions ranged as far as Cyprus and Southern Anatolia.

I go beyond him to argue that the inscription reopens the question
of the historicity of the wide-ranging conquests of Sesōstris reported
by the Greek writers. In fact, even without the inscription, such a revision could have been begun because, as I have stated above, I believe
that where ancient sources converge and are not controverted in Antiquity, one should take their schemes as working hypotheses.

Before trying to assess the plausibility of the Greek writers, it is necessary to try and specify their claims as far as possible. It is clear, for
instance, that when Herodotos reported that Sesōstris had marched
across the 'continent' Asia, he did not mean that he had crossed as far
as Chukhotka and the Bering Straits. In fact, ancient writers challenged Diodoros' claim that the pharaoh had gone to India. It is clear
that, in this context, when Herodotos referred to 'Asia' he meant what
we today call Asia Minor or Turkey. In this case, we should see Sesōstris' campaigns as going through Anatolia and round the north of the
Black Sea to the Caucasus, a route of more than three thousand miles,
an impressive distance, worth remembering for two thousand years.
However, it is considerably shorter than the marches of Alexander
the Great and in modern times it is comparable to the Chinese Communist Long March, which was also made on foot and, unlike those of
Sesōstris and Alexander, did not have the advantages of backing from
a stable state and supplies by sea.

Chapter V includes two sections on chronology. The first of these is
not directly relevant to the chronology of Sesōstris, but it is important
because it provides an excellent illustration of some of the difficulties
caused by archaeologists' desire to establish a 'scientific' basis for their
discipline. It concerns the chronology of Egypt, which until twenty

years ago had to provide the basis for the chronology of the rest of the
Middle East and the Aegean. This was because only Egypt had lists of
kings and their reign lengths going back into the 3rd millennium or
beyond. These lists were far from complete and sometimes contradicted each other and there were the so-called 'intermediate Periods'
between powerful dynasties, when the political confusion in Egypt is
reproduced in the historical records and chronologies. Nevertheless,
with the help of an astronomical dating from the 12th Dynasty, most
scholars accepted that the 1st Dynasty had begun around 3400 BC.

During the mid-20th century AD, there has been a strong urge
among Egyptologists and ancient historians to establish a 'scientific'
status for their disciplines and themselves. The simplest way to
achieve this appeared to be to use scepticism and caution. It became
impermissible to use probabilistic arguments and it was absolutely essential not to appear speculative. This scepticism and caution were
particularly applied to space and time. There was a strong tendency
to restrict the geographical range of ancient activities and an even
stronger one to down-date earlier chronologies. Thus, by taking the
shortest possible reign lengths and insisting upon long co-regencies,
when pharaohs shared the throne with their successors, and upon
overlapping dynasties, the 'new scientific' scholars were able to lower
the founding of pharaonic Egypt to the 29th century BC. Although
there was later a recoil from such radicalism, the new compromise was
established in the 31st century BC, two or three hundred years later
than the old consensus.

Over the last two decades, 'real' natural scientists have arrived on
the scene and with naive open-mindedness they want to solve the
problems that are now amenable to solution by their methods. They
were as surprised as anyone when many of their dates from radio-
carbon and other techniques tended to come out significantly earlier
than they were supposed to according to conventional archaeological
wisdom. The chronological sections of Chapter V, however, are concerned with battles that are still being fiercely fought.

In 1979, the brilliant but erratic archaeologist James Mellaart, who
is generally considered 'unsound' by his colleagues, published an article on chronology in which, in provocative terms, he called for a general revision of Near Eastern chronology upwards to fit with the new
data coming from radio-carbon dating. The article was immediately
attacked by archaeologists for its partial selection of dates and twisting
of data. Although this was successful, the defence of the status quo
was only short-lived. For some time radio-carbon laboratories had
been making continued 'errors' in their datings, which then had to be

repeated until they 'got it right', that is until they found dates that fitted the conventional chronologies. The interesting thing is that, although some of these 'errors' involved scattering in both directions,
the vast majority of datings for the 3rd and 4th millenniums were
simply seen as being 'too high' by from two to five hundred years. In
the case of one eminent laboratory this 'error' persisted for several
years until it was 'corrected' and archaeologists were discreetly told to
lower the previous dates given for their sites by a couple of centuries.
However, no explanation was given for the 'error' *or for the basis of the
correction.*

In the late 1980s a group of scientists from Texas and Switzerland
collected eighty new carbon samples from a number of the pyramids
and their analysis of them has resulted in a series of dates for pharaohs from the Old Kingdom that are, on average, 374 years above
those given by conventional wisdom. This is, in fact, even higher than
the dating proposed by Mellaart and provides powerful support for
his case.

For these reasons, I now accept Mellaart's return to the conventional wisdom of the early 20th century that the 1st Dynasty began
around 3400 BC rather than around 3100 BC, and that the 3rd Dynasty – the first of the Old Kingdom – was founded around 3000
rather than 2686 BC, which is the date given in the *Cambridge Ancient
History*. Because the Aegean ceramic periods have been dated from
Egyptian chronology, this involves raising the beginning of the Early
Minoan/Helladic I period from 3000 to 3300 BC and Early Minoan/
Helladic II from 2500 to 3000 BC.

Mellaart maintained that the raising of the dates for the Old Kingdom necessarily involved raising those of the Middle Kingdom, which
in turn forced the abandonment of the 12th-Dynasty astronomical
date upon which all early Egyptian chronology had depended. On the
other hand, he accepted the conventional dates for the New Kingdom, which he too saw as beginning in 1567 BC. The way in which he
switched from a high chronology for the Old Kingdom to a low or
middle chronology for the New Kingdom was by enlarging the 2nd
Intermediate Period.

The dating and duration of this period will be discussed at length in
Chapter VIII and there is no doubt that there are some problems
with the conventional views on these. Nevertheless, I am extremely
reluctant to abandon the astronomical date for the 12th Dynasty,
which does seem well based. Thus, where Mellaart enlarges the 2nd
Intermediate Period between the Middle and New Kingdoms, I prefer to re-inflate the 1st Intermediate Period between the Old and
Middle Kingdoms. Over the last seventy years, this period has under-

gone an especially radical compression because, as the 'softest' period, its reduction or elimination provided the easiest way in which to achieve the desired low date for the beginnings of the 1st Dynasty and the Old Kingdom. Thus, while I revise Egyptian dating for the Old Kingdom, I stay within conventional bounds for the dating of the Middle and New Kingdoms.

Mellaart did not restrict his raising of dates to Egypt. He insisted that radio-carbon indicated that Mesopotamian dates of the 4th and 3rd millennium should be raised as well. This allowed for synchronisms or parallel datings between the two regions to be maintained. Here his views have been partially supported by scientific work of another kind, that of the statistician Peter Huber. Huber has studied Mesopotamian reports of sightings of Venus and of lunar eclipses for the beginning of the 2nd millennium BC. On the basis of these, he demonstrated that the so-called middle and low chronologies could not be reconciled with this data but that the so-called 'long' chronology fitted it very well indeed. This 'long' chronology should not be confused with the even higher 'high' chronology used by scholars early in the 20th century and required by Mellaart.

Like the scientists and technicians working on radio-carbon, Huber had no apparent axe to grind. He did not care whether his results were high or low, he simply saw the problem as an interesting and soluble puzzle. The same impartiality cannot be attributed to the archaeologists, who had been pushing dates down for decades and who now reject his findings. However, it now appears that they may be reinforced by unpublished and unchecked dates from a palace in Anatolia which tend to support the middle and possibly even the low chronology. Thus, one is forced to be open to the possibility that any of the chronologies could be right.

If one accepts the 'long' chronology it would seem that in the second half of the 20th and the first half of the 19th centuries BC, there was a striking contrast between the peace and prosperity of Egypt, the Levant and the Southern Aegean, on the one hand, and the frequent destructions in Anatolia, the Balkans and the Caucasus, which, according to modern archaeological convention, marked the end of the Early Bronze Age in this region. These are usually attributed to invasions from the north. However, in Anatolia and the Balkans no specifically 'northern' objects have been found at the destruction levels. On the other hand, there have been a number of small 12th-Dynasty Egyptian finds in the former. Such a scenario would be difficult to reconcile with the middle chronology and out of the question with the short.

The possibility that the 'long' chronology is correct and these destructions were the result of Egyptian campaigns is strengthened by the discovery of a treasure hoard from the reign of Amenemhe II found at the temple of Mnṯw at Tôd just south of Thebes. It contained a number of silver vessels from Anatolia as well as other objects including lapis lazuli cylinder seals, the material for which was mined in Afghanistan but which were carved in Mesopotamia and one possibly in Anatolia. The most likely provenance for all of the objects in fact, is Central Anatolia, as the Mesopotamian seals could very probably have reached Anatolia as the result of the Assyrian trading colonies we know to have existed there in the 20th and 19th centuries BC.

The Tôd Treasure could be the result of trade between Anatolia and Egypt. However, its placing in the temple of Mnṯw, the god of conquest especially associated with Stt, would make it seem much more likely that the offering was of booty acquired militarily. This hypothesis is greatly strengthened by a reference in the Mit Rahina inscription to the gift of booty from Stt to the temple of Mnṯw at Tôd. Thus, archaeology would seem to back the ancient claims that Sesōstris made conquests in 'Asia' understood as Asia Minor.

The evidence from the ancient Thrace, the modern Bulgaria, is less clear-cut. There are certainly major destructions during the late 20th and early 19th centuries and a number of precious and semi-precious stones available to Egyptians only from the Balkans first appeared in Egypt in the 12th Dynasty. Nevertheless, these could well have been acquired through long-distance trade. Thus, this section of the pharaoh's 'conquests' is possible but the evidence for it is nowhere near as strong as that for Anatolia. Evidence from Scythia or the South Russian Steppe is even more scanty, though it would be more difficult to establish, as at this time the area was largely inhabited by nomads.

To investigate the claims for conquest in the Caucasus we have to look at another class of evidence that is treated in Chapter VI. This is later tradition. Herodotos believed that the inhabitants of Colchis on the eastern shore of the Black Sea were descendants of troops from Sesōstris' army who had settled there. He based this claim on a number of factors, including that this was what the Colchians claimed to be their origin, and that they were Black with tight curly hair, which was how he identified the Egyptians. Whether or not this is the case, we know from models of Middle Kingdom soldiers that they included stereotypical Nubians as well as Egyptians.

Herodotos' view of Colchian origins was accepted and amplified by a number of later writers, the most notable of whom was Apollonios of Rhodes, an extremely erudite librarian of the great library at Alexandria in the 2nd century BC. Apollonios' epic the *Argonautika* was about Jason's pursuit of the Golden Fleece to Colchis in his magic ship the *Argonaut* with its crew of heroes. Much of the information in the epic on the peoples along the southern and eastern coasts of the Black Sea has been confirmed not for Apollonios' own time but for much earlier periods, showing that the poet had access to accurate historical material. It also suggests that Herodotos was erring on the side of caution when he said that the Egyptians – unlike the Colchians – were unaware of any connections between their two countries. A long passage from the *Argonautika* attributes the foundation of Colchis to an Egyptian pharaoh who had ruled before there was any Greece. This and a number of reported aspects of Colchian culture all tend to confirm Herodotos' picture, at least to the extent that the Colchians in the 5th century BC believed themselves to be descended from soldiers in Sesōstris' army, if not that their tradition was essentially accurate.

A still more remarkable fact is that, even today, there is an African Black local population in from the subtropical coast near the resort of Sukhumi. The people, who survived Stalin's attempts to scatter them and to force intermarriage, speak the local Caucasian language of Abkhaz and are fiercely Muslim. There is no doubt that some of their ancestors migrated there in more recent times when the region was under Turkish control. However, the modern Black Sea Black population can be traced back to the 17th century and the ancient one to as recently as the 4th century AD. Thus the temporal gap here is no larger than the one between Herodotos and Sesōstris and, as Abkhaz and Georgian scholars admit, the possibility of continuity cannot be ruled out.

Other regions too appear to have traditional indications of the passage of a great Egyptian conqueror. There is no doubt that the 2nd-millennium iconography of the Levantine, Hurrian and Anatolian thunder gods Ba'al, Teššub and Tarkhwun was heavily influenced by images of the striking Egyptian pharaoh as portrayed in the Middle Kingdom. The most striking resemblance is that of the tall hats based on the white crown of Upper Egypt, sometimes complicated by images of the guardian snake *uraeus* worn in its front. However, there are also remarkable similarities of stance and posture between the divine and pharaonic images. The possibility that aspects of Herakles may have been influenced by Middle Kingdom pharaohs was raised in Chapter II and the connection between Herakles and these smiting gods is also considered.

Beyond this it would seem likely that the legends of Osiris/Dionysos' civilizing conquest of the East that so influenced Alexander were at least partially a euhemerization – in the original sense of great man to god – of Sesōstris' triumphs. There was also a direct connection between the two: It seems clear that Egyptians of the time saw Alexander as the new Sesōstris and the Alexander legends, which began soon after his death, appear initially to have been modelled on popular stories and epics on Sesōstris current in the Hellenistic period. In fact, the Egyptian tradition of Sesōstris that Herodotos and the other Greek writers reported was clearly old. The 'conquests of Osiris' are attested from the 18th Dynasty.

Apart from the possible indirect survivals of the conquests in the myths of Herakles and Dionysos, two native Greek traditions could well come from them. One of these is the tradition of an Egyptian Kekrops founding Athens. It is possible that Kekrops' name came from the *praenomen* of Sesōstris, Ḫpr kȝrʿ, or that of his great-grandson Sesōstris III, Ḫʿ kȝw Rʿ. Athens was close to the Laurion mines, which we now know were supplying silver to Egypt by the 11th Dynasty. Thus, an Egyptian settlement in Attica would certainly fit the general pattern of the Sesōstris's campaigns, a major motive of which was to acquire metals. This will be discussed further in Volume 3.

The other possible folk memory of the 12th-Dynasty conquests is in the traditions of the activities of the Black hero Memnōn: according to the epic tradition, in the Trojan War Memnōn was summoned to the aid of King Priam, whom Homer described as 'the most handsome man at Troy'. Traditions of Memnōn are in fact most frequent in Northwest Anatolia, where he was seen as both an Osiran deity of fertility mourned by women and birds and as a conquering hero whom Herodotos equated with Sesōstris.

There is no doubt that the Greeks saw Memnōn as an Ethiopian, that is, as a Black. However, there are complications because the Greeks saw two peoples as 'Ethiopians': the Ethiopians to the south of Egypt and the Ethiopians or 'Blacks' who formed the basic population of the ancient kingdom of Elam to the east of Mesopotamia and the Persian Gulf. Elamite civilization was as old as that of the Semitic and Sumerian peoples of Mesopotamia. Its language belonged to the Dravidian family, which now survives most strongly in Southern India and, although there were 'negritic' types in the Elamite population, the majority appear to have been Blacks of the South Indian type. There is no doubt that by the Classical period, Elamites, now under Persian rule, saw Memnōn as a national hero and there was a strong Greek tradition that he came from the Dawn and the East.

On the other hand, there was an equally strong tradition that Memnōn was an African Ethiopian and that he was associated with the Nile Valley. Memnōn was the Greek name for the famous colossal figure, across the Nile from Thebes, of ỉmnḥtp or Amenḥotpe III. However, there are also Greek graffiti on it naming the statue as Amenoth and Phamenoth, which would seem to indicate an awareness of the name of ỉmnḥtp Amenḥotpe.

In fact, however, there are clear indications that the name Memnōn did not come from ỉmnḥtp but from ỉmn m ḥȝt, Ammenemēs, the name both of Sesōstris' father and of his son, who was associated with his conquests in the Mit Rahina inscription and other sources. We also know that the royal family of the 12th Dynasty came from southern Upper Egypt and had some Nubian ancestry. Thus, the tradition of a conquering Black hero called Memnōn arriving in Northwest Anatolia from the east would fit neatly with a historical Egyptian campaign across Anatolia led by Sesōstris' son and heir, ỉmn m ḥȝt II. There is no reason why Homer or the traditions he drew from should have felt any more compunction in placing a hero of the 19th century BC in the Trojan War in the 13th than Virgil did in making the 9th-century Dido, founder of Carthage, a contemporary of the Fall of Troy. It is also clear that factual or fictional Memnōn became an archetypal hero, so that seven hundred years after ỉmn m ḥȝt II a king of Mycenae still used the name Agamemnōn, 'Great Memnōn'.

Thus, a large number of archaeological, iconographic and legendary phenomena from over a large region, which are at present inexplicable, are tied together and make sense if we accept the basic truth of the Greek reports and the Mit Rahina inscription. There is nothing inherently impossible or even implausible about Sesōstris' campaigns if one limits them in the ways suggested. It would, in fact, be more cumbersome to refuse to accept their fundamental historicity.

Although Greek reports and legends have been central to the reconstruction of Sesōstris' conquests, there is no reference in the legends – which are clearly distinct from the stories about the Egyptian Kekrops – to the pharaoh's having gone to Greece. It is striking, for instance, that the legends about Memnōn are centred in Northwest Anatolia, not in Greece itself.

The chief concern of Chapter VII is with the re-dating of the huge eruption of the island of Thera seventy miles north of Crete. This is important for a number of reasons but especially because it leads to a heightening of the Aegean ceramic periods, which makes the traces of Near Eastern influence earlier and synchronizes periods when archaeology suggests close contact with those indicated from documentary sources. It also provides another case study showing the ways in which scholars prefer to stick to established theories rather than to confront the implications of new evidence. In Volume 1, I stuck my neck out and accepted the date of 1628–1626 BC rather than the conventional ones of 1500 or 1450. My reasons for doing so were that the higher date was the one indicated by markings on tree rings in both the Western United States and Ireland and that they fitted better with the evidence from carbon 14. The earlier date also explained the absence of reports from Egypt, about which a good deal is known between 1500 and 1450 whereas the late 17th century BC is a blank there. Above all, I realized that the later dates were merely based on the hunch that the eruption was the cause of the destruction of Minoan rule in Crete and the triumph of the Mycenaean Greeks on the island, which we know from Egyptian records took place at around 1450 BC.

Since I published this, more evidence has appeared to support the higher or earlier date. This comes from tree rings in Germany and England, above all from a study of the layers left by winter snowfalls and summer melts on the Greenland icecap. These have shown that there was a great increase of acidity of the kind one would expect with eruptions of the Thera type at around 1640 BC. This straw of ice has broken the camel's back and nearly all archaeologists of the Bronze Age Aegean now concede that the 17th-century date is correct.

A section of Chapter VII is an inquest on the debates in an attempt to discover why archaeologists should cling so long to such a flimsy hypothesis in the face of so much apparently objective contrary evidence. Such inquests are generally considered to be in bad taste as it is thought in such circumstances that 'anyone can make a mistake'. My purposes in making it are, firstly, to try to warn against such reification of hypotheses in the future and, secondly, to make conventionality have its costs. At present, academic sins of commission are punished ferociously, while there is a great tolerance towards those of omission which involve uncritical acceptance of the status quo. I want to do what I can to lessen the disparity between the treatments of the two kinds of error.

The second half of the chapter is concerned with three traditions that appear to have preserved folk memories of the eruption. The first of these is that of the Bible. In the Book of Exodus, a number of the phenomena associated with the departure of the Israelites from Egypt have long been seen to have strong suggestions of volcanic activity. These are 'the darkness that could be felt' and the 'pillar of cloud' by day and the 'pillar of fire' by night. Above all, there is the parting of the Red Sea and its rushing back to drown the pharaoh's army, which would seem strikingly similar to the effects of a volcanic tidal wave or *tsunami* of the type that appears to have taken place on the Mediterranean coasts of Egypt and Palestine as a result of the Thera eruption.

The tracing back of these legends to 1628 BC rather than to 1450 or 1500 tends to reinforce the already strong and ancient hypothesis that the biblical tradition of an Israelite captivity or sojourn in Egypt is based on a folk memory of the Hyksos rule in Egypt, in which people living in the later Israel clearly played a prominent part. The correspondence is not precise as the expulsion of the Hyksos took place around 1570 BC, that is, over fifty years after the Thera eruption. Thus, the two dramatic events would seem to have been conflated in the legend. Nevertheless, 1628 BC is considerably closer to the Hyksos retreat than the lower dates previously given for the eruption. The notion that these seismic catastrophes were helpful to the Israelites is clearly linked to the fact that their god Yahweh was a god of earthquakes and all kinds of natural disturbances. The Hyksos' dedication to Yahweh's Egyptian counterpart Seth shows that this cult antedates the eruption. Nevertheless, there is every reason to suppose that the eruption provided powerful reinforcement of it.

The second tradition considered is the Egypto-Greek one reported by Plato in his dialogues the *Timaeus* and the *Kritias*. This is the dramatic story and description of Atlantis, allegedly told to the Athenian statesman Solon when he visited the Egyptian capital of Sais around 600 BC. According to this, Atlantis was a rich and magnificent island in the Atlantic, where a confederation of kings had gathered a huge army to conquer all Africa except for Egypt and all Europe except for Athens, which led a heroic resistance to them. Atlantis was dramatically destroyed by earthquakes and floods.

There seem to be two conflations here, one geographical and one historical. For some time scholars have seen a connection between the fiery and watery destruction and the Thera eruption. Nevertheless, Plato is quite explicit that his Atlantis was beyond the Pillars of Hercules – the Straits of Gibraltar – therefore in the Atlantic. I accept that there is a reference to Thera here and that the confusion comes over the name 'Atlantis'. I argue that the stem *Atla-* found in Atlantis, Atlantic and the mountains and giant called Atlas comes from the Egyptian itrw, the name of the Nile and of other large bodies of water, especially the river that was believed to encompass the world. It was, in fact, a close semantic equivalent to Okeanos (ocean), a name which appears to have a Mesopotamian origin. Thus, Atlantis as a sea could well be the setting of Thera in the Mediterranean, though it is possible that this was combined with a vague sense of America beyond the Atlantic Ocean.

The temporal confusion is also linked to this, as *ìtrw* is a synonym for the late Egyptian borrowing *ym* from Semitic *yåm* (sea), used to describe the 'Peoples of the *Sea*' who attacked Egypt in the 12th century BC. Indeed, the passage from Plato portraying the plot against the civilized world in the form of an invasion launched from Atlantis strikingly resembles the inscription written by Ramessēs III describing the 'conspiracy [made] in their islands' by the 'Peoples of the Sea'. If one associates the return of the Heraklids or 'Dorian Invasion' with the Aegean tribal movements in the wake of the invasion of the Peoples of the Sea, then Athens did indeed stand up against the northern invaders, although it would be an exaggeration to claim that it led or saved the world by this. There would seem, then, to be a doubling in Solon's story between what modern Egyptologists call the 2nd and the 3rd Intermediate Periods, between the volcanic destruction of Thera and the Hyksos eruption in the 2nd and the political turmoil of the 3rd.

Interestingly, however, the 3rd Intermediate Period also contained a major volcanic event in the third eruption of the biggest Icelandic volcano Hekla in 1159 BC. Irish and Scottish archaeologists and palaeoclimatologists have recently shown that Northwest Britain was virtually depopulated as a result of Hekla III, although it is also clear that living conditions had been deteriorating for some decades before. Although the situation was less clear-cut and there was no similar overwhelming catastrophe in the sheltered Mediterranean, the climatic pattern may have been similar there – a deterioration leading to migrations and disturbances from the end of the 13th century and a breakdown near the middle of the 12th.

These two eruptions of 1628 and 1159 BC appear to have had an even more dramatic and long-lasting effect on China. Chapter VII contains some excursions there, which focus on the fascinating climatological work of the Chinese American scientist Kevin Pang. Pang and his colleagues have been using Chinese records to help establish meteorological records for the past four thousand years. For the period since the 9th century BC, the descriptions of 'extraordinary' natural phenomena, including many that appear to be the result of volcanic eruptions, can be dated with some accuracy. Before that century, the work is fraught with difficulty because there is considerable controversy over dating. I agree with Pang, however, that it would seem best to date the fall of Xia to the end of the 17th century BC and that of Shang to the end of the 12th.

Pang's chief thesis – based on this chronology – is that the falls of the first two Chinese dynasties, the Xia and the Shang, correlate with the eruptions of Thera and Hekla III. Hence many of the extraordinary phenomena reported in traditional sources in association with dynastic collapse – double suns, pale suns, dry mists, frosts in summer, etc. – should be taken seriously. Until recently, most scholars have understood these reports of unnatural happenings to have been invented or exaggerated with the political purpose of demonstrating that the old dynasty had lost the 'Mandate of Heaven' and therefore deserved to have been overthrown by the new one under whom the reports were written.

Now it would seem that the reports may have contained some truth and that the eruptions and the meteorological 'prodigies' they created, as well as their economic consequences in lost harvests, may indeed have been necessary, though not sufficient – there were of course other social and political factors – causes of the falls of the Xia and Shang.

The probability that the reports are accurate raises the possibility that the basis of the texts describing the fall of the Xia Dynasty and the rise of Shang may come not from around the time of Confucius in the 6th century BC, as is commonly supposed, but from much earlier, in the 12th century after the fall of Shang or even from their purported date the 17th century. In either case, it indicates that Chinese gentlemen were thinking in 'Confucian' terms five hundred years or more before the philosopher's birth. Thus, Confucius should be taken seriously when he claimed that he was a transmitter rather than an originator.

This re-dating has even wider consequences because it removes one of the 'legs' of the theory of the 'Axial Age'. According to this, by chance or providence something extraordinary happened to the world in the 6th and 5th centuries BC. It was then that true religion, philosophy and science were supposed to have begun: in China there were Confucius and Laozi [Laotzu], in India Buddha, in Persia Zoroaster; Judaism was created in Babylonia and most important of all there was the 'Greek Miracle'. Now it seems that Confucius was firmly based in the culture of the Early Zhou in the 12th and 11th centuries and was clearly drawing on still older traditions. Buddha was reacting against Hinduism, which had existed for over a thousand years before his time. Zoroaster himself is now placed in the 2nd millennium BC and much if not most of the Bible was written long before the 6th century. In fact, the only 'revolution' that took place at this time was the Greek one and this, I am convinced, was deeply indebted to much earlier Egyptian and Levantine religious, philosophical *and scientific* traditions.

It is the relative strength of the Greek case that gives the game away. The concept of the 'Axial Age' allows Greece, and hence Europeans, to be in at the beginning of world civilization. Thus, the great Bronze Age cultures of Asia and Africa, upon which not only the techniques but the spirit and reason of Classical civilization depended, were, and had to be, denied.

The role of the eruptions of Thera and Hekla III in the falls of Xia and Shang appears to have had a crucially important long-term effect on Chinese history. I go on beyond Kevin Pang to argue that these two eruptions, roughly five hundred years apart, played a significant role in establishing the historical pattern of the dynastic succession, something that is missing for instance in the other great East Asian empire, Japan. I also believe that the clear signals the eruptions gave indicating that the Mandate of Heaven had been removed were important in establishing the tradition of justified rebellion against 'illegitimate authority' in both China and Vietnam. In these two countries the tradition of the Mandate of Heaven, with its built-in possibility of removal, was accepted and incorporated into a strong peasant tradition of revolt. Thus, whereas peasant millenarian movements have existed in most societies, in China and Vietnam they have been linked to the possibility of political change in this world as opposed to the next.

In the 19th century AD, when Japanese scholars wanted a translation for the European term 'revolution' they chose *kakumei* (Removal of the Mandate), and its Chinese form *geming* maintained the connection between the traditional and the Western concepts. There is no doubt that by the catastrophic late 1940s the Kuomintang was widely considered to have lost the Mandate of Heaven. Thus, the Communists to whom the Mandate had been given, riding on a wave of social and national revolutionary enthusiasm, had a traditional licence or even a duty to remould society. It was this double authority that allowed Mao and his supporters to carry through a successful collectivization of land at breakneck speed and to launch the Great Leap Forward and the Cultural Revolution of unparalleled radicalism. Thus, China today still bears the marks of the Thera eruption over thirty-five hundred years ago.

Chapter VIII is concerned with the Hyksos, the people from the northeast, who invaded or infiltrated Egypt at the end of the Middle Kingdom and who controlled at least Lower Egypt for over a century and a half until they were expelled by the Egypto-Nubian 18th Dynasty at some point near 1570 BC. The first problem considered is that of chronology, which is very uncertain from the Egyptian records. I argue, on the basis of Palestinian ceramic periods, that the Hyksos had arrived in at least the Eastern Delta by 1740 BC. The second problem is that of the ethnicity of the Hyksos. I approach this by considering the historiography of the Hyksos. The standard classical text on this, written by the Egyptian priest Manetho, described the Hyksos as 'from the regions of the East, invaders of obscure race' who invaded and ruthlessly conquered Egypt. As mentioned above, from at least Hellenistic times writers have associated the Hyksos rule in Egypt with the Israelite captivity or sojourn in Egypt so that, until the end of the 19th century, it appears to have been assumed that the invaders were Israelites or Proto-Israelites, in any event Semitic speakers.

With the systematization of anti-Semitism, however, this picture of northerners sweeping down on prosperous river valleys seemed typically Aryan and not at all Semitic, if – as late 19th-century scholars did – one discounts the Arabs for the purpose of this argument. This view of the Hyksos had the backing of Manetho's statement that they were of 'obscure race' and of an 18th-Dynasty inscription which was read as stating that the Hyksos' capital contained ꜥꜣmw, the standard Egyptian term for the Semitic-speakers of Syro-Palestine, with the Šmꜣw, 'wanderers' or 'foreigners in their midst'. This was interpreted as an indication that the Hyksos had a non-Semitic core.

German scholars, struck by apparent similarities with the sudden Mongol and Turkish conquests, suggested that the Hyksos were an 'Inner Asian' nation. This was quickly identified with the newly discovered Hurrians, speakers of a language that was neither Semitic nor Indo-European, who were supposed to have migrated to Northern Mesopotamia at about this time from beyond the Caucasus. We now know that Hurrians were present in Mesopotamia from the 3rd millennium and probably much earlier still. Scholarly enthusiasm for the Hurrian kingdom of Mitanni that was contemporaneous with the 18th Dynasty became even greater when it was discovered that some Mitanni royal and divine names and chariot-driving terms were Indo-Iranian if not Indo-Aryan. This strongly suggested to them that the kingdom had been formed by an Aryan 'master race' whose dominance was associated with chariots. Their suggestions were strengthened by the fact that, while there was little or no information on Syro-Palestine from the 17th century, when the region appears again in Egyptian reports in the 15th century there seem to have been many Hurrians and a certain number of warriors with Indo-Iranian names in the region.

These suggestions were resisted by a number of Egyptologists, who objected to this poaching on their territory and held the new professional dislike of dramatic or far-reaching events. Some of them also disliked the anti-Semitic implications of the introduction of Hurrians and Aryans into the Hyksos. They were able to back their objections

by pointing out that most of the Hyksos names have Semitic etymologies and there were no Indo-European names or, as far as could
be told, Hurrian ones.

The debate continued in the 1920s and 1930s along the general
lines that Middle Europeans and ancient historians believed in Hurrian and Aryan components of the Hyksos, while Egyptologists of
other nationalities stressed their overwhelmingly Semitic nature. Most
of these, however, accepted some Hurrian, though usually not Indo-
Iranian, presence. The revulsion after the Second World War against
anti-Semitism and theories of an Aryan 'master race' appears to have
had a major impact on attitudes towards the Hyksos.

Scholars now tended to dismiss the possibility of Hurrian, let alone
Indo-European, elements among the Hyksos. They also challenged
the belief that there had been an invasion, preferring to postulate a
slow, undramatic Semitic migration or infiltration into Egypt. They
were supported by the current low or middle chronologies, according
to which the admitted Hurrian expansion in Syria and Mesopotamia
took place only in the 17th century, which made it too late to have had
any connection with the original Hyksos movement. This meant that
the few scholars who persisted with the notion of a Hurrian component now had to make a distinction between two types of Hyksos, the
earlier Semitic infiltrators and the later Hurrian-led conquerors.

If one accepts the 'long' chronology for Mesopotamia, the attested
Hurrian expansion is now placed in the first half of the 18th century,
that is, just before the Hyksos arrival in Egypt. Even if one does not,
parallels from the emergences of Islam, the Mongols or the Taiping in
China suggest that it is quite possible for powerful forces to emerge
quite suddenly in a year or two. Either way, much as I applaud the
political inclinations of those who have tried to deny a Hurrian or
Indo-Iranian influence on the Hyksos, I think they are wrong, and the
evidence does indicate a Hurrian and possibly even an Indo-Iranian
element among the Hyksos and, what is more, this element was probably associated with chariotry.

Here, then, we would seem to have a clear case of an 'Aryan Model'.
I have never denied that there have from time to time been conquests
by northern barbarians; indeed, I believe that this was the case in
North India, where there was a strong tradition for it and it fits the
later distribution of languages. The argument in *Black Athena* is simply
that it is implausible for Greece, which has no such traditions or linguistic distribution.

Having accepted the presence of Hurrians and Indo-Iranian speakers among the Hyksos, there is absolutely no doubt that these con-

querors of Egypt were overwhelmingly Semitic-speaking. Most of the Hyksos names are Semitic and excavation of the Hyksos capital at Tell el Daba'a in the East Delta demonstrates that their material culture was Syro-Palestinian, or rather a mixture of Egyptian and Levantine. Thus, just as Attila's hordes were overwhelmingly made up of the Romans' old neighbours the Germans and it was Germanic not Hunnish culture – or barbarism – that came to dominate most of Western Europe, the net effect of the Hyksos invasions in Egypt was to introduce new Hyksos weaponry but Syro-Palestinian culture and language.

Chapter IX is concerned with what I see as the continuation of the Hyksos drive, this time into the Aegean. I am not the first writer to suggest this, as it was proposed by the powerful German ancient historian Eduard Meyer and some others at the beginning of this century. More recently, the Cambridge archaeologist Frank Stubbings has argued that the Shaft Graves at Mycenae were the burials of Hyksos princes. In general, however, this view has been out of fashion over the last fifty years.

In this chapter, I try to revive their contentions in the light of discoveries over the past twenty years. The most important development has been the upward re-dating of many ceramic periods because of the new date for the Thera eruption. These new dates put the breaks in Aegean material culture associated with a very special kind of Near Eastern art and technology in the last quarter of the 18th century BC. This means that these breaks and innovations are to be associated with the Hyksos. Therefore, at this point, I cannot follow the Ancient Model, according to which the Phoenician/Egyptian Hyksos arrived in Greece after they had been expelled from Egypt, which was around 1570 BC. I argue that the Near Eastern settlements in the Aegean took place near the beginning of the Hyksos rule in Egypt around 1730 BC rather than at its end. This adjustment is in fact the second 'revision' of the Revised Ancient Model, the first being the acceptance that the Indo-European basis of Greek speech must have arrived in some way and at some time from the north.

The first section of Chapter IX is concerned with a change that took place in Crete around 1730 BC. At this time, all the palaces of Crete were destroyed and were rapidly rebuilt. Although there was essential cultural continuity, there were sufficient differences to make most historians distinguish between an Old Palace Period and a New Palace Period before and after this break. There is also a general consensus that, although the Old Palaces were themselves heavily influenced by the Near East, the influences appear even more strongly in the New Palaces.

Although most scholars see continuity from Cretan metallurgy, most also agree that the weapons of the new period were heavily influenced by Near Eastern and particularly Syrian technology. It was in the ceramic period Middle Minoan III (1730–1675 BC) that the sword was introduced to Crete. There is some discussion of the plausible Egyptian and Semitic etymologies for the two chief Greek words for 'sword', *xiphos* and *phasganon,* neither of which has Indo-European cognates or related words. At the same time as the sword, the other new 'wonder weapon' of the Late Bronze Age, the chariot, also seems to have arrived in Crete.

In art, one finds a style virtually unknown before in either the Aegean or the Near East. The new style is epitomized by a new convention, the 'flying leap', in which animals give the impression of fast movement by stretching their legs in the air to the front and back. In general there is an emphasis on vitality, flight and speed. This style also appears on some of the few decorated Hyksos objects found in Egypt and Syro-Palestine.

Two important motifs introduced at this time were the winged sphinx and the griffin. Although the sphinx originated in Egypt much earlier, the winged ones appearing in Crete at the end of the 18th century BC were of a Syrian type and have been specifically linked to the Hyksos.

The griffin, a lion with the head of a hawk or eagle, was also introduced to Crete during the ceramic period Middle Minoan III, in a specifically Syrian form. The griffin was frequently represented for the next five hundred years throughout the Aegean, fighting or hunting in the 'flying style'. This is not simply a matter of art history but one with strong suggestions of political importance as griffins flanked the throne at the greatest Cretan palace at Knossos and the Mycenaean one at Pylos. Thus, like the winged sphinx, it would seem to have been a symbol of Hyksos royalty. This could have been borrowed by local Cretan rulers. Borrowing would also explain the greatly increased quantity and quality of weapons belonging to types current in the Near East. It would seem more likely, however, that they were Hyksos themselves. This is not merely because of the destruction of all the Cretan palaces at this stage and the increase of Levantine influence and Hyksos symbols. It is also because at the layer of destruction of the Old Palace at Knossos a number of sealings have been found showing the new, lively artistic style and two – apparently royal – portraits, one of a young prince and the other of a bearded man, the only contemporary parallels for which are a striking vase in the shape of a head from a Hyksos grave in Jericho and the masks found in the Shaft Graves at Mycenae.

All in all, while there is no proof of a Hyksos conquest or conquests of Crete at this time, the number of loose ends such a hypothesis would tie up make it economical to follow Eduard Meyer and the other historians who have postulated it. There is also circumstantial evidence for this from elsewhere in the Aegean.

The second section of Chapter IX is concerned with the city now known as Akrotiri on Thera that was covered by the great eruption. Only a small part of the city has been excavated, but what has been revealed is sensational. It was clearly a prosperous Mediterranean town of a basic type still found today. Houses with two storeys have been recovered, full of what are normally perishable objects. It is thus a Bronze Age Pompeii, but with better preservation. As at Pompeii, the most sensational finds have been a number of frescoes, which tell us a great deal about the artistic techniques but even more fascinatingly about society on Thera in the decades before the eruption. They portray not merely a rich, sophisticated and stratified society but also one that was extremely cosmopolitan, in which there was knowledge not merely of Crete but also of Africa and the Levant. Experts were surprised at the depth of Egyptian influence, particularly in the ceremonial boats. They were also puzzled by the white robes with borders worn by the upper classes portrayed. I believe that good parallels for them can be found from Syria.

The art historians also noted that, although the paintings and the culture they portrayed were heavily indebted to Crete, there was something 'Mycenaean' about them. There were armed men with what were seen as typically Mainland Greek helmets and there were scenes that resembled those portrayed in *niello* – a metal enamelling technique – found in the Shaft Graves at Mycenae. I believe, however, that both the techniques and the scenes are more usefully seen as belonging to the 'Hyksos international' culture.

The cosmopolitan nature of this society was surprising enough when it was believed that the Thera eruption and hence the date of the city were in the late 16th or 15th centuries. With the re-dating of the eruption, we now know that the frescoes have recorded aspects of society in the 17th century, that is to say, approximately a century after the Hyksos conquest of Crete postulated here. Such a hypothesis would in fact fit very well with many of the previously puzzling aspects of the frescoes, the cosmopolitanism and Egyptian influence, the warfare and 'Mycenaean' influence, as well as the royal symbol of the griffin represented in one of the murals.

In Classical times, there were many traditions that the Cycladic islands, of which Thera is one, had been dominated by Crete. There is no reason to suppose that there was only one period in which this was

the case. Nevertheless, a number of scholars do believe that the end of
the Middle and the beginning of the Late Bronze Age was a period of
Cretan domination. This would seem plausible. However, if Crete itself was ruled by Hyksos princes at this time, it would suggest Hyksos
domination of the Cyclades during the late 18th and 17th centuries
BC. Did their activities take them further north?

There is little doubt that the most sensational discoveries of Bronze
Age culture ever made in Mainland Greece were those of the German
entrepreneur and archaeological genius Heinrich Schliemann at Mycenae. His digging of the Shaft Graves at the city produced what were
the first and remain the most spectacular revelations of the culture
that has since become known as 'Mycenaean'. The goods buried with
the early rulers of Mycenae are quite extraordinary. The immediate
and lasting impression is one of violence and barbarism, huge quantities of weapons, some beautifully decorated with *niello* and gold-leaf
masks of striking bearded warriors.

Closer examination reveals an extraordinary eclecticism. The pottery belongs to the local Middle Helladic tradition but almost everything else is exotic and apparently new to Greece. The greatest
influence comes from Crete but some things come from much farther
afield: amber from the Baltic, rock crystal from the Alps, ostrich eggs
from Africa. There are also a number of objects showing Syro-
Palestinian and Egyptian influence. However, the latter are chiefly of
an irregular kind that I believe are best described as 'Off-Egyptian' or
'Hyksos international'. The origins of such a heterogeneous material
culture must clearly have been very complicated and any historical
scheme that attempts to explain them must be equally so.

The pattern proposed here is rather similar to that of the Norman
Conquest of England. Vikings from Scandinavia seized Normandy
and, after a century or more, 'Normans' invaded and conquered England. The effect of this conquest was not to bring Scandinavian language and culture to England but to introduce the languages and
cultures of their French and Italian followers and administrators.
There is a difference in that by 1066 the Normans had become culturally French, whereas it would seem that, as the Hyksos expansion was
much faster, the chiefs and princes still retained many aspects of their
material culture and presumably of their language too. Nevertheless,
the great degree of Semitization of the Hyksos in Egypt strongly suggests that, like other rapidly expanding barbarian 'empires', those for
instance of the Huns, Mongols and Moghuls, their own culture had
very little impact but they introduced that of others. Thus, the Huns
helped bring German culture into Western Europe; the Mongols took

East Asian culture to Iran and Europe; and the Turkic Moghuls brought Persian culture into India. In each case they transformed the cultures of the receiving regions.

The hypothesis proposed here is that the royalty buried in the Shaft Graves and the other early Mycenaean tombs were Hyksos invaders from Syria, who probably spoke Hurrian and possibly even Indo-Iranian. However, the majority of the ruling class were Levantine Semitic-speakers together with significant numbers of Egyptians and Cretans, most of whom probably spoke a Semitic language themselves. All three of these ethnic groups were thoroughly permeated by Egyptian culture, especially in the area of religion. Thus, on the one hand, continuity of pottery styles and the fact that Greek is an Indo-European language demonstrate that the local population and culture persisted. On the other hand, the break of material culture and the new exotic influences, combined with Greek traditions of colonization from Egypt and Phoenicia, indicate that there were foreign conquerors from Egypt and the Levant ruling parts or all of Greece up to the arrival of the Pelopids from Anatolia in the 15th or 14th centuries, and in the case of Thebes the original Phoenician Dynasty survived until the fall of that city in the 13th century.

According to the historical scheme proposed here, although there were native influences and Anatolian ones after 1400 BC, what we consider to be the 'Mycenaean' artistic style is best seen as a survival of the Hyksos international style that arose in Syria in the 18th century. This style largely – but not completely – disappeared in Egypt and Crete where there were rich and sophisticated native traditions. By contrast, less developed Middle Helladic Mainland Greece provided less cultural opposition, so leaving the Hyksos style to become the characteristic style of the Aegean in the Late Bronze Age.

As far as language is concerned, there is little doubt in my mind that Egyptian and Semitic words and names were current in the Aegean in the 3rd millennium BC. It is certain that Greek borrowed massively from these languages during the period of Egyptian dominance of the East Mediterranean in the Late Bronze Age after 1470 BC as well as in the Geometric, Archaic and Classical periods from 950 to 300 BC. Nevertheless, the centuries between 1730 and 1530, which are frequently seen to be the most likely period for the creation of Greek as a language, would seem to be ones when Greece was largely ruled by speakers of West Semitic and Egyptian. There is virtually no doubt that these two languages had high status in the region at that time.

Chapter X is concerned with contemporary documentary evidence, that is to say, Egyptian and Levantine reports of contacts with the Aegean made during the Bronze Age and Aegean references to contacts with Egypt and Syro-Palestine.

The first section is on Egyptian records and, here as elsewhere, it is necessary to determine what the writers meant by various place names they used. For instance, there is the name Mnws used at least since the 12th Dynasty for a foreign country to the northwest, which was once associated with the Fnḫw, probably the Phoenicians. Mnws has been linked by some modern scholars to Minos and Crete. The situation is not at all straightforward. The derivations of Minos from the Egyptian god Min and the first pharaoh Min/Mēnēs are discussed in Chapter IV, and there is the further possibility that many of the place names called Minoa in the Southern Aegean derive from the West Semitic Mᶜnuhåh (resting place). Nevertheless, there is a strong possibility that Mnws does refer to parts of Crete, in which case documentary evidence suggests that princes from Crete accepted the suzerainty of Sesōstris, which is something other evidence discussed in earlier chapters would also seem to indicate.

The name Kftiw or Kaftu is much less problematic. Despite repeated attempts to challenge the location, because the princes of Kftiw portrayed in tomb paintings seem too 'Asiatic', there is no reason to overthrow the conventional wisdom that the name referred to Crete, which has now been confirmed by a statue base of the 18th-Dynasty pharaoh Amenōphis III on which Kftiw has been used as the heading of a number of place names in the Aegean. The earliest reference to Kftiw as a distant trading partner comes from the 1st Intermediate Period 2450–2100 BC. The most frequent use of Kftiw comes in the 18th Dynasty, especially after the 1470s when Tuthmōsis III conquered much of Syro-Palestine and when princes of Kftiw are shown offering tribute to the pharaohs.

This image has caused some discomfort to modern scholars, who have found a number of arguments to deny the truth of such Egyptian claims. I see no reason to doubt them if only because Egyptian dominance of the Levant would require any sophisticated and/or ambitious Aegean ruler to come to terms with the pharaoh.

There may, however, be more to it than that, as Tuthmōsis claimed to have 'trussed the Nine Bows, the isles in the Midst of the W3d wr, the Ḥ3w nbwt and the rebel foreign countries.' From this it would seem that Egyptian naval expeditions – and we know that Egypt had a navy by this time – had sailed to the Aegean. The name W3d wr (Great Green) meant 'sea' from early times, but by the New Kingdom it was restricted to the Mediterranean and often to the Aegean specifically.

Ḥꜣw nbwt (Behind the Islands), which appears in the *Pyramid Texts* in the 3rd millennium, was seen by the Egyptologist Alan Gardiner as 'a sufficiently accurate description of the Aegean Sea'. This was challenged by another Egyptologist and specialist in Egypto-Aegean relations, Jean Vercoutter. Vercoutter argued that this identification was impossible because it required too sophisticated a knowledge of geography at the time when the *Pyramid Texts* were largely composed, in the 4th millennium. I have no difficulty with the idea of Predynastic Egyptians' having this general sense of geography. However, it is possible that the term was interpolated nearer the time that the *Texts* were inscribed towards the end of the Old Kingdom, when it is clear from other evidence, discussed in Chapter III, that Egyptian officials were aware of the Aegean.

In any event, we know that Ḥꜣw nbw was used to describe the Aegean and Greece from New Kingdom times. In fact, after the reign of Tuthmōsis III, in 1450 BC, Ḥꜣw nbw began to replace Kftiw. This, together with the fact that in Ptolemaic times the name Kftiw was used for Phoenicians, suggests that Kftiw was used to describe Crete at a time when a significant, if not dominant, proportion of the island's population was Semitic-speaking.

Another set of names used to represent 'Greece' in New Kingdom Egypt was the cluster Tꜣnꜣy, or Tanaya; Dꜣ-in, Dene or Denyen. There is no doubt that this is the same as Danaoi or Danaan, Homer's most frequent name for the Greeks. There is even a link through the Egyptian sign used with Tꜣnꜣy of a decrepit old man. On the Egyptian side, this is linked to the root *tni* (old, decrepit); on the Greek side, it fits perfectly with the descriptions of Danaos, who, according to tradition, colonized Argos in Greece from Egypt. Danaos was portrayed as old and decrepit. His positive attributes as a colonizer and irrigator also fit a pun with the Egyptian *dni* (allocate, irrigate) which in turn is related to the Semitic *d(y)n(n)* (judge). Although ancient writers clearly perceived these connections, the original name cannot simply be derived from these etymologies as the name Da-ne[ki] appears with apparent reference to the far west in a Mesopotamian text dating back to *c.* 2500 BC.

In the period between 1470 and 1250 Egypt appears to have had both direct dealings with Tꜣnꜣy and indirect ones through Levantine princes. Chiefs of Tꜣnꜣy are pictured in a tomb painting as having brought tribute to Tuthmōsis III and on the statue base of Amenōphis III mentioned above Kftiw and Tꜣnꜣy are the two headings used for a list of Aegean city names.

Dene or Denyen was also the name of one of the Peoples of the Sea

who ravaged Egypt and the Levant in the 12th century BC. This too
has been associated with the Homeric Danaans. It has also been linked
to the biblical tribe of Dan, who can plausibly be seen as having come
originally from the Israelite incorporation of one of the Peoples of
the Sea.

There are also references to the Aegean in Mesopotamian and Syrian texts. The use of the name Da-ne^{ki} has been mentioned above. In
the same position in a parallel list from the Syrian city of Ebla there is
the name Am-ni^{ki} which could well be linked to Amnissos, the name
of the port of Knossos, which is known to be very ancient. An 18th-
century list from the city of Mari on the Upper Euphrates refers to
Kaptara (Crete) as a trading partner and as a centre of manufacture
of luxury goods.

There is a surprising absence of references to Greeks in the considerable 14th- and 13th-century records from the Syrian port of Ugarit.
This, I believe, can partly be explained as the result of a blockade
against the Mycenaean kingdoms by the Hittite kings who at the time
had suzerainty over Ugarit. Not all trade was blocked, however, and
there is a report of an Ugaritic *tamkarum* (officially licensed merchant)
who was trading regularly with Crete.

The Ugaritic texts do, however, point to another type of contact
between the Levant and Greece. Many of the Ugaritic legends and
hymns show striking parallels to early Greek ones and often provide
important 'bridges' between Greek and biblical themes. Thus at this
level too there would appear to have been a common East Mediterranean culture, at least by the Late Bronze Age.

The Aegean has Bronze Age documents, those surviving in Linear
A and Linear B, both of which can now be read. These were the syllabic scripts of Minoan and Mycenaean civilizations, which were used
in many places in the Aegean but particularly in Crete. Although
there is still considerable debate as to the linguistic family of the language written in Linear A, there is no doubt that it contained a considerable number of Semitic words. These do not cover merely luxury
goods, but such staples as grain and grapes and such basic words as
'all' or 'total'. Their presence is either because the language was Semitic, as I am inclined to believe, or because of massive Semitic loans
into the unknown Cretan language. In either event they indicate close
connections between Crete and the Levant.

Linear B is a very similar script used to write Greek. Before the decipherment of Linear B, it was believed that the few admitted Semitic
loan words in Greek, such as *chitōn* (a form of dress) and *chrysos* (gold),
had been introduced in the 7th century BC. Now it is known that they

were already present in the 14th or 13th centuries. Thus, even if one does not accept the many other loan words from Semitic and Egyptian, which I believe to be present in Linear B texts, the texts provide firm evidence of lexical borrowing, and hence cultural contact, during the Bronze Age.

The economy and society of the Mycenaean palaces revealed by the texts also show considerable and detailed correspondences with those of Near Eastern palaces. Even the measurements and bureaucratic formulae used in the texts demonstrate specific borrowings from Egypt and Southwest Asia. Furthermore, there are dozens of personal names in Linear B texts with plausible Semitic, Hurrian and Egyptian etymologies. These include Aikupitio; Aigyptos, 'Memphite' or 'Egyptian'; Misirajo, the Semitic Mṣry, 'Egyptian'; Aradajo, probably 'Man of [the Phoenician city of] Arwad'; and Turijajo and Turijo, 'Tyrian'. Such names confirm the picture provided by an Egyptian papyrus of the 17th century BC on 'How to write the names of Kftiw' which showed a thoroughly heterogeneous population on the island. Similarly the personal name Pꜣ Kfty (the Cretan) appears in Egypt in the 16th century. These scraps of documentary information from Egypt, the Levant and the Aegean all point in the same direction and indicate a considerable amount of contact and ethnic mixture around the East Mediterranean in the Bronze Age at least as early as the 17th century BC but probably from long before that.

Chapter XI is concerned with the later Mycenaean period in Greece. This civilization lasted a long time, from the 18th century BC to the 12th, according to the chronology used in this book. It is also clear there was considerable cultural continuity. Similar artistic styles and motifs, notably the sphinx and the griffin, continued to be used throughout the whole period. The archaeological evidence is spotty so it is impossible to be sure of economic and social structures in Greece during the earlier centuries. We know from the Shaft Graves and other tombs that the early Mycenaeans were concerned with, if not obsessed by, war. However, the Thera murals from the 17th century show a considerable peaceful sophistication of society, at least on the Cycladic islands, where there is also archaeological evidence of relatively rich urbanized society.

Probably because of cultural continuity and rebuilding, which leaves fewer traces of the previous building than destruction, there have been no finds of early Mycenaean royal dwellings – as opposed to tombs. However, a considerable number of palaces have been found from the later part of the period. From the end of the Mycenaean age there are tablets written in Linear B, which, as mentioned

above, provide considerable documentary evidence on the economy
and social structure of the palaces.

The picture emerging from this pattern of evidence might suggest
a violent heroic society settling down to civilian bureaucracy. The actual situation was clearly not so simple, however: not only does the
evidence from Thera indicate peaceful sophistication in the 17th century but also there is the fact that the latest Mycenaean palaces were
normally fortified. Thus it would seem likely that for most of the Mycenaean period Greece was controlled by a number of kingdoms in
which the civil bureaucracies of the palaces coexisted with considerable warfare among the kingdoms and a warrior ethos. The nearest
parallel I can see to this is in Japan after the 8th century AD, where the
exquisite cultivation of the court contrasted with the brutality of the
'feudal' or gangsterlike *bushido*, the cult of military virtue.

Interestingly, despite the later emphasis on the magnificence of the
earlier period, Greek tradition retained a far greater concern with the
warlike activities of the 'heroic age' than it did with any economic or
cultural successes of the Late Bronze Age. This is no doubt partly because bloody deeds of derring-do always make better stories. But it
would also seem to be the result of the lack of civilization and the continuation and intensification of warfare, loyalty and treachery after
the fall of the palaces in the 12th century, in the Dark Ages when most
of the legends were shaped.

There is no doubt that the three centuries with which Chapter XI is
concerned, 1550–1250, are the period in the Bronze Age for which
there are most indications of Egyptian and Levantine contacts with
the Aegean from both the documentary and the archaeological evidence. However, until recently it has been difficult to correlate the
two because the periods in which the Egyptian documents indicate
close relations with the Aegean – the later reign of King Tuthmōsis III (1470–1450 BC) and the reigns of Amenōphis III and his
son Akhenaton (1419–1364 BC) – are not those where conventional
wisdom puts the ceramic periods for which the archaeological evidence indicates the greatest contact. These are Late Helladic IIIA,
conventionally seen as 1400–1275 BC, and Late Helladic IIIB from
1275–1180. Now, however, according to chronologies established on
the basis of new synchronisms with Egypt and the updating of all Late
Bronze Age Aegean ceramic periods required by the re-dating of the
Thera eruption, the beginning of LHIIIA should be raised to between 1490 and 1470 BC and LHIIIB to from 1370 to 1220 BC. As the
chronology of New Kingdom Egypt should stay constant, this means
that the historical and archaeological evidence for close contact of

Egypt and the Levant with the Aegean are now synchronized and present a coherent picture.

The re-dating also requires a change in the periodization of Cretan history. Ancient historians have long been struck by a feature from a tomb painting from the end of the reign of Tuthmōsis III (1460–1450 BC), in which a Cretan bringing tribute to the pharaoh has had his Minoan kilt over-painted with one of a Mycenaean style. Since the recognition from Linear B tablets that Greek was the dominant language in 14th- or at least 13th-century Crete, the repainting has been used to mark the invasion or some other kind of arrival of Mycenaean Greeks in Crete. According to conventional wisdom, 1450 marked the beginning of the Late Minoan II ceramic period. This seemed to tally nicely with the fact that at about this time the provincial palaces in Crete were destroyed and administration for the whole island was centralized at Knossos. Other corroborative arguments which were also used, such as the introduction of Shaft Graves to Crete at this time, have since been abandoned. The arrival of the Mycenaeans c. 1450 was also necessary because Sir Arthur Evans had declared that the palace at Knossos itself had been destroyed at the beginning of Late Minoan IIIA, which was seen as at c. 1380 BC. Thus time was needed for the establishment of Greek as the official language of the island's capital.

However, for several decades a heretical band of scholars led by the linguist Leonard Palmer has been arguing that the palace at Knossos survived until the end of the 13th century and that the Linear B tablets from it should be dated to the end of that century, not two hundred years earlier. Recent interpretations of the archaeological evidence now seem to back Palmer on this, hence this requirement for the arrival of the Greeks in Crete no longer exists, as they could now have come at any time before 1300 BC.

Nevertheless, the Egyptian evidence for a change of rulers, which is also suggested by the dropping of the name Kftiw and the increased use of Tni, makes a strong case for the transfer of power on Crete around the middle of the 15th century. The question still remains, however, at what ceramic period did the change take place. LMII pottery develops from its predecessor LMIB and into its successor LMIIIA. Thus, pottery cannot be used to mark the transfer of power. In any event, all the other forms of evidence suggest an essential cultural continuity on the island at this stage despite any change of language. The simplest thing to do would seem to be to retain the absolute date or shift it slightly up to c. 1470 but to see this in ceramic terms as the beginning of Late Minoan and Late Helladic IIIA. It is the pottery of this pan-Aegean style that has been found throughout the Mediterranean and beyond but particularly in the areas known to have been under Egyptian control or influence after the victories of Tuthmōsis III: Cyprus, the Levant, Egypt and Nubia.

It is interesting to note that the one area in which no Mycenaean pottery has been found is the Central Anatolian Plateau, which at this time was dominated by the Hittites. Several sections of Chapter XI are devoted to relations between the Aegean and Anatolia. One section is concerned with Hittite documents dealing with their neighbours to the west, Arzawa and Assuwa (the name Asia derives from the latter). Towards the end of the 15th century BC a new western power emerges in the Hittite documents, that of Aḫḫiyawa, which a number of scholars since the 1920s have identified with the Achaians, Homer's name for many of the Greeks. The situation is extremely confused but the least implausible picture that can be painted from the Hittite documents and later Greek traditions is that the Aḫḫiyawa/Achaians were a mixture of Hellenized West Anatolians and Greeks, living and raiding both on the fringes of the Hittite Empire and in the Aegean. They should be associated with the Greek legendary hero Pelops, after whom the Peloponnese (Pelops' Island) was named and from whom the great Homeric kings Agamemnon and Menelaos claimed descent. I believe that the name Pelops comes from the Egyptian Pꜣ Rpʿt (Crown Prince). Thus, it is a title not a personal name. It is difficult to date the point at which his chief prototype seized the region of Elis in the Northwestern Peloponnese, which seems to have been the first base of Achaian or Pelopid power. It could be at any point between 1425 and 1300 BC. The difficulty is that it is impossible to detect any differences in material culture between Danaans and Achaians. Documentary and legendary evidence is equally imprecise, just as Homer was not altogether clear in his distinction between the two peoples. The Egyptians seem to have referred to both Tnïw and Iḳwš (Achaians), who were among the Peoples of the Sea who raided Egypt.

The simplest explanation is to see the 'Danaans' as the inhabitants or retainers of the kingdoms established at the end of the 18th century BC by the original 'Hyksos' heroes and the 'Achaians' as those conquered by the new 'Anatolian' dynasties. Just as it is difficult to estimate the date of the establishment of Pelops' kingdom in Elis, it is difficult to say when the other kingdoms such as Mycenae/Argos and Sparta came under Achaian rule. All that does seem clear is that the last of the Hyksos dynasties, that of the Kadmeans at Thebes, survived until the end of the 13th century.

The fact that the Achaians had Anatolian connections does not mean that they were allied to the Hittites. Quite the contrary, like the Danaans, they seem to have been long-term enemies of the central Anatolians. The Hittite documents indicate constant hostilities with the Aḫḫiyawa; the absence of Mycenaean pottery from Hittite territory has been mentioned above. A similar pattern can be seen in the foreign objects from this period found at Mycenae. The American archaeologist Eric Cline has pointed out that, while the finds include a considerable number of Egyptian and Levantine objects, there is only one possible Hittite one and that probably came from a part of Anatolia beyond Hittite control.

We know that Mycenaean goods have been found in a very wide distribution and that the Hittites too were active traders in Mesopotamia and Northern Syria. Why should the two zones have been mutually exclusive? Even if one dismisses the identification of Aḫḫiyawa with Akhaia, it is inconceivable that the two regions were unaware of each other. A slightly less improbable explanation is that, occupying similar geographical niches, they had no need for each other's products. Even if this contains some truth, there is every reason to suppose that such economic independence was strengthened by political will. There is both documentary and archaeological evidence to back this hypothesis. The document is a 13th-century treaty between the Hittites and a subordinate king in Northern Syria, specifically calling for him to prevent ships from Aḫḫiyawa trading through his territories. The archaeological evidence comes from the existence of plentiful Mycenaean pottery from the period LHIIIA in a belt of North Syria, where there is none from LHIIIB. The most plausible explanation for this discrepancy is that it is the result of the known fact that the region came under Hittite overlordship around 1370 BC, which is when LHIIIB began.

Thus, the most probable picture is that from *c.* 1430 to *c.* 1230 BC, there was enmity between Greeks and Hittites. The Hittites' great rivals were, of course, the Egyptians and while Tuthmōsis III may well have sent a punitive expedition to the Aegean around the mid-15th century, both documentary and archaeological evidence indicates that for the next century the leading Greek kingdoms were content to be in the Egyptian sphere and to have 'accepted the breath of life' from the pharaoh.

There is no doubt that there were intimate and trading and cultural contacts in this period. Apart from the documentary references to such contacts discussed in Chapter X, there is considerable archaeological evidence to back this up. As mentioned above, large quantities of Mycenaean pottery of the periods LHIIIA and LHIIIB (1470–1220 BC) have been found throughout the areas of Egyptian control and influence. Similarly, many large Canaanite jars used as containers for all kinds of goods have been found in the Aegean.

By far the greatest hoard of these Levantine containers has been found on a wreck excavated off the Kaş on the southwestern coast of Turkey, which contained over 120 of them. This wreck can be dated to around 1360 BC, at the end of the period of the greatest Egyptian strength. Nevertheless, the richness of the cargo gives a staggering picture of the extent of trade in the East Mediterranean during the Late Bronze Age. As well as ivory and ebony, large numbers of copper ingots were found; these provide confirmation for an extensive trade in copper, mainly mined at this time in Cyprus and Sardinia. There are also suggestions of a smaller but much more far-reaching trade in tin, which came to the Mediterranean from as far away as Afghanistan, Bohemia and Cornwall.

One of the most interesting discoveries of recent years has been that of a trade in lead and silver containing lead, which can now be traced by lead isotope analysis. We now know that the mines at Laurion in Attica to the south of Athens were major exporters of these metals from at least the beginning of the Egyptian Middle Kingdom. During the Late Bronze Age, lead from these mines was found in both Mesopotamia and Egypt.

Another fascinating recent discovery has come from the analysis of a number of faience Egyptian temple foundation plaques with the royal name Amenōphis III found at Mycenae. These are interesting because, if they had been found in Egypt, archaeologists would immediately have begun to search for other signs of the temple built over them. In Mycenae, however, most were found in hoards of precious objects and not in positions that would have marked the four corners of a temple. On the other hand, though ritually of great importance, they have no intrinsic value and are therefore unlikely to have been imported or brought back as souvenirs. Given the other signs of royal contact with Mycenae at this time there would seem to be a reasonable chance that they were intended to mark an Egyptian foundation there, even though such a building could have lasted only a short time or may never have been built at all.

However, it is not merely the symbolism of the plaques that shows the intimacy of contacts between Egypt and Greece at this time. An analysis of the lead in the glaze shows that it came from Laurion. This can be explained in one of two ways: either there was an official Egyptian royal factory in Greece at the time capable of making the plaques or the glaze just happened to be made in Egypt with lead from

Greece. The latter would seem much more likely. Even this solution emphasizes the intricate connections between Egypt and the Aegean at this time, *c.* 1400 BC.

We know that Egypt and the rest of Africa exported ivory, ebony and other tropical goods, like myrrh and other spices, ostrich eggs and probably feathers and papyrus. It is likely that they also sent some gold, though Greece had its own sources. It would seem likely that the predominant flow of slaves went from north to south. The Levant through which much of this trade passed had products of its own such as cedar and fine manufactured goods. On the other hand, we know that the Aegean exported fine pottery and whatever the Mycenaean vessels contained, almost certainly including olive oil. As well as this there were lead and silver.

Such a pattern of trade is not balanced. Now we know that Greece was a major exporter of metals it would seem necessary to explain the apparent imbalance with some other political or economic factor. One possibility would be to postulate that Egyptian political and naval power allowed it to exploit the Aegean. It would seem more likely, however, that the explanation is fundamentally economic and that Egypt was already exporting wheat throughout the East Mediterranean in the way that we know it to have done in the Archaic and Classical periods, 776–325 BC. Both documentary and archaeological sources make it clear that there were already ships with capacities big enough to make a large-scale grain trade feasible. It is also known that Egypt provided famine relief to Anatolia and the Levant *by sea* in the 13th century. It is almost certain that some of the Levantine cities which later made up Phoenicia also had regular grain deficiencies at this time. Both archaeological and documentary evidence from Southern Greece in the same century show both an extremely high population density and surprisingly low grain production. This would suggest frequent famines and/or constant imports of grain. It is possible that some of these already came from the Black Sea region, which also supplied Greece in Classical times, but it would seem much more likely that the bulk of it came from Egypt. Interestingly, a Greek tradition refers to Egyptian relief of a famine in Attika well before the Trojan War. These pointers, together with plausible Egyptian etymologies for a number of Greek words referring to wheat and its baking into bread, suggest that the pattern of Egyptian wheat-exporting to Greece and the rest of the Mediterranean basin that existed in Classical, Hellenistic and Roman times had already been established by the Late Bronze Age.

One of the most bitter scholarly debates of the last two decades has been on the question of who dominated trade in the East Mediterranean during the Late Bronze Age. Since the triumph of the Extreme Aryan Model the predominant view has been that trade was entirely in the hands of the dynamic Mycenaeans. This was justified by the fact that there was much more Aegean pottery in the Levant and Egypt than vice versa. However, pottery is not always a good indicator of who trades in the pots. For instance, it would be wrong to postulate Chinese vessels trading around Western Europe after the 17th century merely because most pottery in the region is Chinese or inferior local imitations. Furthermore, a number of scholars have pointed out the absence of Greeks from the abundant records of trading from Ugarit. This, I believe, can be explained as a local phenomenon arising from the Hittite blockades against its dependants' trading with Aḫḫiyawa. Nevertheless, there is little doubt that Ugarit and the other Levantine cities were much more mercantile than the palace economies in the Aegean as revealed by Linear B tablets. There is also the striking picture given in the Homeric epics of *all* trade being in the hands of Phoenicians.

The first wreck from the end of this period, found off the southern coast of Turkey at Cape Gelidonia, was believed by its excavator George Bass to have been manned by Levantines. His even greater discovery and excavation of the Kaş ship has yielded much more ambiguous evidence on the 'nationality' of its crew. These were probably mixed but almost certainly included some Greeks. The argument, although significant in the struggle between the Extreme Aryan Model, which denied any creative role to West Semites, and the Broad Aryan Model that allowed one, is ultimately futile. This is because it is now clear that between 1470 and 1220 BC the East Mediterranean was thoroughly cosmopolitan. Thus, both Aegean and Levantine as well as Egyptian and mixed crews were sailing with thoroughly mixed cargoes. Some scholars have proposed that this peace and prosperity was the result of a *Pax Mycenaeaca*. This would seem to be an Aryanist putting the cart before the horse. There is no doubt that from 1470 to 1370 BC Egypt was the dominant power in the region and it remained militarily, politically and culturally important until the end of the 13th century. Thus, it would seem better to postulate that the trade and prosperity took place under a *Pax Aegyptiaca*.

The existence during much of the second half of the 2nd millennium BC of such a cosmopolitan society throughout the East Mediterranean, including the Aegean, makes the idea of cultural isolation absurd. There would seem ample reasons to expect cultural and especially linguistic borrowings from Egyptian and West Semitic into

Greek. There would certainly seem no grounds for denying the inherently plausible evidence for them. However, while the archaeological evidence from this period makes the Aryan Model and the Model
of Autochthonous Origin untenable, it could be seen to weaken the
Ancient Model in the narrow sense because such a period of prolonged intimate contact can explain substantial religious, linguistic
and other cultural borrowings without resorting to the idea of conquests or colonies. Against this, however, is the fact that Late Mycenaean Greece was already Greek-speaking, worshipping gods with
their later Greek names. Words and names that I believe to have had
Egyptian or West Semitic origins appear to have been well established
in Greece by this time. Furthermore, we know from the Thera murals
that Cycladic culture at least was already thoroughly cosmopolitan in
the 17th century BC. Thus, despite the close contact between 1470 and
1220 BC, there would seem to be little doubt that Greek culture as
we know it from Archaic and Classical times was already essentially
formed by then. This being the case, we have to look earlier for some
of what I believe to be the *fundamental* Egyptian and Semitic influences on Greek culture. As argued above, some of these can be dated
to the 3rd millennium or still earlier.

Nevertheless, the archaeological evidence would seem to indicate
that the crucial period was the second quarter of the 2nd millennium
and that this influence was associated with Hyksos conquests and
colonizations.

The twelfth and last chapter of this book deals with the end of the
Mycenaean Age in the century from 1250 to 1150 BC. It focuses on
the sieges and destructions of two cities: the Greek Thebes and Troy.
Here, too, chronology has been confused by the low settings of the
ceramic periods. According to conventional wisdom, the relevant periods, Late Helladic IIIB and LHIIIC, began in 1275 and 1180 BC
respectively. Archaeological evidence suggests that Thebes was destroyed in LHIIIB2, which according to this scheme would be *c.* 1200.
There are two candidates for the archaeological city of Troy referred
to by Homer. Troy VI appears to have been destroyed near the beginning of LHIIIB, which, according to the conventional chronology,
would be around 1275 BC. This would put it earlier than the traditional datings for the fall of Troy, which were between 1250 and 1170
BC. More seriously, this date is earlier than that given by conventional
ceramic chronology for the final fall of Thebes, which was universally
supposed, in the tradition, to have occurred before the Trojan War.
There was, however, another destruction, that of Troy VIIa, which
was destroyed by fire in the approved Homeric manner near the

beginning of LHIIIC, which according to conventional wisdom would
be after 1175 BC. While this just fits at the lower end of the Greek
chronologies, it is difficult to reconcile it with the traditional picture of
a massive and well-organized Greek expedition, as we know that Mycenaean civilization was already in steep decline by then.

This confusion and the uncertainty as to which 'Troy' had been destroyed allowed sceptics like Moses Finley, the dominant figure in classics at Cambridge in the 1960s and 1970s, to question the historicity of
the Trojan War in a way that had not been done since Schliemann's
sensational discoveries. However, the new updating of ceramic periods clarifies the situation in two ways. Firstly, the collapse of Troy VI
should now be set at c. 1350 BC, which now allows it over a century of
existence before its destruction at c. 1210 BC. This later date falls precisely at the middle of the traditional chronological range and the nature of its destruction fits that of the epics. This, together with very
suggestive finds on the beach where the Greeks were supposed to
have camped, have triumphantly restored Homer's basic historicity.

Sections of this chapter refer to the complicated history of Troy, as
it can be established through archaeology and Hittite archives. It is
clear that, as an extremely prosperous city, strategically placed at the
point where ships had to wait for a fair wind to sail up the Dardanelles
to reach the Black Sea, during the Late Bronze Age it swayed between
Hittite and Greek power. The complete absence of references to the
Hittites in Homer – and for that matter in the whole of Greek tradition – can be explained by the fact that, although the Hittite Empire
did not finally collapse until the beginning of the 12th century BC, it
appears to have lost power and influence over Western Anatolia by
the 1230s. Thus, it would seem that in some ways the Trojan War was
a Greek attempt to fill a power vacuum resisted by a league of West
and South Anatolian states and Thracians.

Chapter XII also includes sections on Thebes. There is an outline
of what can be reconstructed of its history since what I believe to have
been its second foundation by Hyksos princes represented in tradition by the hero Kadmos. There is some discussion of the arguments
over his dating and of the preference among many scholars for the
later chronologies proposed in Antiquity. These, I believe, were powerfully motivated by the desire to reconcile the tradition that Kadmos
had introduced the alphabet to Greece with the belief that the very
earliest the alphabet could have been introduced was c. 1300 BC. I
have argued on epigraphic grounds that the Semitic alphabet was introduced to Greece no later than 1400 BC and probably nearer to 1800
BC. Thus, there would seem to me no reason to doubt the major an-

cient tradition that Kadmos, or the invasion he represented, arrived at approximately the same time as Danaos and his colonization, that is to say around 1730 BC.

Abundant Classical testimony, which tallies well with earlier iconographic evidence, makes it almost certain that Thebans in the 13th century BC believed their rulers to be the descendants of an ancient line of kings descended from Kadmos and coming ultimately from Phoenicia. I see no reason to doubt that this tradition had a genuine historical basis and that by this time the Theban kingdom alone survived from the Hyksos principalities.

It is also clear that Thebes had kept up or had revived contacts with the Near East. In the Kadmeion or city palace a number of Near Eastern treasures have been found, some of which were being worked or re-worked just as the city fell. This has suggested to one scholar that a colony of Eastern craftsmen was working in the palace. The most startling find of all was a collection of lapis lazuli cylinder seals, most of which were official or religious seals made under the Kassite Dynasty in Babylon. In a wonderful piece of detective work, the senior specialist in West Asian seals Edith Porada has traced these to temples sacked by the Assyrian conqueror of Kassite Babylon, Tukulti Ninurta I. She argued that he had sent them on to Greece either as trade goods or for diplomatic reasons. Porada was aware of the Hittite treaty attempting to prevent trade between Greece and Assyria, but she did not know of the confirming evidence from a large lead ingot stamped with the name of Tukulti Ninurta but made of Laurion lead from Attika.

Thus, while there is no doubt that Thebes was in close contact with the Near East at the time of its fall, it is equally clear that it was not unique among Greek states of the time in this respect. Similarly, while there is no reason to doubt the Kadmean and Phoenician ancestry of the Theban kings, these finds do not in themselves prove that Thebes was a Near Eastern foundation.

The date of the Assyrian conquest of Babylon has been plausibly set at c. 1235 BC. This provides a *terminus post quem* for the final destruction of Thebes, which should now be set in the 1220s. This, according to Greek tradition, took place shortly before the Trojan War, which can now be put in the 1210s culminating in the Fall of Troy c. 1210 BC.

In Chapter XII, I also consider the end of the Mycenaean Age and the general destruction of Bronze Age civilization, which took place in the 12th century but of which the falls of Thebes and Troy can be seen as precursors. The beginning of the 12th century saw the 'Invasions of the Sea Peoples' reported in Egyptian documents. These involved invasions from the north and west of Anatolia, the Levant and Egypt. They brought about the end of the Hittite Empire and the temporary destruction of the Levantine coastal states. Egypt survived but only barely and with much weakened power.

There is no doubt that peoples whom we should now call 'Greek' were involved in these raids and the settlements that followed some of them. On the other hand, it is difficult to tell exactly how these migrations are connected to the turmoil that was taking place in Greece itself at the same time. The major manifestations of this were the raids on and conquests of parts of Southern Greece by the Dorians from Northwest Greece. Whether or not there was any truth in it, the Dorian kings claimed to be 'Heraklids' or descendants of the gods and the earlier Egypto-Phoenician ruling dynasties. In this way, they were able to claim superior legitimacy to the Pelopids they replaced in Argos, Sparta and elsewhere. This Egypto-Phoenician ancestry was also the reason why later Spartan kings believed themselves to be akin to the Jews, whose leaders, like their own real or imagined ancestors, were supposed to have been Hyksos princes expelled by the Egyptians.

The turmoil in Greece appears to have become extreme in the 1150s and it was only then that Mycenae itself appears to have fallen. There were clearly many reasons for the collapse of Bronze Age civilization at this time. One hypothesis states that the underlying cause was a climatic deterioration affecting the whole northern hemisphere from the last quarter of the 13th century. This is discussed in more detail in Chapter VII. However, scholars working along these lines have found no long-lasting deterioration. Furthermore, while they admit that there probably were droughts, sometimes lasting for several years, they plausibly maintain that there were similar droughts in the 14th century when Southern Greece supported a substantial population. I argue that this enigma can be solved by accepting that, in the period from 1470–1220 BC, Egyptian grain was available in Greece to tide the population over periods of famine. Thus, it was the invasions of the Sea Peoples, which both weakened Egypt and cut the possibilities of the maritime transport of grain, that forced the Southern Greek economy to shift from being one of manufacture and specialized agriculture in the ceramic periods LHIIIA and B to become, in LHIIIC, a subsistence economy with a far lower population capable of surviving relatively frequent droughts.

Although the long-term decline in the late 13th and 12th centuries can be attributed to both climatic and political factors, it would seem that the prior and principal cause was the political breakdown of the *Pax Aegyptiaca*. However, in a number of regions the *coup de grâce* that finally overwhelmed the Bronze Age civilization would seem to be the climatic deterioration that took place after the eruption of Hekla III in 1159 BC. It is interesting to note that it was apparently in the following decade that the Prince of Zhou began to overthrow the Shang Dynasty, Northwest Britain was depopulated, the Middle Elamite kingdom in Iran collapsed and palatial society in Greece was destroyed.

While Egypt never succumbed and the Levant quickly regained its wealth and power, the peripheral regions of the Near East took much longer to recover and, when they did, it was in very different social forms. In Greece, the bureaucratic palatial society was replaced by much more primitive tribal society and the recovery in the 9th and 8th centuries was largely along the lines established in Phoenicia in the 11th century of commercial and manufacturing city states, relying on chattel slave labour but with a strong sense of citizens' rights. To put the difference symbolically, where there had been palaces there were now cities dominated by temples to the gods representing corporate identity.

The relationships between this new wave of Near Eastern influence and the indigenous Greek tradition form, however, another story and are not part of this project.

In the introduction to Volume 1, I boldly announced the contents of the then projected Volumes 2 and 3. It will now be clear how wrong I was. Therefore, this time, I shall not go into the projected details of Volumes 3 and 4. In general, they will cover the areas suggested in the introduction to the first volume for Volumes 2 and 3. Apart from changes to the detail of this scheme, the fundamental difference will be that they will be based on the same lines as this volume in that they will be made up of 'thick' description, in which I shall try to demonstrate the fruitfulness of the Revised Ancient Model. This is in contrast to the impartial competition I mistakenly thought possible when I first set out the scheme of this project.

CHAPTER I

CRETE BEFORE THE PALACES, 7000–2100 BC

T HE PLACE TO BEGIN any survey of relations between the Near East and the Aegean is obviously Crete. The reasons for this are, firstly, the evidence that the island had been in contact with Southwest Asia and North Africa since the Neolithic period and that this continued during the Early Bronze Age. Secondly, there is the fact that, after Cretan palatial civilization grew up in the late 3rd and early 2nd millenniums, it acted as a transmitter and filter to later Egyptian and Levantine influences on Mainland Greece. Thus, Cretan influence was central to the formation and development of Mycenaean civilization in the 2nd millennium.

In this chapter we shall consider the earliest stage of the island's history: the long span of the Neolithic and Early Bronze Ages from about 7000 to 2100 BC.

Here I am primarily concerned with archaeology. This is not because I believe that archaeology has any inherent superiority as a discipline nor because it is the only way to find out about the Aegean in the 2nd millennium BC (that is from 2000–1000 BC), with which this book is largely concerned. I focus on archaeology for two reasons: firstly, because it is always an important method of gaining knowledge even in historical or proto-historical times; secondly, because, although information gained from legendary and linguistic sources can be extremely useful, it is usually very difficult to apply with any chronological precision. When dealing with the 3rd millennium, for instance, there are relatively few contemporary documents, so information gained through archaeology is the only type of evidence which we can tie to that period. However, I do not believe that it is desirable or possible to treat the archaeological evidence in isolation even in the very early periods. Therefore, in this chapter I shall try to set it in a context provided by documentary evidence from contemporary cultures, as well as from later legends, mythology, religious cults and sometimes language and proper names.

In addition to these contextual problems there are the difficulties inherent in archaeology as a discipline. I do not intend to go into the complicated philosophical question of whether or not archaeology is an independent science (as opposed to one that uses the scientific methods of others).[1] Here, I should simply like to consider its praxis or low-level theory as it affects the specific problems with which we are concerned. There is often no doubt as to the authenticity of an object or – in a good excavation – as to where and in what stratum it was found. Nowadays it is possible to discover, by scientific study of its material, where it came from. Sometimes through radio-carbon – the measurement of the proportion of radioactive carbon, which begins to decay when an organism dies – and dendrochronology – the counting of tree rings – one can even tell its absolute date. On the other hand, how the object came to be there and what it represents are open only to the archaeologist's or historian's subjective interpretation. Similarly, when looking at buildings or traces of agriculture or industry, which are the major preoccupations of modern archaeologists, there is great leeway in their interpretation, particularly in tracing their relationship to those in other places. In short, the data themselves seldom provide definitive answers; the most they can do is establish limits within which the archaeologist may speculate.

THE 'DIFFUSIONIST' AND 'ISOLATIONIST' DEBATE

Naturally, fashion plays an important role in this largely speculative realm. In Volume 1, I briefly discussed the relationship between colonialism and the preference for 'diffusionism' or the belief that 'higher cultures' were spread through conquest and/or migration.[2] It should be recalled here that the Ancient, Aryan and Revised Ancient Models for Greece are all diffusionist. Isolationism – or 'evolutionism' as its champions rather confusingly like to call it – with its faith in local creativity and initiative, that is to say indigenous development, was seen as a healthy reaction to this and has dominated archaeology since the 1940s.

The most explicit attack on the colonialist aspect of diffusionism came in an article written by William Adams, the distinguished archaeologist at Nubia, but it has been also a major theme in the work of Colin Renfrew and other isolationists.[3] They have put forward powerful arguments against the diffusionist interpretation of archaeological evidence. Adams epitomized these with the plea at the end of his article 'Invasion, diffusion and evolution' which was published in *Antiquity*, one of the central journals in the field:

> As long as there is no ultimate proof in archaeology, every existing interpretation has to be subject to reexamination in the light of fresh discoveries. There is unhappily no point at which we can forget the evidence and accept the interpretation. Since every theory is no more than a probability, any building of theory on theory will significantly reduce the probability. Only solid evidence will significantly reduce the probability. Only solid evidence can ultimately serve as the building blocks of history.[4]

Unfortunately, however, the distinction between 'interpretation' and 'solid evidence' is not so conveniently clear-cut. It is clear that right from the moment archaeologists select their site they must have certain preconceptions and that these preconceptions or their successors remain with the archaeologist in all decisions on where to dig, with what methods, where to stop, what to examine, clean, note and keep. The seeing of *significance* is inevitably subjective. Adams's conclusion might appear to be impartial, but, like that of McNeal, in the article referred to in my Introduction, it is an attack on diffusionism and what he sees to be its racist overtones.[5] In denying the validity of all hypotheses based on archaeological or other 'evidence' about prehistory, scholars like Adams and McNeal leave the presumption in favour of local evolution and isolationism.

My position is that, while I fully accept their criticisms of the 'evidence', I believe that we should make the best of what we have and continue to construct hypotheses, while constantly reminding ourselves of their precariousness. I maintain this because I am convinced that, firstly, research without them produces a meaningless jumble and, secondly, that although they cannot be absolutely 'true' different hypotheses can be more or less heuristically useful and that our job is to concoct and select the least bad. There are also two corollaries to the second point: 1) a prohibition on the establishment of new hypotheses inevitably leaves in place old ones, which are frequently based on much less reliable evidence; 2) the prohibition has a definite isolationist bias in that it is wrongly felt that it is connection rather than isolation that needs to be proved. I think that this is mistaken because I take what has been called the 'modified diffusionist' position, that is, I believe that cultural change can take place as the result either of outside influences or of internal developments, or most commonly from a complex interplay of both.

The present isolationist intellectual atmosphere should be borne in mind when we look at present attitudes towards the Aegean during the Bronze Age (3300–1100 BC). To put it crudely, archaeologists have, until very recently, been in one of two camps. The first of these, as outlined in Volume 1, contained fundamentally conservative scholars like Frank Stubbings and the late Spyridon Marinatos. These, influenced by remnants of the Ancient Model, have maintained that Greece was invaded from Egypt and the Levant near the beginning of the Late Bronze Age c. 1570 BC, but they argue that this had had no significant or long-lasting impact on Greek culture. The second group contains most of the established, middle-aged archaeologists and historians of Ancient Greece, such as John Bintliff and Peter Warren. These tend to be systematically isolationist. They incline towards Renfrew's Model of Autochthonous Origin, the belief that there has been no culturally significant settlement of Greece from the outside since the beginning of the Neolithic period. In particular, they adamantly oppose the idea of any invasion of – or significant settlements in – the Aegean from the Near East.[6] Indeed, Renfrew has gone beyond the founders of the Aryan Model by insisting not merely that the Greeks had no significant major contact with the Near East but that the Pre-Hellenes were equally pure and untouched.

At this point, it is necessary to fill in a serious gap left in Volume 1. I argued there that the Extreme Aryan Model reigned supreme at the turn of the century. I also briefly considered the diffusionist ideas of Elliot Smith, who believed that an energetic Asiatic people had spread culture around the world from Egypt.[7] What was not mentioned, however, was that there was a more moderate and much more influential school of archaeologists who maintained that European culture had been ultimately derived from the Near East and were tagged by their enemies as believers in *ex oriente lux*, 'Light from the Orient'.

The outstanding figure among these 'modified diffusionists' was the Swedish archaeologist Oscar Montelius, but he had many prominent disciples, especially in Britain, of whom the most important were Sir John Myres and the great Australian theoretician of archaeology Gordon Childe.[8] These scholars maintained that the Aegean population had received much, if not most of its technical skills from the

Near East during the 3rd millennium. However, as I mentioned in Volume 1, Myres and Childe were also thoroughly convinced of Aryan racial superiority and that the ancient Greeks had possessed one of the finest Aryan civilizations. The potential contradictions between these fundamental beliefs were avoided by the presumed presence of the 'Pre-Hellenes' who acted as a filter separating the Aryan Hellenes from the Near Eastern elements.[9]

Among the opponents of the modified diffusionists were men like Salomon Reinach, discussed in Volume 1, who had attacked what he called the *mirage oriental* which sought Asian origins for all European developments. There was also Gustav Kossinna, the dominant figure in German archaeology in the early 20th century, who argued that all the master races – the Aryans, the Finns and the Sumerians – had ultimately come from Schleswig-Holstein and that, while inferior peoples benefited from mixing with superior ones, the greatest civilizations arose where the master races were pure and uncontaminated as – it just so happened – was the case in North Germany.[10] While in no way endorsing this kind of racism, the work of Renfrew and Warren has in many ways been an attempt to revive the isolationist or evolutionary opposition to the modified diffusionism of Montelius and Childe and to apply the notion of uncontaminated purity to the Aegean. Thus their ideas, too, have racist overtones in that they see European civilization as the greatest in world history and as having been exclusively created by Indo-European–speaking Europeans. It is extremely significant that Renfrew's massive book has the extraordinary and provocative title *The Emergence of Civilisation: The Cyclades and the Aegean in the Third Millennium B.C.*, although it was paradoxically dedicated 'To the memory of V. Gordon Childe' against whose ideas Renfrew is struggling.

Dealing with Crete before about 1450 BC, when Mycenaeans seem to have become dominant there, we find ourselves in the thick of the battle between isolationists and modified diffusionists. Even the latter, however, tend to maintain that 'Minoan' civilization had a certain European 'freedom' and 'virility' lacking in Near Eastern civilizations.[11]

CRETE BEFORE THE 21ST CENTURY BC
The Neolithic, 7000–3300 BC

According to the geographer Strabo in the 1st centuries BC and AD, Crete was not in the Aegean but set between Greece and Africa.[12] As Keith Branigan, the modern archaeologist and historian of the island, put it, Crete 'sat upon the lines of communication along which the arts and crafts of the great civilizations of the two continents reached the barbarian people of a third.'[13] Archaeological evidence indicates that Crete was influenced by five main regions: Anatolia, the Levant, Egypt, Libya and finally the Cyclades and Greece. There seems little doubt that agriculture came to Crete – as it came to Mainland Greece – from Anatolia, probably in the 8th or 7th millennium BC.[14] During the long Neolithic period that followed, there were both local developments and foreign influences. The American archaeologist Saul Weinberg has argued that the new style of matt-painted pottery found in the Late Cretan Neolithic in the 5th millennium was based on Ubaid ware found in contemporary Mesopotamia and Syria. This could possibly have linguistic significance since, as I tentatively proposed in the introduction to Volume 1, the diffusion of Ubaid pottery in the Middle East could be associated with the spread of Semitic there.[15]

Sir Arthur Evans, the founder of Cretan archaeology, saw Libyan influence on Crete in models of men found in Neolithic levels wearing Libyan penis sheaths. The British archaeologist Sinclair Hood points out, however, that these 'codpieces' also existed in Predynastic Egypt and could have come from there. He also makes a general point from the sheaths' later survival in Crete that 'Conservatism of this kind is a key to many aspects of the Minoan civilization of Crete, where beliefs and customs originally prevalent elsewhere in the Near East tended to linger.'[16] This perception has a number of other fruitful applications which will be examined below.

Following Arthur Evans, J.D.S. Pendlebury, who combined a knowledge of Egyptian and Aegean archaeology, and the Greek archaeologist S. Alexiou both detected Libyan influence on Neolithic Crete and possibly on the type of cairn that later developed into the Cretan *tholos* or domed tomb.[17] Egyptian influence is indicated by a number of Egyptian Predynastic stone bowls and a mace head found at Knossos, from Late or Final Neolithic levels.[18] Arguing against this diffusionist view, however, Warren and Renfrew maintain that the Cretan Neolithic stoneware of this kind, probably produced with a bow drill, was the result of local developments.[19] But the fact that there was large-scale production of similar objects in Egypt at the time and that some of these have been found in Crete, although it does not *prove* diffusion, does make the arguments put forward in its favour by Arthur Evans and other archaeologists seem very plausible.[20] Thus I would suggest that there is enough evidence to indicate that, from the earliest times, many different East Mediterranean cultures met in Crete.

The Early Bronze Age,
c. 3300–2000 BC

Before examining Crete in the Early Minoan Period, it is necessary to look at the beginning of the Bronze Age over the East Mediterranean as a whole. There is little doubt that in general the creation of Early Minoan culture was clearly related to the cultural explosion that took place in Southwest Asia and Egypt at the end of the 4th millennium.

It was in this period that the Semitic-Sumerian culture of Meso-potamia expanded into Syria.[21] Excavations at the Phoenician city of Byblos have shown considerable urbanization there at this time.[22] The 34th century BC also saw the emergence of a united Egypt under the 1st Dynasty. It is clear that these developments occurred on the bases of local Neolithic cultures which went on to become distinctive civiliza-tions. Nevertheless, all of these more or less simultaneous transforma-tions were clearly linked by at least stimulus diffusion (that is, local development stimulated by external activities). This can be shown, not merely by the similarities in contemporary developments, but also by specific stylistic resemblances between, for instance, late 4th-millen-nium Mesopotamia and Egypt at the end of the Predynastic period and the 1st Dynasty.

Furthermore, archaeological evidence shows that there were trad-ing networks at this time connecting Egypt with Iran and Meso-potamia with Afghanistan.[23] The earliest pharaonic tombs found, not in Egypt but in Nubia, contain objects from as far away as the Kor-dofan plateau in the Western Sudan and the Levantine coast.[24] There are also strong archaeological indications of contacts between Egypt and Palestine and Spain at this time, and Mesopotamian tablets from this period have been found in Romania.[25] This is not so startling as it might at first seem, as Transylvania, Hungary and Bohemia contained lead, silver and tin, all of which were extremely prized by and useful to Mesopotamian civilization. In fact, four cups found at Ur from the Jemdet Nasr period in the late 4th millennium appear to have been made with lead from Hungary. It is possible to tell this from lead iso-tope analysis. This is a method of determining the geological age of a particular source of lead from the proportion of uranium and thor-ium in it, as the radioactive isotopes decay at a fixed rate. This process can be applied not only to lead but to other metals, when they appear in conjunction with it, particularly copper and silver.[26]

The demarcation at c. 3300 BC marks not only a technological change but a geographical one.[27] During the Neolithic the richest regions of what later became Greece were the fertile agricultural plains of Thessaly and Macedonia in the north. Crete and Southern Greece appear to have had much smaller, less prosperous communities. This is hardly surprising, given the very limited arable land available and the unreliability of rainfall. At the turn of the 3rd millennium, however, one finds a reversal in which the Southern Aegean appears to have had an economic boom and the north became a backwater. It is this new situation that requires an explanation.

Renfrew argues that this economic expansion was the result of the introduction of new crops, notably grapes and olives, which flourished on the rocky coasts and islands, rather than on the northern plains, which were more suitable for grain.[28] Recently, however, there has been considerable doubt as to whether grapes and olives were 'commercially' exploited – or even present – in the Early Bronze Age (as we shall see below, the linguistic evidence is ambiguous on this). Rather than these new products, Renfrew's followers now tend to stress navigational improvements and the growth of trade in the South Aegean which allowed areas where crops failed because of unreliable rainfall to be supplied from outside. While they stay within Renfrew's school by restricting this hypothetical trade to the Aegean, the picture they draw is of a network of emporia of small but active trading towns.[29] As such trading networks had existed in the Middle East at least since the third quarter of the 4th millennium, it would seem probable that stimulus diffusion, if not direct diffusion, was involved in this economic and social innovation. Material evidence from Crete at this time would make this seem quite likely.

During the Early Bronze/Early Minoan period, the cultures occupying the small plains in Crete varied considerably. In the north, pottery indicates a continuation of the Neolithic tradition and influences from the Cyclades. In the east and south of the island, however, and later even in the north, a new style of pottery, the Agios Onouphrios ware, predominated. There have been suggestions that this originated in Anatolia but, as Branigan writes in his *Foundations of Palatial Crete*,

> The only plausible external source for the red-on-buff tradition is Syria-Palestine, where a very similar style was in being at the end of the fourth millennium B.C. The spirit of the decoration is very similar to that of Minoan ware and several of the shapes are too. Furthermore, some of the preceding [Palestinian] Chalcolithic pottery has affinities in Crete, particularly the so-called bird vases. The author is inclined to see the development of Agios Onouphrios

wares as taking place in the Messara [in Southern Crete] possibly under eastern influence, for which other evidence exists.[30]

The 'other evidence' he was referring to was that of collective burials in caves or *tholoi* and the stacking of skulls. These, and the introduction of bronze working itself, led him to postulate a migration from Palestine through Syria to Crete.[31] Unable to contest the plausibility of Branigan's hypothesis, Renfrew is forced, in rebuttal, to retreat to the requirement of proof. 'Nothing in the Early Minoan I levels unequivocally indicates contact with Egypt or the Near East.'[32]

The American archaeologist Saul Weinberg has also argued that there are a striking number of parallels between the Cretan cultures of the 3rd millennium and the slightly earlier Ghassul culture of Palestine. Weinberg cites 'bird vases, mat impressions on the base of pots, high pedestal feet for chalices, suspension lugs, clay ladles, pattern burnishes, cheese pots, impressed spirals, contracted burial in cist graves, pithos burial, pyxides and incised decoration'.[33] The British archaeologists Branigan and Hood accept these parallels and enlarge upon them.[34] Although Renfrew admits that Weinberg's theory 'is an interesting one', his entire book is based on the assumption that Gordon Childe and his intellectual descendants like Weinberg and Branigan are absolutely mistaken in their advocacy of 'modified diffusion'.[35]

There are also remains of some imports from Egypt and the Levant. Even in the Early Minoan period, Knossos was a considerable settlement and, as we have seen, Egyptian Predynastic and Old Kingdom stone bowls and locally and foreign worked ivory objects have been found there as elsewhere in the Aegean region.[36] But, as Renfrew reassures us, 'Beyond the finds of Egyptian stone bowls in Crete there is little evidence for foreign contact during the third millennium'.[37]

In fact, however, the isolationists do have other problems. For instance, there is the appearance and widespread use of the wheel for pottery in the Early Bronze Age Aegean. Warren and Renfrew have objected to the argument, proposed by Gordon Childe in the 1930s, that this was the result of diffusion. As Renfrew puts it,

The earliest find of a fast wheel comes from the Uruk period at Ur, and certainly nothing in the Aegean is of comparable antiquity. The wheel made pottery of Cilicia could indicate an intermediate step along the diffusion path, since Troy II and Tarsus [in Cilicia] were clearly in some kind of contact. Childe's diffusion theory can be supported in this way. But, on the other hand, the likelihood that a turntable was in use in the Aegean before the emergence of the fast wheel does open, as Warren has suggested, the possibility that the fast wheel developed independently in the Aegean. And whatever its origin . . .[38]

To my mind, here as elsewhere, Renfrew's objections to Childe's hypothesis of diffusion seem strained and do nothing to weaken the Australian's case. They do, however, illustrate the strength of Renfrew's desire to keep the Aegean apart from the Near East. In any event, whether or not one accepts the specifics of Weinberg's and Branigan's schemes, is it possible Crete and the Southern Aegean could have been unaffected by all this long-range trade? As mentioned above, Predynastic stone bowls have been excavated at Knossos. We also know, from widespread finds of obsidian from the Cycladic island of Melos, that many millenniums before 3300 BC overseas trading was taking place in the region. Homer attests that it was common to sail direct from Crete to Egypt in the Early Iron Age and possible to return. As the German Egyptologist and specialist in ancient international relations W. Helck points out in reference to the early obsidian trade, there is no evidence of a loss of navigational skills between the Neolithic and the 3rd millennium.[39] Indeed, it is now generally conceded that navigation in the Southern Aegean, which had better ports then than today, had improved at the end of the 4th millennium, and that the society of the region was deeply involved in trade.[40]

The reason for the implausible picture of isolation does not seem to derive from the evidence – in any event the theory was formulated before the new scientific techniques for determining geographical origins of clay and metals had been applied to archaeology. The isolationist view is essentially an ideological construct. Renfrew writes in the introduction to his *The Emergence of Civilization:*

> I have come to believe that this widely held diffusionist view, that Aegean Civilisation was something borrowed from the Orient, is inadequate. It fails to explain what is actually seen in the archaeological record. We can no longer accept that the sole unifying theme of European prehistory was, in the words of Gordon Childe, 'the irradiation of European barbarism by Oriental civilisation'. . . . Throughout the southern Aegean, for a thousand years [the third millennium B.C.], striking changes were taking place in every field – in agriculture, in craft technology, in social organisation, in art and religion, in trade and in population. These developments evidently owed little to Oriental inspiration. *Yet it was at this time that the basic features of the subsequent Minoan-Mycenaean civilisation were being determined.* (my italics)[41]

It is also clear that Renfrew accepts the view of scholars such as the historian of religion and myth Martin Nilsson that there was an essential continuity from Minoan-Mycenaean civilizations to that of Classical Greece. Thus, the independence of Greek and European culture as a whole is at stake. Where Montelius, Childe and their followers tended to see significant breaks in the culture of the Aegean after 2000 BC, Renfrew like Nilsson sees essential cultural continuity. *Thus, for Renfrew to admit that there was significant Near Eastern influence on the Aegean in the Neolithic and Early Bronze Age would be to place that influence at the centre of all Greek civilization.*

There also appear to have been other borrowings from the Near East in the Early Minoan period. It seems that flax and its product linen were first brought to the Aegean from the Near East at this time.[42] Renfrew maintains that the grape and wine-making seem to have been introduced to Crete during the 3rd millennium but recently some scholars have questioned this. If, as seems likely, they were introduced to the Aegean from the Near East, it is possible that linguistic evidence can help here.

The word *wine* meaning both 'grapes' and 'wine' is described according to conventional wisdom as a 'wandering word', a technical but vague term used to describe verbal similarities in a number of languages, without indicating or wanting to indicate the original source.[43] The root is found not only throughout Indo-European: the Greek *oinos*, the Latin *vinum*, the Armenian *gini* and the Hittite *wiyana* – but also in Semitic *wayn*, in the Arabic for 'black grapes' and the Ethiopic *wăyâne*, 'vine'. There are also the Akkadian *inu*, the Ugaritic *yn* and the Hebrew *yayîn*, 'wine'. The Russian linguists Illič Svitič and A. B. Dolgopolskii did not argue that this cluster was a common heritage from Nostratic (a linguistic superfamily including Afroasiatic and Indo-European as well as a number of other language families), in which both scholars believe. Rather, they saw it as a loan from Semitic into 'proto–Indo-European' in the sense that is referred to in this book, as proto–Indo-Hittite.[44]

When considering Crete, however, we should note that, while the Linear B word for 'wine' is probably *wono* – which is likely to come from the Indo-Hittite root – in Minoan, as written in Linear A, the form is *yane*.[45] This could be an independent development of the general root but it is more likely to come from a specifically West Semitic form in which the initial *w-* has become *y-*. Most scholars maintain that the shift *w-* to *y-* in West Semitic began only in the 2nd millennium.[46] This tends to support the arguments of the younger archaeologists who maintain that, although there were wild grapes in the Aegean since the beginning of the Bronze Age, cultivated vines do not appear in the region until the mid-2nd millennium.[47] However, the linguistic evidence is not altogether clear because the shift *w*- to *y*- had taken place in the marginal West Semitic language, Amorite, which dates back to the 3rd millennium and some traces of it may occur in Eblaite, another West Semitic language of the 3rd millennium.[48] Nevertheless, while it is possible that *yane* could have been a word introduced in the 3rd millennium to describe wild grapes, it was certainly the form of the word used by the Semitic-speakers of the Levantine coast in the 2nd. Therefore, *yane* would be exactly the form one would expect if the term came in with domesticated vines in the 2nd millennium.

All this is not to say that the Early Minoan Cretan culture was exclusively Near Eastern, still less that its prosperous but essentially rural population lived in a society dominated by big cities or states as did their contemporaries in Syria, Mesopotamia, the Levantine coast or Egypt. The position supported here is precisely that of Gordon Childe, 'modified diffusionism' with many cultural items being introduced and absorbed into local cultures that were producing coherence out of mixture and diversity.

CRETAN RELIGION IN THE
EARLY BRONZE AGE

Since Renfrew and Warren staked out their positions against 'modified diffusionism', a fascinating new study of Cretan religious ideas – as revealed through archaeological remains – has shown that they can be quite closely related to contemporary ideas from the Middle East in general and Egypt in particular. Beginning with finds from the 3rd millennium, an Aegean archaeologist, Dr Lucy Goodison, has looked for constant features among the extremely varied imagery concerned with death and burial in Crete and the Cyclades. With great skill, she has demonstrated the centrality of architectural and artistic symbolic representations of women's wombs and pubes as well as other indications of death being seen as a preparation for rebirth.

Further, she firmly denies the conventional view that Minoan religion was originally based on the worship of an 'earth mother' goddess and argues, instead, for one based on a goddess of the sun. The evidence in favour of her interpretation is so strong that she is surprised that other scholars, notably Martin Nilsson, had failed to see the central role of the sun in Minoan iconography – let alone its feminine characteristics.[49]

What Goodison failed to take into account was the *idée fixe* of the Aryanists that Aryan religion was one of the sky, while that of the Pre-

Hellenes was supposedly based on the earth or chthonic. This notion has been associated with a real tension and differentiation in Greek culture between celestial 'Olympian' and chthonic or earthly aspects of religion. On the other hand, its application to 'races' is a modern development. It formed part of the Romantic and racist appropriation of the Manichean categorical division between spirit and matter. This was already apparent in the German Romantic Friedrich von Schlegel's linguistics, according to which the Indo-European languages were 'spiritual' while others, notably the Semitic, were 'animal'.[50] The notion that the Aryans were spiritual and that lesser races were material thrived in late 19th-century Germany and became a linchpin of Nazi ideology.[51] This distinction first appeared in classics in the 1820s, put forward by the man who destroyed the Ancient Model, Karl Otfried Müller. Müller devoted much of his absurd but extraordinarily influential *The Dorians* to stressing that the religion of the superior northern tribe was Apollonian, both heavenly and solar.[52] Until very recently, the view that Greek religion is a mixture of Hellenic sky gods and Aegean chthonic spirits remained canonical and untested. Now, however, the Swiss authority on Greek religion Walter Burkert has very effectively demolished the association between the Olympian gods and the Hellenic invaders. He points out that, if anything, the Greek chthonic cults are closer to those of other Indo-European religions than the Olympian ones are.[53] This incidentally considerably weakens the Aryan Model of northern conquest.

To return to Goodison's ideas on the Cretan solar cult, she argues that some of these features – particularly the vision of a female sun – are distinctive and local.[54] However, she sees others as common to the Aegean and Egypt: specifically, the idea of the sun travelling across the heavens by day and under the world by night on a boat and the image of death and rebirth as vegetation. Both themes find very close parallels in Egyptian religion. In this a number of sacred barks are supposed to sail across the sky with the sun god Re. Similarly, Osiris' murder by his brother Seth and later resurrection and the victory and vengeance of his son Horus are closely linked to the seasonal death and revival of food crops and other plants.[55]

Goodison argues that the 'dancing' floors found near many Cretan tombs were places for festivals, including mourning of the type of the Egyptian goddesses Isis and Nephthys, who mourned for their dead brother/lover Osiris and reassembled his dismembered body. She also sees the Egyptian sisters as possible candidates for two women sometimes represented on seals of the period.[56]

Although they come from a slightly later period, she associates the dedication of beetles at Cretan hill sanctuaries with the Egyptian scarab, the sacred beetle, whose pushing uphill of a ball of dung was seen to represent the solar cycle. She mentions in this connection the find of a Minoan model of a beetle with a sun on its back.[57] The strong possibility that, before the rise of the scarab in the mid-3rd millennium, there were other solar beetles associated with the 'solar' goddess Nēit in Egyptian religion will be discussed below in Chapter II, and also in Volume 3.[58]

Lucy Goodison sets her observations in a context in which she, like Colin Renfrew and Peter Warren, sees considerable cultural continuities in Crete from the Early to the Middle and Late Bronze Ages and even on to the Early Iron Age. However, where Renfrew and Warren see continuities and development occurring in isolation, Goodison has a more complex vision of a continuing and fertile interaction between local cultures and the Middle East.[59]

Walter Burkert has provided another example of this type of interaction. He has traced the religious symbol of the 'double-axe' from Arpachiya in Upper Mesopotamia in the 4th millennium to Sumer and Elam in Central and Eastern Mesopotamia in the 3rd. The cult of the double-headed axe is also found in Troy II in the first half of the millennium and, unlike the bull cult, with which it was later associated, it is also found in Early Minoan Crete.[60] Even closer to Crete, however, was the cult of a double-axe which flourished in Lower Egypt during the Old Kingdom and which has deeper roots still in Upper Egypt.[61] This, I believe, can be related to the 'double belemnite' symbol of the Northeast African god Min, the significance of which will be discussed in Chapter IV. Thus, the double-axe which has been seen as one of the most typical European and Anatolian symbols has far more plausible roots in Africa and the Near East, and there is no reason that the two should be mutually exclusive.[62] Thus, Aryanist remarks like 'If there were any mysterious Oriental ideas to help the Cretans, I imagine they were quickly double-axed to shape'[63] are as inaccurate in detail as they are unpleasant in tone.

CONCLUSION

It seems therefore that there are good reasons for rejecting Renfrew's and Warren's revisionism and for reaffirming the general position, taken by Montelius and Childe and maintained by Weinberg, Branigan and others, that Crete in the Early Bronze Age, even more than in the Neolithic, received massive cultural influences from the Near

East in general and Egypt in particular. This is strongly suggested by the styles and forms of pottery, the introduction of the fast wheel for pottery, flax, linen and possibly viticulture, as well as by burial customs and iconography.

The period in the late 4th millennium when we should now date the beginning of the Early Minoan period was one in which Egyptian civilization was already well established.[64] It was also one in which Syria and the Levant were becoming highly urbanized. The early 3rd millennium saw the apex of the high civilization of Old Kingdom Egypt. By its end, there is evidence that Egyptians and Nubians were trading as far away as Eastern Iran and Afghanistan.[65] Similarly, in the first half of the millennium, the highly commercial urban civilizations of Syria and the Levant had extraordinarily intricate and far-reaching trade networks. Some archaeologists have tentatively proposed that there were migrations to Crete from Palestine at the beginning of the Early Minoan period. Whether or not this was the case, there is every reason to believe, on the basis of both direct and circumstantial archaeological evidence that, during both its initial and later stages of development, Early Minoan culture was permeated by Near Eastern and Egyptian influences.

We shall be looking at the development of the Cretan palaces at the very end of the 3rd millennium in Chapter IV. Before that, however, I want to consider relations between the Near East, especially Egypt, with the Greek mainland and particularly with the key province of Central Greece, Boiotia.

CHAPTER II

EGYPT'S INFLUENCE ON BOIOTIA AND THE PELOPONNESE IN THE 3RD MILLENNIUM, I
The cultic, mythical and legendary evidence

I N THIS CHAPTER I shall be looking at the extraordinarily intricate and dense mass of mythological parallels and connections between Boiotia and Egypt centring on themes of irrigation and drainage. I shall attempt to disentangle some of these myths and legends about Boiotia as well as some of the close parallels to them found in other parts of Greece, particularly in Arkadia in the Peloponnese. These parallels are accompanied not only by similar place names but also by physical evidence of considerable drainage schemes – often thought to have been inspired by Egyptian hydraulic engineering – which have been found in both Boiotia and the Peloponnese, and which will be discussed in detail in Chapter III.

Taken together, the cultic, mythical, toponymic and archaeological evidence strongly suggests that Boiotia and other regions of Greece were massively influenced by Egypt and the Levant during the Bronze Age. It is also extremely likely that these influences began in the Early Helladic period (the ceramic period approximating to the Early Minoan in Crete). However, while there may have been some form of Egyptian suzerainty over some of the Aegean states, there is no evidence to demonstrate that these influences were the result of Egyptian colonization. Thus, while there are many parallels between the situations of the Near East and the Aegean in the Early Bronze Age (c. 3300–2000 BC) and the Late Bronze Age (c. 1700–1200 BC), the only substantial suggestions of direct suzerainty come in the latter.

In Hellenistic and Roman times, writers like Theophrastos, Pliny and Plutarch frequently drew parallels between the shores of the Nile and those of the Kopais. They saw similarities between the floating islands, the water plants, the date palms and the manufacture of linen in the two regions.[1] This accumulation of evidence led Karl Otfried Müller to admit that the idea of a migration of an agricultural people or of Egyptian conquest 'would appear to be not groundless'.[2] Naturally, he went on to demonstrate what he saw as the deceptiveness of appearances in this case.[3] Nevertheless, as Müller knew, it was not only the geographical similarities between the two marshlands that linked Egypt with the Kopais basin. There were also strong mythological and legendary bonds connecting the Egyptian Nile and lakes with the shores of the Kopais and the Boiotian city of Thebes. Plausible Egyptian etymologies for such place names as Thebes, Kopais, Kēphissos and for ethnic names such as Minyans and Lapiths will be discussed below.[4] The Egyptian and West Semitic aspects of many Boiotian myths, such as those around Oedipus and the Sphinx, will be considered in Volume 4. Here, I should merely like to mention some of the cultic, mythological and onomastic evidence for Egyptian influence. This, I hope, will provide a context for Chapter III, where I look at the archaeological evidence from around Lake Kopais, dating from the 3rd millennium, for Egyptian colonization.

SEMELĒ AND ALKMĒNĒ

We shall first turn to Alkmēnē, a legendary princess living in Thebes, who was seduced by Zeus and as a result gave birth to Herakles. Her cult was extremely important on the shores of the Kopais. There are close parallels between the births of two of Zeus' sons, Dionysos and Herakles, from women with strong Theban associations. In support of this connection is the following passage from the *Iliad* where Zeus is reminiscing over past lovers:

> nor of the daughter of far-famed Phoinix who bore me Minos and the godlike Rhadamanthys, nor of Semelē nor of Alcmēnē in Thebes and she brought forth Herakles stout of heart, and Semelē bore Dionysos.[5]

This not only links the two divinities, Herakles and Dionysos, to Kadmos, the legendary Phoenician founder of Thebes, through his sister Europa (the daughter of far-famed Phoinix) but it pairs Europa with Semelē and Alkmēnē.[6] In Volume 1, I noted the derivation of the name of Zeus' paramour Iō from Egyptian words for 'cow'.[7] According to myth, Semelē was a daughter of Kadmos, who was also seduced by Zeus and gave birth to Dionysos. Her name too appears to have a similar Egyptian origin, although others have been suggested. One derivation of the name is from a dubious Phrygian word for 'sky', another is from *selenē*, the Greek word for 'moon'.[8] A stronger possibility, proposed by the Semitist Michael Astour, is a derivation from the West Semitic divinity Ṣml (the Mother of the Eagles) and some versions of the story of the birth and dismemberment of Dionysos do resemble myths about Ṣml and Osiris/Dionysos' Ugaritic equivalent Baʿal and they clearly do share common features.[9] There is thus every reason to suspect West Semitic influence here.

Nevertheless, the most likely fundamental derivation of Semelē would seem to be from the Egyptian *smʒt* (wild cow). The cultural origins of the Egyptians as a cattle people, for whom – like the Silluk and Nuer, who still inhabit the Nile Valley – cows provide a standard of wealth and beauty, can be seen, among many things, from the Egyptian use of the word *smʒt* or *smʒyt* to mean 'royal consort'.[10] Given the royal attributes of the Upper Egyptian ram god Amon and Zeus, whom the Ancient Greeks saw as his Greek counterpart, *smʒ(y)t*, Semelē, would seem a very suitable mate.

It should be noted that the connection between Zeus and Am(m)on in Boiotia was particularly well established. Pausanias, the Greek travel writer of the 2nd century AD, mentions a shrine of Ammon in Thebes with a statue dedicated by the local poet Pindar in the 5th century BC.[11] It will be remembered that Pindar had written a hymn with the line 'Ammon king of Olympos'.[12]

The chief Egyptian etymology for Alkmēnē would give her rather lower status than Semelē. The verb *rḫ*, 'to know', has a biblical or carnal sense. The name Rḫ imn is attested, as are the terms *rḫ nsw* and *rḫt nsw* (male and female acquaintances of the king).[13] Thus, while the Greek names Alkmaiōn, the Argive hero with Theban connections, and Alkma(o)n, the 7th-century Doric poet, may be related to the common Greek onomastic element Alki- (protector), they can also be plausibly derived from Rḫ imn. The name Alkmēnē, the concubine of Zeus, would seem to come from *Rḫt imn. Medial *t*s were unstable in Egyptian and sometimes disappeared in Greek transcriptions of Egyptian names, as with Amenōphis from ᾽Imn ḥtp. We know that in the middle of the 2nd millennium ᾽Imn was vocalized as ᾽Amāna; we also know that initial double or triple consonant clusters in Egyptian always produced prothetic vowels and that unaccented vowels were shortened.[14] Thus, a loan from an Egyptian *aRḫᵉmāna could easily be received in Greek as *Alkmāna and thence in Ionian to Alkmēnē. *Rḫt imn/Alkmēnē would seem entirely suitable for a consort of Amon/Zeus.

Having considered this strong possibility that Alkmēnē's name was Egyptian, we should briefly consider the Egyptian elements in her background. Apart from the connections with Zeus/Amon mentioned above and the fundamentally Egyptian character of her son Herakles, which will be discussed below, Herodotos believed she and one of her husbands, Amphitryon, were Egyptian.[15] The Egyptian aspects of the other husband Rhadamanthys will be discussed in Chapter IV. Here, it is sufficient to say that, as Alkmēnē's husband, hence Herakles' step-father, Rhadamanthys was supposed to have taught the hero how to shoot a bow and arrow.[16] This is interesting, because in Egyptian theology Mntw, who, it will argued in Chapter IV, was Rhadamanthys' Egyptian prototype, was the divine patron of archery.

ATHENA AND ATHENS IN BOIOTIA:
THE CULTS OF ATHENA ITŌNIA
AND ATHENA ALALKOMENA

Alkmēnē had a tomb near Haliartos on the southern shore of the Kopais, the ancient excavation of which will be discussed in Chapter III. It was close to a tomb attributed to Rhadamanthys and to a shrine to Kekrops, the heroic founder of Athens. There are in fact many other 'Athenian' traces in the region. There are shrines to Athena and there were supposed to have been two cities, later flooded by Lake Kopais, called Athenai and Eleusis. Strabo suggests that these, like the major cities of the same names in Attica, were founded by Kekrops.[17] Furthermore, there was a heroic cult of Kekrops in Haliartos itself, though there is some dispute as to whether this Kekrops was the founder of Athens or merely Kekrops son of Pandion, one of the later kings of Athens.[18]

The contemporary specialists on Boiotia, J. M. Fossey and A. Schachter, have argued in support of each other that this 'Athenian motif' in the country to the west of Haliartos arose only much later, when Athens was ruling the territory between 171 and 121 BC.[19] Fossey, in fact, is not quite so extreme and admits that there may be a 'conflating . . . [of] genuine local traditions with an artificial Athenian one'.[20] Even Schachter, however, admits that the two local cults of Athena Alalkomena and Athena Itōnia were 'of considerable antiquity'.[21]

The shrine of Athena Itōnia at Korōnela, 10 kilometres west of Haliartos, was the central cult of Boiotia and was clearly very active in Archaic (776–500 BC) and Classical (500–325 BC) times. It was traditionally supposed to have been established by the Boiotians who conquered the country, which was called Boiotia after them, from the north sometime after the Trojan War (c. 1210 BC). Pausanias reported that the eponymous Itōnos was the father of Boiotos the eponym of the Boiotians. The warlike cult of Athena Itōnia was central in Thessaly throughout Classical and Hellenistic times and Strabo plausibly supposed that it was brought by the conquering Boiotians from their home in Thessaly to the shores of Kopais.[22]

Where does the name Itōnia come from? There appear to be two candidates. The first of these is from the Egyptian *'Itn.t* (the female solar disk). The antiquity of this symbol and concept in the Crete has been discussed in Chapter I. The only attestation of *'Itn.t* for Nēit, whom the ancients saw as Athena's Egyptian counterpart, comes from the 2nd century AD. Thus it may have been the result of Greek influence rather than an authentic Egyptian tradition. However, Nēit's presence on the solar bark and her association with the sun, especially when symbolized by the eye of Re, and the Uraeus – the royal solar disk with a cobra coming out from it – date back at least to the 18th Dynasty.[23] Even earlier than this is Nēit's association with a coleoptera beetle whose iconography seems to have preceded that of the scarab and may well have had a similar solar function, as it was possibly luminous.[24] Nēit's strongest solar associations appear to have been in the Old Kingdom in the first half of the 3rd millennium. What is more, there is the evidence from Crete that the iconography of the solar beetle was already current in Crete in Early Minoan times.[25] The late attestation in Greece may well reflect an extremely ancient Egyptian tradition.

It will be argued in Volume 3 that there is also 2nd-millennium evidence from the Aegean of Athena's association with the solar disk and with snakes in the form of the Gorgon's face, which the goddess almost always wore on her shield or breastplate. This ferocious aspect of the goddess's character would fit very well with the martial nature of Athena Itōnia.

The epithet Itōnia has another origin, however, which is of more immediate concern. When Strabo described the Thessalian origin of the cult of Athena Itōnia at Korōnela, he also stated that there had been punning on the river names Kuralios or Kōralios and Korōnela. This stream, which was supposed to flow from two springs like the breasts of a goddess, was clearly significant in the cult.[26]

This raises another possible etymology for Itōnia. Stephanos of Byzantion, writing in the 6th century AD, maintained that the eponym of the Cretan city of Itanos was a son of Phoinix (the eponym of the Phoenicians). F. C. Movers and Victor Bérard, following up on this indication of Semitic presence, saw an origin for the name in the word *'ētån* or *'êtån* (perennial, ever-flowing) found in Hebrew.[27] Since they wrote, the name has been attested in both Linears A and B as Itano and Utano respectively. The variation Itan-, Itōn- can be explained by the fact that the Semitic *å* seems to have been transcribed into Greek and other languages as *ō* almost as frequently as *a*. See, for example, the name of the small inner harbour at Carthage known in Greek as Kōthōn from the Late Canaanite *qåṭån* or *qåṭon* (small).[28] Given the clear cultic importance of the stream flowing through Itōnia, it is quite likely that this name may have pre-dated the arrival of the Boiotians and have provided a reason for the establishment of the cult there. The great probability of a substantial West Semitic presence in Boiotia in the Late Bronze Age indicates that the name could be Semitic. However, the frequency of Itanos/Itōnos around the Aegean would seem to suggest that the toponym had independent force in the local languages.

Scholars are generally agreed that the cult of Athena Alalkomena is even older than that of Athena Itōnia and, as we shall see, there are arguments for linking the two cults. Homer refers to 'Athena of Alalkomene'.[29] Schachter provides other reasons for accepting its great age: the facts that it was regarded as ancient in Antiquity; attracted legends of the prehistoric period; and existed so close to – only 3 kilometres from – the cult of Athena Itōnia. Both antiquity and an early association with Athena are also suggested by the presence of the name Alalkomenios for the last month of the Boiotian year, which was sometimes repeated for intercalation to adjust the solar to the lunar year.[30] Calendars are generally recognized to preserve archaic nomenclature.

Ōgygos, 'Ôg and Gôg

Relatively little is known about the cult. In a story going back at least to the 4th century BC, Alalkomena or Alkomena was supposed to have been one of the three daughters of Ōgygos, the legendary first ruler of Boiotia.[31] Pausanias also reported that Ōgygos was also the father of Eleusis – in Attica.[32] Ōgygia was the name of Kalypso's far-off island in the *Odyssey*. Linking the insular, the Boiotian and the Attic connotations of the name is the idea that all come from a primal flood. The German ancient historian Eduard Meyer specifically linked Ōgygos to the flooding of the Kopais.[33] A connection with the lake and the flooded cities of Athenai and Eleusis on its western shore would certainly explain the otherwise puzzling association of Ōgygos with both Boiotia and Attica. The double connotation of antiquity and marshland comes in a passage of Aischylos' *The Persians* referring not to the Boiotian but to the Egyptian Thebes.[34]

The clearest etymologies for Ōgygos or Ōgygēs and Ōgygia come from West Semitic. The most common though by no means generally accepted derivation for both Ōgygia and Ōkeanos – the ocean or rim of the world – is from the Semitic root √'wg (to draw a circle).[35] These connotations of the ocean and the associated mountains that surround the world are also present in a West Semitic mythical figure, 'Ōg of Bashan. 'Ōg was strikingly similar to Ōgygos. He was seen in the Bible as the last of the Rephaim, a race of aboriginal giants associated with funerary rites and the spirits of the dead associated with the watery slush of the underworld.[36] In opposition to these characteristics the Rephaim were also associated with healing and the snakes connected in both Greece and the Levant with medicine. They were also linked to life, rebirth and fertility.[37]

In an Ugaritic text, the Rephaim or Rpim were called qdmym (eastern or ancient), the same root from which the name of the founder of Thebes, Kadmos, derived.[38] In the biblical Book of Deuteronomy, it is reported that King 'Ōg of Bashan was the last survivor of the Rephaim living in the general region of Canaan.[39] Thus, his position as the oldest inhabitant is very like that of Ōgygos in Boiotia. Bashan is generally placed to the north of Moab in what is now Northern Jordan. However, unlike this generally arid region, Bashan is also associated with great fertility and fat cattle.[40] In this way it was parallel to the rich marsh grazing lands of Boiotia.

'Ōg was the sole surviving antediluvian creature. According to the Midrash – Jewish biblical commentaries written in Babylonia from the 5th and 6th centuries of the Common Era – 'Ōg had survived the Flood by sitting on top of Noah's Ark.[41] Astour does not associate Ōgygos with 'Ōg. He sees Ōgygos as the counterpart of Noah and his Mesopotamian counterpart Ut-Napištim and his Greek one Deukalion.[42] The name Noah—correctly Noaḥ—is traditionally supposed to derive from the Semitic root √nwḥ (rest, settle). Despite the final ḥ, it is likely that it was influenced by the Egyptian nwy (water, flood). This would explain such anomalies as the term mê noaḥ (flood) found in Isaiah and the rendering of Noaḥ as Nōe in the Septuagint.[43] Thus in some ways Noaḥ was the flood with which he was associated. This ambiguity or double function could also be true for 'Ōg and Ōgygos. In this connection it is interesting to note that in Late Egyptian wgꜣ was a 'type of water or flood'.[44] The toponym Wg(ꜣ) also appears as the name of a body of water, either 'the grand canal or the course of the Nile', in the 3rd nome (or district) of Upper Egypt, that of the city of Esna.[45] Esna was the Upper Egyptian centre of the cult of Nēit. Its association with Troezen Athena's sacred city in the Argolid will be discussed in Volume 3. Here it is simply interesting to note the connection of Wg(ȝ) with water and Athena's Egyptian counterpart Nēit. There are, however, difficulties with this as an etymon for either 'Ôg and Ōgygos. In the first case, the initial ʿayin in the Semitic name does present difficulties. However, there is a close association in Egyptian between w and ʿ so the barrier is not insuperable. The problem with the derivation of Ōgygos from Wg(ȝ) is the second g as there is no evidence of one in any of the Egyptian texts.

There are, however, signs of one in West Semitic. The first of these is suggested by the giant Gôg referred to in the Bible. Gôg, with his brother Magôg, was supposed to have been a son of Japhet and to have lived in the far north. This would seem to make him rather different from 'Ôg, even though 'bulls and buffaloes of Bashan' were prophesied to be eaten at Gôg's funeral.[46] Then there is the possibility that Gôg was simply a West Semitic word for 'giant', the root √gg attested in Akkadian, Ugaritic and Canaanite with the general meaning 'roof, gallery or top'. In Amharic gəgg means 'tooth that pushes under another'. These general connotations of exaggerated height together with the names Gôg and Magôg raise this possibility. In any event, there is no doubt that the Greek gigas (giant) has no Indo-European etymology that respectable lexicographers, such as Julius Pokorny or Pierre Chantraine, cared to repeat. Whether or not gigas comes from Semitic it would seem likely that the double g in Ōgygos was influenced by the Greek word.

Astour argues that Ōgygos derives from the Semitic root √ʾgg (to burn, flame). He links this to the strong tradition that floods are often associated with fire. An example of this is the fact that the wife of the Greek flood hero Deucalion was called Pyrrha (fire).[47] In Chapter VII, I shall argue that this tradition has a historical basis in volcanic events, especially the great Thera eruption of 1628 BC. According to Jewish tradition as preserved in the Talmud, the flood that almost overwhelmed 'Ôg of Bashan was mingled with fire and he would have been scalded to death if it had not been for his gigantic strength.[48]

In short, although the derivation of the West Semitic 'Ôg from the Egyptian wgȝ, 'flood', is weak and that of the Greek gigas from the Semitic √gg is uncertain, the tight network of parallels makes a close relationship of Ōgygēs or Ōgygos to 'Ôg very probable. In any event, there is no doubt that Ōgygos, the Boiotian representative of Greek autochthony, has many intricate relations with the Near East.

Alalkomene

Now I should like to return to Ōgygos' daugher Alalkomena or Alkomena. Alalkomene was supposed to have been the birthplace of

Odysseus, though this may well be a confusion with another Alalkomene on the hero's home island of Ithaca.[49] More importantly, there is the tradition that an eponym, Alalkomeneus, reared Athena by the banks of the river Tritōn below both Alalkomene and Korōnia.

This was an alternative to the other tradition that Athena had been raised by the river Tritōn in Libya.[50] Herodotos placed the Tritōn associated with Athena in 'Libya', in what seems to have been the south of modern Tunisia.[51] Other ancient writers put it in different regions of North and West Africa, but in most cases it was associated with marshes.[52] In a very interesting passage from his epic the *Argonautika*, which will be discussed in Chapter VI, the learned Apollonios of Rhodes, who was a librarian at Alexandria in the 3rd century BC, claimed that Tritōn was an ancient name for the Nile. Apart from linking it to its eponym Tritōn, a son of Poseidon, there has been no satisfactory etymology of the name, though it is vaguely thought to be related to the Greek *tritos* (third). However, the Greek root *trito-* is, I believe, often confused with the Egyptian *tryt-*, a noun from the verb *tr* (respect), frequently used in referring to kings and gods. Adolf Erman and Hermann Grapow, the chief editors of the *Wörterbuch der Aegyptischen Sprache*, derive *tr* from *twr* (respect). The basic sense of this word is, however, 'to purify'. The guide to the soul called the *Book of Going Forth by Day* is more commonly known as the *Book of the Dead*, a title more suitable to the 19th-century image of Egypt. It is one of the most widely attested Egyptian texts and it dates back to the 18th or even the 17th Dynasty, in the 17th century BC. In it ◁𓆓◁𓈖 Twr is the name of one of the rivers in paradise or the Fields of the Blessed, full of rich corn and prosperous agriculture.[53] This etymology for Tritōnis is far from satisfactory, but it should be borne in mind when we consider the associations of Athena and her Egyptian counterpart Nēit with the draining of marshes and the creation of productive land along the banks of the Nile and other rivers and lakes.

Should the Alalkomenian Athena be linked to the cult of the Itōnian Athena, 3 kilometres to the west, and the Tomb of Alkmēnē, about the same distance to the east? Schachter has plausibly argued for fundamental links between the neighbouring cults of Athena. He has even tentatively suggested that the Alalkomeneion was the original site of the cult of Athena Itōnia which was moved west, possibly because of danger from flooding.[54] It is not necessary to go as far as this in order to accept his general argument, for which he has ancient authority – a reference made by the 4th-century African Christian writer Lactantius to Bakchylides, a poet of the 6th-century BC, who had stated that the Itōnian and Alalkomenian Athena signified the same thing.[55]

If we make this parallel, it would seem that interesting characteristics of the cult of the Itōnian Athena may also apply to the Alalkomenian one. For instance, the latter was clearly associated with a
snakelike creature from at least the 6th century BC.[56] Schachter believes that the snake represented on a Boiotian *lekane* (shallow basin)
was an earthy or 'chthonic' Zeus, since Athena Itōnia was paired with
Zeus at Haliartos.[57] There are a few traces of a 'chthonic' or snakelike
'ophic' Zeus, but there are also two possible Egyptian explanations for
this Greek iconography. One is from Nēit's association with the erect
cobra of the *Uraeus*, the ceremonial headdress of the pharaohs, which
was also the determinative or symbolic sign of goddesses. It would appear more probable, however, that the creature from Korōne, like
that found on another 6th-century Boiotian vase and the illustration
of Athena at Priene on the coast of Asia Minor, which has a coiled
snake in front of the goddess, are representations of Nēit's son and
most frequent consort since the Old Kingdom, the crocodile god Sobek.[58] Sobek was a divinity of floods, riverbanks and especially of the
marshy lake Fayum – a huge depression and oasis linked to the Nile
Valley. Such a cult would, thus, seem altogether appropriate for the
marshy shores of Lake Kopais. I shall be looking at the connections
between Alkmēnē and Athena Alalkomena later in the chapter. Here,
however, I should like to consider another aspect of Nēit.

Nēit, the Controller of Water

In Volume 3, I shall discuss the intimate relationship between Nēit
and Athena as well as that between Nēit's city Sais, or Ḥt Nt, and
Athens. At this point, however, it is essential to consider one aspect of
the Egyptian goddess in order to gain some insights into the cults of
Athena on the shores of the Kopais.

Nēit had many functions as a warrior, weaver and a divinity of the
upper air or Ether. Nevertheless, her essential characteristic was as
the bovine divinity – the creative cow ꒽hꜣt Ahet – associated with Mḥt
Wrt, the Great Flood or swamp, the primal water. Details of this are
clearly attested only in texts from the Saite and Ptolemaic periods in
the 1st millennium BC. However, it is clear from references in the *Pyramid Texts* inscribed in pyramids of the late Old Kingdom (2700–2500
BC) but composed many centuries before that, and in the *Coffin Texts*
of the Middle Kingdom (2100–1750 BC) that these ideas were far
more ancient.[59] Her cult at Sais in the marshes of the Western Delta is
known in the 1st Dynasty and may well be even older.[60]

The *Pyramid Texts* describe one of her central aspects: 'Nēit has
come to her lakes which are on the edge of the Mḥt Wrt [Great

Swamp] . . . Nēit makes green the grass on the two banks of the horizon.'[61] In New Kingdom versions of *The Book of Coming Forth by Day*
she is seen as associated with banks and islands.[62] Later texts also specify how Nēit created land out of the waters, 'separating the isles and
the banks'. In the Old Kingdom, she was the goddess who 'opened the
way(s)'. This clearly meant leading religious and funereal processions
often in a bark by water. *Wp(ỉ)* also meant 'opening' waterways.[63]
Thus, she is the goddess who creates channels and disciplines the wild
marshes.

THE BATTLES BETWEEN NĒIT AND
SETH, ATHENA AND POSEIDON

Nēit's role as the divinity of the nourishing flood, of canals, irrigation
and land reclamation would seem to provide a key for understanding
many aspects of Athena's mythological character that have been inexplicable to modern scholars. Take, for example, the Greek goddess's
battles with Poseidon at Athens, Troezen and elsewhere which parallel those fought by Nēit against Poseidon's Egyptian counterpart Seth
and the evil serpent Apopi.[64] Seeking an explanation for this conflict,
Lewis Farnell, the leading orthodox scholar of Greek religion at the
turn of the century, wrote:

> In no part of Greek religion was there any connection between Pal-
> las [Athena] and Poseidon that points to an original affinity of char-
> acter. Where the cults existed side by side, as on the Acropolis
> of Athens, at the deme of Colonus and possibly at Sunium, at
> Troezen, Sparta, Asea [in Arkadia], and probably Corinth we may
> suppose that in some of these places there had been a final recon-
> ciliation of two cults that were often in conflict at first. To say the
> strife of Athena and Poseidon for the Attic land is a symbol of
> physical changes, an allusion to the sea encroaching or the sea re-
> ceding, is very plausible but untrue: we have the analogy of the con-
> test between Helios and Poseidon at Corinth, where the explanation
> appears even more natural and likely; but we know it to be wrong;
> for in the first place the territory in dispute between the two di-
> vinities was Acrocorinthos, a height which never in the memory of
> any Greek had been flooded or threatened by the sea and secondly
> we have abundant evidence of the prevalence of a very ancient
> Helios-cult at Corinth which paled before the later Ionic worship
> of Poseidon. No doubt there were physical reasons why Poseidon
> should be worshipped at Corinth; but the Corinthian legend of this
> strife, the Delphic legend of the conflict between Apollo and the
> Python, of Apollo and Heracles for the Tripod, the Attic legend of

the rivalry of Poseidon and Athena and many other similar the-
omachies, probably all contain the same kernel of historical fact, an
actual conflict of worships – an earlier cherished by the aboriginal
men of the locality, and a later introduced by the new settlers.
Athena was the older goddess of Attica, Poseidon the great god
of the Ionians; the strife and the friendship between the two deities on the Acropolis may have been the religious counterpart of
the conflict and union of the old Attic and Ionic elements of the
population.[65]

The basic flaw in this passage is Farnell's reduction of the problem
to one of 'race' or of 'the ethnic principle' pioneered by Barthold
Niebuhr and beloved by 19th-century ancient historians.[66] Naturally,
Athena was closely tied to Athens. I also accept the ancient view that
Poseidon was the patron of the Ionians and I would go further and
link this to the Mycenaean predilection for the god and to the Hyksos'
worship of Seth. On the other hand, there is no reason to believe that
there was an 'aboriginal Athenian' population which 'paled before'
the Ionian master race.
    Walter Burkert, the modern Swiss authority on Greek religion, does
not mention this racist theory. He places less emphasis on the ethnic
principle than on the two divinities' association with horses.[67] There is
no doubt that a number of such horse cults exist, and I shall argue in
Volume 4 that it would appear that Poseidon had been associated with
chariots since the 18th century BC. On the other hand, there is to
my knowledge no description or representation of the two divinities
fighting from chariots and I hope to make it clear below that the cults
of Athena and Poseidon and their rivalry antedated the introduction
of the chariot to Greece. Burkert also argues – on the analogy of the
struggles between Apollo and Poseidon – that those between Athena
and Poseidon symbolized a generational conflict between young and
old.[68] It is indeed clear that, as a symbol of the rising sun, Apollo, like
his Egyptian counterparts Horus and Khepri, is seen as a young man
and younger than his uncle/opponent Poseidon/Seth. Despite being a
niece of Poseidon, the situation is not so clear for Athena or for Nēit,
both of whom are curiously ageless and not particularly youthful.
    If these schemes break down, what are we left with? First, there is
the argument that Farnell discarded, that the struggle 'is a symbol of
physical changes, an allusion to the sea encroaching or the sea re-
ceding'. He is misled here by his purely maritime view of the Greek
god. Poseidon – like Seth and their Ugaritic equivalent Yam (sea) – is
a divinity of disorder beyond the limits of cultivation. Thus, while
his realm certainly contained the sea, it also included such things as

earthquakes and the donkeys and horses of the nomadic populations of the desert.[69] The chief struggle mentioned by Farnell is between organized land and chaotic water, but the water can be fresh as well as salt. The Egyptian battle between Horus and Seth is usually represented as one between a man and a large, powerful riverine or lacustrine animal, a crocodile or more commonly a hippopotamus. It is interesting to note that since *hippopotamoi* (horses of the rivers) do not look much like horses, the Greek word and concept may well come from their relationship to horses through Seth and his other later Greek counterpart Typhon.

These riverine connotations would explain the cults of Athena and Poseidon at Asea and Sparta, which were at the source and the flood plain of the Eurotas river – the biggest in the Peloponnese. (It is possible that the struggle at Athens was originally over the Thriaisian plain on the coast of Attica.) However, the close associations between Athens and Nēit's marsh-girt city of Sais, and the less certain but still likely pairing of Troezen in the Argolid and Nēit's southern city of Esna, which also required hydraulic work, are sufficient to explain the double cult of Athena and Poseidon in the Greek cities. In many ways the battleground between Athena and Poseidon at Athens was a transposition of one between Nēit and Seth at Ḥt Nt/Sais.

Rather than arguing that the connected worship of such disparate deities must represent religious conflict between different peoples or different generations, it would seem much more plausible to suppose that the struggle was itself central to the cult. Fontenrose and others have shown the universality of such divine battles.[70] Here, I simply want to emphasize that the particular forms of many of these common themes found in Greece are nearly always specifically Egyptian or West Semitic.

In Egypt, as in most other places, it was seen that both the demonic forces of nature and their taming were necessary to human existence. Thus, while I deny that the horse cult was fundamental to that of the struggle between Athena and Poseidon, Walter Burkert is absolutely right to point out that when 'Poseidon sires the horse and Athena invents the bridle and bit, thereby placing the animal at the disposal of man', this represents something much more universal because it 'produced a telling constellation of elemental force and technical wisdom'.[71]

POSEIDON/SETH

We shall return to Athena later, but here we need to consider Poseidon. He too had a cult in the region south of Lake Kopais. Ten kilometres to the east of Haliartos, there was the grove and later the temple of Poseidon Onchestos. As this was situated on the pass separating the Haliartos from Thebes, Schachter has plausibly linked it to other centres of Poseidon's worship on passes or water gaps in the wilds of Thessaly, which he believes date back to the Bronze Age. Schachter also connects the cult at Onchestos to the Kalaurian Amphictiony, or league of cities, set in many of the major plains throughout Southern Greece, which, despite recent scepticism, gives every appearance of having originated in early Mycenaean times.[72] The Onchestian cult was specifically linked to the wildness of the terrain and to horses. The same is true of that of Poseidon Telphousa. This was situated at the spring of Telphousa or Tilphousa, which is generally recognized as being at the bottom of a cliff below the Tilphosian mountain, just one kilometre from Alalkomenai.[73] It was here that Poseidon was supposed to have mated with the fierce goddess Erinys to produce a magic horse, Areion, famous for helping Herakles and for rescuing another hero, Adrastos.[74] The wider significance of this myth is made clear by its appearance at Thelpousa in Arkadia. Here Poseidon was supposed to have ravished Demeter Erinys who gave birth to Areion.[75]

The parallel names of Erinys and Areion seem to be in some way connected to the word *eris* (strife).[76] Here again, Egyptian mythology can provide useful guides for understanding this mythological cluster.

Fontenrose has recognized a close relationship between Erinys and Korē/Persephone.[77] Erinys can, thus, be seen as a Greek version of the Egyptian Nephthys. Nephthys was the sister of Isis (whose Greek counterpart was the earth mother goddess Demeter, mother of Persephone) and the wife of Seth, whose chthonic aspect was in Greek terms Hades.

Like her usual Greek equivalent Persephone, or Korē, Nephthys was seen as both good and evil. The Egyptian goddess helped her sister protect Osiris and Horus but at the same time she was a divinity of death.[78] As a mirror image of her sister, the ever-fertile Isis, Nephthys was normally barren, but she was supposed to have had one child, the jackal god Anubis. As so often in Egyptian mythology – and elsewhere – there was uncertainty as to the father; some sources maintained that it was her brother Osiris and others her husband Seth.[79] The latter version would fit the Greek story very well and link Anubis with Poseidon's offspring, Areion. Anubis' mixed paternity would seem to be the result of his theological character. Despite his intimate connections with death, his role (which will be discussed more fully in Volume 3) was essentially positive. He was the guide and sometimes the carrier of the soul, like his Greek counterpart Hermes Psychopompos. In rescuing the dead and carrying them off to safety, Anubis seems to have resembled Areion. In general then, the story of Poseidon, Erinys and Areion would seem to follow the Egyptian pattern – transposed into hippic or horsey terms.

Delphos and Anubis

The pattern is, however, is extremely intricate in that a number of scholars have plausibly seen a parallel between Telphousa/Tilphousa and Delphos – the son of Poseidon or Apollo and Melantho or Melaina, a dolphinlike daughter of Deukalion (the Flood) – and Delphoussa, the name of one of the three springs at Delphi.[80] The connection was clearly significant because, according to the Homeric *Hymn to the Pythian Apollo,* Apollo considered setting up his temple and oracle at the Telphousian spring before he did so at Delphi.[81] It is further confirmed by the existence of three forms of the Arkadian toponym Thelpousa/Telphousa/Delphousia. This brings us to the identification of Delphos with Apollo and the complications around the latter's cult at Delphi, which will be discussed below and in Volumes 3 and 4. Only some aspects can be raised here.

On the basis of a connection made by the Greek lexicographer of the 5th century AD, Hesychios, between Delephat and the 'Chaldaean' name for the planet Venus, Victor Bérard identified the cluster Thelpousa/Telphousa/Delphousia with a Semitic cult of Dilbat the morning star.[82] If this is so, it is less interesting from our point of view than the fact that Delphos was seen as the son of Poseidon or Apollo and Melaina or Melantho. If one admits the equation of Poseidon with Seth and Osiris' son Horus with Apollo, the ambiguity of Delphos' paternity is remarkably similar to that of Anubis.

Melaina/Nephthys

Delphos' maternity is still more interesting. Fontenrose identifies Melaina with Ge (Earth) and hence indirectly with the earth mother Demeter.[83] There is no doubt that the name Melaina/Melantho is related to the Greek root *melan* meaning 'black', and that earth is frequently called 'black' in Greek writings. It is for this reason that her son Delphos seems to have been considered an African Black and it is apparently his portrait that can be seen on a number of 5th-century coins from Delphi and Athens.[84] However, where does the root itself come from?

There is no common Indo-European root for the colour black, although Chantraine sees an Indo-European cognate for *melan* in the

Baltic root *meln (blue stain).[85] However, it would seem more plausible to derive this from the Egyptian name Mȝnw, the Mountain in the West, where the sun goes down in the evening, and the entrance to the underworld (this is discussed further in Chapters IV and X).[86] A derivation of melan from Mȝnw would have a neat analogy in the Semitic word cluster around the root √ʿrb, with the meanings 'enter', 'the place where the sun sets', 'west' and 'black', found in Homeric Greek as erebos, which is defined in the canonical Greek dictionary of Liddell and Scott as 'a place of nether darkness forming a passage from earth to Hades'. Erebos almost certainly comes from the Akkadian erebu (sunset).

In this case, Melaina/Melantho may mean not merely 'black' but the black of the west and the evening. This could link her to Europa, whose name derives from ʿrb and who played an important role in Boiotian legends and cults.[87] The association with dusk would also associate Melaina/Melantho with one of two Egypto-Greek goddesses – Ḥrt Tmt/Artemis, the ferocious lion goddess of the evening sun, or Nephthys/Persephone, the divinity of the margin between life and death and day and night. Given the associations with Demeter, mentioned above, and the parallel with the Telphousian myths of Poseidon's rape of Erinys, the latter would seem much more likely, and the fit can be made tighter still. In his De Iside et Osiride, Plutarch saw the illicit sex between Osiris and Nephthys as an allegory:

> The outmost parts of the land beside the mountains and bordering on the sea the Egyptians call Nephthys. This is why they give to Nephthys the name of 'Finality' [teleutē] and say that she is the wife of Typhon. Whenever, then, the Nile overflows and with abounding waters spreads far away to those who dwell in the outermost regions, they call this the union of Osiris with Nephthys, which is proved by the upspringing of plants.[88]

As mentioned above, the spring at Telphousa is at the foot of a cliff, a few metres from the historic edge of Lake Kopais but just over a kilometre from the 95-metre contour, which seems to have been the level for most of Antiquity.[89] The spring was at precisely the edge of the flood plain, just as Plutarch described the territory of Nephthys in Egypt. The fundamental difference is that in the Egyptian story Nephthys, the wife of Seth, was seduced by Osiris, the beneficent flood. In Greek mythology, on the other hand, Persephone was seized by Hades and Erinys (Melaina/Melantho) was ravished at Thelpousa/Tilphousa by Poseidon, the symbol of violent water. Nevertheless, the parallel between Plutarch's allegory and the Boiotian myth is remarkable.

For this parallel to be significant, however, two apparently difficult conditions have to be met. Firstly, there has to be an acceptance of the identifications of Poseidon with Seth and Persephone with Nephthys. Although these were not formally accepted in Classical and Hellenistic times, I hope to demonstrate the connections piecemeal in later volumes. The second condition is that, if the Egyptian story is very ancient, as it appears to be, then it must originally have been allegorical or have possessed this allegorical sense over a millenium before Plutarch. This too is not so difficult to accept as it might appear. There have been many examples, the most notable being his telling of the myths around Osiris, where Plutarch can be seen to have been in touch with traditions going back over a thousand years.[90] If one concedes the identification of Nephthys with Persephone/Erinys, the chances that the remarkable parallel between the Tilphousan myth and Plutarch's allegory is an example of 'Interpretatio Graeca' (the term used by Aryanist scholars to describe what they see as the later Greek mistaken interpretation of their own culture as having received profound borrowings from Egypt and Southwest Asia) are negligible. This is both because of the antiquity of the Boiotian cults and precisely because of the failure of Greeks and Egyptians in Classical and Hellenistic times to give public recognition to the identification of Seth and Poseidon.

Areion and Pegasos

As many scholars have noted, the story of the conception and birth of the magic horse Areion is very similar to the story of Bellerophon and Pegasos.[91] Pegasos, the flying horse, was supposedly begotten by Poseidon from Medusa in the mythical Western Hyperborea or Libya, and was especially connected with springs. Caught and tamed by the hero Bellerophon, Pegasos helped his master kill the monstrous Chimaera. After that, while Bellerophon was cast down for his presumption in trying to fly to Olympos, Pegasos reached the heights and remained as a servant to the gods.

Michael Astour has shown that the name Bellerophon comes from the Semitic *Ba'al-râphôn (The Healing Lord) and that many of his ancestors, as well as Pegasos' iconography and some of the themes of the mythical cycle, are clearly Southwest Asian.[92] However, he is unable to explain Pegasos' name and ancestry.

At least from the time of Hesiod, whom I place in the 10th century BC, it was recognized that Pegasos' name was connected to pēgē or pāgā (spring or running water).[93] Strabo, in the 1st century BC, referred to Hippokrēnē (Horse Fountain) as the spring of Pegasos on Mount

Helikon, about 10 kilometres south of Tilphossion and Lake Kopais.[94] Chantraine admits that the etymology is obscure but goes on to specu- late that because fountains are cool, *pēgē* is related to the verb *pēgnymi*, which normally means 'stick or fix upon' in the rare sense of 'congeal or freeze'. This is odd since *pēgē* or its verb *pēgazō* have precisely the sense of the gushing or movement of liquid water, tears, and so on.

It would seem more plausible to derive *pēgē* and Pegasos from the Egyptian semantic cluster which includes such words as *pgȝw* (jugs for washing), *pgȝ* (the opening, for instance of a valley), *pgȝ* (to break out or burst), *pgy* (to open as wounds), all written with the determinative ⌐ *psg* or *pgs* (spittle, to spit out) – it should be noted that Pegasos was supposed to have *spurted out* of the neck of his decapitated mother Medusa. Furthermore, there were the place names Pgȝ and Pgs, also written with ⌐.

It will be shown below that it is very likely that there is paranomasia or punning here in the formation of the name Pegasos, with an Egyp- tian form, **Pȝ gḥ* s (the gazelle), and with *gs* (run) and *gst* (speed).[95]

The Libyan Connection and Horses

A possible derivation of the name Tilphossia from Tȝlbyw (Libya) will be discussed below. Here I shall consider a connection between horses and springs found in Libya, using the name in both the modern sense of the country of Libya and the 'Libya' of Antiquity which included the whole of the Maghreb, the Sahara and further south. In Classical times, as today, the country to the west of Egypt is best known for its sand. Then, however, it was also known for its horses and chariots and oases. Asses and horses appear to have been introduced into Libya, through Egypt, only in the middle of the 2nd millennium and the beginning of the New Kingdom. By the 19th Dynasty, in the 13th century BC, large numbers were being captured there by the Egyp- tians.[96] In Classical times Libya had become the horse country *par ex- cellence*. Pindar called Cyrene in the east of the country 'good horse' and the 3rd-century poet Kallimachos named it 'the best horse bear- ing'.[97] However, as Oric Bates, the early 20th-century writer on the ancient Libyans, pointed out, 'The "horses", it should be said, were little more than ponies, but tough and wiry, and fleet. They were often so well schooled as to follow their masters like dogs.'[98] This is interesting in the light of the equation between the canine Anubis and the horse Areion suggested above.

As well as being good horsemen, Libyans were also reputed to be excellent charioteers. In 1171 BC, Ramessēs III claimed to have captured nearly a hundred chariots from them.[99] Rock paintings – some of them dating to around this period – found across the Sahara as far south as the Niger represent hundreds of chariots.[100] In Classical times nearly all the North African tribes appear to have used them in warfare.[101] According to Herodotos, quadrigas, or four-horse chariots, were introduced to Greece from Libya.[102] As Homer mentions their use, this must have been before 800 BC and may well have been even earlier,[103] the most likely period being the 12th century when Libyans and Greeks were allied as Peoples of the Sea.

The link between horses and chariots on the one hand and springs and oases on the other can be seen from the names given to the nomadic raiders in Libya. One of the most famous of the tribes that raided the coast from the interior, on horseback or using chariots, was the Nigretai or Nigretes – whose beautiful blackness was the source of the Latin word *niger*, from which the Portuguese, Spanish and English 'negro' developed. Their name came from the Semitic root √(n)gr (water to flow into sand) which was the origin of the toponyms Gar, Ger, Nagar and Niger, notably the River Niger, which unaccountably flowed east away from the Atlantic, apparently into the desert.[104]

The Nobatai

The Semitic root √nbṭ meant 'gush forth of water' or oasis. Peoples of the deserts and oases were sometimes called Nabaṭu, Nabati or Nabataeans in Arabia. The situation is confused by the existence of an Egyptian place name, Nbt or Nbyt, referring to two towns in Upper Egypt otherwise known as Ombos and Ombi. Ombos, on the edge of the desert, was the most important cult centre of Seth, who was frequently known as 'He of Ombos' or Nbty.[105] This firmly tied Seth, the god of the desert and its people and animals, to the peoples of the oases. It is therefore impossible, and to some extent uninteresting, to discover which of these formed the origin of the name of the Nobatai, a nomadic people living in the Eastern Sahara. Their city on the Upper Nile, in Nubia, was known as Nabata or Napata.[106] In the Ptolemaic period there was the geographical term Tȝ n Nȝpytw (Land of the Napitu), which the geographer of ancient Egypt Henri Gauthier placed in Libya. These could well be the Nobatai from Eastern Libya, called in by the Roman Emperor Diocletian to defend the southern frontier of Egypt in 294 AD.[107] Various attempts have been made to identify them with particular Libyan tribes but these have been unsatisfactory.[108] Nevertheless, the references are sufficient to demonstrate that Nobatai 'Oasis Dwellers' were reported from Libya as well as from Nubia and Arabia.

Seth and Poseidon, Nbty and Neptune

According to Herodotos, not only the quadriga but its patron god Poseidon came to Greece from Libya: 'for the Libyans are the only people who have always known Poseidon's name and always worshipped him.'[109] Alan Lloyd, who has written a splendid commentary on Herodotos' *Book Two* concerning Egypt, can make nothing of this statement. Working within the Aryan Model, Lloyd maintains that Poseidon's 'Indo-European/Gk. provenance is beyond doubt and the date of his introduction to Greece at least Achaean [Late Bronze Age]'.[110] My tentative hypothesis deriving Poseidon's name from the Egypto-Semitic hybrid Pꜣ(w) Sidôn (He of Sidôn) has been mentioned in Volume 1.[111] Thus, I do not accept that his name was either Indo-European or Libyan. As I have also argued above, I see him as the counterpart of the Egyptian Seth, who by Classical times was considered to be the epitome of evil.

This would explain why Herodotos' Egyptian informants seem to have been so adamant in denying Poseidon, a respectable god in Greece, a place in the Egyptian pantheon and why they saw him as the divinity of the outside wilderness, hence a Libyan god. Possibly following Egyptian informants, Herodotos linked Poseidon to the river Tritôn and Lake Tritônis in Libya or further west.[112] Thus, the god would seem to be associated with inland water within Libya, as well as with the hunting, horses and chariots of the oases' turbulent inhabitants.

At this point, we should consider the name of Poseidon's Italic counterpart Neptune. Let us return, for a moment, to the Semitic root √nbt, used for oases and their inhabitants, which appeared in the place names Nabata and Napata as well as the tribe of Nobatai who lived in Eastern Libya in Late Antiquity. The town of Nepete near Rome had a river and springs and, as the antiquarian George Dennis described it in the 1840s,

> He [the traveller] has left the open wastes of the Campagna and entered a wooded district. It is one of the few portions of central Italy that will remind him, if an Englishman, of home. Those sweeps of bright green sward. . . . The whole forms a lively imitation of – what is most rare on the Continent – English Park scenery.[113]

It was, in fact, an oasis. The existence of many plausible Semitic etymologies of toponyms around Rome – including that of the city itself – will be discussed in Volume 3. Thus, the derivation of Nepete from a Semitic root, which would seem to be extremely appropriate semantically, cannot be easily dismissed. With the West Semitic personal and gentilic suffixes -ån or -ôn, Nepete makes one very plausible origin for Neptune – the other chief candidate being the Egyptian

Nbty, Seth.[114] Thus, the existence of the name Nepete would suggest that some people saw resemblances between desert oases and European water sources and their immediate environs, in dry regions. If one accepts this background, then Poseidon's association with the spring at Tilphousa seems altogether natural.

Poseidon, Tilphousa and Libya

Can anything be made of the name Tilphousa/Telphousa/ Thelpousa itself? At one level there seems to be a connection with Delphousa and Delphos with its basic meaning of 'pair' or 'brother' which has been touched on above and will be discussed further in Volume 4.[115] However, I would argue that there is also a connection between the Egyptian place name Tȝlbyw (Land of Libya) and the frequent Aegean toponymic suffix -s(s)a.[116] Tȝlbyw is a rarely attested variant of Rb or Libu, Libyans. The name itself has been found only from the reign of Ramessēs II in the 13th century BC and at that time appears to have meant a distant tribe to the west of Egypt.[117] During the invasions of the Peoples of the Sea, that is, peoples from the northwest and west, the Libu became – from the Egyptian point of view – the leading people of the Western Desert.

In order to draw out the parallels between Tȝlbyw and the Boiotian Telphusa, it should be remembered that Libya was seen by the Greeks, probably since Homer or earlier, as including all Africa west of the Nile.[118] Most of this area was made up of desert and oases; similarly, the Boiotian Telphousa included the steep cliff and the 'oasis'-like spring below and from it – as in Libya – flowed a river Tritōn, connected to a marshy lake. Telphousa or 'Libyan' would make a very good byname for a goddess parallel to the Egyptian Nepthys, the barren sister of Isis, and the Greek Erinys/Persephone, the fearful sister of Isis' counterpart Demeter.[119] If Erinys' counterpart Melaina/ Melantho is associated with Mȝnw, the Egyptian 'Mountain of the West', as I suggested above, this too would suggest a link with Libya.[120] Furthermore, Libya as Africa would also parallel the blackness of Melaina/Melantho and Delphos.[121] These and the myths of Poseidon's own Libyan associations would make an etymology of Telphousa from Tȝlbyw seem quite plausible.

The Arkadian Thelpousa

The geographical case for identifying Thelpousa in Arkadia with Libya is hardly less clear. The Arkadian Thelpousa was sited on the river Ladōn where it emerged from a gorge and spread out into various channels on a small flood plain. The name Ladōn occurs as an alternative name for the river Ismēnos that flowed past Thebes in Boiotia and also occurs twice in the Peloponnese – once in Arkadia and once in Elis. In the Arkadian case it flows out of 'springs' originating in Lake Pheneos where Athena and Poseidon were jointly worshipped. These springs or channels were and are frequently blocked by earth tremors or quakes, thus leading to sudden stoppages followed by floods.[122] All of these would clearly be attributed to Poseidon, the divinity of earthquakes, and possibly explain the idea of the rape of Demeter Erinys downstream at Thelpousa. In Elis a river Ladōn flows into a river Pēneios at the Elean Pylos or 'Gateway'. The double connection between the two names is interesting, especially as Peneus has a strong Egyptian etymology in Pȝ Nw(y) (the water or the flood).[123]

Astour has pointed out that there was a river Lathōn or Lēton not far from Lake Tritōn in Libya and he links this to the Ugaritic dragon Ltn and the Hebrew Liwyåtån (Leviathan) who has been plausibly identified by modern scholars with the Ugaritic sea god Yam(m).[124] This etymology is strengthened by the mythical Ladōn – the snake that guarded the Golden Apples of the Hesperides – who was killed by Herakles, possibly in Libya. According to Hesiod, this snake could well be a river.[125] The idea of the world being surrounded by a river/snake/dragon, with hell inside it, occurs in an Egyptian Gnostic text, *Pistis Sophia*, of the 2nd or 3rd century AD, which the mythographer Joseph Fontenrose has plausibly linked to earlier Egyptian conceptions.[126] I shall be discussing this further in Chapter VII in connection with Atlas-Atlantos as the ocean that surrounded the world; both the giant Atlas and the Atlantic Ocean were of course intimately connected to Herakles, the Hesperides and Libya.[127]

The scholiast to Apollonios Rhodios described Ladōn as being the dragon Typhōn, who had expired at the springs of the Orontes river in Syria.[128] The Orontes frequently altered its flow and course as a result of seismic movement. Typhōn was the official Greek counterpart of Seth and, as Astour points out in this connection, the Ugaritic Ym(m) or Ṭpṭ Nhr (Judge River), the equivalent of Seth and Poseidon, was also portrayed as a dragon.[129] Thus, in Greece, the Levant and Egypt we find Ladōn/Ltn associated with rivers, dragons and the god of disturbance.

NĒIT/ATHENA AND NEPHTHYS/ERINYS

The Ladōn in Boiotia brings us back to the shores of the lakes in Boiotia, where the presence of Poseidon both as a divinity of the untamed marshes and of the spring is easy to understand. So too is the presence of Erinys, if she can be associated with Persephone and Nephthys, Seth's wife. Similarly, the presence of Athena as the divinity of water regulation and land reclamation is exactly what one should expect in a place where both were going on. There is, however, some difficulty in understanding the relationship between the two goddesses.

One way in which the two were linked was through the Gorgon Medusa, who, as I mentioned above, was closely tied to Persephone/ Nephthys, and incidentally Libya. However, while Athena was mythically involved in the monster's death and decapitation, she also wore her face and was in that way connected to her. This relationship, which dates back to the Bronze Age, will be discussed below and further in Volume 3.

Anukis/Onka

Here we are concerned with another link between the two goddesses Nēit/Athena and Nephthys/Erinys, that found in the name Onka. The shrine of Demeter Erinys at the Arkadian Thelpousa was located in a district of Onkeion. This has an eponymous King Onkos who was supposed to be a son of Apollo Onkaios.[130] These would seem to have gained their names from the location rather than the other way around.

The etymology of Onka almost certainly comes from the name of the Egyptian goddess ꜥnḳt, known to Greeks in Hellenistic times as Anukis. Egyptian and Semitic 'ayins were frequently associated with the back vowels o and u. See, for instance, the Coptic suffix -o from the Egyptian rꜣ (great) and the Coptic ōnh and ōnḫ for ꜥnḫ (life). Final -ts were usually dropped in Egyptian and always in Greek. Thus, there are no phonetic problems in deriving Onka from ꜥnḳt.

Anukis was associated with the world-creating ram god Khnum at Elephantine, on the southern frontier of Egypt, by the rapids of the First Cataract. She was connected with the islands in and near the cataract, notably Sahel, Elephantine and Philai.[131] As a goddess of the place where the Nile burst through into Egypt, she was also associated with the Nile sources – which according to Herodotos were sometimes seen as springs, pēgai – and with the Nile flood.[132] Her sacred animal was the gazelle, *Pꜣ gḥs. This is interesting in the light of one of the etymologies for Pegasos given above. The gazelle was presumably associated with the 'speed,' gst, of the waters rushing past Anukis' islands. In human form Anukis was generally represented with a Nubian headdress and seen as non-Egyptian.[133] She was also closely associated with Nephthys.

Thus the name Onkaios was, if anything, overdetermined. Its setting in Thelpousa where the fast-flowing river Ladōn broke up to form islands and where the seat of Demeter Erinys was located would fit perfectly – if on a much smaller scale – with ʿnḵt's cult centres on the islands of the Nile cataracts and her association with Nephthys.

Nēit/Athena and Anukis/Onka

Far better known than the cult of Onkaios was the cult of Athena Onka or Onga. According to legend, this had been established by Kadmos at the place at the centre of Thebes where the sacred cow had lain down after leading him to found the city.

Accepting the associations between Nēit and Athena and between Anukis and Onka one would expect to find links between Nēit and Anukis. However, no associations between the two Egyptian goddesses have been attested. They are not unthinkable, however, as in Ptolemaic times, Nēit and the ram god Khnum were the divine pair at Esna and were represented as two forms of the same world-creating divinity. Furthermore, Nēit, in her aspect of the divine creative cow ʒḥʒt, Ahet, was seen as Khnum's mother. Ramadan El Sayed, who has written the standard work on Nēit, believes that the association between Nēit and Khnum is much older.[134]

This relationship may well have been reflected in Greek cults. Khnum was widely known as Nb Ḳbḥw (Lord of the Cataracts) and it is possible that he was sometimes referred to simply as Ḳbḥ.[135] It will be argued in the next chapter that the Egyptian Ḳbḥ (Nile cataract or water emerging fresh from a cave) is the origin of the common Greek river name Kēphis(s)os, which was associated with streams that flowed underground.[136] Kēphis(s)os was also a mythological figure and as such, I believe, should be associated with Khnum. In Argos, for instance, Kēphis(s)os was one of the judges who granted the territory to Hera rather than to Poseidon, a myth very close to the conflict between Poseidon and Athena reported elsewhere.[137]

At the city of Argos there was a sanctuary of Kēphis(s)os by which Pausanias reported a head of Medusa.[138] The relationship between Medusa and both Athena and Erinys/Persephone has been mentioned above. Similarly in Upper Egypt, not only Nēit but Anukis, with her associations with Nephthys, were close companions of Khnum. Thus, there could well be a link between Anukis and Nēit through Khnum/Kēphis(s)os.

The association of Athena Onka and the tradition linking her to the cow who lead to the foundation of Thebes with Nēit is made closer by references in inscriptions of the Roman period at her great temple at Esna to Nēit as Ahet, swimming with the sun between her horns to settle at Sais.[139] It would seem that this story of Ahet has great antiquity. As mentioned above, Nēit was identified with the cow of the Mḥt Wrt (Great Swamp) in the *Pyramid Texts* from the early 3rd millennium.[140] We also know that Nēit was identified with her city, Sais or Ḥt Nt (House of Nēit) since the earliest dynastic times. Taken together with the attestation of her as the mother of Re in the *Coffin Texts* of the Middle Kingdom, this makes it overwhelmingly likely that the late inscription at Esna reflected a much older story.[141]

Michael Astour has shown that the story of following a cow to discover where to build a city is found in the Bible and that it was probably known elsewhere in West Semitic culture.[142] However, the parallel between Nēit as Ahet and the foundation of Sais and the story of Kadmos' following the cow, sacrificing her to Athena and establishing both Thebes and the cult of Athena Onka is even closer. Furthermore, the Egyptian myth's focus on Nēit as Ahet is precisely that aspect of the goddess that was closest to Khnum, since Ahet was Khnum's mother, and hence to Anukis. Thus, the context of the foundation myth of any city, but particularly one with the geographical situation of Thebes – see below – would be precisely where one would expect to find a fusion of Nēit/Athena with Anukis/Onka.

Pausanias wrote about the Theban cult of Athena Onga: 'Those who think Kadmos was an Egyptian and not a Phoenician who came to Thebes are contradicted by this Athena called Onga in Phoenician not Sais in Egyptian.'[143] The confusion between Kadmos' Egyptian and Phoenician origin will be discussed in Chapter XII. Here I want to point out that Pausanias was correct to assume that there should be a tight connection between Athena and Sais and was right to be puzzled by Athena Onka. Athena Onka is not a standard name for the goddess; it is a fusion between her and Anukis. Pausanias had good reason to be uncertain as to whether Onka was Egyptian or Phoenician.

The most plausible origin for Anukis' Egyptian name ˁnḳt is from the verb ink (to embrace). This could refer to her islands being embraced by the river branches. However, one finds an even closer parallel in the Semitic root √ˁnq (necklace), the idea being either that the rivers rushing past formed a necklace or that the islands in the cataract resembled a string of jewels. This might seem far-fetched if it were not for two factors. Firstly, there is the geographical situation of Thebes, which is on an escarpment above the Theban plain over which two or three rivers or streams flowed before joining up at the bottom.[144] Thus, the site resembled both the islands of the Egyptian ʿnḳt and the Semitic ʿnq (necklace). Secondly, the fact that the topography was seen in this way in ancient times is shown by the fact that the name of Kadmos' queen was Harmonia, which meant 'stringing together', and that the most famous present given at their magnificent wedding was a *hormon* (necklace).[145]

All these associations can be seen in Euripides' play *The Phoenician Women*. While the city is falling, the chorus of Phoenician Women sing in celebration of its Phoenician foundation.

> And then to Harmonia's wedding came the heavenly gods,
> And the walls of Thebes rose high to the harp's music,
> And at the bidding of Amphion's lyre,
> On ground between two rivers her towers stood straight,
> Where Dirce and Ismenus side by side,
> Moisten the lush green plain.[146]

Note the repeated references to strings. (The derivation of both Harmonia and *hormon* from the Semitic root √ḥrm (string or net) will be discussed in Volume 3.)

Harmonia had, of course, many other mythological attributes. Astour has shown, for instance, her connections to the Sumerian and Semitic goddesses with the title 'Lady of the House or Palace'.[147] This brings her close to Nephthys, or Nbt Ḥt, which also means 'Lady of the House'. Thus, the association of the cults of Onka and Harmonia in the Boiotian Thebes would tally with the Egyptian identification of Anukis with Nephthys. There is another story about Harmonia that she and her husband Kadmos turned into snakes and went to live in the Hesperides at the end of their lives. This myth, too, has many aspects, one of which would seem to be that, as a 'necklace' one strand of which was the river Ismenios/Ladōn (who also lived in the Hesperides), Harmonia was already such a snake.[148] Nevertheless, the central point I want to make here is that Harmonia's name as 'necklace' brings her close to ʿnḳt, ʿnq and Onka.

As we have seen, the most likely etymology for ʿnḳt comes from the verb *ink*. Its existence and its determinative ⟨⟩ raise the possibility that Egyptian too had a word *ʿnḳ, meaning 'necklace'. However, the presence of so many other Semitic names in Boiotia makes the attested Semitic form more likely. Thus Pausanias' confusion between the Egyptian and Phoenician origins of the name Onka would seem to reflect the presence of both languages at the very beginning of the cult.

Athena Onka and Athena Alalkomena

Another Egyptian root that may well be involved in this pattern is ʿrk, which in Egyptian is phonetically close to ʿnk. A similar vocalic pronunciation to Onka can be found in the Greek *horkos* (oath), which comes from the Egyptian ʿrk (swear, oath) and the Coptic *ōrk*.[149] The basic meaning of ʿrk is 'bind' seen in the determinative ⌒, a linen band. This would seem similar to that of ʿnk (embrace, necklace). However, ʿrk was not aways rendered as *ōrk* in Coptic; in the Fayumic dialect, ʿrk (oath) was rendered *ōlk*. The related form ʿrky (the last day of the month), ʿrky rnpt (the last day of the year), was commonly used. Presumably, these came from the sense of the year as a circlet.

The Egyptians had three if not four calendars, but the one that appears to be central to this mythological cluster was that now known as the 'civil' calendar. This was divided into twelve months of thirty days to which were added five 'epagomenal' or 'added' days. The new year began with the heliacal rising of Sirius which was an indicator of the arrival of the Nile Flood in the middle of our July. At least by the 18th Dynasty, the first day of the first month of the flood and of the new year was the feast of Khnum as god of creation and the Nile Cataracts.[150] Thus ʿrky rnpt was linked to his companion ʿnkt/Anukis who was seen as the Nile Flood and, at least in later times, she was identified with Spdt/Sothis, the Goddess of Sirius.[151]

In Coptic, ʿrky was not written only as *ōrk* or *ōlk* but also as *alke*. This leads us back towards Alkmēnē and Alalkomena. The parallel here is not merely phonetic. There are also important calendrical associations. While ʿrky rnpt was the last of the five epagomenal days, dedicated to Isis and Nephthys, as I mentioned above in Boiotia the month sometimes repeated for intercalation to adjust the calendar was called Alalkomenios. The relation between Alalkomena and Athena Alkmēnē will be discussed below. Here we should simply note that -mena and -mēnē were clearly seen to resemble the Greek *mēnē* (month). Schachter claims that in Athens the month equivalent to Alalkomenios was called Athenaios, which would fit nicely with Athena Alalkomena.[152] The calendrical uncertainty in both the Egyptian extra days of ʿrky rnpt and the Boiotian Alalkomenios neatly tallies with the legend of Zeus' having turned one day/night cycle into three when he sported with Alkmēnē to conceive their son Herakles.[153]

Thus, through intricate wordplays between the similar roots ʿnk and ʿrk, there would seem to be parallels between the Theban cult of Athena Onka and ʿnkt/Anukis (hence Nephthys and the latter's Greek counterparts Erinys and Persephone), and those of Athena Alalkomena and Alkmēnē. To complete these, however, we have to establish a relationship between Athena Alalkomena and Alkmēnē.

Athena Alalkomena and Alkmēnē

The name Alkmēnē seems to be overdetermined or based on punning in which it would appear that it has at least two different origins, one from *Rḫt ỉmn (Friend of Amon) and the other from ʿrḳy (last days of the year).

The pairing of Athena Itōnia (whose cultic connections to Athena Alalkomena have been discussed earlier) at Haliartos, and probably at Korōneia as well, with Zeus is interesting, as Athena was so frequently represented as single or as having rivals like Poseidon and Hephaistos. Zeus was worshipped all over Boiotia as Zeus Karaios or Keraios (horned). This suggested to Schachter that there may be some connection here with the Egyptian ram-horned 'Ammon', worshipped in Thebes at least since Pindar's time in the early 5th century BC.[154] However, as he was working within the Aryan Model, Schachter believed this idea is mistaken. On the other hand, for those not using this model, the local worship of Zeus with Athena in conjunction with the fact that Alkmēnē was a consort of Zeus raises the strong possibility that the fact that the shrine of Athena Alalkomena was only seven kilometres from the tomb of Alkmēnē and the extraordinary similarities between their names might well be significant and not just the result of random coincidence.

One possibility is that Alalkomena comes from Alkmēnē with the common Egyptian toponymic prefix R- (entry to), which was mentioned in Volume 1.[155] We have also seen that this may have been transcribed into Greek as La- and that prothetic vowels are possible before single consonants. Furthermore, R- is so widely used that it often simply means 'territory of'.[156] In this case, it could have been 'territory of Alkmēnē'. Given the many indications of Canaanite influence in Boiotia in the Late Bronze Age, it is possible that the initial A- of Alalkomenia comes from the article ha. This is found, for instance, in Atabyrion, the name of the highest and central mountain of Rhodes from the Canaanite *Hatabōr (the highest part centre).[157] On the other hand, the initial A- of Alalkomena could simply be prothetic. If Alalkomena means 'the territory of Alkomenia', Athena Alalkomena would in some sense be a fusion of Athena and Alkmēnē, 'the consort of Amon or Zeus'.

There are a number of associations between Nēit and Amon. As mentioned above, Nēit was sometimes linked to *ỉtn*, the solar disk. She was also seen as the mother of the sun god Re and therefore linked to Amon, who was frequently syncretized as Amon-Re. From at least the 30th Dynasty – the 4th century BC – Nēit was identified with two consorts of Amon, Amenet and the goddess Mut.[158] The antiquity of the latter identification will be considered below. Another interesting feature was Nēit's relationship to Mntw, the Egyptian warrior god especially associated with conquering the north. There are two very interesting reliefs from the 11th Dynasty showing Mntw and Nēit protecting the pharaoh Mntw Htp II, whose possible involvement with the Aegean will be considered in Chapter IV.[159] This notion that Nēit and Mntw and possibly Nēit and Amon were the divine guardians of the pharaohs of the 11th and 12th Dynasties would seem to provide interesting parallels to Alkmēnē's marriage to the mythical judge and lawgiver, Rhadamanthys, who, I will argue in Chapter IV, was the Greek counterpart of both the god Mntw and the 11th-Dynasty pharaoh Mntw Htp. It would also provide interesting parallels to Zeus' consorting with Alkmēnē to produce the hero Herakles, who strongly resembles a Middle Kingdom pharaoh.

HERAKLES
The Sumerian and Semitic origins
of Herakles

Herakles is a mythological figure of such massive richness and complexity that it is difficult to know how to disentangle the different strands that go to make him up. Walter Burkert traces him back as far as the Upper Paleolithic 20000 to 15000 BP (before the present), as a great hunter who kills mighty animals and as a shaman who can enter the world of the dead and return from it. More specifically, he is able to point to images from Sumerian and Akkadian seals of the 3rd millennium showing a hero dressed in a lionskin and with a bow and a club slaying lions, dragons, birds of prey, and so forth.[160] Burkert is careful not to mention the name but it is quite clear that he has the Sumerian hero Gilgamesh in mind, and other scholars have been more explicit.[161] The original Gilgamesh was a ruler of the city of Uruk in about 2600 BC. It is apparent that legends congregated around him in the centuries after his death, but the first texts concerning his exploits appear only in about 2100 BC. The *Epic of Gilgamesh*, as we know it, seems to have been composed in the 1st half of the 2nd millennium.[162]

Gilgamesh was a warlike ruler who, with his companion, the hairy, natural or wild man Enkidu, renouncing marriage and settled life, travelled widely, killing the monster Huwawa and the Great Bull of Heaven. After Enkidu's death Gilgamesh went to visit his friend in the underworld and set out on a quest for immortality. Mythographers have shown that this epic too is immensely complicated. It is made up from the historical Gilgamesh, folkloric themes found in stories from all over the world and literary artifacts, some of which may have astronomical and philosophical significance.[163]

How much influence did the Gilgamesh epic have on the Greek myths surrounding Herakles? It is naturally impossible to tell where the Sumerian cycle drew on world-wide folkloric themes. In the same way, while both of them are on the borderline between mortality and immortality and are concerned with death, this theme is too general to indicate a special relationship between the two heroes. There are, however, a number of particular resemblances – both Gilgamesh and Herakles walked, rather than riding in chariots, and used clubs rather than swords. This would seem to place the Greek hero's origins before 1750 BC, when chariots and swords appeared in the Mediterranean region and quickly became symbols of heroic royalty. Similarly, both Gilgamesh and Herakles usually carried out their deeds alone or in the company of one devoted friend or minion, whose death disturbed them greatly.

The important Phoenician divinity, Melqart or Mlk qrt (King of the City), who was the patron deity of the Phoenician city of Tyre, could provide a bridge between Gilgamesh and Herakles. Both a detailed passage from Herodotos and inscriptional evidence make the identification of Melqart and Herakles absolutely clear.[164]

It is impossible to tell how old the cult of Melqart was at Tyre. Herodotos wrote that Herakles' temple was as old as Tyre itself, which he believed to have been founded 2,300 years before his time, that is, about 2700 BC. This, as the French Semitist Réné Dussaud pointed out, may refer to the cult of Ba'al (Hadad), one of the gods from whom Melqart derived, but that Melqart is a later syncretization of many gods.[165] Most modern scholars maintain that worship of Melqart was much more recent. The most extreme place it at the time of the earliest attested inscriptions in the 10th century BC and suggest that his cult replaced earlier ones in the city.[166] There is also little doubt that Melqart was identified with many divinities including the Mesopotamian god Nergal and, as we shall see below, with the West Semitic god of pestilence Reshef.[167]

The name Herakles would seem to suggest a Near Eastern origin for the hero. Conventional wisdom in Antiquity understood the name Herakles to mean 'glory to Hera'. In any event the ready identifica-

tion of the final syllable of his name with *kleos* (famous) has led etymological researches on his name to be concerned with the first
element of Hēra-, also found in the name Hēra itself and possibly the
word 'hero'. The usual Indo-European etymology for Hēra- is from a
root **ser* (serve or protect). This has been attacked by John Chadwick,
the leading specialist on Mycenaean Greek, on the basis of the Linear
B form Era for the divine name. This lacks a *w* in the reconstructed
form *herwa, which Chadwick believes to be necessary.[168] Whether or
not this criticism is based on misplaced precision, it would seem better
to find an origin for Hēra and *hero*, as well as for aspects of the character of Herakles, from a sacred paranomasia or combination of three
West Semitic roots all based on the consonants √hrr.

The first of the Semitic roots, and the one which would seem central to the characters of Herakles, Hera and heroes is √hrr (noble,
free). *Ḥor* in Hebrew means 'freeborn' or 'noble' and the name Hrr
appears in Ugaritic. In the 20th century AD, we encounter the root
in Ben Hur and the Swahili word of Arabic origin *uhuru* (freedom).
There are problems with the vocalization as the Linear B form Era
shows that the *ē* in Hēra is primary and not a development from *a*, the
vowel one would reconstruct for West Semitic.[169]

The second meaning of √hrr is 'scorch or burn'. The name of an
Akkadian divinity, Erra (the Scorcher), is derived from this. Erra was
known in Sargonic times – in the 3rd millennium – but an epic concerning him seems to have been a product of the early 1st millennium,
which was a peculiarly brutal period in Mesopotamian history. Erra or
'Scorched Earth' was a ferocious and cruel but heroic warrior who
specialized in devastation and causing famine through burning. He
was in many ways identified with Nergal, the much-feared god of
pestilence.[170] This root would seem to appear in the Greek Herakles'
'madness' and destructive urges. It could also be related to the hero's
affinity for fire which was particularly strong in Phoenician Heraklean cults. Here, the phonetic relationship is better than that with
ḥor. There is no doubt that Erra comes from the root √hrr and that
while the initial *ḥ* was dropped in Akkadian it would have been preserved in West Semitic. West Semitic, however, did not tolerate double
r. Therefore, the western counterpart of Erra would have been
*Ḥera, though the exact nature of the *e* is uncertain.

The third Semitic √hrr – etymologically √hrr – means 'to bore and
make holes'. As in √hrr (noble, free), this tends to be vocalized with
the back vowels *o* and *u* in Hebrew. This semantic range would seem
to be reflected in the aspects of Herakles as a tunneller and irrigator

though, as will become evident below, these probably have other origins as well.

A further derivation can be made from the Egyptian name Ḥr, Horus reconstructed as *Ḥāruw. This name was used both for the fierce falcon and solar god and as the symbol and name of the living pharaoh. This will be discussed below.

Despite the confusion and the lack of direct attestation, it is clear that (Ḥ) era was a name used by West Semitic speakers for a Heraclean or Melqart-like hero. The strongest evidence for this comes from the city name Abdēra.

It seems quite plausible to derive Abdēra from the West Semitic *ʿabdera (servant of Era). Although the development of toponyms from personal titles is rare, it does occur. An example of this is Didyma, the name of the city on the Carian coast famous for its oracle from Didymaios (twin), a title of Apollo. I shall argue in Volume 3 that Delphi and Dēlos received their names from Delphos, another word meaning 'twin' used as an epiclesis for Apollo.

In the case of Abdēra there are conclusive links between the cities bearing this name and Herakles. According to legend, Abdēra in Thrace was the place where Herakles' servant, or minion, Abdēros was killed and buried, and both the Thracian city and the Abdēra in Southeast Spain had Herakles as their titulary deity. Even if one neglects the clearly Semitic nature of the prefix Abd-, the name cannot be explained in Greek terms because, not only was the Thracian Abdēra in a region heavily – and at an early date – associated with Phoenicia before it became Greek-speaking, but the Spanish Abdera was at the centre of the band of Phoenician settlements on the southeast coast of the peninsula.[171]

The Egyptian origins of Herakles

Given what seems to be the strong case for a Semitic origin of the name Herakles, it is somewhat puzzling that Herodotos should explicitly state that 'the name' of Herakles came from Egypt.[172] Alan Lloyd suggests that when Herodotos wrote 'name' he meant name and not just 'concept' as other scholars have argued. Lloyd sees Herodotos here – as elsewhere – as a victim of the delusion of *Interpretatio Graeca*, in that the Greek historian really believed that the Egyptian gods were called by their Greek names.[173] As should be clear by now, I do not accept that the *Interpretatio Graeca* is a delusion. I believe that many of the Greek divine names, such as Apollo, Athena and so on, were in fact Egyptian and that when Herodotos said 'name' he usually meant just that, *name*. In this case, however, the evidence is far less clear-cut and it may well be that the cautious scholars who maintain that Herodotos was merely referring to the concept of Herakles are right.

It is just possible, however, that Herodotos' informants had a name in mind. This would have been Ḥr kȝ ⲫⳡ𝑎̊. Ḥr kȝ was a form attested only in the reign of Ptolemy VI in the 2nd century BC of the name generally written Ḥkȝ (magic).[174] Even in the confusing world of Egyptian religion the figure of Ḥkȝ or Heka is particularly dim and slippery. As a personification of magic his basic nature was represented, as Herman te Velde, the expert on Egyptian religion, put it, as 'magic power, divine creative energy, human creativity, vital potential, mysterious efficacy'.[175] This seems altogether too vague a divinity to attach to Herakles. Furthermore, there are severe phonetic problems in that by the late 1st millennium Ḥr kȝ was pronounced in the same way as Ḥkȝ, probably as Hik. This identity seems, in fact, to be a reason for the writing Ḥr kȝ. Thus, to see the *r* and the *ȝ* as liquids would have required an archaizing reading of the name.

Before dismissing this relationship, however, we should consider one or two points in its favour. Firstly, Ḥkȝ was seen as responsible for the subduing of Apopis, the serpentine monster of chaos.[176] Secondly, there was also a close relationship between Ḥ(r)kȝ and a late divinity known as Tutu who was seen in Ptolemaic times as a walking lion and known as 'great in valiance, son of Nēit'. Thus, he resembled Herakles – who was also distinctly leonine – and was the son of Alkmēnē/Athena Alalkomena. The great period for the worship of Tutu was in the first two centuries AD which were also highpoints in the cult of Herakles.[177] Both Ḥ(r)kȝ and Tutu were seen as manifestations of Shu, the god of air, whose undoubted relationship to Herakles will be discussed below. Thirdly, at the Ptolomaic and Roman temple of Nēit and Khnum at Esna, Ḥ(r)kȝ was seen as a divine child, whose mother was Nēit. There is no doubt as to the great significance of Herakles' childhood in the myths surrounding him. This links Ḥ(r)kȝ to the young Horus, known as Ḥr p ḥrd, 'Horus the Child' (Harpokratēs in Greek).[178] The confusion between Herakles and Harpokratēs in Late Antiquity can be seen from a statement by Eratosthenes, the librarian at Alexandria in the early 3rd century BC, in his compilation on the kings of Thebes. Eratosthenes refers to the Pharaoh Semphrukratēs as being 'Herakles Harpokratēs'.[179]

Where does all this leave us? It would seem quite possible that Herodotos and his Egyptian informants had Ḥ(r)kȝ in mind when they said that the name of Herakles came from Egypt. It is much less likely, however, that the name Herakles actually came from Ḥrkꜣ, although it is just possible. All in all, it would seem more plausible to suppose that the final -klēs is merely the Greek suffix meaning 'glory', frequently used with proper names. However, the basis of the name, as well as that of Hera and the word 'hero', would seem to have been influenced by the Semitic roots √ḥrr, especially from √ḥrr (noble, free), but to have come from Horus or *Ḥāruw. There is a phonetic problem here in that the Linear B form Era shows that the ē in the name Hera is Pan-Hellenic and not the result of the shift ā to ē in Eastern Greek dialects. Nevertheless, the semantic parallels are impressive. Firstly, there are the many solar and heroic similarities between Herakles and Horus/Apollo and, more specifically, there are those between Herakles and the Greek heroes, on the one hand, and the Egyptian pharaohs of the Middle Kingdom, whose official titulary always began with Ḥr and the so-called Horus name, on the other.

It is also interesting to note in connection with the name Hera that the 18th-Dynasty woman pharaoh Hapshepsut called herself, among other things, Ḥrt nt ḏꜥm (Female Horus of fine gold).[180]

Given these aspects of his name, it is not so surprising that Greek myths do not place Herakles' childhood in Syria or Mesopotamia. He was seen, however, to have many contacts with Egypt.

Just as modern scholars see Herakles as a composite figure, Ancient writers frequently maintained that there were many different figures called Herakles. Herodotos distinguished between the divine and the heroic Herakles and between the very ancient Egyptian one, the Phoenician one, the one worshipped in the Phoenician colony of Thasos and the Herakles from Thebes in Greece.[181] Diodoros Sikeliotes, the general historian of the 1st century BC, saw three Herakleses. The most ancient of these was born in Thebes in Egypt and subdued the whole world, the second was a Cretan who had founded the Olympic games and the third was the son of Alkmēnē and Zeus and was born just before the Trojan War.[182] Cicero differentiated six Herculeses – the Latin Herakles – of which the Egyptian was second, the Tyrian fourth and the Greek sixth.[183]

Herakles, Ḥry š-f and Reshef

Where in Egyptian tradition can we find this ancient if not the most ancient Herakles? One identification has been made with a ram god Ḥry š-f – Arsaphes in Greek – whose name meant 'He who is on his lake'. Although he had a smaller cult centre in the Delta, Herakleopolis Parva, his chief city was known later as Herakleopolis Magna in the Fayyum, the Egyptian name of which was Nni-nsw(t) (City of the Royal Children). In general, like Herakles, Harsaphes was associated with royal children. He was also identified as a royal god resembling Amon, with whom he was later often assimilated. However, he was also a fertility god like Osiris. This association with fertility, taken together with his name and the situation of his centres in the Fayum and the Delta marshy areas where considerable reclamation had been undertaken, indicates that he was concerned with irrigation and drainage.[184] These aspects of Herakles will be discussed below.

Despite the attestation of the West Semitic god as Ra-sa-ap at Ebla from the middle of the 3rd millennium BC, the name Ḥry š-f would also seem to be the origin of the name of the West Semitic god of war and disease Ršp or Reshef.[185] There is no satisfactory Semitic origin for the latter name.[186] It is known that Ḥry š-f had a temple at Byblos and there is little doubt that there was a confusion between him and and Reshef there and elsewhere.[187] The identification is not invalidated by the fact that the Canaanite god Reshef was worshipped in New Kingdom Egypt. As a parallel to this, it will be argued in Volume 4 that the Egyptian goddess Wȝḏyt became assimilated to the West Semitic goddess Qdšt and was worshipped as such in Egypt.

There are, in fact, some interesting features of the worship of Reshef in Egypt. Firstly, there appears to have been a valley dedicated to him just north of Herakleopolis Magna, the cult centre of Ḥry š-f. An inscription from the Persian period reads either 'Reshef son of the lord of Nni-nsw' (Herakleopolis Magna) or 'the son of Resheph Lord of Nni-nsw'.[188] Either way, there would seem to be a close association between Reshef and Ḥry š-f, whose name had by late times lost its sense of 'on his lake'.[189]

In Egypt – at least since the 18th Dynasty – Reshef was seen as the pharaoh's god of warfare, and archery especially was identified with Mnṯw.[190] This, as we shall see below in Chapter IV, is a parallel to Rhadamanthys' – who, I argue, should be identified with Mnṯw – being the stepfather of Herakles. Rhadamanthys' double Amphitryon – also Alkmēnē's husband and exiled to Thebes – was the hero's teacher in the martial arts.[191]

If Arsaphes' identification with both Reshef and Herakles is clear, the triangle is completed by there being close parallels between Reshef and Herakles. In a posthumously published article, the military general and ancient historian Yigael Yadin demonstrated that, while the West Semitic Reshef was frequently identified with the Greek

Apollo as both were associated with arrows and disease, he was also equated with Nergal and Herakles. He used a lion-headed *rhyton* dedicated to Reshef found at Ugarit to clinch the identification of Reshef with lions. Yadin went on to link this to Herakles' association with lions and to work that he had written previously on the identification of Herakles with Samson – both were essentially solar heroes and had dealings with lions. Yadin plausibly saw Dan, the Israelite tribe to which Samson belonged, as having had its origin from one of the Sea Peoples.

Thus, Yadin saw a fusion between the Aegean Herakles and the Canaanite Reshef.[192] I believe there had been associations between the two long before this and that the oldest figure in the cluster was the Egyptian Ḥry š-f. The characteristics of these deities – that they were solar, wandering, warlike archers, strongly identified with lions and young if not childlike – makes them very close to Horus or Ḫprr, god of the morning sun, and their Greek counterpart Apollo. Thus, for instance, the city in Philistia named Arsuf, from Reshef or Ḥry š-f, was called Apollonia in Greek, and Cypriot inscriptions equate Reshef and Apollo.[193] This, however, does not weaken the identification of Herakles with Reshef.

Herakles, Khonsu and Shu

Many scholars from Sethe to Gwyn Griffiths and Lloyd have identified Herakles with another Egyptian god, Khonsu. Khonsu was the third in a triad of deities worshipped at Thebes, the father being Amon, the mother Mut (mother and/or vulture). Khonsu's name seems to have derived from the verb *ḫns* (travel), and this would fit the travelling hero, or, as Lloyd puts it, 'the Wanderer through the Heavens'.[194] However, the Egyptologist Georges Posener believed that there was paranomasia between *ḫns* and Khonsu's identification as the royal child, for which he reconstructed a name with the form *ḫ-n-nsw (child of the king), thus linking up with Herakleopolis Magna or Nni-nsw(t) (City of the Royal Children). Posener also insisted that Khonsu was not merely associated with Amon, the king of the gods, but also with terrestrial monarchs.[195] Many of these, like Amon, had their principal seat at Thebes. It is interesting to note here that Herakles was born and brought up in the Greek Thebes.

Sethe, Gwyn Griffiths and Lloyd also point out that Khonsu was closely identified with Shu, the air god, who was known as a fierce warrior.[196] Shu's ferocity has been related to the fierceness of the sun at midday; this in turn parallels √ḫrr (scorch) and the demon/hero

Erra.[197] Shu's chief function was to separate earth from heaven or support the sky and this parallels the legend of Herakles and Atlas, in which Atlas first tricks the hero into holding up the sky but Herakles then tricks the giant into taking up his burden again. The Egyptian origin of the name Atlas will be discussed in Chapter 5.[198]

The identification between Herakles and Shu is strengthened by the hero's struggle with Antaios where, like Shu in Egyptian legend, Herakles separates the evil being from earth by raising it in the air. There is a tradition that Antaios lived in Libya and was a son of Poseidon.[199] The Egyptian connotations of this story are confirmed by Gardiner's demonstration that Antaios' Egyptian equivalent, ꜥntywy, was a form of Seth. As he put it:

> Hitherto the identification of the Egyptian 'Antywey with that Antaeus whom the Greeks conceived of as a Libyan giant slain by Herakles has been supposed to rest solely on the identification of names; the equation with Seth-Typhon indicated above shows more resemblance between the Egyptian and Greek legends than had been previously suspected.[200]

The identification with Libya, with its connections with Neptune and Poseidon and Antaios/'Antywey provides a further reason for associating Seth with Poseidon. Interestingly, there was a Renaissance tradition, presumably deriving from Antiquity, of this battle being one between 'Hercules the Egyptian' and Antaeus king of Libya. Machiavelli referred in his *Discourses* to:

> the fables of the poets, in which it appears that Antaeus king of Libya, when attacked by Hercules the Egyptian, was unconquerable while he waited for him in the bounds of his own kingdom, but when he departed from it because of the cleverness of Hercules, he lost his state and his life.[201]

Herakles as the victor over Antaios in Libya resembles both Horus and the Egyptian pharaoh and Shu. The scholars identifying Herakles with Shu do not mention, however, that Tutu and hence Ḥr kꜣ were manifestations of Shu. Thus, their arguments independently tend to strengthen the possibility of the name Herakles deriving from Ḥr kꜣ.

Now let us consider Khonsu's divine mother Mut. This goddess became prominent only during the reign of Hatshepsut in the 18th Dynasty (c. 1503–1483 BC) when a temple to the Royal Triad was erected at Karnak. However, attestations of her name occur in the Middle Kingdom.[202] By the 20th Dynasty (c. 1184–1087 BC) Mut was linked to Nēit and attestations of the assimilation are found in later periods.[203] This leaves open the question of whether Mut was merely a new form of the ancient Nēit, but it does show that the two could be identified in the Late Bronze Age. Here again, it should be noted that Shu, Tutu and Ḥ(r) k3 were all seen as sons of Nēit.[204] Thus the two correspondences, Nēit with Mut and Athena Alalkomena with Alkmēnē would fit nicely with that of Shu and Ḥr k3 with Herakles.

Herakles and the pharaohs of the
Middle Kingdom

At this point, another aspect of Herakles should be considered, that of him as the Greek image of a Middle Kingdom pharaoh (c. 2100–1800 BC). Although, as we shall see below, the Greek hero resembled pharaohs of both the Old and Middle Kingdoms in such things as irrigation, he resembles Middle Kingdom pharaohs more specifically. Herakles was generally seen as coming from the Greek Thebes or in older incarnations from Egypt or more specifically Thebes in Egypt.[205] Like Shu, the Middle Kingdom pharaohs were known to have come from the Theban nome and, according to a widespread Greek tradition, some 12th-Dynasty pharaohs believed by the Greeks to have been great conquerors whose armies ranged from Libya and Ethiopia to Scythia and Colchis in the Caucasus.

Although modern scholars admit the reality of Egyptian conquests in Nubia during the Middle Kingdom and some are prepared to consider an Egyptian suzerainty over parts of Syro-Palestine, they have been unwilling to consider the possibility that any of the wider conquests attributed by Herodotos and Diodoros to Sesōstris, the 12th-Dynasty pharaoh Senwosre I, had any reality whatsoever. However, I shall argue at length for their plausibility in Chapters V and VI. If these arguments are accepted, there would be no difficulty in seeing these real conquests as bases for the conquering aspect of the mythical Herakles. In order to make this connection one need only accept the reality of the southern conquests, although it could be objected that Greeks in the 2nd millennium could not have heard of such distant events. On balance, however, the Middle Kingdom conquests seem to have been great enough to inspire the image of Herakles the conqueror.

Like Herakles and later Greek heroes, the 12th-Dynasty pharaohs were seen as occupying the borderline between humanity or mortality and divinity. Herodotos claimed that Herakles was an Egyptian god of great antiquity and that the hero Herakles was a much later figure.[206]

At another point, he argues that Egyptian religion had no worship of heroes.[207] Alan Lloyd maintains that the Egyptians only deified:

> scholars, wise men or magicians of outstanding ability. Such a difference in attitude is, of course, indicative of a fundamental difference of ethos between the cultures of Ancient Greece and Ancient Egypt.[208]

Lloyd seems a little too eager to make a distinction here. In fact, the Egyptians constantly made gods of a completely different class of men, namely the pharaohs. These, like the Greek heroes, were of royal blood and were frequently seen as carrying out tremendous and valorous deeds. This reverence became particularly strong in the 11th and 12th Dynasties; later generations paid particular homage to the divine figures of Menthotpe II, Ammenemes I and II and Senwosres I and III, and these cults were active in later times.[209] Thus, these divinities, whose titles began with and often repeated the name Ḥr, are relatively similar to Herakles in their mixture of the divine and the human. Furthermore, at the height of the 12th Dynasty it was the practice of pharaohs to rule together with their heirs. Thus the association of Khonsu, Arsaphes and Herakles in Egypt with heroic royal children fits well with both Herakles and the other Greek heroes.

Unlike his half-brother Dionysos (the derivation of whose conquests from those of Senwosret I will be discussed in Chapter VI), who conquered with an army, Herakles is supposed, like Gilgamesh, to have acted on his own or with a single companion. This would seem to distinguish Herakles from the Egyptian pharaohs with their huge armies, except that Egyptian propaganda in texts – and even more strikingly in iconography – portrayed the conquests as if they were those of the pharaoh himself with little if any support from his armies.

Herakles' role as a hunter of huge wild beasts has already been referred to. This too has parallels with Egyptian pharaohs whose magnificent hunts were given great prominence in pictures and reliefs. Sesōstris' great ability in hunting was also noted by Greek writers.[210]

Herakles as a hydraulic engineer

There are also interesting parallels between the activities reported of the Middle Kingdom – and Old Kingdom – pharaohs and a somewhat puzzling aspect of Herakles' character, his role as a hydraulic engineer. Although it is quite common for heroes to suppress enemies and kill monsters, digging canals and tunnels is far less usual. Yet this is one of the most frequent motifs in the myths around Herakles.

It is clear from a Mesopotamian seal that the image of a hero very like Herakles killing a monster with seven heads dates back to the 3rd millennium; Ugaritic myths relate this to the killing of the seven-headed dragon Ltn (Ladōn) who is clearly associated with the Ugaritic sea and river god Yam(m).[211] Nevertheless, Herakles' killing of the many-headed Hydra (water) in his second labour contains the image of damming distributaries or different river mouths and hydraulic engineering.[212] Herakles cleaned the Augean Stables, his fifth labour, by diverting the rivers Alpheios or Peneios through them. The hero's killing of the Stymphalian Birds, who emitted poisonous excrement, has been plausibly linked to other stories involving the draining of foul-smelling marshes. It should be noted here that, as with the Augean Stables, one of the rivers in this legend was called Peneios, which, I shall argue in the next chapter, derives its name from Pȝ nw (the flood) in Egyptian.[213] In his tenth labour, Herakles dammed the river Strymon to drive home his stock. In the eleventh, he kills the monster Ladōn whose riverine character has been discussed above. This may also be an aspect of the story of the infant Herakles strangling the two snakes, which became a symbol of Thebes used on its coins. The two snakes would stand for the two rivers flowing through Thebes, one of which was the Ladōn.[214] In a contrary direction, there was a strong tradition that Herakles had diverted the river Kēphissos to flood Lake Kopais.[215]

The possibility that this aspect of Herakles could be in some way related to the Semitic root √ḥrr<√ḫrr (bore tunnel) has been mentioned above. It is also likely that it is connected to his identification with 'He who is on his lake', Ḥry š-f/Arsaphes. Nevertheless, the clearest parallels would seem to be with the Middle Kingdom pharaohs.

Herodotos reported that King Min had built dikes to protect Memphis at the head of the Delta.[216] He wrote that the great 12th-Dynasty conqueror Sesōstris used prisoners of war for huge works of construction and irrigation.[217] Herodotos also strongly implied that Pharaoh Moeris, Amenemḥet III, the builder of the labyrinth, also of the 12th Dynasty, was involved in irrigation.[218] Diodoros amplified the two latter reports. He described in detail how Moeris had drained the Fayum and used it to regulate the height and flow of the Nile.[219] He also referred to Sesōstris' – Sesoosis as he called him – activities in protecting cities from flooding and improving irrigation.[220]

There are thus striking similarities between the image of Herakles the hydraulic engineer and the Classical Greek perception of the pharaohs of the 12th Dynasty undertaking irrigation and land reclamation. In fact, there is no doubt that there are very strong parallels between the images of these divinized humans held by Egyptians and Greeks in Classical times and those of the hero Herakles. This resemblance was made explicit by the librarian Eratosthenes, who described the 26th king of Thebes as 'Semphroukrates who is Herakles Harpokrates' and the 34th as 'Sistosichermēs, valiant Herakles'. Semphroukrates is difficult to identify but he would seem to belong to the Middle Kingdom. Following references to Amenemes I and II, Sistosichermēs has been plausibly seen by modern scholars as a reference to Sesōstris I, III or both.[221] The 19th-century Egyptologist Reichard Lepsius, when writing a detailed article on what he saw as the identity of the measurements of Sesōstris and Herakles, argued that 'from the standpoint of the ancient critic the mythical connections of both persons [Herakles and Sesōstris] were expressly recognized and indicated'.[222]

It will be remembered that Herakles clearly dates back to the age before swords and chariots. In this way, he was unlike the pharaohs of the New Kingdom (1575–1100 BC) who used the latter both actually and symbolically. Like Herakles, the pharaohs of the 11th and 12th Dynasties wore (and were shown as wearing) lion skins and brandished clubs.[223] The apotheosis, or acquiring of divine status, of the pharaohs of the Middle Kingdom took place during, or immediately after, their reigns.[224] It was not a later construction. Thus, this aspect of Herakles' nature could have been fundamental to the myth as created in the Bronze Age, that is before 1100 BC. While the 12th-Dynasty pharaohs were especially protected by Amon, who as the royal god of Thebes was their divine father, Herakles was the son of Zeus, who in the Greek Thebes was particularly closely identified with Am(m)on. What is more, where the 11th-Dynasty pharaohs called Menthotpe were dedicated to Mont or Mn̠tw, Herakles was in some sense the son of Rhadamanthys, who, it will be argued in Chapter IV, was Mont's Greek counterpart. The identification of Athena with Alkmēnē has been discussed above and there is no doubt that in Greek myths Athena frequently helped and supported Herakles. Similarly, there is explicit evidence of Nēit as a protectress of Menthotpe II and there would seem little reason to doubt that she served the same function for the pharaohs of the 12th Dynasty.

While modern scholars have poured scorn on Herodotos' and Diodoros' reports of the conquests of Sesōstris, detailed evidence from texts and archaeology strongly supports their statements on the tri-

umphs of Middle Kingdom hydraulics. Although the major work in
the draining of the great Lake of Fayyum was in the 12th Dynasty, the
tradition placing the beginning of irrigation in Egypt with the first
pharaoh Mēnēs who ruled around 3400 BC would seem to be accurate; there is also archaeological evidence of damming from the Old
Kingdom (3000–2500 BC).[225] Ample proof has been found of the canal building of the pharaohs Senwosre I–III, who are acknowledged
to be the prototypes for Sesōstris, and the same is true of Moeris.[226]
The name Moeris seems to have had two sources. Firstly, there is the
place name Mr wr (Great Lake or Great Channel), given to a town
near the mouth of the Fayum; secondly, the name Nemaʿ rēʿ, the
12th-Dynasty pharaoh generally known as Amenemḥe III who did in
fact undertake considerable irrigation works in the Fayum.[227]

Thus, the idea that the actual achievements of these pharaohs
played a significant role in the formation of the mythical Herakles
must be taken very seriously.

Herakles as a Middle Kingdom pharaoh in Boiotia

In Greek mythology, Herakles was essentially a Theban hero. Thebes
was his birthplace and the scene of many of his earlier heroic deeds.
There were also a number of sites in Boiotia where he was worshipped. At this stage, it would seem useful to look at some of these
cults for any indications of possible connections with Egypt or the
Middle Kingdom pharaohs in particular – beyond those mentioned in
the general discussion of the myths surrounding Herakles.

Two cities in Western Boiotia had the remarkably similar names
Thespiai and Thisbe and both had major cults of Herakles. As Astour
has pointed out, both of the city names have a plausible origin in the
name of the Hurrian storm god Teššub.[228] The idea of Hurrian influence in Bronze Age Boiotia is likely, firstly, because of the probability
that there were Hurrian elements among the Hyksos, who, it will be
argued, colonized in the Aegean, and, secondly, because of Anatolian
influence at the end of the Bronze Age. These issues will be discussed
in Chapters IX and XI.

Specific links between such Hurrian influence and the cult of Herakles are indicated by the name of the hero's wife, which was Hēbē.
A number of scholars have demonstrated that her name does not
simply mean 'youth'; the German linguist Paul Kretschmer convincingly linked it to Hipta, found in two of the Orphic Hymns, and
showed that both should be derived from the name of Teššub's wife

the Hurrian goddess Ḥebat.[229] The linking of Herakles with Teššub undoubtedly points towards Anatolia and the Southern Caucasus. It does not, however, necessarily point away from the pharaohs of the Middle Kingdom. As I shall argue in Chapters VI and XI, the conquests of Senwosret I in these regions left traces of the pharaoh wearing the White Crown of Upper Egypt on the iconography both of royalty and of the 'Smiting God', most notably Teššub.

> Pausanias found the Sanctuary of Herakles at Thespiai: older than the days of Herakles son of Amphitryon, and to belong to the . . . [earlier] called Herakles, whose sanctuaries I found at Erythrai in Ionia and at Tyre.[230]

The cult of Herakles/Melqart at Tyre has been mentioned above. According to Pausanias, the state of Herakles at Erythrai 'is not like the statues they call Aiginetan or the most ancient Athenian statues, but sheer Egyptian if ever a statue was'.[231] It is worth mentioning that at Thisbe there was a large dike used to control the water and provide land for cultivation.

In both Thespiaia and Thisbe, as well as at Korōneia, Herakles was known as Kharops, Herakles Kharops, or more often Kharops Herakles. The epithet would seem to mean 'flashing eyed'. However, another possibility is that the name is related to Kekrops the legendary founder of Athens, who also had a shrine at Haliartos. Kekrops will be discussed further in Volume 3 but here it is sufficient to say that I shall argue that the name may be related to ḤprkꜣRꜥ, Ḥꜥḫpr Rꜥ or ḤꜥkꜣwRꜥ, the prenomena of Senwosres I, II and III. Thus, there are some possible additional associations of the Boiotian Herakles to the 12th-Dynasty Egypt.

CONCLUSION

This chapter has been concerned with only a small fraction of the evidence suggesting close and long-lasting connections between Boiotia, Arkadia and the Near East during the Bronze Age. Later in this volume, I shall consider the plausible Egyptian and Semitic etymologies for many centrally important Boiotian place names including Kopais, Kēphissos, Orchomenos, Minyan and Thebes itself. In Volume 4, I shall be looking at the equally intricate mythological parallels between such creatures as the Egyptian and Boiotian sphinxes, between the solar cults of Horus/Ḥprr and Apollo and between Tm and Artemis, as well as those between Oedipus and the Egyptian Kꜣ Mwt.f (Bull of his

Mother). Here, we have merely been concerned with those around underground water, irrigation and drainage.

As we have seen, the ancient cults of Athena on the shore of the Lake Kopais and at Thebes would seem to parallel myths surrounding Nēit as a goddess of the marshes and their reclamation. There would also appear to be similarities between her rivalry with Poseidon and the struggles between cultivation and nature in Egypt and Libya. The cult of Athena Onka at Thebes suggests an assimilation of Nēit/Athena with Nephthys/Persephone/Erinys through the Egyptian Anukis and connections with the flow and control of water. There also appear to be relations between ʿnḵt/Onka and ʿrḵ/alke connecting the names Onka and Alkmēnē. The related cults of Athena at Itōnia and Alalkomena indicate an identification of Athena with Alkmēnē, the consort of Amon/Zeus and mother of Herakles; in Egypt, Nēit was represented as the divine mother of the 11th-Dynasty pharaoh Menṯhotpe II.

It is also clear that the Theban hero Herakles is a complicated figure created from many sources and that, although they may not have been the oldest – as the Greeks supposed – the Egyptian sources were fundamental to his formation. On the one hand, there were the gods Shu and Ḥry š-f/Arsaphes and on the other the Middle Kingdom pharaohs. Arsaphes and the pharaohs, as we have seen, provide most of the background to Herakles' exploits as a hydraulic engineer.

Thus, there are not only the parallels between Lake Kopais and Egypt as seen in Hellenistic times, there are also complex similarities between Egyptian mythology and the Boiotian cults of Athena, as well as parallels between the legends of Herakles as a hydraulic engineer and the image and reality of the achievements of Middle Kingdom pharaohs in drainage and irrigation. All in all there would seem to be ample evidence for supposing that the ancient waterworks of Boiotia in general and of Lake Kopais in particular were in some way connected to those in Egypt.

Some of the myths that have been discussed would seem to belong to the Late Bronze Age. They are mentioned by Homer or Hesiod, showing that they at least existed by the 10th century; but they give other indications that they could not be much earlier than the 17th century BC. The clearest examples of this are the myths referring to Poseidon and Erinys as horses, since, as mentioned above, horses were not present in significant numbers in the Middle East and the Aegean before the 17th century BC. The same is probably true of the name Telphousa/Thelpousa with its association with the names Ṯꜣlbyw, Rb and Libu. Although Libya had been known to Aegean peoples since at least the beginning of the 3rd millennium, this name and the country's association with horses could have occurred only in the second half of the 2nd millennium. Similarly, the apparently Hurrian names Thisbe/Thespiai and Hēbē could have been introduced only after the arrival of the Hyksos, which, I shall argue in Chapter IX, took place at the end of the 18th century BC. It is also likely that the fiery myths around Ōgygos developed only after the eruption of Thera in 1628 BC.

For reasons that will become clear below, we are looking for mythic and cultic traces of still earlier ages. Here all that can be said is that it is likely that the basic myths around Herakles, Alkmēnē and Rhadamanthys come from the turn of the 2nd millennium. On the other hand, some, such as the first worship of Athena and Poseidon in Boiotia, could be even older. To assess their probable age it is necessary to look at the archaeological evidence which will be discussed in the next chapter.

EGYPT'S INFLUENCE ON BOIOTIA AND THE PELOPONNESE IN THE 3RD MILLENNIUM, II
The archaeological evidence

I N THE LAST CHAPTER I tried to disentangle some of the myths and legends about Boiotia. These were seen to have close parallels in other parts of Greece, particularly in Arkadia in the Peloponnese. Parallels between the two regions can also be seen in the similarity of place names and in the physical evidence of considerable drainage schemes – often thought to have been inspired by Egyptian hydraulic engineering.

In Volume 1, I argued that the crucial period in which Egypt and the Levant influenced Greece was the 2nd millennium and, in particular, the period between 1730 and 1600 BC, when I maintain that there were Hyksos settlements or 'colonies' in the Aegean. Further enquiry has led me to believe that there were significant influences much earlier. One cluster of these was transmitted to Mainland Greece in the first half of the 3rd millennium BC, the Early Helladic II ceramic period, which coincides with the Egyptian Old Kingdom. Other influences passed chiefly to Crete but also elsewhere in the Aegean during the Egyptian Middle Kingdom between 2100 and 1800 BC, the Cretan ceramic periods EMIII–MMIII. In this chapter, we shall consider the first of these, and we shall look at the others later in the volume.

Although there is no doubt that the irrigation works found in Boiotia go back to the Bronze Age, there is considerable debate as to which period in the Bronze Age they belong. There is increasing evidence suggesting that, in Boiotia, they began to be constructed in the

Early Helladic period. The dating of the Arkadian dams is less secure but they may well be equally old. At Orchomenos to the north of Lake Kopais, what appear to have been granaries of Egyptian type have been found that seem to date from the Early Bronze Age. This picture of a sophisticated Boiotian economy based on irrigation and heavily influenced by Egypt is strengthened by the existence of a massive tomb at Thebes, which its excavator Theodore Spyropoulos sees as a 'Pyramid' dating from the Early Helladic II period.

Although no Bronze Age pyramid has been found in the Argolid in the northeast of the Peloponnese, a massive Egyptian-style granary dating to the Early Helladic period as well as a huge Bronze Age dam have been discovered near Tiryns. These and the considerable remains of a substantial Early Bronze Age building less than 20 kilometres away at Lerna, at the head of the Gulf of Argos, suggest that here too there may have been a sophisticated state heavily influenced by Egypt in the Argolid. The discovery of several 'Houses of Tiles' in different parts of Southern and Central Greece indicates some degree of political organization or at least of social cohesion in these regions.

Taken together, the cultic, mythical, toponymic and archaeological evidence make it quite clear that Boiotia and other regions of Greece were massively influenced by Egypt and the Levant during the Bronze Age. It is also virtually certain that these influences began in the Early Helladic period. However, although there may have been a form of Egyptian suzerainty over some of the Aegean states at this time, there is little apart from some legendary evidence to indicate that the influences were the result of Egyptian or Levantine colonization in the early period. Thus, while there are many parallels between the situation of the Near East and the Aegean in the Early Bronze Age in the 3rd millennium and that of the Late Bronze Age in the 2nd millennium, the only substantial suggestions of direct control by rulers from Egypt or the Levant come in the latter.

SPARTAN ARCHAEOLOGY:
THE TOMB OF ALKMĒNĒ

Before examining the archaeological evidence from the 2nd and 3rd millenniums, I should like to begin with a report of an ancient archaeological discovery.

Plutarch, writing in the 2nd century AD, cited what he claimed to be a contemporary description of a find made over four hundred years earlier. Between 382 and 380 BC, during the Spartan occupation of Boiotia, some Spartans were ordered by their king, Agesilaus II, to dig in what was believed to be the tomb of Alkmēnē situated near the city of Haliartos on the south shore of Lake Kopais.

In the tomb itself no remains were found but only a stone [other interpretations of the text suggest that there may have been a skeleton] together with a bronze bracelet of no great size and two pottery urns containing earth which had then become a petrified and a solid mass. Before the tomb, however, lay a bronze tablet with a long inscription on it of such amazing antiquity that nothing could be made of it, although it came out clear when the bronze was washed; but the characters had a peculiar and foreign conformation greatly resembling that of Egyptian writing. Agesilaus accordingly, it was said, dispatched copies to the king [the pharaoh Nḥt nbf, Nektanebēs 379–363 BC]. . . . The Spartan came to Memphis with a long document from Agesilaus for the Spokesman of the God Chonuphis with whom Plato, Ellopion of Peparethos and I Simmias had many philosophical discussions in these days. He brought orders from the king that Chonuphis should translate the writing if he could make anything of it and send the translation to him at once. Chonuphis shut himself up for three days conning scripts of all kinds in ancient books and then wrote his answer to the king, of which he also informed us. The document, he said, ordered the celebration of a contest in honour of the Muses; the characters had the forms of the script current in the time of King Proteus, which Herakles, the son of Amphitryon, had learned; and the god was using the inscription to instruct and urge the Greeks to live in the enjoyment of leisure and peace by always taking philosophy as their field of contention, laying their arms aside and settling their disputes about right and wrong by an appeal to the Muses and discussion.[1]

What, if anything, can be made of this passage? There is no doubt that the Spartans were in control of Boiotia at this time and that King Agesilaus II commanded their forces. Agesilaus' motives in ordering the tomb opened are unknown, but they were very likely connected to the fact that his patron and lover, the famous and brutal Spartan General Lysander, had been killed at Haliartos sixteen years earlier in 395. Pausanias, the guide, wrote that Lysander's tomb was near Haliartos. However, the contemporary scholar Peter Levi maintains that Lysander's name became attached to an ancient tumulus.[2] Although the logic of the situation is not clear, it is probable that any excavation of the tomb of Alkmēnē would have been in some way connected to the promotion of Spartan interests through the 'heroic' cult of Lysander. In any event, the connection with Lysander adds credibility to this part of Plutarch's citation.

The detailed description and prosaic nature of the objects found in the tomb make the report of their discovery seem very plausible. There is no tale here of serpents, gigantic bones or great treasures. To readers of *Black Athena* Volume 1, it will come as no surprise to learn that Greeks of the 4th century BC – accepting the Ancient Model – should have assumed that the ancient remains and the tablet were Egyptian. Reasons why this should have been particularly likely for the tomb of Alkmēnē in Boiotia will be discussed below. Thus, even the sceptical J. Schwartz, who has written the standard article on the discovery, accepts this part of Plutarch's story.[3]

It is also known that Agesilaus had a lifelong involvement with Egypt. In 396 BC the pharaoh Nepheritēs I had sent supplies to Agesilaus II to aid a Spartan expedition against Persia. At the end of his long, active life, the Spartan king died on a mercenary expedition to help Egypt against the Persians in 364 BC.[4] The biographer of the philosophers, Diogenes Laertios, also reports of the mathematician and astronomer Eudoxos of Knidos that 'he proceeded to Egypt with Chrysippus the Physician bearing letters of introduction from Agesilaus to Nectanabis, who recommended him to the priests'.[5] Eudoxos and Chrysippos were from Knidos, a Spartan colony in Caria which had been taken by Sparta in 390 BC. Thus, despite the fact that Eudoxos had spent time in Athens it is quite possible that the two could have been on a Spartan delegation to the new pharaoh. However, there is a problem with the dating, because, according to Diogenes, Eudoxos went to Egypt immediately after his stay in Athens when he was twenty-three, which must have been before 381 BC. Nevertheless, the dates fit well enough for this to have been the same delegation. The discrepancy could be explained either by a mistake in his age or by the omission of some travel between his stays in Athens and Egypt. It would seem very likely indeed that Agesilaus had communications with Nḥt nb.f, Nektanabēs, 379–363, at the beginning as well as the end of his reign.[6] Indeed, the year 379 BC was particularly significant. It was at this time that Evagoras, tyrant of Salamis in Cyprus who had previously led the opposition to the Persians, submitted to them. In the same year, Nektanabēs overthrew the last pharaoh of the 29th Dynasty, which had been founded by Agesilaus' old ally Nepheritēs I. Thus, in the absence of other allies, it was critical to cement relations between Sparta, the most powerful state in Greece, and the new dynasty in Egypt if the Persians were to be kept at bay.

Connections between Eudoxos, the delegation and the transcribed inscription are tightened by a strong ancient tradition that Eudoxos had studied with a priest named Chonuphis.[7] It is also very likely that Plato had had philosophical discussions with Chonuphis when he was in Egypt *c.* 390 BC.[8] This adds credibility to the reports both of Eudoxos' introduction and of Agesilaus' request for a translation. It would seem overwhelmingly likely that the story is accurate where it refers to the Spartans' sending of a document to the Egyptian pharaoh who referred it to Chonuphis.

All this, however, does not mean that the objects found in the tomb were Egyptian. Indeed, it is unlikely that they were. The bronze bracelet and the pottery urns strongly suggest that they were Early or Middle Helladic (3300–1700 BC) or Mycenaean (1700–1200 BC). The bronze tablet in front of the tomb presents more of a problem because nothing like it has been found from Egyptian, Levantine or Aegean cultures. There is, however, no reason to distrust the report because of this. Any one of these cultures could very well have had bronze tablets in front of tombs. It is also unlikely that the signs on it were in fact hieroglyphs. It would seem most probable that 'the characters [which] had the forms of the script current in the time of King Proteus, which Herakles, the son of Amphitryon, had learned' were in fact Linear B, or possibly Linear A or cuneiform.[9] If the inscription had been in any form of Egyptian hieroglyphs it would be impossible to explain Chonuphis' apparent difficulty in reading the tablet, which should have been relatively easy for an educated Egyptian priest.

The least plausible part of the story is the report of Chonuphis' translation of the text's meaning in that Herakles had

> ordered the celebration of a contest in honour of the Muses . . . and the god was using the inscription to instruct and urge the Greeks to live in the enjoyment of leisure and peace by always taking philosophy as their field of contention, laying their arms aside and settling their disputes about right and wrong by an appeal to the Muses and discussion.

We should not, however, dismiss this as uninteresting. Given the centrality of the cult of the Muses in the region of Haliartos, it would seem likely, if the report is accurate, that Chonuphis knew something about Boiotia. The Egyptian priest's choice of Herakles was also very significant and certainly deliberate. As we have seen, there were fundamental ancient links between Egypt and the Boiotian Herakles. Furthermore, apart from a possible attempt to make a piece of Boiotia 'forever Spartan' by appropriating a Bronze Age tomb for Lysander, it is possible that the reference to Herakles, who was both the hero of Thebes and the legendary ancestor of the Spartan 'Heraklid' kings, could be seen as giving legitimacy to the Spartan presence in Boiotia. The Spartan occupation was in fact extremely shaky from a religious point of view, because of the sacrilege involved in the recent Spartan seizure of the Theban acropolis, which had had Agesilaus' approval.[10] On the other hand, Chonuphis' text does not read like Spartan propaganda, as Sparta was at that stage very active in the internecine warfare. In fact, it reads more like the orator Isokrates' *Panegyric*, made in 380, calling for Pan-Hellenic political and cultural unity against Persia. The least unlikely explanation is that the 'translation' was an Egyptian appeal for Greek unity against Persia, possibly under Spartan hegemony. In the event, however, aid came to Egypt in 377 from the Athenian admiral Chabrias who arrived from having fortified the Boiotian Thebes against Sparta.[11]

It is not difficult to explain why the inscription was thought to be Egyptian. In addition to the prevalence of the Ancient Model in 4th-century Greece, there were specific reasons (as we have seen in Chapter II) for associating Egypt with Alkmēnē, her husband Rhadamanthys, her son Herakles, the location of the tomb at Haliartos on Lake Kopais, as well as with Thebes and Boiotia as a whole.

THE TOMB OF AMPHION AND ZĒTHOS

I want now to turn from ancient to modern archaeology. The fact that Thebes is still a living city makes it extremely difficult to carry out excavations there. This has hampered understanding of all periods of its history and prehistory and it is particularly hard to reconstruct its nature in the Early Helladic period. There are traces of some houses from Early Helladic II (3000–2400 BC) and Early Helladic III (2400–2050 BC) and it is possible that there are the remains of a 'House of Tiles' similar to those found at Lerna in the Argolid' and elsewhere, which appear to have functioned as palaces and/or houses of assembly.[12] Probably Thebes was already a significant centre in the 3rd millennium. This impression is strengthened by the presence at Thebes of a monument that it would be reasonable to describe as a pyramid.

In the early 1970s Theodore Spyropoulos, the *Ephor* or archaeological superintendent of Boiotia, wrote a considerable number of articles on his excavations and surveys. Two of these articles are directly relevant to the possibility of Egyptian presence or influence in Boiotia: the first was entitled 'Egyptian colonization of Boiotia' and the second 'Introduction to the study of the Copaic area'. Spyropoulos's case for Egyptian colonization in Boiotia was based on two important archaeological sites – the so-called Tomb of Amphion and Zēthos and the complicated and sophisticated network of dikes and channels used to drain the Kopais.

The first of these sites, about which Spyropoulos published a book in 1981, is a large mound to the north of the city of Thebes, on the escarpment dominating the junction of two of the streams surrounding the city. The mound was traditionally known as the Tomb of Amphion and Zēthos. Hesiod is supposed to have written that Amphion and Zēthos 'built the walls of Thebes by playing on a lyre'. Given Thebes' links with necklaces and Harmonia mentioned in the last chapter, it is interesting to note the image of a stringed instrument.[13] According to Homer, it was the twins 'Amphion and Zēthos, who first established the seat of seven-gated Thebe, and fenced it with walls, for they could not dwell in spacious Thebe unfenced, how mighty soever they were'.[14] It is clear that their enemies were barbarian tribes – the Aones, Temmikes, Hyantes, Leleges and Pelasgians – who were either indigenous or from Attica just to the south.[15] (There are long discussions on the Pelasgians and a derivation of the names Aones and Hyantes from the Egyptian iwn((t)yw) [barbarian] in Volume 1 of this work.)[16] It would seem likely, then, that in Homer's view Amphion and Zēthos were outsiders colonizing the area. Hesiod and other early writers, as well as the mythographer Pherekydes in the 6th century BC, saw the twins as the first founders of Thebes (Ōgygos, who was discussed in Chapter II, was the first mythical king of the territory later known as Boiotia, but he was not a founder of Thebes).[17] According to Pherekydes' version of Theban history, Amphion and Zēthos' city was built as a defence against the Phlegyans. The Phlegyans appear to have come from Thessaly to the north and destroyed the city after the twins' death. There is in fact a possible Egyptian etymology for the name Phlegyan in Pȝ rḳ(y)w (the enemy). Kadmos and his Kadmeans were then supposed to have *re-founded* Thebes much later on the deserted site.[18]

There was also a strong tradition, however, that Kadmos the Phoenician was not just *a* founder of Thebes but *the* founder of the city. In West Semitic qedem did not mean only 'eastern', it also meant 'ancient'. In any event, there were other traditions only attested later that Kadmos had been the first colonizer of Thebes. These then had the problem of what to do with Amphion and Zēthos. Some, like historian Hellanikos of the 5th century BC and Philochoros of the 4th, simply reversed the order and placed the twins after Kadmos.[19] Pausanias followed this version but claimed that the Thebes constructed by Amphion and Zēthos was below the Kadmeia built by Kadmos.[20] This and similar versions, however, encountered the difficulty that the later kings of Thebes were certainly considered to be descendants of Kadmos, and for this to be possible a restoration of the Kadmids was necessary. This complication was avoided by the early 5th-century writer Hekataios of Miletos and the 4th-century historian Ephoros, who were followed by Strabo in the 1st century BC. These simply denied the Homeric version and claimed that Amphion and Zēthos had not founded Thebes but Eutresis to the southwest.[21]

It seems then that there is no reason for denying the plausibility of the earliest attested version of the tradition of Amphion and Zēthos, despite the clearly folkloric motif of twins founding a city, which is seen, for instance, in the legends of Romulus and Remus' foundation of Rome. Although there is no evidence to show that the later 'Tomb of Amphion and Zēthos' was called that in the Bronze Age, no earlier name for it is known. Aischylos seems to refer to it and it was deeply revered at the time of Pausanias.[22] In fact, as the modern scholars Ioannis and Eveline Loucas emphasize, the site was considered holy throughout Antiquity and was not built on for almost three thousand years.[23] There is also little doubt that it is by far the most ancient large structure in the city. The hill has been dug several times this century and a number of Early and Late Helladic graves have been found in it.[24] Theodore Spyropoulos, who excavated it in 1971, saw the structure as a stepped pyramid with three levels of earth topped by a core of sun-dried bricks in which there was a stone-lined tomb. Startlingly, in the light of the tradition of the twins, Spyropoulos saw traces of two indentations for burial in the tomb.

The tomb had been plundered in Antiquity but three small gold pendants of a necklace, in the form of a lily, with double spirals topped with 'papyroid' forms and some pearls, had escaped the robbers.[25] The jewels' geographical provenance is uncertain. As I shall show in the next chapter, there was considerable Egyptian influence on Cretan and Aegean jewellery in the Bronze Age.[26] Specifically, the papyriform decoration derives ultimately from Egypt, but since this *motif* was widely used in Crete at this time it cannot be used to locate its manufacture in Egypt. There is somewhat less problem with the date, which would also seem to be 3rd millennium. Spyropoulos uses the jewels, together with shards of pottery found there, to place the tumulus in the EHII ceramic period, which in this book is from 3000–2400 BC.[27] Sarantis Symeonoglou, an assistant curator of antiquities of Boiotia, who has written a detailed *Topography of Thebes*, denies this early dating and puts the pottery inside the tomb in the

Middle Helladic period; he does not specify which section of this period.[28] Most scholars, however, have accepted Spyropoulos's conclusion that it is Early Bronze Age and there would seem to me no reason
to challenge this.[29]

While his date for the tomb has been accepted, there has been no
such willingness to accept Spyropoulos's attribution of its origin to
Egypt. Despite its construction before the most common dating of the
arrival of the Indo-Europeans at the end of EHII, Aryanists have attempted to describe it as a *Kurgan* – the kind of burial mound found
in Southern Russia and the Balkans and supposed to have been characteristic of the speakers of Proto–Indo-European.[30] The comparison
is forced because Kurgans are plain tumuli which are always made
with stone and earth. In complete contrast to this pattern, the tomb of
Amphion and Zēthos is carefully stepped, topped with brick-work,
built on an existing hill and has a number of galleries cut into it which
seem to be associated with a funerary cult.[31]

Spyropoulos sees a space in front of the cist containing the two
niches as a vestibule corresponding to the access shaft – or sloping
dromos – which he compares with tombs at Lapithos and Enkomi in
Cyprus.[32] Ingo Pini, who has written the standard book on Cretan
burial, believes that the Cretan tombs with *dromoi* were influenced by
Egypt.[33] Spyropoulos also sees direct relations with Cretan rectangular tombs with shafts, which clearly had their prototypes in Egypt.[34]
Here, however, he is on shakier ground, because the Cretan tombs
come from the Old Palace Period of the early 2nd millennium and
therefore well after his dating of the tomb of Amphion and Zēthos.

Attempts to draw parallels between the tomb of Amphion and
Zēthos and contempory tumuli on Leukas and at Charonea, further
north in Greece, are not very convincing and there seems little doubt
that it is unique in Greece.[35] Strangely enough, the nearest European
parallel is Silbury Hill, just outside the major Megalithic stone circle
of Avebury. This stepped pyramid carefully constructed from chalk is
rather older and seems to date to the 28th or 27th century BC, very
much the same time as the tomb of Amphion and Zēthos, and two or
three centuries after the building of the Great Pyramids in Egypt,
which would now seem to be between 3000 and 2800 BC.[36] Despite the
scorn poured on the idea by scholars of the early and mid-20th century, there is no doubt in my mind that the builders of Silbury were
aware of the contemporary Egyptian pyramids.[37] On the other hand,
it is extremely unlikely – to say the least – that Wessex was colonized
by Egyptians of the 3rd or 4th Dynasties.

In the case of the tomb of Amphion and Zēthos, it is equally clear that its builders knew about the pyramids of Egypt. On the other hand, it has been pointed out that in EHII, when the tomb of Amphion and Zēthos appears to have been built, stepped pyramids were no longer in fashion in Egypt.[38] This objection is not as serious as it might appear. This is, firstly, because it is impossible to say when in the long ceramic period (3000–2400 BC) the tomb was built; if it was at its beginning, it would have been contemporary with the 3rd Dynasty (3000–2920 BC) when the greatest stepped pyramids were constructed. Secondly, there is the fact that stepped pyramids retained their great religious significance after the development of the smooth-sided type. What is more they continued to be built. The sun temple of the 5th-Dynasty pharaoh NiuserrēꞋ (c. 2700) was built in steps and there are good reasons for supposing that the great stepped pyramid of the 3rd-Dynasty pharaoh Djoser (c. 3000) still had exceptional sanctity centuries later in the 5th Dynasty.[39] Thirdly, and simply, it is quite possible for fashions to be taken up abroad when they have been discontinued at home.

Nevertheless, Ioannis and Eveline Loucas are clearly right to consider the possibility of Mesopotamian influence as stepped ziggurats were still being constructed.[40] Like the pyramids, which may have derived from them, ziggurats were sacred constructions which symbolically enabled man to reach heaven. There would seem little doubt that it was in this function and as the real or supposed burial place of royal heroes that the tomb of Amphion and Zēthos retained its extraordinary sanctity for so many millenniums. It would also seem clear that it was seen as a source of the immense fertility of the plains of Boiotia.

According to Pausanias:

> The common memorial to Zēthos and Amphion is a small tumulus of earth. Men from Tithorea in Phokis want to take earth away from it, the idea to take it while the sun is in the bull of heaven (Taurus). If they can take the earth from here and lay it on the tumulus of Antiope [the twins' mythical mother] the ground will bear crops at Tithorea but not at Thebes.

Pausanias then cited the oracle Bakis of the 7th and 6th centuries BC to show the antiquity of this tradition.[41]

In Pausanias' time (the 2nd century AD) Tithorea contained the holiest shrine built in Greece for Isis, where Egyptian rites were strictly followed.[42] There is no way of telling how old this custom was and it may well have been established in the Hellenistic or even the Roman period as part of the Egyptianizing movement mentioned in Volume

1.[43] Nevertheless, it is interesting that this particular cult should have 'gone Egyptian'. Pausanias' quotation from Bakis, however, is paralleled by references from the Homeric *Hymn to Gē* and a fragment from Euripides' lost tragedy *Antiope*, all of which suggest that the tradition of rivalry and the magical power of soil from the tomb of Amphion and Zēthos could well go back to the Bronze Age.[44]

It should be noted here that Middle Kingdom pharaohs were still constructing pyramids, most of them overlooking the marshy lake of the Fayum which they were draining and turning into a plain of extraordinary fertility. Though later than the tomb of Amphion and Zēthos, these pyramids provide interesting parallels with the tomb of Amphion and Zēthos dominating the Theban Plain, though not Lake Kopais, the Greek counterpart to the Fayum. Nevertheless, the fact that the builders of the Theban tomb constructed an imitation pyramid – apparently as a royal tomb – and that this involved considerable wealth and ability to mobilize labour does not prove that they were Egyptian colonists; and, as we have seen, there is no object associated with it that can be definitively derived from Egypt. Spyropoulos, however, does not base his case for Egyptian colonization on the tomb alone; even more important for him are the massive waterworks in the Kopais which he places in the same ceramic period EHII, which he sees as *c.* 2600–2300 BC, but which in this book is put at *c.* 3000–2400 BC.

THE DRAINING OF THE KOPAIS

Lake Kopais is a flat basin of about 350 square kilometres in the northwest of Boiotia. The Kēphissos and other smaller rivers flow into it, but the route to the east and the sea is blocked by the Ptoon massif. However, the limestone mountains are riddled with caves so that with, and sometimes without, human intervention underground channels, or *katavothres*, can drain Kopais into the sea. There is no doubt that for some extended periods during the Bronze Age, much of the lakebed was drained in winter and irrigated in summer, by an intricate series of dams and polders guiding the Kēphissos along the northern edge of the plain to the improved *katavothres* and the sea. This system broke down, probably at the end of Late Helladic III (*c.* 1150 BC), when the northern tribes of Dorians and Boiotians were reported to have swept south. Thus, although some of the polders were repaired in Classical times, during the Iron Age after 1100 BC the basin was flooded and became an unproductive marsh. This explains the contrast between the great wealth and political power of Thebes and the northern Boiotian city of Orchomenos during the Bronze Age and the backwardness of the region in Archaic and Classical times (that is, from the 8th to the 4th century BC).

At the end of the 4th century BC, Alexander the Great tried to drain the lake once more and a huge channel was dug through the middle of the basin. However, the work was not completed, for either political or technical reasons or both. In any event, Kopais remained a marshy lake – or became an even bigger one over the next two millenniums. A French company tried and failed to drain it in the 1870s and it was not until the 1890s that an English company was able to equal the achievements of the Bronze Age and turn the Kopais once more into a productive agricultural region.[45]

It seems that the Bronze Age drainage and irrigation began piecemeal with the building of polders enclosing various 'bays' or 'gulfs' on the northern shore of the lake. Nevertheless, there is no doubt that these operations required hydraulic engineering of great sophistication and involved social stability and large-scale political organization.

One of the greatest question these works pose is the date of their construction. The archaeologists Fossey and Wallace tend to see them as Mycenaean (c. 1700–1200 BC).[46] On the other hand, the German hydraulic engineers and archaeologists who have been working on the constructions for fifty years claim that the earliest works are much earlier. The grand old man of these studies, S. Lauffer, saw them as Early Helladic.[47] His successors, such as Knauss, tend to see them as 'Minyan'. According to tradition, the Minyans were responsible for the drainage (the derivation of this name from the Egyptian Mnîw [herdsmen] will be discussed in Volume 3). In Greek legends, 'Minyan' referred to an early tribe living in Orchomenos, the city north of Lake Kopais. The name was later attached to a style of pottery well represented from Orchomenos that is considered typical of the Middle Helladic period. It should be emphasized that this modern association is entirely arbitrary and there is no reason within the Ancient Model to see the Minyans as exclusively Middle Helladic.

In any event, the first volume of a massive work by Knauss and his colleagues is entitled *The Hydraulic Constructions of the Minyans in the Kopais – the Oldest River Control in Europe,* and the second *The Improvement of the Kopais Basin by the Minyans in the Second Millennium B.C.* Thus there is no doubt in their minds or that of other contemporary scholars that the work started in the Middle Bronze Age (2050–1675 BC), later than Spyropoulos maintains but *before* the Mycenaean Period or the Late Bronze Age.[48] The German scholars are quite rightly very cautious in being more precise than this. In their book published in 1984, Knauss and his colleagues estimated that the drainage began somewhere between 2100 and 1900 BC.[49] In 1987, however, Knauss describes what he sees as the earliest works as beginning at 'sometime, probably in the second half of the Middle Helladic'.[50] This, according to the chronology proposed here, would be somewhere between 1830 and 1675 BC.

However, Knauss does not consider the ceramic evidence presented by Spyropoulos, that pottery found on a bank to the north of the lake dated back to the Early Helladic period possibly contemporaneous with the tomb of Amphion and Zēthos.[51] This earlier dating has been accepted by the Greek archaeologists D. Konsola and Ioannis and Eveline Loucas.[52] Spyropoulos argues that the traditional Minyans should be identified with Minoans and hence Egyptians.[53] While I do not accept his identification of Minyan with the neologism Minoan, Spyropoulos is clearly quite right to suggest that Egypt at the height of the Old Kingdom was the obvious place from which one would expect the high level of hydraulic engineering found around the Kopais to derive.[54] Thus, his argument that the tomb of Amphion and Zēthos and the earliest dikes on the Kopais were in some way connected and date back to the 3rd millennium would seem plausible despite the lack of any definitively Egyptian objects from Boiotia in that period.

There is, however, considerable circumstantial evidence to back Spyropoulos's hypothesis. Firstly, there is the general wealth and riches of the region during the EHII period. Unfortunately, not many settlement sites have been well dug and published for this period. However, during this time there was a largish village at Eutresis, ten kilometres to the southeast of Thebes, and recent excavations at Lithares, seven kilometres north of the city on the shores of Lake Hylike, have revealed a prosperous EHII settlement with clear-cut town planning and proven trading contacts with Anatolia, Macedonia and the Cyclades.[55]

GRANARIES

The possibility that the Boiotian hydraulic works were begun by the middle of the 3rd millennium is increased by the existence at Orchomenos of the remains of a number of round buildings or *Rundbauten*, varying in size from 8 to 2.50 metres in diameter. Spyridon Marinatos, who later became the dominant figure in Greek Bronze Age archaeology, argued in 1946 that these buildings were not tombs, temples or dwellings but granaries closely resembling those illustrated from Egypt and a model found on the Cycladic island of Melos. He argued that their size indicated that they held grain from a large area of land and that such massive storage of grain indicated political organization on a large scale. Marinatos dated them ceramically to Early Helladic I and II. He further pointed out that there seems to have been an even more massive or 'truly gigantic' circular brick building with a circumference of 88 metres and an estimated domed height of 26.4 metres at Tiryns in the Argolid in the Northeastern Peloponnese also dating to EHII. If, as seems likely, it was a granary, it would have served the grain produced in the whole Argive plain.[56]

Marinatos's article seems to have been an embarrassment to the profession. On the one hand, it was written by the scholar who dominated the archaeology of ancient Greece in the 1950s, 1960s and early 1970s; on the other, its suggestions of Egyptian influence and large-scale political and economic organization on Mainland Greece in the 3rd millennium BC went against the whole spirit of Northern European research on Greece in these decades.

Like many others, Colin Renfrew, the champion of isolationism, is clearly confused by the buildings, since their huge size, if they were granaries, would severely weaken his ecological model of small-scale local farming for Early Bronze Age Greek agriculture. At one point in his *The Emergence of Civilisation,* he doubted that the *Rundbauten* were granaries, arguing that 'they should probably be regarded as dwellings'.[57] Elsewhere, however, Renfrew admitted that they and the building at Tiryns may have been grain stores. Nevertheless, he still refuses to see this as damaging to his scheme according to which Greek agriculture in the 3rd millennium was based on a 'subsistence system'.[58]

Given the Kopais draining and the existence of a similar, shorter but more massive dam near Tiryns, it would seem plausible to associate such large granaries with the hydraulic works.

As we have seen, the granaries have dated to EHI and II (c. 3300–2400 BC). The date of the Tiryns dam is debatable. The American scholar Jack Martin Balcer supposes it to be Late Mycenaean by analogies with the Kopais dams.[59] However, Knauss argues that the Tiryns dam is so much bigger than the Boiotian ones that no parallel can be drawn between it and the Kopais dikes. In any event, he puts the Kopais dikes between 1830 and 1680 BC.[60] Interestingly, however, he believes that the Tiryns dam may be earlier, with a *terminus post quem* of Early Helladic II.[61] Thus, this could correspond to the Tiryns granary. On the other hand, Knauss's date for the Kopais polders is long after the EHII date for the granaries. Spyropoulos, however, associates the granaries with the irrigation – going back to EHII.[62] It thus seems likely that the *Rundbauten* were granaries, and that they may well have been influenced by Egypt, and that their early dating may be accurate. On the other hand, because of the uncertainties involved, it can only be suggested that the drainage of the Kopais (and in the Peloponnese) occurred under Egyptian influence during the period of the Egyptian Old Kingdom *c.* 3000–2470 BC, especially since it is just possible that such granaries could have served the rich banks of the Kēphissos river or occasional cropping of the lake-bed in years when it drained naturally.

The existence of a 'House of Tiles' or small palace dating from the EHII period at Lerna a few kilometres from Tiryns provides another piece of circumstantial evidence in favour of agricultural surplus and irrigation at this time. Nevertheless, the presence of 'Houses of Tiles' at Lerna and Thebes should not be taken to mean that such small palaces were exclusively associated with irrigation. There is no trace of damming near the one found in Messenia in the Southwest Peloponnese, though this would be a region where irrigation could be expected. However, there is also a 'House of Tiles' on the island of Aigina, where there is little or no question of irrigation.[63]

IRRIGATION AND SETTLEMENT
IN THE ARGOLID

In Volume 1, I referred to the irrigation supposedly carried out by the colonizing founder of Argos, Danaos, whom I conventionally saw as coming from Egypt in the Hyksos period in the 2nd millennium. The emphasis on Danaos' irrigation may come from his name and its derivation from or paranomasia with the Egyptian *dnỉ* (allocate, irrigate).[64] If this is the case, it could be that some aspects of his character derive from the irrigation of the 3rd, not that of the 2nd millennium. However, for reasons that will be discussed in Chapter IX, I still maintain that the people and events from which his legendary character is compounded belong at least predominantly to the later period.

On the other hand, the legendary if not mythical figure of Inachos, first king of Argos and father of Iō, was generally thought to have lived well before Danaos. Inachos could be interpreted simply as the personification of the river Inachos, which was the largest in Argos. However, this toponym has no conventional explanation and, in Volume 1, I proposed that it came from the Egyptian *ʿnḫ* (life), sometimes used to describe 'living waters' and frequently – in the formula *ʿḥḥ ḏt* (may he live forever) – as an epithet for the living pharaoh.[65] Inachos was generally thought to be autochthonous or locally born.

However, the church father Eusebius referred to a tradition that Inachos, like Danaos, was a settler from Egypt and this tradition was
taken up by the 18th-century French scholars Nicolas Fréret and the
Abbé Barthélemy, who actually argued that Inachos and Phoroneus,
his mythical son, were Egyptian settlers in the Argolid in the 20th century BC.[66] Given the possible Egyptian origin of his name, and its clear
connotations of royalty, water and great antiquity, there may be some
folk memory of Egyptian irrigation and possibly even colonization
connected to the dam and *Rundbau* at Tiryns and the 'House of Tiles'
which seems to have served as a 'palace' of Lerna in the 3rd millennium. This, however, must remain in the realm of speculation.

DRAINAGE AND IRRIGATION
IN ARKADIA

While the drainage and irrigation of the dam above Tiryns and of the
Kopais were the largest operations of their kind, there were other ex-
amples of this type of hydraulic engineering in Greece, not only at
Tiryns but also in Arkadia at the centre of the Peloponnese.

Some of Arkadia's natural features have been mentioned in Chapter II when I discussed Thelpousa and the Ladōn flowing out of Lake
Pheneos. Lake Pheneos also flowed out through a *katavothra* (underground channel) to Lake Stymphalos. According to Pausanias, local
tradition attributed this channel to Herakles.[67] The idea that this was
made or at least improved by man has been strengthened by modern
surveys. These have been carried out most recently by Knauss and his
team, in Lake Pheneos and Lake Stymphalos, as well as at the basins
of Kaphyai and the Peloponnesian Orchomenos just to the south
and Lake Takka near Tegea southwest of the Arkadian Tripoli. All of
these have shown that there was considerable construction of dams
and improvement of natural *katavothres* in the region.[68]

The dating of these works is very uncertain. Some were constructed
in Hellenistic or Roman times. Most, however, existed in the late
Bronze Age. Evidence for this comes from nearby settlements dated
to Mycenaean times.[69] There is also Homer's statement that at the
time of the Trojan War the Arkadian Orchomenos was 'rich in herds'.[70]

In general, the contrast between the wealth of Bronze Age Arkadia
and its backwardness in Classical times would seem to indicate that
drainage and irrigation were more effective in the earlier period. Another indication that the dams and channels date back to the Bronze
Age is their association with the legendary Herakles, who for all the
uncertainties surrounding him clearly belongs to this period.[71] An

even surer indication of the antiquity of the Arkadian hydraulic engineering is the point, made by Knauss and his team, that the dams in Arkadia are very similar to that at Tiryns and those in Boiotia. As these certainly existed in Mycenaean times, there is no reason to suppose that the Arkadian dams are any later. However, as Knauss and his colleagues point out that the Peloponnesian dams resemble the 'Minyan' work in the Kopais, this raises the possibility that they were begun in the Early or Middle rather than the Late Helladic periods.[72]

PARALLELS BETWEEN BOIOTIAN
AND ARKADIAN PLACE NAMES

Modern archaeologists have been struck by the great similarities between the Boiotian and Arkadian techniques of damming and channelling. Even more remarkable, however, are the extraordinary parallels found between the place names around the two areas of waterworks. The presence in both regions of a river Ladōn has been mentioned in Chapter II, as have the similarities of the names Tilphousa and Thelpousa and Onka and Onkaios.[73] Even more striking is the presence of an Orchomenos, close to what seem to be the earliest polders on Lake Kopais and one set strategically above the channel between the ancient lakes Kaphyai and Orchomenos in Arkadia. There was also an Orchomenos on the edge of the plain of Phtiotis in Thessaly.

There is little doubt that the name is an ancient one. The forms Okomeno and Ekomeno appear in Linear B. Although Chadwick insists that these do not refer to the Arkadian Orchomenos – he does not consider the possibility of the Boiotian one – he admits that they fit nicely with the two variants found in Classical times, Orchomenos and Erchomenos.[74] According to Chantraine, the etymology of Orchomenos is 'obscure'. However, there is a general belief that it is derived from the stem orch-, meaning 'a row of vines or fruit trees'. This can be taken in two related senses, as a 'hedge' or 'garden' or as an enclosure. Knauss therefore follows the scholarly tradition that sees the toponym as meaning 'enclosed place'.[75] He admits a problem with this in that both cities were *above* and not in the midst of the irrigation works. However, he argues – on the basis of statements by Strabo and Pausanias – that the original Boiotian Orchomenos was in the Kopaic Plain and was moved to its later site only after the flooding at the end of the Bronze Age.[76] There is, on the other hand, no comparable evidence for the Arkadian Orchomenos.

There is a proposed Indo-European etymology for the root *orch-*

from a reconstructed *wer-gh (close) found in the Lithuanian *veržiu* (enclose) and the Old Norse *virgill* (chord). However, there would seem to be an equally or more plausible etymology for it in the Canaanite root *'rk*. The basic meaning of this verb is to 'arrange in order' to 'set in rows', but it is most frequently used in military organization in the sense of 'draw up a battle line'. There is a slight phonetic problem in that it is uncertain when Canaanite first began to show the phenomenon known as *begadkephat* or spirantization or softening of non-emphatic plosives, stops like *b, g, d,* and *k, p,* and *t* in post-vocalic position, which would render *'rk* as *'rkh*. Nevertheless, the transcription of the Semitic *k* as the Greek *ch* is common enough to justify the equation. The spirantization may well have been promoted by confusion with another Semitic root *'rḥ*, from an earlier *'rḫ* (road, to journey, come, arrive). *'Rḥ* would seem to be the origin of the Greek *erchomai* (journey, come, go) which has no Indo-European etymology.

The two roots *'rk* and *'rḥ* would seem to have many derivatives in Greek. In the sense of 'arranging a 'battle order', *'rk* is probably the origin of the extraordinarily rich Greek cluster of words beginning *arch-*, which have no Indo-European etymologies. Chantraine gives as its basic meaning 'to go first, take the initiative, begin'; he also translates *archein* as 'to command' in a military sense so that from these can be derived the many meanings of *arch-* as 'leading' and 'early'.[77] It thus seems likely that *orcho-* and *ercho-* were loans from the Semitic. This, if anything, strengthens the hypothesis that Orchomenos or Erchomenos means 'regulated' or 'enclosed place' and refers to the dikes and channels of water control. Despite the ultimate Semitic origin of the first element, the final *-menos* would seem to be the Greek passive participle indicating that the toponym itself was Greek. It is possible, however, that there is contamination here from the Semitic *mayîm* in Canaanite – or *mayîn* in Aramaic – 'waters'. As in many other languages, the diphthong *ay* was frequently monophthongized or reduced to *ê* in Semitic.[78] 'Regulated waters' would fit the context exactly.

At this point, we should consider two etymologies of Greek words associated with irrigation. The first of these is the word used by ancient writers for the dams and embankments, *khōma*. This is strikingly similar to the Hebrew *ḥôma* (wall) used for walls surrounding cities and other large areas. However, as *ḥôma* is more isolated in Semitic than *khōma* is in Greek, the loan here is probably from the west to the east. The second word is *gephyra*. The classicist James Hooker has argued for a Semitic origin for this word, which he reasonably takes to have originally meant 'embankment' rather than its later sense of 'bridge'. He suggests deriving it from a Semitic root like √gb which has the meanings of 'dig' and 'dike' and 'bulwark'.[79] I will argue in Volume 3 that it might be better on phonetic grounds to trace *gephyra* to the Semitic *q^wbr (bury). In any event, the Semitic connotations of the word are strengthened by Herodotos' report:

> The Gephyrai . . . came, by their own account, originally from Eretria; but I myself have looked into the matter and find that they were really Phoenicians, descendants of those who came with Kadmos to what is now Boiotia, where they were allotted the district of Tanagra to make their homes in. After the expulsion of the Kadmeans by the Argives, the Gephyrai were expelled by the Boiotians and took refuge in Athens.[80]

Thus, a clan with the name 'Embankment', which had arrived with the invading Kadmos in the Bronze Age, was specifically labelled as a Phoenician one. This provides an interesting hint of the involvement of Semitic-speakers in the irrigation works in Boiotia. These plausibly Semitic toponyms, words and personal names would fit well with the cultic and mythical evidence of Semitic influence on Boiotia and Arkadia in the Bronze Age.[81]

The German scholars Kalcyk and Heinrich point out that Mount Oryxis, close to Orchomenos in Arkadia, is connected to the word *oryssō* (to dig a canal), and means 'Digging Mountain'.[82] The stem *oryg/k* has no satisfactory Indo-European etymology.[83] On the other hand, there is the Semitic root √'rq (to gnaw) attested in the book of Job as 'gnaw the dry ground'.[84] Mount Oryxis was close to Mount Saitis. Nēit/Athena's home city of Sais and its connections with water control have been mentioned above.[85] Both were close to Orchomenos on the shores of Lake Pheneos.

The name Pheneos shows the influence of Egypt on the toponyms of water and irrigation in Boiotia and Arkadia. The derivation of Pheneos and Pēneios from P₃ Nw(y) (the flood) – possibly the Coptic Panau – has been referred to above.[86] Pēneios was the name of the river in Elis in the Northwestern Peloponnese into which the Ladōn flowed. It was also the name of the main river in Thessaly which flowed through the Thessalian plain, believed in Antiquity to have originally been a lake. However, as a result of an earthquake, or Poseidon's work, the Thessalian Pēneios had broken through to the sea.[87] The Egyptian epic poet Nonnos, writing in the 5th century AD – but on the basis of ancient material – linked this dramatic event to the end of the cataclysmic world flood.[88] The suggestions of a flood are equally strong with the Pheneos in Arkadia. The frequent seismic blockages of its outlet to the Ladōn have been mentioned above and the other natural or man-made *katavothres* must have been equally vulnerable.[89] Pliny reported that there had been five floods there in historic times.[90] Pausanias wrote the following about it:

> The Phenean Plain lies below Karyai, and they say it was once flooded and the ancient Pheneos was drowned, so that even today there are signs left on the mountains where they say the water rose to.[91]

James Frazer and later scholars have seen traces of this line, which Knauss and his colleagues attribute to the waterline of a man-made lake.[92] (Pheneos/Pēneios should not be confused with the personal name Phinea/es. This, like the Hebrew Pînḥås, is derived from the Egyptian Pȝ Nḥs [the Nubian or Black], for which see Chapter VIII below.)[93]

Another Arkadian lake that would appear to have an Egyptian etymology is Kaphyai. Ḳbḥ(w) is one of the most common Egyptian toponyms used for streams, rivers and other bodies of water.[94] It is clearly linked to the roots *ḳbb* (cool) and *ḳbḥ* (purify). Ḳbb was one of the names of the two caverns near Elephantine whence the Nile was supposed to spring – the two *pēgai* referred to by Herodotos.[95]

The Egyptian association of Ḳbḥ(w) with cool, pure water springing from caverns in the ground would fit very well with Lake Kaphyai fed by mysterious springs and *katavothres;* with the common Aegean toponymic suffix -*issos,* it would also fit with Kēphissos, the name of the chief river flowing into Lake Kopais and one of the most frequently used river names in Greece. Many – if not most – of these came from caves and were used for ritual purification.[96] Written with the determinatives ⚬ or ⚬, Ḳbḥ(w) was used as a toponym for ponds or lakes on which lived aquatic birds.[97] This may have been applicable for Kaphyai and it was certainly appropriate for Lake Kopais itself.

Knauss, however, has a different proposal. He quotes Pliny's statement that 'Kopai discovered the oar, Plataia the rudder, Ikaros the sail and Daidalos the mast and main-yard.'[98] The statement is clearly learned and cannot be easily dismissed. The wordplay between Plataia and *platē* (oar or rudder) is obvious and the legendary wings of Ikaros would seem to fit the 'sail'. Pausanias and Plutarch describe the cult of Daidala which involved the citizens of Plataia on the border of Boiotia and Attica chopping down the tallest oak trees to make huge wooden idols. This may in fact be related to the Egyptian making of the *Ḏed,* wooden 'stability figures'. These would explain *Daid*alos' alleged invention of the mast.[99] However, the association between Kopais and

the oar is less easy to understand or accept. Knauss links his etymology of Kopai from 'oar' to his belief that the canals in the Kopais
were used not merely for drainage and irrigation but for inland navigation.[100] But the plausibility of this last point does not make up for
the flimsiness of his etymological argument and the unlikelihood of a
place being called 'oar'.

It would seem, therefore, much more plausible to derive the name
Kopais – like Kaphyai – from the amply attested Egyptian toponym
Ḳbḥ, which was precisely appropriate for a shallow marshy lake.
Thus, with Kopais and Kaphyai we have yet another example of the
parallels between place names associated with irrigation in Boiotia
and Arkadia, and one that has a striking connection with Egypt.

What can be made of these various etymologies? The fact that so
many of them appear to originate from Egyptian and West Semitic
would seem to suggest the presence of Egyptian and West Semitic
speakers when the names were given. This, however, is not certain
because the toponyms could have been taken from Egypt and the
Levant without involving any migration. Another problem concerns
dating: were the names given before, during or after the waterworks
were constructed?

This is further complicated by the relative timing of the hydraulic
engineering in Boiotia and the Peloponnese. The discussion above indicates that in Boiotia and the Argolid the hydraulic works may well
have begun in the Early Helladic period and that by analogy the same
could be true for those in Arkadia, though these could have been
started many centuries later. Should we deduce from this that the
similarity of techniques in Boiotia and Arkadia was the result of
the application of Boiotian experience further south, and hence that
the toponyms came to the Peloponnese from Boiotia and not directly
from the Middle East? Furthermore, although at least one of the
toponyms, Orchomenos, was in use in the Late Bronze Age, if the hydraulic systems are dated much earlier, there is no necessary link between the beginning of their construction and the giving of the place
names.

The whole subject of these toponyms is extremely complicated. On
the one hand, as with some of the myths, it is almost certain that some
place names of Middle Eastern origin, such as Thisbe and Thespiai,
were introduced in the Late Bronze Age – that is, after the first construction of waterworks. Others, however, would seem to be earlier.
All I can say with any certainty is that by the end of the Bronze Age
there were a number of place names connected with hydraulic engineering and that most of these have plausible Egyptian and West Se-

mitic etymologies. Thus, while the toponymic evidence is by no means certain, it would seem most economical to suppose that the names came in with the dams and canals themselves and that speakers of West Semitic and Egyptian were involved in their construction, probably in the Early Bronze Age and almost certainly in Mycenaean times.

SOCIAL AND POLITICAL STRUCTURES
IN EARLY HELLADIC GREECE

The first 'state' in Greece I should like to consider is that based on Tiryns and Lerna in the Argolid. It should be emphasized at this point that the Argive Plain is a considerable area and, although it was sometimes disturbed during the middle of the 3rd millennium, it clearly had periods of great prosperity.

Lerna, at the head of the Gulf of Argos, was a considerable settlement with many houses, an elaborate city wall and even 'the House of Tiles', a small 'palace', during EHII.[101] It is also possible that Lerna was smaller than Tiryns itself and there were probably other large cities in the area. Furthermore, as I mentioned earlier, other 'Houses of Tiles' similar to that of Lerna have been found in Messenia, the island of Aigina between Attica and the Argolid and possibly Thebes.[102] Thus, there is little doubt that, when looking at the Argolid in the Early Bronze Age, we are considering a rich and sophisticated society. Furthermore, given the scale of the Tiryns granary and the dam – if it belongs to this period – the region appears to have had some political unity. Emily Vermeule merely suggests that the coordination was 'communal' which leaves the type of social organization vague. However, given the social organization and state formation in the contemporary Near East, it would seem likely that the Argolid was either a kingdom or principality, as in Egypt and Byblos, the great trading city on the Levantine coast, or had an aristocratic or plutocratic 'Venetian' government as at the massive contemporary Syrian city of Ebla.[103]

Although the Kopais was not completely drained at this time and the granaries there were smaller than that at Tiryns, it would seem that there must have been a principality or small 'republic' at the Boiotian Orchomenos. The huge scale and pretension of the tomb of Amphion and Zēthos would suggest that there was also a considerable state at Thebes. The forms of social organization behind the Arkadian dams are even more difficult to speculate about, but in general it would seem clear that Mainland Greece of EHII contained a number of states, some of which were quite considerable.

It is also clear that, at least in Attica and the Cycladic island of Syphnos, there was commercial mining. Lead from mines in both places has been found in sites of the EHII period in Crete and Boiotia.[104] The discovery of two lead ingots from the wreck of the EHII period, at Dokos off the Argolid, points clearly to the lead and silver mines of Laurion near the tip of Attica eighty kilometres away.[105] We shall see in the next chapter that silver from Laurion was being exported to Egypt at the turn of the 2nd millennium.[106] The Dokos ship appears to have been quite substantial and it would seem likely that it was capable of reaching the Levant or Egypt. There is no indication that either of these was its destination, however. Indeed, the locality of the wreck would suggest that the ship was heading for the Argive Plain, Southern Peloponnese or Crete. It can be said, however, that in the first half of the 3rd millennium lead was probably already a commercial product in the Aegean. The recent metallurgical research also indicates that the conventional belief that the Laurion mines began to be worked only in the 5th century BC is wrong by at least two thousand years.[107]

The postulation of large states on the Greek mainland at this time would appear to present a number of problems. Firstly, it would seem difficult to explain why Early Bronze Age Crete, which appears to have absorbed so much more Egyptian and Levantine influence, should – as we have seen in the last chapter – not have had palaces or states, when they seem to have existed far to the north in the Argolid and Boiotia. The most convincing explanation would seem to be geographical in that, with the possible exception of the Messara, Crete had no substantial marshes or plains suitable for drainage and irrigation and so no large social organizations to handle such operations. Thus, while, as we can see, Crete could support a palatial economic structure in the Middle and Late Bronze Age, the prosperity and high culture of Early Minoan or Prepalatial Crete shows it could do very well without one. The Cycladic islands, which also had a flourishing economy and culture in the Early Bronze Age and were in touch with Near Eastern civilizations, had – as far as is known – no palaces at any stage.[108] The drainage of the Kopais and the wealth of Bronze Age Boiotia in fact provide strong cases for the argument that the plains of Mainland Greece required large-scale social organization to make the most of their agricultural potential.

Another problem would seem to be that if such sophisticated states existed and writing was well established throughout the Near East, the 'Greek' states would surely have had to be literate. Yet no traces of script exist. It used to be thought, on the basis of the argument from silence, that seals were not made or used in Early Helladic Greece. It is now clear, however, that they were manufactured there and that there was in fact a lively tradition of glyptic carving on seals.[109] This shows that there was a strong sense of private and/or institutional property in the society. There are also ample examples of potters' marks from the Early Helladic II. None of these signs, however, resemble those of the Linear syllabaries, and there are no other indications of local writing at this period.[110]

I have argued at length elsewhere that we should be particularly wary of the 'argument from silence' when it applies to writing, as this generally consists of slight marks on perishable or fragile surfaces.[111] Thus, I am not troubled by the failure to find traces of script from Early Helladic Greece. However, if there was writing in the area at this period, it would almost certainly have been similar to either the Cretan hieroglyphic or to the prototype of Linears A and B. As will be shown in the next chapter, Linear B cannot be directly derived from Linear A and scholars have argued that Linear B diverged from pre–Linear A around 1600 BC.[112] In order to explain the divergences between the related Cypriot, Linear A and Linear B syllabaries, I argue that their common prototype could hardly have existed later than the middle of the 3rd millennium. In support of my supposition here, given the literacy of neighbouring societies, it is likely that at least the larger states, if not the smaller communities, of the Aegean and Anatolia would have used writing. If – as I argue – the alphabet was introduced to the region in the mid-2nd millennium, these deep roots would explain why the syllabaries should have remained the official scripts in Crete and Mainland Greece.

Such speculation goes against Spyropoulos's theory of Egyptian colonization, which, if it was as sweeping as he seems to suggest, would surely have introduced hieroglyphics or the Egyptian cursive script, hieratic, to Boiotia. The likelihood that the script most commonly used in Early Helladic Greece was either Aegean or Anatolian suggests that other cultural attributes were as well. This I believe was definitely the case with the spoken language. On the other hand, the indications of profound Egyptian influence on the Early Bronze Age states of the Aegean provided by the 'pyramid', the irrigation works and the granaries are not the only archaeological evidence for the argument that Egyptians were present in the region in significant numbers at the time.

OTHER ARCHAEOLOGICAL TRACES OF
OLD KINGDOM EGYPT IN THE AEGEAN

Before looking at Egyptian contacts with the Aegean around the middle of the 3rd millennium, it should be stressed that this was a period of flourishing civilization in the Near East which had diplomatic and trading contacts that spread far beyond it. We know that by this time the Syrian city of Ebla was corresponding with a kingdom in the modern Kurdistan and that Mesopotamia was certainly receiving lapis lazuli and quite possibly tin from Afghanistan.[113] Lead isotope analysis indicates that at this time Mesopotamia was receiving silver and copper from Almeria in Southeast Spain.[114] Given such a scale of operations, contacts between Egypt and the Aegean can be seen in many ways as local traffic.

Third-millennium Egyptian influences on Crete were discussed in Chapter I and possible Egyptian references to the Aegean from the Old Kingdom will be examined in Chapter X, so that here we shall consider only archaeological evidence from elsewhere in the region. Two Predynastic or early dynastic Egyptian stone bowls have been found at Mycenae and Asine in the Argolid – that is, in the same region as Tiryns. However, the one from Mycenae was found in a context of Late Helladic pottery and that from Asine is also probably from the Mycenaean period, that is, 1,500 to 2,000 years after they were made. The Egyptologist and archaeologist of Crete J.D.S. Pendlebury suggested that these extraordinarily beautiful and durable objects may have come by way of Crete or that they came as the result of later Greek tomb robbing.[115] Given the suggestions of Egyptian influence in the Argolid in the 3rd millennium, the possibility that the bowls arrived then and were buried or preserved as heirlooms on Mainland Greece cannot be discounted. Similarly, a button seal, found in an EHIII context at Asine and identified by the excavator as Egyptian, cannot simply be dismissed on the ideological grounds that it is 'much too early for any such contact'.[116] On the other hand, this can only be a possibility and too much weight should not be put on the seal as additional evidence.

Another and undoubted Old Kingdom object is a marble cup inscribed with the name of the sun-temple of the founder of the 5th Dynasty, Userkaf, who probably reigned in the 26th century BC. The cup was found on the island of Kythera, off the southeastern tip of the Peloponnese.[117] The likelihood is that this relatively delicate object was transported to the island not long after its manufacture. Helck argues that it must have arrived after the fall of the 5th Dynasty because an object could never have 'disappeared' from its dynastic temple before then.[118] The strong Semitic associations of the island would allow for its having been transported by Levantines at some point in the 2nd millennium. For instance, there is a cuneiform dedication on the island by the king Naram Sin of Eshnuna, who reigned about the turn of that millennium.[119] The name Ku-te-ra appears in an Egyptian list of Aegean toponyms from the mid-2nd millennium discussed in Chapter X. The Semitic origin of the name Kythera from the *ktrt* (crown), as well as the Egyptian derivation of Kythera's other or 'doublet' name, Skandeia, from sḥmty (the double crown of Egypt), were referred to in Volume 1.[120]

All this, however, does not tell us whether or not the cup can be used as evidence of Egyptian contact with the Aegean in EHII. Here again, the evidence though suggestive remains shaky. It also provides no clear-cut evidence of Egyptian influence on Mainland Greece as it would seem that for that period Kythera was in the Cretan rather than the Mainland sphere of influence.[121]

There are two other finds of Old Kingdom objects from the Aegean that provide a completely different set of difficulties. This is because they are from gold hoards dug up by commercial treasure hunters who have attempted to sell or succeeded in selling them to unscrupulous dealers.

The most notorious of these is the so-called 'Dorak Treasure'. This appears to have been dug up at Dorak near the Sea of Marmara 160 kilometres east of Troy. It is supposed to have contained a number of gold objects of the local Yortan culture, the remains of an iron sword – remarkable for the early Bronze Age – and some gold sheet panels apparently of a throne and with the titulary of the 5th-Dynasty paraoh Sahure*. The 'Treasure' has disappeared since it was described and illustrated with drawings in *The London Illustrated News* in 1959 and some doubts have even been expressed as to its authenticity.[122] However, I am prepared to accept the judgement of James Mellaart, who wrote the original short article and claims to have examined the objects.[123] If they are authentic, the panels would seem to have been an official Egyptian gift to a local ruler, presumably the ruler of Dorak, possibly indicating some kind of Egyptian suzerainty over the area.

This is not the only archaeological evidence indicating Egyptian contact with Anatolia in the Old Kingdom. Jugs from Cilicia were found in an Egyptian 4th-Dynasty tomb at Giza and a 6th-Dynasty Egyptian button seal has been found at Tarsus in Cilicia.[124] While there was a surprising amount of contact between Cilicia in the southeast of Anatolia and Troy and Dorak in the northwest and such finds do indicate Egyptian trading and official contacts beyond Syria, unlike the Dorak Treasure itself, they do not demonstrate Egyptian presence in the Aegean.

Such a presence is indicated, however, by another gold hoard, which would seem to be the grave goods of a princess. Although there seems no doubt that it comes from the Aegean region, the specific provenance of this hoard is unknown. Helck believes that it, like the Dorak Hoard, comes from Northwest Anatolia, possibly Troy itself, and is a single collection dating from the Early Bronze Age.[125] The most sensational object contained in the hoard is a large gold cylinder seal, belonging to a very high official in the reigns of the 5th-Dynasty pharaohs Menkauḥōr and Izozi. How did this personal seal reach the Northern Aegean? Emily and Cornelius Vermeule speculate: 'Did they send an official as a diplomatic or commercial ambassador to the shores of the Mediterranean beyond Egypt. . . . Did he carry his seal as credentials to be married, or murdered or perhaps robbed abroad?'[126] They support their image of Egyptian officials sailing the East Mediterranean in the 3rd millennium BC by pointing out that the names of Menkauḥōr and Izozi as well as that of Saḥureʿ have been found on alabaster jars at Byblos. Thus the idea of Egyptian concern with overseas territories at this time is by no means absurd and the loss of such a precious personal belonging certainly requires explanation. Emily Vermeule has written elsewhere of the extent of Cycladic and other 'Greek' maritime trade in the Early Helladic period, more recent work has demonstrated the flourishing state of Boiotian ports at this time, and now there is the evidence from the Dokos wreck. Thus, there is no reason to suppose that Greece would have been any more backward than Northwest Anatolia.[127]

For those who accept the Ancient Model in general and in particular the idea that the Greek cult of Dionysos derived from that of Osiris in Egypt, there is further evidence of 3rd-millennium contact between Egypt and the Aegean – the existence of the cult of Dionysos as a god of fertility found from late 3rd-millennium strata on the island of Keos, off the point of Attica.[128]

Linking all these scraps of evidence, however, is the strong probability expressed by the Egyptologist and comparative historian of art William Stevenson Smith:

> the expansion of royal trade by land and by sea which we begin to see more clearly in the Fifth Dynasty would suggest that the period from Sneferu [beginning of the 4th Dynasty, c. 2900 BC] to Phiops II [end of the 6th, c. 2450 BC] would have been . . . a propitious time for Egypt to become aware of the Aegean World.[129]

To put it another way, given the wealth of Egypt during the Old Kingdom, the political strength of its pharaohs, their known concern with trading with and plundering their southern neighbours, as well as their constant commercial and political connections with Byblos and the Levantine coast, it would be surprising if there were no contact between Egypt and the Aegean at this time. Furthermore, there would seem little doubt that the consequence of such contact would be Egyptian influence on Greece rather than vice versa. Thus, I believe that one can place some significance on the relatively few Old Kingdom objects found in Crete and elsewhere in the Aegean. Nevertheless, I see the evidence of Egyptian influence from the Theban 'pyramid' and from the irrigation works and granaries as even more impressive.

The End of Early Bronze Age 'High' Civilization

It is generally maintained that the culture and prosperity of Greece in Early Helladic II ended with a series of destructions in the 23rd century BC (I believe this should be dated to the 25th century). It is with this break that most historians associate the introduction of Indo-European speech to the peninsula. Although I am inclined to see the superimposition of an Indo-European language over an Indo-Hittite one as having taken place earlier, I am reluctant to commit myself on this. Nevertheless, there is little doubt that northern tribes were involved in the destructions and successive settlement so that this could have been the time when Indo-European speech was introduced to Greece.[130] There is no doubt that Lerna was destroyed and the Argolid devastated at this time and that, as Emily Vermeule puts it, 'After the House of Tiles [in Lerna] was burned, it took Greece over half a millennium to approach the same level of civilisation again.'[131] Nevertheless, just as in the 'dark ages' following the destruction of Mycenaean civilization in the 12th century BC, the situation was not uniformly bleak. Some districts seem to have been untouched and others actually gained from their neighbours' losses. Furthermore, there appears to have been a general shift of populations in different directions. For instance, the destruction in the 24th century seems to have been less severe in Boiotia, although most authorities see a drop in population and prosperity there after the end of EHII similar to that found in the rest of Greece.[132] Against this, Symeonoglou actually sees a dramatic increase in the population and the level of sophistication of Thebes and Boiotia as a whole in the EHIII period. He tentatively links this to an outside 'intrusion' not from the north but from the south, though – as a convinced 'Aryanist' – he hastens to add that this came from 'population movements within the Aegean'.[133]

Symeonoglou links the 'intrusion' during EHIII with the legends concerning Kadmos, whom he sees as coming from Crete at this time.[134] While I do not wish to contest Sarantis Symeonoglou's archaeological conclusions, there are a number of difficulties with this scheme, as there are with Spyropoulos's belief that the legends of Kadmos and Danaos refer to the foreign, largely Egyptian influences he sees in the Early Helladic period.[135]

Firstly, there are the many specific references in the tradition to Kadmos' being a Phoenician and to the very plausible Semitic origin of his name; these issues will be taken up in more detail in Chapter XII. Secondly, the schemes of both Symeonoglou and Spyropoulos involve the denial of the Homeric tradition according to which Amphion and Zēthos founded Thebes and Kadmos *refounded* it. Pherikydes, the 6th-century logographer, glossed the story to show that the older city had fallen into ruins before Kadmos' arrival.[136] Symeonoglou prefers instead to follow the later traditions according to which the order was reversed and Kadmos was the original founder.[137] The older tradition would agree with the conventional archaeological view that prosperity was at a low ebb during EHIII and the early part of the Middle Helladic period, but this will be discussed in Chapter XII.

The destruction of Early Helladic II in Greece appears to have coincided with the collapse of the Egyptian Old Kingdom and the 1st Intermediate Period of political and social disintegration in Egypt. As with the invasions that ended Late Bronze Age civilization in the 13th and 12th centuries, Egypt and the Levant recovered quickly but peripheral regions like the Aegean went through extended 'dark ages' lasting many centuries.

Conclusion

Seen in the context of the dense and intricate evidence from toponyms, religious cults and local traditions, discussed in Chapter II, it is virtually certain that Boiotia and parts of the Peloponnese received massive cultural influence from Egypt and the Semitic-speaking Levant during the Bronze Age.

It is difficult to be more precise. Some of the myths, possibly including those associated with Athena and Poseidon, which – I believe – relate to the struggle to tame the marshes, could come from the Early Bronze Age and Egyptian involvement in the drainage and irrigation at that time. Others, such as those around Zeus, Alkmēnē and Herakles – in his many aspects – could have arrived only in the 2nd millennium, while others, especially those concerned with horses, must have originated after the actual arrival of horses and chariots in Greece in the 18th century BC. Although they undoubtedly contain much older material, the legends concerning Kadmos would also seem to come from this later period.

Taken together, the myths, legends and toponyms show a massive and sustained influence by Egyptian and West Semitic speakers on Boiotia, the Argolid and Arkadia.[138]

Such a picture would seem to fit the archaeological record relatively well. The likelihood of substantial Egyptian influence on the construction of the 'pyramid' of Amphion and Zēthos and the earliest drainage projects in the Kopais in the Early Bronze Age has been discussed at length, as have the 'Egyptian granaries' in nearby Orchomenos. The Egyptian and Levantine influences on the Mycenaean palace of Thebes and the spectacular hoard of Near Eastern objects found in the Kadmeon from the 13th century, which will be discussed in Chapter XII, attest to the continuity of such contact and influence.

Unfortunately, it is impossible to determine the type of relationship that existed between Boiotia and Egypt in the period with which we are concerned. The chances that it took the form of a direct colonization are very low: despite the dangers of the argument from silence, it has to be noted that not only is there the lack of Egyptian objects, and of Egyptian attestation of such colonies, but there is the strong likelihood that Boiotia's writing system was an Aegean one rather than hieroglyphics or hieratic. Nevertheless, the archaeological indications of Egyptian technology in Boiotia from this period, the depth and density of Egyptian and Semitic penetration of the cult, mythology, legends and toponym of Boiotia and the probability that Egyptian officials were present in the Aegean in the 3rd millennium make some kind of suzerainty quite possible.

To what extent can we extend this picture of Boiotia to the rest of Greece? The archaeological pattern is revealing of a sophisticated co-ordinated polity in the Argolid using an Egyptian-style granary and possibly hydraulic engineering of a style found in Egypt. This would seem to make suzerainty a possibility and diplomatic relations between Argos and Egypt a virtual certainty. The extraordinary parallels between Boiotian and Arkadian drainage and irrigation, as well as between the mythology and toponomy surrounding the constructions in both regions, would suggest that if the Arkadian waterworks began as early as the Early Helladic period there would have been Egyptian and Semitic influence there too. Thus, from very early indeed, possibly even before the arrival of Indo-European – as opposed to Indo-

Hittite – speech, the Bronze Age civilizations of Egypt and the Levant had exerted a massive influence on the Aegean.

The picture in Crete and the Cyclades in the Early Bronze Age is significantly different from that on Mainland Greece. In the islands one sees a very attractive and sophisticated material culture with some traces of urban life but without any indication of strong state power. As I showed in Chapter I, archaeological evidence leaves no doubt, for Crete at least, that there was significant Egyptian and Levantine influence on these cultures. We shall see in Chapter X that evidence from Egyptian documents would seem to back this up. In fact there seems to be a basic similarity between relations between the Aegean and the Near East in the Early Bronze Age at the height of the Egyptian Old Kingdom and those in the Late Bronze Age when the New Kingdom was powerful.

There are also, of course, many striking differences. First of all, there is the fact that – after the disunity and confusion of the 1st Intermediate Period – the revival of Egyptian power with the Middle Kingdom in the 21st century appears to have played an important role in transforming Crete into a territory with palaces and states. By contrast, the impact of the rise of the Middle Kingdom on the Mainland and the more northerly islands seems to have been less significant.

The existence of a culturally and probably politically powerful 'Minoan' Crete after 2000 BC made that island the most important single mediator between the Near East and the Aegean during the first half of the 2nd millennium BC, which, as we shall see, was critical in the development of 'Greek' civilization. The other critical difference between the Aegean in the Early Bronze Age and in the Late Bronze Age is that there is little or no evidence of direct colonization there in the 3rd millennium. On the other hand, as we shall see in Chapter IX, there is a strong possibility that Hyksos princes of Egypto-Semitic culture and language actually established colonies in Greece and set up long-lasting dynasties in the 18th and 17th centuries BC.

CHAPTER IV

THE OLD PALACE PERIOD IN CRETE AND THE EGYPTIAN MIDDLE KINGDOM, 2100 TO 1730 BC

I N THIS CHAPTER we return to consider Crete as it changed from a prosperous and cultivated society of small communities into a group of centralized states ruled from palaces. This change brought it into line with a pattern that had been common through much of the Middle East many centuries earlier. The Cretan development with its own particular features is of great significance, both in itself and because it provided many of the most important components in the later Mycenaean civilization that dominated the Aegean in the Late Bronze Age and formed the basis of the civilizations of Archaic and Classical Greece.

This chapter emphasizes the Egyptian influence behind the rise of the palaces, which, though referred to in the Ancient tradition, has been very much played down in the 20th century since Arthur Evans's finds at Knossos in the years around 1900. The discovery of the startlingly refined and beautiful culture of 'Minoan' Crete made it intolerable for adherents of the Aryan Model to accept it as a mere stepping stone between the 'East' and 'Europe'. Crete thus came to be seen as one of the parents of Hellenic civilization and hence all Western civilization, the other being the steppes and mountains of Central Asia that had produced the virile Indo-Europeans.[1]

EARLY MINOAN III – THE PREPALATIAL PERIOD

The ceramic period Early Minoan III ended and Middle Minoan Ia began some time around the turn of the 2nd millennium. This change also marks the beginning of the Palatial Period in Cretan history. Where in the Early Minoan period Crete was largely rural with relatively little social differentiation, Middle Minoan society was one of states controlled from central palaces.

Not surprisingly, the isolationist Colin Renfrew does not want to stress the extent of any changes that could involve outside influences. Thus, he claims that 'the continuity in the transition from prepalatial to protopalatial Crete must be emphasised.'[2] There is a terminological difficulty here in that the word prepalatial can be used both for the whole Early Minoan Period or – as I use it – for the decades that immediately preceded the building of the palaces. Recently, younger scholars have begun to reaffirm the significance of demarcation between the non-palatial Early Minoan Period and the Prepalatial one. Their doubts about the picture of smooth evolution have been focused on the site of Myrtos on the southern coast of Eastern Crete, which had been seen as a late Early Minoan settlement on the brink of becoming a palace. In a detailed study of the site, a young archaeologist, T. M. Whitelaw, has shown that Myrtos does not provide a bridge between the Early Minoan and Prepalatial Cretan society.[3] Other scholars have tended to accept this. As one Cambridge archaeologist has put it, 'after the reinterpretation of Myrtos it is clear that MM palaces cannot be said to be merely a quantitatively different manifestation of any EM prototype'.[4] John Cherry, another Cambridge archaeologist, appears to have come to the same conclusion. He insists in his article 'Evolution, revolution and the origins of complex society in Minoan Crete' that he is only raising the possibility that 'the transition to palace society in the centuries on either side of 2000 B.C. was in several important respects a quantum leap beyond anything that had gone before'.[5] This caution is hardly surprising in a university where the dynamic Disney Professor of Archaeology is Colin Renfrew. However, it is clear where Cherry's heart lies. Not only does he make a perceptive criticism of the progressive evolutionism of the founder of Cretan archaeology Arthur Evans and his contemporaries and set Renfrew firmly in this tradition, he also places this tradition alongside the greatest Victorian evolutionary system, Darwinism. Thus, he applies to Cretan archaeology the recent biological rejections of Darwinist evolution as a smooth progression in favour of *punctuated equilibria,* sudden changes followed by relative stasis. Cherry's argument is based on the startling differentiation of Cretan society between town and country and social classes, and the sophistication of palatial organization. He also emphasizes the archaeological evidence for a sharp increase at this point of communications between Crete and the Near East.[6]

Before examining this phenomenon, we should look at the relative chronologies of the two regions. Arthur Evans originally established his ceramic chronology of Crete on the basis of the three kingdoms of Ancient Egypt. His Early Minoan Period corresponded to the Old Kingdom, the Middle Minoan Period to the Middle Kingdom and the Late Minoan Period to the New Kingdom. This overall scheme has lasted remarkably well. Over the last fifty years, however, some adjustments have had to be made.[7] One of these came from the recognition that, as William Ward, the American Egyptologist who has devoted much time to East Mediterranean relations, put it, 'The majority of Aegean specialists who use ceramic chronology now place the beginning of MMIa at ca. 2000 B.C., or the beginning of the Twelfth Dynasty.'[8] Thus, according to him, EMIII, which preceded it, seems to have begun in the last decades of the 22nd century. More recently, Professor Cadogan has placed the beginning of MMIa at around 2050 BC, which would seem to fit the carbon dates.[9] However, he and other specialists generally agree that the palaces were first constructed some decades after the beginning of the ceramic period. Either way, it would seem that the great Cretan palaces were built within twenty-five years of the turn of the 2nd millennium.[10] However, there was clearly a Prepalatial Period that lasted approximately a century before this and the line between the ceramic periods is very unclear at this point. There is, in fact, an overlap between MMIa pottery at Knossos and the old EMIII pottery in Eastern Crete. It would seem likely that, as Ward has argued, much of the latter part of EMIII and its architectural equivalent, the Prepalatial Period, does not correspond to the Egyptian 1st Intermediate Period, but, rather, was contemporary with the 11th Dynasty, the first of the Middle Kingdom which began in the middle of the 22nd century and flowered in the 21st.[11]

During EMIII, there was a sharp increase of contact between Crete and the Middle East in general and Egypt in particular. The archaeologist Keith Branigan has noted a new wave of Syrian influence in Crete. For instance, he points out that while there were clear continuities, Cretan metallurgy was at this time 'considerably influenced by types and techniques used in Syria and Cilicia and in this and the following period there are some actual imports of Syrian daggers'.[12] Another archaeologist, O. Krzyszkowska, notes a significant increase during EMIII in the import of elephant ivory which could have come from either Egypt or Syria and possibly of hippopotamus ivory which must have come from Egypt.[13]

Peter Warren has shown that small cylindrical jars and miniature amphorae, found in pottery from EMIII Crete, derive from Egyptian stone prototypes.[14]

The art historian L. Vance Watrous has pointed out that: 'In MMI, a number of new vase shapes, which include the goblet, carinated cup, conical cup, fluted cantharos, and theriomorphic rhyta, appear on Crete in imitation of Near Eastern Vessels with a long prior history.' He also sees connections between the specific cultic uses of these vessels in Crete, Egypt and the Levant.[15] He also makes the interesting and plausible suggestion that the fast (socketed) potters' wheel, which first appears in Southern Crete in MMI–II, was first introduced from the Near East 'to meet the demands for specialization and quantity required by the palace system'.[16]

LEAD AND SPIRALS

Actual Egyptian objects from this period have also been found in Crete. Six Egyptian scarabs have been found in EMIII and MMI contexts in *tholoi* in the Messara in Southern Crete.[17] Their significance is far greater than their size or number would indicate, because they confirm connections made on detailed stylistic grounds between Egyptian and Cretan seals which began in EMIII.[18] As Pendlebury wrote, 'Many of the parallels are too close especially when taken together with the actual imports to be taken to be anything but direct contact between Egypt and the Messara at this period.'[19] Before Pendlebury wrote this, Evans's view of the connections between Egypt and Crete had been attacked by F. Matz in a publication which appeared in 1928 in Berlin. He saw Cretan glyptic art of this period as having Balkan or even Danubian connections.[20] Other German and Austrian scholars have favoured an Anatolian origin for Cretan seal-making.[21] However, Ward, who is also inclined to this view, admits, 'In spite of the arguments of these scholars even in the more recent works there is a surprising amount of support for Evans' original ideas'.[22]

Now to look at connections from north to south, there is the fascinating likelihood – shown by lead isotope analysis – that two 11th-Dynasty statues from the 21st century BC were made with silver from the mines of Laurion in Attica. It is possible that the analysis is wrong or that the silver had been imported some centuries earlier during the Old Kingdom, through possible contacts that were mentioned in the last chapter, and later imports from Laurion to Egypt will be discussed in Chapter XI. The most probable explanation, however, is that there were direct or indirect trading or political contacts between Early Middle Kingdom Egypt and the Aegean.[23]

The most frequently cited example of northern influence is that of spirals. What German scholars have called the *Spiralenproblem* comes from the fact that spiral decorations were frequently used in both Crete and Egypt in the 21st and 20th centuries. One solution to this problem, proposed by German scholars such as Fimmen and Helck, is to suppose that these decorations derived from the north, probably from the Cyclades.[24] Another solution has been more popular in the antidiffusionist atmosphere after the Second World War: it is to postulate independent invention in all three areas.[25] Ward has elaborated on this and, after stressing the ease of independent invention, he tentatively proposes three centres of diffusion – the Cyclades, Eastern Turkey and Iran.[26] This would seem to be acceptable.

However, it should be noted that spirals were in fact common throughout the Middle East and Aegean from at least the middle of the 3rd millennium.[27] Furthermore, motifs with winding lines existed in Old Kingdom Egypt. What is more, two examples of these – the 'winding wall' ⊔ of Mnevis and the 'unwinding spiral and horns' Ⴟ on the ꜣwt or sacred emblem of Min – were specifically linked to bull cults, which on other grounds would seem to have been introduced from Egypt to Crete at this time (see below). Thus, although the forms of the Egypto-Cretan spirals at the turn of the 2nd millennium may well be those of the Cyclades or Anatolia, the significance of their symbolic use may well come from Egypt.

The Cretan Palaces

Before discussing the origins of the Cretan bull cult we should consider the palaces in which it flourished. These palaces were first built in the last decades of the 21st century and seem to have lasted until the 12th century BC, by which time they appear to have been under Mycenaean Greek control for over 250 years.[28]

As Crete is situated in a region of intense seismic activity, there appear to have been many more destructions from earthquakes than one would expect from military activity or accidental burnings. Nevertheless, the only significant cultural break – apart from the arrival of the Greeks *c.* 1450 – seems to have happened near the end of the 18th century BC, between the ceramic periods MMII and MMIII, which has been architecturally demarcated as the division between the Early and Late Palace Periods.[29] Although there were changes in the palaces' structure and use of symbolism, some of which will be discussed below, there seems to have been a remarkable continuity throughout the more than eight hundred years of the Palatial Period. Thus it would seem justified to look at many of their early characteristics by analogy with the considerable amount that we know about the palatial bureaucracy and economy at the end of the Late Palatial Period.

There is no doubt that the building of the Cretan palaces around 2000 BC represented an extension to the Southern Aegean of an economic and social system that had been established over much of the Middle East for over a millennium.[30] Furthermore, their introduction was not merely on a general level but involved specifics. James Walter Graham has devoted much of his scholarly life to the architectural study of the palaces, and in his *The Palaces of Crete*, which remains the standard work on the subject, he writes:

> That resemblances do exist between the Cretan and Near Eastern palaces in some respects can scarcely be denied, and likewise . . . between Cretan and Egyptian architecture.
>
> There are resemblances of a general nature, especially between the Mari palace [on the Upper Euphrates] and the Minoan: rooms are arranged round courts; different quarters of the palaces are used for different purposes . . . there are bathrooms with clay bathtubs, audience halls and so on. But within the limits of this broad likeness the differences are so profound and so deep-rooted that who can say whether one type of palace architecture is really influencing the other to any significant degree? Certain general methods of construction are also widely spread, such as 'half timbering' and the use of orthostats. . . .
>
> There are also some resemblances in detail, between for example the clay pipe sections at Mari and Knossos . . . or between Cretan fluted column shafts and possibly some capitals . . . and Egyptian columns; mural painting is also an area of contact to a limited extent. . . .
>
> The available evidence suggests to my mind, that when the palaces first came into being around 2000 B.C. the Cretan architects though aware in a general way of palace architecture elsewhere, created forms suited to, and determined by, Cretan needs and the Cretan environment, and employed constructional techniques traditional to the eastern Mediterranean and with which they were generally familiar. . . . [They] developed more efficient and more peculiarly local forms, forms which were in some measure affected by the architecture of their overseas neighbors. . . . for new decorative forms they turned especially to Egypt. . . . The possible adoption of the Egyptian type of banqueting hall when Minoan kings wished, in imitation of the pharaohs, to add this luxury feature. . . .[31]

The grudging quality of even this admission of Near Eastern and Egyptian influence can be seen in a later article in which he detailed very specific Egyptian architectural influences on the Late Palatial palace at Phaistos in South Central Crete:

> In a previous article I argued that there is no reason to see strong formative influences from a culture outside the island itself affecting the architecture of Crete at any stage in their development. I am still of this opinion. But the importation of isolated luxury trappings, such as details of decoration, or such splendid features as monumental reception or banquet halls is not only possible but likely.[32]

Luxury trappings and so on are not superfluous to palaces; they and the sense of splendour they produce are essential to the running of the polity and economy.[33] Many such 'details' are found in the Cretan palaces from their first foundation. For instance, the striking resemblances between Egyptian and Cretan jewellery can only mean considerable borrowings in both subjects and techniques which began in the Old Palace Period.[34] Many of the decorative motifs of Cretan painting can be found in Middle Kingdom Egypt. For instance, the 'Minoans' took on the Egyptian convention of painting women yellow/white and men red/brown. Representations of the Egyptian goddess of childbirth T₃ wrt (the Great One) as an upright hippopotamus with a crocodile skin over her back seem to have arrived at this time in Crete to begin her iconographic transformation into kinds of insects known to Aegean archaeologists as 'genii'; these became ubiquitous in Cretan art.[35]

The relationship of other 'Cretan' decorative and religious symbols found in the palaces to those in Egypt will be discussed in this chapter and later in this volume. Similarly, some of the striking and detailed parallels between the official and economic structures of Cretan and Middle Eastern palaces will be considered in Chapter X.

Recently, Watrous has argued that the many artistic and architectural innovations of oriental origin in EMIII, linked to the introduction of the palaces and bureaucratic systems, must be seen as a unified introduction to Crete as 'part of the institution of Kingship'. He explicitly – and to my mind effectively – demolishes Renfrew's isolationism. He also points out that many historical parallels demonstrate that increasing wealth and urbanization do not in themselves lead to the very specific forms of palace society found in both Crete and the Near East.[36] Watrous's ideas are distinctly unfashionable among Aegean archaeologists even though they seem unexceptionable to scholars from other disciplines and the Aegeanists find it hard to argue with his conclusions.[37]

In any event, two major points are clear: firstly, that both the general pattern of the palaces and the societies of which they formed the centres as well as many details came to Crete from the Middle East; and, secondly, that most scholars of the 20th century AD have been reluctant to concede this fact.

I have already cited Graham as being hostile to the notion of Cretan borrowings from the Near East and this is evident throughout his work. A still clearer example of this attitude comes from Keith Branigan, who has been referred to above as remarkably open to the idea of outside influences on Crete:

> But above all, the whole conception of a Minoan palace is totally different from that of the palatial architecture anywhere else in the Bronze Age. A Minoan palace had as its focal point the central court. The palace was laid out around this court and grew from the centre outwards. Thus we find that the architect was not obliged to fit his scheme into a predetermined space or shape.[38]

Here we have clear implications of the ideological belief that in some ways the Minoans were 'Proto-Europeans' and therefore *free* in a way that Asians and Africans were not. The lack of palace walls is frequently referred to in this way; it is also used to illustrate the idyllic and pacific nature of Minoan society, which in many ways can be seen as akin to Winckelmann's picture of serene and childlike Greeks that was so popular in the 18th and 19th centuries. Similarly, it has been shown recently that Arthur Evans was heavily influenced by his cultivated and upper-class background in his reconstruction of the happy and peaceful Cretans.[39]

Having said all this, there *is* something distinctively 'Cretan' about the palaces and the civilization they contained. A similar local distinctiveness, however, is true of all the regions in which there were Middle Eastern palaces: Mesopotamia, Syria, Anatolia, etc. In all of these, the palaces reflected the local geographic, social, economic and cultural conditions. Recent discoveries strongly suggestive of human sacrifice, some of which will be discussed in Volume 3, demonstrate that the Minoan society was not as idyllic as Arthur Evans wanted it to be.[40] Nevertheless, in the Early Palace Period there appears to have been relatively little concern with defence and violence, although this situation seems to have changed considerably in the Late Palace Period. This would suggest relative harmony between the palatial 'states' on the island in the early period, between 2000 and 1730 BC, and also that there was a lack of outside threats.

Other Cretan characteristics, such as the prominence of maritime decorative techniques, can be simply explained by geography. The geographical centrality of Crete is also what distinguishes its palatial culture from those of its contemporaries. In this period the island was a meeting point of Levantine, Egyptian and local influences. For, despite the sharpness of the break at the beginning of the Prepalatial Period, Renfrew is right to point out that there were considerable continuities from the Early Minoan to the Middle Minoan periods. While it should be remembered that these too were not the result of isolation but of frequent cultural mixture, there is no doubt that Early Minoan Crete had been a cultivated society with its own cultural identity.

CRETAN WRITING SYSTEMS

This independence is reflected in the fact that palatial Crete did not adopt Egyptian hieroglyphics, cuneiform or a Byblian script, but used its own hieroglyphic and syllabic systems. The conventional picture of the development of writing in Crete is that in MMI, soon after the foundation of the palaces, signs that had been in use since EMI were regularized to form a pictographic script. The script was used for the next few centuries until the beginning of MMIII, in the later 18th century BC, when it began to be replaced by the phonetic syllabary Linear A. This linear syllabary continued to be written in Crete until replaced by Linear B, a similar script adapted for writing Greek, which came into use at Knossos with the arrival of Greeks there around 1450.

It is admitted that there are some difficulties with this scheme. The first of these stems from the fact that Linear B cannot be derived directly from Linear A. This necessitates postulating that Linear B branched off from a predecessor of Linear A, something not allowed for in the scheme of direct development from pictograph to Linear A given above. It also makes it impossible to hold the attractively simple theory that Linear B was developed in Crete when Greeks conquered the palace at Knossos. To explain the epigraphic evidence, it is necessary to maintain that Linear B existed well before this on Mainland Greece.

The American classicist Sterling Dow suggests that the syllabary was created around 1600 BC. This poses two problems for conventional historians: firstly, why should Greeks have required such a script before they had palaces? and, secondly, how could it have been unattested for so many centuries?[41] Neither of these problems seems serious to me. Societies with quite simple political and economic structures have used and developed quite complicated and sophisticated scripts; see, for instance, the Xixia script developed in Western Xinjiang in the late 1st millennium AD. In any event it was argued in the last chapter that Mainland Greece contained some considerable states as early as the middle of the 3rd millennium BC. As for the lack of attestation for some centuries in 2nd-millennium Greece, to my mind fear of the argument from silence shows a quite unwarranted faith in archaeology; there are many examples of even longer apparent gaps in the record of scripts.[42]

Another difficulty with the conventional scheme comes from the relationship between Linears A and B and the Cypriot syllabary. The last probably derives from an ancestor even more ancient than the prototype of the two Aegean syllabaries. Thus, one has the following scheme:

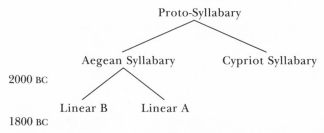

There is evidence from the Southern Cretan palace of Phaistos that a form of Linear A was already in use in the MMIA period at the end of the 3rd millennium.[43] The notion that Linear A itself was already old by the 17th and 16th centuries BC is strengthened by the fact that it was written in several different regional dialects by MMIIIB (c. 1700 BC) from which most of the first surviving tablets come.[44] If Linear A emerged around the turn of the 2nd millennium BC, its prototype from which Linear B derived must have existed in the 3rd millennium. In this case, the ancestor of these and the Cypriot syllabaries must have developed well before this in the middle of the 3rd millennium or earlier. The possibility that it developed before 2500 BC is increased by the fact that cuneiform, which was adaptable and adapted to many languages, was well established in the Levant by then.

The most plausible hypothesis therefore would seem to be that the ancestor of these syllabaries developed somewhere in the range from Cyprus through South Anatolia to Crete soon after the development of pictographic scripts there, near the beginning of the Early Bronze

Age. It was created for a language which – unlike Greek, but like most of those of Anatolia and the Cretan Semitic postulated by the Semitist Cyrus Gordon – made no distinction between voiced and unvoiced consonants.

Thus, despite the lack of attestation, it is probable that both the pictographic and syllabic scripts were well established in Crete by the Prepalatial Period. This would explain why, despite the cultural break between non- and Prepalatial Crete and the massive influences from the Levant and Egypt in the 21st century BC, the Cretan palaces did not adopt cuneiform, hieroglyphics or hieratic. Paradoxically, such a historical scheme would tend – in the important area of script – to confirm Renfrew's argument for cultural continuity from the Early Minoan to the Middle Minoan periods.

CULTIC SYMBOLS IN EARLY PALATIAL CRETE

In other important ways, however, there were significant innovations in the Prepalatial and Early Palatial Periods and it is striking how many of these would seem to have Levantine or Egyptian origins. Among the religious symbols there are the *st* ✹ (shoulder knot) and the tit 🔱 (tie). The latter doubled the Ḍed 🔱 which represented both a cultic construction of reeds and the bull's spinal chord with ribs with the *ʿnh* ☥, the *Ankh* sign of life possibly representing a sandal strap but more plausibly the vertebra of an aurochs.[45] The use of more explicitly bovine Egyptian religious symbols in Crete in the early 2nd millennium can be seen in the 'horns of consecration', a sacred motif used so frequently that its function sometimes seems merely decorative in Cretan palatial culture. These were recognized by the early 20th-century Egyptologists Newberry and Gaerte as coming from the synthesis of two Egyptian symbols: horns, ∪ , *wpt*, and two mountains divided by a valley, ⌣ , *dw*.[46] The visual merging of the two symbols, which first appears in the MMII period, appears to be a local Cretan one. Conceptually, however, the fusion had far older Egyptian roots. In the *Pyramid Texts,* inscribed in the 5th and 6th Dynasties in the 28th and 27th centuries but clearly much older, there is the passage showing this synthesis:

> *Wpy* 'The two mountains are split apart this king comes into being, this king has power in his body.'[47]

Wpy is clearly linked to *wpi*, ∪ ▫ × (open, especially of the womb in childbirth). The relationship with the two mountains would seem to come from another symbol, that of *ȝḫt*, Ωₒ⊏ᴚ or 🦆⊜◠✶, the sun on the horizon between two mountains, the place where the sun sets and the symbol of death and rebirth. The connection between this and the relationship between immortality and the revival of vegetation in Egyptian and Early Minoan religion (see Chapter I) can be seen in the verbal cluster *ȝḥt* (inundation), *ȝḥt* or *ȝḫt* (arable land), *ȝḫ* (papyrus thicket) and *ȝḫ* (to be or become a spirit). This would seem to appear in the Greek root *lakh-* (vegetable, green).[48] *ȝḫ ȝḫ* (to grow green) would seem to appear in Rarian, a name of the sacred fertile plain of Eleusis, more commonly known as the Orgas.[49]

The identification of these Egyptian symbols with the Cretan 'horns of consecration' was rejected by Nilsson, though he conceded a 'similarity of form'. He argued that the Egyptian sign ᗊ was a symbol, whereas the Minoan examples were merely cult objects used to designate places or objects of consecration. He also maintained that the Cretan symbol was not attached to any particular divinity.[50] However, the modern scholar Barry B. Powell points out that the same was true of the two mountains and he rejects Nilsson's other even vaguer objections.[51] There is little doubt, then, that 'horns of consecration' too can be added to the repertory of Egyptian religious symbols found in palatial Crete.

POSSIBLE ANATOLIAN ORIGINS OF THE BULL CULT

From a discussion of horns, we turn to the bull cult of palatial Crete and to considering the possibility that this originated from early Middle Kingdom Egypt. Bulls are attractive and powerful animals both in fact and as symbols. Thus, bull cults exist in many places and seem frequently to be of local origin. However, mountainous Crete, the very name of which may well come from the common Egyptian toponym Ḳȝyt (high land) is a country pre-eminently suitable for goats and wild goats or agrimi rather than bulls.[52] Given this fact, where did the bull cult come from? As is customary, when obliged to find an oriental origin, the favourite candidate is Anatolia.[53] For instance, Walter Burkert writes in his now canonical *Greek Religion:*

> The finds from the Neolithic town of Çatal Hüyük now make it almost impossible to doubt that the horned symbol which Evans called 'horns of consecration' does indeed derive from real bull horns. The serried ranks of genuine bull horns discovered in the house shrines of Çatal Hüyük are hunting trophies won from the

then still wild bull and set up in the precinct of the goddess. . . .
Intermediate stations on the journey from Çatal Hüyük to Crete
are now beginning to appear. Models of sanctuaries from Cyprus
dating from the end of the third millennium . . .[54]

As with the succession he drew up for the derivation of the double-
headed axe, Burkert has serious problems with his scheme for the origins of the Cretan bull cult.[55] The bull cult at Çatal Hüyük is indeed
impressive but he fails to make the point that it flourished and disappeared in the 6th millennium BC, that is, over three thousand years
before the 'horns of consecration' are first attested in Cyprus or Crete.
Indeed, there appears to have been an equally striking tradition – or
sporadic occurrences – in Egypt of marking human burials with bulls'
heads with the horns sticking out of the ground from the 11th millennium BC to the early dynastic period in the 4th millennium.[56]

I have frequently argued that one should not pay too much attention to the 'argument from silence' and it is possible that the cultic use
of bulls' horns existed in Anatolia without any attestation for three
thousand years. Nevertheless, Anatolia seems far-fetched as a source,
not merely for the 'horns of consecration' for which a reasonably
plausible Egypto-Cretan origin has been given in the last section, but
also for the Cretan bull cult as a whole.

There is an almost complete absence of any bovine iconography in
Neolithic or Early Bronze Age Crete.[57] In Cyprus there are bull cults
at the end of the 3rd millennium. During the same centuries, at the
beginning of the Palatial Period, bulls become centrally important to
Cretan religious life.

THUNDER AND SEX: MIN, PAN AND Bᵂ̈ÄZÄ

In this section, we shall make an excursion away from archaeology
and examine another possible origin for the Cretan bull cult that appears to have sprung up so suddenly on the island in the 21st and
20th centuries BC. I maintain that this did not derive from an Anatolian tradition, attested only three thousand years earlier, but from
contemporary 11th-Dynasty Egypt. Before going into the bull cult of
the Early Middle Kingdom, however, we should look at some earlier
African bull cults and their Cretan connections.

We shall begin with the Egyptian god Min, the counterpart of the
Greek Pan, who, Herodotos maintained, 'is very ancient and of the
eight gods who existed before the rest'.[58] The historian Diodoros
Sikeliotes, writing in the 1st century BC, named the gods of the Ethio-

pians of Meroe – the great political and cultural centre on the Upper Nile, a hundred miles north of the present Khartoum – as Isis, Pan, Herakles and Zeus.[59] His younger contemporary the geographer Strabo maintained that they worshipped Herakles, Pan, Isis and another barbarian god.[60] The precise identities of the others will be discussed in Volume 4. Our concern here is with Pan, the Egyptian Min.

Min can be traced back to the oldest stages of Egyptian history at the two southern cities of Koptos and Akhmin. However, from very early times, Min, whose name was probably first pronounced *Minw, was also associated with Nubia, the country immediately up the Nile from Egypt, and Punt, an East African territory still farther south, reached by sea.[61] In the Middle Kingdom Min was called the 'young stranger' and the direction he came from was clearly the south.[62] In Ptolemaic texts, Min was frequently linked with the Mḏз, the Beja people who lived and still live in the deserts east of the Nile in what is now Southern Egypt and the Eastern Sudan, as well as with Punt, and he was seen as a dispenser of tropical luxuries. As the French Egyptologist Chassinat and others have postulated, the Beja may well have acted as middlemen in trade between the coast and the Nile Valley.[63]

Min was associated with fertility and growth in Egypt, which does not appear to fit his cult as a divinity of the desert. I believe that this can be reconciled by drawing parallels between him and the modern East African divinity Bᵂäzä, who represented the fertilizing power of thunder followed by rain.

With the possible exceptions of the Yazidis and the Alawi, in Iraq and Syria, the non-Christians or non-Muslims among the Gurage of South-Central Ethiopia are today the only Semitic-speaking 'pagans'. Among them, Bᵂäzä or Bazo is still worshipped for his arbitrary violence and his sexual appetite. As a Gurage hymn puts it:

Oh Bᵂäzä, is there a place you do not descend to,
A *Keyae* [household] you do not visit,
Where you do not slay father and son,
Where you do not elope with the mother and the daughter?[64]

Interestingly, these two apparently contradictory aspects seem to be reflected etymologically in the name Bᵂäzä itself. This comes from a Semitic or Afroasiatic biconsonantal root √BZ with many different forms, which the lexicographer David Cohen groups into two semantic clusters, 'split, divide, distribute' and 'inflate, inseminate and abound'.[65]

I shall argue in Volume 3 that the name Bᵂäzä appears in Canaanite culture as Bō'az. In the Book of Ruth Bō'az was the name of Naomi's kinsman whose association with fertility is shown by his consummation of his marriage to Ruth, on a threshing floor at harvest time in Bethlehem, 'House of Bread'.[66] The thundering aspect of Bʷäzä is paralleled in the biblical use of the name Bō'az as the name of one of the pair of pillars placed in front of the temple of Yahweh. Bō'az was presumably also the name of the similar pillars known to have been placed before other Canaanite temples.[67] The practice of placing free-standing pillars in front of temples has a counterpart in the cult of Bʷäzä among the Gurage. The priests of Bʷäzä called *maga* – a name that is interestingly but inexplicably close to the Iranian *magi* – distribute for profit small strips of wood, *šäna*, from trees struck by lightning. These are placed on the ground close to the entrance of a compound or outside a hut and, as the anthropologist William Shack puts it, 'Wherever the *šäna* is displayed, it symbolizes that the land and property is blessed and others respect it for fear of Boza's (Bʷäzä's) reprisals'.[68] This type of spiritual lightning conductor in front of houses would seem to be a Gurage parallel on a domestic scale to the Bō'az placed in front of temples. The need for protection from this fierce but creative divinity in West Semitic religion can be seen in the Ugaritic hymns and epics of Ba'al, who punishes without mercy while fertilizing the land and, like a storm, tears out and brandishes trees.[69]

There are interesting possible Cretan connections to this cult. Klearkhos, a pupil of Aristotle, wrote that in the 5th century BC the people of Tarantum in Southern Italy conquered the nearby city of Kausina, inhabited by a people called Iapyges. As a punishment for this they were struck by lightning. The Tarantines, therefore, set up pillars in front of their doors for those who had been struck and made sacrifices to the pillars dedicated to Zeus Katabaites, 'the Descender'.

The English classicist A. B. Cook plausibly argued that this type of worship 'points in the direction of Crete'. In fact, Klearkhos gave a number of details to support the legendary belief that Iapyx, the eponym of the Iapyges, originated from Crete.[70] Cook also suggested that the thunderbolt wielded by Zeus Katabaites could well be related to the Cretan double-axes, which he believed should be seen as symbols of Zeus Katabaites.[71]

The iconographic trail of the double-axe Burkert followed to 4th-millennium Mesopotamia gives no clear indication of its religious meaning. However, as I mentioned in Chapter I, there also appears to have been a cult of the double-axe in Archaic Egypt.[72] If one accepts Cook's suggestion, it could be that at least one of the religious purposes of the Cretan double-axes, some of which lined parapets while others were free-standing, was that of the Iapygian pillars, to ward off actual and spiritual thunderbolts. We shall see below that the shape of the double-axe loosely resembles that of Zeus's thunderbolt. Thus, rather in the way the Gurage use the *šäna* taken from a tree struck by lightning to serve as a protection from Bᵂäzä, the double-axe would have symbolized both the striking and protection from it.

It is not clear that Zeus' Egyptian counterpart Amon had thunder-bolts. However, Min, who was early and often associated with both Amon and Mntw, clearly possessed one, the Ḥm, ⚬⚬. The Ḥm was a symbol of Min, used in the names of two of his cult cities, Akhmin/Panopolis and Koptos, and also possibly for the name of the 9th nome of Upper Egypt, known in Greek as Khemmis. The significance of this mysterious sign, which dates back at least to the 1st Dynasty (3400–3200 BC) is obscure. Gardiner tentatively called it 'two fossil belem-nites'. However, he pointed out that 'the earliest [examples of the symbol] resemble a double-headed arrow'.[73] The Egyptologist G. A. Wainwright claimed that the Ḥm was a conventionalized thunderbolt taken over from Min by Amon after the fusion of the bull with the ram thunder god.[74] Thus, belemnites, which were inexplicable in terms of contemporary natural history, were probably interpreted in the same way in both Egypt and Greece – as thunderbolts. In Greece, an Archaic status of Zeus holds a belemnite 'thunderbolt' in one hand and a crook looking very like an ammonite in the other.[75] The Ḥm, 'two or double belemnites', also closely resembles representations from the 7th century of Zeus about to hurl his thunderbolt.[76]

It is interesting to note that, while many of the Egyptian gods had flags, Min was the one in front of whose temples ceremonial poles were erected. These were the ḫt or ḫwt Ⳇ. The symbol seems to rep-resent a bull's head or horns on a staff together with an unwinding spiral, as already mentioned above. The spiral's significance is un-clear. It could be a herder's crook and/or, more likely, an ammonite, one of the commonest fossilized gastropods, shaped like a coiled – though naturally headless – snake which may itself have been seen as a thunderbolt. The ammonite was named after Amon and it is almost certain that others saw the resemblance and hence connection be-tween the ram's horn of Am(m)on and the ammonites before medi-eval scholars called the fossil *Cornu Ammonis* from which the modern name comes.[77] The ḫt could also have symbolized the uterus, written ⳿, and hence possibly the spiral and labyrinth.[78]

There are also interesting indications that the double belemnite Ḥm may have been used in similar ways. Although the words *ḥm* (shrine) and *ḥm* (sacred image) have been attested as being written with a ⚬⚬ only since the Middle Kingdom, there would seem to be a possibility that the phonetic *ḥm* meant 'sacred', and the 'two belem-nites' as a sign of divine power was used more as a general symbol of sanctity rather in the way the double-axe was used in Crete.[79] This raises the possibility that the ritual double-axes found in Predynastic and Old Kingdom Egypt were developments or variants of the Ḥm which became an important source if not the most important origin of the Cretan 'double-axe'.

To return to Min, the Egyptologists Gauthier and Chassinat, who studied his cult, have tried to explain his two aspects, as the god of the dry wilderness and of fertility of the cultivated soil, by claiming that his worship began in tropical Punt and was transmitted through the Eastern Desert to Upper Egypt, where it became assimilated to that of the ancient fertility god of Koptos, K₃ mwt.f (Bull of his Mother).[80] If such a merger took place, it would have had to have been in the 4th millennium, as there are statues of Min at Koptos dating back to before the beginning of the Old Kingdom.[81] I believe that, in this case, one should avoid misplaced precision and simply agree that there was a cult of a god of the Min type over a wide belt of East Africa, including Upper Egypt, associated with livestock, and that in wet areas this cult tended to be associated with fertility in crops and in dry ones with the constant rainless thunder of the region. Min had a special association with the mountainous countries of strangers.[82]

There is no doubt that Min's principal animal was a bull. Not only was he called K₃ mwt.f but also K₃ nfr (Beautiful Bull) and K₃ nḫt (Mighty Bull). He was also sometimes represented with bull's horns.[83] Furthermore, his massive phallus came like that of a bull not from his groin but from his abdomen. Nevertheless, as the German Egyptologist Eberhard Otto put it, there has always been a 'fundamental affinity' between Min and the ram god Amon.[84] The two gods were associated at Thebes since the 11th Dynasty and by the New Kingdom Amon and Re seem in many cults to have been fused with Min as a single massively endowed ithyphallic figure.[85]

The Greek god Pan's identification as a goat can be explained as a result of this fusion with Amon the ram/goat. Pan's derivation from Min would seem to be confirmed, not only by his great phallus, his association with the fertility of stock and his living in the wilderness, but also because of the whips both carried and the negroid blackness with which he, like his attendant satyrs, was often portrayed. The Egyptian name and theological position of his mother Kallisto will be discussed in Volume 4.

In the early 19th century, Niebuhr's patron the Romantic poet and mythologist Johann Heinrich Voss speculated that the name Pan derived from a European root *pa(s) (to guard, protect) from which we derive 'pasture', 'pastor', etc.[86] The French classicist Philippe Borgeaud, who has written a book on Pan, believes that Voss's view is confirmed by the discovery of a 6th-century dedication to Pan addressed as Paoni. This, Borgeaud claims, came from *Pāwōn and ultimately *Pa(s)ōn which provides the required s.[87] Chantraine is sceptical of this and follows a proposal made by the Dutch scholar C. H. Rujgh that the name Pan is 'Pre-Hellenic' and may well simply be a doublet of the name Paiáōn seen as an ancient name for Apollo.[88] The relation between the names Iōn, Iaōn and Paiōn and their derivation from the Egyptian iwn and pȝ iwn, 'barbarian' and 'the barbarian', have been mentioned in Volume 1.[89] Such a name would seem altogether suitable for the wild Pan.

However, this would seem not to be the only source of the name, and the abbreviation of *Paiáōn to Pan may well have been influenced by sacred, mysterious paranomasia or puns with which ancient Near Eastern and Mediterranean cultures were riddled.[90] The first of these is from the Greek pan (all, everything). Two others, however, may well be Egyptian, linking him to Min. For instance, it could be related to Pȝ ḥm, 'The Ḥm' itself. Another and stronger possibility is that the development of the name Pan was influenced by the Egyptian pȝ ỉm (the groan). A phonetic parallel comes in the derivation of the Greek word pan, panos (a Nile fish) from the Egyptian pȝ ỉn (the fish).[91] Semantically, there is a similarity between pȝ ỉm (the groan) and ꜥš (groan) and ꜥš (cedar); both were applied to Osiris in the mythical scenes in which he was in a tree.[92] The association of a divine name with groans can also be seen in the names Bakchos, from the Semitic Bâkûi (bewailed), and his counterpart Pentheus (bewailed) from the Indo-European.[93] The association of Pan with groaning can be seen from the words panikos and panismos (panic and terror). Plutarch made the link explicit in his story about Thamus. Thamus is clearly Dumuzi/Tammûz, the Mesopotamian and Syrian god of fertility of crops and herds who was bewailed annually for his premature death.[94] He was in many ways equivalent to the Egyptian Osiris. According to Plutarch, Thamus was instructed to go in his boat to Palodes and call out 'Great Pan is dead!' He did so and 'even before he had finished there was a great cry of lamentation, not of one person but of many, mingled with exclamations of amazement'.[95]

MIN AND MINOS

Following this digression on the relationship between the Egyptian lecherous bull Min and the Greek lecherous goat Pan, let us now look at the possible presence of Egyptian 'Mins' in the Aegean under the name of Minos.

According to a Greek tradition dating back at least to Hesiod,

Minos was a Cretan king and lawgiver, 'the most kingly of mortal kings'.[96] Homer too saw him as a judge of the dead.[97] This very Egyptian role would seem to equate him with Osiris. However, by the New Kingdom, Amon was seen as an aspect of or, to be more precise, as the *bꜣ* or 'spirit' of Osiris. A Saite version of the *Book of the Dead* of the 7th century BC contains appeals to Amon, who by this time was assimilated with Osiris, as the judge of the dead man.[98] In this respect then, the Cretan Minos resembled both Osiris and Amon; he also resembles Min, through Min's assimilation with Amon.

In Chapter X, I shall consider the hypothesis suggested by Albright that the Egyptian toponym Mnws, used for a foreign country, should be identified with Crete through Minos; I shall also be looking at the possibility that Minos might be related to Mꜣnw, the mountain of the sunset, with which Re, who was also assimilated to Amon, was directly associated.[99] Unfortunately, however, we have no vocalization for Mnws and Mꜣnw so their identification with Minos must remain tentative, especially as the Greek name did not refer directly to the island of Crete but merely to its legendary king.

A more plausible derivation of the name Minos is from that of the first Egyptian pharaoh Mn (*c.* 3400 BC), generally known by the later Greek transcription of his name as Mēnēs, but whom Herodotos some centuries earlier had called Min.[100] There is considerable difficulty over this name, as the official Egyptian king-lists of the New Kingdom used one kind of name (the Nbty-name) for the early rulers of the 1st Dynasty, while contemporaries referred to living monarchs by another, their Horus-name. Thus, although the Nbty-name Mni appears in the king-lists, the name Mn has been found on only one or two contemporary inscriptions. It is therefore difficult to know which Horus name to attach. Gardiner and Lloyd are probably right to identify Mn with the first pharaoh of the Dynasty whose Horus-name was Narꜥmer.[101]

This problem, however, does not concern us as the name was clearly used by an important pharaoh early in the 1st Dynasty and in later times Mn(i) was universally considered to be the founder of dynastic rule. It is also possible that there was punning here with the word *mn* (be firm, established) which was sometimes used transitively (to establish). In this case, the Cretan Minos could just have been the title of the local 'founder' and unifier.[102] In classical times it would seem that Mn was seen not only as the first pharaoh but as a pioneer of coherent government anywhere. Diodoros drew an explicit parallel between Mn and the Cretan Minos. According to him, the Egyptian was:

. . . a man not only great of soul but also in his life the most public-spirited of all lawgivers whose names are recorded. According to the tradition he claimed that Hermes had given the laws to him with the assurance that he would be the cause of great blessings, just as among the Greeks they say that Minos did in Crete and Lycurgus among the Lacedaimonians, the former saying that he had received his laws from Zeus and the latter his from Apollo.[103]

Interestingly, as we are now considering the Cretan bull cult, a late tradition associated Min/Mēnēs with bulls. Aelian, the Roman writer of the 2nd and 3rd centuries AD, claimed that Mēnēs had founded the bull cult of Apis.[104] The Egyptian historian Manetho maintained that this was established in the 2nd Dynasty, but this has been disproved by a reference to the cult from the reign of the 1st-Dynasty pharaoh ʿḥ.[105] Furthermore, there are many connections between Min/Mēnēs and Mn nfr, Memphis, the site of the Apis cult.[106] Thus, there would seem every reason to accept Aelian's claim, even though the foundation of the cult took place over three thousand years before he wrote. This is a remarkable, and I believe instructive, example of the strength and durability of traditions over this huge expanse of time. In short, given the similarity of name, the connection with a bull cult and the image of the Egyptian ruler as the political founder it would seem plausible to derive Minos as a lawgiver and judge of the dead from Min/Mēnēs.

However, Min/Mēnēs was not the only source of King Minos; there are at least two others. The first of these is Mnevis. In the passage quoted above from Diodoros, the writer was clearly referring to Mēnēs. The name he used, however, was Mnevis. This was the Greek name for the sacred bull at iwn or Heliopolis, now a suburb of Cairo, which was discussed in Volume 1.[107] The bull's name was normally written in Egyptian as Mr Wr, 'Great Mr'. In the *Coffin Texts* of the Middle Kingdom, however, it appears as Nm Wr.[108] The early 20th-century German Egyptologist Kurt Sethe derived Mnevis from a postulated Egyptian form *Mnewe, which has since been confirmed by the discovery of a late writing Mnỉ.[109]

In fact, from the earliest times, there has been considerable confusion in Egyptian among the three biconsonantals *mr*, *mn* and *nm*. It should be noted that during the Middle Kingdom *l*s in Semitic names were transcribed into Egyptian almost indiscriminately as *r*, *ꜣ*, and *n*. The best-known example of the last is the Egyptian name Kbn for the city known to its Semitic-speaking inhabitants as Gubla and to the later Greeks as Byblos.[110] All three sounds, *mr*, *mn* and *nm*, have associations with cattle: *mrw* means 'bulls' and *mry* 'fighting bull'. Apart from Mnì there are the words *mnìw* (herdsmen), *mnˁt* (milch cow) and *mnmnt* (cattle). Mnmn mwt.f (Bull of his Mother) was an epithet of Min. *Nmìw*, which looks very much like *mnìw*, means 'Bedouin'.[111] *Nmnm* means 'quake' as does *mnmn*, but the former also signifies 'go back and forth like herds'. It is interesting to note that two meanings for *nmì* [hieroglyphs], 'traverse' – 'travel around' in Late Egyptian – and [hieroglyphs] (lowing of cattle) both contain [hieroglyph] which Gardiner believes should be read 'for some unknown reason' as the phonetic *nm*. However, the same sign occurs in the writing of *mrrt* [hieroglyphs] (street) and of the name Mnevis Bull Mr Wr [hieroglyphs] or [hieroglyphs]. However, the phonetic *nm* and the meaning of 'winding wall' are seen together in the Late Egyptian *nmˁ* (set out, lay down walls). The origination from this Egyptian semantic cluster around *nm* of the Greek one surrounding the root *nom-*, found in both *nomaditēs* (nomads) and *nomos* (law) will be discussed in Volume 3.[112]

Putting this altogether, we see a triple parallel: in Egypt there was a bull cult associated with the name Mn, the founding pharaoh and a winding wall. In Crete there was a bull cult associated with a founding king Minos and a labyrinth. The parallels can be made even closer. The classicist and Egyptologist Alan Lloyd has shown that a description by Strabo of fights between bulls in a *dromos* by the temples of Apis and Hephaistos (Ptah) in Memphis was of an Egyptian tradition going back to the Old Kingdom, which seems to have symbolized the struggles between Horus and Seth.[113] Translation of *dromos* into English is difficult. It is clearly a place for running but its shape is indeterminate. It could be a circular theatre but more often it was an avenue or racecourse – with winding walls? The fighting bulls were often called *mry*, a term that was clearly linked to Mr Wr. What is more, Mr Wr/Mnevis was sometimes represented as a bull but also, though possibly only in later times, as a man with a bull's head, thus strikingly resembling the Minotaur in his labyrinth.[114]

There was an ancient tradition that Minos' architect Daidalos built the labyrinth at Knossos on an Egyptian model.[115] It is also noteworthy that the earliest extant use of the word *labyrinthos*, in Herodotos, is in reference not to the Cretan edifice but to the huge complex built as funerary temple by the 12th-Dynasty pharaoh Ammenemēs III (Amenemhe III, 1859–1814 BC) at the present Hawwâra, a few miles west of El Lâhûn at the mouth of the Fayum. Remarkably, the massive building was still standing even after Herodotos' time and may possibly have been seen by Strabo in the 1st century BC.[116]

Heinrich Brugsch, an Egyptologist employed by the Egyptian

Khedive Ismaiʻil (1866–1879 AD), became the first professor of Egyptology at Göttingen after Champollion. He also wrote a magnificent *Dictionnaire géographique de l'ancienne Égypte*, which was published in 1879. In this, he proposed that the Greek *labyrinthos* derived from a name of the Egyptian building *R-pr R-ḥnt (Temple at the mouth of the lake).[117] The name is not attested but *r-pr* is a common term for 'temple' and R-ḥnt was the name for the region which appeared in Coptic as Leḥōne or Liḥōne, preserved today in the village name El Lâhûn. For obvious reasons, this hypothesis did not find favour in the following decades and it was energetically denied in the 1930s by Gauthier in his *Dictionnaire géographique*.[118] At the turn of the century, the derivation from *R-pr R-ḥnt was completely ousted by an etymology from the Lydian word *labrys* (double-axe) which increased in plausibility when that symbol was found with great frequency at Knossos.[119] As mentioned above, it is true that the double-axe was an important religious symbol in Minoan Crete, but it is not so easy to see why it should give the name to a building. In any event, it is far from certain that Lydian or any other Anatolian language was ever spoken in Crete. There is certainly no major tradition connecting the labyrinth with Lydia. The reason for this far-fetched hypothesis would seem to come from the sociology of knowledge and the unthinkability of Egyptian or Semitic origins among most German and British scholars after 1880 and their preference for Anatolian 'Asianic' influences over anything from the Near East.

In Volume 1, I accepted Brugsch's proposal of a derivation from *R-pr R-ḥnt which had been recently revived by the Semitist Robert Stieglitz.[120] I still believe that this name may have influenced the Greek word. However, I now prefer an etymology endorsed by Maspero, Spiegelberg and Arthur Evans but treated sceptically by the historian H. R. Hall in 1920 and rejected more recently by Alan Lloyd.[121] This is that the origin of *labyrinthos* lies in the prenomen Ny-mꜣꜥ t-Rꜥ of the pharaoh Amenemḥe III, the builder of the original Egyptian 'labyrinth'. Classical writers rendered Ny-mꜣꜥ t-Rꜥ in a number of different ways which include Marēs, Lamarēs, Lamaris and Labarēs and Labaris.[122] The coincidence of the name of the building labyrinth and the name of the pharaoh to whom it was dedicated seems to me too remarkable for chance. I believe that the widespread final *-nthos*, commonly believed to be Pre-Hellenic, has many different sources, including simple nasalization before dentals. In some cases, however, as with the word *anthos* (flower, growth) itself, I think that it comes from the Egyptian *nṯr* (divine [in a pantheist sense] growth).[123] This could well be the case with the final *-inthos* of *labyrinthos*.

As has been mentioned above, there are strong connections between labyrinths and Egypt. Furthermore, there are the many clear
Egyptian influences on the construction and decoration of the Cretan
palaces. By contrast, there are only tenuous connections between
Bronze Age Crete and Anatolia and none at all with Lydia. It is for
these reasons, as well as for the better semantic fit, that I prefer an
Egyptian etymology for *labyrinthos* to a Lydian one.

Even if the name 'labyrinth' did not come from Egypt, and despite
the obvious confusion among later Greeks and others between a
dromos for the bulls, a funerary temple and the Cretan palaces themselves, it is clear that there are striking similarities between the Egyptian bull cults and those of palatial Crete. There is also no doubt
which cult developed first, as in Egypt it went back to the 4th millennium, whereas in Crete it seems to have begun only around 2000 BC.
Before going on to the specifics of transmission, it would be useful to
tie up some more mythological parallels.

The Cretan Minos had certain qualities that do not fit his image as a
majestic lawgiver. He was renowned for his rapes and seductions of
nymphs and mortal women.[124] In this, of course, he could be compared to Zeus, but Minos was not so clearly an immortal and above
human morality. These aspects do however correspond to the Egyptian god Min rather than to the pharaoh of the same name.

First of all there are the apparent correspondences referred to above
between the god Min's emblem, the Ḥm (double belemnite) and the
double-axe so prevalent in Minoan Crete. There is, furthermore, the
story of Minos' dazzling white bull, which he admired and took as the
chief of his herd. It then impregnated his wife Pasiphai, who crouched
in a contraption she had commissioned Daidalos to construct for her.
It was from this union that the Minotaur was born. The Egyptian bull-
god Min had a white bull consecrated to him which has been associated with his epithet Kɜ mwt.f (Bull [who impregnates] of his mother).
Thus, to the extent that Minos and Pasiphai's son the Minotaur *were*
his white bull, they can be identified with Min. It is also striking that
Min's cult contained a sacred black cow, iḥt kmt.[125] Given the close
pairing between Min and Amon in Egypt and Zeus and Minos on
Crete it is also interesting to note the strong possibility, discussed in
Volume 1, that Zeus' paramour Iō derived her name from iḥt (cow).[126]

The synthesis of the two Mins, the god and the pharaoh, would not
be a purely Cretan phenomenon. There were occasions in Egypt
when the two were worshipped together. In the great feast of the god
Min at Thebes as celebrated in the 19th Dynasty (13th century BC),
the first statue to follow that of the divinity was that of Min/Mēnēs.[127]

Thus, if there was not an actual connection between the two, as some scholars maintain, the ancient spirit of punning led worshippers to see a significant religious connection.[128] It would seem, therefore, that between them the royal Min/Mēnēs, the divine Min and the sacred bull Mnevis make up all the legendary characteristics of Minos.

THE CASE AGAINST EGYPTIAN INFLUENCE

Demonstrating the striking similarities between Min and Minos has been a matter of comparative mythology rather than one of archaeology. Furthermore, there is a considerable time gap between Greek legends about Crete extant in the Geometric ceramic period 1000–700 BC and the Archaic age 776–500 BC and the appearance of the bull cult in the Cretan palaces a thousand years earlier. Taken together, it would seem possible to argue with Karl Otfried Müller and his many followers that the parallels between Crete and Egypt were merely the result of later 'combinations' and 'liaisons' between Greek and 'barbarian', that is, Egyptian, priesthoods.[129]

There are, however, two major difficulties with this interpretation. Firstly, there is the extraordinary intricacy of the parallels. Secondly, there is the fact that, although fuller versions of the legends about King Minos appear only later, fragmentary references to them in the works of Hesiod and Homer make it clear that they were known in their time. Thus, modern proponents of the view that the parallels were later inventions – if, unlike Müller, they are systematic – would have to place the concoction before the 10th century, when I place Hesiod, whom I believe to be the earlier poet.[130] That is to say, the chief concoctions must have taken place either in the sub-Mycenaean period c. 1150–1000 BC which was one of little sophistication and relatively little friendly contact between the Aegean and the Middle East, or in the Late Bronze Age. In the latter case it would have meant the weaving of a tissue of fabrication when not only were there highly literate priesthoods in Egypt and the Levant but the Cretan and/or the Mycenaean palaces were still flourishing and presumably had some kind of historical records. This would seem likely to limit the possibilities of historical fiction. Nevertheless, there is no doubt that the creation of such myths is possible at this period. Furthermore, given the close relationship between Egypt and the Aegean in the 15th and 14th centuries BC, one could even detect motives for such fabrications so as to link the two regions and establish Egypt's pre-eminence over the north.

However, there is further evidence to support the simpler case that the legends reflected some historical reality and that, just as the Cretan palaces evolved as a result of Near Eastern influences, the bull cult that played such an important role in the palaces derived from Egypt specifically at precisely the same time, the 21st century BC.

MONT AND RHADAMANTHYS

To examine this other source of evidence, it would seem useful to begin by considering one of Minos' legendary brothers, King Rhadamanthys. Robert Graves tentatively suggested that this striking name came from *Rhabda Mantis (He who rules with a wand) and Wilamowitz rather vaguely that it was Carian.[131] Chantraine, on the other hand, dismissed this and other speculations as 'baseless'. I believe that one can fruitfully see the name as deriving from the Egyptian *Rdi Mntw ('Mntw or Mont gives' or 'whom Mntw or Mont has given'). Although this form is unattested, the construction is standard and both elements, Rdi + divine name and the divine name Mntw, are very common in the extant Egyptian onomastica.[132] The very form Rhadamanthys suggests that the hypothetical loan is early because the verb rdi began to drop its initial r- even in the Middle Kingdom, although one should never underestimate the power of archaistic revival in Egyptian culture.[133]

Let us first consider the possibility that Rhadamanthys/Rdi Mntw stood for the divinity Mntw or the syncretic Mntw Rˁ (Re) himself. Mntw was yet another solar god associated with Amon and Re. He was mentioned as a solar or stellar deity in the *Pyramid Texts*.[134] He was the god of the Theban nome, or province, in Upper Egypt. His rise came with that of his territory in the 11th Dynasty (2153–1979 BC). During the later half of this period, his cult, attached to the royal court, became dominant throughout the whole country. With the beginning of the 12th Dynasty, however, it began to be superseded by that of Amon, with whom Mntw tended to be identified. Nevertheless, even after this, Mntw remained important in the Theban nome and was generally popular as a god of war associated with the reunification of Egypt in the 11th Dynasty, after the three hundred years of disunity of the 1st Intermediate Period. As we shall see in more detail in Chapter V, the god also remained particularly associated with the subjugation of northern barbarians.[135]

Mntw originally had two consorts. The first was iwnyt (She of the southern iwn), this being the name of his cult centre, the city of Armant or Hermonthis, twenty kilometres upstream of Thebes. It was the counterpart to iwn, Heliopolis in Lower Egypt.[136] The second consort was Tnnyt, whose name is the feminine of Tnn, the ancient chthonic creator god who merged with the creative smith god Ptah. iwnyt and Tnnyt later lost their separate identities and were replaced by Rꜥt ꜣwy (Ria of the two lands).[137] Rꜥt is clearly a feminine form of Rꜥ and it is equally clearly the Egyptian prototype for the name Rhea. The phonetic fit is perfect, as we know that in the New Kingdom Rꜥt was transcribed into Akkadian as Riya or Ri'a.[138] Ria became assimilated with Nut, who in Hellenistic times was seen as the Egyptian counterpart of Rhea.

The apparent discrepancies between the Nut's character as a sky goddess and Rhea's as pre-eminently an earthly deity protecting the young in caves and grottoes are resolved by the fact that in Egyptian ritual the starry Nut's chief function was to arch over the mummy inside the coffin and to guard tombs and coffins. Some scholars claim to have traced her descent from being a sky goddess to being one of death with strong chthonic associations; others, however, believe that the subterranean associations were there from the earliest times.[139] When looking at Mnṯw's consort Rꜥt in relation to Rhadamanthys, it is particularly interesting to note that Rhea was one of the most important divinities in Crete, thus strengthening the Egyptian god's connections with the island.

The commonly used name Mnṯw Rꜥ shows the links between him and the sun as Re; and the name Mnṯw Ḥr demonstrates the connection with the young warrior god Horus. Like the latter and as a predatory war god, Mnṯw was sometimes portrayed with a hawk's head. From the 11th Dynasty, however, he was identified with a raging bull and his worship as a bull, or with bulls, is attested at all his cult centres by the 12th Dynasty. By this time, the sacred bull's colour was often seen as white and Mnṯw's bull was closely associated with the white bull of Min. Mnṯw too was linked to the 'black cow', iḥt km, whose correspondence to Iō has been considered above.[140] In late times after 700 BC, there were four bull cults of Mnṯw. One of these was oracular and all of them appear to have included rituals, processions and fights involving bulls.[141] It has been suggested that such a warlike deity could not have played an important role as a judge of the dead in funerary religion. However, ferocity has seldom been a disqualification for judges anywhere, especially in the underworld, and in fact the *Book of Coming Forth by Day*, commonly known as the *Book of the Dead*, does include Mnṯw among the other gods in Elysium.[142]

How do these characteristics tally with those of Rhadamanthys? The Cretan was known as a lawgiver. His stepson Herakles was supposed to have invoked one of his laws on murder, which seems to have been on the principle of 'an eye for an eye'. Together with Minos, Rhadamanthys was seen by Hesiod, Homer and later writers as a judge of the dead.[143] In the *Odyssey* he was called *xanthos* which, it will be argued in Volume 3, should often be rendered as 'sacred' rather than 'fair-haired'.[144] 'Sacred' would certainly fit better with *antitheos* (godlike), the epithet given him in the *Iliad*.[145] In the *Odyssey*, Rhadamanthys was seen as able to go to the furthest point in the west and return in one day, which strongly suggests solar associations.[146]

It should be reiterated here that Rhadamanthys' reputation as a lawgiver and judge did not make him pacific. He was supposed to have gained empire over the Ionian islands, not only because of his reputation for justice but also because of his 'inexorable punishment upon . . . malefactors'.[147] Rhadamanthys' legendary flight from Crete to Boiotia and his associations with Zeus and his 'fatherhood' of Herakles were discussed in Chapter II. Thus, to the extent that Herakles was a Middle Kingdom pharaoh, Rhadamanthys parallels Mntw as patron of 11th-Dynasty and later pharaohs.[148]

In general, therefore, there are good grounds for associating Rhadamanthys and Mntw: both were warlike and in some way father to a wandering hero/pharaoh. In Chapter II, I noted the representation of Mntw as the protector of Mntw Htp II.[149] Both Rhadamanthys and Mntw were closely connected to Amon/Zeus and were more or less connected to bulls. Phonetically, there is no difficulty in deriving the element -*manthys* from Mntw. We know from the Assyrian transcription of the personal name Mntw m ḫȝt as Mantimeḫe that Mntw was originally vocalized with an *a*.[150]

Mntw's connections with Crete are not restricted to Rhadamanthys. Given the centrality of Rhea in the island's later religion, it is striking to find that Rˁ t/Ria, who was not a prominent figure in Egyptian theology, should have been Mntw's consort. There is also the coincidence of the white bull, which would seem to link Mntw and Rhadamanthys to the latter's brother Minos and the divine Min. Furthermore, there is the possibility that Mntw like Mnevis was represented as a man with a bull's head. This was certainly the case in late times.[151] A unique three-sided seal from Karnak near Thebes, dated to the 1st Intermediate Period or the 11th Dynasty, portrays a man with a bull's head.[152] Given the prominence of Mntw at this time it could well represent him, but there is no way of being certain. It is also interesting to note that 'bull men' are represented on two of the Mesopotamian seals in the Tôd Treasure from the reign of Amenemḥe II (1917–1882 BC) found under a sanctuary of Mntw, which will be discussed in Chapter V. It is worth speculating whether they were considered especially suitable for Mnṯw.[153]

Nevertheless, although firmly associated with bulls in the Middle Kingdom, Mnṯw was at that time generally represented with the head of a falcon.[154] However, in Crete there are no representations of a tau- rocephalus Minotaur from the Palatial Period and the image which is so powerful in Greek tradition may have emerged only after the mas- sive contact with Egypt in the 15th century BC. In any event, there is no doubt that Mnṯw's raging bull, which like that of Min was indirectly identified with Amon, would fit nicely with the Minotaur, son of Minos, nephew of Rhadamanthys and grandson of Zeus.

At this point it would seem useful to consider the possibility that Rhadamanthys did not derive merely from an Egyptian god but from an Egyptian monarch as well (it will be remembered that Minos would seem to have been identified with both the divine Min and the royal Min/Mēnēs).

Min/Mēnēs, as the official founder of the 1st Dynasty, was always renowned as a conqueror and a lawgiver. The only other Egyptian rulers who came close to equalling his reputation were the reunifiers of the country and the founders of the Middle Kingdom. Although Mnṯw ḥtp I who flourished around 2150 BC does not appear tech- nically to have been a pharaoh, he was honoured as an ancestor of the 11th Dynasty and as one of the Black family who had reunited Egypt from their base in the Theban nome.[155] Mnṯw ḥtp II, who ruled in the 21st century, was the most effective ruler of the Dynasty and during the fifty-one years of his reign, Egypt once again became a major power as it had been under the Old Kingdom.[156] As Gardiner put it,

> Menthotpe, a name that signifies 'Mont is content': And contented the local god had good reason to be for . . . [he] witnessed, after many years of conflict, the reunion of all Egypt under a single ruler.[157]

In Egyptian tradition the two great Mnṯw ḥtps were frequently merged as the founder of the Middle Kingdom and paralleled with Min/Mēnēs. For instance, statues of Min/Mēnēs and Mnṯw ḥtp were given special prominence at the great festival of the god Min held at the Ramesseum near Thebes in the reign of Ramessēs II in the 19th Dynasty.[158] Thus we find the pharaohs Min/Mēnēs and Mnṯw ḥtp playing important roles specifically in the bull cult of the god Min.

The theological parallels between the Egyptian and Cretan cults are both intricate and neat. In Egypt, Min and Mnṯw are associated with white bulls and identified with Amon. In Crete Minos and Rhada-

manthys are brothers, the former is associated with a white bull
and both are sons of Amon's counterpart Zeus. An identification of
Rhadamanthys with Mnṯw ḥtp would elegantly complete the square.
Where Minos combined the bull god Min with the pharaonic founder
Min/Mēnēs, Rhadamanthys would combine the bull god Mnṯw with
the founding pharaoh Mnṯw ḥtp. In Egypt the two pharaohs were
stern rulers and lawgivers just as Minos and Rhadamanthys combined
both characteristics in Crete. There was also the Cretan view of the
two royal heroes' role in that essentially Egyptian institution, the Court
of the Dead.

Although such a conflation of god and monarch might seem
strange, as we have seen in the case of Min, it was perfectly normal in
Egypt and a very close parallel can be seen in a reference to the 12th-
Dynasty pharaoh Sesōstris I, who will be considered in detail in Chapter V. Sesōstris is described as the 'White Bull' who puts the 'intyw
[barbarians] to flight'.[159] The German Egyptologist Otto, who has written extensively on Egyptian bull cults, commented on this:

> This would seem to provide a connection to the warlike character of
> the Month (Mnṯw) bull and similarly a new proof of how tight the
> connection was between the warlike king and the Upper Egyptian
> bull cult.[160]

What is striking about these elaborate cultic parallels between Egypt
and Crete is that the cult of the royal white bull flourished in Egypt in
the 21st century BC, precisely when, on the archaeological grounds
given above, the Cretan palaces were first founded and the Cretan
bull cult is first attested.[161] As mentioned above, it is also a period in
which several scholars have noted Egyptian and Levantine influence
on the island. Pendlebury argued that Crete was heavily influenced by
Egyptian and Levantine culture via the Nile Delta, parts of which
were dominated by Semitic speakers in the 1st Intermediate Period.[162]
William Ward prefers – on what seem to be good grounds – to see the
phenomenon as having taken place in the early Middle Kingdom with
the Egyptian influence coming to Crete by way of Phoenicia in general
and particularly Byblos.[163] Byblos was always heavily Egyptianized:
many Egyptian inscriptions from the Middle Kingdom have been
found there and at that time Egyptian texts refer to its prince as ḥȝtì
(mayor), not as ḥḳȝ ḥȝswt, 'Hyksos' or 'foreign princes', as the other
rulers of Syro-Palestine were called.[164]

We know that not merely did Mnṯw ḥtp II reunite Egypt but that
his generals campaigned abroad in Nubia, Sinai and possibly further
north. We also know from documentary sources that at least one

official maritime expedition was sent to Byblos.[165] This picture is confirmed by archaeological evidence. Syrian wood was used in 11th-Dynasty boxes and coffins. Furthermore, the 'Montet Jar', a huge hoard of mainly Egyptian objects found at Byblos, has been dated to the 21st century.[166] Evidence that Egyptians of the 11th Dynasty may have penetrated the Aegean, together with suggestions of a motive for such voyages, comes from the silver from the mines of Laurion in Attica found in the two Egyptian statues of this period mentioned above.[167] It seems likely, then, that Crete received considerable Egyptian and West Semitic influence from the Levant in the 21st century, when the dominant figure in both Egypt and Syro-Palestine was Mnṯw ḥtp whose royal cult was that of Mnṯw and his ferocious bull.

There is no documentary evidence of any Egyptian expeditions to the Aegean at this time, but the Mit Rahina inscription, with its descriptions of previously unknown Egyptian expeditions by both land and sea – discussed in detail in Chapter V – provides a dramatic warning against the argument from silence in this kind of situation. There is no need of conquest, however, to explain such an expansion of cultural influence: the fact that pharaohs with the name Mnṯw ḥtp had reunited Egypt and established it as the dominant power in the Levant, and that they desired metals unavailable in Northeast Africa and Southwest Asia would be quite sufficient for this. If one accepts an identification of Rhadamanthys with Mnṯw ḥtp there are even some legendary indications that there was an expansion of political power. Diodoros wrote about Rhadamanthys: 'He came also to possess no small number of islands and a large part of the seacoast of Asia, all men delivering themselves into his hands of their own free will because of his justice'.[168] At another point, Diodoros specified the islands of Caria and Ionia.[169] The probable origin of the Greek ethnic name Ionian from the Egyptian iwn (bowman, barbarian) has been described in Volume 1.[170] It is interesting to note in this respect that Mnṯw, who was specifically concerned with warfare against northern barbarians, had the title Nb ḥsf iwntyw (Lord who represses the barbarians).[171] Apart from the Laurion silver, there is no archaeological confirmation of any 11th-Dynasty penetration of the Aegean. As far as I am aware, the only Egyptian objects from the Middle Kingdom found around the Aegean outside Crete are a scarab from Sparta and a wooden figure from the Heraion on Samos.[172] These, however, are much more likely to have been imported during the Archaic period (776–500 BC) of intense Samian trade with Egypt. Rhadamanthys was also associated with Boiotia, and, as we have seen in Chapters II and III, this area was strongly influenced by Egypt in the 3rd millennium.

THE SURVIVAL OF THE BULL CULT –
CRETAN CONSERVATISM

Although the bull cults in general and that of Mṇtw in particular remained important in Egypt until the collapse of its religion in the 2nd
and 3rd centuries AD, there is no doubt that they reached a peak in
the 11th Dynasty but diminished during the 12th with the rise of the
new royal cult of the ram- or human-headed Amon. In the Cretan
bull cult we seem to have an example of the important point made by
the Aegean archaeologist Sinclair Hood: 'Conservatism . . . is a key to
many aspects of the Minoan civilization of Crete, where beliefs and
customs originally prevalent elsewhere in the Near East tended to linger'.[173] By retaining the centrality of the bull cult for many centuries
throughout the Palatial Period, the Cretans preserved the religion of
Early Middle Kingdom Egypt. A parallel for such a pattern can be
seen in East Asia. Korea and Japan borrowed massively from China in
the Sui and Tang dynasties. They preserved many aspects of this culture while Chinese civilization moved on. Within a few hundred
years, these Chinese archaisms, modified by the local culture, came to
be considered as peculiarly Korean or Japanese. For example, even
today the Korean 'national dress' for women preserves Chinese fashions of the 7th and 8th centuries AD. A more immediately relevant religious parallel can be seen in the virtual disappearance of Buddhism
in its original home in India and its survival in Sri Lanka, Tibet and
Southeast Asia, in all of which it has become thoroughly distinctive
and local.

CONCLUSION

To return to the topic of this chapter, what does the archaeological
evidence from Crete before c. 2000 BC lead us to believe? Let me begin by reminding the reader of my arguments in Chapter I. Firstly,
the evidence strongly suggests that Neolithic Crete received its agriculture and pottery from Anatolia but that it was already in contact
with North Africa and the Levant. Secondly, the culture of Late Neolithic and Early Bronze Age Crete was an amalgam formed by local,
Libyan, Egyptian, Levantine, Anatolian and northern influences. It is
probable but unprovable that the new form of trading society which
developed in the Southern Aegean at the turn of the 3rd millennium
was stimulated directly or indirectly by similar and earlier developments in the Near East. In any event, there is little doubt that the
Aegean region received the potter's wheel, as well as pottery styles

and burial customs, from the Near East. Work on material remains of religious symbolism of Early Minoan Crete indicates very close parallels to Egyptian religion of the contemporary Old Kingdom.

It is clear that the Cretan palaces did not emerge gradually and spontaneously from Early Minoan society but represent a break from what went before. The introduction of the palaces and their methods of social organization from patterns that had existed several centuries earlier in the Near East in itself shows clear evidence of Levantine influence. Furthermore, many of the specifics of the construction and decoration of the palaces can have come only from Egypt. It is also striking that in the 21st century BC, just as palatial society was emerging in Crete, the bull cult which was to remain central to it was the state cult of 11th-Dynasty Egypt.

Archaeology can show this only as an array of remarkable coincidences. However, when evidence from it is combined with information preserved in Greek tradition and Egyptian inscriptions, a number of intricate and detailed parallels emerge that can be satisfactorily explained only if the cult was in fact borrowed from Egypt at that time. Thus, it is from this contemporary Egyptian royal bull cult and not from any dim chain leading back to Çatal Hüyük in Anatolia more than three thousand years earlier that palatial Crete seems to have gained its most characteristic cult around which the legends of Minos and the Minotaur were woven.

The social and cultural transformations of Crete in the 21st century BC coincide with the reunification of Egypt under the 11th Dynasty and the spread of Egyptian influence to the Levant and possibly beyond. The apparent adoption of the dynastic cult would seem to suggest direct Egyptian influence at this critical stage. Some legends, recorded only in Hellenistic times, seem to suggest that there could have been Egyptian rule or suzerainty over Crete and some of the islands at this time, but, given their lateness and the indirectness of the indications contained in them, such a suggestion must remain purely speculative. There is no doubt, however, that Crete was heavily influenced by Egypt in the 21st century.

The massive Near Eastern and particularly Egyptian influence postulated here does not mean that the 'Minoans' merely copied from their neighbours. Like most other peoples, the Cretans had considerable cultural originality. There is no doubt that, just as they seem to have developed the 'horns of consecration' out of two Egyptian symbols, they made their own developments of the bull cult. For instance, there is only slight evidence that Egyptians practised bull leaping, which became so common in Crete.[174] Similarly, while styles and motifs were frequently borrowed from Egypt and the Levant, no one has any difficulty in identifying Cretan art, particularly when it contains representations of marine life which were largely absent from the artistic repertoires of the continental Near East. Nevertheless, the evidence given in this chapter shows that, although like other regions it had a number of distinctive local characteristics, Early Palatial Crete was definitely part of the civilized world of the Middle East, borrowing most heavily from Egypt and the Levant.

CHAPTER V

Sesōstris, I
The archaeological and documentary evidence for the Greek accounts of his conquests

> *The odd figure of Sesōstris is one of the problems of the second book of Herodotos.*
>
> (Levi, 1971, vol. 1, p. 117, n. 245)

AS I HOPE I HAVE SHOWN, there are many methods available for studying the Ancient Mediterranean, including archaeology, language, proper names and traditions current among peoples of the region in later times; there are also contemporary documents. These are particularly relevant here because by the beginning of the 3rd millennium BC Egypt was certainly, and the Levant was almost certainly, literate. It is also clear that writing was used in both Anatolia and the Aegean during the 2nd millennium, the period with which we are largely concerned.

Here again, it should be made clear that, as with the archaeological evidence, there are no 'smoking guns'. There are no contemporary documents of the type '*X* the Egyptian/Phoenician arrived at this place in Greece and established a city/kingdom (t)here', explicitly confirming the Ancient Model. Nor, for that matter, are there others denying it. All one can do in their absence is to look at the circumstantial evidence that Bronze Age documents can provide concerning contacts between the Levant and the Aegean during the Middle and Late Bronze Age.

This chapter focuses on a single text from the richest source of documentary evidence, that from Egypt. This text does not mention Greece directly; we shall be considering documents that do so in Chapter X. Nevertheless, the Mit Rahina inscription and its relationship to the reports by Herodotos and others about the huge conquests

of the Pharaoh Sesōstris is, I believe, one of extraordinary importance
not only for checking the credibility of Classical sources but also for
understanding changes in Anatolia, the Balkans, the Caucasus and
the Aegean at the end of the Early Bronze Age.

The Discovery of the
Mit Rahina Inscription

For some years, Gerhard Haeny, director of the Swiss Archaeological
Institute in Cairo, had suspected that there was a large inscription
under one of the colossi of Ramessēs II (1290–1224 BC) which had
stood in front of the Temple of Ptah, built – or enlarged – by the
pharaohs of the 19th Dynasty on the site of a 12th-Dynasty one, at
Memphis near the present village of Mit Rahina. In 1974 Sami Farag,
the inspector of antiquities, extracted the inscription carved on a large
slab of stone.

When he saw it, Labib Habachi, the doyen of Egyptian Egyptology,
immediately recognized the inscription as resembling a much smaller
fragment discovered nearby and published by Flinders Petrie in 1909.
It was quickly accepted that both belonged to the same 'exceptionally
long' inscription. Even though the new 'fragment' was 2 by 2½ metres
square, the two pieces make up only a portion of the whole. Both the
beginning and the end of the original inscription are missing, as are
the tops of all the lines. The text is made still less clear by the fact that
the left side of the photograph from which the transcription has been
made was out of focus, and it has been impossible to take a new one.
Nevertheless, Farag and the Belgian Egyptologist Georges Posener
quite rightly believed that the inscription was so important that, despite these imperfections, it should be published as soon as possible,
and this was done in the *Revue d'Égyptologie* in 1980.[1]

Not surprisingly, there has been no complete translation but
Posener and Farag have both written notes on some of the inscription's contents. The text refers most frequently to the two Middle
Kingdom pharaohs Senwosre I and his son Amenemḥe II in the early
12th Dynasty between 1959 and 1882 BC and it was almost certainly
made soon after the reign of the latter.[2] It is largely concerned with
expeditions beyond Egypt by both land and sea. Some of these were
to Africa but most were to Asia. One expedition went to Sinai, two
went to Ḥnty-š (Lebanon) but another, in which the pharaoh himself
took part, was to Stt.

Stt is the name of a country in the far north. It was used during the
New Kingdom to represent Nahrin, or the Kingdom of the Mitanni in

Northern Syria and Mesopotamia, but its use for an Asiatic country has been attested since the 11th Dynasty.[3] The Mit Rahina inscription also referred to expeditions that destroyed other countries to the north, the names of which have not appeared elsewhere in Egyptian geographical texts. The results of these campaigns or raids was the sending back to Egypt of huge quantities of special goods, most frequently livestock, slaves and metals.

THE SIGNIFICANCE OF THE INSCRIPTION AS EVIDENCE FOR AN EGYPTIAN EMPIRE IN ASIA DURING THE MIDDLE KINGDOM

What is so startling about this text? Firstly, as we shall see, it appears to provide strong evidence to support much later Greek traditions that Senwosre I and Amenemḥe II did conduct major campaigns far to the north of Egypt. Secondly, it greatly strengthens the case of those Egyptologists and ancient historians who have argued that Middle Kingdom Egypt had an empire or at least a sphere of influence in the Levant. Thirdly, it provides a salutary chastening to Egyptology and ancient history as disciplines because this new and remarkable evidence of many massive campaigns comes from a period that was generally thought to be well reported in both official and literary documents. From these it was known that Egypt was rich and powerful during the early 12th Dynasty, after the seizure of power by its founder Amenemḥe I.

The dynastic family was from the extreme south. Amenemḥe's father seems to have come from the Theban nome, or district, and his mother from Tꜣ Sty, the border city of Elephantine or Nubia beyond. Either way, there is little doubt that the Dynasty came from places where, as Gardiner put it, 'the population was at least partly of Nubian race'.[4] Thus, it would seem reasonable to accept the accuracy of sculptures portraying these pharaohs as Blacks, although there are others that give them a more Asiatic appearance. Despite their southern origin, the Dynasty moved their capital away from Thebes, the capital of the 11th Dynasty, to Lisht in Northern Upper Egypt.

Under Senwosre I there was a extraordinary amount of construction. As the Egyptologist W. K. Simpson puts it: 'Few sites do not attest the extensive monument-building activity of the king.'[5] It is particularly interesting that the inscription would seem to have been connected to the great temple of Ptah at Memphis, with which – as we shall see below – the Greek writers specifically linked Sesōstris.[6]

We know that the generals of Amenemḥe I were active in major campaigns in Nubia and to the west against the Libyans. Senwosre I himself appears to have been leading one of the latter when there was an attempt on the life of his father. It is not clear exactly when this took place or even whether it was successful, though it probably was.[7] If this was the case and it took place at the end of the ten-year co-regency between the two, Senwosre quickly restored order and the wealth and power of Egypt continued to expand.

Scholars have been divided on the interests and power of the 12th Dynasty in Asia. Up to now, the only direct documentary evidence of conquests in Asia was the stela – or commemorative pillar – of the general Nsw Mnṯw, recording a victorious campaign against Asiatics and the destruction of their fortresses during the co-regency of Amenemḥe I and Senwosre I.[8] There is, however, considerable indirect evidence of such conquests. Interestingly, Egyptologists' information about Egyptian relations with Asia at this time comes primarily from a literary text of this period, the *Story of Sinuhe*.[9]

This vivid story, which for many centuries remained one of the most popular in Egypt, is about Sinuhe, a courtier who overheard state secrets on the death of Amenemḥe I. Fearing for his life, he fled into Canaan. He went north as far as Byblos. He then turned 'homewards' and finally settled in Upper Rṯnw, which seems to have been inland in Southern Syria.[10] There he became first an adviser to the local king and then a rich chief in his own right. After many years there, the pharaoh Senwosre I gave him permission to return to Egypt and welcomed him back to the court, and his body was buried in Egypt.

No one doubts that the story contains both historical fact and creative fiction; the difficulty lies in distinguishing the two. The story of Sinuhe's life in Rṯnw contains few descriptions of warfare; in fact, the generally friendly relations between Egyptians and the natives of the region, the comings and goings of Senwosre I's messengers through Rṯnw and the Syrian princes' humble approaches to Egyptian authority would all seem to indicate some kind of Egyptian suzerainty over the region. On the other hand, the *Story* describes Senwosre I as being 'created to smite the Bedouin and to crush the sandfarers' and as 'the one who severs the neck of those who are among the Asiatics'. Scenes from the funerary temple of Senwosre I show livestock and booty from vanquished foreigners with files of prisoners including a Syrian.[11] How can one reconcile these contrasting pictures of war and peace? One possibility would be to postulate peace within the sphere of Egyptian suzerainty and warfare beyond it. Before developing this idea, however, we should look at the very different interpretations that have been made from the archaeological evidence as to whether Middle Kingdom Egypt did or did not have an Asiatic empire. We know that there was intense activity in the mines of Sinai. More monuments of Egyptian activities there have been found from the 12th Dynasty than from all the other dynasties put together. Furthermore, relations seem, in contrast to those of other periods, to have been friendly. Unlike the monuments from the Old Kingdom, there are few indications from the Middle Kingdom that the mining expeditions were armed.[12]

But archaeological evidence of contact with Egypt exists far beyond Sinai. Large numbers of objects from the reign of Senwosre I have been found not only in Syro-Palestine but also in Anatolia. Their significance has, however, been hotly debated during the 20th century AD, as we shall see in this and the following chapter. The Semitist and archaeologist of Palestine William Foxwell Albright summarized the conclusions of British and American archaeology between the wars when he wrote:

> Western Palestine, Phoenicia and parts of Syria were dominated by Egyptian power and material culture. . . . Monuments attesting to direct connections with the Egyptian court as far back as the early 19th century B.C. [which is when Albright places the 12th Dynasty], have been found far north at Ugarit and far east at Qatna north east of Hums. The finds at Byblus give a vivid idea of the extent to which the art and craftsmanship of Phoenicia were influenced by Egypt. The Execration Texts [from the end of the 12th Dynasty denouncing enemies of Egypt] even enable us to draw the boundary of the direct sphere of Egyptian control across central Syria north of Damascus to the Eleutherus Valley in central Phoenicia.[13]

This general picture has been maintained and developed by Georges Posener and the Israeli archaeologist Raphael Giveon.[14] Posener drew attention to indications of an Egyptian 'empire' in Syro-Palestine with regular communications and transport of booty. He quotes a line from Sinuhe while the latter was living in Rtnw: 'the messenger who went to the north or to the south towards the residence (of the Pharaoh) stopped because I was there.'[15] Posener pointed out that Sinuhe found Egyptians in many of the places he visited. Posener also refers to the famous contemporary text generally known as the *Satire of the Trades*. This school text, which encouraged boys to study by describing the unpleasantness of all occupations except for that of the scribe, contains the following verse:

The courier goes into the desert,
Leaving his goods to his children;
Fearful of lions and Asiatics [ʿꜣmw],
He knows himself [only] when he is in Egypt.[16]

The name ʿꜣmw is generally conceded to be non-Egyptian and is probably Semitic. However, specialists are uncertain of its origin. The most likely source would seem to be ʾărāmî (Arami in Assyrian texts), the nomad Aramaeans. There is a semantic difficulty in that the ʿꜣmw appear in Egyptian texts for over a thousand years before we first hear of Aramaeans from Semitic sources in the late 12th-century BC annals of the Assyrian conqueror Tiglath-Pileser I.[17] This, I believe, is overcome by the known persistence of ethnic names and by the striking similarities between the two groups. Both the ʿꜣmw and the ʾărāmî appear as nomads inhabiting the deserts of Syria and Northern Mesopotamia. As the term ʿꜣmw is first found at the end of the Old Kingdom and is common in the Middle, when we know that ꜣ was used to transcribe foreign r's and l's, this provides no problem. The distinction between the Egyptian ʿayin and the West Semitic ʾaleph at the beginning of the names is more serious. Nevertheless, there are many examples of interchange between them within Semitic, so confusion in a loan would seem quite possible, especially with the possibility of contamination of the Egyptian name from ʿărāb, another Semitic name for desert nomads.[18]

As the mythologist Fontenrose has pointed out, Homer seems to have known about Aramaeans when he referred to the Arimoi. The context in the *Iliad* in which this occurs is particularly fascinating:

the earth groaned beneath them [the Achaean host] as beneath Zeus that hurleth the thunderbolt in his wrath, when he scourgeth the land about Typhōeos in the country of the Arimoi, where men say is the couch of Typhōeos.[19]

The extreme Aryanist Francis Vian, in his systematic attempts to remove all Semitic influences on Greece, placed Homer's Arimoi in a completely mythical fairyland.[20] Fontenrose is much more plausible when he links the land of Typhōeos or Typhōn to Cilicia or Northern Syria, where Aramaeans did become dominant in the 9th century BC.[21] In this context, it is interesting to note that Typhōeos was the counterpart of the Egyptian (Stḫ) Seth, who was the god of disturbance and the desert, notably in the land of Stt. There seems to have been a punning relationship between the two names. Stt was generally seen as Syro-Palestine and points north (see p. 231) – the land of the ꜥ꞉mw. Seth's struggle with Horus is clearly reflected in the Greek myths about one between Typhōeos/Typhōn and Zeus.[22]

The likelihood of early Greek knowledge of ꜥ꞉mw/Aramaeans is increased by the attestation in Homer of the word *erēmos* from the root *erēmo*, meaning 'solitary or abandoned of place or persons' with special connotations of deserts and their inhabitants; one of its derivatives was *erēmitēs*, from which comes our 'hermit'. The plausibility of an Afroasiatic etymology for this word is increased by the inability of lexicographers to find an Indo-European one.[23]

To return to Posener's arguments in favour of Egyptian control over Syro-Palestine at this time, he interpreted the 12th-Dynasty golden pectorals or jewels for the chest and royal sphinxes, found not merely in Byblos and Beirut but also at Ugarit, Aleppo and other places, as ceremonial gifts to vassal kings.[24] Stevenson Smith and William Ward have pointed out that there are also statues of private Egyptians from Palestine and Syria and as far away as Crete and southern Anatolia dedicated to local temples and therefore suggesting some long-term presence in these regions.[25] On the other side of the coin, Posener showed that the Asiatics in a tomb painting from Beni Hasan in Central Egypt of the early 19th century BC were not starving Bedouin, as they are commonly supposed to have been, but a prosperous chief with his entourage, probably on a trading and/or official mission. He connected this to the many Asiatic imports and slaves in Egypt during the 12th Dynasty. Other paintings from early in the reign of Senwosre I show not merely Egyptian and Nubian but also Asiatic soldiers.[26]

Other scholars, however, have been more more sceptical of this Asiatic 'empire'. Wolfgang Helck, who has dominated German Egyptology for the last thirty years, dismisses any information about Syria from Sinuhe's claims, suggesting that the author may have merely been in South Palestine.[27] Disregarding the idea of an Egyptian 'empire' in Asia, Helck admitted there were close contacts of an almost colonial type with Byblos but believes the undoubted exchange of material goods with places as far away as Afghanistan and the considerable number of Asian slaves in Egypt during the 12th Dynasty were the result of indirect trade largely through Syrian middlemen.

The American scholar and great champion of the Lebanese and Phoenicians, William Ward, is equally sceptical of any Asiatic 'empire' of the Middle Kingdom. He concedes that evidence from Sinuhe indicates the presence of Egyptians in Palestine, but makes the point that Sinuhe wrote that he had to sneak past a defensive wall built on the eastern frontier of Egypt, which would make Egyptian control of the territory many miles beyond this line seem unlikely.[28] However, even when they were well maintained and guarded, the walls of traditional empires such as China and Rome seldom marked their frontiers but usually divided their settled from their nomadic zones. I see no reason to deny this possibility in Egypt.

There seemed to be stalemate on this issue, with the leading figures of French and German Egyptology fixed in opposition to each other. Posener immediately recognized the help the discovery of the Mit Rahina inscription could give to his case and wrote in his note describing it:

> Besides much interesting information in the fields of vocabulary, geography and economy, the inscription from Mit Rahina casts a new light on the foreign policy of the early kings of the twelfth dynasty. I would like to insist on this point. Some scholars like Helck and recently Frandsen, writing on the relations of Egypt with the neighbouring countries, have strongly reduced the impact of the twelfth dynasty on Syria and Palestine.
>
> We do not know the exact nature of the relations. Even if they were strictly reduced to commerce, the parties were not equal. A big and powerful state such as Egypt inevitably exercised a strong pressure on the small principalities of Asia. This led to a certain degree of domination propped up by some military expeditions.
>
> Now with the testimony of the Mit Rahina inscription, we see that we should not minimise the hold of Egypt over Syria and Palestine from the beginning of the twelfth dynasty.[29]

Unfortunately, Posener has since died and never published any development of the implications of the discovery. Wolfgang Helck, however, has shown an open-mindedness and disinterested commitment to the pursuit of knowledge, which is rare even among the greatest scholars. In a short article he accepted that Posener's challenge to him and other minimalists on the basis of the Mit Rahina inscription was correct, 'at least in the geographical extent' of Egyptian power in Syria and Palestine during the Middle Kingdom. What is more, Helck now maintains that Senwosre I or at least his son and heir Amenemhet II made expeditions still further north.[30]

SENWOSRE AND SESŌSTRIS

The Mit Rahina inscription raises even more important issues than the existence or non-existence of a Middle Kingdom 'empire' in Syro-Palestine. These concern the strengthening of the identification of Senwosre I with Sesōstris. Sesōstris was described by Herodotos and other Greek writers as the great Egyptian conqueror and was placed by Manetho, the Egyptian priest and historian of the 3rd century BC, in the 12th Dynasty.

The ordering of signs within cartouches, the ovals of rope drawn round the names of pharaohs, is very irregular. Initially Egyptologists rendered the common pharaoh's name of the 12th Dynasty as Wsrt sn. Champollion and a number of his students were unable to see a resemblance between this and Sesōstris, Sesoōsis or Sesonchōsis and the other variants of the name given by the Greeks to the Egyptian world conqueror.[31] Thus, they maintained that Sesōstris was fictitious and that his supposed conquests were exaggerations of those made by the later pharaohs Ramessēs II in the 13th century BC and Sheshonk in the 9th. Such a solution was congenial for a number of reasons. Firstly, it confirmed the *Besserwissen* or 'knowing better' of scientific modern Egyptologists over Herodotos and the credulous 'late' Greeks. Secondly, it limited the number and scope of foreign conquests by the African and supposedly passive Egyptians. It is also possible that the reluctance to link the names came from the early 19th-century Christian dislike of early Egyptian history, where it threatened biblical chronology; this attitude was expressed by the German ancient historian Barthold Niebuhr, when he denied the actuality of Egyptian history before the Hyksos.[32]

However, there were different opinions and a number of scholars, including Niebuhr's secretary Christian Bunsen, were impressed by the fact that Manetho, the Egyptian priest and historian of the 3rd century BC, had clearly placed Sesōstris in the 12th Dynasty. Thus, they wanted to identify him with one or all of the three pharaohs thought to be called Wsrt sn.[33] In 1900, the German Egyptologist Kurt Sethe solved the problem by reading the royal name not as Wsrt sn but as S-n Wsrt (Man of the Goddess Wsrt). He argued that this name, conventionally rendered as Senwosre, was the origin of Sesōstris.[34] The plausibility of this identification of Sesōstris with Senwosre was so overwhelming that it was accepted almost immediately and it has not been challenged in the last seventy-five years.[35]

While the name imn m ḫ3t (Amon to the fore) is an obvious one for pharaohs whose known cult was of Amon, S-n Wsrt is both puzzling and interesting. The name Wsrt was derived from the adjective *wsr* meaning 'strong, wealthy and influential'. She was an ancient but obscure goddess, probably a local Theban form of Hathor, the cow goddess of beauty: both goddesses were associated with far-away places and Hathor was specifically the patron deity of precious minerals and their sources.[36] The pharaoh's association with Hathor would seem to be preserved by Diodoros when he refers to Sesōstris' daughter Athyrtis who guided her father on his conquests.[37]

As we shall see, an association with Hathor/Wsrt would be particularly appropriate in the light of Senwosre's later conquests and concern with precious metals and stones. It is unclear, however, whether the name Senwosre was given before or after these activities had begun. Technically, Senwosre was what Egyptologists call the *nomen* within the pharaoh's long titulary. Usually this was given to him before his accession to the throne and this was certainly the case with later pharaohs with the same *nomen*.[38] This could be the case here, as it seems that Amenemḥe I was also very concerned with foreign conquest. It is also possible that the name was given after some of Senwosre's conquests, while ruling in conjunction with his father. At the very least the name was a remarkably apt precursor of the most notable activities of his reign.

Manetho's Sesōstris

At this point, in order to examine the identification further, I shall first look at the Greek and late Egyptian writers' descriptions of Sesōstris before turning to the Egyptian archaeological and inscriptional evidence about Senwosre I.

This identification has, however, left some problems. Firstly, Manetho had placed Sesōstris as the third pharaoh in the 12th Dynasty. According to him, the great conqueror had been preceded by Ammenemēs, the founder of the Dynasty, then Sesonchosis, then Ammanemēs, who was murdered by his own eunuchs.[39] Here he seems to have garbled a rather confusing sequence of monarchs which can now be roughly established as follows:

Amenemḥe I	1979–1950 BC
Senwosre I	1959–1914
Amenemḥe II	1917–1882
Senwosre II	1884–1878
Senwosre III	1878–1859
Amenemḥe III	1859–1814
Amenemḥe IV	1814–1805
Sebeknofru	1805–1801

Manetho appears to have confused Senwosre I, whom he called Sesonchosis, with Senwosres II and III. Senwosret III was indeed a powerful ruler and he seems to have made more conquests in Africa than any of his predecessors.[40] The possibility must therefore be faced that later writers such as Herodotos may have attributed achievements of Senwosre I's descendents, especially Senwosre III, to their ancestor.[41]

The second problem that Manetho poses comes from his description of Sesōstris:

> In nine years he subdued the whole of Asia and Europe as far as Thrace, everywhere erecting memorials of his conquests of the tribes [*ethnē*]. Upon *stelae* [pillars] he engraved for a valiant race the secret parts of a man, for an ignoble race those of a woman. Accordingly he was esteemed by the Egyptians as the next in rank to Osiris.[42]

This image, seemingly created to attract the readers' interest if not prurience, and linked to Sesōstris' great and godlike reputation, would seem to strengthen modern classicists' image of Manetho as typical of the inconsequential and unreliable Hellenistic historians. However, as I shall try to show below, there is some reality behind both of these reports.

Herodotos' Sesōstris

Before dealing with these, we should look at two other similar descriptions of the conqueror, those of Herodotos in the 5th century and of Diodoros Sikeliotes in the 1st century BC. The former wrote:

> As none of the other kings on the priests' roll left any memorial at all, I will pass on to say something of Sesōstris, who succeeded them. Sesōstris, the priests said, sailed first with a fleet of warships from the Arabian gulf along the coast of the Indian Ocean, subduing the coastal tribes as he went, until he found that shoal water made further progress impossible; then on his return to Egypt (still according to the priests' account) he raised a powerful army and marched across the continent, reducing to subjection every nation [*ethnos*] in his path. Whenever he encountered a courageous enemy who fought valiantly for freedom, he erected pillars on the spot inscribed with his own name and country, and a sentence to indicate that by the might of his armed forces he had won the victory; if, however, a town fell easily into his hands without a struggle, he made an addition to the inscription on the pillar – for not only did he record upon it the same facts as before, but added the picture of a woman's genitals, meaning to show that the people of that town were no braver than women. Thus his victorious progress through Asia continued, until he entered Europe and defeated the Scythians and Thracians; this, I think, was the furthest point the Egyptian army reached for the memorial columns are to be seen on this part of the country but not beyond. On his way back Sesōstris came

to the river Phasis [in Colchis], and it is quite possible that he here
detached a body of troops from his army and left them behind to
settle – or, on the other hand, it may be that some of his men were
sick of their travels and deserted. I cannot say with certainty which
supposition is the right one, but it is undoubtedly a fact that the
Colchians are of Egyptian descent. . . .

Most of the memorial pillars which King Sesōstris erected in conquered countries have disappeared, but I have seen some myself in
Palestine, with the inscription I mentioned and the drawing of a
woman's genitals. In Ionia also there are two images of Sesōstris cut
on rock, one on the road from Ephesus to Phocaea, the other between Sardis and Smyrna; in each case the carved figure is nearly
seven feet high and represents a man with a spear in his right hand
and a bow in his left, and the rest of his equipment to match – partly
Egyptian partly Ethiopian. Across the breast from shoulder to
shoulder runs an inscription, cut in the Egyptian sacred script: *by
the strength of my shoulders I won this land* . . .

The priests went on to tell me that Sesōstris, on his return home
with a host of prisoners from the conquered countries, was met at
Daphnae, near Pelusium, by his brother, whom he had left to
govern Egypt during his absence, and invited with his sons to a banquet. While they were at dinner, his brother piled faggots round
the building and set them on fire . . . with the result that two of his
sons were burnt to death, while the others together with their father, were saved. . . .

Sesōstris was the only Egyptian king to rule Ethiopia. As memori-
als of his reign he left stone statues of himself and his wife, each
forty-five feet high, and statues thirty feet high of each of his four
sons. They were erected in front of the temple of Hephaestus
[Ptah]. Long afterwards the priest of Hephaestus would not allow
Darius king of Persia to erect a statue of himself in front of these,
because (as he put it) his deeds had not been as great as those of
Sesōstris the Egyptian; the conquests of Sesōstris, no less extensive
than those of Darius, included the Scythians, whom Darius had
been unable to subdue; it was not right therefore, that he should
put his statue in front of those dedicated by a monarch whose
achievements he had failed to surpass. Darius, they say, admitted
the truth of this.[43]

Diodoros' Sesōstris

Diodoros' still longer description of the pharaoh, whom he calls Sesoōsis, is similar to that of Herodotos and would seem to derive from

the earlier historian directly as well as from the same Egyptian sources. The passage on his conquests is as follows:

First of all Sesoōsis, his companions also accompanying him, was sent by his father with an army into Arabia, where he . . . conquered the entire nation of the Arabs, which had never been enslaved before his day; and then, on being sent to the regions of the west, he subdued the larger part of Libya though in years still no more than a youth. And when he ascended the throne upon the death of his father, being filled with a confidence by reason of his earlier exploits he undertook to conquer the inhabited earth. . . .

After he had made ready his army he marched first of all against the Ethiopians who dwell south of Egypt, and after conquering them he forced the people to pay a tribute in ebony, gold and the tusks of elephants. Then he sent out a fleet of four hundred ships into the Red Sea, being the first Egyptian to build warships, and not only took possession of the islands in those waters, but also subdued the coast of the mainland as far as India, while he himself made his way by land with his army and subdued all Asia. Not only did he, in fact visit the territory which was afterwards won by Alexander of Macedon, but also certain peoples into whose countries Alexander did not cross. For he even passed over the Ganges and visited all of India as far as the Ocean, as well as the tribes of the Scythians as far as the river Tanais, which divides Europe from Asia; and it was at this time, they say, that some of the Egyptians who were left behind near the Lake Maeotis [the Sea of Azov] founded the nation of Colchi. . . . In the same way he brought all the rest of Asia into subjection as well as most of the Cyclades Islands. And after he had crossed into Europe and was on his way through the whole length of Thrace he nearly lost his army through lack of food and the difficult nature of the land. Consequently he fixed the limits of his expedition in Thrace, and set up stelae in many parts of the regions which he had acquired. . . . He dealt gently with all conquered peoples and, after concluding his campaigns in nine years, commanded the nations to bring presents each year to Egypt according to their ability, while he himself, assembling a mass of captives that has never been surpassed and a mass of other booty . . .

Although many great deeds have been credited to Sesoōsis, his magnificence seems best to have been shown in the treatment which he accorded to the foreign potentates when he went forth from his palace. The kings whom he had allowed to continue their rule over the peoples which he subdued and all others who received from him the most important positions of command would present themselves in Egypt at specified times bringing him gifts, and the king would welcome them and in all other matters show them honour and special preferment; but whenever he intended to visit a temple or city he would remove the horses from his four-horse chariot and in their place yoke the kings and other potentates, taking them four at a time.[44]

THE REAL AND THE FANTASTIC
IN THE SESŌSTRIS STORIES

How many of these apparently extravagant stories should we believe? Most scholars today accept the identification of Sesōstris/Sesoōsis with Senwosre I and III and believe that there is a historical kernel to the stories. However, they maintain that this kernel is relatively small and very deeply buried. According to them, the legendary figure of Sesōstris has been massively contaminated by features borrowed from later conquering pharaohs – notably Ramessēs II of the 19th and Sheshonk of the 22nd Dynasty – and he has been built up into a pharaonic ideal, an Egyptian conqueror who could rival the later triumphs of the Persians and Greeks. Herodotos wrote when the Persian Empire was still flourishing and Manetho and Diodoros after the extraordinary conquests of Alexander the Great.[45] It would seem likely that there is some truth in these interpretations, although they clearly smack of *Besserwissen* (readers of the first volume of *Black Athena* will know I see explanations illustrating this as less reliable than the ancient sources).

However, other scholars, notably Georges Posener, have insisted that much of the Sesōstris legend dates back to the Middle Kingdom in two senses: firstly, the stories have a considerable factual basis and, secondly, from the end of the Old Kingdom there was a conscious use of propaganda for many purposes but in particular for the creation of a royal myth.[46]

The Egyptian word for this was *md.t* (speech, discourse) from which the Greek *mythos* derives. *Mdw* or *mwdw* (Demotic *mt*, Coptic *moute* or *mout*) means 'speak or advise' as a verb or 'speech or words' as a noun. *Mdw nṯr* means 'word of god' or, in plural, 'sacred writings'; the expression *ḏd mdw*, Demotic *ḏd md(t)*, Coptic *ḏe mtau*, is 'speaking words' or 'magic'. *Mdt* is 'speech, words or legal plea'. However, it is attested as being vocalized as *mēt* or *met*. Thus the exact form from which the Greek word *mythos* was borrowed is obscure. Nevertheless, the loose phonetic fit should be seen in the light of the tight semantic correspondence between *mdw/mdt* and *mythos* and the many words with that stem.[47]

To return to the reports on Sesōstris, instead of denigrating or dismissing the claims of 'credulous ancients', it would seem worthwhile to test them in the light of other sources of information. I argued in Volume 1 that it would be helpful to take widespread and uncontested ancient traditions as working hypotheses. However, it seems sensible to take only those elements of the stories that were generally accepted in Antiquity and I therefore now want to examine what those elements were.

As far as I am aware, the only one that was challenged at the time was that of Sesōstris having conquered India, although it is interesting that Herodotos makes no mention of Sesōstris having been to Mesopotamia.[48] It would seem, therefore, that Sesōstris' supposed northern conquests should be limited to 'Asia' (the boundaries of which will be discussed below), Colchis (Georgia), Thrace (the Southeastern Balkans) and Scythia in South Russia; but there is some doubt about the last two of these.

Modern writers have made a plausible case that the conquests of Thrace and Scythia should not be treated as factual because, just as Hellenistic Egyptians exaggerated the conquests of Sesōstris to make them surpass those of Alexander, claims made during or after the Persian conquest of Egypt would try to outdo the conquests of the great Persian conquerors, Cyrus and Darius. This would seem to be supported by the legend of Darius being refused permission to have his statue erected in front of the temple of Ptah at Memphis because the Persians had failed, where Sesōstris had succeeded, in conquering Scythia.[49] The same argument could also be made for Nubia, which the Persians were unable to conquer, except that in this case there is clear inscriptional, archaeological and cultic evidence to show that Senwosre I and III were successful there. Thus, an Egyptian passage through Thrace and Scythia must remain less probable than that through 'Asia'. Even so, such a possibility will be examined.

This brings us to the difficulty posed by the ambiguity of the term 'Asia'. The Greek name derives from an early local name found in the kingdom of Assuwa, reported in Hittite texts as being in Western Anatolia, and the city name Assos in the Troad, the region around Troy. When the Lydian kingdom of Western Anatolia was incorporated into the Persian Empire in the 6th century BC, Ionian geographers extended the meaning of 'Asia' in two ways, to cover the whole of Anatolia and also to be the name for one of the three continents, with Europe and Libya (Africa).

There is no doubt that Herodotos followed his predecessors in using the second meaning and, given the absence in his writings of any term for Anatolia, it would seem quite probable that, like both earlier and later geographers, he also used 'Asia' as the name for what was later called 'Asia Minor'.[50] Thus, when Herodotos wrote about Sesōstris' 'victorious progress through Asia [having] continued, until he entered Europe', he may well have been referring merely to a march through Anatolia. I believe that it was this ambiguity of the name 'Asia' that allowed Diodoros and other later writers to make Sesōstris' conquests continental in scope.

This later expansion of Sesōstris' conquests must be seen in the light of the need of Diodoros and/or his sources to compete with the achievements of Alexander the Great. We shall see below the close parallels in the 'romances' about the two.[51] Here it is simply worth noting that Diodoros' description of the young Sesōstris' ambitions to conquer the world after his father's death sounds very much like Alexander's attitude to his father Philip. On the other hand, this probably fictional element is tied to Sesōstris' subduing 'the larger part of Libya though in years still no more than a youth', which would seem to have sound historical backing. Similarly, Manetho's report that Sesōstris' predecessor Ammanemēs had been 'murdered by his own eunuchs' seems to have been confirmed by modern Egyptology.[52]

We can trace this same mixture of the fantastic and the factual in many of the stories told by Herodotos and Diodoros. For instance, the one of Sesōstris' brother trying to burn him to death would seem incredible because of its folkloric character.[53] Yet other stories, which could seem equally or more fantastic, may surprisingly have a factual basis. For instance, the descriptions of the pharaoh placing on stelae inscriptions with male and female genitals, which appears in Herodotos, Manetho and Diodoros, would seem to have a basis in fact. We know that the word $ḥm$ ⊃🦅〜 (coward) contains the signs for both the female and male genitalia; and it had clear connotations of male homosexuality in a pejorative sense and was related to $ḥmt$ ⊃🦅⌒ (woman). $Ḥm$ was used to refer to enemies and to cowards in the Egyptian army in military documents during the Middle Kingdom, and also in the frontier stelae set up by Senwosre III at Semna and Uronarti on the Nubian Upper Nile.[54]

Another 'extravagance' of Diodoros was his reference to Sesōstris' chariot having been pulled by Egyptian potentates and foreign kings. Sethe, Malaise and Burton object to this, arguing that there is no evidence of chariots or horses in the Middle Kingdom and that they were in fact introduced to Egypt by the Hyksos invaders.[55] But the situation is not quite as clear-cut as they make out. The burial of a horse that had worn a bit has been found near the Middle Kingdom fortifications at Buhen in Nubia and, if the claims for Sesōstris' widespread conquests to the north are justified, Egyptians would have been in contact with peoples using at least simple chariots. Evidence from cylinder seals shows that these were known in Eastern Anatolia by the end of the 20th century BC.[56] However, since this is a circular argument, it is not satisfactory. Thus, it is probable that the reference to a chariot with horses was a later gloss.

On the other hand, Diodoros' claim that Sesōstris was pulled by high officials and foreign kings is extremely plausible given the long-standing Egyptian tradition of carrying or pulling the statues of gods on religious visits to towns. It should be stressed that Senwosre I, unlike his predecessors, who were merely 'divine', manifestations of a god or 'god*like*', *was* a god.[57] Further support for the story that he was pulled by high officials and foreign kings comes from the fact that Diodoros refers to the pharaoh's visiting 'a temple or city'.

If even some of the most 'fantastic' claims Herodotos made about Sesōstris seem to contain an element of truth, what are we to make of the more substantial ones of his vast conquests? Before tackling these directly, we should consider why they should have been dismissed by modern scholarship.

The claims for extensive conquests were not rejected on the basis of detailed archaeological or historical research but because they were 'known' to be inherently absurd. This was suspected by scholars even before the destruction of the Ancient Model. In Volume 1, I mentioned that Edward Gibbon's first historical essay, written in 1752 at the age of fifteen, was on 'the Age of Sesōstris' but that by 1780 he had torn it up because, as he wrote, 'at a riper age I no longer presume to connect the Greek, the Jewish and the Egyptian antiquities which are lost in a distant cloud'.[58] By the 1820s and 1830s, the racial hierarchy was established and the image of the Egyptians as a peculiar isolated people was securely in place. These stereotypes completely precluded the notion of Egyptian empires in Asia or Europe.[59]

Thus, despite the confirmation of 12th-Dynasty conquests in Africa and of some details of the Greek stories about the pharaoh, for the past 150 years it has been taken as axiomatic that the Greek stories of Sesōstris' northern conquests were essentially false.[60] As so often, it was only the French classicist Paul Foucart who stood out against this trend, arguing that there was no justification for dismissing the widespread ancient belief out of hand.[61] No attempt has been made to assess the likelihood of these stories in the light of the mass of new information that has become available since then.

If one excludes Diodoros' claims that Sesōstris reached India and beyond, one is left with a scheme which begins with his conquests of Ethiopia and Libya and the naval expeditions to the 'Red Sea', by which Greeks generally meant the Indian Ocean. These were followed by his overland campaigns for nine years through Anatolia, Thrace and apparently around the Black Sea through Scythia to Colchis. There are also imprecise suggestions of conquests in Mesopotamia and Persia.

What does 'conquer' mean in such contexts? Despite Egyptian claims of Sesōstris' benevolence, the conquests would seem to have been horrible experiences for the peoples who experienced them. Both the Egyptian and the Classical reports are of destructions, seizures of people and wealth and the imposition of regular tribute. The erection of stelae suggests some attempt to maintain control but there is no suggestion of his having established a long-lived empire. Nevertheless, there was also a tradition, discussed below, that colonies were established.

MIDDLE KINGDOM EGYPT'S MILITARY CAPABILITY

We know from the contemporary story of 'the shipwrecked sailor' that Egyptians were sailing south to tropical lands during the Middle Kingdom.[62] We also know from the famous frieze of Queen Ḥashepsowe at Deir el Bahri, across the Nile from Thebes, that by the 15th century BC official fleets were sailing to the coasts of East Africa.[63]

Nevertheless, Burton maintains that, while Egyptians had used ships 'for purposes of war' since the Old Kingdom, no illustrations of ships specially designed for war appear until the great battle against the Peoples of the Sea in the reign of Ramessēs III near the beginning of the 12th century BC. However, we know from documentary evidence that the navies of the 18th Dynasty were specialized and competent.[64] Since our knowledge of Middle Kingdom fleets is far from complete, we cannot preclude the possibility that such ships existed some centuries earlier. Even so, there is some reason to doubt Diodoros' statement that Sesōstris was 'the first to build ships of war'. Furthermore, it would seem unlikely – though in view of the known scale of his military operations not impossible – that he sent 400 ships to the Red Sea or Indian Ocean. Similarly, there are problems with Herodotos' statement:

> [he] sailed first with a fleet of warships from the Arabian gulf along the coast of the Indian Ocean, subduing the coastal tribes as he went, until he found that shoal water (*brachys*) made further progress impossible.[65]

This would seem to indicate some confusion between ocean voyages and those up the Nile, where we know that shoal water did cause difficulties to 12th-Dynasty military expeditions.[66] Even so, there is no intrinsic reason for doubting the first part of Herodotos' statement.

At first glance the reports about Sesōstris' campaigns by land would seem unlikely because his armies lacked the chariots, horses and even the swords one normally associates with ancient warfare and the conquests of the Assyrian Tiglath Pilesar, the Persian Cyrus the Great or Alexander. It should be remembered, however, that some three hundred years before Sesōstris, the Mesopotamian Sargon the Great had made vast conquests over some of the same terrain with no better equipment. Furthermore, the presence of horses did not mean that later armies relied on them for transport. In fact, it was not until the 19th century AD that any substitute for marching was found for moving soldiers and many of their supplies overland.

We know from the Mit Rahina inscription that ships were used to bring booty back to Egypt. Therefore it would seem possible that supplies to armies on the coast could be brought the same way. We also know that donkeys were already in use as pack animals in both Syria and Anatolia and were thus available to the Egyptian armies. If the reports of Sesōstris' campaigns are reliable, most supplies seem to have been seized from the local populations. It is interesting to note that the only difficulties Diodoros reported for Sesōstris' armies were in relatively poor and remote Thrace and Scythia, where 'he almost lost his army through lack of food and the difficult nature of the land'.[67]

There are many representations from this period of uniformed Egyptian, Nubian and Asiatic troops who are well armed with spears, bows and maces.[68] However, the most impressive picture of the scale and effectiveness of the armies of the 12th Dynasty came from the remains of their fortifications in Nubia, most of which are now flooded by the Aswan High Dam. William Adams, the authority on Nubia, writes about these:

Not content with the spoil of the southern lands, the pharaohs proceeded to fortify the Nile in the northern *Batn el Hajar* with a chain of the mightiest fortifications ever erected in the ancient world. Four thousand years after their building, and three thousand years after their final abandonment, the mud walls of these gargantuan relics still rose in places forty feet above the desert sand. . . . The Second Cataract forts were apparently built over a period of about a hundred years, in the reigns of Senwosre I, Senwosre II and Senwosre III. They were evidently conceived as forming a single complex, and may have been under unified command. Similarities of plan suggest that several of the forts were designed by the same architect and were built almost simultaneously. . . . Buhen staggers the imagination not only by its size but by the complexity of its defences. Bastions, loopholes, fosse, drawbridge, glacis – virtually all of the classic elements of medieval fortification are present in this structure. . . . To a greater or lesser degree, the same features are incorporated in most of the other Middle Kingdom fortresses.[69]

Given the known wealth and centralization of Egypt in the reign of Sesōstris and the evidence from Nubia of the ability to concentrate these resources for military purposes, there would seem no intrinsic reason why such a state with such a military machine should not have made considerable conquests in Asia. However, this ability does not mean that such conquests actually took place, for that we need more evidence. It is this which I hope to provide below.

THE BACKGROUND
Egyptian chronology for the 4th and 3rd millenniums BC

Before searching for any archaeological traces of Sesōstris' conquests, it is necessary to sort out, as far as is possible, the dating of the supposed campaigns. The 12th Dynasty has clear records of the lengths of the reigns of its pharaohs but it also would seem to have a relatively firm temporal anchor. This is based on the coincidence of the beginning of the solar new year with the rising of the star Sothis which announced the Nile Flood, recorded in year 7 of the reign of Senwosre III. If the observation were made in Memphis this would have been in 1872 BC. This correspondence has been recognized by Egyptologists for many years and a chronology for the whole dynasty from 1991 to 1786 was established by the Egyptologist and specialist in Egyptian astronomy R. A. Parker in 1950.[70] Over the next decades, however, Parker and others began looking at the traditional reign lengths of the pharaohs so as to compress these and lengthen every co-regency. In this way the dynasty was shortened by twelve years and is now set between 1979 and 1801 BC.[71]

At the same time, a number of German scholars began to argue that the observation of the rising of Sothis had not taken place at Memphis or Heliopolis, on or near the 30° latitude, but 6 degrees further south, on the frontier at Elephantine. The coincidence of the rising with the beginning of the solar new year would, then, have taken place in 1830 BC, putting the dynasty – with *a further* reduction of forty-two years – between 1937 and 1759 BC.[72] Because of the raising of the Greek ceramic dates, which will be discussed in later chapters, this now seems unlikely, though it cannot be ruled out.

The chronology of the Egyptian
Old Kingdom

The difficulties of lower or 'short' chronologies in general and the
forces within scholarship that have led to their being proposed are
made very clear by 20th-century dating of earlier Egyptian history. To
understand this process at work in academia, I believe it is helpful to
make a digression to consider the dating of the Egyptian Old Kingdom, even though this is not strictly speaking necessary for the dating
of the 12th Dynasty.

By the beginning of this century, all the Egyptian chronologies that
we now possess were available to scholars and the Sothic date had
been calculated. Thus, all chronologies since then have been calculated by combining the Sothic date with Egyptian records.[73]

The pharaonic reigns of the 11th Dynasty are less well established
than those of the 12th but here there is evidence that the dynasty as a
whole seems to have lasted for 160+ years, although modern scholars
prefer a length of 143.[74]

This duration of the 11th Dynasty comes from the so-called *Turin
Canon*. The *Canon* is a list of pharaohs and their dates drawn up during the 19th Dynasty in the 13th century BC. Its listing strikingly resembles what we know from Manetho's history written for the Greek
rulers of Egypt about one thousand years later. The *Turin Canon*
seems to have been complete when it was acquired by the French
consul in Egypt, Drovetti. However, it was in fragments by the time
Champollion was able to see it, in Turin, where it has been for the past
180 years and from which it gets its name. Immense thought and
labour has been put into the reassembling of these tiny and fragile
pieces. Not only the text and its obverse, a tax document, but the
fibres of the papyrus have been used to make joins and establish relationships.[75] Nevertheless, one key figure does appear to be relatively
well established. It is that of 955 years from the beginning of the reign
of the first pharaoh Mēnēs to the end of the 6th or 8th Dynasty,
the last dynasty of the Old Kingdom and its epigonoi or degenerate
successors.

Accepting this, there is still a problem with the so-called 1st Intermediate Period after the fall of the 6th or 8th Dynasty. The specialist
in intermediate periods, Hans Stock, writing in the 1930s, argued for
the following:

7th Dynasty (*c.* 27) 2190–2163 BC
8th Dynasty (*c.* 65) 2175–2110 BC
9th Dynasty (*c.* 45) 2175–2130 BC
10th Dynasty (*c.* 90) 2130–2040 BC.[76]

This pattern is very different from that given at the beginning of the 20th century AD. The American Egyptologist James Breasted proposed the following chronology in 1906:

7th Dynasty 2475 BC
8th Dynasty 2475 BC
9th Dynasty 2445 BC
11th Dynasty 2160 BC.[77]

Breasted's contemporary, the ancient historian and polymath Eduard Meyer, put the whole 1st Intermediate Period between 2440 ± 100 years and 2160 BC.[78] As shown above, with Stock's chronology, recent scholarship has minimized the length of this break. At the end of his life Gardiner saw the Intermediate Period as having lasted between one hundred and two hundred years.[79] William Hayes, writing in the *Cambridge Ancient History*, put it at a mere forty-eight years and he saw the 11th-Dynasty unification of Egypt as having taken place only in 2040 BC; there is no doubt that most Egyptologists today would agree with him.[80]

This compression of the 1st Intermediate Period must be seen as part of the general drive to lower the dates of Egyptian history. Why should scholars want to down-date, if, as has been mentioned above, no new Egyptian chronologies have been discovered since the time of Breasted and Meyer? I think the trend is best explained in terms of the sociology of knowledge. Since the First World War, archaeologists and ancient historians have intensified their struggle to achieve 'scientific' status. Their drive can be expressed as the desire to be 'sounder than thou'. Cautious and conservative scholars became terrified above all of the accusation of being speculative. At the same time, they were expected to be innovative. In this situation, the only room for innovation was to be hypercritical of every form of evidence but particularly of that from ancient documentary sources. Thus, they have tended to limit all ancient claims in both space and time.

Ironically, this tendency is now being checked by information from the 'hard' sciences, which the Egyptologists and archaeologists have tried to emulate. As seen throughout this book, the new sources of information have tended to increase the historical depth and geographical breadth of ancient activities.

In this case, the challenge has come from radio-carbon. In 1979, the broad-ranging archaeologist of Anatolia James Mellaart published a startling article in the standard British journal *Antiquity*, entitled 'Egyptian and Near Eastern chronology: a dilemma?' He argued in it that the convention that maintained that radio-carbon dating could not be used in Egypt and Mesopotamia, where there were other sources for chronology, was no longer valid since the recalibration and refining of the chronology of carbon dates. Mellaart proposed, therefore, to assess their chronologies in the light of this new evidence. His conclusion for Egypt was that carbon datings indicated that the 1st Dynasty began around 3400 BC. Thus, all dates in Egyptian history should be raised by three hundred years until one reached the foundation of the New Kingdom, for which he agreed that the conventional date of 1567 BC was credible.

The point at which he 'crossed over' from his high chronology to the conventional one was during the 2nd Intermediate Period, for much of which Egypt was dominated by the Hyksos invaders from the north.[81] He maintained that this period was far longer than was usually supposed. Where the *Cambridge Ancient History* estimates the gap between the fall of the 12th Dynasty and the rise of the 18th to be 219 years, between 1786 and 1567 BC, Mellaart put it at 379 years, between 1946 and 1567 BC. This topic will be taken up in greater detail in Chapter VIII, but it should be noted here that he was able to back his argument for a long 2nd Intermediate Period by pointing out that the Hyksos were in Egypt in the 18th century and that both Manetho and contemporary monuments indicate that there were a large number of pharaohs from the 13th Dynasty that preceded the Hyksos arrival.

Mellaart admitted that his placing the 12th Dynasty from 2155 to 1946 BC could not be reconciled with the Sothic date but he saw no way of reconciling that with what seemed to him to be the irrefutable evidence from radio-carbon.[82]

Mellaart's arguments on the Egyptian and Palestinian dating upset the whole Egyptological establishment, which up to then had been divided between supporters of the 'middle chronology' and those who were trying to establish even lower chronologies. His article was immediately challenged by two Egyptologists, Barry Kemp and James Weinstein, and the arguments quickly became too technical and acrimonious for most readers to follow.[83] Nevertheless, the attacks had the effect of discrediting Mellaart's revision.

Eight years later, in 1987, a detailed report of new carbon datings from the pyramids was published. A group of Swiss and American scholars led by Herbert Haas collected sixty-four fresh organic samples from the pyramids and tested them in laboratories in Texas and Switzerland. Their results were amazing, for they required that the periodization of the *Cambridge Ancient History* be raised by 374 years.[84]

In their discussions of previous radio-carbon dating, which had tended to support the conventional chronology, Haas and his colleagues drew attention to the fact that the previous samples were far from fresh and that earlier researchers had used less advanced and precise techniques and that calibrations had been irregular.[85]

The Texans and the Swiss do not raise another difference that exists between their work and that of many other researchers, for example that of the Cambridge archaeologist Ian Shaw in his article 'Egyptian chronology and the Irish oak calibration' published in 1985.[86] While Shaw and the others worked closely with Egyptologists and were eager to accommodate their findings into conventional chronology and appear to have been disappointed when this was not possible, Haas and his colleagues were much more concerned with technicalities and appear to have gone into the question with open minds, though they were surprised at the extent to which their dating differed from that of the *Cambridge Ancient History*.[87] Responses to the work of Haas and his colleagues have so far been muted. One objection is that the Texans and Swiss have failed to pay due attention to the difference between short-lived and long-lived material and the lack of precision in dating when the sample comes from a substantial log in which the central tree rings may have died decades or centuries before it was built into the pyramid. Haas and his team attempt to counter this by claiming that the pyramids often took decades to build.[88] Furthermore, it would seem that only a minority of the samples were long-lived and thus *could* be older than the pyramids. Nevertheless, I believe that the team's claim that the dates given in the *Cambridge Ancient History* should be raised by 374 years needs to be reduced somewhat.

Interestingly, however, the chief argument against the Texan and Swiss high datings is that they do not accord with earlier radio-carbon dates for Egypt and the chronology based on historic sources. Furthermore, they do not fit with Palestinian chronology, which is itself based on Egyptian parallels and radio-carbon.[89]

Against this, it can it be argued that Haas and his colleagues have in fact taken the earlier Egyptian radio-carbon dates into account. Furthermore, while their dates do not fit with the historic chronology as it is reconstructed today, if one rounds them down for the reasons stated above, they do accord with those of Breasted and his contemporaries, which were based on the same Egyptian annals. As I stated above, I believe that Breasted's chronology is more trustworthy than those of his successors, or epigoni, because of later pressures to down-date. Palestinian chronology has been almost entirely based on synchronisms with Egypt. Thus it is circular to use it to control Egyptian chronology for these periods. As for the Palestinian carbon dates, the argument between Weinstein and Mellaart on this shows that their interpretation is extremely uncertain.

The chronology of Ebla

One advantage of restoring Breasted and Meyer's chronology for the Egyptian Old Kingdom is that it solves a difficulty in the chronology of the great Syrian city Ebla. The excavation of this city has been the greatest sensation of Near Eastern archaeology in the last quarter of a century. Rich finds have been discovered from many periods but attention has been focused on the palace found at the level labelled IIB1 in which a massive archive has been found. The revolutionary impact of these tablets on the study of the economy, society, religion and language of the ancient Near East is too great and complex to go into here.[90]

Thus, I shall consider only the issue of chronology and the question of the date of the destruction of the palace in which the archive was found and hence the date of the tablets themselves. Two Mesopotamian rulers, Sargon the Great and his grandson Naram Sin, claimed to have conquered Ebla. Paolo Matthiae, the archaeologist who selected the site and has excavated its many treasures, initially argued, on grounds of architecture and artistic style, that the destruction was that of Naram Sin in the 23rd century BC.[91]

Giovanni Pettinato, the epigrapher who first read the texts and reconstructed the new Semitic language of Eblaite, the local language in which many of the tablets were written, argued against Matthiae's dating and proposed that the archive at Ebla had been destroyed much earlier, well before the reign of Sargon. His case for this was based on a number of facts. Firstly, the texts contain a mass of geographical information but no mention of Sargon or of his city Akkad, which would seem extraordinary given the conqueror's overwhelming importance in Mesopotamia and his devastation of Syria. Secondly, there were the parallels in script and language between the Ebla tablets and 'pre-Sargonic' texts from Mesopotamia dating from around 2500 BC. This led him initially to attribute the destruction of the archive at Ebla to the Sumerian king Eannatum of the South Mesopotamian city of Lagash, who was known to have conquered the city of Mari on the Upper Euphrates 170 miles to the east of Ebla. However,

Pettinato later lowered this to around 2400 BC and the considerable campaigns of Lugalzaggizi, the Sumerian ruler of the Mesopotamian city of Kish.[92] Pettinato's case for a pre-Sargonic destruction has been overwhelming and Matthiae and his supporters have quietly shifted to a destruction by Sargon around 2350 BC, though they still do not go back as far back as Pettinato.[93]

Matthiae did appear to have one piece of evidence in favour of the Naram Sin destruction. It was that Palace IIB1, in which the archive was found, also contained two fragments of diorite vessels with the name of the 4th-Dynasty pharaoh Chephrēn and an alabaster lid of a jar with the name of Pepi I of the 6th Dynasty. According to the *Cambridge Ancient History*, Pepi I reigned from 2331 to 2283 BC and Naram Sin from 2291 to 2255 BC. Although he put the latter somewhat later, Matthiae originally argued from this that, while the Chephrēn pieces were already antiques when the palace fell, Pepi's jar was a contemporary gift. Hence, he maintained, this Eblaite palace could not have been destroyed by Sargon or any earlier Mesopotamian ruler. Even today, although Matthiae now accepts a Sargonic destruction, he is clearly uncomfortable with what he sees as the lateness of the Egyptian synchronism.[94]

Astronomical data now seem to back the *Cambridge Ancient History* for the Mesopotamian rulers of this period and raise Sargon's dates by a mere nine years. Thus, Sargon should now be seen as having ruled between 2380 and 2324 BC and Naram Sin from 2300 to 2263 BC.[95] According to the Egyptian chronology proposed here, Pepi I reigned c. 2614–2565 BC. This would accommodate even Pettinato's initial and earliest date for the destruction of Ebla palace IIB1 at c. 2500 BC, which most scholars see as preferable in terms of epigraphic parallels with Mesopotamia.

It is also possible that two other problems are solved by returning to Breasted and Meyer's chronology for the Egyptian Old Kingdom. The first of these is the absence of any reference to Egypt in the Ebla texts. Accepting the orthodox dates for the Egyptian Old Kingdom and believing that the great 4th Dynasty was flourishing during the fifty to seventy years covered by the texts, Pettinato was puzzled by this.[96] Now, however, it would seem that by 2500 BC the 6th Dynasty and the Old Kingdom were crumbling, and, if the destruction of Ebla were lowered by some thirty years, to c. 2470 BC, it would coincide with one of the most chaotic periods of Egyptian history. Thus, there would be no reason to be surprised at the absence of Egypt from the Eblaite texts.

This argument cannot, however, be taken too far as there is now considerable argument as to how far the archive contained geographical information about anywhere to the west of the city.[97]

The second problem possibly resolved by the higher dating of the Egyptian Old Kingdom is that, if the Mesopotamian Dynasty of Akkad was not contemporary with the Egyptian Old Kingdom but rather with the 1st Intermediate Period, it would explain the absence of any Egyptian objects found in Mesopotamia or vice versa indicating synchronisms, which one might well have expected between these two powerful and far-reaching empires.

These last two points are of course based on the argument from silence, which I have attacked many times in this work. Nevertheless, with these additional advantages and the plausible Eblaite synchronism, I can see no reason to doubt that the chronology of the Old Kingdom is considerably higher than that given in the *Cambridge Ancient History* and that the new radio-carbon dating appears to have confirmed the Egyptian chronologies for the Old Kingdom of Breasted, Meyer and Mellaart.

Egyptian chronology before
the Old Kingdom

Does this extend to the whole of early Egyptian chronography? One obvious way in which to reconcile these new results and the 'heightened' Old Kingdom with the conventional amalgam of the Sothic date with the *Turin Canon* was to shorten the Proto-Dynastic period before it. In this way, even if the 3rd Dynasty began *c.* 3000 BC, the 1st Dynasty could be placed *c.* 3200 BC. Unfortunately, this solution is barred by another source for Egyptian history, the Palermo Stone, which is at least a thousand years earlier than the *Turin Canon*. This stone, now in Palermo, is a fragment of a tablet apparently inscribed in the 5th Dynasty, listing earlier pharaohs and some of the outstanding events of their reigns. As with the *Turin Canon,* it can provide only tantalizing scraps of information. One of these is that the first two dynasties lasted for 444 years. This number may have more numerological and arithmetical than historical significance. Nevertheless, the latest study of the Palermo Stone plausibly puts the length of the first two dynasties at between 405 and 486 years.[98] Thus it is impossible to reduce the length of this period to less that two hundred years, despite the relatively few pharaohs whose names have been preserved from it. Thus, there would seem no doubt that Mellaart has been right to restore the date of the foundation of pharaonic Egypt at around 3400 BC, which is where Breasted put it. The 3rd Dynasty should now be seen as having started at approximately 3000 BC and the Old Kingdom as having ended at around 2470 BC, thus following the *Turin Canon*'s claim that this was 955 years after the foundation of the first dynasty.[99]

The dating of the Middle Kingdom

If Mellaart was right about the Old Kingdom, does that mean that one has to accept his high dating for the Middle Kingdom? I believe not. Barry Kemp made a good defence of the overwhelming plausibility of the Sothic date.[100] Thus, the only way to combine the new high dating for the Old Kingdom with the Sothic dating for the Middle Kingdom is to lengthen the 1st rather than the 2nd Intermediate Period. There is little doubt that there were many pharaohs, apparently as many as eighteen after the death of the 100-year-old Pepi II. These belong either to the end of the 6th Dynasty or to the 8th. The *Turin Canon* named a further eighteen for the 9th and 10th Dynasties.[101] What is more, it is clear that not all of these reigns were short and anarchic; a number of papyri portray life as quite peaceful and prosperous, at least for some periods in some regions of the country. There also appear to have been considerable dynasties of nomarchs, 'rulers' of districts or nomes.[102]

The art historian William Stevenson Smith, who stood out against the fashion for low dating in many of its aspects, saw major cultural differences between the Old and Middle Kingdoms and was concerned about the tendency to compress this Intermediate Period.[103] Although traces of Middle Egyptian, the official written language of the Middle Kingdom, appear in the Old Kingdom, the very change of official dialects suggests a substantial political and cultural break between the two kingdoms.[104] This would be unlikely to have occurred in one century and almost impossible with no time gap.

In short, I believe that we should go back to Breasted for our early Egyptian chronology. This means a fundamental revision of the dating of the Archaic Period, the Old Kingdom and the 1st Intermediate Period, but relatively little change in the chronology with which this chapter is concerned, that of the Middle Kingdom and the reign of Sesōstris.

Mesopotamian chronology

In order to assess any possible impact of Sesōstris' campaigns in Mesopotamia and Anatolia it is necessary to have some idea of Mesopotamian chronology in the early 2nd millennium BC. There has, in fact, been considerable debate on this question over the past fifty years. This has centred on competition among a 'long', a 'middle' and a 'short' chronology for such dates as the reign of Hammurabi, the famous king of Babylon, and the later Hittite conquest of that city. These chronologies were based on four possible dates that fitted reports of astronomical observations of Venus found in a Babylonian tablet. During the past decade the earliest date, hence the 'long' chronology, has been powerfully championed by Peter Huber, a statistician from MIT. Huber maintains that not only Babylonian observations of the eight-year cycle of Venus, but also certain lunar eclipses, as well as the lengths of months, all point to the 'long' chronology rather than the other two. He concludes his most recent writing on the subject by stating:

> In my opinion, the problem of the chronology of the early 2nd millennium has thereby shifted in a very significant fashion. It is no longer a question of picking one of several Venus chronologies on the basis of historical or other non-astronomical arguments, but a question of either accepting or refuting one single chronology.
>
> While 99% confidence of course is different from certainty, I believe this margin of error is narrower than in most historical arguments, and a potential refutation would have to be based on exceptionally strong contrary evidence.[105]

Huber's conclusion fits with the predominant and long-standing trend among the archaeologists of Anatolia.[106] The problem is that there now appears to be just the 'strong contrary evidence' Huber required. This comes from dendrochronology. The dendrochronologist Peter Kuniholm now believes that the palace at Açem Hüyük in central Anatolia in which a sealing from Iakhtun-Lim king of Mari has been found can be dated to 1792/1 BC ± 37 years.[107] Iakhtun-Lim appears to have been an older contemporary of the Assyrian king Šamši-Adad, who according to the long chronology reigned in the middle of the 19th century BC. Thus, it is extremely difficult to reconcile this dating with this chronology. However, it can fit easily with the middle and with not too many problems with the low chronology.[108]

On the other hand, there are several a number of difficulties with the date from Açem Hüyük. The first is that the dating is not the result of 'pure' dendrochronology, that is to say that there is no continuous set of parallel rings from Central Anatolia going down to the present. The date was arrived at from radio-carbon datings of tree rings matched with those from places where there are such continuous series. Hence, although this method is far more reliable than simple radio-carbon dating, there are possibilities of error. The second problem is that the excavations of palace at Açem Hüyük from which the timber and sealings were taken have not been published. Because of these uncertainties, we cannot simply abandon the long chronology. Equally, however, we cannot share Huber's near absolute confidence in it.

Thus, just as we have to consider Parker's high and the German low dates for the 12th Dynasty, we have to work with high middle and low dates from Mesopotamia. From the Egyptian end, we are looking for destructions in Anatolia during the reigns of Senwosre I and Amenemhe II the periods 1958–1883 BC or 1912–1841 BC. It is not likely that any Egyptian campaigns in Anatolia could have taken place near the beginning of the reign of Senwosre I. We know that there was a political crisis when he came to the throne and that he was fighting in Libya at the beginning of his reign. It would seem unlikely, then, that he would have begun such an undertaking as the 'conquest' of Asia until he had built up a strong enough political, economic and military base to do so. If one accepts the traditional sources, they argue that his naval and land expeditions to the south came before those made to the north. Finally, there are the references to his son Amenemḥe II on the Mit Rahina inscription. All of these would make it more likely that the latter was involved and that the campaigns took place in the last portion of Sesōstris' reign. Thus, we are looking for archaeological evidence of a powerful army in Anatolia and beyond somewhere between 1930–1916 or 1898–1884 BC.

ARCHAEOLOGICAL EVIDENCE
FOR THE CAMPAIGNS

If we hypothesize Sesōstris' conquests, what should we expect to discover in the archaeological record? Primarily one should find widespread destructions in that period in the regions mentioned, Anatolia, Thrace, Scythia and the Western Caucasus. As tradition does not specify the establishment of a long-lasting empire, one would not expect to see many traces of Egyptian rule but there could be some Egyptian objects. With great luck, it might be possible to find some of the booty sent back from the conquered territories to Egypt. Economically, one would probably see a relatively rapid restoration of the status quo, after the destructions, in prosperous central regions though less economically secure ones would take longer to recover. Politically, the short-lived incursions of Mongols into Southeast Asia or Europeans into sub-Saharan Africa provide analogies for such 'conquests' in having stimulated massive migrations and the formation of new states and ethnic identities. Finally, the tradition of long-lasting colonies having been established might lead one to expect to find new areas of prosperity alongside the devastated regions.

Archaeologically, there does seem to be an indicator of the 12th-Dynasty 'empire' as interpreted by Albright, Posener and the 'maximalists' – those who emphasize its extent – in the distribution of the Syro-Cilician Middle Bronze Age I painted pottery. The material culture of this region around the turn of the 2nd millennium clearly unites Cilicia, in what is now Southeast Turkey, to Syria and, as James Mellaart has pointed out, this culture should be related to Egypt because of the Egyptian 12th Dynasty objects found there.[109] As we shall see below, it is very likely that Cilicia was conquered by Senwosre I and/or his son Ammenemēs II and it is probable that it remained under Egyptian political influence for many decades after that. Though raided by nomads from the east, even before that Western Syro-Palestine formed a relatively stable basis of Egyptian protectorates from which Sesōstris and his son could have launched their campaigns. This would explain the archaeological record of stability in this region during the 20th and early 19th centuries BC, in striking contrast to the situation elsewhere in the Middle East.

Perhaps dealing only with the period from the end of the reign of Senwosre I, Mellaart sharply distinguishes Syro-Cilicia, with its Egyptian connections, from Central and Northern Anatolia where trading links tended to be with Assyria to the east.[110]

Early Anatolia: a brief history

Geographically, Anatolia is an extraordinarily broken up and climatically diverse region with lush Mediterranean plains and high continental mountains, plateaus and inland lakes. The present relative cultural uniformity of Turkey is a misleading exception. For most of its known history, Anatolia has been more like the Caucasus today, a cultural and linguistic mosaic combining isolated spots of local conservatism with areas radically affected by innovation and invasion. This was certainly the case at the beginning of the 2nd millennium BC.

As far as it can be reconstructed from contemporary names and later distribution, the linguistic pattern was as set out in map 13. Several of these languages – Hittite, Luvian, Palaic, Lydian and possibly Carian – belong to the Anatolian branch of the Indo-Hittite family; Phrygian and Proto-Armenian are Indo-European. There were also Hattic, Proto-Kartvelian – from which the Georgian languages are descended – and Hurrian. All of these were non–Indo-European.[111]

Much historical reconstruction and explanation of destructions in Anatolia has been concerned with the perceived problem of the 'arrival' of the speakers of the Hittite and other Anatolian languages from the north. I have stated in Volume 1 that I follow Georgiev and Renfrew in believing that these, like the non–Indo-European languages, were indigenous to the region.[112] Therefore their introduction is not a problem here. On the other hand, it is possible that Hurrian came in from the southeast and Phrygian and the Indo-European component of Armenian clearly arrived from the north. There is no attestation of the latter two languages at the beginning of the 2nd millennium, but from linguistic evidence it would seem likely that they had arrived in Anatolia before then, although Phrygian expanded into the centre of the peninsula only in the first part of the 1st millennium. The most probable time for their original entry would seem to be in the upheavals we know from archaeology and Akkadian records to have taken place in the 23rd century BC.

It is generally accepted that it was in this period that the so-called Kurgan culture, represented north of the Caucasus by the great Maikop Barrow, appears to have penetrated Eastern Anatolia and fused with the local civilizations.[113] It is possible but less likely that the disturbances in Western Anatolia at approximately the same time, which used to be associated with a 'Luvian invasion', were triggered by the arrival of Proto-Phrygians from the northwest.[114]

In any event, after about 2100 BC, Central and Eastern Anatolia began a period of economic expansion and prosperity based largely on abundant mineral resources and trade with the Middle East, which lasted, with some significant interruptions, until the end of the Bronze Age in the 12th century. The earliest examples of the so-called 'Hittite Hieroglyphic' come from around 2000 BC; however, it would seem likely that this script originated after Anatolians knew of writing but before they had come in contact with cuneiform, which was probably around the turn of the 3rd millennium. The type of cuneiform used by the Hittite Empire, which was founded after the disturbances with which we are concerned, was not Assyrian but Syrian. How and when it was transmitted is unknown but an opening to Syria in the 20th and 19th centuries is one possibility.

Destruction in Anatolia: Kültepe II and Karum Kanesh

Although there is, so far, no trace of local literacy in 3rd-millennium Anatolia, there is a source of historical information about its central region from the middle of the 20th century BC. This is the many thousands of tablets found at an Assyrian trading station at Karum Kanesh at a site now called by the common Turkish village name Kültepe. Unfortunately, as is nearly always the case in Assyriology, perfectionism and scholars' sense of private property have prevented most of these tablets from being published. Nevertheless, a great deal has been learnt from those that have been made available about the structure of the *karum* (meaning commercial colony), about its relations with other Assyrian colonies in Anatolia and with the city of Assur, 500 miles away over extremely difficult terrain. They also tell us much about trade in the ancient world and the importance of the private merchant. Specifically, they show the large quantities of Anatolian silver, gold and lead being exported to Assyria in exchange for textiles from Mesopotamia and tin, which came from further east, probably Afghanistan.[115]

The tablets also reveal a little about the society in which the foreign merchants were operating. Most of the cities had kings, many of them with Hittite names. There was a 'Great King' at Burushattum, a hundred miles to the west. Hittite histories refer to their first king as Anitta, king of Kussara, to the north of Kanesh, who moved his capital to Nesha or Nisha, which is probably Kanesh. He is reported as having conquered a number of cities and as having forced the king at Purushkhanda/Burushattum to submit to him. Anitta is mentioned in the Assyrian texts and a dagger or arrowhead with his name has been found in the ruins of a destroyed palace at Kanesh. However, there is dispute among scholars as to whether he was contemporaneous with the late 20th-century BC period of Kültepe II or the 19th-century BC period, Kültepe Ib.[116] In any event, there is a considerable and almost complete gap between him and the next 'founder' of the Hittite Empire, Labarnas, in the mid- or late 18th century BC.

This leads us to the critical problem of dating the texts at Kültepe. The two periods with which we are concerned are Kültepe II and Ib. Both of these periods were prosperous ones, in which there was considerable trade between Kanesh and Assur, and they have produced great numbers of tablets. At the end of Kültepe II, however, both the city and the suburb, where the Assyrians lived, were utterly destroyed with little or no warning, and it was several decades before they were restored and the Ib period began.

In his splendid work on the economy and social structure of the *karum*, the Danish Assyriologist Mogens Trolle Larsen wisely did not tackle the question of dating. Thus the most detailed work on the *karum*'s dating is still that published by the Turkish ancient historian

Balkan in 1955. Reading the references in the tablets to Assyrian kings, he was able to link them with the contemporary kings of Babylon. The Assyrian *karum* seems to have begun near the beginning of the reign of King Erisum I. However, the documents only refer to the last fourteen years of his forty- or forty-one-year reign. They cover the reigns of Erisum I's successors, Ikūnum and Šarrum-kîn, and end in that of Puzur-Aššur II. Unfortunately, the Assyrian king-lists do not give the length of these kings' reigns so here we are reduced to speculation. We seem to be back on firm ground, however, with the rebuilding of the *karum* in the tenth year of King Šamši-Adad.

Assyrian chronologies give 159 years for the period between the accession of Erisum I and the death of Šamši-Adad. Looking at Karum Kanesh, Balkan allocates twenty-six of these to the undocumented period at the *karum* and another eighty to the rest of Kültepe II. A further twenty-three are taken up with the period of Kültepe Ib in the reign of Šamši-Adad, leaving a gap of thirty years between the two periods which would put the destruction of Kültepe II about 1890 BC.[117]

There are, however, a number of problems with this. Balkan himself makes several points in favour of a longer interval between the periods; there was over a metre of debris between the two strata, the orientation and plans of the houses had changed, which means that the new settlers were unaware of the layout of the old settlement; there had been changes in the types of object and techniques used in making them; and, finally, there had been a number of significant linguistic changes in the interim.[118] The second point seems particularly telling, for even if the whole Assyrian population of the *karum* were killed with its destruction, in a mobile mercantile population there must have been others surviving elsewhere who knew about its layout. For these reasons, the excavator Özgüç argued, such changes would have taken fifty years. I believe that this is the bare minimum.[119]

The gap between the two periods covered the reigns of two kings, Naram-sin and Erisum II, and the first ten years of Šamši-Adad. Professor Balkan conjectures that the destruction took place at the end of the reign of Puzur-Aššur II, but there seems no reason for this and he may well have continued to rule longer. We know that Naram-sin reigned for at least fifteen years. Therefore, a thirty-year gap would allow only five years for any further years of his reign or that of Puzur-Aššur II, let alone the whole reign of Erisum II. The compression seems too great.

At the same time, there would seem to have been too much time given for the documented period of Kültepe II. It is true that some merchant families appear to have been there for four generations, but in the case used as an example by Larsen, in his detailed study of the *karum*, the great-grandfather is dead before the correspondence begins and the great-grandson is supposed to have been very young.[120]

It would seem likely, then, that documented Kültepe II should be shortened and the gap lengthened by from twenty to forty years. If we accept the Assyrian king-list's total of 159 years from the accession of Erišum I to the death of Šamši Adad and subtract thirty years from Erišum's reign before the *karum* correspondence begins and the twenty-three further years of the reign of Šamši Adad, we are left with 108 years for Kültepe II and the destruction period. If we further estimate that the literate period of Kültepe II lasted some forty to fifty years, we should estimate that Kültepe II was destroyed fifty to seventy years before the tenth year of Šamši Adad. Thus, everything hangs on this date, which is 1859, 1803 and 1792 BC, according to the long, middle and short chronologies respectively. These dates plus sixty to seventy years give the ranges 1929–1909, 1873–1853 and 1799–1779 for the destruction. The long chronology would provide a perfect synchronism with the later part of the reign of Senwosre I, according to Parker.

The middle chronology would not fit this but would fit the German low Egyptian chronology for the reign of Amenemḥe II, 1875–1842 BC. One could reconcile the possible synchronism by suggesting that the hypothetical Egyptian destruction took place during the reigns of Senwosre II and III. This would lower the Egyptian range to 1830 or 1788, and despite Mellaart's preference for the early part of the dynasty there is nothing in the 12th-Dynasty Egyptian objects found in the Anatolian destruction levels restricting them to it. On the other hand, no letter in the *karum* correspondence refers to Egyptians, making it unlikely that Egyptians had been campaigning in the region for a long time. Furthermore, there is the evidence from the Tôd Treasure, to be discussed below, that objects similar to those found at Kültepe II arrived in Egypt during the reign of Amenemḥe II.

To repeat, there is a synchronism between the destruction of Kültepe II and Parker's dating of the later reign of Senwosre I, if one accepts the Mesopotamian long chronology backed by Huber's astronomical computations. There is one between the German chronology for the reign of Amenemḥe II and the middle chronology, but there is none if one accepts the low Mesopotamian chronology.

Mellaart, when working with the high chronology and on the basis of the 12th-Dynasty objects, puts the destruction between 1940 and 1900 BC.[121] This also puts it close to the period of Sesōstris' hypothetical northern campaigns, which we have dated to between *c.* 1930 and 1916 BC.

I hope the reasons why I have devoted so much space to determining the date of the destruction of Kültepe II will now become clear. Kanesh or Nesha or Nišili, as the Hittites called it, was a key cultural and military centre. Hittites called their own language after the city of their founder Anitta, long after the capital had moved north to Hattus. Kanesh, which at the end of Kültepe II had a very considerable population of 20–30,000, was also a key junction for trade routes from Mesopotamia and Syria north to the rich silver and lead mines, near the present Sebinkarahisar and the Black Sea, and west to the Aegean Coast and Troy (see map 12). It is in this context that we should read the following from Mellaart's classic article 'The end of the Early Bronze Age in Anatolia and the Aegean', which appeared in 1958:

> In Central Anatolia, the prosperous Assyrian *karum* or trading settlement below the walls of the great city of Kanesh . . . was reduced to ashes *c.* 1900 B.C. (level II) and not reoccupied for half a century. The contemporary city of Alishar Hüyük, another trading centre, suffered the same fate, but the destruction of Alacar Hüyük V is definitely earlier. Among the many sites of the Kirşehir basin, Has Hüyük, the only one excavated, was burnt, and south of the river Halys, the destruction layers of the great mound of Acemköy near Aksaray indicate a conflagration about 1900 B.C. or a little later.
>
> In the hill country between the Halys and the Sangarius, widespread destruction occurs; Karaoğlan, Bitik, Polatli and Gordion are burnt, and Etiokuşu, Cerkes and several other sites are deserted. Within the great bend of the Sangarius, the plain of Eskişehir was studded with Early Bronze Age villages of the Demirci Hüyük culture, and at least half of the number were deserted after 1900 B.C. and not reoccupied. Further westward still, the two large mounds of Köprüören and Tavşanli, west of Kütahya, are littered with burnt bricks of the destroyed city walls, in either case associated with pottery of the E.B.A. (Troy V type) and the neighbouring site of Tepecik appears to have been deserted after the end of the period.
>
> Between this region and the Troad lies the Balikesir plain, now famous as the centre of the Yortan culture, the knowledge of which is almost entirely drawn from its cemeteries. None of these contained any pottery later than the end of the E.B.A.
>
> In the Troad, Troy V was not destroyed by fire, but the next pe-

riod shows a change of culture and two other sites, Kumtepe II and Karaağaçtepe, the so-called mound on the Thracian Chersonese are deserted. On Lemnos the last E.B.A. settlement of Poliochni is said to have been destroyed by earthquake, but the site is not re-occupied in the Middle Bronze Age.[122]

The boldness of this baleful roll-call and the shortened version of it Mellaart gave a decade later in the *Cambridge Ancient History* has been a challenge to more cautious scholars ever since. The powerful American archaeologist James Muhly saw the destruction at Karum Kanesh simply as 'some sort of local event'.[123] One writer on Hattus claimed that the Assyrian *karum* there was not destroyed, but later research seems to contradict this.[124] Mellaart had not, in fact, claimed that it had been destroyed. Even so, he allowed for such corrections when he wrote 'even if later research eliminates some of the sites from our list, it will undoubtedly add others'. Indeed, the important city later known as Aphrodisias in Western Anatolia now seems to have been destroyed at about this time.[125] There is no doubt that there was, as he put it, 'a long line of burnt or deserted sites, which demonstrate some disturbance in the northern half of Anatolia at the end of the Early Bronze Age'.[126]

WAS SESŌSTRIS THE DESTROYER?

In 1958 Mellaart argued that the destructions were the result of a Hit-tite invasion into central Anatolia, which had led to westward migra-tions and further chaos. To do this, he had not merely to insist that the spearhead with the name of the Hittite king Anitta belonged to Kültepe Ib – after the destructions – but to deny the Hittite names found in Kültepe II.[127] He was also puzzled by the lack of any material culture of his hypothetical invaders. This suggested to him that 'they came from beyond the area of Middle Eastern Civilization'. In the 3rd millennium, however, there had been ample material evidence of Anatolian contacts with trans-Caucasian cultures. The implausibility of these parts of his scheme seems eventually to have led to his aban-donment of the whole, *but the band of destruction remains and becomes more mysterious with Mellaart's failure to explain it.*

Is it permissible to associate them with Sesōstris and accept the statements of Herodotos, Manetho and Diodoros that he conquered 'all of Asia', a term generally used for Anatolia, 'from east to west'? I believe that, despite the chronological difficulties, that it may well be. While Mellaart notes the absence of 'northern' objects, he later recorded the presence of a number of Egyptian 12th-Dynasty ones found at key places along the route. As mentioned above, it was partly from these that he established the date for the destructions.[128] Further archaeological evidence in favour of an Egyptian campaign in Central Anatolia at this time comes from Egypt itself.

The Tôd Treasure

The Tôd Treasure was discovered in the 1930s in the foundations of a sanctuary of Mont built at Tôd, seventeen kilometres upstream from Luxor, in the Theban nome of which Mont was a local god and which was the original home of the 12th Dynasty. The temple complex dates back to the 11th Dynasty, which ruled from the nome and whose chief divinity was Mont, but Senwosre I demolished this earlier structure and built a new sanctuary. The treasure itself was placed in four copper caskets which were inscribed with the name of Amenemḥe II.[129]

These caskets were Egyptian but their contents were all foreign. They included gold ingots, chains of rings and bracelets and ornaments of gold, silver and electrum as well as 143 flattened and 10 unfolded silver bowls. Other caskets were filled with lapis lazuli and contained a number of cylinder seals. As the excavator Bisson de la Roque pointed out, there is no doubt that the objects came from Asia. Gold from Nubia and the Red Sea coast came in bags – not caskets – and these regions did not produce silver, which at this time was equally or more valuable than gold.[130] The nearest silver came from Anatolia, the Caucasus and Laurion in Greece, though there were still greater sources in the Balkans.

As there are Egyptian assayers' marks of quality on some of the pieces, the treasure was clearly prized for its metal content. Nevertheless, although some of the bowls were crushed, the fact that they were not melted down would seem to indicate that their form and, I believe, their provenance added to their value.[131] If there was any doubt about the metal's place of origin, it is resolved by their forms, which are not Minoan, as has sometimes been suggested. Although the Aegean appearance of some of them might come from an origin from the west of the peninsula, the group as a whole clearly come from Anatolia or the Caucasus. One cup is even seen to have its closest parallels with another found at Kültepe II.[132]

The cylinder seals indicate the same general origin. Most are Mesopotamian but they include at least one from Cappadocia in North-Central Anatolia and another from Iran. As with all collections of seals – or coins – they come from a long time period but bunch to-

wards its end. In this case, they go back to the end of the Akkadian
period in the 23rd century BC but most come from early in the 1st
Dynasty of Babylon, which ruled either in the 20th or the early 19th
centuries BC. Acceptance of the long chronology for Mesopotamia
would make Porada's ingenious attempts to demonstrate that these
glyptic styles existed before the 1st Dynasty unnecessary.[133] Their origin and date fit perfectly with the hypothesis that Egyptians and their
allies were plundering Anatolia, and its Assyrian traders, in the late
20th century BC.

The other great component of the treasure was lapis lazuli, which
ultimately came from Afghanistan. Although I would not absolutely
deny that Egyptian forces could have reached there, it would seem
much more plausible to suppose that the lapis lazuli came through
Mesopotamia, the Caucasus and Anatolia. We know that during the
New Kingdom Assyria was a particular source of the material.[134]

How did the treasure reach Tôd? One of the silver cups is marked
as having been brought by an Egyptian conveyor, whose position
Posener has connected to that of the messengers moving up and down
Syro-Palestine referred to in *Sinuhe*.[135] He quotes from a dedicatory
inscription of the temple of Sesōstris at Tôd describing the presentation of offering tables made of precious materials:

> twice as beautiful and twice as numerous as all one was accustomed
> to see in this country before, and representing what foreigners and
> explorers, who travel across the lands, have delivered.[136]

Sesōstris was living up to the promise of his name, S-n Wsrt (Man of
Wsrt), patron of foreign mines.[137] Apart from the indication – which
neatly parallels the Greek writers and the Mit Rahina inscription –
that something quite exceptional was going on in the later part of the
reign of Sesōstris, the dedication also indicates that the material was
brought by both tribute-bearing foreigners and Egyptian officials.
This fits the descriptions and paintings from the New Kingdom of
tribute arriving in Egypt. Kemp and Merrillees describe the latter
gifts in the following way: 'whilst some was plunder or tax from conquered territories, some had been sent to Egypt as diplomatic gifts.'[138]
This may have been the case with the Tôd Treasure but in the light of
the other indications of military activity, emphasis should be put on
the component of plunder and tax.

Furthermore, it should be remembered that the dedication was
made to Mntw or Mont, who, as well as being the god of the Theban
nome and of central importance to both the 11th and 12th Dynasties,
was a god of warfare and specifically of foreign conquests and the

suppression of barbarians. In particular, Mont was associated with the land of Stt in Asia.[139] It is striking that Mont of Tôd is specifically mentioned in the Mit Rahina inscription as the recipient of foreign booty from Stt (*sic*).[140]

We shall return later to the location of Stt – more correctly Stt – and its connections with the temple of Mont at Tôd. Meanwhile, we should consider the probable function of the treasure. Kemp and Merrillees place emphasis on its raw materials and its economic value. Although this was undoubtedly a function, one should not forget that many of the objects were not reduced to ingots of their basic metals and that they were dedicated and preserved in a temple to Mont. Thus, it would seem that, like many other temple treasuries, it had what we, though not the ancients, would see as two functions, one secular and the other religious. The treasure of Tôd was not just bullion; the crushed exotic objects that made it up were altogether suitable representations of the subjection of foreigners. It was also an offering to Mont and the Egyptian military triumphs that could be attributed to him.

Thus, there is nothing in Egyptian, Levantine and Anatolian archaeology to preclude the Greek writers' descriptions of Sesōstris' conquests in Anatolia. Indeed, such campaigns would explain a number of previously inexplicable phenomena, notably the belt of destructions and the Tôd Treasure containing objects from Anatolia and further east. On the other hand, if one accepts the middle or low Mesopotamian chronologies, the destructions could have been the result of any number of other causes. Before considering the Mit Rahina inscription and other sources of evidence on the conquests in Anatolia, however, it would seem useful to look at evidence for the campaigns in other regions.

Sesōstris in Thrace and Scythia?

In the quotation from Mellaart on the belt of destruction in Northern Anatolia given above, there was a reference to the desertion of a major site just across the Hellespont on the Thracian Chersonese. He continued:

> Turkish Thrace (also called Turkey in Europe) and the coastal province and Macedonia (Greek Thrace) are blanks on the archaeological map, but in Bulgaria there is evidence that the disturbance in Northern Anatolia made itself felt there also. Bulgarian scholars date the end of their Early Bronze Age (Yunacite, Salcutza, Esero, etc.) to *c.* 1900 and the sudden desertion of these sites added to the

complete absence of a Middle Bronze Age certainly indicates some catastrophe.[141]

Mellaart went on to describe the much more complicated situation in Greece, to which we shall return in the next chapter. We will not describe it here because it was not on Sesōstris' itinerary as described by the Greek writers.

It should be emphasized that the Early Bronze Age culture of the Mariça Valley in Bulgarian Thrace was far richer and more developed than that of its neighbours to the north, even though it shared many cultural features with them. Thus what Bulgarian archaeologists refer to as the Early Bronze Age is called the Aeneolithic or 'Copper/Stone Age' by their Romanian, Yugoslav and Russian colleagues. This is because, although rich in copper and gold, these peoples were still using stone not bronze for their tools and weapons.[142] There is no doubt that c. 1900 BC marks a watershed in the history of the Balkans.

As far as I am aware, there is no archaeological evidence of a Middle Kingdom Egyptian presence in the region. However, there have been some interesting indications from Egypt. It appears to have been during the Middle Kingdom that the alloy electrum, made up of 30 per cent silver and 70 per cent gold, was first used in Egypt. It seems that the only mines in the world where this proportion occurs naturally is in the Apusini mountains in Transylvania. The region also produces amethyst, jasper, cornelian and chalcedony. These, too, first appear in Egypt in the Middle Kingdom, as does a clear red and yellow jasper, used in inlays, which came from elsewhere in Romania. These types of jasper do not occur in Egypt nor does amethyst of this quality.[143] It would seem quite likely then that the electrum and these semi-precious stones did come from the Balkans. This, of course, does not necessitate an Egyptian conquest of the region; as we know, trading chains have stretched far further than this without any political or military control. On the other hand, the desire for such luxuries would provide a motive for Egyptian expeditions in the region and their presence in Egypt at this time provides yet another piece of circumstantial evidence for the historicity of the traditions around Sesōstris' conquests.

The Russian Steppe also went through a break around 1900 BC. As in Thrace, this is the conventional date for the end of the Aeneolithic and the beginning of the Bronze Age there. However, archaeologists do not report widespread destructions comparable to those seen by Mellaart in Bulgaria. Tracing these would be more difficult because much – though not all – of the population of these regions was nomadic. It should be noted that the prosperous Tripolye agricultural culture of South Russia had been broken up several centuries earlier. It is difficult to imagine how well an essentially African army would have coped with the weather of the steppes. In his account of Sesōstris, Diodoros mentions the problems of hunger rather than cold: 'And after he had crossed into Europe and was on his way through the whole length of Thrace he nearly lost his army through lack of food and the difficult nature of the land'.[144] Thus, we are presented in Scythia with two difficulties. The first of these is the absence of any archaeological trace of Egyptian presence there. The second is the clear-cut motive, mentioned above, for Egyptians to have invented a story of Sesōstris' having conquered Scythia in order for the Egyptian hero to have outdone the Persian rulers, who had not succeeded in conquering it.[145] Nevertheless, as I mentioned earlier, Sesōstris' conquests in Nubia, which served the same anti-Persian purpose, have been proven true. Thus, the use of the pharaoh's conquest of Scythia for propaganda does not in itself remove its historicity.

SESŌSTRIS IN COLCHIS?

The case for Sesōstris having been in Colchis on the eastern shore of the Black Sea is rather stronger. During the 3rd millennium BC, despite what must have been enormous linguistic divergences, there was a remarkable unity in material culture over the whole of the Western Caucasus in what is known as the Kuro-Araxes culture. The splendid pottery from this culture, known in the Levant from its first find-site Khirbet Kerak, has been found as far south as Palestine, though not in Central Anatolia. The culture was already exploiting the rich mines of the Southwest Caucasus both for local use and for export to the south and north.[146]

This civilization broke up around 2300 BC, apparently under pressure from the northern Kurgan culture, associated with the Indo-European language, and the invasion or infiltration of the peoples best known from the royal burials at Maikop and the first barrows at Trialeti in Georgia. This radical change has been seen in ceramic terms as the shift from Early Bronze II to Early Bronze III.[147]

There seems to be some confusion among archaeologists on the dating of the destructions and cultural innovations. Professor Burney tried to link them to the series put forward by Mellaart as cited above.[148] However, this involves stretching the Indo-European invasions over four hundred years from 2300 to 1900 BC, as there seem to have been waves of destruction in both of these periods. This problem could be resolved by postulating, instead, a northern invasion c. 2300 and Sesōstris' campaigns in the 1930s or 1920s BC. This would fit with a passage Burney and Lang wrote concerning the turn of the 2nd millennium:

> . . . the long continuity of the third millennium BC had at last vanished. Though the population had not radically changed, new elements were making their appearance. New forces were at work throughout Trans-Caucasia and in most of the Urmia basin too.[149]

Elsewhere, Lang noted the following:

> That some major movement of population brought to an end the Armenian and East Anatolian Early Bronze Age is suggested by the layers of ashes and other evidence of sudden disturbance that occur at several sites in this region. In Armenia we observe a shift in population from the fertile lowlands,with their settled village communities, to the upland pastures usually favoured by owners of the large herds and flocks which are a feature of the pastoral life of the early Indo-European tribes from the steppe.[150]

This retreat to the mountains could equally well have been the response to an invasion by an organized army. Evidence in the same direction comes from the very heavily Egyptianized Byblos where evidence of Caucasian metal-workers has been found. The French archaeologist Claude Schaeffer attributed this to a movement of Caucasian bronze-workers which he believed had been caused by 'earthquakes of exceptional violence' which had shaken the region around 2000 BC. Much of Schaeffer's chronology has had to be revised because of new finds and new scientific methods. Nevertheless, the basic point he made still holds:

> It is a fact that the countries of Asia Minor, which during the last period of the 3rd millennium had possessed a metallurgic industry in advance of all those of all the countries of West Asia and Protohistoric Europe, were, at the beginning of the 2nd millennium, dispossessed of their monopoly and deprived of their best artisans. The absolute poverty of metal types in Asia Minor between 2000 and 1500 has always struck archaeologists and it is even more remarkable in that it contrasts with the richness of production in the surrounding countries.[151]

It is striking that in 1978 Mellaart indicated that the whole region of Northeast Anatolia – the later Armenia and Western Georgia – which had enormous mineral deposits and intense metal-working has 'no known Middle Bronze Age Settlements'.[152] It should be emphasized that regions to the east, including the famous site of Trialeti in inland Georgia, continued to flourish. The 'invasions' at the end of Early Bronze II *c.* 2300 BC enriched the Kuban and the north of the Caucasus but did not destroy the prosperity and technology of Northeast Anatolia. The disturbances in the 20th century BC were locally devastating but appear to have benefited regions all around, especially to the south. Throughout the Levant one finds traces of northern workmanship and a great improvement in metallurgy.[153]

Egypt itself began to use metal on a large scale only in this period. It is also interesting to note how quickly the armies of the 12th Dynasty took on the new weapons made possible by the new metallurgy – daggers, distinctive fenestrated axes and the sickle sword. In fact, it is remarkable to what an extent there was a *koinē* or common standard of military equipment and techniques around this time, from Nubia to the Caucasus.[154]

As far as I am aware, no confirmed Egyptian objects from this period have been found in the Caucasus, although a couple of maceheads found in Armenia could well be Egyptian. On the other hand, there is little doubt that objects of Caucasian provenance have been found in Egypt.[155]

Thus, the archaeological evidence from the Southwest Caucasus allows for an invasion, in that, like Bulgarian Thrace, it seems to have suffered major destructions and long-lasting devastation. Neither archaeology nor documentary sources will allow us to explain the southern spread of Northern Anatolian and Caucasian metallurgy during the 12th Dynasty in terms of an invasion from the north. By contrast, the picture given by the Greek writers of Sesōstris sending back huge numbers of captives would explain this phenomenon very well.

THE EVIDENCE FOR SESŌSTRIS' 'CONQUESTS' FROM THE MIT RAHINA INSCRIPTION

I should now like to return to the Mit Rahina inscription and the light that it can throw on these traditions. The Mit Rahina inscription gives very much the same picture as these do of the pharaoh's glorious and profitable campaigns. Most of it is taken up with the sending back to Egypt of livestock, slaves and precious goods, especially metals. There are frequent references to silver and one to lead, which was previously known to have been imported only in the New Kingdom.[156] These can have come only from Anatolia, the Caucasus or Greece. There are also references to the land of Stt<Stt.[157]

A conjunction of the Mit Rahina inscription with the Tôd Treasure strongly indicates that Stt included Anatolia. Two fragmentary lines from the inscription give a parallel between offerings – including metal – from Stt to the royal temple of Mont at ỉwny, Armant, on the west bank of the Nile twenty kilometres upstream from Thebes, and other offerings from Stt given by Amenemḥe II to Mont at Ḏrty, Tôd. The precise reference is obscure but, given the parallel with the temple at ỉwny and the well-known temple of Mont at Tôd, this would seem the most likely recipient.[158] The objects described are not those of the Treasure; nevertheless, the conjunction of the archaeological find of metal objects from Anatolia dedicated by Amenemḥe II at the temple of Mont at Tôd with the offerings from Stt dedicated by the same pharaoh is startling. Thus, it would seem almost certain that, at least in the Middle Kingdom, Stt included Anatolia just as Stt's later equivalent 'Asia' did.

In this case, what seems to be the bꜣ (destruction or subduing) of Stt under Amenemḥe II, referred to on the line before the offerings to Mont, takes on a different meaning.[159] These are the only references to Stt but the inscription contains three previously unknown Asiatic place names.

The first of these is ═𝔄𝕏ꟻ﹏, Ṯmpꜣw. One possibility for this is ═□ꟻ﹏, Ṯnpw, or ○ꟻ﹏(ⅾ) 𝕏, Twn(y)pꜣ, Tunip, a city in central Syria. This important city is known in Babylonian texts from the reign of Hammurabi and would seem likely despite the interchange of n and m.[160] There is, however, another phonetic difficulty in that while 𝕏, pꜣ, was used vocalically in the New Kingdom simply for pa, ꜣ retained its liquid quality, sounding like an r or an l, in the Middle Kingdom. The semantic difficulties are even more serious in that Ṯmpꜣw is described as producing 'lead', none of which is known in Syria.[161] A less unlikely candidate is the land of Tabalu or Tubal, a name known from Assyrian texts and the Bible as a territory in Central or Northeastern Anatolia famous for its metal-working: in Genesis, its eponym Tûbal Qayîn (smith) was known as 'the master of all coppersmiths and blacksmiths'. Iron had been worked in small quantities in Anatolia since the 3rd millennium.[162] Thus, the bringing of lead from Ṯmpꜣ would seem to be an indication here of Egyptian power at this time in Anatolia.

The other new names in the inscription are those of two 'cities' destroyed or subdued by Egyptian armies, ⟨𝔄⟨⟩, ỉwꜣỉ, and ⟨𝕏⟨⟨⟩, ỉꜣsy. Wolfgang Helck sees ỉwꜣỉ, or, as he reads it, 'ꜣur-a, as the name Ura, found in Hittite and Ugaritic and Egyptian texts six hundred years later in the 13th century BC referring to an important city on the coast of Cilicia.[163] This may well be the case. However, iwȝi also looks somewhat like 𓆑𓏤𓇯𓏏𓇋𓇋𓈖, wȝ iwr y, an Aegean name found on a column base of Amenhotep III from around 1400 BC, which a majority of scholars have identified with (W)Ilios – Troy.[164] The identification would be better if the name could be read as wȝy but this seems unlikely. As I mentioned in Chapter III, politically significant Egyptian objects from as far back as the Old Kingdom may well have been found in the Troad so there is no inherent impossibility of involvement there.[165]

Mellaart included Troy in his list of destructions from *c.* 1900 BC, but he admitted that Troy V, which ended at this time, was not burnt. Nevertheless, he seems justified in claiming that there was a categorical break at this time.[166] If iwȝi were Troy, the fact that the Mit Rahina inscription claimed that the city was bȝ, literally 'hacked up' or 'destroyed', does not provide an insuperable difficulty, as – at least in the New Kingdom – the word seems to have been used to mean merely 'to subdue'. The connections between iwȝi and Ilios are too tenuous for anything substantial to be based on them. This does not mean, however, that we should exclude Troy from the band of destruction that swept Anatolia at the end of the 20th century BC, and we shall return in Chapter VI to the image of an African army at the walls of Troy.

Helck's argument that iwȝi should be identified with Ura is strengthened by the association of the other name, isy, with Cyprus, 150 kilometres across the sea to the south. The name isy leads to great complications, as it falls between two names, both of which are themselves the subjects of great dispute. The first and less controversial of these is 𓊪𓄿𓏏𓇯𓇋𓈇, irs, commonly vocalized as Alasia on the basis of Akkadian and Hittite transcriptions. irs is generally accepted as the name for Cyprus, though some scholars identify it as a stretch of coastline in South Anatolia.[167] This name is attested from Egypt and elsewhere only in the New Kingdom. Given the fact that during the Middle Kingdom the ȝ was a liquid, the suggestion made by Meltzer and Helck that isy was the earlier form of Alasia seems plausible, and this would also fit evidence from the Mit Rahina inscription.[168]

As Posener points out, iwȝi and isy must have been in Asia because 1,546 ꜥȝmw (Asiatic) prisoners were taken from them. The other booty would fit either Anatolia or Cyprus as it included bronze axes, daggers and knives, and Cyprus is known to have been a major source of copper in the Late Bronze Age. However, many scholars accept that it had been producing the metal since the Early Cypriot III period around 2000 BC.[169] There appear to have been strong Egyptian

influences on ECIII Cyprus, and Middle Kingdom beads and amulets
have been found in contemporary strata in Cyprus, though no Cypriot material of this time has been identified in Egypt.[170] Evidence of
destructions in 20th-century Cyprus is unclear but it is probable that
nothing on the scale of those in Anatolia took place.

There is also a slight problem in that both iwȝi and iȝsy are written
with the battlemented cartouches used for cities – nearly always conquered – and not with the sign for mountain, ⌒⌒, generally employed
for foreign countries and in this inscription for Tmpȝw. However, the
line between a territory and its chief city is not always clear-cut and in
this case there has been a frequent alternation between irs/Alasia as
city and a country. Thus iȝsy may refer to Enkomi or another of the
chief cities of Cyprus.[171]

The close parallel drawn between iwȝi and iȝsy suggests that that the
two 'cities' were geographically adjacent as are Ura and Cyprus. This
would not be the case if iwȝi were Troy and iȝsy Cyprus. The tangle
around iwȝi grows even thicker, however, when we consider another
name recorded in the New Kingdom, that of 𓇌⸺𓏤𓏏𓏏⌒⌒ , isy. This
name, which looks remarkably like iȝsy, has been the subject of much
debate, some scholars seeing it as an earlier form of irs/Alasia. However, in 1946 the specialist in ancient Anatolia H. T. Bossert clearly
identified isy with Assuwa, the Hittite name for a kingdom in Western
Anatolia from which, as mentioned above, the Greek name 'Asia' is
derived.[172] As long ago as 1886, the Egyptologist and ancient historian
Gaston Maspero had derived the name Asia from an extension of isy
which he saw as originally having been a name for Cyprus.[173]

One possible solution of this complex problem comes from the Mit
Rahina name iȝsy. This is to suppose an Egyptian adoption of a local
or Levantine name, iȝsy, for Cyprus, which was extended to cover
points further to the northwest. Analogies for this would be the European use of the name Indies in the 16th century or the Greek expansion of Asia itself. Thus in Cyprus, where the name had authentic
roots, the phonetics were preserved and iȝsy was rewritten irs/Alasia;
in Western Anatolia the graphic form iȝsy, pronounced and later written isy, came to dominate. This hypothesis would correspond well
with the conclusions arrived at by the ancient historian G. A. Wainwright in 1915, that isy was located on a seacoast and had affinities
with Syria and Asia Minor, and connections with the Cilicia, and was
never called an island.[174]

On the other hand, the Hellenist D. J. Georgacas, in his detailed
study of the name 'Asia', has two objections to this kind of argument. The first is that Egyptians already had a name for Asia in Stt.

However, given the vagueness of the first term as set out above, I see no reason why specific regions in West Anatolia should not have had their own names. Georgacas's second argument is far more powerful: it is that Assuwa is well established in Anatolian languages and there is no need to propose an Egyptian origin for it.[175]

Thus, while the connections between ìsy, Assuwa and Asia are clear, their origin is not. Similarly, while it is very likely that ìɜsy was an early form of ìrs/Alasia/Cyprus, it could also be the origin of ìsy/Assuwa/Asia. The report of ʿɜmw prisoners and booty of metalwork would fit either. Cyprus is closer to Egypt and would seem more likely on that count. In any case, the names Stt, Ṭmpɜw, ìwɜì and ìɜsy and their products listed in the Mit Rahina inscription clearly indicate that Sesōstris' expeditions went well beyond Syro-Palestine and into Cyprus and Anatolia.

CONCLUSION

The traditions about Sesōstris' northern campaigns were discredited from the beginning of the 19th century AD, long before there was any archaeological or inscriptional evidence on the subject. They were rejected firstly because the new scepticism would not tolerate speculations about such an early period about which there was so little evidence. There were also religious objections to Egyptian history before the Hyksos, which came dangerously near to the Creation. To these must be added the increasingly systematic racism which found it inconceivable that an African monarch could have made military expeditions not merely to the Levant but to Asia Minor and Europe.

Thus, all the later discoveries that might have some bearing on the issue have been viewed in the 'knowledge' that the traditions concerning Sesōstris' northern campaigns were utterly absurd. If one questions this preconception, several pieces of evidence that were previously considered unrelated fit a relatively coherent pattern. These include the massive strength and great military sophistication of 12th-Dynasty armies revealed by their extraordinary fortifications in Nubia, the destructions quite possibly at the appropriate time in Anatolia and the Balkans, the Tôd Treasure of northern and eastern precious metals and jewels dedicated to Mont the god of northern conquest, and the inscriptions and reliefs from buildings dedicated to Senwosre I or his son Amenemḥet II.

The Mit Rahina inscription is not concerned with any possible Egyptian colonization in Greece. Even if interpreted in the broadest possible way and linked to the traditions about Sesōstris, it affects only the neighbouring regions of Anatolia and Thrace and not the Greek peninsula and archipelago themselves. Why then should it be examined in this work in this and the next chapters? The answer to the first question lies in its relation to the Ancient Model. The Mit Rahina inscription supports what is generally thought to be the most absurd set of stories told by Herodotos and Hellenistic Greek writers. If there are substantial elements of truth in these, the Ancient Model should be taken much more seriously in general.

The Mit Rahina inscription also demonstrates, specifically, that the Egyptians were not always the 'stay-at-home', conservative people they are usually thought to have been by proponents of the Aryan Model. Early this century, the classicist Paul Foucart had argued that the discovery of portrayals of the maritime expeditions under Queen Hashepsowe to Africa, found on reliefs at Deir el Bahri, had destroyed that image completely and that there was no reason why the Egyptians should have restricted this kind of enterprise to the south.[176] Supporters of the Aryan Model, unable to refute his point, ignored it. Now the Mit Rahina inscription with its reports of land *and sea* expeditions beyond Syro-Palestine raises this problem in a more acute form at a more propitious time when supporters of the Aryan Model can no longer maintain that they possess a monopoly of the 'scientific truth'.

Just as in the first four chapters it seemed necessary to set the archaeological evidence from Crete and Boiotia in a legendary, cultic and toponymic context, to examine the Mit Rahina inscription and its implications I have had to introduce more evidence from different sources, notably archaeology. Despite the lack of rigour in this eclectic procedure, I am convinced that the overall picture produced in this way indicates that – on this topic and presumably on others – we should have less faith in conventional wisdom and more trust in the Ancient Model. There is, however, another possible source of information which could test the Greek reports, that of myths, legends and folk memories in the ancient world. It is to these that I shall turn in the next chapter.

CHAPTER VI

Sesōstris, ii
The cultic, mythical
and legendary evidence

I N THIS CHAPTER I shall look at some cults, myths and traditions
in a number of cultures – Egypt, the Levant, Anatolia, Thrace,
Colchis on the eastern coast of the Black Sea and finally Greece –
to see if they contain elements that can be understood to refer to actual conquests by the historical Sesōstris.

I believe that there are a surprising number of such indications and
that, in fact, the supposition of such a historical conqueror would
make sense of many previously inexplicable features in a number of
traditions. This combines with the evidence from documents and archaeology, discussed in the last chapter, to make the idea of Sesōstris
as something like the figure portrayed by Herodotos, Manetho and
Diodoros if not certain, at least more likely than not. As these portraits are considered to be among the 'most fantastic' of their works,
the restoration of historicity to some if not the majority of the Egyptian conquests of the 12th Dynasty should have a significant positive
impact on the credibility of the Greek and Egyptian historians.

THE EGYPTIAN TRADITION

Whether or not one believes that the descriptions of Sesōstris given by
Herodotos, Diodoros and Manetho refer to a historical figure, no one
accuses these writers of having invented them. As we have seen, the
standard view is that they mix together traditions about Senwosres I
and III and Ramessēs II and lace these with oriental hyperbole. The

German Egyptologist Wilhelm Spiegelberg, whose lecture in 1925 is still seen as a defence of Herodotos, but who was fully imbued with the 19th- and 20-century spirit of condescension and *Besserwissen*, said:

> Among his [Herodotos'] tales are many that are purely Egyptian, for instance the famous story of the treasury of Rhampsinitus (ch. 121), or the legends of the world conqueror Sesōstris (chs. 102 ff.), under cover of whose name are enumerated the deeds of several Egyptian kings. They are so genuine in their local colouring, that they might have come straight out of an Egyptian papyrus and Maspero was quite right to include them in his delightful collection of Ancient Egyptian folktales.[1]

Thus, there is no difficulty in admitting that there were Egyptian stories about Sesōstris' vast conquests current during the 1st millennium BC. The fact that Sesōstris/Senwosre I was worshipped during the New Kingdom strongly suggests that the tradition of his special qualities was older still.[2] Posener even suggests that, as well as having a strong historical component, the legendary qualities of Sesōstris date back to the Middle Kingdom.[3] Despite the massive rebuilding programmes of later pharaohs, notably Ramessēs II, it is also likely that the Mit Rahina inscription and/or others like it were available for much of this period, not to mention the chronographies and chronicles written on papyrus.

In general it would seem that, when Herodotos and the later authors were writing, there had been a rich and continuous tradition about Sesōstris for some considerable time. It is also almost certain that Diodoros and/or his informants embroidered the tradition, presumably to keep up with Alexander, and that modern writers may well be right when they argue that the legends were inflated to satisfy competitive feelings against the Persians.[4] Nevertheless, there is little doubt that the core of the tradition was much older and that much of it came from sources contemporary to the Egyptian 'conquests' and was therefore subject to some check.

Thus, it would seem likely that a careful historian in the 5th century BC who wanted to report the truth about Sesōstris would have had the means to do so. Thus, the question to answer is whether Herodotos had the time or the inclination to do so? I believe, on the basis of most of what we know about his reporting on other areas, that the answer to both questions is 'yes'. The situation with the reports of Manetho and Diodoros is less clear but here too, despite the pressures of Egyptian nationalism during the Hellenistic period, there is no reason to dismiss them and their sources without checking counter or corroborative evidence.

Sesōstris and Osiris/Dionysos

There is another possible trace for Sesōstris' conquests in the Egyptian traditions of the world-wide conquests of Osiris. Diodoros reported that, according to the Egyptians, Osiris had left certain gods to rule Egypt and set out with an army of musicians and dancers. After going through Ethiopia and India, he

> took an interest in hunting elephants and everywhere left behind him inscribed pillars telling of his campaign. And he visited all the other nations of Asia as well and crossed into Europe at the Hellespont. In Thrace he slew Lycurgus. . . . Finally Osiris in this way visited all the inhabited world and advanced community life by the introduction of the fruits that are most easily cultivated. And if any country did not admit of the growing of the vine he introduced the drink prepared from barley. . . . On his return to Egypt he brought with him the very greatest presents from every quarter and by reason of the magnitude of his benefactions received the gift of immortality with the approval of all men and honour equal to that offered to the gods in heaven.[5]

Over a century later, around 100 AD, Plutarch wrote along the same lines:

> One of the first acts related of Osiris in his reign was to deliver the Egyptians from their destitute and brutish manner of living. This he did by showing them the fruits of cultivation, by giving them laws and by teaching them to honour the gods. Later he travelled over the whole earth civilising it without the slightest need of arms, but most of the peoples he won to his way by the charm of his persuasive discourse combined with song and all manner of music. Hence the Greeks came to identify him with Dionysos.[6]

The first problem encountered in considering these passages is their antiquity. Just as in Diodoros' descriptions of the conquests of Sesōstris, the references to India and riding elephants show that the accounts of Osiris have clearly been influenced by Alexander. On the other hand, as seen in Volume 1, the stories of the world conquests of Osiris' Greek counterpart Dionysos antedate Alexander, and the traditions of Osiris' conquests go back at least to the 18th Dynasty.[7] Thus, the parallel traditions can only have originated in Egypt.

It is clear that these stories contain aetiological myths for the origins and spread of agriculture and civilization, as well as for the foundation of orgiastic fertility cults. The conquests are less easy to explain but the structural similarities between Diodoros' description of them and of those of Sesōstris suggest that the latter may have provided the inspiration for the former.

This leads us to the problem of euhemerism. In Volume 1, I used this term in the commonly used sense of the turning of gods or spirits into mortals.[8] I now see that this was very much in the spirit of *Besserwissen*, that is to say knowing better than Euhemeros, when he said that the gods were apotheoses of great men.[9] However, there are many examples to justify the modern reversal of the ancient idea described in Volume 1 and it is clear that the 'rationalization' of mythical beings into 'historical' figures is a relatively common process, which goes back a long way. In this case, it is interesting to note that the tradition that Osiris – and other gods – were originally kings of Egypt is attested in the *Turin Canon* from the 19th Dynasty.[10] On the other hand, we know that many pharaohs and later monarchs deified their predecessors or themselves and there is the argument I made in Chapter II on the influence of Middle Kingdom pharaohs on Greek heroes. Thus, mortals sometimes became gods in the way Euhemeros described.[11]

If the actual conquests of Senwosre/Sesōstris were the model for the mythical ones of Osiris/Dionysos, we should have a good example of euhemerization in the original sense. There is, however, no reason why the two processes should be mutually exclusive and it was quite possible for mortals to become gods and vice versa. In fact, this particular historic and mythical cycle would seem to provide an excellent example of this two-way process. The splendid reign and conquests of the deified Senwosre merge with the attributes of Osiris/Dionysos. The latter's mythical conquests and spreading of civilization became an inspiration for Alexander the Great whose actual achievements embellish both the legends around Sesōstris and the myths about Osiris/Dionysos, as well as beginning a whole new cycle of myths and legends.[12] Thus, in Egypt there would seem to have been two related but distinct traditions based on Senwosre's conquests, the first claiming to be historical and the second a mythical association with Osiris.

Sesōstris did not influence the life and legend of Alexander merely indirectly through Osiris/Dionysos. There is clear evidence of direct influence. This can be seen, for instance, in the *Alexander Romance* – the first in the massive tradition of legendary embroidery on Alexander's life – the earliest versions of which were written in Egypt not long after the Macedonian's death in 323 BC.[13] In this, Alexander is supposed to have encountered the great Egyptian conqueror Sensonchōsis during a vision in an Ethiopian cave. The name Sensonchōsis was taken from the first pharaoh of the 22nd Dynasty 945–730 BC called Shōshenk and Sechōnsis or Sesonchōsis by Greek writers, and Shishak, in the Bible, who conducted campaigns in Palestine and Syria. However, there is no doubt that the name and the attributes became confused or merged with those of Sesōstris. Manetho, for instance, used the names alternately.[14] At another point, Alexander was explicitly called the 'new Sesonchōsis' and when Alexander's body was brought to Memphis he was received as "Sesonchōsis Demigod Ruler of the World'.[15] There is, in fact, no reason to doubt the historicity of these epithets. In general, there are many parallels between the *Alexander Romance* and a *Sesonchōsis Romance* outlining the vast achievements of the Egyptian conqueror. Both of these romances were extremely popular in Ptolemaic and Roman Egypt and almost certainly elsewhere as well.[16]

THE TRADITIONS OF THE LEVANT AND ANATOLIA

No Levantine or Anatolian texts report Sesōstris' or any other Egyptian 'conquests' there. Nevertheless, there are indications of traditions and folk memories which could well refer to them.

The most impressive of these is the emergence in the 18th and 17th centuries BC of the image of a striking god armed with a hammer or axe and wearing the ⟨, *ḥdt*, white crown of Upper Egypt, or the ⟨, *shmty*, double crown of Upper and Lower Egypt. At times, however, this is combined with symbolic horns which have an older Mesopotamian tradition.[17] While the imagery is clearly largely Egyptian, the figures are associated with the local thunder gods Baʿal and Tessub and Tarkhun.

These figures are also identified with the Canaanite god Reshef, god of thunder and disease. This foreign god was incorporated into the Egyptian pantheon during the 18th Dynasty, but Reshef appears as a divine element of names in the Middle Kingdom. It is also possible that his name, which is difficult to explain in West Semitic, derives from the Egyptian, Ḥry š.f, Arsaphes in Greek (On his lake), whose association with Herakles has been mentioned in Chapter II, as has the fact that there has been some confusion between Ḥry š.f and Reshef in the dedication of a temple to the Egyptian god at Byblos.[18] It is fascinating to note that, after Reshef's adoption into the Egyptian pantheon, he was particularly linked to Mont, whom we have seen above to have been associated with northern conquest and whose Greek counterpart was – if my hypothesis on this is right – the Cretan ruler Rhadamanthys, a stepfather of Herakles.[19]

In a stela from Ramessēs II, there is the passage: 'His Majesty crossed the Orontes [in North Syria] over the tempestuous waters like Reshef.'[20] Thus there would seem little doubt that, in Egyptian eyes at least, Reshef was associated with royal conquest of the north – directly through the pharaoh and Mont – and indirectly through Ḥry š.f and Herakles.

The theological identification is also apparent in the iconography. The 'striking god' figures are strongly reminiscent of Middle Kingdom representations of the pharaoh striking down foreigners.[21] Edith Porada, the expert on seals, admits a similarity between representations of Sesōstris I dancing at his Heb Sed or jubilee festival and that of a Syro-Palestinian weather god found at Tell el Dabaʿa from a century or two later. But she claims that there are important differences in that

the heel of the king's backward foot is raised from the ground, whereas the weather god's feet are placed flat above the mountains on which he stands. Moreover, the upright torso of the Egyptian king appears unmoved by the wide stride of his legs, whereas the torso of the weather god is slightly inclined forward.[22]

Nevertheless, the parallels are noteworthy.

Such Levantine figures are not attested from the third millennium and therefore probably cannot be attributed to the influence of the Egyptian Old Kingdom. On the other hand, they are well established before the New Kingdom conquests in Syria in the 15th century. Thus, although the image of the powerful godlike destructive pharaoh may well have been intensified by the activities of Tuthmōsis III in the 15th and Ramessēs II in the 13th centuries BC, it cannot have been created as a result of them. It is possible that the Hittite tall pointed hat was influenced by the *ḥdt* or the *ʒtf* 𓋔 (crowns) even though the shapes are very different. Even without this link, however, the emergence of an image of a striking god with the characteristics of an Egyptian pharaoh at this particular time could be conveniently explained if Sesōstris had campaigned in these regions.

In this respect, it is worth repeating part of Herodotos' report quoted earlier:

Most of the memorial pillars which King Sesōstris erected in conquered countries have disappeared, but I have seen some myself in Palestine, with the inscription I mentioned and the drawing of a woman's genitals. In Ionia also there are two images of Sesōstris cut on rock, one on the road from Ephesos to Phocaea, the other between Sardis and Smyrna; in each case the carved figure is nearly seven feet high and represents a man with a spear in his right hand and a bow in his left, and the rest of his equipment to match – partly Egyptian partly Ethiopian. Across the breast from shoulder to shoulder runs an inscription, cut in the Egyptian sacred script: *by the strength of my shoulders I won this land.* The name and country of the conqueror are not here recorded.[23]

This is to the south of Mellaart's belt of destructions but, since he wrote, another destruction of the same period has been discovered at Aphrodisias, inland from Miletos about midway along the west coast of Anatolia.[24] Thus, given the assumption that Sesōstris made conquests in Anatolia, it is possible that he could have left monuments there. On the other hand, it is almost certain that the reliefs were not Egyptian but Hittite; one such has been identified precisely on the road from Ephesos to Phokaea. There is, however, an Egyptian connection in that the royal figure is wearing the Hittite tall hat, which could well have been derived from the Egyptian crown and is holding a 'flail', a typical Egyptian emblem of royalty.[25]

As with the Egyptian stories of Sesōstris, I think it unlikely that Herodotos invented the Egyptian connection with the reliefs. It is much more likely that he was following local West Anatolian or Ionian Greek traditions to that effect.

Toponyms provide another source of evidence for Egyptian influence in Anatolia. Sinope on its northern coast was confused in Hellenistic times with Se(s-t)-n Hʿpy (Place of the Nile god Hʿpy) near Memphis. This led to the view that the obviously Egyptian composite god Serapis had been brought from Sinope in Pontos in Anatolia. Here, however, there was also punning with S-t n Ḥp, the Temple of the bull god Apis, at Mephis. We have seen paranomasia or confusion between the two names Ḥp and Hʿpy in the discussion of Danaos and the *Suppliants* in Volume 1.[26] Thus, the Anatolian name could well be Egyptian in origin.

An even more striking example is the city of Abydos at the key narrows of the Hellespont, which in ancient times was seen as identical with the Egyptian ꜣbdw, Abydos in Greek transcription, the name of the religious centre, famous for its tomb of Osiris. The name of Byzantium on the European side of the Bosphoros is a mystery but, according to Nonnos, the learned Hellenized Egyptian of the 5th century AD, Byzas (the eponym and founder of the city) was similar to Kadmos and his brothers: Kilix, eponym of Cilicia in Southeastern Anatolia, and Thasos, that of Thasos in the Northern Aegean, both of whom settled down after giving up their search for their sister Europa:

For another man also who carried his home upon his back, one of the divine stock of Iō, a heavenly sprout dropt from Zeus, named Byzas, who had drunk the seven-mouth water of the self-begotten Nile, inhabited the neighbouring land, where along the Bosporos shore flows the water once traversed by the Inachian heifer. To those who dwelt about he showed a light, when he turned about the neck of that mad bull unbending.[27]

As usual with ancient poetry, this passage is full of learned allusion and double meanings. The 'light' would seem to refer to the city of *Lamp*sakhos at the head of the Hellespont. The intricate connections between Iō, the cows, the Nile and Inachos have been discussed in Volume 1.[28] Here it should be added that the Bosphoros was traditionally seen as the place of 'bull carrying', over which Zeus, as a bull, carried Europa to the west; he is clearly the 'mad bull' referred to. It is just conceivable that this may also contain an allusion to Sesōstris as the personification of the patron deity of the Egyptian northern expedition, the bull god Mont.

Byzas himself seems to parallel another mythological figure – Phineus – a son of Agenor and brother of Kadmos who settled at the same place as Byzas on Cape Thynia, which separates the Sea of Marmora from the Black Sea. The derivation of Phineus and Peneus from the Egyptian pȝ nw(y) (the [masc.] water or the flood) was discussed in Chapter III.[29] In this case, the parallel between Phineus and Thynia can be explained by deriving the latter from Tȝ nwt (the [fem.] stretch of water), a toponym attested in Egypt itself.[30] These would seem altogether suitable names for the Golden Horn through which the voyager from the Mediterranean enters the Black Sea.

This toponymic evidence is made very uncertain by the fact that, even if these names were ultimately Egyptian, it is impossible to tell at what stage or by whom they were introduced. They could date back to Sesōstris' 'conquests' but equally or more likely they could come from later contacts, either directly or through Phoenicians or Greeks aware of the principles of Egyptian toponymy. By Classical times it is clear that Egyptian influences were felt along the coast, since cities from Mytelene on Lesbos to Lampsakos and Kyzikos on the southern shore of the Sea of Marmora all issued coins with the head of Ammon.[31] The only name which does appear to point to Egyptian influence at precisely the period with which we are concerned is that of the tomb of Memnōn on the shores of the Sea of Marmora, and this will be discussed below.

The same ambiguity on timing holds for the striking religious

parallels between Egypt and Northwest Anatolia, notably those concerning the dying fertility gods – the Egyptian Osiris, the Semitic
Adonis and the Phrygian Attis of North Anatolia – which will be discussed in some detail in Volume 3.[32] Herodotos tells the story of the two
children brought up without hearing any speech (on the instruction of
the pharaoh Psammetekhos) whose first word was *bekos*, the Phrygian
for 'bread', thus *proving* that Phrygian was the oldest language in the
world – even older than Egyptian.[33] According to modern linguistics,
Phrygian is an Indo-European language – in the narrow sense of the
term – and far more recent than Egyptian. Nevertheless, it is interesting that Phrygia could have been seen as a competitor to Egypt's antiquity. A plausible reason for this would be the similarities between the
religions of the two countries. Here, too, there is the question of when
the Egyptian influence originated. A short and violent invasion by
Sesōstris would seem rather unpropitious for this. Nevertheless, unlike the place names for which we have no way of determining a chronology, the Anatolian cults do appear to have been very ancient and
very probably date to the 2nd millennium, so that contact in the 20th
century BC would be quite possible.

THRACE AND SCYTHIA

Further Northwest Anatolian traditions concerning an Egyptian conquest in the 20th century BC will be discussed with those from Greece
later in this chapter. Meanwhile, we shall glance at traces of Egyptian
influence on the other side of the Bosphoros in Thrace.

Herodotos and later authors wrote about the Thracian cults of Dionysos among remote tribal groups called Satrai and Bessoi.[34] I shall
argue in Volume 4 that the name Satrai, like Satyroi, is derived from a
form *Snṯrw from the Egyptian verb *snṯr* (consecrate); similarly, the
name Bessoi can be plausibly derived from an Egyptian *Bsw (initiates)
from the verb *bs* (initiate). I shall also propose that other Thracian divine names, such as Bendis and Sebazios, may well have Egyptian origins and will draw attention to the parallels between the Thracian and
Egyptian aspects of Orphism. I should add that I am not the first to
see these parallels. A number of scholars have referred to a 'Libyan,
Thracian substratum' to explain the many parallels they have seen between the Thraco-Phrygians and Africa, but these would seem to me
more plausibly explained as the results of Egyptian influences.[35]

As with the cultic parallels with Phrygia, however, it is difficult to
date such influences. The cult of Osiris, from which that of Dionysos
seems to have been derived, was flourishing in the 12th Dynasty, as
was the cult of Ammon from which came, I believe, the ram cults asso-

ciated with Zeus. These then could have been introduced at the time of the 'conquests'. Many of the other Egyptian elements, like the cults of Bes, god of initiations, and Geb/Orpheus, would seem to come from much later periods, when we know from the striking of coins in Thrace with the head of Ammon that there was Egyptian cultic influence.[36] The idea of such influence in the early 1st millennium BC would tally well with the considerable Phoenician presence in the Northern Aegean in this period, which can be demonstrated, historically, archaeologically and toponymically as well as through cultic parallels. The Phoenicians, then as in other millennia, absorbed and promoted much Egyptian civilization.[37] Thus, although there is clear evidence of Egyptian cultural influence on Thrace, it is impossible to show that any of it goes back to the beginning of the 2nd millennium and Sesōstris' conquests.

There are, to my knowledge, no traditions concerning Sesōstris or Egyptians of any sort in Scythia in South Russia. Even if the African army had passed through, it is unlikely that folk memories could have been preserved, given the political turmoil in the Steppe and the complete absence of written records for the next two millenniums. However, the situation is very different on the eastern side of the Black Sea.

COLCHIS: AN EGYPTIAN COLONY?

Colchis is an area of long cultural and linguistic continuity. Two types of Caucasian languages – Kartvelian, of which Georgian is the best-known member, and Abkhaz, one of the Northwest Caucasian languages – have been spoken there since the earliest times. The only major shift to have taken place was the breakthrough, during the period of Arab domination in the 9th century AD, of the inland Iberian-Georgians of the mountains to the coast; this left the original West-Kartvelian–speaking inhabitants of subtropical coastal Colchis both in the south and to the north, where they mingled with Abkhaz speakers.[38] However, more recent linguistic groups – Armenian, Iranian and Turkish – are also present. Partly as a function of its continuity and partly because of many migrations through the Caucasus, but essentially because of its geographical isolation in the mountainous country, the region seems always to have been one of extraordinary linguistic variety. In the 1st century BC Strabo reported that seventy different tribes mingled in the markets of Dioskyrias, the modern Sukhumi.[39] On the coast, this mixture is reflected today in the extraordinary variety of physical types, which Lang plausibly sees as the result of 'several millennia of ethnic mingling'.[40]

With this background in mind, we should return to Herodotos' description of Sesōstris' conquests:

> On his way back Sesōstris came to the river Phasis, and it is quite possible that he here detached a body of troops from his army and left them behind to settle – or, on the other hand, it may be that some of his men were sick of their travels and deserted. I cannot say with certainty which supposition is the right one, but it is undoubtedly a fact that the Colchians are of Egyptian descent. I noticed myself before I heard anyone else mention it, and when it occurred to me I asked some questions both in Colchis and in Egypt, and found that the Colchians remembered the Egyptians more distinctly than the Egyptians remembered them. The Egyptians did, however, say that they thought that the original Colchians were men from Sesōstris' army.[41]

Jason and the Golden Fleece:
evidence for a Black population in Colchis

By far the best-known Greek tradition concerning the Black Sea region was that of Jason's search for the Golden Fleece. This was set forth most coherently by Apollonios Rhodios in his *Argonautika,* written in the Egyptian Alexandria in the 3rd century BC. The legend begins with a father, King Athamas of Orkhomenos in Boiotia, reluctantly offering his children Phrixos and Helle to Zeus on the top of a mountain. Zeus then sent a ram to save them, and it took them on its back across the Hellespont – where Helle dropped off – and the Black Sea to Colchis. There the ram was sacrificed and his golden fleece was preserved until Jason stole it.

Michael Astour has demonstrated the striking and intricate parallels between this story and that of the *Akedah,* or Abraham's binding or offering of Isaac. Astour convincingly maintains that the Athamas legend is the result of Semitic influence on Greece.[42] However, the great champion of diffusionism, R. A. Jairazbhoy, points out the importance of the themes of rams and their fleeces in Egyptian religion and refers to the following passage in Herodotos. After explaining why the Thebans, whose god was the ram Amon, never sacrifice rams, the historian went on to say:

> Nevertheless on the festival of Zeus [Amon] which occurs once a year they break this custom and do, in fact, slaughter a ram, but only one. They cut the animal in pieces, skin it and put the fleece on the statue of Zeus, just as Zeus once put it upon himself.[43]

In his detailed commentary on this passage, Lloyd concludes that Herodotos' description of this ritual was 'probably correct'.[44] The close and intricate relations between Amon, Zeus and rams will be discussed in Volume 4. The only further point I should like to mention here is that there is a tradition, first attested in Thebes in the New Kingdom, but probably going back to the Middle Kingdom, of Amon as a ram and oracle.[45] This leads us back to Colchis where Strabo reports that at the oracle founded by Phrixos a ram was never sacrificed.[46]

The parallels between the traditions surrounding the Colchian ram/fleece and the Egyptian cults of Amon as a ram would seem to be extremely close. Jairazbhoy draws attention to the passage in the *Argonautika* which describes the fleece being guarded by a serpent. He relates this to images of Amon-Re' of a royal ram's head of Amon surmounted by the solar disk and uraeus with a snake's head of Re'. However, if they are related, it would seem to indicate later influence as this writing of Re' has been found only from the 18th Dynasty and the example given by Jairazbhoy comes from the 19th.[47] In general, as with the Anatolian cults, there is no indication when these putative Egyptian influences arrived.

Ostensibly, Jason was supposed to have sailed in the 13th century BC.[48] Whether or not the legend has any historicity, it belongs to the earliest epic cycles and surviving writings. Hesiod, who was writing in the 10th century BC, refers to both Phrixos and the Golden Fleece.[49] Thus, the tradition goes back at least to this time.

It is, of course, impossible to assess Apollonios' accuracy in his reports of Colchis. Nevertheless, Lang has written: 'It is remarkable how many details in the *Argonautica* corroborate the findings of archaeology, as well as the scattered references in the Hittite, Assyrian and Urartian sources.' Lang then goes on to give specifics on the peoples the Argonauts encountered on their way to Colchis. He is even more emphatic on the ways in which Soviet excavations have confirmed Apollonios' descriptions of Colchis itself.[50]

Thus, the ancient writer's descriptions of the Southern and Eastern Black Sea seem reliable not merely in his own time but for many centuries before. Whether this is true of his reports of Colchian traditions referring to events 1,600 years earlier is another story. Nevertheless, it would be foolish to dismiss out of hand the following passage from the epic about the history of Colchis or Aea:

> Think of a time when the wheeling constellations did not yet exist; when one would have looked in vain for the sacred Danaan race, finding only the Apidanaean Arkadians, who are said to have lived before the moon itself was there, feeding on acorns on the hills.

These were the days before the scions of the noble Deukalion ruled
the Pelasgian land, when Egypt mother of an earlier race was
known as the corn rich country of the dawn, and the Nile that
waters all its length was called the Triton, a generous river flowing
through a rainless land yet by its floods producing crops in plenty.
Now we are told that from this country a certain king set out, supported by a strong and loyal force, and made his way through the
whole of Europe and Asia, founding many cities as he went. Some
of these survive though others have succumbed to the burden of
the years. But to this day Aea stands with people in it descended
from the very men whom that king had settled there.[51]

This passage is full of interest. 'The wheeling constellations' seems to
refer to the precession of the equinoxes and the 'great year' of some
26,000 solar years.[52] Like Plato's dating of Atlantis, this and Apollonios'
other astronomical references seem to be a combination of mathematical symbolism and poetic hyperbole used to refer to a period before
the beginning of the oldest Greek tradition. The choice of the name
Triton for the Nile will be discussed below. The Api- in 'Apidanaan'
would appear to refer to the esoteric name for the Peloponnese, the
intricate Egyptian origins of which were discussed in Volume 1.[53]

The references to the Egyptian king who 'made his way through the
whole of Europe and Asia' have long been seen as referring to Sesōstris.[54] What we therefore need to consider is whether Apollonios
based this on Herodotos' reports of the Egyptian colonization of Colchis, supplemented from contemporary Egyptian fictional material,
or whether he was referring directly to a historical tradition.

As stated above, Apollonios lived most of his life in Alexandria.
What is more, he was considered learned enough to be appointed director of the great library there. The accuracy of his other reports on
the Black Sea region shows he knew a good deal about it, independently of Herodotos. Thus, I think it is likely that both men were reporting a real Colchian tradition that their city had been colonized
from Egypt. Whether there was any truth to it or whether it was
merely an attempt by a remote people to provide themselves with a
central and ancient heritage is much more difficult to say.

Herodotos believed that he had found independent confirmation
of this claim:

My own idea on the subject was based first on the fact that they have
black skins and woolly hair (not that that amounts to much, as other
nations have the same), and secondly, and more especially, on the
fact that the Colchians, the Egyptians, and the Ethiopians are the

only races which from ancient times have practised circumcision. The Phoenicians and the Syrians of Palestine themselves admit that they adopted the practice from Egypt, and the Syrians who live near the rivers Thermodon and Parthenius, as well as their neighbours the Macronians say they learnt it only a short while ago from the Colchians. . . .

And now I think of it, there is a further point of resemblance between the Colchians and Egyptians: they share a method of weaving linen different from that of any other people; and there is also a similarity between them in language and way of living. The linen made in Greece is known as Sardonian linen; that which comes from Egypt is called Egyptian.[55]

It is interesting to note that this manufacture of linen was also a characteristic of the shores of the Kopais where, as we have seen in Chapters II and III, there are strong suggestions of Egyptian influence.[56] Nevertheless, there is no way of telling at what date the technique spread to Boiotia and Colchis, even if it was a case of diffusion. Unfortunately also, Herodotos' statements of Colchian linen and the distribution of circumcision, which are in themselves of the utmost importance, are impossible to check.

There is, however, some fascinating evidence on the blackness. Herodotos was not the only ancient writer to refer to it. His older contemporary Pindar referred to Jason's expedition attacking the dark-skinned Colchians. Some later writers also refer to the darkness of the Colchians, although they could have been influenced by Herodotos on this.[57]

Physical anthropology provides no help. The population of the mountains inhabited by Ibero-Georgians shows considerable physical continuity. It was, as Georgians are today, brachycephalic, 'short-skulled', or hyperbrachycephalic, which is typically Caucasian. By contrast, the coastline of Colchis shows a considerable mixture, including some dolichocephalic, 'long-skulled', types which could be from Africa.[58] The Abkhaz linguist and ethnographer Dmitri Gulia, who believes that the Colchians had Abyssino-Egyptian origins, claims to have found traces of Egyptian influence in Abkhaz geographical, divine and personal names.[59]

The most tantalizing evidence of all is the existence in the 20th century AD of a Black African population around Sukhumi in Abkhazia, to the north of the ancient Colchis. It is clear that some of these Blacks came as slaves from Africa when Abkhazia was part of the Turkish Empire, from the 16th to the 18th centuries AD. However, the community, which still seems to survive despite Soviet attempts to dissipate it through intermarriage and dispersion, has deep roots in the region and most of its members speak nothing but Abkhaz.[60]

The debate as to whether some of the Blacks are descendants of those Herodotos saw has been going on in Russian and Georgian scholarship for more than a century. More recently, an American writer, Patrick English, has supported this contention in an erudite and important – if uncritical – article. In this, he shows that a belief in a Black population in Colchis was still present in the writings of St. Jerome and Sophronius around the end of the 4th century AD, that is over eight hundred years after Herodotos.[61] This reduces the gap between the ancient and modern reports of Blacks in the region to about twelve hundred years which, given the persistence of other small groups in the Caucasus, makes continuity possible. On the other hand, it is equally possible that the subtropical climate of Colchis made it attractive to Africans at different periods.

Spiritual geography

Let us now look at a very intricate set of what one might call 'sacred' or 'spiritual-geographical' parallels between Egypt and Colchis. To do this we should return to the passage from Apollonios:

> These were the days before the scions of the noble Deukalion ruled the Pelasgian land, when Egypt mother of an earlier race was known as the corn rich country of the dawn, and the Nile that waters all its length was called the Tritōn, a generous river flowing through a rainless land yet by its floods producing crops in plenty.[62]

As we have seen in Chapter II, the name Tritōn seems to have been linked to the Egyptian *tryt* (respect) and was the name given to a number of river systems in Libya. Tritōn was possibly a son of Poseidon.[63] Apollonios continued:

> But to this day Aea stands, with people in it descended from the very men whom that king settled there. Moreover they have preserved tablets of stone which their ancestors engraved with maps giving the outlines of the land and sea and the roots in all directions. On these is shown a river the furthest branch of the Ocean Stream broad and deep enough to carry merchantmen. They placed it at a great distance from Aea, giving it the name of Ister [generally accepted as the Danube]. Far away beyond the North Wind, its headwaters come rushing down from the Rhipaean mountains.

Then it flows for a time through endless plains as a single stream, but when it reaches the borderlands of Thrace and Scythia it divides one branch running down into the Ionian [Black] Sea the other [the Rhone?] flowing south into a deep gulf that stretches up from the Sicilian Sea – a sea that washes your own shores if I am right in thinking that the river Achelous flows into it from Hellas.[64]

From this point on the *Argonautika* changes from a relatively staid and precise itinerary along the Black Sea into a mad rush across Europe and the Mediterranean. Clearly the cosmological aspects of the poem have transcended the geographical.

The references here to the two great rivers, the Nile and the Danube, are significant. In the next chapter, I shall argue that the Egyptian name ỉtrw for the Nile and the great water or 'ocean' around the world, which I believe appears in Greek as the root Atla-, is found not merely in 'Atlantic' but also as a name for the Danube. But in this passage, as in his poem as a whole, Apollonios is referring to a geography that is simultaneously real, celestial, infernal and spiritual in the sense that the souls of the dead have to navigate through it.

The most detailed description of this kind of geography comes in the *Phaedo*, where Plato reports of Sokrates' last speech on his death and immortality:

I believe that the earth is very large and that we who dwell between the Pillars of Hercules and the river Phasis live in a small part of it about the sea, like ants or frogs about a pond, and that many other people live in many other such regions.[65]

Crudely put on the geographical plain, the cosmology is self-consciously limited. It is centred on the Mediterranean and Black Sea basins into which four or more great rivers pour water from the heavenly or terrestial ocean surrounding it. The mystery of solar evaporation in the Mediterranean was explained in terms of a flow into 'the lowest abyss beneath the earth', as Plato quoted Homer.[66] The four streams generally include the Nile from the south, the inflow from the Atlantic through the Pillars of Herakles from the west, the Danube [and/or the Rhone and Po] from the north and the Phasis from the East.

Kȝš and Colchis: an Egyptian derivation?

Given that the land up the Nile from Egypt and the rich valley of the river Phasis in Colchis were two of the extreme points of 'this earth' and that they seem to have been inhabited by Blacks, could these two territories have shared the same name Kȝš/Kolkhis (Colchis)? Before examining this, however, I want to look at a few examples which show that Egyptian toponymy on the Black Sea is not impossible. I have already mentioned the cases of Sinope and Abydos, but there is another even more striking example.

The name Pontos was given in Classical times to the Black Sea as well as to the northern coast of Anatolia and the southern coast of Russia. It was also one of the many Greek words for 'sea'. It is conventionally thought to derive from an Indo-European root, √pent (to walk, way), from which among many others we obtain the Latin *pons–pontis*, 'bridge' and our 'path.' Although, it will be argued below, it is more common for even maritime peoples to see the sea as a barrier or a frontier, and there is no analogy in Indo-European for the root being used in this way, there is no reason why a sea should not be viewed as a 'path' or 'passage'. Indeed this would fit very well with the Helles*pont*, linking the Aegean and Black seas.

However, its use for the land on either side of the Pontos (the Black Sea) presents a problem. In this respect there would seem to be a better parallel with the Egyptian place name Pwnt. This was a country reached by sea travel down the Red Sea and Indian Ocean from which tropical products were brought to Egypt. Although there is no record of the name having been used for a northern locality, it was standard in Egyptian cosmology and toponymy for places to exist in matching pairs. In Greek and Roman geography the frequent *coincidentiae oppositorum* were usually east and west;[67] we shall see this below in the case of the two Ethiopias. In Egypt, however, set along the axis of the Nile, the opposition was usually north–south. Nearly every city of Lower Egypt had its namesake in Upper Egypt. The same was sometimes true for external place names; see, for example, the northern and southern Stts, mentioned above. Similarly, the territory Tȝ ntr (Holy Land) either stretched from Anatolia to East Africa or it represented another southern and a northern pair.

In this way, the idea of a Kȝš or a Pwnt in both the remote south and the remote north would seem very possible, even though they are not attested and therefore cannot be used as independent evidence. Nevertheless, they provide more depth to the overall pattern suggesting Egyptian involvement in the region.

The etymology of the name Colchis or Kolchis is unknown. It could come from Chalk-, seen in the place names Chalkis or Chalkidike coming from the root Chalk-, 'bronze' or 'metal' in general, which is, I believe, derived from the Semitic root √ḥlq (smooth, make smooth, forge, fabricate).[68] Given the kingdom's famous mineral resources and metallurgy, Colchis could come from either the Semitic or the Greek forms of this word and it could also come from any of the many languages spoken in the West Caucasus.

However, there is another possibility. St. Jerome and Sophronius in the 4th century AD referred to Colchis as 'a second Ethiopia'. Thus, it could be that the name Kolchis came from K3š, the Egyptian name for Upper Nubia on the Egyptian southern frontier. The Hebrew rendering of this was Kûš, translated in the Septuagint as Xous, Khus or Aithiopia. The early value of ꜣ as a liquid r or l has been frequently mentioned above. As there was a frequent interchange between š and ḫ in Egyptian and other languages and the Hebrew vocalization suggests a back vowel o or u, the phonetic fit of *Kolš/ḫ with Kolchis is excellent.

If one accepts an Egyptian etymology, the form Kolchis would suggest the Middle Kingdom form of K3š in which the ꜣ was sounded as a liquid r or l rather than the New Kingdom pronunciation preserved in the Hebrew Kûš. Thus, it would point to the 12th Dynasty – the only period before the New Kingdom when it is likely that Egyptian political and cultural influence spread so far north. Semantically, both Nubia and Colchis shared a rich production of gold and had climatic similarities, in that K3š was lush after the desert reaches of Lower Nubia; even today it has slight but significant rainfall.

The Blacks of Colchis and Elam

The possibility that K3š and Colchis are a south–north pair is hugely complicated by the fact that many modern scholars maintain that, while the biblical name Kûš generally referred to Nubia or Ethiopia, it was also used for two other regions and their peoples: the Midianites in Western Arabia and the Kaššû or Kassites to the east of Mesopotamia who controlled Mesopotamia for much of the middle of the 2nd millennium.[69]

There do, in fact, seem to have been two independent similar names. In both cases, however, they would seem to have been for dark or black peoples. Thus, Kûš became a generic title for them. In this way, it was used for the darker Midianites to the southeast of Canaan, many of whom, like the South Arabians of today, resembled Somalis and other Northeast Africans.

The Kassites, who originated on the fringe of Mesopotamia, are an elusive people. In order to try to place them it is necessary to consider the major independent civilization of Elam. The Elamites inhabited Susiana – the modern Khuzistan in Iran – the plain to the east of the

Tigris, as well as parts of the Iranian highlands before the arrival of the Iranian speakers in the 2nd millennium BC.[70] It is now almost certain that Elamite belongs to the Greater Dravidian language family.[71] It is also likely that many of its speakers were 'South Indian' in appearance and therefore darker than the peoples to the west. There may even have been negro or 'negritic' types in the population.[72] Professor Hinz, the doyen of Elamite studies, writes about the glazed brick reliefs of Elamite bodyguards of the Persian king Darius around 500 BC:

> Some guards are white-skinned and are obviously intended to represent Persians, although in Elamite garb. A second group is brown-skinned and a third is very dark, almost black. These must be Elamites from the hinterland. Even today dark-skinned men, in no way negroid, are seen in Khuzistan.[73]

Herodotos, writing about the same army twenty years after these reliefs, may well have been referring to upland Elamites when he wrote:

> The Eastern Ethiopians – for there were two sorts of Ethiopians in the army – served with the Indians. These were just like the southern Ethiopians, except for their language and their hair: their hair is straight, while that of the Ethiopians in Libya is the crispest and curliest in the world.[74]

Note the clear distinction he made between their hair and the tight curls of the Kolchians, upon which he laid such great stress. This makes it extremely unlikely that he was referring to the latter here.

The tradition of two Ethiopias is much older than Herodotos. In the *Odyssey* the Ethiopians are described as dwelling 'sundered in twain, the farthermost of men, some where Hyperion sets and some where he rises'.[75] Thus, there were Black men, Aithiopes (the name means 'burnt face'), from Western Libya (Africa) to Eastern Mesopotamia.

Were the two Ethiopias paralleled by two Kûss? The attempt by some writers to link the name Khuz – as in Khuzistan (Elam) – with Kûš is possible but implausible. Nevertheless, there are links between Elam and the name Kûš. Herodotos wrote, describing Aristagoras of Miletos looking at a map of the provinces of the Persian Empire, 'Again, further East lies Kissia, you can see the Choaspes marked, with Susa on its banks'.[76] This Kissia is also referred to by Strabo. There is only one possible local attestation of the name, the modern river name Kashghan in Khuzistan/Elam. However, Hinz attributes this to Kassite influence.[77]

Let us therefore, return to the Kassites. They were called Kaššû in Akkadian and Kuššû in its Nuzi dialect. The Greek version was

Kossaioi, which the Mesopotamian and biblical specialist E. A. Speiser claimed indicated that it contained the same back vowel of the biblical Kûš. However, the people seem to have called themselves Galzu, Galdu or Galšu – hence the Akkadian Kaššû – indicating an a.[78]

The geographical origin of the Kassites is extraordinarily difficult to locate, beyond saying that they came from the mountain rim of Mesopotamia.[79] However, their later stronghold was in the Zagros Mountains to the east of Mesopotamia and therefore they were close to Elam and definitely within the sphere of Elamite influence. There seems little doubt that in later times there were Kassites in Elam, although scholars debate whether there are Elamite traces in what little can be found of their language.[80] On the other hand, the 'blackness' of many Elamites leaves open the possibility that Kassites themselves may have been seen as Black. The question must remain moot.

The biblical Mesopotamian conqueror Nimrod the Mighty should also be considered in this context. He was specifically called a son of Kûš.[81] Speiser, who is still considered the major authority on this field, dismissed outright the theories of Eduard Meyer and Kurt Sethe that Nimrod could have been an Egyptian. Sethe had proposed a derivation of the conqueror's name from Nibmuaria, an attested cuneiform transcription of Nb Mȝʿt, a name of Amenhōphis III, who certainly had political if not military power in Mesopotamia.[82]

I agree with the earlier scholars that, despite the existence of an Eastern Kûš, one should not dismiss an African connection so peremptorily. However, I believe that the title Nb r-dt (Lord of the Universe), which was given to Senwosre I, is a more attractive derivation, as the ambitious title to which few gods were entitled was especially appropriate for a ruler described in the Bible as 'a man of might on earth' and known for his arrogance in setting himself up as a god.[83]

Nb r-dr is certainly more plausible phonetically than Speiser's ingenious but far-fetched derivation of Nimrod from Tukulti Ninurta.[84] Leaving aside the major phonetic difficulties, this hypothesis has considerable semantic problems. Firstly, Tukulti Ninurta was not a Kassite but an Assyrian who drove the Kassites out of Babylon. Secondly, he reigned in the 13th century BC, which is uncomfortably close to the date of the composition of Genesis. Nimrod's position early in Genesis and Talmudic tradition that he was the 'first' conqueror strongly suggest that he was a very early figure, which would weigh against Tukulti Ninurta, Amenhōphis III or even the Kaššû or Kassite kings.[85]

However, I am not trying to argue here that Nimrod was simply a Hebrew version of Sesōstris. The description of the great hunter's conquest from Southern Mesopotamia to the north would in fact fit Sargon of Akkad or his grandson Naram Sin much better than they

would any Egyptian. Thus, I propose that Nimrod is a composite figure made up of the early great conquerors, Sargon, Naram Sin *and*
Sesōstris. However, as neither of the Akkadians were in any way associated with Elam or the Kassites, Nimrod's name and parentage would
come most plausibly from the last.

A summary of the arguments
for Egyptian colonizing of Colchis

Let me now sum up this extremely complicated argument. There appear to have been two Black populations in Southwest Asia in the 2nd
and 1st millenniums BC. One was of African appearance and possibly
African origin in Colchis, which may be derived from the Egyptian Kȝš
(Ethiopia). These people were not called Aithiopes by the Greeks but
may have been called so by the church fathers. The second population
was of Asian Blacks in Elam, who were called Aithiopes. Among
these, forms of the name Kûš were used, but these probably came
from the neighbouring Kassites, whose name seems to be an independent local development.

    In general, it is certain that Herodotos, Apollonios and Diodoros
were convinced that Colchis had been settled by Black expeditionaries
from Sesōstris' army. Herodotos claims that he gained this knowledge
in Colchis not in Egypt – according to him the Egyptians did not know
much about their 'Colchian colony'. It is possible that Diodoros based
his account on Egyptian sources. Apollonios' sources of information
are unknown; he probably drew both from Herodotos and from
Egyptian priests and earlier writings. On the other hand, much of Apollonios' epic shows a considerable and accurate knowledge of the
southern coast of the Black Sea, so that it is very likely that, in part, his
belief in the early colonization, like Herodotos', came from Colchis.

    Thus, it is extremely probable that, at least in the 2nd half of the
first millennium BC, there was a local belief in Colchis that their country had been founded by an Egyptian pharaoh, probably Sesōstris. It
is possible that the tradition was mistaken and arose from a desire to
have a respectable cultural ancestry or, more likely, to explain not
only cultic parallels but the African appearance of some of the population. However, if this was the case, one is still left with the problem
of that population itself. Burton outlined this when discussing the
Blacks in Abkhazia in the 20th century:

> This may well be the only negro community in the Old World
> outside Africa and the Coastlands of the Indian Ocean. Obviously
> they cannot be descendants of Sesōstris' army, since none of the

XIIth Dyn. kings penetrated to this area, but their origins remain obscure.[86]

There is, of course, no proof that Colchis was in some way the result of Sesōstris' expedition. However, the simplest way to clear this tangle of evidence would be to take the Colchians and Greeks at face value and to accept that the African army did reach the Eastern Black Sea in the 20th century BC.

MESOPOTAMIA AND IRAN

Herodotos made no claim that Sesōstris had conquered Mesopotamia or Iran. As we have seen, Diodoros' belief in these conquests would seem to be based on an Egyptian need to compete with Alexander – naturally not felt by Herodotos writing in the middle of the 5th century, almost a century before Alexander was born. Diodoros lived after the shift in meaning of the term 'Asia' from Anatolia to the whole continent. The traditions around Memnōn (discussed below), which are considerably older, do refer to the Ethiopian army being active in Nineveh and Susa but these can, I believe, be largely explained in terms of the Elamite 'Ethiopians' discussed above. A conquest of Mesopotamia is made very unlikely by the complete absence of any reference to Egyptian invaders, in either contemporary records or later traditions.

This is not to say, however, that Mesopotamia was unaffected by Egypt. It would seem very likely that the weakness of Assyria around the turn of the 19th century BC was connected to the disruption of Assur's commercial network in Eastern Anatolia and the Southern Caucasus at that time.

An Egyptian invasion of Iran bypassing Mesopotamia is just possible, but there, too, one would expect some local Elamite or Mesopotamian record. Thus it would be simpler to see the Central Asian lapis and Iranian seals found at Tôd (see Chapter V) as coming from Assyrian traders in Anatolia.

THE GREEK LEGENDS OF MEMNŌN
AND HIS CONQUESTS OF ANATOLIA

When describing the conquests of Sesōstris, the Greek writers Herodotos, Apollonios and Diodoros drew from Egyptian and Colchian sources; they were not relying on their own traditions. Similarly, it is generally recognized that the *Romance of Sesonchōsis* was basically Egyptian.[87] This is not surprising, not only because of the breaks in Greek history – notably that of the 'Dark Ages' from 1150–800 BC –

but also because, according to these writers, Sesōstris' conquests were not supposed to have affected Greece, according to Herodotos, or only peripherally, as when Diodoros mentioned that the pharaoh had brought the Cyclades under subjection.[88]

Nevertheless, there is a Greek tradition which I believe can be related to the conquests; it is centred, not surprisingly, in Asiatic Ionia on the western coast of Anatolia. This region was supposed, in the Egyptian tradition, to have been conquered by the Egyptian army. The categorical distinction between the Ionian legends and the Egyptian tradition is made by the complete absence from the former of the name Sesōstris. In its place, one finds the name Memnōn. The clash between the Egyptian and Western Anatolian traditions can be seen in Herodotos' description of one of the 'Egyptian' or 'Ethiopian' carved figures in Western Anatolia: 'some who have seen the image suppose it to represent Memnōn; however, they are wide of the mark, for Sesōstris has made the truth plain enough elsewhere'.[89] I shall argue below that Memnōn was Sesōstris' son Ammenemēs II. Before coming to that, however, I should like to examine the Greek traditions about him.

The earliest extant reference to him seems to be that of Hesiod, who wrote in his Theogony (The Birth of the Gods): 'Eōs bore to Tithōnos brazen-crested Memnōn king of the Ethiopians.'[90] Even earlier than this, there is the tradition of Memnōn, wearing a splendid suit of armour, going to the help of Troy. He killed Antilochos, son of Nestor, but was killed in his turn by Achilles. This outline comes from the epitome of an epic entitled Aithiopis, written by Arktinos of Miletos.[91] Arktinos was supposed to have lived in the early 8th century BC. However, it is clear that both Hesiod and Homer knew the story. Thus it must date back to the 10th century BC, when Hesiod was writing, or earlier. The 20th-century classicists Clark and Coulson pointed out the striking parallels between the deaths of Memnōn and of the mythical figure Sarpedon. Sarpedon was the name of both the brother of Minos and Rhadamanthys who founded the South Anatolian kingdom of Lycia, and the leader of the Lycians and all the allies who came to the aid of Troy in the Trojan War and was killed by Achilles' beloved companion Patroklos. Clark and Coulson argued that 'The poet of the Iliad is obviously familiar with the events concerning Antilochos and Memnōn in the Aithiopis but has decided not to include these heroes . . . but instead has constructed the Sarpedon episode to replace the Memnonis.'[92] The modern classicist Gregory Nagy denies the derivation of Sarpedon's fate from that of Memnōn and explains the parallels as the results of belonging to a single tradition. Nevertheless, he accepts that the Memnōn myth is more fundamental than that of Sarpedon.[93]

It is more difficult to determine which of the details given in later reports belong to the original story and which are later accretions. However, certain themes seem, from circumstantial evidence and their widespread appearance in the iconography of the 6th century BC and in 5th-century writings, to be very early indeed. Memnōn was always the son of Eos and Tithonos; the story of the competition between Eos and Achilles' mother Thetis pleading to Zeus for their sons' lives, and of the heroes' souls being weighed in a balance, is also very ancient.[94] As *Aithiopis*, the title of the lost epic, and early representations of scenes from it indicate, Memnōn's being Ethiopian and hence Black was central to the story.[95]

On the other hand, doubt as to which 'Ethiopia' he came from seems to have existed from very early on.[96] There is no doubt that he came to Troy from the east and, by the 5th century, Herodotos was describing Susa in Elam as the 'city of Memnōn'.[97] Some decades after Herodotos wrote, the Persian monarch Ataxerxes II called himself Memnōn, presumably to consolidate his legitimacy among the Elamite population of his winter capital (Susa) and its surrounding region. Thus, by then at least, Memnōn would seem to have been a national hero of Elam. The Belgian classicist Goosens also cites Strabo's quotation from Aischylos' lost drama *Memnōn* that Memnōn's mother was 'Susienne' (i.e., from Susa). In point of fact, the quotation merely says that she was 'Kissian' and, while this is clearly what Strabo believed, it could also indicate that she was a Cushite or simply a Black.[98]

Goosens claimed that the Susian tradition was the original one and that the southern one came much later, and in this he has been followed by Snowden.[99] Against this, however, is the general portrayal of Memnōn as Black with 'African' tight curly hair and the confusion between him and Sesōstris reported by Herodotos, cited above.[100] Finally, and to my mind this is critical, there seems little doubt that for the Greeks the principle Ethiopia was always the African one. For instance, it seems likely from the Thera frescoes that African Blacks had been present in the Aegean at least since the 17th century BC.[101] However, the evidence is flimsy on either side, and it would seem that the traditions of the two locations of Memnōn's Ethiopia are equally old.

Furthermore, attempts to reconcile them started very early. Ktēsias of Knidos, a Greek who was a physician at the court of Artaxerxes Memnōn around 400 BC, is supposed to have written:

For when Teutamos was ruler of Asia . . . the Greeks made an expedition against Troy with Agamemnon . . . and Priam, who was king of the Troad and a vassal of the king of the Assyrians . . . sent an embassy requesting aid; and Teutamos despatched ten thousand

Ethiopians and a like number of the men of Susiana along with two hundred chariots, having appointed as general Memnon son of Tithonos.[102]

Memnōn's parents

Later writers followed both traditions, but with increasing emphasis on the African Ethiopia and Egypt.[103] However, before going on to look at this and the name Memnōn, it would seem useful to investigate some of the mythical aspects of the legends, beginning with the hero's parentage. Memnōn's mother, Eos, was the female personification of dawn and hence the East. His father, Tithōnos, was a much more complicated figure. According to Homer, he was a brother of King Priam of Troy and, as mentioned above, Ktēsias seems to have linked him to the king of Assyria.[104] For Homer, Tithōnos was clearly associated with the East. The poet twice used the formula: 'Now Dawn rose from her couch beside lordly Tithōnos.'[105]

However, the situation becomes more complicated if one looks at possible Afroasiatic etymologies for the name. These will be examined in more detail in Volume 4, but to put it crudely they seem to come from two sources. The first of these was the Semitic word *ṭiṭ* (mud) with a gentilic suffix -n, 'mudmen' or 'the dead buried in the west', from which, incidentally, the Greek infanticidal monsters Titias, Tityos and Titan derive. The second, which had a long-standing tradition of punning with the first, was Tdn/Dtn/Ddn, a cardinal point, and a barbarian people who lived to the west of Mesopotamia and to the south of Syro-Palestine. These Semitic-Sumerian names seem to be related to the deity Ddwn, found in Nubia to the south and Libya to the west of Egypt.[106] The cult of Ddwn was very closely related to that of ỉmn/Amon, who himself had strong Nubian, Ethiopian and Southern Egyptian connections, seen in Greek tradition in Zeus' special relationship with the Ethiopians.[107]

The ambiguities arising from the possibility of Tdn/Tithōnos having come from any or all directions except the north were to some extent eased by agreement that he lived on the shores of the stream or 'ocean' that surrounded the world which was, as we have seen, considered in Greek cosmology to be the home of the Ethiopians. Returning to the connections with ỉmn/Amon/Zeus, it is important to note that *ỉmn* in Egyptian also meant 'west', the Semitic cognate of which is √ymn, 'right hand' or 'south'.[108] It could be that Tithōnos' identification as an easterner, or more specifically as an Assyrian, came from the Tidnu, a barbarian people living in the desert west of Mesopotamia. It is much more likely, however, that, as with the image of the Ethiopians, Tithōnos was simply a man from the edge of the world. Thus, Tithōnos was a man from the distant east and south like his son. We should now look at the clearly mythical elements of the latter.

Memnōn and Osiris

The great 19th-century pioneer of comparative religion Robertson Smith saw one aspect of the legendary hero as resulting from confusion between Memnōn and the Canaanite Nå'åmån (Darling), an epithet commonly used for the young dying god known in Greek as Adonis, from the Canaanite 'ădônî (My Lord). The Greek flower name *anemōnē* is probably derived from Nå'åmån.[109] Whether or not there was such paranomasia, such an occasion would tally well with the conquests of Memnōn and those of the dying gods Osiris and Dionysos, the counterparts of Adonis.[110] It should also be noted here that Northwest Anatolia had its own young dying god of vegetation, Attis, whose cult was strikingly similar to those of Osiris and Adonis.[111]

Tombs of Memnōn were reported in the Troad (the region around Troy in Northwest Anatolia and at Paltos in Syria) where they were associated with black birds called Memnōides. These were supposed to have been girl companions of the hero, whose laments so moved the gods that they were changed into birds.[112] On the level of natural history, their congregation around his tomb in the Troad represented the annual migrations from Central Africa about which Greeks since Homer appear to have been aware.[113] On the mythical plane, this closely resembles the stories of Isis and Nephthys mourning for Osiris and their metamorphosis into birds.[114]

Even Memnōn's blackness could be explained in these cultic terms, as Osiris was represented as Black.[115] It is also interesting to note that while Osiris' most important tomb and cult centre in Egypt was at Abydos, the Troad contained both a tomb of Memnōn and a city called Abydos, although they were more than fifty miles apart. The report of a tomb at Paltos in Syria brings us back to the Canaanite Nå'åmån or Adonis and the image, preserved in Greek tradition, of his great beauty. This parallels Homer's description of Memnōn as the 'most handsome' man at Troy.[116] Furthermore, Memnōn, like most Greek heroes, resembles Osiris in that he both dies and is made immortal.

However, not all the myths about Memnōn can be explained by the connections with Osiris. Contrary to the Osiran myth of the resurrection of the body, there was a tradition that Memnōn's body had been burnt and that the Memnōides were formed from the smoke. This could be a parallel to the story of the Phoenix rising from the ashes and thus relate Memnōn to the sun cult at Heliopolis, which will be discussed in Volume 4. It is also significant that both the smoke and the birds were black.[117]

This is, of course, suitable for an Ethiopian, although black was also the national colour of Egypt. Kmt (the black land) meant 'Egypt' and *kmt* with the determinative for 'people' meant Egyptians. Finally, Osiris was not the only Egyptian god represented by that colour, as Amon too was Black. These connections will be discussed below.

Heroes in the balance

Another clearly mythological element in the Memnōn legend is the tradition of the *psychostasia* or *kērostasia*, the weighing of souls. The image of the souls of two heroes being weighed to determine which shall win a mortal combat is described explicitly in the final battle between Hector and Achilles:

> Then the Father (Zeus) lifted on high his golden scales, and set therein two fates [*kēre*] of grievous death, one for Achilles and one for horse-taming Hector; then he grasped the balance by the midst and raised it; and down sank the day of doom [*aisimon ēmar*] of Hector and departed unto Hades.[118]

This theme was used elsewhere for the Greeks and Trojans collectively. Homer's other allusions to weighing souls are even more interesting and significant. The German scholar Dietrich has plausibly argued that their very abbreviation shows that the concept was of long standing and familiar to Homer and his readers.[119] The German classicist G. E. Lung mentions in this connection – but with some scepticism – the find of scales made of gold leaf in one of the tombs at Mycenae.[120]

It is quite clear that there was a *kērostasia* between Memnōn and Achilles. An allusion is made to the 'balance' (*talanta*) in the death of Sarpedon, which Clark and Coulson have shown to be closely parallel to that of Memnōn.[121] Furthermore, Aischylos featured this scene in his lost drama *Memnōn*.[122] Any doubt about there having been a *kērostasia* in the case of Memnōn and Achilles is removed by iconography. As well as the many representations of Achilles' mother, the nymph Thetis, and Eos pleading for their sons, Lung was able to identify seven vase paintings of a *kērostasia* involving Memnōn and Achilles, and Clark and Coulson have been able to add three more.[123]

The parallels between this scene and that of the weighing of the

souls of the dead to assess which should be blessed and which damned
– one of the most common images in Egyptian theology, literature
and art – are so striking that they were seen even in the early 20th
century. The mythologist Otto Gruppe drew a parallel between the
two, pointing out that in the Greek representations Hermes has a central role in the weighing, just as his counterpart Thoth is always shown
recording the balance in the Egyptian scenes.[124] Lung put this poten-
tially dangerous idea into proportion. 'In this form [Gruppe's theory]
is untenable because it is not possible to detect any Egyptian influence
in the Greek psychostasia, one should rather say that Hermes con-
forms somewhat to Thoth.'[125] This confusion is an excellent example
of what happens when a paradigm – in this case the Aryan Model – is
unable to cope. There is, of course, an important difference between
the two scenes in that in Egypt it is not a competition between two
souls, but the weighing of a single soul against a feather $\int$⌒l *šwt*. On the
other hand, Gruppe's case can be strengthened by noting that Hermes
is not merely the counterpart of Thoth but also of Anubis and that in
the *Book of Coming Forth by Day* Anubis is also always present at the
weighing. Indeed, I believe that a good argument can be made that
their fusion in Late Egyptian and Greek religion comes from their
close cooperation in this key scene.[126] In the case of Memnōn's *psychostasia*, Hermes is sometimes represented in Anubis' chief role of passing between life and death and guiding the soul to immortality.[127]

Egyptian and Greek souls

The Alexandrian scholiasts or commentators on earlier texts claimed
that there was an opposition between the *kērostasia* of Homer and the
psychostasia of Aischylos. German scholars of the 19th century took
this as unnecessary Hellenistic elaboration and argued economically
that 'Ker is really only the older form of psyche and represents the
same thing'.[128] Looked at from Greece, it is indeed difficult to distinguish between the two, but the scholiasts were writing in Egypt and I
believe that they may well have been aware of a distinction in Egyptian
metaphysics. To investigate this, it is necessary to look at the Egyptian
etymologies for the two Greek terms.

The Greek *kēr*, sometimes *kār* in the Dorian and Aeolic dialects, is
a term of rich and complex religious significance. There is no doubt
that it came to mean 'fate, doom, or violent death'. However, as we
have seen above, Homer was also using it in a different sense of individual fate or 'soul'. This, according to one passage in the *Iliad*, it was
appointed to a man at birth to meet him at his death.[129] This same

sense was preserved in the ancient formula used in the Athenian festival of Anthesteria – in which the souls of the dead revisit the living – 'get out *kēres* the Anthesteria is over'.[130] Thus, this sence of *kēr* as an individual soul would seem to be central to its original meaning. The word has no Indo-European etymology.

The concept of *kꜣ*, commonly written *ka*, which is central to Egyptian theology, has an even richer semantic field. As the hieroglyph ⊔, representing open or embracing arms, the original meaning of *kꜣ* would seem to be one of relations between beings: god and god; god and man; man and man. In the sense of father and son it gained connotations of personal and institutional continuity and immortality, especially in royal contexts. It seems to be from this that the later sense of *kꜣ* as a ghost came about. Even in the Old Kingdom *kꜣ* had developed the sense of spiritual companion or doppelgänger whom one met at the point of death, and it is from here its widespread use to denote 'fate' seems to have arisen.[131]

The beauty of the semantic fit between *kꜣ* and *kēr* is not matched by the phonetic parallels but they are still good. An Akkadian rendering of an Egyptian name gives the vocalization *ku*, while the later Greek and Coptic transcriptions of *kꜣ* are *ke*, *ki* or *choi*.[132] This would seem to indicate an earlier *kʷer*, which would provide a reasonable basis for *kēr* – the *kār* could be explained as a back formation – but only after the breakdown of the Greek labiovelars. However, the sounding of *ꜣ* as a liquid would suggest an earlier loan. Despite this problem and the uncertainty of the vocalization, the phonetic similarities are easily sufficient to confirm the semantic equation.

The Egyptian etymology of *psyche* does not have the same precision. It is a paradox of language that the same words are often used to describe both 'sun' and 'shade'. The two meanings are shared by the Indo-European root *skāi*, *skǝi* and *ski*, from which it would seem that the Greek *skia* (shadow) and its synonym *skotos* are derived.[133] The latter may well come from an Indo-European root with a final dental that is found in our 'shade'. Equally, however, it could derive from the Egyptian *šw(y)t* with the same meaning. The Egyptian root *šw* has the same ambiguity as its Indo-European equivalent: *šw*, 𓇳 , 'sun and its light' and 'dried'; *šw*, 𓈙𓏏 (parasol, shelter); *šw(t)*, 𓈙𓃀 (empty). Particularly relevant for us are *šwyt*, 𓈙𓏭𓏪 , or *šwt*, 𓈙𓏏 (shadow, shade), and *šw(y)t*, 𓏏𓂝 (shade as a part of a man's personality, spirit of a god).

The Egyptian *šw* with the masculine article *pꜣ* may well be the origin of the Greek *psyche*. The semantic fit between *psychē* and *pꜣ šw(t)* is excellent. Furthermore, the phonetic difficulties are more apparent than real. During the late 2nd millennium there was an increasing tendency to replace the feminine definite article *tȝ* with the masculine *pȝ*. Thus, for instance, Middle Egyptian 'neuter' abstracts like *ḏwt* (evil) became 'masculine' in Late Egyptian.[134] If the *š* in *pȝ šw(t)* preserved its alveopalatal quality, the resulting sound would be in Greek terms the nearly unpronounceable **pschy*. Thus, it would seem justifiable to postulate a metathesis to *psych*. The etymology is strengthened by the cluster of words *psychros, psychos* and *psychō* with the same semantic range – 'shady, cold, lifeless, empty' – as that of *šw*. There are even some later uses of *psychō* in the sense of 'aeration' and 'drying' thus pointing to the other contradictory meanings of the Egyptian term.[135]

If these etymologies are right, *kēr* and *psychē* represent *kȝ* and *šw(t)*, two different souls or aspects of the personality. Some Egyptologists like Gardiner have maintained that the Egyptians were wrong in their treatment of souls in two ways. Firstly, because they 'conceived of such notions in a more personal and tangible way than we do' and secondly because the *ka*, for instance, 'remained a shadowy and ill-defined concept variously regarded in different contexts'.[136] Thus, as usual, non-Europeans get it wrong in both directions. In fact, however, one person's confusion is another's subtle metaphysics or theology. There is, therefore, no doubt that Egyptian priests took the distinction between the two very seriously. On the other hand, it is very unlikely that this distinction was understood by the common people or by uninitiated foreigners like the Greeks.

The phonetics of the loans would seem to confirm the pattern discerned by Lung for reasons other than that *kēr* is the older form. As noted above, the liquid quality of *ȝ* disappeared early in the New Kingdom. Thus, though the possibility of conscious archaism remains, it is likely that the loan from the Egyptian took place before 1500 BC. If the weighing of souls was – as seems very likely, given the scales found in a funerary context in a Shaft Grave – known in Greece by the middle of the 2nd millennium, the term *kērostasia* would have become established then. It has been argued in Volume 1 that Aischylos had relatively recent and erudite Egyptian sources as well as ancient ones. This could explain his replacement of Homer's term by *psycho-stasia*.[137] The appropriateness of using a term based on *psycho* would seem to come about because in the Egyptian weighing the soul of the dead man is weighed against a feather *šw, ꜥ*!

Memnōn's links with Northwest Anatolia

Although suggestive, the intricate pattern of mythological and lexical parallels with Egypt tells us nothing specific about the Memnōn legends. This is especially so if, as I am asserting throughout this work, all Greek culture is permeated by Egyptian influence. The best parts of legends from which to gain historical insight are not the folk or mythic themes but geographical specifics and proper names. This is clearly the case where there is a historical control to test against, as with the fantasies of the Welsh *Mabinogion* and the Germanic *Nibelungenlied* which contain heroes with the names of known historical figures.

The 'Ethiopian' origins of Memnōn have been discussed at length. Here, I should just like to emphasize his attachment to Northwest Anatolia and the Troad in particular. Memnōn's links to Troy and his 'tomb' some seventy miles to the east have already been mentioned. In a very interesting passage on the weapons of Antiquity being made of bronze, Pausanias wrote that 'Memnōn's sword in the temple of Asklepios in Nikomedea [80 miles east of his 'tomb'] the blade, a butt of the spear and the whole of the sword were made of bronze.'[138] This offers hints of great antiquity, but, given the notorious unreliability of relics, the weapons are very unlikely actually to have been those of the historical prototype of Memnōn. Furthermore, if he is to be identified with Sesōstris' expedition, as I shall be seeking to show, there were few if any swords in the 20th century BC.

At another point Pausanias reports that 'the Phrygians still point to the road he took [from Susa] choosing the shortcuts across country; the road cuts from halt to halt'.[139] This tallies with Herodotos' report that the local people in Lydia, in Northwest Anatolia to the south of the Troad, thought that the statues he believed to be of Sesōstris were of Memnōn.[140] All in all, there is a strong association between Memnōn and Northwest Anatolia.

Memnōn's Egyptian identity

Memnōn was also the Greek name for the famous colossal figure, across the river from Thebes, of imn ḥtp III, called Amenhotep by modern scholars and Amenōphis by Manetho.[141] The figure was renowned in Roman times for the strange sounds it made – appropriately for the son of Eos – at dawn.[142] It is not known when this sound was first heard but it is possible that it may have influenced the choice of Memnōn's mother and strengthened his attachment to the East. I have mentioned earlier that, even when the hero was identified as an Egyptian, Memnōn was associated with Tithōnos. One of the many Greek graffiti on the colossus addresses it as: 'Memnōn son of Tithōnos or Amenoth'. The same hesitancy seen in this epithet appears more directly in another inscription which called the colossus 'Memnōn or Phamenoth'.[143] The alternation would seem to indicate the source of the confusion. However, many of the Greek travellers appear to have had a pretty good idea who the figure represented. Amenoth, Phamenoth and Phamenoph would seem reasonable renderings of (pɜ) imn ḥtp, i.e., Amenōphis. Other forms such as Phamenos appear to be either drastic reductions or simply pɜ imn, 'The Amon'. Pausanias summed up opinions on the matter in this way:

> In Egyptian Thebes where you cross the Nile to the Reeds, as they call it, I saw a sounding statue of a seated figure. Most people call him Memnōn who marched into Egypt and as far as Susa out of Aithiopia; on the other hand the Thebans say that this is not Memnon, but a statue of Phamenoph who lived in their region. I have also heard him called Sesōstris.[144]

The image of the Ethiopian king who marched into Egypt and on to Susa would seem to be based on the Ethiopian conquerors of Egypt Shabaka (716–695 BC) and Taharḳa (689–664 BC). These, of course, came after Hesiod, Homer and Arktinos and therefore cannot have been the inspirations for their Memnōn.

How can we explain the name Memnōn for this statue? The two major studies on the topic believe that the name of a Greek hero became confused with local names. Working within the Aryan Model neither considers the possibility that the name itself could have come from Egypt.

Goosens argues that Memnōn was confused with an Elamite god named Humban or Umman or possibly Amman.[145] Gardiner derives the name of the statue from the term Memnonion which Strabo, the Greek geographer of the 1st century BC, used as the name for the funerary temple in front of which sat the two colossi, one of which became 'the Memnōn'. According to Gardiner, the confusion came from the praenomen of Amenōphis III, Nb mɜʕt Rʕ – mentioned above in connection with Nimrod – transcribed in the Late Bronze Age as Nibmuaria or Nimmuria. The name of the so-called Memnonion at Thebes was contaminated by the title of the temple complex at Abydos which Greeks called by the same name. This was not built by Amenōphis but by the 19th-Dynasty pharaoh Sethos I and, in Egyptian, Sethos' praenomen Mn mɜʕt Rʕ was used in the formula tɜ ḥwt Mn mɜʕt Rʕ ib ḥr m ɜbdw (the Mansion of Mn mɜʕt Rʕ, contented heart in Abydos).[146] The idea that there was a confusion between Memnōn or Memnonion with Nimmuria is distinctly implausible on phonetic grounds, though one with Mn mɜʕt Rʕ is less so.

To my mind, however, Strabo provided a clue not to the Egyptian name Amenhotep for which that of the 'Greek' hero was mistaken, but to the origin of the name Memnōn itself. He wrote that the Labyrinth of El Lâhûn in the Fayum, built by Ammenemēs III – discussed in Chapter IV – might be a Memnonium because Egyptians said that Ismandēs was Memnōn. He had written earlier that Imandēs was buried in the labyrinth.[147] Thus, while some Egyptians appear to have objected to the name Memnōn being applied to a statue of Amenōphis, others identified it with Ammenemēs. imn m ḥt/Amenemḥe/Ammenemēs is a more plausible origin for Memnōn than imn ḥtp/Amenhotep/Amenōphis. The phonetic fit between imn m ḥt and Memnōn is reasonable, better, in fact, than that of Sesōstris and Sesoōsis from S-n Wsrt. However, if Manetho had difficulty in sorting out the different imn m ḥts (see Chapter V), it is certain that Greeks trying to follow Egyptian sources were in equal or greater confusion as to which imn m ḥt/Ammenemēs they were referring at any given time.[148] However, the most plausible candidate for the Memnōn of Greek tradition is Sesōstris' son, successor, co-regent and fellow campaigner, imn m ḥt/Amenemḥe II.

Despite the danger of charges of circularity, this would seem a sufficient basis upon which to postulate a sequence of events which could have provided a core around which the myths about Memnōn could have accreted.

If, around 1900 BC, an Egyptian army, many of whom were Black and led by a prince who was Black – the Deep Southern origin of the 12th-Dynasty pharaohs has been noted – had marched through Anatolia from east to west, how would this have been remembered? Memories of his great force and splendid accoutrement would persist. His being the son of Eos would come from his arrival from the east. This and his blackness would explain the Susian (Elamite 'Ethiopian') connection and possibly the identification of his father as Tithōnos, who also came from the east and south. The Osiran parallels would come from his being both Black and Egyptian, from the strength of the cult of Attis (mentioned above) in Northwest Anatolia and the possibility, considered above, that the myths of Osiris/Dionysos' world conquests could have been stimulated by or at least influenced by the campaigns of the pharaohs of the 12th Dynasty.[149] Memnōn's struggle with Achilles would be a matching of heroes from different periods. This is a frequent phenomenon in many mythologies, especially in that of Greece; see, for instance, the chronologically disparate crew of Jason's ship the *Argos* and the range of heroes at the Siege of Troy, such as Sarpedon mentioned above.[150]

Reference has been made above to the close connections between the two world conquerors Sesōstris/Sesonchōsis and their romances, and it seems that the *Sesonchōsis Romance* had a major formative influence on the earliest *Alexander Romance*.[151] The latter, which was found throughout Eurasia for more than two thousand years after his death in 323 BC, provides an excellent parallel on which to postulate the widespread variation and survival at the popular level of fantastic stories based on the real achievements of a conquering ruler.[152] In fact, given the far greater general cultural continuity during the last two millenniums BC than in the 1st millennium AD, it would seem very likely that tales about Sesōstris and Memnōn should have survived from the beginning of the Middle Bronze Age in the 20th century BC to the 10th century, when we seem to pick them up in the Greek tradition.

In conclusion, I should like to make it clear that I believe that it would be absurd to postulate an Egyptian expedition to Northwest Anatolia solely on the basis of the fragmentary traditions around the legendary Memnōn. However, given the other information suggesting 12th-Dynasty military activities in Anatolia, these traditions would seem to provide further evidence in this direction. In short, the Memnōn legends provide a prop that could not stand on its own but provides extra strength to the larger structure.

THE CASE FOR AN EGYPTIAN
CONQUEST OF TROY C. 1900 BC

Greek tradition makes it clear that, for all his magnificence, Memnōn was killed at Troy by the Greek hero Achilles. The possibility that Egyptians took the city should be considered, however. There is no doubt that Troy V ended and Troy VI began about this time (these numbers refer to different cities on the site of Troy). Troy V was not destroyed by fire, but Mellaart maintained that the radical shift in culture there should be seen as part of the general series of destructions of *c.* 1900 BC, including some very close to Troy, which – as discussed above – he attributed to invaders from the east.[153]

From the Mit Rahina inscription we have Sesōstris' and Amenemḥe's destruction – *bꜣ*, a word that does not necessarily involve burning – of a city called iwꜣì; this could possibly be an earlier form of the name Wꜣiwry which some scholars have identified with (W)ilios (Troy).[154]

To these tenuous pieces of evidence can be added three more. Firstly, there are the reports from Egypt of Trojan prisoners. However, these may well be, as Sethe and Gardiner propose, the result of punning with the Egyptian toponym T3 R-3wy – known today as Turah – ten kilometres upstream from Cairo, which was equated with Troy. Nevertheless, the idea of Northwest Anatolian slaves in Egypt should not be ruled out of the question.[155]

Secondly, there is the tradition found in Homer and later writers that Herakles had taken Troy *before* the famous seige. As Robert Graves points out, if this has any historical foundation it must refer to the fall of Troy V. In Homer, the Herakles portrayed is clearly Greek and all the reports are of his arriving by sea.[156] However, as we saw in Chapter II, the Greek Herakles was a conglomerate of many different origins. Although he was a solar – east to west – conqueror, unlike Osiris/Dionysos who went west to east, there are parallels which could link the two and hence Sesōstris/Memnōn. I also argued in Chapter II that Herakles was sometimes seen as an Egyptian from the Egyptian Thebes.[157] Herodotos clearly thought so and described Herakles as one of the 'Twelve Gods' of Egypt.[158] Diodoros also wrote of

> the most ancient Herakles who, according to the myths, had been born in Egypt, had subdued with arms a large part of the inhabited world, and had set up the pillar which is in Libya.[159]

There are even some suggestions that he was Black.[160] This and the association of Ḥry š.f/Herakles with the 'striking god' and Sesōstris discussed above provides further indication of the strong likelihood that the conquering pharaohs of the Middle Kingdom played an important role in the construction of the mythical Herakles.[161]

The third suggestion of an Egyptian conquest of Troy is more far-fetched. It comes from Apollonios Rhodios' report of the Colchian statement:

> Now we are told that from this country a certain king set out, supported by a strong and loyal force, and made his way through the whole of Europe and Asia, founding many cities as he went. Some of these survive though others have succumbed to the burden of the years. But to this day Aea stands with people in it descended from the very men whom that king had settled there.[162]

If we take this as serious historical statement, could prosperous Troy VI, which lasted over five hundred years, from *c.* 1900 to the 14th century BC, have been one of these? On their own, these very ambiguous scraps of information would be totally useless as historical indications. However, in a general context indicating a 12th-Dynasty presence in Anatolia, they do gain some value as circumstantial evidence.

Sesōstris/Senwosre and
Amenemḥe's Conquests:
A Summary of the Evidence

I now want to try and draw together the evidence we have looked at in this and the preceding chapter on the bearing of new information from various sources on the Greek and Egyptian writers' reports of the northern conquests of Sesōstris. The discovery of the Mit Rahina inscription describing the expeditions beyond Syria made by the two pharaohs Senwosre I and Amenemḥe II provides a remarkable fillip to the claims made by Herodotos and later writers for the conquest of 'Asia' by Sesōstris – who was Senwosre I. Archaeological evidence of fortification and military planning in Nubia now shows that 12th-Dynasty armies had the capacity to undertake such major operations. Possible evidence comes from a wave of destructions across Anatolia and finds of Egyptian objects there from what may be the appropriate period. There has also been the discovery of Anatolian objects in a treasure at Tôd in Southern Egypt dedicated to Mont, the god of conquest with special associations with Asia.

There is iconographic evidence in favour of military expeditions in Syria and Anatolia from the appearance there, soon after this time, of a smiting god resembling an Egyptian pharaoh. There are also traditions, recorded both in the locality itself and in Greece, of Memnōn, a Black prince with a large army marching through Western Anatolia. These could well represent a folk memory of Senwosre's son Amenemḥe II who is reported on the Mit Rahina inscription as having played a role in the foreign expeditions. Thus, if one understands 'Asia' to mean Anatolia – as Herodotos seems to have done at times – there is a strong case for believing the Greek writers' claims that Sesōstris marched through 'Asia'.

There is much less confirmatory evidence of an expedition through Europe. However, the claimed conquest of Thrace would seem plausible because of the widespread and long-lasting destructions in that region in the second half of the 20th century BC, the most likely period for Senwosre's campaigns there. There is no archaeological or legendary evidence to back the Egypto-Greek claims that the army marched through Scythia – the modern South Russia – but there would have been fewer visible destructions in this nomadic country and traditions would have been harder to preserve. By contrast, in Colchis, in Soviet Georgia, Greek writers reported strong local traditions of that state's having been established by Sesōstris' army and there is the tantalizing possibility that the long-standing Black population in the area arose, in part, from this army.

Other parts of the Caucasus seem to have been devastated at the time of Senwosre's alleged expedition there. Further evidence in favour of its having taken place would seem to come from the destruction of old, highly advanced regions of metallurgy there and the apparent movement of Caucasian metal-workers to cities in the Levant under Egyptian influence. This would fit with the reports from Mit Rahina and other Egyptian texts, as well as from the Greek writers, that Senwosre I, true to his name of s-n Wsrt, sent or brought back unprecedented quantities of booty, especially metal and slaves. Such a pattern would provide the explanation for the expeditions not only in the Caucasus but in Western Anatolia and Thrace as well. All of these regions were rich in metallic ores and many of them had very advanced metallurgy. Thus Senwosre and Amenemḥe would have been using the strong economic base and efficient state and military organization of Egypt to seize the superior technology of less politically centralized societies. In this it would seem that they were successful. There is no doubt that in the following centuries, while Anatolia stagnated, Levantine and Egyptian metalwork, at least partially based on Anatolian and Caucasian techniques, flourished. Egyptian jewellery, for instance, was heavily influenced from the east at this time. The art historian Cyril Aldred writes: 'It may well be that with the more intimate contacts between Egypt and Asia in the Twelfth Dynasty, new techniques were introduced by immigrants and adopted by native goldsmiths'.[163]

In many ways, it was only in this period that Egypt fully emerged from the Stone Age to become a society using metal as a commonplace material. It is also interesting to note that it was at this time that the Assyrian monopoly of trade with Central Anatolia was broken and commercial contacts between that region and Egyptian-dominated Syria were established. These could well have been intentional or unintentional results of Egyptian expeditions.

The contact with the Balkans can be similarly explained in terms of the search for precious metals and stones mentioned above.[164] An expedition through South Russia would be less easy to explain. Possibly the Egyptians were hoping for significant quantities of booty. It would seem more likely that, like Alexander, they went further than was militarily or politically justified, and that their successes generated a spirit of *hybris* – to use the Egypto-Greek term – to explore and to round the Black Sea to reach the good pickings of the Caucasus.[165] Thus, there would seem little that is strategically implausible in the campaigns as described by Herodotos or the time-scale of nine years attributed to them by Diodoros.

The explicit arguments used by the mature Gibbon for not studying Sesōstris' 'conquests' were 'that I no longer presume to connect the Greek, the Jewish and the Egyptian antiquities which are lost in a distant cloud'.[166] This cloud has been at least partially dispelled by linguistic and archaeological advances since the 1770s. However, we are left with what may have been implicit in Gibbon and was certainly present among later northern scholars, that is an ideological objection to the very idea of a 'civilized' African marching in triumph not only across Southwest Asia but also through regions of a 'barbaric' Europe. The notion that there was any truth to the tradition has been literally unthinkable to the 19th and most of the 20th century. It is now time to reassess it.

CHAPTER VII

THE THERA ERUPTION:
FROM THE AEGEAN TO CHINA

THIS CHAPTER IS concerned with the great eruption on the island of Thera or Santorini in the middle of the 2nd millennium BC. I shall begin by considering the question of re-dating the eruption from 1450 or 1500 to 1628 BC. This change is important for a number of reasons. Firstly, it is important from the point of view of the sociology of knowledge. The debate over the re-dating provides a splendid illustration of the tenacity of an academic convention in the face of massive contrary evidence from outside scholars using independent sources, who have no particular interest in causing trouble and often a strong reluctance to upset the status quo. The extraordinary slowness to accept the new evidence demonstrates the way in which scholars tend to rally to the structures they have been taught, and upon which they have spun their hypotheses; they demand absolute proof from challengers without pausing to reconsider the bases of their own beliefs, which in this case were extremely flimsy.

The re-dating is also of the utmost importance in establishing an absolute chronology of the middle of the 2nd millennium BC for the Aegean and the Eastern Mediterranean as a whole. This is because the eruption was fitted into ceramic dating from the pottery styles of these centuries. All of these now have to be shifted many decades upwards.

While there is a rather surprising lack of historical information on this gigantic event, there are a number of legends that appear to refer to the Thera eruption. In this chapter, I will be considering two of the most plausible of these: the 'volcanic' aspects of the biblical story of the Exodus and Plato's myth of Atlantis. I shall argue that one of the interesting aspects of the latter is the way in which the events of the 18th and 17th centuries BC – the Hyksos invasion and the Thera eruption – may have been confused with those of the 12th century BC – the invasions of the Peoples of the Sea and the massive third eruption of the Icelandic volcano Hekla in 1159 BC. These two sets of events, approximately five hundred years apart, seem to have led to a belief in the historical pattern of events that Plato states was held by Egyptian priests. According to this, history was punctuated by catastrophes, which destroyed not only the civilizations but the historical memories of all countries except Egypt, which was saved by the constancy and life-giving power of the Nile.

Later in this chapter I will be considering the possibility that Chinese tradition was also affected by these two world-wide events. I shall argue that the concept of the 'Mandate of Heaven', according to which Heaven removed the right of one dynasty to rule and gave it to another – manifesting this shift by extraordinary natural phenomena – may have originated under the influence of these two massive series of events. This view of a long-term historical cycle has had a fundamental impact on dynastic change in China. Today it continues to influence Chinese political thought and politics, because China – unlike other Asian countries such as India and Japan – has an indigenous tradition of revolution, *geming*, or 'Removal of the Mandate'.

THE CONTROVERSY OVER DATING

Thera, otherwise known as Santorini, is a spectacular island seventy miles north of Crete. Today one sails through the punctured rim into the crater of a huge volcano in which there are still small bubbling and fuming islands. Originally it was a whole mountain which exploded some time during the 2nd millennium BC.

The scale of the event was enormous. It was larger than the eruption of Krakatoa between Sumatra and Java in 1883. That explosion broke windows in Batavia (Jakarta) over 120 miles away, caused tidal waves which drowned people in Ceylon (Sri Lanka) and the dust it put into the atmosphere created, for several subsequent years, glorious sunsets, which are plausibly supposed to have had an impact on the development of Impressionism. More importantly, the Krakatoa eruption reduced world temperature, apparently causing temperature falls of 2–4° C for several months as far away as the Western United

States.[1] Similarly, geologists and physicists have demonstrated the massive scale of the Thera explosion, the huge amounts of ash and dust it must have put into the atmosphere and the strong likelihood that there was a *tsunami*, or gigantic tidal wave, caused by the huge displacement of water following the eruption and the sea's breaking into the crater.[2]

Until 1988, there was considerable controversy over the dating of the explosion. In 1939, Spyridon Marinatos, who was later to dominate Greek archaeology, put in academic form the widespread belief that Minoan civilization had been destroyed by the eruption in about 1450 BC and that this had allowed the Mycenaeans to conquer the region. As the Egyptian evidence indicated that the 'Mycenaeans' replaced 'Minoans' as rulers of Crete in the middle of the 15th century, he argued that the Thera eruption should be dated to about 1450 BC.[3] Marinatos was unable to test the hypothesis until the 1960s. He then began a well-funded and well-equipped excavation of the site he believed to be the most promising, at Akrotiri on the southern slope of the island.

The results were sensational: within hours, the archaeologists discovered a city below the ash and lava of the eruption. Over the subsequent years, they have excavated and preserved a dozen or so buildings, though technical difficulties and archaeological scrupulousness have prevented further digging of what is clearly a much larger site.[4] The huge boost the sensational discovery gave to Marinatos' reputation, together with his intellectual power and imagination and his friendship with some of the key political figures in Greece, meant that his generally very plausible theory was unassailable for many years.

Almost from the beginning of his excavation, however, there were difficulties with his dating. Firstly, the pots found in Akrotiri were all from the ceramic period Late Minoan IA or earlier. Since the next ceramic period, Late Minoan IB, was then thought to have begun in about 1500 BC, the explosion had to have been before that date. This was accommodated by a compromise according to which the eruption was put between 1550 and 1500 BC. The fact that acceptance of the earlier dates invalidated the original premise of Marinatos' hypotheses, that is, that the eruption had shattered Minoan power at around 1450 BC, was played down.

For many years, Leon Pomerance, a retired businessman, had attacked the 15th-century BC date for the eruption. His objections to it were on three grounds. The first was that the Thera eruption seemed to provide a historical explanation for many of the signs and portents described in the biblical Exodus: 'hail and fire mingled', the 'darkness that could be felt', the 'pillar of smoke by day' and the 'pillar of fire by night' and the *tsunami*-like effects of the parting of the sea followed by a huge wave. It is widely believed that the Exodus has a firm historical basis, clearly associated with the pharaoh Ramessēs. Since this would date the Exodus to the 13th or 12th centuries BC, Pomerance argued that the eruption must have taken place in these centuries.[5]

Pomerance's second objection to the dating was that the 15th century BC was one of general prosperity in Egypt and showed no historical break in the way one would expect after such a major catastrophe. By contrast, the break at end of the 13th and the beginning of the 12th centuries which marks the division between the Late Bronze Age and the Early Iron Age did provide exactly that kind of rupture. His final argument against the 15th-century date was that it was a period for which there were not only good Egyptian records but also specific information about Egyptian–Cretan relations. Pomerance believed it was virtually certain that volcanic ash from the Thera eruption would have reached Egypt and that a *tsunami* would have hit the low-lying Egyptian Delta and had devastating effects there. He was convinced that, even if it had not, Egyptians would surely have noted the Aegean catastrophe and that records of it would have been preserved.[6]

Apart from his amateur status and his unorthodox ideas, Pomerance had other things telling against him. These were that he was a Jew and that he had linked an Aegean explosion to the Bible. In the eyes of his opponents this brought about two unpleasant conjunctions: firstly, that between religious myth and 'scientific' archaeology and, secondly, one between Greeks and Levantines – the taboo against which is one of the themes of *Black Athena*. With all these handicaps, the surprise is not that Pomerance and his ideas were marginalized but that they were heard at all. As it was, his intelligence, determination and money gained him a hearing, but he was kept firmly on the sidelines. He attended the Second International Conference on Thera in 1977 but his talk was scheduled at an early hour when there could be little or no attendance and his paper was put at the end of the enormous conference volume.[7]

Nevertheless, some of Pomerance's ideas have fared well. It is now generally conceded that a *tsunami* from Thera hit Kos, Rhodes, Cyprus, Syria and Israel and may well have struck Lower Egypt.[8] Furthermore, there is no doubt that Thera ash fell on the Egyptian Delta. As the sedimentologists Daniel Stanley and Harrison Sheng, who have studied the evidence on this, conclude:

The presence of Santorini volcanic ash provides a powerful non-archaeological argument that lends further support favouring an important natural phenomenon as recorded in diverse early documents. Of particular note are the 'plague of darkness' in the Biblical book of Exodus ('there may be darkness over the land of Egypt, even darkness that . . .' *Ex.* 10: 21).[9]

Apart from linking the eruption to the biblical report, the new work showing the impact of the explosion on Egypt strengthens one point in Pomerance's argument: the implausibility of the absence of any record of what would have been a major catastrophe, given the relatively high number of Egyptian texts from the 15th century BC. On the other hand, where Pomerance seems to have been mistaken is in taking the Exodus tradition too literally and specifically by accepting a date around 1200 BC for this event (the historicity of the Exodus will be discussed below). In any event, Pomerance placed the eruption after, not before, the improbable 15th century.

The challenge of radio-carbon

While Pomerance was promoting his hypothesis, powerful evidence in favour of an early date for the Thera eruption was beginning to emerge. In the 1970s, the American archaeologist Philip Betancourt and others published papers showing that the many short-lived radiocarbon samples from immediately below the eruption levels on the site tended to indicate that the eruption took place in the 17th century BC.[10]

Only short-lived samples are useful in pinpointing a date because carbon 14 begins to decay when the living matter dies, which in the centre of a tree is when that particular ring dies. Thus, a piece of a timber beam may well come from the centre of a tree which 'died' several centuries before the tree was chopped down and the building constructed in which it was placed, and there may be a longer time-lag still before the destruction of the building. For this reason, carbon from brushwood and olive stones, which are contemporary with the destruction, is a much more accurate guide.

Despite this, the 17th-century BC date for the short-lived samples flew straight in the teeth of conventional wisdom. The Swedish Aegean archaeologist Åström wrote in 1978:

> The average corrected Carbon-14 dates for a short-lived sample of seven samples from the time of the destruction of Thera, or a little earlier, is 1688 ± 57 B.C. These results are obviously quite ridiculous, as there is general agreement on other grounds that the eruption occurred sometime in the first half of the 15th century B.C. (*c.* 1475 in my opinion).[11]

In the same year, the English archaeologist Gerald Cadogan wrote an article entitled 'Dating the Aegean Bronze Age without radiocarbon'. In this, he argued that since the carbon dates were clearly wrong on this issue, archaeologists should simply ignore them.[12] Other scholars were more open-minded. In 1980, the Egyptologist Barry Kemp and the Mediterranean archaeologist James Merrillees argued on the basis of synchronisms between Egypt and the Aegean and radio-carbon dates that the Thera eruption should be dated 1600/1575 BC 'or even earlier'.[13] Interestingly, in 1979, the Aegean archaeologist Peter Warren had proposed raising the date of the beginning of the ceramic period LMIA, in which the Thera eruption took place, from 1550 to 1600 BC on the basis of synchronisms with Levantine pottery. Thus, while he still refused to reconsider the radio-carbon data for the eruption itself, he came very close to tolerating the date of 1628 later proposed on the basis of dendrochronology.[14]

In 1980, another weakness in the low dating was revealed when the Greek archaeologist M. Marthari pointed out that pots from the destruction level at Thera resembled those of the Middle Helladic tradition in Mainland Greece.[15] The *Cambridge Ancient History* puts the end of the Middle Helladic at 1600 BC but, as is far too often the case, Northern Europeans and Americans paid very little attention to this work of Greek scholarship.

In any event, the orthodox view still had considerable resilience. From the beginning, the scholars who published the radio-carbon dates were unhappy about the discrepancy between their own results and conventional wisdom. Betancourt has since written that in 1978 he had 'agreed completely with the view that the absolute dating of the Aegean Late Bronze Age was already established'.[16] Two of his colleagues, H. N. Michael and Gail Weinstein, tried to explain their findings in terms of a distortion by volcanic gases, though they had to admit that this could not explain all the examples.[17] They also stressed that the carbon datings were very scattered and therefore very unreliable. Their conclusion, therefore, was extremely timid:

> At most it can be said that the LMIA radiocarbon dates suggest an early trend. Yet both Theran series are problematical. Whatever the explanation, we must proceed carefully, especially in attempting to utilize the Theran dates for chronological purposes.[18]

Given this hesitation and the tenacious opposition by the champions of conventional wisdom, the challenge from radio-carbon evidence seemed to have been contained. However, apart from the defections

of Kemp and Merillees, there was a weakness in the orthodox argument on another front – the evidence from dendrochronology.

The evidence from dendrochronology

During the 1960s and 1970s, there had been great developments
in dendrochronology. Dendrochronology is the method of establishing chronologies over more or less extensive geographical regions by
counting and measuring tree rings, and matching similar sequences
on different trees. The longest tree-ring sequences have been found
in very long-lived bristlecone pines in the American West and the
most interesting are those near the snow line. From the breadth and
colour of the annual tree rings quite small temperature differences
can be noted – summer frosts are an especially distinctive feature.
These markings have been correlated with historically attested volcanic explosions, with their known effects of throwing dust into the
atmosphere and lowering world, or at least hemispheric, tempera-
tures. Scientists noted that many summer frosts occurred in the three
years following such world-scale events and that this was six times
more than the number of frosts that could be expected to occur by
chance. Thus they established what they called the 'Krakatoa effect' to
explain this phenomenon.[19]

In the mid-1970s, Valmore Lamarche, one of the founders of the
new discipline, noted that there had been no Krakatoa effect of the
type one would expect for an eruption the size of Thera in the 15th or
14th centuries BC. The only such effect in the mid-2nd millennium
appeared in 1628 BC. He therefore concluded that this must have
been the date of the Thera eruption. However, as the issue was not of
particular importance to Lamarche, and since he may have been worried by the threat of opposition from the archaeologists, he did not
publish his conclusion at the time, although he did mention it casually
in an article in the *National Geographic Magazine* published in 1976.[20]
Thus, although word of this sensational discovery soon got about
in 'dissident' archaeological circles, where it was related to the high
radio-carbon dates, it could not be the subject of formal debate.

The situation changed in the mid-1980s with the official publication
of Lamarche's conclusion in *Nature* in 1984.[21] Soon after this, new dendrochronological evidence in favour of a 17th-century date began to
emerge. Michael Baillie of Queens University, Belfast, discovered that,
while there were no noticeable events of the Krakatoa type marked on
the oak trees preserved in Irish bogs for the 15th or 16th centuries BC,
there was a major break in 1628; in this year, in fact, several of the

oaks had died.[22] Although Baillie's work on this was not published until 1989, it was known about for three or four years before that.

Thera: The Chinese connection

The evidence from radio-carbon and dendrochronology indicating a higher date for the Thera eruption was now supplemented from another surprising direction, China. Before investigating the Chinese evidence on the Thera eruption, however, it is necessary to take a long detour to consider the traces in China of two later European eruptions.

In 1984, the Chinese American scholars Kevin Pang, a meteorologist, and Hung-hsiang Chou, a sinologist, gave a joint paper entitled 'A correlation between Greenland ice core climatic horizons and ancient meteorological records'.[23] The two events they correlated with Chinese records were the eruption of Etna in Sicily in 44 BC and the third major eruption of the Icelandic volcano Hekla in about 1120 BC (this would now appear to be 1159 BC).

The effects from the Etna eruption would seem to appear in reports in the following year of red dust surrounding a comet; in the West this was supposed to have marked the death of Caesar.[24] A 'blue sun that cast no shadow' and had no warmth was recorded by Chinese astronomers and historians, who also noted unseasonable frosts.[25]

Pang and Chou associated the 12th-century eruption with meteorological phenomena reported in later Chinese works. However, these associations encounter a debate that has been raging for more than two thousand years concerning the dating of the fall of the Shang Dynasty. The standard view, maintained by Sima Qian, the founder of Chinese historiography who lived in the 2nd century BC, has been that the Shang fell and its successor the Zhou Dynasty came to power in 1122 BC. But there is a minor tradition associated with the so-called *Bamboo Annals* which gives a different date. The *Annals* were chronological records written on bamboo strips which were unearthed from the tomb of a local ruler in 281 AD, having been buried some six centuries earlier. They placed the fall of Shang around the middle of the 11th century BC.[26]

This debate has had its latest revival in the 1980s AD. The American sinologists David Nivison and David Pankenier and the Chinese ancient historian Chen Mengjia argue for a date between 1050 and 1020 BC.[27] They support the accuracy of the *Bamboo Annals* and stress the significance of the rare conjunction of the five visible planets Mercury, Venus, Mars, Jupiter and Saturn, which occurred in 1059 BC. Such a conjunction was supposed – at least by the 3rd century AD – to have taken place shortly before the fall of the Shang.[28] Kevin Pang counters this by pointing out the known fabrication of dates of the five-planet conjunction in periods when it can be accurately checked and accepts the earlier conventional wisdom that the conjunction was computed back by later scholars.[29] Pang prefers to emphasize what he sees as the certain dating of a lunar eclipse in the 35th year of King Wen of Zhou, who reigned just before the defeat of Shang, to 1137 BC. This would mean that the Shang Dynasty fell in 1117 BC.[30] Pankenier, however, placed the same eclipse in 1065 BC.[31]

Despite my inability to follow the detailed astronomical and mathematical arguments involved, there is, to my mind, little doubt that Pang and his colleagues have the more plausible case. The external reason for this preference is the fact that, as discussed in Chapter V, the general inclination towards low dating found among 20th-century archaeologists and ancient historians has tended to be discredited by information from radio-carbon, dendrochronology and other scientific measures. Linked to this is my greater trust in the judgement of natural scientists, who are less encumbered by the scholarly traditions of the archaeologists and historians, which in this case are for low dating. Pang and his colleagues have demonstrated the simple arithmetical errors involved in the work of proponents of the 'short' (1027 BC) and 'middle' (1045 BC) chronologies.[32] Furthermore, they claim – with some plausibility – that radio-carbon dates from the early Zhou Dynasty are consistent with their higher dating.[33]

Pang and his colleagues have shown that a solar eclipse that took place in the reign of the Zhou king Yi occurred in 899 BC, which it is not possible to accommodate in the short and middle chronologies.[34] They have used this date, together with an earlier conjunction of the five planets, which occurred in 1953 BC in the reign of Yü, the first ruler of the Xia Dynasty (the dynasty preceding the Shang), to construct a rough scale of the difference between this and 899 BC (1,054 years) against the number of generations counted – with some accuracy – between Yü and Yi, which is thirty-seven. This, they point out, comes out remarkably close to the traditional standard length for a generation of thirty years.

Using this measure, the knowledge that there were seven generations between the reign of King Yi and the original Zhou conquest and that there were nine generations between it and a regency known as Gonghe which is generally acknowledged to have been in 841 BC, Pang and Chou arrive at a date of c. 1100 for the Zhou conquest.[35] This would not fit the 'short' or 'middle' chronologies but it would tally reasonably well with the date of 1117 arrived at on the basis of the eclipse in the thirty-fifth year of the Zhou king Wen given at 1137 BC.[36]

Once one accepts 1117 as the date of the fall of Shang, a number of meteorological events reported at the end of the Dynasty would seem to fit the phenomena one would expect to see after a major eruption. For instance, a fall of ash reported at the Shang city of Bo took place in the fifth year of the last Shang king, Shou, which would have been in 1164 BC. This is five years away from 1159, the year in which Michael Baillie now places the third eruption of Hekla, which, while not perfect, is a tolerable distance.[37]

Pang and Chou also provide evidence for this event from an 'oracle bone'. These were the shoulder blades of oxen or sheep or tortoise shells, heated to produce cracks which were then interpreted as oracular (they will be discussed further below). Pang and Chou cite a newly discovered bone with a radio-carbon date of 1095 BC (plus or minus ninety years). The inscription mentions a year without harvest and with stunted seedlings.[38] This could refer to a year near the end of the Shang Dynasty but it is very imprecise. Similarly, there is a report of two suns appearing together in the forty-eighth year of Shou's reign, that is, 1121–1120 BC. The sighting of 'mock suns' created by refraction caused by dust is one of the phenomena generally associated with large-scale eruptions.[39]

There is no doubt that the meteorological evidence is scattered. Nevertheless, the protracted dynastic struggle between Shang and Zhou probably began in the years between 1159 and 1140, which, Baillie argues, were those affected by Hekla III. Furthermore, Zhou partisans claimed that Duke Wen of Zhou received the 'Mandate of Heaven' (see above) nine years before his death in 1128, that is, in 1137, the year of the eclipse, and relatively soon after the disasters associated with Hekla III.[40]

Against this meteorological explanation of the dynastic overthrow, however, is the fact that the propaganda put out by the first emperor of the new dynasty, Wu of Zhou, to justify his conquest of Shang contains no emphasis on this kind of natural calamity. This is striking because Wu claimed parallels with Tang of Shang, who had overthrown that dynasty's predecessor the Xia, and Tang was supposed to have placed great emphasis on the presence of such natural disasters surrounding the transfer of power. It is also possible that some of Tang's speeches on this were at least rewritten at the beginning of the Zhou Dynasty.[41]

In 1985, Pang and Chou gave another paper in which they restated their claims about these eruptions and discussed another eruption, that of Santorini. This, they maintained, should be correlated with the fall of the Xia Dynasty. In this case, there is no doubt that there was a whole range of meteorological phenomena – dry fog, dimmed sun, severe, unseasonably cold weather and failed harvests – that can be plausibly explained as the results of a major eruption.[42] In a further paper in 1985, Pang reinforced his case by citing the reports of exceptional floods followed by years of drought, which he argued could have been caused by the eruption, that extended into the beginning of the Shang Dynasty.[43]

At this point, Pang and Chou were very imprecise as to when exactly these climatic changes took place, because of the uncertainty as to the dating of both the eruption and the fall of the Xia Dynasty. They placed the Thera eruption between 1400 and 1600 BC and the change of dynasties in the 16th century. In the case of Thera, this was a compromise between the conventional dates of 1450 and 1500 and the dendrochronological evidence for 1628 BC, of which they were aware. For the Chinese dynastic shift, they were influenced by the range allowed by the two dates for the dynasty's beginning given in the traditional chronography, 1765 and 1557 BC. These were backed by radio-carbon dates from early Shang strata indicating the early 16th century.[44]

However, Pang has since become convinced that the change of dynasty took place around 1600 BC. This was partly because of the shift of opinions on Thera but there were also other reasons. The first of these came from his growing conviction that the end of the Shang Dynasty took place around 1100 BC, discussed above. According to computations based on Sima Qian's Shiji, 'Records of the Grand Historian', the Shang Dynasty lasted 471 years, which gives a date for its foundation at the beginning of the 16th century BC. The other chronology based on the Zhushu Jinian (Bamboo Annals) gave 508 years for the Shang Dynasty, which fits with the '500 and more' years suggested by the Confucian philosopher Mengzi, known in the West as Mencius, who was writing in the 4th century BC.[45] This would put the fall of Xia at around 1600. Pang's generational scale produced the same result.[46] If one accepts the astronomically derived date of 1117 for the Zhou conquest of Shang, the 508 years takes us to 1625 BC for the fall of Xia, which tallies almost too neatly with the revised date for the Thera eruption – 1628 BC.

Between 1984 and 1987, Pang and his colleagues were to provide still more evidence in favour of a late 17th-century or early 16th-century date for the eruption.

The Eruption Re-dated

By 1986, the radio-carbon data, the dendrochronological evidence from the United States and Ireland, the indications from China and the absence of signs of the eruption from 18th-Dynasty Egypt seemed quite sufficient to me to indicate that it took place in 1628, rather than *c.* 1500 or *c.* 1450, especially because the later dates were based only on a tenuous connection with the destruction of 'Minoan' power. As I wrote in the introduction to Volume 1:

> The huge scale of the catastrophe allows me to make an exception to my general opposition to the 'argument from silence'. However, I acknowledge that this type of argument is inherently weak. Furthermore, the dendrochronological, the carbon and the 'Chinese' datings are all open to doubt. Nevertheless, given the extreme weaknesses of the case for a 15th-century date, the four sources together make 1626 BC [I now accept that it was 1628] seem much more plausible.[47]

Although the logic of this argument seemed irrefutable to me, I put it forward with some trepidation, because at an emotional level I questioned how I could go against the considered opinion of so many experts, who had spent their scholarly lives dealing with this and similar problems. In this, as in so many things surrounding the publication of Volume 1, I was very lucky, because the scholarly consensus in favour of the 15th-century dating collapsed in 1987.

The first shot was fired by Philip Betancourt. He now recanted his earlier acceptance of conventional wisdom and the attempts to reconcile the radio-carbon datings with it. He argued that any possible volcanic distortion of the datings would be overcome if, as was the case in Thera, 'large groups of dates were averaged'. Furthermore, he completely denied the vague 'island effect' which had also been supposed to lead to distortions.[48] He went on to argue that the new ceramic periodization necessitated by updating the eruption did not clash with synchronizations with Egyptian dynasties or Levantine pottery.

Betancourt's only difficulty came from the stone lid with the name of the Hyksos ruler Khyan, which Arthur Evans claimed to have found in an MMIII deposit at Knossos. Accepting a mid- or late 17th-century date for this pharaoh, Betancourt could not reconcile this with his new sequence, which put the end of MMIII in 1700.[49] Fortunately for him, however, Evans's published data had been challenged – on the basis of the stratum's mixed nature and the uncertainty in Evans's excavation notes – by the Indo-European linguist Leonard Palmer and by Pomerance.[50]

In his response to Betancourt, Peter Warren came to Evans's defence and blasted the 'tendentious' nature of the attacks on his dating of the lid's context. (I shall argue below that this problem is not so serious as they suppose, because it is possible to update this Hyksos ruler by several decades, thus making an MMIII context for Khyan quite feasible.) Warren's challenge to the radio-carbon dating was simply to say that the dates of short-lived specimens, adjusted to exclude those that were grossly deviant, gave a range 1σ (standard deviation) from 1620–1520 but that it would be sounder to give one of 2σ, which would give 1670–1510 for the Thera eruption.[51] However, Warren's case for the lower end of this range was weakened not only by his failure to take the dendrochronological evidence into account but also by his own admission that a new series of short-lived samples from LMIB strata at Myrtos-Pyrgos in Crete suggested a much higher chronology.[52] Thus, he failed to stop Betancourt's challenge. In fact, the writing was on the wall for the orthodox view. Betancourt's reopening of the issue of the radio-carbon dating was quickly reinforced by evidence of a completely different kind.

For some decades, scholars have been attempting to duplicate the work of dendrochronologists by looking at annual winter snowfalls followed by summer thaws in the Greenland Icecap. The changing seasons produce sequences of differing layers or laminations which provide an independent source of information about early climatic conditions. There are three different parameters: radioactive isotopic composition, dust content and acidity.

For more than a decade a Danish team of geophysicists led by C. U. Hammer have been working on cores drilled from the Greenland ice sheet. In 1980, they published an article in which they claimed that the Thera eruption must have taken place c. 1390 BC on the basis of ice cores taken from North Greenland.[53] This result, which went against all the other sources, was welcomed by no one except for Pomerance and very little attention was given to it in the literature.

In 1987, Hammer and his colleagues published a new article in which they dismissed their earlier claim. Using new cores from South Greenland, which was more suitable than North Greenland both because of more substantial summer melts and greater sensitivity to events in the northern hemisphere as a whole, they now came out in favour of an acidity peak at 1644 BC. They tied this in with Betancourt's radio-carbon dating and their own summary of his evidence which gave a weighted mean of 1σ 1630–1530 and 2σ 1675–1525.

The longer band fitted their dating of the eruption to 1645 and the acidity peak to the following year. They allowed for a standard deviation of ±7 years and an estimated error limit of ±20 years.[54]

The orthodox response to this was given by the archaeologist Gerald Cadogan. He now stressed the general uncertainties involved and the difference between the ice-core date of 1645 and the dendrochronological one of 1628. Cadogan admitted that the radio-carbon dates made the conventional 1500 for the eruption untenable but still stuck out for a 16th-century date because of Egyptian correlations. He clearly objected to Betancourt's high chronology.[55]

In a volume of *Nature* published in March 1988, the young archaeologist Sturt Manning firmly established the 1628–1626 date. He attacked Cadogan's 16th-century date as:

> . . . not correct. Only traditional pottery studies support this view. Moreover, there are several plausible contrary interpretations using traditional archaeological evidence. . . . Cadogan argues that because three independent scientific techniques (icecore, dendrochronology and radiocarbon) produce results which vary by only 30 years over 3,600 years, they should all be rejected. Instead, he asks us to accept a subjective archaeological date a century later.[56]

Manning then went on to reconcile the three scientific methods. That is to say, he accepted the dendrochronology but claimed that earlier scientists had failed to remove an aberrant radio-carbon date, which if done led to a 1σ range of 1675–1609, with a calibrated mean of 1629–1622 BC. He maintained that the margin of error of ±20 years from 1645, allowed by Hammer and his team, also fitted with the 1628–1626 BC date.[57] Hammer and Clausen replied to this that Manning, like Betancourt and Michael before him, had been too ready to cut out aberrant radio-carbon dates, and they felt it unjustified, even though such excision helped the writers' own higher date. The crux of the matter was that they were convinced that:

> the acidity signal in the 1645–44 BC ice layers is clearly related to a major volcanic eruption, whereas the frost damage at 1628–26 BC, though carrying a statistical probability of being related to a volcanic eruption, could have been caused by climatic impacts other than volcanism. We consider it premature to fix the date more precisely than in our paper, by radio-carbon or other methods. This is why we left a question mark at the proposed date of 1645 ± 7 yr BC.[58]

Such caution would seem to be irreproachable. However, in asserting the primacy of their own method, they failed to mention that it is far more difficult to handle cores of ice than those of wood, as exemplified by their own mistake with the core samples from North Greenland. They also did not deal with the problem that if the dendrochronological Krakatoa effect was not the result of the Thera eruption, then the effects of the other eruption – which was a hemispheric event – did not show up elsewhere. They do not seem to have been aware of Baillie and Munro's work on the Irish bog oaks, which clearly points to 1628 or 1627, not the 1640s. Finally, there is no doubt that Manning was correctly quoting them as having allowed for an estimated error limit of ±20 years.

While this debate was going on in *Nature* another was being conducted in *Archaeometry*. This was between Betancourt – and his old colleague Michael – and Warren, with the English archaeometrist M. J. Aitken holding the ring. Here again, it is clear that the proponents of the higher dating were victorious, the only point gained by Warren being on the stratigraphical position of the Khyan lid.[59] Thus, by the end of 1988 there was little doubt that the archaeological establishment had accepted a late 17th-century date and probably 1628 as the precise date of the Thera eruption.[60] In 1989 the evidence in favour of 1628 BC from Northern Ireland has been confirmed by new material from the Eire, England and Germany.[61]

THE IMPLICATIONS OF THE RE-DATING

I have given this blow-by-blow account of the arguments over dating for three reasons: firstly, to establish the overwhelming probability that the eruption did take place in 1628; secondly, to show the dangers of reification of hypotheses and the ways in which a vested academic interest can defend its position so successfully for so long; and, thirdly, to show how the 1500 and 1450 dates were embedded in a whole chronological fabric. This fabric was, in fact, the most effective means of defending the orthodoxy. With the establishment of the higher date, we have to reconsider the chronology of the Late Bronze Age, not merely in the Aegean but throughout the East Mediterranean basin.

In fact, the tendency to raise dates for this period began before the new dating. In 1980 the Egyptologist Barry Kemp and the Australian diplomat and specialist in Cypriot archaeology Robert Merrillees had begun this process in a massive study, *Minoan Pottery in Second Millennium Egypt*. In this, the authors argued, on the basis of Egyptian synchronisms from the New Kingdom, that the dates of the Cretan ceramic periods LMIA, LMIB and LMII should be raised approximately seventy-five years above the previous convention. As I mentioned earlier, this chronology allowed for the Thera eruption in 1628 because it placed LMIA – the period in which the eruption took place – as running not from 1600 to 1500 BC, as conventional wisdom held, but from 1675–1650 to 1600–1575 BC.

In the introduction to Volume 1 of *Black Athena* (written in 1986), I discussed the need for LMIA to have been established by 1628, and I cautiously raised the dates to 1650–1550. At the same time, Betancourt raised the period more boldly by approximately a century. Convinced by Kemp and Merrillees and, to some extent, by Betancourt's arguments, I have now revised my dating upwards, though often not as far as Betancourt, Kemp and Merrillees.[62] This incidentally solved a problem which had previously worried me – the fact that various motifs, such as the abstract sign for water, that appeared only on LMIB pottery, were already present on the murals from Thera before the eruption.[63] If LMIA is now taken as running from 1675 to 1600, the painting of these motifs in the decades before 1626 would have been in 'mature' LMIA.

As mentioned above, the one point where the traditionalists scored over the proponents of the radio-carbon dating was on the lid with the name of the Hyksos pharaoh Khyan, which Evans claimed to have found in a MMIII context at Knossos. Betancourt, Kemp and Merrillees end this ceramic period in 1700 or 1675–1650 respectively, while the conventional date for Khyan is in the second half of the 17th century. The radicals have tried to get round the discrepancy by following the rather shaky work of Palmer and Pomerance to discredit Evans's considered stratigraphy for the lid. It seems to me that this is the wrong way to tackle the problem. We now have to estimate the competitive plausibility of Evans's dating and that conventionally given to Khyan. I am convinced that, although Evans's conclusion is open to some doubt, it is far more reliable than the chronology now given for the Hyksos period.

THERA AND KALLISTE

According to Herodotos, the original name of Thera was Kalliste. It was called this when it was settled by the Phoenician Membliaros 'eight generations' before it was settled by the later eponymous colonist Theras, a Lakonian of Kadmean or Phoenician descent.[64] The Semitic origin of the name Membliaros will be considered below. Kalliste could mean simply 'Most Beautiful', which, like the name Formosa ('Beautiful' in Portuguese) for China's volcanic island province Taiwan, would be altogether appropriate for its rich volcanic soils, or it could be related to the nymph Kallisto, the connotations of whose name will be discussed in Volume 4. One possible explanation for the change of name from Kalliste to Thera is the change of the island's form following the eruption.

The name Thera, or to be more accurate Thēra, is conventionally supposed to come from *thēr-* (wild animal, game), which in turn is not altogether convincingly derived from a reconstructed Proto–Indo-European form traditionally rendered *$ghw\bar{e}r$.[65] However, the name Thēra does not appear on the Linear B tablets although the gentilic Qerajo (He of Qera) does. On this basis, the Mycenaean linguist John Chadwick maintains that Thēra comes from a labiovelar *Q^wera.[66] It will be argued in Volume 3 that, although the series of signs transcribed with an initial *q*- originally represented labiovelars, after the breakdown of this series they were used to transcribe the labials, velars or dentals which the sounds had now become. We are then faced with the origin and meaning of *$Q^w\bar{e}ra$ and, while the general solution to this problem is simple, the specifics are immensely complicated. There is no doubt that a word pronounced *k^wer, *q^wer or *$kior$, meaning 'kettle' or 'cauldron', was current in the East Mediterranean in the 2nd millennium BC. The root's origin and development, however, are extremely difficult to trace. Johannes Friedrich, a linguist who wrote about Phoenician and Anatolian languages, saw the Hebrew *kiyôr* as deriving from the Urartian *kiri*.[67] Against this, William Albright argued that *kiyôr* came from the Akkadian *kiuru* which in turn derived from Sumerian *ki.ur*.[68] Friedrich was clearly right to draw attention to the Urartian, and more recently Soviet scholars have reconstructed a form *k^war V for the Proto–East-Caucasian word for 'vessel'.[69] The Jewish scholar Aron Dolgopolskii saw this, the Urartian (a Northeast Caucasian language related to Hurrian, spoken in East Anatolia) and the Proto–Indo-Hittite for *k^wer as all being derived from a Proto-Semitic root $\sqrt{q^cr}$, often vocalized *qu^car-, meaning 'to be deep, hollowed out'. This was then loaned back into Akkadian and Hebrew as *kiuru* or *kiyôr* with a *k*.[70] This may or may not be the answer but some such complex scheme is necessary to explain the obvious but not simple relationship.

The root $\sqrt{q^cr}$ was not restricted to Semitic within Afroasiatic. In Egyptian one finds *krr* or *kr*, meaning 'hole, cave or vessel'. Furthermore, there is a word *krḥt* (vessel) written with the determinative ʊ. This is very similar to the archaic ʊ 'cauldron'. Thus it is possible that *krht* was used in this sense.[71] However, the most probable origin for the place name *Kʷera > Thēra is from the Canaanite *kûr,* which had the specific sense of 'smelting pot' or 'furnace'. The strong possibility that this may well have been pronounced *kʷer* will be discussed in Volume 3.

The meaning 'smelting pot' would seem a far more appropriate name than 'wild animals' for an island whose dominant feature was a volcanic crater. If there were a loan from Semitic it would have had to have taken place before the breakdown of labiovelars in Greek, which is generally agreed to have occurred in the 16th or 15th centuries BC. As mentioned above, it is very likely that by the 13th century, when (I shall argue in Chapter X) both the Knossos and the Pylos tablets appear to have been written, Qerajo was already being pronounced *T(h)eraio.

It is impossible to reconstruct the shape of the island before the great eruption and it may be that a giant crater was an important feature before this took place. If, however, this only happened after the eruption, the new dating at 1628 BC allows for the island to have been named from the crater after the explosion but before the breakdown of the labiovelars. This would also support the notion that the island was called 'most beautiful' – *Kalliste* in Greek – before the eruption.

VOLCANIC ALLUSIONS
IN THE EXODUS STORY

In this and the next few sections, I shall be looking at a number of traditions that seem to refer to the Thera eruption. In much of *Black Athena* I have been trying to use myth and legend to help understand historical events and processes. Here I shall be attempting to do the reverse, that is to use known and datable events – the Thera eruption, the expulsion of the Hyksos and the invasions of the Peoples of the Sea – to interpret myths and legends. Apart from its intrinsic interest, such a procedure can also be useful in assessing the historical reliability of ancient traditions and the permissibility of using them to help reconstruct the past in cases where historical and archaeological evidence is not available.

As mentioned above, Leon Pomerance championed the view that the Book of Exodus contains passages referring to the Thera eruption. But he was by no means the only person to do so.[72] There is no doubt that, as he pointed out, some of the passages from the book do appear remarkably 'volcanic'. For example, among the seven plagues with which Yahweh and Moses afflicted Egypt were: 'the darkness over the land of Egypt, darkness that can be felt . . . and it became pitch dark throughout Egypt for three days.'[73] This would be very much the kind of effect one would expect at such a distance from an eruption of this scale. The second 'volcanic' reference is equally striking:

> They [the Israelites] set out from Succoth and encamped at Etham on the edge of the wilderness. And all the time the Lord went before them, by day a pillar of cloud . . . by night a pillar of fire.[74]

This, too, is how an eruption like that of Thera would appear from many miles away. However, there is a problem in that the Eastern Delta is over five hundred miles away from Thera so that the curvature of the earth would make it impossible to see the column.[75] Thus, while it would seem clear that contributors to the tradition were aware of the phenomenon, there is nothing to link the passage specifically to Thera. Indeed, there is a clear biblical tradition not restricted to this section of Exodus that God lived in fire and cloud.[76] On the other hand, this would seem altogether appropriate if, as I shall argue in Volume 4, although he made a covenant with his people to treat them gently – if they behaved – and he had more pacific and benevolent manifestations, Yahweh is chiefly to be seen, with Seth, Yam and Poseidon, as a divinity of unpredictable disruption and especially of volcanic disturbance.

Pomerance maintained that the most suggestive passage is that concerning the destruction of pharaoh's army:

> the Lord drove the sea away all night with a strong east wind and turned the sea bed into dry land. The waters were torn apart and the Israelites went through the sea on the dry ground, while the waters made a wall for them to the right and the left. The Egyptians went into pursuit of them far into the sea, all pharaoh's horses, his chariots and his cavalry. In the morning watch the Lord looked down through the pillar of fire and cloud . . . and at daybreak the water returned to its accustomed place, but the Egyptians were in flight as it advanced and the Lord swept them into the sea.[77]

The early date of this image if not of the text itself is suggested by the song Moses is supposed to have sung in triumph, which is generally conceded to be very old. This contains the verses:

> At the blast of thy anger the sea piled up:
> the waters stood up like a bank:
> out at sea the great deep congealed . . .
> Thou didst blow thy blast; the sea covered them.[78]

Although there is no explicit mention in the song of the parting of the waters referred to in the later prose passage, as with the volcanic nature of the image of the two columns, it is overwhelmingly likely that the composer of Moses' song knew about *tsunami*. In this case the most likely *tsunami* would be that of Thera, which, as we have seen above, almost certainly did strike the coasts of Lower Egypt.[79] Furthermore, if one can rely on the prose passage there is a specific connection made with the pillars of fire and cloud. On the other hand, if we accept the date of 1628 BC for the eruption, even the song must have been written many centuries after the event as it refers to Philistia, which existed only after the first invasions of the Sea Peoples at the end of the 13th century BC.

As Pomerance and others have pointed out, this has caused difficulties for those scholars, like the Egyptologist Hans Goedicke, who have tried to reconcile the Exodus with the Thera eruption dated to 1450 or 1500.[80] Dating the Exodus to the end of the 13th century BC also raises difficulties for those who take seriously an Egyptian reference to the so-called 'Israel Stela' from the reign of the 19th-Dynasty pharaoh Merneptaḥ in 1219 BC. In this the name Israel clearly refers to a people living in Palestine at a time when, according to most traditional chronologies, the Israelites were just beginning the Exodus.[81] They must, therefore, have set off earlier. It is to accommodate this that scholars like Albright tried to demonstrate that the Exodus took place before the middle of the 13th century.[82] The reference to Philistines is, of course, not a problem if, like Pomerance, one accepts both the mainstream biblical tradition and the fact that the Thera eruption took place in the 12th century.[83]

I am inclined to see the basis of the Exodus tradition as a loose folk memory of what the Egyptians described as the Expulsion of the Hyksos (the relations between the Exodus and the Expulsion of the Hyksos will be discussed further in the next two chapters). Even in this case, however, it is impossible to tie these political events in with the Thera eruption and its associated *tsunami* since the Hyksos were driven out – at the earliest – in the 1570s, over fifty years after the eruption.[84]

In summary, the nature of the descriptions does suggest that the Exodus tradition contains some memories of the Thera eruption. Furthermore, it would seem that these have been in some way incorporated with folk memories of the Expulsion of the Hyksos. Nevertheless, the descriptions do not form a coherent legend. For instance, the 'darkness that can be felt' is placed among six other 'non-volcanic' plagues of Egypt, and there would seem to be no reason to try to tie the Thera eruption and the Expulsion/Exodus too tightly together.

MEMBLIAROS AND THE
PALL OF DARKNESS

We shall see in later chapters that the Israelites were not the only Canaanite speakers to be associated with Thera. Here, however, we are
concerned with legends that may refer to the eruption; some of these
seem to have been preserved in Western Semitic tradition. According
to this passage from Herodotos, which I have cited earlier:

> This island used to be known as Kallista, and certain descendants of
> Membliaros, son of the Phoenician Poikiles, were living on it. Kad-
> mos son of Agenor touched at it during his search for Europa and,
> whether because he liked the place or for some other reason, left
> there a number of Phoenicians with his own kinsman Membliaros
> among them.[85]

As Michael Astour has pointed out, just as Theras is clearly the eponymous ancestor of Thera, the name Membliaros clearly comes
from the toponym Membliaros or Bliaros – the old name of Anaphe,
the island closest to Thera. He has demonstrated that the form
Bliaros makes it impossible for Membliaros to derive – as has been
suggested – from *memblomai,* a secondary present middle form of *melô*
(to take care), which is in any event extraordinarily implausible on
semantic grounds. Instead, he proposes that it 'represents a very
accurate transliteration of Ugaritic or archaic Phoenician *mêm bli-ʾår*
"waters without light" or shorter *bli-ʾår* "without light, darkness"'.[86]
The Aryanist Francis Vian objected to Astour's hypothesis because
mêm bli-ʾår is unattested. However, Astour replied that records of
West Semitic languages are very incomplete and the cosmogony of
Philo of Byblos – a Phoenician of the 1st and 2nd centuries AD who
plausibly claimed to be translating ancient Phoenician sources – is full
of otherwise unknown combinations of known words.[87] Astour does
not answer the objections that nothing like this place name exists in
the Canaanite-speaking Levant and that there are no parallel borrowings of phrases into single names in the Aegean.

Nevertheless, the phonetic fit is perfect and the association with the
Phoenicians is clear, and Astour goes further by citing Apollonios of
Rhodes of the 3rd century BC, whose erudite *Argonautika* was consid-
ered in the last chapter.[88]

> But straightway as they sped over the wide Cretan sea night scared
> them, that night which they name the Pall of Darkness: the stars
> pierced not that fatal night nor the beams of the moon, but black
> chaos descended from heaven, or haply some other darkness came,
> rising from the nethermost depths.[89]

The Argonauts escaped from the darkness by calling on Apollo:

And quickly, O son of Leto, swift to hear, didst thou come from heaven to the Melantian rocks, which lie there in the sea. Then darting upon one of the twin peaks, thou raisedst aloft in thy right hand thy golden bow; and the bow flashed a dazzling gleam all round. . . . and straightway dawn arose and gave them light: and they made for Apollo a glorious abode in a shady wood, and a shady altar, calling on Phoibos the 'gleamer' [*Aiglētēs*] because of the gleam far-seen; and that bare island they called Anaphe, for that Phoibos had revealed it to men sore bewildered.[90]

This reference to Anaphe is supported by evidence from inscriptions and from Strabo which shows that there was a cult of Apollo Aiglētēs on the island.[91]

Astour points out the similarities between Apollo's bow and that shown to Noah lighting up the world after the Flood.[92] His main concern is to demonstrate the parallels between this description of Membliaros and the 'Pall of Darkness' and the biblical and other Canaanite cosmogonies in which before the world begins:

the earth was without form and void, with darkness over the face of the abyss and a mighty wind that swept over the surface of the waters. God said let there be light and there was light.[93]

There is little doubt that Astour has made his point and that not only the name Membliaros but the legends surrounding his island indicate West Semitic cosmogonies. (In Volume 4, I shall be looking at ways in which the latter resemble and to some extent derive from Egyptian ones.) However, Astour fails to explain why these Greek myths should be localized north of Crete around Thera and Anaphe. The reason would seem to be that there was a memory of the great Thera eruption. Thus, as well as symbolizing the chaos before creation, Membliaros and 'the Pall of Darkness' which neither the stars nor moon could penetrate record the massive dust cloud emanating from Thera in 1628.

THE MYTH OF ATLANTIS

Plato's report of a dialogue between the Athenian statesman Solon and Egyptian priests has been referred to in Volume 1.[94] It was noted both for its assertion of the identity of Athena and Nēit and their/her cities of Athens and Sais and for the aged priest's statement beginning 'O Solon, Solon, you Greeks are always children; there is no such thing as an old Greek.' When Solon questioned this, the priest continued:

You are young in soul, every one of you. For therein you possess not a single belief that is ancient and derived from old tradition, nor yet one science that is hoary with age. And this is the cause thereof: There have been and there will be many and divers destructions of mankind, of which the greatest are by fire and water and the lesser ones by countless other means.

The priest then gave a rationalized view of the myth of Phaeton and Helios as the shifting of heavenly bodies causing destructions on earth by fierce fire.[95] He went on:

At such times all they that dwell on the mountains and in high and dry places suffer destruction more than those that dwell near to rivers or the sea: and in our case the Nile, our saviour in other ways, saves us from this calamity by rising high. And when, on the other hand, the Gods purge the earth with a flood of waters all the herdsmen and shepherds that are in the mountains are saved but those in the cities of your land are swept into the sea . . . it leaves none of you but the unlettered and uncultured, so that you become as young as ever, with no knowledge of all that happened in old times in this land or your own.

After pouring scorn on Greek traditions he continued:

For verily at one time Solon, before the greatest destruction by water, what is now the Athenian State was the bravest in war and extremely well organised also in all other respects.[96]

After expatiating on the glories of Ancient Athens, the priest continued:

it is related in our records how once upon a time your state stayed the course of a mighty host, which, starting from a distant point in the Atlantic Ocean, was insolently advancing to attack the whole of Europe and Asia to boot. For the ocean there was at one time navigable; for in front of the mouth which you Greeks call . . . 'the pillars of Heracles' there lay an island which was larger than Libya and Asia together; and it was possible for the travellers of that time to cross from it to the other islands, and from the islands to the whole of the continent over against them which encompasses that veritable ocean. For all that we have here, lying within the mouth of which we speak, is evidently a haven having a narrow entrance; but that yonder is a real ocean, and the land surrounding it may most rightly be called and in the fullest and truest sense, a continent. Now in this island of Atlantis there existed a confederation of kings, of great and marvellous power, which held sway over all the island, and over many other islands also and parts of the continent; and moreover, of the lands here within the Straits they ruled over Libya as far as Egypt, and over Europe as far as Tuscany. So this host, being all gathered together, made an attempt one time to enslave by one single onslaught both your country and ours and the whole of the territory within the Straits. And then it was that the manhood of your State showed itself conspicuous for valour in the sight of the world . . . whereby it saved from slavery such as were not yet enslaved, and all the rest of us who dwell within the bounds of Heracles it ungrudgingly set free. But at a later time there occurred portentous earthquakes and floods, and one grievous day and night befell them, when the whole body of your warriors were swallowed up by the earth, and the island of Atlantis in like manner was swallowed up by the sea and vanished.[97]

A German writer has recently estimated that there are over 20,000 relevant writings, including 7,000 books, on these passages from Plato.[98] Therefore, even if it were desirable, it would be impossible to cover all the secondary literature on Atlantis. For these reasons I shall restrict the discussion here to some of the recent academic work on the subject and to the primary sources.

A sceptical tradition, possibly dating back to Plato's pupil Aristotle and firmly re-established at the time of George Grote in the 1840s, has viewed the whole story as an ahistorical myth.[99] On the other hand, there have been others who have believed the story to be entirely true.[100] The majority of those writing about it, however, have taken positions between these two poles, either hesitating between the extreme positions or accepting that there is some historical truth in the myth although history was far from the only reason for his recounting of the story.

I belong to the moderate majority on this issue. I believe that the narrative does not form a single historical whole. On the other hand, it would appear equally certain that some sections do refer to actual places and events. The problem is how to sort them out.

The Irish classicist John Luce has established a very strong case that Solon did go to Egypt shortly after 600 BC, and that he probably had both a nephew and a great-grandnephew called Kritias and that the latter Kritias, who was the figure of that name in Plato's dialogues, was the philosopher's great-grandfather. This fits well with the words Plato put in Kritias' mouth. Thus, despite the two hundred years and more between Solon's visit and Plato's composition of the dialogues,

Plato could well have been drawing on a family tradition. However, as
Luce points out, he could have gained additional information from
his own visit to Egypt.[101]

Atlantis and the 'Atlantic'

There is no doubt that when Plato referred to the 'Atlantic Ocean',
Atlantikon Pelagos, he meant what we call the Atlantic Ocean. This is
because he is quite explicit that it lay beyond the Pillars of Herakles,
the Straits of Gibraltar. On geological grounds, it is equally clear that
the island there that was 'larger than Libya [Africa] and Asia together'
was not some lost continent lying in the middle of the Atlantic, where
the Atlantic Ridge now is.

On the other hand – as scholars have suggested since soon after Columbus's discovery – Atlantis could have been America.[102] In Volume 1,
I considered the possibility of African contacts with Mexico at the beginning of the 1st millennium BC.[103] We also know from Herodotos
that Phoenicians employed by the pharaoh Necho (610–595 BC) had
circumnavigated Africa and that in the 5th century BC Carthaginians
had sailed down the coast of West Africa as far as the Gulf of Guinea.[104]
Therefore, the chances of sightings or landings on Brazil, while avoiding the African coastal winds and currents – in the way that the Portuguese sailor Cabral did in 1500 AD – would seem quite high. Thus,
I see no reason why educated Egyptians should not have known of
America at the time of Plato in the early 4th century or that of Solon
in the late 6th.

While at one level the *Atlantikon Pelagos* is the Atlantic Ocean and
the huge island in it could be America, there are other levels at which
they clearly cannot be equated. It would be extraordinarily implausible to suggest that an American 'confederation of kings' ruled over
Africa as far as Egypt and Europe as far as Tuscany, and it is quite out
of the question to suppose that anyone seriously imagined that America could have been 'swallowed up by the sea'.

I shall be returning to these issues and to the relationship between
Atlantis and Thera but, before that, I believe it would be helpful to
investigate the origin and the meanings of the Greek root *Atla-*.

Atlantis and Atlas and his Mountain(s)

The most widely accepted theory for the origin of the name of the
Atlas Mountains in Northwest Africa is that proposed by the French
geographer Vivien Saint Martin in 1863, and put in a suitably esoteric

linguistic form by Walter Steinhauser in 1936: that the mountains get their name from the native Berber word *adrār* (mountain).[105] *Adrār* is attested only from the 19th century but there is no reason to suppose that it is not an ancient word. Although Steinhauser's reconstruction of a Proto-Berber *atlār* is open to doubt, there is no serious phonetic difficulty with deriving Atlas from *adrār*. Semantically, however, there are some problems in that *adrār* is not the local name for the Atlas Mountains; this has been Deren or Durin sometimes compounded as Adrār n Deren.[106] Deren could have been the local name that led Strabo to refer to the mountain as Duris and Pliny as Addiris.[107] There are indirect references to the 'Atlas' Mountains in the *periplous* (description of voyage) of the 5th-century Carthaginian traveller Hanno and the geographical name 'Atlas' was widely known in later Antiquity.[108]

Steinhauser argued that the giant's name came from the toponym. This could be so, but we cannot neglect the much earlier attested personal name and its mythological connotations. The name Atlas is first attested in Hesiod and Homer as the name of the Titan or giant who separated the earth from the sky which he continued to support by tall pillars.[109] In this function, he would seem to derive from the Egyptian god Shu, the god of dryness and air who holds Nut the sky up away from Geb the earth.[110] Interestingly, there are two associations between Shu and the west. Firstly, there is his name, ⌐. The ⌐ clearly refers to the possibly related words *šwỉ* (air, empty, free) and *šwt*, ⌐ (feather), but the sign ⌐ is also the symbol of Libya and the Libyans – the people to the west of Egypt – who seem to have worn large feathers on their heads. The second connection between Shu and the west is his close association with the god Tm, the divinity of the evening or western sun.[111]

The first reference to Atlas as a toponym comes in Herodotos who refers to it not as a mountain range but as a single mountain with a slender cone, whose peaks are always covered in cloud. According to Herodotos the local inhabitants were named Atlantes after the mountain which they called 'the Pillar of the Sky'.[112] Thus, the original meaning seems to have been 'edge of the world' or Pillar of Herakles. In the myth-cycle of the Twelve Labours of Herakles there is the well-known story of Atlas' tricking the hero into holding up the sky and of Herakles' trick to hand the burden back. The parallel or connection between Atlas and Herakles has been touched on in Chapter II and the notion of Atlas holding pillars that keep the sky up at the gates of the world is already present in Hesiod.[113]

The connection between the giant and the Atlas Mountains would fit the name of the Atarantes – a tribe that, according to Herodotos, inhabited the deserts of Northwest Africa – as well as the Atlantes he referred to as inhabiting the mountains.[114] In short, it would seem quite possible that one source of the name Atlas/Atlantis was the Berber Adrār.

Atlas and Ocean

It would seem unlikely to be the only source for Atlas/Atlantis, however, as Adrār cannot explain a number of aspects of the name. For instance, the name Atlas was given by Herodotos to a major tributary of the Danube and the mountains from which this river flowed were called Athrys.[115] These could hardly be Berber, but they could come from a sense of *coincidentiae oppositorum* or at least an affinity between cardinal points, as discussed in the last chapter. In some ways both the Atlantic and the Danube were seen as edges of the world.[116] The notion of Atlas as a river raises the possibility that *atla* refers not to mountains but to 'rivers' or bodies of water. In which case the Atlantic would not derive its name from the Atlas Mountains but the mountains would take their name from that of the ocean.

There is no doubt of the intimate relations between Atlas and the Okeanos – the ocean or river that circles the world – according to Greek cosmologies dating at least from the time of Hesiod and Homer. Hesiod saw Atlas as the father of the Peleiades or Pleiades, the stars of storm; their mother was Pleione, who was herself the daughter of Okeanos.[117] The Pleiades were, in fact, sometimes known as the Atlantides.[118] Atlas was also known as the father of the Hyades and the stars/islands of the western ocean, the Hesperides. The 'ocean' that goes round the world and forms the rim between earth and heaven would seem a much more likely source of constellations than a range of mountains. This would seem especially true of the Pleiades which have been seen since ancient times as *the* stars of navigation – *plein* in Greek.[119]

In Homer's eyes Atlas was a figure 'of baneful mind, who knows the depths of every sea, and himself holds the tall pillars which keep heaven and earth apart'.[120] According to Homer, Atlas was also the father of Kalypso, the nymph who lived in a grotto on the island of Ōgygia set in the distant ocean. On the other hand, Hesiod referred to Kalypso as the daughter of Okeanos.[121]

Overall, it is clear that Atlas' essential function was to separate earth from sky. However, there were two ways in which this could be done – by mountainous pillars at the edge of the world or by the *ocean* which formed the rim between the two spheres. Judging from the mythological evidence, it would seem that his fundamental nature was watery and that the 'Atlantic' Ocean was primary and the Atlas Mountains were secondary. In short, Atlas-Atlantos was an equivalent of Ōkeanos. This would explain both the Atlantic Ocean and the name Atlas for the Danubian tributary on another edge of the world.

There is no Indo-European etymology for the name Ōkeanos and it is generally acknowledged to be a non–Indo-European loan possibly related to the name of Kalypso's island Ōgygia. Ōgygia has already been discussed in Chapter II in its relations to the Semitic root √'wg (to draw a circle) and the name 'Ôg, king of Bashan. Its links to Okeanos, the river/dragon/snake that surrounds the world and separates it from heaven, can be argued through the names Ōgenos, mentioned by the early 5th-century mythographer Pherekydes, and Ōgên, referred to by the lexicographer Hesychios.[122] Although, I believe, there is another candidate for the etymology of Ōgygia in the Egyptian Wgʒ (flood), the link between √'wg and Ōgygia is semantically and phonetically possible.[123] However, it is not possible to make more than a loose connection between them.

Another possibility is the derivation of Ōkeanos from the Sumerian *A ki an(u) (Water of the Land and Heaven).[124] The concept of both earth, *ki*, and heaven, *an*, having wet rims that were parallel or ran into each other was well established in Mesopotamian religion.[125] Furthermore, there is no doubt that Mesopotamian cosmologies and cosmogonies did have a significant impact on Greek theology and thought, and there are especially close parallels in the image of the snakelike oceanic rim of the world.[126] Nevertheless, the term *Akian is unattested and the etymology must remain tentative.

One way or another, it is likely that Okeanos is a Levantine or Mesopotamian name. Could *Atla-* simply be its Egyptian doublet or counterpart? The Egyptian word *itrw* is generally translated as 'river'. Whether or not it is genetically related to the Indo-European root *wet* (wet, flowing) which frequently had a final -r as in the Hittite *wa-a-tar* (our 'water') there is no doubt that *itrw* had a wider semantic range beyond river.[127] With the adjective *rʒ* (great), *itr(w)rʒ* (great river) was also widely used. In later times, this referred to one or more of the distributories of the Nile Delta. However, it was also used for the 'whole or main course of the Nile'; and the Coptic forms Eiero or Iaro were applied to other great rivers like the Euphrates and the Jordan and – interestingly from our point of view – the Danube.[128] The Canaanite borrowing from the Late Egyptian form – the -t- in *itrw* seems to have been dropped by the 18th Dynasty – is the Hebrew Yeʾôr. Like *itr(w)rʒ*, this is used both for the Nile as the river *par excellence* and for other great rivers.[129]

In the *Book of Coming Forth by Day*, more commonly known as the

Book of the Dead (a guide to the soul, dating back to the 18th Dynasty, 1575–1300 BC), *itr(w)* in the plural was used for rivers in eternity. In later times at least it would even seem to have been used for the river or ocean that surrounded the earth. Diodoros Sikeliotes wrote that 'in their language the Egyptians speak of the Nile as Okeanos'.[130] Horapollo, the Upper Egyptian writer of the 5th century AD, also identified the Nile with the ocean as the *noun* 'abyss' or 'deep' from which the world was created.[131] Thus, *itr(w)* or *itr(w)ʿȝ* could refer to either the Nile or the ocean or any other substantial body of water.

Although the Greek borrowing from *itr(w)* or *itr(w)ʿȝ* to Atlas-Atlantos would seem to have been in this sense of river/ocean, in either language there must have been considerable room for confusion with any body of water. Thus, although there is no attestation of *itr(w)* or *itr(w)ʿȝ* as an equivalent of *Wȝḏ wr*, the name used by the Egyptians for sea in general and the Aegean in particular, or of *yam*, the later Egyptian borrowing from the Canaanite *yȃm* (sea), the use of *itr(w)* or *itr(w)ʿȝ* in this way would seem very likely.

Plato's Atlantis and the Thera eruption

Now we come to the frequent association made in modern scholarship between Plato's Atlantis, with its fiery destruction, and Thera.[132] The most plausible explanation for the geographical confusion between the vast island in the Atlantic and Thera in the Aegean is to suppose that, given the specific links between *itr(w)* or *itr(w)ʿȝ*, *Atla-* and Okeanos, Solon, or Kritias in Plato's dialogue, found it useful to associate the lost island with Atlas, Okeanos and Poseidon in the ultimate sea, the Atlantic.

As well as the geographical confusion between the Atlantic and the Mediterranean in Plato's text, there appears to be a temporal one between what in Egyptological terms would be called the 2nd and the 3rd Intermediate Periods, that is to say, the 18th and 17th centuries BC on the one hand and the 12th on the other. Plato's kings of Atlantis, with this generalized sense itr(w), look very much like the Egyptian chieftains of the Peoples of the Sea, the confederation that attacked Egypt in the early 12th century BC. This confederation is referred to in the famous inscription of Ramessēs III: 'as for the foreign countries, they made a conspiracy in their islands. No country could stand before their arms. Hatti, Qode, Karkamesh Arzawa and Alashiya . . . Their League was . . .'[133] This looks remarkably like the quotation from Plato given above:

> Now in this island of Atlantis there existed a confederation of kings, of great and marvellous power, which held sway over all the island,

and over many other islands also and parts of the continent; and moreover, of the lands here within the Straits they ruled over Libya as far as Egypt, and over Europe as far as Tuscany [Tyrēnias]. So this host, being all gathered together, made an attempt one time to enslave by one single onslaught both your country and ours and the whole of the territory within the Straits.[134]

The geographical names cited above give further indications of a close connection in that, although not mentioned in the Ramessēs' text itself, two of the best-known confederates of the Peoples of the Sea were the Libyans and the Trš or Tursha who have been plausibly identified with the later Tyrēnoi/Etruscans.[135] If Plato's text was referring to the 12th century and some parallel were drawn between the invasion of the Sea Peoples and the 'Dorian Invasion' of Southern Greece which took place some decades later, a historical basis could be found for the description of Athens reported by Plato, despite the obvious fulsome praise and hyperbole:

acting partly as a leader of the Greeks, and partly standing alone by itself when deserted by all others, after encountering the deadliest of perils, it defeated the invaders and reared a trophy; whereby it saved from slavery such as were not yet enslaved and all the rest of us, who dwell within the bounds of Herakles.[136]

According to both Greek tradition and archaeological evidence, Athens and Attica did resist the Dorians and other northerners and provided a refuge for others fleeing from them.[137]

But Plato was not merely describing the 12th century. In his dialogue the Kritias, which is a sequel to the Timaios, Plato referred to 'the war of that period' in connection with the names of the Athenian kings Kekrops, Erechtheus, Erichthonios and Erysichthon.[138] These were not the names of the kings at the time of the Dorian invasion, who were Melanthos and Kodros. It is, of course, very uncertain how much weight one can put on such information. These chronologies and even the royal names themselves are extraordinarily inconsistent and unreliable. Nevertheless, as I have stated repeatedly, I believe that one should sift through these traditions for possible nuggets of historicity.

According to the most complete ancient Greek chronology, the Parian Marble – inscribed in 264 BC – which seems to correspond to the chief Athenian tradition, Kekrops began to reign in 1582 BC and the others mentioned in the Kritias were among his successors over the next century or so.[139] The possibility that the name Kekrops refers to the much older figure of Sesōstris will be discussed in Volume 3. Even discounting this, it would seem that the Parian chronology may be too low. Tradition reported that the greatest flood in Greek history, that of Deucalion, took place in the reign of Kekrops' immediate successor Kranaos.[140] It is possible that there is a connection between this flood and the Thera eruption, either through a *tsunami* or through the years of heavy rainfall which seem to have succeeded it in China and may well have done elsewhere. If the two events are connected, then we should have to place Kekrops before 1628.[141] Whether or not this is the case, and despite the lack of any description that would fit the latter, Plato would seem to have conflated reports of the wars and invasions of the Peoples of the Sea with those of the Hyksos, whose invasion of Egypt in the 18th century BC will be discussed in the next chapter. One could even take seriously Plato's report:

> But at a later time there occurred portentous earthquakes and floods, and one grievous day and night befell them, when the whole body of your warriors were swallowed up by the earth, and the island of Atlantis in like manner was swallowed up by the sea and vanished.[142]

Can Atlantis in this passage be identified with Thera? In *Kritias* Plato gave a detailed description of the island. The name he attributed to its first king was Atlas, the eldest son of Poseidon – yet more evidence of his oceanic nature. Here, as in the *Timaeus*, the island is set beyond the Pillars of Herakles in the Atlantic. Poseidon constructed a complicated succession of land and sea circuits around the island linking the outside to the centre by an underground tunnel.[143] It is possible that some elements of Plato's descriptions derive from the actual wealth and fertility of Thera or Kalliste before the eruption. However, the symbolic importance of these constructions, and the detailed and intricate mathematics and harmonics used in the description of the island's wonderful arrangements and extraordinary wealth, thickly overlay any such kernel of historicity.[144]

It is also possible that the island's association with Poseidon is in some way connected with the facts that Poseidon was the most widely worshipped divinity in Mycenaean Greece and that he was the counterpart of Seth, to whom, according to the Egyptians, the Hyksos were passionately devoted. Furthermore, Poseidon was the patron of chariots which were introduced into Egypt and probably into the Aegean by the Hyksos.[145] Here too, however, any possible historicity is obscured by the mythological importance of the story of Poseidon as the father of Atlas, the patron of the sea and of the earthquake that destroyed it.

THE HEKLA ERUPTION IN ICELAND

Having discussed the conflation of the 2nd with the 3rd Intermediate Periods on political and military grounds, it would seem useful at this point to reconsider Plato's – or the Egyptian priest's – first point: 'There have been and there will be many and divers destructions of mankind, of which the greatest are by fire and water and the lesser ones by countless other means.' There is a good case for claiming that there were two events to which the Egyptian priests were especially referring: the Thera eruption of 1628 and its aftermath and the eruption of Hekla III in 1159 BC. The results of this pair of disasters in China have been touched on above and will be discussed below. At this point, I want to consider the impact of the 12th-century explosion in Western Eurasia.

As the Hekla eruption was in Iceland, it is not surprising that its most dramatic affects were in Britain. According to the paleo-climatologists Chris Sear and Mick Kelly:

> The dust veil [put up by the volcano] may well have created an area of low pressure and low temperature over the British Isles. This, the research indicates, led to extremely high rainfall, which, combined with cold weather, would have made agricultural life impossible in areas such as the Scottish Highlands, the southern uplands, the Pennines, the Lake District and Wales.[146]

The archaeologist John Barber now postulates catastrophes and major depopulation in Northern Britain in the mid-12th century BC, which he and Baillie tentatively link to Hekla III.[147] They also suggest that the breakdown of the economy of the Highlands led to social disruption:

> The catastrophe was so sudden and severe that it appears to have forced hundreds of thousands of people to leave their upland homes to seek a new life in the already inhabited valleys and lowlands. Widespread warfare would have followed and in the later half of the twelfth century BC, valley settlements start to be fortified.[148]

However, the drama had a background. Barber and Baillie agree that for several centuries before the eruption the Scottish Highlands had been under severe environmental stress as a result of long-term climatic changes. Nevertheless, they insist that the final breakdown occurred only after the eruption.

To what extent can one apply these data elsewhere? It is clearly impossible to maintain that the social collapse of the East Mediterranean basin occurred only after 1159 BC. The invasions of the Sea Peoples, their destruction of Hatti (the Hittite Empire in Central Anatolia) and other states began decades earlier and the disturbances around the Aegean began in the late 13th century. These facts would seem to fit the theory proposed over thirty years ago by the American classical archaeologist Rhys Carpenter and revived in the 1970s, in a different way, by the archaeologists Bryson, Lamb and Donley.[149] However, more recent studies have been unable to detect any long-term deterioration. What is more, while the scholars working on this admit that there must have been droughts in Southern Greece, some of which may well have lasted for several years in a row, they also insist that similar disasters would have occurred in earlier centuries but were overcome without any drastic reduction of population.[150]

In Chapter XI, I shall argue that during the period of the *Pax Aegyptiaca*, from *c.* 1470–1220 BC, Egyptian grain was shipped to the Aegean at least for famine relief.[151] In Chapter XII, I maintain that it was the political collapse of this structure and the trading pattern dependent on it that led to the breakdown of the Mycenaean economy and consequently the high population density supported by it being unable to survive climatic adversity. Now it may be that the Invasions of the Peoples of the Sea were at least partially precipitated by long-term climatic deteriorations in regions beyond the Mediterranean of the type noted above for Britain, but in the East Mediterranean itself the prime cause of the end of the Bronze Age seems to have been political rather than climatic.[152]

Nevertheless, there is little doubt that the situation deteriorated sharply after 1159. It is after this that Mycenae and Tiryns were destroyed, and the Southern Aegean islands were settled by Dorians, Western Anatolia by Ionians, and the Phrygians spread destructively through much of Central Anatolia. At the same time, Middle-Elamite power in what is now Iran mysteriously collapsed.[153] While one cannot attribute the social, economic and political collapse at the end of the Bronze Age to Hekla III, there would seem little doubt that some of what Michael Baillie has shown to be the world-wide effects of this massive volcanic activity would have been present during the worst years of the crisis.[154]

Thus, just as the Thera eruption seems to have been associated, by later tradition, with political and military events surrounding the Hyksos, it would seem that the eruption of Hekla III was seen as a manifestation of the social and political chaos of the 12th century.

Plato and his predecessors Kritias and Solon were therefore connecting not only the Hyksos and the Peoples of the Sea but Thera and
Hekla III.

CHINA:
THE HISTORIOGRAPHICAL IMPACT

The plausible suggestion, made earlier in this chapter, that the Thera
eruption took place just before the overthrow of the Xia Dynasty and
may have facilitated the triumph of its successor the Shang Dynasty
has interesting implications for the influence of the eruption, in conjunction with that of Hekla III, on the course of Chinese history over
the last 3,600 years. Before considering such long-range impacts, however, I should like to investigate the impact of the relation of the
Thera eruption to the fall of the Xia Dynasty on historiography.

As mentioned above, Pang and Chou collected sources on the fall of
Xia, some of which purported to be contemporary documents from
the *Shujing* or 'Book of History' while others were drawn from different sources from up to one thousand years later. These describe a
dimming sun and moon, the appearance of many suns, a dry fog, fall
of ashes, frosts in summer and destructions of crops. All these would
fit well with a mini 'nuclear winter' of the type which seems to have
taken place in 1628 BC and which it is assumed would have followed
the eruption on Thera.[155]

The claims of Pang and Chou must be put in the perspective that
the meteorological events they draw attention to are not the only ones
in the Chinese records of the periods concerned. Furthermore, there
is no answer to the charge that this synchronizing of European eruptions with Chinese dynastic changes is merely based on a series of
unverified suppositions. On the other hand, as I have repeated throughout this work, the same is true of all general hypotheses in pre- or
proto-history, including those that deny connections. In these and
many other areas it is unfair to demand *proof* for any new scheme
when *proof* is not available for most conclusions in natural science and
is certainly not the basis of conventional wisdom on these nebulous
areas. The best one can hope for in such cases is competitive plausibility. Here I think Pang and Chou have made a sufficiently strong
case for the relation between the Thera eruption and the fall of the
Xia for it to be taken as a working hypothesis.

If they are correct, the apparent accuracy of some ancient Chinese
metereological reports suggests that we should take a number of early

historical sources more seriously. Notable among these is the *Shujing* (Book of History), which was supposedly edited by Confucius in the 6th century BC. The tendency of 20th-century scholarship has been to see the *Shujing* as essentially made up of pious forgeries uttered by Confucius and later writers. The new meteorological evidence now indicates that in many cases Confucius may well have been, as he said, merely editing some truly ancient documents and that several of its texts do indeed date back to the early Zhou and possibly even the Shang Dynasty.

This confirmation for a number of its sections, as well as for the Shang chronology of the *Zhushu Jinian* (Bamboo Annals), comes in addition to that provided by the results of modern archaeology and from the 'oracle bones' which will be discussed below. Put together, the new sources of information indicate that there should be a major reassessment of the antiquity and accuracy of many Chinese classics.

Chinese tradition had no doubt about the existence of the first two dynasties, the Xia and the Shang. However, in the late 19th century Western and Chinese scholars, carried away by the prevailing positivism and scepticism, considered them as largely or wholly figments of the imagination of the Confucian and other later philosophical schools, concocted for moral and didactic purposes. Thus, as with that towards Western Asia and the Eastern Mediterranean, the 'scientific' approach to Chinese history has been to down-date traditional periods and to reduce the geographical scale of the ancient claims for travel, conquest or contact.

In the West, the approach of *Besserwissen* has continued more or less unchecked, but in China it was rudely shaken in the late 1920s by the large-scale discovery of what has now become a huge corpus of inscriptions on 'oracle bones'. These were bones heated to form cracks; the cracks were then interpreted as answers to inquiries put to the ancestral spirits and were then inscribed on the bone. The bones, usually excavated in the context of sites traditionally associated with the Shang, were found to contain the names of the emperors of that dynasty and the relationships recorded between them fit very well with the traditional historical sequence. Since 1949, extensive archaeology has continued to strengthen the credibility of the tradition. Furthermore, as elsewhere in the world, dates from carbon 14, though they do not indicate as high a dating as some of the traditional claims, tend to point away from the low dating of sceptical scholars.

However, the spirit of the 20th century is not to be balked so easily. The oracle bones are now the only accepted source on the Shang. The traditional materials on the dynasty, notably those in the *Book of His-*

tory, are considered virtually unusable and there continues to be a tendency to deny the historicity of the Xia altogether, despite the increasing archaeological evidence to back it.

Scepticism about the *Shujing* is, in fact, very ancient. As Confucius' disciple Mencius put it in the 4th century BC, 'It would be better to be without the Book of History than to give entire credit to it.' [156] Nevertheless, for Mencius as for many later scholars the best course was clearly to believe some sections and reject others. H. G. Creel, writing in the 1930s, at the height of the sceptical period, denied that the corpus had existed at the time of Confucius, but argued that a number of books, including 'the Oath of Tang', 'are undoubtedly Pre-Confucian'.[157] 'Pre-Confucian' is a deliberately vague term and essentially means simply that Confucius referred to, or quoted from, the document. However, the meteorological confirmation of apparently fantastic phenomena must be added to astronomical backing for observations quoted in other texts dealing with the period of the 'Three Dynasties', Xia, Shang and Zhou. Taken together, these give considerable credibility to the authenticity of some sections of the *Shujing*, not merely as 'Pre-Confucian' but as dating from at least the 12th or 11th century BC in the early Zhou and possibly even from the early Shang in the 17th, which is the period from which they are purported to come.

The Fallacy of the Axial Age

Scepticism about the date of these sections of the *Shujing* and the *Zhushu Jinian* should be seen in the light of late 19th- and 20th-century *Besserwissen* and the related appeal of the widespread notion expressed most clearly by the German historian and philosopher Karl Jaspers of an 'Axial Age'.

According to this scheme, in the middle of the 1st millennium BC, by some mysterious osmosis, there was supposed to have been a simultaneous cultural breakthrough in Greece, with Sokrates, Plato and Aristotle, in Iran, with Zoroaster, in India, with Buddha, and in China, with Confucius and Laozi [Laotzu] the founder of Taoism.[158]

Because it includes Iran, India and China, this scheme is less Eurocentric than most of those current when it was established. Interestingly, though not surprisingly, the nature of this breakthrough is rather unclear. The sinologist Benjamin Schwartz has provided a working definition used by the two latest conferences on the Axial Age:

> If there is nevertheless some common underlying impulse in all these 'axial' movements, it might be called the strain towards

transcendence. . . . What I refer to here is something close to the etymological meaning of the word – a kind of standing back and looking beyond – a kind of criticial, reflective questioning of the actual and a new vision of what lies beyond. . . . In concentrating our attention on these transcendental breakthroughs . . . we are stressing the consciousness of small groups of prophets, philosophers, and wise men who may have had a very small impact on their immediate environment.[159]

This description would seem to fit to a tee what we know of the priesthoods of Egypt and Mesopotamia of the 3rd and 2nd millenniums. Why should there have been such an insistence on a transformation in the 6th and 5th centuries? In some ways, the whole scheme can be seen as the result of as well as a reinforcement to the Aryan Model. By denying the scientific and philosophical and religious significance of all the great Bronze Age civilizations, the idea of an Axial Age eliminates Mesopotamia, the Levant and Egypt as sources of Greek and hence European civilization. It also sets Archaic and Classical Greece in the vanguard, at the centre of 'true civilization'.[160]

In Volume 1 of this work, I put forward some of my objections to the idea of an Axial Age as it affects Greece.[161] It is also very dubious when it comes to Iran; a strong case is now being made for the great religious reformer Zoroaster's having lived in the 2nd millennium.[162]

The great Chinese philosopher Confucius claimed that he was a transmitter of ancient culture and he seems to have had no difficulty in envisioning the existence of an élite class acting in a very 'Confucian' way almost a thousand years before his birth in about 550 BC.[163] The increased credibility of some of the claims to antiquity of the *Shujing* makes it likely that there was a thoroughly 'Confucian' worldview in the late and possibly even the middle of the 2nd millennium BC. Thus, the Chinese 'leg' of the 'Axial Age' now appears equally shaky.

The chronology of the Xia and Shang Dynasties

Now that it seems very likely that the fall of the Xia Dynasty was within a decade or two after 1628, it is interesting to look at previous attempts to date the change of dynasty. Kevin Pang's conclusion that the Xia fell *c.* 1600 BC was anticipated in the 1950s by Perceval Yetts, working from the two chronologies of Sima Qian and the *Bamboo Annals*.[164] On the other hand, one of the leading Western historians of the Shang, David Keightley, tentatively postulated the year 1460 on the basis of astronomical data recorded on oracle bones.[165] However, K. C. Chang, an equally eminent expert on the Shang, disagreed about the astronomical data and held out for the early 17th century on the basis of very early Shang radio-carbon datings.[166] As mentioned earlier in the chapter, later information from the first Shang capital points to the Shang Dynasty as being in place in the first half of the 16th century BC.[167]

The religious impact
of the Thera eruption

In China the eruption would seem to have had an impact on both religious and political thought. That on religion, in the strict sense of the word, would seem to have been shorter lasting. Immediately after the fall of the Xia Dynasty around 1620 BC, there would seem to have been a real awe of heaven and Shangdi, the high god. Tang, the founder of the Shang Dynasty, is reported by contemporaries or writers some five hundred years later as having said in a passage that has an almost biblical flavour:

> High Heaven truly showed its favour to the inferior people (referring to himself), and the criminal has been degraded and subjected. Heaven's appointment is without error; – brilliantly now like the blossoming of flowers and trees the millions of people are reviving. It is given to me the one man, to give harmony and tranquillity to your States and Families; and now I know not whether I may not offend the powers above and below. I am fearful and trembling as if I should fall into a deep abyss . . .[168]

Fung Yu-lan, the most famous 20th-century historian of Chinese philosophy, has pointed out that 'Here in a speech of less than a hundred and fifty characters, we find heaven and God referred to three times.'[169] It is no wonder that Tang was a great favourite of Protestant missionaries. For example, the 19th-century German K.F.A. Gützlaff wrote: 'From his frequent invocations of Shang-te, we might be led to believe that he was a pious prince who knew something of the true God.'[170]

Nevertheless, in China, this transcendent power of heaven was reduced in some significant ways. Firstly, it was insisted, from the beginning and throughout, that the reason for the withdrawal of the Mandate of Heaven – discussed below – was the dissolute behaviour of the last ruler of the dynasty, which had caused an imbalance of nature. Thus, there was a clear anthropocentrism. However, as by the end of the Shang Dynasty in China only the imperial clan had access to heaven, it was the dynasty – not the people as, for instance, in Israel – that was reponsible for the disaster. Secondly, and in sharp distinction to the Israelite tradition, there was an attempt in China to remove the arbitrary power of heaven by stressing the regular, cyclical, almost 'seasonal' nature of such happenings.

The political impact:
the Mandate of Heaven

The long-term impact of the Thera eruption, in conjunction with that of Hekla III, was seen in the formation of the Chinese religio-political concept of *Tianming*, 'Mandate of Heaven'. Before examining this concept and its possible relation to the eruptions we should consider ancient Chinese thought on the role of the emperor and the nature of *Tian* (heaven).

In a recent survey of what he calls 'early cultural orientations', the American intellectual historian Benjamin Schwartz sees the salient characteristics of China before *c.* 1000 BC as a powerful ancestral cult and the model of a hierarchical family in which the kinship roles are extremely important, though he hastens to reassure us that this did not diminish the individual. He sees the family model not only as central to the extended clan but also as imposed on society at large and even on nature. He suggests that, in China, the concept of a competitive and equal 'civil society' between the hierarchical family and the state was weaker than elsewhere.[171]

Associated with the direct conjunction of family and state was the image of the emperor and the imperial clan as the epitome of the world and as the only link between man and heaven. Schwartz believes that the great historian of Chinese science Joseph Needham – whose views on this he rather simplifies – has exaggerated the immanence or pantheism of Chinese religion and thought and underplayed the transcendental role of Di or Shangdi, the high god, and Tian, heaven.

Schwartz maintains the emperor's monopoly over the connection between man and heaven by insisting on the weakness in Chinese tradition of shamanism or cults of possession in which – in other cultures – the shaman's soul leaves the body and soars above the earth. One major qualification to this view seems to be needed, that is that the image of the emperor as the sole ruler seems to date only from the middle of the Xia Dynasty; earlier rulers appear to have been hegemons or first among equal lords.[172] Similarly, the idea of the emperor as the sole communicator between heaven and earth seems to have emerged only in the middle of the Shang Dynasty. Before then, he appears to have been assisted by a 'college' of 'sorcerer-scribes' but their role was almost completely subordinated to his by the end of the dynasty.[173]

Even for later periods, I think that Schwartz is too quick to dismiss Chinese shamanism and it seems that a shamanist tradition there is stronger than he claims. Furthermore, he fails to make a connection – made clearly by Needham – between shamanism and the 'gnosis' seen in Taoism and elsewhere, through which an enlightened philosopher can rise up to heaven.[174] Nevertheless, for the period after the late Shang, Schwartz is clearly right to stress the central mediating role of the emperor and to emphasize that, in this respect, China went beyond other ancient societies in which the people or at least the priesthoods had direct access to celestial forces.[175]

At this point, we should consider three related concepts that have dominated Chinese history for the past three thousand years. They are *tian* (heaven), *Tianzi* (the 'Son of Heaven' or emperor) and *Tian-ming* (Mandate of Heaven). Modern Chinese and Western scholars have had long debates on the meaning of *tian*. Some have argued that it was merely the sky and others that it represented a transcendental being analogous to the Jewish, Christian and Moslem 'God'. The Swedish sinologist Bernhard Karlgren, who dominated Western studies of early China in the mid-20th century, saw a form of the character for *tian* 夨 found on Shang oracle bones as that of an 'anthropomorphic deity'.[176] This would seem plausible from the shape of the character but the Japanese specialist on the oracle bones Shima Kunio has denied this adamantly and Shima's view predominates today.[177]

It would seem that, during and after the Shang Dynasty, the Chinese concept ranged from sky to transcendental god, but was centred on the image of *tian* as 'the solemnity of the dome of the sky'.[178] Some scholars imply that the concept of heaven as a divinity was impossible during the Shang because the oracle bone inscriptions often fail to distinguish between the character for *da* 大 (great) and *tian* 天, which is the same with a bar over the top. This, however, should not be taken too seriously as it would seem probable that the script used on the oracle bones was already archaic when it was used in the 2nd millennium. Furthermore, most Shang examples of *tian* are written with a circular 'head' rather than a single stroke.[179] Nevertheless, most scholars today believe that *tian* with a religious sense was a concept developed during the Shang Dynasty in the western state of Zhou, which emerged only with the triumph of the Zhou Dynasty, which arose from that state. They base their case on what they see as the absence of *tian* in a religious sense in Shang oracle bones.[180] While Shang concern with divine *tian* was probably wider than this, there is no doubt of its special worship in the state of Zhou and an explosion of interest in it at the beginning of the Zhou Dynasty.

The Shang emperors were known as *Di* divinities and, at least at the end of the dynasty, were seen as powerful gods in their own right, subordinated only to the *shangdi* (Upper *Di*) who was the Shang ancestors' ancestor or the '*Di* of *Dis*'.[181] This divinization was modified in the Zhou when the term *Di* seems to have become less current and the deceased Zhou rulers were seen to be living in heaven. Furthermore, by the early reigns of the Zhou Dynasty, the living emperor began to be called the *Tianzi* (Son of Heaven). The traditional reason for this was because he served heaven as a father.

The title *Tianzi* was also closely linked to the notion that the emperor had received the *Tianming*, the 'Mandate of Heaven'. This concept was well established by the beginning of the Zhou Dynasty. *Tianming* or the *Ming* of *Tian* appears repeatedly in the Hymns of Zhou in the *Shijing* (The Book of Poetry), the early date of which is generally accepted.[182] According to the *Book of Poetry*, 'The Mandate of Heaven is not constant'.[183] It was believed that misrule by an emperor could so upset the course of nature that *tian* – as a high god or agent, or merely as an inert reaction – could manifest the disruption by prodigies: floods, droughts, earthquakes, the birth of freaks, etc.

The general modern interpretation of this tradition has been that it was essentially a political ploy designed to give legitimacy to the new usurpers to whom the mandate was supposed to have been transferred. Furthermore, in a large country like China one can always find plenty of such 'unnatural' events to justify such a claim.

There is no doubt that the concept of a change in the Mandate of Heaven was well established early in the Zhou Dynasty. Given the uncertainty about Shang thinking about *tian*, it is not surprising that it is not generally believed to have existed during that dynasty. Nevertheless, David Keightley has speculated interestingly on the possibility that there may have been the concept of a *'Mandate of Di' during the Shang.[184] I am not so certain that the attestation of *tian* in the state of Zhou and the Zhou Dynasty limits the concept to that region and that period, and the parallel drawn by the early Zhou rulers, who claimed to have been given the Mandate of Heaven [*tian*], and Tang of Shang suggests that we should be careful before ruling out the authenticity of the texts allegedly from the early Shang, in the *Book of History*, which are in fact obsessed with *tianming*.

If there were major natural catastrophes near the ends of the Xia and Shang dynasties, how does this alter our picture of the Mandate of Heaven? It would make sense of the puzzling but key statement attributed to the people of Xia: 'When will this sun expire? We will all perish with thee.'[185] This now could be seen as a moving attestation of loyalty in the face of what we should now see as a natural 'nuclear winter'.

The existence of mid- or late 2nd-millennium texts about natural catastrophes and dynastic change lessens our scepticism about the protestations of the founders of the new dynasties that they would never have rebelled if heaven had not removed the mandate from the previous ruler and given it to them. This, in turn, would help explain the central paradox of how a civilization so focused on the royal clan as the sole bridge between heaven and man could make such radical breaks. Nevertheless, there is little reason to suppose that natural ca-tastrophes on their own could bring dynasties down. The destruction of the Xia seems to have required the conjunction of three conditions: political crisis, an alternative 'royal' family *and* the catastrophe. The lack of any one of these would have made the shift impossible. All three conditions existed at the falls of both the Xia and the Shang dy-nasties. There were princes and principalities of Shang and Zhou from the beginning of the Xia, the political crises were detailed in the ancient chronicles of the events and now we know about the natural catastrophes.

Thus, the Thera eruption seems to have been necessary but not suf-ficient condition for the Shang triumph. As we have seen, the situa-tion is not so clear when it comes to the fall of the Shang Dynasty itself. Nevertheless, the fact that the Shang themselves were over-thrown some five hundred years later and their fall was rightly or wrongly associated with natural anomalies seems to have set the pat-tern of a 500-year cycle. In Han times, in the last centuries BC, this was clearly seen to relate to the conjunction of the five planets which seems to have come every 516 years and it is possible that Mencius was referring to this when he maintained that a new king should be born every 500+ years.[186] As mentioned above, the conjunction did appear in 1953 BC, near the beginning of Xia, and dates of its occurrence were manipulated to fit with the beginnings of the Zhou and Han dy-nasties.[187] Thus, despite the short-term religious impact described above, by the middle of the 1st millennium BC the principle of imma-nence, with heaven as part of nature rather than dominating it, seems to have been largely established or re-established. Such a cyclical pat-tern would seem to be appropriate for a non-tropical agricultural civi-lization like that of China, where the basic temporal structure was that of the repetitive 'rhythm' of the seasons.

Another piece of evidence that would seem to confirm the 'volcanic hypothesis' is the fact that some late Zhou thinkers were surprised that, after much more than five hundred years, there had been no change of the Mandate.[188] What had happened instead was that powerful lords in the 7th century BC became *ba* (political hegemons), leaving the emperor with a small state and his central 'religious' position intact. This can be explained in purely political terms because the emperors lacked the military and economic power to dominate the other feudal rulers. Nevertheless, there was no discrediting of the Zhou comparable to that of the later Xia and Shang, and this may well have been due to the absence of a world-shattering natural event.

Interestingly, the pattern of secular hegemony was that adopted by Japan in the institution of the 'Shogunate'. In Japan, the concept of the Mandate of Heaven does not exist and it is claimed that there has been no break in the imperial family. This could be explained by the fact that – despite frequent eruptions and other natural disasters in Japan – there have been no overwhelming events of the order of Thera and Hekla III coinciding with an acute political crisis since the foundation of the Japanese Empire early in the 1st millennium AD.

In China, however, the tradition of the removable Mandate was sufficiently strong for Qin Shi Huangdi to be able to use it to seize religious as well as secular power from the last Zhou emperor in 249 BC, and these precedents established a tradition of dynastic succession that has lasted in China ever since.

In the 4th century BC, Confucius' disciple Mencius discerned another sign of the Mandate of Heaven, and argued that its loss was signalled by the people's turning away from the unrighteous ruler and towards the new one as water flows downhill.[189] Mencius' picture of the people's preference as an expression of Heaven's removal of the Mandate – *vox populi vox dei* – established an orthodox Confucian tradition according to which a popular revolt could set up a new and legitimate dynasty.

The choice of the word *Kakumei* (Removal of the Mandate) to represent the Western term 'revolution' was originally made in Japan. However, in a culture where the concept was viewed only at second hand, it lacked the potency of its Chinese translation, *geming*. Twentieth-century revolutionaries from the time of the Nationalist Sun Yat Sen have seen themselves, and have been seen by others, as bearers of a new Mandate and therefore legitimate in a traditional sense.[190]

When Mao Zedong rose to power, his image was easily assimilated into that of a Son of Heaven – and more specifically to that of Qin Shi Huangdi, the founder of the Qin Dynasty and reunifier of China. This gave him enormous traditional licence to change the world to fit the new era. The Chinese Revolution of 1949 was the result of the interaction of many different forces: national disunity in the face of imperialism, the desperate economic and unequal position of the peasants, and its offensiveness to traditional values of equality, Marxist-Leninist theory and the brilliant mind of Mao himself. Nevertheless, the traditional political implications of the Mandate of Heaven and its removal played an important part in the Chinese Communist revolution.

However, the link between political and social shifts and natural catastrophes has never disappeared. The tradition's continued vitality is shown by the widespread rumours in 1976 that the three deaths, of Zhou Enlai, Zhu De and Mao Zedong, were related to three earthquakes, including the one that devastated the coal-mining centre of Tangshan causing the death of hundreds of thousands if not millions of people. Together, they were seen to signal the end of an era and possibly the removal of the Mandate of Heaven. Nevertheless, conditions of possibility for the extraordinary transformations between 1949 and 1976 lay in the paradox of the double traditions of the 'Son of Heaven' and the movable Mandate expressed by natural disasters and popular movements, which go back more than three thousand years to the fall of the Xia Dynasty and thence partially to the Thera eruption.

THE WORLD-WIDE IMPACT
OF THE THERA ERUPTION

Positing the world-wide effects of the Thera eruption provides a fascinating example of the responses of different cultures to the same event. The Chinese case has interesting parallels and contrasts with those in Western Asia. Whether or not one can follow Pomerance in linking the traditions around the Exodus to Thera, there is no doubt that Israelite culture was acutely aware of the devastating effects of natural catastrophes. In a tradition that almost certainly antedates 1628, the god of Israel was fundamentally a divinity of turbulence of the type of the Egyptian Seth and the Greek Poseidon. He had a direct responsibility for earthquakes, tidal waves and disasters of fire and water. Thus catastrophes of this type would confirm his might – and that of his people even if they were the victims! Furthermore, it was within his power to strike wherever and whenever he chose. Nevertheless, the Israelite scheme was anthropocentric to the extent that the disasters were thought to have been brought about by the sinfulness of the peoples affected.

In the Israelite tradition the possibility of unpredictable disaster from on high is held strongly. Not surprisingly, in Mesopotamia there was generally more concern with floods than with volcanoes. Myths about floods long antedate the time of Thera. As we have already considered earlier in the chapter, there were Greek legends of catastrophic floods many elements of which were borrowed from earlier Near Eastern ones. The most notable of these, which was generally placed in the 2nd millennium BC, was that of Deukalion, whose wife was called Pyrrha (fire).

Another Greek tradition that may reflect Thera, among other seismic events, is that – discussed in Chapter II – of the battles between Athena, the goddess of order, and Poseidon, the god of disturbance in general and the sea and earthquakes in particular.[191] Nevertheless, the Greek tradition of major catastrophes was generally weaker than those of Israel and China.

Paradoxically, however, the relative weakness of a Greek catastrophic tradition could be the result of the catastrophes themselves. As the Egyptian priests were reported to have told Solon, there were serious discontinuities in the Greek tradition which they attributed to the disasters. Other reasons for the relative weakness of the catastrophic tradition in Greece, where after all there are frequent earthquakes and the Thera explosion itself took place, were the pleasant consistency of the Mediterranean climate and the great dependence of Greek tradition on Egypt. In Egypt, the principle of uncontrolled transcendence was at its weakest. If we can believe Plato, Egyptian priests of the 6th century BC were well aware that periodic disasters of fire and water devastated other countries but they were smugly confident that Egypt itself was always saved by the Nile.

In ancient Egyptian culture as a whole, the movements of sun, the stars and the Nile floods were all complicated but regular, predictable and generally beneficent. In Greece, despite the tragic or 'Nietzschean' view of man and the caprices of Zeus and Poseidon, it seems to have been this generally positive attitude that dominated views of nature.

CONCLUSION

We can now see that the huge eruption of Thera has had a massive and long-lasting impact on world history. The fact that its influence seems to have been most persistent in China many thousand miles away is not surprising when one considers that only China has had a continuous cultural history since 1628 BC. All the other major contemporary civilizations – in Egypt, Mesopotamia and Elam – have disappeared. Some legends referring to the eruption have been preserved in both Greece and Israel, but, as the Egyptian priests pointed out, the Greeks had no long-term cultural memory. We must now return to the central theme of this book and consider what our new knowledge of the nature and date of the eruption can tell us about East Mediterranean history around the middle of the 2nd millennium BC.

CHAPTER VIII

THE HYKSOS

I N THE PREVIOUS CHAPTERS, I have drawn attention to what could be called the two 'anchors' of the chronology of the 2nd millennium. The first of these was discussed in Chapter V. It is the establishment of a chronology for the 12th Dynasty based on the co-incidence of the beginning of the Egyptian solar new year with the rising of the star Sothis – which announced the Nile Flood – recorded in year 7 of the reign of Senwosre III. If, as would seem reasonable, the observation was made in Memphis, this would have been in 1872 BC. This correspondence has been recognized by Egyptologists for many years, and a chronology for the whole Dynasty from 1991 to 1786 was established by Parker in 1950. More recently, however, Parker and others re-examined the traditional reign lengths of the pharaohs with the result that he compressed these and lengthened every co-regency. In this way the Dynasty was shortened by forty-two years and now set between 1979 and 1801. As mentioned above, the new movement of German Egyptologists prefer to lower this date by forty-two years, citing the observations at Elephantine.[1]

The second 'anchor' is the establishment of 1628 rather than 1450 or 1500 BC as the date of the Thera eruption, which was discussed at length in the last chapter.

The chronology for the Egyptian 12th Dynasty has been generally accepted for several decades. The high Thera dating tends to discredit the low chronolgies given by the mainly Central European scholars who have dominated the historiography of Egypt in the 2nd Intermediate Period, that is to say between the end of the 12th Dynasty and the Middle Kingdom around 1800 BC and the rise of the 18th Dynasty and the New Kingdom in the 1570s BC.

There is little doubt that the Eastern Nile Delta was being heavily infiltrated or invaded from the Levant by the late 18th century BC. This chapter is concerned with the nature of these migrations and with that of the 'Hyksos'. These foreigners were given the name 'Hyksos' by the Egyptian priest Manetho in the 3rd century BC. However, the Egyptian prototype for this name, *ḥḳз ḫзst* (chieftains of the hill country), is attested before, during and after the 'Hyksos' period.

In this chapter, there will be an extended discussion of the historiography of the problem of the ethnic composition of the Hyksos. The chief struggle here has been between those who maintain that the Hyksos were merely the neighbouring Canaanite-speaking inhabitants of Palestine and those who believe that they contained Northern Hurrian or even Aryan elements from Northern Syria and the Eastern Caucasus. The champions of the Canaanites argue that the title 'Hyksos' or *ḥḳз ḫзst* always retained the meaning of chief or ruler and never had any special ethnic connotation. Against these, the 'Hurrianists' and 'Aryanists' follow Manetho, who had described the Hyksos as 'invaders of obscure race' from presumably distant 'regions of the east'.

By the 1880s, attempts were being made to identify the Hyksos with the Hurrians, speakers of a language that is neither Semitic nor Indo-European. At that time, the Hurrians were seen as analogous to the later Turks and Mongols in having come from as far away as Central Asia. Since then, it has been established that by the 2nd Intermediate Period Hurrians had lived for many centuries, if not millenniums, in Northern Mesopotamia and its surrounding mountains.

There is no doubt that, in the rising anti-Semitism of the late 19th century AD, the view that the dynamic, aggressive Hyksos came from the north was far more appealing than the image of them as local 'Semites'. Interest in the Hurrians and their kingdom of Mitanni, which flourished in Northern Mesopotamia and Eastern Syria in the middle of the 2nd millennium, became still more intense when it was discovered that the Mitanni swore by Indian gods, some of their kings had Aryan Indian names and, even more sensationally, some of their charioteering terms – the Mitanni were famous for their horses and chariots – were found to be very close to those in Sanskrit. The most plausible explanation of this situation was to suppose that speakers of Indo-Aryan, that is to say of an Indo-Iranian language that resembled Indian not Iranian, had conquered the Hurrians and retained a dominance over Hurrian society, which gave the latter the dynamism to sweep through Southwest Asia.

This view was widely stated, especially by Indo-Europeanists and general historians of the ancient world. But it was resisted by some archaeologists of Palestine and by many Egyptologists. These could not see archaeological evidence of a 'northern' presence in either Palestine or Egypt at this time. They also seem to have had the professional dislike of sensational or widespread events, and to have disliked outside intervention in their academic provinces. What is more, as anti-Semitism became more virulent in the 1920s and 1930s, many liberal scholars hated the ideological implications and uses of such an historical scheme.

This 'professional-liberal' current of thought became dominant in the anti-racialist atmosphere after the Second World War. After 1950, the Hyksos 'invasion' was generally demoted to a slow and undramatic infiltration of Semitic speakers, who had had the collaboration of many Egyptians. One of the most effective ways of discrediting the old Hurrian hypothesis was to use the generally accepted middle or low chronologies for Mesopotamian history to show that, as there were no Hurrian movements in Northern Mesopotamia until the late 17th century BC, Hurrians could hardly have been involved much farther south in Egypt a hundred years earlier. However, the acceptance of the 'long' or high chronology for Mesopotamia removes this objection to the Hurrian hypothesis.

Hurrians and Indo-Aryans have also been linked to the development and use of the light war chariot, and diffusionists have tended to see this as the secret of their military success. This seemed plausible as there is little or no trace of horses and chariots in Middle Kingdom Egypt, while they played an important role in the 18th and later Dynasties. Against this attempt to link the Hurrians and Hyksos scholars were able to argue, until recently, that, as chariots were first mentioned in Egypt at the *end* of the Hyksos period, there is no reason to suppose that they had been present at its beginning. In the 1960s, however, horses or at least 'equids' were found buried in association with Hyksos graves dating from the second half of the 18th century BC. Thus, there would seem no reason to deny the inherently plausible notion that horses and chariots came in with the Hyksos, and that the Hyksos 'invasion' was directly or indirectly connected to the Hurrian expansion and further that there may have been Indo-Aryan speakers involved in the movement.

All this looks disturbingly like the Aryanist or even Nazi image of the Indo-Europeans as a 'master race'. However, I am convinced that one should clearly distinguish between what one likes and what is likely. I argued in Volume 1 that the fact that arguments suit or are even created for distasteful or immoral reasons does not in itself falsify them. Here, as in Northern India but unlike in Ancient Greece, there seems to be a case where the Aryan Model works.

However, 'works' is a relative term: the importance of the presence of any Hurrians and Indo-Aryans in the Hyksos migration seems to have been largely confined to military technology; the Huns had no long-term influence on Europe and the Turks who formed the core of the Moghuls in India left virtually no trace there. What these far-ranging movements did achieve was the breakdown of existing political structures and the mixing of neighbouring cultures – German language and 'culture' entered the Western Roman Empire and Persian civilization came into India. Similarly, the material and linguistic culture introduced by the Hyksos into Egypt seems to have been overwhelmingly that of the neighbouring Canaanites and it was this Egypto-Levantine civilization with some 'barbaric' elements that dominated Lower Egypt between 1750 and 1570 BC.

The Chronology of the 13th Dynasty: Chaos in Egypt

In Chapter V, I mentioned our good fortune in having such a relatively well-established chronology for the 12th Dynasty. In stark contrast to this, the period that followed was one of the most confused periods of Egyptian history. This problem is all the more acute because, until very recently, Egyptian chronology has been the one upon which all those of the East Mediterranean – Levantine, Cypriot, Anatolian and Aegean – have been based. Thus, up to now any attempt to reconstruct Egyptian history on the basis of ceramic evidence from these areas has required circular reasoning. Now, however, the situation has improved somewhat with the anchors provided by the independent datings from Thera, though this does not by any means eliminate the many problems involved.

There is even dispute about the beginning of this Intermediate Period. As mentioned in Chapter V, in this book I use the compromise of 1801 BC.[2] The end of the 2nd Intermediate Period and the beginning of the 18th Dynasty and the New Kingdom are also debated. Conventional wisdom, as represented by Gardiner in his *Egypt of the Pharaohs*, put it at 1575 BC. However, the *Cambridge Ancient History* places it at 1567, most German scholars have it at 1550 and one radical puts it as low as 1539 BC.

Whichever date one accepts, the gap we are considering was one of between 211 and 260 years. Somewhere within this period we have to fit the 13th Dynasty and the dynasties of Hyksos invaders from the north. In his *History*, written in the 3rd century BC, Manetho or his copyists distributed the Hyksos dynasties – with a great deal of repetition – among the 15th, 16th and 17th dynasties. The so-called 14th Dynasty seems to have consisted of local rulers in the West Delta. Modern Egyptologists have appropriated the title of '17th Dynasty' for the Egyptian lords of Thebes, whose descendants later drove out the Hyksos, reunited the country and established the 18th Dynasty.[3] Thus, it is possible that the 13th Dynasty overlapped some of the Hyksos rulers and it is certain that at least the latter co-existed with the 14th and '17th' dynasties for many decades.

The chaos of the period meant not only that many kings ruled simultaneously but that their power tended to be unstable and their reigns short-lived and that therefore they built few monuments from which one can establish the lengths of their reigns. Furthermore, the Abydos and Saqqara king-lists inscribed on stone in the 13th century BC avoid the period. The Karnak Table from the 18th Dynasty and the 15th century contains the names of pharaohs from this period but mixed up with many other real and imagined names.[4] The *Turin Canon*, the king-list dating from the 19th Dynasty in the 13th century BC, covers the period, and is taken seriously by most archaeologists. However, the portion concerned with the latter part of the 2nd Intermediate Period is extremely fragmentary. It is virtually certain that the *Canon* originally contained a continuous list of pharaohs with their reign lengths for this period, though some of these appear to be fanciful. As it is, we are now left with small fragments with one or more names, which were put in some sort of order in the 1920s and 1930s by the charming and meticulous Heinrich Ibscher, whose 'feel' for papyrus was quite extraordinary, although he could not read Egyptian.[5]

There are also apparently insuperable difficulties with Manetho's *History*. In the first place, the fragments of the work preserved in later historians' works are frequently at odds with each other. Secondly, many of the figures they give for the length of dynasties are longer than the whole period between the 12th and the 18th Dynasties and some, though not absolutely impossible, seem improbably long. Finally, where we are able to check monuments and contemporary documents at the end of the 15th Dynasty, the sequence of pharaohs is completely different from that given by Manetho. Thus, Manetho, whose generally reliable work has formed the basis for the reconstructing of Ancient Egyptian history, is internally inconsistent and of only very limited value for this period.[6]

The only relatively secure datings we have for this period come from before the complete political breakdown of order, that is to say, in the very earliest years of the 13th Dynasty. At the beginning of the dynasty there were two pharaohs, who controlled the whole of Egypt for three or more years each. This was followed by a period of six years without a pharaoh. After that we are at sea, or have been until very recently.

The only major outside indicator for the dating of the 13th Dynasty would seem to come from the identification of a prince of Byblos named Yantin, who paid homage to the pharaoh Neferhotpe, with Yantin Hammu, prince of Byblos, who was a contemporary of Zimri Lim, king of Mari on the Upper Euphrates. William Albright put this plausible double synchronism at about 1730 BC and he has been followed in this by many Egyptologists.[7] However, Albright was working on the low Mesopotamian chronology and this has caused problems for the majority of scholars, who have felt obliged to take the middle chronology into account. Thus, in an article published in 1967, the Egyptologist K. A. Kitchen gave Yantin a twenty-five- to thirty-year reign so as to reconcile his subordination to Neferhotpe with the 'middle' or 'low' dates for Zimri Lim, 1775–1762 or 1705–1685 BC.[8] Wolfgang Helck felt this was impossible and, though happy with the synchronism if made with the low Mesopotamian chronology, he felt obliged to separate Yantin from Yantin Hammu if he followed the middle chronology.[9] The situation was made still more complicated by the new low chronology for Egypt devised by Krauss. Thus, when writing about the subject twenty years later, Kitchen had to carry out permutations for high and low Egyptian datings with the middle and low Mesopotamian ones. Nevertheless, by giving Yantin twenty-five to thirty years, he was still able to maintain the synchronism.[10]

All of these computations were based on the assumption that Neferhotpe ruled about 1730 BC. This fitted relatively well, though by no means perfectly, the ordering of the names on the *Turin Canon*. However, it presented historical problems in that Neferhotpe seems from his monuments to have been a powerful ruler controlling the whole of Egypt as well as having influence in Byblos. This would seem unlikely on the eve of what many historians believe to have been the invasion or infiltration of the Hyksos from Syro-Palestine into Egypt. Therefore, before Albright proposed his synchronism, there had been a tendency to adjust the ordering of the *Turin Canon* and to put Neferhotpe, and the relatively powerful pharaoh called Sebekhotpe

who preceded him, towards the beginning – rather than the end – of
the 18th century.[11]

Acceptance of the long Mesopotamian chronology would create
even more acute problems for Albright's synchronism. This is because
it puts the reign of Zimri Lim of Mari between 1831 and 1818 BC,
near the end of the 12th Dynasty. We know that two other princes of
Byblos were contemporaries of two of the last pharaohs of the 12th
Dynasty – Amenemhe III and IV – who, according to Parker, reigned
from 1859–1814 and 1814–1805 BC. Thus, Yantin Hammu would
have ruled before the end of the 12th Dynasty, that is to say in the 1830s
and 1820s. Tempting though the identification is, this can hardly be
the same as the Yantin who paid homage to Neferhotpe during the
13th Dynasty. The only way of reconciling the two Yantins is to break
loose from the Sothic dating upon which the chronology of the 12th
Dynasty is based and to raise it by several decades to end, say, in 1830
BC. While the Sothic date is the weaker of the two chronological anchors mentioned above and it should be questioned more seriously
than Huber's 'long' chronology or the 17th-century date for the Thera
eruption, there is no doubt that chronological chaos would ensue if
we were to remove it. It would seem simpler to do what Helck did for
different reasons and postulate two Yantins, thus abandoning the synchronism. There is no particular difficulty in two princes of Byblos
having similar or even the same name. We know, for example, that
there were two called Abishemu in the 18th century.[12]

Even though the synchronism did not necessarily require it, all scholars since Albright's first article have placed Yantin's overlord Neferhotpe at around 1730. Although this may be the case, there is no
reason to dismiss the proposal made by Stock in the early 1940s that
Neferhotpe and the Sebekhotpe pharaohs belong between 1780 and
1760 BC.[13] This would have the advantage of allowing some decades of
weakened or non-existent Egyptian power in the Levant before the
advent of the Hyksos. Whatever precise chronology one follows, there
is no doubt that for much of the 13th Dynasty and the 18th century
BC, Egyptian government was extremely weak and ineffectual. At this
point, we should consider a set of problems that are still thornier than
the chronology of the 13th Dynasty – those surrounding the Hyksos.

THE CHRONOLOGY OF THE 15TH
DYNASTY: THE BEGINNINGS
OF HYKSOS RULE

The nature of the Hyksos invasion or infiltration will be discussed below. Here, we are merely concerned with chronology and the question

of when the Hyksos period began. One solution is to suppose that it began at the end of the 13th Dynasty.

Thus, Hyksos rule would have begun around 1650 BC. Manetho refers to a 15th Dynasty of 'six foreign kings from Phoenicia', but there are two different versions of the names and order of these kings in the epitome of his work by the early Christian chronographer Africanus and in a long quotation from it by the Jewish historian Josephus which will be discussed below. The reign figures for these rulers add up to from 284 to 250 years, which is clearly impossible.[14] However, the Christian church father and chronographer Eusebius, referring to a Hyksos 17th Dynasty with some similar names and a scholia or commentary on Plato's *Timaeus*, gave a shorter length to this dynasty – 103 years.[15] This, in fact, corresponds well to the period of 108 years given to the kings in the *Turin Canon*. It has therefore led a number of Egyptologists to postulate absolute dates for the Hyksos 15th Dynasty of *c.* 1650–*c.* 1540.[16]

Such an interpretation requires a very low dating for the end of the 2nd Intermediate Period and the beginning of the 18th Dynasty. As with the 12th Dynasty, the anchor for the 18th is based on an observation of the rising of Sirius or a Sothic date, which in this dynasty is recorded as having taken place in the ninth year of the pharaoh Amenhotpe I. Until recently, Egyptologists have assumed that this observation was made at Memphis, as was customary, and deduced – on the basis of reign lengths – that the Dynasty began around 1570.[17] More recently, however, scholars have argued that, since Thebes was the administrative capital at the time the observation was made, and the papyrus recording the Sothic date was found at that city, this should be seen as the point of observation. Such a site would lower the ninth year of Amenhotpe I and the beginning of the Dynasty by some twenty years to 1550. The German scholar Krauss has gone even further and argued that the observation was made at Elephantine, still further to the south, thus bringing the start of the dynasty to 1539.[18]

There is something to be said for this last argument in that the Nile Flood was believed to have started at Elephantine. Nevertheless, it and Thebes would seem less likely than Memphis or neighbouring Heliopolis, which are the conventional sites for astronomical observations.[19] Thus, we should consider both *c.* 1570 and *c.* 1550 as possible dates for the beginning of the 18th Dynasty. Either of these make it difficult to squeeze in 103–108 years for the 15th Dynasty after 1650.

In any event, how much can we trust this figure of a century plus given for the 15th Dynasty? Very little of the *Turin Canon* survives for this dynasty, though what there is would seem reliable. Like Manetho, it states that there were six Hyksos rulers. We also know from contemporary sources that the last king was, as the *Canon* states, called Ḥmwdy or Khamudi. The ruler before Khamudi is not preserved on the *Canon* but, according to Manetho, he was the king named Apōphis, who clearly had a long reign of over forty years. This would seem likely, although there is some confusion about the name, which may have been used by a number of Hyksos rulers.

Apōphis' rule seems to have started with prosperity and with the Hyksos sovereigns on good terms with the native Egyptian rulers of Thebes. However, his rule ended with the revolt of these Egyptian rulers which led, after Apōphis' death, to the expulsion of the Hyksos.[20] If, as some versions of Manetho maintain, Apōphis reigned for sixty-one years and we accept the conventional date of *c.* 1570 for the end of the dynasty and allow Khamudi a reign of six to eight years, this would place the beginning of Apōphis' rule in the 1630s – that is, before the Thera eruption and its impact on Egypt in 1628. This chronology receives some support from a note on the back of the Rhind Mathematical Papyrus which was copied in the thirty-third year of the pharaoh's reign. The note refers to the 'voice of Seth' and the 'precipitation of Isis' in the eleventh year of an unnamed pharaoh's reign. The Egyptologist Hans Goedicke has argued, with some plausibility, that this could refer to volcanic action, given Seth's role as the lord of disturbance, and has specifically linked the report to the Thera eruption. However, he maintains that the pharaoh whose eleventh year was referred to was Ahmose, the first ruler of the 18th Dynasty. Such a solution could not refer to Thera, given the re-dating of the eruption. On the other hand, 1628 as the eleventh year of Apōphis would fit nicely with the chronology proposed here. There are, however, many uncertainties with the text and Goedicke's interpretation of it.[21]

Even if one accepts such risky hypotheses, Apōphis' survival for so many decades after the event makes it impossible to argue that Hyksos rule was destroyed by the eruption, though it is likely to have been weakened by it, whichever individual ruler was on the throne.

Before Apōphis, in the absence of any names from the *Turin Canon*, the history of the Dynasty is almost impossible to trace. Some scholars have identified Salitis or Saitis, whom Manetho referred to as the first ruler, with the king Šꜣrk (Sharek), mentioned in a genealogy of Memphite priests one generation before Apōphis.[22] This seems very unlikely, for, apart from the phonetic difficulty, there is Manetho's insistence that Salitis was the founder of the Dynasty, if not the leader of the original Hyksos conquest. In fact, as the American Egyptologist H. Winlock pointed out, Salitis is very like the Semitic root √slṭ and even the vocalization *salîṭ* found in Hebrew, meaning 'ruler'. This is the root from which the Arabic Sulṭan derives and, like the latter, it may well have been a general Semitic title used for Hyksos rulers which became interpreted as a personal name.[23] In any event, there seems very little to be gained from identifying Salitis with Šꜣrk.

Similarly, the ruler referred to by Manetho as Iannas or Staan is believed by many modern Egyptologists to be the pharaoh Ḥy ꜣn, Khyan, who is listed as either the second, the third or the fourth of the Hyksos rulers.[24] On the other hand, the Israeli scholar Kempinski identifies Ḥy ꜣn with Apachnan, a different name on Manetho's list.[25] The uncertainty surrounding Khyan is still more tantalizing because he appears to have been a powerful and long-lived monarch. Official cartouches with his names have been found throughout Egypt, in Palestine and possibly in Mesopotamia. Furthermore, as mentioned in Chapter VII, the lid of an alabaster bowl has been found inscribed with his name at Knossos. The geographical issues raised by these finds will be discussed below; here, we shall focus on the chronological ones. According to Arthur Evans, the lid was found in a context of the ceramic period MMIII. We have seen that this date has been contested and defended.[26] Nevertheless, if Evans is to be believed, this would put Khyan's lid before 1675 BC, according to the new dating of the Aegean ceramic periods. In this case, either Khyan cannot be identified with either Iannas or Apachnan as the close predecessors of Apōphis, or the Hyksos 15th Dynasty began several decades before 1650, or Manetho was not listing the six rulers of any one dynasty but simply the six best-known Hyksos rulers.

Another Hyksos leader, whose identification and date have caused some difficulty, is called Mꜣꜥ ib Rꜥ / Ššy, and scarabs with his name have been found in Egypt, Palestine and Kerma on the Third Cataract in the Sudan. Some scholars have identified him with Manetho's pharaoh Assis but others have denied this and have linked him to Salitis.[27] On the basis of pottery found in the same context at Kerma, Mꜣꜥ ib Rꜥ / Ššy has been dated to the mid-17th century BC. Given that the Sudanese sequence should probably be updated to tally with the raising of Levantine and Aegean ceramic periods to fit with the higher date for the Thera eruption and the 'long' Mesopotamian chronology, one should now think in terms of the first half of the century or even earlier.[28]

An even more interesting and puzzling Hyksos ruler was Mr wsr Rꜥ /Yꜥḳb hr. This name has not been connected to any in the *Turin Canon* or in Manetho, though it has been related to the biblical Jacob (see below). Stylistic similarities between his scarabs and those of

Mȝꜥ ib Rꜥ / Ššy have led scholars to associate the two very closely.[29] Thus, von Beckerath sees Mr wsr Rꜥ /Yꜥḳb hr as the direct predecessor of Mȝꜥ ib Rꜥ / Ššy, while Kempinski puts them the other way round.[30]

However, Kempinski has discovered what he sees as an anomaly here. He has found a scarab of Yꜥḳb hr in a tomb at Shiqmona near Haifa, which he dates to the very beginning of the Levantine ceramic period Middle Bronze Age (MB)IIB. He dates this between 1750 and 1720. Thus, Kempinski is forced to postulate two different rulers – Yꜥḳb hr, the local Palestinian ruler contemporary to the 13th Dynasty, and Mr wsr Rꜥ /Yꜥḳb hr, the Hyksos pharaoh, who reigned over Egypt and Palestine some eighty to a hundred years later.[31] Although, as we have seen in the case of Yantin and Yantin Hammu, it is sometimes helpful to postulate two different figures with the same name, in this case there seems to be no such necessity. It would be simpler to suppose with von Beckerath that Mr wsr Rꜥ /Yꜥḳb hr was a close predecessor of Mȝꜥ ib Rꜥ / Ššy, but that both reigned in the 18th rather than the 17th century.

THE HYKSOS CAPITAL
AT TELL EL DABAꜤA

At this point it would seem useful to consider the archaeological breakthrough made since 1965, and especially in the 1970s, by Manfred Bietak and his Austrian team in excavating at Tell el DabaꜤa, in the Eastern Delta. He has demonstrated that this is the site of the Hyksos capital Avaris. With meticulous archaeological technique in the very difficult digging conditions of the water-logged Egyptian Delta, Bietak has established clear stratigraphies for his site. As one would expect, given earlier knowledge of the Hyksos, the city contained a mixture of Egyptian and Syro-Palestinian material, indicating the place of origin of most of the Hyksos.

Apart from that Tell el DabaꜤa tells us about Hyksos culture, it also provides some interesting data on chronology. Unfortunately, Bietak has tried to fit this information into the low or ultra-low dates preferred by German-speaking scholars, neither of which fit the higher Aegean and Mesopotamian chronologies. Even in terms of orthodox Syro-Palestinian archaeology, his dates are disconcertingly low. Where, for instance, conventional wisdom places the transition of the Syro-Palestinian Middle Bronze Age IIA to IIB in the middle of the 18th century BC, Bietak placed it about 1700.[32] As he sees LBIIB as ending at around 1590, this involves considerable compression of what had clearly been a very long ceramic period in Palestine. It saw, for instance, five substantial rebuildings of the city defences of Shechem, near the modern Nablus.[33] In Bietak's latest article on the subject, he based his low dating on three pieces of evidence, which he claimed have provided dates that could not be raised. All of these are from styles of scarabs.

Scarab typology, seriation and dating are extraordinarily difficult subjects and theories based on them are notoriously liable to be overturned. Bietak himself has already destroyed one of his props. Since 1984, he has found a so-called *Rhy-R'* scarab – which he had previously claimed were not made before 1650 – in a stratum that even by his own chronology comes before that date. Thus, this cannot be used as evidence.[34] Bietak sees another indicator in the 'lotus back' scarab found in his Stratum G.2–3. This type, he claims, was uniquely a product of the reigns of the Sebekḥotpe pharaohs and Neferḥotpe and therefore to be dated after 1730.[35] As we have seen above, however, the dating of these pharaohs is extremely uncertain and they may well have reigned some thirty or forty years earlier.[36] The third diagnostic type of scarab was that 'deeply cut' with animal or human figures, found in Stratum F of Tell el Daba'a. These scarabs, he claims, began only in the reign of M3' ib R' / Ššy. Therefore, according to his chronology, this can be no earlier than the beginning of the 17th century.[37] However, as mentioned above, a case can be made for this ruler's having reigned in the 18th century.

In any event, the extreme unreliability of Bietak's use of scarabs for dating has been shown in a detailed argument by the specialist in ancient relations between Egypt and the Levant, William Ward. In a recent article Ward has used the corpus of Egyptian and Levantine scarabs to argue in favour of a date in the early 19th century BC – in the reigns of Sesōstris II and III – for the shift from MBIIA to MBIIB, that is to say 150 years before that claimed by Bietak.[38] Bietak argues that:

> Palestinian chronology is dependent on Egyptian absolute chronology. Therefore, it would be methodologically wrong to date the Tell el Daba'a sequence according to Palestinian dates in order to find its proper setting within the Egyptian framework.[39]

As mentioned above, this sentiment may be true in general, but it is certainly false for the 2nd Intermediate Period, for which Egyptian chronology needs all the outside help it can get. Given the newly established higher chronology for the Aegean, there can now be no question of lowering the conventional dates of the Syro-Palestinian ceramic periods; the likelihood is, in fact, that they should be raised, though, if one accepts Parker's dating of the 12th Dynasty, this process cannot be taken too far. Ward's dating of the key transition from MBIIA to MBIIB to the early 19th century BC is untenable if, as he does, Ward accepts the accuracy of Bietak's stratigraphy. The application of Ward's chronology to Tell el Daba'a would mean that Stratum F should be placed before 1850 and Stratum G some decades earlier than that. At the centre of Tell el Daba'a, there was an Egyptian palace before Stratum G which appears to have been destroyed and the area settled by Syro-Palestinians for two centuries. The idea that such a thing could happen at the height of the powerful 12th Dynasty is unthinkable. Thus, it is impossible to reconcile Ward's chronology, Bietak's stratification and any of the conventional datings of the 12th Dynasty.

It would seem better to take a date for the transition from MBIIA to MBIIB closer to the conventional 1750 or a little earlier. This would be Bietak's Stratum F, which he sees as the beginning of the Hyksos period at Tell el Daba'a. There have been only two radio-carbon dates from Tell el Daba'a Stratum G but, for what they are worth, they have 'central dates' in the mid-18th century BC. Bietak himself admits that the first of these 'fit very well into the absolute chronological scheme generally accepted by Palestinian archaeology'.[40] There is no destruction layer associated with Stratum F. As mentioned above, however, a thick layer of ashes separates its predecessor from the one before that. Thus, according to the chronology proposed here, the Egyptian palace of the 12th Dynasty would have been destroyed and replaced by a predominantly Asiatic population late in the 19th or early in the 18th century BC, that is to say near the end of the 12th or the beginning of the 13th Dynasty.

THE 400-YEAR STELA
AND THE TEMPLE OF SETH

The notion that Syro-Palestinians or Hyksos were in power – at least in the Eastern Delta – during the 18th century BC is made more credible by a stela found at Tanis to the north of Tell el Daba'a commemorating the 400th anniversary of the foundation of a temple of Seth. There has been considerable debate as to whether or not this has any connection with the establishment of Hyksos power at Avaris. No one contests that the Hyksos were especially devoted to Seth or that there was an important temple dedicated to him at Avaris. Although there were arguments in favour of Tanis being the site of Avaris, these have now been silenced by Bietak's discoveries at Tell el Daba'a.

The stela at Tanis was erected by Seti (an ancestor of the pharaohs of the 19th Dynasty) who was an official under Ḥaremḥeb, the last ruler of the 18th Dynasty. Ḥaremḥeb is generally thought to have ruled between 1348 and 1320 BC. There have been some questions about the exactitude of the period of 400 years inscribed on the stela but most scholars have accepted that the figure should be taken at face value.⁴¹ Thus there is a range of dates for the temple's original foundation between 1748 and 1720 BC.

Despite the great general uncertainty, there is widespread agreement that this cult of Seth was in some ways linked to a king Neḥesy, whose name appeared in the *Turin Canon*. This is because a fragment has been found with the inscription 'Neḥesy beloved of Seth, Lord of R-ʒḥt'; R-ʒḥt, meaning 'Entry into the Fertile Land', was probably used for Avaris, the Hyksos capital.⁴² Conventional wisdom has seen Neḥesy as a king belonging to the 14th Dynasty.⁴³ However, all versions of Manetho insist that that dynasty was based at Xois in the West Delta, while inscriptions with the name of Neḥesy come from Tanis and Tell el Dabaʿa in the East. It would seem better to follow the Canadian ancient historian John van Seters's more modest claim that Neḥesy was simply a local ruler in the region of Avaris.⁴⁴ Given the proven Hyksos dedication to Seth at the end of their period of dominance, van Seters is plausible when he speculates that one reason for establishing the cult at Avaris was that there was already a strong Asiatic presence in the region. However, like other scholars, he assumes that, as Neḥesy's name meant Nubian (Nḥs), he must have been an Egyptian official and this precludes his having been Asiatic.⁴⁵

Neḥesy may well have been Nubian. On the other hand, we know that Semitic speakers used the same name. The biblical name Pînḥås comes from the Egyptian Pʒ Nḥs, 'The Nubian' or 'The Black'. It is particularly interesting to note that the first attested use of this name was for a grandson of Aaron referred to in Exodus (the connections with the Hyksos will be explored below).⁴⁶ There is, of course, no way of telling the age of this name. However, as names tend to be the elements most resistant to change in myth and legend, it could well date back to the 2nd millennium or even to the period of the Exodus itself.

This is in no way to propose a connection between Neḥesy and Pînḥås. It is merely to indicate that the name Pînḥås (The Black) was in use among Canaanite speakers with no direct contact with Nubia. The name Pînḥås also casts an interesting light on the 'racial' make-up of this population with its indication that there were people with pigmentation darker than the Mediterranean norm, but that this feature was uncommon enough to be remarkable.⁴⁷ Thus, given our knowledge of the Syro-Palestinian presence in 18th-century Tell el Dabaʿa and the later Hyksos dedication to Seth, I see no reason to deny the possibility that Neḥesy (Black) was himself an Asiatic dynast. We also know from another inscription and scarabs that Neḥesy claimed to be a king's son and was therefore probably not the first of his line. It is generally assumed that his father founded the 'dynasty', but this is by no means certain.

Bietak has found a limestone fragment with the name Neḥesy that he believes come from a major temple. In admitted contradiction to his other datings, he places the temple in the 18th century and believes this necessitates forcing his Stratum F up to about 1715 BC.[48] If, following the archaeologists of Palestine, we push Stratum F to before 1750, we arrive at a date for the foundation of the major temple at Tell el Dabaʿa quite compatible with the period 1748–1720 specified by the stela's 400th year anniversary of the foundation of the Temple of Seth at Avaris. Furthermore, as van Seters has pointed out, even before Neḥesy there were probably cults of Seth in the northeast frontier region.[49] These were not necessarily Asiatic. However, the chances that they were are increased by the fact that Tell el Dabaʿa was inhabited by people using a Syro-Palestinian material culture many decades before Neḥesy, which if we take the chronology proposed here means from the early 18th century BC.

A CHRONOLOGICAL SUMMARY

To sum up this section on Egyptian chronology in the 2nd Intermediate Period, I propose the following working hypothesis. Around the time of the fall of the 12th Dynasty in 1800 BC there was political collapse during which some regions in the Eastern Delta fell into Asiatic hands – where they remained for the next two centuries. Despite this, however, the 13th Dynasty rallied in the 1770s and under the Sebekhotpe pharaohs and Neferhotpe re-established at least nominal power throughout Egypt and some of the traditional spheres of influence beyond.

This goes against the conventional wisdom that these powerful monarchs ruled in the 1730s. However, as mentioned above, the conventional late dating is largely based on Albright's indirect synchronism with Zimri Lim of Mari; as the synchronism may be mistaken and Zimri Lim could well have ruled eighty to a hundred years earlier, it is almost certainly wrong.[50] The earlier dating for Neferhotpe is difficult, though not impossible if one follows the *Turin Canon*, although this in itself is too shaky to be used as evidence. However, the advantage of the higher dating is that it allows time for the

consolidation of Syro-Palestinian power in Lower Egypt during the
second half of the 18th century shown by archaeology, particularly at
Tell el Daba'a. It is to this period that the Hyksos ruler Ykb ḥr would
seem to belong. There seems little doubt, however, that the 13th Dynasty continued in a reduced state at Memphis and later in Upper
Egypt for many decades, possibly until the middle of the 17th century, and it was probably under Hyksos suzerainty for the later part of
that period. The 14th Dynasty lasted on a small scale in the Western
Delta over approximately the same period.

The group of six Hyksos kings with a total of 108 years referred to
in the *Turin Canon* ruled from about 1680 to 1570 BC. These would
seem to correspond to Manetho's 17th Dynasty. It should be emphasized that, even though some of their names appear in the *Turin
Canon*, the succession of native Egyptian rulers of Thebes, who are
today called the 17th Dynasty, were not called that by Manetho. There
is no doubt that the last pharaoh of the later Hyksos dynasty was
Khamudi and it is almost equally certain that his immediate predecessor was Apōphis. Before that, although Manetho was probably referring to real names – with the exception of Salitis, which was almost
certainly a title – it is impossible to be sure which dynasty they belonged to. The same is true of the jumbled names on the *Canon*, some
of which may correspond to those in Manetho. However, while there
is clearly confusion in their sequence, all the versions of Manetho
refer to two dynasties of Hyksos pharaohs. This would suggest that
there were Hyksos rulers in Egypt before *c.* 1680 BC and this indication is reinforced by the archaeological evidence of Syro-Palestinian
material culture from the Eastern Delta. Thus, powerful Hyksos rulers such as Khyan, who are well attested from monuments, could have
well have reigned in the early 17th century BC or even at the end of
the 18th.

The idea that sections of Lower Egypt were dominated by Hyksos
rulers from the second half of the 18th century would also fit well
with the genealogy of priests at Memphis inscribed on a stela from
that city. As mentioned above, one of these came from the reign
of Apōphis and one from his otherwise unknown predecessor, Šꜣ rk
(Sharek). Then there are the priests who correspond to five rulers before the sixth, who was called ꜥ kn, who was the immediate successor
of a king called Ibi (one with this last name appears in the *Turin
Canon*). Gardiner claimed that:

> The important point about this Memphite Stela is that it covers the
> whole Hyksōs period and can accordingly have envisaged no more

than six reigns provided that these were of no more than normal length.[51]

This is uncharacteristically sloppy thinking. If, as is not entirely clear, the intervening rulers were not Egyptian, the priesthoods covered five generations before the third to last Hyksos monarch, Sharek. Thus, if the priestly generations were as long as the royal reigns, there would have been a total of eight Hyksos pharaohs – more than specified in the *Canon* or by Manetho. There is every reason to suppose that the priestly generations were like those of most privileged groups, approximately twenty-five years. Hence if Šȝ rk was reigning in the 1620s or 1630s, ʿkn and Ibi would have ruled approximately 125–150 years earlier, that is to say around the mid-18th century. In such a case Memphis would have been under Hyksos control seventy or eighty years before the beginning of Manetho's 17th Dynasty – or the modern 15th Dynasty. Thus, Hyksos rulers would seem to have controlled most of Lower Egypt from the mid-18th century. In this way Egyptian chronology can be brought into line not merely with Palestinian archaeology but also with the new high datings for the Aegean.

WHO WERE THE HYKSOS?

Although I believe it is essential to establish a temporal framework at the outset, in many ways treating the chronology first has put the cart before the horse by describing the dating of the Hyksos, and using the name interchangeably with 'Syro-Palestinian' without considering whom the title 'Hyksos' was used to designate, where they came from or even how they arrived.

Some of the longest extant passages – as opposed to epitomes – from Manetho's history are those concerning the Hyksos. These were preserved in Josephus' polemic against the anti-Semitic writings of the Alexandrian Greek Apion in the 1st century AD. The key passage begins:

> Toutimaios. In his reign, for what cause I know not, a blast of God smote us; and unexpectedly, from the regions of the East, invaders of obscure race marched in confidence of victory against our land. By main force they easily seized it without striking a blow; and having overpowered the rulers of the land, they then burned our cities ruthlessly, razed to the ground the temples of the gods, and treated all the natives with a cruel hostility, massacring some and leading into slavery the wives and children of others. Finally, they appointed as king one of their number whose name was Salitis. He

had his seat in Memphis, levying tribute from Upper and Lower Egypt, and always leaving garrisons behind in the most advantageous places . . . in the Saite (Sethroite) nome he found a city very favourably situated on the east of the Bubastite branch of the Nile, and called Avaris after an ancient religious tradition. This place he rebuilt and fortified with massive walls. . . . After reigning for 19 years, Salitis died; and a second king Bnōn succeeded and reigned for 44 years. Next to him came Apachnan, who ruled 36 years and 7 months; then Apōphis for 61, and Iannas for 50 years and 1 month; then finally Assis for 49 years and 2 months. These six kings, their first rulers, were ever more and more eager to extirpate the Egyptian stock. Their race as a whole was called Hyksōs, that is 'king-shepherds'; for *hyk* in the sacred language means king and *sōs* in common speech means 'shepherd' or 'shepherds': hence the compound word 'Hyksōs'. Some say that they were Arabs. In another copy the expression *hyk*, it is said does not mean 'kings': on the contrary, the compound refers to 'captive-shepherds'. In Egyptian *hyk*, in fact, and *hak* when aspirated expressly denotes 'captives'.[52]

Egyptologists and ancient historians have described this passage as derived from Egyptian folktales, thereby implying its untrustworthiness.[53] Although this is certainly the case, no one doubts that the text also contains some historical facts. As I have argued elsewhere, names tend to be more resistant to change than other elements of traditions and we should, therefore, consider their authenticity here.

It is certain, for instance, that some version of the name Hyksos was used at the time. The term *ḥkꜣ ḫꜣst* (chief of the hill country) had been used to describe Bedouin sheikhs since the Middle Kingdom and it was a title used to describe the 'Hyksos' leaders and kings during the 2nd Intermediate Period.[54] The first part of Manetho's etymology is correct and the second is based on the fact that there was a Coptic word *šōs* from the earlier *šꜣsw*, meaning 'Bedouin northeast of Egypt and their land'. Josephus' alternative – that *hyk* meant 'captive' – seems, at one level, to have been created to tie the story of the Hyksos in with the biblical tradition of a captivity in Egypt. Even here, however, there is a basis for the etymology in the word *ḥꜣkw*, 𓏏𓄿𓏤𓀀 (captives). The pun between *ḥkꜣ* and *ḥꜣkw* may in fact be quite ancient because written as 𓏏𓈙𓄿𓆟𓀀, *ḥꜣkw* meant 'plunderer', a title very much in keeping with the New Kingdom view of the Hyksos.

There has also been considerable speculation linking the name Toutimaios to a pharaoh called Ddw-ms, whose names are inscribed on monuments from Upper Egypt and who may be the '???-ms' whose name appears in the *Turin Canon*. The Egyptologists Hans Stock and William Hayes argue that they should be identified with each other.[55] Gardiner and his most talented student Battiscombe Gunn denied the identification in a very influential article, maintaining that the Egyptian name element *-ms* was transcribed into Greek only as *-mosis* or *-mbis*.[56] This seems to me to be a case of misplaced precision and, although the rendition of the name may have been modified by the name Timaios, after whom Plato's most famous – and thoroughly Egyptian – dialogue was named, this does not provide sufficient grounds to dismiss the striking similarity between Toutimaios and Ddw-ms. Thus, I believe that Stock and Hayes were right to stand by the identification.

DIFFERENT VIEWS ON THE ORIGIN AND THE ARRIVAL OF THE HYKSOS

Until the end of the 19th century AD, most scholars took Josephus' extract of Manetho literally and saw the Hyksos as a people who had entered Egypt in a single violent invasion. On the other hand, many writers, seeing the parallels between Manetho's report and the biblical 'sojourn' or 'captivity' in Egypt, assumed that the invaders were Israelites or Proto-Israelites, and in any event of Semitic type.[57] At the end of the 19th century, however, the idea of a people sweeping down on the rich valley lands in a way generally associated with the Aryans did not seem at all 'Semitic', at least in the Jewish sense; there was an increasing tendency to believe that they had come from further north, and were possibly Aryan.

Such a view had the backing of Manetho's statement that the Hyksos had come 'unexpectedly, from the regions of the East, invaders of obscure race'. This did not seem to refer to the neighbouring 'Semites', with whom Egyptians had long been familiar. For example, in the first edition of his quickly canonical *History of Antiquity,* published in 1884, Eduard Meyer argued that, while the Hyksos were basically Semitic and specifically Canaanite, they 'possibly belonged to an Inner Asian nationality'.[58] By Inner Asia, Meyer meant Inner Asia! In the 1880s, it was decided that the faces on certain sphinxes which had Hyksos names written on them had definite Mongol features. Soon after that, however, it was realized that, even if there were similarities, the sphinxes were 12th Dynasty and predated the Hyksos.[59] In point of fact, the sphinxes do not look European or East Mediterranean. Could it be that, like some other portraits of 12th-Dynasty pharaohs, they have African features?

By the end of the 19th century AD, an ancient text was found that seemed to support the view of the Hyksos as a separate 'master race'. In 1898 the aged polymath Friedrich Max Müller, who had dominated English Oriental, Indian and Indo-European studies since the 1840s when he had been appointed to a chair for these fields at Oxford at the behest of Christian Bunsen, published an article on Near Eastern history.[60] The text he examined was an inscription made by the woman pharaoh Hashepsowe in the early 15th century BC at Speos Artemidos in Northern Upper Egypt. In this – according to Müller – she described the ˁꜣmw as having lived in the Northlands, in Avaris with the Šmꜣw in ther midst'. Müller interpreted ˁꜣmw conventionally, as meaning the Semitic nomads, who had always been to the north of Egypt. By contrast, he saw Šmꜣw, which is normally understood as simply 'wanderer' – from šm (travel) or 'foreigner', as referring to Manetho's 'obscure race' from the regions of the East. He also speculated that this 'master race' could be Aryan.[61]

This view gained more plausibility – and ideological baggage – with the discovery that the Hittites were Indo-European–speaking and the discovery of the Mitanni kingdom of speakers of Hurrian (a language that is neither Semitic nor Indo-European), which flourished in Northern Mesopotamia during the Egyptian New Kingdom. We now know that Hurrians were living in Northwestern Mesopotamia in the 3rd millennium and they could well have been there since the 7th millennium BC.[62] However, at the turn of the 20th century AD, the Hurrians tended to be seen as nomadic forerunners of the Aryans. Excitement about them became still more intense when it was recognized that some Mitanni divine and royal names and chariot-driving terms were 'Aryan', that is to say they belonged to the Indian branch of the Indo-Iranian family.

These discoveries could scarcely have been more welcome. They seemed and still seem to suggest that the Hurrian-speaking Mitanni Kingdom was founded, or at least dominated, by Indo-European chariot-driving lords.[63] This fitted perfectly with the 19th-century view of the Aryans as the 'master race' which had expanded from central Asia or the Steppe with the chariot. In 1908 Eduard Meyer published an article on the Indic names among the Mitanni and on evidence for some Indo-European divine names among the Kassites, the people from the mountains to the east who had conquered Mesopotamia at approximately the same time that the Hyksos had invaded Egypt.[64] The following year, he wrote in the second edition of his *History* that the Hyksos 'came from much further away, from Asia Minor. They overran both Syria and Egypt, probably they were associated with the Hittites'.[65] In 1910 the Egyptologist Kurt Sethe published an article discussing the Hyksos. In this, he demonstrated that *ḥḳꜣ ḫꜣst* was used as a term for Bedouin chiefs in the Middle Kingdom and that Hyksos leaders had used the term to describe themselves. Thus, he suggested that it referred to a rank rather than a 'people'. On the other hand, he pointed out that at least by the reign of Tuthmōsis III in the 15th century BC, Ḥḳꜣ ḫꜣswt referred to a whole people. This provided a pedigree of at least twelve hundred years for Manetho's claim. Sethe, however, left open the question of whether *ḥḳꜣ ḫꜣst* had been used with both meanings in the 2nd Intermediate Period.[66]

In general, as professional specialists, the Egyptologists disliked wide-ranging speculation on the Hyksos as an exotic people. The American Egyptologist James Breasted, in his massive compendium *Ancient Egyptian Records* published in 1906, challenged Müller's reading of the Speos Artemidos inscription. He argued that instead of reading it as 'the *ʿꜣmw* as having lived in the Northlands, in Avaris with the Šmꜣw in their midst', *ʿꜣmw* and Šmꜣw should be understood as synonyms and the lines should be read in parallel: 'their' *sn* referred not to the *ʿꜣmw* but to the Northlands.[67] Forty years later, Gardiner translated an improved copy of the inscription in which, although he did not explicitly reject the translation made by his old friend Breasted, he clearly followed Müller's version.[68] In 1912, M. Burchardt published a response to Meyer in a note called 'The racial affiliations of the Hyksos'. Burchardt went over the clear Semitic etymologies of many of the Hyksos names and insisted that the *ʿꜣmw* were always seen as Semitic, though he admitted that some Hyksos names were not readily explicable as Semitic and that there was probably a Hittite or Aryan influence on the Hyksos.[69]

Despite this professional response, the idea of the Hyksos as a 'master race' from the east retained considerable appeal in the increasingly racist and anti-Semitic atmosphere of the 1920s. This was especially true among general historians. In his article on 'The Semites' in the first edition of the *Cambridge Ancient History*, S. A. Cook interpreted the Speos Artemidos Inscription as saying of the Hyksos, 'They brought many Amu (Bedouins) but were themselves foreigners.' He approved of the Mitanni who had what he called a 'strikingly virile organisation', and he thought that the Hittites and other Indo-Europeans were involved.[70] H. R. Hall's chapter on 'The Middle Kingdom and the Hyksos conquest' in the same volume was more cautious, but he too saw the Hyksos invasions as the result of movements of the Indo-Europeans, whose influences he detected among the Mitanni and the Kassites.[71]

The following year, 1925, Eduard Meyer published a new article on early Indo-European expansion, in which he emphasized the crucial impact of the Indo-Europeans upon the Mitanni and Kassites. He also saw both Indo-Europeans and Hurrians – he tended to confuse the two – as dominant over the Semitic Hyksos' movements into Syria, Egypt and – interestingly from the point of view of this book – into the Aegean.[72] In the 1928 edition of his *History,* Meyer linked together the widespread finds of objects with the name of Khyan to postulate a Hyksos empire stretching from Crete and Syria to Egypt and the Sudan, which, with the Central Asian image still in his mind, he likened to 'the ephemeral empires of the Huns or the Mongols'.[73] Even in the intensifying anti-Semitism of the late 1920s, there were opponents of this view and in 1929 the Egyptologist W. Wolf published an article emphasizing the Semitic nature of the Hyksos and denying any Aryan influence, though he conceded that there might be a Hurrian one.[74]

In 1933 the White Russian Indologist N. D. Mironov tried to reinforce the Aryan hypotheses for both the Kassites and the Hyksos not only by finding Indian etymologies for names that had not been explained in terms of Semitic or Hurrian but also by even challenging some of those given in these languages.[75]

All these writings mentioned so far belong to what would generally be considered to be the 'prehistory' of Hyksos studies. Its 'history' began with the dissertation of the Egyptian Egyptologist Pahor Labib on *The Hyksos Rule in Egypt and Its Fall,* which was published in 1936. It was a detailed study of the epigraphic and literary sources on the subject. Labib concluded from the Semitic royal names that the Hyksos were Semitic.[76] The Danish-American Egyptologist R. M. Engberg took a less clear-cut line in his monograph *The Hyksos Reconsidered,* which appeared in 1939. Engberg accepted Manetho's use of 'Hyksos' as an ethnic term and argued that there was 'the certainty that there was other than Semitic blood among the Hyksos'. In general he concluded that:

> It is clear that the Semitic element was strong. Hurrians too seem to have played a major part in the movement . . . among other possible participants Indo-Iranian elements appear to have made important contributions.[77]

Germans in the Third Reich found the situation simpler and felt less need for academic equivocation. The Egyptologist Hermann Junker saw the Hyksos as the result of an Aryan push in the 18th century BC, with a mix of 'different races'.[78] As the younger Egyptologist Hans

Stock put it in his *History and Archaeology from the 13th to the 17th Egyptian Dynasties,*

> Nevertheless, it appears doubtful to think of the Hyksos as purely or predominantly Semitic. *The leaders of the whole movement doubtless had a non-Semitic origin.* . . . The Hyksos are above all not to be seen as Canaanites or princes from Palestine. . . . this population never displayed the necessary military might and force (emphasis in original).[79]

Later, while he admitted Semitic influence on Egypt during the period, Stock insisted

> Nevertheless, one must turn to characteristics of an invasion from the north with a non-Semitic layer. Therefore like Götze one should think of a movement led by Aryan lords of Hurrians and also Semites.[80]

Stock's language, like that of his contemporaries Götze and von Soden, was academic, but, as will be discussed below, there are some internalist grounds for seeing 'northern' influences on the Hyksos.[81] Even so, there is no doubt that these conclusions were heavily influenced by the *Weltanschauung* in which the 'Semites' and at least those from Palestine (Arabs had to be excluded), were 'known' to have been essentially passive and incapable of large-scale political organization throughout history. Nor was this attitude restricted to Nazi Germany: it is evident in the writings of Max Müller and Eduard Meyer, as well as in the English authors of the *Cambridge Ancient History* cited above.

Given the power of anti-Semitism in the period, it is more surprising that the notion was fought so fiercely. The opposition came from various sources. There was a parochialism in the suspicion felt by Egyptologists and archaeologists of Palestine towards attempts to invade their fields from Asia Minor and the Caucasus. There was their positivism in that, as the remains and records of the Hyksos were overwhelmingly Syro-Palestinian and Semitic, they saw no need to speculate more widely. They also, as I have mentioned, had the professional dislike of the reconstruction of dramatic and far-reaching events as promoted so often by general historians and amateurs. Finally, however, there was their scepticism towards racism as a principle for organizing history and – after 1933 – this was reinforced by their distaste of its political implications.[82]

For these reasons, there was an essential shift with the exposure of the Holocaust and the creation of Israel. Before the 1940s the lines had been drawn between most professional Egyptologists on the one hand and, on the other, general historians with their views of the broad sweep of history and some Egyptologists who retained a respect for Manetho and were sustained by the prevalent racial interpretations of history and anti-Semitism. By 1950, the boot was on the other foot – the narrow professionals were now supported by the widespread revulsion among academics against anti-Semitism.

In 1951, the Swedish scholar T. Säve-Söderbergh published an extremely influential article in which there was no room for 'Northerners' or even for an invasion. According to him, the Hyksos domination in Egypt was the result of an internal rising by Asiatics, who had settled in Egypt over the previous centuries in collaboration with native Egyptians.[83] It is interesting that the same healthy atmosphere of revulsion against 'master races' and their conquests, and the preference for social revolutions over ethnic conflicts in the late 1940s and 1950s, produced George Mendenhall's denial of the Israelite 'conquest' of Canaan and his argument that in reality the 'conquest' had been a popular rising.[84] Gardiner, who as late as 1947 still believed that Hurrians 'contributed a large ingredient to the Hyksos invaders of Egypt', accepted Säve-Söderbergh's arguments fourteen years later in his *Egypt of the Pharaohs*.[85]

Säve-Söderbergh's position was also backed by the leading French and German Semitists Roland de Vaux and Albrecht Alt, who argued that the new activity among the Semitic-speaking Syro-Palestinians was the result of the Semitic-speaking Amorites moving into the Levant and Canaan from the Syrian desert. Alt believed that traces of this could be seen in the so-called 'Execration Texts' from the 13th Dynasty in which Egyptians had cursed the names of princes of inland Syro-Palestine, who threatened Egyptian power there.[86]

This view of the Hyksos as an exclusively Semitic and largely Palestinian local movement still predominates today, at least outside Middle Europe. It has been forcefully maintained by the German specialist on the 2nd Intermediate Period Jürgen von Beckerath and the Canadian Egyptologist and ancient historian John van Seters, as well as by William Hayes in the *Cambridge Ancient History*.[87]

However, Wolfgang Helck, who has written the standard work on Egyptian–Near Eastern relations in the 3rd and 2nd millenniums, has stood out against the new trend and has argued forcefully that there were Hurrian elements among the Hyksos. Helck believes that one should not dismiss Manetho's description of the Hyksos as an 'obscure race', 'from the regions of the East'. He has made a sharp distinction between the Semitic-speaking infiltrators of the East Delta and their kinglets and the later pharaohs who were called Hyksos. He argued, and maintained against the objections of the dominant school, that many of the Hyksos pharaohs' names cannot be explained in terms of Semitic or Egyptian.[88] Helck's need to make such a sharp distinction between the 'Semitic' and the 'High Hyksos' periods came from his acceptance of the low chronology for Mesopotamia. This appears to have prevented him from postulating the presence of Hurrians in Egypt before the middle of the 17th century BC, which in turn leaves him with the Semitic invaders or infiltrators of the 18th. If one accepts the 'long' chronology it becomes possible to admit 'northern' elements in Palestine by the beginning of MBIIB, c. 1760. With the middle chronology they can be there in the 1740s. It is only with the low chronology that Helck's apparently clumsy two-stage solution is necessary.

Even though he did not believe that they were there in the 18th century, Helck still argued that the presence of Hurrians in Syro-Palestine should be dated earlier than was commonly accepted. At this point, we encounter one of the strongest arguments for a Hurrian and possibly Indo-Aryan presence among the Hyksos. This is based on the fact that, while there is no indication of their presence among the Syro-Palestinian population in Egyptian documents from the Old and Middle Kingdoms, Hurrians are reported in considerable numbers in those of the New Kingdom, to such an extent that by the Ramessid period in the 13th century, one of the names of Palestine was 'Land of the Ḫurru'.[89] Furthermore, both Egyptian and Ugaritic documents attest the names of princes in the region with Indic names. These Hurrians and Indo-Aryans clearly placed a great cultural emphasis on chariot warfare.[90] Nevertheless, the New Kingdom references to Hurrians and Indo-Aryan warriors or 'Maryannu' begin only with the conquests of Tuthmōsis III in the 15th century, that is, two centuries later than Helck posits his Hurrian-Hyksos invasion of Egypt.[91] Van Seters maintains that the fact that the Egyptians knew the name of the Hurrians and used it from the 15th century means that their use of the old term ʿꜣmw for the Hyksos indicates the absence of Hurrians among the outsiders.

Van Seters also believes that the Hurrian presence in Palestine in the 15th century can best be explained as the result of early 18th-Dynasty attacks on the Semitic-speaking Amorite principalities in Syria leaving a power vacuum then filled by Hurrians.[92] For instance, Van Seters and other writers have pointed out that the archives from Level VII of the Syrian coastal city of Alalakh refer to horses and chariots but give no indication of Hurrians or Indo-Aryans.[93] However, if one accepts the 'long' chronology for Mesopotamia, one can see the Hurrian and Kassite movements (the latter was into Mesopotamia from the northeast) back into the early 18th century. Furthermore, Alalakh VII would be placed not in the 17th or 16th but in the 18th century BC, as the city was destroyed by the Hittite king Ḫattusili I, who according to the 'long' chronology reigned before 1700, and in the second quarter of the 17th century according to the middle chronology.

The linguist and ancient historian Anneliese Kammenhuber points out that the westernmost expansion of the Hurrians in Anatolia took place in the reign of the Hittite king Ḫattusili I, which she dates to the 16th century.[94] But this evidence has a very different significance if one accepts the long or middle chronology and places him decades or more than a century earlier. It would then seem to strengthen the case that there were Hurrians in the Levant by the 18th century.

The Hyksos as a Multinational Corporation

In recent years, Manfred Bietak, the excavator of Tell el Dabaʿa, has developed a new picture of the Hyksos. He has noted the huge quantity of Syro-Palestinian storage jars for wine and oil found at his site and has shown that in Hyksos times there must have been a massive trade up and down the Nile and into the Mediterranean. On this basis he argues that the ancient sources and previous archaeologists must have been wrong in seeing the Hyksos as land-based conquerors. Instead, he postulates that there was a sea-borne migration of Semitic-speaking Levantines from Byblos to Avaris and that the rise at the latter can be corellated with a decline at Byblos. Thus his vision of the Hyksos is of an essentially unwarlike commercial network with power like that of the Phoenicians in the 1st millennium BC.[95]

Bietak's evidence for the massive trade carried out under Hyksos auspices is incontrovertible. However, the conclusions he draws from it are much less secure. Firstly, there is no Egyptian or later reference to a migration from Byblos to Avaris at this or any other period. Furthermore, it seems risky to ignore the widespread tradition in Antiquity which stated clearly that there was a major invasion by land from the northeast – the only one referred to in Egyptian history before that of the Assyrians in the 7th century BC. This view is not contradicted by archaeology and, as we shall see below, some archaeologists believe they have found material evidence to back it. Bietak himself has found destructions at Tell el Dabaʿa congruent with conquest and tombs with armed men with pairs of 'equids' buried in front of them.

I do not accept that any decline of Byblos during the period at which
Avaris was flourishing has to be explained as having been caused by a
sea-borne migration from the Levant to the Nile Delta. It would seem
much more plausible to explain it as the result of a land invasion
as described by tradition, which opened up to Syro-Palestinians the
opportunities of controlling the trade of Egypt and the Nile as well
as that of the Levant. This led to a new commercial concentration at
Avaris, possibly at the expense of Byblos.

The most important point is, however, the general one that military
conquest and riverine or maritime trade are by no means mutually
exclusive. There are a number of parallel examples, such as that of
the Islamic Arabs, who combined desert raiding and mobile land warfare with a profound commercialism and a later dominance of the
trade of the Eastern and Southern Mediterranean. In Northern Europe there were the Vikings who combined their well-known raiding
with extensive trade and the urbanization of much of Northern Europe. Thus I see no reason to throw out the traditional images of the
Hyksos. Instead, I think that one should simply add the evidence of
their riverine and maritime commercial activities revealed by Bietak's
excavations, and – as I shall argue in the next chapter – by their remains in the Aegean.

HORSES AND CHARIOTS:
HURRIANS AND ARYANS

It is not at all clear that Helck had just Hurrians in mind when he
argued against the Hyksos being purely Semitic. As he wrote in his
History of Ancient Egypt:

> [The Hurrians] in their thrust to the South, had subjugated Syria,
> Kizzuwatna [Cilicia] and Palestine and broke into the Delta. They
> were later partly under an Indian aristocracy [*Oberschicht*], who in
> their migrations had brought with them the horse and the light war
> chariot from the Steppes of South Russia. Naturally the horse was
> known much earlier in Mesopotamia . . . but in conjunction with
> the newly appearing light war chariot its significance and worth
> were greatly raised.[96]

There is no doubt that four-wheeled vehicles were in use in Mesopotamia by 3000 BC. These were first drawn by cattle or buffaloes and
later by onagers or asses. It is also recognized that horses and carts
existed in Mesopotamia in Old Babylonian times (20th and 19th centuries BC), though it is not certain how they were used.[97] It is almost

certain that horses themselves were introduced to the Middle East from the Eurasian Steppe, but this does not mean that their use for war chariots first arose there or was associated with the speakers of Indo-European or its subsets, Indo-Iranian or Indo-Aryan.

Mary Littauer and Joost Crouwel, who have written the latest book on the subject, argue that the evolution of the four-wheeled vehicle into the fine-spoked two-wheeled war chariot took place long before there was any trace of Indo-Europeans in the region.[98] The Russian linguist and ancient historian I. M. Diakonoff has argued forcefully that, as Indo-Aryans are attested in the Near East only after 1600, and this was long after the use of chariots there, horses and chariots should not be used as markers of an Indo-European presence.[99] This is clearly correct, as shown, to take an extreme case, by the presence of the bones of a horse that had worn a bit near the 12th-Dynasty fort at Buhen in Nubia.[100]

Nevertheless, at least in a loose way, there is clearly some association between the Indo-European speakers who originated on the Steppe, for whom horse and wagon travel were of central importance, and the development of the chariot in the Middle East. The Russian archaeologist Roman Ghirschman proposed that Indo-Aryan (or at least Indo-Iranian) speakers with domestic horses and horse-drawn vehicles had been living in Northeastern Iran since the early 3rd millennium. He also argued that, around 1800 BC, Indo-Aryan speakers mixed with the Hurrian population of the Zagros Mountains – the present Kurdistan – and that it was this symbiosis that formed the Mitanni society that dominated Upper Mesopotamia and its northern fringes in the middle of the 2nd millennium BC.[101]

There have been a number of acute challenges to the archaeological evidence he gives to support this Indo-Aryan movement. However, they do not to my mind destroy the plausibility of the overall scheme.[102] One challenger, the German archaeologist Annelise Kammenhuber, has claimed that the notion of a conquest by Aryan charioteers is a myth. She argues that the Indic words in the Mitanni were relics rather than part of the spoken language, which was clearly Hurrian, and that the Aryan names of kings and gods were merely the result of casual contact between Hurrians and Indo-Aryans in the middle of the millennium.[103] The first part of her argument is persuasive; however, it suggests that the contact between Hurrian and Aryan speakers was earlier and therefore more likely to be involved with the introduction of chariots. The second part of her argument, the idea that the names of gods and kings are picked up casually, is extremely unconvincing.

In short, while the exact form of the symbiosis is unclear, the fact that the later texts specify that some Mitanni gods, royal names and some charioteering terms are Indo-Aryan, while the basic vocabulary was Hurrian, does suggest the Aryanists' dream of a conquering élite. As the contemporary Indo-Europeanist J. P. Mallory puts it, it seems that

> an element of Indic-speaking chariot warriors superimposed themselves on a native Hurrian-speaking population to form a ruling dynasty that endured for many centuries. The precise mechanism with which this Indic element fused with the Hurrians is unknown.[104]

Despite considerable ideological reluctance, I find this a very plausible picture. This does not, however, rule out the point made by Littauer and Crouwel that the light war chariot may have been developed in Northern Mesopotamia, rather than in Iran or the Steppe.[105] Nevertheless, the Aryan association with Mitanni chariots and the fact that Indo-European speakers were involved in their use from Central Asia to Ireland would make it seem quite likely that Indo-Aryan speakers were involved in its development, wherever it took place.[106] The most plausible scenario is that proposed by the German archaeologist Gertrude Hermes in the 1930s: that the light chariot was developed at a point of contact between horse and cart, using Indo-European speakers and Near Eastern technologists.[107]

Thus, while it is quite clear that, as Diakonoff argues, there was no Indo-European monopoly of the chariot and that its use spread to many peoples speaking many different languages, I see no reason to deny its first development to Indo-Aryan speakers.

HURRIANS AND HYKSOS

The further question remains of whether or not the formation of the Mitanni amalgam of Hurrians and Indo-Aryans had anything to do with the Hyksos. References to the state in Mesopotamian, Anatolian and Egyptian sources appear only in the 15th and 14th centuries BC. However, as Mallory points out,

> Our dating of the Indo-Aryan element in the Mitanni texts is based purely and simply on written documents offering datable contexts. While we cannot with certainty push these dates back prior to the fifteenth century BC, it should not be forgotten that the Indic ele-

ments seem to be little more than the residue of a *dead* language in Hurrian, and that the symbiosis that produced the Mitanni may have taken place many centuries earlier.[108]

As mentioned above, many scholars have dismissed Hurrian – and even more strongly Indo-Aryan – influences on the Hyksos purely on the grounds of date. As the Belgian Assyriologist J. R. Kupper argued in the *Cambridge Ancient History,*

> It is generally allowed that the Hyksos period opened towards the end of the eighteenth century. . . . At the time when these were moving into the Delta the Hurrians were just beginning to spread into North Syria, the only route they could have followed into Egypt. This being so, it is impossible, without pushing Hammurabi's [the famous king of Babylon upon whose reign much of Mesopotamian chronology depends] date considerably further back, to connect the Hyksos with the Hurrian migration. In the same way there can be no influence of Indo-Aryans, who appear distinctly later, certainly after the period of level VII at Alalakh.[109]

If one follows the long chronology, Hammurabi's date *is* pushed considerably further back, to 1848–1806 BC, and the Hittite king Hattusili I was fighting Hurrians in central Anatolia around 1700 BC. Following the middle chronology, Hammurabi reigned in the first half of the 18th century and Kassites, whose migrations appear to have paralleled those of the Hurrians, appear in the reign of his successor Šamšuiluna. In both cases, a Hurrian presence in Syro-Palestine in the second half of the 18th century BC becomes a very real possibility. This is only prevented by the low chronology. Thus, even if one accepts the argument from silence from the Mesopotamian and Syrian states, there is no cause to dismiss the presence of Hurrians or even Indo-Aryan speakers in the Levant in the 18th century BC. In all these discussions, I think there is an underestimation of the suddenness with which new military, political or religious forces can arise. Islam, the Mongols and the Taiping sprang into widespread action, to be greeted with a shock of the kind Manetho expressed about the Hyksos.

The archaeological and linguistic
evidence for a Hurrian presence

Does the supposed Hurrian presence in 18th-century Syro-Palestine show up in the archaeological record? In general, the only possible

line of demarcation that could indicate the putative arrival of Hurrians is that between Middle Bronze IIA and IIB, which, as argued
above, should probably be dated to the second quarter of the 18th
century BC. Twentieth-century scholars have emphasized the lack of
change involved. As Dame Kathleen Kenyon put it in the *Cambridge
Ancient History,*

> As far as Palestine is concerned . . . From the first beginnings of the
> Middle Bronze Age down to its end, and long past it, all the ma-
> terial evidence – pottery, weapons, ornaments, buildings, burial
> methods – is emphatic that there is no break in culture and basic
> population . . . this is the Canaanite culture of the Mediterranean
> littoral.[110]

There is absolutely no doubt of the essential truth of this statement.
Even so, there were changes in pottery styles, most notably the widespread use of the distinctive Tell el Yehudiyeh ware, named after a
Hyksos settlement in the Eastern Delta. This has been found throughout the Levant and Northeastern Egypt. There has been some question as to its beginnings, but at Tell el Daba'a it first appears in
Stratum G, which Bietak puts as 13th Dynasty and before the transition from MBIIA to MBIIB.[111] Nevertheless, there is little doubt that
it first appeared among a Syro-Palestinian population in the Eastern
Delta in the second quarter of the 18th century, and that it remained
in use throughout the Hyksos period. There is, however, no question
of its having been introduced by Hurrian or Indo-Aryan invaders
from the north.

Some scholars have drawn attention to what they see as a change in
fortification styles, namely great ramparts with sloping glacis of *terre
pisée* or battered stone. This has commonly been linked with chariot
warfare and then with the Hyksos and sometimes with a Hurrian invasion from the north.[112] However, these 'improvements' had already
appeared in the 12th-Dynasty fortifications in Nubia and were clearly
widely used in Syro-Palestine in the MBIIA period of the 20th and
19th centuries.[113] On the other hand, there is an unprecedented form
of construction in the fortified enclosures found – sometimes with a
raised acropolis in one corner – at a number of sites from Northern
Syria, through Palestine to Tell el Yehudiyeh in the Eastern Delta and
Heliopolis, now a suburb of Cairo.[114] Petrie speculated that they could
be enclosures for chariots, and no one to my knowledge has come
up with a better idea.[115] Whether or not this is the case, there is little
doubt that their purpose was military.

This leads us to consider the spread of chariots into Palestine and

Egypt. The possibility of ceremonial chariots in Egypt at the time of Sesōstris has been considered in Chapter V.[116] The earliest Egyptian reference to horses, *ḥtr*, and chariots, *t3 nt ḥtry*, comes in the inscription celebrating the campaigns against the Hyksos by the Theban ruler Kamose, in the early 16th century.[117] Van Seters points out that there is no mention in the inscription of their being used for a warlike purpose, but an inscription from some fifty years later mentions Kamose's successor, ʿAḥmose I, riding a chariot in the siege of Avaris. Van Seters claims that this was an anachronism on the grounds that the inscription also mentions, at another point, the capture of a chariot in Naharayin in Upper Mesopotamia, which, he maintains, could have happened only in the 15th century.[118] This would seem to be special pleading and there is virtually no doubt that war chariots were in use not only in Palestine but in Egypt by the beginning of the 16th century BC.

There is some debate on the origins of the vocabulary of this semantic field. The word *ḥtr* itself is clearly an adaptation of an Old Egyptian term for a pair, or span, of ploughing oxen. This was used for the new technology as a pair of horses for a chariot and hence a horse itself. Another word for 'horse' that appears for the first time in the 18th Dynasty is *ssmt*. This has been linked to the Hebrew *sûs* (horse) and the Akkadian, *sîsû*. This cluster is still debated but it has commonly been derived from the reconstructed Proto–Indo-European form found in the Sanskrit *ašva* (horse); the etymology has been made even more plausible with the discovery of the Ugaritic form *ś ś w*, which would probably have been pronounced *$*s^w as^w a$. On the other hand, although the words are clearly related, the possibility remains that they originate from another unknown language.[119] *ibr*, the Egyptian word for 'stallion', which also first appeared in the 18th Dynasty, is clearly derived from a Semitic form found in the Hebrew *ʾabîr* and the Ugaritic *ʾibr*.[120] One Egyptian word for 'chariot', *mrkbt*, is clearly derived from the Semitic form seen in the Hebrew *merkȧvȧh*, or in the construct form, *merkebet*. The other word, *wr(r(y))t*, was supposed by the Semitic linguist and early specialist in Hurrian E. A. Speiser to have come from the Hurrian *waratušhu*, but the existence of this form is uncertain.[121] Despite the uncertainty, however, there would seem to have been not only native Egyptian terms adapted to the new needs, but also Semitic and possibly some Hurrian terms, and ultimately Indo-Aryan ones for the new species and technology.

Apart from the Buhen horse, there have been other indications that horses were present in Palestine and Egypt well before the end of the Hyksos period. Petrie found bronze horse bits at Gaza at what he described as a Hyksos level. In 1936, the specialist in ancient horses Gertrud Hermes dated them to *c*. 1700 BC.[122] Since then, other scholars have tended to lower these dates, but they do not – as the contemporary classicist Robert Drews puts it – 'confront Hermes's arguments'.[123] Given the general confirmation of the higher dating outlined earlier in this chapter there would seem no reason to doubt that the bits were from the 18th century.

Evidence from Tell el Daba'a tends to confirm the picture that horses – or at least equids – were introduced into the Levant and Lower Egypt before 1750 BC. The skeletons of seventeen donkeys or equids have been found at the site from Stratum G to Stratum D3, that is to say between *c*. 1800 and 1570.[124] Most are buried in pairs in front of tombs and it is assumed that they were harnessed together. Looking at the ground plans of these tombs one has the strong impression that they were seen as symbolic wagons or carts being pulled by equids.[125] In Stratum F.9 (in the early or mid-18th century) in front of the grave of an important armed personage, the bones of two youths and five 'equids' were found. Bietak believes that both men and animals were probably sacrificed.[126] Horses' teeth have been found from Stratum E.2 from the late 18th century.[127] The practice of burying donkeys or horses near or in human graves also occurred in MBII sites at Inshas, Tell el Farasha and Tell el Maskhutha in the Eastern Delta and Tel el Ajjul and Jericho in Palestine, and there appears to have been a general association with armed persons, presumably warriors.[128] Thus, while there is no direct evidence of chariots it would seem that the newcomers into the Delta treated equids and carts very seriously, either at a religious or at a practical level or both.

The introduction to Palestine and Egypt of equids and vehicles associated with warfare from Syria, and/or further north, at this time clearly strengthens the hypothesis that Hurrians and Indo-Europeans were involved in the Hyksos migration.

HYKSOS MATERIAL CULTURE

Before the excavation of Tell el Daba'a very little was known about the material culture of Hyksos Egypt. This was partly because of the conscious destruction of Hyksos remains by the rulers of the 18th Dynasty, who were violently hostile to them; but it was even more that 'Hyksos' material remains were not recognized as such because the culture revealed at Tell el Daba'a was in fact one already well known to archaeologists of Egypt and Palestine – a mixture, or rather a range of mixtures, of the MBII culture of Syro-Palestine and that of the Late Middle Kingdom in Egypt.

Some features – like burials under house floors – seem to have developed in MBIIA in the Levant, while others – like the Tell el Yehudiyeh ware – arose either there or in the Canaanite Eastern Delta. On the other hand, both phenomena became characteristics of the Hyksos culture and period.[129] The graves at Tell el Daba'a contain many bronze weapons, especially axes, daggers and knives, made with the fine metal-work styles that had been developed in Syro-Palestine since the Egyptian 12th Dynasty.[130] Although they have so far not been found at Tell el Daba'a, swords, clearly developed from earlier daggers, have been found throughout Syro-Palestine during the MBIIB-C periods.[131] Thus, the Syro-Palestinian Hyksos culture of the second half of the 18th century BC already possessed the new weapons that were to dominate the Late Bronze Age – certainly donkeys, horses, carts and fine daggers and very probably chariots and swords.

The archaeologist and art historian Helene Kantor described the art of the Hyksos period as a *Mischkunst,* a 'mixed art'.[132] The only specific object that could suggest a contact between the Hyksos upper classes and the north is a striking electrum headdress with four gazelle heads and one of a stag that looks distinctly Anatolian. This came from the so-called Salhiya treasure found some ten kilometres from Tell el Daba'a and thought to be from a Hyksos royal tomb there.[133] There is also a kind of barbaric quality not found in other periods in the striking bearded male portrait on a pot from the Hyksos period at Jericho.[134]

Furthermore, there is the appearance in many representations of the 'flying gallop', in which the impression of speed is given by showing the animal with its legs stretched out forward and back. This posture was often given to the fantastic new creature the griffin (the griffin and the flying gallop will be discussed further in Chapter IX).[135] In her pioneering monograph on 'The Aegean and the Orient in the second millennium BC', published in 1947, Kantor suggested that the 'flying gallop' came to the Near East from the Aegean. Her chronological arguments were extremely imprecise and the basis for this opinion seems to have come from earlier authorities, who reasoned purely archaeologically that such 'vivacity' must have a European source. Nevertheless, Helck continues to support the same hypothesis.[136]

The carving of cylinder seals and ivories seems to have borrowed heavily from North Syria, although many Egyptian motifs were added.[137] Even more widespread than the seals and ivories, in both

Lower Egypt and Palestine, were the Hyksos scarabs. Some of these followed or even copied patterns established in Middle Kingdom Egypt; others, while keeping the basic shape, developed their own distinctive designs on the flat surface showing the influence of Syro-Palestinian art.[138]

One of the major sources for Hyksos fine arts was clearly Byblos, where for centuries there had been an eclectic Egypto-Levantine tradition. A striking example of this is in the *niello* work or metal inlay in bright colours which had been manufactured there since the Middle Kingdom. Van Seters described a spectacular example of this work on a Hyksos dagger with an embossed hilt and sheath:

> On one side of the hilt is a figure done in Egyptian style with short skirt and a crown resembling the 'White Crown' of Egypt. On the other side of the hilt are two antelope standing on their hind legs, standing back-to-back, but with their heads turned facing each other. This is certainly an Asiatic motif and is common on Syrian glyptic. Above the two antelope is a third in a more natural pose, grazing. The design on the sheath is also a mixture. There are Egyptian motives, such as a boy with a baboon, the wild dog and the fish; the two men are also dressed in Egyptian style. But the theme of the antelope, lion and hunter, as well as the man on a donkey carrying a scimitar are clearly Asiatic.[139]

The same style is also found on what is frequently seen as the archetypal example of Hyksos art. This is a dagger found in a tomb at Saqqara in the coffin of a man named ʿabd, a clearly Semitic name. The dagger had the Hyksos pharaonic name Apōphis on one side. On the other is written 'the henchman of his lord Neḥmen', presumably the West Semitic name seen in the Hebrew Naḥămânî (Compassionate). The sword type is 'Asiatic' and the design on the hilt in electrum on ebony portrays

> a man in an energetic pose attacking a lion. He is dressed in a short Egyptian kilt but has Asiatic armlets, a torque, and bands with discs crisscrossing his chest. The two animals, a lion and a gazelle, are also portrayed in 'flying gallop'.[140]

Van Seters follows this description with the statement:

> In many ways this piece sums up the technical achievements, the artistic eclecticism and the political and economic interdependence common to Syria-Palestine and Hyksos Egypt in the MBIIB-C Period.[141]

What he does not go on to mention is the remarkable number of these techniques and mixed artistic themes that are to be found in the precious objects from the contemporary Shaft Graves at Mycenae. Some of these parallels will be discussed in the next chapter.

THE HYKSOS AND THE BIBLICAL
CAPTIVITY OR SOJOURN IN EGYPT

Before concluding with a general survey of the eclectic nature of Hyksos culture, I should like to consider one of the two non-Egyptian traditions that preserve some folk memories of the Hyksos conquest and of an expulsion from Egypt. The Greek version in the stories of the rivalry between Danaos and Aigyptos has been discussed in Volume 1 and will be looked at further in the next chapter of this volume.[142] Here we shall consider the other tradition, that of the sections at the end of the Book of Genesis and the beginning of Exodus.

Genesis tells, with some diversions and many folkloric flourishes, the story of Joseph's being sold into slavery in Egypt and his rise to power as seal bearer or vizier there. Then, in a period of hunger in Canaan, his father Jacob and his brothers seek food in Egypt and Joseph settles them there as serfs to the pharaoh.[143]

The story is taken up again in Exodus approximately three generations later. By this time the Hebrews have multiplied greatly and a new pharaoh saw them as a threat and used them to build his new cities in the Eastern Delta. Moses, a Hebrew boy brought up as an Egyptian, identified himself with his people and became involved – with his god's backing – in a political/magical struggle to allow the Jews to leave Egypt and return to Canaan. Some of the plagues God and he inflicted on Egypt have been described in the last chapter because of their volcanic nature, but there were many others, culminating in the killing of all the first-born in Egypt, from which the Israelites were spared. This broke down the pharaoh's resistance. He allowed the Jews to go and they immediately slipped away, being guided by the pillar of smoke by day and fire by night. Pharaoh then changed his mind and set out with all his chariots to bring them back. After some hesitation the Israelites went on and God parted the sea for them to bring it crashing down on the Egyptian army. However, the Israelites' problems were not over and it took them forty years in the wilderness before, under Moses' successor Joshua, they were able to enter the Land of Canaan.[144]

The Bible gives conflicting evidence on the date of the Exodus. The

Book of Kings puts it 480 years before the building of the Temple in *c.* 965, that is, *c.* 1445 BC.[145] If one adds up the years mentioned chronologically in the books of Exodus, Judges, Samuel and Kings one arrives at a total of 554 years, with considerable periods unaccounted for.[146] This would give a date in the 16th century. In the Book of Exodus itself, however, there are references to the building of the 'store cities' of Pithom and Ramesses, which point to the 19th Dynasty between 1308 and 1194.[147] This later date seemed to fit the statement that a grandson of Moses was alive around 1150 BC. Thus, conventional wisdom tended to prefer a reign near the end of the 19th Dynasty, probably that of Mereneptah 1224–1214. Even this, however, did not accommodate the reference in Exodus to the Philistines who are mentioned in Egyptian sources only from the 12th century BC. Nevertheless, as discussed in the last chapter, the dating to the reign of Mereneptah was ruled out by the discovery of a stela from this time which referred to Israel as a people already settled in Palestine.[148]

The early confusion has been confounded by modern archaeology. Arguments about the dates of the likely destructions of Canaanite cities mentioned in the conquest narrative have raged for over a century.[149] Essentially, however, controversy has been between a 15th-century date backed by the quotation from Kings and a 13th-century one that would fit the genealogies.[150] The latest round of this has come in the work of the British biblical archaeologists John Bimson and David Livingston. They have revived the Kings 15th-century dating, and have shown conclusively that there are no 13th-century destructions to match those of the Bible. The only band of sufficient scale to satisfy them comes at the demarcation between MBIIC and LBI. This is conventionally put at around 1550 but they have brought it down to 1420 to fit the Kings dating.[151]

The incompatibility of this chronological shift with all other evidence, and particularly the compression of the LBI period that would be involved, has made this hypothesis unacceptable to other scholars.[152] On the other hand, the defenders of the 13th-century date have failed to answer Bimson's and Livingston's basic criticism that there is no archaeological evidence to back the hypothesis of a conquest of Canaan in the 13th century. Against the latter, however, is the fact that the 16th- and 15th-century destructions in Palestine can best be explained as the results of Egyptian campaigns which we know to have taken place from Egyptian records.

Thus, just as an immense amount of wasted time and effort has gone into tracing with misplaced precision the geographical track of the Exodus, it would seem equally futile to attempt to pinpoint its date. Clearly many different strands have been used or fabricated to create the legend as a whole. Nevertheless, it seems to me that the most important single base for the stories of the sojourn in Egypt and the Exodus are the historical facts of the Hyksos' occupation of Egypt and their expulsion from it. The relationship between the Hyksos and the Israelites is uncertain; that is to say, it is impossible to discover whether or not Israel existed as an ethnic identity in the 17th and 16th centuries or, if it did, what role it played among the invaders. If, as would seem more likely, Israel developed later, did some of the elements from which it was constructed come from a Hyksos alliance? Or was it simply that the Israelites borrowed from the legends of other peoples?

Apart from the general suggestion of a connection by the fact that the majority of the Hyksos were, like the later Israelites, West Semitic speakers from Canaan, there are two specific reasons for supposing a more direct relationship. Firstly, there is the attestation in both Palestine and Lower Egypt of the name Yꜥkb hr or Yꜥkb as a Hyksos ruler in the late 18th century. This name is remarkably similar to Jacob, Ya'ăqov.[153] Jacob Israel was not only the eponym and the specific ancestor of Israel, he was also the patriarch who, according to tradition, led the Israelites into Egypt. Secondly, there is the archaeological evidence from the fact that by far the highest density of Hyksos scarabs is to be found in the territory now known as the West Bank, which at the end of the Bronze Age was the Israelite heartland.[154] It is also interesting to note that the computation of the chronology of the Book of Judges, mentioned above, gives a date that is compatible with a mid-16th-century expulsion of the Hyksos.

The equation of the Hyksos and Israelites is not new. Hekataios of Abdera, writing at the end of the 4th century BC, maintained that the Jewish tradition of the Exodus – and the Greek traditions of the migrations of Danaos and Kadmos – both came from the expulsion of the Hyksos.[155] In one version of his history, Manetho saw the first pharaoh of the 18th Dynasty, whom he called Tethmôsis, as having expelled the 'shepherds'. In another they are called 'Jews' under their leader Moses.[156] It is uncertain if it was Manetho who made the equation, rather than the later excerpters, but it would seem very likely. There is absolutely no doubt that Apion, the Alexandrian anti-Semite of the 1st century AD, and his polemical opponent Josephus treated the Hyksos and the Jews as identical; Josephus in fact described them as 'the so-called Shepherds, our ancestors'.[157] According to the Byzantine monk Syncellos it was the 4th-century church father Eusebius who – presumably under biblical influence – placed the Exodus at the end rather than the beginning of the 18th Dynasty, thus separating the Israelites from the Hyksos.[158] Since then there has been a tendency to treat the equation of the two as anti-religious if not anti-Semitic.[159]

With the seculization at the end of the 19th century, many scholars returned to the earlier equation. Most of the agnostic or atheist ancient historians and Egyptologists, including Michael Astour, James Breasted, René Dussaud, Alan Gardiner, H. R. Hall, Salomo Luria and Raymond Weill, treated the period of the Hyksos domination as the direct or indirect basis for the biblical sojourn or captivity in Egypt and the Hyksos expulsion as the basis for the Exodus.[160] This view has also been taken by some more broad-minded religious scholars.[161] Thus, there is no reason to doubt that the Exodus story was – at least in part – a folk memory of the expulsion of the Hyksos.

CONCLUSION

Barbarian attacks or conquests are always confusing affairs; they tend to take place suddenly and disappear or are assimilated almost equally quickly. If their temporal range is short, their geographical one is huge and dispersed, making systematic excavation difficult. The 'barbarians' usually do not leave permanent monuments and, being nomads or at least in a nomadic phase, they tend to have relatively few material belongings. Those they do possess are generally made by the craftsmen of the local or other sedentary peoples. Thus, it is extremely difficult to use archaeology to trace the migrations or analyze the nature of such historically attested movements as the Hunnish conquests of the 5th century AD or those of the Mongols and Moghuls from the 13th to the 15th centuries AD.

What one does notice, however, is a certain mixture of styles and the faster diffusion of techniques at such periods. One can see, for instance, the intricate interplay of Chinese and Persian art in the 13th and 14th centuries AD.[162] This leads to a breakdown of earlier local technical or artistic traditions. It is from this eclecticism and the presence of some of the original 'barbaric' traditions that any distinctively barbarian style tends to develop. However, it tends to disappear even before the barbarians' political power disappears or is assimilated. After this, the older sedentary civilizations tend to reassert themselves, sometimes with conscious archaism but usually with some modification.

Another characteristic of barbarian conquests is for the 'outer' barbarians directly or indirectly to encourage 'inner' barbarians, who have often lived adjacent to richer civilizations for centuries, to invade them. Thus, very few Huns or Turkish speakers penetrated the Roman Empire, while Goths and Germans, who had been set in motion by the appearance of the Huns, poured in. Similarly, although the leaders of Moghuls, who conquered and ruled India, were Turkish-speaking, the culture their invasion introduced to India was not Turkish or Central Asian but Persian, that of the highly civilized people who had lived to the northwest of India for centuries.

Such a model of cumulative impulses would appear to fit the archaeological evidence from Syro-Palestine and Lower Egypt between 1750 and 1570. As mentioned above, there was a basic continuity of material culture throughout the MBII period. Nevertheless, there are some changes in the 18th century, most of which involve a combination of Mesopotamian, Syrian, Levantine and Egyptian styles; there are also a few traces of northern or barbaric influences, that is to say, a new emphasis on motion and violence. But, even so, the culture that arrived in Lower Egypt in the 18th century BC was essentially that of Syro-Palestine.

There is no reason to suppose that the balance of linguistic influence was any different. From their names it would seem that the overwhelming majority of the Hyksos in Egypt were Semitic-speaking and it is equally clear from names that, just as the material culture of the Hyksos at Tell el Daba'a became increasingly Egyptian in the 17th century BC, the Egyptian language reasserted itself in the face of Semitic. Despite the fact that these two were undoubtedly the dominant languages, others may well have been spoken.

There is no doubt that it has been difficult to explain any of the apparently non-Afroasiatic Hyksos names in terms of Hurrian and Indo-European. Nevertheless, given the Manethonian tradition, the Speos Artemidos inscription, the Hurrian expansion in Syria in the 18th century BC, the Mitannian association with horses and chariots, and the attestation of the presence of Hurrian and Indo-European speakers in 15th-century Palestine, I see no scholarly reason to deny that they could well have formed part of the Hyksos invasion of Egypt. I find it difficult to admit this, because – as can be seen from my survey of the historiography of this problem – I feel a strong ideological sympathy with those who object to this apparent confirmation of the image of the Aryans as a 'master race'.

On the other hand, as I insisted earlier in this chapter, I am convinced that a scholar should try as far as possible to detach her or his historical interpretation from any ideological preferences. In this case, where I accept the Aryanists' interpretation, I refuse to accept their basic Social Darwinist premise that conquest or domination through violence somehow makes a people or linguistic group morally or creatively *better* than those who are conquered or dominated. I certainly would not accept a hierarchy Hun > German > Gallo-Roman or Mongol > Turk > Persian > Indian any more than I would put the German Nazis *above* the Jews, gypsies, homosexuals and Communists they had power over and murdered.

CHAPTER IX

CRETE, THERA AND THE BIRTH OF MYCENAEAN CULTURE IN THE 18TH AND 17TH CENTURIES BC
A Hyksos invasion?

THIS CHAPTER IS concerned with contacts between the Near East and the Aegean in the middle of the 2nd millennium BC. It is a critical period, not only because of the archaeological evidence, but also because, according to the most comprehensive ancient chronology – the Parian Marble – it was during the 16th century BC that the Egyptian and Phoenician princes established their rule in Greece. Thus, the Ancient Model in the narrow sense (that is, that Greek culture was the result of Egyptian/Phoenician colonization) depends on the evidence from this period. The contacts during this period seem to have been both directly from Egypt and the Levant to the Aegean and Mainland Greece and indirectly through Crete and the Southern Aegean.

The eclectic and highly cosmopolitan nature of Cretan culture has been discussed in Chapters I and IV and the strong possibility of Egyptian and Levantine influences on Mainland Greece during the centuries in the 3rd millennium has been considered in Chapters II and III. Although the previous four chapters contain information about Greece, their chief concerns – Sesōstris' conquests in Asia Minor, the chronological implications of the re-dating of the Thera eruption and the nature and rise of the Hyksos – were apparently peripheral subjects. Nevertheless, it has been necessary to consider them in order to understand the central issue of this chapter, the possible colonization of regions in the Aegean from Egypt and the Levant between 1750 and 1500 BC.

The archaeological evidence of extensive contact in the middle of the 2nd millennium provides powerful support for many of the ideas set out in *Black Athena*. If there was such extensive contact during the formative period of Mycenaean civilization on the material plane, objections to massive cultural and specifically linguistic and religious Greek borrowings from the Near East are substantially weakened. On the other hand, the archaeological evidence does not help the Ancient Model in the narrow sense. There is no hoard of purely Egyptian and Levantine objects – including weapons – from the last Middle Bronze Age settlements or palaces overlying a destruction level below which there are earlier primitive Hellenic artifacts.

Furthermore, as we shall see in Chapter XI, most of the Egyptian and Levantine objects found in Bronze Age contexts in the Aegean come from the 15th, 14th and 13th centuries. It is also probable that some Egyptian religious institutions were established in Greece in this later period. On the other hand, there is no doubt that the 'Greek' Mycenaean kingdoms were well established by then, and although there is a strong tradition, which will be discussed in Chapter XI, that the Pelopids arrived in the Peloponnese from Anatolia in the 15th or 14th centuries, the 'Egyptian' and Phoenician colonizations were always traditionally placed before that.

This raises the possibility that many if not most of the Near Eastern cultural traits found in Greek culture were not the result of the military conquests referred to in the Greek tradition but come from the long-standing relationship between Egypt, the Levant and the Aegean.

During the four years that have passed since completing Volume 1 in 1986, I realize that I probably overestimated the extent of Near Eastern cultural penetration during the 'colonizations' and underrated the extent to which this took place in later periods, particularly during the peak of the international power and prestige of the Egyptian 18th Dynasty.

There is, in fact, a historically attested parallel for this pattern of greater cultural borrowings after the establishment of independence rather than during the period of political domination. It comes from East Asia. There is no doubt that the Red River Delta, which later became the heartland of Vietnam, received cultural influences from China both before and during direct Chinese colonization by the Han and later dynasties from the 1st century BC to the 10th century AD. However, the most intense sinification of Vietnam was imposed by a powerful native dynasty, the Nguyen, during the 19th century.[1] A similar pattern may well be true of Greece, with the major reception of Egyptian and Levantine influence having taken place in periods after 1450 BC.

While the case for the eclectic nature of Mycenaean civilization and hence that of Iron Age Greece, which itself had further Phoenician and Egyptian admixtures, is overwhelming, the presence of this cultural amalgam does not, in itself, prove that there were Hyksos colonies in Greece between 1750 and 1500 BC. However, I believe that there is enough linguistic and other evidence from or concerning these two and a half centuries to indicate that significant cultural borrowing took place in this early period.

In the period between 1750 and 1500 BC, with which this chapter is concerned, much of the archaeological evidence of contacts between Egypt and the Levant and the Aegean has a distinctly military flavour. This tallies well with the period known in the Classical Greek tradition as the 'heroic age', in which heroes from the east founded their cities in Greece. Thus, there would seem to be a plausible case in favour of at least indirect Egypto-Levantine colonization in these centuries. However, archaeology is too blunt a tool to provide clear answers to such problems and we shall see that the evidence can be explained in a variety of ways. That is to say, the archaeological evidence can be used to support both the Ancient and the Aryan Models. In this chapter, as in its predecessors, we will see that there appears to be clear evidence in favour of early cultural influences from the Near East. Here, however, I believe one can go further and find persuasive archaeological evidence indicating the presence of dynasties of foreign origin, who transformed the cultures of the Aegean basin.

The first revision of the Ancient Model I propose in *Black Athena* is to accept the 19th-century philologists' demonstration that Greek is essentially Indo-European and hence the implication that at some stage there must have been one or more invasions or infiltrations from the north. The second revision is the one that arises in this chapter. In Volume 1, I discussed the ancient writers' belief that the colonizations of Greece took place in the 16th century and the specific links they made between Danaos' acquisition of the Argolid and the Egyptian defeat of the Hyksos, which we know took place in the second quarter of that century.[2] This chronology, which had always been difficult to maintain in the face of the archaeological evidence, with the updating of the Thera eruption and Aegean ceramic periods now becomes impossible. Therefore, I am forced to part company with the ancient historians and argue that the colonizations, or the wave of Egypto-Levantine influence, took place at the beginning of the Hyksos period in the late 18th century not at the period's end in the early 16th.

In the introduction to Volume 1, I touched on various possible reasons why the ancient writers should have lowered the dates of these events. One possible cause is that it is not only modern historians who feel that understatement makes them seem more sober and reasonable and that these pressures were also in operation in Antiquity, alongside the opposite desire to astound their audiences with spectacularly high dates.

Another possible cause for down-dating is that it was less painful for patriotic Greek writers to see their country as a hospitable receiver of refugees than as the victim of conquest. This was reinforced by a resemblance seen between the name Hyksos and *hiketēs*, adjective *hikesios* (suppliant). In Hellenistic times, there was also a desire to tie in the migration of Danaos with the biblical Exodus, which, as argued in the last chapter, gained much of its historical basis from the Egyptian expulsion of the Hyksos.

THE CRETAN NEW PALACES

In the treatment of Cretan archaeology so far, I have tended to use Evans's chronology based on ceramic periods from Early to Late Minoan. As mentioned above, Evans based his periods on Egyptian chronology, with Early Minoan corresponding to the Old Kingdom, Middle Minoan to the Middle Kingdom and Late Minoan to the New. One problem with this was that the significant changes in Egyptian – and Cretan – culture often appeared at the end of a kingdom, before or during an Intermediate Period, rather than at the formation of the next strong dynasty.

Since the 1950s, however, a new scheme has come into use, which attempts to deal with this problem and to broaden the cultural range of the periods by paying special attention to architecture. According to this, the chronology of Bronze Age Crete should be divided into the Pre-Palatial, Early Palace, Late Palace and Post-Palatial periods. There is some argument about the boundary between the first two, some scholars seeing the ceramic MMIA as Pre-Palatial and others as belonging to the Early Palaces.[3] On the other hand, there is no dispute about the break in the middle of the Palatial Period. It is generally agreed that this took place between the ceramic periods MMII and MMIII. This has generally been put at 1700 BC, but because of the updating required by the new date for the Thera eruption it would now seem to be rather earlier, around 1730.

The break was marked by the destruction of all three of the major palaces on Crete, at Knossos in the north, Mallia in the east centre and Phaistos in the Messara Plain in the south. These destructions are generally attributed to a massive earthquake. There is no doubt that Crete is situated in a zone of extreme seismic instability and there have been frequent and widespread destructions by earthquakes throughout Cretan history and prehistory. On the other hand, the palaces built after these particular destructions show slight but clear differences that have led scholars to see the break as the watershed between the 'Early' and the 'Late' palaces.

The great extent of Near Eastern influences on Early Palatial Crete has been discussed in Chapter IV. However, it is generally and convincingly maintained that such influences – and especially those from Egypt – increased with the building of the New Palaces in the late 18th century BC.[4] For instance, it was in the MMIII period (that is, 1730–1675 BC) that Egyptian-style bathrooms and elaborate banquet halls were built in the Cretan palaces.[5]

Most of the surviving paintings from Knossos belong to the later period. As discussed in Chapter V, Egyptian conventions appear to have dominated painting at least from the beginning of the Palatial Period.[6] Thus, one cannot be certain exactly when particular Egyptian motifs arrived on the island. Furthermore, while some of the themes first attested in the MMIII period appear to be Egyptian or Levantine, many other motifs, such as those of dolphins, octupuses and other marine life, are distinctively Cretan.

Nevertheless, there is little doubt that there was an intensification of Near Eastern and especially Egyptian influence on Cretan painting at the beginning of MMIII.[7] Some of the new foreign motifs, such as the winged sphinx, the griffin and the 'flying leap', will be discussed in detail below. Others, with less direct 'political' significance, can be considered here. These include partridges and hoopoes, portrayed almost exactly as they were in Egypt. There are also reeds, which are painted precisely according to the Egyptian convention, and papyrus, which if it was grown in the Aegean was not common there, as it was along the Nile; here too there was close conformity to their representation in Egyptian paintings.[8] The 'Nile scene' with a cat stalking or catching birds is attested in Egypt only from the New Kingdom.[9] In the Aegean, however, it appears even earlier, in MMIII/LMI in Crete and, as we shall see, in 17th-century contexts from Thera and Mycenae. Nevertheless, the gradual development, since the Old Kingdom, of the different elements that make up the scene make it virtually certain that it originated in Egypt.[10] Blue monkeys may have existed in captivity in the 18th- and 17th-century Aegean. This in itself would be an interesting indication of Cretan relations with Egypt and the rest of Africa. However, it would seem equally if not more likely that the Aegean artists were imitating representations of monkeys in Egyptian art.[11]

The general increase of wealth and splendour at the beginning of the Late Palace Period also seems to be reflected in the great decline in the standard of pottery from the sensationally beautiful Kamares Ware of MMI and II. This has been plausibly explained as the result of increased use of metal, especially gold and silver.[12] New styles of pots also show Egyptian influence and it was in this period that the fast wheel for pottery making first came into general use in both Egypt and Crete.[13] It was also in MMIII that objects made of faience become common in Crete. The earlier centres of production were in Egypt and Syria.[14] Finally, there is the famous lavishly decorated 'royal gaming board' found in the palace for which there are close parallels from 18th-Dynasty Egypt.[15]

It is a striking fact that, while tombs provide one of the staples of Egyptian and Mycenaean archaeology, they are hardly considered in 2nd-millennium Crete. The reasons for this are twofold: firstly, there is the mass of information provided by the palaces and, secondly, there is the confusion about the extraordinarily varied burial practices. There are, however, some major tombs.

The 'Temple Tomb' just south of the palace at Knossos dates to MMIII–LMIa. This splendid building had a court, a crypt and a sepulchral chamber, with a temple built above the crypt. As Arthur Evans pointed out, this pattern was neatly paralleled by Diodoros' descriptions of a tomb of Minos in Sicily in which there was a tomb concealed beneath a temple of Aphrodite.[16] Although there are no strict parallels between this and any Egyptian funerary complex, there is no doubt that the Cretan construction belongs to the general class of mortuary temples, which had been built – often quite close to the tomb itself – in Egypt throughout the 3rd millennium. As well as this general similarity of plan, there are also some details of the Temple Tomb, such as the painting of the ceiling of the crypt in blue to represent the sky, which are purely Egyptian. In Volume 4, I shall attempt to link this to the Egyptian sky goddess Nut, who was portrayed above the mummy in the sarcophagus and on the ceiling above the sarcophagus. Nut's Greek equivalent Rhea, whose name came from R'␣t, the female counterpart of Ra, was also an underground divinity of tombs and she remained a central figure in the Cretan pantheon of the Iron Age.

There is also a cemetery containing some rich tombs at Isopata, between Knossos and the modern Herakleion, dating back to MMIII. The largest 'royal tomb' there had a *dromos* or broad sloping passage to the tombs and a huge burial chamber; it probably had a corbelled vault eight metres high, which implies it rose above the ground to form a considerable mound.[17] Corbelling had been used in Egypt and the Near East at least since the beginning of the 3rd millennium, yet there is no evidence of any considerable use of it earlier in Crete. However, this may be simply because stone masonry was used only for the bases of buildings.[18] Other tombs at Isopata have shafts two or three metres deep from which the tomb chamber was approached.[19] This appears to have been a new type of tomb in the Aegean but was well known in much of the Near East, most outstandingly at Byblos where there is a royal cemetery of shaft graves dating back to the Egyptian Middle Kingdom, which formed a grave circle of very much the same type that we shall consider below at Mycenae.[20]

THE WEAPONS OF CRETE IN MMIII

Ever since Evans first created it, the attractive image of the peaceful, childlike Minoans has been enormously influential.[21] This theory has at its basis the fact that there is no evidence for palace or city walls. However, it should be remembered that Sparta had no walls and their absence in Crete indicates merely a lack of outside military threat rather than a lack of interest in violence. In any event, a number of Cretan tombs of the MMIII period contain fine bronze weapons, strongly suggesting that the tombs' owners were concerned with fighting and warfare.[22] There was, in fact, a striking development in MMIII of sophisticated daggers and swords.

It has long been noted that the bronze weapons of this period show a remarkable uniformity throughout the Middle East and Aegean. So much so that the archaeologist Rachel Maxwell-Hyslop, who catalogued the various types of daggers and swords, proposed that they must have been made by bands of wandering smiths, 'trained in the same school of metallurgy'.[23] Helck, however, convincingly dismisses the probability of this notion on the grounds that, firstly, there is no attestation of wandering smiths in Bronze Age texts and, secondly, the deportation of artisans reported in the 1st millennium BC never referred to free workers and in Egypt weapon-makers were employees of the state.[24] Indeed, in Chapter V I argued that one of the consequences – if it was not one of the intentions – of Sesōstris' conquests in the 20th century BC was to transfer East Anatolian metal-workers to Egypt and the Levant.[25]

To return to developments in Crete two centuries later, as Pendlebury wrote more than fifty years ago in his *The Archaeology of Crete*, which remains the standard work,

> The bronze weapons show a distinct advance on those of MMI. The great sword of Mallia must certainly be regarded as an exception to that date and we are justified in saying that the sword as such is first found in MMIII.[26]

The question of the origin of MMIII weapons manufacture in general and sword-making in particular has been considered very difficult. Nancy Sandars, who has written on the origin of the sword in the Aegean, argues that the sword was invented in the Aegean under Syrian influence.[27]

The archaeologist and expert in ancient metallurgy Keith Branigan, who has studied the problem in great depth, maintains that the situation was especially complicated because – as I mentioned in Chapter IV – he believes that Minoan weapon-making had been substantially influenced by the Levant since EMIII.[28] When it comes to the change between MMII and MMIII he finds no single origin and concludes with the compromise:

> It is rarely that the mixture [of weapons during MMIII–LMI] does not contain some Syrian or Levantine element. . . . Despite these features' inspiration the weapons still have an Aegean rather than a Levantine appearance.[29]

There are three types of daggers and swords that seem to be at issue here – those catalogued by Maxwell-Hyslop as 31, 32 and 33. Type 31 is characterized by 'flanged hilts'. The flanges allowed for decorated inlaid hilts held in by rivets. The basic type is attested from the Hyksos levels at Tell Ajjul and Tell Fara in Palestine. It is impossible to be certain but this type of dagger also appears to be illustrated on some Middle Kingdom coffins, sometimes labelled *mꜣsgw*, that is *bꜣsgw*, the word for dagger written with the determinative 𓏏.[30] Thus, it may well have been part of the *koinē* (common standard) of military technology of the late 20th and 19th centuries BC.[31] A similar type of sword also appears in MMIII Crete and was later improved upon there.

Maxwell-Hyslop's type 32 was generally found among daggers and short swords. These lacked the rivets of 31 and had a rather different ridged shape. They appear to have originated in Byblos in the 18th century and, although they have been found throughout the Middle East and in the Aegean, they are most common in Syro-Palestine.

Maxwell-Hyslop described type 33 as having a 'pointed blade with straight sides, plain flanged hilt cast together with blade; the sides of the hilt are concave, the base practically flat, and the ricasso rectangular shaped'.[32] This type was the one which most commonly had inlaid blades, as, for instance, on the dagger decorated with a lion hunt of Nḥmn who served the Hyksos pharaoh Apōphis, described in the last chapter.[33] Maxwell-Hyslop saw this type as having originated in North Syria and its popularity in Hurrian-speaking regions during the Egyptian New Kingdom led her to believe it to be a Hyksos weapon, though later than types 31 and 32.[34]

What is clear from this is that, even within the close world of weapon types referred to above, there was a 'province' containing the Hyksos areas of Syro-Palestine, Lower Egypt and MMIII Crete in which there was a near identity of forms. It would also seem virtually certain that after the beginning of LMI innovations were made in the Aegean, some of which were exported to the Levant. It is also likely that the metallurgy of MMI and II played some role in the flowering of MMIII. Nevertheless, I believe the probability remains that the basic weaponry of MMIII derived from the Hyksos zone in the Levant.

This view is drawn partly from the fact that it would fit with the direction of cultural diffusion in other areas, some of which have already been mentioned while others will be considered below. It is also because of evidence that can be retrieved from the Greek vocabulary of swords.

The Afroasiatic vocabulary
of swords and daggers

The most common word for sword in Greek is *xiphos*. This name may appear in Linear B as *qi-si-pe-e*.[35] The broad-minded Indo-Europeanist Oswald Szemerényi sees this as indicating a form with a labiovelar initial *k^wsiphos*. However, he admits some surprise that this does not result in a later form *$psiphos$*.[36] I think that postulating a labiovelar here may be a case of misplaced precision. It may simply be a rhyming velar and sibilant – as in *ke-se-ne, xenos* (stranger) and *ku-su xyn* or *syn* (with) – to indicate the presence of a velarized sibilant in a loan word.[37]

In the 1850s, before the Aryan Model had triumphed over Egyptology, both Samuel Birch and Heinrich Brugsch proposed that *xiphos* was derived from the Egyptian *sft*, the Coptic *sēfe* (sword, knife).[38] The neatness of the fit has led several Egyptologists to preserve the etymology despite its being anomalous to the Aryan Model; but others have not been so happy.[39]

In 1912 the Egyptologist M. Burchardt tried to dismiss it on the grounds that *xiphos* could not have an Egyptian etymology because the Egyptians did not possess double-edged swords of the Greek type.[40] However, both his premise and his reasoning were faulty. There is now absolutely no doubt that there were double-edged blades in Egypt during the 2nd Intermediate Period.[41] Even if this had not been the case, it is a commonplace that innovations almost always borrow and change meanings from previously known similar objects. For example, there is the use of 'corn' by English settlers in America to describe the previously unknown maize, or the application of the horse-drawn 'car' for the new automobile. More closely related to this is the origin of the Egyptian word for 'dagger' *bꝫgsw* from the earlier *bꝫgs* (thorn). The weakness of Burchardt's arguments would seem to indicate his ideological difficulties with the derivation. These seem to be shared by most classicists, who, while perfectly willing to accept Phoenician names for luxury goods, have preferred not to discuss the possibility that a word for the super-weapon of the heroic age could have an Egyptian origin.[42]

There is virtually no doubt that *xiphos* is a loan word, for not only is there the lack of an acceptable Indo-European origin, but there are a number of irregularly similar words in a pattern that is typical of loaning.[43] Firstly, there is the dialect form of *skiphos*, showing the common Greek uncertainty over complex sibilants. Secondly, there is the word *sēpia* (cuttlefish). The usually resourceful Julius Pokorny was unable to find an Indo-European etymology for *sēpia*, and Chantraine cannot accept Fraenkel's proposal to derive it from *sēpomai* (be putrid) because of its ink.[44] It would seem more likely that the gastropod gained its name from its internal 'blade' which looks remarkably like a Hyksos or Mycenaean dagger. This of course would be analogous to the English 'cuttle' of 'cuttlefish' which was influenced by, even if it did not derive from, 'cut' or its extensions, 'cutler' or 'cutlass'. Thus, *sēpia* could well be another loan from the Egyptian *sft*, the Coptic *sēfe*, though both the initial *s* and the long *e* would suggest a later borrowing. The shift from Egyptian *f* to Greek *p* is paralleled in the derivation of the Greek *kēpos*, *kēbos* or *keibos* from the Egyptian *gf* (monkey) and in the origin of the Greek stem *kapn-* (smoke) from the Egyptian *gfn* (bake) written with the determinative 𓊶 ('a brazier with flame [and smoke?] rising from it').[45] Similarly, the equation of the Egyptian *f* with the Greek *ph*, which would seem to occur in the borrowing of *xiphos* from *sft*, occurs elsewhere, for example in the transcriptions of such names and titles as *-thphēnis* from *tfnt*, Kamēphis from Kꝫ mwt.f, Onnōphris from Wnn wfrw and Memphis from Mn nfr.

However, in 1971 an Egyptologist challenged this plausible picture. The English scholar Richard Holton Pierce attacked the etymology on three grounds. The first of these was based on Burchardt's criticism. The second was almost equally improbable. Pierce argued that 'while the Coptic *sēfe* shows that *sf. t* had a long stressed vowel in its first syllable, the alleged loan of *xiphos* has a short vowel in the corresponding position'.[46] This demonstrates an extraordinary faith in the reconstruction of Ancient Egyptian vowels from Coptic. The more usual view is that of Gardiner who wrote:

The disadvantage of Coptic is, however, its remoteness in time from the language upon which it is required to shed light; it would be as little legitimate to transfer the Coptic pronunciation of such a word as ōbᵉt 'goose' to the old Egyptian equivalent *ɜpd* as it would be to use modern English pronunciation as our authority for pronouncing Anglo-Saxon. The vowels and consonants of the older language have usually become modified in the course of time, so that the more recent equivalents *can at best only serve as a basis for inference.* (my italics)[47]

Pierce's third argument, which is the only one with any value, is to question why the Egyptian initial *s* should have been considered a cluster of *ks*, which is what both *qi-si* and *xi* indicate. This again would seem to be a case of misplaced precision. Firstly, there is no doubt that there has been considerable interchange between the different Greek sibilants.[48] Secondly, there is the objection that Pierce failed to distinguish between the Egyptian *s* and *z*. This is partly excusable because many Egyptologists consider that the two sibilants had merged in Middle Egyptian and there are confusions between *s* and *z* in the writing of *s/zft*. On the other hand, it is striking that in Babylonian and Assyrian transcriptions of Egyptian made from the 14th to the 8th century BC distinctions are made between *s* and *z*.[49] Thus, it is quite possible that at the time of loaning the form was *zft*, making the initial *x* rather more likely.

Nevertheless, while there is an undoubted equation between the Egyptian *š* and the Greek *x* in the transcription of the Libyan tribe the Mšwš as Maxyes, apart from *s/zft* to *xiphos* there is no other accepted loan or transcription from Egyptian or Semitic *s* as *x*. In Volume 3, however, I shall argue in some detail that there are a number of loans involving this kind of transcription – notably *xen-* (strange, foreign) from the Semitic *śn'* (hate) and *xyn* or *syn* (with) from a Semitic stem found in the Eblaite *ši-in* (movement to, up to) and the preposition *sə'n* (up to, until, as far as) found in the Gunnan Gurage Semitic languages of Southern Ethiopia.

There is also *xanth-*, not 'blond' but 'chestnut brown' and the 'colour and aroma of cooked meat' and 'sacred', which, I shall argue in Volume 3, comes from the Egyptian *snṯr* (cense or consecrate). Sometimes confused with *xanthos* as a word of colour is *xouthos*. *Xouthos'* other and probably primary meaning is 'rapidly moving to and fro, nimble', used of bees, grasshoppers, etc. The Egyptian *swtwt* (to walk about, stroll, promenade) would seem to fit this very well. A possibility that the Egyptian word was not always reduplicated comes from the

Coptic *sōt* or *sot* (return or repeat) which has no other etymology and would seem to be related to *swtwt*.[50] Thus, there would seem to be quite a number of likely cases in which an Egyptian *s* appears in Greek as an *x*.[51] Not one of the Greek words referred to here has an acceptable Indo-European etymology.[52]

Whether or not any of the derivations I propose holds up, the loaning of sibilants is far too uncertain a matter for Pierce's objection on these grounds to block the conventional and thoroughly plausible derivation of *xiphos* from *sft*.[53]

If *xiphos* comes from Egyptian, *phasganon*, the other Homeric word for 'sword', which is attested in Linear B as *pa-ka-na*, has no acceptable Indo-European etymology and would seem to be Semitic.[54] Without the final *-(a)n*, which is one of the commonest Semitic suffixes with very imprecise functions, the root is √*psg*.[55] *Psg* (cut in two) is found in the biblical place name Pisgâh, a mountain with a cleft. Although the medial is written with the letter *sameḥ* rather than with the letter *śin*, it would seem probable that *psg* is a reflex of a fricative lateral *pśg*, which in turn is related to the root *plg* (divide, split), which is well attested throughout Semitic.[56] The latter stem seems to occur in Late Egyptian as *png* (detach or divide), written with the knife determinative ⟍. Thus, there would seem to be a high probability that the Greek *phasganon* came from a Semitic derivative of the root *√pśg*, and meant 'cleaver'.

It should be noted that the signs in Linear B with which the two words were written, *qi-si-pe-* and *pa-ka-na*, both indicate that if they are loans they were introduced before the breakdown of labiovelars in Greek; otherwise, *qi-si-pe-* would have been pronounced *ti-si-pe-*, and I also maintain that later loans from Afroasiatic sounds *pa* or *ba-* were transcribed into Linear B with the sign for *qa* which was already a homophone with *pa*.

The dating of the breakdown of labiovelars is uncertain and controversial, but it is generally considered that, although it may have taken place before the vowels *u* and *y*, the other labiovelars were still pronounced as such when the Linear B tablets were written.[57] However, I shall argue in Volume 3 both that the spelling conventions of Linear B were established well before the 14th and 13th centuries to which the extant texts belong and that by that time the labiovelars had been transformed in most Greek dialects.[58] In such a case, the introduction of the words *xiphos* and *phasganon* would seem to have taken place by 1400 BC and possibly several hundred years before that. This would bring the introduction of the words into the same span as the first appearance of swords and advanced daggers in the Aegean.

It should be noted at this point that the situation is complicated by the fact that the dominant language in Crete during the first half of the 2nd millennium BC may well have been a Semitic one; and, if not, there is no doubt that dialects of West Semitic as well as Egyptian were widely spoken on the island.[59] This leaves open the possibility that even if the words *xiphos* and *phasganon* derive from Egyptian and Semitic roots they could have originated in Crete and therefore tell us little about the development of swords on or off the island. However, the fact that *sft* became a standard word for 'sword' in Egypt and was earlier used to mean 'knife' makes it very probable that it developed in Egypt itself. This is less clear in the case of *phasganon,* where there is no attestation of *psg, pšg* or *plg* being used as the name of a sharp implement or weapon in the Levant. Thus, it is possible that *phasganon* has a Cretan Semitic origin, although a Mainland one would seem more probable.

In any event, taken together, the etymologies would seem to support the archaeological evidence in suggesting that Cretan swords and advanced daggers were introduced to the island from the Hyksos-dominated regions of the Levant in the second half of the 18th century BC.

The composite bow, horses and chariots

It was in MMIII that the 'composite' bow, in which the wooden stave is reinforced by strips of horn, first appeared in Crete.[60] This too seems to have had a Syrian origin. In Egypt, it appears to have been present from the 12th Dynasty but was reserved for the king and high personages and appears to have retained its association with 'Asiatics' in Egyptian representations.[61] Thus, its presence in MMIII would fit well with a Hyksos invasion.

The original introduction of the chariot to the Aegean will be looked at in more detail when we come to consider Mainland Greece. Here, however, it should be pointed out that the first Cretan representations of horses and chariots occur in MMIII. A sealing with a chariot drawn by two horses has been found from that period at the small palace at Aghia Triada in the Messara Plain in the south of the island.[62] The significance of horses in the New Palace Period is also shown by the discovery in an apparently royal tholos tomb at Archanes south of Knossos of the sacrificed and dismembered body of a horse.[63]

THE FLYING GALLOP,
THE SPHINX AND THE GRIFFIN

There is little doubt that the 'flying gallop' came late to Egypt as the first examples of its use are attested only from the 15th century BC.[64]

On the other hand, it seems to have appeared almost simultaneously in Crete and Syria. In Crete it appears at the beginning of MMIII but it is also seen in Hyksos art from the Levant.[65] Kantor's argument that such vitality had to be European seems to me less convincing than to associate the 'flying gallop' and a taste for hunting and combat scenes with the Hyksos way of life as we know it from other sources. The appearance of the 'flying gallop' was only one aspect of a development of movement and naturalism in Cretan art that began with the start of MMIII.[66] Thus, in art as in architecture and metallurgy we gain a picture of the creation of striking new forms that drew from both Minoan tradition and the contemporary Hyksos Near East.

Now let us examine two specific motifs both connected with royalty and conquest. The name 'sphinx' probably comes from the Egyptian *šsp ʿnḫ* (living statue) possibly used in the *Story of Sinuhe* for sphinxes guarding the palace of Sesōstris.[67] The composite of lion and man is first attested in Crete in MMII but its adoption and the appearance of the earliest winged sphinx dates only from MMIII. Obviously, however, its origins in Egypt, Syria and Mesopotamia go far further back.

Although the monster is represented in both Egypt and Mesopotamia from the first half of the 3rd millennium, there seems little doubt that it began as a solar symbol in Egypt and that it was there that its winged form developed, probably by analogy with the griffin. It is certain, however, that Syria always played a very important role in its iconographic development and dissemination.[68] It is also clear that, as André Dessenne, who has written a substantial monograph on the sphinx, described the situation during what he saw as the anarchy of the Hyksos period, 'Not only does it [the sphinx] not disappear, but it takes, can one say, new forces.'[69] Given the undoubtedly close relations between Egypt and Syro-Palestine during the Middle and New Kingdoms, Dessenne was surprised how seldom sphinxes appeared then, in comparison with during the 2nd Intermediate Period. This led him to the conclusion that the monster had a special significance for the Hyksos. He described the extraordinary frequency with which sphinxes appear on Hyksos scarabs. Dessenne also remarked on the wide variety of types, without wings, with wings, moving, still, standing, lying, crowned and uncrowned. Nevertheless, he emphasized how Syrian and un-Egyptian most appeared. He considered this surprising given the undoubtedly close contacts with Egypt.[70]

Dessenne maintained that the sphinx arrived in Crete at the beginning of MMIII. Furthermore, the forms it took in that period had Syrian origins.[71] Dessenne demolished the old Aryanist claim that there was a fundamental distinction between the male Egyptian sphinx and the female Aegean one by demonstrating the great confusion of gender in both regions.[72] However, he was reluctant to claim that the sphinx had been brought to Crete by Hyksos invaders. Writing in the 1950s, when the idea of a Hyksos invasion of Egypt was unfashionable and one of Crete unthinkable, he had to resort to the hypothesis of two simultaneous events:

> . . . after the catastrophe that brutally put an end to the existence of the Early Palaces, one sees the arrival of an orientalizing wave – which it would be interesting to study – which brought with it a number of oriental motifs and themes including the sphinx and the griffin. Why should Crete have shown itself more receptive then? One can only speculate. It is possible even though there appears to be no break in continuity between the first and the second palaces, that there the shock created a vacuum. . . . As we said in our first section, it is probable that relations between Crete and the Orient were greater in the Hyksos period than is generally believed.[73]

This picture of the Cretan sphinx coming from regions under Hyksos control is repeated when it comes to the griffin. The griffin – a lion with the head of a hawk or eagle – also dates back in Mesopotamia, Elam and Egypt to the 4th millennium.[74] Its existence in Egypt and Syria throughout the Old and Middle Kingdoms meant that it could have been borrowed by Cretans at almost any time. The first example of the creature's representation on the island comes from two seal impressions found at latest levels of the old palace at Phaistos. The Austrian ancient historian Fritz Schachermeyr argued that this was probably the result of Egyptian influence.[75] However, Anna Maria Bisi, who has written a monograph devoted to the griffin, maintains that:

> Two firm points seem already established in the development of the Cretan griffin, that it does not appear on the island before Middle Minoan III 1700–1580 [1730–1675 in this book] BC and that from the beginning it was not an autonomous creation but an import from outside the region, Syria in the 2nd millennium.[76]

Reconciliation of these two statements is not as difficult as it might appear. Firstly, as with so many 'breaks' in history or the archaeological record, there are a number of instances in which phenomena associated with the new period appear in small numbers at the end of the previous one. Secondly, Schachermeyr's preference for Egyptian influence, which follows that of Arthur Evans, as opposed to Bisi's for Syria, which was also that of Henri Frankfort, is just another example of an uncertainty expressed about this period in many different areas of archaeology, art history and, for that matter, in the Ancient Model itself; Herodotos, for example, was uncertain as to whether the ancestors of the Spartan kings were Egyptian or 'Assyrian'.[77] The answer is clearly that during MMIII both Southern Syria and Lower Egypt were under Hyksos control. This combination can be seen clearly in the case of the griffin. In a brilliant article written in 1936, Henri Frankfort compared the iconography of the griffin in the Aegean and New Kingdom Egypt, and on seals from Mitanni and Middle Assyria, and established that it was a creation of the Hyksos period.[78] Bisi completely accepts this view.[79]

The representation of the griffin is not a trivial matter of concern only to art historians; it has a vital political significance. Like the sphinx, the griffin seems to have started as a creature that protected the pharaoh. Nevertheless, it always had its aggressive, rapacious aspects and – while it kept its royal connotations – these became dominant in Syria in the first half of the 2nd millennium. This aspect of its nature, together with its temporal and spatial coincidence with the Hyksos, make it virtually certain that the griffin was a symbol and supporter of Hyksos royalty. This would correspond with the functions of what seems to be its Canaanite equivalent, the $k^e r\hat{u}b$ (cherub), which in the Bible is a fantastic and varied creature supporting the throne and chariot of God.[80]

The word $k^e r\hat{u}b$ is well-rooted in Semitic, being found in the Akkadian $kar\hat{u}bu$ or $kar\hat{i}bu$, and the idea that it is connected to the Greek *gryps grypos* (griffin) was proposed by many 19th-century scholars.[81] It later fell into disfavour despite the inability of lexicographers to find an Indo-European etymology.[81] In 1968, however, the classicist and Semitist John Pairman Brown used a massive corpus of biblical, Greek and Latin texts to demonstrate that the Greek *gryps* and the Hebrew $k^e r\hat{u}b$ had strikingly similar appearances and functions and that there was no possible reason to deny the etymology.[82] However, Brown did not speculate on the date of the loan. The word 'griffin' does not occur in Hesiod or Homer and it is possible that the borrowing took place during the 'orientalizing' period in the 6th century BC, when, in fact, the griffin was a very frequent motif.[83] In the light of the considerable iconographic evidence from the Bronze Age, the linguistic loan probably took place in the 2nd millennium.

Given the predominantly Semitic-speaking composition of the Hyksos, it is very likely that the beast was already called $kar\hat{u}bu$, $kar\hat{i}bu$ or $k^e r\hat{u}b$ in the 18th century BC.[84] The use of the name in the Aegean during the Late Bronze Age is made more likely because, running, flying or hunting, the griffin was one of the most frequent images in Late Minoan and Mycenaean art. Most striking of all is the evidence that pairs of griffins were painted on the walls on either side of the throne in both Late Palatial Knossos and Mycenaean Pylos.[85] This suggests that they were a standard symbol of royalty throughout Late Palatial Crete and Mycenaean Greece. The Cretan pair probably belong to the LMII period and should be dated to the first half of the 16th or 15th centuries and the Pylian ones were even later. Thus, it could be suggested that the griffin was a purely Mycenaean symbol. However, it will be argued in Chapter XI that the Greek takeover of Central Crete did not take place until the beginning of LMIIIA, that is, after the Knossian griffins. Furthermore, there is enough attestation from smaller objects to show the importance of the motif in MMIII and LMIA and enough circumstantial evidence to indicate its royal connotations in those periods.[86]

Thus, with the griffin as with the sphinx, there appears to have been a direct influence on the iconography of Cretan royalty in MMIII from Hyksos-controlled Syria and Egypt.

WAS THERE A HYKSOS INVASION OF CRETE C. 1730 BC?

At the beginning of the ceramic period MMIII, all three palaces on Crete were destroyed and rapidly rebuilt. Although there was clearly continuity from before to after the destruction, there were enough changes to justify archaeologists and ancient historians in describing it as the only break in Cretan palatial culture. Most of these changes – in architecture, tomb construction, painting, minor arts as well as in the making of bronze weapons – indicate a combination of local developments with the borrowing of styles and techniques from Egypt and Syria. Some of them, such as the introduction of the chariot – or at least the knowledge of it – suggest specific contact with the Hyksos. This Hyksos connection is further indicated by the introduction of the flying gallop and of the two royal emblems, the sphinx and the griffin, in their Hyksos forms.

What explanation is there for these new features and the destruction of all three palaces? There is no doubt that during the 20th century there has been a strong preference to explain these and other destructions in any way rather than that of an invasion. Such 'sound' and undramatic explanations have sometimes turned out to be mistaken. For instance, the archaeologist Leonard Woolley made an extremely plausible case in 1953 that the seventh city of Alalakh in

Northwestern Syria could not have been destroyed by foreign invasion.[87] However, a Hittite text discovered in 1957 showed that the city
had been destroyed by the Hittite king Ḫattusili I around 1700 BC.[88]
In Crete, the seismic explanation remains predominant, although the
archaeologist Sinclair Hood has tried to explain the destructions in
terms of internal warfare.[89] Would it not be more economical to propose that the palaces were destroyed by Hyksos 'princes' who established themselves as rulers in Crete?

Arthur Evans saw the changes at this time as evidence of 'new ethnic ingredients', but he insisted that they were not enough to suggest a
'foreign yoke'.[90] Most modern scholars would not even accept this degree of infiltration and insist on the continuity between 3000 BC and
the 'Greek' invasion of the island around 1400 BC.[91] Although Frank
Stubbings maintained that Hyksos princes had settled the Argolid in
the early 16th century in his article on the early Mycenaeans in the
Cambridge Ancient History, which itself was generally unpopular, the
idea that there should have been Hyksos rule of Crete in the 18th and
17th centuries is unthinkable today.[92]

There are a number of examples of land-based 'barbarian' conquerors adapting to the sea. While it is true that the Mongols did not
conquer Japan, there is no doubt that they were able to muster and
construct large fleets and mount major expeditions. Despite strong
Roman prohibitions against any subject instructing barbarians in
ship-building or navigation, the Germanic tribe of Vandals were able
to seize much of North Africa and dominate the Western Mediterranean by naval force for many decades in the 5th and 6th centuries AD.[93]

In the case of the Hyksos – as discussed in the last chapter – Bietak's
excavations at Tell el Daba‘a have revealed that they were deeply involved in navigation and he himself has linked this activity to Cyprus
and Crete.[94] This new light on the Hyksos has not yet been absorbed
by historians who still tend to consider as absurd the suggestions
made by Eduard Meyer and other ancient historians of the early 20th
century that there was Hyksos rule in the Aegean. Meyer is supposed
to have based his case largely, if not exclusively, on the alabaster lid
found in a MMIII level at Knossos with the name of the Hyksos pharaoh Khyan.[95] However, it is a travesty of their thinking to reduce the
foundation of their hypothesis to this single object. Their overall concept was based on what they saw as similar transformations of Egypt
and Crete at the same time.[96]

Nevertheless, the main challenges to Meyer's ideas are based on the
lid, especially since a parallel find of Khyan's name on an obsidian
cosmetic box at the Hittite capital. As the latter has been plausibly

explained as a gift from the pharaoh to the Hittite king, it has been argued that the Cretan find was the same and that, far from demonstrating the existence of a Hyksos empire, it indicates a concert of independent powers; thus the find merely indicates the existence of contacts and not of an empire.[97] The Egyptologist and art historian Stevenson Smith accepted this but was unwilling to discredit Meyer and wrote: 'Meyer's penetrating intuition nevertheless gave imaginative emphasis to the signs of increasing contact [of Egypt] with the Aegean and Syria which are even more evident today'.[98] It would seem to me plausible to take Meyer slightly further than this and to see the 'increasing contact' as a sign of some kind of confederation of Hyksos princes at times under the hegemony of the Egyptian Hyksos pharaoh. However, given the wealth and splendour of the Knossos palace, it would seem likely that the rulers of MMIII–LMIA Knossos were kings or hegemons over the other princes in the Aegean.

Archaeological evidence, discussed below, indicates that there was close attachment if not direct rule of at least some of the Cyclades. The massive Cretan influence on the material objects found in the shaft and other graves of the Early Mycenaean Mainland would seem to strengthen the legends of Theseus and the annual Athenian tribute to King Minos and the Minotaur; these legends indicate some kind of Minoan 'thalassocracy' or maritime empire with some kind of suzerainty over Mainland states. At a recent conference on 'The Minoan thalassocracy: myth or reality?', the majority of the participants, while rightly not wanting to see an absolute equation between the two, believed that the legends chiefly referred to the beginning of the New Palace Period.[99]

As mentioned above, Stubbings maintains that there was a conquest of parts of Mainland Greece, though not of Crete, by Hyksos princes. I believe that the same probably took place in Crete. In their attacks on Meyer's image of a Hyksos empire, Schachermeyr and Helck pointed out that gifts similar to the ones found at Knossos and the Hittite capital were sent during the Middle Kingdom to the rulers of Byblos and other Syro-Palestinian princes. This leads us back to the arguments discussed in Chapter V on the nature and extent of Egyptian power or influence over the Levant in the Middle Kingdom. Nevertheless, no one doubts that Byblos, which was a dependency of Egypt during most of the 12th Dynasty, received gifts from its pharaohs.[100] Thus, it is quite clear that the pharaoh could send personal gifts to rulers under his suzerainty.

To sum up this section, we know that all the Cretan palaces were destroyed at some time around 1730 BC and that when they were rebuilt they showed slight but significant changes, many of which resemble contemporary trends in the Hyksos-dominated Levant and Lower Egypt. In particular, we know that the symbols of the sphinx and the griffin, which have plausibly been associated with the Hyksos royalty and conquest, appeared for the first time in Crete in MMIII. We also know that there was contact between Crete and the 'Hyksos region' in the succeeding decades.

There is another piece of evidence pointing in this direction, the so-called 'Hieroglyphic Deposit'. This is a number of sealings found at the palace at Knossos precisely on the destruction level between MMII and MMIII. The name comes from the Cretan hieroglyphs found on them, but as Friedrich Matz put it in the *Cambridge Ancient History*,

> Apart from seals with decorative designs and hieroglyphic characters, there are some with pictures which have no precedent in Crete, Egypt or the East for the directness of their reproduction of nature.[101]

It is likely, as Matz suggested, that some precedent for these could be found in Cretan gems from the preceding MMII. Nevertheless, it would seem that a major ingredient was the eclectic and vital 'Hyksos international' style discussed in the last chapter.[102] Two of the most remarkable of the sealings were the naturalistic portraits of a mature and fully bearded man generally known as 'the ruler' and of a young beardless man, 'the prince'. The portrait of 'the ruler' resembles the portrait (mentioned in the last chapter) found on a pot found in a 'Hyksos' grave from Jericho and a seal from a Shaft Grave and the golden royal masks from Mycenae, which will be discussed below.[103] If these were, as has been generally supposed, the portraits of rulers, the possibility that they were Hyksos barbarians would seem quite high.

All in all, while there is no direct *proof* that Crete was conquered in the late 18th century BC by Hyksos warriors from Lower Egypt, it would seem more economical to employ this hypothesis than to agree with André Dessenne that there had been two events – a mysterious destruction of the palaces at the end of MMII followed by an openness to foreign influence – especially given what we know of the newly established and very aggressive Hyksos.[104]

THE HYKSOS IN THERA?

There is no doubt that, if the Hyksos conquered Crete, they formed only a thin veneer over what was already a well-established and sophisticated civilization. Thus, almost immediately after the hypothetical conquest, the Hyksos barbaric influence on material culture disappeared into the Minoan tradition and that of the cultivated East Mediterranean as a whole.

The situation would have been rather different to the north of Crete. While, as discussed in Chapters II and III, there seems to have been considerable Egyptian and Levantine influence and a high level of local civilization there in the 3rd millennium, the indigenous culture was at a rather low ebb at the beginning of the 2nd millennium. Thus, the cultural influence of any Hyksos colonizations on the Greek Mainland would have had a much more lasting impact.

Furthermore, just as the greatest 'Hyksos' influence on Egypt was the introduction of neighbouring Palestinian culture, it would seem likely that in the Aegean the greatest influence of a 'Hyksos invasion' would come from Crete. Thus, while the Egyptian Hyksos would seem to have been Indo-Aryan-Hurrian-Semitic and those in Crete would be Indo-Aryan-Hurrian-Semitic-Egyptian, those in the Cyclades and Mainland Greece would have been Indo-Aryan-Hurrian-Semitic-Egyptian-Cretan. If such complexity seems improbable, one has only to look at the Hunnish-Turkish-Iranian-Gothic nature of the invasions of the Western Roman Empire or the Viking-French (Italian) combination behind the Norman Conquest. It should also be noted that in each of the historically attested cases, the neighbouring culture was the most influential. Thus, in terms of material culture in the Aegean as a whole, one would expect to see an expansion of Minoan forms and styles and to the extent that Crete had been Semitized and Egyptianized one would expect to find an introduction of these cultures in the realms of myth, religion and language.

Archaeological
evidence from Thera

The Thera eruption and its dating have been discussed at length in Chapter VII. Here we shall simply consider some aspects of the considerable remains of the culture destroyed by the explosion. Before coming to the sensational finds at Akrotiri, it would seem useful to mention the two finds from elsewhere on the island that would seem to indicate some contact with the Hyksos.

The first of these are three juglets in the Tell el Yehudiyeh style, exhibited at the Thera museum. The identification of the Tell el Yehudiyeh style with the Hyksos has been contested, but despite dubious cases the overlap between the two is overwhelming. There is also doubt about the provenance of the juglets, which could have been brought from Egypt to Thera in modern times. As they are undecorated and not characteristically Egyptian, this would seem unlikely; it would seem best to accept the judgement of the Swedish archaeologist Åström that they were taken to the island in ancient times, as were the similar juglets found in Cyprus.[105] There is also a sword said to have been found on Thera which is decorated with the Syrian technique of niello referred to in the last chapter in connection with Hyksos art.[106]

Among many other things that the Thera eruption destroyed was the town now known by the modern village name of Akrotiri. This was overwhelmed by volcanic debris and created what the archaeologist Christos Doumas has appropriately called a 'Pompeii of the Ancient Aegean'. As mentioned in Chapter VII, in 1939, Spyridon Marinatos put into academic form the widespread belief that Minoan civilization had been destroyed by the Thera eruption in about 1450 BC. It was this, he maintained, that had allowed the Mycenaeans to conquer the region. Marinatos was unable to test the hypothesis until the 1960s, but then he began a well-funded and equipped excavation of the site he believed to be the most promising. The results were sensational. Within hours, the archaeologists discovered a city, and over the subsequent years they have excavated a dozen or so splendidly preserved buildings sometimes two storeys high; technical difficulties and archaeological scrupulousness have, however, prevented further digging of what is clearly a much larger site.[107]

Nevertheless, the town has shown the high level of sophistication of life in the South Aegean in the 17th century BC. Its culture shows close affinities to that of Crete. The scanty remains of writing of the period, from Thera and other Cycladic islands, are in the Cretan Linear A. Weights from Akrotiri mostly conform to Cretan and hence Middle Eastern metrology.[108] There were many Minoan stone vessels at Thera and it is estimated that 6.5 per cent of the pottery was imported, mainly, as one would expect, from the northern and eastern parts of Crete.[109]

There appear to have been rather fewer contacts with the Greek Mainland, with only 2.5 per cent of the pottery coming from there. Even so, there are parallels with pottery found in Shaft Graves and there appear to have been special connections between Thera and the Argolid in the Northeastern Peloponnese and the islands of Melos, Kea and Kythera in the ceramic period MHIII between 1730 and 1675.[110]

Cycladic container vessels have also been found in MMIII Knossos. However, it has been plausibly argued that from the Cretan point of view the Cyclades were essentially stepping-stones to Mainland Greece.[111] On the other hand, wider contacts on at least a commercial basis would seem likely in the light of the facts that Cretan lead weights from the MMIII period contain lead from the Laurion mines in Attica and that other metal objects contain copper from there and from Laconia as well as gold from the latter.[112] Thus, there would seem ample archaeological evidence to back the many Greek legends concerning a Minoan 'thalassocracy', and the particular tradition of a Minoan settlement and distribution of land on the Cycladic island of Keos.[113]

Egyptian and Near Eastern objects have also been found at Akrotiri just below the eruption level. There are nine gypsum vases, which are probably Syro-Palestinian, and a number of tripod stone mortars that may also be so.[114] There is also a Levantine 'Canaanite Jar' with the standard shape and volume common over much of the East Mediterranean throughout most of the 2nd millennium. In addition, there is one possibly Egyptian alabaster jar and two ostrich egg *rhyta* of, at least ultimately, African origin.[115]

In her massive study of the Thera murals, Lyvia Morgan makes the interesting and crucially important though paradoxical point about the greater number of Levantine objects:

> . . . the iconographic evidence suggests a slightly different emphasis, there being more connections with Egypt than with the Near East. Ideas may have infiltrated from the one via the other or, indeed, via Crete, but the possibility of direct contact between Therans and Egyptians should not be ruled out. 'Invisible' imports/exports are inevitably a spectral presence and among them are ideas and images.[116]

The apparent paradox of the greater number of material finds from the Levant and the greater extent of Egyptian intangible influence is a general phenomenon throughout the Bronze Age Aegean. As Lyvia Morgan suggests, it is best explained as the result of contacts through Byblos and the other Semitic – though heavily Egyptianized – Levantine ports in the counter-clockwise trade we shall be looking at in Chapter XI. Meanwhile, we should turn to the fascinating and important iconographic evidence from Thera.

The Theran frescoes

The most sensational finds at Akrotiri were a number of frescoes, which were even better preserved than those found by Arthur Evans at Knossos. From the Theran paintings, it has been possible for the first time to gain some understanding of their overall structure and –

with the use of Egyptian parallels – to speculate interestingly on their function. There is now little doubt that they were not merely decorative but had general religious and specifically cultic significance.[117] Furthermore, scholars are agreed that the Theran murals have both local and more general features. They are similar but not identical to the Cretan frescoes. They also have close relations to the Near East. As Nanno Marinatos puts it in her study of the frescoes,

> Naturally, there were important difference between Crete and the Orient but the similarities were more basic. An Egyptian would not have felt totally alien in Crete. . . . if we are going to approach Minoan mentality at all, and that is all we can do in the absence of written records, we have to see Crete and Thera as part of the larger world of the Ancient Orient.[118]

I shall be looking at the implications of the frescoes for Egyptian influences on Greek mythology in the fourth volume of this series. Here we are concerned with what they reveal about Theran society at the time when they were painted.

In this respect, the most revealing murals are two narrow bands, which have been interpreted in a number of ways. Most of these distinguish the two, along the general lines that one portrays an urban and rural scene and what seems to be a naval battle and the other a ceremonial flotilla of ships moving from a city sited at the mouth of a river flowing from mountains to a welcome at another city, which is generally thought to be Akrotiri itself.[119]

The art historian and Aegean archaeologist Karen Pollinger Foster sees the two panels as an integrated whole. She draws many precise parallels to back her contention that the whole scene is an Aegean version of the Egyptian Heb Sed festival in which there were a number of competitions and ceremonies to celebrate the jubilee and rejuvenation of the pharaoh.[120] This may be a case of misplaced precision, but even so the frescoes contain many indubitable features of Egyptian ceremonies.

The frescoes' most outstanding features are the portrayal of sophistication and luxury of life and a high degree of social stratification. There are clear social 'class' contrasts in dress, in positioning and, most strikingly, between the oarsmen and paddlers and the idle passengers seated under palanquins or in private cabins.[121]

The detailed pictures also reveal for the first time a great deal about the construction and rigging of a number of different ships. These show many features that are Egyptian and some that are Levantine and local Cycladic. Distinguishing these strands is extremely difficult as there had been borrowing of forms and equipment among these regions at least since the 3rd millennium. In general, all that can be said is what the Israeli maritime archaeologist Avner Raban concluded in his detailed study of the Thera ships:

> The Theran ships represent a fusion of Cycladic, Cretan and Egyptian naval traditions. Many Egyptian elements appear in the ships; some are characteristic of contemporary Egyptian vessels, while others can be traced back to Predynastic times.[122]

Another interesting feature of the ships in the 'nautical procession' is that the ships in it are not sailed or rowed but paddled from a standing, bent-over position. As a number of writers have pointed out, this method of propulsion of such large craft was both inefficient and out of date by the 2nd millennium. The nearest parallel of such paddling of a large boat comes from a 5th-Dynasty (c. 2700 BC) relief from Saqqara. From these features, they plausibly conclude that the ships were going only a short distance on a religious procession for which there was a desire for archaism appropriate to a Heb Sed or other ceremony.[123]

Despite this strong Egyptian presence, there is no doubt that the chief cultural influence on these paintings is that of Crete, seventy miles to the south. There are, however, interesting and probably significant differences between the Theran and Cretan pictures. The most striking of these is the representation in Thera of warfare that is absent from the paintings so far discovered in Crete. What is more, the warriors are wearing helmets made of boars' tusks, a feature that had previously been seen as distinctively Mycenaean.[124] However, as Lyvia Morgan points out, the boars'-tusk helmets here are of a 'zoned' type found in both Crete and Mainland Greece and 'marginally more' in the former, where they date back to the MMIII period.[125] No swords are represented on the Theran murals but the association of swords with royalty in archaeological finds from the Middle East and the Aegean at this time, as well as in Greek legends of the heroic age, would make this absence unsurprising.[126] The 'tower' shields which the soldiers in the murals are often seen as using have also been found in Crete, especially from the MMIII and LMIA periods.[127] In general, Lyvia Morgan points out how difficult and arbitrary it is to try to distinguish between the Minoan and Mycenaean features of the people portrayed on the Theran frescoes.[128] The idea of Mycenaean features at Thera at this time is especially striking, when we realize that the frescoes date from before 1628, not to around 1450 or 1500 BC as Marinatos and other archaeologists have supposed.

Some garments resemble the shaggy coats of Near Eastern and Aegean shepherds. Karen Pollinger Foster relates these to the designation of some of the royal entourage as rustics at the Heb Sed festival.[129] Unlike Minoans, Mycenaeans and Egyptians, many of the men in the Thera murals are represented as wearing long, enveloping garments, which in their most elaborate forms had single or double bands around the hem and a band around the neck.[130] Somewhat similar robes, also with coloured piping, are found in the portraits of princes of Tunip and Kadesh in Syria on Egyptian tomb paintings from the reign of Tuthmōsis III in the 15th century.[131] Despite the temporal and geographical gaps between Thera in the 17th century and 15th-century Syro-Palestine, this resemblance in clothing, together with the representation of a 15th-century 'prince of Keftiw' (Crete) as a fully clothed Levantine, would suggest the possibility of Hyksos prestige if not rule in pre-eruption Thera.[132] Morgan does not note this parallel. She does, however, record that a number of scholars have pointed out that the additional piece of fabric hanging behind the shoulders of certain significant – possibly priestly – Theran figures 'has a long history in the Near East' going back to Sumerian gods.[133]

There has been considerable debate on the locality of the town from which the procession of ships sets out. Peter Warren and other scholars maintain that all its features can be found in the Aegean.[134] Other scholars can find no Aegean parallels for a town at the mouth of a river flowing down from the mountains, or for the flora and fauna, especially the lion which is portrayed hunting deer in the mountains. While there were lions at this period in continental Greece, as Nanno Marinatos points out, 'it is unlikely that lions roamed on the dry Aegean islands'.[135] It is also interesting to note that the Greek words for lion, *leōn-*, the Mycenaean *rewo-* and *lis* come from the Egyptian *rw* and the Canaanite *layîs* respectively.[136]

Spyridon Marinatos argued on these geographical and biological grounds that the first city was in Libya and he was supported in this by the English classicist Denis Page and the Italian archaeologist S. Stucchi.[137] They maintained that the spectacular mountainous coast, full of exotic flora and fauna, with a river tumbling down to the sea around the city, could not have been set in the Aegean. Marinatos reinforced this with parallels he saw with Herodotos' descriptions of the appearance of Libyan tribes: the shaven head with hairlock; large earrings; circumcision; armour; clothing and the nakedness of drowning figures.[138] Marinatos drew attention to the African characteristics of two boys boxing, portrayed on another mural.[139]

These arguments have been attacked from the isolationist stand-point by Lyvia Morgan. She argues that the painting is nothing like the flat East Libyan coast and even the mountainous coast of Cire-naica lacks the capes and islands, let alone the major river. On the hu-man characteristics, she points out that, although Libyan children and youths had shaven heads and hairlocks, so did Egyptian ones; that large earrings were present in the Aegean; that the pictorial evidence that Therans were circumcised is fanciful, and, in any event, the Li-byans were not circumcised; that the similarities of armour and clothing are wrong; and that it was a common convention to portray the enemy dead as naked.[140] Most of these points are valid.

However, in denying a specifically Libyan connection, Lyvia Mor-gan is admitting a more general African connection in the hairlocks and the negroid appearance of many figures in Thera and elsewhere in the Aegean. Thus, there would seem little doubt that the Theran artists were familiar with Blacks either at home – as personal names discussed in the next chapter would suggest – or in Africa or, most likely, in both. Similarly, while Lyvia Morgan weakens the case for a Libyan landscape, she is unable to argue against the distinctively Af-rican animals and plants. However, neither Morgan nor Marinatos and his allies have considered another coast that would seem a much more likely prototype, that of the Levant. There sacred rivers poured down from mountains to the sea near such major cities as Byblos and Sidon.

Nevertheless, while Morgan is clearly right to point out that there is something fantastically exotic about the landscape, there is no escap-ing the conclusion that directly and indirectly Therans had not only considerable knowledge of Crete, Egypt and the Levant but also some awareness of other parts of Africa.

As mentioned above, the various boats that make up the flotilla pro-cessing between the two cities are strikingly similar to Egyptian ves-sels. Lyvia Morgan has made a very convincing case that the Theran fresco portrays a celebration of spring and the opening of the naviga-tion season. This, of course, has no strict parallel in Egypt with its very different seasonal pattern. However, she goes on to point to the pre-cedents of the Babylonian Zagmuk festival on the Euphrates and the Egyptian New Year 'Opet' festival of boats along the Nile. In all of these as well as in the nautical processions of the Heb Sed, ships were put in perfect trim decorated with garlands and the whole population came out in festival, as on the Thera mural.[141]

Another miniature fresco in the same room is known as the 'river scene'. The archaeologist Doumas describes it as follows:

On both banks of a meandering river wild beasts are shown among palm trees and other exotic plants and bushes. Predominant among the beasts is a griffin at a flying gallop, a spotted panther-like feline stalks a group of ducks and below the griffin there is a galloping deer. . . . Both the flora and the fauna led Marinatos to recognize a North African landscape, which further supported his Libyan theory.[142]

The presence of both the griffin and its flying gallop is fascinating. As argued in the last chapter and above, both the mythical animal and its motion appear to have been hallmarks of the Hyksos princes in Syria and the Aegean.[143] Although there were some rivers in Libya in the 2nd millennium BC, the river in the fresco would seem more likely to be an idealized vision of the Nile. In support of this is the fact, mentioned above, that the feline stalking or catching ducks is a common theme in Egyptian painting.[144] Thus it would seem that Spyridon Marinatos has put forth a convincing case for his claim of an African prototype for this scene.

Egyptian themes can also be found in the paintings from other buildings at Akrotiri. These contain representations of Egyptian plants, such as the papyrus, which – as in Crete – is not represented realistically but according to Egyptian convention.[145] There are also many representations of East African antelope and monkeys. Although these may just possibly have existed on Thera and Crete, their general association with Africa is undoubted. Here, as with the lion, there is a common word for monkey – the Egyptian *g(w)f*, the Akkadian *ukupu*, the Canaanite *qôp*, the Sanskrit *kapih* and the Greek *kēpos* or *kēbos*. The lexicographer Chantraine follows the 19th-century Semitist Lewy in deriving all of these from the Egyptian.[146]

Spyridon Marinatos was convinced that the painters of the frescoes were intimately in touch with Libya, Egypt and the Levant. He saw this as evidence for his hypothesis that Greece had been invaded – by Greeks – from these regions in the early 16th century, at the end of the Hyksos period. Since he dated the eruption at least half a century after the defeat of the Hyksos he had some difficulty with this. As he wrote in 1974,

We cannot as yet suggest definite dates. All antiquities unearthed at Thera show that the town was buried about 1520 to 1500 B.C. under the ashes of the tremendous volcanic explosion that took place then. The 'African' fresco should be assigned for preference to the turbulent Hyksos period with which some scholars have connected the legend of Danaos and Aigyptos.[147]

We now know that the eruption was in 1628, which, of course, puts it before the traditional date for the arrival of the heroic colonists. Given the earlier contacts referred to above, there is, in fact, no need to associate this detailed knowledge of the Near East with any putative settlements. Nevertheless, the military connotations of the frescoes still make Marinatos' association with the Hyksos attractive. This is possible if one accepts the Revised Ancient Model's dating of the colonizations, not at the end of the Hyksos period *c.* 1575, but at its beginnings at the end of the 18th century BC.

THE ORIGINS OF MYCENAEAN CIVILIZATION

It has been mentioned above that there appear to have been special connections between Thera and the Argolid, in the Northeastern Peloponnese, and the islands of Melos, Kea and Kythera in the ceramic period MHIII between 1730 and 1670 BC. It has also been suggested that these led on to a relationship between Crete and the Greek mainland.[148] This is, of course, the period in which the earliest of the famous Shaft Graves of Mycenae in the Argolid must be dated.

The Shaft Graves were first discovered by Heinrich Schliemann in 1876 AD. Disregarding current academic opinion and following Pausanias' precise description of the site, Schliemann dug inside the citadel of Mycenae, where he very quickly hit on the extraordinarily rich remains of what later came to be called Grave Circle A. He immediately identified them with Agamemnon and his family, but the 'barbaric' 'unHellenic' nature of the art immediately made this attribution unpopular and in fact it is now universally acknowledged that the richest tombs belong to the beginning of the Mycenaean period, not the end when Agamemnon was supposed to have flourished.[149] For many decades, this circle was believed to be unique, but in the 1950s a second cemetery called Circle B was discovered and excavated.[150]

Although the cemeteries in which the Shaft Graves are found contained some cist graves – or stone-lined boxes – for contracted bodies from the earlier Middle Helladic period, the Shaft Graves themselves seem to date from MHIII. Unlike the earlier cist graves they were larger, ranging from 4.5 metres to 6.4, and much deeper, from 1 to 5 metres. Some way down the shaft a wooden roof was set across it. The dead were laid full length and, especially in Circle A, they were covered with rich ornaments and some had striking gold masks. Many were also surrounded with an extraordinary profusion of bronze spears, swords and daggers, gold, silver and bronze vessels, as well as ones of alabaster, rock-crystal and pottery.[151]

Unfortunately, there are no traces of buildings associated with these early graves at Mycenae. This may be because of the considerable construction in Mycenae at the end of the Late Bronze Age. On the other hand, some scholars, influenced by what they see as the nomadic style of some Mycenaean art, have suggested that the rulers buried there lived in temporary wooden structures and that the lavishness of their burials should be compared to those of the nomadic Scyths a millennium later.[152]

This idea would seem to be reinforced by a Semitic etymology for the toponym. The traditional origin of the name Mykēnai is from *mykēs*, 'mushroom' and by implication 'knob', which would be appropriate for the hill upon which the citadel is built. This, however, is generally dismissed today.[153] In the 1890s, the American Assyriologist W. Muss-Arnolt derived it from the Semitic *mᵉkonåh* (fixed resting place, base). The form *mknt* is found in Ugaritic and the masculine *mkn* is attested in Phoenician.[154] A more plausible candidate would seem to be the Ugaritic toponym Mḫnt (the Hebrew Maḥăneh), 'camp', or Mḫnm (Hebrew Maḥănayîm), 'two camps'. In West Semitic, settlement names often appear in the dual form, apparently reflecting an upper and a lower city. This suffix, *-ayîm*, would seem the most plausible origin for the common Greek practice of referring to cities – with their duality of the acropolis and the lower town – in the plural with *-ai:* for example, Athēnai, Thēbai, etc. Either of these Semitic etymologies would seem better than the vague one put forward by the German writer of the latest book on Ancient Greek place names, Adolf Fick. Fick proposed in 1905 that Mycenae was related to Mykale and Mykalessos and was Carian. He could not divine any meaning for them, and the relation between these words would seem simply to be that all have the Semitic and Egyptian locative prefix *m-*.[155]

Even if the name Mycenae originally meant 'base' or 'camps', the density of early Middle Helladic pottery at Mycenae itself makes it unlikely that any hypothetical invaders were camped away from the native population centres and there is no doubt that there were towns in the Argolid in the 17th century BC. Despite the fact that there are no archaeological traces of urbanization in Early Mycenaean Mainland Greece, there are village sites from Central and Northern Greece. Furthermore, we know from representations in contemporary Crete and Thera and from the actual remains at Akrotiri, as well as ones on the islands of Kea and Melos, that there were many multi-storeyed 'Mediterranean' cities around the Aegean at this time.[156] Indirect evidence comes from Mycenae itself, where a battered and fragmentary silver *rhyton* has been found decorated with the picture of the siege of a city of this type; the city could possibly be Mycenae itself.[157]

Nevertheless, there is no physical evidence of any palace or major city on Mainland Greece during the ceramic periods MHIII and LHI, that is, between 1730 and 1600 BC. Apart from the unreliable chances of preservation, the most likely reason for this absence would seem to be the continuity of Mycenaean civilization; that is to say, the sites of the first Mycenaean cities continued to be built on – and frequently – for the next five hundred years, thus obliterating the earlier structures.

In order, therefore, to reconstruct society on Mainland Greece in the late 18th and 17th centuries, we have to rely very heavily on graves and their contents. The Shaft Graves are not the only spectacular tombs from this period. Substantial tholos tombs, sometimes with rich grave goods, have been found in Sparta and Messenia in the Southern Peloponnese. More recently, splendid 'royal' tumuli with pottery from the MHIII period have been excavated at Thorikos and Marathon in Attica. At one of the Marathon group it appears that, as sometimes occurred in Central Asian tombs, a horse had been killed on its roof, and at another, later one, a team of horses had been sacrificed in front of the tomb.[158]

Shaft graves, *tholoi* and tumuli

Shaft graves were not restricted to Mycenae. Examples from the Late MHIII, and LHI – the 17th century BC – have also been found at Lerna in the Argolid, Eleusis in Attica, the island of Skopelos north of Euboia and Leukas in the Ionian islands to the northwest. It is commonly but mistakenly believed that the earliest Cretan shaft graves were dug in LMII, after what has been seen as the 'Mycenaean invasion' of the island, whereas in fact they date back to MMIII.[159] Outside the Aegean, there are close parallels in the royal shaft graves that have been found from the 3rd millennium at Alaca Hüyük in Central Anatolia.[160] Shaft graves sunk into the ground or slanted into rock faces were common in Syro-Palestine in Middle Bronze Age IIB *c.* 1760– 1600 BC – the Hyksos period – and they became common in New Kingdom Egypt.[161] These did not have wooden roofs, but, as the archaeologist Oliver Dickinson put it,

> The essential feature of the grave-type is not that it is cut into rock or roofed with wood, but that the grave is constructed in the lower part of the shaft, which after the earliest examples was always of considerable depth.[162]

The classicist and archaeologist N.G.L. Hammond, who has consistently championed the importance of northern influences on Greece, has argued that shaft graves and the walled circles of shaft graves originated from the wall round single tumuli found in what is now Albania and Epiros.[163] This theory has not been well received because of stratigraphical difficulties and major differences not merely between tumuli and shaft graves but between Albanian and Greek tumuli.[164]

Some scholars believe that the Shaft Graves developed out of the cist burials of the early Middle Helladic period, maintaining that the relatively poorer graves in the somewhat earlier Circle B helped bridge the enormous gap between the very poor, crouched, shallow cist burials of the Middle Helladic and the deep and spacious splendour of the Shaft Graves. To take a recent example, the Belgian archaeologist Oliver Pelon sees them, and the circles within which they were set, as the result of a meeting of two traditions – the Cretan monumental circular tombs and family burials and the native Helladic traditions of cist graves and occasional high-status tumuli.[165] To my mind, this conclusion demonstrates the futility of refusing to look beyond the Aegean. Although set in a circle, which was possibly walled, the Shaft Graves are neither circular nor monumental, nor does a single cist grave resemble larger chambers frequently containing a number of bodies. Other scholars also find such continuity difficult to accept. For example, Frank Stubbings argued in his article in the *Cambridge Ancient History:*

> Whether this collective use of a tomb by itself is a significant departure from the Middle Helladic practice of a single burial is debatable; the personal grave and the family vault can exist side by side in one period and culture. Again, the change from contracted to extended posture might simply be the result of using larger graves. But still the access of grandeur, the prodigal use of hitherto unparalleled riches, has to be explained; and in the grave goods themselves there are numerous innovations of form and decoration that hardly allow us to regard these burials as a natural development and elaboration of Middle Helladic practice.[166]

Or, as Emily Vermeule put it with wonderful succinctness, 'Speaking honestly, there is nothing in the Middle Helladic world to prepare us for the furious splendor of the Shaft Graves'.[167] If the Shaft Graves came, or were at least stimulated, from elsewhere, where should we look? The archaeologist of Anatolia Machteld Mellink, and James Muhly see the connection with the very similar graves at Alaca Hüyük and postulate influence across Anatolia to the Aegean, which they see reflected in other aspects of material culture and language.[168] There are both temporal and spatial difficulties with relating Alaca Hüyük to

Mycenae, as the Anatolian tombs are at least five hundred years earlier than the Greek ones and there are no other similar tombs geographically between them. On the other hand, the resemblances are striking, and it might well be possible to see an Eastern Anatolian tradition, transmitted to the Aegean. Though the transmission could have occurred through Anatolia or around the north of the Black Sea, the most likely route would be with the Hyksos, through Syria and Egypt and Crete to the European Mainland (this will be discussed further below).

Stubbings and Marinatos, who on other grounds prefer to see the influences as coming from Egypt and the Near East, are interestingly silent on the question of the graves themselves.[169] Although they lack the wooden roofs of Alaca Hüyük, the shaft graves of 'Hyksos' Syro-Palestine and those of New Kingdom Egypt and Crete do offer some interesting parallels. Van Seters points out that those of Hyksos Palestine appear to have been restricted to the rich and that, as at Mycenae, the burials were nearly always multiple, though there were some single ones.[170] Another striking parallel is that with the royal cemetery at Byblos, which started during the Egyptian 12th Dynasty in the 19th century and continued for seven hundred years, and was made up of shaft graves set in a semi-circle.[171] This would fit well with the plausible theory that at least the later tombs in Circle A at Mycenae were those of the kings of a distinct dynasty, or members of a restricted elite.[172] In general, then, this type of burial could possibly reflect earlier Anatolian influence and certainly indicates contemporary Syro-Palestinian influences.

The other type of princely or royal burial common in early Mycenaean Greece were the *tholos* and the tumulus.[173] The origins of the *tholos* in Crete have been discussed in Chapter I. Despite some differences in form, there would seem no reason to doubt that its appearance at the end of MHIII in Mainland Greece and its increasing popularity and construction on a massive scale there in succeeding centuries was the result of the Cretan influence, evident in other aspects of Mycenaean material culture. As mentioned in Chapter I, *tholoi* were first built in Crete in Neolithic times and they continued to be constructed as late as MMII and to be used in LMIA. Thus, there is no problem in arguing that they were introduced to Greece from the island in MMIII.[174] However, the similarity of *tholoi* to pyramids may indicate some indirect Egyptian influence.[175] The tumuli may possibly reflect some native Helladic survival. On the other hand, their apparent links to the Shaft Graves' Circles, which some scholars rather implausibly argue were originally covered by tumuli, would seem to show that they too were the result of Eastern influences.[176]

Burials and grave goods

Before coming on to the specific nature of the burials and grave goods of the Shaft Graves, it would seem useful to consider them and their social implications in general. The expense and elaboration of the graves would seem to indicate two things: the wealth available in the society and striking social differentiation. As has been mentioned above, the latter is also shown by the exclusive circle of graves. The huge quantities of weapons makes it clear that whether or not the individual buried was an outstanding warrior, warfare and military prowess were important and desirable features. Thus, we are clearly considering the burials of a martial elite.

The only information to be gained from the physical anthropology of the skeletons is of their extraordinary variety. This is true for all social strata at Mycenae although the privileged appear to have been slightly taller. This could have been the result of better nutrition, of elite interbreeding or selection for size.[177]

The gold-leaf death masks are the most distinctive objects from the Shaft Graves. The idea for them may well have come from knowledge of Egyptian mummies. However, their most striking features, which are distinctly un-Egyptian, are their strong beards and moustaches. The nearest contemporary parallels to these are the Hyksos pot from Palestine and the sealing from the 'Hieroglyphic Deposit' precisely between MMII and MMIII at Knossos.[178]

One almost universal characteristic of early Mycenaean burials is that the bodies were stretched at full length. They were not crouched like those of the Early Middle Helladic nor cremations like those of what seems to be the Indo-Aryan tradition or of the Homeric heroes at the end of the Mycenaean period.[179] As mentioned above, the bodies were lavishly bedecked with ornaments and jewels and heavily armed with bronze weapons. In at least one case, the body appears to have gone through some primitive mummification and this, together with the use of gold masks, has suggested to many scholars some knowledge of Egyptian burials.[180] On the other hand, they are clearly not Egyptian mummies and sarcophagi.

The Shaft Graves do, however, show some striking resemblances to the much poorer contemporary Hyksos graves found at Tell el Daba'a. These too had inhumation and the unmummified bodies were buried wearing their bronze weapons, which were very similar to those from Mycenae.[181]

The Mycenaean tombs in Circle A had stelae, often with representations of chariots, set in front of them and the early Marathon tumulus had the bones of a small horse, while a later one had a pair of horses sacrificed in its *dromos*. Similarly, the grander of the tombs at Tell el Daba'a had equids and carts buried in front of them. The major difference between the deep Shaft Graves, cut into soft rock or earth, and those at Tell el Daba'a is that the latter were shallow and brick-lined. On the other hand, this was inevitable given the fine soil of the Delta and the high water table. Thus, there would seem no reason to doubt that the rock-cut Shaft Graves of Palestine represented the major Hyksos style of burial.

The grave goods at Mycenae came from an extensive geographical range. There are ostrich eggs from Nubia, lapis lazuli from Afghanistan through Mesopotamia, alabaster and faience from Crete, raw ivory from Syria, silver from Anatolia, Hungary and Spain, rock-crystal from the Alps and amber from the Baltic.[182] There are many Cretan objects and Stubbings and other scholars have identified some Egyptian pieces, in addition to the ostrich egg. These include a crystal bowl in the form of a duck, a sycamore box with appliqué ivory figures of dogs, and a faience vase.[183] The bowl, the vase and the duck seem to be Egyptian, but the ivory appliqué, which looks more Syrian, is more problematic. There is also a splendid lapis lazuli scarab of the Hyksos period of undoubted Egyptian provenance.[184] At a more practical level the grave goods included flint arrowheads, which, according to H. L. Lorimer, 'were almost certainly imported from Egypt'.[185] All these goods show that there were direct or indirect trading or other contacts between Mycenae, Egypt and the Near East in the 17th century BC. If we want to investigate the origins of Mycenaean culture, however, we must examine the sources of the Mycenaean objects themselves.

The sources of Early Mycenaean material culture

These have in the words of one scholar 'a promiscuous quality'.[186] They appear to draw on a huge range of artistic styles, some known and others not. Nevertheless, three of these seem to predominate: Minoan or Cycladic, native Helladic and 'barbaric off-Egyptian'.

The Minoan and Cycladic influence on Mycenaean Mainland Greece is present from the beginning and increases until the 15th century with the Mycenaean domination of Crete.[187] Despite this and the strong Greek tradition of King Minos' domination of parts of Mainland Greece, no scholar since Arthur Evans has proposed a purely Minoan invasion to explain the culture of the Shaft Graves.[188]

This would seem to be because of the apparent lack of Cretan precedents for the 'barbaric off-Egyptian' style.

There is no doubt about the continuity of pottery styles. MHIII continues during the Shaft Grave period and although Late Helladic shows Minoan and other 'Mycenaean' traits, there seems no doubt of some continuity from the earlier period. Some scholars have used this to argue that the developments at Mycenae and elsewhere were indigenous ones based on local agriculture and trade with an increasingly prosperous Europe.[189] Against this, however, are not only the extraordinary changes in all the other aspects of material culture, but also what several archaeologists believe to be signs of widespread destructions during MHIII. This is true of the two key regions of the Argolid and Attica, and as the excavators of Kirrha and Krisa in Phocis have written, 'In many places the constructions of MHIIIb rest on a layer of ashes, the presence of which fits well with the hypothesis of an invasion'.[190] Spyridon Marinatos tried to reconcile the continuity of pottery with what he was convinced had been an invasion by the strange argument that there had been 'an identity of blood' between the natives and an invading group.[191] There would seem to be no need for such contortions. Pottery is a technique or art form of the poor and therefore this survival of Middle Helladic material culture can easily be accommodated in theories, which have been widespread over the past century, of invasion by a warrior élite.

The German ancient historian E. Grumach, who argued for the late arrival of the Greeks, pointed out, in support of an Aryan invasion at this time, that the word for potters' clay *keramos* and those for a range of vessels – *kantharos, aryballos, lekythos, depas, phiale* – were non–Indo-European.[192] However, the original stem *keram-* is concerned not with the clay but with the potter and metal-worker as a craftsman. It has a plausible etymology in the Egyptian *ḳзm*, an attested variant of *ḳm з* (hammer out, create). The Greek *kantharos* is a word with an extraordinary multiplicity of meanings, including 'scarab' and a 'mark on the tongue of the Apis Bull'. It would seem to come from an Egyptian form *kз nṯr* (holy spirit). *Depas* must derive from the Egyptian *dpt* (boat or vessel).[193] As no one suggests that the original population of Greece spoke Egyptian, this part of Grumach's argument must fall. Nevertheless, his general point on the fundamental and conservative nature of pottery remains.

In the areas of higher art and technology, there are complete breaks from the native tradition. As mentioned above, there is a strong Minoan influence on many of the jewels and smaller objects found in the tombs as well as on decorative motifs, such as 'inverted pillars', 'horns of consecration' with birds, bulls' heads and double-axes, women with open bodices, the dolphin and the octopus.[194]

Other decoration, however, is 'barbaric off-Egyptian' or, as it was described in the last chapter, 'Hyksos international'. Early Mycenaean ivories are full of leaping and rapacious lions, griffins and distinctive 'Mycenaean' sphinxes of the Syrian type that appeared in Crete in MMIII.[195] Emily Vermeule has pointed out how similar many of the motifs – stags and other animals back to back, mythical beasts with curly manes, etc. – are to Scythian and other art of the Steppe from the 1st millennium BC.[196] James Muhly does not claim any direct connection with Scythian art but he is convinced of and convincing about the 'common nomadic background' it shares with some of the Mycenaean motifs.[197] His discussion, in this connection, of the arrival of the horse and chariot will be taken up below.

The Syrian origin of the technique of niello was discussed in the last chapter and there are some magnificent examples of it from Mycenae.[198] The motifs of the Mycenaean niello are those familiar from Hyksos Syro-Palestine and Egypt, as well as MMIII Crete – lion hunts, animals in flying gallop and the 'Nilotic scene' of a cat catching birds referred to in the discussion of the Thera murals.[199] Although there are some unique swords and daggers, the metallurgy and basic patterns of the many weapons found in the Shaft Graves belong to the Syro-Cretan school discussed above.[200] The question of the arrival of the chariot on Mainland Greece at this time will be discussed below.

In summary, the grave goods from Mycenae and early Mycenaean art both indicate extraordinarily varied origins – from the Aegean, Eastern Anatolia, Syro-Palestine and Egypt. Such a complicated pattern requires equally complicated answers.

THE ARYANIST MODEL OF INVASION
Greek mercenaries

Despite the continuities from the native Helladic tradition, and the emphasis laid upon them by isolationist scholars, there are simply too many discontinuities which cannot be explained without a massive outside stimulus.[201] Given the extraordinarily military orientation of Mycenaean society, the most plausible explanation for this is a violent invasion from abroad. As Spyridon Marinatos put it:

All these radical innovations can be explained only by external causes: just before 1600 BC [I would put it a century earlier] a few well organised groups of professional warriors invaded Greece.

They possessed a new weapon, which had a tremendous effect upon the simple agricultural people of Greece; the chariot and the horse [I would add the sword].[202]

If one accepts the premise of an invasion, one has to postulate its place of origin. Given the proximity and striking similarities between Shaft Grave Mycenae and Cretan culture of MMIII and pre-eruption Thera, the most likely base would seem to be Crete and the Cyclades. Nevertheless, as mentioned above, no modern scholar has argued for a purely Minoan invasion, because there are simply too many other influences involved.[203]

Probably the most popular hypothesis was that held by Marinatos himself: that the new invaders were Greeks who had returned from Egypt after helping the 18th-Dynasty pharaoh Amōsis expel the Hyksos.[204] Evidence for this is seen in the statements of the pharaoh that the Ḥ3(w)-nbw were his followers and that his queen Aḥḥotpe was 'mistress of the Mediterranean islands'.[205] The plausible identification of Ḥ3(w)-nbw with the Aegean will be discussed in the next chapter but here it would seem useful to note that Amōsis' statement would seem more likely to be a claim of suzerainty than a reference to any mercenaries.

This 'mercenary' hypothesis would satisfactorily explain both the Helladic continuities and the 'barbaric off-Egyptian' element of the Shaft Graves and ideologically it would provide the least painful kind of Near Eastern invasion. However, the re-dating of the Thera eruption to 1628 makes it utterly untenable. The Hyksos were expelled between 1575 and 1550 BC and the earliest Shaft Graves were dug in the MHIII ceramic period, which ended c. 1675 BC, that is, nearly a century before the Greek mercenaries allegedly arrived. The same chronological considerations make the association between the arrival of Danaos and the expulsion of the Hyksos seen by proponents of the Ancient Model equally untenable (see below).

Indo-Europeans

Before discussing this second set of hypotheses, it is necessary to point out that, as with the mercenary hypothesis, they were formulated before the establishment of the high date for the Thera eruption. Thus, all of them are approximately a century too low in their reconstructions.

The possible links between the royal tombs at Alaca Hüyük and the

Shaft Graves have been discussed above, but, when proposed by Muhly and Drews, they have to be seen as part of an irregular variant of the Aryan Model. Instead of envisaging the Indo-Europeans as arriving in Greece *c.* 2200 BC at the end of EHII or in 1900 BC (conventionally seen as the start of the Middle Helladic), this variant sees them as descending on Greece in the 17th century. Such a 'heresy' – unlike the one that sets the arrival of the Indo-Europeans with the 'Dorian Invasion' or 'Return of the Heraklids' in the 12th century – could, according to some contemporary scholars, be accommodated in present theories of Greek and Indo-European historical linguistics.[206] The scheme appears untenable to me, because I believe conventional wisdom is plausible when it maintains that by 1700 BC the language of the Steppe was not proto–Indo-European but distinctively Iranian.[207] Furthermore, we know that the language associated with chariotry in the Hurrian kingdom of Mitanni was Indo-Iranian or, more specifically, Indo-Aryan.[208] Thus, if this region is seen as the origin of the Shaft Grave culture or the latter's arrival is to be linked to chariots, this cannot explain the origin of Greek as a language which is neither Iranian nor Indo-Aryan.[209]

Despite this fundamental difficulty, the appeal of linking the arrival of the Indo-Europeans to the arrival in Greece of the chariot – that symbol of the 'master race' – has proved irresistible. As the Indo-Europeanist William Wyatt put it in his article on 'The Indo-Europeanisation of Greece',

> My conclusion is inextricably bound up with the chariot: if a chariot, or evidence for a chariot, is found in Greece dating from before 1600, then my argument will lead me to assume that the Greeks arrived at that earlier date.[210]

Wyatt is not the only scholar to be overwhelmed by this appeal. It was proposed by the classicist C. D. Buck in 1926 and was strongly supported by Martin Nilsson, the historian of religion, in 1933.[211] More recently, it has been revived by Wyatt, James Muhly, Leonard Palmer, the Dutch ancient historians R. A. van Royan and B. H. Isaac and most recently the classicist Robert Drews.[212] Nilsson based his case on such arguments as the *megaron* or hall with a pitched roof of an allegedly northern type having first appeared at the beginning of the Late Helladic (this has now been disproved) and on the presence of Baltic amber beads in the Shaft Graves. However, these were also widespread in New Kingdom Egypt and no one would propose a northern conquest of that country on this basis.[213]

Nilsson and the later scholars relied most heavily on the culture of

the rulers buried in the Shaft Graves. They argued that the veneration of the graves in later Mycenaean times showed that the early
kings must have been 'Greeks'.[214] This by no means follows. In the
quotation from Herodotos with which I opened Chapter I of Volume 1, the historian maintained that the Spartan kings, for whom legitimacy was of extreme importance, were believed to have been of
Egyptian or Syrian ancestry.[215] This is more than a significant analogy,
since the Spartan kings saw themselves as Heraklids, that is, descendants of the pre-Pelopid dynasty at Mycenae.

However, the chief arguments of these scholars, which do retain
some force, are that not only do the Shaft Graves resemble the East
Anatolian and Caucasian royal graves but also the barbaric style of
Mycenae does bear striking if intangible resemblances to the nomadic
styles of the Steppe. In addition there is the important point that the
chariot, the Indo-European and Indo-Aryan involvement in which
has been discussed in the last chapter, undoubtedly first appeared in
Mainland Greece about the same time as the Shaft Graves. What is
more, the stelae engraved with chariots that marked many of the royal
graves clearly demonstrate that in Greece, as in Southwest Asia,
chariots were associated with nobility if not royalty.[216] This association
helps solve another great problem of the Aryan Model, the massive
survival of Pre-Hellenic in the later Greek language and culture, since
it is more easily explained in terms of a small-scale élite conquest than
by the mass migrations proposed by the supporters of an earlier
invasion.

In his article on the subject, James Muhly postulates a first invasion
of Greece from the northeast around 1700 BC. Muhly understands
the essential point that the Anatolian languages are not Indo-European in the narrow sense. So he argues against an invasion from
Anatolia and for one coming from the Caucasus, the Steppe and the
Eastern Balkans.[217] He also knows that by 1700 BC the Steppe was
Iranian-speaking, but he believes that this difficulty can be overcome
by what he sees as a special relationship between Greek and Indo-
Iranian.[218]

Here, Muhly based himself on the hypothesis of a number of Indo-
Europeanists, that there is a special relationship between the Greek
and Indo-Iranian branches of the Indo-European language family.
Despite considerable uncertainty on the significance of the different
isoglosses, there is a general view that at one time speakers of the languages that became Greek, Armenian, Phrygian and Indo-Iranian
lived in proximity to each other.[219] On the other hand, it is also believed that Indo-Iranian divided into Indo-Aryan and Iranian in the

late 3rd millennium. If this is the case, the divisions between Indo-Iranian and proto-Greek must have been earlier still.[220] Thus, the argument that the speakers of proto-Greek arrived in Greece from the Steppe, where they had been in contact with Indo-Iranians, with the break in MHIII around 1700 BC is untenable on linguistic grounds.

On the archaeological side, although Muhly can point to Mycenaean contact with the Balkans, Northern Europe and with the Trialeti culture in the Southern Caucasus further to the north, he can find no physical trace of his hypothetical migratory route.[221] There is of course no legendary support for such a scheme.

Drews explains the lack of archaeological evidence by postulating that the chariot-riding Indo-Europeans moved from Armenia to Greece by boat. He is able to argue convincingly that, as there appears to have been no difficulty about shipping horses and chariots at the end of the Late Bronze Age, there is unlikely to have been any five hundred years earlier, given the same technology; it should be noted that light chariots could be relatively easily dismantled.[222] Drews is able to back his argument with iconographic evidence from a LMII seal which shows a horse in a ship. He could further have strengthened his case by pointing out the fact, discussed above in Chapter II, that Poseidon was the god not only of the sea but of horses and chariots. Furthermore, just as his Egyptian counterpart Seth received passionate devotion from the Hyksos, Poseidon appears to have been the most frequently worshipped deity in Mycenaean Greece.[223] In general, however, as with the Buck and Nilsson theories in the 1920s and 1930s, the theories of Muhly and Drews fail not only because they have no traditional backing but because Greek is not an Indo-Aryan or even an Indo-Iranian language and because there is no evidence of any kind showing the path of migration from the Caucasus to Greece. Nevertheless, they do contain the tantalizing truths that there are artistic parallels between the two regions and that the chariot, which appears to have been crucially important in warfare and social structure, developed somewhere to the south of the Caucasus and reached Greece in the period of the Shaft Graves.

It was to preserve these advantages and to try to overcome the difficulties that the Dutch ancient historian Jan Best hit upon the desperate expedient of claiming that the Hyksos were the original Greeks. In an erudite pamphlet he issued in 1973, Best argued that the population of Greece from 2100 to 1600 BC was Thracian, that is, speaking an Indo-European language, but that there was a real cultural break during MHIII, which he puts around 1600. This he attributes to a Hyksos invasion. Omitting the Hurrians, he uses Helck's very cautious opinions to argue that the Hyksos were 'intermingled' Semites and Indo-Europeans and then quotes an unpublished paper of Marija Gimbutas claiming that they could have been Indo-Europeans. Best also cites Eduard Meyer on the possible Hyksos conquest of Crete and from there goes on to postulate a conquest of Mainland Greece.[224]

It will be noted that there are many points in this scheme with which I agree, but there are even more on which I do not. Firstly, it suffers from the same flaw as those of Muhly and Drews, that, even if there were Indo-Aryan speakers among the Hyksos, Greek is not an Indo-Aryan language. Secondly, there is no doubt that any putative Indo-Aryan speakers among the Hyksos were certainly outnumbered by Hurrians. Thirdly, as I have argued at length in the last chapter, there is absolutely no doubt that the vast majority of the Hyksos in Lower Egypt were Levantine in material culture and Semitic in language.[225] Any one of these objections would be enough to sink Best's scenario. The three together make it a complete non-starter.

Between Aryan and Ancient: Frank Stubbings

Stubbings's hypothesis set out in his article on 'The rise of Mycenaean civilization' in the *Cambridge Ancient History* has been treated in Volume 1.[226] Unlike the scholars discussed above, Stubbings believes that Greece was Greek-speaking long before the 17th century BC and therefore he is not obliged to go through their contortions to get the Greeks into Greece. Also, unlike many modern archaeologists, Stubbings takes the Ancient Model very seriously. He believes that it is necessary to look at both archaeology and the ancient traditions simultaneously:

> Thus the legendary conquest of Danaus, and the arrival of the new dynasty at Mycenae, which seems necessary to explain the efflorescence of material culture we observe in the Mycenae Shaft Graves, may be regarded as one and the same thing. That is to say that, in tune with the tradition, we may postulate the conquest of the Argolid by some of the displaced Hyksos leaders from Egypt in the early 16th century B.C. By so doing we can readily account for the Egyptian imports or influences in the graves, and for the introduction of war-chariots.[227]

In this way then Stubbings was working within the Ancient Model. Indeed one of the chief flaws in his scheme is his fidelity to its canon that the Hyksos arrived in the Argolid as 'suppliants' after their expulsion from Egypt by the 18th Dynasty. The 16th century BC is when the ancient chronology of the Parian Marble set the arrival of Danaos and when modern chronology puts the expulsion of the Hyksos.[228] This perfect conjunction is marred by the fact that even before the re-dating of the Thera eruption, it was generally acknowledged that the earliest Shaft Graves came from the 17th century. Now, we know that they have to have been dug even earlier, nearer 1700 than 1600 BC. Thus, this part of his scheme and of the Ancient Model is untenable; this will be discussed further below. His mistaken chronology has another important consequence. As there is no significant break in Cretan culture in the 16th century, Stubbings cannot, as Eduard Meyer did, see the Hyksos as having conquered Crete. Thus, his scheme has no mention of the island and leaves the implausible picture of the Hyksos having bypassed it on their way to Mainland Greece.

While these failings come from too rigid adherence to the Ancient Model, Stubbings's other flaw comes from his fidelity to the Aryan one. He continues the passage quoted above:

> That their arrival is not accompanied by any more wholesale Egyptianizing is perfectly compatible with what we know of the Hyksos in Egypt. There they introduced little but new military techniques and organization; they do not represent a mass movement of population; rather they were a military caste, taking over the highly developed Egyptian civilization as a going concern. They introduced no new language; for their few official inscriptions the native Egyptian served.[229]

I think there are real problems with his analysis of the impact of the Hyksos in Egypt. Despite the new discoveries, we still know very little about the Hyksos period there. In the long term, however, there is no doubt that, despite the resurgence of Egyptian nationalism and culture in the 18th Dynasty, a major cultural transformation did take place during the Hyksos period. Furthermore, the excavations at Tell el Daba'a show that Stubbings's image of the Hyksos as purely a warrior caste has to be discarded. While Hurrian and Aryan elements were small, the Hyksos invasion also involved a mass movement of Syro-Palestinians into at least the Northeastern Delta.[230] Nevertheless, numbers are likely to have been smaller when it came to overseas voyages to Crete and beyond.

Furthermore, as stated above, I do find the common analogy between the Hyksos and the Mongols a fruitful one. Like the later peoples of the Steppe, the Hyksos seem to have had their own vital but 'barbaric' art forms. However, their chief long-term cultural impact seems to have been in transmitting other civilizations – Semitic into Egypt and 'Minoan', Levantine and Egyptian into Greece, etc. Thus, the Shaft Graves reflect both the barbaric style and the cultural mixture. While these elements tended to disappear in Egypt and Crete with their strong traditions of civilization, Helladic Greece was much more susceptible to change and therefore the Hyksos would be likely to have had an altogether greater influence in both material and non-material culture. Nevertheless, for Stubbings, as for any scholar reared in the Aryan Model, any profound Greek borrowings from Egyptian or Semitic culture or language were unthinkable.

Historiographically, Stubbings's position is a return to the arguments of Thirlwall and Holm, that, though there may have been Egyptians and Semites in Greece, it did not matter because they had had no long-term effects. It was a break with the crude racism of the period 1885–1945. Nevertheless, Stubbings, like Thirlwall and Holm, firmly rejected the essential aspect of the Ancient Model, which saw Egyptian- and Semitic speakers as having played a central role in the formation of Greece.

CONCLUSION: A REVISION
OF THE ANCIENT MODEL

At the outset of this section, I want to stress that at this point I depart from the Ancient Model, according to which there is no doubt that Danaos and his fellow voyagers settled in Greece in the 16th century BC and that this settlement was associated with the Egyptian expulsion of the Hyksos.[231] This is because the archaeological and contemporary evidence will not allow for any such invasion at this time. Although I have a great respect for the historical knowledge and judgement of the Greeks in Classical and Hellenistic times, I do not believe that they were infallible. Sometimes they were clearly too credulous and exaggerated the age and geographical extent of conquests and migrations to impress their readers. At others they seem to have minimized both, presumably for some of the same reasons that caused Marco Polo to tell only half of what he had seen and that make scholars cautious today – to avoid awkward gaps, to appear sober and reasonable and to be believed by their audience.

On the other hand, if one revises the Ancient Model in this respect and maintains that the Hyksos arrived in the Aegean about 1730 BC, at the beginning not the end of their rule in Egypt, a remarkably coherent picture emerges that is able to explain many, if not most, of the puzzling features of the events in Crete and the extraordinary material culture of the Shaft Graves and other Greek tombs of the Early Mycenaean period. However, while disagreeing with its chronology, I want to insist on the essential plausibility of the Ancient Model's scheme of colonization. Archaeological evidence does indeed tend to strengthen its case that there were landings on Greece in general and the Argolid in particular by fleets from Egypt of Egyptians, Syrians or Hyksos and that the outsiders established long-lasting heroic dynasties.

I now want to emphasize the positive features of the schemes of Best, Muhly and Drews and the other scholars. It is clear that the break represented by the Shaft Grave culture is too great to be explained without postulating a major stimulus from outside Greece and that, given the warlike nature of the society and the traces of destructions that have been discovered, it is most likely that the stimulus took the form of an armed invasion. It is also clear that the invaders were armed with two important new weapons – the chariot and the sword – and that these originated in the region south of the Caucasus and Syria respectively. Associations with these regions would seem to be confirmed by the techniques and styles of many of the objects found in the Shaft Graves and contemporary *tholoi* from late 18th- and 17th-century Greece and possibly by the form of the Shaft Graves themselves.

As Muhly, Stubbings, Best, Drews and the others are agreed, the key question is how and by what means these were transmitted. The northern routes have a triple disadvantage: firstly, there is no archaeological evidence to back them; secondly, they cannot explain the considerable Syrian, Egyptian and 'off-Egyptian' elements in the Shaft Grave culture; and, thirdly, there is no ancient mention of them. Their only advantages would seem to be ideological in that they allow for the introduction of 'Eastern' culture without involving Egyptians or Semites.

Best saw that all of the disadvantages could be overcome if one identified the transmission of sub-Caucasian culture to Greece with the Hyksos migrations, for which there was both historical and archaeological attestation. Furthermore, such an identification would explain the 'southern aspects' of the culture of the Shaft Graves. Unfortunately, these perceptions were vitiated by his linking the Hyksos movement to the arrival of the Greeks. Apart from its inherent absurdity, discussed above, this led to a huge exaggeration of the role of the Aryans within the Hyksos.

Although there are, of course, many differences, I think that perhaps the best analogy to the Hyksos conquest of Greece is the familiar one of the Norman Conquest of England. Danes and Norwegians had seized Normandy and formed an independent duchy; their own military ethos and élan together with French and Italian civilian skills then created a powerful combination of forces that was able to conquer many parts of Europe, notably England, where they established a relatively long-lasting dynasty. The important point to note is that the Normans did not introduce Norse culture and language; they introduced French and Latin and a modification of the French feudal system. It was from these long-term linguistic and cultural contacts that the modern English language and culture emerged. Similarly, I argue that the middle-range result of the Hyksos conquests in the Aegean was the introduction of the Near Eastern palatial system to Mainland Greece, probably in the form already present in Crete. In the long run, I believe, their chief function was to introduce Egyptian and West Semitic culture and language, which in the succeeding centuries mixed with the native Indo-European–speaking population to form what we now know as Greece and Greek.

What I propose is that at least some of the owners of the Shaft Graves, and the long-lasting dynasties that succeeded them, originated in what we should now call Kurdistan, covering Eastern Anatolia, Northern Syria and Mesopotamia and possibly the Southern Caucasus. In the first half of the 18th century BC, people there, speaking Indo-Aryan and Hurrian, formed the nucleus of the grouping that the Egyptians called the Hyksos. Although the archaeological evidence is ambiguous, it seems likely that by the middle of the century they had dominated large areas of Syro-Palestine and that the movement very quickly became 'Semitized'. Thus, it would seem very likely that, though some of the leaders may have continued to speak Hurrian and possibly even Indo-Aryan, the *lingua franca* was West Semitic (with Egyptian as the language of high culture). This was the native language of the vast majority of those in the migrations. In the 1740s or 1730s the Hyksos moved into Lower Egypt, where a pharaonic dynasty was set up, to which most, if not all, the Hyksos princes owed some allegiance. Very soon after this, expeditions set out for and conquered Crete, the Cyclades and the fertile plains of Southern Greece.

The speed of the movement was such that even in the short life-spans of the time, one man or woman could have seen the whole process. Rapidity would also explain, for instance, why several gold diadems from the Shaft Graves have no Syrian, Egyptian or Cretan models but have as their closest parallels similar types found at Assur in the north of Mesopotamia from between 2000 and 1700 BC; it would also explain why another diadem resembles Kassite work.[232] It will be remembered that the Kassites overwhelmed Babylonia at very much the same time as the Hyksos entered Egypt.[233]

Such rapid movement, which was far faster than the Norman migration to Normandy and conquest of England, would provide a general explanation for the relative purity of the 'barbaric' style of Mycenae. We know that the Hyksos had been substantially Egyptianized by the end of their rule, so that Hyksos refugees fleeing to Greece at that time would have had a very different material culture. This provides yet another argument against the theories of a 16th-century invasion. On the other hand, the Hyksos rulers clearly had at their disposal considerable numbers of skilled craftsmen, especially metallurgists, using the most advanced Syrian techniques to make and decorate the things that meant most to them – weapons. They also had Egyptian, Syrian and Cretan goldsmiths to make vessels and jewels both in their native styles and motifs but also according to the new rulers' tastes and with the motifs of the sphinx and the griffin that they had appropriated.

There is no doubt that the camps and cities of such 'barbarian' conquerors would have been polyglot. Written evidence indicates that in every region the Hyksos ruled the native script remained in use. A Linear A sign was inscribed on a cauldron found in a Shaft Grave.[234] This suggests that the Semitic or other language of the Minoan palaces was at least written at Mycenae around 1700 BC. The only possible scriptural innovation is the introduction of the West Semitic alphabet to the Aegean, which, I argue on epigraphic grounds elsewhere, took place between 1800 and 1400 BC.[235] There would seem little doubt, however, that the dominant scripts remained Linears A and B. As argued in the last chapter, Egyptian evidence suggests that most Hyksos leaders had Semitic names and we can assume that West Semitic and Egyptian were the two dominant languages. Just as Marco Polo heard virtually no Mongol, and spoke a Turki *lingua franca*, it is unlikely that much Aryan or Hurrian was spoken in Egypt or the Aegean, although, as has been mentioned in Chapter II, there are Hurrian traces in Greek toponyms and mythological nomenclature.[236]

Whether or not the language of Linear A was Semitic, it would seem very likely that by 1700 BC the languages of the ruling classes in the towns of the Southern Aegean were West Semitic and Egyptian, or a mixture of the two with the language of the native Indo-European population, which later became Greek. Interestingly, though such a situation is the last way in which they would conceive of the situation, such a pattern would fit well with the views of most historical linguists specializing in ancient Greek dialects, who see Greek as having developed somewhere around the 17th century BC and in Greece itself rather than somewhere to the north.[237]

After a time, the 'barbaric' Hyksos warriors of the Shaft Graves were succeeded by more cultivated rulers and traders. For over a century between c. 1720 and c. 1570 BC there was a cosmopolitan mercantile 'Hyksos world' – represented by the Theran frescoes – which included Egypt, parts of the Levant, Crete, the Cyclades and the richer areas of Mainland Greece. Thus, in many ways, what is known today as 'Mycenaean' material culture could usefully be seen as 'Hyksos' or at least the 'Hyksos of the non-Cretan Aegean'. Although there were clearly many later developments and influences from abroad, especially from 18th-Dynasty Egypt, it was from this society that not only the cultivation of the later Mycenaean palaces but also Greek language and culture – as they survive until today – first took shape.

CHAPTER X

EGYPTIAN, MESOPOTAMIAN
AND LEVANTINE CONTACTS
WITH THE AEGEAN
The documentary evidence

U NLIKE THE MIT RAHINA inscription, discussed in Chapter V,
the documents discussed in this chapter deal with direct
Egyptian and Levantine contacts with the Aegean during the
Bronze Age. Only a few of them are from the 18th and 17th centuries, when, according to the Revised Ancient Model, the colonizations were supposed to have taken place. Most evidence on the
contacts comes from the 15th to the 13th centuries BC. The obvious
reason for this discrepancy is that the period from 1750 to 1575 BC
was one of considerable disturbance in the Middle East, from which
there is relatively little documentary information of any sort. By contrast, the period from 1500 to 1250 BC was one of great prosperity in
which most of the Levant was politically and culturally dominated by
Egypt. In the last twenty years, an overwhelming quantity of documentary and archaeological evidence has convinced most scholars
that the Aegean was included in this 'world'. Most, however, have not
thought through the cultural and linguistic implications of such intimate contacts. Furthermore, there remain a number of scholars,
trained during the prime of the Extreme Aryan Model, who still insist
on the essential autonomy of the Aegean at this, and almost all other
times, and see the new discoveries as representing only superficial
contacts on the material plane.

This chapter and the next are concerned with testing two propositions. The first, which is becoming less and less controversial, is that
there were significant contacts between the Near East and the Aegean
during the Bronze Age. The second, against which there is still con-

siderable resistance, is that we should believe the Classical and Hellenistic Greeks when they said that their country had several times
been colonized from the south and east. It is certainly possible to hold
the one without the other, that is, to accept most of the evidence put
forward here on the depth and significance of Greek cultural borrowings from Egypt and Canaan as being the result of peaceful contacts
in the Late Bronze Age. There is, in fact, an excellent parallel for this
in the extraordinary extent to which Japan borrowed from Chinese
culture over more than a thousand years without ever having been
conquered by China.

However, I am convinced of the truth of both propositions and,
while I accept that there must have been massive cultural borrowing
during the years between 1500 and 1250 BC, I also believe that the
legends of early colonizations contain factual kernels. My reasons for
this are, firstly, my increasing confidence in ancient sources and distrust of 19th- and early 20th-century historiography on this subject
and, secondly, my conviction that the Theran murals show that it was
not merely Crete that had been 'Levantinized' in the first half of the
2nd millennium BC. There is also the fact that texts in Linear B make
it clear that Mycenaean society was Greek-speaking by the 13th century BC and that many Semitic and Egyptian words were already in
place by then. Finally, a significant number of linguistic and mythological borrowings seem too archaic in Egypt and the Levant to have
been introduced to the Aegean after the 16th century.

Much of the evidence for the truth of these propositions will be
concerned with the 15th, 14th and 13th centuries. This is partly because, despite the growth of a consensus on the Late Bronze Age contacts and borrowings, the case for them still has to be made. Study of
this later period can also provide direct evidence on the earlier one as
well as giving information on the credibility of Archaic, Classical and
Hellenistic sources.

EGYPTIAN PLACE NAMES
REFERRING TO THE AEGEAN

Any use of Egyptian texts and paintings depends on the identification
of place names. In Egyptian, as in many other cultures, the names of
distant places tended to shift geographically and especially tended to
alternate between having general and specific significance. What we
are interested in here is not the original sense of the name or what it
came to mean later, but the meaning of certain toponyms in the periods with which we are concerned – the 2nd Intermediate Period
c. 1730–1570 and the New Kingdom c. 1570–1090 BC.

Egyptian names of foreign places were written and can be read in two different ways. They frequently appear simply with their consonantal structure like other Egyptian words or proper nouns. However, from the Middle Kingdom on, certain hieroglyphs were used in the transcription of foreign names, to represent not merely the consonant but the vowel that followed it. There are difficulties with this because the Egyptian writers were not consistent in their use of the signs and because specialists disagree on their interpretation. The American Semitist William Albright pioneered this work in the 1930s but today the most commonly used transcription is that of the German Egyptologist Wolfgang Helck. This latter transcription will be used here but only in brackets, as it is clearly unsatisfactory in many ways and the primary form will remain the normal reading of the hieroglyphs.[1]

Mnws and Minos

The first name to be considered is 𓎛𓊝𓏤 Mnws. The earliest attested reference to this comes in the 12th-Dynasty *Story of Sinuhe* mentioned in Chapter V. It is used as the name of a prince of the Fnḥw (a Syrian people, probably the Phoenicians). Posener argues that this represents literary licence and that other personal names in the context are in fact the names of countries, so that Mnws too should be understood as a place name.[2] Such an interpretation would certainly fit with the later use of the name with the determinative 𓈉 (foreign land).

This seems very likely but there is more difficulty in locating the territory. Its position on lists of countries was usually between Kftiw, now accepted as Crete (see below), and Syria. Sometimes it appears between Syria and Mesopotamia, suggesting a region there. However, the name is unattested in contemporary Akkadian and Hittite sources. Pictures of tribute-bearers from Mnws seem to represent Syro-Palestinians, though there are signs of Aegean influence.[3] Furthermore, as we shall see below, men from Kftiw itself include Syro-Palestinians.

The name Mnws and its association with Crete strikingly parallel the Greek traditions of King Minos of Crete and the place name Minoa, which was common in Crete and the Southern Aegean in Classical times. In 1934 Albright tentatively proposed a link between them.[4]

The origins of the names Minos and Minoa are immensely rich and complicated, quite apart from Arthur Evans's coining of the neologism 'Minoan' for the pre-Greek people of Crete.[5] In Chapter IV, I discussed the relations between the 'Cretan' king Minos, the lawgiver, and the Egyptian Mn(y), founder and lawgiver of the 1st Dynasty, called Mēnēs by Manetho and Min by Herodotos; I also looked at the relations between King Minos, the lecher, and the strikingly well-endowed Egyptian fertility god Min, with whom Mn(y) may well be associated.[6] As for the place name Minoa, Victor Bérard plausibly associated it with the West Semitic Månahat or Mənuḥå (resting place) which seems to have been used as a toponym.[7]

The confusion is confounded by the possibility of a relationship between Mnws and Mȝnw, a legendary mountain to the west of Egypt, where the sun was supposed to set. References to Mȝnw are late, so that the ȝ may have been purely vocalic, which would make the identification possible. However, Mȝnw may be older and originally have sounded *Mrnw. In the 5th century AD Stephanos of Byzantium described the god Marna worshipped at Gaza in Philistia, which had strong Cretan connections, and saw him as Zeus Krētogenes 'born in Crete'.[8] While the older phonetic value of Mȝnw weakens the association with Mnws, it suggests that, although Mȝnw is generally thought to have been located in Libya, the name may have also applied to the other high mountains in the west, those in Crete.[9]

In short, Mnws was probably to the north and west of Egypt and its princes may have accepted Sesōstris' suzerainty and certainly brought tribute to New Kingdom pharaohs. Thus, despite its appearance in lists at the same time as Kftiw, it is possible that the name Mnws was at different times used for part or all of the island. If this was so, the Egyptian inscriptional evidence on Mnws would tend to confirm the Revised Ancient Model. Firstly, the pictures of the tribute-bearers from Mnws would show there was Egyptian suzerainty over parts of the Aegean during the 18th Dynasty and possibly in the 12th as well; secondly, the association between Mnws and Fnḫw in *Sinuhe* would suggest relations between Crete and the Semitic-speaking Levant as early as the 20th or 19th centuries BC, when the story was written. Finally the 'Semitic' and Asiatic appearance of some men of Mnws would support the picture of the Aegean as cosmopolitan in the Late Bronze Age. However, despite the tempting parallels between Mnws and Crete, there is not enough evidence to demonstrate Albright's hypothesis that the two names are equivalent.

Kftiw, Kaftu and Crete

The identification of Kftiw (Kaftu) with Crete is more straightforward. The earliest reference to it would seem to come from the 1st Intermediate Period between 2450 and 2100 BC and, though it cannot be dated with any security, it is certainly very early. It reads as follows:

No one goes down to Byblos today. What shall we do for the coffins imported for our mummies in which the priests are buried and the oil with which [kings] are embalmed as far away as the country of Kaftu.[10]

This suggests regular trade between the Levant and Crete in the 3rd millennium, which would fit with the archaeological evidence discussed in Chapter I. Jean Vercoutter, who wrote the standard work on Egyptian relations with the 'Pre-Hellenes', maintains, largely on the basis of this text and the absence of others, that before the end of the Hyksos period there was no direct contact between Egypt and the Aegean, that is to say, all communication and trade between them went through the Levant. The art historian William Stevenson Smith, in his massive work *Interconnections in the Ancient Near East,* was 'inclined to doubt' Vercoutter's use of the argument from silence, and archaeological evidence since 1965, when Stevenson Smith wrote, clearly justifies his scepticism.[11]

The next text mentioning Kaftu comes from the Hyksos period or just after. It is entitled 'To make names of Kftiw', and consists of typical names from Kaftu that a young scribe was likely to encounter.[12] Kaftu also appears frequently in texts of the 18th Dynasty, especially during the reign of Tuthmōsis III *c.* 1504–1450, but it is not used after the reign of Amenōphis IV/Akhenaton *c.* 1379–1362.[13]

Noting the resemblance to the Akkadian Kaptara, a name that may date to the 3rd millennium, and the Hebrew Kaptôr, which was traditionally believed to have been a name for Crete, Egyptologists have for a long time tended to see this as the location of Kaftu.[14] The identification was made with much greater confidence after striking parallels were seen between remains and murals found at Knossos and Egyptian tomb paintings of tribute-bearers and tribute from Kaftu. In the 1960s the equivalence was finally confirmed by its use at the head of a list of Cretan and Greek place names on the statue base of Amenōphis III from Kom el-Hetan, which will be discussed below.

Even so, scholars working in the Aryan Model with its image of a somehow European 'Pre-Hellenic' Aegean population have encountered great difficulties in accepting that Kaftu was Crete. There are several pieces of evidence suggesting that Kaftu was Levantine. The list of names from Kftiw contained some that can be plausibly seen as Semitic or Hurrian and others that were clearly Egyptian. Accepting the premise that the Aegean was 'racially' European, the contemporary scholars Strange and Merrillees have used the list's heterogeneity to deny the identification of Kaftu with Crete. This is, in fact, one of the chief planks in Strange's argument that the Egyptian name referred to Cyprus, not the island to the south of the Aegean. He does not, however, mention the Linear A and Linear B personal names or onomastica from the 15th, 14th and 13th centuries (discussed below) which give the impression of a thoroughly cosmopolitan population at Knossos. Nor does Strange consider the frescoes at Thera which also indicate the presence of different ethnic groups in the Southern Aegean in the 17th century, the time at which the list was probably drawn up.[15]

Evidence from Egyptian tomb paintings of the 15th century BC has been equally unsettling. While the famous murals from the tomb of Rḥ mi Rˁ (Rekhmire) clearly indicated Aegean figures as men from Kaftu, those with the same label in other tombs often seem Syrian, though sometimes with an Aegean admixture. These can be explained away as the inaccuracies of ignorant painters and the supposed phenomenon of 'hybridism' which will be discussed below. However, this is more difficult in the case of the tomb of Mn ḥpr Rˁ snb (Menkhepre seneb). In this, the bearer and the goods are Cretan but the figure, clearly labelled Wr n Kftiw (king or chief of Kaftu), is typically 'Syro-Palestinian'. The early 20th-century archaeologist Furumark, who believed that Kaftu was in Cilicia, argued that the details of such precise painting could not be ignored.[16] But for those who maintained that Kaftu was Crete, any accuracy in this label was impossible within the Aryan Model and the paradigm of European supremacy. As Vercoutter put it:

> Unless one admits that a Syro-Palestinian could have been king over Aegean populations, it is absolutely necessary that one or other of the texts accompanying the Aegean tribute in the tomb of Rḥ mi Rˁ or the tomb of Mn ḥpr Rˁ snb must be wrong. This is an alternative that one cannot avoid.[17]

This difficulty, like the one of the Egyptian list of names, vanishes if one accepts that the population of the Southern Aegean was thoroughly mixed and the common view in Antiquity that the Cretan population was Semitic-speaking.[18] Specifically, this tends to support the hypothesis of a Hyksos conquest.[19]

Some light may be shed on this problem by discussing another anomaly in the equation of Crete with Kaftu. In Ptolemaic times, Kaftu did not mean Crete but Phoenicia.[20] Furthermore, the Classical Greeks referred to what we should now call 'Minoans' as Phoinikes. Thus, the confusion was not confined to Hellenistic Egyptians. As has been mentioned above, Kaftu was not mentioned in New Kingdom documents later than 1350 BC. The issue of when Greek speakers came to dominate Crete will be discussed below. Here it is sufficient to say that it was sometime around 1450 BC. Thus, the Egyptian dropping of the name Kaftu would have been either a delayed or a rapid recognition of the change.[21] In any event, it would seem reasonable to associate the name Kaftu with the island's pre-Greek inhabitants.

Thus, Cyrus Gordon's interpretation of Linear A and Eteo-Cretan (the non-Greek language spoken in Eastern Crete in Classical times) as West Semitic would seem to be supported not merely by Semitic words in Linear A and onomastica from Crete recorded in documents in Egyptian and Linear A, but also by the shift of Kaftu from Crete to Phoenicia after the island became predominantly Greek-speaking.[22] Before that, it is clear that the island was culturally and linguistically heterogeneous. Nevertheless, it is still plausible to suppose with Gordon and the archaeologist Saul Weinberg that the early Minoan culture, as it emerged in the late 4th millennium BC, was predominantly Semitic-speaking.[23]

Wȝḏ wr and Ḥȝw nbw:
the Aegean Sea and the Mycenaeans

Other Egyptian toponyms commonly associated with the Aegean are less securely identified, for example 'Isles in the Midst of the Wȝḏ wr' (great green). The contemporary writer Alessandra Nibbi argues that even during the Invasion of the Sea Peoples at the turn of the 12th century BC, Wȝḏ wr referred to the marshes of the Nile Delta.[24] This proposal and its corollary that the invasion came from the Delta are clearly absurd, as they require the dismissal of a huge quantity of plausible information concerning the much more distant origins of the invasions. The Egyptian inscriptions describing the invasions are extremely valuable, but even without them it would still be possible to detect many of the tribal movements and conquests of the period which affected the whole of the East Mediterranean from archaeological evidence, Canaanite texts and the biblical and Greek traditions.[25]

Nevertheless, Nibbi's argument rests on the plausible case that Wȝḏ wr did signify the swamps of the Delta in Predynastic times. Wȝḏ, which will be discussed below, appears to have meant 'green' not 'blue' and it was written with 𓇅, 'papyrus plant' with a ḏ or a 'snake', a pun which will be discussed in Volume 4. What is more, the original sense may have persisted into early dynastic times.[26]

As Vercoutter has demonstrated, however, from the period of the Old Kingdom Wȝḏ wr meant 'sea'. During the Middle Kingdom it was used for the Red Sea but by the New Kingdom it meant Mediterranean and often – though not always – the Aegean.[27] Vercoutter has also shown that, at this time, W3d̠ wr was used in conjunction with Kftiw in a way that would suggest a nearby and similar country and that W3d̠ wr continued to be employed in the later New Kingdom after Kaftu had fallen into disuse. Furthermore, it was from these islands that the Sea Peoples were supposed to have planned their invasions.[28] All in all, it would seem plausible to associate the Isles in the Midst of the W3d̠ wr with non-Cretan Aegean peoples and probably with Mycenaeans.

Another possible name for these is H3w nbw, the people who came from the H3w nbwt – from h3 (behind) the nbwt (islands). H3w nbw has been considered to mean 'Greek' ever since it was read as a translation of 'Hellene' on the Rosetta Stone, the famous tablet inscribed during the Ptolemaic period in Hieroglyphic, Demotic and Greek, which provided the basis for the decipherment of Hieroglyphics and Demotic.[29]

Sethe, followed by Gardiner, maintained that the formula dbn phr h3 nbwt (the circle which turns around the islands), which appears three times in the Pyramid Texts, indicated the Aegean. It was referred to by Gardiner as 'a sufficiently accurate description of the Aegean sea'.[30] The term is also attested on a bas-relief of cattle from the funerary temple of Cheops, on another 4th-Dynasty block and a text from the funerary temple of the 5th-Dynasty pharaoh Sahureˁ with the formula 'I bring to you the iwntyw the Mntyw, all the foreign countries and the H3 nbwt' – a formula that was repeated many times later. It will be remembered that objects with the titulary of Sahureˁ are supposed to have been found in the Dorak Treasure.[31]

The identification of H3 nbw with the Aegean was attacked by the Egyptologist Vercoutter on the grounds that it was used in the 7th century BC to describe mercenaries, who included Carians as well as Greeks, and that therefore before that date it merely meant people from far away.[32] Vercoutter was particularly eager to discredit any idea that there was any Egyptian knowledge of the Aegean in the Old Kingdom. He pointed out that the construction of a place name with h3 (behind) was unique and that the idea of a people 'behind the islands' was very sophisticated indeed. If one accepted this, it would, as he put it,

> be necessary to admit that since the *fourth* millennium the inhabitants of the Nile already had a precise idea not only of the islands of the East Mediterranean but also of the continental coasts that surrounded them.[33]

I do not consider such a possibility out of the question. On the other hand, even though the Pyramid Texts were clearly ancient when they

were inscribed, they do, in fact, date only from the the 3rd millennium. There seems no reason to push the use of the term Ḥꜣ nbwt as a
specific designation of the continents behind the Aegean into the 4th
millennium. Its use in this sense at the height of the Old Kingdom
would seem much more likely. As Stevenson Smith wrote about this,
after discussing Old Kingdom objects found around the Aegean,

> Vercoutter has shown that it is unlikely that the Aegean or its inhab-
> itants were meant by the term 'Haunebut' (Ḥꜣ nbwt) in the Pyramid
> Texts or in inscriptions of the time of Cheops and Sahure. He also
> questions contacts with Crete that have been made for the Old
> Kingdom. On the other hand, the expansion of royal trade by land
> and sea which we begin to see more clearly in the 5th Dynasty
> would suggest that the period from Sneferu [1st pharaoh of the 4th
> Dynasty] to Phiops II [Pepi II, the last effective pharaoh of the 6th]
> would have been a more propitious time for Egypt to have become
> aware of the Aegean world than the impoverished days of politi-
> cal discontent in the First Intermediate Period which Vercoutter
> suggests.[34]

Despite these plausible doubts, there is no question that Vercoutter's
ideas on the Ḥꜣ nbwt prevail today. His arguments were made with
such force that Gardiner changed the view he expressed as late as
1947 that the Ḥꜣ nbwt of the *Pyramid Texts* were near the Aegean, to
stating in the second edition of his *Egyptian Grammar* in 1950 that
it merely meant 'distant and indeterminate regions' and their inhabitants, though in Graeco-Roman times interpreted to mean the
Greeks.[35] This, in fact, is going further than Vercoutter himself who
claimed that it was a 'vague term for the populations of the distant
Asiatic shore'.[36] However, if the term 'behind the islands' has any substantial content, it would seem more appropriate for the coasts of
Mainland Greece and Western Anatolia than the coast behind the one
island of Cyprus.

There is no doubt that Vercoutter destroyed the French Egyp-
tologist Montet's far-fetched notion that Ḥꜣw nbwt was the name for
Hellenes – Greeks, who, Montet maintained, had inhabited the Nile
Valley in Predynastic times.[37] However, there would seem reasonably
strong grounds for supposing that Ḥꜣw nbwt was used to refer to the
Aegean long before the Ptolemaic period, possibly as early as the Old
Kingdom and almost certainly by the 18th Dynasty.

As with her treatment of Wꜣḏ wr, Alessandra Nibbi's attack on the
identification of Ḥꜣw nbwt with the Aegean lacks historical sense. On
the other hand, her suggestion largely drawn from Vercoutter that *nb*
▽ (basket) became associated with the concept of 'island' because of

floating matted papyrus seems a plausible answer to a problem that puzzled Sethe and Gardiner.[38] This Predynastic etymology, however, does not mean that the *nbwt* of the Old Kingdom, still less of the New Kingdom almost two thousand years later, had the same significance.

THE ETYMOLOGY OF DANAAN

The widespread cluster of ethnic names – Tìnȝy, Tanaya, Dȝ-ỉn, Dene, Denyen, Danuna, Danaan, Danaos and Dan – occurring in Egyptian, Akkadian, Canaanite and Greek during the Late Bronze Age is extremely difficult to disentangle, but, before attempting to do this, it is essential to establish their unity. This can be achieved through the fact that the same statue base that confirmed the equation between Kftiw and Crete also firmly established the equation between the Egyptian name Tìnȝyw and Danaoi – Homer's most frequent name for the Greeks. The identification of the foreign country Dȝ-ỉn (Dene) is only slightly less secure. Gardiner accepted that the Dene, a People of the Sea who had plotted their attacks on the civilized world in the isles of the Wȝd wr, were the Greek Danaoi. He also linked Dene to the land the Egyptians called Tanaya through the determinative 🖼, which is attested with it and is that of tnỉ < ṯnỉ, 'old, decrepit' (for the association of tnỉ < ṯnỉ with the 'decrepitude' of Danaos, the Greek eponym of the Danaans, see below).[39] However, Gardiner rejected any association with the Danuna mentioned by Abimilki, king of Tyre, in his letter to the pharaoh at his capital at Amarna in the 14th century, because the *u* in Danuna did not tally with the group writing of Dene and because it was specified as being part of Ki-na-aḫ-na, Canaan.[40] After Gardiner published this in 1947, a new candidate for Danuna was found on a bilingual inscription at Karatepe in Cilicia, which referred to a people called Adanawa in the Anatolian language Luvian and Dnnym in Phoenician. The Dnnym were also mentioned in a 9th-century inscription from the nearby kingdom of Sam'al in North Syria.[41] There were also Assyrian references to Cyprus as Yadna or Ya-ad-na-na, which has been plausibly translated as Island of the Danana.[42] However, apart from the possible reference from Tyre, there is no mention of a country of Danuna in Cilicia before the invasion of the Sea Peoples. This is somewhat surprising in view of the numerous geographical references given by the Hittites, who frequently campaigned in this region, and the substantial Late Bronze Age archives found at Alalakh and Ugarit, both of which were within one hundred miles of Eastern Cilicia. Furthermore, during this period this region appears to have been occupied by a kingdom called

Kizzuwatna by Hittites and Qode by Egyptians. On the other hand, the name of a city, attested in the 17th century, at its centre was Adana.[43]

Accepting the likelihood of a link between the Luvian Adanawa and the Phoenician Dnnym, the Anatolian specialist Laroche has claimed that the Denyen/Danun were Anatolians and this has been accepted by a younger scholar, Yoël Arbeitman.[44] Albright and Astour, however, reject the parallel. They point out that Dnnym could easily have been written with an initial ʾaleph as the toponym ʾdn is used for Adana in the Karatepe Inscription.[45] If the link between the city of Adana and the Adanawa is not accepted, the only possible evidence for a kingdom of Danuna in Cilicia before 1200 BC comes from the Amarna letter. This is sufficient for Astour and Helck.[46] Albright, on the other hand, believed that the name Danuna referred to in the Amarna letter was the same as the Dene/Denyen Sea People and the Danaoi. He argued against Gardiner on the problem of the middle u, claiming that Danuna simply represented the Akkadian rendering of a Canaanite form *Danôna which was the result of an original Danana being transformed by the Canaanite phonetic shift $â > ô$, this shift having taken place in the previous century.[47] Albright did not, however, deal with the problem raised by Gardiner that Abimilki began his letter to the pharaoh:

> The king, my lord has written to me 'What thou hearest from Kinaḥna write to me'. The king of Danuna is dead and his brother has become king in his stead and his land is quiet. And fire has consumed Ugarit . . .[48]

Gardiner, as we have seen, claimed that this strongly implied that Danuna was in Kinaḥna/Canaan and, as he put it,

> . . . there is nothing in the context to suggest that Abimilki was able to provide information from outside Palestine and Syria and it is highly unlikely that at so early a date Danaans were anywhere in the neighbourhood of those countries.[49]

The seriousness of these objections to Albright's hypothesis is mitigated by the wide range of evidence, which is particularly strong for the New Kingdom, suggesting that much of Egypt's contact with the Aegean was through the Levant and Levantines. I do not believe that all Egyptian trade and other contact with the Aegean was 'counterclockwise', that is to say, went from Egypt to the Levant and then along the southern coast of Anatolia to the Aegean. Nevertheless, there is no doubt that this was the predominant direction (the archae-

ological aspects of this will be discussed in the next chapter). The frequent juxtaposition of, not to say confusion between, Levantine and
Aegean country names, evident in the discussions of Mnws and Kftiw
above, shows that the two regions were frequently associated in Egyptian geographical thinking. It is also interesting to note that during
the reign of Tuthmōsis III, just over a century before the Amarna letter, the Egyptian viceroy in Syria was also responsible for the Isles in
the Midst of the Wȝḏ wr.[50] Thus, Aegean affairs could well have been
reported to the pharaoh from Tyre and Mycenaean Greece might
have been at least loosely included in Kinaḫna.

Given the relative weakness of Gardiner's objections and the problems in the identification of Adanawa with Dnnym, Albright's hypothesis that the Dnnym in 9th-century Cilicia were descendants of Greeks
who had settled there during the migrations of the Sea Peoples remains
extremely attractive.[51] It would explain the absence of references to
Dana/una in the area before 1200. It would also fit the association
made on the Karatepe Inscription between the Dnnym and the house
of Mps. This seems remarkably close to the Greek hero Mopsos who,
at about the time of the Trojan War (that is, c. 1210 BC), was supposed
to have established colonies in Pamphylia and Cilicia. A Lydian Mopsos, who may or not have been the same, is alleged to have gone to
Ashkelon in Palestine.[52] If the two legends do refer to the same historical figure, they would provide not only a link between the Aegean
and the Cilician and North Syrian Dnnym but also one with the biblical tribe of Dan.

The Semitists and ancient historians Cyrus Gordon, Yigael Yadin
and Allen Jones have all identified Dan with Danuna, Dnnym and the
Danaoi.[53] The linguist and biblical scholar Gary Rendsburg has given
an excellent summary of the biblical grounds for their claim. The
Danites were described as living on ships, they were admitted late into
the Israelite amphictyony or tribal league, they were the last tribe to
establish their own territory and they were originally settled on the
coast between two known Sea Peoples, the Philistines and the Tjeker.[54]
There is also the lack of any detailed genealogy for Dan which re-
inforces the hypothesis that the tribe was not an original member of
the Israelite amphictyony. Finally, there are the strong associations
between the Danite hero Samson and the Philistines.

This evidence seems to me to be quite sufficient but one can go further by looking at the parallels between the Samson cycle of stories
and the Greek myths around Herakles. The most striking parallel is
that between Samson's death and Herodotos' story that Herakles was
taken quietly to be sacrificed in an Egyptian temple but then exerted

his strength and killed all the Egyptians.[55] As I argued in Chapter II, and shall be discussing further in Volume 3, there is a very fundamental Egyptian component in the 'Greek' myths of Herakles.[56] Nevertheless, the Samson stories would seem to come from Greek branches of the tradition. Both heroes are strong; like the sun with which they are associated – Samson's name comes from the Semitic Sms (sun) – both have strange rages and temporary losses of power; both kill lions and wear their skins. The closeness of the parallels suggests that the stories were taken from the Aegean to Palestine by Sea Peoples. The ethnic reversal involved in the biblical form has a neat parallel in the way in which native Christian writers appropriated and reversed a Muslim story with the hero, who retained the clearly Islamic name Aucassin, becoming Christian while his love Nicolette was turned into a Muslim.

With the exception of the similarity of the city name Adanawa to the basic stem, all the evidence suggests that Tanaya and the other names were first associated with the Aegean rather than the Levant. According to Gordon the name Danane appears in Linear A texts. He explains the final -ne as a suffix common to Cretan and Ugaritic names and perhaps related to the adjectival and sometimes specifically gentilic (concerned with peoples) suffix -n, common among Indo-European languages.[57] As Rendsburg points out, this suffix and its absence explain the two forms Dn and Dnn.[58]

This leaves open the question of how the name came to be used in the West. Astour, who believes in a Semitic Cilician origin, argues that the ethnic name Dana(na) came to Greece with the Hyksos invaders. He also draws parallels between the Danaans' eponym Danaos and the West Semitic hero Danel or Daniel, the epitome of wisdom in the Bible.[59] The name comes from the Semitic root $\sqrt{dyn}$ (judge, govern, allocate). However, as mentioned in Volume 1, there is a related Egyptian root dnỉ (share out, allocate, and more specifically dam and irrigate). Dnỉ has a very close relationship to the Greek Danaos, and together with the verb ṯnỉ (grow old, decrepit), dnỉ or a derived form *dnỉw (he who colonizes, irrigates) can explain all the 'Greek' hero's aspects as a feeble old man who colonized – allocating land – and irrigated.[60]

Although, as discussed in Volume 1, some of the legends surrounding the arrival suggest that the hero had non-Egyptian, possibly Hyksos and Semitic, origins, there is no doubt that, according to the tradition, Danaos came from Egypt and that the cults attributed to him and his daughters were Egyptian.[61] Thus, it would seem more plausible that Danaos' name should be Egyptian rather than Semitic.

There are two linked Indo-European candidates for the origin of Danaan. The first of these is the name of the Irish legendary people the Danann, who arrived in Ireland from the south. It is very unlikely but just possible that this is a memory of Mycenaeans in Northwest Europe. However, it is impossible to see how this could be the origin of the Aegean term.[62]

The second Indo-European hypothesis is that Danaan comes from the common Indo-European river name 'Dan-', found in Danube, Dnieper, and Don both in the Ukraine and Yorkshire. This is linked to the traditions of Danaos and his daughters as irrigators.[63] However, the Egyptian links are not merely with water but with irrigation, and there are no traditions linking Danaos to the north whereas there are many connecting him to Egypt and the southeast. Thus, the primary origin of the name Danaos is less likely to be Indo-European than Afroasiatic.

Despite the heavy influence of punning or paranomasia from Egyptian, on the character of Danaos there is no reason why the Egyptian source should be the only one. The relationship between Danaos and Danaans is not straightforward. It would seem unlikely that the Danaans simply meant people of Danaos (the colonizer). There is, in fact, a piece of evidence suggesting that the geographical and gentilic name Dane may be primary and pre-date any possible Hyksos settlement in the Aegean. This comes from a geographical list found at the Mesopotamian site of Abu Salabikh dating to the middle of the 3rd millennium. In this, in a position that could well be in the far west, there is the name DA-ne[ki] which in the parallel list from Ebla is called am-ni[ki].[64] Pettinato, who published the latter list, has tentatively identified am-ni[ki] with Amnissos, the port of Knossos in Crete, which is clearly an old name because it appears in both Linear A and hieroglyphic texts from the middle of the 2nd millennium.[65] Thus DA-ne[ki] could well be an ancient name for the 'Far West' and specifically Crete and the Aegean.

To sum up this section, there is a dense tangle of paranomasia around the name Danaan, which it is impossible to tease out. At this point, the best working hypothesis would seem to be that Dane was an ethnic or place name in Crete from the 3rd millennium. After the Hyksos settlement in the Western Peloponnese in the 2nd millennium, punning with the Egyptian words *dnì* and *t̠nì*, and possibly the Semitic *dyn*, led to the naming of an eponym Danaos. By the 15th century BC Danaioi had become a common name for the people we should call Mycenaeans and, as Dnnym and Dan, this spread to Cilicia and Palestine during the invasions of the Sea Peoples. However, despite the uncertainty of this hypothesis, there is vritually no doubt that when Egyptians used the ethnic names Tinȝy, Tanaya, Dȝ-in, Dene and Denyen, they were referring to Greeks.

DOCUMENTARY EVIDENCE FOR
EGYPTIAN RELATIONS WITH THE
AEGEAN IN THE LATE BRONZE AGE

If we accept these identifications, what picture do the Egyptian documents give of Egyptian relations with the Aegean? There is a possibility that documentary references to Hȝ nbw can be linked to Egyptian objects and structures in the Aegean to indicate contacts in the 3rd millennium. There are much more substantial indications that there was trade between Egypt and Crete during the Middle Kingdom. Relations seem to have been particularly close at the end of the Hyksos period and the beginning of the 18th Dynasty.

We know, from the list of 'names from Kftiw' and the name Pȝ Kftiwy (the Cretan) found in Egypt from the start of the 18th Dynasty, that there were Egyptians in Crete and Cretans in Egypt.[66] Amōsis, the Dynasty's first pharaoh, claimed that the Hȝw nbw were his followers and his mother Queen Aḥḥotpe was described as 'Mistress of the regions of the Hȝw nbwt'.[67] It would seem more likely that these are claims of suzerainty rather than any reference to Greek mercenaries as some scholars have suggested.[68] In general, as Helck writes, 'Certainly the beginning of the Eighteenth Dynasty should be seen as the period when the Aegean influence was strongest.'[69]

ACCURACY AND HYBRIDISM
IN EGYPTIAN INSCRIPTIONS
AND TOMB PAINTINGS

Before looking at the content of the 18th-Dynasty tomb paintings, we have to consider their reliability as representations of reality at the time they were painted. There is no doubt that many of the pictures of plants and animals are meticulously accurate in terms of modern botany and zoology. Archaeological finds – most startlingly the recent discoveries from the Kaş shipwreck – have also provided clear evidence of the accuracy of the representation of many objects.

Nevertheless, many experts have cast doubts on the veracity of the pictures. In the first place, they suspect the timing of the paintings, arguing that artists may not have drawn from life but copied earlier tomb paintings or even that they based their work on 'pattern books'.

Although many tombs were sealed and no pattern book or reference to one has been found, their existence would seem very likely, given what we know about artistic canons and the regulation of artistic production in Egypt as well as the frequent repetitions of themes and images in the surviving corpus of paintings.[70]

On the other hand, suspicions about the originality and contemporaneity of the paintings of exotic nature and human artifacts are largely based on the modern stereotype of Egypt as an essentially isolated, conservative and inward-looking civilization with the corollaries that Egyptians travelled rarely and that there were very few exotic objects and plants, animals and people available in Egypt. These seem to me very debatable propositions. The presence of Egyptians in foreign cities during the Middle Kingdom was mentioned in Chapter V, and there is every reason to suppose that there were even more Egyptians abroad at the height of the New Kingdom.[71] It is even clearer that there were large numbers of foreigners living in Egypt in the same period.[72] Furthermore, the Egyptian tradition of copying earlier work or patterns does not necessarily exclude the artists' desire or ability to copy from life or to alter standard patterns in order to conform to reality. A striking example of this can be seen in the famous correction of a fresco in the tomb of the court official Rḥ mri Rꜥ (Rekhmire), painted between 1470 and 1450, in which the 'Minoan' kilts of Aegean envoys appear to have been over-painted with 'Mycenaean' loin-cloths.[73] Here – for the moment accepting that Mycenaeans conquered Crete in this period – we would seem to see the stereotype corrected to conform to the exact representation of reality. At least in later times, this principle seems to have been fundamental to Egyptian art.[74]

This leads on to the second and major difficulty modern historians have with the Egyptian tomb paintings, which they call 'hybridism'. The Israeli archaeologist Shelley Wachsmann opens his discussion of this in the following way:

> Hybridism is the name given here to the phenomenon in Egyptian art by which subjects, be they human figures, objects or even entire scenes, were composed by uniting elements originally belonging to two or more separate entities. . . . Erroneous conclusions were derived by Wainwright and others concerning figures of foreigners due to their inability to take hybridism into consideration.[75]

There is no doubt that hybridism is a feature of Egyptian art. Representations of gods with animal heads and human bodies, or vice versa, sphinxes and griffins, are commonplace. Even more striking was the artistic convention of a typical 'hybrid' Egyptian, which played down the huge physiological variety which we know from human remains always to have existed among the Egyptian population. The reason for this 'hybridism' would seem to be the overriding need to maintain the unity of Upper and Lower Egypt despite their different predominant physical types. Such a desire would fit very well with the image of Egyptian art as a whole, about which the architectural historian Earl Baldwin Smith wrote: 'Egyptian art was persistently ideographic, dealing always with the fundamental, communal ideas rather than with the transient and personal experience'.[76] It is also possible that, as Wachsmann and his predecessors claim, hybrid objects and plants, though not animals, were concocted. Nevertheless, one should also be alert to the strong possibility that Wachsmann and earlier historians of ancient art have used the notion of hybridism to dismiss Egyptian representations of things they cannot understand or do not like. In particular, any mixture of foreign cultures or human types portrayed in the paintings is not accepted as a representation of reality. Interestingly, because Egyptian artists knew that the outside world was varied, and was supposed to be so, it is likely that they represented varied humanity more realistically when portraying foreign populations than when portraying Egyptian people themselves. Thus, pictures of people who combine Syrian with Aegean physical characteristics and dress or uncomfortably dark Cretans are often dismissed as figments of the artists' imagination. Modern scholars also emphatically deny the portrayal of Egyptian motifs and artistic elements in foreign artifacts.

The denial seems to me to be based on two fallacies. The first is that we know enough about the ethnic nature and cultural habits of the inhabitants of the East Mediterranean in the 15th and 14th centuries BC to be able to rule out a significant number of portraits as 'impossible'. The second is the belief that there were distinct cultures of uniform physical type in fixed regions of the Mediterranean basin. This seems to me to be a projection of early 20th-century ethnicity and racism into a time and place where it is singularly inappropriate. In fact, the more we learn about the region, during the New Kingdom, the more we discover its diversity and cosmopolitanism. Furthermore, archaeological evidence discussed earlier shows the penetration of aspects of Egyptian culture well beyond the Levant into Anatolia and the Aegean and vice versa. Thus, while there may be instances of artificially 'hybrid' foreigners, it would seem to me more reasonable to accept the mixed and complex cultural pattern portrayed in the tomb paintings than to reject it.

Why Did Cretan Princes
Bring Tribute to Egypt?

I now want to look at the political context in which the tomb paintings were made. The reign of the powerful woman pharaoh Ḥashepsowe (1503–1483 BC) is well known for its uniqueness and for the famous expedition to Pwnt in East Africa, undertaken apparently at her behest. It is also clear that, despite later vilification, her reign was prosperous and formed the basis for many of the later triumphs of her stepson, co-ruler and rival Tuthmōsis III. Tuthmōsis ruled for a further twenty-two years after her death.[77] Tuthmōsis III was one of the greatest pharaohs of Egyptian history, overshadowed, in my opinion, only by Sesōstris five hundred years earlier. Tuthmōsis appears to have been benevolent – apart from his hatred of Ḥashepsowe – and enormously talented. There is no doubt that during his reign Egypt became more prosperous and better administered. However, he was best remembered for his expeditions and conquests, in all directions but particularly to the north.[78]

In his twenty-second year, probably 1482 BC, he personally led an expedition through Syria, which was followed by frequent campaigns over the next sixteen years.[79] These culminated in his thirty-second year (c. 1472) with an expedition into the Hurrian or Mitannian kingdom of Naharin in the Upper Euphrates. He withdrew from here with some prisoners but the campaign impressed neighbouring monarchs from Babylonia, Assyria and Hatti, the territory of the Hittites.[80] This is the context in which the tomb paintings described above were painted. The Egyptian military triumphs and the pharaoh's control of both the Egyptian Levantine ports would be quite sufficient to explain why, as the description of the foreign tribute put it,

> When they [the princes of Kaftu] hear of his victories over all the countries, they bring their gifts on their backs in order to obtain the breath of life in order to submit to his majesty [Tuthmōsis III] in order that his power could protect them.[81]

Receiving the *ṯ3n ʿnḫ* (breath of life) is a term used in connection with Kaftu and other foreign countries in contexts where it can only mean suzerainty. However, it is possible that there was also more direct pressure on the princes of Kaftu. In an inscription from Napata or Jebel Barkal in the Sudanese Upper Nile, Tuthmōsis claimed to have 'trussed the Nine Bows, the Isles in the Midst of the W3ḏ wr, the Ḥ3w nbwt and the rebel foreign countries',[82] and with a confusing use of personal pronouns:

I came and I made you strike those who are in the Isles and those that live in the Midst of the Wȝd wr, hearing your war cry, I made them see your majesty like the millstone pressing on the back of its victims.[83]

Vercoutter pointed out that these texts appear to be highly symbolic, stressing the universality of Tuthmōsis' conquests and rule, and he argued strongly that they should not be taken in a literal sense.[84] On the other hand, as mentioned above, the highest frequency of the name Kftiw on Egyptian documents came in Tuthmōsis' reign. A considerable number of Aegean pots from this period LHIIIA1 have also been excavated in Egypt. These and the Egyptian objects from the first half of the 15th century found in the Aegean will be discussed in the next chapter.[85]

Furthermore, the fact that such expeditions are unknown to modern Egyptology should not make us dismiss the possibility that they took place. We know from the Mit Rahina inscription not merely that 12th-Dynasty pharaohs, over four hundred years earlier, had launched naval expeditions into the Mediterranean, but also that Egyptologists were completely unaware of them. We also know, from the reliefs at Deir el Bahri, that Hashepsowe had sent out a major fleet far down the Red Sea.

Even more to the point, we know that, in the reigns of Tuthmōsis III and his successors, campaigns were supplied and supported by a substantial navy. This organization, which was considered important enough to have its chief dockyard at Memphis administered by the pharaoh's eldest son, consisted of specially designed warships and merchantmen used for supplying and freight. Among other ships were the so-called *kbnwt* or *kpnwt* (Byblites) and *kftiw* (Cretans), which, as William Hayes wrote in the *Cambridge Ancient History*,

are now generally conceded to have been ships designed and built by Egyptians for journeys *to* Byblos and Crete or journeys of similar type and duration. Furthermore, it is evident that in ship design and construction and in seafaring knowledge in general the Egyptians of the New Kingdom owed little or nothing to their Minoan and Phoenician neighbours, but were, in fact, the originators of at least one type of ship adopted and used by the latter (italics in original).[86]

All in all, we can no longer be as sure as Vercoutter, who, it should be stressed, was working at the height of the Aryan Model, that no Egyptian expeditions went to the Aegean during Tuthmōsis' reign in the

first half of the 15th century. Indeed, given our knowledge of Tuthmōsis' habits and inclinations and of the capacity of his navy, together
with the certainty that Cretan princes came to Egypt to offer tribute,
I see no reason to doubt the strong implication that Egyptian naval
forces were in the Aegean in the 1470s.

In any event, there is no doubt that 'princes of Kftiw and the Isles in
the Midst of the Wȝḍ wr' visited the pharaoh's court in what the Egyptians, at least, interpreted as an act of submission. It is possible that
the rulers of Kaftu felt threatened by the 'Mycenaeans' to the north;
on the other hand, it would seem equally possible that the latter's conquest relatively soon after could have been facilitated by the Egyptian
disruption of Cretan power.

Suzerainty is a vague concept and we have no clear idea of the political meaning of 'receiving the breath of life'. Its economic significance will be considered in the next chapter. The possibility that
Amōsis, the founder of the 18th Dynasty, claimed suzerainty over
the Aegean has been mentioned above.[87] All that can be said is that
the ceremony of bringing rich gifts, which was interpreted by the
Egyptians as an act of submission, was repeated for almost a century
after Tuthmōsis' conquests. In the 12th year of Akhenaton, c. 1369 BC,
men from the 'Midst of Wȝḍ wr' offered tribute before the pharaoh's
throne. Vercoutter pointed out that the phraseology used indicated
that the islanders had a less subordinate position than the envoys
from Syria and Nubia. Even so, the northerners too offered tribute to
'receive the breath of life'.[88] As has been mentioned above, the name
Kaftu was mentioned much less often after the beginning of the 14th
century. The change in nomenclature from Kaftu to 'the Midst of the
Wȝḍ wr' and Tanaya seems to reflect the new Mycenaean dominance
of Crete.

DATING THE MYCENAEAN
DOMINATION OF CRETE

At this point it is necessary to make a digression on the date at which
the Mycenaeans came to dominate Crete. Some reference was made
to this in Chapter VII, when describing the theory that this occurred
as the result of the alleged devastation of Crete by the Thera eruption.[89] However, here we must consider an even more widespread, but
doubly mistaken, belief that 'Greeks' conquered Crete at the beginning of the ceramic period LMII around 1450 BC.

The enormous influence of Arthur Evans on Minoan studies, particularly in matters concerning relative and absolute chronology, has
been referred to frequently above. According to him a big change

came over Crete at the end of his ceramic period LMIB. At this point, all but one of the Cretan palaces were destroyed. Only that of Knossos itself survived for a few more decades until it too succumbed at the end of LMII, which Evans saw as about 1400 BC. After that a new age of degeneracy began and the palace was inhabited by poor, illiterate squatters. According to Evans, Cretan palatial civilization, and for that matter that of the Greek mainland, was and remained 'Minoan'.[90] That is, it was non- or Pre-Hellenic to the end of the Bronze Age. By the end of his long life – in the 1930s at the height of the Extreme Aryan Model – Evans was being challenged by Mycenologists, notably A. J. B. Wace. These, while admitting the heavy Minoan influence, argued for the racial uniqueness of Mycenaean civilization and in 1939 even claimed that they saw Mycenaean influences on Evans's last palace at Knossos, that of LMII.[91]

Their speculation seemed dramatically confirmed thirteen years later, when Michael Ventris read as Greek the Linear B tablets which Evans claimed to have found in the LMII palace. Thus, it was now generally believed that sometime around 1450 BC Mycenaean invaders had conquered Crete, destroying all the palaces except for that at Knossos from which they had ruled the whole island for the next seventy years, until the destruction of their palace by unknown invaders at the end of LMII. This scheme would fit perfectly with the change of kilt in the painting of the tomb of Ḥ mrỉ Rˁ (Rekhmire) which was completed between 1470 and 1450 BC. It would also tally, with some allowance for time lag, with the disappearance of the term Kaftu.

However, the situation is not so simple. During the 1950s large numbers of Linear B tablets began to be excavated on the Greek mainland, notably at the palace at Pylos in Messenia. These did not come from LMII or its approximate equivalent LHIIB, but from LHIIIB, which was then supposed to have begun c. 1275, approximately a century after 1380 BC, when Evans saw the final destruction of the the palace at Knossos. Although there were some differences between the Pylian and the Knossian scripts, the similarities were so striking that several of the linguists reading them became convinced that they must be contemporary with each other and that, as the dating of the Mainland tablets was irrefutable, the Cretan texts must themselves be from LMIIIB.

This was first seen in 1955 by the English linguist Leonard Palmer, who then began a campaign to show that the palace at Knossos had lasted as long as those on the Mainland, and like them had been destroyed by the Dorians during the early 12th century.[92] He had ancient authority for this, in that Homer described Crete on the eve of the Trojan War, *c.* 1220 BC, as rich and powerful, contributing eighty ships, the third greatest number, to the expedition to Troy, and as ruled by a single king, Idomeneus.[93] Seeing this fundamental flaw, Palmer plunged in to attack Evans's conclusions, using as his chief weapons the archaeological 'Day Books' of Evans's assistant D. Mackenzie, which showed how uncertain the basis of Evans's magistral schemes were.

Palmer received some support from Blegen, the excavator of Pylos.[94] Nevertheless, his ideas were considered distinctly cranky by the majority of Aegean archaeologists. One reason for this was professional: there was distaste at a linguist 'poaching' in archaeology. There was also a certain trepidation in the face of Palmer's challenge to Evans's ceramic schemes. It was not so much affection for the founder of Minoan archaeology as a fear of the chronological chaos that would follow any fundamental upheaval. Another difficulty was that Palmer's re-dating of the Linear B tablets was commonly associated with his belief in a Luvian invasion, which had very little to recommend it.[95]

Meanwhile, however, evidence was accumulating to back Palmer's contention that the Linear B tablets from Knossos were written during LHIIIB. For one thing, a number of stirrup jars from this period inscribed in Linear B, which were found on Mainland Greece, have been shown by clay analyses to have been made in Crete.[96] Even more impressive has been work showing the prosperity of Crete throughout the LHIIIA and B periods, which made it impossible for the island to have been devastated at the end of LMII.[97] Later work on the palace itself indicates that the distribution of LHIIIB pottery there does not fit the pattern of 'squatting' envisioned by Evans and that, although some parts of the earlier buildings may not have been used in LHIIIB, the archaeological evidence indicates that it was still a functioning administrative centre. Another piece of evidence pointing in this direction comes from the obvious importance of Cretan trade.[98] Most if not all of the extant Linear B tablets from Knossos come from the destruction at the end of the period, *c.* 1200. Such a scheme would also fit the Homeric evidence mentioned above.

This, however, does not answer the problem of when Linear B, and presumably Greek, were first introduced to the island. LMII is a style of limited distribution and apparently short duration. It shows connections to both LMIB that preceded it and LMIIIA which followed. However, it does not have the clearly 'Mycenaean' characteristics claimed for it by Blegen.[99]

It has been shown in the last chapter that the militarization of society and the introduction of Shaft Graves to Crete that had previously been attributed to this period should now be pushed back into MMIII.[100] It is now also clear from inscriptional evidence that Linear A continued to be used at Knossos in this LMII.[101] While not conclusive, these facts make it unlikely that the destruction of the 'provincial' palaces, which did take place at the beginning of LMII, can be linked to the arrival of the Mycenaeans. It would seem best to envisage the centralization of power as an internal process, though possibly in the face of external pressures from the north and the south.

There is no evidence for a destruction of the palace at the beginning of LMIIIA. This too would seem to be an unlikely point for a military invasion of, though not a peaceful migration to, Crete. On the other hand, there was a substantial though not total destruction some decades later, at the beginning of what is cumbersomely called the LMIIIA2 ceramic period. This would seem the most probable point for the Mycenaeanization of Knossos and Crete, though it is possible that the process began with LMIIIA1 and that the destruction should be associated with an Achaean intrusion.[102]

In all this, however, Palmer and his supporters have been ignoring the evidence from Egypt – the disappearance of the name Kaftu for the island and the systematic over-painting of Cretan kilts with Mycenaean loincloths in the murals on the tomb of Rḫ mri Rˁ, which took place between 1470 and 1450.[103] The reluctance to consider this evidence is overdetermined. In the first place, for reasons that have been discussed in Volume 1, scholars who postulate Luvian invasions are unlikely to turn to the Levant and Egypt for anything.[104] Secondly, these scholars, whose general preference has been to down-date, have tended to accept the standard absolute chronology for the Minoan ceramic periods, rather than revise it upwards. Thus, for them, LMII began in 1450. This date makes the evidence from the tomb of Rḫ mri Rˁ fit the conventional belief in the Mycenaean conquest at that date. However, it is difficult to reconcile with a conquest during LHIIIA, dated between 1380 and 1275, if one accepts the chronology of the *Cambridge Ancient History*.

The discrepancy is removed, however, if one uses the new higher chronologies necessitated by the re-dating of the Thera eruption to 1628 BC. Kemp and Merrillees put the beginning of LMII between 1500 and 1475, although they do not commit themselves on the date of the start of LMIIIA. Thus, their scheme would not allow for the Mycenaean takeover at the beginning of LMII. Betancourt goes still higher, starting LMII in 1550 and LMIIIA in 1490 BC. Even though he puts the break between LMIIIA1 and LMIIIA2 as 1430–1410, it

would be quite possible to compress the earlier period so as to allow
for the destruction of Knossos at the end of LMIIIA1 to have taken
place during the span of Rḥ mrì Rˁ between 1470 and 1450. In fact,
such a high chronology for the beginning of LMIIIA is not necessary
and it could be allowed for even if one puts this at *c.* 1470 as I do.
Thus, it would seem likely that the Mycenaean takeover at least began
with the start of LMIII, although it is just possible that the destruction
at the end of LMIIIA1 was the result of conquests or raids from Asia
which will be discussed in the next chapter.[105]

CRETAN AND MYCENAEAN MISSIONS TO EGYPT

The dating of the Mycenaean takeover to the decades between 1470
and 1450 is also strengthened by evidence from Egyptian court annals. In the forty-second year of Tuthmōsis III, *c.* 1462, these record
'[tribute of the chief] of Ti nȝy, Ta-na-yu; a worked silver 'Shuabt'
from the country of Kftiw'.[106] The tomb of Mn ḥpr Rˁ snb, in which
the king or chief of Kaftu is depicted as a Syro-Palestinian, appears to
have been painted near the end of Tuthmōsis' reign; the pharaoh
died *c.* 1450. The German Egyptologist Wegner argued on stylistic
grounds that this tomb antedated that of Rḥ mrì Rˁ, but Vercoutter,
who wrote the standard work on the subject, maintained that, if anything, the tomb of Mn ḥpr Rˁ snb was earlier.[107] Thus, as the Danish
archaeologist Ingrid Strøm has suggested, the picture of the arrival of
a 'Syro-Palestinian' king of Kaftu, begging for 'the breath of life' near
what appears to have been the end of the old Cretan regime, might
well be interpreted not merely as a need to come to terms with the
Egyptian conqueror of the Levant and actual or potential raider of
the Aegean, but also as an appeal for diplomatic or military protection
from northern enemies.[108] Similarly, the presentation by a chief of
Tanaya of a precious object of Kaftuy workmanship could well represent the presence of the new rulers of Crete, possibly trying to secure
their legitimacy through relations with Egypt. These interpretations
are, of course, unproven but there is no reason to doubt that Cretan
and Greek missions, which the Egyptians at least interpreted as ex-
pressing submission, were sent to Egypt in the middle of the 15th century BC.

THE STATUE BASE OF AMENŌPHIS III

There is further evidence of Egyptian contacts with the Aegean some
eighty years later, from the reign of Amenōphis III *c.* 1419–1381.[109]

This comes from one of five bases of what appear to have been statues of the pharaoh from his funerary temple at Kom el-Hetan near
Thebes. Each of the bases is inscribed with toponyms in cartouches
surmounted with the figure of a bound prisoner. Four of the bases
refer to places in Syria and Mesopotamia but the fifth refers to ones in
the Aegean under the headings Kftìw and Tìnȝyw.

Some of these names are lost but twelve remain. They are:
ìmnšȝ ('amniša), Bȝyš(ȝ)y (Biyaš-), Kȝ tw nȝy (Kútunaya), Mwk ìnw
(Muk'ánu), Dyȝkȝìȝs (Diqaês), Mydȝnìȝ (Miṣanê), Kȝtìyr (Kútíra), Nupyryy (Nupirayy), Kȝnywšȝ (Kúnúša), Rykȝtì (Rikatá) and Wȝìwry
(Wìliya). Nine scholars have published on these names and they have
agreed on the following identifications: ìmnšȝ as Amnissos, Kȝ tw nȝy
as Kydonia, Mwk ìnw as Mycenae, Nupyryy as Nauplia, Kȝtìyr as
Kythera, Kȝnywšȝ as Knossos, Mydȝnìȝ as Messenia and Rykȝtì as Lyktos. There is some argument over Bȝyš(ȝ)y, which some scholars see as
Phaistos and others as Pisaia, and Faure believes that Dyȝkȝìȝs is a supposed Tegeai in West Crete, Sergent has it as Tegea in Arcadia but
Astour maintains that it is Mount Dikte in Crete. This could also be
the name of the palace and city known archaeologically as Kato Zakro
in Eastern Crete.[110] Wȝìwry was mentioned in Chapter V, in the discussion of the name ìwȝì, a city destroyed by Senwosre I and Amenemḥe
II.[111] Four scholars had their own individual candidates, while three
plumped for (W)ilios or Troy, despite the fact that it is far to the north
of the other cities.[112]

This list provides us with a mass of extremely important information. It provides evidence of many place names four or five hundred
years before their earliest other attestation. This strengthens the case
for a strong cultural continuity from the Bronze to the Iron Ages in
Greece. It also shows that Egyptians had specific knowledge of the
Southern Aegean, at least in the early 14th century. As the city names
are inscribed in cartouches surmounted by the image of a bound prisoner, the base could be interpreted as a claim to Egyptian dominance
over the area.[113] On the other hand, as many scholars have pointed out,
binding is merely a New Kingdom convention for indicating a foreigner, and other states, such as Hitti, Assur and Mitanni, which were
clearly independent at the time were represented in the same way.[114]

The idea that the names of the statue base do not merely represent
symbolic power has been strengthened by the work of the archaeologists Vronwy Hankey and Eric Cline, who have correlated the inscription with archaeological discoveries of Egyptian objects from the
reign of Amenōphis III in the Aegean region and with Aegean objects found in Egypt. These and their implications will be discussed
further in the next chapter. Here it is sufficient to state that Hankey

and Cline have made a plausible case for the list's representing an itinerary of one or more official voyages to the Aegean.[115] On the other
hand, the Australian archaeologist Merrillees makes a strong case
when he argues that, by the 14th century BC, the name Kftiw was an
anachronism and that the figures above the cartouches are 'of Semitic
type', indicating that they could not be portraying Mycenaeans, who
were in control of the Aegean by the time of Amenōphis III. As
he is when he considers the period of Tuthmōsis III, Merrillees is
extremely unwilling to entertain the notion that Cretans or Greeks
could have been politically subordinate to Egypt.[116]

It seems to me that the hypotheses of Hankey and Merrillees are
not mutually incompatible. The phonetics of the transcriptions of the
Aegean place names show that they cannot antedate the New Kingdom. There is no reason, however, why they should not come from
the reigns of Ḥapshesowe and Tuthmōsis III in the early 15th century, when Kftiw was still the appropriate name for Crete. On the
other hand, Hankey and Cline have made a powerful circumstantial
case for supposing that there was Egyptian political activity in the
Aegean during the reign of Amenōphis III. Given the economic, military and cultural inequality between the two regions, there would
seem to be good grounds for accepting the Egyptian claims for some
sort of hegemony over the Aegean at this time.

CONTACTS BETWEEN EGYPT
AND THE AEGEAN IN THE LATE 18TH
AND 19TH DYNASTIES

As mentioned above, tribute from the 'Isles in the midst of the
Wȝḏ wr' is recorded from the reign of Amenōphis III's successor
Amenōphis IV/Akhenaton.[117] There are also reports of imports of
precious stones from Kftiw. These would confirm what we know
about the exchange of luxury goods between the two regions in the
first half of the 14th century from the Kaş shipwreck. However, both
the wreck with the considerable Levantine cargo and the Amarna letter, in which the pharaoh was informed of the situation in Danuna
by the king of Tyre, seem to suggest that in the middle of the 14th
century, Egypt was not communicating with the Aegean directly but
through Levantine and possibly Cypriot middlemen. Documents from
the late 18th and 19th Dynasties refer to goods and possibly slaves
from Kftiw and the name pȝ Kftiwy (The Cretan) is found from this
period too.[118] A fragment from the late 19th or early 20th Dynasty, c.
1200 BC, states: 'I [came back] and I brought back a Kftiwy.'[119] Thus,
there appears to have been direct as well as indirect communication

between Egypt and Crete. The revival of Egyptian power in Syro-Palestine at the beginning of the 19th Dynasty in the first quarter of the 13th century seems to have had some effect in Greece. Ramessēs II, who reigned for sixty-six years from 1304–1237 BC, claimed that 'the islands in the midst of the Wȝḍ wr' had returned to Egypt, or, more specifically, 'Ramessēs II, your prestige has crossed the Wȝḍ wr and the islands in its midst are in fear and the envoys of her chiefs come to him for fear governs their hearts'.[120] How close the relationship was at this time is more difficult to say and we shall see in the next chapter that there is much less archaeological evidence of contacts between Egypt and the Aegean for the 13th century than there is for the 14th. By the end of the 13th century the boot was on the other foot and there are the reports, mentioned above, of the plots and invasions of the Peoples of the Sea, many of whom, including the Prst, the Ṯkr, the Trš and the Dnn, came from the Aegean.[121] Thus, it is likely that by the 12th century cultural influences flowed in both directions.

A SUMMARY OF THE EVIDENCE FROM EGYPTIAN DOCUMENTS AND PAINTINGS

The picture we gain from this evidence is that Egyptians had been aware of Crete since the 3rd millennium. There is no sign from the documents of any Middle Kingdom contact with the Aegean, but the recent discovery of the Mit Rahina inscription warns us against putting too much trust in the argument from silence on this. There are indications of knowledge of Crete during the Hyksos period. There are also hints that there was some kind of alliance between the rising 18th Dynasty and the people of Hȝw nbw. After c. 1570 there seems to have been a gap in relations until the reign of Tuthmōsis III (1504–1450), when there are Egyptian claims of expeditions to the Aegean and reports of tributary missions to Egypt from both Kftiw (Crete) and Tinȝ (Mycenaean Greece). The statue base from the funerary temple of Amenōphis III (1419–1381) shows that Egyptians of this time had quite a detailed knowledge of at least the Southern Aegean. There is a report of another tributary mission in the reign of his successor Amenōphis IV/Akhenaton (1381–1364) and a report on the situation in Danuna (Greece) to the pharaoh from the king of Tyre. There are occasional later references to Greece but contacts between the two regions appear to have lessened by the middle of the 13th century. Soon after this, however, there are several Egyptian references to Aegean Peoples of the Sea, who raided Egypt and the Levant in the late 13th and 12th centuries BC.

These references tell us nothing about the Aryan Model. However, the relatively intense and protracted nature of Egyptian contacts with the Aegean they reveal both weakens and strengthens the Ancient Model. In the narrow sense it is weakened because these contacts would seem sufficient to explain the deep cultural borrowings from Egyptian to Greek culture proposed in these volumes without needing the settlements postulated in the Ancient Model. However, as mentioned in the last chapter, there are reasons for postulating earlier borrowings. The contacts strengthen the Ancient Model historically by showing the relative ease of contact between Egypt and the Aegean during the Bronze Age. The spottiness of the record indicates how easy it would be for other contacts to have taken place without leaving any trace. Finally, the lack of emphasis these admitted contacts have received in the historiography of Ancient Greece throws a very interesting light on the ideology of 19th- and 20th-century historians.

MESOPOTAMIAN AND UGARITIC DOCUMENTS

Most of the Egyptian documents referred to above were known by 1930, when the Extreme Aryan Model became enshrined as the objective interpretation. Since then, a number of new sources of documentary evidence from the Semitic-speaking Near East have become available, which have substantially altered the picture. The first of the new sources are the tablets from Ugarit on the Syrian coast near the northern end of the Levant. Some of these are in Akkadian and Hurrian but most are written in the local West Semitic language now called Ugaritic. Before looking at the Ugaritic texts, however, we should examine other sources from Syria and Mesopotamia, many of which are newly discovered.

The reference to DA-ne^{ki} in the geographical list found at the Mesopotamian site of Abu Salabikh dating to the middle of the 3rd millennium has been mentioned above. The parallel list from Ebla, dating to approximately the same period, appears to call the same place am-ni^{ki}.[122] This toponym may well be related to Amnissos, the port of Knossos, which appeared on the statue base of Amenōphis III as ỉmnš; ('amniša) and thus clearly existed in the Bronze Age. If Amnissos really does date back to the 3rd millennium, the name can hardly refer, like many Egyptian toponyms, to the god Amon, as his cult emerged only in the 12th Dynasty in the 20th century BC. On the other hand, it would be quite plausible to derive it from the Egyptian ỉmn (west), even though in place names this always appears with a final -t.[123]

A Mesopotamian text ostensibly dating back to the reign of Sargon the Great in the 24th century, but probably from much later, refers to 'Kaptara beyond the Upper Sea'; the Upper Sea was the conventional name for the Mediterranean. Lists from the city-state Mari, on the Upper Euphrates, in the early 18th century BC mention Kaptara as a trading partner and centre of craftsmanship. There is also a specific mention of a consignee of goods in Ugarit known as a Kaphtorite.[124] From these documents, it is clear both that there was frequent trade between Mesopotamia and Syria on the one hand and Crete on the other and that, during the 2nd millennium, Cretan goods were much admired in the Near East, as they were in Egypt. This, and the distance and isolation desirable for a divine residence, would explain why the Ugaritic god of metal-work and craftsmanship Ktr w ḥss was supposed to dwell in Crete.[125]

Like other Levantine ports, such as Alalakh, Ugarit was an extraordinarily commercial society.[126] As Michael Astour put it:

> In Ugarit, the big merchants were the upper class – they owned the largest land estate, they surrounded the throne as advisers and administrators, and they served in the elite corps of the army as *mariannu* – charioteers. . . . if we look for a parallel to the Ugarit *mariannu*, it would be the patriciate not of early Rome but of Medieval Venice, except that the social relations in Ugarit were far from the rigidity and exclusiveness of the Venetian mercantile oligarchy.[127]

Given the extraordinary activity and geographical range of Ugaritic trade, it is surprising how little contact there appears to have been with the Aegean. It is clear that the Ugaritic authorities were extremely concerned about the ethnic identities of the merchants with whom they traded, yet, as the archaeologist and social historian Anita Yannai put it,

> the fact remains that although Canaanites, Assyrians, Hurrians, Egyptians, Alasiotes (Cypriots) and inhabitants of virtually every city up and down the Syro-Palestinian coast are mentioned in the abundant archives, these have not yielded any ethnic, geographic or personal names that are indisputably Greek, nor any Linear B texts.[128]

Yannai was, of course, referring to the texts in the second rather than the first half of the 2nd millennium, when we know that there was a Kaphtorite in the city. Even in the later period, however, there is the exception of the geographical name Kaphtor itself. Another apparent exception is the name Bn Dnn found in the records. Astour argues that the man of that name had relatives with West Semitic names, indicating that it had indigenous roots there.[129] This is indeed a puzzle but it is clear that the Hittite and Indo-European gentilic -*n* was used in Ugaritic, for example in the name 'arwdn, the Arwadite. Thus it is possible that, despite the Semitic connections, Dnn meant 'Greek'.

The clearest link between Ugarit and Crete comes in a tax document from the 13th century concerning a *tamkarum* (officially licensed merchant) called Sinarenu, who was regularly trading with the island.[130] By this time, however, Ugarit was in the Hittite sphere of influence. It may well be that after about 1366 BC there was a politico-economic blockade between this zone and Mainland Greece. This will be discussed further in Chapter XI.[131] A blockade would help explain the absence of Greeks from Ugaritic texts, most of which come from after 1366 BC, and the apparently limited direct contact of Ugaritic merchants with the Aegean. Furthermore, as we shall see in the next chapter, it is very likely that Cyprus on or beyond the fringes of the Hittite empire served as an entrepot between the two zones.[132] Although there are no mercantile documents from there, archaeological evidence indicates that there was considerable trade between the Aegean and the Southern or Egyptian sector of the Levant.[133]

More germane to the Ancient Model and the extent of Levantine influences on Greece are the poetical and mythological texts found at Ugarit. These reveal a 2nd-millennium West Semitic mythology that in many ways provides a bridge between that of Greece and what we can glean of Israelite and Canaanite mythology from the rationalizations of the Bible.[134] It is largely on these texts that Cyrus Gordon and Michael Astour based their claims for the derivation of much Greek mythology from the West Semitic.

The classicist and Semitist Ruth Edwards has shown that, in some instances, Astour's claims are founded on very flimsy evidence. However, while she is right to challenge their certainty, she is very far from damaging their probability and, as I argued in Volume 1, competitive plausibility not certainty is all that one can or should require in these areas. Thus, for instance, when Edwards points out the unreliability of the reading of the Ugaritic texts on which Astour bases his claim that there was an Ugaritic divinity of the morning star or dawn called Qdm and one of the evening star or dusk called ʿrb, she does not destroy the cumulative circumstantial case he has made for this; still less does she weaken the overwhelming plausibility of a link between the Greek legendary figures Kadmos and Europa, who travel from Phoenicia in the east to Greece in the west, with the Semitic words *qdm* (east) and *ʿrb* (west and sunset).[135]

Furthermore, the striking number of parallels between West Semitic and Greek mythology brought out by Astour and Gordon should be taken as a whole and in the light of the fundamental question 'why not'? What is so unlikely about the idea of Greek culture having borrowed heavily from one of its most sophisticated neighbours? However, I am running ahead of myself. All that can be claimed at this point is that a number of scholars have seen striking parallels between some West Semitic myths and legends preserved on Ugaritic tablets and Greek myths that appear in later sources.

Thus, both the economic and cultural texts from Ugarit suggest sustained contact between the Levant and the Aegean during the Bronze Age. The cultural borrowings could well be the result of intense and frequent trade and they do not prove the case for Levantine conquests of, or settlements in, the Aegean. Nevertheless, they would certainly fit very well with the Ancient Model.

AEGEAN DOCUMENTS

Although the Aegean syllabaries, Linears A and B, were discovered by Arthur Evans at the turn of the century, they were not deciphered until the 1950s. Thus, like that of the Ugaritic tablets, the content of the Aegean ones became available to scholars only after the Extreme Aryan Model was firmly in place. However, like the Ugaritic texts, the Aegean ones have, in the long run, proved subversive to the model.

Tablets written in the Linear A syllabary have been found in Crete, the Cylades and Mycenae in strata dated from the beginning to the middle of the 2nd millennium. It is now generally acknowledged that it can be read by using known sound values from the related syllabary Linear B. As the doyen of Mycenaean studies John Chadwick puts it, 'Granted some uncertainties about the identification of individual signs, it seems clear that in the main the Linear B syllabic values hold good also for Linear A.'[136] When Cyrus Gordon read it in this way in the 1950s, disbelief in this was used as a weapon to attack his ideas of close cultural contacts in the Bronze Age East Mediterranean. Now, however, this part of his hypothesis is uncontroversial. On the other hand, the interpretation of the language for which Linear A was used is still hotly debated. Nevertheless, whether or not the language was basically Semitic, there is no doubt that it contained Semitic words. Gordon cites *kunisu*, written with the ideogram for wheat, which he relates to a Semitic form found in the Akkadian *ku(n)išu* (emmer wheat); he also relates *qapa* and *supu*, types of pots, to the Hebrew *kp* and the Hebrew and Ugaritic *sp* (vessel), and *yane* (wine) to the

Hebrew *yayîn*.[137] Helck adds to these *kumina* (cumin), the Akkadian *kammūnu*, Sumerian *gamun*, Hebrew *kammōn; sasame* (sesame), the Akkadian *šamašama*, the Ugaritic *ssmn; samuku* (raisin), the Hebrew *ṣimmuq; sarinu* (saffron), the Akkadian *šurnu* (saffron), which Helck associates with the Greek *selinon* (celery/iac); *karopa* (a 'type of vase'), the Akkadian *karpatu* and Ugaritic *krpnm;* and *akanu*, Akkadian *aggânu* (a peel).[138] Thus, either the 'Minoans' were originally Semitic speakers or their culture received considerable cultural influence from the Levant or both.

Here, however, we shall deal only with the uncontroversial and restrict ourselves to the many personal and some place names which can be identified with near certainty. The personal onomastica tend to parallel the roughly contemporary Egyptian 'list of names from Kftiw' and indicate a population with Egyptian, Semitic, Hurrian and Anatolian names, as well as the name Danane discussed above. Thus, the Egyptian texts and pictures, as well as the 'Minoan' documents in Linear A, indicate that, at least *c.* 1700–1470 BC, the population of Crete was thoroughly mixed and contained considerable numbers of people with Egyptian and Semitic names.

Linear B

Tablets written in this syllabary have been found at Knossos and in Mainland Greece from the 13th and possibly the 14th century BC. Despite the fact that many texts still cannot be translated satisfactorily, there is now no doubt that Ventris and Chadwick correctly interpreted Linear B as Greek.[139]

Proof that at least late Mycenaean society was Greek-speaking has confirmed the work of those scholars, like the historian of Greek religion Martin Nilsson, who had argued that there was a strong continuity between the Late Bronze and Early Iron Ages. Specific evidence of this has been found in the many names of people, places and divinities in Linear B texts for which there are Archaic and Classical Greek parallels. On the other hand, some scholars were disconcerted to find several words of admitted Semitic origin – notably *kuruso, chrysos* from *ḥ < ḥârûṣ* (gold); *kito, chitōn* or *kitōn* from the Semitic *ktn,* the Hebrew *kətonet* (tunic) and *rita, lita* in later Greek (garment linen) from the Semitic *lṭ* (covering), the Assyrian *liṭu* and the Hebrew *lōṭ.*

The introduction of these words had previously been attributed to Phoenician traders in the 8th or 7th centuries BC.[140] Even today, there is a tendency to play down their significance by linking them to the names of the spices, most of which are already attested in Linear A (see above): *kumino*, the Greek *kyminon*, *sasama*, the Greek *sēsamon*, and *kuparo*, *kypairos*, the Ugaritic *kpr* and the Hebrew *kōper*. These were then classified merely as 'contact borrowings', which could have been picked up through casual trade.[141]

In fact, however, they cannot be dismissed so easily. Clothes are not unnecessary luxuries in the European climate and archaeological evidence shows that gold, *the* precious metal, was of cultural significance in Greece even in the Neolithic. Thus, the absence in Greek of a word for 'gold' belonging to the widespread Indo-European family – for which the root **ghel* has been postulated – and its replacement by a Semitic word would seem to indicate very substantial contacts.[142]

The Linear B tablets also show that the Aegean palatial economy followed oriental models.[143] As Ventris and Chadwick argued, when they compared the Aegean and Levantine versions,

> These contemporary records [from Mesopotamia and Syria] present the most useful and significant analogies with the Mycenaean tablets, and will often be found quoted in our commentary. In spite of some differences of climate and culture, the similarities in the size and organization of the royal palaces and in the purposes for which the tablets were written ensure close parallels, not only in the listed commodities and their amounts, but even on occasion in phraseology and layout. Some direct knowledge of each other's scribal methods through the medium of Mycenaean traders cannot be ruled out.[144]

The ideological implications of the last sentence are fascinating. The idea that Mycenaeans could have had a significant impact on the structures of long-established Near Eastern palace administrations shows the extraordinary force of 'Aryanism'. What is more, although it is possible that there were Greeks at Ugarit, and it is very likely that there were some further south, there is far stronger evidence (see below) that there were Levantines in the Aegean. Thus, it is clear that the authors' insistence on the medium of Mycenaean traders comes from their Graeco-centrism. Nevertheless, the striking parallels they note are clearly there. There are, for instance, specific parallels in the systems of measurement, even though Chadwick and Ventris try to play these down:

> It will be noted that the ratios and the volumes of the biblical system for liquids show some analogy with the Mycenaean: there are reasons for regarding the former as survivals of a general Canaanite system, traces of which can be seen in use at Ugarit, *but a direct influ-*

ence on Mycenae is perhaps doubtful. The primary dry unit also corresponds *perhaps accidentally* with the Babylonian *imêru* or 'donkey load', which is similarly subdivided into ten. (my emphasis)[145]

On the other hand, the Semitist and mathematician Robert Stieglitz points out that Linear A texts show that they were primarily influenced by Egyptian decimal practices, while those of Linear B bear a closer resemblance to Mesopotamian sexagesimal practices.[146] This could be explained by the hypothesis that the methods used in the Old Palaces, which were heavily influenced by Egypt, survived in the New Palaces in Crete, but that further north, Canaanite 'Hyksos' practices were established. However, such hypotheses are purely speculative.

Overall, however, the best explanation for the striking parallels between the Mycenaean Aegean and Syro-Mesopotamia is to suppose that, along with the palaces and the script, the Mycenaean rulers took over the bureaucratic traditions of their predecessors in Crete, which in turn belonged to the general institutional patterns of the Near East. This does not, however, rule out the likelihood of later borrowing.

There is one way in which the society portrayed in the Linear B tablets is very unlike that revealed by the texts from Ugarit, which was probably very similar to that of other Levantine cities. It is that there is no indication of merchants in the Mycenaean palaces. This is particularly puzzling because most archaeologists have assumed that most if not all of the very widespread Mycenaean pottery was transported by Mycenaeans.[147] Thus Emily Vermeule writes of the Mycenaean merchants: 'They are an anonymous, adventurous, essential element in empire society, whose lives will not be completely illuminated until some Mycenaean harbor installation is discovered and excavated.'[148] Although this statement is true in an absolute sense, it is misleading when comparison is made with the Levantine cities. The Mycenaean merchants do not lack complete illumination archaeologically; however, the Linear B tablets throw no light whatsoever on them. There seems to be an essential difference in the fact that, where the palace at Ugarit has provided information about the city's merchants, the Mycenaean palaces have not.

From the written evidence, we know that overseas trade was extremely important at Ugarit and there is no reason to suppose that it was any different from the other cities on the Levant in this respect. The Aegean records tell us nothing about Mycenaean trade. Thus, we know, from the tomb paintings discussed above, that Cretans and Mycenaeans arrived in Egypt bearing valuable goods. We also know from a Hittite document that ships of Aḫḫiyawa were quite usual on the Levant in the mid-13th century and we shall see in the next chapter that there is archaeological evidence to suggest this.[149] Furthermore, we shall see from the archaeological evidence that it is possible that some important merchant ships were sailed by Greeks. Nevertheless, it is clear that trade was less central to Mycenaean society than it was to that of the cities of the Levant. It may be that the Aegean was less dependent on Egyptian grain. But it is likely that both regions required at least aid to overcome crop failures in order to maintain their high populations and economic specialization.[150]

While the Danaans and Achaians described in Homer were thoroughly maritime in their long ships, in his view most trade and most luxury manufacture seems to have been carried out by Phoenicians.[151] It is impossible to solve the question of whether the poet was here referring to his own time in the 10th or 9th centuries or to that of the Trojan War in the 13th or to an amalgam of both. There is, in fact, little doubt that Phoenicians did fulfil this function in Homer's lifetime but I see no reason why this should not have been the case in the Late Bronze Age itself.[152]

Thus, it would seem clear from documentary evidence that both Levantine and Mycenaean ships were travelling between the Near East and the Aegean during the Late Bronze Age and it is likely that Egyptian ones were too. The archaeological evidence for major and continuous contacts will be discussed in the next chapter. However, indications of intense contact with the Near East also appear from the documents too, from the Semitic vocabulary and lists of ivory and other exotic materials which have been recorded. Thus, there is little doubt that the earlier cosmopolitanism in the Aegean, indicated by the Egyptian paintings and the list of names from Kftiw, persisted into Mycenaean times.

Onomastica in Linear B contain dozens of names with plausible Semitic, Hurrian or Egyptian etymologies, for example, Aikupitijo, Aigyptos. This came originally from Ḥt kȝ Ptḥ (Temple of the Spirit of Ptah), an Egyptian name for Memphis. Thus, the personal name means 'Memphite' or 'Egyptian'. (This etymology and the attestation of the name Aigypios of his twin and enemy Danaos are mentioned above.)[153] There are also such names as Misarajo from the Semitic Mṣry (Egyptian); Aradajo, probably a gentilic from the Phoenician city Arwad, written Arados in Greek, and Turijajo and Turijo, Tyrian.[154] There is also the name Kupirajo, which would seem to be a gentilic from Cyprus.[155]

Onomastica also suggest the presence of African Blacks in the Ae-

gean. A₃tijoqo, which Chadwick plausibly links to the Homeric Aithiopes, appears several times, and Chadwick and Chantraine plausibly
associate the Mycenaean names Sima and Simo to the later ones
Simos, Simōn, Simmos and Simmias and to the word *simos* (snub-
nosed). Xenophanes, a poet of the 6th century BC, referred to the
Aithiopes as *simoi*.[156] Chadwick and Chantraine also accept the hypothesis that these are linked to a lost form that was borrowed into
Latin as *simia* (monkey).[157] All of these and quite possibly the Hebrew
name of Simʿôn would seem to derive from the Egyptian *šmʿ(w)*,
'Upper Egyptian' or 'musician'.[158] The acceptance of this etymology
has interesting and not altogether pleasant consequences. Firstly, it
would suggest that Upper Egyptians were seen in ancient as well as
medieval times as Blacks. Secondly, it would also imply the antiquity
of the common white or brown European association of African Blacks
with negroid features with monkeys. There is no doubt that, while
Greeks and Romans were by no means as obsessed with racism as
Northern Europeans have been since the institution of racial slavery
in the 17th century AD, they were far from free of racial prejudice.[159]

In general, the evidence from the Linear B tablets indicates that society in the 14th and 13th century Aegean was less mercantile than
that of the cities of the Levant. Nevertheless, the structure of palatial
society was strikingly similar to that in the Near East, and it is clear
that there were many Egyptians, Blacks and Levantines, and/or their
descendants, in Crete and the Peloponnese at the time.

CONCLUSION

The evidence from the Egyptian, Mesopotamian, Levantine and Aegean documents all points in the same direction. Firstly, there are
suggestions that these regions were in some sort of contact in the 3rd
millennium. Secondly, it is clear from the tablets in Linears A and B
that Cretan palatial culture was thoroughly permeated with the bureaucratic practices of the Near East and it would seem likely that this
was so from their first establishment in the 21st century BC. Evidence
from Crete and Thera shows that there continued to be close contact
between at least the Southern Aegean and Egypt and the Levant in
the succeeding centuries; we have no documentary information about
the situation further north. It would seem that with the beginning
of the 18th Dynasty in the early 16th century there was some kind of
alliance between it and some forces in the Aegean. Furthermore,
there appear to have been Egyptians and Semitic-speakers in Crete
and Cretans in Egypt.

With the expansion of Egyptian power in the 15th century there was increasing contact between the two regions. There is no doubt that the Egyptians believed they were receiving tribute from the region and it seems that the Egyptians sent expeditions, possibly punitive ones, to the Aegean. It is quite clear that, at least by 1400 BC, Egyptian officials had a reasonable notion of the region's geography and that both Cretans and northerners continued to send tribute to Egypt until the end of the 14th century. In this period, however, there is some doubt as to the extent to which contact between Egypt and the Aegean was direct and how much was transmitted through the Levant and Levantines. There is an interesting hiatus during the 13th century; that is to say, the documents suggest that contact lessened not merely during the period of the Sea Peoples in the 12th but also during the apparently flourishing reign of Ramessēs II in the 13th century.

The intensity and long duration of these contacts, which is far greater than scholars working within the Aryan Model were, until recently, prepared to accept, makes the extent and depth of Egyptian and Semitic influence on Greek culture proposed in these volumes very plausible. This very fact, however, makes the colonizations proposed by the Ancient Model redundant and here again I should insist that I am not arguing that all or even nearly all Egyptian and Semitic elements of Greek culture are the results of these hypothetical settlements. Nevertheless, the documentary evidence of close contact – particularly between the upper classes – if anything increases the likelihood of earlier colonization.

CHAPTER XI

EGYPTIAN AND LEVANTINE
CONTACTS WITH THE AEGEAN,
1550–1250 BC
The archaeological evidence

W E NOW COME ON to much firmer terrain. In the last chapter
we have seen that there is considerable documentary evidence of contacts between the Near East and the Aegean
during these centuries. After 1500 the Near East and East Mediterranean were dominated by a system of 'Great Powers' – Egypt, Babylonia, the Mitanni, Assyria and the Hittites. From the 14th and 13th
centuries, a significant amount of diplomatic correspondence among
these powers has survived. This provides a remarkably good framework in which to place and understand the considerable quantity of
archaeological material available.

Until recently, however, the match between the two types of evidence had been obscured by the dating of the Greek ceramic periods.
Thus, for instance, it was difficult to tally the Cretan LMII, in which
there appeared to have been relatively little contact between the island
and Egypt, with the reign of Amenōphis III, whom Egyptian records
showed to have been an extremely powerful pharaoh with an active
and wide-ranging foreign policy which included the Aegean. Furthermore, many objects with his cartouche have been found at Mycenae
and elsewhere in Greece. I hope to show in this chapter that, with the
updating of ceramic periods called for by Kemp and Merrillees, on
the basis of Egyptian synchronisms, and by Betancourt, in order to
keep in line with carbon dates and the re-dating of Thera, the whole
pattern makes much better sense.[1]

There is a tradition that the hero Pelops settled in Greece from
Anatolia, and that his descendants overthrew the Heraklid 'Hyksos'

dynasties and established kingdoms in the peninsula, which was called the Peloponnese after him. The dates at which such a colonization could have taken place and the great difficulties in tracing it archaeologically will be discussed below. Here it should simply be noted that he was universally reported to have arrived considerably later than Danaos and that, unlike the legends around the latter and Kadmos, there are no traditions of Pelops having introduced any new technique or institution other than chariot-racing.[2]

Accepting the shifts in chronology proposed in previous chapters, there are no reports of any colonizations or invasions from Egypt or the Levant during these centuries. It is possible, however, that, as some of the documents discussed in the last chapter suggest, there were Egyptian or Egypto-Canaanite punitive expeditions to the Aegean in the 15th century and that rulers in the region offered what the Egyptians took to be tribute and a recognition of the pharaoh's suzerainty at other points in the following 150 years.[3] Nevertheless, there would seem little doubt that most of the contact between the regions in this period took the form of state or private trading, certainly in luxuries and very probably in staples. This took place within a civilized world stretching out in all directions, well beyond the Fertile Crescent and the East Mediterranean, but particularly within the region that appears to have been directly or indirectly under Egyptian power. All this came to an end with migrations and tribal movements, possibly precipitated by climatic deterioration in the late 13th century and exacerbated by the eruption of Hekla III in the 12th century BC.[4]

The central areas, Egypt, Mesopotamia and the Levant, recovered from the crisis relatively quickly. By contrast, while the name 'Dark Age' should not be taken to mean a complete extinction of culture, it took peripheral regions like Iran, Anatolia and the Aegean longer to revive and, when they did so, it was in very different forms. The Hittite Empire was replaced by the Phrygian and other kingdoms and in the Aegean the palaces of the Bronze Age were replaced by the *poleis* or city-states following the new patterns developed in Phoenicia at the end of the Bronze and beginning of the Iron Age.[5] This chapter, however, is not concerned with the collapse and the period of the so-called invasions of the Sea Peoples but with relations among the three regions during the high civilization of the Late Bronze Age.

LATE MYCENAEAN GREECE

While not so dramatic as the expansion of documentary evidence, the archaeological evidence for the period after 1470 BC is substantially greater than that for the early Mycenaean period. Similarly, though they were not so spectacular as the grave goods of the Shaft Graves, tumuli and early *tholoi*, the grave goods from later tombs provide considerable information about upper-class material culture. There is also evidence of several palaces and many remains of settlements and fortifications from all over Mainland Greece and the islands. In addition to this, there is archaeological as well as documentary evidence from the palace at Knossos for the fact that, somewhere around 1450, Greek-speaking mainlanders took over Crete.

As mentioned in Chapter IX, while the Mycenaean palaces may have had certain 'northern' features like the *megaron* or hall with fireplace, they were generally cut-down versions of the greater and more luxurious palaces of the Middle East and Minoan Crete.[6] Like those of the Middle East, and unlike the Cretan palaces, many of those of Mainland Greece were fortified. In the 14th century, presumably after the Pelopid invasion, the architectural style of these fortifications followed the Anatolian 'Cyclopean' style of gigantic irregular stone works.[7] At the same time, the long-standing Cretan and Mainland tradition of *tholos* tombs was developed to create the massive and splendidly decorated 'beehive' tombs of which the best known is the so-called 'Treasury of Atreus' at Mycenae.[8]

From the tablets, it is known that there was a massive amount of metal-work in the palaces of which very little indeed survives; the same is true of the wood and ivory work and jewellery. What has survived indicates a persistence of early Mycenaean 'Hyksos' motifs – lion hunts, sphinxes and griffins – and if anything an increase of the Minoan influences, as well as traces of earlier and contemporary Near Eastern art.[9] These motifs also occur on the seals which follow the Minoan and early Mycenaean traditions closely.[10] There are also some fragmentary murals which resemble Cretan and even more clearly Theran prototypes.[11]

However, a much larger and more original corpus of Mycenaean painting comes from pots. The Mycenaean palaces and even more the tombs have produced a mass of pottery, which has also been found in huge quantities in Cyprus and to a lesser extent in Egypt and the Levant.[12] Many of these pots were painted in a much more distinctively Mycenaean way. While clearly derived from earlier Cretan and to a lesser extent Middle Eastern styles, they are definitely 'Mycenaean' in their attractive naiveté and heaviness. Though many of the scenes on them are of animals and birds, a considerable number are of chariots and their riders and of armed warriors.[13] The same is true of scenes found on pottery from the palace at Pylos in the Southwestern Peloponnese.

There is very little to be surprised at in Mycenaean art and architecture. Everything fits with the picture painted by tradition and revealed by the Linear B tablets of petty kingdoms following Cretan palatial bureaucratic customs and 'Hyksos' and native habits of frequent if not constant warfare with each other. The neatest parallel I can find to Mycenaean Greece is that of Fujiwara and Kamakura Japan between the 9th and 14th centuries AD. In these periods the bureaucratic civilian court system of ultimately Chinese origin coexisted uneasily with an increasingly turbulent military caste which was pushing towards gangsterism or, to give it its more elegant title, feudalism.

THE RELATIVE ISOLATION
OF THE AEGEAN 1550–1470 BC

In the last chapter I mentioned that Queen Aḥḥotpe, the wife of Seḳenenrʿe Taʿo II of the 17th Dynasty and mother of Amōsis, founder of the 18th, was called 'Mistress of the regions of the Ḥꜣw nbwt'. It is especially interesting to note, therefore, that some of the jewels found buried with her have been plausibly linked to contemporary Minoan work.[14]

Given the wide provenance of the jewels' materials and the other artistic styles involved, it would seem useful to consider these as belonging to the Hyksos cultural zone discussed in Chapters VIII and IX. The same would seem to be true of the dagger found in her tomb with the name of her son Amōsis. Its metal-work and decoration both belong to this non-Egyptian East Mediterranean tradition. An axe of Amōsis himself with the inscription 'beloved of Mntw', which, as we know from Chapters IV and V, was altogether appropriate for the expeller of the Asiatic Hyksos, was paradoxically engraved with a griffin and a sphinx.[15] Here, as with his mother's jewellery, it would seem that there was a lag between the political and the artistic revival of native Egyptian as opposed to Hyksos power. Very quickly, however, the traditional forms and motifs of the Middle Kingdom were re-established in their traditional dominance, although, as we shall see, the Hyksos motifs never disappeared altogether during the 18th Dynasty and admiration for Minoan art continued. The prevalence of the Hyksos artistic *koinē* seems to have lasted for only a few years after the establishment of the native dynasty. It is largely for this reason, as well as because of the inscriptional evidence, that Helck described the beginning of the 18th Dynasty as 'the period when the Aegean influence was strongest'.[16]

According to the chronology used in this book, the 16th century corresponds to the Cretan LMIB and the Greek LHIIA. Interestingly, fewer Egyptian and Levantine objects have been found in these strata than before or later. On the other hand, a number of Cretan vessels of LMIB have been found in Egypt, some of them in contemporary Egyptian late Hyksos and early 18th-Dynasty contexts. There is also some Mycenaean IIA (1600–1520) pottery in Cyprus and some of the major cities in Syro-Palestine, which Helck plausibly argues indicates some import of ointments and oil from the Aegean.[17] The possibility that metals were being exported from Greece at this time will be discussed below. In any event, there appears to have been less trade in the later part of the century. This would seem to indicate that after the break-up of the Hyksos common culture, which included the opponents of the Hyksos, around 1570, there was a period of some decades of relative isolation for the Aegean.

EGYPTIAN EXPANSION
FROM C. 1520 TO 1420

In his short reign *c.* 1528–1518, the pharaoh Tuthmōsis I campaigned widely in territories both to the south and the north of Egypt. It is possible that, in the immediate aftermath of these successes, there were diplomatic and trading contacts between Egypt and the Levant, with Crete and the rest of the Aegean. Some Mycenaean IIB and Minoan II (1520–1470 BC) pottery, though not so much as in later centuries, has been found in Cyprus and the Levant but none has been found in Egypt.[18] There are also a number of finds of Egyptian objects in the Aegean, which could have arrived at that time. An Egyptian object that may date from this time is an alabaster amphora found at the royal *tholos* at Vaphio in Lakonia in a LHII context. This tomb also contained the famous gold 'Vaphio Cups' with men and wild and tame oxen.[19] At *tholos* tombs at the Prosymna, three miles from Mycenae, a considerable number of Egyptian objects have been found from LHI to LHIII (1675–1220 BC). Of these, many Egyptian beads, some fragments of a faience bowl and two fitting pieces of an alabaster vase are also associated with LHII pottery, and therefore arrived between 1600 and 1520.[20]

The alabaster vase bears a resemblance to ten such vases found with small objects in the Cretan Royal Tomb at Isopata, two miles north of the palace at Knossos. Pendlebury put this between LMI and LMII, that is, around 1520 BC.[21] However, it may be that the tomb belongs, as the archaeologist and specialist in Egyptian relations with the Aegean Eric Cline claims, to between LMII and LMIII, that is, *c.* 1470.[22]

It is at this latter point that traces of contacts in both directions pick up dramatically. There are a large number of high-quality Egyptian stone vessels from cemeteries around Knossos from this later period.[23] The best known of these is a superb alabaster amphora with an engraved cartouche of Tuthmōsis III.[24] The absolute dating here of 1470–1430 for the LMIIIA1 context in which this was found would mean that it was buried soon after its manufacture and import rather than a century later, as would be required by the chronology of the *Cambridge Ancient History;* this is a pattern of alleged delay that we shall see with a number of other Near Eastern finds in the Aegean. Thus, the evidence from the named and the other stone vases would fit with the period of great contact in the full or effective reign of Tuthmōsis III from 1470 to 1450 BC.

The history of Egypt during his reign and that of his stepmother Ḥashepsowe was outlined in the last chapter,[25] and it will be remembered that there appears to have been a considerable difference between Ḥashepsowe's reign, in which there seems to have been little Egyptian activity to the north, and that of Tuthmōsis III, in which the pharaoh launched repeated attacks on the rulers of Syro-Palestine and his fleets may well have sailed in the Aegean.

As we saw in the last chapter, the century 1475–1375 BC seems to have been one of Egyptian suzerainty over the Aegean. Egyptian finds at or near Knossos, from the ceramic period LM/LHIIIA which covers the same century, confirm the accuracy of tomb paintings, with their detailed pictures of Cretan metal-work being offered to the Egyptian throne.[26] Confirmation can also be provided from other finds, although most of this evidence is difficult to assess. For instance, a considerable number of scarabs with the cartouches of Tuthmōsis III have been found on Mainland Greece. However, most if not all of these are reproductions made during the Saite Dynasty from 664–525 BC.[27] There are also many Egyptian objects found in LHIIIA contexts from Mycenae and elsewhere. Similarly, Mycenaean pottery from this period is found widely in the Levant.

This increase in the number of finds must be seen in a larger context. In the first place, LHIIIA pottery has been found over a wide geographical range, stretching from Italy and Malta to Cyprus, Syria and Egypt.[28] Unfortunately, however, this ceramic period covers not only the later reign of Tuthmōsis III but also those of his successors Amenōphis II (1450–1427); Tuthmōsis IV (1427–1419); and, more importantly, those of Amenōphis III (1419–1381) and the first half of that of Amenōphis IV, better known as Akhenaton (1381–1364). As it is likely that most of this pottery came from the last two reigns and belonged to the subdivision LMIIIA2, this will be discussed below after some consideration of the international situation after *c.* 1420 BC.

PELOPS AND THE ACHAIANS: EVIDENCE FROM ANATOLIA

After the death of Tuthmōsis III, there was some recession in Egyptian power. This was not accompanied by a resurgence of Egypt's old enemy in the north, the Mitanni, but by a revival of the Hittite empire under its king Tudhaliyas II, who may have had Hurrian ancestry and certainly introduced considerable amounts of Hurrian civilization into Hittite culture. During the 1440s and 1430s Tudhaliyas II asserted Hittite power against both Egyptians and Mitanni and became predominant not only in Cilicia but over much of North Syria. Even more interesting from our point of view was the Hittite expansion to the west.[29]

The discussion in the last chapter omitted a set of Bronze Age documents which was not directly relevant to relations between Egypt, the Levant and the Aegean – that of the Hittites. Hittite records report that sometime in the second half of the 15th century BC King Tudhaliyas II defeated a coalition of states in Arzawa, the old enemy of the Hittites in the west of Anatolia. However, this specific league was subsumed under the title Assuwa.[30] The origin of this name and the derivation of 'Asia' from it have been discussed above in Chapter V, where the immense complexities of the Egyptian names ḭsy and ḭsy were also considered.[31] Envoys from ḭsy were among those offering tribute to Tuthmōsis III. Wolfgang Helck is adamant that this cannot be Assuwa, but the Hittitologist Gurney is not so sure, and there would seem to be some plausibility in the notion of a confederation under threat from the Hittites offering tribute to the pharaoh.[32]

Given the name Assuwa and its connection to Asia, it is interesting to note the Greek traditions that Pelops came from Asia.[33] Pindar connected Pelops' father Tantalos to Lydia, others maintained he came from Phrygia and Pelops himself was supposed to come from Paphlagonia.[34] The precise location of Pelops' origins is difficult to pin down but the general region is clearly Northwest Anatolia.

Tradition maintained that Pelops was the father of Atreus, who was in turn the father of Agamemnon and Menelaos. These heroic kings were supposed to have reigned at the time of the Trojan War in the second half of the 13th century. Thus a precise acceptance of the tradition, which – estimating thirty years for a generation – would have Pelops born around 1330, cannot be reconciled with an emergence of the Pelopids before 1400 BC. Furthermore, the spread of Pelops and his descendants from his base in Elis to rule Mycenae, Sparta and other cities in the Peloponnese, would seem to have been a process over more than sixty years. Thus, some degree of compression would seem to be involved in the traditional story. Stubbings goes as far as to argue that Pelops should be seen as belonging to the Shaft Grave period, which he put in the 16th century BC – in this book it is seen as in the early 17th.[35] Either way, this is excessive, if only because of the clear traditions that the Danaan Dynasty, associated with the hero Perseus, ruled Mycenae a long time before being replaced by the Pelopids.

It would seem to me plausible to place if not Pelops, then the beginning of the invasion or invasions he represented at the end of the 15th century with the Aḫḫiyawa or the Achaioi (Achaians). In the early 20th century AD, the Achaians were seen as the 'tall, fair-haired, grey-eyed' 'master race' of Greece.[36] In Homer, they are rather less dramatically distinct. Nevertheless, the Homeric Achaians were clearly associated with the Pelopid kings Agamemnon and Menelaos and the expedition they led to Troy.[37] Pindar made explicit what was implicit in Homer, that Pelops was their ancestor.[38] Even so, it is difficult to make an altogether clear distinction between them and the Danaans in the *Iliad*. In later times, the name Achaia came to be associated with particular localities, notably Achaia Phthiotis in Thessaly, the home of Achilles, and Achaia in the Northern Peloponnese. There were other smaller settlements, usually described as refuges from the later Dorian conquest of the Peloponnese.[39] There was also a strong and early tradition that there had been Achaians in Crete.[40]

The association with the Pelopids and the tradition that Pelops had come from Asia, as well as Hesiod's belief that, as sons of Xouthos, they were closely connected to the Ionians, who in Classical times inhabited the central section of the west coast of Anatolia, led 19th-century scholars to see the Achaians as having come with Pelops from Anatolia.[41] This hypothesis was strikingly strengthened in 1924 with the discovery by the German linguist Emil Forrer of the reference in Hittite texts to a people living to the west of Anatolia called Aḫḫiyawa, whom he immediately identified with the Achaioi.[42] This inherent plausibility has been increased by the discovery of striking parallels between legends about Pelops and Hittite texts, which will be discussed below.

Nevertheless, 'sound' and sceptical scholars demanded 'proof' for Forrer's claim. It is possible that they were partially motivated by a distaste for the establishment of a link between the 'European' Homeric heroes and the cuneiform-using Near East, even though the affront was mitigated by the fact that the Hittites were speaking a language close to Indo-European. The topic became one of violent controversy and even today there are occasional sputters of opposition. However, the decipherment of Linear B, the indubitable establishment of the Mycenaeans as Greek-speaking and the confirmation from a Linear B tablet that the term Achaian dates back to the Bronze Age have tilted the battle decisively in favour of the identification of the Aḫḫiyawa with the Achaioi.[43]

With this connection established, it is possible to begin to reconstruct the history of Pelops and the Achaians. The name Aḫḫiyawa or Aḫḫiya first appears in Hittite texts referring to the reign of Tudhaliyas II, who, as mentioned above, had defeated the confederacy of Assuwa in the same region.[44] It would seem likely, though by no means certain, that there is some connection between the two, and that the Aḫḫiyawa were survivors or incorporated survivors of the earlier opponents of the Hittites. The text refers to the activities of two freebooters in Western Anatolia, one Madduwatas, who flourished nominally within the Hittite Empire and the other Attarassiyas, an Aḫḫiyawa, or to be precise an Aḫḫiya.

According to one episode in this text, Attarassiyas drove Madduwatas out of his country, but Tudhaliyas prevented further pursuit and granted Madduwatas the land of Mt. Zippasla, a name not known elsewhere in the Hittite records.[45] It is fascinating to compare this with the Greek legend of Pelops who, as ruler of Paphlagonia, was expelled by Ilos of Phrygia and retired to the Lydian Mt. Sipylos.[46] This is a wonderful example of how legends can both preserve and garble. Greek tradition appears to have preserved no memory of the huge and long-lasting Hittite Empire, which never recovered from its defeat by the Sea Peoples in the 12th century. Nevertheless, the specific idea of refuge around Mt. Zippasla/Sipylos associated with a man of Aḫḫiya(wa)/Achaia must be a genuine survival, even if, as so often happens in such cases, the roles are reversed and the refuge, which according to the early sources was given to the opponent of the Aḫḫiya(wa), was given in the legend to Pelops the ancestor of the Achaians.

There is another even more striking Greek mythological parallel with a Hittite text – a letter written by a Hittite king – from around 1300 BC. This is concerned with the brother of the king of Aḫḫiya(wa) called Tawagalawas, who lived in the city of Millawanda, generally considered to be Miletos in Western Anatolia. Tawagalawas appears to have considered becoming a vassal of the Hittite king but in the end did not do so. The letter contains a curious passage in which the Hittite king writes to the king of Aḫḫiya(wa): 'This charioteer used to step on the chariot with me and with your brother Tawagalawas'.[47]

This idea of sharing an enemy's chariot also occurs in a legend about Pelops, in which there is a complex story about his alliance, and quarrel with and murder of his charioteer Myrtilos.[48] As Wolfgang Helck points out, the similarities to charioteers' changes of alliances are made stronger still by the parallel between Myrtilos and the Hittite royal name Mursilis.[49] Hans Güterbock, the Hittitologist who has written most extensively on the Aḫḫiyawa texts, believes that the letter containing references to Tawagalawas was probably written by King Ḫattusilis III, who reigned c. 1286–1265 BC. The evidence for this preference is by no means clear-cut and the readiness with which the later dating has been accepted must be seen in the context of the general enthusiasm for low dating. Thus it remains quite possible that the king in whose reign it was written was Mursilis II (c. 1346–1320 BC), the father and indirect predecessor of Ḫattusilis III, who conquered Western Anatolia and whose influence may have brought about the end of Troy VI.[50] Whether or not this is the case, there would seem little doubt that the Greek legends were preserving a garbled version of what we now know to have been historical reality or at least the contemporary propaganda version of it.

It would seem, then, that we have two sources of written evidence about the Aḫḫiyawa/Achaians between 1450 and 1200 BC – the Hittite documents and the Greek legends which we can put in conjunction with the evidence from archaeology. It was noted above that sometime around 1430 BC the Hittite king Tudhaliyas II defeated an alliance of states in Northwest Anatolia under the general name of Assuwa. Given the first appearance of the name Aḫḫiyawa shortly after this and the association of Pelops with Asia, it would seem plausible to suggest that elements of the Assuwa alliance formed or were incorporated into the Aḫḫiyawa.[51] As a working hypothesis it would seem best to view the Aḫḫiyawa initially as a category of inhabitants of Western Anatolia and the Aegean beyond Hittite royal control. Fairly soon, however, it seems to have denoted people in that category who spoke Greek. Greek tradition is quite clear that the power of the Pelopids spread gradually in Greece and never encompassed the whole territory. Thus, although Aḫḫiyawa meant 'Greek' to the Hittites, in Greece itself 'Achaian' meant only the Hellenized West Anatolians from the Hittite marches who came to dominate Southern Greece. This confusion means that when the Hittite texts mention the king of Aḫḫiyawa, they are almost certainly referring to the king of Argos in Mycenae, but we cannot be sure whether he was a Danaan Perseid or an Achaian Pelopid.

Pelops 'The Crown Prince'?

The Greek legends parallel to the Hittite texts show that the name Pelops was used to refer to a number of historical figures from a considerable period. Given the long-term Egyptian influence in both the Aegean and Northwestern Anatolia, I would tentatively propose an etymology for the name from Pꜣ rpꜥ(t) (the hereditary noble or heir). In 13th-century Egypt it meant 'Crown Prince'.[52] Such a title would certainly fit the 'royal' descent from Tantalos. It would also tally nicely with the legend concerning Tantalos, who sacrificed his son Pelops to entertain the gods; Zeus later reassembled and revived him.[53]

This theme of a kingly father offering his most precious belonging by sacrificing his eldest son and heir has been touched on in Volume 1.[54] As such, I think deriving Pelops from Pꜣ rpꜥ(t) would be parallel to deriving the name of another sacrificed or nearly sacrificed heir, Isaac, Yiṣḥâq or Yiśḥâq, from the Akkadian iššaku – Sumerian ensi – 'prince', rather than from the folk etymology 'he will laugh', yiṣḥâq. Although there is a phonetic difficulty in the distinction between q and k, the semantic basis for the identification is strengthened by the fact that Isaac's mother was called Sarah which means 'queen'. This increases the likelihood of the son's being called 'prince'. Martin Nilsson provides further support for this in his discussion of the names Hera and Herakles. 'The folk tale (unlike the myth) gives commonly no individual name to its heroes but only one which denotes his class or social standing e.g. "the king", "the princess" etc.'[55] In Volume 4, I shall try to make the case that this distinction is often not one between noble myths and peasant folktales but one between traditions which have preserved titles of class or social standing in their own languages and those that continued to use titles in old languages, which the tellers of the tales or mythographers do not know. Both Pelops and Isaac appear to fit the latter case.

The Achaians and the Danaans

Whether or not these etymologies are correct, we should not take the Greek genealogies too literally and it is quite possible that there were Achaians not merely in Western Anatolia but in the Aegean area as a whole from the end of the 15th century rather than merely in the 13th century as suggested by Greek tradition. The Homeric picture of a powerful Achaian king based on Mycenae and with family control is given historical substance from the existence of a mid-13th-century treaty between King Tudhaliyas IV (c. 1265–1240) and the king of

Amurru in Syria. In this, the Hittite monarch listed as his equals the rulers of Egypt, Babylonia and Assyria, and named and then crossed out the title of the king of Aḫḫiyawa. This negation was clearly not the result of moral obloquy, because Assyria, the constant enemy of the Hittite Empire, was included. Some scholars have argued that the deletion was because destructions in Greece had lessened or annihilated the power of the Achaian king.[56] This could possibly refer to the first war between Thebes and Argos, which seems to have taken place about this time. It would seem unlikely to relate to the final destruction of Thebes, which, as will be argued below, must have taken place after 1235. Still less could it refer to the Trojan War which was even later. We shall see in the next chapter that there may well have been interesting connections between Thebes and Assyria. Another possible reason for the deletion of Aḫḫiyawa is that, though it was important, it was not sufficiently powerful or was simply too disunited to rate as a 'world power'. In this case the Achaian kingdom at that time would have been at the bottom of the first league and the top of the second.

There are no Hittite reports of Danaans although, as mentioned in the last chapter, Egyptians referred to Tanaya at least until the 12th century, when they are included among the Peoples of the Sea.[57] The iḳwš, who are generally equated with the Aḫḫiyawa and the Achaians, appear among those who invaded Egypt in the 5th year of Merneptah c. 1231 BC.[58] There are difficulties with the chronology of the following story from Homer, because this raid by the iḳwš would seem to be two decades too early. It is remarkable that Homer described a violent and bloody raid on Egypt by Achaians soon after the Trojan War, which according to this book ended c. 1210 BC. Furthermore, just as Merneptah claimed to have crushed the invaders, Odysseus reported that, defeated by the Egyptians, his comrades 'were led up to their city alive to work perforce'.[59] This fits the abundantly attested Egyptian practice of using foreign prisoners in construction work. Odysseus himself was treated very differently:

> [I] went towards the chariot horses of the king. I clasped and kissed his knee and he delivered me and took pity on me, and setting me in his chariot took me weeping to his home. Verily full many rushed upon me with their ashen spears, eager to slay me for they were exceeding angry. But he warded them off. . . . There then I stayed for seven years, and much wealth did I gather among the Egyptians.[60]

H. L. Lorimer, in her encyclopaedic *Homer and the Monuments*, pointed out that Odysseus' experience had been paralleled many decades earlier by a certain Ynn Trš of the Turša/Tyrsanoi – probably Etruscan barbarians – who repeatedly attacked Egypt, but went on to become a high official under the pharaoh Sethos I (1309–1291).[61] The fact that Odysseus was lying when he told this story makes it even more interesting, as it means that Homer at least believed that it was a plausible common experience.

Despite the use of iḳwš (Achaians) by Merneptah, we saw in the last chapter that the Dnn (Danaans) reappear in the invasion of the 8th year of Ramessēs III *c.* 1174.[62] Thus, just as Homer appears to have used Danaans and Achaians with at least some degree of interchangeability, by the end of the 13th century BC the Egyptians seem to have been very uncertain as to the precise meanings of these names, although the fact that Tanaya was usually seen as an organized kingdom and the iḳwš only as invaders would appear significant. Nevertheless, it would seem that, by the 13th century, Achaians ruled the Argolid and had gained a pre-eminent place in Greece as a whole.

ARCHAEOLOGICAL TRACES
OF THE ACHAIANS

From the middle of the 15th century (LHIIIA), the Cretan settlements in Southwest Anatolia, notably at Miletos and Rhodes but also at Kos and a nearby peninsula as well as other islands, begin to be replaced – sometimes with and sometimes without destructions – by Mycenaean ones.[63] These new settlements remained in touch with Crete but there was also considerable trade with Mainland Greece throughout this period. Given the explicit reference to Milawanda (that is, Miletos) in the Hittite text concerning Tawagalawas, there is little doubt that the people of this region comprised part or all of the Aḥḥiyawa during the period 1470–1370.

It is hard to find archaeological traces of the Asiatic Achaians in Greece or Crete. It is possible that the partial destruction of the palace at Knossos was the result of an Achaian conquest at the end of LMIIIA1, around 1425 BC. According to both Hesiod and Homer, Crete was supposed to have Achaians as part of its population, although there is no explicit mention of Danaans on the island. However, it may well be that they were indicated by the name Pelasgian, the Pelasgians being 'Hellenic' according to Hesiod and 'goodly' according to Homer.[64] Thus, a number of possibilities remain open. Firstly, the Danaans may have dominated the island at the beginning of the LMIIIA and have ruled it for only a few decades before the arrival of the Achaians. This would certainly fit with the evidence from the Egyptian tomb paintings.

Alternatively, Danaans may have conquered Knossos with the destruction of LMIIIA1 and the Achaians then slipped in imperceptibly at a later stage. Given the likelihood that the expansion of the Achaians took place in the 15th century, this would require raising the destruction to before 1450, which would be difficult. Yet another possibility is that the Egyptians were unable to distinguish between the two and that they called Achaians Tanaya. This would mean that there was no Danaan conquest of Crete and that there had been only one Greek invasion, that of the Achaians. All that is certain is that Greek speakers came to rule Knossos during the LMIIIA period between 1475 and 1375 BC and, given their later prominence, it is probable that Achaians dominated the island for most of that period until the invasion of the Dorians in the 12th century.

Tradition is clear that the Pelopids' first area of control on Mainland Greece was Elis – in the Northeast of the Peloponnese – and that their rule of Mycenae and the Western Peloponnese came later. The use of Cyclopean masonry, which has plausibly been derived from Anatolia, would seem to have begun in Greece during LHIIIA. However, the technique was clearly spread far beyond the regions controlled by the Pelopids and cannot be used as an indicator of their presence.[65]

Frank Stubbings argues that the destruction of the palace or palaces at Thebes at the end of LHIIIB1 was the work of the new masters of Mycenae.[66] According to the chronology used here LHIIIB1 ended about 1300 BC, but Stubbings believed that this was about 1250 BC and, in making this assessment, he was basing himself at least partly on tradition. According to the legends mentioned in Homer and widespread in Athenian tragedy, the war of the 'Seven against Thebes', which took place a generation before the city's final destruction, involved Adrastos the king of Argos, who had many Anatolian connections and might therefore have been the first Pelopid to rule Argos. However, Adrastos and the Seven against Thebes have so many mythic characteristics it is hard to believe in their historicity or base substantial historical constructions upon them.[67] Nevertheless, I see no reason to doubt that there were two sieges of Thebes in the 13th century and that some of the heroes involved were historical figures and that the second siege ended in the city's destruction.

To return to the general topic of this section, there seems to be no archaeological evidence to indicate the arrival of the Pelopids and the establishment of their new dynasties. It would seem that there was no difference of material culture between Danaans and Achaians. Similarly, linguists have not detected an Achaian dialect. However, it will be tentatively argued in Volume 3 that this was what was later known as Ionian. It is interesting to note that in Antiquity it was believed that there was a close though complicated relationship between the Achaians and the Ionians.[68]

MYCENAEANS AND HITTITES

One indication that the Achaians were influential in Greece from the middle of the 15th century BC is the surprising lack of evidence of any trade between the Aegean and the areas of Hittite control during the ceramic periods LMIIIA and LMIIIB (c. 1470–1230 BC). As we shall be discussing below, Mycenaean pottery of these periods has been found over a huge geographical range from Sardinia to Syria and Nubia. In particular, as mentioned above, it has been found in considerable quantities along the western coast of Anatolia, in states that were generally hostile to the Hittite Empire. However, the only site where it has been found in the Anatolian Highlands is Masat in the northeast and Eric Cline argues that this too was beyond Hittite control at the time.[69] It would be plausible, in fact, to link it to the Mycenaean connections with the Trialeti culture in the present-day Georgia.[70] In any event, the general point is irrefutable – not a single shard of Mycenaean pottery has been found at the Hittite capital at Boğazköy. Equally, only one Anatolian object from this period has been found at Mycenae. It is a steatite hemispheroid semi-bulla or seal, engraved with hieroglyphic Luvian. There is no doubt that the piece is Anatolian and most of the territories using Luvian script were usually under Hittite control. Even so, Cline is quite right to point out that it does not come from the Hittite heartland.[71]

Mycenaean pots travelled far and documentary sources make it clear that Hittites were active traders.[72] Thus, the lack of archaeological evidence for exchange of material goods would seem to be significant, even though we know that at least one king of Aḫḫiyawa sent a present to King Ḫatusilis III c. 1280 BC.[73] A number of explanations have been suggested for this absence. Some scholars have proposed that it was because Mycenaeans and Hittites were unknown to each other. This, however, is preposterous. Even if one does not accept that the Aḫḫiyawa texts, indicating intimate and frequent confrontations, refer to Greeks, there is no doubt that there was contact between the two in Western Anatolia in general and at Miletos in particular. There, for instance, a Hittite cap was found drawn on a locally made Mycenaean shard.[74] It is also inconceivable that people from the two societies did not come into contact in Cyprus, which was often under Hittite suzerainty during their period but contains masses of Mycenaean pottery made in the Peloponnese.

A more plausible explanation is that there was trade between the two but that it was in perishable commodities, such as textiles and metals that were not carried in pots.[75] Even more probable is the likelihood that neither side felt the need to trade extensively with the other. Although the Mediterranean agricultural products of the Aegean, like the olive and the grape, could not be grown in Highland Anatolia, Hittites could obtain them more easily from Cyprus and Syria which were closer and more susceptible to their political control. Similarly, neither region had significant amounts of gold or tin but both had their own supplies of copper, silver and lead, and, while the Hittites were using iron, the Mycenaeans were still in the Bronze Age, though they made amulets and jewels of iron.[76]

It would seem likely, however, that this economic independence was reinforced by political will. The bitter rivalry between the Hittites on the one hand and Arzawa and the Aḫḫiyawa on the other has been mentioned above. Thus, there would seem every reason for there to have been political blockades or boycotts. We know from letters from the Hittite king to officials in Ugarit that the activities of merchants were of great concern to the political powers and that the latter tried to regulate their activities very closely.[77]

Even more interesting is a treaty between Tudhaliyas IV (c. 1265–1240) and the king of Amurru in Northern Syria. The treaty is directed against Assyria but one line reads: 'Let no ship of Aḫḫiyawa go to him.'[78] There is little doubt that this was chiefly directed against Tukulti-Ninurta I of Assyria (1244–1208), the conqueror of Babylon, who had seized Commagene, north of Mesopotamia, which had been a protectorate of the Hittites. Nevertheless, it is also a directive to blockade Aḫḫiyawan ships and block the overland transport of their goods.[79] There is no doubt that the blockade was not merely symbolic; for example, the lead in a huge block of some thirty kilos found at the Assyrian capital of Ashur, inscribed with the name Tukulti-Ninurta, came from Laurion in Attika.[80] Thus, significant amounts of metal must have been transported, before the blockade or in spite of it. The possibility of diplomatic relations, including the sending of precious gifts, between the Assyrian king and Thebes in Greece will be discussed below.

Both Machteld Mellink and Frank Stubbings have tried to link the Hittite blockade of Aḫḫiyawa to the relative lack of Mycenaean LHIIIA and LHIIIB pottery in Cilicia in Southeastern Anatolia, which was usually under Hittite control.[81] More recently Sherratt and Crouwel have made the argument still tighter by showing that, while very little Mycenaean pottery has been found at Kazanli and Tarsus from the 14th and 13th centuries when the Hittites dominated the region, there were considerable quantities of Mycenaean pottery in the post-Hittite levels.[82] This, however, might indicate not trade but the actual presence of Greek raiders and settlers in Cilicia in the migrations of the Peoples of the Sea.[83] However, their conclusion that 'in Anatolia there appears to be a strong inverse relation between the amount of Late Helladic IIIA-B pottery and [the] degree of Hittite control' is very convincing.[84]

Eric Cline goes on from this to make another critically important point which had already been raised by Stubbings in 1951:

> Furthermore, in Northern Syria, in an area midway between the coastal and extreme inland regions, one finds LHIIIA Mycenaean pottery but little or no LHIIIB pottery. At least six sites are involved: Khan Sheikhoun, Hama, Qatna, Ebla, Carcemish, and Qadesh. All have LHIIIA pottery but only two, Qadesh and Carcemish, report any LHIIIB pottery; and each of these has only one or two identifiable LHIIIB sherds. This is the only area in the entire Syro-Palestinian region where such a discrepancy is immediately apparent. It is also the only major region in Syro-Palestine which came under direct Hittite control. This event happened about 1370 B.C.[85]

Cline appears to see the break between LHIIIA and LHIIIB as at around 1300 BC. Using an adjusted chronology, however, I see the break at *c.* 1365, which then serves as a double demarcation, reflecting both the change of pottery styles and the change of political control of this region.

UGARIT AND CYPRUS

While inland North Syria came under direct Hittite control, Ugarit came under Hittite suzerainty. From the time of the conquests of Tuthmōsis III around 1470 to the weakening of Egyptian power after Akhenaten around 1360 BC, the city was in the Egyptian sphere of influence. At the end of this period, the palace was destroyed and a magnificent new one was built for wealthy and powerful kings, who, nevertheless, acknowledged the suzerainty of the Hittites.

While it is true that Egyptian cultural influence seems to have survived the city's change of political sphere for some time and that it revived after the peace treaty between the Hittites and Egypt in 1284, there is no doubt that there was hostility between the two powers for most of this period.[86]

The absence of Greek names from the extensive corpus of Ugaritic texts was noted in the last chapter. However, a considerable quantity

of LHIII pottery has been found in the city, so much in fact that
the earlier excavators of the site used it to postulate Greek colonies
there. This is now generally discredited, as the tombs in which they
were found belong to a Levantine tradition going back to the 3rd
millennium.[87]

Anita Yannai has suggested that one reason for the absence of
Greek names may have been the Hittite blockade.[88] This may well be
true for the LHIIIB period after 1365, and the treaty between Tudhaliyas IV and Amurru discussed above makes it likely that a boycott
of Aḥḥiyawa shipping continued as an anti-Assyrian move after hostilities had ended between the Hittites and Egypt in 1284. It would
not, however, explain the situation when Ugarit was under Egyptian
influence from 1470 to 1370. One possibility, mentioned in the last
chapter, is that Greeks were present in the city at that time, but there
are no direct records from this period.[89]

Regardless of the local situations in Syria, a general economic pattern appears to have been established throughout the East Mediterranean from the beginning of LHIIIA that lasted until the end of
LHIIIB c. 1220 BC. For example, the amount of Mycenaean pottery
found on Cyprus is quite staggering, especially after the beginning
of LHIIIA2 (c. 1420). As the archaeologist of Cyprus H. W. Catling
wrote:

> If we take the island as a whole, the quantity of Mycenaean pottery
> of the IIIA2 and IIIB phases is enormous. . . . Rich as the sites in
> Egypt and along the Syro-Palestinian littoral may be in the same
> material, I doubt whether the sum of all their finds would approach
> that of Cyprus.[90]

Åström has even given the precise figure of 3,445 for the number
of Greek pots found there.[91] The quantities have been so huge that
scholars have quite rightly suggested that many of them could have
been made in Cyprus itself. However, both spectrographic and neutron activation analysis have consistently shown that the overwhelming majority were made in the Peloponnese. (The same is also true for
a sample taken in Israel.)[92] Thus, there is every reason to suppose that
the Mycenaean pots found in Egypt and elsewhere in the Levant were
made in Greece.

MYCENAEAN EXPANSION AND THE
CONQUESTS OF TUTHMŌSIS III

Although Mycenaean pots found in the Near East were plentiful, as
the archaeologist and specialist in ancient Mediterranean relations

Vronwy Hankey and Anita Yannai have noted, they were always accompanied by larger numbers of Cypriot ware, and Cypriot pots were sometimes found on their own. Thus, there was a huge increase of trade from both Cyprus and Greece to the Levant and Egypt from around 1470 BC.[93] Hankey, assuming that LHIII began c. 1400, argued that the Cypriot ware appeared first in the reign of Tuthmōsis III.[94] However, now that it would seem that the Mycenaean ceramic period began c. 1470, the arrival of the two would seem contemporary.

Although some large, coarse Minoan stirrup jars found in Cyprus and at Ugarit could have been used only as containers, most of the Mycenaean pots were small and fine and were probably valued in their own right. How are we to explain their presence and likely functions? The conventional view is that this could all be explained in terms of Mycenaean enterprise. As H. W. Catling put it in the *Cambridge Ancient History*,

> Whatever the historical facts may be that are represented by the sack of Knossos c. 1400 BC, that catastrophe seems to have cleared the way for a great Mycenaean trading expansion into the east Mediterranean, of which Cyprus became the focus. What had been a trickle in the late fifteenth century became a flood in the fourteenth. . . . Mycenaean Greece maintained a great demand for Egyptian and Levantine merchandise and a regular trading association was built up between the two areas. In the process, Aegean merchants learnt the value of the ports in South and East Cyprus both as markets and as bases of operations for their trafficking further afield. The dealings of these merchants can be traced from the 'Amūq plain in north Syria to the Second Cataract in Egypt.[95]

While Catling is undoubtedly right to see the pottery as indicative of a market area which had Cyprus as an important centre, his other constructions are very flimsy. In the first place, pots do not have to be transported by their makers and this is especially true when, as in this case, the ware is not coarse and varied for domestic use but is fine and restricted to a limited number of types. Thus, in itself the spread of Mycenaean pottery around the East – and Central – Mediterranean is no more a sure indicator of Mycenaean presence or colonization than the world-wide spread of Chinese pottery in the 17th and 18th centuries AD indicated an expansion of Chinese military or political power. It does, however, indicate a trading system in which Chinese products played an important role.

The second major problem in Catling's scheme, which is shared by all other writers on this, comes on the question of dating. It is based on the convention that LHIIIA began *c.* 1400 and that the 'last' palace of Knossos fell *c.* 1380. It has been argued above that LHIIIA began *c.* 1470 and that the palace at Knossos survived to the last half of the 13th century.[96] Thus, while Mycenaeans took over Crete during the period 1470–1370, this is unlikely to have been the cause of the extraordinary expansion of trade networks that took place around the middle of the 15th century. A much more plausible reason for this would be the conquests of Tuthmōsis III and the establishment of an Egyptian empire in the Levant with a penumbra of states accepting Egyptian suzerainty, including Tanaya, Asy (Cyprus) and Ugarit. A text from the Amarna period in the 14th century refers to a similar relation with Arzawa in Western Anatolia.[97]

Thus, while the presence of Mycenaean pottery clearly went beyond the Egyptian sphere of influence in the Central Mediterranean, it stayed within it in the East: LMIIIA pottery is found in the Levant and Nubia but not in the Hittite Highlands of Anatolia. The French scholar Jean-Claude Courtois has suggested that this took place in a *Pax Mycenaica*.[98] Given the complete lack of evidence to back such a notion, the proposal can only be a testimony to the power of the Aryanist imagination. Nevertheless, in order for such a substantial trade network to flourish a zone of relative tranquillity would be necessary. The obvious candidate for this, for which we have considerable documentary evidence, is a *Pax Aegyptiaca* established by Tuthmōsis III and maintained by his successors for over a century.

THE MERCHANTS OF THE
MEDITERRANEAN IN THE
LATE BRONZE AGE?
Bass's challenge

I now want to consider the question of who transported the pottery and other goods. As I have made clear above, conventional wisdom has been that, since Mycenaean pots were transported, it must have been Mycenaeans who transported them. However, an equally strong case can be made for Levantine traders at this time and for Egyptians. In the last chapter we saw that Egypt had powerful fleets in the mid-15th century.[99] There is certainly no doubt that Egyptian tomb paintings of this time portray Syro-Palestinians bringing what appear to be Aegean as well as Levantine goods to Egypt.[100]

The idea that West Semites dominated trade at this time in the East Mediterranean was argued on the basis of the distribution of Canaanite jars by Virginia Grace, in an article in 1956, and more forcefully by

Jack Sasson ten years later in 1966. Sasson pointed out that these undecorated objects were clearly used as containers for other goods and
that their increasing appearance throughout the Aegean provided
sufficient archaeological backing for the knowledge of Levantine trade
found in the Ugaritic texts and their omission of any reference to a
Greek presence.[101] The argument was clearly very plausible. Nevertheless, as a Jewish Semitist and pupil of Cyrus Gordon, Sasson was
seen as partisan and not to be taken seriously.

The following year, however, new evidence for this thesis came
from an unimpeachably gentile source. George Bass, from Texas
A & M University, is now the leading American marine archaeologist;
then he was, as he describes himself, a naive graduate student 'with no
axe to grind'.[102] In 1967 Bass published his considered opinion that
the Late Bronze Age boat he and his colleagues had been excavating
off Cape Gelidonya in South Turkey was crewed by Levantines. He
based his conclusion on the Levantine origins of most of the pottery, weights, cylinder seals and other personal objects found on the
wreck.[103] The Gelidonya boat was quite small, 8 to 10 metres, and
seems to have belonged to a maritime bronze-smith functioning at the
very end of the period we are considering *c.* 1220. Nevertheless, Bass
added the evidence from it to what he saw as the mounting evidence
in favour of a major role for the Phoenicians in the Late Bronze Age:

> The distribution of Syrian cylinder seals, therefore, may be stronger
> evidence for Near Eastern trading ventures than the distribution of
> Mycenaean pottery for a monopoly of Mycenaean shipping.
>
> Phoenician merchant ships, including that at Gelidonya, would
> not have returned with empty holds to Cyprus and the Near East,
> and it is reasonable to assume that their cargoes consisted largely
> of Mycenaean pottery which often contained perishable goods. But
> what had the ships originally carried westward on their outbound
> voyages? No longer must we 'resort to guessing the nature of the
> Syrian merchandise received in exchange' for Mycenaean goods.[104]
> No longer can we say that 'few actual oriental objects have actually
> been found in Mycenaean Greece'.[105] It was metal above all, that ar-
> rived in Greece on ships such as that which sank at Gelidonya while
> carrying its cargo to the Aegean.
>
> I have shown that copper oxhide ingots were dealt with by Sem-
> ites, and not by Aegean merchants as commonly supposed. Buch-
> holz has suggested that bun ingots also were associated with Syrians,
> but that primitive form of bronze seems too widespread to be as-
> signed to any one people.
>
> Hoards of bronzes on the Greek Mainland, often containing
> fragments of oxhide ingots, may now be accepted as Phoenician

merchandise. The ingots and broken tools were, to be sure, usually picked up in Cyprus, but the bronzes were most often non-Aegean types which originated in the Near East, and we have further shown good cause to believe that the oxhide ingots were made to Phoenician specifications.[106]

Ivory and gold and cloth and spices also came from the East, as indicated by Semitic words for these items found on linear B tablets, and at least the latter may have formed part of the contents of the Canaanite jars which arrived in Greece during the fourteenth and thirteenth centuries.[107]

The absence of greater amounts of Near Eastern pottery in Greece is explained by the nature of this merchandise, for metals and cloth and ivory do not require pottery containers. Indeed we should expect to find few traces of any of these goods in the Aegean, for the cloth and spices have long since disappeared, and the metals and ivory would be found in altered form if preserved at all. This is borne out by excavation; Near Eastern ingots and implements appear mostly in founders' hoards which had, for one reason or another, been lost before being hammered or recast into typically Aegean forms. We may conclude that the extent of Mycenaean shipping has been highly overrated simply because her chief export commodities, pottery and goods shipped in pottery, left such durable remains. Although the goods received by the Mycenaeans are no longer so immediately apparent, they were certainly of equal value to the people who traded them.

I do not suggest that the Phoenicians held a monopoly on maritime trade during the Late Bronze Age, but that they played a major part in it.[108]

While later research would question some specifics in this statement, there is very little question today about the correctness of his overall conclusions. However, at the time, Bass's work was considered very startling and generally unwelcome.[109] This was especially the case as it seemed to provide empirical archaeological evidence to back two more abstract and schematic works: Astour's *Hellenosemitica* and a more cautious but distinctly 'orientalist' work *Agäis und Orient* by the Austrian archaeologist and ancient historian Fritz Schachermeyr, which came out at approximately the same time.

Bass's final statement was:

Further study is necessary, but our findings support the recent statement by Stubbings that 'there is no anachronism in Homer's Phoenicians; his picture of the heroic age would indeed be less true without them'.[110]

Muhly's response

It was against this and the general trend of orientalism represented by
Astour that James Muhly, the one Mediterranean archaeologist with a
background in Akkadian studies, wrote his passionate and learned article 'Homer and the Phoenicians: the relations between Greece and
the Near East in the Late Bronze and Early Iron Ages'. This article
has already been touched upon in Volume 1.[111] In it, rather than confront Bass's detailed arguments, Muhly took it as axiomatic that Mycenaean pots were shipped by Mycenaeans. Thus, according to Muhly,
the pottery indicated that Greeks had ample knowledge of the Levant
and this would explain any cultural borrowings. Furthermore, the
finds of Levantine and Egyptian objects in the Levant were merely
oriental bric-à-brac. In attempting to deal with the Ugaritic emphasis
on trade and implicitly with the lack of reference to any Greeks there,
he launched a violent attack on Jack Sasson:

> Reference has already been made to some of the questionable con-
> clusions of his study, which is also marred by numerous factual
> errors. . . . The author, Jack Sasson, certainly does show that the
> Ugaritic and Akkadian texts from Ras Shamra [Ugarit] deal with
> matters of trade and commerce. This does not establish the impor-
> tance of Canaanite shipping in the eastern Mediterranean. Sasson
> feels that the Ugaritic and Alalakh texts do not mention any Ae-
> gean proper, ethnic or geographical names. He also remarks that
> 'Linear A and B documents record names that greatly resemble
> those that were current in Northern Syria at the same epoch'. His
> conclusion is: 'that Mycenaean trade, at least with Syria, was either
> maintained by Canaanites or, more likely, conducted in places such
> as Rhodes and Cyprus.' Yet, assuming that the above observations
> are valid, does it not logically follow that the trade was controlled by
> the Mycenaeans? The Near Eastern texts betray no knowledge of
> the Aegean world. The Mycenaean texts demonstrate a knowledge
> of Near Eastern languages and perhaps even of Near Eastern place
> names. This makes Greece the active participant, the Near East the
> passive partner in the trade relations of the Late Bronze Age.[112]

I am afraid to say that Muhly's logic escapes me. Although it is just
possible that they were all slaves, the presence of Semitic and Egyptian
gentilic names in Crete and Greece would suggest to me – as it does to
Astour and Sasson – that there were Near Easterners in the Aegean
rather than vice versa. As mentioned above, I think that in the late
14th and 13th centuries, Ugarit may have had fewer Greeks than

other parts of the Levant. Nevertheless, Astour and Sasson are quite right to point out that the textual evidence as it stands gives no indication of Greek presence in the region.

Muhly is also wrong when he claims that the 'Near Eastern texts betray no knowledge of the Aegean world'. In the last chapter I mentioned the Ugaritic *tamkarum* Sinarenu, who had licence to trade with Crete [Kptr] and in fact Kptr, the biblical Kaphtor, appears quite frequently in Ugaritic theological texts as the dwelling place of the craftsman god Ktr w Ḥss.[113] Muhly does not mention the Egyptian texts which betrayed a considerable knowledge of Aegean geography at this time. Given the close relations between the Levantine coast and Egypt in these centuries and the fact that much if not most of Egyptian contact with the Aegean went via the Levant, it is inconceivable that the Canaanites knew less.

Muhly's linguistic arguments are equally improbable. The Semitic names for luxury goods found in the Aegean indicate influence from the Near East to Greece not the other way around. While this does not tell us who transmitted this influence, the etymologies cannot be used to make 'Greece the active participant'.

The relative academic power of Muhly, as opposed to that of Astour, Bass and Sasson, meant that for many years his arguments (despite their inherent implausibility) were not seriously scrutinized or challenged. After such rough treatment, all three men moved on to safer scholarly pastures. However, as we shall see, Bass much later returned to his work on the Bronze Age.

Yannai's negative synthesis

In the late 1970s, there was a recovery of the Broad Aryan Model and the beginnings of an acceptance of a significant 'Semitic' role in the ancient Mediterranean, and Muhly's conclusions began to be questioned. In Volume 1, I referred to the thesis by Muhly's student Randolph Peyton Helm (passed in 1980) in which he tentatively suggested that in the Early Iron Age 'the Oriental trade was largely, if not exclusively, in the hands of [Phoenician] merchants from Cyprus (and probably the Levantine coasts as well).'[114] This hypothesis was also suggested in a thesis completed in Oxford in 1983 by an Israeli scholar, Anita Yannai. Yannai is, as we shall see below, an archaeological positivist, believing that if a thing has not been found it cannot have existed in significant quantities. On these grounds she demolished the earlier idea that there had been Mycenaean colonies at Ugarit or elsewhere on the Levant. The presence of Aegean pottery in Levantine tombs of local style, in the absence of Ugaritic textual evidence to suggest the presence of Greeks, made her doubt that there had ever been any Mycenaeans there.[115] She also pointed out the lack of Linear B material on mercantile activities which was discussed in the last chapter.[116] Approving the detailed arguments put forward by the British archaeologist H. W. Catling against the existence of Mycenaean colonies in Cyprus, she argued that ones on the Levant were still less probable.[117]

Anita Yannai was equally scornful of the idea of Near Eastern colonies in the Aegean. In general she saw the number of Levantine and Egyptian objects in the Aegean from this period as insignificant. As for the latter, 'It is difficult to see in them more than occasional 'bric à brac' objects that could be picked up in the course of any overseas contact, not necessarily with Egypt.'[118] Yannai used the fact that the Egyptian tomb paintings of Aegean gifts – she too did not like the term tribute – from the mid-15th century corresponded to LMIB/LHIIA in her chronology to dismiss any connection between these formal presentations and Aegean pottery. Although Merrillees had suggested this connection earlier, Yannai pointed out that there was very little pottery of this period to be found anywhere in the Near East.[119] As noted above, this discrepancy is removed once one accepts Betancourt's high chronology, according to which the tomb paintings correspond with the beginning of LHIIIA. Pots from this period are abundantly represented in Egypt and the Levant. Anita Yannai, however, used the mismatch to play down the significance of both the paintings and the pottery and to deny that there had been any significant trade between Egypt and the Aegean in the Late Bronze Age.

She went on to investigate the various types of Levantine and Mesopotamian objects found in the Late Bronze Age Aegean – cylinder seals, ivories, Canaanite jars, smiting god statuettes. In each case (they will all be discussed below) she emphasized the paucity of the finds and argued that they could just as well have come from Cyprus as from points further east or south. She was similarly dismissive of any argument based on Semitic words found in Linear B, insisting that there was only an extremely small number of such loan words, perhaps just four. She argued that two of these – 'cumin' and 'sesame' – were too widespread for any significance to be placed on them, and the remaining *kurusu* (gold) and *kito* (clothes) could equally well have been transmitted indirectly as directly.[120]

Yannai then turned to the Mycenaean pottery found in the Levant, which she admitted was substantial. As has been mentioned above, however, she insisted that it was even more substantial on Cyprus and re-emphasized that the Mycenaean pottery in the Levant was always accompanied by Cypriot ware.[121]

Thus, Anita Yannai was convinced that there was no significant My-cenaean trade of any sort, let alone any colonization. She also believed that there was little evidence of direct influence on the Aegean from the Semitic Levant. However, she still needed to explain the signifi-cant quantities of Mycenaean pottery excavated in the Levant, which must have found their way there through trade. Thus, she took the line that everything hinged on Cyprus, arguing that Aegean goods had been shipped to the island and then reshipped to be transported to the Levant and beyond.

In this she followed her predecessors. The British archaeologist and interestingly original thinker on ancient Mediterranean connec-tions Vronwy Hankey had proposed that Mycenaean ships had sailed to Cyprus, where they had exchanged most of the goods held in their pots for the island's copper and some other goods contained in Cyp-riot containers. They had then sailed on to dispose of their remaining goods and the Cypriot ones in exchange for oriental goods, possibly the bric-à-brac discussed above.[122] Cumbersome though it was, this scheme explained the material evidence in terms of what Vronwy Hankey, like every one else at the time, assumed to be the Mycenaean dominance over trade. Yet, as Anita Yannai has pointed out, it pro-vides no reason for the Greeks to have sailed beyond Cyprus.

The Israeli archaeologist provided a different scheme. She saw Cy-prus as the 'terminus' of the Aegean trade. The Aegean needed Cyp-riot copper and the Levant had developed a taste for Mycenaean and Cypriot pottery. The exchange took place in Cyprus through 'middle-men'. Yannai, as we have seen, adamantly denies that there was any Levantine or Semitic influence on the Aegean: 'The two cultural spheres ultimately concerned in the exchange of goods had in effect minimal contacts with each other.'[123] At the same time, however, she was inclined to see these Cypriot 'middlemen' as Levantines. She pointed out that there is archaeological evidence of a Syro-Palestinian 'colony' or quarter of the town at Enkomi near the present Fama-gusta, which she plausibly saw as having a mercantile function.[124] While she rejected the Helleno-centrism of the Aegean archaeologists and was willing to accept the presence of Semitic-speaking seamen in the East Mediterranean, her goal has been essentially the same as theirs – how to reconcile the undoubted trading contacts demon-strated by archaeology with what at the time was the equal certainty that there had been no substantial oriental cultural influence on the Aegean. Yannai, however, was unable to square the circle and was forced to admit that Semitic-speaking Levantines would have had to have been central to both sections of her categorically divided trading network.

THE KAŞ SHIPWRECK: THE SAILORS

Anita Yannai has been exceptionally unlucky. Many of her hypotheses, like most of those of her predecessors, have been quickly proved wrong by the sensational discovery and excavation of a Late Bronze Age ship off Ulu Burun near Kaş in Southwestern Turkey in 1984. Some of the many critically important aspects of this find will be discussed in later sections. Here it is sufficient to say that the huge scale and magnificence of the cargo show that all previous attempts to assess the extent and significance of trade in the Late Bronze Age East Mediterranean have been hopelessly underestimated.

The ship should be dated to the very end of the LHIIIA2 period, or the reign of Akhenaton, 1381–1364. Most of the objects can be dated only roughly, to between the 15th and the 13th centuries BC. However, the Turkish underwater archaeologist Cemal Pulak has shown that the latest tolerable date for the pottery is the end of LHIIIA2, which he puts at c. 1350, although, following Betancourt, I would put it a decade or two earlier. The discovery of a gold scarab with the inscription 'the exquisite beauty of Aten, Nefertiti' would also seem to indicate this date. The American Egyptologist James Weinstein plausibly suggests that the discovery of the scarab strengthens the case that Akhenaton's famous wife Nefertiti became pharaoh at his death and that she should be identified with the ruler otherwise known as Smenkhkare. Weinstein prefers the lower datings for Akhenaton's reign, which, for reasons given above, I do not; I put his dates at 1381 to 1364 BC.[125] Thus the scarab was probably made between 1364 and 1361 BC. The fact that another gold object in frequent use was well worn and was found near the ship's scrap gold, suggesting that the scarab might have been lost decades after it was made, weighs less heavily with me than the pottery dating of LHIIIA2, which would fit perfectly with the scarab's having been in current use.[126] This earlier date for the Kaş wreck in turn would strengthen the argument that the scarab was not scrap metal but was an indication of some kind of official status to the voyage, which is what one would expect given the size of the vessel and the value of the cargo.[127]

Given this date and the association with royalty, George Bass's tentative connection of the wreck with the Amarna letter, in which the king of Alasia (he denies the common identification with Cyprus – though it would seem to fit very nicely here) promised the pharaoh: 'I will bring to thee as a present two hundred talents of copper as a present', seems quite plausible. Bass argued that this amount, which probably surpasses any other recorded in Bronze Age documents, would fit well with the estimated two hundred ingots on the Kaş wreck. He also pointed out that further letters refer to the offering of other luxury goods, of the type found at Kaş, from Alasia to Egypt.[128]

At this point we should consider the question of the origin of the ship and its crew. Cemal Pulak tentatively suggests that they were Mycenaean Greeks on the basis of Mycenaean pots found in the ship:

> [they] must have been personal drinking cups, for the forms are hardly suitable for use as containers. Along with a few other coarse-ware bowls not yet studied, it is almost certain that these Mycenaean ceramics constituted shipboard items; were they being reused by a Near Eastern crew or did they belong to a Mycenaean crew aboard the ship? The purpose of this pottery is uncertain, but the Mycenaean merchant's seal suggested to Bass the presence of a Mycenaean on board. The recently discovered globe pin (KW 570), so far unparalleled in the Near East, is of a type worn by Mycenaeans as part of their clothing. Cast of bronze and of negligible scrap value, the pin probably belonged to a Mycenaean, perhaps even the person who owned the seal. Was this person an official on a royal mission, a wealthy merchant returning from a successful trade venture, or was he only a passenger merchant of moderate means, perhaps with a small share of the cargo? . . . Whether or not the presence of a Mycenaean on the Ulu Burun ship suggests a like origin for the vessel itself remains unknown, but, for the time being, available evidence may slightly favor a Mycenaean home port for the Ulu Burun ship.[129]

While admitting the force of this argument, Bass believes that the discovery at Ulu Burun of twenty-three stone anchors of a Levantine or Cypriot type and of the 'oriental' wooden *pinax* of diptych (see below) makes a stronger case for a Near Eastern origin.[130] This ambiguity is also reflected in the finding of two adjacent swords, one Canaanite and the other Mycenaean. Thus, it would seem likely that there was a mixed crew.

The Greek component of the crew provides archaeological evidence of Mycenaean maritime activity to back the documentary evidence for it which, if lacking from the Aegean itself, is available from the Near East. There are tomb paintings showing men of Kftiw and Mycenaeans bringing tribute that must have come from overseas. The Hittite king Tudhaliyas IV in the 13th century saw it as normal to find ships of Ahhiyawa coming to the Syrian coast. In addition, the Egyptian records of Ikwš invasions by sea are echoed by Homer's description of Odysseus' sea-borne raid.[131]

On the other hand, the Levantine element in the crew of the Kaş ship should be combined with the archaeological evidence from the Gelidonya wreck and the Syrian trading colony in Enkomi. There are Canaanite jars and other pots found in Greece. Recent excavations have also revealed Cypriot and Levantine pottery of the period 1470–1200 BC at Marsa Matruh in Libya and Sardinia and some has been found on the sea-bed near the Aeolian islands just north of Sicily.[132] These no more prove the presence of Levantines in the Central Mediterranean than the Mycenaean pottery indicates the presence of Greeks in the Near East. However, a 14th-century bronze statuette of a Canaanite deity found off Cape Selinunte in Southwest Sicily is more suggestive.[133]

There is also the documentary evidence from the tomb painting of Syro-Palestinian merchants unloading their ships and the active and extensive maritime trade reported in the Ugaritic texts, as well as the specific mention of a *tamkarum* trading with Crete. Furthermore, there are the mercantile traditions of Byblos, Sidon and Tyre and the picture given by Homer that all trade between the Aegean and the Levant was in the hands of Phoenicians.[134]

The picture that emerges is that both peoples were engaged in considerable trading activities; and the special situation of Ugarit after 1370 could explain the complete absence of Greeks from the records there. Nevertheless, the greater stress on commercial affairs at Ugarit and other Syro-Palestinian cities as compared to in the Aegean, in combination with the Homeric picture, strongly suggests that most trade in the East Mediterranean during the Late Bronze Age was carried out by Levantines.

The Kaş ship merely provides archaeological proof for what was already evident from documentary sources, that at least in the 14th century BC there was massive trade in both luxuries and metals around the East Mediterranean. The region was dominated at the time by Egypt, and the only other power there, that of the Hittites, was clearly outside the trading system. Within it, there was a thoroughly cosmopolitan society with upper-class tastes for foreign goods and presumably some knowledge of other regions. Before looking at some particular indicators of this trade, as demonstrated in the Ulu Burun wreck, I think it would be useful to consider what we know of the relationship between the two capitals, the Egyptian Thebes and Mycenae.

THE EGYPTIAN THEBES
AND MYCENAE, 1420–1370 BC

The conventional view of the origin of the Greek name Thebes for the Egyptian southern capital known in Egyptian as Niwt ỉmn (City of

Amon) is that it came from a confusion between the Greek Thēbai with a local name *tȝ ipȝt, hypothesized from a name for Luxor near Thebes – ipȝt rst (Southern Harem) – which was later abbreviated to ipt; no example has been found with the definite article tȝ.[135] This explanation is flimsy and it does not explain the name of the Boiotian Thebes or, for that matter, the one in Mysia in Northwestern Anatolia. In the introduction to Volume 1, I outlined a counter-argument which I intend to make in more detail in Volume 3:

> . . . before the advent of the Extreme Aryan Model it was generally accepted that the Greek city name Thēbā came from the Canaanite tēbâh (ark, chest). This itself came from the Egyptian tbi, or dbt (box). These two were often confused with another and possibly related word ḏbȝ (wicker float, ark of bullrushes) and ḏbȝ t (coffin, shrine) and hence (palace). Ḏbȝ, written Tbo or Thbo in Coptic, was an Egyptian city name. Interestingly, however, there is no record of its having been used for the southern capital of Egypt which the Greeks called Thēbā. Nevertheless, it may well have been used for the Hyksos capital at Avaris. If this were the case, Ḏbȝ/Thēbā could have become a Greek term or name for 'Egyptian capital' which was attached to the Egyptian Thebes when the 18th Dynasty established their capital there. In any event, there is no reason to doubt that the Greek city name came from the West Semitic tēbâh and the Egyptian cluster mentioned above.[136]

In Homer's time in the 10th and 9th centuries BC, Thebes had ceased to be the capital of Egypt for almost two hundred years. However, memories of the city at its height in the time when a black pharaoh received tribute from the known world can be seen in Achilles's rejection of Agamemnon's placatory gifts:

> . . . not though it were all the wealth that goeth into Orchomenos, or to Thebes of Egypt, where treasures in greatest store are laid up in men's houses, – Thebes which is a city of an hundred gates wherefrom sally forth through each two hundred warriors with horses and cars.[137]

Thus, Greek tradition raises the possibility of an Egyptian influence, if not hegemony, over Mycenae, the greatest city in Greece, during the height of the 18th Dynasty, 1470–1370, or at least during the reigns of Amenōphis III and Akhenaton, 1419–1364.

Now I should like to turn to the archaeological evidence. As stressed above, Mycenaean trade with the Near East increased greatly at the beginning of LHIIIA, which I see as having begun at the same time as Tuthmōsis III's consolidation of power in the Levant and his establishment of hegemony over the Aegean around 1470 BC.[138] However, the high point for the distribution of Mycenaean pottery in the Levant and Egypt comes in LHIIIA2, which I believe roughly corresponds with the reigns of the pharaohs Amenōphis III and Akhenaton. From the documentary evidence of the statue base of Amenōphis' funerary temple near Thebes, discussed in the last chapter, it is certain that Egyptian officialdom of the time knew a considerable number of Greek towns and principalities, and it is likely that Egypt exercised some kind of hegemony over the region.[139] 'Tribute' had been offered in the reign of Tuthmōsis III and we know that, at the end of the period, in the 12th year of Akhenaton (1369 BC), Aegean representatives came to offer precious gifts in exchange for the 'breath of life'.[140]

In 1981, Vronwy Hankey published an article in which she tried to relate the Aegean place names found in the statue base to the faience plaques with the cartouche of Amenōphis III found at Mycenae. She postulated that the list represented the route of the itinerary of an official Egyptian embassy and tentatively suggested that the faience plaques could have been presented by this embassy.[141] Two years earlier in 1979, Wolfgang Helck had proposed the same without linking the objects to the list.[142]

In 1980 J. Strange proposed that the list was an itinerary of a My-cenaean embassy to Egypt. However, as Eric Cline points out, this is less likely because the ordering of the names from east to west to east again indicates a journey from Egypt to the Aegean and back.[143] As I argued in the last chapter, I do not accept that the Egyptians were aware of these places only through one embassy and believe that many if not most of the toponyms may well have been known in Egypt from the time of Tuthmōsis III or even earlier.[144] Cline put forward his argument against Strange in an article which enlarged on Han-key's scheme. While he is anxious to dissociate himself from the idea of Egyptian hegemony, Cline clearly believes that the relationship was unequal and that this imbalance was formalized by the giving of gifts.

There is no doubt that more objects have been found around the Aegean with cartouches of Amenōphis III and his wife, Queen Tiyi, than with those of any other pharaoh. Cline estimates there to be eleven of these two as opposed to ten for all the rest of the pharaohs combined.[145] If one takes the reading of the toponym Bjs to be the Cretan Phaistos, as the majority of scholars do, and equates one Pha-istos with Agia Triada two kilometres away, four of the six findspots of these inscribed objects also appear on the statue base.[146] This is ex-tremely suggestive. Whether or not one can tie the list to the itinerary of a particular embassy, the correlation does show that there is both documentary and archaeological evidence of contact between these particular cities – Kydonia, Knossos, Phaistos and Mycenae – and the Egyptian court at around 1400 BC.

Cline points out that, while two of the eleven inscribed objects were buried in an LM/HIIIA1 context and two in LM/HIIIA1–2, one was buried in LM/HIIIA–B and five in LHIIIB. This, he argues, would suggest that they arrived in LHIIIA1.[147] As I see this ceramic period as ending in *c.* 1415 and the reign of Amenōphis III beginning in 1419 BC, I find the chronological squeeze tight but not unbearable. In any event, I see no reason why they should all have arrived at the same time. However, Cline is convincing when he claims that not enough of the objects were buried during or soon after the reign of Amenōphis III for them to have arrived casually through intermediaries or as touristic bric-à-brac.

Cline does, however, admit a difficulty over the fact that relatively little pottery has been found in Egypt from LHIIIA1, which he sees as corresponding to the reign of Amenōphis III. He explains it simply on the grounds that the known distribution is based only on the hazards of finds. If, however, one sees LHIIIA2 as corresponding to the reigns of Amenōphis III and Akhenaton, large quantities of this ware have been found at the latter's capital at El Amarna, and at the artisans' village near Deir el Medina near Thebes, as well as at Sesebi, in Nubia far to the south of Aswan.[148]

THE FOUNDATION DEPOSIT PLAQUES
Egyptian temple cults at Mycenae?

Cline would seem right to distinguish between objects exchanged through trade and some of the inscribed pieces he was concerned with, which he saw as symbols of diplomatic exchanges. Both he and Vronwy Hankey were particularly interested in the fragments of six to nine rectangular faience plaques inscribed with the nomen and prenomen of Amenōphis III, discovered over the last century at Mycenae. They seem similar or identical to the plaques found in so-called foundation deposits in Egypt, buried under the corners of temples and secular buildings which were constructed 'at the royal command or at least with the king's approval'.[149] On the basis of a comment by the Egyptologist G. T. Martin that similar finds in Egypt would lead scholars to look for a temple or shrine, Vronwy Hankey proposed that they could have had that function at Mycenae as well.[150] Cline mentioned another 'intriguing possibility' that they could have been intended for a statue of the pharaoh.[151]

This would seem less likely than their use for the foundation of a temple. Plaques of this type have been found elsewhere outside Egypt, in Nubia and at Beth Shan and Aphek in Palestine. The latter have led Israeli archaeologists to postulate the building of Egyptian temples there.[152] Thus, it would seem likely that Egyptian temples were established in areas of Egyptian influence and control beyond the country itself. Can Greece around 1400 BC be considered in the same category?

None of the fragments have been excavated in a context that can be seen as a foundation deposit; they were generally found in LMIIIB strata, which could be well over a century after their arrival in Greece. It seems likely, however, that they, like the other royally inscribed objects, were treated with a reverence divorced from their original purpose.[153] This would suggest that, if they were at the foundations of buildings, such constructions could not have lasted long. It is also possible that the buildings to match the deposits were never erected.

An Egyptian temple was not merely a building; it was a substantial institution, with many priests in complex hierarchies. Is there any reason to suppose that such a body could have existed in Mycenaean Greece? A possible answer to this comes from the cult of Demeter and Korē at Eleusis in Attika. This cult will be discussed in detail in Volume 4, in which I hope to show, not merely that it has clear roots in the Bronze Age and that its cult and mysteries strikingly parallel those of Isis, Nephthys and Osiris in Egypt, but also that its two families of priests – the Eumolpids and the Kerykes – resemble the two ranks of Egyptian priests.

This identification was universally accepted in Antiquity. It is also interesting to note that the Egyptian informants of Diodoros Sikeliotes told him that the mysteries had been introduced to Eleusis by Erekhtheus of Athens, a king of Egyptian descent, during his reign, c. 1408/9 BC.[154] The Parian Marble also gives this date. Apollodoros, however, put the arrival of Demeter and Dionysos in Greece somewhat earlier, during the reign of King Pandion, c. 1462–1423 BC.[155] As I mentioned in Chapter II, it is likely that cults of Dionysos existed in Keos just off the coast of Attika in the 21st century BC.[156]

Thus, what we are considering here is not simply the worship of the god but would seem to be the introduction of a religious institution. The temporal coincidence with the reign of Amenōphis III (1419–1381) is remarkable. It is also true that, while Mycenae suffered from the change from the Perseid Danaan dynasty to the Pelopid Achaian one and later the Return of the Heraklids or the 'Dorian Invasion', Attika had no such radical upheavals and the Athenians frequently boasted of the continuity and antiquity of their institutions and religion. Thus, the survival of an Egyptian cult at Eleusis and its collapse at Mycenae would fit very well with what we know of the general historical pattern.

In any event, the possible foundation of one or more Egyptian temple cults at Mycenae has a possible parallel. If the plaques were not intended as foundation deposits, it is difficult to see what purpose they could have had; they cannot be worn as decorations and have little intrinsic value, and they are unlikely to have been on the souvenir market during the New Kingdom. The simplest solution is to interpret their function in the way that similar objects have been in Egypt, Palestine and Nubia – as temple deposits that were at least intended to be placed under temples of the Egyptian type.

The plaques and other royally inscribed objects and Egyptian material evidence of this period, in conjunction with the documentary evidence, make it very likely indeed that there were close diplomatic relations between Thebes and Mycenae and that the relationship was unequal.

The trading circuit

In 1970, the glaze on one of the fragments from Mycenae, known as Taylour's plaque, was subjected to lead isotope analysis from which R. H. Brill of the Corning Museum of Glass startlingly concluded:

> The lead in the glaze is definitely of type L. Most type L leads in the ancient world came from the mines in the Laurion region. The lead in the glaze differs markedly from leads found in numerous examples of 18th Dynasty yellow glasses, glazes and kohls. Improbable as it may seem, the most straightforward interpretation of these findings would be that the object was glazed (and presumably fabricated) somewhere near Mycenae and not in Egypt.[157]

If this analysis is correct, and we shall see below other reasons for thinking that it is, it leaves two possibilities. The first is the one proposed above, that the plaque was made in Greece. However, the manufacture and the hieroglyphs are of the high standard required by Egyptian workshops, and no one has previously considered the possibility that it could have been produced anywhere but Egypt. The idea that such a workshop existed at or near Mycenae is extremely implausible. It would have needed Egyptian royal licence and would have further required resident Egyptian workmen, or Mycenaeans with long apprenticeship in Egypt.

As Eric Cline argues, the second possibility, that it was manufactured in Egypt using lead imported from Greece, would seem much less unlikely. He is able to draw on analyses by the metallurgist N. H. Gale which indicate that the material of three other 18th-Dynasty Egyptian lead artifacts also came from Laurion near the southern tip of Attika.[158] He also cites Gale's comment that 'the Egyptian artefacts with Laurion composition . . . suggest some sort of contact between the Mycenaean and Egyptian cultures at this time'.[159] Further confirmation of the hypothesis that there was a regular export of metals from Attika to Egypt around 1400 BC comes from the analysis of the copper in a bronze dagger with an inscription of Amenōphis III found at Beth Shan in Palestine, which indicates that it probably came from Laurion.[160] The economic cosmopolitanism of the age is also shown by the fact that the copper in a contemporary spear from Beth Shan – also with the cartouche Amenōphis III – seems to have come from Sardinia![161] There is also documentary evidence to support the idea of metals from Greece, as 'the Isles in the Midst of . . . [the Wȝd Wr]' are included in a 19th-Dynasty list of mining countries at the temple at Luxor.[162]

The idea that there was a substantial export of metals from Attika to Egypt in the 2nd millennium BC blows the isolationist model of Greek development sky high. Since Gale wrote his analysis of the lead, his wife, Z. A. Stos-Gale, has announced that two statues from the 11th Dynasty were made of silver from Laurion![163] This shows that the metal trade, though flourishing at the height of the 18th Dynasty, was not restricted to that time and may well have existed at other periods when economic and political conditions permitted. Together they indicate that, when looking at the material archaeological finds, we are seeing less than the tip of the iceberg of contact between the regions.

Here, however, we will concentrate on the later period for which there are substantial material remains. Further evidence has emerged which has put the information on lead exports in context. The massive cargo of metals – six tons of copper, a considerable amount of tin and some gold – on the Kaş ship makes it clear that bulk shipment of metals was taking place around the Mediterranean during the 18th Dynasty. Furthermore, evidence from Kaş and elsewhere makes it clear that the ingots were of standard shapes and many scholars believe that there was 'a central authority over the production of and trade in this important commodity [copper]'.[164] Not surprisingly, scholars have differed as to where such a centre would have been. Catling proposed the Aegean and Bass Syria, while Muhly and his colleagues see it as having been in Cyprus.[165] As Cyprus seems to have been the major centre of copper production at the time, this would seem the most plausible.

There is further evidence in its favour in that many of the smaller ingots were marked with the Cypriot – and not the Cyprus – form of a sign read as *na*. However, it is not only copper ingots that are marked with this sign, since one made of tin appears to have the same sign.[166] This cannot have originated from Cyprus as the tin in the ancient Mediterranean world came either from Afghanistan or Malaya or from Bohemia or Cornwall, though Bronze Age tin mines have now been found in Turkey. Muhly has maintained that the Aegean was using the European metal.[167] However, Bass and Pulak believe that the fact that the Kaş ship, loaded with tin, appears to have been heading west indicates that this tin at least came from Asia.[168] If the sign *na* is not specifically concerned with copper, what does it mean? One possible answer is that it was a Cypriot or Levantine rendering of the Egyptian *nꜥr* (smooth or fine) used in the compound *nb nꜥr* (especially fine gold). In the 18th Dynasty *nꜥr* was also used as 'the best'.

Whether or not this is the case, there is little doubt that the metal and other trade of the East Mediterranean of the 15th and early 14th centuries BC took place in the spheres of Egyptian political influence. The extent to which Italy and the metal-producing regions of Sardinia and Spain, which were clearly integrated economically, were politically involved is much more uncertain. Nevertheless, there is abundant evidence of commercial relations including the find, mentioned above, of a spear made of Sardinian copper with the cartouche of Amenōphis III.[169]

We also know that the scope of the East Mediterranean trading area extended further across the whole of Europe from Britain to the Ukraine. Throughout this huge northern region, small numbers of weapons and beads from the south have been found in sites from this period. Some of these objects are specifically Mycenaean and others clearly Egyptian and others still have specific origins that are difficult to trace.[170] All indicate the wealth of the East Mediterranean after the beginning of LHIII or the establishment of a *Pax Aegyptiaca* by Tuthmōsis III. This evidence of trading networks would fit well with the spreading of the alphabet to the West Mediterranean and Northern Europe, which, I have argued elsewhere on palaeographical grounds, took place near the middle of the 2nd millennium BC.[171]

Here, however, we shall concentrate on the East Mediterranean. From the Kaş ship and the Ugaritic written evidence we gain evidence of a grand circle going 'counter-clockwise' with the predominant currents, taking ivory, hippopotamus teeth, ebony, spices and other tropical products, fine goods, papyrus and possibly wheat from Egypt to the Levant, boarding tin, glass, resins and spices from there on to Cyprus. This exported copper and local pots. In the Aegean, the boats took on silver, lead and Mycenaean pottery and its contents and, passing through Crete, the circuit went on to the African shore at the present Mersa Matruh in Western Egypt and back to the Nile.[172]

THE VOCABULARY OF TRADE

Although this circuit is only fully attested for this period, it is extremely likely that elements of it existed much earlier. This is indicated by the way in which the Greek vocabulary seems to reflect such a trading pattern. The Semitic names for spices have been referred to in the last chapter. The Egyptian origins of such words as *papyros; ebenos* from *hbnì; annēs-* (anis); *kiki* from *kȝkȝ* (castor oil – used for lamps); *kommi* (gum) from *ḳmìt; sindōn* (fine tissue) from *šnḏwt* (kilt of fine cloth) and *nitron* from *nṯr* have been accepted even by Aryanist scholars who believe that 'Egyptian culture stands to Hellenic as Chinese to European. It is in many respects so alien that Greeks could find little to borrow in the philological sense.'[173] I would add to this vocabulary of trade 'ivory' *elephas, erepa* in Linear B, from the Egyptian *ȝbw* (elephant) with the elephant determinative 𓃰 and 'ivory' with that of 'bone' �￢. The Greek word *elephas* serves the same double purpose. It is generally recognized that *elephas*, like the Latin *ebur* (ivory) is a loan.[174] The specialist in Anatolian languages Emmanuel Laroche has argued that *elephas* comes from a Hittite form *la-ah-pa-aš*, meaning 'tooth of elephant', and a hypothetical form *lahpant* with a Hittite suffix of animation *-n(t)*. This he derives in turn from the Semitic *alpu(m)* (ox), linking this to the Syrian elephants and ivory that survived well into the 2nd millennium.[175] While there might be contamination from these sources, *ȝbw*, which specifically means 'elephant', would seem a more probable source for both the Greek and Hittite words. Despite the Syrian ivory, Egypt and the rest of Africa would seem to be the most likely point of origin. Chantraine dismissed an etymology from *ȝbw*, apparently unaware that the initial *ȝ* was originally a liquid.[176] Given the correspondence *b > ph*, seen in the transcription of Nbt ḥt as Nephthys and the name Wȝḥ ib Rˤ as Ouaphris, and the Egyptian propensity for prothetic vowels, I see no serious phonetic difficulty with this etymology, which has a perfect semantic fit. The Latin *ebur* would seem to come from a later pronunciation seen in the Coptic *ebu*, the final *-r* being added 'after the analogy with *femur; robur* etc.'[177]

The generally accepted cases of word loans for exotic goods from Egyptian to Greek provide very little evidence as to when they were borrowed. The derivation of *elephas* from *ȝbw*, however, must have taken place in the early 2nd millennium or earlier. This is indicated not only by its attestation in Linear B but also by the retention of the consonantal value of *ȝ*.

Another possible Egyptian etymology in Greek is much more fundamental – it is that for *sitos* (wheat), defined not as a plant but as the cereal used for food. This word has no Indo-European cognates. Furthermore, the initial *s-*, which, in Greek, did not survive from Indo-European, makes it a likely candidate for a loan. The Assyriologist and linguist W. Muss-Arnolt proposed that *sitos* was 'connected' to the Assyrian *še'u*, feminine *še'atu* (grain, corn).[178] The German semitist Heinrich Lewy linked it to the Sumerian *zid* with the same meaning.[179] The Italian linguist Nunzio Maccarone argued that, while *še'atu* and *zid* were phonetically and semantically plausible etyma for *sitos*, as there was much more direct contact between Greece and Egypt than there was between Greece and Mesopotamia, it was more likely that it came from the Egyptian *s(w)t* (wheat).[180] Maccarone admitted some difficulty with the vowel, which remains as *sw* in Demotic and *suo* in Coptic. However, he postulated a form *sᵉʷot* from which *sit-* could derive. He pointed out that the loan must have been made before the dropping of the final -*ts* from Egyptian in the New Kingdom.[181] This early range would seem confirmed by the presence of *sito* in Linear B. The Semitic and Egyptian forms *še'u* and *s(w)t* are clearly related, and *zid* is a loan word, and it may be that a West Semitic form will be discovered. In the meantime, I believe that Maccarone's arguments are plausible and should be tentatively accepted.

Interestingly, there are two other possible loans from Egyptian on related subjects. The first of these is the Greek *art-* (bread baked from wheat). In their etymological dictionaries both Prellwitz and Boisaq are inclined to see *artuō* (prepare food) as the fundamental meaning of the cluster, which would fit quite nicely with the Egyptian *rtḥ* (bake, especially bread).[182] The semantic overlap with *artos* (wheaten bread) is not perfect, as 'baked bread' is *t rtḥ* in Egyptian. Nevertheless, both the semantic and the phonetic correspondence with *artuō* are reasonably good. The Italian linguist Pisani derived *artos* from a reconstructed Iranian root *arta* (flour) and he has been supported in this by Georgacas but Chantraine is sceptical.[183] He is equally doubtful about the hypothesis that *artos* comes from a substrate language found in the Basque, *arto* (bread made of maize).[184] Such a connection would seem very distant in space and time and could well be a loan from Greek into Basque directly or indirectly through Spanish. *Artos* itself is a very old word; not only does it occur in Hesiod but it also appears in Linear B in the compound *atopoqo*, which Chadwick sees as *artopoq^u oi* (bakers).[185] Thus, here too there could well be an early loan.

The standard Egyptian corn measure the *ḥḳ3t* was written with the determinative ⸗⊓. This measure had a curious characteristic in that, written with a numeral, it stood for 100 *ḥḳ3t*, with a half, 50 *ḥḳ3t*, etc.[186] Thus, there was a very close relationship between it and the number 100. The Greek word for 'hundred' is *hekaton*. This is explained as coming from the proto–Indo-European **dkṃt-om*, from which the Latin *centum* and the Germanic *hund* are supposed to derive. However, the initial *he-* in the Greek form has caused a considerable problem for linguists.[187] It would seem plausible to suggest either that this was the result of contamination from *ḥḳ3t* or, more likely, that the Greek word is a straightforward borrowing from the Egyptian.

There are both phonetic and semantic parallels to strengthen this hypothesis. The ugly old Egyptian frog goddess of fertility was called *Ḥḳt* and there was a clear relationship between this name and *ḥḳ3* (magic). In Greek mythology there was the old crone goddess of magic Hekatē, whose name has no Indo-European etymology.

The semantic parallel for a borrowing of *hekaton* from *ḥḳ3t* is with the Greek stem *khili-* (thousand). This is conventionally supposed to come from a hypothetical proto–Indo-European root **kheslioi*, seen in the Sanskrit *sahásram* (thousand). As Chantraine admits, there are many formal difficulties with this derivation. He is adamant, however, that there is no case to be made for borrowing. As far as I am aware, no one has attempted to derive it from the Egyptian *ḥ3* (thousand). As it is vocalized with an *o*, an *a* and an *e* in different Coptic dialects, it is difficult to determine the vowel. However, the consonantal structure and the semantic field fit perfectly.

The Greek word *khilos* or *kheilos* (fodder) is of unknown origin. It would seem to come from the Egyptian *ḥ3 w* (vegetables, plants). This brings us back to the plausible Egyptian etymologies for key Greek words in the vocabulary of wheat, *sitos*, *art-* and possibly *hekaton*. These etymologies suggest a possible answer to a question that has become even more acute since it has become clear that Greece was exporting metals to Egypt and the Levant: what materials was Egypt providing in exchange for these and the goods provided in or with Mycenaean pottery?

Egypt produced and presumably exported high-quality gold, papyrus and linen and possibly cotton.[188] We know from the Kaş wreck that ebony was shipped in bulk and it is virtually certain that both elephant and hippopotamus ivory was another major Egyptian export.[189]

It is likely that other tropical goods – ostrich feathers and eggs as well as gums, ointments and spices – were sent north from Egypt. Slaves, however, were more likely to have been shipped from Greece to the Near East than vice versa.[190]

It will be noticed that with the exception of *chrysos,* the word for gold which has a Semitic etymology, the Greek names of all the other Egyptian exports have plausible Egyptian origins. Is it possible that the plausible Egyptian etymologies for the Greek vocabulary of wheat indicate that this too was exported from Egypt?

There is, to my knowledge, no contemporary documentary mention of this and archaeological traces of such a trade would be difficult to find. Nevertheless, a reasonable circumstantial case can be made for the Egyptian export of wheat during the Bronze Age. In the first place, we know that Egypt, which was proverbial for its agricultural richness, was a substantial wheat producer and that the crop was easily accessible by water. The Bible describes with some plausibility South Syrian nomads buying grain from Egypt: 'The whole world came to Egypt to buy corn from Joseph, so severe was the famine everywhere.'[191] There is also no doubt that grain was shipped in bulk during the Late Bronze Age, at least for famine relief. A letter found at Ugarit from the late 13th century contains a request from the Hittite king to the king of Ugarit asking for 2,000 measures of grain to relieve the famine at the city of Ura in Cilicia, which he estimated could be done in one or two trips. The French Assyriologist Jean Nougayrol tried to work out the capacity of such a ship and concluded that the king of Ugarit must have possessed ships capable of carrying 500 tons.[192] Astour, in his discussion of this issue, points out that such voyages were not limited to creeping around coasts, as Columbus's flagship, the *Santa Maria,* was 233 tons.[193]

The Kaş ship has confirmed Nougayrol's estimate of the capacity of late Bronze Age ships. These particular shipments of grain supposedly came from Mukis to the north of Ugarit. However, it would seem that in the 13th century BC Ugaritic agriculture was highly commercialized. The Semitist and economic historian Michael Heltzer stresses the fact that land prices were far higher at Ugarit than they were in Mesopotamia and suggests that one reason for this may have been that 'A large part of the agricultural lands in Ugarit was covered in olive-groves, date palms and vineyards etc.'[194] It is interesting that the usual Ugaritic word for 'estate' or 'farm' was *gt* (wine or olive press). This situation would seem likely to have led to frequent or constant shortages of grain, which seems to have been considerably more expensive in Ugarit than in Egypt.[195] We know that Ugarit itself was receiving grain from Egyptian granaries. A tablet of the same period, found at Tel Aphek just outside Tel Aviv, refers to a missing delivery of approximately fifteen tons of grain from Joppa, the site of the chief Egyptian granary in South Canaan, due for Ugarit apparently by ship.[196]

The local food shortage referred to in the Hittite letter to Ugarit appears to have been part of a widespread famine affecting much of Central Anatolia; indeed, the pharaoh Merneptah (1236–1223 BC) boasted of having provided grain to the Hatti.[197] Diodoros Sikeliotes reported an Egyptian tradition that Erechtheus, a Bronze Age king of Athens, secured his position there by bringing a large quantity of grain from Egypt to relieve a famine. It was this in fact that was supposed to have led to the introduction of the cult of Demeter.[198]

How far should famine relief be distinguished from regular trade? Most economic historians would argue that the line between the two is easily crossed, especially in the ancient East Mediterranean, where 'years of dangerously low rainfall occur with frightening regularity, and there is a high statistical probability that several such years should run successively'.[199]

We know that at least by the 10th century BC Phoenician cities were regularly deficient in food supplies.[200] Given the scale of urbanization and manufacture, and the constricted arable land around the coastal cities, there is little reason to doubt that this was also the case in the Late Bronze Age, when it is clear that Canaan was already exporting cedar wood, 'Tyrian' purple dye and finished metalwork and it is very likely that it was manufacturing and sending out large quantities of raw glass as well as decorated containers in that material.[201]

There is no doubt that during Classical times (500–320 BC), except during periods of Persian occupation of Egypt and hostility to Greece, there was a major trade between Greece and Egypt based on an exchange of Greek silver for Egyptian grain, although it has rightly been insisted that other commodities were involved. The classicist M. M. Austin has made a strong case that the trade was already functioning the Archaic Age.[202] Richard Brown, who has written a thesis on Egyptian objects found in Greece, maintains that there was no similar export of grain from Egypt to the Aegean in the Bronze Age. He argues that such imports would have been unnecessary 'for a population considerably smaller than that of Classical Greece'.[203] The evidence on relative populations in Mycenaean and Classical Greece is uncertain but it seems likely that, in some key regions at least, the density was quite similar.[204] In the Late Bronze Age there was a specialization in wool, metal and pottery production and agricultural emphasis on olives and vines, in which shortfalls of grain would seem likely. Although imports are not mentioned in the Linear B texts, scholars working on Pylos, the Mycenaean kingdom about which most is known, are surprised at the relative lowness of acreage put to wheat.[205]

There is also the argument by analogy with the situation during much of the 1st millennium BC when shipping had not significantly improved since the Bronze Age and Egyptian wheat, transported by sea, provided food reserves for Greece and much of the Mediterranean basin.[206] Most significant of all is the discovery, made since Brown argued against the Bronze Age trade, that there is now archaeological proof of one half of the exchange, the export of silver and lead to Egypt, thus – and given the circumstantial evidence cited above – the export of grain from Egypt to Greece in the Bronze Age would seem very likely. It would seem very probable then that the dense population and prosperity of Mycenaean Greece during the ceramic periods LHIIIA and LHIIIB (1470–1220 BC) was dependent on a sophisticated, and fragile, trading network covering the Eastern Mediterranean. Local agriculture could not support such a population through the inevitable cycles of bad harvests and therefore relied on Egyptian grain for relief.

There is a common identification of wheat or bread with life, as in the Hebrew *matēh lehem* (staff of bread, the food supply upon which life depends). In Middle Egyptian Egyptian *iri* (make) *ꜥnḫ* was 'to provision' and *ꜥnḫt* with the determinative ⸗▭ meant 'corn'. In late Egyptian, the language spoken during the period with which we are concerned, *ꜥnḫ(w)* was used with the same writing to mean 'life, sustenance and victuals'. Thus, it is probable that the Egyptian formula *tꜣ n ꜥnḫ* (the breath of life), given by the pharaoh to foreign tributaries, had the tangible sense of promised grain supplies, as well as a political and spiritual meaning.[207] This would have given Egypt an economic as well as a politico-military and cultural hold over Mycenaean Greece.

Even if Egyptian wheat was not included in the exchange of commodities, there is no doubt that during the period from 1470 to 1220 BC there was a dense network of trade around the East Mediterranean and extending to the West Mediterranean and Black Sea. While the trading pattern of the 15th and 14th centuries clearly resembled and was probably built on earlier ones, it had its own characteristic features which appear to reflect the political situation of the time. While the lead in some weights for some fish-net sinkers come from the Bolkardağ region of the Taurus mountains in Southern Anatolia, there is nothing else from the zone of Hittite control.[208] Nor, apart from what Bass sees as the eastern tin, was there anything from Mesopotamia.

Thus, the trade goods came either from regions known to have been under Egyptian control, like Nubia, the Levant and Egypt itself, or from Crete, Mainland Greece and Arzawa in Western Anatolia. This pattern is clearly not the result of chance. Eric Cline has found the same pattern, indicating that Greece belonged to the Egypto-Levantine world rather than the Hittite Anatolian one, in a survey of foreign objects found at Mycenae from the LHIII period. He lists 22 objects from Egypt, 19 from Syro-Palestine, 2 from Mesopotamia and 1 each from Cyprus and Anatolia. The balance is still more striking when one remembers that, as pointed out above, the Anatolian object is unlikely to be Hittite.[209]

The foreign objects were largely found in LHIIIB contexts – 26 out of 45 – with another 5 coming from LHIIIA–B. This can partly be explained by the length of the later period, c. 150 years as opposed to c. 100 for LHIIIA. Furthermore, as mentioned above, the finding of objects inscribed with the name of Amenōphis III in LHIIIB contexts indicates that some foreign objects probably arrived in Greece several decades before they were buried.[210]

In this section, I have argued that there is a general correspondence between Semitic and Egyptian etymologies for Greek words for goods and the import of these goods into Greece during the Bronze Age. The only surprise here is that the etymologies indicate that, at the end of the Bronze Age, wheat was exported from Egypt not merely to the Levant but to the Aegean. There is documentary evidence that Egyptian wheat was sent north by sea for famine relief in this period and I argue that there is circumstantial evidence to suggest that such relief was given easily enough for local economies and populations to develop beyond the subsistence levels imposed by bad harvests.

Wheat is of course very difficult to detect through excavation, but now, thanks to land and underwater archaeology, we have a much clearer idea of many other items that were traded around the Mediterranean between 1470 and 1220 BC.

The picture given by these objects fits relatively well with that from the distribution of Mycenaean pottery and what we know of Egyptian and Aegean history from documentary records: that is to say, there was some increase in contacts after Tuthmōsis III's domination of the Levant and possibly around the Aegean c. 1470, the approximate point at which LHIIIA began. Around 1420, with the accession of Amenōphis III and the beginning of LHIIIA2, relationships intensified greatly. They remained high for some decades but began to fade somewhat after the waning of Egyptian power in the Levant after 1370, even though, as mentioned above, Greek trade does not appear to have been present in North Syria after Hittites took control of the region around that date.

THE DECLINE OF EGYPTIAN INFLUENCE
ON THE AEGEAN 1370–1220 BC

Anita Yannai maintains that 'after the Amarna period [*c.* 1370] Mycenaean imports virtually cease'.[211] If, however, one takes LHIIIB as beginning at that time, there are plenty of shards of that ware throughout Egypt and the Levant not to mention their abundance in Cyprus.[212]

As indicated above, a relatively large number of Egyptian and Syro-Palestinian objects discovered in Greece have been found in LHIIIB contexts but at least some of these must have arrived earlier. The ceramic period is so long that it is difficult to tell whether the contacts were uniform throughout the period or whether they reflected the changes of Egyptian power, notably the revival of Egyptian influence over the Levant and possibly the Aegean during the first twenty-five years of the 19th Dynasty.

In the last chapter, I mentioned Ramessēs II's claims that chiefs from the Wȝḏ wr had been sent to him and the implications of Egyptian suzerainty.[213] However, there is no archaeological confirmation for any official Greek presence in Egypt at this time. What is more, there is a somewhat surprising lack of royally inscribed objects from Ramessēs II's long reign in Greece (those from its very end will be described below). On the other hand, the same is true of the 18th-Dynasty pharaoh Tuthmōsis III, whose claims of suzerainty have the backing of very plausible tomb paintings.

PHI AND PSI FIGURINES
AND SMITING GODS

At this point it would seem useful to examine two types of figurines from the LHIII period, the Phi and Psi figurines from Greece found in the Levant and the smiting god figurines from the Levant found around the Aegean. The Phi and Psi terracotta figurines are named after their shapes, which resemble the letters φ and ψ.

The function of the figurines is not at all clear. They have been seen as votives, divine nurses or toys. The latter two would seem more likely, as their appearance has been correlated with child burials. On the other hand, deposits of these figurines at the shrines at Delphi and Amyklai in Sparta would suggest that they were votives there.[214] It seems to me that these categories are not mutually exclusive and they could well have served all three functions. However, I believe their origins, like those of the earlier Cycladic and Cypriot figurines, are related to the Egyptian *Shuabtis*, figurines buried with the dead to act as servants and protectors in the afterlife.

A number of the Phi and Psi figurines have been found in Cyprus and the Levant, especially Ugarit. As Elizabeth French, who has studied the distribution, writes,

> The presence of Mycenaean figurines does seem to presuppose the presence of Mycenaeans or those who have consciously adopted their ways, and this makes the overseas distribution particularly interesting. The scarcity of examples is again striking, as is the small number of finds in proportion to the other Mycenaean remains from Rhodes and Cyprus.[215]

Anita Yannai rejects this indication of a Mycenaean presence on the Levant. She makes the most of the inconsistencies pointed out by Elizabeth French as well as the facts that the figurines are frequently accompanied by those of animals, the virtual absence of Greek personal seals on the Levant and the non-attestation of Greek names at Ugarit.[216] I fail to understand the significance of the presence of the animal figures, one way or the other. Furthermore, while it is true that only one Greek seal from LHIII has been found in the Levant, at Tell Abu Hawam in Palestine, there are very few Syro-Palestinian seals in the Aegean, though we know through onomastica or lists of personal names that they were present there. Finally, the lack of personal names at Ugarit reflects the situation there only after 1370 and I see no reason to believe the situation was the same before the city entered the Hittite sphere of influence or that there were no Greeks in the Southern Levant still under Egyptian suzerainty. All in all, despite the difficulties, I find French's argument persuasive and accept that the figurines do indicate that there were some Mycenaean Greeks present in the Levant between 1470 and 1220 BC.

The smiting god figurines are altogether more formidable. They represent 'a striding figure with tall headgear holding a weapon in the right hand'.[217] These are the figures of the thunder gods Tarkhun, Teššub, Ba'al and Reshef mentioned in earlier chapters. However, as I argued in Chapter VI, these were derived from images of the striking pharaoh wearing the crown of Upper Egypt.[218] The closeness of the iconography was also mentioned in the discussion of the seal of Ba'al discovered at Tell el Daba'a which had parallels to images of Sesōstris dancing at the Heb Sed Festival.[219] It is also clear that, as late as Ramessēs II in the 13th century, pharaohs identified themselves with Mont and his Semitic counterpart Reshef in their northern conquests.[220]

Smiting god figurines have been found in Late Bronze Age contexts at Mycenae, Tiryns, Delos and at Phylakopi on Melos. Others have been found in Iron Age strata or without clear contexts at Dodona, Lindos, Nezero, Patsos, Samos, Thermon and Sounion.[221] The figures cannot all be described as bric-à-brac since the only ones found in a controlled excavation, those at Phylakopi, were in clearly cultic positions in a shrine dating to the beginning of LHIIIB.[222] There is no doubt that the cult was extraordinarily widespread and that it was derived from the Levant which was the centre of the figures' distribution.[223]

Their presence is particularly interesting because it is the only Levantine cult of which there is any archaeological trace in the Aegean. One explanation could be that the ambiguity between the pharaoh as warrior and the gods of warfare, storm and pestilence that was undoubtedly present in Egypt, and may well have been seen in the Levant, also existed in the Aegean. In such a case, the statues represented not only Reshef's Greek counterparts – Apollo the archer of pestilence and Herakles – but the pharaoh himself. Thus, the Homeric idea of the king 'honoured by the people like a god', which would seem inappropriate to what we know about Mycenaean or Homeric kings, would fit the image of the deified pharaoh quite well.[224] Examples of the ambiguity between the pharaoh and a Syrian weather god can be seen at the very end of the Late Bronze Age on cylinder seals found around the Aegean. Both the seal found on the Gelidonya wreck and another from Perati in Attica portray gods with Egyptian crowns and Egyptian attributes.[225]

Whether or not there is anything to such speculation on a pharaonic cult, the smiting god statues make it quite evident that there was a considerable Levantine cultural penetration into the Aegean by the 14th century BC.

CANAANITE JARS

The clearest archaeological indicator of Levantine economic penetration into the Aegean are the Canaanite jars. As with the smiting gods, there is no doubt that they developed in the Syro-Palestinian region, which is where they have their widest diffusion. They became the standard jar used for transport from the Late Bronze Age to the 6th century BC. Anita Yannai reported fourteen of these from the Aegean – those found at Menidi, Mycenae, Argos, Athens, Pylos, Asine, Thebes and Thera. The earliest was the one from Thera, which she put in the early 15th century, but which, as mentioned in Chapter VI, we must now see as 17th century, thus pushing back the development of the form two centuries. Fragments of a Canaanite jar have been found off Pseira on the northern coast of East Crete in an LMIB context from the 16th century.[226] Yannai sees the number of jars as far lower than one would expect if there had been intense commercial contact between the Levant and the Aegean and she concludes her discussion of them:

> To sum up, not much can be learnt from these storage jars. The twelve jars are spread chronologically over nearly three centuries, and two sites in Greece have produced 75% of the evidence so far known. Although foreign, and from the Levant, it is hard to see in them an important item of trade as suggested for instance by Vermeule, with contents of wine, oil or spices.[227] Were they indeed such, there could not have been much demand for their contents. As they were found in the only shipwreck of the period found to date, off Cape Gelidonya, they are more likely to have served as containers for commodities needed aboard ships heading West, where they remained.[228]

This turns out to have been a case of 'the argument from silence' and the common-sense view of Emily Vermeule and others that the Canaanite jars were containers for cargo has not merely been strengthened by the recent discovery of Canaanite jars from Late Bronze Age contexts at Pseira, Knossos, Kato Zakro and Kommos in Crete but has been spectacularly vindicated by the discovery of the Kaş wreck. This ship contained over 120 'Canaanite amphoras'. Their contents are difficult to analyze, though it is clear that some contained fruits and others resins, including ones of terebinth, pistachio and frankincense. Still others contained organic detritus, which may have come from stoppers for the mouths of the jars but could also possibly have come from impurities among olives, figs or other fruit or possibly even in wheat whose export from Egypt has been suggested above. Most surprisingly, one jar was found to be full of Cypriot pottery. Thus, there is no doubt that they were used as general containers and not just for liquids.[229]

The discovery of all these jars underlines – once again – the dangers of the argument from silence. The fourteen previously excavated should never have been seen as representing a significant proportion of those shipped to Greece. Their chance survival should more plausibly be seen as representing thousands, if not hundreds of thousands of the jars used in hundreds or thousands of voyages, which did not sink or whose wrecks have disintegrated or not been found.

IVORY

The Kaş wreck also contained sections of ivory and two hippopotamus teeth.[230] Even at this time there were some elephants left in Syria. Nevertheless, it is virtually certain that, as the Egyptian etymology of *elephas* would suggest, this, like the teeth, came from Africa in general and from or through Egypt in particular. The fact that it was unworked, taken together with the discovery of unworked ivory at Kato Zakro in Eastern Crete, would suggest that Mycenaean rulers had a taste for their own local styles.[231]

There is some debate as to the relationship between these Aegean styles and those of the Levant. Emily Vermeule has stated that there was 'a more accentuated orientalism of style [in the ivories] since the raw material came from the East'.[232] Anita Yannai disagrees and argues that there are fundamental differences in both techniques and motifs. She maintains that the Mycenaeans preferred relief in the round while the Syro-Palestinians generally used engraving or inlay. However, she admits exceptions to both rules: the animal scenes from Delos are engraved, while the examples of relief work from the Levant are more numerous.[233] When it comes to motifs, Yannai admits the parallels but plays them down, rightly pointing out:

> the problem in this instance is in determining whether the influence is direct or through intermediaries, in which case the intermediate could be another place or another medium. In the first case, the question is whether the oriental motifs detected in some Mycenaean ivories have their origin in Pre-Mycenaean Crete; in the second rather than contacts between schools of ivory carvers, it could be influence through another field such as metalwork or glyptics.[234]

This is absolutely right, since by the 15th and 14th centuries Mycenaean Greece was a fully fledged member of the Near Eastern world, sharing a common heritage but with its own characteristics. There was, as Anita Yannai points out, the Cretan tradition, which itself, as we have seen, drew heavily on Egyptian and Levantine culture. More important, the ivories depicted the hunting and struggling lions and griffins of the 'Hyksos international' tradition, which had now become the 'national' one of Mycenaean Greece. Nevertheless, there was further artistic mixture in the LHIIIB period, as the French art historian Jean-Claude Poursat, who has made a study of the ivories, admits. However, he sees it in terms of an exchange of styles at Cyprus, which certainly led to the introduction of oriental motifs in Mycenaean ivories; on a smaller scale there was an influence in the other direction from Mycenae to the Levant.[235]

There is no doubt from the archaeological evidence cited above that, after its copper came into large-scale production in the 15th century, Cyprus played a central role in the trade of the East Mediterranean. On the other hand, it is equally certain that it plays a key role in the ideology of Aryanist and isolationist archaeologists by providing a screen or filter between East and West, allowing them to be in contact *without actually touching*. It seems to me that both the documentary and archaeological evidence show that there were many other ways in which the peoples of Egypt and the Levant were able to reach and influence those of the Aegean and vice versa.

CONCLUSION

There is now every reason to suppose that dense and far-reaching networks operated in the East Mediterranean at least after 1470 with the establishment of the *Pax Aegyptiaca* following the victories of Tuthmōsis III. Given the documentary and archaeological evidence for close contacts, it would be extremely surprising if there had not been extensive linguistic, religious and other cultural exchange during these centuries. Furthermore, because of the greater age and sophistication of the Egyptian and Levantine cultures, it would seem overwhelmingly likely that the predominant cultural flow was from the East Mediterranean to the Aegean rather than the other way around.

On the other hand, the evidence indicates that already in the 15th century BC not only was Egypt, Egypt and the Levant, the Levant, but Greece was Greek. The Mycenaeans were speaking Greek and worshipping gods with Greek names and it is overwhelmingly likely that many of the Greek cults and myths found in later times were already current in the Late Bronze Age. Thus, the formative period of Greek culture must be pushed back beyond this to the 18th and 17th centuries BC, in Hyksos times – the age portrayed in the Thera murals. It is most likely that it was in this period that the amalgam of local Indo-European with Egyptian and Levantine influences that we call Greek civilization was first and lastingly formed.

CHAPTER XII

THE HEROIC END TO
THE HEROIC AGE
The fall of Thebes, Troy and
Mycenae 1250–1150 BC

B Y THE MIDDLE of the 13th century BC the concert of powers that had dominated the Middle East since 1500 was beginning to crumble. The 'victories' of Ramessēs II around 1300 BC may have prolonged Egyptian influence in the Levant by a few decades, but unlike those of Tuthmōsis III they had no lasting effect. The Mitanni kingdom had disappeared and was replaced by a revived power in Assyria, which dominated Mesopotamia. In *c.* 1280 there was peace between the Egyptians and the Hittites, and during the second half of the century the latter became embroiled with Assyria. By the 1230s, Hittite power began to disintegrate. There was a famine in Central Anatolia which was possibly part of the general climatic deterioration discussed in Chapter VII.[1] The Hittite Empire appears to have lost control of Western and Southwestern Anatolia where there was a resurgence of local independence. It seems to have been in this situation that the Trojan War was fought.

In Greece, Thebes, the seat of the last of the original Hyksos dynasties, the Kadmeans, was besieged in the 1250s and appears to have been destroyed around 1230 BC. Pelopid rule was not secure as there appear to have been threats from the northern Greek tribes, the Dorians, Boiotians and Thessalians, on or beyond the fringes of Mycenaean palatial civilization. Even so, Pelopid kings appear to have been able to mount a considerable expedition against Troy, which in turn appears to have rallied a number of West and South Anatolian as

well as Thracian allies. This conflict appears to have ended around
1205 BC.

At least since the time of Thucydides, it has been conventional to
suggest that Greece never recovered from the disruption of the Trojan War. In fact, however, many of the palaces and cities, including
Mycenae, survived for another fifty years and some, like Athens, much
longer than that. The collapse in the 12th century is in some way
linked to the migrations and destructions of the Peoples of the Sea
reported in Egyptian records. It was argued in Volume 1 that many of
these came from the Aegean and spoke Greek.[2] Homer makes Odysseus say that he took part in a raid on Egypt and it is likely that 'Greeks'
from both Mycenaean states and fringe tribes, including some aligned
with the Trojans, were involved.[3] It is interesting, however, that the
main Dorian conquest, that of most of the Peloponnese, took place in
the 1150s. This, as we saw in Chapter VII, was the decade following
the eruption of Hekla III, which seems to have had a devastating
effect on Northern Europe and may have been a factor in the defeat
of the Shang Dynasty and rise of the Zhou in China.[4] It would seem
possible, therefore, to make a tentative link between this eruption and
the final collapse of the Near Eastern Bronze Age and Mycenaean
civilization.

CYLINDER SEALS

One important class of Near Eastern object found in the Bronze Aegean, which was not considered in the last chapter, was the cylinder
seal. Cylinder seals were in use in Mesopotamia and Syria from the
4th millennium and they continued to be used there for the next
three thousand years as markers of personal and corporate property.
Made out of hard or semi-precious stone, they also appear to have
had a talismanic quality, and the fact that they were often preserved
for several centuries indicates how highly valued they were. It is
known, for instance, that owners were sometimes obliged to report
the loss of a seal to the authorities.[5] Mycenaeans used clay as a surface
for writing and they too made and used cylinder seals imitating eastern patterns; an unfinished one made of local stone has been found at
Mycenae.[6] Nevertheless, Anita Yannai is right to point out that they
were not used in Greece as extensively as in Mesopotamia.[7]

In this section I want to concentrate on cylinder seals from Mesopotamia, Syria and Cyprus, although the latter two are sometimes
hard to distinguish from each other. These foreign finds are particularly interesting because of their personal and institutional value.
Their presence at a particular site is extremely significant.

In 1967 Hans-Günter Buchholz published a list of just over one hundred Near Eastern cylinder seals found in Greece (Yannai reported four more discovered in the following decade).[8] Of those that Buchholz could date, 14 came from before 1600 [or, according to my chronology, 1670] BC, 36 from between 1600 [1670] and 1200, and 13 from later than that. In some ways their provenance resembles that of the objects found at Mycenae, notably in the absence of Hittite seals and the presence of a large number from Syria or Cyprus: the difference lies in the fact that there were none from Egypt. This is not surprising, because Egypt used cylinder seals only at the beginning of the dynastic period in the late 4th millennium BC. The other difference is that a number of seals came from Mesopotamia, that is, from the Mitannian and Kassite kingdoms that ruled there until their overthrow by the Assyrians in the second half of the 13th century. By far the biggest cache of these was that found in the Kadmeion or palace at Thebes, but, before discussing this exceptionally rich and significant find, it would be helpful to consider the history of the city.

THE BOIOTIAN THEBES AND
THE PHOENICIANS' ARRIVAL

In Chapter II, some consideration was given to the early history of Boiotia and the argument was put forward that we should accept the tradition preserved in Homer and by the 6th-century mythographer Pherekydes that there had been two foundations of Thebes. This is not merely because of some mythical need for binary Jungian or Lévi-Straussian foundations but also because I believe that the tradition was accurately reporting two actual foundations, those of the Egyptian or Egyptianizing Amphion and Zēthos in the middle of the 3rd millennium and of Kadmos the Phoenician in the 2nd.[9] It should be emphasized here again that I am not insisting that any such individuals ever existed; even if they had done, they are so encrusted with myth that it would be impossible to extricate any historicity from them. Nevertheless, I believe that the stories do serve a historical function as they would seem to symbolize or represent historical processes and in this case migrations and conquests that actually took place.

As mentioned in Chapter II, it is virtually certain that the name Kadmos comes from the West Semitic qdm, 'Easterner' and 'ancient one'.[10] This is shown by the derivation of Europa, the name of Kadmos' sister, from the Semitic ʿrb (west or evening).[11] The outline of the standard version of the myth is that Europa had been playing on the beach of her father Agenor's kingdom of Tyre. There Zeus saw her and, turning himself into a bull, persuaded her to ride on his back. He then carried her off to Crete and the west. Europa's brothers Kadmos and Phoinix and others pursued their sister without success. However, they settled down and built cities at various places, all of which later had special associations with Phoenicians. The most notable of these was Kadmos' establishment of Thebes.[12] The existence of such stories since the times of Hesiod and Homer, in the 10th and 9th centuries BC, and of the legends of Kadmos the Phoenician as the founder of Thebes was discussed in Volume 1.[13]

Our confidence in the Bronze Age origin of these legends is strengthened by archaeological confirmation of a number of Classical reports about early Thebes. Late Bronze Age Thebes had seven gates, precisely as the Classical tragedies described it; LHIIIB iconography from Boiotia emphasizes a royal figure and a sphinx, suggesting that the stories of Oedipus and the Sphinx, in which the hero answers the monster's riddle which relieves the city of her depredations, were current in the 14th or 13th centuries, when he was reported to have ruled Thebes.[14] Because of such finds and the widespread and relative consistency of the legends, I see no reason to doubt that there were strong surviving traditions from the Bronze Age into Archaic and Classical times – especially in Thebes. Thus, Hesiod and Homer, who were generally well informed about the past, were almost certainly right when they portrayed the last rulers of Thebes in the 13th century as seeing themselves as Kadmids, whose ancestors had come from Phoenicia. The issue of whether or not these rulers were right to think this is not so clear. Nevertheless, this self-image and the fact that the probably Afroasiatic name Thebes appears in Linear B texts rule out any possibility of a Kadmean Phoenician conquest or settlement of the city after the end of the Bronze Age.

The credibility of the Bronze Age tradition depends on a number of factors, the first of which is at what point in the 2nd millennium it is plausible to see a Phoenician or West Semitic migration or conquest. Ruth Edwards has pointed out that a LHIIIB settlement would not allow enough time for the many events recounted in Theban historical legends before the city's fall.[15] Furthermore, we know that the official language of the city in the 13th century was Greek. Thus, it is clear that any Phoenician domination must have taken place earlier and cannot be directly connected to the hoard of oriental objects found in the last palace, although, as will be discussed below, it is quite likely that there was an 'enclave colony' of Levantine craftsmen in the city at the time.

It is possible that there was a Phoenician invasion or settlement

during LHIII, that is, after 1470 BC when there are at least two destructions.[16] However, the reconstructions give no evidence of any
'orientalization'. The fact that there is no archaeological sign of a
settlement or conquest does not provide an insuperable objection; as
we have seen, the Achaian takeover elsewhere in Greece left no tangible trace. On the other hand, one would expect the Kadmeans to
have left more evidence than the Pelopids, both because of the innovations they were supposed to have introduced and because, according to tradition, their migration would seem to have been much more
substantial.

There is no doubt that there are many more signs of Semitic speakers having been in Boiotia than there are of Anatolian speakers in the
Peloponnese. Apart from the name Thebes itself and those of its
founders Kadmos and Europa, there are those of the river Ladōn as
well as the Gephyroi – all of which, as mentioned in Chapter III, have
plausible Semitic etymologies. Similarly, the city names Thisbe and
Thespiae can be derived from the Hurrian god Teššub.[17] Scholars
since Bochart in the 17th century AD have seen Elieus, an epithet of
Zeus at Thebes, as deriving from the Phoenician Eliun, which Philo of
Byblos rendered as Hypsistos (Most High) in Greek; the name appears as ʾEl ʿElyōn in the Bible.[18] This would fit well with the cult
at Thebes of Zeus Hypsistos which was associated with the Hypsistoi
Gate.[19]

Another name is Ismenos, the alternative name for the river Ladōn,
which is linked by the cult of Apollo Ismenios to the god Apollo.
Apollo's role as a healer would correspond well with the Canaanite
healing god Ešmun. The Semitic root šmn, with the two meanings
'eight' and 'fat' or 'fertile', was suitable for the land through which the
river Ismenos flowed. The number eight is significant because, according to Philo of Byblos, Ešmun was the eighth brother of the seven
Kabiroi or Kabeiroi, mysterious underground pygmy smiths. The
derivation of their name from the Semitic kabîr (Great) is confirmed
by their Greek and Roman names Megaloi Theoi and Magni Dei. The
Kabiroi were worshipped in Beirut in Phoenicia and in Boiotia and
Samothrace. According to tradition, Kadmos was involved in both the
latter cults.[20]

Victor Bérard proposed another plausible Semitic etymology for
the mountain name Kithairon, upon which a holocaust with strong
Syrian parallels was carried out, from the Semitic root qṭr, which has
the Piel form qiṭṭēr (offer burnt sacrifices).[21]

Having accepted these Semitic etymologies, I am not convinced that
they make Boiotia extraordinary. In the first place, there are also sev-

eral names with plausible Egyptian origins – possibly Thebes itself and Kopais, Kēphissos, Alalkomenai and Athēnai as well as the Sphinx Mountain.[22] Secondly, many of the Boiotian Semitic, and Egyptian, place names occur elsewhere in Greece. In Chapter II, I discussed the toponomy of irrigation and mentioned 'Semitic' names, such as Orchomenos and Ladōn, and Egyptian ones, such as Peneus, being found not only in Boiotia but also in Arkadia and Thessaly. There are others such as Kēphissos, Athēnai and Harma, as well as Thebes itself, that occur elsewhere around the Aegean. In short, while there is a high incidence of names and cults with plausible Egyptian and Semitic origins in Boiotia, too much emphasis cannot be laid on this fact because they appear so frequently elsewhere.

The same impression that Boiotia was not especially different from other parts of Greece is also conveyed by the archaeological evidence. This suggests that Boiotia in general and Thebes and Orchomenos in particular were extremely prosperous during the Late Bronze Age and that irrigation works on Kopais and other lakes were considerably expanded during this period. The tombs, palaces and fortifications built on the basis of this wealth and considerable trade seem to have been very much like those found in other rich parts of Mainland Greece, such as the Argolid and the Southern Peloponnese. As mentioned above, there is strong evidence of Boiotia having been in close contact with Crete, especially during LHIIIB, but Cretan influence was widespread throughout Greece in the Mycenaean Age.[23] Thus, apart from the oriental hoard in the palace, the material culture of Thebes seems no more 'oriental' than that of the rest of Greece.

Similarly, while it is certain that Linear B was used there in the Late Bronze Age and Herodotos tells us that alphabetic Kadmean letters were too, there is every reason to suppose that both scripts were in use elsewhere in Greece.[24] The Boiotian inscriptions in both scripts make it clear that, at least by the 13th century, the official language was Greek and here again there is little reason to suspect that this situation had developed any later here than elsewhere. Thus, to sum up, if there was any truth in the Kadmean tradition of arrival from the East it would have to date from before the beginning of the age of the Mycenaean palaces we know.

ANCIENT CHRONOGRAPHIES

The idea that the Kadmean settlement was as old as that of Danaos is not new. The Parian Marble put Kadmos' arrival at Thebes at the equivalent of 1518/17 BC, while that of Danaos was set at 1511.[25] How-

ever, as Ruth Edwards insists, this was not the only ancient chronography and she lists Kastor of Rhodes from the 1st century BC, who
placed Kadmos' arrival at the equivalent of 1307 BC.[26] The church
father Eusebius gave, in his different writings, dates ranging from
1455 to 1285 BC. He put Danaos from 1492 to 1467 BC.[27]

Scholars who maintain a 2nd-millennium date of transmission of
the alphabet to Greece, and who accept the traditional association of
the introduction with Kadmos, have tended to prefer the later dates or
even the one of 1313 BC spuriously attributed to the Hellenistic scientist Eratosthenes.[28] However, most contemporary historians deny any
possibility of a 2nd-millennium transmission of the alphabet. The few
who have accepted some historical basis for the traditions of settlement have liked the Parian Marble's 16th-century dates for both arriv-
als, if only because they fit with the Ancient Model's linkage between
them and the expulsion of the Hyksos and their own association of
these with the beginning of the Late Bronze Age.[29] But, as we have
seen in Chapter IX, these scholars were working before the shifting of
MMIII to the period 1730–1675 and indeed before the proposal put
forward in this book that the first Hyksos colonizations of Greece
should be seen in the 18th not the 16th century BC.[30]

Kadmos and the Alphabet

While unorthodox in their attraction to the Ancient Model in general,
the scholars arguing for a 15th- or 14th-century date for the arrival of
Kadmos have accepted the conventional wisdom, established in the
1930s, that the alphabet was introduced to Greece in the 1st millennium, probably the 8th century BC.[31]

I reject this convention and have argued on epigraphic grounds not
merely that the alphabet was introduced to Greece in the late 2nd millennium, but that the transmission can have been no later than 1400,
though it was probably after 1800 BC. Thus, while accepting an overall association between the movement that Kadmos represented and
the introduction of the alphabet, I do not feel obliged, as the historians of the alphabet B. L. Ullman and David Diringer did, to lower
the date of his arrival.

Similarly, while I accept their attachment to the Ancient Model – in
general – one of my revisions of it is to shift the arrival of the Hyksos
in Greece from the period of their expulsion from Egypt in the 16th
century to the period of their general expansion in the 18th. This association between the transmission of the alphabet to Greece and the
Hyksos receives further traditional backing from the fact that the ear-

liest report of the introduction of the alphabet to Greece, that of Hekataios of Miletos in the 6th century, refers not to Kadmos but to Danaos.[32]
The relationship between the two and their Hyksos connections will be
discussed below. Thus the epigraphic arguments for the spread of the
alphabet coincide with the historical one for the spread of the Hyksos
in the Eastern Mediterranean, as well as with the Greek tradition.

The diffusion of Mycenaean influence in the Western Mediterranean, the Black Sea and Northern Europe during the 15th century,
after the establishment of what I see as the *Pax Aegyptiaca,* would explain the diffusion of early alphabets beyond Greece to Numidia and
Spain as well as the existence of runes in Northern Europe and Central Asia.[33] Nevertheless, they could well be earlier and the spread to
the Aegean must antedate this, despite the fact that historically the
idea that the alphabet spread in the East Mediterranean in the century of Egyptian hegemony (1470–1370 BC) is very attractive, because
of the abundant evidence of frequent contact, much of it through
trade, for which a convenient script like the alphabet would be extremely useful. However, this later period is difficult if not impossible
to reconcile with the archaic nature of the scripts that appeared in
Anatolia and Greece. Thus, it is possible to retain the association between Kadmos and the alphabet and to put him in the Hyksos age,
even if this has to be raised to the 17th or 18th centuries.

KADMOS AND DANAOS:
HYKSOS RULERS

This would also tally with the report of Danaos as the transmitter of
the alphabet and the strong tradition that Kadmos was related to
Danaos. At different times, the Hellenistic mythographer Apollo-
doros, basing himself on traditions going back at least to Homer, saw
Kadmos as a cousin or as a brother of Danaos.[34] At first blush this may
seem strange, given the clear attachment of Danaos to Egypt, while
Kadmos was the most famous Phoenician. In Classical and probably
in Archaic times too, Kadmos was often specifically associated with
Tyre.[35] However, it is unlikely that this association dates back to the
Bronze Age.

Evidence from archaeology and Egyptian texts leaves little doubt
that Tyre was an ancient city dating back at least to the beginning of
the 2nd millennium.[36] There is Herodotos' informed statement that it
was founded *c.* 2750 BC.[37] Furthermore, we know that Tyre was in
touch with the Aegean in the 2nd millennium BC. The gentilic Turijo
exists in Linear B and the Greek form Tyros shows that the city name

was introduced to the Aegean earlier than 1400 BC, when its name was Ṭor, before the sound-shift *ṭ* > *ṣ*, which made the Phoenician name Ṣor. Friedrich put the *terminusante quem* of the loan in the middle of the 2nd millennium and this would be confirmed by the dates of *c.* 1500 and the 14th century put forward for the sound-shift by the American Semitists Zellig Harris and W. L. Moran.[38]

Nevertheless, in Homer and the Pentateuch, Phoenicia was epitomized by Sidon not Tyre.[39] Furthermore, there are also traditions that Kadmos came from Sidon and there is little doubt that, for most of the Bronze Age, the Levantine city *par excellence* was Byblos.[40] Thus, it would seem likely that the connection of Kadmos the Phoenician and his family with Tyre should be dated only to the period after Tyre's rise to pre-eminence in the 11th or 10th centuries BC and that both this association and those with Sidon were simply cited to establish Kadmos' credentials as a Phoenician.

There is no doubt that by Archaic times there was a close identification between Kadmos and his brother Phoinix, the eponym of Phoenicia. Kadmos' other brothers were Kilix and Thasos, the eponyms of Kilikia or Cilicia in what is now Southeastern Turkey and Thasos, an island in the Northern Aegean. These, like that of another kinsman Membliaros, clearly served the aetiological function of explaining Phoenician influence in Kilikia, Thasos and Thera – where Membliaros was supposed to have settled.[41] Kadmos was also associated with other places where Phoenician influence was strong – Thrace, Samothrace and Rhodes – all of which were worked into the story of his pursuit of Europa.[42]

Phoenicia was not the only country associated with Kadmos' origins. Many sources linked him to Egypt.[43] Some of these were undoubtedly trying to make a connection between the two cities named Thebes and they are consistent in that most viewed him as a foreigner in Egypt. Thus, there are parallels between Kadmos and Danaos in being foreigners in Egypt, through mythical kinship and the invention of the alphabet. There were other links in such things as the close association of both heroes with Rhodes, particularly the city of Lindos where both were reported to have made votive offerings to the temple of Athena.[44] Danaos' origin from the Hyksos Semitic speakers in Lower Egypt has been discussed in Volume 1 and again in Chapter IX above.[45]

All this would point to a common origin for both heroes in the Hyksos movement in the 18th and 17th centuries BC. Hekataios of Abdera, whose writings at the end of the 4th century BC were discussed in Volume 1, specified that both Danaos and Kadmos were expelled from Egypt as Hyksos leaders.[46] If Kadmos were a Hyksos ruler of

Semitic and Hurrian speakers from Egypt, it would explain much of the toponymic evidence of these languages in Boiotia, although, as we saw in Chapter III, some of the place names may be earlier.[47] I should add that this view of Kadmos as a Hyksos leader and as a contemporary or near contemporary of Danaos is not new or original. It is held by Emily Vermeule, Frank Stubbings, George Huxley, Michael Astour and others.[48]

Since the re-dating of the Thera eruption, however, we have to adjust their chronology and place the establishment of the Kadmeans at about the same time as that of the Danaans in the late 18th and early 17th centuries. Thus both movements contributed to the formation of Mycenaean Greece, which would explain the similarities in the material cultures of the Peloponnese and Boiotia in the Late Bronze Age. What made Thebes different was that there was no Pelopid takeover and the original dynasty appears to have held power there until the middle of the 13th century BC.

PROBLEMS IN THE WRITING OF LINEAR B

The only major difficulty for the historical scheme that the Semitic influence on Boiotia came in with the Hyksos in the 18th and 17th centuries comes from the name Thebes or Thēbai itself. As stated above, this name would seem likely to come from the Canaanite *tēbåh* (ark or chest), which itself came from the Egyptian *tbi* or *dbt* (box). These two were often confused with one another and with the possibly related word *ḏbꜣ* (wicker float, ark of bullrushes) and *ḏbꜣt* (coffin, shrine and hence palace).[49]

The problem is that Thebes or Thēbai was not written as *Tepa in Linear B but as Teqa. This would appear to make it difficult to derive the Greek city name from the Egyptian *ḏbꜣt* or Canaanite *tēbåh*. Interestingly, there are two comparable cases. The first of these is *basileus*, which originally meant 'high officer' rather than 'king' and has a plausible etymology in the Egyptian *pꜣsr* (the officer or the vizier) which was transcribed in Akkadian of the late 2nd millennium as *pašia(ra)*. However, it is written in Linear B as *qasireu* not *pasireu. Finally, there is the Greek river name Pamissos which would seem to have come from the Egyptian Pꜣ mw (the water) which was a frequent toponymic element in Egyptian. However, Pamissos appears to have been written in Linear B as Qamisijo.

I believe that the simplest explanation for all of these terms is to suppose that they were introduced into Greek after the Greek labiovelars had broken down and the Proto–Indo-European sound k^w had disappeared and become p or t or k depending on the vowel that followed it.[50] There is no doubt that when Linear B was devised labiovelars were still pronounced in Proto-Greek and that the series of signs now transcribed with an initial q was borrowed from a language which also had these sounds to represent them. However, it is almost equally clear that the Linear B syllabary was used to represent the language we should now call Greek by the 17th century BC at the very latest. Thus, as the broad-minded Indo-Europeanist Oswald Szemerényi wrote about the series of signs beginning with q: 'a much more difficult question is whether the sounds so denoted were still labiovelars [when they were written]'.[51] The point at which the Linear B tablets were written is still very uncertain. Some may be as early as the 14th century. However, as I argued in Chapter X, I accept the case made by Palmer and Niemeier that most of the tablets date from the end of the 13th century.[52]

No one now seems to doubt that the labiovelars in front of u and y had been delabialized to become ku and ky before that time.[53] The problems of dating the palatalization of the labiovelars before e and i to become te and ti and of their labialization before a and o to become pa and po are more complicated. There is no doubt that k^wo could be written as po where there was another labiovelar in the same word, which indicates some instability here.[54] Nevertheless, the consensus among Mycenologists is that the original k^w was still present in the 13th and 12th centuries in these cases.

The bases for this judgement, however, seem very slight. The survival of labiovelars or their 'unorthodox' reflexes in later Greek dialects tells us nothing about the date of their breakdown in the standard language represented in Linear B. Lejeune has shown that the Linear B sign for a labiovelar before o is the same as that in *equos (horse) where the kw is not a labiovelar. This would suggest that the Linear B sign qo was pronounced as k^wo. It could, however, merely reflect an earlier situation when the spelling convention was established. Furthermore, there are two possible cases of early labialization in the Linear B texts.[55] There is no evidence about qa specifically. Ventris and Chadwick initially read qa as a labial pa_2, but Chadwick later retracted this reading.[56] However, even if one accepts Chadwick's discrediting of his and Ventris's earlier etymologies indicating this, it still does not establish that qa was heard as k^wa.[57]

The linguist Michel Lejeune has argued that the lack of alphabetic letters to represent the labiovelars demonstrates that they had disappeared before the alphabet's establishment, which he, following conventional wisdom, takes to be in the 8th century BC.[58] Today, however, the date of the transmission of the alphabet from the Levant to Greece is being raised to the 11th century, or, as I claim, to between 1800 and 1400 BC.[59] Accepting these dates would indicate that labiovelars had disappeared by the 11th century or the middle of the 2nd millennium. However, the situation is still further complicated – in my disfavour – because I see the letter *phi* ϕ as having originated from a Semitic *qup* used to represent labiovelars before their breakdown.[60] Nevertheless, there is no trace of the labiovelars in Hesiod or Homer, who not only lived in the 10th and 9th centuries BC, but – if I am right on the introduction of the alphabet – were following spelling conventions that went back into the Bronze Age. This indicates that there had been no labiovelars in their dialects for some considerable time.

Finally, there is the admittedly circular argument that Qamiso and *qasireu* have good etymologies from the Egyptian name P꜠ mw and word *p꜠sr*. The transcription of these two with *qa* rather than *pa* would fit a very common pattern according to which foreign loans are transcribed by rare or redundant signs. This practice provides the additional information that the word was foreign. This phenomenon can be seen in the Japanese use of the less common *katakana* syllabary for foreign words and the Modern Hebrew use of *tet* and *quph* to reproduce foreign *ts* and *ks* rather than the standard *tav* and *kaph*.[61]

These arguments make a good case for a scheme in which P꜠ mw and *p꜠sr* were introduced to the Aegean in the 15th or 14th centuries after the breakdown of k^wa in Greek. This would in fact fit the fact that the term *p꜠sr* seems to have come into official use only in the 18th Dynasty. However, the name Thebes or Thēbai would seem to be much earlier. Indeed, if we are to follow tradition associating the Kadmean migration with the introduction of the alphabet, the former must have come before the breakdown of the labiovelars.

The name Thēbā was sometimes linked to the earliest Kadmean stories or even earlier to those around Amphion and Zēthos.[62] On the other hand, there was another tradition that the city had originally been called Kadmeia and that Thēbā was a later name.[63] The simplest way to explain the problem away is to say that Teqa has nothing to do with *tēbåh* or *ḏb꜠*. Failing that, one could argue that the use of *qa* and *pa* was random in names or postulate that Thēbā still sounded foreign in the 15th or 14th centuries and was therefore transcribed that way. Finally, one could follow the tradition that Thēbā was a later name. None of these suggestions is satisfactory. Nevertheless, the depth of plausible Semitic and Egyptian cultic and linguistic influence and the strength of the tradition of the settlement of Kadmos the Phoenician are overwhelming. Furthermore, the difficulties in proposing any later colonizations and the intricate legendary links between Kadmos and Danaos and the Hyksos make the end of the Middle Bronze Age the only possible time for the Kadmean arrival.

Such early traditions and the legitimacy they bestowed would explain the emphasis on the Kadmean and Phoenician ancestry given in the many tragedies written about the decline and fall of the city. This is especially emphatic in Euripides' *The Phoenician Women* in which the chorus cries:

From the Tyrian seacoast,
From an island of Phoenicia,
I have come . . .
But now raging war,
Stands at this city's ramparts,
With a blaze of blood.
Threatening death to Thebes, which God forbid!
Friend suffers with friend,
If these seven towers should fall,
Our country too is struck to the heart,
We and they are one family,
Descended alike from Iō;
Their fate, then, is ours too.[64]

Or later:

When Kadmos came from Phoenicia to this country
An untamed heifer bounded before him . . .
You too Epaphos son of Zeus,
Born long ago to Iō our ancestress,
I invoke with a song of the east,
With prayers in the Phoenician tongue:
For you Thebes was founded by your descendants . . .[65]

Such passages not only emphasize the Phoenician ancestry of the Kadmeans, they also stress the connections with Danaos the descendant of Iō.

THE TREASURE OF THE KADMEION

If the 13th-century rulers of Thebes held a belief in their Phoenician origins and legitimacy, did this affect their actual contacts with the Near East? It is interesting that, despite the fact that Thebes was, as has been stated above, essentially Mycenaean, a significant number of

Levantine objects have been found in and around the city. For instance, a Canaanite jar has been discovered in a rich Late Helladic
tomb outside the city.[66] Much more sensational are the finds from the
Kadmeion or palace of Thebes itself. These include two ivory throne
legs that have no parallel in the Aegean and an extraordinary collection of cylinder seals. The cylinders, together with some Aegean seals,
some agate, onyx and lapis jewellery, were found in a LHIIIB context. Although it is uncertain whether they come from LHIIIB1 or
LHIIIB2, the second would seem more likely because they appear
to have been buried in the final destruction of the palace, probably
around 1230 BC. As with the discovery of the 120 Canaanite jars
on the Kaş wreck, the find of thirty-eight cylinder seals in one spot,
where only sixty others had been found from all previous excavations
in the Aegean, should give pause to those who want to believe that the
quantity of objects present in Antiquity can be determined from those
that have been excavated in modern times.

The sensational discovery of the oriental seals in the Kadmeion, the
palace of the Phoenician Kadmeans, has led to a great deal of loose
thinking. Suggestions were made that they represented the invasion
of Kadmos himself or were proof of a Canaanite or even Babylonian
metropolis in Greece.[67] Despite the exaggeration of such claims, the
seals do indicate that relations between Greece and the Levant were
much closer than has generally been supposed.

The archaeologist Connie Lambrou-Phillipson has argued cogently
that the treasure found in the palace came from a workshop of Levantine craftsmen. She points out that eleven of the cylinder seals were
'abraded' or deliberately ground away, and on one there appeared to
be the beginnings of a Mycenaean design.[68] However, she also points
out the presence of other techniques of jewellery and gold work that,
according to her, have seldom if ever been encountered in Aegean
craftsmanship: the inlaying of jewellery with lapis lazuli, gold-wire
making and the inlaying of metal articles with gold, niello. She herself
admits a number of other examples of these techniques from the Aegean. Nevertheless, there is no doubt that they were better and earlier
established in the Levant, especially at Byblos, and I think that there is
little doubt that this was the origin of their use in the Aegean.[69]

Lambrou-Phillipson also draws attention to the ivory carving on the
throne legs, which has no parallel in the Aegean and does suggest
craftsmen from a school of Levantine ivory carving for furniture
parts that flourished from the 17th to the 7th centuries BC.[70] Her most
impressive example of the latest Near Eastern technology is the iron
drill found at the Kadmeion with a collection of ivories. There was a

scarcity of iron in the Aegean at this time, while, as she stresses, it was being used in the Levant.[71] Although Connie Lambrou-Phillipson has not made a conclusive case for an enclave colony of Levantine crafts-men at Thebes, she has made a good one or at least a case for the presence of a number of individual Levantine craftsmen. Either of these hypotheses would fit well with the evidence of Near Easterners in the Linear B onomastica. Furthermore, Lambrou-Phillipson has shown without doubt how closely in touch the makers of luxuries were with each other in the Late Bronze Age, which is precisely what one would suppose from other archaeological evidence, most notably that of the Kaş ship.

THE KASSITE CONNECTION

If some of the seals found in the Kadmeion had been abraded, others had not and from the latter it is possible to learn a considerable amount. Seven of the seals were made in Cyprus or Syria – it is very difficult to tell the styles apart – from the 15th to the 13th centuries BC. Another four seals were originally engraved elsewhere but had been re-engraved in Cyprus or Syria in this period.[72] There is also one Hittite cylinder seal. However, although it comes from the 'Hittite world', there are some features that are not purely Hittite. In fact, the seal most closely resembles a sealing found at Ugarit of an official from Carcemish in North Syria. Thus, it may well come from the re-gion of Commagene seized by Assyria in the 13th century.[73] There were eight Mesopotamian seals from the Old Babylonian period early in the 2nd millennium or earlier, two of which had been recut in Cyprus; three seals were Mitannian from Northern Iraq in the late 15th and 14th centuries, showing both local and Egyptianizing influ-ences; and a further two are of mixed style but may be Assyrian.[74]

The most splendid pieces in the collection were the cylinder seals from the period of Kassite kings of Babylon, some of them in the purest lapis lazuli. These date from the 14th to the 13th centuries.[75] It will be remembered that the Kassites were the people who conquered Babylonia from the northeast at approximately the same time that the Hyksos conquered Egypt in the 18th century BC.[76]

Edith Porada, the expert in ancient seals, has thought long and hard about these cylinders and the significance of the hoard. Apart from arguing that they show the sophistication of the workshops in which they were made, she is unable to give any special significance to the Cypriot seals. However, her considered opinion of the Kassite seals and how they got to Thebes is elaborate and fascinating.

Among the Amarna letters of Egyptian diplomatic correspondence, there was a letter from the Kassite king Burna Buriaš II (1375–1347 BC) to Akhenaton (1381–1364 BC) in which the writer said that he was sending the pharaoh a *mina* of lapis lazuli.[77] The *mina* was the standard Mesopotamian weight of about 510 grams. Edith Porada contends that the use of one *mina* of lapis lazuli as an acceptable gift is confirmed by this being the weight of a number of vases listed in the temple archives at Nippur during the Kassite period.[78] She and Evi Touloupa, one of the archaeologists who discovered them, weighed the Kassite seals from Thebes and found them to be 496 grams. Porada believes this to be close enough to one *mina*. The idea that ancient Near Eastern monarchs would have been casual about such things is implausible. On the other hand, there may be one missing and it should be remembered that some weight would have been lost through the abrasion.

Edith Porada maintains that the Kassite seals were too splendid for personal use but were used especially for dedications to gods. She postulates, without direct evidence, that these had been dedicated to the Temple of Marduk in Babylon, whose cult was already central at that time. Her circumstantial evidence comes from the use by the 7th-century Assyrian kings Sennacharib and Esarhaddon of a Kassite cylinder seal that was probably dedicatory but which had been partially reinscribed by Tukulti Ninurta I five centuries earlier. She also shows that a son of Burna Buriaš had dedicated a block of lapis lazuli to the temple of Enlil.[79]

There is no doubt that Tukulti Ninurta I pillaged the temple of Marduk at Babylon after he captured the city and overthrew the Kassite rulers. Furthermore, Porada is able to show that some consideration was given to the disposition of the booty.[80] From all this, she concludes that the Kassite seals found at Thebes had been seized by Tukulti Ninurta I from the temple of Marduk at Babylon, when he took it *c.* 1235, and that they were sold or given to the ruler of the Greek city.

How can the presence of the seals in Thebes be explained? Porada is fully aware of the Hittite treaty of the 1240s, referred to above, in which there was an attempt to block trade between Aḫḫiyawa (the Achaians) and Assyria.[81] She was not, however, aware of the block of Laurion lead stamped with the seal of Tukulti Ninurta I, which indicates the importance of such trade before, and/or during or after the blockade.[82] Furthermore, there is the political angle, in that, as we have seen, the basic strategy of Aḫḫiyawa was anti-Hittite. This provides an explanation for the Achaians' good terms with the Hittites' major enemy Egypt in the late 15th and 14th centuries, and it would also seem plausible to extend this principle to the Hittites' new enemy Assyria in the mid-13th century.

THE DESTRUCTION OF THEBES

There are, however, some problems with the scheme of explaining the Kassite seals at Thebes in terms of an Aḫḫiyawa–Assyrian alliance. In the 13th century, Kadmean Thebes appears to have been the mortal enemy of the Pelopid rulers of the Argolid, who are generally supposed to have been the kings of Aḫḫiyawa referred to by the Hittites. There are no surviving records in the Hittite archives of different powers in the realm of the Aḫḫiyawa, although, as mentioned above, one possible reason for deleting the name of the King of Aḫḫiyawa in the text of King Tudhaliyas IV (c. 1265–1240) may have been internal struggles.[83]

The discovery of the Kassite cylinders would have been much easier to explain on diplomatic grounds had they been found at Mycenae, the presumed capital of Aḫḫiyawa, rather than at its rival Thebes. As it is, they would seem to be best explained as the result of trade and it is possible that Theban or Boiotian vessels played some role in the shipping of Attic metals to Syria for the Assyrian market. If we accept Edith Porada's scheme as a working hypothesis, as it would seem reasonable to do, despite the large number of suppositions upon which it is based, it provides some indication for the date of the destruction of the Argive forces of Thebes or at least that of its palace.

In his general survey of Thebes, Sarantis Symeonoglou puts this in the ceramic period at the end of LHIIIB1, which, according to the chronology proposed here, would be c. 1300 BC.[84] In his earlier study of the palace itself, however, he stated that there were some elements of LHIIIB2 and that 'a date later than this is possible'.[85] The Canadian classicist Robert Buck, in his *A History of Boeotia*, agrees with this second view and puts the consensus for final destruction of the palace 'near the end of LHIIIB'.[86] In this book that would be c. 1220 BC.

The *Cambridge Ancient History* puts the fall of Kassite Babylon at 1235 BC. Porada points out that the fact that work on abrading the cylinders found in the Kadmeion had not got very far would seem to indicate that they had not been in Thebes long. There is no way of telling how quickly Tukulti Ninurta I would have disposed of his loot or how fast or directly it travelled from Babylon to Thebes, possibly past a Hittite blockade. However, it is unlikely that the total was less than five years. Thus, it would seem likely that the destruction of

Thebes took place sometime between 1230 and 1225 BC. If, as tradition emphasizes, the war of the seven heroes against Thebes, which is so widely described in Greek drama, took place a generation earlier, this would then be around 1250 BC.[87] From these two points we can begin to examine possible dates for the Trojan War. Before doing this, however, we should look back at what is known of Trojan history.

A Brief Survey of Trojan History

The site of Troy on the southern end of the Dardanelles, where boats would have to wait for a south wind to blow them, against the current, north to the Sea of Marmara and the Black Sea, gave the city a crucial economic and strategic importance. As is well known, there were seven Bronze Age cities of Troy, dating back to the beginning of the Early Bronze Age in the late 4th millennium. In Chapter V, I looked at the possibilities that the ʾIwȝі mentioned in the Mit Rahina inscription was (W)Ilios or Troy and that the site known archaeologically as Troy V, which was replaced with a change of culture *c.* 1900 BC, had been taken by the armies of Sesōstris and Ammenemēs II [Memnōn].[88] We also saw, in Chapter X, that the majority belief is that the Wȝiwry shown as submitting to the pharaoh on the statue base of Amenōphis III was (W)Ilios. Opinion is, however, divided as to whether this and the other names referred to a single Egyptian expedition or had been used earlier in the New Kingdom.[89]

Archaeologically, the period dated by imported Mycenaean pottery to LHIIIA1 [1470–1415] was one of the most prosperous in Troy's history, and it was one in which the city was in close contact with Greece.[90] Sometime in the middle of the 14th century the city was destroyed, possibly by earthquake, but soon after that a new Troy (VII) was constructed, which, however, seems to have had less contact with Greece.[91] This lessening has been plausibly supposed to be the result of increased Hittite influence.

Before looking at this, we should consider reports of earlier contacts with Wilusa – the country names Wilusa and Taru(ú)isa are widely agreed to be Ilios and Troy – preserved in the Hittite archives.[92] The most informative text is a treaty between the Hittite king Mutawališ and Alakšanduš king of Wilusa just before 1300 BC.[93] The distinguished Hittitologist Hans Güterbock renders the first few lines as follows:

> After my forefather Labarnas had long ago subjugated all the lands of the Arzawa [and] the land of Wilusa, Arzawa began hostilities but Wilusa defected from Hatti – since the matter is long past, I do not

know from which king. (But even) when they had [defec]ted from Hatti they (its people) were at peace with Hatti and kept sending [messengers]. But when Tudhaliyas came to Arzawa he did not enter Wilusa: [it was] at peace and kept sending messengers.[94]

Labarnas reigned in the 18th or 17th century BC and the loss of suzerainty about which Mutawališ is ignorant probably occurred after the collapse of the Hittite Old Kingdom with the Hurrian pressure on the east of Hatti (the country of the Hittites) in the second half of that century. The Tudhaliyas mentioned was probably Tudhaliyas II, whose defeat of the Arzawa alliance around 1430 BC has been referred to above. The section of the text dealing with further relations in the 14th century is badly damaged but it seems that, while Hatti continued its struggles with Arzawa until the latter's destruction c. 1340, it remained on good terms with Wilusa, possibly protecting it from its immediate neighbours.[95]

Hittite suzerainty over Wilusa seems to have been confirmed with the treaty between Mutawališ and Alakšanduš at the very end of the century. It is generally agreed that the contingent of Drdny – the Classical Dardanians, close associates of the Trojans – who fought with Mutawališ against Ramessēs II at the battle of Qadesh in the fifth year of the latter's reign c. 1300 BC were from Wilusa.[96] After that, Egypt seems to have been out of the picture.

In the middle of the 13th century, there is evidence from the so-called Millawanda letter written by a Hittite king, probably Tudhaliyas IV (c. 1265–1240), to a vassal in or near Millawanda (Miletos). According to this, the vassal was sheltering Walmus, a ruler of Wilusa, who had been overthrown. The Hittite king asked him to send Walmus so that he could reinstate him as ruler and as his vassal.[97] This, as Itamar Singer has plausibly argued, marks the end of direct Hittite influence over Western Anatolia.[98]

In the Late Bronze Age, Troy was in the zone of conflict between the land powers of Anatolia, usually the Hittites, and the sea powers of the Aegean, notably Greeks, who after the 15th century were known to the Hittites as Aḫḫiyawa. We know that there was a considerable import of Mycenaean pottery during late LHII and LHIIIA down to the beginning of LHIIIB, that is from c. 1500 to c. 1350, suggesting close relations. This is also the period when Egyptian documents indicate contacts with W3iwry and Arzawa.[99] The picture is somewhat puzzling because this includes the period around 1430 of Tudhaliyas II's defeat of the Assuwa Alliance and it is possible that the recession in Mycenaean pottery imports in LHIIIA2 seen by some scholars reflects this.[100]

In any event, there is no doubt that there was a striking diminution in the amount of Greek pottery found in Troy VIIA, which raises the possibility that although there was no fiery destruction of Troy VI, its collapse and rebuilding may have been the result of a change of power, tipping the balance towards the Hittites. This probably occurred with the conquests of the West Anatolian kingdoms and the destruction of Arzawa by the Hittite king Mursilis II in his third year, c. 1340. There are indications that these were co-ordinated with a Hittite alliance with Wilusa.[101]

The so-called Tawagalawas letter is nowadays generally thought to have been written by Hattusilis III in the 13th century. Earlier scholars, however, attributed it to Mursilis II, and the mythological grounds for preferring this have been given above.[102] If such were the case, the war between Hatti and Ahhiyawa over Wilusa and the peace settlement that followed it, referred to in the letter, should be placed in the second half of the 14th century about the time of the end of Troy VI and the beginning of Troy VII.[103] If this correlation is accepted, it would seem that the settlement was in favour of the Hittites or at least against the interests of Ahhiyawa. This 'Pan-Anatolian' alliance was consolidated at the end of the century, as we have seen, with the battle of Qadesh.

Despite the lack of Greek pottery in Troy VIIA, there is no doubt that by this time there was a strong Greek influence on the town, an influence which had presumably existed for some time previously. The name of Alakšanduš, the ruler who signed the agreement with Mutawalliš, has been seen by many scholars to be a Hittite orthography for the Greek Alexandros.[104] The Indo-Europeanist Calvert Watkins also points out that the Homeric Trojan prince Paris had the alternative name Alexandros. The Hittitologist Laroche derives Paris from a Luvian name Pari-LU or Pari-zitis Pari (man).[105] Watkins draws a parallel between this and the Greek Alex-andros or Alex-'man'.[106] Pari(ya) seems to have been a family name and Laroche and Georgiev have independently derived the name of Paris' father Priamos from Pariyamuwas, a name attested from Cilicia.[107] Such an intricate linguistic interplay suggests that Homer may not arbitrarily have given Greek names to many Trojans but that they may have actually possessed them. Thus, although it was not as Hellenized as Millawanda/Miletos to the south, it would seem reasonable to suppose that Troy as a trading city reflected profound cultural influences from both Central Anatolia and the Aegean.

In the 1230s, Hatti appears to have been seriously threatened by the famine in Central Anatolia and it seems likely that its control of western and southern regions had been lost.[108] Hence, the absence of any mention of the Hittites in Homer and the geographical range of the Trojan alliance as portrayed in the *Iliad* may well reflect the actual situation, not as it was following the destruction of the Hittite Empire after 1200 BC, but after its loss of control of Western and Southern Anatolia *c.* 1235. It was from these regions and Thrace that the Trojan allies were reported to have assembled.[109] Thus, the Trojan War could well be seen as a Greek attempt to move into the power vacuum left by the recession of Hittite power.

THE DATE OF THE TROJAN WAR

For the last fifty years attempts to date the Trojan War have been baffled by the Swedish scholar A. Furumark's authoritative dating of Mycenaean pottery. His *The Chronology of Mycenaean Pottery*, which was written at the height of archaeological positivism and German influence in the late 1930s, put the beginning of LHIIIB at 1300 and its end at 1200.[110] Scholars have used this framework to date the cities of Troy VI and VII. The Mycenaean pottery from the former is mostly from LHIIIA but there are some 'elements' of LHIIIB.[111] Following Furumark, this would put the end of Troy VI at around 1280–1275 BC. This is too early for the traditional range of dates given for the fall of Homer's Troy, 1250–1170 BC. Thus, scholars have generally preferred its successor Troy VIIa, which was destroyed by fire in the approved Homeric manner. The rather scanty Mycenaean material in Troy VII comes from LHIIIB with a few shards from LHIIIC.[112] According to Furumark's chronology, this would put the destruction after 1180 BC. Such a date would fit the lower end of the traditional dating but, given the collapse of Aegean civilization which began around 1200, it is difficult to see how such a mighty expedition could have been launched so late.

The unsatisfactory nature of both destructions – in terms of the Homeric story – has caused great perturbation among those who take the ancient sources seriously. This agonized confusion can be seen most recently in the popular but informed and thoughtful BBC television series by the journalist Michael Wood.[113] On the other hand, these difficulties have been a boon to sceptics like Moses Finley who have used the archaeological confusion to cast doubt on the historicity of the Trojan War and hence on all Greek legends.[114]

The situation is now made much more straightforward by the raising of the ceramic periods – for reasons that have nothing to do with the Trojan War. As mentioned above, the ceramic chronology adopted in this book would make the fall of Troy VI about 1340 BC, which would correspond well with Mursilis II's re-establishment of Hittite power in Western Anatolia; Troy VIIa was destroyed shortly after the beginning of LHIIIC, which is seen here as *c.* 1220 BC. Thus, on archaeological grounds, the siege of Troy would seem to have taken place between that date and *c.* 1200.

This would also fit the Egyptian record of a major invasion of the Sea Peoples that took place in the fifth year of the pharaoh Mereneptah *c.* 1231. This alliance included both the ı̣kwš, almost certainly the Achaians, and the Trš, the Tyrsenoi referred to in Greek documents, probably the ancestors of the Etruscans.[115] These almost certainly came from Northwest Anatolia and so would have belonged to the Trojan alliance against the Greeks. Hence, it would seem impossible that such an alliance could have taken place after the beginning of the Trojan War. A date between *c.* 1220 and 1210 BC would fit very well within the traditional range from 1250 to 1170 BC. It would also make it possible for a massive expedition on something like the scale that Homer described to have been organized. Such a time-scale would lengthen the life of Troy VIIa to over 120 years, making it much more than a squatters' camp, as has sometimes been supposed. And, as mentioned above, the layer of ashes and burnt matter found above Troy VIIa would fit the fiery destruction of Troy described in tradition.

There is no doubt that some of the aspects of the Homeric story are folkloric. For instance, Cyrus Gordon has provided plausible Ugaritic antecedents to many aspects of it, including that of the story of the stolen bride for whom it is necessary to besiege a city.[116] Similarly, Emily Vermeule has shown both that many descriptions refer to techniques of warfare that were no longer in use in the 13th century and that some verses can be scanned properly only in a 'pre-Mycenaean' dialect. Her response to this is to suggest that the siege may have taken place long before the end of LHIIIB, in LHIIIA or LHII, which she puts in the early 14th century. While it is clear that LHIIIA does mark a high point of Mycenaean contact with Troy, her archaeological evidence for a Greek destruction of the city is slight.[117] It would seem far more plausible to suppose that when Homer or, as Mark Twain put it, someone of the same name, composed the *Iliad* and *Odyssey* around 900 BC, he drew from a Mycenaean epic tradition as a whole, as well as from that concerning the Trojan War. This would explain the presence of pre–13th-century elements.

Calvert Watkins has now found reference to a Luvian epic, specifically referring to the city, which apparently began with the line 'When they came from Steep Wilusa'; this strikingly resembles the 'steep

Ilios' of Homer.[118] This startling parallel and the possibility that many of the epithets and descriptions of the city may refer to Troy VI not Troy VIIa do not damage the credibility of the war itself. For while, like many other epics, the *Iliad* and *Odyssey* contain a large number of extraneous elements, some of which antedate the destruction of Troy VIIa by many centuries, there seems no reason to doubt the core of the story. Thus, the mobilization of a considerable Greek army, which besieged and eventually took Troy some time around 1210 BC, would seem on archaeological grounds to have a historical basis.

While the denial of the historicity of Homer's Trojan War would have a devastating effect on the credibility of less well-attested traditions, its re-establishment does not have such dramatic repercussions. It was much more central to ancient historiography than, for example, the colonizations of Kadmos and Danaos. Even so, the confirmation of the historicity of the Trojan War does give some credibility to other Greek traditions such as these.

THEBES AND TROY

It has been argued above on archaeological grounds that the destruction of Thebes took place sometime between 1230 and 1225 BC and that of Troy sometime around 1210. There is also literary evidence to back this view. The 'Catalogue of Ships' contained in Book II of the *Iliad* is a list of contingents sent to join Agamemnon's expedition, which even the most extreme believers in the epics as oral compositions believe to be based on very ancient, if not Mycenaean information.[119] The catalogue begins with Boiotia and gives great detail about it, to such an extent indeed that some scholars believe it – or its original – to have been composed there. It contains no mention of Kadmeians, and Hypothēba (Lower Thebes), though described as 'well built', has no especial importance, let alone dominance.[120] Thus, there is no doubt that the text was – or was meant to appear to be – after the destruction of Kadmean Thebes.

One difficulty in the credibility of this report comes with the name 'Boiotians' itself. As mentioned in Chapter II, the Boiotians were supposed to have been a tribe living in Thessaly who were pushed out of their home and invaded 'Boiotia'.[121] Thucydides put the date for this migration some sixty years after the Trojan War.[122] This would make it around 1150 BC, which – apart from Thucydides' explicit statement that the migration was later – is far too late for the launching of the expedition to Troy. Some scholars have tried to get around this by postulating two Boiotian migrations.[123] Furthermore, it would make a short gap between the falls of Thebes and Troy difficult to sustain. However, this explanation seems less plausible than the suggestion that 'Boiotian' was an anachronism in the 'Catalogue of Ships'. In a recent paper the archaeologist and ancient historian John Fossey has argued that the 'Boiotian Catalogue' contained a mixture of Mycenaean and Archaic material and he backed his contention by pointing out that the Homeric numbers indicated later tribal organization.[124] While I do not accept that the *Iliad* was composed in Archaic times, that is, after the 8th century, the idea that Homer was influenced by contemporary society around 900 BC seems very plausible.

Another possibility is that there were Boiotians in Boiotia in the Bronze Age. The similarity between Boiotian with its strong connotations of 'cattle' (*bous*) is strikingly similar to my interpretation of the name Minyan – the other inhabitants of Boiotia – which is from the Egyptian *mniw* (herdsmen). Both names would be very suitable for the rich plains and marshes of Boiotia and that name could well be a calque for *mniw*.[125] This is not to deny Thucydides' description of the tribal migration but merely to question his nomenclature.

One way and another, this objection to the close conjunction of the two sieges does not seem insuperable. Other traditions in fact indicate that they took place in the same generation. Homer maintained that the Diomedes and his companion Sthenelos who were at Troy had been involved in the final destruction of Thebes and that they were the sons of Tydeus and Kapaneus, who had fought in the first Theban War, with Polyneikes of Thebes.[126] Many of Homer's genealogies are clearly mythological. This one, however, has considerable apparently historical detail. Hesiod, in the 10th century, may have been implying the closeness of the two destructions when describing the end of Mycenaean civilization in his *Works and Days:*

> But when the earth had covered this generation [the Bronze one] also, Zeus, the son of Cronus, made another the fourth upon the fruitful earth, which was nobler and more righteous, a god-like race of hero-men who are called demi-gods, the race before our own, throughout the boundless earth. Grim war and dread battle destroyed a part of them, some in the land of Cadmus at seven gated Thebe, when they fought for the flocks of Oedipus, when it had brought them in ships over the great sea gulf to Troy for rich-haired Helen's sake: there death's end enshrouded a part of them.[127]

Whether or not there was any connection between these two wars is even harder to determine. It may be, however, that the Argive and Achaian final triumph over the earlier 'Hyksos' dynasties led to overseas ambitions, though, as mentioned above, the recession of Hittite power was probably more significant.

THE COLLAPSE OF
MYCENAEAN CIVILIZATION

If the Trojan War took place between 1220 and 1210, it signalled the end of Bronze Age civilization. Even before then, tradition reports that the Dorians had made their first attack on Southern Greece. The Egyptian inscription describing the sweeps of the Peoples of the Sea, the Prst, Ṭkr, Šklš, Dnn and Wšš, by land and sea in year 8 of Ramessēs III, c. 1190, has been mentioned in Volume 1.[128] In this the Egyptians claimed, credibly, that Hatti, Qode [Cilicia], Karkemesh [Upper Euphrates], Arzawa and Alashia had been destroyed.[129] Despite the participation of Greeks among the Sea Peoples argued in Volume 1, the Mycenaean states did not survive the crisis long.

The recent discoveries at Kaş and elsewhere have made it clearer than ever that the Mycenaean palaces and their economies were integrally connected to those of the Near East. We know that such trade survived the Fall of Thebes and the Trojan War. The Cape Gelidonya wreck with its Syrian crew and international cargo of metal and metalwork is not of the same scale or splendour as the Kaş ship but it shows that, when it sank just before 1200 BC, there was still trade around the East Mediterranean.[130]

Further evidence of the continuation of trade is provided by the grave-goods from the cemetery at Perati in Eastern Attica. These date from LHIIIB/C to well into LHIIIC. From the earliest strata of these come several scarabs of Horemheb, last king of the 18th Dynasty (1348–1320 BC), and Ramessēs II (1304–1237).[131] The re-dating of the beginning of LHIIIC to c. 1220 would make the Ramessēs II scarabs almost contemporaneous and therefore imported and buried in a relatively short time. There are also figures of the Egyptian god Bes and faience crocodiles, as well as two Mitanni cylinder seals.[132] It is impossible to say whether these were acquired through trade or robbery, though trade would seem more likely, given the graves' proximity to the lead and silver mines of Laurion. In any event, they show that contacts between Greece and the Near East survived into the 12th century.

Nevertheless, the sieges of Thebes and Troy symbolically marked the end of the heroic ages, as Hesiod and Thucydides specified, and there may have been disturbances in Greece soon after that time.[133] There is also strong evidence of a major social and economic upheaval after the beginning of the ceramic period LHIIIC. These changes, which have been touched upon in Chapters VII and XI, appear to have involved a considerable decline of population over most of Greece. The decline seems to have been less steep in Western Greece, which a number of scholars have plausibly explained in terms of the higher rainfall there, which would make these regions less susceptible to drought.[134] There was also a change in the pattern of settlements from dispersed houses or clusters of houses into 'nucleated' centralized villages, a transformation that is generally associated with social uncertainty and depressed economic conditions. In general, the archaeological evidence points to a shift from a prosperous specialized agricultural and manufacturing society to a much reduced subsistence economy.[135]

Many scholars have linked this to the breakdown of trade in the East Mediterranean at this time.[136] The argument made in the last chapter for an export of grain to the Aegean from Egypt – at least to relieve famine – provides some precision to this hypothesis.[137] It is that the removal of this support occurred after the repeated raids by the Peoples of the Sea had weakened Egypt and made maritime transport increasingly dangerous. This in turn made at least Eastern Greece vulnerable to famine following the inevitable droughts. Therefore, the Mycenaean states were forced to turn to subsistence agriculture.

Nevertheless, the Mycenaean palaces seem to have survived for another two generations. It was only sixty years after the fall of Troy that they were overrun by Greek tribes from the north, notably the Dorians but also the Thessalians and the Boiotians. These movements are clearly connected in some way to the Invasions of the Sea Peoples, especially the invasion of c. 1190. But they would also seem to be related to the weakness of the Mycenaean states. However, it is also interesting to note that the invasions of c. 1150 happened very soon after the eruption of Hekla III in 1159, given what we know to have been its devastating effects in Northwestern Europe, and what may have been its harmful impact on Elam in the Iranian highlands. Thus, it is possible that it was a short-term climatic variation caused by this that stimulated the most powerful tribal movements and finally destroyed the Mycenaean state system and its palaces.[138]

Thus, the collapse of Mycenaean civilization seems to have been overdetermined. Mycenae was damaged firstly by local wars at Thebes and Troy and the subsequent dynastic feuds described in the epics and tragedies; secondly, by the breakdown of trade and civilization around the East Mediterranean after the Invasions of the Sea Peoples c. 1190 BC, with the consequent lack of the staples necessary for a specialized food-deficient economy. Thirdly, there were the migrations of northern Greek tribes around 1150 BC, which were possibly precipitated by the Hekla volcanic disaster. In any event, 1150 BC marks the end of the Greek Bronze Age with which this book is concerned.

CONCLUSION

The events of the second half of the 13th century BC discussed in this chapter linked Thebes with Aššur and Babylon, and the Aḫḫiyawa based at Mycenae with Central Anatolia, Syria and Egypt, providing glimpses of the dense network of trade and diplomacy that existed over the whole of the Middle East and East Mediterranean at this time. Paradoxically, we know rather more about this period, because the destructions that brought it to an end have preserved documents and objects from it that are lacking for earlier centuries. There is thus no reason to suppose that such far-reaching networks did not operate in earlier centuries, at least after 1470 when the victories of Tuthmōsis III appear to have led to the establishment of a *Pax Aegyptiaca*. The flourishing society of late Mycenaean Greece appears to have arisen as the result of this Egyptian hegemony and there is no doubt that the two fell at the same time.

CONCLUSION

ᴛ

T HE PURPOSE OF THIS volume has been to show how the documentary and archaeological evidence from the Bronze Age supports the two hypotheses that Egypt and the Levant had a fundamental impact on the Aegean in this period and that the Classical and Hellenistic writers knew what they were talking about when they referred to colonizations of Greece from Egypt and Phoenicia. I believe that this purpose has been achieved. It could be argued, however, that this has been achieved only by committing what many modern scholars would consider to be 'outrages'.

Indeed, in many ways, this volume is more outrageous than the first. On the other hand, as fewer readers will be aware of the extent of the 'outrages', it would seem useful to indicate some of them here. A significant number of these 'outrages' fit into the interesting general pattern of a return to older scholarly beliefs or, to be more specific, those of the early 20th century.

There would seem to be an extreme paradox here, as the main thrust of my whole project has been against the influence of racism and anti-Semitism on scholarship. Yet in this volume I have frequently found myself championing the views of scholars working at the high tide of racism 1880–1940, though it must be said that these are generally on issues in which racism is not directly involved.

These are also issues where the conclusions of the older generation of scholars fit better with the results of modern scientific techniques than do the views of contemporary scholars. To take two instances discussed in this volume, lead isotope analysis shows that lead from Central Europe was being used in Mesopotamia around 3000 BC. This is exactly what Gordon Childe would have expected, as he believed that Sumerian prospectors had gone up the Danube at this period. Similarly, the latest radio-carbon datings put the beginning of the Egyptian Old Kingdom to around 3000 BC, which fits the chronology of James Breasted, but that is far earlier than any accepted by conventional wisdom today.

I believe that this pattern is not the result of random coincidence and that the modern archaeologists have been led astray for reasons that can be relatively easily explained in terms of the sociology of knowledge. Firstly, there has been the turn away from diffusionism. As I argued in Volume 1, I believe that on one level this represents an admirable rejection of the uses of diffusionism to justify imperialism and colonialism. However, it also indicates the desire of new professionals to appear sober and responsible and not indulge in the spectacular theories to which amateurs are so attracted.

This is connected the second tendency that appears to have misled modern scholarship. In a surprisingly large number of areas of Western ancient history, there was no great increase of information between 1920 and 1960. This period was one in which there was a powerful drive among archaeologists to acquire 'scientific' status. This in turn produced a double effect. In the first place, archaeologists wanted, above all, to avoid being considered as speculative and irresponsible. However, they also needed to show that the discipline was progressing and innovative. Thus, the only alterations they could make were those that demonstrated their greater scepticism and caution. For this reason all 'progress' in these disciplines since 1920 has tended to restrict the geographical scope and lower the historical dating of ancient activities. Recent evidence from scientific techniques, however, points in precisely the opposite direction and this has led to the paradoxical situation that the archaeologists who have proclaimed their scientific status most loudly are in the greatest conflict with the results of the new scientific techniques when applied to archaeology. What is more, the results of the new techniques often fit better with the ideas of earlier or more conservative scholars.

Thus, a number of the controversial ideas in this volume are only 'outrageous' in the light of modern conventional wisdom. An example of this comes in the attempt I make in Chapter I to reverse the present isolationist current among archaeologists with a return to modified diffusionism, and in particular to the belief that early European Bronze Age civilization derived in some way from the still earlier metalworking cultures of Southwest Asia and Northeast Africa.

If I am right here, it means that the sustained attack on the positions of the early 20th-century archaeologists Oscar Montelius and Gordon Childe launched by Colin Renfrew and his colleagues has not merely been a complete waste of time but has been positively harmful to our understanding of the origins of Greek civilization. I also go beyond Montelius and Childe by arguing that Crete and possibly the Cyclades may well have become Semitic-speaking at this time.

Another example of my revisionism comes in Chapter III, where I champion the views of two very unfashionable Greek archaeologists, the late Spyridon Marinatos and Theodore Spyropoulos, when they claim that there were strong traces of Egyptian influence on Greece in general and Boiotia in particular during the 3rd millennium. If they are right, and I believe they are, Greece at this time must have contained some substantial states capable of massive irrigation works and collection and storage of considerable amounts of grain. Furthermore, these works and buildings look so 'Egyptian' that Egyptians may well have been involved in them, either in positions of authority or as experts or both.

In the fourth chapter, I propose that the Cretan palaces and the bull cult associated with them were at least indirectly derived from the contemporary Egyptian 11th Dynasty and that it is possible that there was Egyptian suzerainty over Crete and the Cyclades during the Egyptian Middle Kingdom. Here I am going beyond early 20th-century scholarship, but it is a picture that Sir Arthur Evans would have found less scandalous than most specialists in Cretan archaeology today.

Probably the greatest single outrage in this volume of *Black Athena* is the elaborate effort to resuscitate the northern campaigns of the 12th Dynasty pharaoh Sesōstris. Stories of his magnificence and his far-reaching conquests were believed until the late 18th century. After that time, however, the idea of two black pharaohs, Sesōstris and his son Ammenemēs II, having led an Egyptian army as far as the Balkans and the Caucasus seemed completely preposterous. I maintain that this extraordinarily widely attested legend has been strikingly strengthened by the newly discovered Mit Rahina inscription from the 12th Dynasty. Even if it had not, however, I think that there is sufficient other evidence to suggest that the pharaohs did lead campaigns to the north on this scale. Such a proposal goes flat against the dominant trend in Egyptology, which is to limit the scale of any Egyptian operation or foreign contact and to see as boastful or purely symbolic any claim to have dominated any foreign region, especially those to the north.

The most unconventional aspect of the treatment of the Thera eruption in Chapter VII is the post-mortem on the fierce defence of the conventional dating of 1450 or 1500 BC for the eruption based on an earlier hunch. This was in the face of substantial evidence from comparative styles of pottery, radio-carbon, dendrochronology and analysis of the Greenland Icecap, all of which indicated that the eruption was more than a century earlier. The bad taste here is to dig up an issue that many people now consider decently buried. I believe that such an investigation is useful because it is important to understand the sociology of knowledge and the processes by which historical arguments are decided.

The main point of Chapter VIII is the conclusion I came to, with some surprise and distress, that there may well have been not merely Hurrian speakers among the Hyksos invaders of Egypt, but also Indo-Aryan or at least Indo-Iranian speakers. This shows not only that Aryan Models may sometimes be useful or 'true' but that the anti-Semitic scholars who denied on principle that the Semitic speakers of Syro-Palestine could have provided the drive for such an invasion may this time have hit on the better historical explanation for morally reprehensible reasons.

Nevertheless, I insist that the fact that barbaric invaders from northern and barren lands have – as appears in this case – sometimes conquered more prosperous and cultivated regions does not mean that all historical changes can be explained by such processes. In particular, I am still convinced that in the case of Greece such a model is definitely unhelpful.

In Chapter IX, the 'outrage' is once again my support of early 20th-century scholars against their descendants or *epigonoi*. The ancient historian Eduard Meyer made a case for a Hyksos conquest of Crete which I believe has better support than the isolationist arguments against it. Similarly, the distinctly old-fashioned archaeologists Spyridon Marinatos and Frank Stubbings insisted that Greek legends should be taken into serious account when assessing ambiguous archaeological data. They concluded that, although not straightforwardly Egyptian, the goods found in the Shaft Graves and contemporary burials showed strong signs of Egyptian and Levantine influence. On this basis, they concluded that the legends had been essentially accurate when they reported, if not Egyptian colonization, colonization from Egypt, at this time.

It must be pointed out, however, that both Marinatos and Stubbings belong firmly to the Aryan Model and deny that these invasions introduced any long-term Egyptian or Semitic influences into Greece. I believe, on the contrary, that the period after these settlements, c. 1700–1500 BC, was the one in which Greek as a language and the 'Greek' cultural or national identity were formed and that, during much of this period, considerable areas of Greece were dominated by

Semitic- and Egyptian-speaking dynasts and that these high-status cultures and languages had a critical impact on the formation of both Greek and Greece.

There is nothing particularly outrageous about Chapter X. It is a survey of the written and pictorial evidence for contacts between Egypt and the Levant on the one hand and the Aegean on the other. The only controversial aspect of my work here is to take the Egyptian claims of knowledge of, activities in and suzerainty over the Aegean more literally and seriously than has been customary.

Chapter XI is, in some ways, even less controversial. Although many non-specialist readers may be surprised at the extent of the archaeological evidence for contacts between the Near East and the Aegean between 1550 and 1200 BC, scholars concerned with the period are fully aware of them. There are three new features here. The first of these is the insistence that the intimacy engendered by this degree of contact must have had important and long-lasting effects on Greek language and culture. The second is the relating of the recent heightening of ceramic periods – brought about by new work on synchronisms with Egypt and the re-dating of the Thera eruption – to evidence from Egyptian documents. This makes the ceramic periods in which there was massive trade between the Aegean and the Near East tally neatly with the periods of maximum Egyptian power and influence over the East Mediterranean. Thus the expansion of Mycenaean trade would seem to have taken place within a *Pax Aegyptiaca*. The third innovation in this chapter is my suggestion that the new proof that Aegean lead and silver were exported to Egypt during the New Kingdom raises the possibility that the trade of such metals for Egyptian grain, known to have existed in Archaic and Classical times, was already taking place in the Late Bronze Age. Such a supply of grain, at least as a buffer against famine, allowed Mycenaean Greece to develop a specialized and sophisticated food-deficient economy capable of supporting a large population.

The vulnerability of such a system led to the collapse of Mycenaean civilization after 1200 BC, which came with the weakening of Egyptian power and increasing difficulties of marine transportation, following the Invasions of the Sea Peoples, all of which are described in Chapter XII. In this chapter, the new ceramic datings provide a plausible chronology for the sieges and falls of the Greek Thebes and Troy. This confirms the veracity of Homer and the Classical Greek writers, which in turn provides support for the credibility of the Ancient Model which they maintained.

Although there are exceptions, such as my belief in the northern campaigns of Sesōstris, most of my revisions to today's conventional wisdom are in tune with the views of scholars in the early part of this century. Where I differ from them, of course, is in my non-acceptance of the principle of ethnic history and permanent racial hierarchy. However, if one subtracts that crucial element from their thinking something remarkably close to the Revised Aryan Model emerges.

Oscar Montelius and Gordon Childe saw the whole scheme I am proposing when they talked about 'the irradiation of European barbarism by Oriental civilisation'. Without in the least meaning to, Eduard Meyer laid down a crucial way in which Egyptian and Semitic civilization and languages could have been introduced to the Aegean when he suggested Hyksos control of Crete. Similarly, Frank Stubbings and Spyridon Marinatos indicated another way of transmitting West Semitic and Egyptian culture to the Aegean when they argued that the grave goods of the Shaft Graves indicated a migration from Egypt. None of these scholars, however, was able to see the logical consequences of their hypotheses, namely that Greek culture and language were permeated by those of Egypt and the Semitic-speaking Levant. It is these consequences that I want to underline.

To conclude this conclusion: if a significant quantity of what I claim in this volume is correct, much of contemporary work on the archaeology and ancient history of the East Mediterranean will have to be rethought. Having said that, however, the 'outrages' in this book are nothing to those I propose for the next volume, Volume 3, for there I shall attempt to challenge the linguists on language, which is, for romantic positivist scholars, the holy of holies, the *sanctum sanctorum* or, to use the Afroasiatic prototype for this phrase, *qōdeš haqqŏdāšîm.*

MAPS AND CHARTS

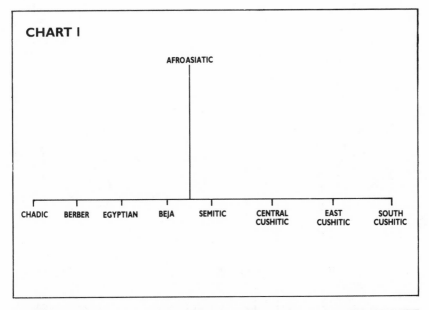

CHART I

AFROASIATIC

CHADIC   BERBER   EGYPTIAN   BEJA   SEMITIC   CENTRAL
CUSHITIC   EAST
CUSHITIC   SOUTH
CUSHITIC

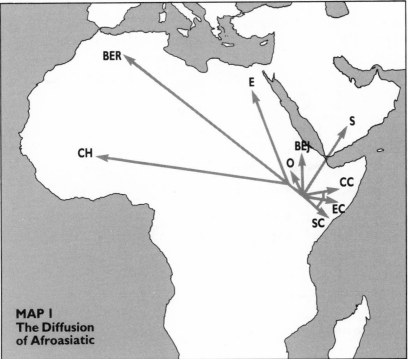

**MAP I
The Diffusion
of Afroasiatic**

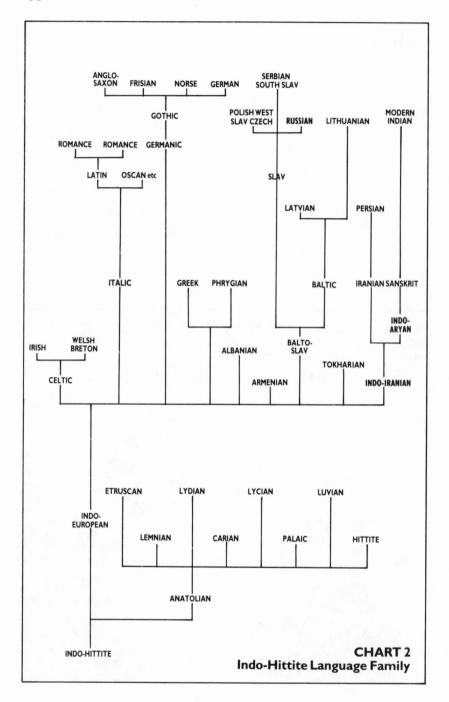

CHART 2
Indo-Hittite Language Family

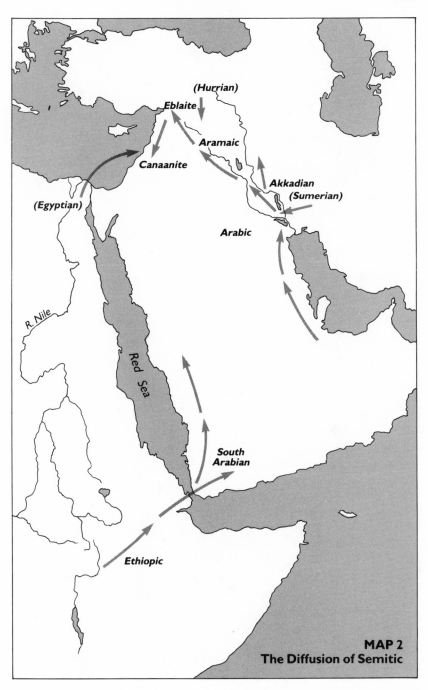

**MAP 2
The Diffusion of Semitic**

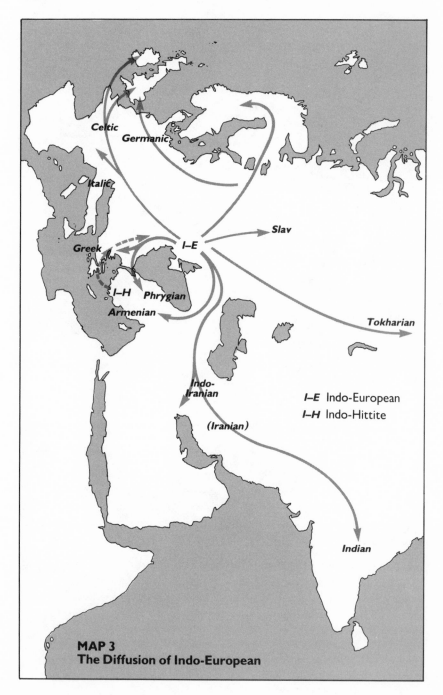

MAP 3
The Diffusion of Indo-European

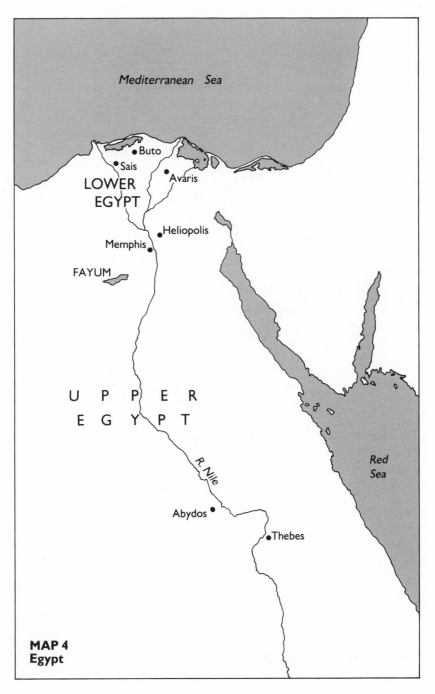

**MAP 4
Egypt**

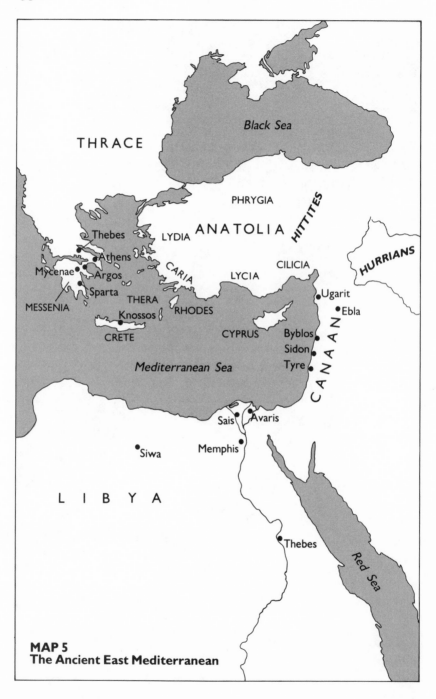

MAP 5
The Ancient East Mediterranean

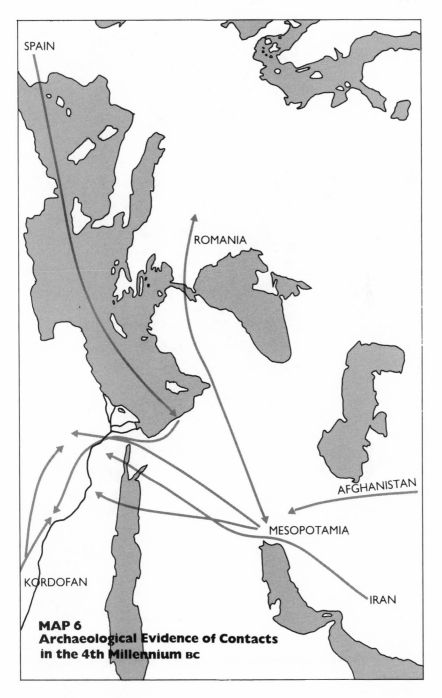

SPAIN

ROMANIA

AFGHANISTAN

MESOPOTAMIA

KORDOFAN

IRAN

MAP 6
Archaeological Evidence of Contacts
in the 4th Millennium BC

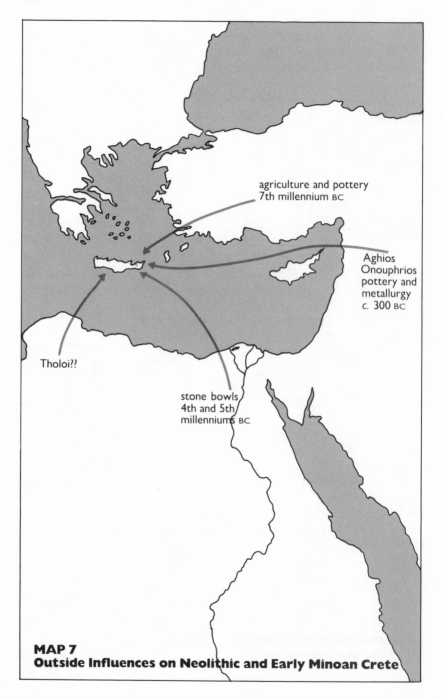

agriculture and pottery
7th millennium BC

Aghios
Onouphrios
pottery and
metallurgy
c. 300 BC

Tholoi??

stone bowls
4th and 5th
millenniums BC

MAP 7
Outside Influences on Neolithic and Early Minoan Crete

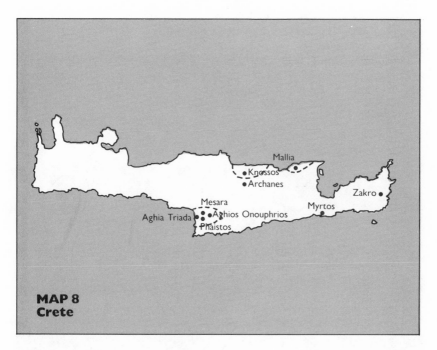

MAP 8
Crete

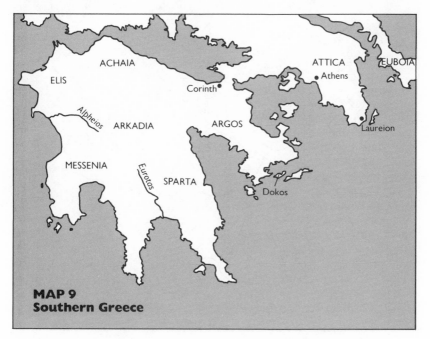

MAP 9
Southern Greece

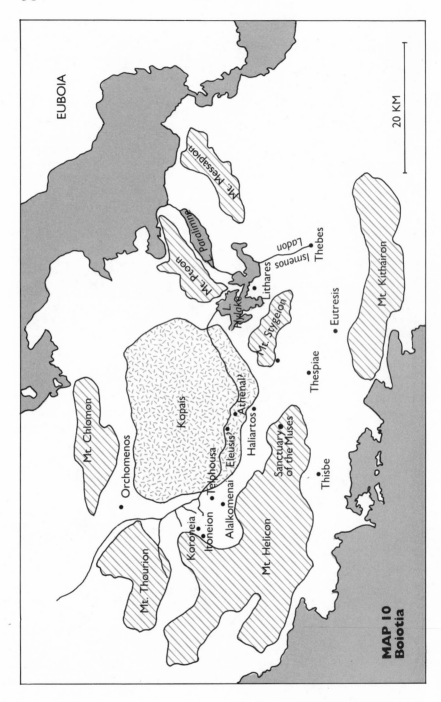

MAP 10
Boiotia

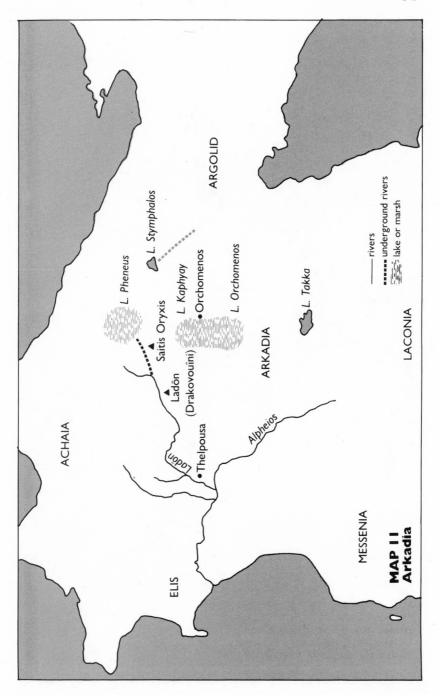

ARGOLID

L. Stymphalos

L. Pheneus

Saitis Oryxis

L. Kaphyay

Orchomenos

L. Orchomenos

Ladōn
(Drakovouíni)

ACHAIA

ARKADIA

L. Takka

LACONIA

Thelpousa

Alpheios

Ladōn

ELIS

MESSENIA

rivers
underground rivers
lake or marsh

**MAP 11
Arkadia**

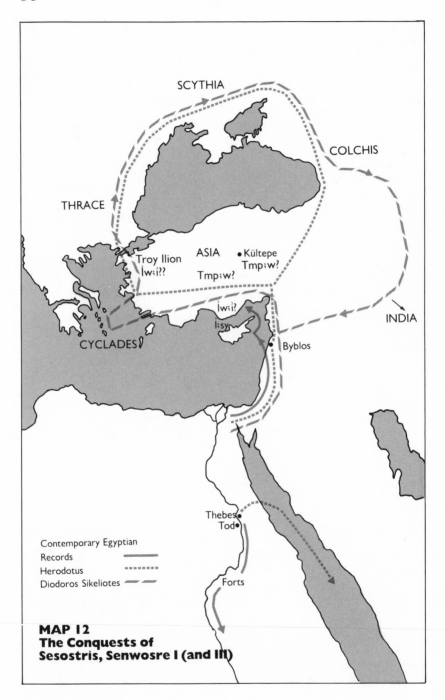

SCYTHIA

COLCHIS

THRACE

Troy Ilion   ASIA   ● Kültepe
Iwꜣi??   Tmpꜣw?
          Tmpꜣw?

          Iwꜣi?
          Iꜣsy   INDIA

CYCLADES   ● Byblos

Thebes ●
Tod ●

Contemporary Egyptian
Records
Herodotus
Diodoros Sikeliotes

Forts

MAP 12
The Conquests of
Sesostris, Senwosre I (and III)

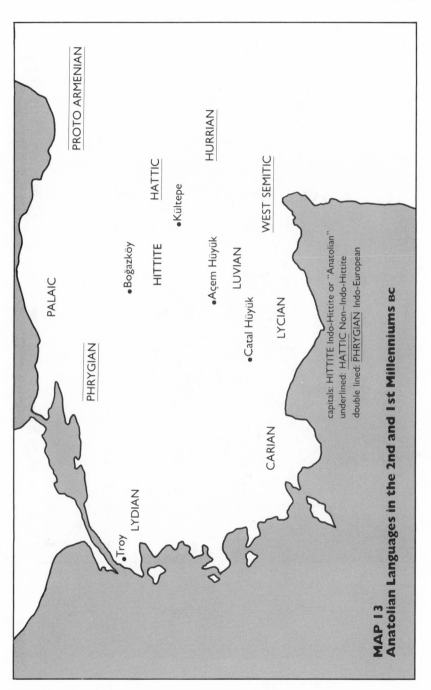

MAP 13
Anatolian Languages in the 2nd and 1st Millenniums BC

capitals: HITTITE Indo-Hittite or "Anatolian"
underlined: HATTIC Non–Indo-Hittite
double lined: PHRYGIAN Indo-European

PROTO ARMENIAN

PALAIC

PHRYGIAN

HITTITE   HATTIC

•Boğazköy

•Kültepe

HURRIAN

•Açem Hüyük

LUVIAN

WEST SEMITIC

•Çatal Hüyük

LYCIAN

CARIAN

LYDIAN

•Troy

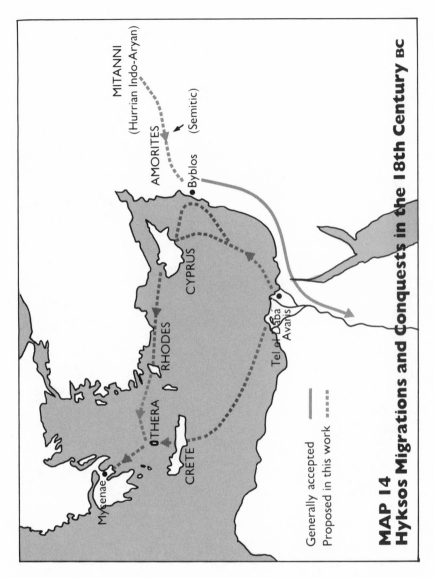

MAP 14
Hyksos Migrations and Conquests in the 18th Century BC

MITANNI
(Hurrian Indo-Aryan)

AMORITES
(Semitic)

• Byblos

CYPRUS

RHODES

THERA

CRETE

Mycenae •

Tel el-Daba
Avaris

Generally accepted ———
Proposed in this work = = = =

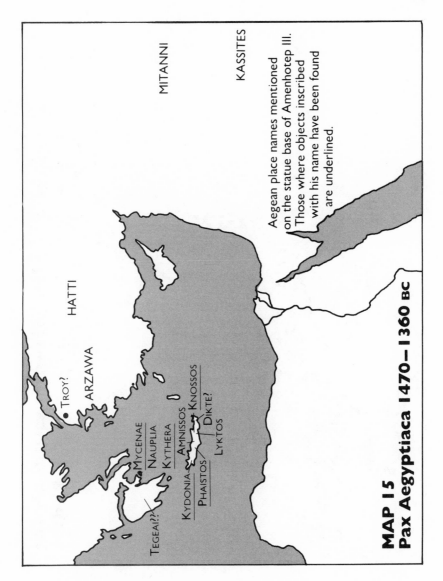

MAP 15
Pax Aegyptiaca 1470–1360 BC

Aegean place names mentioned on the statue base of Amenhotep III. Those where objects inscribed with his name have been found are underlined.

KASSITES

MITANNI

HATTI

ARZAWA

TROY?

MYCENAE
NAUPLIA
KYTHERA
AMNISSOS
KYDONIA
KNOSSOS
PHAISTOS
DIKTE?
LYKTOS
TEGEA??

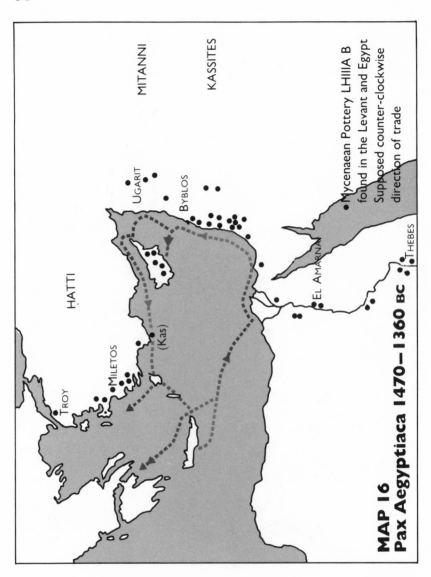

MAP 16
Pax Aegyptiaca 1470–1360 BC

MITANNI

KASSITES

• Mycenaean Pottery LHIIIA B
  found in the Levant and Egypt

  Supposed counter-clockwise
  direction of trade

UGARIT

BYBLOS

HATTI

(Kas)

MILETOS

TROY

EL AMARNA

THEBES

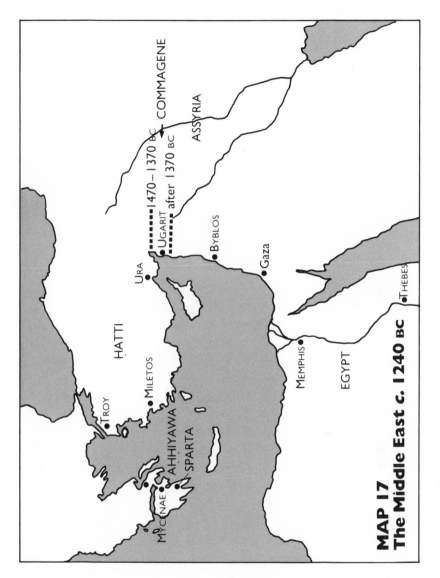

MAP 17
The Middle East c. 1240 BC

Notes

Preface

1. Peradotto and Myerowitz Levine (1989).

Introduction

1. Vol. 1, pp. 442–3.
2. McNeal (1972, p. 20). I admire the article for its bold attack on the subjective linguistic underpinnings of the Aryan Model and its use of Goethe's important dictum 'The most important thing to understand is that everything factual is already theory.' My objections are to its faith in professionalism and refusal to accept anything less than certainty.
3. Edwards (1979, pp. 65–89).
4. Nilsson (1932). Burkert (1985, pp. 47–53) is more cautious but he does not deny Nilsson's basic case.
5. Naveh (1973, pp. 1–8); Bernal (1987, pp. 1–19); Bernal (1990).
6. For Cyprus, see Jensen (1969, pp. 138–41) and Friedrich (1957, pp. 124–31). For Crete, Davis (1967, p. 26); Gordon (1966, p. 13); Steiglitz (1976, p. 85); Marinatos (1958, p. 228); Raison and Brixhe (1961, p. 130); Brown (1978, p. 44); *pace* Brice (1959, p. 330).
7. Thucydides I.1; Pausanias, III.3.3; and Plutarch *De Gen. Soc.* 5–7.
8. Josephus, *Contra Apionem,* I.12–21. For Philo, see Baumgarten (1981) and Attridge and Oden (1981). For Manetho, see Waddell (1940, pp. vii–xxx).
9. Josephus, *Contra Apionem,* I. 14, Walcot (1966, pp. 18–19) and Kirk, Raven, and Schofield (1983, pp. 48–72).

10. Many commentators have pointed out that Herodotos' chronology of Egyptian history can be straightened out by a single textual emendation (de Selincourt, 1954, p. 166).

11. Josephus, *Contra Apionem*, I.28, trans. p. 175.

12. Josephus, *Contra Apionem*, I.107–111, trans. pp. 205–7.

13. See below, ch. VII, nn. 2–62.

14. Åström (1978, pp. 87–90).

15. See ch. VII.

16. Petrie (1890, 1891, 1894). See also Cadogan (1978, p. 209).

17. Plato, *Timaios* 22D.

18. Bernal (1989a, pp. 22–5).

19. Gardiner (1961, p. 309); Wilson (1969, p. 27). For the continuities of material culture, see Prausnitz (1985, p. 191).

20. (1975, p. 52).

21. See Herrin (1987, pp. 19–53).

22. Volume 1, pp. 303–5.

23. Especially pp. 281–330 and Bernal (1988).

24. *Pace* Leach (1986) and Thapar (1975, 1977), both of whom have written brilliant and devastating ideological criticisms of 19th-century Indology and Indo-European studies.

25. Kuhn (1977, p. 463). For the division of Kuhn's earlier 'paradigms' into 'exemplars' and 'disciplinary matrices', see Suppe (1977, pp. 135–51).

26. Barnes (1982, p. 11).

27. Kuhn (1970, p. 169).

28. Lacatoš (1970, pp. 106–11).

29. Volume 1, pp. 407–8.

30. Volume 1, pp. 326–30 and Bernal (1988).

31. Renfrew (1972, p. xxv).

32. Volume 1, p. 64.

Chapter I
CRETE BEFORE THE PALACES, 7000–2100 BC

1. See M. H. Salmon (1982, esp. pp. 19–30) and the papers in Renfrew, Rowlands and Seagraves (1982).

2. Volume 1, pp. 407–8.

3. Adams (1968) and Renfrew (1987, esp. pp. 86–94).

4. Adams (1968, p. 213).

5. McNeal (1972, p. 19). See Introduction, n. 2.

6. See Volume 1, pp. 407–12.

7. See Volume 1, pp. 270–2.

8. For a good survey of these archaeological trends, see Trigger (1980, pp. 24–31, 44–9).

9. For Myres's racism, see Volume 1, p. 389. For Gordon Childe's early love of the Aryans, see Volume 1, pp. 388–9 and Trigger (1980,

pp. 49–53). Childe of course later played a distinguished role in opposing Nazi racism and anti-Semitism. See Trigger (1980, pp. 91–2).

10. For Reinach, see Volume 1, pp. 370–3. For Kossinna, see Trigger (1980, pp. 24–6). It will be remembered that the Sumerians were seen as the originators of Mesopotamian civilization. For some of the ideological aspects of this, see Volume 1, pp. 364–5.

11. See, for instance, Trigger (1980, p. 50).

12. Strabo, *Geography* 10.4.2.

13. Branigan (1968a, p. 7).

14. Branigan (1968a, p. 7); Renfrew (1972, pp. 63–4). Hood (1971, p. 28) raises the possibility that the earliest pottery came from further east, possibly even from Palestine.

15. Weinberg (1965b, p. 47). Renfrew (1972, p. 67) is clearly suspicious of this idea but he does not raise any objections to it. For the association of Ubaid ware with Semitic speech, see Volume 1, p. 12.

16. Hood (1971, p. 31).

17. Evans (1928, p. 34); Pendlebury (1963, p. 74); Alexiou (1967a, p. 484). See also Branigan (1970a, p. 141). The same idea was proposed by the Greek archaeologist Xanthoudides (1924, p. 128). Objections to this have been raised by Banti (1933, pp. 244–5) and Hood (1971, p. 173).

   The word *tholos*, for which Chantraine can find no satisfactory Indo-European etymology, would seem likely to come from the Egyptian *dw3t, t(w)3t*, in Demotic the 'underworld' or the 'inner chamber of a tomb'. This seems to be derived from *dw3w* (dawn, morning). For the connections between Aegean tombs of the 3rd millennium and sunrise, see Goodison (1985, pp. 70–2).

18. Warren (1965, pp. 30–1). See also Pendlebury (1930a, pp. 20–1) and Hood (1971, p. 29).

19. Warren (1965, p. 8); Renfrew (1972, p. 347).

20. Evans (1921, pp. 64–70; 1928 (Volume 2), pp. 21–59; 1925, esp. pp. 11–23).

21. Oates (1979, pp. 21–2 and 29–30).

22. Jidejian (1968, pp. 11–15).

23. Gardiner (1961, pp. 396–7); Hoffman (1979, pp. 293–4). For the Lapis see Biggs (1966); Herrmann (1968) and Kulke (1976).

24. Williams (1980; 1985, pp. 32–5 and 1986).

25. For the trade patterns in general, see Helck (1979, pp. 12–13). For the evidence from Spain, see Monteagudo (1985, pp. 36–41). For Romania, see Helck (1979, pp. 9–12) and Dumitrescu (1982, p. 84). The radiocarbon dating for this is much higher, suggesting a date in the 5th or 6th millennium. Given the lack of carbon datings for early Mesopotamian tablets, I do not think this can be completely disregarded and the possibility remains that there may have been writing in this very remote period. Nevertheless, the likelihood remains that it should be placed with the trade in the 4th millennium. Similarly, the cylinder seals, of

undoubted Mesopotamian inspiration, and the pottery forms resembling those of Anatolia found in the Maliq II period in Albania, should probably be updated to the beginning of the 3rd millennium if not the 4th. For the objects, see Prendi (1982, p. 204) and Eggebrecht and Eggebrecht (1988, p. 186).

26. The idea of Near Eastern prospectors on the Danube by the end of the 4th millennium is an old one. See Childe (1949, esp. pp. 239–40) and Dayton (1982a, p. 154). An Extreme Aryanist, J. E. Dayton, sees the initiative as coming from Europe. For the lead cups, see Dayton (1982a, p. 166).

27. This dating is rather earlier than that of conventional wisdom but reflects the general updating of Near Eastern chronologies suggested by the recent carbon dates from the Egyptian Old Kingdom. See ch. V, nn. 71–87 and 96–7.

28. See Renfrew (1972) and, more recently, (1984, pp. 248–57). See also Trump (1981, pp. 75–7) and Andel and Runnels (1988, pp. 240–2).

29. See Andel and Runnels (1988, pp. 242–5). However, it is interesting to note that they are not so Eurocentric in their title as Renfrew himself. They refer merely to 'the emergence of civilization in the Aegean'.

30. Branigan (1970a, pp. 199–200). The name Onouphrios is generally accepted as coming from the common title for Osiris, Wn nfr, 'The good or beautiful being'. This, of course, has nothing to do with the pottery which is named after the place name Agios Onouphrios, 'Saint Onouphrios'.

31. Branigan (1970a, pp. 199–200).

32. Renfrew (1972, p. 89).

33. Weinberg (1954, p. 95; 1965a, pp. 302–8). There are also striking parallels around 3300 BC between styles of fortification in Palestine and the Cyclades and Spain. See de Vaux (1971, pp. 214–18), Trump (1981, pp. 100, 126) and Renfrew (1972, pp. 392–9).

34. Branigan (1970a, pp. 199–203); Hood (1971, pp. 36–8). While Branigan (1970a, pp. 181–2) lists the finds of Egyptian objects from the Old Kingdom, in his article (1973b) he plays down their quantity. This would seem to be to emphasize the great expansion of contacts between Egypt and the Aegean after EMIII. Warren too (1965, p. 38) admits that there are remarkably close resemblances between Early Minoan and Ghassulian objects.

35. Renfrew (1972, p. 347). This argument is referred to in Volume 1, pp. 15–16.

36. Helck (1979, pp. 13–15) and Renfrew (1972, pp. 444–9). For the ivory, see Krzyszkowska (1983, pp. 163–70).

37. Renfrew (1972, p. 449).

38. Renfrew (1972, p. 57).

39. *Odyssey*, XIV. 252–8; Helck (1979, p. 4).

40. See n. 29 above.

41. Renfrew (1972, p. xxv).

42. Renfrew (1972, p. 269).
43. Masson (1967, p. 9, n. 1); Chantraine (1968–75, p. 785).
44. Dolgopolskii (1987, pp. 5, 9). The Georgian *kvini*, which is sometimes believed to be the original one, is now generally seen as a loan. For a detailed study of this word, see Brown (1969, pp. 147–51).
45. For *yane*, see Gordon (1966, pp. 28–9). See also below, ch. X, n. 137. For the monphthongization of *ay > a* in this case, see Rendsburg forthcoming.
46. Harris (1939, pp. 8–9); Moran (1961, pp. 34–72); Moscati *et al.* (1969, p. 46).
47. See Zohary and Hopf (1988, pp. 140–1).
48. This, at any rate, is the belief of Lipinski (1981, p. 201).
49. Goodison (1985, pp. 159–60; 1988, p. 169). For Goodison the most important cult object here is the earthenware so-called 'frying pan'. For a detailed survey of these, see Coleman (1985).
50. See Volume 1, pp. 230–1.
51. See Katz (1986, pp. 168–9) and Pois (1986, pp. 43–5). I am grateful to Glenn Ayala for this reference.
52. Müller (1820–4); *Black Athena*, Volume 1, pp. 310–11.
53. Burkert (1985, pp. 200–1).
54. As Goodison (1985, p. 50) points out, however, many cultures, like Japan, have sun goddesses and they were also found around the Mediterranean in Anatolia and Ugarit so that even this is not necessarily a local Aegean phenomenon. It is also interesting to note that the Hebrew *šemeš* (sun) is both feminine and masculine. I believe that there may even be Egyptian connections in the case of Crete, as Rhea, the leading goddess in later Crete, seems to have gained her name from the Egyptian Rˁt(Riyat) ʒy, the Egyptian female personification of the sun. See below, ch. IV, nn. 137–8. For ways in which this Aegean preference for a female sun affected the Greek adoption of Egyptian solar theology in respect of Artemis and Europa, see Volume 3.
55. Goodison (1985, pp. 84–5; 1988, p. 169).
56. Goodison (1985, pp. 85, 101).
57. Goodison (1985, p. 110). Watrous (1987b, p. 67) also sees a connection between Cretan figurines of beetles and Egyptian solar beetles.
58. See ch. II, n. 25, and Volume 3.
59. Renfrew (1972, pp. 44–60); Goodison (1985, pp. 120–3).
60. Burkert (1985, pp. 37–8).
61. Newberry (1909, pp. 27–30); Hall (1929).
62. See ch. IV, nn. 72–86.
63. Cadogan (1986, p. 171). For the Northern European attachment to the double-axe, see Volume 1, p. 467.
64. See n. 27 above.
65. See Porada (1982, p. 291).

Chapter II
EGYPTIAN INFLUENCE ON BOIOTIA AND THE PELOPONNESE
IN THE 3RD MILLENNIUM, I

1. Theophrastos, *Peri phytōn historias,* IV.10.1; IV.59; *Peri phytōn aitiōn,* II.12.4; Pliny, *Natural History* II.95 and XIX.1.2.2; Plutarch *Sulla* 20.3– 5. These should be seen in relation to Herodotos II.156. It should also be noted that Sarapis, Ammon, Isis and Anubis were all worshipped in Thebes in Hellenistic and Roman times and that there was a cult centre of Sarapis at Tanagra in Southern Boiotia. See Spyropoulos (1972a, p. 25). Such cults were so widespread in Greece at the time that it is difficult to make much of these.
2. Müller (1820–4, I, p. 92).
3. Müller (1820–4, I, p. 93).
4. For the Kopais and Kēphis(s)os, see ch. III, nn.94–7. For Minyan, see ch. III, n.48, and Volume 3. For Thebes, see ch. XII, nn.49–52.
5. *Iliad,* XIV.321–5, tr. A. T. Murray, II, p. 91.
6. Schachter (1981, p. 16) sees the cults of the two as being seen as parallel in Thebes.
7. Volume 1, p. 95.
8. Chantraine plausibly derives this from the Greek *selas* (fire or torch light). However, he can find no acceptable etymology for this. There would seem to be a link between *selas* and the Egyptian Demotic *sl–sol* in Coptic, meaning 'wick' or 'torch'. This root does not exist in Ancient Egyptian and Černy plausibly suggests that *sol* comes from the Semitic **sᶜl. Šaᶜala* in Arabic means 'kindle', 'blaze'. Thus the most likely hypothesis is that both Demotic and Greek borrowed from an unattested West Semitic **šaᶜl,* meaning 'fire', 'flame', 'torch' or 'beacon'.
9. Astour (1967a, pp. 170–2). For sharp criticisms of this, see Burton (1972, pp. 102–3).
10. For the importance of cattle herding in the origins of Egyptian civilization, see Hoffman (1979, pp. 236–8).
11. Pausanias, IX.16.1.
12. See Volume 1, p. 114.
13. See Ranke (1935–52, I, p. 226).
14. Gardiner (1957, pp. 428–30).
15. Herodotos, II.43.
16. Tzetzes, *Scholiast on Lykophron.* This may also have been accepted by Apollodoros, II.4.12; see the discussion in Frazer (1921, I, p. 183, n.1).
17. Strabo, IX.2.18.
18. Pausanias, IX.33.1. The idea that this Kekrops was the later king of Athens is challenged by Roesch (1982, p. 214) and supported by Schachter (1986, p. 113). I believe that Roesch could well be right and that Pausanias was rationalizing here.
19. See Fossey (1974, p. 15, n.40) who cites Schachter's thesis and Schachter (1981, p. 114, n.3) who cites Fossey's article.

20. Fossey (1974, p. 15, n.40).
21. Schachter (1981, p. 113).
22. Strabo, IX.2.29. See also Pausanias, I.13.1 and X.1.10 and Farnell (1895–1909, I, pp. 402–3, n.61).
23. Sayed (1982, I, pp. 71–2, 106–14).
24. Keimer (1931, pp. 151–9); Hollis (1988, pp. 1–3).
25. See ch. I, n.58. For more, see Volume 3.
26. Strabo, IX.2.29.
27. Movers (1841–50, II, 1, p. 258) and Bérard, *Les Phéniciens et l'Odyssée*, 2nd. ed., II, p. 337, not in (1902–3). See Astour (1967a, p. 140).
28. The use of the *kōthōn* to mean a 'large drinking cup' could either refer to the Carthaginian harbour or be an example of soldiers' humour. For more on this etymology, see Brown (1969, p. 157).
29. Schachter (1981, p. 113); *Iliad*, IV.8 and V.908.
30. Schachter (1981, p. 113).
31. Pausanias, IX.5.1.
32. Pausanias, I.38.7. Varro, *Res rusticae*, 3.1.2.
33. Meyer (1928–36, II, p. 194). See also Fontenrose (1959, pp. 236–7).
34. Aischylos, *The Persians*, ll. 37–40.
35. See below, ch. VII, nn. 122–3.
36. See Pope (1981, p. 170). In Volume 4 there will be further discussion of the relationship between the Rephaim with their slushy abode and the Greek Titans (*Titanes*), whose name has been reasonably linked to the Greek *titanoi* (men of mud or gypsum). Astour (1967a, pp. 196–7, n.3) plausibly suggests it comes from a Semitic word for 'mud or clay' found in the Akkadian *ṭiṭu*. I am indebted to Scott Noegel for the whole section on the relationship between Ōgygos and ʿŌg.
37. Astour (1967a, pp. 236–7) shows the relationship between the Rephaim √rpʿ (heal) and the archangel Raphael on the one hand and snakes on the other.
38. Pope (1981, p. 170).
39. Deuteronomy 3.11.
40. Ezekiel 38, 39 and elsewhere.
41. Midrash Bereshit Raba 31.13; Sanhedrin 108b; Targum Yerushalmi Dt. 2.11, 3.10; Yalkut Reubeni on Gn. 7.22.
42. Astour (1967a, p. 212).
43. Isaiah 54.9.
44. Erman and Grapow (1982, I, p. 376). It is not, however, in Lesko and Switalski-Lesko, 1982–90.
45. Gauthier (1925–31, I, p. 208).
46. Ezekiel 39.18.
47. Astour (1967a, p. 212).
48. Zebahim 113b; Sanhedrin 108b; Rosh ha-Shanah 12a; Yerushalmi Sanhedrin 10, 29b; Yelmmadenu in Yalkut 11508 on Isaiah 64.11.
49. Schachter (1981, p. 113) dismisses the association with Odysseus as complete fantasy and he is probably right. However, as Odysseus' name

may well simply mean 'voyager', *wḏ(yt)w from the Egyptian wḏyt (expedition, journey, campaign). This could also be applied to Herakles whose possible association with the cult will be discussed below.

50. Pausanias, IX.33.7. Pausanias, VIII.26.5–6, reports that the Arkadians also had a river Tritōn near their cult of Asklepios and Athena. Interestingly, it was placed at Peneos, which we shall see below derives its name from the Egyptian pᵢnw (the Flood). For other references to Athena's birth and other activities near Tritōn see Farnell (1895–1909, I, pp. 266–9; 385–6, n. 16). Farnell, of course, believes that the Libyan Tritōn was named from a Greek one.

51. Herodotos, IV.178.

52. Apollonios Rhodios, IV.149; Diodoros, III.53.4; Pliny, *Natural History*, V.28.

53. For the derivation of tr from twr, see Erman and Grapow (1925–31, V, pp. 255 and 318).

54. Schachter (1981, p. 113).

55. Lactantius on Statius, *Thebaid*, VII.330. See Schachter (1981, p. 112).

56. See Farnell (1895–1909, I, pl. xv) and Schachter (1981, p. 122).

57. Schachter (1981, pp. 120–1).

58. Sayed (1982, I, pp. 101–6). For the coin and the statue at Priene, see Farnell (1895–1909, I, p. 338).

59. Sayed (1982, I, pp. 51–62).

60. Sayed (1982, I, pp. 31–2).

61. *Pyramid Texts* 508–9. Sayed, Doc. 196 (1982, I, pp. 31–2). He provides references for all the published translations.

62. Sayed (1982, I, pp. 61–2; II, pp. 319–20, Doc. 287).

63. Sayed (1982, I, pp. 67–9). See also Hollis (1987b, pp. 8–9).

64. For Nēit's warlike triumph over Seth and Apopi, see Sayed (1982, I, pp. 72–6). For the identification of Seth with Poseidon, see Volume 1, pp. 66–7). It will be discussed further in Volume 4.

65. Farnell (1895–1909, I, pp. 270–1).

66. See Volume 1, pp. 303–6, 320.

67. Burkert (1985, p. 221).

68. Burkert (1985, p. 221).

69. For Seth's characteristics, see Rundle-Clark (1959, pp. 114–15).

70. Fontenrose (1959).

71. Burkert (1985, p. 221).

72. Schachter (1986, pp. 211–14).

73. Pausanias, IX.33.1; Strabo, IX.2.36.

74. Thebais schol. on *Iliad*, XXIII.346–7.

75. Pausanias, VIII.25.4–7 and 42.1. See also Bérard (1894, pp. 136–7).

76. The connection would seem to be confirmed by the existence of the variant Eriōn on an Arkadian coin. See Schachter (1986, p. 222, n.5). *Eris* (strife) which has no Indo-European etymology, may well derive from the West Semitic root √ḥrr (scorch, kindle), which is used in the sense of 'kindle strife' in Proverbs 26.21. For more on this root, see below under Herakles.

77. Fontenrose (1959, p. 368, n. 5).
78. This and the parallels with Mary Magdalene will be discussed in more detail in Volume 4.
79. For the Osiran version, see Plutarch, *De Iside...*, 356F and 366B–C. For Seth's paternity, see Budge (1904, p. 378) and Graefe on unpublished sources (1984, IV, col. 459, n. 20).
80. See Bérard (1894, pp. 136–7) and Fontenrose (1959, pp. 47, 421).
81. *Hymn to the Pythian Apollo*, 244–76.
82. Bérard (1894, pp. 136–7).
83. Fontenrose (1959, p. 47, esp. n. 5). For the relationship between *gē* and Demeter, see Volume 1, p. 57.
84. For a full bibliography on this, see Snowden (1970, pp. 307–8, n. 6).
85. André (1948, pp. 44–53).
86. See ch. IV, n. 99 and ch. X, n. 9.
87. Lewy (1895, p. 139) and Astour (1967a, p. 130). The Indo-Europeanists prefer to derive *erebos* from a root $*reg^u os$ (dark) found in Sanskrit and Armenian. Another Semitic word for 'West', 'aḥărôn, appears in the place name Acherōn, the river associated with death in cult and mythology and located geographically in the far northwest of Greece. See Astour (1967a, p. 314).
88. Plutarch *De Iside...*, 366B. Trans. Babbit, p. 93.
89. Knauss (1987a, pp. 43–6; 1987b, p. 3).
90. See, for instance, Fontenrose (1959, pp. 177–81).
91. Fontenrose (1959, pp. 370–2).
92. Astour (1967a, pp. 226–7; 250–71).
93. Hesiod, *Theogony*, 282–3.
94. Strabo, IX.2.25.
95. Bérard (1894, p. 116) followed Bochart in deriving the name from √pgh (rein). This would seem plausible in the light of the myth that Athena put reins on Pegasos. This form is not attested in biblical Hebrew. However, *pag*, which sometimes has the meaning 'halter', and *pagă'* (bit) do occur in Aramaic and Neo-Hebrew from the first centuries AD and it is quite possible that the root did exist much earlier. Given the Semitic etymology of Bellerophon it would seem likely that this root for Pegasos also played a part in the creation of the myth.
96. See Breasted (1906, III, § 589 and IV, § 111).
97. Pindar, *Pythian Ode*, IV.2; Kallimachos, quoted in Strabo, X.5.1 and XVII.3.21. For others, see Bates (1914, pp. 96–7).
98. Bates (1914, p. 97).
99. Breasted (1906, IV, § 111).
100. See Lhote (1959, pp. 122–8).
101. Herodotos, IV.170–93.
102. Herodotos, IV.189.
103. *Iliad*, VIII.184–5, and *Odyssey*, XIII.81–5.
104. Bernal (forthcoming).
105. See Gardiner (1947, II, pp. 5, 28–9).
106. Procopius, *History*, I.19.29; Pliny, *Natural History*, VI, 35; Arkell (1961,

p. 178); André (1948, pp. 44–53). It is generally accepted that the Greek word *oasis* comes from the Egyptian *wḥ̣t, uahe* in Coptic.

107. Procopius, *De Bello Persico*, I.19.29–31, cited in Bates (1914, p. 236).
108. Gauthier (1925–31, V, p. 21).
109. Herodotos, II.50.
110. Lloyd (1976, pp. 237–8).
111. See Volume 1, p. 67.
112. Herodotos, IV.180 and 188.
113. Dennis (1848, I, p. 109).
114. For the gentilic suffix *-n*, see Gordon (1966, § 8.60). There is no reason why the Etruscan form Nethun should be older than the Latin Neptune. Nethun would seem more likely to derive from Neptune than vice versa. For Roman awareness of the significance of Nbty, see Winkler (1985, pp. 309–18).
115. For Delphos see n. 84 above. For the meaning of the stem *Delph-* see Volume 4.
116. Gauthier (1925–31, V, p. 27).
117. For Rb, Libu, see Gardiner (1947, I, pp. 121–2).
118. See *Odyssey*, IV.85 and XIV.295.
119. For a bibliography on references to Tilphousa/Telphousa/Thelpousa, see Fontenrose (1959, p. 367, nn. 3–4).
120. See above n. 86.
121. See above nn. 83–4.
122. Frazer (1898, IV, 262–3; 286).
123. For more on this, see below, ch. III, nn. 85–6.
124. Astour (1967a, p. 214). For the Ugaritic parallels, see Gray (1956, p. 32); for the biblical ones, see Pope (1973, p. 30). The tradition linking the Arkadian Ladōn to a snake or dragon would seem to have survived in the modern place name Drakovouni, 'Dragon Mountain', for a mountain near the source of the river.
125. Hesiod, *Theogony*, 333–5. The snake is not actually named in the *Theogony* but for the identification with Ladōn, see West (1988, p. 258, l.334).
126. See *Pistis Sophis*, 287–9; Budge (1934, pp. 357–79) and Fontenrose (1959, pp. 234–7).
127. See ch. VII, nn. 107–18.
128. Scholiast on Apollonios Rhodios, IV.1396.
129. Astour (1967a, p. 214).
130. See Fontenrose (1959, p. 369).
131. For Anuket(is), see Otto (1975c, cols 333–4). For this derivation of Onka, *pace* Bérard (1894, p. 140).
132. Herodotos, II.28. For some of the immense complexity surrounding these supposed springs, see Lloyd (1976, pp. 107–17).
133. For Nephthys and Anukis, see Graefe (1982, cols 458–9).
134. Sayed (1982, I, p. 125).
135. For Khnum being known as Nb ḳbḥw, see Gardiner (1947, II, p. 4), though his reference to Gauthier (1925–31, V, 170) does not mention

Khnum. For the possible use of the title Ḳbḥ alone, see Budge (1904, II, p. 5).

136. See ch. III, nn. 94–7.

137. See Pausanias, II.4.5.

138. See Pausanias, II.20.6.

139. Inscription at Esna, Sayed, Doc. 1024 (1982, II, pp. 634–5).

140. See n. 60 above.

141. For Nēit as cow and mother of Re, see Sayed, Doc. 260 (1982, II, pp. 308–9).

142. I. Samuel 6.7–12; Astour (1967a, pp. 157–8).

143. Pausanias, IX.12.2.

144. Symeonoglou (1985, pp. 7–11).

145. Euripides, *The Phoenician Women*, 822–33, trans. Vellacott (1972, p. 265), and Scholiast on [l].71; Pherikydes quoted in Apollodoros, III.4.2; Pindar, *Pythian Odes*, III.94 (167); Diodoros, IV.65.5 and V.49.1; Pausanias, IX.12.3. For further bibliography, see Frazer (1921, I, p. 317, n. 4).

146. Euripides, *The Phoenician Women*, 822–7, trans. Vellacott (1972, p. 265).

147. For other reasons for their snaky or ophic natures, see Astour (1967a, pp. 154–8, 392).

148. Astour (1967a, p. 160).

149. This was seen by Barthélemy (1763, p. 226). Chantraine, writing two hundred years later, calls the etymology of *horkos* 'obscure'.

150. Sethe (1906–9, IV, l. 823).

151. Hintze (1975, col. 333).

152. Schachter (1981, p. 113). Bickerman (1980, p. 20), however, saw the equivalent as Poseidonios.

153. Apollodoros, II.4.8, and Diodoros, IV.9.2.

154. Schachter (1981, p. 121, n. 3).

155. Volume 1, p. 76.

156. See the eighty-nine place names beginning with *R*- in Gauthier (1925–31, III, pp. 112–28).

157. Lewy (1895, p. 194, n. 2).

158. See Sayed (1982, p. 141).

159. Sayed (1982, pp. 282–3, Docs. 220 and 221).

160. Burkert (1985, p. 209).

161. See, for instance, Kirk (1974, p. 257).

162. Jacobsen (1976, p. 195).

163. Jacobsen (1976, pp. 208–19).

164. Herodotos, II.44, and Levy (1934, p. 48).

165. Dussaud (1946–8, p. 208).

166. For a full bibliography on this, see Lloyd (1976, pp. 205–6).

167. See Seyrig (1944–5); Dussaud (1946–8). See also Brundage (1958). Brundage effectively demonstrates the relationships between Herakles and Gilgamesh and Melqart. He then goes on, with what would appear to be misplaced precision, to tie the Greek hero to 7th-century Southwest Anatolia.

168. Chadwick (1976, pp. 87, 95).
169. There may also be some punning with the Akkadian *šarrum*, which is not present in Eblaite, and the Hebrew *šar* (king). Going through the shift *s* > *ḥ* will be discussed in Volume 3.
170. See Roberts (1971) and Jacobsen (1976, pp. 226–32). Interestingly, Walter Burkert sees a connection between Erra and Thebes. However, he connects the Mesopotamian divinity to Adrastos, the mythical king of Argos and enemy of Thebes, who led the seven heroes against Thebes (1984, pp. 97–104). Thus, to the extent that Herakles is identified with Erra, he would here be the enemy of Thebes rather than its champion. Nevertheless, Herakles' violence and unreliability make this quite possible.
171. Apollodoros, II.5.8. For further bibliography, see Frazer (1921, p. 201, n. 2). For the cult of Herakles at the Spanish Abdēra and the difficulties Aryanist scholars have in dealing with its purely Phoenician nature, see Farnell (1921, pp. 145, 167).
172. Herodotos, II.43.
173. Lloyd (1976, pp. 203–4).
174. Sauneron (1968, p. 18).
175. te Velde (1970, p. 186).
176. te Velde (1970, p. 175). In fact, Budge notes a variant form of Ḥrkȝ p ḥrd, 'Ḥrkȝ the Child' (1904, I, p. 463).
177. See Budge (1904, I, p. 463) and Sauneron (1960).
178. Budge (1904, I, p. 463, n. 3).
179. See Syncellus (1719, p. 81). For Lepsius' interpretation of this, see below, n. 222.
180. See Gardiner (1957, pp. 71–3).
181. Herodotos, II.43–4. Lloyd (1976, pp. 207–11) denies that there was any Phoenician cultic connection. This case had already been demolished by Van Berchem (1967) – not cited by Lloyd – who looked at the problem throughout the Mediterranean.
182. Diodoros, III.74.4.
183. *De Natura Deorum*, III.42.
184. See Altenmüller (1977, cols. 1015–18) and Yadin (1982).
185. For a bibliography on this see Yadin (1982, p. 266).
186. For the unsatisfactory nature of the proposed Semitic etymologies, see Fulco (1976, pp. 64–5).
187. For his cult at Byblos, see Fulco (1976, p. 55, nn. 292–4). For the confusion between the Egyptian and West Semitic gods, see Leclant (1960, p. 53, nn. 7–10), Simpson (1960, p. 68) and *pace* Fulco (1976, p. 55). For the Egyptian cities, see Gardiner (1947, II, pp. 113–14, 176).
188. Fulco (1976, p. 20).
189. Gardiner (1947, II, p. 114).
190. Fulco (1976, pp. 3–21).
191. Diodoros, IV.10.2. See also ch. IV, nn. 132–58.

192. Yadin (1982, pp. 269–74). For his arguments on Dan, see Yadin (1968) and, below, ch. X, nn. 53–9. For the Aegean origins of the Sea Peoples, see Volume 1, pp. 445–50.
193. Fulco (1976, p. 50) and Yadin (1982, p. 270).
194. Lloyd (1976, p. 195).
195. Posener (1966).
196. Sethe (1929, pp. 30–4); Bonnet (1952, p. 142); Griffiths (1955, p. 23). For a full bibliography, see Lloyd (1976, p. 195).
197. See above, n. 170. There is a Hebrew root √ršp with the same meaning, 'burn over, pestilence', but Fulco (1976, pp. 64–5) sees this as deriving from the divine name.
198. Sethe (1929, pp. 30–4); Bonnet (1952, p. 142); Griffiths (1955, p. 23); Lloyd (1976, p. 195).
199. Apollodoros, II.5.11.
200. Gardiner (1947, II, p. 55).
201. Machiavelli (Gilbert, 1964, p. 354). For a full bibliography of Herakles and Antaios, see Frazer (1921, I, pp. 222–3, n. 2).
202. te Velde (1982, cols. 247–8).
203. Sayed (1982, pp. 139–40).
204. Sayed (1982, pp. 116, 128).
205. See n. 181 above.
206. Herodotos, II.44.
207. Herodotos, II.50.
208. Lloyd (1976, p. 239).
209. For Menthotpe's divinity, see ch. IV, n. 158. For that of Senwosre I, see ch. V, n. 57.
210. Diodoros, I.55.5.
211. Rachel Levy (1934) pointed out the parallels between the Tel Asmar Seal and the Heraklean Labour over fifty years ago. For a detailed study of the seal, the Ugaritic texts and the Greek legends on this theme, see Rendsburg (1984).
212. Servius, the commentator on Virgil in the 4th century AD, pointed this out in his commentary on *Aeneid* VI.287.
213. See Diodoros, IV.18.6, and Graves (1955, II, p. 120).
214. See nn. 122–7 above. Astour (1967a, p. 392) points out that the image of a god strangling two snakes is found on one of the Kassite seals found in Thebes (see below, ch. XII, nn. 75–87). Although this shows that the iconography goes back to the Bronze Age in the Middle East, I believe that its presence in Thebes can only be a coincidence.
215. Pausanias, IX.38.7, and Strabo, II.4.11.
216. Herodotos, II.99.
217. Herodotos, II.108.
218. Herodotos, II.13, 101.
219. Diodoros, I.51.5–52.
220. Diodoros, I.57.1–4.

221. See Waddell (1940, pp. 223, 225). See also n. 209 above.
222. Lepsius (1871, p. 54). Burton (1972, pp. 171–3) points out some of the technical difficulties of the measurements.
223. Wildung (1984, p. 40, ill. 33).
224. For more detail on this, see ch. V, n. 57.
225. Stevenson Smith (1971, p. 169).
226. Burton (1972, pp. 175–6). The name Ny-mꜣꜥ t-Rꜥ was rendered in a number of different ways which include Lamarēs, Lamaris and Labarēs and Labaris (Waddell, 1940, p. 224, n. 1).
227. For two excellent surveys of the complicated literature on this, see Burton (1972, pp. 162–3) and Lloyd (1976, p. 34).
228. Astour (1967a, pp. 215–16). See also Levin (1989).
229. Kretschmer (1927, pp. 76–8), Hrozný [Civ. of Hittites and Subaraeans] and Graves (1955, p. 206).
230. Pausanias, IX.27.8. He refers specifically to Herakles as 'the Idaian Daktylos', that is, a 'finger' of Mount Ida, in Crete and Northwest Anatolia used as protector of the infant Zeus. The name Ida in connection with the fingers was clearly derived from, or at least punned with, the Semitic root √yd (hand) and possibly from the proto-Egyptian word d indicated by the sound value of d given to the sign ⇌ even though it is not attested with this meaning in Egyptian texts. See Gardiner (1957, p. 455) and Greenberg (1986, p. 287).
231. Pausanias, VII.5.5. Astour (1967a, p. 215) seems to overstate the case here by saying that there was a similar statue at Thespiai.

Chapter III
EGYPT'S INFLUENCE ON BOIOTIA AND THE PELOPONNESE IN THE 3RD MILLENNIUM, II

1. Plutarch, *De Genio Socratis;* de Lacy and Einarson pp. 389–97. For textual difficulties with this passage, see Schachter (1981, p. 14). For more on the tomb and its excavation, see Persson (1932, pp. 295–307).
2. Levi (1971, I, p. 380, n. 190).
3. Schwartz (1950, p. 81).
4. Cartledge (1987, pp. 328–9).
5. Diogenes Laertios, VIII.87, trans. Hicks (1925, pp. 401–3).
6. The problem is not quite so great as Schwartz (1950, p. 78) imagined, because Nektanabēs began to reign in 379 not 378 as Schwartz supposed. See Lloyd (1983, p. 281).
7. Plutarch, *de Iside,* 10; Clement of Alexandria, *Strom.,* I.15, 69; Diogenes Laertios, VIII.90; Schwartz (1950, p. 78).
8. For bibliographies of discussions of the credibility of Plato's trip to Egypt, see Volume 1, p. 459, n. 148.
9. This is the opinion of many authors. See, for instance, Persson (1932, p. 303) and Schwartz (1950, p. 81).
10. Cartledge (1987, pp. 296–7).

11. Schwartz (1950, p. 79).
12. See Symeonoglou (1985, pp. 15–19) and Shaw (1987, p. 60).
13. Hesiod, Merkelbach and West, 1983, frg. 182. Palaephatos c. 42 in Loeb, p. 214, no. 96.
14. *Odyssey*, XI.262–4.
15. Fragment of Hecataeous, Jacoby (1923–9, I, F.119).
16. Volume 1, p. 83.
17. See Hesiod, Merkelbach and West, 1983, frg. 182. Palaephatos c. 42 in Loeb, p. 214, no. 96. For a general survey of this evidence, see Buck (1979, p. 46) and Symeonoglou (1985, pp. 76–7).
18. Fragment of Pherecydes, Jacoby (1923–9, III, F.41). According to the scholia on Euripides, *The Phoenician Women*, 638, the man from whose herd Kadmos took the heifer that led him to Thebes was called Pelagon. Could it be that this name too came from P; rkw?
19. For detailed discussions of these sources, see Buck (1979, p. 46) and Symeonoglou (1985, pp. 76–7).
20. Pausanias, IX.5.1–3.
21. Strabo, IX.2.28; Buck (1979, p. 46); Symeonoglou (1985, pp. 76–7).
22. Aischylos, *Seven Against Thebes*, 526–9, and Pausanias, IX.17.2. For Symeonoglou's identification of this site in these references see (1985, pp. 83, 192).
23. Loucas and Loucas (1987, p. 100).
24. Keramopoullos (1917, pp. 381–92) see also Symeonoglou (1985, p. 273).
25. Spyropoulos (1972a, pp. 18–23). See also Konsola (1981, p. 100) cited in Loucas and Loucas (1987, p. 96).
26. See Pausanias, IX.34.3. Higgins (1979, pp. 25–7).
27. Spyropoulos (1972a, p. 20). The higher dates given here for the Greek ceramic periods are because the Egyptian synchronisms on which they have been based have been raised by radio-carbon dating. See ch. V, nn.84–8.
28. Symeonoglou (1985, p. 273).
29. For scholars who accept this conclusion, see, for instance, Treuil (1983, p. 441); Konsola (1981, p. 140) and Loucas and Loucas (1987, p. 96).
30. See Schachermeyr (1967, pp. 269–70) and Konsola (1981, pp. 231–4, 238) cited in Loucas and Loucas (1987, p. 97).
31. Loucas and Loucas (1987, pp. 97–8).
32. Spyropoulos (1981a, pp. 84–6).
33. Pini (1968, p. 39).
34. Spyropoulos (1981a, pp. 117–24).
35. *Pace* Treuil (1983, p. 441).
36. Burl (1979, pp. 130, 254).
37. Burl (1979, p. 129). This does not mean that I go all the way with J. Ivimy (1974, pp. 68–80) that Silbury Hill and other 3rd-millennium Megalithic monuments were built by Egyptian colonists, but that I do agree that the builders had sophisticated mathematical knowledge and

certainly were aware of Old Kingdom Egypt. Ivimy's problem that Silbury Hill appeared to pre-date the pyramids has now been resolved by the higher dating for the Egyptian Old Kingdom.

38. Loucas and Loucas (1987, p. 99).
39. Edwards (1947, pp. 136–7).
40. Loucas and Loucas (1987, pp. 99–100).
41. Pausanias, IX.17.3; Levi (1971, I, pp. 342–3). For sources on Bakis, see Kern (1896, II, cols 2801–2).
42. Pausanias, X.32.9.
43. See Volume 1, pp. 117–20.
44. Homeric Hymn to Gē, 11.6–7, and Euripides, Nauck frag. 195.
45. For a bibliography on the draining of the Kopais, see Hope-Simpson (1965, pp. 113–20). See also Spyropoulos (1972a, pp. 22–6, 1973a); Fossey (1974); Wallace (1979); Knauss, Heinrich and Kalcyk (1984); and Knauss (1986, 1987a, 1987b).
46. See Fossey (1974, p. 7) and Wallace (1979, p. 8). Fossey admits, however, that 'the initial construction' could be earlier.
47. Lauffer (1981, pp. 245–6).
48. Knauss, Heinrich and Kalcyk (1984); Knauss (1986, 1987a, 1987b).
49. Knauss, Heinrich and Kalcyk (1984, p. 56).
50. Knauss (1987a, p. 103).
51. Spyropoulos (1981, pp. 133–4).
52. Konsola (1981, p. 39); Loucas and Loucas (1987, pp. 102–3).
53. Spyropoulos (1981, pp. 135–6).
54. It is surprising how little recent research has been published on the important subject of the 12th-Dynasty water management of the Fayum, but see Arnold (1977, cols 87–93).
55. See Tzavella-Evjen (1984).
56. Marinatos (1946). See also Vermeule (1964, p. 35).
57. Renfrew (1972, p. 110).
58. Renfrew (1972, p. 288).
59. Balcer (1974), who does not consider the possibility of a Middle or Early Helladic date.
60. Knauss (1987a, pp. 103–4).
61. Knauss (1987a, p. 206, n. 33).
62. Spyropoulos (1973a, p. 209).
63. Shaw (1987).
64. Volume 1, pp. 88–98.
65. Volume 1, p. 94.
66. Volume 1, pp. 83, 186.
67. Pausanias, VIII.14.2.
68. Kalcyk and Heinrich (1986); Knauss (1987c); Knauss, Heinrich and Kalcyk (1986).
69. Hope-Simpson (1965, p. 81).
70. *Iliad*, II.605. See also Knauss, Heinrich and Kalcyk (1986, p. 604).
71. For Herakles' associations with Arkadian lakes, see ch. II, nn. 213–14.

72. Knauss, Heinrich and Kalcyk (1986, p. 604).
73. See ch. II, nn. 122–4.
74. Ventris and Chadwick (1973, p. 543).
75. Knauss, Heinrich and Kalcyk (1986, p. 611).
76. Knauss, Heinrich and Kalcyk (1986, p. 611). See Strabo, IX.2.18, and Pausanias, IX.24.1–3.
77. It is possible that there is some contamination here from the verb *erchomai*.
78. See, for instance, Moscati *et al.* (1969, p. 47).
79. Hooker (1979).
80. Herodotos, V.60, trans. de Selincourt (1954, pp. 360–1).
81. See, for instance, Astour (1967a, pp. 138–224) and Bérard (1894).
82. Kalcyk and Heinrich (1986, p. 12).
83. Chantraine tentatively links it to the Lithuanian *rūkēt* (dig).
84. Job 30.3–8.
85. See ch. II, nn. 59–71, and 139–41.
86. See ch. II, nn. 123–4. For Panau, see Gardiner (1947, II, p. 177).
87. Herodotos, VII.128–9.
88. Nonnos, *Dionysiaka*, VI.366–80.
89. See ch. II, n. 122.
90. Pliny, *Natural History*, XXXI.54.
91. Pausanias, VIII.14.1; Levi (1971, II, p. 405).
92. Frazer (1898, IV, pp. 231–3); Kalcyk and Heinrich (1986, p. 12). I am unable to see this line in the photograph they reproduce on p. 11.
93. See ch. VIII, nn. 48–9.
94. See Brugsch (1879–80, pp. 823–5) and Gauthier (1925–31, V, pp. 169–72).
95. See ch. II, nn. 135–8.
96. For *-issos*, see Volume 3. See, for instance, Pausanias, I.37.3 and II.20.6 for the site of Theseus' purification by the Attic Kēphissos where there was a sanctuary to Kēphissos, where the river could be heard running underground.
97. See Gauthier (1925–31, V, p. 171).
98. *Natural History*, VII.209. See Knauss (1987a, p. 199, n. 22).
99. See Pausanias, IX.3.3–4, and Plutarch, *Daedala*, in Eusebius *Praeparatio Evangelica*, III.1.6. For the Ded, see ch. IV, n. 45 below.
100. Knauss (1987a, pp. 194–9).
101. Caskey (1956, 1957, 1960, 1971); Vermeule (1964, pp. 29–44).
102. Shaw (1987).
103. Vermeule (1964, p. 35). For the constitution of Ebla, see Pettinato (1981, pp. 69–95).
104. Gale and Stos-Gale (1981) and Stos-Gale and Gale (1984b).
105. Vichos and Kyriakopoulou (1989); Bass (1990a).
106. See ch. IV, n. 23.
107. See, for example, Dayton (1982a, p. 158).
108. See Vermeule (1964, pp. 45–58) and Renfrew (1972).

109. Vermeule (1964, pp. 37–9).
110. For the potters' marks, see Vermeule (1964, pp. 40–1).
111. See Bernal (1990, pp. 54–6).
112. See ch. IV, nn. 43–4.
113. Pettinato (1981, pp. 103–9). See also Biggs (1966), Herrmann (1968) and Kulke (1976, pp. 43–56).
114. Dayton (1982a, pp. 159, 163)
115. Pendlebury (1930a, pp. 53, 57, 64–5).
116. Brown (1975, pp. 8, 106. For the original attribution, see Frödin and Persson (1938, p. 234).
117. The cup is item 4578 at the Athens Museum. See Stevenson Smith (1971, p. 180).
118. Helck (1979, p. 15).
119. For a transcription and discussion of this text, see Astour (1967a, pp. 142–3).
120. See Volume 1, pp. 382, 501.
121. Coldstream (1973) and Coldstream and Huxley (1984).
122. For a sensational view of this undoubtedly sensational subject, see Pearson and Connor (1968).
123. For Mellaart's assurance, see, for instance, (1967, p. 394).
124. See Mellaart (1967, p. 401).
125. Helck (1979, p. 16). See also Vermeule and Vermeule (1970).
126. Vermeule and Vermeule (1970, pp. 36–7).
127. Vermeule (1964, pp. 64–6) and Konsola (1981, p. 182) cited in Loucas and Loucas (1987, p. 103).
128. See Caskey (1980).
129. Stevenson Smith (1971, p. 181).
130. See Howell (1973), Caskey (1986, pp. 22–3). For a recent survey of arguments on this, see Drews (1988, pp. 17–20).
131. Vermeule (1964, p. 59).
132. See Buck (1979, pp. 35–6).
133. Symeonoglou (1985, pp. 69–70).
134. Symeonoglou (1985, pp. 70–5).
135. Spyropoulos (1981, pp. 133–7).
136. See n. 18 above and Buck (1979, p. 47).
137. Symeonoglou (1985, pp. 76–7).
138. See Volume 1, pp. 51–4 and 88–101. The cases of Athens and Sparta will be discussed in greater detail in Volume 3.

Chapter IV
THE OLD PALACE PERIOD IN CRETE AND THE
EGYPTIAN MIDDLE KINGDOM, 2100 TO 1730 BC

1. For a discussion of the new desirability of ancient Crete after 1900, see Volume 1, pp. 385–6.
2. Renfrew (1972, p. 98).
3. Whitelaw (1983, pp. 323–40).

4. Lewthwaite (1983, p. 172).
5. Cherry (1983, p. 33).
6. Cherry (1983, p. 41).
7. Matz (1973a, pp. 141–3).
8. Ward (1971, p. 72). Ward went on (pp. 74–82) to demolish Åström's low chronology for this. Åström does not recover from this in his later writing (1978, pp. 87–90). It is, of course, based on his low chronology for Mesopotamia, for which see below ch. V, n. 105.
9. Cadogan (1978, pp. 209–14). The situation is complicated by the fact that there was a temporal overlap between the pottery styles known as MMIA at Knossos and the end of those called EMIII in the rest of the island. See Merrillees (1977, p. 37).
10. Matz (1973a, pp. 141–5).
11. Ward (1971, pp. 72–125).
12. Branigan (1970a, p. 81).
13. Krzyszkowska (1983, p. 168). Similarly, imports of faience which increased in EMIII could have come from Egypt or Syria. Karen Pollinger Foster prefers Syria on the circular grounds that this was where conventional wisdom maintains that Near Eastern goods were coming to Crete from, but also because the techniques of the faience found in Crete seem closer to those of Syria than those of Egypt (1979, pp. 56–9).
14. Warren (1965, pp. 7–43; 1967, pp. 37–48; 1969, pp. 41–5, 71–91).
15. Watrous (1987b, p. 67): for a demolition of an isolationist view on these pottery styles see his discussion on p. 70.
16. Watrous (1987b, p. 70).
17. Ward (1971, pp. 92–5).
18. Evans (1921–35, I, pp. 117–25).
19. Pendlebury (1963, p. 83).
20. Matz (1928, pp. 30–42). Despite his denial of connections between Crete and Egypt at this time, Matz believed that the swastika motif was taken from Crete to Northeast Africa. Given the association of the swastika with the Aryan 'race' – which was not restricted to Nazis – it was unthinkable that the pattern could have passed from Africa to Europe. Ward (1971, pp. 85, 89) avoids the issue by maintaining that the simultaneous occurrence of the swastika in both Crete and Egypt was the result of independent invention.
21. Fimmen (1921, pp. 154–60); Biesautl (1954, pp. 33–41); Helck, (1979, p. 20).
22. Ward (1971, p. 86). For a bibliography on the controversy over the seals, see his n. 347.
23. Comment by Z. A. Stos-Gale on Poursat (1984, p. 87).
24. Ward (1971, pp. 107–25); Helck (1979, pp. 21–2).
25. Kantor (1947, pp. 21–4).
26. Ward (1971, pp. 108–10). It is interesting to note in this connection that the 'reef-knot' design seems to have been introduced from Egypt to Crete in the 19th or 18th centuries BC. Higgins (1979, p. 37).
27. See, for instance, Vermeule and Vermeule (1970, p. 33).

28. For a justification of this unconventional chronology see ch. X, nn. 91–105.

29. The *Cambridge Ancient History* dates the break to 1700, in line with the ceramic updating required by the re-dating of the Thera eruption to 1628 BC. I put this at *c.* 1730 BC; see below, ch. VII.

30. For ways of playing this fact down, see, for example, Trump (1981, p. 175).

31. Graham (1962, pp. 231–2).

32. Graham (1970, pp. 238–9).

33. For a good description of this principle as it applied to Ancient Egypt, see Springborg (1990, pp. 73–88).

34. Higgins (1979, pp. 22–37).

35. Schachermeyr (1967, p. 47) argues that this convention was only established in Crete at the beginning of MMIII. However, the basis for his argument is from pots where the convention never held. For Thueris see Schachermeyr (1967, p. 31 and plates 63–9).

36. Watrous (1987b, pp. 65–6, 70).

37. Bennet (1990, p. 194, n. 70).

38. Branigan (1970a, p. 52).

39. Bintliff (1984).

40. Warren (1981); Sakellerakis and Sapouna-Sakelleraki (1981).

41. Dow (1973, p. 602).

42. Dow is particularly sensitive on this issue because he wants to use 'the argument from silence' to establish that there was a long period of illiteracy separating the Bronze Age from the Archaic one. This can be seen from his anxiety to show that 'Cyprus may have been crucially different' from Greece in preserving its Bronze Age script into the Classical period (1973, p. 606). For this argument and its relationship to supporting the Aryan Model and discrediting the Ancient one, see Volume 1, p. 398, and Bernal (1990, pp. 57–8).

43. Godart (1983).

44. Ventris and Chadwick (1973, p. 31).

45. Evans (1921–35, II, p. 49). See also Rundle Clark (1959, p. 237). For the plausible hypothesis that both signs derive from the vertebra of an aurochs or wild bull, which was seen as the source of sperm and hence life, see Schwabe, Adams and Hodge (1982). This is not to say that they did not accrete many other symbolic meanings.

46. Newberry (1909, pp. 24–31); Gaerte (1922, pp. 72–5).

47. *Pyramid Text*, Utt. 685. Faulkner (1969, p. 295).

48. For the Early Minoan cult, see ch. I, n. 55. *Lakh-* has no Indo-European etymology. Other derivatives of ꜣḫ would seem to include *leikhēn* (tree moss, lichen). This seems more plausible than to take it from the Indo-European root **leigh* found in our 'lick' and the Greek *leikhō*. Another strong possibility is the Greek *lasios* (hairy). The alternation between ḫ and š̮ was frequent in Egyptian.

49. For a bibliography on the Rarian Plain, see Frazer (1898, II, pp. 514–15). For the etymology of Orgas, see Volume 4.

50. Nilsson (1950, p. 189).
51. Powell (1977, pp. 72–3). Powell gives an excellent survey of the earlier literature on this. He maintained his Aryanist orthodoxy on this by arguing that symbols can be transmitted between completely alien cultures without affecting fundamental systems of thought.
52. K₃yt is not attested in connection with the island. For discussions of the known Egyptian names for Crete, see ch. X, nn. 2–23, below.
53. For a discussion of this preference for Anatolia, see Volume 1, pp. 391–2.
54. Burkert (1985, p. 37).
55. See ch. I, n. 60, above.
56. Hoffmann (1979, p. 91).
57. The only possible evidence of an Early Minoan bull cult comes from two vases – from Porti and Kumasa in the Mesara – representing bulls which seem to have human forms attached to the horns. Branigan (1970b, p. 81) writes about these: 'Some may plausibly be attributed to Early Minoan II. We cannot be certain about the date of these. They could be later, and certainly some bull-vessels, like those of Agios Kyrillos, are of Middle Minoan I date'. (I am indebted to Lyvia Morgan for this reference.) The same uncertainty of date is true of the clay models nos 4126 and 5052 at the Herakleon museum. These do not appear to form a very strong foundation for a case in favour of an early or indigenous origin of the bull cult of palatial Crete.
58. Herodotos, II.145.
59. Diodoros, III.8.
60. Strabo, XVII.2.3.
61. Chassinat (1966–8, II, p. 676); Gundlach (1982, cols 135–9).
62. Chassinat (1966–8, II, p. 676).
63. Chassinat (1966–8, II, pp. 676–7). See also Gardiner (1947, I, pp. 80–6).
64. Shack and Habte (1974, p. 26). For more on Bʷäzä, see Leslau (1950, pp. 54–5).
65. Cohen (1970–6, II, p. 53). The orthodox interpretation of this name is to derive it from b₃ + aʿaz (with strength), a problematic construction; see Mulder (1986, pp. 19–25).
66. Ruth 3.1–18. Other aspects of the extraordinarily rich myth will be discussed in Volume 3.
67. I Kings 7.21. For other examples, see Herodotos, II.45, and for a bibliography on this, see Lloyd (1976, p. 200).
68. Shack and Habte (1974, p. 175).
69. See, for instance, Gordon (1962b, pp. 178–205).
70. Klearkhos, fr. 9, in *Frag. Hist. Gr.* II. See Cook (1914–40, II, pp. 28–32). For more on the Iapyges, see Bernal (1990, pp. 44–7).
71. See Cook (1914–40, II, p. 30). Jane Harrison (1927, pp. 176–7) too saw this identification of the double-axe with Zeus *katabaites* and thunder. It was not only double-axes that were identified with thunderbolts. Harrison (1927, pp. 56–7) pointed out that stone axes or celts have also

been seen in this way and that modern Greek peasants called them *astropelekia* (star axes).

72. See ch. I, nn. 61–2.
73. Gardiner (1957, p. 503, R-22).
74. Wainwright (1931, pp. 185–95). Wainwright also associates the missile with Horus and his counterpart Apollo.
75. Cook (1914–40, I, pp. 84–6). The etymology of the recent word 'belemnite' from the Greek *belemna* (missiles) shows how easy it is to see them as projectiles.
76. Cook (1914–40, I.1, pp. 85–6).
77. See Gardiner (1957, p. 487) and Gundlach (1982, p. 136).
78. The Egyptian symbol represents the uterus of a heifer rather than that of a woman. This reflection of the centrality of cattle, particularly cows, has been referred to above. Schwabe, Adams and Hodge (1982, p. 445) maintain that the belief that it was the shape of the human uterus survived in European thought until the work of Vesalius in the 16th century AD. I have no reason to doubt this, but I have not been able to find the reference they give to Gardiner (1947). For a moving linkage of wombs and intestines with spirals and labyrinths, see Eco (1989, pp. 362–3).
79. *Ḥm* written with other determinatives increases the interest of the cluster. With ⤵ (falling wall) and ⎯ (beat, force), *ḥm* meant 'demolish buildings and harm someone', but it also was used in the sense of 'debar and exclude'. In Late Egyptian, this word signified 'demolish, force open, break through'. With the determinative ⌐ (motion) it seems to have meant 'wild, of animals'. *Ḥmʿ* meant 'seize, grasp' or 'penetrate' or 'drive off'. Taken together, the cluster seems semantically very close to the Semitic *bʷaz* with its double sense of destruction and penetration and protection from it. *Ḥm(w/y)* also meant 'dust'. Its having been written with ⛵ (sail) suggests that it was associated with winds. Given the parallels with the storm god *bʷäzä*, and the storm god Min's *Ḥm*, it is possible that this is the origin of the Greek *kheima*, in the sense of 'storm'. *Kheima* meaning 'winter' has a clear Indo-European origin, but although winter in Greece can be stormy, the word does seem to have two relatively distinct semantic fields which could be the result of the conflation of two different roots.
80. Gauthier (1931, pp. 149–50); Chassinat (1966–8, II, pp. 684–91).
81. Gundlach (1982, col. 136).
82. Gauthier (1931, p. 197). For a detailed survey of inscriptions concerning the god in these regions, see Bernand (1977).
83. Gauthier (1931, p. 176).
84. Otto (1966, p. 118; n.d., p. 123).
85. Budge (1904, II, p. 18); Gauthier (1931, pp. 180–1); Otto (n.d., p. 123).
86. Voss (1827–34). For Voss and Niebuhr, see Volume 1, p. 298.
87. Borgeaud (1979, p. 263). For even wilder speculation, see the appendix by Alfred Willy (Borgeaud 1979, pp. 283–5).

88. Ruijgh (1967, s. 86, n.40).
89. Volume 1, p. 454, n.50.
90. For a discussion of this, see Volume 1, pp. 91–2.
91. Both the Egyptian *in(t)* and the Greek *pan* referred to *Tilapia Nilotica*.
92. See Sethe (1908, pp. 11–14; 1910a, pp. 71–8). See also Hani (1976, p. 69). For more on this, see Volume 4.
93. See Astour (1967a, pp. 174–5). There is also a possibility that the mysterious Greek fish-name *bakkhos* is a pun on *pan-panos*.
94. See, for instance, Frazer (1911, I, pp. 6–121) and Jacobsen (1976, pp. 25–73).
95. Plutarch, 'On the Obsolescence of Oracles', 419, trans. Babbit (1936, p. 403).
96. Quoted by Plato in *Minos* in Loeb, *Hesiod*, p. 204.
97. *Odyssey*, XI.586.
98. Rubric to chs. CLXII and CLXIII cited in Budge (1904, II, p. 10). See also Otto (1975b, cols. 245–6).
99. See ch. X, nn. 2–8.
100. Herodotos, II.7 and 99. Possibly the two vocalizations point to an earlier *Mayn, but this is purely hypothetical.
101. See Lloyd (1988, pp. 6–10).
102. The situation is made still more confusing by the fact that the legendary Indian founder of political order and lawgiver was called Manu.
103. Diodoros, I.XCIV 1–2, trans. Oldfather (1935, I, p. 319).
104. Aelian XI.10, cited in Otto (1938, p. 5, n.2).
105. Manetho fragments 8, 9 and 10; Vercoutter (1975, col. 338). See also Lloyd (1976, p. 171).
106. Herodotos, II.99, claimed that Min had founded it. See also Gardiner (1961a, p. 408).
107. For iwn, iwnw or 'On, see Volume 1, pp. 176–7.
108. *Coffin Texts*, V.1916. See also Kakosy (1982, col. 165).
109. Sethe (1923, p. 191). See also Otto (1938, p. 34).
110. Apart from those mentioned in the text, one finds such parallels as *mniwt* (harbour) and *mrw*, *mr* and *mrgt*, all meaning 'harbour, shore, run aground'; and *mr* and *mn*, both meaning 'sick man'. Interestingly, in modern Maghrebi and Egyptian Arabic, final *l*'s are often pronounced as *-n*, as in *futban* (football).
111. *Mniw* will be discussed below under Minyans.
112. See Volume 3.
113. Lloyd (1978, pp. 609–26). For a discussion of the word *mtwn*, the name of the site of such bullfights, and its relationships to the word *mothos*, -acc. *mothon* (sound of animals fighting) and the place names Mothone, Methana, etc., see below n. 174 and Volume 3.
114. Erman (1934, p. 27); Otto (1938, p. 36). The figure of a bull-headed Mnevis reproduced by Lanzone (1881–6, vol. I, pp. 170–2, pl. 55.3) is Ptolemaic and, as far as I know, there is no earlier attestation.
115. See Diodoros, I.61.1–3, and Pliny, N.H. XXXVI.90.

116. See Herodotos, II.148–49, and Strabo XVII.1.37. When Petrie looked at the site in 1889 and 1911 he found only a vast area of limestone chips, and there seems to have been a considerable amount of lime burning there in Roman times. Diodoros, I.61.1–3, and Pliny (36.90) stated that it had been destroyed by their times. See Gardiner (1961a, pp. 139–40). For sceptical but unconvincing attempts to deny the testimony not only of Herodotos but of Strabo and Petrie on this, see Armayor (1978, p. 70; 1985). Very few of the scholars who since Late Antiquity have identified Herodotos' Lake Moeris with the Fayyum have accepted his description of the lake and the building of the labyrinth by the Moeris or Ammenemēs III in detail. Nevertheless, they have plausibly seen the association of the labyrinth with what appears to have been an exceptionally large and elaborate mortuary temple, confirmed by archaeological and inscriptional evidence. For a good survey, see Lloyd (1988, pp. 121–7). It is noteworthy and indicative of the sceptical Aryanist approach, which tends to see Greek descriptions of Egypt very largely in terms of a fevered Greek imagination, that Armayor takes the much murkier origins of the Cretan labyrinth as given.

117. Brugsch (1879–80, II, p. 501). Brugsch is also mentioned in Volume 1, pp. 258, 261.

118. Gauthier (1925–31, III, p. 119).

119. See Kretschmer (1896, p. 404) and many others on this hypothesis, for which see Hester (1965, pp. 358–9). Frisk and Chantraine do not mention Brugsch's hypothesis. For the cult of the double-axe and its Near Eastern origins, see ch. I, nn. 61–3 above.

120. Volume 1, p. 64, and Stieglitz (1981b, pp. 195–8).

121. Hall (1905, pp. 320–4) in 1920 (pp. 153–5); Lloyd (1970, pp. 92–6; 1988, pp. 120–1).

122. Waddell (1940, p. 224, n. 1). Diodoros, I.61, would seem to have reproduced both of the pharaoh's names when he called him 'Mendēs or Marrus'. I would derive these from ỉmn m ḫȝt and Ny-mȝʿ t-Rʿ. However, Vergote (1962) maintains that they are both different forms of Ny-mȝʿ t-Rʿ. For the relationship between ỉmn m ḫȝt and Memnōn, see ch. VI, nn. 147–8.

123. See Volume 3.

124. Apollodoros, II.5.9 and III.1.2, and Nonnos, XIII.222 and XL.284. For an extensive bibliography of ancient sources on Minos' sexual adventures, see Graves (1955, I, p. 301).

125. Gauthier (1931, p. 83).

126. Volume 1, p. 95.

127. Gauthier (1931, pp. 83, 205). Sethe's reading of names 47 and 52 of the Abydos list as Nfr-kȝ Min and Nfr-kȝ Min ʿnnw (see the discussion in Stock, 1949, p. 35) is interesting in this regard. These pharaohs of the mysterious 8th Dynasty, from the middle of the 25th century, could have helped link Min and royalty in Crete four hundred years later.

128. Gundlach (1982, col. 136).

129. See Volume 1, pp. 310–11.
130. See Volume 1, pp. 85–8.
131. Graves (1955, I, p. 298); Wilamowitz-Moelendorff (1931–32, I, p. 56, n. 3).
132. Ranke (1935–52). I am not the first to propose an Egyptian etymology for Rhadamanthys. Bérard did so (1902–3, pp. 68–9), deriving it from the Egyptian 'amenti', imnty, which he points out was transcribed by Plutarch as 'Amenthys'. This was the western land where the dead were judged. There may have been some punning with this (see below, n. 143), but Bérard could not explain the initial Rhada-.
133. Gardiner (1957, p. 217, § 288).
134. *Pyramid Texts*, Utt. 503.
135. For a good general survey of his cults, see Bourghouts (1982, cols 200–4).
136. Jahnkuhn (1980, col. 212).
137. Bourghouts (1982, col. 201).
138. Budge (1904, I, p. 328); Mercer (1949, p. 125).
139. Rusch (1922); Frankfort, de Buck and Gunn (1933, p. 27). For the contrary view, see Hollis (1987a, pp. 7–8).
140. Otto (1938, p. 47); Bourghouts (1982, col. 201); Drawer (1940 pp. 157–9).
141. Bourghouts (1982, col. 202).
142. *Book of Coming Forth by Day*, CXI, 6 and CLXX. See Budge (1904, II, p. 26).
143. Hesiod, in Merkelbach and West 1983, frs 140–4. *Odyssey*, IV.564; Diodoros, V.79; Nonnos, XIX.190. See also Marinatos (1949, p. 11). Victor Bérard (1902–3, pp. 68–9) links this to 'amenti'; see above, n. 132. There may well be some punning on this in this aspect of Rhadamanthys' character.
144. *Odyssey*, IV.564 and VII.323. Marinatos (1949, p. 11) interprets it as 'blond' and uses this to support his connection of Rhadamanthys to Boiotia, which he sees as famous for the blondness of its inhabitants.
145. *Iliad*, XIV.322.
146. *Odyssey*, VII.323.
147. Diodoros, V.79.1–2.
148. Ch. II, nn. 190–1.
149. See ch. II, n. 159.
150. Ranke (1935–52, I, pp. 54, 57). For further indications that Mntw was vocalized with an 'a', see Gardiner (1947, II, p. 22).
151. Drioton (1931, pp. 260–1); Lanzone (1881–6, vol. 1, pp. 293–9, pls 99.2 and 4).
152. Ward (1971, p. 138).
153. Contenau (1953, p. 17, plate 40). The treasure will be discussed in detail in ch. V, nn. 126–37.
154. Bourghouts (1982, col. 200).
155. For the parallel, see, for instance, Maspero (1884, p. 462, n. 1). If the

head is attributed to him, Min/Mēnēs' features are, as Sheikh Anta Diop pointed out, early African. The face of Mntw ḥtp II is less obviously Negro, but the colouring of his famous statue in the Cairo Museum leaves no doubt whatsoever about his Blackness. See Diop (1974, plates 5 and 9).

156. Beckerath (1982a, col. 66; 1982b, cols 66–8).
157. Gardiner (1961a, p. 120).
158. Gauthier (1931, p. 205).
159. Inscription from Wadi Halfa cited by Otto (1938, p. 47).
160. Otto (1938, p. 47).
161. See above, nn. 28–39.
162. Pendlebury (1963, pp. 120–1).
163. Ward (1971, pp. 119–20).
164. For a bibliography on this, see Helck (1975a, cols 889–91).
165. Ward (1971, pp. 58–65).
166. Ward (1971, pp. 62–3).
167. See n. 23 above.
168. Diodoros, V.77.1, trans. C. H. Oldfather (III, p. 313).
169. Diodoros, V.84.1–4.
170. Volume 1, p. 83.
171. Reisner and Reisner (1933, pp. 35–46).
172. Pendlebury (1930a, p. 109); Burleigh and Hewson (1979).
173. See ch. I, n. 16.
174. See the curious markings suggesting movement over the bull's back on the determinative 𓄹 in the word *mtwn* (arena) (Erman and Grapow, 1982, II, p. 175), which is attested from the Old Kingdom. See also nn. 107–12 above.

Chapter V
SESŌSTRIS: THE ARCHAEOLOGICAL AND DOCUMENTARY EVIDENCE FOR THE GREEK ACCOUNTS OF HIS CONQUESTS

1. Farag (1980, p. 75); Posener (1982, p. 7); Petrie and Walker (1909, pp. 6–7, 17–18).
2. Farag and Posener assume the inscription should be taken at face value and be dated to the 12th Dynasty, as does Giveon (1985, p. 16, n. 34). William Ward, who is equally expert in the Middle Kingdom, dismisses their opinions and that of Petrie on the other fragment and maintains that it is 'Ramesside', that is to say dating from the 13th rather from the 19th century BC (1987, p. 528). He points out that the names given are not those of living kings but those on funerary monuments. However, he admits that they could be 'early 12th Dynasty'.

　　Against Ward it can be argued that the foreign place names are unknown in New Kingdom texts and seem plausible in terms of Middle Kingdom pronunciation. It is for this reason and the circumstantial evidence presented below that I prefer to follow Farag and Posener and accept the 12th-Dynasty date, which is what the text indicates. This view is now generally accepted by Egyptologists; see O'Connor (1990). The most striking example of this is Helck (1989).

3. Farag (1980, pp. 78–9); Posener (1982, p. 8). For Ṣtt, see Gardiner (1947, I, p. 177) and Gauthier (1925–31, I, p. 95).

4. Gardiner (1961a, p. 126).

5. Simpson (1984a, col. 891).

6. See Herodotos, II.110, and Diodoros, I.57.5. Lloyd (1988, pp. 36–7) – not discussing the inscription – admits that there are 12th-Dynasty remains there but insists, with some plausibility, that the statues the Greeks believed were of Sesōstris and his family were in fact of Ramessēs II.

7. For scepticism on this, see Simpson (1984b, col. 950). For belief that the assassination was successful, see Posener (1956, pp. 66–73) and Blumenthal (1983, pp. 105–6).

8. For bibliographies on this stela and on Nsw Mnṯw himself, see Posener (1971, p. 538) and Simpson (1984a, col. 899).

9. See Lichtheim (1975, I, pp. 222–35). For bibliographies of the many translations of this famous story, see Lichtheim (pp. 222–3) and Simpson (1984b, col. 953).

10. For a long discussion on the location of Rṯnw, see Gardiner (1947, I, pp. 142–9).

11. Posener (1971, p. 538).

12. Posener (1971, p. 539).

13. Albright (1960, p. 85).

14. Posener (1940, 1956, and 1971); Giveon, (1978a, pp. 61–72; 1981; 1985). Weinstein, who is very much opposed to the idea of a Middle Kingdom 'Empire' in the Levant, has admitted that there are many scarabs of Senwosre I in Palestine and that a statue of a woman who may be his daughter has been found at Tell Gezer (1974, p. 52). The archaeological grounds upon which he argued that this princess was a daughter of Amenemḥe III have since disappeared.

15. Posener (1956, p. 109).

16. Posener (1971, p. 540). For the quote, see Lichtheim (1975, I, 188). She discusses the term Sḫꜣḫꜣty, which she and Brunner translate as 'courier', but Helck as 'caravaneer'.

17. Giveon (1975, cols 462–63). See also the short bibliography on the name in Helm (1980, p. 229, n. 5).

18. Confusion between the two names is shown in the difficulties surrounding Homer's reference to a people called Eremboi in the passage from the *Odyssey* describing Menelaos' wanderings: 'Over Cyprus and Phoenicia I wandered, and Egypt, and I came to the Ethiopians and the Sidonians and the Eremboi and to Libya...' (IV.82–5).

In Antiquity, this was seen as a reference to Arabs (Strabo, I.41), but, as Helm (1980, p. 217), points out, this may have been contaminated by the name Aramaean so that Erimboi may simply have meant Near Eastern nomads.

There is an even earlier Greek reference to Arabs in Hesiod's *Cata-*

logue of Women: 'The daughter of Arabos, whom worthy Hermaon begat with Thronia, daughter of the lord Bēlos', frg. 15 (137), trans. Evelyn-White (1914, p. 167). Frg. 137 in Merkelbach and West (1983).

Bēlos provides a clearly Semitic context for this. If, as argued in Volume 1, pp. 86–8, we should date Hesiod in the 10th century BC, this reference is earlier than any from the Near East, the first attestation being from an inscription of the Assyrian monarch Shalmaneser III of 853 BC. The earliest biblical references to the name come in prophetic writings of the 6th century. For all the sources on this, see Eph'al (1982, pp. 6–9).

Eph'al (p. 7, n. 24) dismisses any connection between ʿărăb (Arab) and ʿărăbăh (desert). Although he is right to deny ʿărăbăh as the etymon for ʿărăb, the two words must be connected. To my mind, the most plausible etymology for Arab is from the Semitic root √ʿrb or √ġrb (enter, sunset, west). Thus the gentilic – or name of a people – would be a Mesopotamian name for the people living in the desert to their west.

19. *Iliad*, II.782–85.
20. Vian (1960, pp. 19–24).
21. Fontenrose (1959, p. 71, n. 2) and against Vian (1963, pp. 64–82).
22. Fontenrose (1959, pp. 82, 177–93). For Seth's association with Ṣṭt and Syro-Palestine, see Van Seters (1966, p. 99).
23. Chantraine (1968–75, p. 371) wrote about this *'rien de clair'* and rightly dismissed Pokorny's (1959–69, pp. 332–3) attempt to derive *erēmo-* from an I.E root *er* (loose).
24. Posener (1971, pp. 540–1). For a list of these statues, see Helck (1971, pp. 68–9).
25. Ward (1961, pp. 17–38); Stevenson Smith (1965, pp. 14–150). See Stevenson Smith (1965, p. 15, n. 48) for a full bibliography on these.
26. Posener (1971, pp. 540–1). For the pictures, see Davies and Gardiner (1936, plates X and XI).
27. Helck (1971, p. 41).
28. Ward (1971, p. 68).
29. Posener (1982, p. 8).
30. Helck (1989, p. 27).
31. Maspero (1901, p. 593).
32. Volume 1, pp. 252, 306.
33. Bunsen (1848–60, I, 309–24); Maspero (1901, p. 593).
34. Sethe (1900, 1904). Burton (1972, p. 164) misdates Sethe's articles to 1902 and 1905 respectively.
35. Maspero (1901, pp. 596–7) accepted Sethe's reading of the name Senwosre, but initially claimed that Sesōstris came from a biname of Ramessēs, Rʿ s s t sw. Sethe demolished his case in 1904.
36. Burton (1972, p. 166).
37. Diodoros, I.53.8.
38. Gardiner (1957, p. 74).
39. Manetho, frs 32, 34–6, trans. Waddell (1940, pp. 64–73).

40. For details, see Delia (1980, pp. 24–107).
41. *Pace* Hayes (1971, p. 505), who sees Senwosre III as the prototype.
42. Manetho, Frs 32, 34–6.
43. Herodotos, II.100–110, trans. de Selincourt (1954, pp. 166–9).
44. Diodoros, I.53.5–58.2, trans. Oldfather (1933, pp. 187–95).
45. See Sethe (1900, 1904); Maspero (1901); Rattenbury (1933); Braun (1938, pp. 13–18); Lange (1954); Malaise (1966); West (1977); Lloyd (1982; 1988, pp. 16–18).
46. Posener (1956, p. 15).
47. The Soviet Egyptologist and Coptologist Petr Viktorovitch Ernshtedt established the Egyptian etymology of *mythos* in 1953 (pp. 55–7). Chantraine gives the original meaning of *mythos* as 'succession of words which have a direction, proposal, discourse', 'the content of words'. There is also the fact that there is no Indo-European etymology for the word.
48. Megasthenes, cited in Strabo, XV, 686, and Arrian, *Indica*, V.4.
49. See Herodotos, II.110, and Diodoros, I.58.4. For a modern discussion of this, see Lloyd (1982, p. 37).
50. Georgacas (1969, pp. 34–7). See also Helm (1980, p. 23, n. 23). For Egyptian etymologies or renderings of Asia, see nn. 164–72 below.
51. See ch. VI, nn. 12–14.
52. For a bibliography of this, see Posener (1956, pp. 68–9).
53. Spiegelberg's explanation of Sesōstris escaping from the fire over the bodies of two of his sons, as the result of 'a dragoman's tale based upon a frequently recurring representation of the triumphant Pharaoh. He is often depicted with his feet placed on two heads symbolizing the foreign enemies of Egypt, the Negroes and the Syrians' (1927, p. 25) is far-fetched but possible.
54. The parallel was first pointed out by Iversen (1961, p. 149, n. 16). See also Burton (1972, p. 171). For details, see Delia (1980, pp. 54–6). The sign ♡ (well) was used for *ḥm* (female organ) from Middle Kingdom times.
55. Sethe (1900, p. 3); Malaise (1966, p. 250); Burton (1972, p. 178).
56. Emery, 1960, p. 6; Clutton-Brock (1974, pp. 92–3). For the 'chariots' illustrated on cylinder seals from Kültepe II, see Drews (1988, pp. 93–6). Drews (n. 48) accepts a 'middle chronology' dating of 1910–1840 for Kültepe II.
57. For official involvement in the transport of gods, see, for instance, the Stela of Ikhernofret (Berlin Museum 1204), translated in Lichtheim (1975, pp. 123–9). For the newness of Senwosre I's title of 'God', see Blumenthal (1985, pp. 108–9). See also Springborg (1990, pp. 46–7).
58. Volume 1, pp. 170, 185.
59. See Volume 1, p. 326.
60. For acceptance of the stories of Sesōstris' conquests in Africa and Arabia, see, for instance, Sethe (1900, pp. 16–20), Malaise (1966, pp. 260–4) and Lloyd (1988, p. 36). Lloyd gives a full bibliography of the secondary literature on this point.

61. Foucart (1914, p. 4) cited by E. Meyer (1928–36, I, p. 263). For more on Foucart, see Volume 1, pp. 264–5, 314, 380, 383.

62. See Lichtheim (1975, I, pp. 211–15).

63. Naville (1894–1908, III, plates 69–71); Stevenson Smith (1958, pp. 136, 138; 1965, p. 7).

64. For Ramessēs' fleets, see Burton (1972, p. 169). For the 18th-Dynasty navies, see Hayes (1973, pp. 367–9) and Säve-Söderbergh (1946, pp. 33–50). See also ch. X, n. 86.

65. Herodotos, II.100.

66. See the inscription from the 19th year of Senwosre III (c. 1864 BC) from Uronarti (Khartoum 2683) discussed in Delia (1980, pp. 77–9). For a literary explanation of Sesōstris' having been checked by shoals, see Lloyd (1988, p. 19). Lloyd accepts that the text was referring to the sea not the Nile.

67. Diodoros, I.55.6.

68. See, for instance, Wildung (1984, plates 140, 150–1).

69. Adams (1984, pp. 176–81). For a comparative view of these fortifications, see van Seters (1966, pp. 33–7).

70. Parker (1950, p. 69).

71. Parker (1976, pp. 178–84); Kitchen (1987, p. 43).

72. Krauss (1985, pp. 73–82); Kitchen (1987, p. 43).

73. Meyer (1904, pp. 45–51).

74. Modern convention since Farina's transcription of the hieratic text into hieroglyphic of col. V.1.18 in the *Turin Canon* (1938, p. 35), backed by a somewhat hesitant claim by Winlock (1940, p. 118, n. 2), has been that the dynasty lasted 143 years. Gardiner (1959, p. 16) copied it in the same way in his transcription. Sethe (1905), however, read it as 160+ and this was accepted by Meyer (1907b, p. 21) and by Breasted (1906, I, p. 41). It is impossible to make a firm judgement on this issue, which is extremely obscure. The line appears made up of two or three unclear sections of different fragments (63, 64 and ?). As Meyer put it, 'out of these miserable fragments [Sethe] had established with his usual acuteness' the total of 160+ he found. There is no doubt that when Winlock wrote and Farina and Gardiner were working on the text, the trend in Egyptian chronology was sharply downwards (see below). Thus, it is impossible to say whether they and their contemporaries saw the number 143 in the text because it was there or because they believed it should be. With the greater general credibility given to the chronology of the earlier scholars by new radio-carbon dates, I am inclined to follow them rather than their successors in this too.

75. Gardiner (1959, pp. 11–13).

76. Stock (1949, p. 103).

77. Breasted (1906, I, pp. 40–5).

78. Meyer (1907b, pp. 68, 178).

79. Gardiner (1961a, p. 67).

80. Hayes (1971, p. 996). For a bibliographical survey of the trend to diminish or annul the 1st Intermediate Period, see Kemp (1980, p. 27).

81. Mellaart (1979, pp. 7–11).
82. Mellaart (1979, p. 7).
83. Kemp (1980) and Weinstein (1980).
84. Haas *et al.* (1987). Their results also appear to have been supported by work on a different sample processed with the latest methods at Hanover, Haas *et al.* (1987, p. 597).
85. Haas *et al.* (1987, pp. 586–7).
86. Shaw (1985).
87. Shaw (1985, p. 304); Haas *et al.* (1987, pp. 596–7).
88. Haas *et al.* (1987, pp. 588–9).
89. See Weinstein (1989b, p. 103). See also Harding and Tait (1989, pp. 151–2).
90. For a survey of the finds at Ebla and some of their implications, see Pettinato (1981).
91. Matthiae (1981, p. 9).
92. Pettinato (1981, p. 107).
93. Matthiae (1988, p. 76).
94. Matthiae (1988, p. 77). Synchronisms in Byblos also indicate that Sargon reigned during the Egyptian 1st Intermediate Period.
95. Huber (1987b, p. 9).
96. Pettinato (1981, p. 107; personal communication, Cornell, 1983).
97. Steinkeller (1986, pp. 31–40).
98. See Gardiner (1961a, pp. 62–3); O'Mara (1979, addendum).
99. Mellaart (1979, p. 9).
100. Kemp (1980, p. 25).
101. See Mit Rahina, col. 5+x.
102. Gardiner (1961a, pp. 112–16).
103. Smith (1965, p. xxiv).
104. See Callender (1975, p. 1). He even suggests that Middle Egyptian was the spoken language of the late Old Kingdom and the 1st Intermediate Period. It is true that the differences between New and Middle Egyptian are far greater than those between Old and Middle Egyptian and the time gap of 230 years for the 2nd Intermediate Period is rather less than the 310 years postulated here for the 1st. However, even more important than any linguistic impact of the Hyksos invasions is the fact that while Old and Middle Egyptian both appear to have been based on the spoken language of Memphis in Lower Egypt, New Egyptian was the spoken language of Thebes in Upper Egypt (see Greenberg 1986, pp. 282–3). Thus there was a major regional as well as a temporal distance in the second case.
105. Huber (1987a, p. 17). See also Huber (1982). The 'long' chronology is not the higher chronology proposed by Landsberger and Nagel (see Strommenger, 1964, chart). This is some eighty years earlier still. It should, however, be pointed out that Huber has not checked his figures against higher chronologies as thoroughly as against the lower ones. For his dismembering of objections see Åström (1987–9, III, pp. 61–3).
106. Mellaart (1957, 1958, and 1967).
107. Personal communication from Peter Kuniholm, Cornell, October 1990.

108. See Maps and Charts.
109. Mellaart (1982, pp. 31–2).
110. Mellaart (1982, pp. 31–2).
111. Gurney (1973, pp. 229–32); Watkins (1986, pp. 45–8).
112. Volume 1, pp. 13–14.
113. Lang (1966, pp. 43–4; 1977, p. 76); Burney and Lang (1971, 78–85); Bosch-Gimpera (1980, p. 171); Mellaart (1967, pp. 36–8).
114. For the old view, see Mellaart (1967, pp. 29–31).
115. Larsen (1976, pp. 80–105).
116. For a bibliography of the debate, see Gurney (1973, pp. 232–3). Macqueen (1975, p. 21) and Mellaart (1978, p. 57) plump for the later date.
117. Balkan (1955, pp. 58–63). Dendrochronology seems to be on the brink of establishing a date for the destruction, but the tree-ring sequences have not yet been anchored to an absolute chronology. See Kuniholm and Newton (1989).
118. Balkan (1955, pp. 42–3, 58–63).
119. Cited by Mellaart (1957, p. 58).
120. Larsen (1976, pp. 81–4).
121. Mellaart (1958, p. 9) and (1967, p. 37) – c. 1900 BC; (1978, p. 49) – c. 1940 BC.
122. Mellaart (1958, p. 10).
123. Muhly (1973b, p. 326). For Mellaart's repetitions of his thesis see (1967, pp. 44–5). However, he omits it in 1978.
124. Bittel (1970, pp. 46–7). For the report of burning, see Mellink (1977, p. 293).
125. Kadish (1971, p. 123).
126. Mellaart (1958, p. 10).
127. Mellaart (1958, p. 14).
128. Mellaart (1978, map on pp. 46–7).
129. Bisson de la Roque et al. (1953, pp. 7–14); Helck (1971, p. 382). For a bibliography on this, see Kemp and Merrillees (1980, p. 290, n.690). See also Vandier (1972, pp. 260–1).
130. Bisson de la Roque et al. (1953, p. 10).
131. Pace Kemp and Merrillees (1980, p. 296).
132. Davis (1977, pp. 69–78, esp. p. 72; 1974, pp. 46–81); Kemp and Merrillees (1980, p. 290).
133. Porada (1950, pp. 155–62). It is significant that Kemp and Merrillees make no mention of the seals which put the cap of futility on their ingenious attempt to downdate the treasure, which mars their otherwise splendid work.
134. Bisson de la Roque et al. (1953, p. 9 and plates XLIII–XLIX); Kemp and Merrillees (1980, p. 295).
135. Posener (1971, p. 540).
136. Unpublished but quoted by Posener (1971, p. 543).
137. See nn. 36–7 above.
138. Kemp and Merrillees (1980, p. 295).

139. Erman and Grapow (1982, II, p. 92).
140. Farag (1980, p. 78, line 9+x); Borghouts (1982, cols 200–4). See below. Helck (1989, p. 29) makes the general connection between the Mit Rahina inscription and the Tôd Treasure.
141. Mellaart (1958, p. 11).
142. Dumitrescu (1982, pp. 37–43); Garašanin (1982a, pp. 142–52).
143. Dayton (1982a, p. 155).
144. Diodoros, I.55.6–7.
145. See n. 49 above.
146. Lang (1966, pp. 43–5; 1978, pp. 70–3); Muhly (1973b, pp. 202–6); Mellaart (1982, pp. 22–3).
147. Burney (1958, pp. 169–75); Lang (1978, p. 78); Burney and Lang (1971, p. 95).
148. Burney (1958, p. 178); Lang (1978, p. 78).
149. Burney and Lang (1971, p. 85).
150. Lang (1978, p. 76).
151. Schaeffer (1948, pp. 544–5).
152. Mellaart (1978, p. 47, map). For the high development of metalwork in EBIII Anatolia see Yakar (1985).
153. Maxwell-Hyslop (1946).
154. Tylecote (1976, p. 21); Yadin (1963, I, pp. 60–2, 153–75); Maxwell-Hyslop (1946). See also ch. IX, nn. 22–34 below.
155. Lang (1978, p. 77). See, for instance, the two splendid 12th-Dynasty gold-mounted ointment jars made from Caucasian obsidian illustrated in Wildung (1984, p. 93, plate 82).
156. Helck (1971, p. 389). The main silver and lead mines are those near Sebinkarahisar some fifty-five miles south of Giresun on the Black Sea and Ergani Maden near Diyarbakir on the Upper Euphrates in Central Turkey. See Dayton (1982a, p. 166).
157. Gardiner (1947, I, p. 177).
158. Farag (1980, p. 78, lines 9+x and 10+x). Not only the transcription but the style of these passages is obscure. See, for instance, the use of *dy* instead of the more usual *rdi*, and ⌐▭|ʘ, -*ds* not *ds*-, not for 'beer jugs' but offerings in general as in the determinative for *inw* ʃ̄ʘ (tribute). For this, see Gardiner (1957, p. 530). The reading I propose also involves using ○ *n(y)w* for 'of' rather than *n* or *nt* as was common in the Middle Kingdom. The reason for reading ⱶ⊨ as the foreign country rather than as a 'cake' is the reference earlier in the line to ⱶ (▱=𝄑) ▵▵ (copper or bronze of Stt). I am deeply indebted on this point, as for so much else, to Edward Meltzer. He of course bears no responsibility for my conclusions. For another discussion of the writing of Stt and a reference to ⱶ in the term *sttyw* (Asiatics) in an 11th-Dynasty inscription, see van Seters (1966, p. 107).
159. Farag (1980, p. 77, lines 8+x). I follow Posener (1982, p. 8) in reading the 'bird' before Stt as *bꜣ*.
160. Helck (1971, pp. 295–7, 571).

161. Muhly (1973b, pp. 209–11) doubts even the reports of copper mining in the region.
162. Genesis (4.22). For the iron-working see Tylecote (1976, p. 40). See also Yakar (1985). See also ch. XI, n. 76. For a discussion of the exchanges between *m*, *p* and *b* with especial reference to Anatolia, see Bernal (1990, pp. 92–3). See also Helck (1989, p. 28).
163. Helck (1989, p. 28).
164. Cline (1987, p. 28). For further discussion see ch. III, nn. 122–4 above.
165. See ch. III, n. 122 and Macqueen (1975, p. 18).
166. See above n. 121.
167. See Gardiner (1947, p. 131) and Helck (1971, pp. 282–3). Strange (1980, pp. 169–83) argues that Alashia is not Cyprus, but Wachsmann (1987, pp. 99–102) argues powerfully in favour of conventional wisdom. Wachsmann's main point – which had been made almost fifty years earlier by Power (1929, p. 156) – was that Alashia could not be a city to the north of Byblos because, in the Amarna Letter 114, Byblos' king Rib-Addi saw Alashia as a way of reaching Egypt by avoiding his enemies. Merrillees (1987, p. 59) claims, not altogether convincingly, that this argument resembles one put forward by Astour, when the latter mistakenly denied the identification of Tell Mardikh with Ebla on the grounds that the Tell was not on an itinerary described for Ebla. Merrillees is quite right to point out that the identification of Alashia with Cyprus is not as secure as those for cities like Ebla and Ugarit, where the name is attested by abundant local documents. On the other hand, he and his faction provide no alternative location for Alashia and there is no other 2nd-millennium Egyptian, Levantine, Mesopotamian or Hittite toponym for Cyprus. Thus the identification remains extremely plausible. It is strange that Merrillees should refer so frequently to Astour's demand for certainty and his refusal to recognize the plausibility of the identification of Tell Mardikh with Ebla, when he himself makes the same kind of argument over the plausible linkage of Alashia with Cyprus.
168. Meltzer (personal communication, 22 October 1987) and Helck (1989, p. 28). Vercoutter (1956, p. 93, n. 4), noting that irs appeared only after the reign of Akhenaten, argued that it must have been preceded by isy. İsy seems more probable, though isy may also have been used.
169. Farag (1980, p. 79, line 16+x); Posener (1982, p. 8).
170. Catling (1971, pp. 818–22); Merrillees (1977, pp. 44–6).
171. Ward (1961, p. 30). Merrillees (1987, pp. 67–71) gives a thorough survey of the previous literature surrounding this ambiguity. See also Helck (1989, pp. 27–8).
172. Bossert (1946, pp. 5–40, 177).
173. Maspero (1886, pp. 361–8).
174. Wainwright (1915, pp. 1–36).
175. Georgacas (1969, pp. 39–41). Vercoutter (1956, p. 181) avoids this problem by simply denying any connection between isy and Assuwa. As

Merrillees (1987, p. 36) points out, Vercoutter does this 'not on philological but on historical grounds'.

176. Foucart (1914, pp. 2–3). For more on Foucart, see Volume 1, pp. 70, 264–5, 314, 380, 383, 495. Foucart's ideas will be discussed in some detail in Volume 4.

Chapter VI
SESŌSTRIS: THE CULTIC, MYTHICAL AND LEGENDARY EVIDENCE

1. Spiegelberg (1927, p. 20). While Spiegelberg was very much a scholar of his time, his attitude was – to my mind – far more open than that of Diels (1887, p. 423) or of Sayce (1885) or, for that matter, of Armayor (1985).
2. Simpson (1984a, col. 891).
3. Posener (1956, pp. 141–4).
4. See ch. V, n. 45.
5. Diodoros, I.20, trans. Oldfather, pp. 63–5.
6. *De Iside...*, 356A, trans. V, p. 35.
7. Volume 1, pp. 115, 461, n. 193.
8. Volume 1, pp. 142–5.
9. Dörrie (1979).
10. Gardiner (1961a, pp. 47–8).
11. For discussions of this, see Posener (1960, p. 43); Bell (1985a, p. 274; 1985b); Springborg (1990, pp. 209–14). For pharaohs and heroes, see ch. II, nn. 208–10.
12. See Volume 1, pp. 115–16, and n. 16 below.
13. For the date of the first fragments of the *Alexander Romance*, see Rattenbury (1933, pp. 220–1).
14. For the 22nd Dynasty, see Gardiner (1961, pp. 326–34). For Manetho's uncertainty on the names, see Frs 34 and 35, trans. Waddell (1940, pp. 66–9).
15. *Alexander Romance*, Pseudo Kallisthenes, I.34.2, I.34.4 and III.24.
16. For parallels between the two traditions, see Rattenbury (1933, pp. 219–23), Braun (1938, pp. 13–18, 41–2) and West (1977, pp. 47–8). The Sesonchōsis and Alexander 'Romances' were not the only ones of this type. There were many others, notably that of King Ninos and Queen Semiramis, embroideries on the deeds of Assyrian monarchs of the 9th century. See Rattenbury (1933, pp. 221–6), Braun (1938, pp. 6–18) and, most recently, Pettinnato (1985).
17. Simpson (1953, p. 86). For examples of these 2nd-millennium figures from Byblos and Ugarit, see Amiet (1977, plates 73–7). For the horns, see the war helmet worn by Naram Sin in the famous stela now in the Louvre, Amiet (plate 49). This, however, is clearly a helmet rather than a crown: its peak is much lower than that of the White Crown of Upper Egypt.
18. See ch. II, n. 187.

19. Simpson (1960, p. 64).
20. Simpson (1960, p. 65); Grdseloff (1942).
21. For an Egyptian example, see Wildung (1984, p. 40, plate 33). For Levantine ones, see Amiet (1977, pp. 390–3). For Hittite and Neo-Hittite ones, see Amiet (1977, p. 399). There is a discussion of these figures in the Aegean in ch. XI, nn. 217–24.
22. Porada (1984, p. 486).
23. Herodotos, II.106.
24. Kadish (1971, p. 123).
25. See the models and relief in the Cairo Museum in Wildung (1984, pp. 175–6, plates 150–1).
26. Amiet (1977, p. 395, plate 518); Spiegelberg (1927, p. 24). See also Volume 1, pp. 92–5. For S-t n Ḥp, see Gauthier (1925–31, V, p. 83). The identification of Sinope with Se n Hᶜpy was first proposed by Guignant (1828) but, like Griffiths (1970, pp. 396–7), I have been unable to see this.
27. Nonnos, III.1s.365–71, trans. Rouse (1940, I, p. 127).
28. See Volume, 1, pp. 94–5.
29. See ch. II, n. 123, ch. III, nn. 86–92 and Apollonius, II.11.178–533.
30. Gauthier (1925–31, III, p. 75).
31. Parke (1967, p. 220).
32. Frazer (1914).
33. Herodotos, II.1–2.
34. Herodotos, VII.107–109, trans. de Selincourt (1954, pp. 478–9). Strabo, Geography, VIII.319 and frg. VII. Pliny, Natural History, IV.18, 11, 40. Paulinus cited in Harrison (1903, p. 371).
35. Cook (1914–40, I, pp. 400–1); Parke (1967, p. 159).
36. Cook (1914–40, I, p. 371); Parke (1967, p. 220).
37. See Volume 3. This is not to deny that some of this influence may well have entered the region in the second half of the 2nd millennium.
38. Lang (1966, pp. 20–2). Just as the Albanians of the Caucasus have nothing to do with the Albanians in the Balkans, the Georgian Iberians have nothing to do with the Iberians of Spain. The local explanation for the name Iberian comes from an Armenian and Persian name Virkᶜ given to the Georgians (Lang, 1966, p. 18). However, I find it more plausible that both Iberians and the Hebrews derive their name from the name ʿp/bri, common in the Levant in the 2nd millennium. Although Moshe Greenberg, in his meticulous study of the name, does not mention it and demonstrates that many ʿp/bri were settled in or near cities (1955, pp. 86–7), I find the traditional derivation of the name from the verb 'âbar' (to cross over) and 'êber' (region across), and the general association of ʿp/bri with outlaws, persuasive. It is interesting to note that in both Spain and the Caucasus, Iberians were the unassimilated inland people in contradistinction to the 'civilized' coastal population living in the maritime economy. The basis of the etymology of these place names had been established by Bochart in the 17th cen-

tury. The name Albanian, like Albany, the old name for Scotland, and Albion from the white cliffs of Dover, and Lebanon, simply comes from the root common to Semitic and Indo-European √(a)lbn (white) and hence limestone or snow-covered mountains.

39. Strabo, XI.2.16.
40. Lang (1966, p. 18).
41. Herodotos, II.104–5, trans. de Selincourt (1954, pp. 167–8).
42. Lloyd (1967, pp. 164–5, 282–3).
43. Herodotos, II.41, trans. de Selincourt (1954, p. 146); Jairazbhoy (1985, p. 60).
44. Lloyd (1976, pp. 192–5).
45. See Volume 3 and Borghouts (1980, pp. 33–46).
46. Strabo, XI.2.17–18.
47. *Argonautika*, II.402; Jairazbhoy (1985, pp. 59–60).
48. According to Eratosthenes, 1225 BC and 1263–1257 BC according to Eusebius: Bacon (1925, p. 143).
49. Hesiod (Merkelbach and West, 1983, frgs 68 and 255) from the *Catalogue of Women* and the *Great Eoii*, Loeb, p. 177.
50. Lang (1966, pp. 65–9).
51. Apollonios, IV.260–80.
52. See Santillana and von Derchend (1969, pp. 58–9). For the precession of the equinoxes, see Volume 1, p. 126.
53. Volume 1, pp. 92–3.
54. See Riew intro. to Apollonios, pp. 27–8.
55. Herodotos, II.104–5.
56. See ch. II, n. 1.
57. Pindar, *Pythian Odes*, 4.11. See Vradii (1914, pp. 116–17). Prokopios, *Wars*, VIII.3.10–12.
58. Lang (1966, pp. 19–20); English (1959, pp. 49–50).
59. Tynes (1973); Blakely (1986, pp. 10–11).
60. Blakely (1986, pp. 5–12, 75–80).
61. English (1959, p. 53). The references are cited by Bochart (1646, IV.XXXI, p. 286).
62. See n. 51 above.
63. See ch. II, n. 53.
64. Apollonios, IV.270–93, trans. Riew, p. 154.
65. *Phaedo*, 109B, trans. Fowler, p. 375.
66. *Iliad*, 8.14; *Phaedo*, 112.A. For a fascinating and exciting, though ultimately not very illuminating discussion of these issues, see Santillana and von Derchend (1977, pp. 179–212).
67. See Nagy (1979, pp. 206–7).
68. Chantraine has no explanation for the root. Pokorny sees an Indo-European root *ghelĝh borrowed from a foreign culture. The stem ēlek[t] *ālek[t] (brilliant), the origin of which Chantraine calls 'obscure' would also seem to come from √ḥlq in one of two ways. The first is that the root was common to Semitic and Proto–Indo-European and that

ālek[t] came as a result of the loss of the laryngal ḥ. The second that it was a loan from the Canaanite √ḥlq after the merger of ḥ with ḫ in that language.

69. Sasson (1980, p. 212, n.3); Speiser (1967, pp. 25–6).
70. See Hinz (1973); Carter and Stolper (1984).
71. McAlpin (1974, pp. 89–101; 1975, pp. 105–15).
72. See Rashidi (1985, p. 20).
73. Hinz (1973, pp. 21–2). The 8th-century Elamite version of the Gilgamesh legend found recently in Urartu, the present Armenia, indicates that Elamites shared the general culture of Southwest Asia, including the 'theatrical' convention of actor and chorus. See Diakonoff and Jankowska (1990, pp. 109–10).
74. Herodotos, VII.71, trans. de Selincourt (1954, p. 468). He does not seem to have been referring to Susian Elamites here, as he refers elsewhere to a Kissian contingent. It is strange, however, that while Hinz points out that the Elamites in Darius' army were dressed in Elamite costume, Herodotos describes the Kissians in Xerxes' army as being dressed like Persians, except that they wore turbans (VII.62). Still, uniforms and national costumes can and do change suddenly.
75. *Odyssey*, I.22–5.
76. Herodotos, V.50, trans. de Selincourt (1954, p. 358).
77. Strabo, XV.3.2; Hinz (1973, p. 99).
78. For possible connections between Kassite and Elamite see Speiser (1930, pp. 122–3). For the vocalization of Kassite/Kossaioi see Speiser (1967, p. 25). For Galzu, etc., see Balkan (1954, pp. 131–2). Galšu is uncomfortably close to Kₓš in that they could all belong to the same cluster, while the Akkadian rendering of the -ld- of Galdu as -šš- looks disturbingly like the later barbarian conquerors of Mesopotamia, the Chaldaeans, Kaśdîm in Hebrew, but Kaldu in Assyrian and Kalday in Aramaic. Steiner (1977, pp. 137–43) plausibly posits a fricative lateral ḷ or South Semitic s² for the original sound. In languages that lacked this consonant, this sound was sometimes rendered as ś and sometimes as l. Were both Kassites and Chaldaeans originally called ka ḷ/śu? The coincidence is remarkable. However, unlike the Kassites, the Chaldaeans seem to have come from the south and were originally Semitic-speaking.
79. Gadd (1973, pp. 224–5).
80. Delitzsch (1884, pp. 39–47).
81. Genesis X.8–9. Nimrod played a prominent if villainous role in Jewish folklore and Rabbinical writings. In these, he is credited, among other things, with having built the Tower of Babel. Ginzberg, in his *Legends of the Jews* (1968), lists 195 citations to Nimrod in his index.
82. Speiser (1967, pp. 41–2). For other Mesopotamian etymologies, see Gesenius (1953, p. 650).
83. Gardiner (1957, p. 79, 100.1). It is interesting to note that the name is transcribed *Nebrōd* in the Septuagint and *Nebrōdēs* in Josephus. Burton

(1972, p. 167) sees a survival of nb-r-ḏr in Diodoros' phrase *pros tēn tōn holōn dynasteian* (acquire empire over the whole world).

84. Speiser (1967, pp. 47–52).

85. Ginzberg (1968, V, pp. 199–201).

86. Burton (1972, p. 170). Blakely (1986, p. 11) points out there were small Negro communities in Yugoslavia and Iran.

87. See Lloyd (1982, pp. 37–40).

88. Diodoros, I.55.6.

89. Herodotos, II.106, trans. de Selincourt, 1954, p. 168.

90. Hesiod, 1.984, trans. Evelyn-White (1914, p. 153).

91. From Proklos, *Krestomanthia*, II, in Kinkel (1877, pp. 32–4).

92. Clark and Coulson (1978, p. 73).

93. Nagy (1979, p. 205, 42 n. 3). I believe that the two traditions are even closer than Clark and Coulson and Nagy imagine because, as I shall argue in Volume 4, I see Apollo as deriving his name and some of his nature from the Egyptian Ḫprr, the god of dawn, and thus strictly parallel to Eos, Memnōn's mother. This would tend to strengthen Clark and Coulson's case.

94. See Lung (1912, pp. 13–27).

95. Lung (1912, pp. 10–12) admits that Memnōn was Ethiopian and that he is always represented as being accompanied by Blacks. However, he claims that some early vases show the prince himself as a Greek though many others portray him as a Negro. I do not think that too much significance should be put on this point as another 'barbarian' hero, Orpheus, known as a Thracian, was portrayed as a Greek while surrounded by Thracians. See Guthrie (1966, pp. 45–6, plates 4, 6).

96. Lung (1912, p. 10).

97. Herodotos, V.54; VII.151.

98. Strabo, XV.3.2; Goosens (1939, p. 337).

99. Goosens (1939, pp. 377–8); Snowden (1970, pp. 151–5).

100. Lung (1912, pp. 10–13); Snowden (1970, pp. 45–9, plates 15, 16, 18 and 19).

101. See ch. IX, n. 139.

102. Cited in Diodoros, II.22.1–3.

103. For an excellent bibliography of these, see Snowden (1970, pp. 151–3).

104. *Iliad*, XX.239; Diodoros, II.XXII.3.

105. *Iliad*, XI.1; *Odyssey*, V.1.

106. For this tangle and the derivation of the name and cult of Dōdōna from Ddwn and his cult at the oracle of Siwa in the Libyan desert, see Volume 3.

107. *Iliad*, I.423. The adjective used for the Ethiopians, *amymonas* (blameless), would seem to be a paranomasia for Amun, with whom, as mentioned in Volume 1, p. 114 and as will be given in more detail in Volume 3, he was generally identified. This, of course, would strengthen the case that Homer was thinking principally of the African Ethiopia.

The root -*mym*- (blame) in *amymonas* would appear to come from the West Semitic *mûm* (blemish, disfigurement). The derivation is complicated by the Middle English 'maim' which has exactly the same meaning. However, 'maim' has no known etymology and the whole problem remains unresolved.

108. See Rendsburg (1981, p. 198). He claims that the West Semites oriented themselves to the source of the sun in the east while the Egyptians looked to the source of the Nile to the south. Thus √*ymn*, the right hand, was the south and west respectively.

109. Robertson-Smith (1894, p. 507). For the association of these gods with spring flowers, see the passages on Hyakinthos in Volume 3.

110. For an outline of this see, Volume 1, pp. 115–16. For more detail, see Volume 3.

111. For details on this, see Frazer (1914).

112. Strabo, XII.I.2; XV.II.2; Aelian, *Nat. Anim.*, V.I; Servius on *Aeneid*, I.751. For a general survey, see Frazer (1898, V, p. 387).

113. Homer described 'the clamour of cranes ariseth before the face of heaven, when they flee from wintry storms and measureless rain, and with clamour fly toward the streams of Ocean, bearing slaughter and death to Pygmy men.' *Iliad*, III.3–7.

The Greek word for 'dwarf', *nanos*, has no Indo-European cognates and probably comes from the Egyptian *nm(w)* (dwarf). There is no doubt that Egyptians had a considerable knowledge about Central Africa. Not only are there the Deir el Bahri reliefs, but there is the fact that 12th-Dynasty eye paints have been shown to come from Busumbi in Uganda. See Dayton (1982a, p. 164). *Pygmē* (pygmy or boxer) has been derived from *pyx* (fist), the origin of which is itself completely obscure. The possible illustration of African boxers in the Thera murals and the certain later associations between Africans and the sport, together with the undoubted ancient location of the pygmies in Ethiopia, would make it likely that the Greek word came from Egyptian or a language from further south. It could be related to the name 𓂝𓈖𓃒𓏤𓏏, usually read *gnb(tw)* (a Negro people from Pwnt [Africa reached by sea] with tight curly hair). This could be either by assuming a transposition **bgn(tw)* or with the definite article p₃ *gnb(tw)*. In any event, the legend of the cranes slaughtering the pygmy men is likely to be related to a pun in *(p₃)gm* 𓅢, not actually a crane but a black ibis. The paranomasia involved in the legend would seem to be increased with *gmì* 𓅢𓃀 (find, control, destroy) and *gmgm* 𓅢𓃀𓅢𓃀 (smash, tear up, etc.).

114. See Griffiths (1980a, pp. 49–50).

115. Plutarch, *De Iside*, 359E. Griffiths (1982a, col. 628) stresses the greenish tinge of the blackness in some of the portraits.

116. *Odyssey*, XI.522.

117. Ovid, *Metamorphoses*, XIII; Aelian, *Nat. Anima*, V.1.

118. *Iliad*, XXII.208–13. Murray trans., 1925, II, pp. 469–71. The root aisa in *aisimos*, which is present in Mycenaean and means 'part accorded'

and by extension 'destiny', is supposed to have an Indo-European cognate in the Oscan *aetis* (portion). The Greek root would seem equally or more likely to come from the Egyptian isw, Coptic 'asou' and 'esou' (reward, compensate). The Greek dialect forms *wiswos* or *hisos* would seem to indicate uncertainty but do not provide substantial objections to the derivation of *isos* or *eisē* (equal in share, number or right) from isw. The English learned prefix *'iso-'* comes from this. The Indo-European etymologies proposed for *isos* in Chantraine are hopelessly obscure and cumbersome.

119. See also *Iliad*, VIII.60–70, and Dietrich (1964, p. 108) cited in Clark and Coulson (1978, p. 67).

120. Lung (1912, pp. 20–1) Tomb 3 (Schliemann, 1878, pp. 196–8).

121. *Iliad*, XVI.658; Clark and Coulson (1978). While *talant-* has a clear cut Indo-European etymology, Mḫꜣt, the standard Egyptian word for a balance and the beam across it, appears in the Greek *mochlos* (lever or beam), which occurs in Homer.

122. Plutarch, *De audiendis poetis*, 2, and schol. on *Iliad*, VIII.70.

123. Lung (1912, pp. 13–19); Clark and Coulson (1978, pp. 70–1).

124. Gruppe (1906, II, p. 681, n. 7).

125. Lung (1912, p. 20).

126. For this fusion, see Volume 1, p. 141.

127. Clark and Coulson (1978, p. 71).

128. See Lung (1912, p. 14).

129. *Iliad*, XXIII.78. This sense of *kēr* is emphasized by Malten (1924, col. 885). Pârvulescu (1968) demonstrates clearly that *kēr* cannot simply mean 'doom' or 'death', but he is less convincing when he argues that it means 'suffering'.

130. For the Anthesteria, see Parke (1977, pp. 116–17). See ch. IV, n. 123, for the Egyptian origin of the stem *anth-* in Anthesteria.

131. For a survey of this immensely dense semantic field, which was further contaminated by the word kꜣ (bull strength), see Kaplony (1980, cols 275–82). He provides a substantial bibliography in his notes. For a discussion of the political function of kꜣ in Egypt and later European political thought, see Springborg (1990, pp. 89–117).

132. See Erman and Grapow (1925–31, V, p. 86).

133. Pokorny (1959–60, I, pp. 917, 957). He transcribes them as *skāi*, *skəi* and *ski*.

134. Gardiner (1957, p. 417, 511.4).

135. Chantraine (1968–75, pp. 1295–6) admits this group has no known Indo-European origin, but the resourceful Pokorny (1959–60, I, p. 146) invented a root, **bhes* (breath, blow) upon it. It is of course possible that some or all of these etymologies came simply from šw, without the article, as it seems clear that the letter Ψ was used to represent several indistinct sibilants and that the initial *p-* was added as a hypercorrection to words that sounded Egyptian. See Bernal (1990, pp. 118–19).

Coptic contains the word *šoou* (incense, perfume). Černy (1976, p. 257) derived it from *ḥrw* (flowers). However, given *šooue* (dry) and *šouo* (empty), both of which come from *šw*, *šoou* must have been at least contaminated by them. In any event, this provides a neat analogy for the Greek word *thumos* (spirit or soul) which derives from an Indo-European root for 'smoke', found in our 'fume'. For the Egyptian *snṯr* (to cense) and what I believe to be its Greek derivative *xanthos*, see below.

136. Gardiner (1957, p. 173).
137. Volume 1, p. 93.
138. Pausanias, III.3.8; Levi (1971, II, p. 17).
139. Pausanias, X.31.3; Levi (1971, I, p. 487).
140. See above, n.89.
141. See Goosens (1939) and Gardiner (1961b).
142. For a bibliography on this, see Frazer (1898, II, pp. 530–1).
143. *Corpus Inscriptionum Graecarum*, nos. 4731 and 4727.
144. Pausanias, I.42.1; Levi (1971, I, pp. 116–17).
145. Goosens (1939, p. 339).
146. Gardiner (1961b, pp. 95–6).
147. Strabo, XVII.1.37, 42. Gardiner (1961b, p. 96) assumes that there was confusion between the Greek word labyrinth and Egyptian names. For the argument that the name labyrinth comes from another title, Ny-mꜣꜥ t-Rꜥ, used for Amenemḥe III, see ch. IV, nn. 117–19.
148. For the many different versions of Manetho on this, see Waddell (1940, pp. 62–73).
149. For the Egyptian origins of this myth, see Volume 1, p. 115.
150. See above, n.92.
151. See ch. V, n.51, and above, nn. 12–16.
152. Lane Fox (1980, pp. 38–46, bibliography for ch. 1).
153. See ch. V, nn. 121–5.
154. See ch. V, nn. 163–6.
155. Strabo, XVII.1.34; Diodoros, I.56.4. See Gardiner (1947, II, pp. 126–7).
156. *Iliad*, V.640–5; Diodoros, IV.32; Apollodoros, II.6.4. For other ancient sources, see Frazer (1921, I, pp. 244–5) and Graves (1955, II, p. 174).
157. See ch. II, nn.172–83.
158. Herodotos, II.42–5. For a denial that the Egyptians ever had a system of twelve gods and sceptical analysis of the passage, see Lloyd (1976, p. 202).
159. Diodoros, III, 74.3, trans. Oldfather (1935, p. 331).
160. Servius on *Aeneid*, V.30; Tzetzes on Lykophron 472; Hyginus Fabula 89. For an iconographic representation of him as an African Black, see the portrait of him attacking King Busiris on the famous Caeretan *hydria*.
161. See above, nn. 13–15.
162. See n.51 above.
163. Aldred (1971, p. 113).
164. See ch. V, nn. 142–3.
165. *Hybris* is unexplained in terms of Indo-European, although Szemerényi (1974a, p. 154) sees it as coming from an unattested Hittito-Luvian

form *Hu(wa)ppar. It would seem to me altogether more plausible to derive it from the attested Egyptian *wr ỉb*, literally 'great heart' but with the meaning 'insolent'. One is reminded of Aesop's fable of the frog and the bull. The initial aspiration in Greek is automatic with *upsilon*.

166. Gibbon (1794, p. 137). See Volume 1, p. 185.

Chapter VII
THE THERA ERUPTION

1. La Marche and Hirschbeck (1984, pp. 124–6). Kelly and Sear (1985, pp. 740–3) claim that the temperature drops were rather less.
2. McCoy (1980); Stanley and Sheng (1986).
3. See Marinatos (1939). For surveys of earlier theorizing along these lines, see Ramage (1978, pp. 39–41) and Vitaliano (1978, pp. 143–4).
4. See Doumas (1983, pp. 11–14, 29–42).
5. Pomerance (1970; 1978).
6. Pomerance (1970; 1978).
7. Personal communication, New York City, December 1983.
8. Stanley and Sheng (1986, p. 733).
9. Stanley and Sheng (1986, p. 735).
10. Betancourt and Weinstein (1976); Betancourt, Michael and Weinstein (1978).
11. Åström (1978, p. 88).
12. Cadogan (1978).
13. Kemp and Merrillees (1980, p. 259).
14. Warren (1979a, pp. 106–7).
15. Marthari (1980).
16. Betancourt (1987, p. 45).
17. Michael (1977, p. 794).
18. Weinstein and Michael (1978, p. 208).
19. Lamarche and Hirschbeck (1984, pp. 124–5).
20. Matthews (1976, p. 610).
21. Lamarche and Hirschbeck (1984).
22. Baillie and Munro (1988); Baillie (1988a; 1988b; 1989b).
23. Pang and Chou (1984).
24. Plutarch (*Caesar*, 53.1) reports very much the same phenomena after the death of Caesar in 44 BC. There is a discrepancy in the years here, but there is very little doubt that they are describing the same phenomena.
25. Ban Gu (1959, IX, pp. 297–9; 1959, XXVII.2.2, p. 2377; 1959, XXVII. 3.2, p. 2452).
26. For a survey of this debate, see Shaughnessy (1985–7). See also Nivison (1983), Pang (1987, pp. 142–3) and Hsu and Linduff (1988, pp. 387–90).
27. Chen Mengjia (1977, p. 53); Nivison (1983); Pankenier (1981–2).
28. Pankenier (1981–2, p. 25).
29. Pang (1987, pp. 147–8).

30. Pang (1987, pp. 147–8). He cites Chen Zongguei (1984, p. 1009).
31. Pankenier (1983, p. 5).
32. Pang, Espenak, Huang, Chou and Yau (1988, p. 9).
33. Pang, Espenak, Huang, Chou and Yau (1988, p. 10); Shaanxi Zhouyuan Kaogu Dui (1979).
34. Pang, Yau, Chou and Wolff (1988, pp. 6–8).
35. Pang, Espenak, Huang, Chou and Yau (1988, p. 19).
36. A date of *c.* 1100 would also fit the chronology of the Japanese historian Shirakawa Shizuka, who puts the Zhou Conquest at 1087 BC; see Hsu and Linduff (1988, p. 390). But this does not have either the astronomical backing or the traditional authority of that of Pang and his colleagues.
37. Baillie (1989a); Keys (1988).
38. Pang and Chou (1984).
39. See *(Gu) Zhushu Jinian* (Bamboo Annals), in Wang Guowei (1941, XXVI.I, p. 7b).
40. See the *Songshu, Furuizhi* cited by Wang Guowei (1941, XXXVI.II, p. 27a).
41. 'Taishi', 'Great Speech', and 'Wucheng', 'Successful War', in 'Zhoushu', 'The Book of Zhou' in the *Shujing* (Book of History).
42. *Shujing* (Book of History). 'Tang shi', 'Speech of Tang' I.3.; 'Zhonghui zhi Gao', 'Announcement of Zhonghui', II.2. 'Tang gao', 'Announcement of Tang' V. Pang and Chou (1985).
43. Pang (1985, p. 10; 1987, p. 145).
44. Keightley (1983, p. 525). See also the personal communication from the archaeologist Gao Ming to Kevin Pang in 1985, cited in Pang (1987, p. 146).
45. Mencius, VII.2.38.
46. Pang (1987, pp. 144–6); Pang, Espenak, Huang, Chou and Yau (1988, p. 10).
47. Volume 1, pp. 42–3.
48. Betancourt (1987, pp. 45–6).
49. Betancourt (1987, p. 46).
50. See Palmer (1969, pp. 63–4) and Pomerance (1984). Evans was defended by Hood and supported by Helck, though the latter maintained that MMIII began in 1610 BC. See Helck (1979, pp. 48–9). For further bibliography on the lid and its context, see Cline (1987, p. 31).
51. Warren (1987, pp. 209–10).
52. Warren (1987, p. 210).
53. Hammer, Clausen and Dansgaard (1980, pp. 230–5).
54. Hammer, Clausen, Friedrich and Tauber (1987).
55. Cadogan (1987).
56. Manning (1988).
57. Manning (1988).
58. Hammer, Clausen, Friedrich and Tauber (1988). Manning has now

(1990) come round to their view on this. Nevertheless, he is more convinced than ever that the radio-carbon dating points to the 17th century.

59. Aitken (1988); Michael and Betancourt (1988a,b); Warren (1988).

60. Personal communication, Colin Renfrew, Cambridge, December 1988.

61. Baillie (1989b).

62. See chart 1.

63. See the discussion in Morgan (1988, pp. 166–7).

64. Herodotos, IV.147.

65. Chantraine (1968–75, I, p. 436) and Pokorny (1959–69, I, p. 493). The labiovelar is deduced from the existence of the word *phēr*, which in Homer occurs only in the plural forms *phērsin* (*Iliad*, I.268) and *phēras* (*Iliad*, II.743), meaning 'centaurs' but later seen as cognate with *thēr-*. This suggests that both came from an earlier labiovelar. It would seem more plausible to me to derive a Greek **phērs* (centaur) from the Semitic *prs* (horseman) and to link *thēr* to an Indo-European root, **dēr* or, conventionally, **dhēr*, cognate with the root **deures* or **dheures* from which we would obtain our 'deer' and the German *Tier* (wild animal).

66. Ventris and Chadwick (1973, p. 577).

67. Friedrich (1933, p. 67).

68. Albright (1942, pp. 151–3, 216); Ellenbogen (1962, p. 84).

69. Diakonoff and Starostin (1986).

70. Dolgopolskii (1987, p. 5).

71. Egyptian also has *kwr* (miner; dig a hole). the Demotic *gwrì* and Coptic *kour* (pivot, hole drilled in the door base) strengthen the idea that it was commonly vocalized with a *u* in Egyptian.

72. Pomerance cites some of his predecessors (1970, p. 19). Since he wrote, the Egyptologist Goedicke has joined in. See n. 80 below.

73. Exodus 10. 20–3.

74. Exodus 13. 20–1.

75. Pomerance (1970, p. 19) does not address this problem.

76. See, for instance, Exodus 3. 2, 19.18 and 34. 5, Deuteronomy 4. 24 and 9. 3 and many other instances.

77. Exodus 14. 21–8.

78. Exodus 15. 8–10.

79. See n. 8 above.

80. Pomerance (1970, p. 19) and Khramalkov (1981, p. 52). Goedicke (1986, pp. 40–1) read into a note on the back of the Rhind Papyrus a reference to the 'Voice of Seth' followed by the next day of Isis by a precipitation of the sky. These phenomena took place in the 11th year of an unnamed pharaoh, whom Goedicke takes to be Ahmose, the first ruler of the 18th Dynasty, whose reign he sets very low in the 2nd half of the 16th century. The 'Voice of Seth' and the precipitation associated with Isis do suggest volcanic events, the noise of the explosion followed a day later by the fall of *tephra*. He points out that this cannot refer to the normal epagonomenal or extra days dedicated to the gods. However,

the passage is extremely obscure and I shall argue in the next chapter (n. 22) that the 11th year is more likely to tally with the reign of the Hyksos pharaoh Apopi, in whose reign it is generally accepted that the Rhind Papyrus was copied. In any event, Goedicke's specific hypothesis falls with the re-dating of the Thera eruption.

81. For a translation of the crucial passage in the text and a discussion, see Gardiner (1946, p. 46 and 1961a, p. 273). See also ch. VIII, n. 148.

82. Albright (1957, pp. 255–6).

83. See Pomerance (1970, p. 20).

84. Volume 1, p. 107.

85. Herodotos, IV, 147, trans. de Selincourt (1954, p. 319).

86. Astour (1967a, p. 114).

87. Astour (1967a, p. 389).

88. See ch. VI, nn. 42–54.

89. *Argonautika*, IV. 1694–98. Seaton, 1912, pp. 408–11.

90. *Argonautika*, IV. 1706–18. Seaton, 1912, pp. 411–13.

91. See Farnell (1895–1909, IV, 365) and Strabo, X.5.1.

92. Genesis 9. 11–14.

93. Genesis 1. 2.

94. *Black Athena*, Volume 1, p. 107.

95. This is told most fully in Ovid's *Metamorphosis*, I.755–80. For a rich survey of this myth, see Ahl (1985, p. 394). It recounts that Phaethōn son of Helios (the sun) yoked his father's chariot but was unable to keep it on its proper course and drove it too high, causing the earth to freeze, and too low, scorching it. Enraged, Zeus killed him with a thunderbolt and Phaethōn fell to earth. As the Egyptian priest claimed, the substance of the myth was to explain meteorological abnormalities. The name Phaethōn would seem to come from an intricate network of Egypto-Greek paranomasia or punning. *Phaethōn*, presumably from the Greek root *phae-* (shine), is used by Homer as an epithet for Helios (the sun). However, Phaethōn in the myth would also seem to derive from a number of Egyptian titles. The first of these is Pꜣ idn(w), or the Demotic Pꜣ itnw (the deputy). The derivation of *pha-* from pꜣ can also be seen in the month name Pharmuthi from Pꜣ rnnwt. The second title, which also appears as an aspect of the story, is Pꜣ itn, with the probable vocalization *pa 'atun (the solar disk), the third is Pꜣ itn (the rival or the enemy). Finally, there is the phrase found in Coptic *e-p-itn*, which was substantivized into the word *epitn* (space leading downward). Thus the whole of the Greek myth would seem to be contained in the interplay of these roots.

96. Plato, *Timaeus*, 22–3, trans. Bury pp. 33–5.

97. Plato, *Timaeus*, 24–5, trans. Bury pp. 41–3.

98. Steuerwald (1983, p. 11).

99. Ramage (1978, pp. 23, 32–3).

100. The tradition of complete belief can be seen as early as Plato's first commentator Krantor (335–275 BC) – see Ramage (1978, pp. 23–45) for

this and later credulity. In 1987 the American writer Mary Settegast set out the same position in a beautifully produced book.

101. Luce (1978, pp. 76–7), *pace* Fredericks (1978) who combines extreme scepticism towards any suggestion of a connection between Plato's story and the remarkably congruent *reality* of the Thera eruption with utter credulity towards Aryanist classical scholarship.

102. The first recorded identification of America as Plato's Atlantis was by Francesco López de Gómara in 1553 (see Ramage 1978, p. 30), but the connection must have been made sooner.

103. Volume 1, p. 486, n. 168.

104. Herodotos, IV.42. See also Bartolini (1988, pp. 74–5).

105. Saint Martin (1863, p. 154) and Steinhauser (1937, pp. 229–36).

106. Steinhauser (1937, pp. 233–5).

107. See Strabo, 17.825, and Pliny, *Nat. Hist.*, 5.5–16.

108. Hanno, *Periplous*, 7.14.

109. Hesiod, *Theogony*, 509.746, and *Odyssey*, I.52.

110. See, for instance, Evelyn-White (1914, p. 93).

111. Budge (1904, II, pp. 85–94). There will be a more detailed discussion of Tm in the section on Artemis in Volume 4. For Herakles and Shu, see ch. II, nn. 185–90. For the cluster of words written *šw*, see ch. VI, nn. 134–5.

112. Herodotos, IV.184, trans. de Selincourt (1954, p. 333), is slightly misleading when he refers to the Atlantes being named after 'the mountains'; the word is in fact in the singular.

113. Hesiod, *Theogony*, 746–50. For the relation between Shu and Herakles, see above ch. II, nn. 198–203.

114. Herodotos, IV.187–8.

115. Herodotos, IV.50. Georgiev (1966, p. 134) derives Athrys from the Germanic *attel*.

116. See ch. VI, n. 66.

117. Hesiod, *Works and Days*, 383, and *The Astronomy*, frg. 1, trans. Evelyn-White (1914, p. 66). See also Apollodoros, III.10.

118. For a survey of the scholiast literature on this, see Frazer (1921, II, pp. 2–3, n. 1).

119. Servius on Virgil, *Georgics*, I.138.

120. *Odyssey*, I.52.

121. *Theogony*, 359–64.

122. Ch. II, nn. 35–6. See also Roscher (1884–1937, III, col. 816) and Onians (1988, pp. 248–50, 315–17).

123. Ch. II, nn. 35–6.

124. Astour has proposed this orally (personal communication, David Owen).

125. See Jacobsen (1976, pp. 168–71).

126. Walcot (1966, pp. 27–53); Onians (1988, pp. 247–9, 316–18).

127. There is clearly a great deal of confusion about this final -*r*. See Pokorny (1959–69, I, pp. 78–80). Bomhard's solution is to postulate two distinct stems in Indo-European: *ħḫụer* (to rain, sprinkle) and *wet* (to be wet).

However, he admits that the two stems 'overlap semantically' (1984, p. 121). There would seem to be another example, apart from ìtrw, of the root in Afroasiatic in the Arabic *oued* or *wadi* (water course). See Partridge (1958, p. 798).

128. For an extended discussion of this, see Gardiner (1947, II, pp. 156–68).
129. Ellenbogen (1962, p. 80).
130. Diodoros, I.96.7.
131. Horapollo, I.21. See Budge (1904, I, p. 284).
132. See Luce (1969, 1978); Ramage (1978) and Fredericks (1978).
133. See Sandars (1978, p. 119), Astour (1967a, p. 11) and Volume 1, p. 446.
134. Plato (*Timaeus*, 25, trans. Bury, pp. 41–3). Luce (1978, p. 62) points out the general parallel, though he is more inclined to see it as the influence of the well-known relief of the defeat of the Peoples of the Sea rather than as indicating any knowledge of the text.
135. See Gardiner (1947, I, pp. 197–9).
136. Plato, *Timaeus*, 25, trans. Bury, p. 43.
137. Helck (1979, pp. 146–7) puts the chief destructions of Mycenae, Tiryns and Pylos in the early 12th century. While Snodgrass (1971, pp. 28–34) would accept these dates for the Southern Peloponnese he sees them as too early for Mycenae. The Greek tradition puts the final attack around 1120 BC. See Hammond (1975, pp. 682–706).
138. *Kritias*, 110B.
139. *Parian Marble*, II.1–18. See also Apollodoros, III.14. For a discussion, see Frazer (1921, pp. 88–96).
140. *Parian Marble*, II.4–7.
141. See Luce (1969, pp. 145–7; 1978, pp. 70–1) [I do not accept his chronology here.] For China, see n. 32 above, also Baillie (1989b).
142. Plato, *Timaeus*, 25, trans. Bury, p. 43.
143. *Kritias*, 113–21.
144. For the numerology, see McClain (1976, pp. 161–201).
145. See ch. VIII, nn. 111–26.
146. Keys (1988).
147. Keys (1988); Baillie (1989a).
148. Keys (1988).
149. Carpenter (1966, esp. pp. 14–21); Bryson, Lamb and Donley (1974).
150. Bintliff (1977, I, p. 51); Shrimpton (1987, pp. 140–4).
151. See below, ch. XI, nn. 191–9.
152. See below, ch. XII, nn. 135–7.
153. Labat (1975, pp. 500–3).
154. Baillie (1989a).
155. See nn. 37–52 above.
156. Mencius, VII.II.iii.1.
157. Creel (1951, p. 111, n. 7).
158. Jaspers (1949).
159. Schwartz (1975, pp. 4–5).

160. The priority and centrality of Greece to the concept of the Axial Age can be seen from the latest major volume on the subject. In this, the first 126 pages (out of 483) are devoted to Greece. See Eisenstadt (1986).
161. Volume 1, pp. 276–80.
162. Boyce (1979, pp. 18–19) places Zoroaster in the first half of the 2nd millennium. Sir Harold Bailey puts him at around the 11th century (personal communication, Cambridge, December 1988). For a further bibliography of works in favour of a 2nd-millennium date, see Kingsley (1990, p. 245, n.4). Kingsley also argues convincingly that it was the Greek legend of Pythagoras' having studied with Zoroaster rather than any native Iranian traditions that led to the 6th-century dating of the Iranian prophet.
163. For a sceptical view of Confucius' reliance on the past, see Fung (1952, I, pp. 56–7). For a more open one, see Creel (1951, pp. 153–9).
164. Moule and Yetts (1957, pp. xii–xvi).
165. Keightley (1983, p. 524).
166. Chang (1980, pp. 322–9).
167. See n.44 above.
168. 'The Announcement of Tang', Shu-ching, IV.III.5–6, trans. Legge (1972, p. 188).
169. Fung (1952, I, p. 30).
170. Gützlaff (1838, p. 306), cited in Legge (1972, III, p. 190).
171. Schwartz (1985, pp. 23–55).
172. Hsu and Linduff (1988, p. 11).
173. Hsu and Linduff (1988, p. 26).
174. Needham (1954–, II, pp. 132–9).
175. Schwartz (1985, pp. 32–6).
176. Karlgren (1957, p. 104).
177. Shima (1958, p. 214); Hsu and Linduff (1988, p. 106).
178. Hsu and Linduff (1988, p. 106).
179. Karlgren (1957, p. 104).
180. For a bibliography of these arguments, see Hsu and Linduff (1988, p. 107, n.90).
181. Hsu and Linduff (1988, p. 106).
182. Shijing, III.i.1,6–7 and IV.i.3.1. Karlgren (1950, pp. 186–9; Odes 235–6). David Keightley points out that the term Tianming does not appear on bronze inscriptions dating to the beginning of the Dynasty and argues that they should be dated only to the reign of the Dynasty's third ruler King Kang some thirty years later (personal communication, Berkeley, April 1989). This is interesting but would seem to me to be a case of misplaced precision to deny that the odes containing the term were written shortly after the Zhou conquest.
183. Shijing, III.1.I 3.
184. Quoted in Schwartz (1985, p. 46).
185. 'Speech of Tang', Shu-ching, IV.I.3, cited by Mencius, I.II.iv.4.

186. Mencius, II.II.xiii.3. See Shaughnessy (1985–7, p. 38).
187. Needham (1954–, III, p. 408); Pang (1985, p. 21; 1987, pp. 151–2).
See also Pang, Espenak, Huang, Chou and Yau (1988, p. 17).
188. Mencius, II.II.xiii.3. See Shaughnessy (1985–7, p. 38).
189. Mencius, I.I.vii.6.
190. Schiffrin (1968, pp. 99–100).
191. Ch. II, nn. 64–71.

Chapter VIII
THE HYKSOS

1. See ch. V, nn. 70–2.
2. See ch. V, n. 70.
3. von Beckerath (1965, p. 165).
4. von Beckerath (1965, p. 70); Gardiner (1961a, p. 440).
5. See Gardiner (1959, p. 17 and plate III). For an appreciation of Ibscher, see Gardiner (n.d., pp. 47–50).
6. Van Seters (1966, p. 155); Kempinsky (1985, pp. 132–3).
7. Albright (1945; 1965, pp. 54–7); Hayes (1973a, p. 49); von Beckerath (1965, p. 222); Helck (1971, pp. 95–6).
8. Kitchen (1967, pp. 50–3).
9. Helck (1971, pp. 64–6).
10. Kitchen (1987, p. 48).
11. Stock (1955, p. 62).
12. Kitchen had already seen the necessity of distinguishing the two if one accepted a high Mesopotamian chronology (1967, p. 53).
13. Stock (1955, p. 62) was working from the base-line of the end of the 12th Dynasty in the 1780s. Thus, working with a final date of c. 1801, I have raised Stock's dates by approximately ten years.
14. Manetho, frgs 43–4, trans. Waddell (1940, pp. 90–5).
15. Manetho, frgs 48–9, trans. Waddell (1940, pp. 95–9).
16. von Beckerath (1965, p. 223); Helck (1971, pp. 95–6); Bietak (1979, pp. 235–6; 1980, col. 101; 1984, p. 473); Kitchen (1987, p. 44).
17. Parker (1976, p. 186).
18. Krauss (1985, pp. 63–7; 109–10).
19. Kitchen demolishes Krauss's argument; see (1987, p. 42).
20. Hayes (1973, pp. 60–4).
21. For the irregularities of the dating and the uncertainties of the translation, see Goedicke (1986, pp. 37–8). The second line in the note refers to one entering Heliopolis and seems to mention an attack on the frontier fortress of Sile. Goedicke maintains that this refers to the expulsion of the Hyksos. Apart from the great uncertainty as to whether Hyksos are mentioned at all it is interesting that the references are to Heliopolis and Sile rather than the Hyksos capital Avaris, the siege of which played a great role in the 18th Dynasty myths of reconquest. All in all, it seems

unlikely that the text refers to the expulsion of the Hyksos. However, Goedicke's hypothesis that the third line is a meteorological report – based on earlier work by Erman – is given greater credibility by the strong possibility that the 11th year of Apophis was approximately 1628 BC. See ch. VII, n. 80. However, the whole scheme remains extremely uncertain.

22. von Beckerath (1965, pp. 133–4).
23. Winlock (1947, p. 96, n. 21).
24. von Beckerath (1965, pp. 130–1) calls him the 2nd. Gardiner (1961a, p. 158) and Hayes (1973, p. 60) place him as the 3rd, while Bietak (1980, col. 95) saw him as the 4th. Later, however, Bietak (1984, p. 474) accepted Kempinski's view that Khyan should be identified with Apachnan and was therefore the 3rd Hyksos pharaoh.
25. Kempinski (1985, pp. 131–4).
26. See ch. VII, nn. 49 and 59.
27. Stock (1955, p. 69); von Beckerath (1965, p. 134); Bietak (1984, p. 474); Kempinski (1985, p. 132).
28. For the matching of the strata of Kerma and Tell El Daba'a, see Bietak (1984, p. 475). Bietak of course still holds to the low absolute chronology for both.
29. Stock (1955, pp. 66–7); von Beckerath (1965, pp. 134–5); Kempinski (1985, pp. 132–3).
30. von Beckerath (1965, pp. 134–5); and Kempinski (1985, pp. 132–3).
31. Kempinski (1985).
32. Bietak (1984, pp. 476–7).
33. Kenyon (1973, p. 111); Cole (1984).
34. Personal communication, J. Weinstein, 30 January 89. In fact, Rdi Rꜥ scarabs have been found in late 12th-Dynasty contexts at El Kubaniyeh South; see Kemp and Merrillees (1980, p. 218).
35. Bietak (1984, p. 479).
36. See n. 13 above.
37. Bietak (1979, p. 235; 1984, p. 479).
38. Ward (1987, pp. 531–2).
39. Bietak (1984, p. 472).
40. BM–1165 and BM–1225. See Shaw (1985, p. 312) and Bietak (1979, p. 255).
41. For a discussion of this debate up to the 1960s, see Van Seters (1966, pp. 98–103). See also von Beckerath (1965, pp. 161–2). Parker's (1957) low and Kitchen's still lower dates (1987, p. 52) for the 18th Dynasty would now seem to be untenable in the light of Casperson's work (1986) on the lunar dates of Tuthmōsis III.
42. See von Beckerath (1965, pp. 262–3). Van Seters (1966, pp. 101–2) misprints R-ꜣht for what should be R-ꜣht. For the possibility that R-ꜣht (entry into the fertile land) is the origin of the common Greek toponym Laris(s)a, see Volume 1, pp. 76 and 452.

43. For a survey of that conventional wisdom, see von Beckerath (1965, p. 82).
44. Van Seters (1966, pp. 101–2).
45. Van Seters (1966, p. 101, n. 22).
46. Exodus 6.25 and elsewhere. Another Pînḥås, also a priest's son, appears frequently in I Samuel. See nn. 140–7 below.
47. For Simeon as another name for African Black, see ch. X, nn. 155–9.
48. Bietak (1979, p. 255).
49. Van Seters (1966, p. 101).
50. See above, nn. 9–14.
51. Gardiner (1961, p. 160).
52. Josephus, *Contra Apionem*, I.14, trans. as Manetho, frg. 42, Waddell (1940, pp. 79–85).
53. See, for instance, Meyer (1928–36, I.2, p. 313).
54. See, for instance, Gardiner (1961a, pp. 156–7) and Van Seters (1966, p. 3). See also the discussion of the name in Volume 1, p. 97.
55. Stock (1955, p. 63); Hayes (1973a, pp. 52–3).
56. Gardiner and Gunn (1918, p. 38, n. 5).
57. For a survey of 19th-century views on the Hyksos, see Griffith (1911). See below for the discussion of the relation between the Hyksos and the Exodus.
58. Meyer (1884, I, pp. 133–4).
59. For descriptions of this controversy, see Petrie and Walker (1909, I, pp. 237–40) and Hall and King (1906, p. 136).
60. For Müller's life and attitudes, see Chaudhuri (1974).
61. See Müller (1898, p. 7) For the text of this inscription at Speos Artemidoros, see Sethe (1906–9, IV.2, p. 390).
62. There was a debate on this in the 1930s – on the possible link between the Halafian ware found in Northern Mesopotamia and Syria from the 6th and 5th millenniums and the Hurrians of the 2nd – the general conclusion of which was that the gaps were far too great to tolerate any connection. See, for instance, von Soden (1937, p. 9) and Albright (1939, p. 121). While it is virtually impossible that there was any continuity from the early Halafian ware to the painted pottery of the Hurrians in the 2nd millennium, the attestation from Ebla of the presence of Hurrian speakers in 3rd-millennium Syria and the general association between Semitic speech and the Ubaid ware that replaced the Halafian, argued in Hrozný (1947, pp. 47–9), seem to me to open up the question again (see also Volume 1, p. 12). For Hurrian in the 3rd millennium, see Kammenhuber (1977, pp. 133–5) and Pettinato (1981, p. 27).
63. It is not just racists like Wolfram Nagel (1987, pp. 169–70) who see it in this way. The respectable Indo-Europeanist Mallory (1989, pp. 37–8) agrees too.
64. For the Kassites, see ch. VI above, nn. 79–80. The Indic names of their gods is disputed. See Mallory (1989, p. 38).

65. For the Mitanni, see Meyer (1907a). For the quotation, see Meyer (1909, I.ii, p. 291).
66. Sethe (1910b).
67. Breasted (1906, II, p. 125).
68. See also Gardiner (1946, pp. 47−8). Gardiner's translation runs: 'Even from the time when the Asiatics were in Avaris in the Northland (with) roving hordes in the midst of them overwhelming what had been made . . .'
69. Burchardt (1912a).
70. Cook (1924, pp. 232−3).
71. Hall (1924, p. 317).
72. Meyer (1925, p. 253).
73. Meyer (1928−36, I.ii, pp. 315−19). The association between the Hyksos and Central Asia was still tempting other scholars in the 1920s; see, for instance, Peake and Fleure (1927, p. 202).
74. Wolf (1929).
75. Mironov (1933, especially pp. 150−70).
76. Labib (1936, pp. 3−8).
77. Engberg (1939, pp. 47, 49).
78. Junker (1933, p. 105).
79. Stock (1955, p. 71).
80. Stock (1955, p. 74). The reference to Götze's work was to his (1936, p. 99).
81. The Hittitologist Götze was in fact a refugee from Nazism but he too was influenced by the same forces. See his (1936, pp. 99, 105−6) and von Soden (1937, pp. 14−17).
82. For a good example of this, see Albright's splendid review of *Der Aufstieg des Assyrerreichs...* by then Nazi Assyriologist Wolfram von Soden (1939). I am grateful to Peter Daniels for this reference.
83. Säve-Söderbergh (1951).
84. Mendenhall (1962).
85. See Gardiner (1947, I, p. 185; 1961a, pp. 156−7).
86. de Vaux (1967, pp. 481−503); Alt (1954). For the 'Execration Texts', see Posener (1940, 1975) and Helck (1971, pp. 44−67).
87. von Beckerath (1965, pp. 114−19); van Seters (1966, pp. 181−90); Hayes (1973, pp. 54−5).
88. Helck (1971, pp. 101−3).
89. For references to this, see Gardiner (1947, I, pp. 181−7).
90. Examples of this can be seen in the name of the Mitannian king Tushratta (chariot of terror), the name Bardashwa (many horses) in Indic, used among Hurrians in Nuzi, and the name Zurata (one who owns a good chariot), used by a prince of Accho in Palestine. For a discussion of these, see Drews (1988, pp. 150−1).
91. For a list of Egyptian and other references to Mariannu in the 15th and 14th centuries, see Helck (1971, pp. 482−7).
92. Van Seters (1966, pp. 186−7).
93. Van Seters (1966, p. 185).

94. For Hattusili I, see Kammenhuber (1977, p. 133). A similar argument is made for the absence of Hurrian names during the reign of Hammurabi's successor at Babylon, Šamšuiluna. See Kammenhuber (1977, p. 132). However, following the long chronology his reign would now be put as beginning in 1806, rather than at 1750 or 1686 BC as according to the middle and low chronologies.
95. Bietak (1983). For Bietak's latest ideas on this, see the interview with Neil Asher Silberman (1989, pp. 147–52).
96. Helck (1968, p. 132).
97. See Mallory (1989, pp. 40–1) and Yadin (1963, pp. 36–8, 74).
98. Littauer and Crouwel (1979, pp. 51, 61). See also Drews (1988, pp. 96–7).
99. Diakonoff (1972, pp. 91–120).
100. See ch. V, nn. 55–6.
101. Ghirschman (1977, pp. 3–10, 25–32).
102. For a discussion of these arguments, see Mallory (1989, pp. 39–41).
103. Kammenhuber (1977, pp. 220–3).
104. Mallory (1989, p. 41).
105. Littauer and Crouwel (1979, pp. 51–68).
106. This is the position taken by Drews (1988, pp. 136–57).
107. Hermes (1936, pp. 393–4).
108. Mallory (1989, p. 42).
109. Kupper (1973, p. 36).
110. Kenyon (1973, p. 115).
111. Bietak (1984, p. 476). See also Kemp and Merrillees (1980, pp. 96–8).
112. See the extended discussion on this in Van Seters (1966, pp. 27–37).
113. See ch. V, n. 69, and Van Seters (1966, pp. 33–7).
114. Van Seters (1966, pp. 28–9).
115. Petrie (1952, p. 3).
116. Ch. V, nn. 55–7.
117. Gardiner (1916, p. 107).
118. For this inscription, see Sethe (1906–9, IV, pp. 1–3) and Pritchard (1955, pp. 233–6). See also Gardiner (1961a, pp. 168–9) and, for Van Seters's argument, his (1966, p. 184, n. 25).
119. Ellenbogen (1962, p. 123) and Gordon (1966, p. 451). For objectors, see Littauer and Crouwel (1979, p. 59, n. 52) and Drews (1988, p. 141). They have on their side the fact that the Assyrian word *sisu* or *sisi e* was in use in 19th-century Anatolia before the likely arrival of Indo-Aryan speakers. On the other hand, the connection is strengthened by Segert's reading of the Ugaritic *ś* as *s^w* (1983, pp. 202, 215).
120. Gardiner (1957, p. 459 (E5)) and Gordon (1966, p. 350). It is interesting to note here that, like the Egyptian *ḥtr*, the West Semitic *ibr* also originally had bovine connotations, meaning 'bull (humped) buffalo'.
121. Speiser (1933, pp. 49–52). I have, however, been unable to find *waratašhu* in Laroche (1977).
122. Hermes (1936, pp. 379–81).

123. Drews (1988, pp. 102–3).
124. Van den Brink (1982, pp. 46–7).
125. See, for instance, Bietak (1968, pp. 91, 98).
126. Bietak (1968, pp. 90–2).
127. Boessneck (1976, p. 25); Bietak (1979, p. 247).
128. Van den Brink (1982, pp. 74–83).
129. For the burials, see Van den Brink (1982, pp. 74–83); for the Tell el Yehudiyeh ware, see Kemp and Merrillees (1980, p. 97, n. 252).
130. Bietak (1968, pp. 106–9).
131. Van Seters (1966, pp. 56–7).
132. Kantor (1956, p. 153).
133. Bietak (1979, pp. 242–3).
134. In the Jerusalem Museum, illustrated in many places, including Amiet (1977, plate 77).
135. Bisi (1965, p. 167); Frankfort (1970, pp. 263–4).
136. Kantor (1947, pp. 92–5); Helck (1979, pp. 80–1). For further discussion of Cretan or Hyksos priority for this and other motifs, see the next chapter.
137. Van Seters (1966, pp. 67–70); Porada (1984).
138. Van Seters (1966, pp. 61–7); Ward (1987, pp. 517–32).
139. Van Seters (1966, p. 71).
140. Van Seters (1966, pp. 71–2). See also Hayes (1975, p. 64).
141. Van Seters (1966, p. 72).
142. Volume 1, pp. 94–8.
143. Genesis 37–50.
144. Exodus.
145. I Kings 6.1.
146. See the computation in Rowley (1950, pp. 87–8).
147. Exodus 1.11.
148. See ch. VII, nn. 81–3.
149. For a good survey of these up to the Second World War, see Rowley (1950, pp. 10–19).
150. See Rowley (1950, pp. 10–11).
151. For their latest views on this, see Bimson and Livingston (1987, pp. 40–53, 66–7).
152. Halpern (1987, pp. 56–71).
153. See n. 31 above. Astour (1967a, pp. 193, 393) points out that the name Ykbʿr is probably not a misreading of Yqbir but comes from a form Yakke Baʿal (Let Baʿal strike).
154. Weinstein, 1981, pp. 8–10.
155. Diodoros Sikeliotes, XL.3.2.
156. Frg. 50 from Josephus, *Contra Apionem*, I.15, and frg. 51 from Theophilus, *Ad Autolycum* III, 19, as well as frg. 52, Syncellus.
157. *Contra Apionem*, I.14–16.
158. Manetho, frg. 53. See Waddell (1940, pp. 114–15).
159. See, for instance, the attitude of Schwartz (1950).

160. Astour (1967a, pp. 98–9); Breasted (1912a, p. 220); Dussaud (1946–8, pp. 45–7); Gardiner (1961a, p. 156); Luria (1926, p. 97); Weill (1923, pp. 185–91).
161. See, for instance, Baron (1952, I, pp. 35–9).
162. See Ashton and Gray (1935, pp. 246–8) and Grousset (1959, pp. 287–8).

Chapter IX
CRETE, THERA AND THE BIRTH OF MYCENAEAN CULTURE IN THE 18TH AND 17TH CENTURIES BC

1. Woodside (1971).
2. See Volume 1, pp. 84–101.
3. For the former view, see Platon (1956). For the latter, see Matz (1973a, pp. 141–3). There is also dispute about the nature of the 'post-palatial period'. See ch. X, nn. 89–95.
4. Pendlebury (1963, p. 173); Higgins (1979, p. 60).
5. Graham (1962, pp. 125–8); 1975; 1977).
6. See ch. IV, n. 34.
7. See Schachermeyr (1967, pp. 47–8).
8. See Morgan, who generally is a strong advocate of Aegean isolation (1988, pp. 20–4).
9. See Davies and Gardiner (1936, plates 54 and 65).
10. Morgan (1988, pp. 146–50). For other Egyptian artistic motifs adopted and adapted in Crete in MMIII, see Higgins (1979, pp. 22–9).
11. Morgan (1988, pp. 39–40) and see, for instance, Davies and Gardiner (1936, plates 16 and 33).
12. Pendlebury (1963, p. 158); Betancourt (1985, pp. 103–4).
13. Pendlebury (1963, pp. 159, 165).
14. Pollinger-Foster (1979, pp. 153–5).
15. See Pendlebury (1963, pp. 166–7) and Sakellerakis (1981, p. 39).
16. Diodoros, IV.79.3; Evans (1921–35, IV, pp. 960, 965).
17. Pendlebury (1963, pp. 193–4).
18. See Graham (1962, p. 160).
19. See Pini (1968, p. 45).
20. Montet (1928–9, pp. 143–238).
21. See ch. IV, n. 39.
22. Pendlebury (1963, p. 164). See also Hiller (1984).
23. Maxwell-Hyslop (1946, esp. p. 15).
24. Helck (1979, p. 55).
25. Ch. V, nn. 153–4. See also ch. VI, n. 163.
26. Pendlebury (1963, p. 164). See also Shaw (1978, p. 444; 1980, p. 246).
26. Sandars (1961).
28. See ch. IV, n. 12.
29. Branigan (1968b, p. 201).

30. Lacau (1904–6, I, plate 43, nos. 255, 257, 259, 261), cited in Gardiner (1957, p. 511, item 8, n. 2).
31. Ch. V, n. 151.
32. Maxwell-Hyslop (1946, pp. 33–41). Although this author wrote over forty years ago, the chronology she used is more compatible with the one followed in this book than those found in most later works.
33. See ch. VIII, nn. 140–1.
34. Maxwell-Hyslop (1946, pp. 38–41).
35. See Heubeck (1968). Pierce (1971, p. 106) expresses some scepticism about this.
36. Szemerényi (1966b, p. 36). He tries to explain the discrepancy as the result of a dissimilation of the labial element in k^w caused by the following labial. This is possible, although the example he cites to justify this is *kapnos* (smoke) from $*k^wap$. Apart from the completely hypothetical nature of this etymon, there is, as will be argued below, a good case for deriving the Greek *kapn-* (smoke, fumigate) from an Egyptian alternative.
37. The rather complicated proposed derivations of *xen-* from the Semitic *śn'* (hate) and *xyn* (with) from a Semitic stem found in the Eblaite *ši-in* (movement to, up to) and the Gunnan Gurage preposition *sə'n* (up to, until, as far as) will be discussed in Volume 3.
38. Birch (1853, p. 62); Brugsch (1855, p. 40).
39. For a bibliography on this, see Pierce (1971, p. 106). Since Pierce wrote, the etymology was accepted in Černy (1976, p. 171).
40. Burchardt (1912b, pp. 61–3).
41. Apart from the finds at Tell el Daba'a, Bietak (1968, p. 106; 1979, p. 261), there are the well-known daggers described in the last chapter, see nn. 139–41.
42. The exception to this is Hemmerdinger (1969, p. 239).
43. For a dismissal of Benveniste's derivation from a root $*kšipra$, allegedly found in the Ossetic *aexsyrf* (scythe), see Szemerényi (1966b, p. 36, n. 3).
44. Fraenkel (1910–12, II, p. 174, n. 1). A Semitic etymology for *sēpomai* will be proposed in Volume 3.
45. The etymology of *kēpos* will be discussed further in the next chapter. See also n. 146 below.
46. Pierce (1971, p. 106).
47. Gardiner (1957, p. 428).
48. This will be considered further in Volume 3.
49. Erman and Grapow (1982, VI, pp. 241–2).
50. Černy (1976) does not provide an etymology for *sōt* nor does he list it among those for which no etymologies are given.
51. Another remote possibility is that the Greek word *xylam-* derives from the Egyptian *srmt*, found in the Coptic *sorm, sarm, sorem*. As *xylam-*, which has no Indo-European etymology, is attested only in Egypt and is clearly connected to agriculture, there have been unsuccessful attempts

to find an Egyptian origin. The difficulty in attempting to connect *xylam-* to *srmt* or *sorm* is that the meanings of both words are extremely uncertain. *Xylam-* is a process carried out before the planting to prepare the soil. If this was some sort of fertilizing, it could be connected to *srmt l sorm*, which later had the meaning 'dregs' or 'lees' but earlier was some sort of processed granule that could be eaten (Gardiner, 1947, II, pp. 234–5). Whether it could also be used as fertilizer is as uncertain as the rest of this messy problem.

52. For the dismissal of the tentative Indo-European etymologies for these, see Chantraine (1968–75, pp. 763–8).

53. Rendsburg (1989b, p. 76) sees the derivation of *xiphos* from *sft* as 'perfectly reasonable'.

54. For the dismissal of the tentative Indo-European etymologies for this, see Chantraine (1968–75, p. 1180). Another 'sword' found in the military *koinē* of the 20th and 19th centuries BC was that known to the Egyptians as ḫpš written with the determinative ⌣. This was an extended sickle. Brown (1968a, pp. 178–82) has suggested that the Greek word *harpē* (sickle) derives from the West Semitic √ḥrb found in the Hebrew *ḥereb* which derived from the earlier vocalization *ḥarb* seen in the Aramaic *ḥarba* (sword). This seems attractive. However, as Burkert (1984, p. 41, n. 32) points out, there is a satisfactory Indo-European etymology for *harpē*. (There is a typographical error in Burkert's text which reads *ḫäräb* instead of *ḥäräb* which is also etymologically √ḥrb not √ḫrb.) I see no reason to give priority to Indo-European roots and I have no doubt that there was some 'contamination' involved. Nevertheless, Brown's case for a Semitic etymology does seem to be weakened.

55. For the suffix *-(a)n*, see Gordon (1965, p. 63 [8.58]) and Moscati *et al.* (1969, p. 82 [12.21]).

56. For the alternation between *š* and *l*, see Steiner (1977). One of the most common uses of *plg* is as a dividing stream or canal: see the Akkadian *palgu* and the Hebrew *pᵉlagåh* and *pᵉlugåh*. Despite the meaning of the Greek *pelagos* as the 'open sea' rather than a 'strait or channel', I am not convinced by Muss-Arnolt's (1892, p. 69) rejection of a Semitic origin from *plg* as proposed by 19th-century scholars. This would seem a good deal closer than its current European competitor *plak-* (stretch, flat) (Chantraine, 1968–75, p. 872). Furthermore, the image of the sea as a division would also seem to be strengthened by what I see as the most plausible etyma for the Greek *thalassa* (sea) and *isthmos* (isthmus or neck) in the Egyptian *tꜣš* (boundary) and *sdmỉ* (attach). Neither has an Indo-European etymology and both will be discussed further in Volume 3.

Muss-Arnolt did, however, accept the Greek *pallakē* (concubine) came from the Semitic *pᵉlagåh*, in the sense of 'cut off from the family'. However, he saw the Hebrew *pilegeš* (concubine) as a borrowing from *pallakē*. These two words are clearly related but the precise manner of the relationship is very elusive. For an exhaustive 19th-century bibliography on this, see Muss-Arnolt (1892, pp. 65–6). For more up-to-date discussions, see Ellenbogen (1962, p. 134), Rabin (1974) and, above all, the elegant work of Brown (1968a, pp. 164–9).

57. See Szemerényi (1966b) and Lejeune (1972, p. 46 [33]). See also ch. XII, n. 51.

58. See also Bernal (1989b, pp. 35–7).

59. See ch. X, nn. 14–23.

60. Lorimer (1950, pp. 276–80).

61. Wolf (1926, pp. 14–26); Lorimer (1950, pp. 278–80).

62. Pendlebury (1963, p. 172); Crouwel (1981, p. 122).

63. Herakleion Museum Case 75A; see Sakellerakis (1981, p. 60).

64. Helck (1979, pp. 80–1). See also ch. VIII, n. 136.

65. Matz (1973a, p. 157); Stock (1955, pp. 31–2). See also, above, ch. VIII, nn. 135–6.

66. Matz (1973a, p. 157).

67. Dessenne (1957, p. 76).

68. Dessenne (1957, pp. 27, 175–6).

69. Dessenne (1957, p. 178).

70. Dessenne (1957, pp. 35–43, 178–9).

71. Dessenne (1957, p. 124).

72. Dessenne (1957, pp. 112, 149). See also Helck (1979, p. 75).

73. Dessenne (1957, p. 187).

74. Bisi (1965, pp. 21–42).

75. Schachermeyr (1967, p. 32, plate 76).

76. Bisi (1965, p. 167).

77. Evans (1921–35, I, pp. 709–13); Frankfort (1936–7). See also Morgan (1988, pp. 50–1) and Herodotos, VI.53–4.

78. Frankfort (1936).

79. Bisi (1965, pp. 72–3).

80. See the short essay in Gesenius (1953, pp. 500–1).

81. For the 19th-century scholars, see Muss-Arnolt (1892, p. 100), who accepts it. For the 20th-century, see Brown (1968a, p. 185, n. 3). See also Grimme (1925, p. 17) and Chantraine (1968–75, p. 75).

82. Brown (1968a, pp. 184–8).

83. Bisi (1965, pp. 197–246).

84. The possibility that a griffin at Pylos was called po-ni-ke is considered unlikely by Ventris and Chadwick (1973, p. 136). It may be an alternative name. The enormously complicated subject of phoinix and similar words will be considered in Volume 3.

85. Bisi (1965, pp. 167–95). For the pairs of griffins in both the megara at Pylos and a comparison between them and the pair at Knossos, see Lang (1969, pp. 99–103, 194–211).

86. Bisi (1965, pp. 167–77); Morgan (1988, pp. 49–51).

87. Woolley (1953, pp. 80–5).

88. Kupper (1973, p. 31). See also ch. VIII, n. 93.

89. Hood (1967, p. 80).

90. Evans (1921–35, I, p. 316).
91. Warren (1973, p. 43).
92. Stubbings (1973). This issue will be considered below.
93. See Courtois (1955).
94. See ch. VIII, n.95.
95. See, for examples, Schachermeyr (1967, p. 43) and Helck (1979, p. 49). For the lid, see also ch. VII, nn.51–2 and 61, and ch. VIII, n.26.
96. Meyer (1928–36, II, pt. 1, pp. 40–58, 162–75).
97. Schachermeyr (1967, p. 43) and Helck (1979, p. 49).
98. Stevenson Smith (1965, p. 28).
99. See Wiener (1984), Hiller (1984), Stos-Gale and Gale (1984a), Korres (1984) and others.
100. Ch. V, nn.8–30.
101. Matz (1973a, p. 157).
102. Ch. VIII, nn.132–9, 162.
103. See ch. VIII, n.134.
104. Dessenne (1957, p. 178).
105. Åström (1971).
106. Thorpe-Scholes (1978, p. 40). See also ch. VIII, nn.139–41.
107. Doumas (1983, pp. 11–14, 29–42). For more on ancient Akrotiri, see Barber (1987, pp. 201–16).
108. Barber (1987, pp. 191–6). For more on the weights, see ch. X, nn.145–6.
109. Niemeier (1980); Morgan (1988, p. 171).
110. Morgan (1988, p. 171). While she puzzlingly sticks to a low date for the eruption, she honestly admits that these parallels to Theran pottery are of, as Marthari puts it, the 'Middle Helladic tradition' (1988, p. 211, n.17).
111. Barber (1987, pp. 156, 196). Barber also claims that these stopped at the end of the period and suggests that this represented a Cretan political takeover of the islands. I think it is hard to make so much of an argument from silence.
112. Stos-Gale and Gale (1984b); Hiller (1984); Barber (1987, p. 197).
113. Vermeule (1964, p. 116).
114. Immerwahr (1977, p. 189); Buchholz (1980, p. 228); Morgan (1988, p. 171). The systematic isolationist Peter Warren claims that the mortars are local Theran (1979a, p. 108).
115. S. Marinatos (1976, p. 30, plate 49b). For a survey of Canaanite jars, see ch. XI, nn.225–8.
116. Morgan (1988, p. 171).
117. N. Marinatos (1984, pp. 31–3).
118. N. Marinatos (1984, p. 32).
119. Pollinger-Foster (1987, p. 13).
120. Pollinger-Foster (1987, p. 16).
121. Morgan (Brown) (1978, pp. 631–41); Morgan (1988, pp. 116–17); N.

Marinatos (1984, pp. 52–60). For a bibliography on the friezes, see N. Marinatos (1983, p. 2, n. 2).

122. Raban (1984, p. 19). Morgan (1988, pp. 116–42) comes to very much the same conclusion.

123. For a bibliography on this, see Raban (1984, p. 19, n. 36). See also Casson (1975, p. 7) and Morgan (1988, p. 127).

124. For different interpretations of the scene, see Doumas (1983, pp. 84–104) and N. Marinatos (1984, p. 38).

125. Morgan (1988, p. 119).

126. The most striking example of this comes from the legends around the royal Theseus whose possession of a sword is of great significance, but whose enemies employed their arms, feet, rocks, pine trees and even beds! Anything, in short, except for swords. See Graves (1955, I, pp. 327–32).

127. Morgan (1988, pp. 107–9).

128. Morgan (1988, pp. 118–20).

129. Pollinger-Foster (1987, p. 16).

130. Morgan (1988, p. 93).

131. From the tomb of Mn ḥpr Rˤ snb, reproduced in Davies and Gardiner (1936, I, plates 21 and 24). For more details on their clothing, see Vercoutter (1956, pp. 287–8). See also Helck (1971, pp. 154–5).

132. For more on this, see ch. X, nn. 15–19.

133. Morgan (1988, p. 94).

134. Warren (1979b, pp. 116–29). For another example of Warren's preference for indigenous development in the most unlikely situations, see Volume 1, p. 16. For the others, see Doumas (1983, pp. 83–4) and Immerwahr (1983, p. 147).

135. N. Marinatos (1984, p. 41). Morgan (1988, pp. 44–5) agrees.

136. Masson (1967, pp. 85–7) tries to explain these striking parallels by postulating a common Mediterranean origin for these two words, thus avoiding the possibility of Greek borrowings from Semitic or Egyptian. I agree with her and Astour (1967a, p. 338) that it is difficult – though not impossible – to derive *rewo* from the Ugaritic *lbu* or the Hebrew *låbî*. The Egyptian etymology, however, would seem much more plausible, especially as we know that the Egyptian *û* frequently 'broke' to form *ew*. See Albright (1923, p. 66). The attestation of the Egyptian *rw* since the Old Kingdom and the probability – in view of the Semitic forms – that it derives from a Proto-Afroasiatic *lbu* makes it far more likely that Greek and hence other Indo-European languages borrowed from the Egyptian. Masson's denial of the etymology of *lis* from *layîs*, proposed by Muss-Arnolt (1892, p. 96), Lewy (1895, p. 9) and Boisaco (1950), in favour of the notion of a *mot voyageur* shows only the strength of Aryanism in 20th-century scholarship.

137. Doumas (1983, p. 105); N. Marinatos (1984, p. 41); Page (1976); Stucchi (1967).

138. Morgan (1988, pp. 89–91).
139. S. Marinatos (1969, pp. 374–5; 1974, pp. 199–200). There are also representations of negroid Blacks from Late Bronze Age Cyprus. See Karageorghis 1988, esp. p. 10, n. 2.
140. Morgan (1988, pp. 89–91).
141. Morgan (1988, pp. 144–5) and Pollinger-Foster (1986, 1987).
142. Doumas (1983, p. 105).
143. Stevenson Smith (1965, p. 155).
144. See nn. 9–10 above and Higgins (1979, p. 25). Morgan (1988, p. 44) seems to concede this, though she insists that the Theran representation has significantly different features.
145. N. Marinatos (1984, pp. 94–6); Morgan (1988, pp. 23–4).
146. Lewy (1895, p. 6). Masson (1967, p. 87, n. 5) follows Mayrhofer (1953, I, p. 156) in being uncertain of the point of origin. There is no doubt that the Egyptian form is attested much earlier than the rest, but the case is not clear-cut; it may be a proto-Afroasiatic root. The alternation *kēposl kēbos* makes it almost certain that the Greek forms are loans. Another Greek word for monkey, *pithēkos*, also has a plausible Egyptian etymology. The root for this is *tḥ* (drink beer or beer jug) ठ with the derivatives *tḥw* (drunkard) and *tḥt* (drunkenness). With the definite article, *pꜣ tḥ* would seem a plausible origin for the Greek *pithos* (large jar, usually for wine), which has no clear Indo-European etymology. In Demotic there is the term *pr tḥ* (house of drunkenness) which would seem cognate to the Greek *pithōn* (cellar). *Pithos* has many derivatives, some of which have the suffix *-ak*. It would seem probable that *pithēkos* is one of these. The best Indo-European etymology found for this is to relate it to the Latin *foedus* (ugly), but Chantraine sees it as a loan. The association of monkeys and apes with drunkenness is proverbial in most cultures, for instance 'as giddy as an ape'. The common name for islands in the West Mediterranean, Pithekusa, should not be seen as 'monkey island' but as 'wineland'.
147. Marinatos (1973b, p. 200).
148. See nn. 109–14 above.
149. For a good short survey of this, see Ceram (1952, pp. 44–55). For a sceptical if not hostile view see Calder (1986).
150. See Vermeule (1964, p. 84).
151. Vermeule (1964, pp. 86–90); Stubbings (1973, pp. 630–3); Dickinson (1977, pp. 42–50).
152. See below, nn. 196–7.
153. Chantraine (1968–75, p. 720).
154. Muss-Arnolt (1892, p. 48).
155. Fick (1905, pp. 128, 131). One possible origin for Mykale and Mykalessos is from the West Semitic *miklâh* (enclosure, fold).
156. Vermeule (1964, pp. 116–20); Dickinson (1977, pp. 87–100); Barber (1987, pp. 58–64, 203–16).
157. Vermeule (1964, pp. 100–4).

158. For these and the literature on them, see Drews (1988, pp. 187–90).
159. See nn. 19–20 above.
160. Mellink (1956); Hooker (1976, p. 45).
161. Kenyon (1973, pp. 93–5); Van Seters (1966, p. 47).
162. Dickinson (1977, p. 51).
163. Hammond (1973).
164. Dickinson (1977, p. 51).
165. Mylonas (1973, I, 117); Dickinson (1977, p. 51); Pelon (1987, p. 115).
166. Stubbings (1973, p. 631). Mellink (1956, pp. 55–6), Vermeule (1964, p. 108; 1975); Muhly (1979a, p. 317); Drews (1988, p. 185) and others take the same view.
167. Vermeule (1964, p. 81).
168. Mellink (1956, pp. 55–6); Muhly (1979a, p. 317); Drews (1988, p. 185).
169. S. Marinatos (1973a); Stubbings (1973).
170. Van Seters (1966, p. 47).
171. Montet (1928–9).
172. See Wace (1964, pp. 21–2). For a bibliography of the recent debate on this issue, see Wilkie (1987, p. 127, n. 1).
173. See ch. I, n. 17, and Branigan (1970b).
174. See Dickinson (1977, p. 61).
175. Vermeule (1964, pp. 120–6).
176. Pelon (1976). He maintains that they should be linked to the Kurgan tradition of the 3rd millennium. See also Drews (1988, p. 184).
177. Angel (1957) and Dickinson (1977, p. 52).
178. See ch. VIII, n. 134, and n. 101 above.
179. For ancient traces of Indo-Aryan cremation, see Mallory (1989, pp. 47–8).
180. Dickinson (1977, pp. 49, 57–8); Taylour (1964, p. 76); Stubbings (1973, p. 633).
181. See ch. VIII, nn. 123–36. For the weapon types, see above nn. 21–34.
182. Vermeule (1964, pp. 89–90); Dayton (1982a, pp. 164–6).
183. Stubbings (1973, p. 633); Pendlebury (1930a, p. 55 [89]).
184. Boufides (1970).
185. Lorimer (1950, p. 278).
186. Hooker (1976, p. 46).
187. Hooker (1976, p. 48).
188. Evans (1929); Dickinson (1977, p. 53).
189. Cadogan (1971); Hooker (1976, pp. 38–9); Dickinson (1977, pp. 107–9). The re-dating of the Thera eruption and the lowering of carbon dating for the Wessex culture in Southern Britain invalidates the work in this area of such scholars as Butler (1963) and McKerrell (1972) and confirms the commonsense view held by Bouzek (1973) that Mycenaean culture spread to Northern Europe rather than the other way around. See also Trump (1981, pp. 195–7).
190. See Van Royen and Isaac (1979, pp. 26–8), and Dor et al. (1960, pp. 32–3).

191. S. Marinatos (1973a, p. 109).
192. Grumach (1968/9, pp. 85–6).
193. These etymologies will be considered further in Volume 3.
194. For a survey of this influence, see Evans (1929). See also Vermeule (1964, pp. 96–7) and Dickinson (1977, p. 52).
195. See ch. VIII, nn. 139–41 and above nn. 67–75.
196. See Vermeule (1975, pp. 23–6). For examples of this Steppe art and a survey of what can be reconstructed of the society that produced them, see Phillips (1965).
197. Muhly (1979a, pp. 317–19).
198. See ch. VIII, nn. 139–40.
199. For illustrations of these, see, for instance, Vermeule (1964, plates xii and xiii) and Hood (1967, plates 54–6). For the earlier discussion, see above, nn. 133–9.
200. See Vermeule (1964, p. 98) and Dickinson (1977, p. 52). See also above nn. 25–33.
201. *Pace* Cadogan (1971) and Dickinson (1977, pp. 108–9).
202. S. Marinatos (1973a, p. 108).
203. See n. 188 above.
204. See Persson (1942, pp. 178–96) and Marinatos (1960, pp. 81–2).
205. See ch. X, nn. 67–8.
206. Mallory (1989, p. 51).
207. Mallory (1989, pp. 35–41).
208. See ch. VIII, nn. 102–4.
209. See nn. 219–20 below.
210. Wyatt (1970, p. 107).
211. Buck (1926); Nilsson (1933, pp. 71–82).
212. Wyatt (1970); Best and Yadin (1973); Muhly (1979); Van Royen and Isaac (1979); Drews (1988).
213. Nilsson (1933, pp. 71–82).
214. Drews (1988, p. 23).
215. Herodotos, VI.55. See Volume 1, p. 75.
216. Ch. VIII, nn. 102–29.
217. Muhly (1979a, pp. 319–20). The Greek archaeologist George Mylonas (1962) took the more moderate position that, although Greece had been Greek since about 2100 BC, a Luvian invasion was responsible for the changes around 1600.
218. Muhly (1979a, p. 319).
219. For special connections between Greek and Indo-Aryan, see Porzig (1954b, pp. 61–83) and Sakellariou (1986, p. 128). For a survey of recent linguistic schemes, see Mallory (1989, pp. 20–1).
220. For arguments that Indo-Iranian had already split by the first half of the 2nd millennium, see Szemerényi (1964, pp. 90–6) and Mallory (1989, pp. 38–9).
221. Muhly (1979a, pp. 320–3). The absence of evidence for any invasion at

this time was used by Mylonas to deny any possibility of there having been one then (1962, p. 301).

222. Drews (1988, pp. 181–3).
223. See ch. II, nn. 112–29.
224. Best and Yadin (1973, pp. 29–31).
225. See ch. VIII, nn. 108–41.
226. Volume 1, pp. 410–11.
227. Stubbings (1973, pp. 636–7).
228. See Volume 1, pp. 88–97 and 109–10.
229. Stubbings (1973, p. 637). This passage is quoted in Volume 1, p. 411.
230. See ch. VIII, nn. 31–40.
231. See Volume 1, pp. 95–8 and 109–110.
232. See Hooker (1976, p. 47).
233. For the Kassites, see ch. VI, nn. 78–85.
234. See Vermeule (1964, p. 89).
235. Bernal (1987, pp. 9–10, 1990).
236. See ch. II, nn. 228–30.
237. See Risch (1949, pp. 1928; 1955, pp. 61–75); Porzig (1954a, pp. 147–61); Wyatt (1972); Chadwick (1973b, pp. 817–19). These questions will be discussed further in Volume 3.

Chapter X
EGYPTIAN, MESOPOTAMIAN AND LEVANTINE CONTACTS
WITH THE AEGEAN: THE DOCUMENTARY EVIDENCE

1. Albright (1934); Helck (1962, pp. 567–8).
2. Posener (1940, pp. 83, 93). See also Vercoutter (1956, p. 161).
3. Vercoutter (1956, pp. 159–82).
4. Albright (1934, p. 9).
5. See Volume 1, p. 385, n. 47.
6. See ch. IV, nn. 60–1 and 80–114.
7. Bérard (1902–3, I, pp. 215–24).
8. See Volume 1, p. 449.
9. For the identification with Libya, see Gauthier (1925–31, III, p. 7). For Mꜣnw's religious significance, see Kurth (1980, cols 1185–6). Crete's height would be reflected in a possible etymology for its name from the common Egyptian toponym Ḳꜣ(y)t (height). There is, however, no attestation of Ḳꜣ(y)t as a name for the island. Thus this etymology must remain tentative, despite the absence of any alternative. See also ch. IV, n. 52. For the name Mꜣnw for the mountain in the west and entrance to the underworld, which could well be the origin of the Greek root *melan-* (black), see ch. II, nn. 85–7.
10. Vercoutter (1956, doc. 3, pp. 43–5); Strange (1980, text 21, pp. 71–3).
11. Stevenson Smith (1965, p. 92). For the archaeological evidence, see ch. III, nn. 115–27.

12. British Museum 5647; Vercoutter (1956, doc. 4, pp. 45–51); Helck (1979, p. 100); Strange (1980, text 39, pp. 94–6).
13. Vercoutter (1956, p. 136). Here, I follow the dates of Wente and Van Siclen (1976, p. 218) and the *Cambridge Ancient History*, 3rd ed., II.2, p. 1038.
14. Vercoutter (1956, pp. 33–124); Helck (1979, pp. 27–8). Gardiner (1947, I, p. 203) is clear that the absence of the final -*r* in the Egyptian form 'need not be a serious obstacle . . . since there are many analogies for the intrusion of this letter'.
15. Strange (1980); Merrillees (1982; 1987, p. 51); Vercoutter (1956, pp. 45–6); Helck (1979, pp. 100–2); Astour (1964a, pp. 240–54). For the debate on the identification of Alashia, the ancient place name that is widely accepted as designating Cyprus, see ch. V, n. 164.
16. Furumark (1950, p. 240).
17. Vercoutter (1956, p. 220).
18. For the ancient view, see Volume 1, p. 385.
19. Evans (1921–35, I, p. 316), *pace* Warren (1973, p. 44).
20. Vercoutter (1956, pp. 100–1).
21. See below, nn. 91–105.
22. For Gordon's work on this, see Volume 1, pp. 416–19.
23. *Pace* Warren (1973, p. 42). Weinberg (1954, pp. 94–6; 1965a, pp. 302–7). Branigan (1970a, pp. 198–200) equivocates on the issue but he too sees major influences from Palestine at the beginning of the EMI. See next chapter.
24. Nibbi (1975).
25. Sandars (1978).
26. Nibbi (1975, pp. 35–44).
27. Vercoutter (1956, pp. 152–3).
28. Vercoutter (1956, pp. 57–8, 144–7). For the invasions, see Volume 1, pp. 445–50.
29. Gardiner (1947, I, 208).
30. Utterances 366, 454 and 593; Text 629, 847 and 1631. Sethe (1937, III, pp. 168–9); Gardiner (1947, I, p. 206).
31. Gardiner (1947, I, p. 206); Nibbi (1975, pp. 53–4). For the Dorak Treasure, see ch. III, n. 122.
32. Vercoutter (1956, pp. 16–17).
33. Vercoutter (1954, p. 40).
34. Smith (1971, pp. 180–1). Part of this is also quoted in ch. III; see n. 129.
35. Gardiner (1950, p. 573); Vercoutter (1956, pp. 20–32).
36. Vercoutter (1956, p. 32).
37. Vercoutter (1956, pp. 20–31).
38. Vercoutter (1956, p. 26); Nibbi (1975, p. 52).
39. Gardiner (1947, I, p. 126). See also Volume 1, p. 96. For *tni* as the origin of the Greek *thnē-* (die) and *thanatos* (death), see Volume 1, pp. 457–8. Here it should be noted that in epic poetry the negative *athanatos* is frequently paralleled with *agēros* (unageing). See Faraone (1987, p. 258,

n. 4). The parallel would be tighter if *athanatos* originally had the same meaning.

40. Gardiner (1947, I, 124–5). The letter, Knudzon 151. See Moran (1987, p. 386). It is quoted in Akkadian and English in Astour (1967a, pp. 4–5).

41. Astour (1967a, pp. 1–2).

42. Albright's hypothesis to this effect (1950, pp. 171–2) seems more plausible than that of Astour (1967a, pp. 48–9).

43. Astour (1967a, pp. 22–3, 36, 387).

44. Laroche (1958, pp. 252–83); Arbeitman and Rendsburg (1981, pp. 152–3). Rendsburg dissociates himself from this particular conclusion.

45. Albright (1950, p. 172); Astour (1967a, p. 12).

46. Astour (1967a, p. 12); Helck (1979, p. 138).

47. Albright (1950, pp. 171–2; 1975, p. 508).

48. Knudzen 151. See Moran (1987, p. 386). Trans. Astour (1967a, p. 5).

49. Gardiner (1947, I, 124).

50. Vercoutter (1956, pp. 129–30).

51. *Pace* Astour (1967a, pp. 53–67). Astour (1967a, pp. 67–9) conscientiously adds a further argument against his case, when he points out that Herodotos (VII.91) refers to a people called Hypachaioi in Cilicia. He dismisses the hypothesis that this is a mistake for Hylachaioi from Ḥilakku (Cilicia) and admits that the Hypachaioi were Achaioi or Greeks from Cyprus who had settled in Cilicia in the 8th century. Surely it would be simpler to admit that Greeks had arrived here in the 13th century, when they settled in Pamphylia to the west and Cyprus.

52. For more on this, see Volume 1, pp. 445–8.

53. Gordon (1963b, p. 21); Yadin (1968, 1973); Jones (1975).

54. Judges 5. 17; Genesis 49. 16; Judges 18. 1, cited in Arbeitman and Rendsburg (1981, pp. 151–2). For the Philistines and Tjeker, see Volume 1, pp. 445–8.

55. Herodotos, II.45.

56. Ch. II, nn. 172–215.

57. Gordon (1966, p. 38).

58. Arbeitman and Rendsburg (1981, pp. 150–2).

59. Ezekiel 28. 3; Astour (1967a, pp. 69–80).

60. See above, n. 38. *dnì* clearly comes from *dn* (cut off), from the cutting and sharing of the portions of a killed or sacrificed animal. This suggestion would be strengthened if the obscure determinative for *dnì* (share out) is ꜥ (limb, flesh).

61. Volume 1, pp. 96–8.

62. See Cook (1914–40, III, pp. 362–70). For a recent survey of the literature on this, see Sakellariou (1986, pp. 130–2).

63. See Sakellariou (1986, pp. 130–2) and Arbeitman and Rendsburg (1981, pp. 149–50).

64. Pettinato (1978, p. 69, n. 188); personal communication, Cornell, December 1986. The suffix [-ki] is the sign for 'land'.

65. For a discussion of the name Amnissos and its connections to the Egyptian word *imn* (west) and the name Amon, see Volume 3.
66. Vercoutter (1956, pp. 96–7, docs 21–2); Helck (1979, p. 103).
67. James (1973, p. 303).
68. See ch. IX, n. 204.
69. Helck (1979, p. 81).
70. Wachsmann (1987, pp. 11–26).
71. The Amarna Letters are full of references to the Pharaoh's Egyptian and Nubian soldiers in the Levant and the presence of Egyptian civilians there is also attested. See, for example, E.A. 67.
72. Vercoutter (1956, p. 97, doc. 22ʰ); Helck (1971, pp. 342–69; 1979, p. 103).
73. Vercoutter (1956, pp. 256–7); Wachsmann (1987, pp. 44–6).
74. Davis (1979, pp. 126–7). For a discussion of the point at which Mycenaeans came to dominate Crete, see below nn. 90–105.
75. Wachsmann (1987, pp. 4–5).
76. Smith (1968, p. 241).
77. Gardiner (1961a, pp. 181–9).
78. Hayes (1973, pp. 319–22).
79. For the date, see Casperson (1986, pp. 147–8). For the campaign, see Gardiner (1961a, pp. 188–93) and Drower (1973, pp. 444–59).
80. Gardiner (1947, I, pp. 127, 191; II, p. 209); Gardiner (1961a, p. 193); Drower (1973, pp. 456–7).
81. Vercoutter (1956, p. 57, doc. 9b). Merrillees (1972, p. 288) tries to detach this inscription from the paintings that accompany it. Of course, retouching or changing is possible, but why should it have been so? The reason for Merrillees's objection to the inscription's referring to the painting is easier to fathom. While he has no objection to Aegean peoples trading with Egypt, he clearly has a great distaste for the idea that they were in any way subordinate to them. He writes: 'it should be noted that there is not one Aegean foreigner in the Theban tomb paintings who is depicted in any but a normal upright position' (1972, p. 287). This is not surprising as they are nearly all portrayed as carrying what the Egyptians saw as tribute.
82. Stela of Gebal Barkal, Vercoutter (1956, p. 132, doc. 33). The term 'Nine Bows' is the translation for the term usually transcribed as *pḏt 9*. However, ⟝ɑ⎮⎮⎮⎮⎮ could also be read *iwnt*. For the relation of iwn(tyw) to Ionian, see Volume 1, pp. 83–4.
83. Vercoutter (1956, pp. 132–3, doc. 34).
84. Vercoutter (1956, pp. 132–3); Pendlebury (1930b, pp. 75–92).
85. See ch. XI, nn. 18–28.
86. Hayes (1973, p. 368; see also pp. 367–9); Säve-Soderbergh (1946, pp. 33–50). See also ch. III, nn. 125–6.
87. See n. 68 above.
88. See Vercoutter (1956, pp. 134–5, doc. 36).
89. See ch. VII, n. 5.

90. Evans (1929, p. 49). For a survey of this, see Niemeier (1982a, pp. 220–1).
91. Wace and Blegen (1939, pp. 138–9).
92. Palmer (1956; 1965; 1984b).
93. *Iliad*, II.645–54 and elsewhere.
94. Blegen (1958).
95. Palmer (1958, p. 75); Huxley (1961). For criticisms, see Schachermeyr (1962b, p. 27) and Vermeule (1964, pp. 62–3).
96. Catling, Cherry, Jones and Killen (1980); Niemeier (1982a, p. 260).
97. Kanta (1980).
98. Niemeier (1982a, pp. 224–57); Palmer (1984b). For evidence on this from Ugarit, see Heltzer (1988).
99. Betancourt (1985, pp. 149–55).
100. See ch. IX, nn. 22–63.
101. Niemeier (1982a, p. 271).
102. See ch. XI, nn. 63–5.
103. See nn. 73–4 above.
104. See Volume 1, p. 365.
105. See ch. XI, nn. 56–68.
106. Vercoutter (1956, p. 55, doc. 8). The words in brackets represent a reconstruction by Sethe.
107. Wegner (1933, pp. 46, 82, 100, 142); Vercoutter (1956, p. 21).
108. Strom (1984, p. 193).
109. For a discussion of the datings of this reign, varying from 1420–1385 BC to 1386–1349 BC, see Cline (1987, p. 13, n. 60). As Cline points out, the low dates are very difficult to reconcile with the chronology of the Aegean. Here again, I follow the dates of Wente and Van Siclen (1976, p. 218) and the *Cambridge Ancient History*, 3rd ed., II.2, p. 1038, which would not seem to be far off.
110. See Kitchen (1965, p. 5; 1966a, pp. 23–4), Astour (1966, pp. 313–16), Edel (1966, pp. 37–40), Faure (1968, pp. 139–48), Goedicke (1969, p. 7), James (1971, pp. 144–5), Sergent (1977, pp. 128–67), Helck (1979, pp. 26, 30–2) and Strange (1980, p. 21).
111. Ch. V, nn. 163–4.
112. Faure (1968, p. 143) proposed a hypothetical Elaia in Northwest Crete, Goedicke (1969, p. 10) advocated Aulis in Boiotia, Astour (1966, p. 315) hypothesized a Waero in the kingdom of Pylos, while Sergent (1977, pp. 152–61) saw it as Helos in Lakonia. Edel (1966, p. 52), Kitchen (1966a, p. 24) and Strange (1980, p. 21) all believed it to be Ilios.
113. Cline (1987, p. 5) attributes this view to Merrillees, but the latter (1972, p. 290) insists that the list suggests purely symbolic power over the whole world.
114. Merrillees (1972, p. 290). For the criticism, see Cline (1987, p. 5). The same objection can be made to the two other inscriptions from this reign including Kftiw as a subject nation. See Vercoutter (1956, pp. 78–9).
115. Hankey (1981, pp. 45–6); Cline (1987, p. 23).

BLACK ATHENA

116. Merrillees (1972, pp. 291–2).
117. Vercoutter (1956, pp. 134–5).
118. Vercoutter (1956, pp. 86–97).
119. Vercoutter (1956, p. 97, doc. 22^h). See also his discussion of the complications of this fragment.
120. Vercoutter (1956, p. 139, doc. 40; p. 137, doc. 38).
121. See Volume 1, pp. 445–50.
122. See n. 65 above.
123. Gauthier (1925–31, I, pp. 73–6). See nn. 64–5 above.
124. Strange (1980, text 8, pp. 32–5; texts 33–6, pp. 90–2). See also Sasson (1971, p. 172) and Helm (1980, p. 45, n. 23).
125. Astour (1967a, p. 110, n. 3); Smith (1965, p. 91); Gordon (1966, pp. 424–5).
126. Wiseman (1953, p. 12); Yannai (1983, p. 80).
127. Astour (1972b, p. 26).
128. Yannai (1983, p. 78). The inner quotation is from Riis (1969, p. 435).
129. Astour (1967a, p. 48).
130. Astour (1967a, p. 107), Heltzer (1978, p. 134; 1988); Yannai (1983, p. 79). For a discussion of the meaning of *tamkarum*, see Yannai (1983, pp. 15–18).
131. For the rapid shifts of political and military power in North Syria in the 1360s BC, see Astour (1981, pp. 19–23).
132. Yannai (1983, p. 112); Cline (forthcoming a).
133. See ch. XI, nn. 28, 93–7.
134. See Gray (1957), Gordon (1962b, 1963b), Astour (1967a) and Caquot, Sznycer and Herdner (1974).
135. Edwards (1979, pp. 139–46). These myths will be discussed in more detail in Volume 4.
136. Ventris and Chadwick (1973, p. 388); Astour (1967b, p. 291); Duhoux (1978, pp. 65–129); Gordon (1966, p. 26); Peruzzi (1959–60, p. 34). For *leōn* from *rw*, see Billigmeier (1975, pp. 1–6) and Burkert (1984, p. 41). For *lis* from *layiš*, see Masson (1967, p. 86).
137. For the language of Linear A being Semitic, see Gordon (1966, pp. 26–32; 1981, pp. 761–72) and Astour (1967b, p. 291). For an a priori argument against, see Ruijgh (1968, pp. 198–9) and, for an apparently pragmatic one, see Duhoux (1978, pp. 223–3). It should be noted, however, that his very critical discussion of Gordon's proposal of Semitic is placed after six far less substantial claims for different origins of Eteo-Cretan. For a discussion of Gordon's proposal and its reception as well as the Ancient belief that the earliest language on the island was Semitic, see Volume 1, pp. 417–18. For more on *yane/yayîn* and the root *woino/*weino (wine), see nn. 45–9 to ch. I.
138. Helck (1979, p. 124).
139. See ch. XI, nn. 94–8.
140. Astour (1967a, pp. 337–8). Chantraine, like Masson, accepts the Semitic origins of *chrysos* and *chitôn*. However, he follows the Indo-Euro-

peanist interpretation of *lita* as deriving from an Indo-European root *li* of indeterminate meaning. The many derivations of Greek words from the Semitic *lṭ* will be discussed in Volume 3. The discovery of these words in Linear B was a key factor in convincing Astour of the importance of West Semitic influence on the Late Bronze Age Aegean (Astour 1987).

141. Ventris and Chadwick (1973, p. 134).
142. For the family, see Pokorny (1959–69, I, pp. 429–30).
143. For a Marxist view on this, see Suret-Canale (1974, pp. 178–82). See also Bernal (1989a, pp. 20–1).
144. Ventris and Chadwick (1973, p. 106). For similarities in the organization of textile manufacture, see Killen (1964, pp. 1–15).
145. Ventris and Chadwick (1973, p. 60).
146. Stieglitz (1978; 1982, p. 260).
147. For a history of this research, see Yannai (1983, pp. 51–7).
148. Vermeule (1964, p. 257).
149. Güterbock (1983, p. 136) and ch. VIII, n. 73.
150. See ch. XI, nn. 198–207; ch. XII, nn. 135–7 and Bernal (1989a, pp. 23–4).
151. *Iliad*, VI.290–1 and XXIII.742–5; *Odyssey*, IV.618, XIII.272–85, XIV.288–301, XV.117–19 and 415–80.
152. *Pace* Muhly (1970a).
153. See nn. 53–65 above and Volume 1, p. 95.
154. Astour (1967a, pp. 340–4); Ventris and Chadwick (1973, p. 588).
155. This is likely – see Yannai (1983, p. 80) – but Godart (1968) believes it to be an occupation.
156. Xenophanes 16.
157. Ventris and Chadwick (1973, pp. 537, 582); Chantraine (1968–75, p. 1005).
158. There is no problem with the derivation of a Greek initial *s* from an Egyptian *š* which has been attested frequently in transcriptions such as Sōs for the god Šw. Chantraine has no explanation for the Greek word. He does not seem persuaded by Pokorny's derivation of *simos* from a root *suě (bend, twist, swing), an interesting indication of the phonetic and semantic lengths Indo-Europeanists are sometimes prepared to go. Note the ʿayin in both the Egyptian word and the Hebrew name. Simʿôn has no known etymology. The idea that Jacob could have a son with the name 'snub nose' or 'black' is not so shocking when one realizes that it is generally accepted that Pînḥås, the name of a grandson of Aaron, comes from the Egyptian Pȝ Nḥsy (The Nubian or Black), ch. VIII, nn. 48–9.
159. *Pace* Snowden (1970, 1983), but see the fascinating work of Thompson (1989).

Chapter XI

EGYPTIAN AND LEVANTINE CONTACTS WITH THE AEGEAN
1550–1250 BC: THE ARCHAEOLOGICAL EVIDENCE

1. Hankey and Warren (1974) and Betancourt (1987, p. 47).
2. Thucydides, I.5. See also Stubbings (1973, pp. 638–40) and Taylour (1964, pp. 170–2).
3. See ch. X, nn. 59–60.
4. See ch. VII, nn. 148–53.
5. For this process, see Bernal (1989a, pp. 21–8).
6. Graham (1977, pp. 114–15).
7. Higgins (1981, pp. 82–6); Stubbings (1975, pp. 172–3). For the Anatolian origins of Cyclopean fortification, see Scoufopoulos (1971, pp. 101–6) and Sandars (1978, pp. 62–8).
8. Higgins (1981, pp. 87–90).
9. Higgins (1981, pp. 129–36); Taylour (1964, pp. 126–34).
10. Higgins (1981, pp. 179–88).
11. Higgins (1981, pp. 98–101).
12. Vermeule and Karageorghis (1982, pp. 1–9).
13. Vermeule and Karageorghis (1982).
14. Smith (1958, p. 126).
15. See ch. IV, nn. 134–5 and ch. V, nn. 9–40. Schachermeyr (1967, p. 33 and plate 77); Helck (1979, pp. 57–8).
16. Helck (1979, p. 81).
17. Helck (1979, p. 111); Kemp and Merrillees (1980, pp. 226–45).
18. Helck (1979, p. 111); Kemp and Merrillees (1980, p. 245).
19. Pendlebury (1930a, p. 44), object 74.
20. Pendlebury (1930a, p. 59), objects 103 and 104. Pendlebury pointed out that the closest Egyptian parallel to the faience bowl comes from the reign of Ḥashepsowe. However, he cautiously claimed only that it was 18th Dynasty. However the Helladic ceramic period could equally well be wrong and the bowl could date from c. 1490 rather than c. 1520 BC. A still greater number of the Egyptian beads at Prosymna date to LHIII – see Brown (1974, pp. 65–9).
21. Pendlebury (1930a, pp. 23–5), objects 31–45.
22. Cline (1989). See also Warren (1969, p. 105) and Kemp and Merrillees (1980, p. 283).
23. Some of these are now on display in the Herakleion Museum. See Case 72, no. 611, and Case 75, nos. 600, 601 and 3050. Sakellerakis (1981, p. 52).
24. Case 82, no. 2409. For a bibliography, see Cline (1987, p. 32, chart D.4).
25. Ch. X, nn. 77–8.
26. Ch. X, nn. 16–17 and 81–5.
27. Cline (1987, p. 32).

28. Stubbings (1975, pp. 181–5). For the western contacts see Pålsson-Halagger (1983).
29. Gurney (1973, p. 677); Güterbock (1986, p. 40).
30. Güterbock (1986, pp. 39–40).
31. See ch. V, nn. 167–75.
32. Helck (1971, pp. 283–4); Gurney (1973, p. 677, n. 3).
33. Thucydides, I.9.
34. Strabo, XII.8.21. Pausanias, II.22.3 and V.13.7.
35. Stubbings (1973, p. 639).
36. Ridgeway (1911).
37. *Iliad*, II.104–40.
38. Pindar, *Olympian Odes*, III.23.
39. For a good short survey of this, see Thomson (1949, pp. 385–7).
40. The fragment attributed to Hesiod or Kerkops of Miletos cited in Evelyn-White (1914, p. 274) is not included in Merkelbach and West (1983, pp. 210–12). However, their frg. 204 does imply the same. See also *Odyssey*, XIX.175.
41. Evelyn-White (1914, p. xxii); Ridgeway (1911). For Xouthos see Volume 1, pp. 83–4.
42. Forrer (1924a, 1924b).
43. For this parallel, see Helck (1979, p. 300, n. 19). For the Mycenaean attestation, see Knossos C914. For up-to-date bibliographies on the 'Aḫḫiyawa question', see Bryce (1989, pp. 3–4) and Cline (forthcoming b, n. 36).
44. For a survey of the debate, see Güterbock (1983, p. 133).
45. Güterbock (1983, pp. 134; 1986, pp. 39–40).
46. Pindar *Olympian Odes*, I.24; Apollonios Rhodios II.358 and 790; Pausanias II.22.4.
47. See Güterbock (1983, p. 136).
48. Strabo, X.1.7; Sophokles, *Elektra*, 508–15; Apollodoros, *Epitome*, II.7–9; Pausanias, VIII.14.7.
49. Helck (1979, p. 300, n. 19).
50. Güterbock (1983, p. 136).
51. See Cline (forthcoming b, p. 25).
52. See Gardiner (1947, I, pp. 14–19). Another derivation of the extended form iry p't, Orpheus, is mentioned in Volume 1, pp. 71–2 and will be discussed further in Volume 4.
53. Pindar, *Olympian Odes*, I.26; Hyginus, *Fabula*, 82–3; Servius on *Aeneid*, VI.603.
54. Volume 1, pp. 358–9. The 2nd edition of this volume will contain much more on this crucial and frightening theme.
55. Nilsson (1972, p. 189).
56. See Yannai (1983, p. 113) and Bryce (1989, p. 5). Bryce maintains that the name was crossed out because of what he believes to have been the conquest of Millawanda from Aḫḫiyawa by the Hittites at that time. I

disagree with this, following the argument proposed by Singer that the
so-called 'Millawata Letter' comes from this period and indicates the
Hittite loss of control of Western Anatolia in the mid-13th century. See
ch. XII, nn. 97–8.

57. See Volume 1, p. 446, and ch. X, nn. 39 and 64.
58. Helck (1979, p. 133).
59. This part of the story is told twice in almost identical words: *Odyssey*,
XIV.272 and XVII.441.
60. *Odyssey*, XIV.275–86.
61. Lorimer (1950, p. 93). For the identification of Trš with Tyrsenoi and
Etruscan, see Gardiner (1947, I, pp. 197–8).
62. See ch. X, nn. 51–3.
63. Mee (1982, pp. 83–7). He doubts that there was a Cretan settlement at
Miletos. Mellink (1983, p. 139) believes that there was one.
64. See n. 40 above. For a discussion of the meaning of Pelasgian and why it
could be used for Danaan, see Volume 1, pp. 75–83.
65. Stubbings (1975, p. 173).
66. For the destruction, see Symeonoglou (1985, pp. 47–50). See also Stubbings (1975, p. 171).
67. See Burkert (1984, pp. 97–104) and ch. XII, n. 87, below.
68. See Pausanias, VII.1.
69. See Cline (forthcoming b). This is interpreting the six fragmentary vessels as LMIIIB, not LMIIIA2-B.
70. Lang (1966, pp. 46–8).
71. Cline (forthcoming a and b).
72. Cline (forthcoming b, n. 40).
73. References for this are given by Zaccagnini (1987, pp. 58, 64).
74. Cline (forthcoming b, n. 50).
75. Cline (forthcoming b, nn. 53–4).
76. For a detailed survey of iron objects found in Mycenaean sites before
1950, see Lorimer (1950, pp. 111–17). For an update see Varoufakis
(1982). This is not to accept the conventional wisdom that the Hittites
had a monopoly of the manufacture of iron during the Late Bronze
Age. There is considerable evidence that non-meteoric iron was in use
in Egypt at that time – see, for instance, the magnificent iron dagger
found in the tomb of Tutankhamen. The fact that we name the period
the 'Bronze' Age does not preclude the use of iron in it. If we are to
believe Mellaart's testimony, there was an iron dagger in the Dorak
Treasure which we should date to the 28th century and there is little
doubt that in Egypt the use of iron dated back to the Old Kingdom – see
Dows and Dunham (1942) and Diop (1973).
77. Cline (forthcoming b, n. 61).
78. Güterbock (1983, p. 136).
79. Yannai (1983, pp. 112–13); Cline (forthcoming b, n. 63).
80. Dayton (1982a, p. 164).
81. Stubbings (1951, p. 110) and Mellink (1983, pp. 140–1).
82. Sherratt and Crouwel (1987, p. 341).

83. See Volume 1, p. 446.
84. Sherratt and Crouwel (1987, p. 345).
85. Cline (forthcoming b, n. 67); Stubbings (1959, p. 104). Cline answers Liverani's (1987, p. 407) objections to this argument. For the Hittite dominance in North Syria after 1370 BC, see also ch. X, n. 131.
86. Drower (1975, pp. 133–9).
87. For a survey of this theory see Yannai (1983, pp. 52–6). The only archaeological evidence to suggest the presence of Greeks at Ugarit are the Mycenaean clay animal figurines, which seem to have been used as votive offerings. I have been unable to discover whether these are LHIIIA or LHIIIB. See Yannai (1983, pp. 81–3). Schaeffer does not give a ceramic date for the pottery but places them absolutely as 'late 14th or early 13th century'. This would seem to be LHIIIA according to the low chronology current in the 1930s. Against this, however, is Schaeffer's belief that the 'Mycenaean' tomb was cut in the library indicating a Greek incursion (1933, pp. 103–19).
88. Yannai (1983, p. 111).
89. Ch. X, nn. 131–2.
90. Catling (1964, p. 38).
91. Åström (1973, p. 122).
92. See Åström (1964, p. 38); Catling, Richards and Blin-Stoyle (1963, p. 111); Catling and Millet (1965, p. 219); Asaro and Perlman (1973). For the debate as a whole, see Yannai (1983, pp. 73–4).
93. Yannai (1983, p. 75).
94. Hankey (1970–1, p. 146).
95. Catling (1975, pp. 199–201).
96. See ch. X, nn. 92–8.
97. For Tanaya, see ch. X, nn. 39–65; for Ugarit, see Drower (1975, pp. 133–4); for ỉsy, see Catling (1975, pp. 203–4); for a discussion of the complications of this name, see ch. V, nn. 165–71. For Arzawa, see the Amarna Letter in Hittite to Amenōphis III, E.A. 31, 32. See also Yannai (1983, p. 127, n. 137).
98. Courtois (1973, p. 137).
99. For the Mycenaean explanation, see Taylour (1958, pp. 81–137; 1964, pp. 148–65). For a more Levantine view, see Culican (1966, pp. 42–50). For the Egyptian fleets, see ch. X, n. 86.
100. See, for instance, the Syrians painted in the tomb of Sbkḥtp from the reign of Tuthmōsis IV. Tomb 162. For a bibliography on this, see Bass (1967, p. 135, n. 1). See also Culican (1966, plate 42).
101. Grace (1956) and Sasson (1966a).
102. Bass (1967, pp. 163–7).
103. Bass (forthcoming).
104. Albright (1950, p. 327).
105. Barnett (1956, p. 214).
106. I do not accept Bass's claim that the metal trade was all one way. See below for more on Greek exports of metal.
107. For more on Canaanite jars, see below. The finding of Semitic names

for some spices in Linear A (see ch. X, n. 137) means that the naming and hence the trade must have existed well before the 14th century.

108. Bass (1967, pp. 165–6).
109. See, for instance, Cadogan (1969b) and McCann (1970).
110. Wace and Stubbings (1962, p. 543). Bass gives a substantial but incomplete bibliography of contrary views on this question (1967, p. 167, n. 41).
111. Muhly (1970b); Volume 1, p. 422.
112. Muhly (1970b, pp. 43–4).
113. See ch. X, n. 129.
114. See Volume 1, p. 427.
115. Yannai (1983, pp. 51–4).
116. See ch. X, n. 147.
117. Catling (1964, pp. 53–4); Yannai (1983, p. 55).
118. Yannai (1983, p. 61).
119. Yannai (1983, p. 60); Merrillees (1972, pp. 281–94).
120. Yannai (1983, pp. 60–70).
121. See nn. 89–92 above.
122. Hankey (1967, pp. 20–2; 1970–1, p. 146).
123. Yannai (1983, p. 103).
124. Schaeffer (1971, p. 521); Courtois (1973, p. 137); Yannai (1983, p. 102).
125. Weinstein (1989a, p. 27).
126. Bass (1987, p. 732); Weinstein (1989a, p. 24).
127. Pulak (1988, pp. 33–4).
128. E.A. 33 and E.A. 34 and 35. The 500 'talents' mentioned in E.A. 35 may well not be ingots. See Bass (1986a, pp. 293–4; 1987, p. 709) and Pulak (1988, p. 34). For Bass's denial that Alasia is Cyprus, see (1990b, pp. 19–20).
129. Pulak (1988, p. 37).
130. Bass (1990b, pp. 17–18).
131. See nn. 78 and 58–60 above.
132. For Marsa Matruh, see White (1986, pp. 76–8). For the Aeolian Islands and Sicily, see Bass (1990b, p. 17).
133. Purpura, (1981, pp. 15–35).
134. See ch. X, n. 151 and above nn. 101–10.
135. Gardiner (1947, II, p. 25).
136. Volume 1, p. 51. I have altered Thēbai to Thēbā as Thēbē is the common Homeric form. The relationship between Thēba and the West Semitic Tēbåh has been known for a long time. Hesychios, the lexicographer of the 5th or 6th century AD, wrote that Thēba 'was a city of Boiotia' and 'a chest' (kibotos). Kibotos is used to translate the tēbåh (ark) in the Noah story in the Septuagint. See Astour (1967a, p. 158, n. 2).
137. Iliad, IX, 380–4. For the attack on these lines, which are disturbing to the Aryan Model, by Heyne at Göttingen, see Volume 1, p. 478, n. 119.
138. See above, n. 25 and ch. X, nn. 77–8.
139. See ch. X, nn. 110–16.
140. See ch. X, nn. 87–8 and n. 207 below.

141. Hankey (1981).
142. Helck (1979, p. 97).
143. Strange (1980, p. 25); Cline (1987, p. 6).
144. See ch. X, nn. 109–16.
145. Cline (1987, pp. 24–6 and 30–2).
146. Cline (1987, p. 7).
147. Cline (1987, p. 1; 1990, p. 209, nn. 39–40).
148. Cline (1987, pp. 13–16).
149. Weinstein (1973, pp. 430–2).
150. Hankey (1981, p. 46).
151. Cline (1987, pp. 10–11).
152. Giveon (1978a, nos. 3–4, plates 54, and 2–4).
153. Cline (1990, pp. 208–9, nn. 35–40).
154. Diodoros, I.29, 1–5. The scholiast Aristeides, XIII.95, also calls Erechtheus Egyptian but seems to be confusing him with Kekrops. See Tzetzes, *Lykophron* 111. The Greek scholar Alexandra Lambropoulou (1988, pp. 77–8) derives the name from the Egyptian Ḥr-ȝḫty or Ḥr-ȝḫti (Horus of the Horizon). These issues will be discussed further in Volumes 3 and 4.
155. Apollodoros, III.14.7. For a thorough but thoroughly Aryanist discussion of these sources, see Burton (1972, pp. 124–5). Astour (1967a, p. 343) identifies the name Pandion with the Linear B Padijo and hence with the Ugaritic names Pdy, Padiya or Pdyn from the common Semitic root *padâ* (ransom, redeem).
156. See ch. III, n. 128.
157. See letter quoted in Cline (1990, p. 209, n. 42).
158. Gale (1980, pp. 178, 180–1). He also cites Buchholz (1972) and Stos-Gale and Gale (1982).
159. Gale (1980, p. 178).
160. Dayton (1982a, pp. 159, 164).
161. Dayton (1982a, p. 166).
162. Vercoutter (1956, p. 139, doc. 41; pp. 89–90, doc. 19).
163. See ch. IV, n. 23.
164. Pulak (1988, p. 8).
165. Catling (1964, p. 271); Bass (1986a, pp. 294–5); Maddin, Wheeler and Muhly (1977, p. 46).
166. Pulak (1988, p. 9).
167. Muhly (1979b, p. 95).
168. Pulak (1988, p. 36).
169. See n. 161 above.
170. See Harding (1984, pp. 261–6).
171. See Bernal (1990, pp. 35–40).
172. For a map of this, see Bass (1987, pp. 697–8). See also Bass (1986a, 1986b), Pulak (1988) and Knapp and Stech (1985). Bass does not mention the wheat from Egypt or the lead and silver from Greece.
173. McGready (1968, pp. 252–3); see also Hemmerdinger (1968). Hbni

may be a loan into Egyptian from some other African language. *Kytisos,* a false ebony probably found in the Linear B *kuteso,* is also generally acknowledged to be a loan into Greek from an African language. See Lucas and Harris (1962, p. 434) and Brown (1975, p. 143). However, no Egyptian etymon has been found.

174. Chantraine (1968–75, p. 338). Nineteenth-century scholars were divided on this. See Muss-Arnolt (1892, p. 93).

175. See Laroche (1965). Chantraine (1968–75, p. 338) points out that the Hittite form *laḫpas* is also a loan. See also the discussion in Masson (1967, pp. 80–3). In deriving *elephas* from the Semitic *alpu* Laroche was following a long tradition that goes back as far as Bochart. See Hemmerdinger (1970, p. 52). The possibility that the Hittite animating suffix *-nt* and several Greek finals *-nthos* come from the Egyptian *nṯr* (divine or living) will be discussed in Volume 3.

176. Chantraine (1968–75, p. 338).

177. Muss-Arnolt (1892, p. 93).

178. Muss-Arnolt (1892, p. 92, n. 3).

179. Lewy (1895, p. 81).

180. Maccarrone (1939, p. 102).

181. Maccarrone (1939, p. 102).

182. Chantraine does not put *artos* and *artuō* in the same family.

183. Pisani, p. 141. Georgacas (1957, p. 115).

184. Hubschmid *Sardische Studien;* see Georgacas (1957, p. 115).

185. Ventris and Chadwick (1973, p. 535).

186. Gardiner (1957, p. 198, § 266.1).

187. Szemerényi (1960) does not mention it in his comprehensive studies of Indo-European numbers.

188. See Brown (1975, p. 143). For the possibility of cotton production in Egypt this early, see Volume 3.

189. Bass (1987, p. 728) points out that this was not the wood we now call ebony but *Dalbergia melanoxylon* (African blackwood), which is what the Egyptians called *hbnì.* See also n. 173 above.

190. For a brief discussion and bibliography on the ancient slave trade with a special reference to the Phoenician role in it, see Bernal (1989a, pp. 18–26).

191. Genesis 41. 57.

192. Nougayrol (1957, p. 165).

193. Astour (1967a, p. 348).

194. Heltzer (1978, p. 119).

195. Heltzer (1978, p. 100).

196. See Singer (1983b).

197. Singer (1983b, pp. 4–5).

198. Diodoros I.29. For a bibliography of arguments as to whether this story dated from the 6th or the 4th century, see Brown (1975, p. 149, n. 23). I see no reason to doubt that the overall tradition, if not the specifics, dated back to the Bronze Age. Erechtheus, whom a significant tradition

considered to be Egyptian, was supposed – according to the Parian Marble – to have reigned around 1400 BC, which was in fact a high point of Egyptian contact with the Aegean. See *Schol. Aristides*, XIII.95, and Burton (1972, pp. 124–5).

199. Bintliff (1977, pt. 1, p. 51).

200. See Bernal (1989a, p. 23).

201. For the glass ingots found on the Ulu Burun ship and their plausible Levantine origin, see Bass (1987, pp. 716–17) and Pulak (1988, p. 14). Dayton (1982b) argues that the cobalt blue colouring of much of the glass came from Schneeberg in Bohemia and that it was first manufactured in Mycenaean Greece. Linear B tablets record the presence of *kuwanokoi* (glass paste workers) in Mycenae (see Pollinger-Foster, 1979, pp. 10–11). Nevertheless, the Greek tradition clearly associated lapis lazuli and its manufactured imitation, faience, as coming from Egypt or possibly Phoenicia. Theophrastos, *De Lapidibus*, 55. The Greek word for blue glass, *kyano – kuwano* in Linear B – is clearly cognate to the Hittite *ku(wa)nan*, the Akkadian *uqnu* and the Ugaritic *iqnu*. However, this is simply a general word for lapis lazuli and its imitation, which is interestingly not present in Egyptian. Thus, while there is no doubt that blue glass was widely used in Egypt and this may well have led to its having been associated with it, it is much more likely that it was first manufactured in Phoenicia or possibly in Greece.

202. Austin (1970, pp. 35–7). The speeches of Demosthenes refer only to grain coming to Athens from the Black Sea and not that coming from Egypt. This absence can be explained by the second Persian occupation of Egypt 343–332 BC.

203. Brown (1975, p. 143).

204. Renfrew (1972, pp. 232–3).

205. For a survey of this, see Ventris and Chadwick (1973, pp. 236–8).

206. For references on Egyptian exports of wheat to Greece in Classical times, see Austin (1970, pp. 35–7) and Brown (1975, pp. 149–50).

207. For the relationships between *ꜥnḫ* and *ꜥnḫt* and between life and victuals in other cultures, see Ember (1917, p. 89).

208. Bass (1990b, p. 16).

209. Cline (forthcoming a). See also n. 72 above.

210. See n. 146 above.

211. Yannai (1983, p. 59).

212. See Hankey (1967) and the chart at the end of Cline (forthcoming b).

213. Ch. X, n. 120.

214. See Blegen (1937, pp. 255–9); Mylonas (1956, pp. 119–25); French (1971, p. 142) and Yannai (1983, p. 82). Fragments of a Levantine flask with legs and a Canaanite jar have been found at Pseira, off the coast of Northeast Crete from LMIB, but Canaanite pottery is found far more frequently in LMII and LMIII contexts. See Lambrou-Phillipson (1990, p. 6).

215. French (1971, p. 131) quoted in Yannai (1983, p. 83).

216. Yannai (1983, pp. 82–3).
217. Yannai (1983, p. 68).
218. Ch. II, nn. 185–93 and ch. VI, nn. 17–21.
219. Ch. VI, n. 21.
220. Ch. II, nn. 185–93; ch. VI, nn. 19–21.
221. For a bibliography on these, see Yannai (1983, p. 123, n. 83a).
222. Renfrew (1978, plates 4a and b).
223. See Negbi (1976) and Seeden (1980). *Pace* Canby (1969).
224. Webster (1958, p. 11) argues for the phrase being taken literally. Astour (1967a, p. 359, n. 2) denies this.
225. Buchholz (1967, pp. 148–50, 157, n. 55).
226. For the jars, see Grace (1956), Sasson (1966a), Åkerström (1975) and Yannai (1983, pp. 66–7). For the Thera Canaanite jar, see ch. IX, n. 115.
227. Vermeule (1964, p. 255).
228. Yannai (1983, pp. 66–7).
229. For a bibliography on the recent Cretan finds see Lambrou-Phillipson (1990, p. 6). For other recent discoveries of Canaanite jars in the Aegean see Shaw (1981, p. 246). For Kaş see Bass (1987, pp. 708–9); Pulak (1988, pp. 10–11).
230. Bass (1987, pp. 726–7).
231. For the Zakro tusk, see the Herakleion Museum Case 113.
232. Vermeule (1964, p. 218).
233. Yannai (1983, pp. 63–4).
234. Yannai (1983, p. 64).
235. Poursat (1977, pp. 244–6). Poursat follows Furumark to take LHIIIB as beginning in 1300 BC. Thus what he sees as 13th-century developments I see as developments of the 14th *and* 13th centuries.

Chapter XII
THE HEROIC END TO THE HEROIC AGE

1. See ch. VII, nn. 151–2.
2. See Volume 1, pp. 445–50.
3. See ch. XI, nn. 59–62.
4. Ch. VII, n. 42 and nn. 148–56.
5. Hallo (1977, p. 58).
6. Buchholz (1967, pp. 151, 159).
7. Yannai (1983, p. 63).
8. Buchholz (1967, pp. 152–8); Yannai (1983, p. 120).
9. See ch. III, nn. 13–21.
10. The etymology from *kekasmai* (excel) proposed by Vian (1963, pp. 154–7), though not as good as that from *qdm*, is possible semantically but far weaker phonetically. Astour (1967a, pp. 147–52) gives a fascinating portrait of the contortions of Aryanist scholars to avoid the obvious but unwelcome evidence for Kadmos' Semitic connections. For these, see ch. II, nn. 6 and 143.

11. Europe, the western continent, as well as its eponym Europa, comes from ʿrb but this time, in contrast to the etymology of erebos discussed in ch. II, n.87, from the Canaanite infinitive construct form ʿărôb: Astour (1967a, p. 130). There will be further discussion of the Boiotian cult of Europa in Volume 4.

12. This comes from Ovid, Metamorphoses, II.836–52. For a detailed discussion of the various variants of this legendary cycle and its treatment by 19th- and 20th-century scholars, see Edwards (1979, pp. 17–86).

13. Volume 1, pp. 85–6.

14. For the gates, see Symeonoglou (1985, pp. 32–8). For the sphinx, see the larnax in the Thebes Museum no. 14.

15. Edwards (1979, p. 173, n.185). I believe that this holds true even if one begins LHIIIB in 1370 rather than 1275 BC.

16. Edwards (1979, p. 105, n.105).

17. See ch. II, n.228.

18. Bochart (1646, II.17). Philo, History, 809:14 (Baumgarten, 1981, pp. 184–6). See also Astour (1967a, p. 216). Astour also suggests the alternative that the name simply comes from ʿēly, an epithet of Baʿal. See also Genesis 14. 18.

19. See Pausanias, IX.8.5. See, further, Symeonoglou (1985, p. 125).

20. Philo, History, 809:14 (Baumgarten, 1981, pp. 184–6); Astour (1967a, p. 155). This cult and its Egyptian and Phoenician roots will be discussed in more detail in Volume 4. The Semitic etymology of Kabiroi has been known at least since the time of Scaliger (1565, p. 146). George Eliot's Mr. Casaubon knew of the 'Cabiri' (Middlemarch, ch. 20). She learnt about the Semitic etymology from her friend Mark Pattison – from whom she took the name Casaubon itself. Pattison had written biographies of both Scaliger and Isaac Casaubon. See Hertz (1985, pp. 75–96) and La Capra (1987, pp. 56–82). This is also discussed in Volume I, p. 483, n. 113. For Aryanist attempts to disconnect the Kabiroi from Phoenicia, see Edwards (1979, p. 81, n.75).

21. Bérard (1902–3, II, pp. 411–16). See also Astour (1967a, p. 214). I do not find Astour's etymologies for Zēthos, Dirkē, Asōpos, Tanagra or Gephyroi semantically tight enough to be convincing.

22. See ch. III, nn.77–94.

23. See ch. X, n.96.

24. For the Theban Linear B, see Chadwick (1969), Olivier (1971) and Godart and Sacconi (1978). For the alphabetic inscriptions, see Herodotos, V.59–61. For arguments in favour of the widespread use of the alphabet in Greece in the Late Bronze Age, see Bernal (1990, pp. 53–70).

25. Parian Marble L1.12–15.

26. Jacoby (1923–9, IIB, p. 250, frg. 4.8).

27. Bérard (1952, pp. 7–8). See also Edwards (1979, p. 167).

28. See Ullman (1927, p. 326) and Diringer (1968, p. 358). Edwards and Edwards (1974) have shown that this date does not go back to Eratosthenes but merely to the 19th century.

29. See n.45 below.

30. See ch. IX, nn. 148–84.
31. For the establishment and maintenance of this ultra low dating, see Bernal (1990, pp. 7–15).
32. Jacoby (1923–9, IA, p. 1, frg. 20). See also Edwards (1979, p. 66). For the relationships among the different traditions, see Edwards (1979, p. 268) and Dörpfeld (1935, II, pp. 401–4).
33. See Bernal (1990, pp. 38–52).
34. Apollodoros, II.14–4.8 and III.4.1–5.5–8. For a clear survey of this confused situation, see Edwards (1979, p. 166).
35. Herodotos, I.2, II.49, IV.45; Euripides, *The Phoenician Women*, 639, etc. For other references, see Edwards (1979, p. 47, n. 50).
36. See Katzenstein (1973, pp. 18–20).
37. Herodotos, II.44. For Lloyd's reasons for accepting Herodotos' statement, see (1976, pp. 206–7).
38. Friedrich (1923, p. 4); Albright (1950, p. 165); Harris (1939, p. 40); Moran (1961, p. 59).
39. *Iliad*, VI.290, XXIII.743; *Odyssey*, IV.84, 618, XIII.326, XV.118, 425; Joshua 13. 4, 6; Judges 3. 3; I Kings 5.6.
40. See Euripides, *Bacchae*, 171 and 1025, *Phrixos*, frg. 819, and Isokrates, X.68. See Edwards (1979, p. 47, n. 50) for other references. See also Garbini (1979, p. 54).
41. See Herodotos, II.44, for Thasos. For a sceptical view of Phoenician influence there, see Lloyd (1976, pp. 207–11). Neither he nor Birgitta Berquist, whose monograph on Thasos was published in 1973, refer to the article by Denis Van Berchem, who sets the cult of Herakles at Thasos firmly in a Phoenician context. See Van Berchem (1967, pp. 88–109). For Membliaros, see ch. VII, nn. 85–93.
42. For a general study of the whole mythological tangle, see Edwards (1979, pp. 23–32).
43. See Diodoros, I.23; Konon, in Jacoby (1923–9, IA, p. 26, frg. 1); Kharax of Pergamon, in Jacoby (1923–9, IIA, p. 103, frg. 14); Nonnos, *Dionysiaka*, IV.265–70; Tzetzes *Scholia to Lykophron*, 1206; *Scholia to Euripides Phoenissae*, 638; Hyginus, *Fabulae*, 277. See also Edwards (1979, p. 48, n. 51).
44. Jacoby (1923–9, IIIB, p. 532, frg. 1B-C). See also Diodoros, V.58.
45. Volume 1, pp. 88–98; ch. IX, this volume, nn. 227 and 228.
46. Volume 1, p. 109.
47. Ch. III, nn. 73–100 and 138.
48. Vermeule (1964, p. 239); Stubbings (1973, pp. 637–8); Huxley (1961, p. 37); Astour (1967a, pp. 220–4). For a full bibliography on this, see Edwards (1979, pp. 167–9).
49. See ch. XI, n. 136.
50. For the labiovelars and their breakdown, see Volume 1, pp. 56–8, and Bernal (1989b, pp. 35–6). This problem will be discussed in more detail in Volume 3.
51. Szemerényi (1966b, p. 29).

52. See ch. X, nn. 92–8.
53. Lejeune (1972, pp. 46–7).
54. Ventris and Chadwick (1973, p. 389).
55. Lejeune (1958, p. 302) and *pace* Szemerényi (1966b, p. 35).
56. Ventris and Chadwick (1973, p. 386).
57. *Pace* Szemerényi (1966b, p. 29).
58. Lejeune (1972, p. 51).
59. See Bernal (1987, 1990).
60. Bernal (1987, p. 14; 1990, pp. 115–6). The preference for *ṭet* and *quph* over *tav* and *kaph* is also influenced by the fact that, according to the rule of *begadkephat*, the latter are spirantized in many contexts and therefore not such accurate representations of the stops.
61. See Bernal (1987, pp. 13–14; 1990, pp. 115–16).
62. *Odyssey*, XI.262–4. See ch. II, n. 212.
63. Pausanias, IX.5.1.
64. *The Phoenician Women*, 231–46, trans. Vellacott (1972, pp. 243–4).
65. *The Phoenician Women*, 638–82, trans. Vellacott (1972, pp. 259–60).
66. For a bibliography of this, see Symeonoglou (1985, p. 289, site 191).
67. See Fontenrose (1966b, p. 189), Sasson (1966a, p. 135, n. 53), Hammond (1967, p. 654) and Hemmerdinger (1966, p. 698; 1967).
68. Lambrou-Phillipson (1987, p. 6). See also Porada (1981, p. 4).
69. Lambrou-Phillipson (1987, pp. 7–8).
70. Lambrou-Phillipson (1987, p. 8). For the Levantine craft, see Winter (1976).
71. Lambrou-Phillipson (1987, p. 8). See also Symeonoglou (1985, pp. 231–2, site 4). For the iron, see ch. XI, n. 76.
72. Porada (1981, pp. 9–29).
73. Porada (1981, pp. 46–9).
74. Porada (1981, pp. 36–46).
75. Porada (1981, pp. 49–66).
76. For the Kassite conquest of Babylonia, see ch. VIII, nn. 64 and 93. For unsatisfactory speculations about their name and origins, see ch. VI, nn. 69 and 78–9.
77. E.A. 2. Knudtzon (1915, pp. 88–9, l. 43). Porada actually accepted low datings for both of these rulers. Given the general fate of 2nd-millennium low dating in the face of evidence from carbon 14 and dendrochronology – and what this reveals about Middle European scholarly tendencies – as well as difficulties it would make for the dating of the Trojan War, I think it is better to stick with the conventional dating of the *Cambridge Ancient History* here.
78. Porada (1981, p. 68, n. 175).
79. Porada (1981, p. 70).
80. Porada (1981, p. 69, n. 180).
81. See ch. XI, n. 78.
82. See ch. XI, n. 80.
83. See ch. XI, n. 56.

84. Symeonoglou (1985, pp. 67 and 227).
85. Symeonoglou (1973, p. 21).
86. Buck (1979, p. 40).
87. See Aischylos, *Seven Against Thebes*, Sophokles, *Electra, Antigone* and *Oidipos at Colonos*, and Euripides, *The Phoenician Women*. Burkert (1984, pp. 100–2), following a number of German sceptics, doubts that Late Bronze Age Thebes had seven gates. However, the existence of the Homeric epithet of *heptapylio* (Seven-Gated Thebes) in Homer, *Iliad*, 4.406 and *Odyssey*, 11.263, strengthens the position of the Greek archaeologists, who see seven gates in the remains of Late Bronze Age Thebes. (See the bibliography in Burkert [1984, p. 100, n.6] and Symeonoglou [1985, pp. 34–8].) Burkert's doubts seem reasonable, however, when he questions the historicity of the seven heroes who were supposed to have attacked the city, one for each gate, and shows the parallels of these stories with Mesopotamian legends of the seven 'heroic plagues' led by Erra. For Erra, see ch. II, n.170. Indeed, I would go further and link the seven plagues heroes to the seven underground Kabiroi – see n.20 above. On the other hand, I see no reason to doubt that there were two sieges of Thebes in the 13th century BC and that some of the seven were historical figures.
88. See ch. V, nn.164–6, and ch. VI, nn.102 and 138–40.
89. See ch. X, nn.111–12.
90. Korfmann (1986, pp. 27–8); Vermeule (1986, pp. 87–8).
91. Güterbock (1986, p. 36); Mellink (1986a, p. 96).
92. For a recent discussion of the identification of these names, see Güterbock (1986, pp. 35, 41–3).
93. Güterbock (1986, p. 35) puts it about 1280 BC. I follow the chronology of the *Cambridge Ancient History* here against the enthusiasts for low dating. This is what Mellink (1986a, p. 93) does in this case.
94. Güterbock (1986, p. 36).
95. See ch. XI, nn.30, 44, and 51.
96. Helck (1971, pp. 195–8); Mellink (1986a, pp. 96–7).
97. Güterbock (1986, p. 38).
98. Singer (1983a, p. 215).
99. For Arzawa, see ch. XI, n.97, and, for W3iwry, see ch. X, nn.111–12.
100. Vermeule (1986, p. 88). The difficulty with this scheme is that it is in this period that we have the Egyptian documentary evidence.
101. See Güterbock (1986, p. 36).
102. See ch. XI, n.50. For a bibliography of the scholars preferring the earlier dating, see Singer (1983a, p. 210, n.3).
103. For the references to war and peace, see Güterbock (1986, p. 37).
104. Laroche (1966, p. 26); Watkins (1986, p. 57).
105. Laroche (1966, pp. 325, 364); Watkins (1986, p. 57).
106. Watkins (1986, p. 57).
107. Laroche (1966, p. 325); Georgiev (1972, p. 7).
108. See ch. XI, n.192.

109. *Iliad*, II.820–78.
110. Furumark (1941).
111. Blegen *et al.* (1950–8, III, pp. 386–8).
112. See Korfmann (1986, p. 27). Korfmann deals with the ultra low dating of Podzuweit (1982).
113. Wood (1987, pp. 224–31).
114. Finley *et al.* (1964).
115. See ch. XI, n.61.
116. Gordon (1955; 1962b, pp. 132–55).
117. Vermeule (1986, pp. 85–91).
118. Watkins (1986, p. 58).
119. Kirk (1985, pp. 168–70).
120. *Iliad*, II.504.
121. See ch. II, n.22.
122. Thucydides, I.12.
123. See, for instance, Snodgrass (1971, p. 300).
124. Fossey (1989b).
125. This will be discussed in more detail in Volume 3.
126. *Iliad*, IV.370–410.
127. Hesiod, *Works and Days*, 156–66, trans. Evelyn-White (1914, p. 15).
128. Volume 1, p. 446.
129. It is possible that the Hittite monarchy lingered on for two more decades but there is no doubt that its power was broken.
130. Bass (1967, pp. 163–7).
131. Charles (1965); Yannai (1983, p. 58).
132. Vermeule (1964, pp. 302–3).
133. Hesiod, *Works and Days*, 156–66, and Thucydides, I.12.
134. See Shrimpton (1987, pp. 149–50).
135. Bintliff (1977, I, p. 115); Cherry (1985, pp. 20–8).
136. Desborough (1964, esp. p. 226; 1975, pp. 658–71); Kilian (1985). See also the bibliography in Shrimpton (1987, pp. 154–55, n. 1).
137. See ch. XI, nn. 191–9.
138. See ch. VII, nn. 151–4.

GLOSSARY

Abkhaz
: A language belonging to the Northwest Caucasian linguistic family and ethnic group living along the Black Sea coast to the west of Georgia.

Afroasiatic
: Otherwise known as Hamito-Semitic, a linguistic superfamily consisting of a number of language families including **Berber,** Chadic, **Egyptian, Semitic** and East, South and Central Cushitic.

Akkadian
: The **Semitic** language of ancient Mesopotamia, heavily influenced by and influencing **Sumerian.** It was replaced by **Aramaic** around the middle of the 1st millennium BC.

Anatolia
: Ancient region, more or less coextensive with modern Turkey.

Anatolian
: The **Indo-Hittite** but non–**Indo-European** languages of Anatolia. They include **Hittite,** Palaic, Luvian, **Lycian, Lydian** and probably **Carian** and **Etruscan.**

Aramaic
: A West Semitic language, originally spoken in parts of what is now Syria, that became the lingua franca of the **Assyrian, Neo-Babylonian** and much of the **Persian** empires. It replaced the **Canaanite** dialects of **Phoenician** and **Hebrew** in the East Mediterranean in the middle of the 1st millennium BC. It was in its turn replaced by Greek and Arabic.

Archaic Greece Greek historical period from the first Olympic
                Games in 776 BC to the beginning of the **Clas-
                sical Age** around 500 BC.
Armenian   Indo-European language of an ancient people
                of Eastern Anatolia. It is sometimes supposed
                to be especially close to Greek. However, as
                the earliest surviving texts go back to only the
                4th century AD, the similarities may be the re-
                sult of Greek influence or common contacts
                with Semitic.
Aryan   Term used to describe the speakers of the
                Indo-Iranian branch of the **Indo-European**
                language family. They appear to have invaded
                Iran and India in the first half of the 2nd mil-
                lennium BC. In the late 19th century AD the
                term came to be used for the Indo-European
                'race' as a whole.
Assyria   An ancient kingdom in Northern Mesopota-
                mia dating back to the middle of the 3rd mil-
                lennium. Its greatest periods were at the end
                of the 2nd millennium and between 900 and
                600 BC. Its language was originally a dialect of
                Akkadian.
autochthonous   Native or aboriginal.
Axial Age   The period between 700 and 500 BC in which
                it is believed, by some, that Greeks, Israelites,
                Iranians, Indians and Chinese made the re-
                ligious, philosophical and scientific break-
                throughs that led to the modern age.
Babylon   Ancient city in South-Central Mesopotamia.
                Seat of several important kingdoms and finally
                of the Neo-Babylonian Empire between 600
                and 538 BC.
Berber   The languages spoken by the original inhabi-
                tants of Northwest Africa. They are still spoken
                from the Western Desert in Egypt to Morocco.
Besserwissen The German for 'knowing better', a scholarly
                approach based on the belief that the 'science'
                and alleged 'historical method' of 19th- and
                20th-century historians make their conclusions
                categorically superior to those of Ancient
                writers.
Bohairic   **Coptic** dialect originally spoken in the Western
                Delta, later standard throughout Christian
                Egypt.
Book of Coming Commonly known as *Book of the Dead*. Com-
Forth by Day   pilation of prayers, spells and instructions to

guide the soul of the dead person through the journey of the afterlife.

Byblos · Ancient port city in what is now Southern Lebanon. In close touch with Egypt since the 4th millennium, it was the most important Levantine city until it was eclipsed by the rise of **Sidon** at the end of the 2nd millennium.

byname · A subsidiary name.

calque · The literal borrowing of an expression or idiom from another language.

Canaanite · A Semitic language, heavily influenced by Egyptian, spoken in Southern Syro-Palestine between 1500 and 500 BC, when it was displaced by **Aramaic. Phoenician** and **Hebrew** are the best-known later Canaanite dialects. 'Canaanite' is also used to describe the material culture of Southern Syro-Palestine in the Late Bronze Age c. 1500–1100 BC.

Caria · Region in Southwest Anatolia. Its language was probably **Anatolian** but may have been non–**Indo-Hittite.** Alphabetic inscriptions in Carian date from the 6th century BC.

ceramic period · A period of time reconstructed by archaeologists on the basis of pottery styles.

Chaldaean · A name used in the 8th century BC to describe a people from the South of Mesopotamia. It was later used for the whole of Mesopotamia and its language between 500 BC and 500 AD was usually known as **Aramaic.**

Classical Greece · Greece in the 5th and 4th centuries BC, the period which is generally held to have seen the greatest and 'purest' products of Greek genius.

Colchis · Ancient country at the eastern end of the Black Sea in the present **Georgia** and **Abkhazia.**

Common Era · Term used by non-Christians in general, and Jews in particular, to avoid the sectarianism of the term AD, Anno Domini.

Coptic · The language and culture of Christian Egypt. Spoken until the 15th or 16th centuries AD, it remains the liturgical language of Egyptian Christians. Written in the Greek alphabet, with some additional letters derived from **Demotic,** it is the latest form of the Egyptian language.

cuneiform · A script system developed in Mesopotamia in which nail-shaped wedges were pressed into wet clay.

Dark Ages (Christian) · Name conventionally given to the period after the fall of the Western Roman Empire in the 5th century AD and before the Middle Ages which are generally seen as beginning in the 9th or 10th.

Dark Ages (Greek) Name given to the period of Greek history after the fall of the Mycenaean palaces in the 12th century BC and before the rise of **Archaic Greece** in the 8th.

Demotic Strictly speaking, Demotic is the script derived from **Hieroglyphic** and **Hieratic,** used in Egypt after the 7th century BC. The word is also used to describe the language of this period.

dendrochronology The method of determining the age of wood and its archaeological context by counting tree rings.

dentals Consonants formed with the tongue against the teeth, as, for example, d and t.

determinative Element in the hieroglyphic representation signifying the meaning of a word as opposed to its sound.

diffusionism The belief that cultural characteristics can be transmitted from one culture to another.

Diodoros Sikeliotes Greek historian from Sicily, $c.$ 80–20 BC, known for his *Library of History.*

Dorians A Greek tribe originating from Northwestern Greece who overran much of Southern Greece in the 12th century BC. The most famous Dorian state was Sparta.

Dravidian Independent language family which extended in ancient times from Southern India to Eastern Mesopotamia. It was probably the language of the civilization of **Harappa.** The best-known members of the family are Tamil and Telugu, which still flourish in Southern India, and **Elamite,** the language of the ancient Elamite civilization.

Early Helladic **Ceramic period** applied to Mainland Greece in the Early Bronze Age $c.$ 3300–2000 BC.

Early Minoan **Ceramic period** in Crete in the Early Bronze Age, $c.$ 3300–2000 BC.

Ebla An ancient Syrian city first excavated in the 1970s. It had a massive trading network and empire throughout Syro-Palestine, around 2500 BC.

Eblaite The language of **Ebla,** an independent Semitic

language that can usefully be seen as a predecessor of **Canaanite.**

Egyptian   This is is often used to refer, not to the Arabic dialect spoken in Egypt today but to the language of Ancient Egypt, which was an independent **Afroasiatic** language. It is subdivided into Old Egyptian, spoken during the Old Kingdom from *c.* 3400 to 2400 BC, and Middle Egyptian, spoken during the Middle Kingdom from 2200 to 1750 BC, which remained the official language for the next fifteen hundred years. When 'Egyptian' is used without epithet it usually refers to this. Late Egyptian was spoken by the 16th century, but it was not commonly used in writing until the end of the millennium. It was, I argue, Late Egyptian that had the greatest influence on Greek. For the later stages, **Demotic** and **Coptic,** see above.

Elam   Ancient civilization in the East of Mesopotamia from the 4th millennium to *c.* 300 BC.

Elamite   The language of Elam, belonging to the **Dravidian** language family.

epiclesis   Surname or additional name.

Eratosthenes   *c.* 275–195 BC. Greek scholar and librarian of the great library at Alexandria. The first Greek to calculate the circumference and tilt of the Earth.

Ethiopia   Name given by the Ancient Greeks to two regions inhabited by Black people. One approximated to **Elam,** and the other, much better known, was the African territory south of Egypt.

Ethiopic   Name of a number of branches of the Semitic language family spoken in **Ethiopia.** These include Ge'ez, the ancient church language; Amharic, the national language of Ethiopia today; and the Gurage languages, some of which appear to exhibit the most archaic forms of any Semitic language.

Etruscan   Civilization of ancient Italy. The predominant view in Antiquity was that the Etruscans came from **Lydia** in Northwest Anatolia. The language – which is not well understood – could well be **Anatolian.** A very closely related language has been found on inscriptions from the nearby island of **Lemnos. Etruscan** seems to have been heavily influenced by Phoenician civilization from the 9th to the 6th centuries BC. It was itself a central influence in the formation of Latin culture.

Eudoxos Greek astronomer and mathematician from Knidos on the Anatolian coast. Studied in Egypt. Born *c.* 400, died *c.* 350 BC.

euhemerism Doctrine of **Euhemeros** according to which what were commonly worshipped as gods were actually deified heroes. By extension the word has been used in modern times to mean the explanation or reduction of religious beliefs in rational terms.

Euhemeros Philosopher of around 300 BC.

genetic A 'genetic' relationship between languages is one in which they are supposed to come from a single ancestor. For example, French and Romanian have a 'genetic' relationship because, for all their differences, both derive from the Vulgar Latin spoken in the Roman army.

Georgian People who have inhabited the Central Caucasus since earliest times. The Georgian language belongs to the **Kartvelian** language family.

Han Chinese dynasty that succeeded the **Qin** in 206 BC and lasted until 220 AD.

Harappa The names of this site or another, Mohenjo Daro, are used for the ancient civilization that flourished in Northwest India from *c.* 2500 to 1700 BC, when it was destroyed, probably by the invading **Aryans** from the north. The writing of this civilization has not been deciphered, but it is likely that its language belonged to the **Dravidian** language family dominant today in South India and still spoken in pockets in Western Pakistan.

Hatti Ancient name for a territory in Central Anatolia. The homeland of the **Hittites.**

Hebrew **Canaanite** dialect spoken in the kingdoms of Israel, Judah and Moab between 1500 and 500 BC. For religious reasons it is often treated as a distinct language.

Helladic Name given to three **ceramic periods** on Mainland Greece, roughly approximating to the **Minoan ceramic periods** in Crete.

Hellenic Greek or Greek-speaking, but particularly as-

	sociated with Thessaly in Northern Greece. Since the late 18th century, the word has gained many connotations of nobility and of northern and Aryan 'blood'.
Hellenistic	The name given to Greek culture throughout the East Mediterranean from the conquests of Alexander the Great in the late 4th century BC until the incorporation of the region into the Roman Empire in the 1st century BC.
Hellespont	Strait linking the Mediterranean and Black Seas and dividing Asia from Europe.
Herodotos	Earliest Greek historian from Halikarnassos in Asia Minor, born *c.* 485 BC, died *c.* 425 BC.
Hesiod	Greek poet from Boiotia of the 10th century BC, most famous for his **Theogony.**
Hieratic	Egyptian script gradually developed from **Hieroglyphic** about 2700 BC. It changed the formal pictorial Hieroglyphic into a cursive script that was still based on the same principles.
Hieroglyphic	Egyptian script first attested in the late 4th millennium. It is made up of phonetic signs for letters, double letters, triple letters and 'determinatives' which indicate the category of the word's meaning.
Hittite	Empire in Central **Anatolia** during the 2nd millennium BC. Its language was an **Anatolian** one and was written earlier in a form of cuneiform and later in its own hieroglyphic system.
Hurrian	Name of a people who lived in Syria and Eastern Anatolia in the 3rd and 2nd millenniums BC. Their extinct language, like that of **Urartu,** belongs to the linguistic family now represented by the Northeast Caucasian languages. It was neither **Afroasiatic** nor **Indo-Hittite.** The most important Hurrian-speaking state was that of Mitanni, which flourished in Western Mesopotamia and Northern Syria in the second half of the 2nd millennium BC.
Hyksos	These were invaders from the northeast, who dominated Egypt between *c.* 1725 and *c.* 1575 BC. The bulk of the Hyksos spoke a West Semitic language, but they seem also to have contained **Hurrian** and possibly Indo-Aryan speakers.
Indo-European	Language family including all European lan-

guages – except for Basque, Finnish and Hungarian – the Iranian and North Indian languages and **Tokharian.** Although **Phrygian** and **Armenian** were situated in **Anatolia,** they are Indo-European languages not **Anatolian** ones.

Indo-Hittite
A language superfamily including both the **Anatolian** and **Indo-European** families.

inflected languages
Languages like Greek, Latin and German that rely to a great extent on the inflection or changing word shapes or morphology to convey meaning.

interdentals
Consonants formed by putting the tongue between the teeth, as in *th*.

Ionians
Central and Southern Greek people who survived the **Dorian** conquest, some of whom migrated to the western coast of **Anatolia.**

isolating languages
Languages like Chinese and English that have relatively little inflection but rely heavily on syntax or the positioning of words in a sentence.

isolationism
The belief that cultures cannot be fundamentally affected from elsewhere.

Kartvelian
A Caucasian language family of which the best known member is **Georgian.**

Kassites
A people from the mountains to the east of Mesopotamia, who conquered the whole region in the late 18th century BC and held it until the second half of the 13th.

Kekrops
Legendary founder and king of Athens. He was generally portrayed as **autochthonous,** although a minority tradition saw him as coming from Egypt. Some evidence supporting the latter will be given in Volume 3.

labials
Consonants formed with the lips: *b, p, m,* and so on.

labiovelars
Velars completed with a rounding of the lips, as for instance in our *qu-*.

laryngeals
Sounds made in the larynx or throat as a whole; more precisely they can be divided into velar fricatives – *ḫ* and *ġ* – pharyngeals – *ḥ* and ʿ – and the laryngeals in the narrow sense – ʾ and *h*. All of these, except for *ġ*, exist throughout Semitic and **Egyptian,** but all except *h* have disappeared from **Indo-European.**

Late Helladic or Mycenaean
Ceramic period in Mainland Greece from *c.* 1675–1100 BC.

Late Minoan	**Ceramic period** in Crete from *c*. 1675–1450 BC when the island became dominated by Greeks.
lead isotope analysis	The measurement of the proportion of radioactive isotopes in lead, from which it is possible to determine the geological age of a lead deposit and hence the origin of lead objects.
Lemnos	Island in the Northwest Aegean where a non–Indo-European language related to **Etruscan** was spoken in Classical times.
Linear A	**Syllabary** used in Crete and elsewhere before the establishment of Greek on the island.
Linear B	**Syllabary** derived from a prototype of **Linear A,** attested from about 1400 BC but probably written long before that date.
liquids	Consonants like *l* and *r* which flow.
Lycia	Region in Southern **Anatolia.** The Lycian language was **Anatolian** and was an indirect descendant of **Hittite.** Alphabetic inscriptions in it date from the 5th century BC.
Lydia	Region of Northwest Anatolia. The Lydian language belonged to the Anatolian family. Tradition maintained that the Etruscans came from Lydia. Alphabetic inscriptions in it date from the 5th century BC.
Mandate of Heaven	*Tianming* in Chinese. An ancient political theory according to which a dynasty ruled only so long as it held the Mandate of Heaven, which would eventually be removed and handed to new challengers.
metathesis	Alternation or switching of consonantal or vocalic position in language.
Middle Helladic	**Ceramic period** for Mainland Greece for the period *c*. 2000–1675 BC.
Middle Kingdom	Period containing the 11th, 12th and 13th Dynasties from *c*. 2150 to 1750 BC, during which Egypt was united and powerful, and upon which the **Middle Minoan** and **Helladic ceramic periods** were loosely based.
Middle Minoan	**Ceramic period** for Crete for the period *c*. 2000–1675 BC.
Minoan	Name – derived by Arthur Evans from Minos, the legendary king of Crete – applied to the cultures of Crete before the arrival there of Greek speakers, and to three **ceramic periods,** also established by Evans.
modified diffusionism	The belief that cultures can be altered or transformed by outside forces, but that in most

cases the changes take place only after considerable interaction with the local culture.

monism In this book 'monism' is used to indicate the
notion that all things have single fundamental
causes.

monogenesis The belief in single origins, largely restricted
in this book to humanity and language. The
opposite of **polygenesis.**

Mycenae City near Argos in the Northeastern Peloponnese, famous as the leading city in the Late
Bronze Age.

Mycenaean Name of Bronze Age material culture first discovered at Mycenae and, by extension, Greek
culture of the Late Bronze Age.

nasals Consonants like *m* and *n* formed in the nasal
passage. Nasalization is the common phenome-
non of the introduction of nasals before stops:
m before *b, p* or *f; n* before *d, t,* or *th;* and *ng*
before *g, k* or *ch.*

Old Kingdom Period of Egyptian strength and prosperity
from the 3rd to the 6th Dynasties *c.* 3000–
2500 BC.

Olympic Games Religious festival and games held at Olympia
in the Northwest Peloponnese every four years
from 776 BC until they were discontinued by
the emperor Theodosius at the end of the
4th century AD. They were revived in a spirit
of European ethnicity and élitism from which
the Aryan Model emerged at the end of the
19th century.

Orphics Followers of the divine Orpheus. Very much
like the Pythagoreans, the Orphics promoted
Egyptian religious beliefs and were especially
concerned with personal immortality.

pantheism Belief that God is in all things and all things
are God. This world-view, which closely resembled that of Egyptian and Greek religion,
became significant in the 17th century, especially after the publication of the works of
Spinoza.

Pausanias Writer of an extensive *Guide to Greece,* who
lived in the 2nd century AD.

Pelasgians According to Classical tradition, the earliest inhabitants of Greece.

Persian Empire Founded by Cyrus the Great in the mid-6th
century BC, it dominated the Middle East, Asia

Minor and the Aegean until pushed back by the Greeks. It was finally destroyed by Alexander the Great in the second half of the 4th century BC.

Philistines   Invaders of Egypt and the Levant from the Aegean and **Anatolia** in the late 13th and 12th centuries BC.

Phoenicia   Cities along a strip of coast stretching from the present-day Lebanon to Northern Israel, the most famous of which were **Byblos, Tyre** and **Sidon.** The name Phoenicia refers to this region throughout Antiquity. However, it generally indicates the greatest period in the cities' history, between 1100 and 750 BC. The Phoenician 'language' was, like **Hebrew,** a dialect of **Canaanite.** The alphabet is often refered to as a Phoenician invention. It may well have originated in the region, but it was developed long before the Phoenician period.

phoneme   The minimal significant unit of sound within a language.

phonetic correspondences   Sounds that are actually or etymologically similar.

Phrygia   Region in Northern **Anatolia.** It was a powerful state in the first half of the 1st millennium BC. Its language, which was written alphabetically, was not **Anatolian** but **Indo-European,** and closely related to Greek.

pictogram   Writing in which the object signified is pictured or directly represented.

polygenesis   The belief in multiple origins, in particular of humanity or language. The opposite of **monogenesis.**

prothetic or prosthetic   Vowels placed at the beginnings of words to avoid initial consonants. The placing of prothetic vowels is particularly common before double consonants.

Proto-Greek   The unattested language or people reconstructed as having been the origin of Greek or the Greeks.

Ptolemaic   Name given to Egyptian culture under the rule of the Ptolemies.

Ptolemy   Name of a succession of descendants of Ptolemy I, a general of Alexander the Great who seized power in Egypt after Alexander's death. The last ruler of this dynasty was Kleopatra

VII, loved by both Caesar and Anthony, who
died dramatically in 30 BC.

Pythagoras   Greek philosopher and mathematician *c.* 582–
500 BC. He studied in Egypt and brought back
Egyptian mathematical and religious principles, and founded the Pythagorean brotherhood.

Pythagoreans   Followers of Pythagoras organized into a
'brotherhood' along what were generally seen
to be Egyptian lines. The Pythagoreans played
an important political, religious and scientific
role in the Greek society of Sicily and Southern Italy in the 5th and 4th centuries BC.

Qin (Ch'in)   Chinese dynasty, 256–207 BC, from which we
probably acquired the name China. As a 'national' dynasty, it was founded by the unifier
of China, Qinshihuangdi, but survived only a
few years after his death, to be followed by the
Han Dynasty.

root   Essential part of a word which remains after
all the others have been removed.

Seleucid   The name of a dynasty established in Syria
and Mesopotamia by Alexander's general
Seleukos.

semantic   Relating to signification or meaning.

Shang   Chinese dynasty, *c.* 1600–1100 BC. Prince
Tang, the first emperor of the dynasty, overthrew the **Xia** and the Shang were in turn
overthrown by the **Zhou.**

sibilants   Consonants with hissing sounds like *s, š, ṣ* and *z.*

Sidon   Ancient Phoenician city dedicated to the sea
god Sid. Its apogee was in the very early Iron
Age. Therefore 'Sidonian' is used for Phoenician in general in the early historical books
of the Bible and Homer. Its dominance was
replaced by that of its rival **Tyre** in about the
9th century BC.

stele   Upright slab with sculptured designs or
inscriptions.

stem   Verbal form derived from the root by special
vocalization or the addition of various prefixes
or suffixes.

stop   A complete consonantal explosion of breath,
as in the sounds represented by our letters *b,
p, d, t, g* and *k.*

Strabo   Greek geographer of the 1st century BC and
1st century AD.

theogony	Ancestry or birth of the gods; it was the name and subject of a number of poems, the most famous being that of Hesiod.
Thera	Volcanic island seventy miles north of Crete. It suffered a major eruption during the 2nd millennium BC, which is now dated to 1628 BC.
Thucydides	Greek historian of the Peloponnesian War, born *c.* 46 BC, died *c.* 400 BC.
Tokharian	Indo-European language spoken in the 1st millennium AD in the now Turkic-speaking, Western Chinese 'autonomous region' of Sinkiang. Tokharian shares several features with Western Indo-European languages which are not present in the Indo-Aryan languages. It therefore provides critical information on the nature of early **Indo-European.**
toponym	Place name.
Tyre	Ancient Phoenician city. Its period of greatest glory was from the 9th to the 10th centuries BC. But it remained an important political and cultural centre until its destruction by Alexander the Great in 333 BC.
Ugarit	Major port on the Syrian coast, which flourished in the second half of the 2nd millennium BC.
Ugaritic	The West Semitic language spoken at Ugarit and recorded in an alphabetic form of **cuneiform** on many of the tablets found in the city.
Urartu	Kingdom in the Southern Caucasus in the first half of the 1st millennium BC. Its language was related to **Hurrian** and the present Northeast Caucasian languages.
velars	**Stops** formed with the tongue at the back of the mouth, as, for example, *k* and *g*.
vocalization	Infusing a consonantal structure with vowels.
Xia (Hsia)	Chinese dynasty, *c.* 1900–1600 BC, overthrown by the **Shang.**
Zhou (Chou)	Chinese dynasty that succeeded the Shang, *c.* 1100 BC. It lost political power in the 8th century BC but survived with the title of emperor until finally overthrown by Qinshihuangdi in 221 BC.
Zoroaster	Iranian religious reformer who lived in the 2nd millennium BC.
Zoroastrianism	Religion founded by Zoroaster, which became the state religion of the Persian Empire. It maintained that the universe was the scene of

a perpetual and finely balanced struggle between good and evil. It was largely destroyed
in Iran after the Islamic conquest, but is still
flourishing elsewhere in the world among the
Parsee community.

BIBLIOGRAPHY

Abel, L. S. (1966) *Fifth Century B.C. Concepts of the Pelasgians*. MA thesis, Stanford University.

Abou-Assaf, A., Bordreuil, P. and Millard, A. R. D. (1982) *La Statue de Tell Fekheriyé: et son inscription bilingue assyro-araméenne*. Paris: Études Assyriologiques, Éditions recherche sur les civilisations no.7.

Adams, W. Y. (1968) 'Invasion, diffusion and evolution', *Antiquity* 42: 194–215.

—— (1984) *Nubia: Corridor to Africa*. London: Allen Lane & Unwin; Princeton, NJ: Princeton University Press.

Ahituv, S. (1984) *Canaanite Toponyms in Ancient Egyptian Documents*. Jerusalem: Magnes; Leiden: Brill.

Ahl, F. (1982) 'Amber, Avallon and Apollo's singing swan', *American Journal of Philology* 103: 373–411.

—— (1985) *Metaformations: Soundplay and Wordplay in Ovid and Other Classical Poets*. Ithaca, NY: Cornell University Press.

Aitken, M. J. (1987) 'The Minoan eruption of Thera, Santorini: a reassessment of the radiocarbon dates', in R. E. Jones and H. E. Catling, eds. *Science in Archaeology: Proceedings of a Meeting Held at the British School at Athens*.

—— (1988) 'The Thera eruption: continuing discussion of the dating, 1, resumé of dating', *Archaeometry* 30: 165–9.

Åkerström, A. (1975) 'More Canaanite jars from Greece', *Opuscula Athensiensa* 11: 185–92.

Akurgal, E. (1968) *The Art of Greece: Its Origins in the Mediterranean and the Near East*. New York: Crown Publishers.

Albright, W. F. (1923) 'The principles of Egyptian phonological development', *Recueils de Travaux* 40: 64–70.

—— (1934) *The Vocalization of the Egyptian Syllabic Orthography*. New Haven, Conn.: American Oriental Society series, vol. 5.

—— (1939) 'Review of Wolfram Freiherr von Soden, *Der Aufstieg des Assyrerreichs als geschichtliches Problem*', Orientalia N.S. 8: 120–3.

—— (1942) *Archaeology and the Religion of Israel*. Baltimore, Md.: Johns Hopkins University Press.

—— (1945) 'An indirect synchronism between Egypt and Mesopotamia *circa* 1730 BC', *Bulletin of the American Schools of Oriental Research* 99: 9–18.

—— (1950) 'Some Oriental glosses on the Homeric problem', *American Journal of Archaeology* 54: 160–76.

—— (1957) *From the Stone Age to Christianity: Monotheism and the Historical Process*, 2nd. edn. Garden City, NY: Doubleday.

—— (1960) *The Archaeology of Palestine*, rev. edn. London: Penguin.

—— (1961) 'The role of the Canaanites in the history of civilization', appendix to *The Bible and the Ancient Near East (Essays in Honor of William Foxwell Albright)*, ed. E. G. Wright. Garden City, NY: Doubleday, pp. 328–62.

—— (1965) 'Some remarks about the archaeological chronology of Palestine before about 1500 BC', in R. W. Ehrich, ed., *Chronologies in Old World Archaeology*. Chicago: University of Chicago Press, pp. 54–7.

—— (1968) *Yahweh and the Gods of Canaan: A Historical Analysis of Two Contrasting Faiths*. London: Athlone Press.

—— (1970) 'The biblical period', in L. Finkelstein, ed., *The Jews Their History*. New York: Schocken, pp. 1–71.

—— (1975) 'Syria, the Philistines and Phoenicia', *Cambridge Ancient History*, 3rd edn, Vol II, pt. 2, pp. 507–13.

Aldred, C. (1971) *Jewels of the Pharaohs: Egyptian Jewellery of the Dynastic Period*. London: Thames & Hudson.

Alexiou, S. (1967a) 'Arkhaiotetes kai Mneimeia Kentrikes kai Anatol. Kretes', *Archaiologikon Deltion* 22: 2.2.

—— (1967b) *Hysterominōikoi taphoi limenos Knōsou Katsamba*. Athens: Bibliothēkē tēs en Athēnais Archaiologikēs Etairias 56.

Allen, T. G. (1974) (trans.) *The Book of the Dead or Going Forth by Day*. Chicago: Oriental Institute.

Alt, A. (1954) 'Die Herkunft der Hyksos in neuer Sicht', *Berichte über die Verhandlungen der sächsischen Akademie der Wissenschaften zu Leipzig. Phil.-Hist. Klasse* 101: 6.

Altenmüller, B. (1975) 'Anubis', in W. Helck and E. Otto, *Lexikon der Ägyptologie*, vol. I, cols 327–33.

—— (1977) 'Harsaphes', in W. Helck and E. Otto, *Lexikon der Ägyptologie*, vol. II, cols 1015–18.

Amiet, P. (1977) *The Art of the Ancient Near East*, trans. J. Shepley and C. Choquet. New York: Harry N. Abrams Inc.

Andel, T. van and Lianos, N. (1983) 'Prehistoric and historic shorelines of the southern Argolid peninsula', *Journal of Nautical Archaeology and Underwater Exploration* 12: 303–24.

Andel, T. van and Runnels, C. N. (1988) 'An essay on the "emergence of civilization" in the Aegean world', *Antiquity* 62. 235: 234–47.

André, J. (1948) *Étude sur les termes de couleur dans la langue latine*. Paris: Klincksieck.

Angel, J. L. (1957) 'Kings and commoners', *American Journal of Archaeology* 61: 181.

Apollodoros (1921) *The Library*, J. G. Frazer, trans., 2 vols. Cambridge, Mass.: Harvard University Press (Loeb).

Apollonios of Rhodes (1959) *The Voyage of Argo: The Argonautica*, trans. with intro. E. V. Riew. Harmondsworth: Penguin.

Arbeitman, Y. and Bomhard, A. R., eds. (1981) *Bono Homini Donum: Essays in Historical Linguistics, in Memory of J. Alexander Kerns*, 2 vols. Amsterdam: John Benjamins.

Arbeitman, Y. and Rendsburg, G. (1981) 'Adana revisited: 30 years later', *Archív Orientální* 49: 145–57.

Aristotle, *De Caelo*.

Metaphysica.

Meteriologica.

Politics, T. A. Sinclair, trans. Harmondsworth: Penguin, 1962.

Arkell, A. J. (1961) *History of the Sudan to 1821*. London: University of London, Athlone Press.

Arktinos, *Aithiopis*, see Kinkel (1887, pp. 33–6).

Armayor, O. K. (1978) 'Did Herodotos ever go to Egypt?', *Journal of the American Research Center in Egypt* 15: 59–73.

—— (1985) *Herodotus' Autopsy of the Fayoum: Lake Moeris and the Labyrinth of Egypt*. Amsterdam: Gieben.

Arnold, D. (1977) 'Fajjum', in W. Helck and E. Otto, *Lexikon der Ägyptologie*, vol. II, cols 87–93.

Arrian (1929) *Anabasis of Alexander*, E. I. Robson, trans. New York: Putnam.

Artzy, M. (1985) 'Supply and demand: a study of second millennium Cypriot pottery in the Levant', in A. B. Knapp and T. Stech, eds., *Prehistoric Production and Exchange: The Aegean and East Mediterranean*. Los Angeles: Institute of Archaeology, Monograph 25, University of California, pp. 93–9.

Asaro, F. and Perlman, I. (1973) 'Provenance studies of Mycenaean pottery using neutron activation analysis', in V. Karageorghis, ed., *The Mycenaeans in the Eastern Mediterranean*, Acts of the International Symposium, Nicosia, 1972, pp. 213–24.

Ashton, L. and Gray, B. (1935) *Chinese Art*. London: Faber.

Assmann, J. (1984) 'Politik zwischen Ritual und Dogma: Spielräume politischen Handelns im pharaonischen Ägypten', *Saeculum* 35: 97–114.

Astour, M. C. (1964a) 'The second millennium B.C. Cypriot and Cretan onomastica reconsidered', *Journal of the American Oriental Society* 84: 240–54.

—— (1964b) 'Greek names in the Semitic world and Semitic names in the Greek world', *Journal of Near Eastern Studies* 23: 193–204.

—— (1966) 'Aegean place-names in an Egyptian inscription', *American Journal of Archaeology* 70: 314–17.

—— (1967a) *Hellenosemitica: An Ethnic and Cultural Study in West Semitic Impact on Mycenaean Greece*. Leiden: Brill.

—— (1967b) 'The problem of Semitic in Ancient Crete', *Journal of the American Oriental Society* 87: 290–5.

—— (1972a) 'Some recent works on Ancient Syria and the Sea Peoples', *Journal of the American Oriental Society* 92.3: 447–9.

—— (1972b) 'The merchant class of Ugarit', *Bayerische Akademie der Wissenschaften Abhandlungen* 75: 11–26.

—— (1981) 'Ugarit and the great powers', in G. D. Young, ed., *Ugarit in Retrospect: Fifty Years of Ugarit and Ugaritic*. Winona Lake, Ind.: Eisenbrauns, pp. 3–29.

—— (1987) Personal letter, 5 March.

Åström, P. (1971) 'Three Tel el Jahudieh juglets in the Thera Museum', *Acta of the 1st International Congress on the Volcano of Thera, 15–23 September 1969*. Göteborg: Paul Åströms Förlag, pp. 415–21.

—— (1973) 'Comments on the corpus of Mycenaean pottery in Cyprus', in V. Karageorghis, ed., *The Mycenaeans in the Eastern Mediterranean*, Acts of the International Symposium, Nicosia, 1972, pp. 122–7.

—— (1978) 'Methodological viewpoints on Middle Minoan chronology', *Opuscula Atheniensia* 12.4: 87–90.

—— (1987–9) *High, Middle or Low? Acts of an International Colloquium on Absolute Chronology Held at the University of Gothenburg 20–22 August 1987*, 3 pts. Göteborg: Paul Åströms Förlag.

Attridge, H. W. and Oden, R. A. (1981) *Philo of Byblos, The Phoenician History: Introduction, Critical Text, Translation, Notes*. Washington, DC: Catholic Biblical Quarterly Monograph Series, 9.

Austin, M. M. (1970) *Greece and Egypt in the Archaic Age*. Cambridge: Proceedings of the Cambridge Philological Society, Supplement 2.

Bacon, J. R. (1925) *The Voyage of the Argonauts*. London: Small, Maynard & Co.

Baillie, M. G. L. (1988a) 'Irish oaks record volcanic dust veils drama!', *Archaeology Ireland* II. 2: 71–4.

—— (1988b) 'Marker dates', *Archaeology Ireland* II. 4: 154–5.

—— (1989a) 'Hekla 3 – just how big was it?', *Endeavour* 13.2: 78–81.

—— (1989b) 'Irish tree rings and an event in 1628 BC', in *Thera and the Aegean World III: Papers to Be Presented at the Third International Congress at Santorini Greece. 3–9 September 1989*. Thera Foundation, pp. 1–9.

Baillie, M. G. L. and Munro, M. A. R. (1988) 'Irish tree rings, Santorini and volcanic dust veils', *Nature* 332. 24/3: 344–6.

Baillie, M. G. L. and Pincher, J. (1984) 'Make a date with a tree', *New Scientist* 17.3: 48–51.

Baker, J. R. (1974) *Race*. London: Oxford University Press.

Balcer, J. M. (1974) 'The Mycenaean dam at Tiryns', *American Journal of Archaeology* 78: 141–50.

Balkan, K. (1954) *Kassiten Studien 1. Die Sprache der Kassiten*, trans. from Turkish by R. Krauss. New Haven, Conn.: American Oriental Series, vol. 37.

—— (1955) *Kaniš Kārum'unun Kronoloji Problemeri Hakkinda Müşahedeler: Observations on the Chronological Problems of the Kārum Kaniš.* Türk Tarih Kurumu Yayinlarindan, *VII*, seri no. 28. Ankara: Türk Tarih Kurumu Basimevi.

Ban Gu (1959) *Hanshu*, ed. Wang Xianqian, 8 vols. Shanghai: Shangwu Yinshuguan.

Banti, L. (1931) 'La grande tomba a Tholos di Hagia Triadha', *Annuario de la Scuola Archeologica di Atene* 13: 155–251.

Baramki, D. (1961) *Phoenicia and the Phoenicians.* Beirut: Khayats.

Barber, R. L. N. (1984) 'The status of Phylakopi in Creto-Cycladic relations', in R. Hägg and N. Marinatos, eds., *The Minoan Thalassocracy: Myth and Reality: Proceedings of the 3rd International Symposium at the Swedish Institute in Athens 31 May–5 June 1982. Skrifter utgivna av Svenska Institutet i Athen*, 4, pp. 167–78.

—— (1987) *The Cyclades in the Bronze Age.* London: Duckworth.

Barnard, K. (1981) *The Paradigm of Race and Early Greek History*, paper for an undergraduate course, Government 352, Cornell University.

Barnard, N. (1975) *First Radio Carbon Dates from China.* Canberra: Australian National University, Institute of Advanced Studies, Department of Far Eastern History, Research School of Pacific Studies, Monographs on Far Eastern History 8.

Barnes, B. (1982) *T. S. Kuhn and Social Science.* New York: Columbia University Press.

Barnett, R. D. (1956) 'Ancient Oriental Influence on Archaic Greece', in S. S. Weinberg, ed., *The Aegean and the Near-East, Studies Presented to Hetty Goldman.* Locust Valley, NY: Augustin, pp. 212–38.

—— (1960) 'Some contacts between Greek and Oriental religions', in O. Eissfeld, ed., *Éléments orientaux dans la religion grecque ancienne.* Paris: Presses Universitaires de France, pp. 143–53.

—— (1975) 'The Sea Peoples', *Cambridge Ancient History*, 3rd edn., vol. I, pt. 2, pp. 359–78.

Baron, S. W. (1952) *A Social and Religious History of the Jews*, vols. 1–2. New York: Columbia University Press.

—— (1976) *The Russian Jew under Tsars and Soviets*, 2nd enl. edn. New York: Macmillan.

Barthélemy, J.-J. (1763) 'Réflexions générales sur les rapports des langues égyptienne, phénicienne et grecque', *Recueils des Mémoires de l'Académie des Inscriptions* 32: 212–33.

Bartolini, P. (1988) 'Ships and navigation', in Sabatino Moscati, ed., *The Phoenicians.* Milan: Bompiani, pp. 72–7.

Bass, G. F. (1961) 'The Cape Gelidonya wreck: preliminary report', *American Journal of Archaeology* 65: 267–86.

—— (1967) 'Cape Gelidonya: a Bronze Age shipwreck', *Transactions of the American Philosophical Society* 57.8.

—— (1970) 'A hoard of Trojan and Sumerian jewellery'. *American Journal of Archaeology* 74: 335–41.

—— (1986a) 'A Bronze Age shipwreck at Ulu Burun (Kaş): 1984 Campaign', *American Journal of Archaeology* 90: 269–96.

—— (1986b) 'Underwater excavation of the Ulu Burun shipwreck', *Kazu Sonuçlari Toplantisi*, Ankara; T.C. Kültür ve Turizm Bakanliği Eski ve Müzeler Genel Müdülüğü. VII. II.

—— (1987) 'Oldest known shipwreck reveals splendors of the Bronze Age', *National Geographic* 172.6: 693–733.

—— (1990) Personal communication, 6 January.

—— (forthcoming) 'Evidence of trade from Bronze Age shipwrecks', *Proceedings of the Oxford Conference on Bronze Age Trade*.

Bass, G. F., Pulak, C., Collon, D. and Weinstein, J. (1989) 'The Bronze Age shipwreck at Ulu Burun: 1986 campaign', *American Journal of Archaeology* 93: 1–29.

Bates, O. (1914) *The Eastern Libyans: An Essay*. London: Frank Cass.

Baumgarten, A. J. (1981) *The Phoenician History of Philo of Byblos: A Commentary*. Leiden: Brill.

Beattie, A. J. (1962) 'The Aegean languages of the Heroic Age', in A. J. B. Wace and F. H. Stubbings, eds., *A Companion to Homer*. London: Macmillan, pp. 311–24.

Beckerath, J. von (1965) *Untersuchungen zur politischen Geschichte der Zweiten Zwischenzeit in Ägypten*. Ägyptische Forschungen Heft 23. Glückstadt, New York: Augustin.

—— (1975) 'Amenemhet I-VI', in W. Helck and E. Otto, *Lexikon der Ägyptologie*, vol. I, cols 188–93.

—— (1980) '*Kalender*', in W. Helck and E. Otto, *Lexikon der Ägyptologie*, vol. II, cols 297–9.

—— (1982a) 'Mentuhotep I', in W. Helck and E. Otto, *Lexikon der Ägyptologie*, vol. IV, col. 66.

—— (1982b) 'Mentuhotep II', in W. Helck and E. Otto, *Lexikon der Ägyptologie*, vol. IV, cols 66–8.

Bell, L. (1985a) 'Luxor Temple and the cult of the royal Ka', *Journal of Near Eastern Studies* 44: 251–94.

—— (1985b) 'Aspects of the cult of the deified Tutankhamen', in *Mélanges Gamal Eddin Mokhtar*. Cairo: Institut français d'archéologie orientale, pp. 31–61.

Beloch, J. (1893) *Griechische Geschichte*. Strasburg: Trübner.

—— (1894) 'Die Phoeniker am aegischen Meer', *Rheinisches Museum* 49: 111–32.

Bennet, J. (1990) 'Knossos in context: comparative perspectives on the Linear B administration of LMII–III Crete', *American Journal of Archaeology* 94: 193–211.

Benz, F. L. (1972) *Personal Names in the Phoenician and Punic Inscriptions*. Rome: Biblical Institute.

Bérard, A. (1971) Préface, in V. Bérard, *Les Navigations d'Ulysse*, 3 vols. Paris: Librairie Armand Colin.

Bérard, J. (1951) 'Philistines et préhellènes', *Revue archéologique*, série 6. 37: 129–42.

—— (1952) 'Les Hyksos et la légende d'Io: recherches sur la période prémycenienne', *Syria* 29: 1–43.

Bérard, V. (1894) *De l'origine des cultes arcadiens: Essai de méthode en mythologie grecque*. Paris: Bibliothèque des Écoles Françaises d'Athènes et de Rome.

—— (1902–3) *Les Phéniciens et l'Odyssée*, 2 vols. Paris: Librairie Armand Colin.

—— (1927–9) *Les Navigations d'Ulysse*. Paris: Librairie Armand Colin.

Bernal, M. (1986) 'Black Athena denied: the tyranny of Germany over Greece', *Comparative Criticism* 8: 3–69.

—— (1987) 'On the transmission of the alphabet to the Aegean before 1400 B.C.', *Bulletin of the American Schools of Oriental Research* 267: 1–19.

—— (1988) 'The British Utilitarians, imperialism and the fall of the Ancient Model', *Culture and History* 3: 98–117.

—— (1989a) 'First by land then by sea: thoughts about the social formation of the Mediterranean and Greece', in E. Genovese and L. Hochberg, eds., *Geographic Perspectives in History*. Oxford: Blackwell.

—— (1989b) '*Black Athena* and the APA' in J. Peradotto and M. Myerowitz Levine, eds., 'The Challenge of "Black Athena"', *Arethusa* special issue: 17–37.

—— (1990) *Cadmean Letters: The Transmission of the Alphabet to the Aegean and Further West before 1400 BC*. Winona Lake, Ind.: Eisenbrauns.

—— (forthcoming) 'Nig(g)er is beautiful'.

Bernand, A. (1977) *Pan du désert*. Leiden: Brill.

Berquist, B. (1973) 'Herakles on Thasos: the archaeological, literary and epigraphic evidence for his sanctuary, status and cult reconsidered', *Acta Universitatis Upsaliensis, Boreas: Uppsala Studies in Ancient Mediterranean and Near Eastern Civilisation* 5.

Best, J. G. P. and Yadin, Y. (1973) *The Arrival of the Greeks*. Amsterdam: Publications of the Henri Frankfort Foundation, Hakkert.

Betancourt, P. P. (1984) 'The Middle Minoan pottery of Southern Crete and the question of a Middle Minoan thalassocracy', in R. Hägg and N. Marinatos, eds., *The Minoan Thalassocracy: Myth and Reality: Proceedings of the 3rd International Symposium at the Swedish Institute in Athens 31 May–5 June 1982. Skrifter utgivna av Svenska Institutet i Athen*, 4, pp. 89–92.

—— (1985) *The History of Minoan Pottery*. Princeton, NJ: Princeton University Press.

—— (1987) 'Dating the Aegean Late Bronze Age with radiocarbon', *Archaeometry* 29.1: 45–9.

—— (1989) 'High chronology and low chronology: Thera archaeological evidence', in *Thera and the Aegean World III: Papers to Be Presented at the Third International Congress at Santorini, Greece, 3–9 September 1989*. Thera Foundation, pp. 9–17.

Betancourt, P. P., Michael, H. N. and Weinstein, G. A. (1978) 'Calibration and the radiocarbon chronology of late Minoan 1B', *Archaeometry* 20: 200–3.

Betancourt, P. P. and Weinstein, G. A. (1976) 'Carbon-14 and the beginning of the late Bronze Age in the Aegean', *American Journal of Archaeology* 80: 329–48.

Beth, K. (1916) 'El und Neter', *Zeitschrift für die alttestamentliche Wissenschaft* 36: 129–86.

Bickerman, E. J. (1980) *Chronology of the Ancient World*, rev. edn. London: Thames & Hudson.

Biesautl, M. (1954) *Kretisch-mykenische Siegelbilder*. Marburg: Hinrich.

Bietak, M. (1968) 'Vorläufiger Bericht über die erste und zweite Kampagne der österreichischen Ausgrabungen auf Tel el-Daba'a im Ostdelta Ägyptens (1966, 1967)', *Mitteilungen des Deutschen Archaeologischen Instituts, Abteilung Kairo* 23: 79–114.

—— (1970) 'Vorläufiger Bericht über die dritte Kampagne der österreichischen Ausgrabungen auf Tell el Daba'a im Ostdelta Ägyptens', *Mitteilungen des Deutschen Archäologischen Instituts Abteilungen Kairo* 26: 15–42.

—— (1975) *Tel el-Dab'a II: Die Fundort im Rahmen einer archaeologischgeographischen Untersuchungen über das ägyptische Ostdelta*. Vienna: Österreichischen Akademie der Wissenschaft Verlag.

—— (1979) *Avaris and Piramesse: Archaeological Exploration in the Eastern Nile Delta*. *Proceedings of the British Academy* 65. London.

—— (1980) 'Hyksos', in W. Helck and E. Otto, *Lexikon der Ägyptologie*, vol. III, cols 93–103.

—— (1983) 'Some news about trade and trade warfare in the Ancient Near East', *Marhaba* 3.83: 41–3.

—— (1984) 'Problems of Middle Bronze Age chronology: new evidence from Egypt', *American Journal of Archaeology* 88: 471–85.

Biggs, R. D. (1966) 'Le Lapis lazuli dans les textes sumériens archaïques', *Revue d'Assyriologie et d'Archéologie Orientale* 60: 175–6.

Bikai, P. M. (1978) *The Pottery of Tyre*. Warminster: Aris & Phillips.

—— (1983) 'Imports from the East', in V. Karageorghis, ed., *Paleopaphos-Skales: An Iron Age Cemetery in Cyprus*. Konstanz: Kevalaer, pp. 395–405.

—— (1987) *The Phoenician Pottery of Cyprus*. Nicosia: Leventis Foundation.

Billigmeier, J. C. (1975) 'The origin of the Greek word ΛΕΩΝ', *Talanta* 6: 1–6.

—— (1976) *Kadmos and the Possibility of a Semitic Presence in Helladic Greece*. Ph.D. dissertation, University of California, Santa Barbara.

Bimson, J. G. and Livingston, D. (1987) 'Redating the Exodus', *Biblical Archaeology Review* 13.5: 40–53 and 66–7.

Bintliff, J. L. (1977) 'Natural environment and human settlement in prehistoric Greece', *British Archaeological Reports* 28, 2 pts. Oxford.

—— (1984) 'Structuralism and myth in Minoan studies', *Antiquity* 58: 33–8.

Birch, S. (1853) 'The Annals of Thothmes III, as derived from the hieroglyphic inscriptions', *Archaeologia* 35: 116–66.

Bisi, A. M. (1965) *Il Grifone: Storia di un motivo iconografico nell' antico oriente mediterraneo*. Rome: Centro di studi semitici, Istituto di studi del vicino oriente-Università.

Bisson de la Roque, F., Contenau, G. and Charpoutier, F. (1953) *Le Trésor de Tôd*. Cairo: L'Institut Français d'Archéologie Orientale.

Bittel, K. (1970) *Hattusha: Capital of the Hittites*. New York: Oxford University Press.

Blakely, A. (1986) *Russia and the Negro: Blacks in Russian History and Thought*. Washington, DC: Howard University Press.

Blegen, C. W. (1937) *Prosymna*. Cambridge: Cambridge University Press.

—— (1958) 'A chronological problem', in *Minoica, Festschrift zum 80. Geburstag von Johannes Sundwall*. Berlin: Deutsche Akademie der Wissenschaften zu Berlin; Schrifter der Sektion für Altertumswissenschaft 12.

Blegen, C. W., Boulter, C. G., Caskey, L. and Rawson, M. (1950–8) *Troy*, 4 vols. Princeton: Princeton University Press.

Blegen, C. W. and Haley, J. (1927) 'The coming of the Greeks: the geographical distribution of prehistoric remains in Greece', *American Journal of Archaeology* 32: 141–52.

Blegen, C. W. and Wace, A. (1939) 'Pottery as evidence for trade and colonization in the Aegean Bronze Age', *Klio* 32: 131–47.

Bloch, M. (1924) *Les Rois Thaumaturges: Étude sur le caractère surnaturel attribué à la puissance royale particulièrement en France et en Angleterre*. Strasburg and Paris: Publications de la Faculté des Lettres de l'Université de Strasbourg.

Blumenbach, J. F. (1795) *De Generis Humani Varietate Nativa*, 3rd. edn. Göttingen.

Blumenthal, E. (1982) 'Die Prophezierums des Neferti', *Zeitschrift für ägyptische Sprache und Altertumskunde* 109: 1–27.

—— (1983) 'Die erste Koregenz der 12 Dynastie', *Zeitschrift für ägyptische Sprache und Altertumskunde* 109: 104–121.

—— (1984) 'Die Lehre des Königs Amenemhet (teil 1)', *Zeitschrift für ägyptische Sprache und Altertumskunde* 110: 85–107.

—— (1985) 'Die Lehre des Königs Amenemhet (teil 2)', *Zeitschrift für ägyptische Sprache und Altertumskunde* 111: 104–15.

Boardman, J. (1964) *The Greeks Overseas: The Archaeology of Their Early Colonies and Trade*. London: Penguin.

Boas, G., trans. (1950) *The Hieroglyphics of Horapollo*. New York: Pantheon.

Bochart, S. (1646) *Geographia Sacræ Pars Prior: Phaleg seu de Dispersione Gentium et Terrarum Divisione Facta in Ædificatione Turis Babel etc. Pars Altera: Chanaan, seu de Coloniis et Sermone Phœnicum*. Munich.

Boessneck, J. (1976) *Tell el-Dabʿa III, die Tierknochfunde*. Vienna: Verlag der Österreichischen Akademie der Wissenschaft.

Boisacq, E. (1950) *Dictionnaire étymologique de la langue grecque*, 4th edn. Heidelberg: Winter; Paris: Klincksieck.

Bomhard, A. (1976) 'The placing of the Anatolian languages', *Orbis* 25.2: 199–239.

—— (1984) *Toward Proto-Nostratic: A New Approach to the Comparison of Proto-Indo-European and Proto-Afroasiatic*. Amsterdam and Philadelphia: John Benjamins.

Bonnet, H. (1952) *Reallexikon der ägyptischen Religionsgeschichte*. Berlin: de Gruyter.

Bordreuil, P. (1982), see Abou-Assaf.

Borgeaud, P. (1979) *Recherches sur le dieu Pan*. Rome: Institut Suisse de Rome.

Borghouts, J. F. (1980) 'The ram as a protector and prophesier', *Revue d'Égyptologie* 32: 33–46.

—— (1982) 'Month', in W. Helck and E. Otto, *Lexikon der Ägyptologie*, vol. IV, cols 200–204.

Bork, F. (1909) 'Die Mitanni Sprache'. *Mitteilungen den vorderasiatischen Gesellschaft* 14: 1–126.

Borsi, F. *et al.* (1985) Fortuna degli etruschi. Florence: Elekta.

Bosch-Gimpera, P. (1980) *Les Indo-Européens: Problèmes archéologiques*. Paris: Payot.

Bossert, H. T. (1946) *Asia*. Istanbul: Literarische Fakultät der Universität Istanbul no. 323, Forschungsinstitut für altvorderasiatische Kulturen no. 2.

Boufides, N. (1970) 'A scarab from Grave Circle B of Mycenae', *Archaiologika Analekta Athēnōn* 3: 273–4.

Bouzek, J. (1973) 'Bronze Age Greece and the Balkans: problems of migrations', in R. A. Crossland and A. Birchall, eds., *Bronze Age Migrations in the Aegean: Archaeological and Linguistic Problems of Greek Prehistory*. London: Duckworth.

—— (1985) *The Aegean, Anatolia and Europe: Cultural Interrelations in the Second Millennium BC*. Göteborg: Paul Åströms Förlag, Studies in Mediterranean Archaeology 29.

Boyce, N. M. (1979) *Zoroastrians: Their Religious Beliefs and Practices*. London: Routledge & Kegan Paul.

Boylan, P. (1922) *Thoth the Hermes of Egypt: A Study of Some Aspects of Theological Thought in Ancient Egypt*. London: Oxford University Press.

Brady, T. H. (1935) 'The Reception of Egyptian Cults by the Greeks (330–300 BC)', *The University of Missouri Studies* 10.1.

Branigan, K. (1968a) *Copper and Bronze Work in Early Bronze Age Crete*. Lund: P. Åströms Fölag.

—— (1968b) 'A transitional phase in Minoan metallurgy', *Bulletin of the British School in Athens* 63: 185–203.

—— (1970a) *The Foundations of Palatial Crete*. London: Duckworth; New York: Praeger.

—— (1970b) *The Tombs of the Mesara: A Study of Funerary Architecture and Ritual in Southern Crete, 2800–1700 BC*. London: Duckworth.

—— (1973a) 'Radio-carbon and the absolute chronology of the Aegean Bronze Age', *Kretika Chronika* 15: 352–74.

—— (1973b) 'Crete, the Levant and Egypt in the early second millennium BC', *Pepragmena tou 3 Diethnous Kretologikou Synedriou* [Athens] 11: 22–7.

—— (1984) 'Early Minoan society: the evidence of the Mesara Tholoi', in C. Nicolet, ed., *Aux Origines de l'Hellénisme: La Crète et la Grèce; Hommage à Henri Van Effenterre*. Publications de la Sorbonne, Histoire et Médiévale Paris 15, pp. 29–37.

—— (1987). 'Ritual interference with human bones in the Mesara Tholoi', in R. Laffineur, ed., *Thanatos: Les coutumes funéraires en Égée à l'âge du bronze: Actes du Colloque de Liège (21–23 avril 1986)*. Université de l'État à Liège: Histoire de l'art et archéologie de la Grèce antique, pp. 43–51.

Braun, M. (1938) *History and Romance in Graeco-Oriental Literature*. Oxford: Blackwell.

Braun, T. F. R. G. (1982) 'The Greeks in the Near East', in *Cambridge Ancient History*, 2nd edn., vol. III, pt. 3, pp. 1–31.

Breasted, J. H. (1901) 'The philosophy of a Memphite priest', *Zeitschrift für ägyptische Sprache und Altertumskunde* 39: 39–54.

—— (1904) 'The Eleventh Dynasty', in E. Meyer, ed., *Aegyptische Chronologie*, in *Abhandlungen der Königlich Preussischen Akademie der Wissenschaft, Philosophische-historische Classe* I, pp. 1–212.

——, coll., ed., trans. (1906) *Ancient Records of Egypt: Historical Documents from the Earliest Times*, 5 vols. Chicago: University of Chicago Press.

—— (1912a) *The Development of Religion and Thought in Ancient Egypt*. New York: Scribner's.

—— (1912b) *A History of Egypt from Earliest Times to the Persian Conquest*, 2nd. edn. London: Hodder & Stoughton.

Brice, W. C. (1959) 'Compte rendu de *Minoica*', *Gnomon* 31: 330–2.

Broshi, M. and Gaphna, R. (1986) 'Middle Bronze Age Palestine: its settlements and population', *Bulletin of the American Schools of Oriental Research* 26: 173–90.

Brown, J. P. (1965) 'Kothar, Kinyras and Kytheria', *Journal of Semitic Studies* 10: 197–219.

—— (1968a) 'Literary contexts of the common Hebrew Greek vocabulary', *Journal of Semitic Studies* 13: 163–91.

—— (1968b) 'Cosmological myth and the tuna of Gibraltar', *Transactions of the American Philological Association* 99: 37–62.

—— (1969) 'The Mediterranean vocabulary of the vine', *Vetus Testamentum* 19: 146–70.

—— (1971) 'Peace symbolism in ancient military vocabulary', *Vetus Testamentum* 21: 1–23.

—— (1979/80) 'The sacrificial cult and its critique in Greek and Hebrew, pt. 1', *Journal of Semitic Studies* 24: 159–74; 'pt. 2', *Journal of Semitic Studies* 25: 1–21.

Brown, R. (1898) *Semitic Influences in Hellenic Mythology*. London: Williams & Norgate.

Brown, R. (1978) 'The Eteocretan inscription from Psychro', *Kadmos* 17: 43–6.

Brown, R. B. (1975) *A provisional catalogue of and commentary on Egyptian and Egyptianizing artifacts found on Greek sites*. PhD. dissertation, University of Minnesota.

Brugsch, H. (1855) *Grammaire Démotique, contenant les principes généraux de la langue et de l'écriture populaires des anciens Égyptiens*. Berlin: Dümmler.

—— (1879–1880) *Dictionnaire géographique de l'ancienne Égypte*, 2 vols. Leipzig: Hinrichs.

Brundage, W. (1958) 'Herakles the Levantine: A comprehensive view', *Journal of Near Eastern Studies* 17: 225–36.

Brunner, H. (1957) 'New aspects of Ancient Egypt', *Universitas* 1.3: 267–79.

Brunner-Traut, E. (1971) 'The origin of the concept of the immortality of the soul in Ancient Egypt', *Universitas* 14.1: 47–56.

Bryce, T. R. (1989) 'The nature of the Mycenaean involvement in Western Anatolia', *Historia* 38: 1–21.

Bryson, R. A., Lamb, H. H. and Donley, D. (1974) 'Drought and the decline of Mycenae', *Antiquity* 48: 46–50.

Buchholz, H.-G. (1959) 'Keftiubarren und Erzhandel im zweiten vorchristlichen Jahrtausend', *Praehistorische Zeitschrift* 37: 1–40.

—— (1965) 'Review of H. Schleimann, *Ithaka, der Peloponnes und Troja; Mykenae* (1869, 1878; reprints Darmstadt, 1963, 1964), ed. E. Meyer', in *Gymnasium* 72: 569–73.

—— (1967) 'The cylinder seal', in *Cape Gelidonya: A Bronze Age Shipwreck. Transactions of the American Philosophical Society* 57. 8: 148–57.

—— (1972) 'Das Blei in der mykenischen und bronzezeitlichkyprischen Metallurgie', *Jahrbuch des Deutschen archaeologischen Instituts* 87: 1–59.

—— (1973) 'Grey Trojan ware in Cyprus and Northern Syria', in R. A. Crossland and A. Birchall, eds., *Bronze Age Migrations in the Aegean: Archaeological and Linguistic Problems in Greek Prehistory*. London: Duckworth; Park Ridge, NJ: Noyes Press, pp. 179–87.

—— (1980) 'Some observations concerning Thera's contacts overseas during the Bronze Age', in C. Doumas, ed., *Thera and the Aegean World*, vol. II, pp. 227–40.

Buck, C. D. (1926) 'The language situation in and about Greece in the second millennium BC', *Classical Philology* 21: 1–26.

Buck, R. J. (1979) *A History of Boeotia*. Edmonton: University of Alberta Press.

Budge, E. A. W. (1904) *The Gods of the Egyptians; or Studies in Ancient Egyptian Mythology*, 2 vols. London: Methuen.

—— (1934) *From Fetish to God in Ancient Egypt*. London: Oxford University Press.

Bunnens, G. (1979) *L'expansion phénicienne en méditerranée: essai d'interpretation fondé sur une analyse des traditions littéraires*. Brussels and Rome: Institut historique belge de Rome.

Bunsen, C. (1848–60) *Egypt's Place in Universal History*, C. H. Cotrell, trans., 5 vols. London: Longman.

Burchardt, M. (1912a) 'Hyksos Rassenangehörigkeit', *Zeitschrift für ägyptische Sprache* 50: 6–8.

—— (1912b) 'Zwei Bronzeschwerter aus Ägypten', *Zeitschrift für ägyptische Sprache* 50: 61–3.

Burkert, W. (1983) *Homo Necans: The Anthropology of Ancient Greek Sacrificial Ritual and Myth*, P. Bing, trans. Berkeley, Los Angeles and London: University of California Press.

—— (1984) 'Die orientalisierende Epoche in der griechischen Religion und Literatur', *Sitzungberichte der Heidelberger Akademie der Wissenschaften, Philosophische-historische Klasse* I.

—— (1985) *Greek Religion*, J. Raffan, trans. Cambridge, Mass.: Harvard University Press; Oxford: Blackwell.

—— (1987) *Ancient Mystery Cults*. Cambridge, Mass., and London: Harvard University Press.

Burl, A. (1979) *Prehistoric Avebury*. New Haven, Conn., and London: Yale University Press.

Burleigh, R. and Hewson, A. (1979) 'Radiocarbon measurements 12', *Radiocarbon* 34.

Burney, C. A. (1958) 'Eastern Anatolia in the Chalcolithic and Early Bronze Age', *Anatolian Studies* 8: 157–209.

Burney, C. A. and Lang, D. M. (1971) *The Peoples of the Hills: Ancient Ararat and Caucasus*. London: Weidenfeld & Nicolson.

Burns, A. R. (1949) 'Phoenicians', in *Oxford Classical Dictionary*, pp. 687–8.

Burton, A. (1972) *Diodorus Siculus, Book 1: A Commentary*. Leiden: Brill.

Bury, J. B. (1900) *A History of Greece to the Death of Alexander the Great*. London: Macmillan.

—— (1950) *A History of Greece to the Death of Alexander the Great*. 3rd edn., rev. R. Meiggs. London: Macmillan.

Burzachechi, C. (1976) 'L'adozione dell' alfabeto nel mondo greco', *Parola del Passato* 31: 82–102.

Butler, J. J. (1963) *Bronze Age Connections across the North Sea: A Study of the Prehistoric Trade and Industrial Relations between the British Isles, the Netherlands, North Germany and Scandinavia, c. 1700–700 B.C.* Groningen: Palaeohistoria IX.

Cadogan, G. (1969a) 'Mycenaean trade', *Bulletin of the Institute of Classical Studies* 16: 152–4.

—— (1969b) 'Review of G. F. Bass, *Cape Gelidonya: A Bronze Age Shipwreck*', *Journal of Hellenic Studies* 89: 187–9.

—— (1971) 'Was there a Minoan landed gentry?', *University of London Institute of Classics, Mycenaean Seminar* 19 May, pp. 367–71.

—— (1973) 'Patterns of distribution of Mycenaean pottery in the East Mediterranean', in V. Karageorghis, ed., *The Mycenaeans in the Eastern Mediterranean*, Acts of the International Symposium, Nicosia, 1972, pp. 166–74.

—— (1978) 'Dating the Aegean Bronze Age without radiocarbon', *Archaeometry* 20: 209–14.

—— (1986) 'Why was Crete different?', in G. Cadogan, ed., *The End of the Early Bronze Age in the Aegean*. Leiden: Brill, pp. 153–71.

—— (1987) 'Unsteady date of a big bang', *Nature* 328. 6/8: 473.

—— (1988) 'Reply', *Nature* 332. 31/3: 401–2.

Cagni, L. ed. (1981) *La Lingua di Ebla: Atti del convegno internazionale (Napoli, 21–23 aprile 1980)*. Naples: Istituto Universitario Orientale, Seminario di Studi Asiatici 14.

Calder, W. M. (1984) 'Schliemann's discovery of Priam's Treasure: A re-examination of the evidence', *Journal of Hellenic Studies* 104: 95–115.
—— (1986) 'A new picture of Heinrich Schliemann', in W. M. Calder and D. A. Traill, *Myth, Scandal and History: The Heinrich Schliemann Controversy and the First Edition of the Mycenaean Diary*. Detroit: Wayne State University Press, pp. 17–47.
Calder, W. M. and D. A. Traill (1986) *Myth, Scandal and History: The Heinrich Schliemann Controversy and the First Edition of the Mycenaean Diary*. Detroit: Wayne State University Press.
Callaway, J. A. and Weinstein, J. M. (1977) 'Radiocarbon dating of Palestine in the Early Bronze Age', *Bulletin of the American Schools of Oriental Research* 225: 1–16.
Callender, J. B. (1975) *Middle Egyptian*. Malibu: Undena.
Canby, J. V. (1969). 'Some Hittite figurines in the Aegean', *Hesperia* 38: 141–9.
Capart, J. (1942) 'Egyptian art', in S. Glanville, ed., *The Legacy of Egypt*. Oxford: Clarendon Press, pp. 80–119.
Caquot, A., Sznycer, M. and Herdner, M. (1974) *Textes Ougaritiques'*, Tome I; *Mythes et légendes*. Paris: Éditions du Cerf.
Carpenter, R. (1933) 'The antiquity of the Greek alphabet', *American Journal of Archaeology* 37: 8–28.
—— (1938) 'The Greek alphabet again', *American Journal of Archaeology* 42: 58–69.
—— (1958) 'Phoenicians in the West', *American Journal of Archaeology* 62: 25–53.
—— (1966) *Discontinuity in Greek Civilization*. Cambridge: Cambridge University Press.
Carter, E. and Stolper, M. W. (1984) *Elam: Surveys of History and Archaeology*. Berkeley: University of California Press.
Cartledge, P. (1979) *Sparta and Laconia: A Regional History 1300-362 BC*. London: Routledge & Kegan Paul.
—— (1987) *Agesilaos and the Crisis of Sparta*. London: Duckworth.
Caskey, J. E. (1956) 'Excavations at Lerna', *Hesperia* 25: 147–73.
—— (1957) 'Excavations at Lerna', *Hesperia* 26: 142–62.
—— (1958) 'Excavations at Lerna', *Hesperia* 27: 125–44.
—— (1960) 'The Early Helladic Period in the Argolid', *Hesperia* 29: 285–303.
—— (1971) 'Greece, Crete and the islands in the Early Bronze Age', in *The Cambridge Ancient History*, 3rd edn., vol. I, pt. 2, pp. 771–807.
—— (1986) 'Did the Early Bronze Age end?', in G. Cadogan, ed., *The End of the Early Bronze Age in the Aegean*. Leiden: Brill, pp. 9–30.
Caskey, M. E. (1980) 'Dionysos in the temple of Agia Irini, Keos', *American Journal of Archaeology* 84: 200.
Casperson, L. W. (1986) 'The lunar dates of Thutmosis III', *Journal of Near Eastern Studies* 45: 139–50.
Casson, L. (1971) *Ships and Seamanship in the Ancient World*. Princeton, NJ: Princeton University Press.

—— (1975) 'Bronze Age ships: the evidence of the Thera wall paintings', *International Journal of Nautical Archaeology* 4: 1–10.

Cassuto, U. (1971) *The Goddess Anath: Canaanite Epics of the Patriarchal Age.* I. Abraham, trans. Jerusalem: Magnes.

Catling, H. W. (1964) *Cypriot Bronze Work in the Mycenaean World.* Oxford: Oxford University Press.

—— (1971) 'Cyprus in the Early Bronze Age', in *Cambridge Ancient History*, 3rd edn., vol. I, pt. 2, pp. 808–23.

—— (1975) 'Cyprus in the Late Bronze Age', in *Cambridge Ancient History*, 3rd edn., vol.II, pt. 2, pp. 188–216.

Catling, H. W., Cherry, J. F., Jones, R. E. and Killen, J. T. (1980) 'The Linear B inscribed jars and West Crete', *Bulletin of the British School in Athens* 75: 49–113.

Catling, H. W. and Millet, A. (1965) 'A study of the composition patterns of Mycenaean pictorial pottery from Cyprus', *Annual of the British School in Athens* 60: 212–24.

Catling, H. W., Richards, E. E. and Blin-Stoyle, A. (1963) 'Correlations between composition and provenance of Mycenaean and Minoan pottery', *Annual of the British School in Athens* 58: 109–27.

Ceccherelli, I. M. (1986) *Alle fonte della civiltà: Viaggio storico linguistico attraverso i secoli.* Florence: Il Fauno.

Ceram, C. W. (1952) *Gods, Graves and Scholars: The Story of Archaeology*, trans. E. B. Garside. London: Gollancz and Sidgwick & Jackson.

Černy, J. (1952) *Egyptian Religion.* London: Hutchinson.

—— (1976) *Coptic Etymological Dictionary.* Cambridge: Cambridge University Press.

Chadwick, J. (1969) 'Linear B Tablets from Thebes', *Minos* 10: 115–37.

—— (1973a) 'The Linear B tablets as historical documents', in *Cambridge Ancient History*, 3rd edn., vol. II, pt 1, pp. 609–26.

—— (1973b) 'The prehistory of the Greek language', in *Cambridge Ancient History*, 3rd edn., vol. II, pt 2, pp. 805–19.

—— (1976) *The Mycenaean World.* London: Cambridge University Press.

Champollion, J. F. (1811) *L'Égypte sous les Pharaons: ou Recherches sur la géographie, la religion, la langue, les écritures et l'histoire de l'Égypte avant l'Invasion de Cambyse.* Grenoble.

—— (1909) see H. Hartleben.

Chandler, R. (1769) *Ionian Antiquities, Published with Permission with the Society of Dilettanti.* London.

Chang, K. C. (1980) *Shang Civilization.* New Haven, Conn.: Yale University Press.

Chantraine, P. (1928) 'Sur le vocabulaire maritime des grecs', in *Étrennes de Linguistique: offertes par quelques amis à Émile Benveniste.* Paris: Guethner, pp. 1–25.

—— (1968–75) *Dictionnnaire étymologique de la langue grecque.* 4 vols. Paris: Klincksieck.

Charles, R. P. (1965) 'Note sur un scarabée égyptien de Perati (Attique)', *Bulletin de correspondance hellénique* 89: 10–14.

Chassinat, E. (1966–68) *Le Mystère d'Osiris au mois de Khoïak.* 2 vols. Cairo: Institut français d'archéologie orientale.

Chaudhuri, N. C. (1974) *Scholar Extraordinary: The Life of the Professor the Right Honourable Max Müller PC.* London: Chatto & Windus.

Chen Mengjia (1977) *Xi Zhou Niandaikao* [*Western Zhou Chronology*]. Hong Kong: Huaxia.

Chen Zongguei (1980–) *Zhongguo Tianwenxue shi* [*History of Chinese Astronomy*]. 3 vols. to date. Shanghai: Shanghai Renmin Chubanshe.

Cherry, J. F. (1983) 'Evolution, revolution, and the origins of complex society in Minoan Crete', in O. Krzyszkowska and L. Nixon, eds., *Minoan Society: Proceedings of the Cambridge Colloquium 1981.* Bristol: Bristol Classical Press, pp. 33–46.

—— (1985) 'Islands out of the stream: isolation and interaction in early East Mediterranean insular prehistory', in A. B. Knapp and T. Stech, eds., *Prehistoric Production and Exchange: The Aegean and East Mediterranean.* Los Angeles: University of California, Institute of Archaeology, Monograph 25, pp. 12–29.

Childe, G. F. (1926) *The Aryans.* London: Kegan Paul.

—— (1949) *The Danube in Prehistory,* 2nd edn. London: Oxford University Press.

—— (1958) *A New Light on the Ancient Middle East.* London: Routledge & Kegan Paul.

Cicero. *The Nature of the Gods.*

—— *Tusculanae Disputationes.*

Clapham, L. R. (1969) *Sanchuniaton: The First Two Cycles.* Ph.D. dissertation, Harvard University.

Clark, M. E. and Coulson, W. D. E. (1978) 'Memnon and Sarpedon', *Museum Helveticum* 35: 65–73.

Clement of Alexandria, *Stromateis.*

—— *Protrepticus.*

Cline, E. (1987) 'Amenhotep III and the Aegean: a reassessment of Egypto-Aegean relations in the 14th century BC', *Orientalia* N.S. 56: 1–36.

—— (1989) Personal letter, 22 February.

—— (1990) 'An unpublished Egyptian faience plaque from Mycenae: a key to a new reconstruction', *Journal of the American Oriental Society* 110: 200–12.

—— (forthcoming a) 'Hittites in the Aegean world and vice versa', *American Journal of Archaeology.*

—— (forthcoming b) 'International trade in the Amarna period: Egyptian and Near Eastern imports at LHIII Mycenae', in B. J. Beitzel and G. D. Young, eds., *Tell el-Amarna 1887–1987.* Winona Lake, Ind.: Eisenbrauns.

Close, A. (1980) 'Current research and recent radiocarbon dates from Northern Africa', *Journal of African History* 21.2: 145–67.

—— (1984) 'Current research and recent radiocarbon dates from Northern Africa II', *Journal of African History* 25.1: 1–24.

Clutton-Brock, J. (1974) 'The Buhen horse', *Journal of Archaeological Science* 1: 89–100.

Cohen, D. (1970–6) *Dictionaire des racines sémitiques: ou attestées dans les langues sémitiques.* Fasc. 1–2. Paris, The Hague: Mouton.

Coldstream, J. N. (1973) 'Kythera, the change from the Early Helladic to the Early Minoan', in R. A. Crossland and A. Birchall, eds., *Bronze Age Migrations in the Aegean: Archaeological and Linguistic Problems of Greek Prehistory.* London: Duckworth, pp. 33–6.

Coldstream, J. N. and Huxley, G. N. (1984) 'The Minoans of Kythera', in R. Hägg and N. Marinatos, eds., *The Minoan Thalassocracy: Myth and Reality: Proceedings of the 3rd International Symposium at the Swedish Institute in Athens 31 May–5 June 1982.* Skrifter utgivna av Svenska Institutet i Athen 4, pp. 89–92.

Cole, D. P. (1984) *Shechem I: The Middle Bronze Age II B Pottery.* Winona Lake, Ind.: Eisenbrauns.

Coleman, J. E. (1974) 'The chronology and interconnections of the Cycladic Islands in the Neolithic Period and the Early Bronze Age', *American Journal of Archaeology* 78: 333–43.

—— (1985) 'Frying pans' of the Early Bronze Age Aegean', *American Journal of Archaeology* 89: 191–219.

Collon, D. (1972) 'The Smiting God', *Levant* 4: 111–33.

—— (1989) 'Cylinder seals from Ulu Burun', in G. F. Bass, C. Pulak, D. Collon and J. Weinstein, 'The Bronze Age shipwreck at Ulu Burun: 1986 campaign', *American Journal of Archaeology* 93: 12–16.

Contenau, G. (1953) 'Cylindres-Sceaux', in F. Bisson de la Roque, G. Contenau and F. Charpoutier, *Le Trésor de Tôd.* Cairo: L'Institut d'Archéologie Orientale, pp. 15–20.

Cook, A. B. (1914–40) *Zeus: A Study in Ancient Religion,* 3 vols., 5 pts. Cambridge: Cambridge University Press.

Cook, R. M. (1937) 'Amasis and the Greeks in Egypt', *Journal of Hellenic Studies* 57: 227–37.

Cook, S. A. (1924) 'The Semites', in *Cambridge Ancient History,* 1st edn. vol. I, pp. 181–237.

Corpus Hermeticum (1945–54), text established by A. D. Nock, trans. (into French) by A.-J. Festugière, 4 vols. Paris: Le Coffre, Gabalda *et al.*

Cory, I. P. (1832) *Sanchuniaton, Ancient Fragments of the Phoenician, Chaldaean, Egyptian, Tyrian, Carthaginian, Indian, Persian and other writers, with an introductory dissertation and an inquiry into the Philosophy and Trinity of the Ancients.* London: Pickering.

Courtois, C. (1955) *Les Vandals et l'Afrique.* Paris: Arts et Métiers Graphiques.

Courtois, J.-C. (1971) 'Le sanctuaire du dieu au l'ingot d'Enkomi-Alasia', in *Mission archéologique d'Alasia dirigée par Claude F. A. Schaeffer,* vol. I. Paris: Mission archéologique d'Alasia, pp. 151–356.

—— (1973) 'Sur divers groupes de vases mycéniens en Mediterranée orientale (1250–1150 av. j. c.)', in V. Karageorghis, ed., *The Mycenaeans in the Eastern Mediterranean*, Acts of the International Symposium, Nicosia, 1972, pp. 137–65.

Cramer, M. (1955) *Das altägyptische Lebenszeichen (Ankh) im christlichen (koptischen) Ägypten*. Wiesbaden: Harrassowitz.

Creel, H. G. (1937) *Studies in Early Chinese Culture*. London: Routledge & Kegan Paul.

—— (1951) *Confucius, the Man and the Myth*. London: Routledge & Kegan Paul.

Cross, F. M. (1968) 'The Phoenician inscription from Brazil: a nineteenth-century forgery', *Orientalia* 37: 437–60.

—— (1974) 'Leaves from an epigraphist's notebook', *The Catholic Biblical Quarterly* 36: 490–3.

—— (1979) 'The early alphabetic scripts', in F. M. Cross, ed., *Symposia, Celebrating the Seventy-fifth Anniversary of the American Schools of Oriental Research (1900–1975)*. Cambridge, Mass.: Harvard University Press, pp. 97–123.

—— (1980) 'Newly found inscriptions in Old Canaanite and early Phoenician scripts', *Bulletin of the American Schools of Oriental Research* 238: 1–21.

Crossland, R. A. (1971) 'Immigrants from the North', in *The Cambridge Ancient History*, 3rd edn., Vol. I, pp. 824–76.

Crossland, R. A. and Birchall, A. (1973) *Bronze Age Migrations in the Aegean: Archaeological and Linguistic Problems of Greek Prehistory*. London: Duckworth.

Crouwel, J. H. (1981) *Chariots and Other Means of Land Transport in Bronze Age Greece*. Amsterdam: Allard Pierson.

Crum, W. (1939) *A Coptic Dictionary*. Oxford: Clarendon Press.

Culican, W. (1966) *The First Merchant Venturers: The Ancient Levant in History and Commerce*. London: Thames & Hudson.

Dahood, M. (1981a) 'The linguistic classification of Eblaite', in L. Cagni, ed., *La Lingua di Ebla: Atti del convegno internazionale (Napoli, 21–23 aprile 1980)*. Naples: Istituto Universitario Orientale, Seminario di Studi Asiatici, 14, pp. 177–89.

—— (1981b) 'Afterward: Ebla, Ugarit and the Bible', in G. Pettinato, ed., *The Archives of Ebla*. Garden City, NY: Doubleday, pp. 271–321.

Daniel, C. (1962) 'Des emprunts égyptiens dans le grec ancien', *Studia et Acta Orientalia Bucarest* 4: 13–23.

Davies, N. M. and Gardiner, A. H. (1936) *Ancient Egyptian Paintings Selected, Copied and Described by Nina M. Davies with the Editorial Asistance of Alan H. Gardiner*, 3 vols. Chicago: Oriental Institute.

Davis, E. N. (1977) *The Vapheio Cups and Aegean Gold and Silver Ware*. New York and London: Garland.

Davis, J. L. (1984) 'Cultural innovation and the Minoan thalassocracy at Agia Irini Keos', in R. Hägg and N. Marinatos, eds., *The Minoan Thalassocracy: Myth and Reality: Proceedings of the 3rd International Symposium at the Swedish Institute in Athens 31 May–5 June 1982, Skrifter utgivna av Svenska Institutet i Athen* 4, pp. 159–66.

Davis, S. (1967) *The Decipherment of Minoan Linear A and Pictographic Scripts*. Johannesburg: Witwatersrand University Press.

Davis, W. M. (1979) 'Plato on Egyptian Art', *Journal of Egyptian Archaeology* 66: 121–7.

—— (1981) 'Egypt, Samos and the Archaic style in Greek sculpture', *Journal of Egyptian Archaeology* 67: 61–81.

Davison, J. M. (1987) 'Egyptian influence on the Greek Legend of Io', paper given to the Society for Biblical Literature.

Dayton, J. E. (1982a) 'Geology, archaeology and trade', in J. G. P. Best and N. M. W. de Vries, eds., *Interaction and Acculturation in the Mediterranean: Proceedings of the Second Congress of Mediterranean Pre- and Protohistory, Amsterdam, 19–23 November 1980*, vol. 2. Amsterdam: Grüner, pp. 153–68.

—— (1982b) 'The Mycenaeans and the discovery of glass' in J. G. P. Best and N. M. W. de Vries, eds., *Interaction and Acculturation in the Mediterranean: Proceedings of the Second Congress of Mediterranean Pre- and Protohistory, Amsterdam, 19–23 November 1980*. vol. 2. Amsterdam: Grüner, pp. 169–78.

Deïlaki-Protonotariou (1980) *Oi tumboi tou Argous*. Ph.D. dissertation, Athens University.

Delatte, A. (1922) *La vie de Pythagore de Diogène Laerce*. Brussels: Académie Royale de Belgique, Classe de Lettres, etc.

Delia, R. (1980) *A Study in the Reign of Senwosret III*, Ph.D. dissertation, Columbia University.

Delitzsch, F. (1881) *Wo lag das Paradies?* Leipzig: Hinrich.

—— (1884) *Die Sprache der Kossäer: linguistisch-historische Funde und Fragen.* Leipzig: Hinrich.

Dennis, G. (1848) *The Cities and Cemeteries of Etruria*, 2 vols. London: John Murray.

Desborough, V. R. d'A. (1964) *The Last Mycenaeans and Their Successors*. Oxford: Oxford University Press.

—— (1975) 'The end of the Mycenaean civilization and the Dark Age: the archaeological background', in *Cambridge Ancient History*, 3rd edn., vol. II, pt. 2, pp. 658–76.

Dessenne, A. (1957) *Le Sphinx: Étude iconogaphique*. Paris: Bibliothèque des Écoles françaises d'Athènes et de Rome, 186.

Diakonoff, I. M. (1972) 'Die Arier im Vorderen Orient-Ende eines Mythos-Zur Methodik der Erforschung verschollener Sprachen', *Orientalia* N.S. 41: 19–120.

—— (1985) 'On the original home of the speakers of Indo-European', *Journal of Indo-European Studies* 13: 92–174.

Diakonoff, I. M. and Jankowska, N. B. (1990) 'An Elamite Gilgameš text from Argištihelene, Urartu (Armarvir-blur, 8th century BC)', *Assyriologie* 79.2: 107–120.

Diakonoff, I. M. and Starostin, S. A. (1986) *Hurro-Urartian as an East Caucasian Language*. Munich: Kitzinger.

Dickinson, O. T. P. K. (1977) *The Origins of Mycenaean Civilisation*. Göteborg: Studies in Mediterranean Archaeology, 49.

Dietrich, B. C. (1964) 'The judgement of Zeus', *Rheinisches Museum für Philologie* 107: 97–125.

Dietrich, M. and Loretz, O. (1976) 'Die Keilalphabetischen Texte aus Ugarit, einschliesslich der keilalphabetischer Texte ausserhalb Ugarits', *Alter Orient und AltesTestament*, Suppl. 24.

Diodoros Sikelos (1933–67) *The Library of History*, 12 vols. C. H. Oldfather, trans. (vols 11 and 12, F. R. Walton and R. M. Geer, trans.). Cambridge, Mass.: Harvard University Press (Loeb).

Diogenes Laertios (1925) *Lives of Eminent Philosophers*, R. D. Hicks, trans., 2 vols. Cambridge, Mass.: Harvard University Press (Loeb).

Diop, C. A. (1973) 'La métallurgie de fer sous l'empire ancien égyptien', *Bulletin de l'Institut Fondamental d'Afrique Noir* 35, Série B, 3: 532–48.

—— (1974) *The African Origin of Civilization: Myth or Reality?* M. Cook, trans. Westport, Conn.: L. Hill.

Diringer, D. (1968) *The Alphabet: A Key to the History of Mankind*, 2 vols., 3rd. edn., rev. with the help of R. Regensberger. London: Hutchinson.

Dolgopolskii, A. B. (1973) *Svratinel'no-istoričeskaya fonetika Kusšitikix Jazykov*. Moscow: Nauka.

—— (1987) 'Cultural contacts of Proto-Indo-European and Proto-Indo-Iranian with neighbouring languages', *Folia Linguistica Historica* 8. 2. 3–36.

Dor, L., Jannoray, J., van Effenterre, H. and van Effenterre, M. (1960) *Kirrha, Étude de préhistoire phocidienne*. Paris: Boccard.

Doresse, J. (1960) *The Secret Books of the Egyptian Gnostics*. London: Hollis & Carter.

Dörpfeld, W. (1935) *Alt Olympia: Untersuchungen und Ausgrabungen zur Geschichte des ältesten Heiligtums von Olympia und der älteren griechischen Kunst.* Reprint. Osnabruck: Zeller, 1966.

Dörrie, H. (1979) 'Euhemeros', in K. Ziegler and W. Sontheimer, eds., *Der kleine Pauly: Lexikon der Antike*. Munich: Deutscher Taschenbuch Verlag, cols. 414–15.

Dothan, M. (1973) 'Philistine material culture and its Mycenaean affinities', in V. Karageorghis, ed., *The Mycenaeans in the Eastern Mediterranean*, Acts of the International Symposium, Nicosia, 1972, pp. 187–8.

Dothan, T. (1982) *The Philistines and Their Material Culture*. Jerusalem and New Haven, Conn.: Yale University Press.

Doumas, C. (1978 and 1980) *Thera and the Aegean World: Papers Presented at the Second International Scientific Congress, Santorini, Greece, August 1978*, 2 vols. London.

—— (1983) *Thera: Pompeii of the Ancient Aegean: Excavations at Akrotiri 1967–79*. London: Thames & Hudson.

Doumas, C. and Papazoglou, L. (1980) 'Santorini tephra from Rhodes', *Nature* 287. 25/9: 322–4.

Dow, S. (1937) 'The Egyptian cults in Athens', *Harvard Theological Review* 30.4: 183–232.

—— (1973) 'Literacy in Minoan and Myceaean lands', in *Cambridge Ancient History*, 3rd edn., vol. II, pt. 1, pp. 582–608.

Dows, D. and Dunham, W. J. (1942) 'An occurrence of iron in the Fourth Dynasty', *Journal of Egyptian Archaeology* 28: 57–9.

Drake, S. C. (1987) *Black Folk Here and There*. Vol. 1. Los Angeles: Center for Afro-American Studies, University of California.

Drawer, M. S. (1940) 'The Inscriptions' in R. Mond and O. Myers, eds., *The Temples at Armant: A Preliminary Survey*. London: The Egypt Exploration Society, pp. 157–96.

Dreihaus, J. (1957) 'Praehistorische Siedlungsfunde in der unteren Kaikoseben und an dem Golf von Çandarhli', *Istanbuler Mitteilungen*. 7: 76–101.

Drews, R. (1983) *Basileus: The Evidence for Kingship in Geometric Greece*. New Haven, Conn., and London: Yale University Press.

—— (1988) *The Coming of the Greeks: Indo-European Conquests in the Aegean and the Near East*. Princeton, NJ: Princeton University Press.

Drioton, E. (1931) 'Les Quatre Montou de Medamoud', *Chronique d'Égypte* 9: 259–70.

—— (1948a) 'Le Monothéisme de l'ancienne Egypte', *Cahiers d'histoire égyptienne* 1: 49–68.

—— (1948b) 'Preface', in J. F. Lauer, *Le Problème des pyramides d'Égypte*. Paris: Payot.

Drioton, E. and Vandier, J. (1949) *L'Égypte*. Paris: Clio, Introduction aux études historiques.

Drower, M. (1973) 'Syria *c.* 1550–1400 BC,' in *Cambridge Ancient History*, 3rd edn., vol II, pt. 1, pp. 417–525.

—— (1975) 'Ugarit IV. Ugarit in the fourteenth and thirteenth centuries BC', in *Cambridge Ancient History*, 3rd edn., vol II, pt. 2, pp. 130–48.

DuBois, W. E. B. (1975) *The Negro*. New York: Kraus-Thompson Organisation.

Duhoux, Y. (1978) 'Une analyse linguistique du linéaire A', *Études minoennes* 1: 65–129.

—— (1982) *L'Eteocretois: Les textes la langue*. Amsterdam: J. C. Gieben.

Duke, T. T. (1965) Review, *The Classical Journal* 61.3: 131–6.

Dumitrescu, V. (1982) 'The prehistory of Romania: from the earliest times to 1000 BC,' in *Cambridge Ancient History*, 2nd edn., vol. III, pt. I, pp. 1–74.

Dunand, F. (1973) *Le culte d'Isis dans le bassin de la méditerranée*, 3 vols. Vol. II, *Le culte d'Isis en Grèce*. Leiden: Brill.

Dunbabin, T. J. (1957) *The Greeks and Their Eastern Neighbours*. London: Penguin.

Dussaud, R. (1907) *Les Arabes en Syrie avant Islam*. Paris: Leroux.

—— (1931) 'Victor Bérard (nécrologue)', *Syria* 12: 392–3.

—— (1946–8) 'L'origine de l'alphabet et son évolution première d'après les découvertes de Byblos', *Syria* 25: 36–52.

—— (1947) 'Melqart', *Syria* 25: 205–30.

Earp, F. R. (1953) 'The date of the Supplices of Aeschylus', *Greece & Rome* 22. 66: 118–23.

Eco, U. (1989) *Foucault's Pendulum*. London: Secker & Warburg.

Edel, E. (1966) *Die Ortsnamenlisten aus dem Totentempel Amenophis III*. Bonn: Peter Hanstein.

Edwards, G. P. (1971) *The Language of Hesiod in Its Traditional Context*. Oxford: Blackwell.

Edwards, G. P. and Edwards, R. B. (1974) 'Eratosthenes and the date of Kadmos', *Classical Review* 24: 181–7.

Edwards, I. E. S. (1947) *The Pyramids of Egypt*. London: Penguin.

—— (1971) 'The Early Dynastic Period in Egypt', in *Cambridge Ancient History*, 3rd edn., vol. I, pt. 2, pp. 1–70.

Edwards, R. B. (1979) *Kadmos the Phoenician: A Study in Greek Legends and the Mycenaean Age*. Amsterdam: Hakkert.

Eggebrecht, A. and Eggebrecht, E. *et al.* (1988) *Albanien: Schätze aus dem Land der Skiptaren*. Mainz: Philipp von Zabern.

Eisenstadt, S. N. (1986) 'The Axial Age breakthroughs – their characteristics and origins', in S. N. Eisenstedt, ed., *The Origins and Diversity of Axial Age Civilizations*. Albany, NY: State University of New York Press, pp. 1–39.

Eissfeldt, O. (1935) 'Molk als Opferbegriff im Punischen und Hebräischen und das Ende des Gottes Moloch', *Beiträge zur Religiongeschichte des Altertums*, vol. III.

—— (1939) 'Ras Shamra und Sanchuniaton', *Beiträge zur Religionsgeschichte des Altertum*, vol. IV.

—— (1960) 'Phönikische und Griechische Kosmogonie', in O. Eissfeldt *et al.*, eds., *Éléments Orientaux dans la Religion Grecque Ancienne*. Strasburg and Paris: *Colloque de Strasbourg 22–4 mai 1958*, pp. 1–15.

Ellenbogen, M. (1962) *Foreign Words in the Old Testament: Their Origin and Etymology*. London: Luzac.

El Sayeed, see Sayeed.

Ember, A. (1917) 'Kindred Semito-Egyptian Words', *Zeitschrift für ägyptische Sprache und Altertumskunde* 53: 83–90.

Emery, W. B. (1960) 'A preliminary report on the excavations of the Egypt Exploration Society at Buhen', *Kush* 8: 7–16.

Engberg, R. M. (1939) *The Hyksos Reconsidered*. Chicago: The Oriental Institute, Studies of the Ancient Oriental Civilizations 18.

English, P. T. (1959) 'Cushites, Colchians and Khazars', *Journal of Near Eastern Studies* 18: 49–53.

Eph'al, I. (1982) *The Ancient Arabs: Nomads on the Borders of the Fertile Crescent 9th–5th Centuries BC*. Jerusalem: Magnes.

Erman, A. (1934) *Die Religion der Ägypter*. Berlin/Leipzig: Teubner.

Erman, A., and Grapow, H. (1925–31) *Wörterbuch der ägyptischen Sprache*, 7 vols. Reprint. Berlin: Akademie Verlag, 1982.

Ernshtedt, P. V. (1953) *Egiptskie Zaimstvovaniia vgrechskom iazyke*. Moscow and Leningrad: Akademij Nauk.

—— (1954) 'Iz oblasti drevnejshikh egiptizmov grechskogo Yazyka', *Palestinskij Sbornik* 83: 29–40.

Evans, A. (1909) *Scripta Minoa*. Oxford: Clarendon Press.

—— (1921–35) *The Palace of Minos*, 4 vols. in 6. London: Macmillan.

—— (1925) *The Early Nilotic, Libyan and Egyptian Relations with Minoan Crete* (The Huxley Memorial Lecture for 1925). London: Royal Anthropological Institute.

—— (1929) *The Shaft Graves and Bee-Hive Tombs of Mycenae*. London: Macmillan.

Evans, J. D. (1964) 'Excavations in the Neolithic settlement at Knossos 1957–60, Pt. I', *Annual of the British School in Athens* 59: 132–240.

Evelyn-White, H. G., trans. (1914) *Hesiod: The Homeric Hymns and Homerica*. Cambridge, Mass.: Harvard University Press (Loeb); London: Heinemann.

Fan Xiangyong (1962) *Guben Zhushu Jinian Jixiao Dipu*. Shanghai: Shangwu chubanshe.

Farag, S. (1980) 'Une inscription memphite de la XIIe dynastie', *Revue d'Égyptologie* 32: 75–81.

Faraone, C. A. (1987) 'Hephaestus the magician and Near Eastern parallels for Alcinous' watchdogs', *Greek, Roman and Byzantine Studies* 28. 3: 257–80.

Farina, G. (1938) *Il Papiro dei Re restaurato*. Roma: Pubblicazioni Egittologiche del R. Museo di Torino.

Farnell, L. R. (1895–1909) *The Cults of the Greek States*, 5 vols. Oxford: Clarendon Press.

—— (1921) *Greek Hero Cults and Ideas of Immortality*. Oxford: Clarendon Press.

Faulkner, R. (1969) *The Ancient Egyptian Pyramid Texts*. Oxford: Oxford University Press.

—— (1976) *A Concise Dictionary of Middle Egyptian*. Oxford: Oxford University Press.

Faure, P. (1968) 'Toponymes créto-mycéniens dans une liste d'Amenophis III', *Kadmos* 7: 138–49.

Fazzini, R. (1982) 'Mut-Tempel Karnak', in W. Helck and E. Otto, eds., *Lexikon der Ägyptologie*, vol. IV, cols. 248–51.

Fears, R. J. (1978) 'The historical perspective: Atlantis and the Minoan thalassocracy: a study in modern mythopeism', in E. S. Ramage, ed., *Atlantis: Fact or Fiction*. Bloomington: University of Indiana Press, pp. 103–36.

Ferron, J. (1972) 'Un traité d'alliance entre Caere et Carthage', in H. Temporini and W. Haase, eds., *Aufstieg und Niedergang der römischen Welt: Geschichte und Kultur Roms im Spiegel der neueren Forschung*, 21 vols. Berlin and New York: de Gruyter, vol. I, pt. 1, pp. 189–216.

Fick, A. (1905) *Vorgriechische Ortsnamen als Quelle für die Vorgeschichte Griechenlands*. Göttingen: Vandenhoeck & Ruprecht.

Fimmen, D. (1921) *Die kretisch-mykenische Kultur*. Leipzig and Berlin: Teubner.

Finley, M. I. (1959) 'The Mycenaean tablets and economic history', *Economic History Review* 10: 128–41.

—— (1978) *The World of Odysseus*, rev. edn. New York: Viking.

—— (1980) *Ancient Slavery and Modern Ideology*. New York: Viking.

—— (1981) *The Legacy of Greece: A New Appraisal*. Oxford: Clarendon Press.

Finley, M. I., Caskey, J. L., Kirk, G. S. and Page, D. L. (1964) 'The Trojan War', *Journal of Hellenic Studies* 84: 1–20.

Fishman, B. and Lawn, B. (1978) 'University of Pennsylvania radiocarbon dates', *Radiocarbon* 20: 205–31.

Fontenrose, J. (1959) *Python: A Study in Delphic Myth and Its Origins*. Berkeley: University of California Press.

—— (1966a) 'Typhon among the Arimi', in L. Wallach, ed., *The Classical Tra-*

dition: Literary and Historical Essays in Honor of Harry Caplan. Ithaca: Cornell University Press, pp. 64–82.

—— (1966b) 'Review of Vian, *Les Origines de Thèbes*', *Classical Philology* 61: 189–92.

Forrer, E. (1924a) 'Vorhomerische Griechen in den Keilschrifttexten von Boghazköi', *Mitteilungen der deutschen Orientgesellschaft* 63: 1–22.

—— (1924b) 'Die Griechen in den Boghazköi-Texten', *Orientalische Literaturzeitung* 27: 113–18.

Forrest, W. G. G. (1982) 'Central Greece and Thessaly', in *Cambridge Ancient History*, 2nd edn., vol. III, pt. 3, pp. 286–99.

Fossey, J. M. (1972) 'Tilphossaion?' *Teiriseias* suppl. 1: 1–16.

—— (1974) 'The end of the Bronze Age in the South West Copaïc', *Euphrosyne* 6: 7–21.

—— (1988) *The Topography and Population of Ancient Boiotia*, 2 vols in 1. Chicago: Ares.

—— (1989a) 'Later prehistory of Boeotia: an overview', paper given at the 6th International Conference of Boeotian Studies, Bradford, 26–30 June.

—— (1989b) 'The Boeotian Catalogue of Ships, Mycenaean or Archaic?' paper given at the 6th International Boeotian Conference, Bradford, 26–30 June.

Fossey, J. M. and Schachter, A., eds. (1979) *The Proceedings of the Second International Conference on Boiotian Antiquities* (held in Montreal).

Foucart, G. (1914) *Les Mystères d'Eleusis.* Paris: A. Picard.

Fraenkel, E. (1910–12) *Geschichte der griechischen Nomina agentis auf τήρ, -τωρ, -της.* Strasburg: Trübner.

Frankfort, H. (1936–7) 'Notes on the Cretan griffin', *Annual of the British School of Archaeology in Athens* 37: 106–22.

—— (1970) *Art and Architecture in the Ancient Orient.* London: Penguin.

Frankfort, H., de Buck, A. and Gunn, B. (1933) *The Cenotaph of Seti I at Abydos*, 2 vols. London: Egypt Exploration Society.

Frankfort, H. and Frankfort, H. A. (1946) 'Myth and Reality', in H. Frankfort and H. A. Frankfort, eds., *The Intellectual Adventure of Ancient Man.* Chicago: University of Chicago Press.

Frazer, J. (1890–1915) *The Golden Bough: A Study in Magic and Religion*, 9 vols. London: Macmillan.

—— (1898) *Pausanias's Description of Greece*, 6 vols. London: Macmillan.

—— (1914) *Adonis Attis Osiris: Studies in the History of Oriental Religion (Golden Bough IV)*, 3rd edn., 2 vols. London: Macmillan.

—— (1921) *Apollodorus; The Library*, 2 vols. Cambridge, Mass.: Harvard University Press (Loeb).

Fredericks, S. C. (1978) 'Plato's Atlantis: a mythologist looks at myth', in E. S. Ramage, ed., *Atlantis: Fact or Fiction.* Bloomington: Indiana University Press, pp. 82–99.

French, D. H. (1971) 'The Development of Mycenaean terracotta figurines', *Annual of the British School of Archaeology at Athens* 66: 101–84.

—— (1973) 'Migrations and 'Minyan' pottery in Western Anatolia and the

Aegean,' in R. A. Crossland and A. Birchall, eds., *Bronze Age Migrations in the Aegean*. London: Duckworth, pp. 51–4.

Fréret, N. (1784) 'Observations générales sur l'origine et sur l'anciennes histoires des premiers habitans de la Grèce', *Académie des Inscriptions, 1784–1793* 47 (published 1809), Mémoire de littérature, pp. 1–149.

Friedrich, J. (1923) 'Zum Phönizisch-Punischen', *Zeitschrift für Semitistik* 2: 1–10.

—— (1933) 'Einführung ins Urartäische', *Mitteilungen der vorderasiatisch-ägyptischen Gesellschaft* 37, Heft 3.

—— (1951) *Phönizisch-punische Grammatik*. Rome: Analecta Orientalia.

—— (1957) *Extinct Languages*, F. Gaynor, trans. New York: Philosophical Library.

—— (1968) 'Die Unechtheit der phönizischen Inschrift aus Parahyba', *Orientalia* 37: 421–4.

Frödin, O. and Persson, A. (1938) *Asine, Results of the Swedish Excavations 1922–1930*. Stockholm: General Straben Litografiska Förlag.

Froidefond, C. (1971) *Le Mirage égyptien dans la littérature grecque d' Homère à Aristote*. Paris: Ophrys.

Fronzaroli, P. (1959) 'I rapporti fra la grecia e l'oriente in alcuni studi recenti', *Athene e Roma*, ser. IV. 2: 65–79.

Frothingham, A. (1891) 'Archaeological news', *American Journal of Archaeology* 6: 476–566.

Fulco, W. J. (1976) *The Canaanite God Rešef*. New Haven: Yale University Press.

Fung Yu-lan (1952) *A History of Chinese Philosophy*, D. Bodde, trans., 2 vols. Princeton, NJ: Princeton University Press.

Furumark, A. (1941) *The Chronology of Mycenaean Pottery*. Stockholm: Kungl. Vitterhets Historie och Antikvitets Akademien.

—— (1950) 'The settlement at Ialysos and Aegean history, c. 1550–1400 BC', *Opuscula Archaeologica* 6, Lund.

Gadd, C. J. (1973) 'Hammurabi and the end of his dynasty', in *Cambridge Ancient History*, 3rd edn., vol. II, pt. 1, pp. 176–228.

Gaerte, W. (1922) 'Die 'Horns of Consecration', *Archiv für Religionswissenschaft* 21: 72–5.

Galanopulos, A. (1963) 'Die Deukalionische Flut aus geologischen Sicht', *Das Altertum* 9: 3–7.

—— (1964) 'Die ägyptischen Plagen und der Auszug Israels aus geologischen Sicht', *Das Altertum* 10: 131–7.

Gale, N. H. (1980) 'Some aspects of lead and silver mining in the Aegean world', in C. Doumas, ed., *Thera and the Aegean World: Papers Presented at the Second International Scientific Congress, Santorini, Greece, August 1978*, vol. 2. London, pp. 161–95.

Gale, N. H. and Stos-Gale, Z. A. (1981) 'Lead and silver in the ancient Aegean', *Scientific American* 244: 176–92.

Gamer-Wallert, I. (1977) 'Fische, religiös', in W. Helck and E. Otto, *Lexikon der Ägyptologie*, vol. II, cols. 228–34.

Garašanin, M. (1973) 'Ethnographic problems of the Bronze Age in the Central Balkan peninsula and neighbouring regions', in R. A. Crossland and A. Birchall, eds., *Bronze Age Migrations in the Aegean*. London: Duckworth, pp. 115–28.

—— (1982a) 'The Eneolithic Period in the Central Balkan area', in *Cambridge Ancient History*, 2nd edn., vol. III, pt. 1, pp. 136–62.

—— (1982b) 'The Bronze Age in the Central Balkan area', in *Cambridge Ancient History*, 2nd edn., vol. III, pt. 1, pp. 163–86.

Garbini, G. (1977) 'Sulla datazione dell' iscrizione di Ahiram', *Annali dell' Istituto Orientale di Napoli* 627: 81–9.

—— (1978) 'La lingua di Ebla', *La Parola del Passato* 181: 241–51.

—— (1979) *Storia e problemi dell' epigrafia semitica*, Supplemento (19) agli *Annali dell'Istituto Universitario Orientale di Napoli* 39.

—— (1981) 'Considerations on the language of Ebla', in L. Cagni, ed., *La Lingua di Ebla*. Naples: Istituto Universitario Orientale, Seminario di Studi Asiatici, 14, pp. 75–82.

Gardiner, A. H. (1916) 'The defeat of the Hyksos by Kamōse: the Carnarvon Tablet No. 1'. *Journal of Egyptian Archaeology* 3: 95–111.

—— (1927) *Egyptian Grammar*. Oxford: Clarendon Press.

—— (1942) 'Writing and Literature', in S. R. A. Glanville, ed., *The Legacy of Egypt*. Oxford: Clarendon Press, pp. 53–78.

—— (1946) 'Davies's Copy of the Great Speos Artemidoros Inscription', *Journal of Egyptian Archaeology* 32: 43–56.

—— (1947) *Ancient Egyptian Onomastica*, 3 vols. Oxford: Oxford University Press.

—— (1950) *Egyptian Grammar*, 2nd edn. Oxford: Clarendon Press.

—— (1957) *Egyptian Grammar*, 3rd edn. Oxford: Clarendon Press.

—— (1959) *The Royal Canon of Turin*. Oxford: Griffith Institute.

—— (1961a) *Egypt of the Pharaohs*. Oxford: Clarendon Press.

—— (1961b) 'The Egyptian Memnon', *Journal of Egyptian Archaeology* 47: 91–99.

—— (1945–55) *My Early Years*, ed. J. Gardiner. Reprint. Isle of Man: Andreas, 1986.

—— (n.d.) *My Working Years*. London: Coronet Press.

Gardiner, A. H. and Gunn, B. (1918) 'New renderings of Egyptian Texts. II. The Expulsion of the Hyksos', *Journal of Egyptian Archaeology* 5: 36–56.

Gardner, P. (1880) 'Stephani on the tombs at Mycenae', *Journal of Hellenic Studies* 1: 94–106.

Garnsey, P. and Whittaker C. R. (1983) 'Trade and famine in Classical Antiquity', *Cambridge Philological Society Supplement* 8: 1–44.

Garvie, A. F. (1969) *Aeschylus' Supplices: Play and Trilogy*. Cambridge: Cambridge University Press.

Gaster, T. H. (1964) *The Dead Sea Scriptures: In English Translation*. Garden City, NY: Anchor Books.

Gauthier, H. (1925–31) *Dictionnaire des noms géographiques contenus dans les textes hiéroglyphiques*, 5 vols. Cairo: L'Institut français d'archéologie orientale.

—— (1931) *Les Fêtes du dieu Min.* Cairo: L'institut français d'archéologie orientale.

Gelb, I. J. (1944) *Hurrians and Subarians.* Chicago: Oriental Institute Studies in Ancient Oriental Civilization, No. 22.

—— (1977) 'Thoughts about Ibla: a preliminary evaluation, March 1977', *Syro-Mesopotamian Studies* 1.1: 1–26.

—— (1981) 'Ebla and the Kish Civilization', in L. Cagni, ed., *La Lingua di Ebla.* Naples: Istituto Universitario Orientale, Seminario di Studi Asiatici, 14, pp. 9–73.

Georgacas, D. J. (1957) 'A contribution to Greek word history, derivation and etymology', *Glotta* 36: 100–22; 161–93.

—— (1969) 'The name *Asia* for the continent; its history and origin', *Names* 17.1: 1–90.

Georgiev, V. I. (1952) 'L'origine minoenne de l'alphabet phénicienne', *Archiv Orientalni* 20: 487–95.

—— (1966) *Introduzione alla storia delle lingue indeuropee.* Rome: Edizione dell' Ateneo.

—— (1972) 'Die ethnischen Verhältnisse im alten Nordwestkleinasien', *Balkansko Ezikoznanie/Linguistique Balkanique* 16. 2: 5–34.

—— (1973) 'The arrival of the Greeks in Greece: the linguistic evidence', in R. A. Crossland and A. Birchall, eds., *Bronze Age Migrations in the Aegean.* London: Duckworth, pp. 243–54.

Georgius Syncellus (1719) *Chronographia.* Venice.

Gesenius, F. H. W. (1953) *A Hebrew and English Lexicon of the Old Testament*, E. Robinson, trans., ed. F. Brown, S. R. Driver and C. A. Briggs. Oxford: Clarendon Press.

Ghirschman, R. (1977) *L'Iran et la Migration des Indo-Aryens et des Iraniens.* Leiden: Brill.

Gibbon, E. (1776–88) *The Decline and Fall of the Roman Empire*, 6 vols. London.

—— (1794) 'Memoirs of my life and writings', in *Miscellaneous Works of Edward Gibbon Esquire with Memoirs of his life and writings, composed by himself: Illustrated from his Letters with Occasional Notes and Narrative by John Lord Sheffield*, 2 vols. London, vol. I, pp. 1–185.

Gilbert, A. (1964) *Machiavelli: Chief Works and Others.* Durham, NC: Durham Press.

Giles, P. (1924) 'The peoples of Europe', in *Cambridge Ancient History*, 1st edn., vol. II, pp. 20–40.

Gillings, R. J. (1973) *Mathematics in the Times of the Pharaohs.* Cambridge, Mass.: M.I.T. Press.

Gimbutas, M. (1970) 'Proto-Indo-European culture: the Kurgan culture during the fifth, fourth and third millennia', in G. Cardona, H. M. Hoenigswald and A. Senn, eds., *Indo-European and Indo-Europeans: Papers Presented at the Third Indo-European Conference at the University of Pennsylvania.* Philadelphia: University of Pennsylvania Press, pp. 155–97.

Ginzberg, L. (1968) *The Legends of the Jews*, Paul Radin, trans., 7 vols. Reprint. Philadelphia: Jewish Publication Society of America.

Giveon, R. (1975) 'Asiaten', in W. Helck and E. Otto, eds., *Lexikon der Ägyptologie*, vol. I, cols. 462–71.

—— (1978a) *The Impact of Egypt on Canaan: Iconographical and Related Studies*. Freiburg: Universitätsverlag; Göttingen: Vandenhoek & Ruprecht.

—— (1978b) 'Two unique Egyptian inscriptions from Tel Aphek', *Tel Aviv* 5: 188–92.

—— (1981) 'Some Egyptological considerations concerning Ugarit', in G. D. Young, ed., *Ugarit in Retrospect: 50 Years of Ugarit and Ugaritic*. Winona Lake, Ind.: Eisenbrauns, pp. 55–8.

—— (1985) *Egyptian Scarabs from Western Asia, from the Collections of the British Museum*. Freiburg (Switzerland): Universitätsverlag.

Glanville, S. (1942) *The Legacy of Egypt*. Oxford: Clarendon Press.

Godart, L. (1968) 'Kupirijo dans les textes mycéniens', *Studi Miceni ed Egeo-Anatolici* 5: 64–70.

—— (1983) 'Le Linéaire A et son environnement', *Studi Miceni ed Egeo-Anatolici* 20: 30–3.

—— (1984) 'Le Linéaire A au Linéaire B', in *Aux origines de l'Hellénisme: La Crète et la Grèce: Hommages à Henri van Effenterre*. Paris: Publications de la Sorbonne, pp. 121–8.

Godart, L. and Sacconi, A. (1978) 'Les tablettes en Linéaire B de Thèbes', *Incunabula Graeca* 71. Rome: dell'Ateneo & Bizzarri.

Goedicke, H. (1969) 'Ägäische Namen in ägyptischen Inschriften', *Wiener Zeitschrift für die Kunde des Morgenlandes* 62: 7–10.

—— (1986) 'The end of the Hyksos in Egypt', in L. H. Lesko, ed., *Egyptological Studies in Honor of Richard A. Parker*. Hanover and London: Brown University Press and the University Press of New England, pp. 37–47.

Gomme, A. W. (1913) 'The legend of Cadmus and the Logographi', *Journal of Hellenic Studies* 13: 53–72; 223–45.

Goodenough, W. H. (1970) 'The evolution of pastoralism and Indo-European origins', in G. Cardona *et al.*, eds., *Indo-European and Indo-Europeans: Papers Presented at the Third Indo-European Conference at the University of Pennsylvania*. Philadelphia: University of Pennsylvania Press, pp. 253–65.

Goodison, L. (1985) *Some Aspects of Religious Symbolism in the Aegean Area during the Bronze and Early Iron Ages*. Ph.D. dissertation, University College, London.

—— (1988) 'A female sun deity in the Bronze Age Aegean?', *Bulletin of the Institute of Classical Studies of the University of London* 35: 168–73.

—— (1989) *Death, Women and the Sun: Symbolism and Regeneration in Early Aegean Religion*. London: Institute of Classical Studies.

—— (1990) *Moving Heaven and Earth*. London: Women's Press.

Goosens, G. (1939) 'Memnon était-il éthiopien ou susien?', *Chronique d'Égypte* 14: 337–8.

—— (1962) 'La Légende de Sésostris', *La Nouvelle Clio* 10–12: 293–5.

Gordon, C. (1955) 'Homer and the Bible', *Hebrew Union College Annual* 26: 43–108.

—— (1962a) 'Eteocretan', *Journal of Near Eastern Studies* 21: 211–14.

—— (1962b) *Before the Bible: The Common Background of Greek and Hebrew Civilizations.* New York: Harper & Row.

—— (1963a) 'The Dreros Bilingual', *Journal of Semitic Studies* 8: 76–9.

—— (1963b) 'The Mediterranean factor in the Old Testament', *Supplements to Vetus Testamentum* 9: 19–31.

—— (1965) *Ugaritic Textbook, Analecta Orientalia* 18. Rome: Pontificum Institutum Biblicum.

—— (1966) *Evidence for the Minoan Language.* Ventnor, NJ: Ventnor Publishers.

—— (1968a) 'The present status of Minoan studies', *Atti e memorie del congresso internazionale di micenilogica, Roma, 27 settembre–3 ottobre 1967*, pp. 383–8.

—— (1968b) 'Northwest Semitic texts in Latin and Greek letters', *Journal of the American Oriental Society* 88: 285–9.

—— (1968c) 'The Canaanite text from Brazil', *Orientalia* 37: 425–36.

—— (1968d) 'Reply to Professor Cross', *Orientalia* 37: 461–3.

—— (1969) 'Minoan', *Athenaeum* 47: 125–35.

—— (1970a) 'Greek and Eteocretan unilinguals from Praisos and Dreros', *Berytus* 19: 95–8.

—— (1970b) 'In the wake of Minoan and Eteocretan', *Praktika tou 1 Diethnous Anthropistikou Symposiou en Delfois* 1: 163–71.

—— (1971) *Forgotten Scripts: The Story of Their Decipherment.* London: Penguin.

—— (1973) 'The Greek unilinguals from Praisos and Dreros and their bearing on Eteocretan and Minoan', *Pepragmena tou 3 Diethnous Kretologikou Synedriou*, 3: 97–103.

—— (1981) 'The Semitic language of Minoan Crete', in Y. Arbeitman and A. R. Bomhard, eds., *Bonum Homini Donum.* Amsterdam: John Benjamins, pp. 761–82.

Gossman, L. (1983) 'Orpheus Philologus: Bachofen versus Mommsen on the study of Antiquity', *Transactions of the American Philosophical Society* 73. 5.

Götze, F. (1936) *Hethiter, Churriter und Assyrer: Hauptlinien der vorderasiatischen Kulturentwicklung im II. Jahrtausend v. Chr. Geb.* Oslo: Aschehoug.

—— (1973) 'Anatolia from Shupililuliumash to the Egyptian War of Mutawalish', in *Cambridge Ancient History*, 3rd ed., vol. II, pt. 2, pp. 117–29.

Grace, V. (1956) 'The Canaanite jar', in S. S. Weinberg, ed., *The Aegean and the Near East (Studies Presented to Hetty Goldman).* Locust Valley, NY: Augustin, pp. 80–109.

Graefe, E. (1982) 'Nephthys', in W. Helck and E. Otto, *Lexikon der Ägyptologie*, vol. IV, cols. 457–60.

Graham, A. J. (1986) 'The historical interpretation of Al Mina', *Dialogues d'histoire ancienne* 12: 51–65.

Graham, J. W. (1962) *The Palaces of Crete.* Princeton, NJ: Princeton University Press.

—— (1964) 'The relation of the Minoan palaces to the Near Eastern palaces of the second millennium', in E. L. Bennett, ed., *Mycenaean Studies* pp. 195–215.

—— (1970) 'Egyptian features at Phaistos', *American Journal of Archaeology* 74: 231–40.

—— (1975) 'The banquet hall of the Little Palace', *American Journal of Archaeology* 79: 141–4.

—— (1977) 'Bathrooms and lustral chambers', in K. H. Kinzl, ed., *Greece and the Eastern Mediterranean in Ancient History and Prehistory*. Berlin: de Gruyter, pp. 110–25.

Grapow, H. (1944) 'Ägyptisch. Vom Lebensverlauf einer afrikanischen Sprache', in H. H. Schaeder, ed., *Der Orient in deutscher Forschung*. Leipzig: Harrassowitz, pp. 205–16.

Graves, R. (1948) *The White Goddess*. London: Faber.

—— (1955) *Greek Myths*, 2 vols. London: Penguin.

Gray, J. (1956) *The Canaanites*, 2nd ed. London: Thames & Hudson.

—— (1957) *The Legacy of Canaan: The Ras Shamra Texts and Their Relevance to the Old Testament*, suppl. to *Vetus Testamentum* V.

Grdseloff, B. (1942) *Les Débuts du culte de Rechef en Égypte*. Cairo: Institut français d'archéologie orientale.

Green, A. R. W. (1975) *The Role of Human Sacrifice in the Ancient Near East*. Missoula, Mont.: Scholars Press for the American Schools of Oriental Research.

Greenberg, J. H. (1986) 'Were there Egyptian Koines?', in J. H. Fishman *et al.*, eds., *The Fergusonian Impact: In Honor of Charles A Ferguson on the Occasion of His 65th Birthday*, vol. I, *From Phonology to Society*. Berlin, New York and Amsterdam: Mouton & de Gruyter, pp. 271–90.

Greenberg, M. (1955) *The Ḥab/piru*. New Haven, Conn.: American Oriental Series, vol. 39.

Griffith, F. Ll. (1896) 'The Millingen Papyrus', *Zeitschrift für ägyptische Sprache* 34: 35–51.

—— (1911) 'Hyksos', in *Encyclopedia Britanica*, 11th edn., vol. 14, pp. 174–5.

Griffiths, J. G. (1955) 'The orders of gods in Greece and Egypt', *Journal of Hellenic Studies* 75: 21–3.

—— (1970) *Plutarch's De Iside et Osiride*. Cambridge: Cambridge University Press.

—— (1975) *Apuleius of Madauros, The Isis Book (Metamorphosis, Book XI)*. Leiden: Brill.

—— (1980a) 'Interpretatio Graeca', in W. Helck and E. Otto, *Lexikon der Ägyptologie*, vol. III, cols. 167–72.

—— (1980b) *The Origins of Osiris and His Cult*. Leiden: Brill.

—— (1982a) 'Osiris', in W. Helck and E. Otto, *Lexikon der Ägyptologie*, vol. IV, cols. 623–33.

—— (1982b) 'Plutarch', in W. Helck and E. Otto, *Lexikon der Ägyptologie*, vol. IV, cols. 1065–7.

Grimm, G. (1969) *Die Zeugnisse Ägyptischer Religion und Kunstelemente im römischen Deutschland*. Leiden: Brill.

Grimme, H. (1925) 'Hethitisches im griechischen Wortschatze', *Glotta* 14: 13–25.

Grondahl, F. (1967) *Die Personennamen der Texte aus Ugarit*. Rome: Pontifical Institute.

Grousset, R. (1959) *Chinese Art and Culture*, Haakon Chevalier, trans. London: Andre Deutsch.

Grumach, E. (1968/9) 'The coming of the Greeks', *Bulletin of the John Rylands Library* 51: 73–103; 400–30.

Gruppe, O. (1906) *Griechische Mythologie und Religionsgeschichte*, 2 vols. Munich: Beck.

Guignant, J. (1828) 'Mémoire insérée au tome V du *Tacite de Burnouf*', Paris, pp. 531–5.

Gundlach, R. (1982) 'Min', in W. Helck and E. Otto, *Lexikon der Ägyptologie*, vol. IV, cols. 135–9.

Guralnick, E. (1985) 'Profiles of Kouroi', *American Journal of Archaeology* 89: 399–409.

Gurney, O. R. (1973) 'Anatolia *c.* 1750–1600 BC'; 'Anatolia 1600–1380 BC', in *Cambridge Ancient History*, 3rd edn., vol. II, pt. 1, pp. 228–55; 659–82.

Güterbock, H. G. (1983) 'The Hittites and the Aegean world, part 1, the Ahhiyawa problem reconsidered', *American Journal of Archaeology* 87: 133–8.

—— (1986) 'Troy in Hittite texts? Wilusa, Ahhiyawa, and Hittite history', in M. Mellink, ed., *Troy and the Trojan War: A Symposium Held at Bryn Mawr College October 1984*. Bryn Mawr, Pa.: Department of Classical and Near Eastern Archaeology, pp. 33–44.

Guthrie, W. K. C. (1966) *Orpheus and Greek Religion: A Study of the Orphic Movement*, rev. edn. New York: Norton.

Gützlaff, K. F. A. (1838) *A Sketch of Chinese History Ancient and Modern*. 2 vols. London: T. Ward.

Haas, H., Devine, J., Wenke, R., Lehner, M., Wolfi, W. and Bonani, G. (1987) 'Radiocarbon chronology and the historical calendar in Egypt', in O. Aurenche, Jacques Evin and Francis Hours, eds., *Chronologies du Proche Orient/ Chronologies in the Near East: Relative Chronologies and Absolute Chronology 16,000–4000 BP: CNRS symposium, Lyon (France), 24–28 November 1986*, 2 vols. Oxford British Archaeological Reports, International Series 379, pp. 585–606.

Hall, H. R. (1905) 'The two labyrinths', *Journal of Hellenic Studies* 25: 320–4.

—— (1920) *The Ancient History of the Near East*, 6th edn. London: Routledge.

—— (1924) 'The Middle Kingdom and the Hyksos conquests', in *Cambridge Ancient History*, 1st edn., vol. I, pp. 299–325.

—— (1929) 'A Pre-Dynastic Egyptian double-axe', in S. Casson, ed., *Essays in Aegean Archaeology: Presented to Sir Arthur Evans in Honour of His 75th Birthday*. Oxford: Clarendon Press, p. 42.

Hall, H. R. and King, L. W. (1906) *History of Egypt, Chaldea, Syria, Babylonia and Assyria*. London: Grolier Society.

Hallo, W. W. (1977) 'Seals lost and found', in M. Gibson, and R. D. Biggs, eds., *Seals and Sealings in the Ancient Near East*. Malibu: Undena, pp. 55–60.

Halpern, B. (1987) 'Radical Exodus dating fatally flawed', *Biblical Archaeology Review* 13.6.56–61.

Hammer, C. U., Clausen, H. B., and Dansgaard, W. (1980) 'Dating from the Greenland Icecap', *Nature* 288: 230–35.

Hammer, C. U., Clausen, H. B., Friedrich, W. L., and Tauber, H. (1987) 'The Minoan eruption of Santorini in Greece dated to 1645 BC', *Nature* 328. 6/8: 517–9.

—— (1988) 'Dating of the Santorini eruption', *Nature* 332.31/3: 401.

Hammond, N. G. L. (1967) *A History of Greece to 322 BC*, 2nd. edn. Oxford: Clarendon Press.

—— (1973) 'Grave circles in Albania and Epirus', in R. A. Crossland and A. Birchall, eds., *Bronze Age Migrations in the Aegean*. London: Duckworth, pp. 189–95.

—— (1975) 'The literary tradition for the migrations', in *Cambridge Ancient History*, 3rd edn., vol. II, pt 2, pp. 678–712.

—— (1976) *Migrations and Invasions in Greece and Adjacent Areas*. Park Ridge, NJ: Noyes Press.

Hani, J. (1976) *La Religion égyptienne dans la pensée de Plutarque*, collection d'études mythologiques. Centre de Recherche Mythologique de l'Université de Paris. Paris: 'Les Belles Lettres'.

Hankey, V. (1967) 'Mycenaean pottery in the Middle East: notes on finds since 1951', *Annual of the British School at Athens* 62: 107–46.

—— (1970–71) 'Mycenaean trade with the south-eastern Mediterranean', *Mélanges de l'Université St-Joseph, Beyrouth* 46: 11–30.

—— (1973) 'The Aegean deposit at El Amarna', in *The Mycenaean in the Eastern Mediterranean*, Acts of the International Archaeological Symposium, Nicosia, 1972, pp. 128–32.

—— (1981) 'The Aegean interest in El Amarna', *Journal of Mediterranean Anthropology and Archaeology* 1: 45–6.

—— (1982) 'Pottery and people of the Mycenaean IIIC period in the Levant', in *Archéologie au Levant. Recueil à la mémoire de R. Saidah*. Lyons: Maison de l'Orient, pp. 167–72.

Hankey, V. and Warren, P. (1974) 'The absolute chronology of the Aegean Late Bronze Age', *Bulletin of the Institute of Classical Studies of the University of London* 18: 142–52.

Hansberry, L. W. (1977) *Africa and the Africans as Seen by Classical Writers: The Leo William Hansberry African History Notebook*, J. E. Harris, ed., 2 vols. Washington, DC: Howard University Press.

Harden, D. (1971) *The Phoenicians*. London: Penguin.

Harding, A. F. (1984) *The Mycenaeans and Europe*. London: Academic Press.

Harding, A. F. and Tait, W. J. (1989) 'The beginning of the end': progress and prospects in Old World chronology', *Antiquity* 63: 147–52.

Harris, Z. S. (1939) *The Development of the Canaanite Dialects: An Investigation in Linguistic History*. New Haven, Conn.: American Oriental Society.

Harrison, J. (1903) *Prolegomena to the Study of Greek Religion*. Cambridge: Cambridge University Press.

—— (1927) *Themis: A Study of the Social Origins of Greek Religion*, 2nd rev. edn. Cambridge: Cambridge University Press.

Hartleben, H. (1906) *Champollion sein Leben und sein Werk*, 2 vols. Berlin: Weidmann.

—— (1909) *Lettres de Champollion le Jeune recuelliés et annotées*, 2 vols. Paris: Bibliothèque Égyptologique.

Havelock, A. E. (1982) *The Literate Revolution in Greece and Its Cultural Consequences*. Princeton, NJ: Princeton University Press.

Hayes, W. (1971) 'The Middle Kingdom in Egypt', in *The Cambridge Ancient History*, 3rd edn., vol. I, pt. 2, pp. 464–531.

—— (1973a) 'Egypt from the death of Ammenemes III to Seqenere II', in *Cambridge Ancient History*, 3rd edn., vol. II, pt. 1, pp. 42–76.

—— (1973b) 'Egypt: Internal Affairs from Tuthmosis I to the Death of Amenophis III', in *Cambridge Ancient History*, 3rd edn., vol. II, pt. 1, pp. 313–416.

Heath Wienke, M. (1986) 'Art and the world of the Early Bronze Age', in G. Cadogan, ed., *The End of the Early Bronze Age in the Aegean*. Leiden: Brill, pp. 69–92.

Helck, W. (1962) 'Osiris', in *Pauly Wissowa*, suppl. 9: 469–513.

—— (1968) *Geschichte des Alten Ägypten*. Handbuch Orientalia pt. 1, vol. 1, issue 3. Leiden and Cologne: Brill.

—— (1971) *Die Beziehungen Ägyptens zu Vorderasien im 3. und 2. Jahrtausend v. Chr.*, 2nd improved edn. Wiesbaden: Harrassowitz.

—— (1975a) 'Byblos', in W. Helck and E. Otto, *Lexikon der Ägyptologie*, vol. I, cols. 889–91.

—— (1975b) *Propyläen Kunstgeschicht 15*.

—— (1975c) *Wirtschaftgeschichte des alten Ägypten im. 3. und 2. Jahrtausend vor. Chr.: Handbuch der Orientalistik I.IV.* Leiden, Köln.

—— (1979) *Die Beziehungen Ägyptens und Vorderasiens zur Ägäis bis ins 7. Jahrhundert v. Chr.* Darmstadt: Wissenschaftliche Buchgesellschaft.

—— (1989) 'Ein Ausgreifen des Mittleren Reiches in den zypriotischen Raum?', *Göttinger Miszellen: Beiträge zur ägyptische Diskussion* 109: 27–30.

Helck, W. and Otto, E. (1975) *Lexikon der Ägyptologie*, vol. I, Wiesbaden: Harrassowitz.

—— (1977) ——, vol. II.

—— (1980) ——, vol. III.

—— (1982) ——, vol. IV.

—— (1984) ——, vol. V.

Helm, P. R. (1980) *'Greeks' in the Neo-Syrian Levant and 'Assyria' in Early Greek Writers*. Ph.D. dissertation, University of Pennsylvania.

Heltzer, M. (1978) *Goods and Prices and the Organization of Trade in Ugarit*. Wiesbaden: Harrassowitz.

—— (1988) 'Sinarenu, Son of Siginu, and the trade between Ugarit and Crete', *Minos* 23: 8–13.

Hemmerdinger, B. (1966) 'Trois notes: I. Kadmos, II. Emprunts du grec mycénien à l'Akkadien, III. L'infiltration phénicienne en Béotie', *Revue des Études Grecques* 79: 698–703.

—— (1967) 'La Colonie Babylonienne de la Kadmée', *Helikon* 7: 232–40.

—— (1968) 'Noms communs grecs d'origine égyptienne', *Glotta* 46: 238–47.

—— (1970) 'De la méconnaissance de quelques etymologies grecques', *Glotta* 48: 40–66.

Herm, G. (1975) *The Phoenicians: The Purple Empire of the Ancient World*, C. Hillier, trans. New York: Morrow.

Hermes, G. (1936) 'Das gezähmte Pferd im alten Orient', *Anthropos* 30: 364–94.

Herodotos, (1954) *Herodotus: The Histories*, A. de Selincourt, trans. London: Penguin.

Herrin, J. (1987) *The Formation of Christendom*. Oxford: Blackwell.

Herrmann, G. (1968) 'Lapis lazuli: the early phases of its trade', *Iraq* 30: 24–35.

Hertz, N. (1985) *The End of the Line*. New York: Columbia University Press.

Hesiod (1914) *Hesiod: The Homeric Hymns and Homerica*, H. G. Evelyn-White, trans. Cambridge, Mass.: Harvard University Press (Loeb).

Hester, D. A. (1965) 'Pelasgian a new Indo-European language?', *Lingua* 13: 335–84.

Heubeck, A. (1958) 'Mykinisch *qi-si-po* = ξίφος', *Minos* 6: 55–60.

Higgins, R. (1979) *The Aegina Treasure: An Archaeological Mystery*. London: British Museum Publications.

—— (1981) *Minoan and Mycenaean Art*, rev. edn. London: Thames & Hudson.

Hiller, S. (1984) 'Pax Minoica versus Minoan thalassocracy: military aspects of Minoan culture', in R. Hägg and N. Marinatos, eds., *The Minoan Thalassocracy: Myth and Reality: Proceedings of the 3rd International Symposium at the Swedish Institute in Athens 31 May–5 June 1982, Skrifter utgivna av Svenska Institutet i Athen*, 4, pp. 17–31.

—— (1987) 'Palast und Tempel im Alten Orient und im minoischen Kreta', in R. Hägg and N. Marinatos, eds., *The Function of the Minoan Palaces: Proceedings of the Fourth International Symposium at the Swedish Institute in Athens, 10–16 June 1984*, pp. 57–63.

Hintze, F. (1975) 'Anuket', in W. Helck and E. Otto, *Lexikon der Ägyptologie*, vol. I, cols. 333–4.

Hinz, W. (1973) *The Lost World of Elam: Recreation of a Vanished Civilization*, J. Barnes, trans. New York: New York University Press.

Hodge, C. (1976) 'Lisramic (Afroasiatic): an overview', in M. L. Bender, ed., *The Non-Semitic Languages of Ethiopia*. East Lansing, Mich.: African Studies Center, Michigan State University, pp. 43–65.

Hoffman, M. A. (1979) *Egypt Before the Pharaohs*. New York: Knopf.

Hofmann, A. and Vorbichler, U. A. (1979) *Der Äthiopenlogos bei Herodot*. Vienna: Beiträge zur Afrikanistik.

Hollis, S. T. (1987a) 'Nut in the Pyramid Texts', paper given to the American Research Centre in Egypt Annual Meeting. Memphis, Tenn., April.

—— (1987b) 'The Goddess Neith in Ancient Egypt through the end of the third millennium BC', paper given to the American Academy of Religion Annual Meeting.

—— (1987c) 'Women of Ancient Egypt and the Sky Goddess Nut', *Journal of American Folklore* 100: 496–503.

—— (1988) 'Neith: bees, beetles and the red crown in the third millennium BC', paper given to the American Research Centre in Egypt Annual Meeting, Chicago.

Homer. (1925) *The Iliad*, A. T. Murray, trans., 2 vols. London: Heinemann.

Hood, S. (1960) 'Tholos tombs of the Aegean', *Antiquity* 34: 66–76.

—— (1967) *Home of the Heroes: The Aegean Before the Greeks*. London: Thames & Hudson.

—— (1971) *The Minoans: Crete in the Bronze Age*. London: Thames & Hudson.

—— (1978) 'Discrepancies in ¹⁴C dating as illustrated from the Egyptian New and Middle Kingdoms and from the Aegean Bronze Age and Neolithic', *Archaeometry* 20: 197–9.

—— (1986) 'Evidence for invasions in the Aegean area at the end of the Early Bronze Age', in G. Cadogan, ed., *The End of the Early Bronze Age in the Aegean*. Leiden: Brill, pp. 31–68.

Hooker, J. T. (1976) *Mycenaean Greece*. London: Routledge & Kegan Paul.

—— (1979) 'γέφυρα: a Semitic loan-word?', in B. Brogyanyi, ed., *Studies in Diachronic, Synchronic, and Typological Linguistics: Festschrift for Oswald Szemerényi on the Occasion of his 65th Birthday*, pt I. Amsterdam: John Benjamins, pp. 387–98.

—— (1983) 'Minoan religion in the Late Palace Period', in O. Krzyszkowska and L. Nixon, eds., *Minoan Society: Proceedings of the Cambridge Colloquium 1981*. Bristol: Bristol Classical Press, pp. 137–42.

Hope-Simpson, R. (1965) *Gazetteer and Atlas of Mycenaean Sites*. University of London, Institute of Classical Studies Bulletin Supplement 16.

Hopfner, T. (1922/3) *Fontes Historiae Religionis Aegyptiacae*, 2 vols. Bonn: Mark & Weber.

—— (1940–1) *Plutarch über Isis und Osiris*, 2 vols. Prague: Orientalisches Institut.

Hornung, E. (1971) *Der Eine und die Vielen: Ägyptische Gottesvorstellungen*. Darmstadt: Wissenschaftliche Buchgesellschaft, trans. J. Baines (1983) as *Conceptions of God in Ancient Egypt: The One and the Many*. London: Routledge & Kegan Paul.

Horton, R. (1967) 'African traditional thought and western science', *Africa* 37: 50–71; 155–87.

—— (1973) 'Lévy-Brühl, Durkheim and the scientific revolution', in R. Horton and R. Finnegan, eds., *Modes of Thought: Essays on Thinking in Western and Non-Western Societies*. London: Faber.

Howell, R. J. (1973) 'The origins of Middle Helladic culture', in R. A. Crossland and A. Birchall, eds., *Bronze Age Migrations in the Aegean*. London: Duckworth, pp. 75–99.

Hrozný, B. (1947) *Historie de l'Asie antérieure de l'Inde et de la Crète*. Paris: Payot.

Hsu, C.-y. and Linduff, K. M. (1988) *Western Chou Civilization*. New Haven, Conn., and London: Yale University Press.

Huber, P. J. (1982) 'Astronomical dating of Babylon I and Ur III', *Monographic Journals of the Near East*. Occasional Papers 1/4 (June).

—— (1987a) 'Astronomical evidence for the long and against the short chronologies', in P. Åström, *High, Middle or Low*, pp. 5–17.

—— (1987b) 'Dating by lunar eclipse omina: with speculations on the birth of omen astrology', in J. L Berggren and B. R. Goldstein, eds., *From Ancient Omens to Statistical Mechanics: Essays on the Exact Sciences Presented to Asger Aaboe.* Copenhagen: University Library. *Acta Historica Scientiarum Naturalium et Medicinalium* 39: 3–13.

Hubschmid, J. (1953) *Sardische Studien das mediterrane Substrat des Sardischen: Seine Beziehungen zum Berberischen und Baskischen sowie zum euroafrischen und hispanokaukasischen Substrat der romanischen 1 Sprachen.* Bern: A. Francke.

Hutchinson, R. W. (1962) *Prehistoric Crete.* London: Penguin.

Huxley, G. (1961) *Crete and the Luvians.* Oxford: Author.

Iakovides, S. (1979) 'Thera and Mycenaean Greece', *American Journal of Archaeology* 83: 101–2.

Illič Svitič, V. (1964) 'Drevneyschie indoevropeysko Semitiskie Yazygkovye Kontakty [The most ancient contacts between Indo-European and Semitic]', *Problemy Indoevropeyskogo yazykoznaniya* 6.

Immerwahr, S. A. (1977) 'Mycenaeans at Thera: some reflections on the paintings from the West House', in K. H. Kinzl, ed., *Greece and the Eastern Mediterranean in Ancient History and Prehistory: Studies presented to Fritz Schachermeyr on the Occasion of His Eightieth Birthday.* Berlin and New York: de Gruyter, pp. 173–91.

—— (1983) 'The people in the frescoes', in O. Krzyszkowska and L. Nixon, eds., *Minoan Society: Proceedings of the Cambridge Colloquium 1981.* Bristol: Bristol Classical Press, pp. 143–54.

Isokrates. (1928–44) *Works.* 3 vols. 1 & 2 trans. G. Norlin; 3, trans. L. Van Hook. Cambridge, Mass.: Harvard University Press (Loeb) and London: Heinemann.

Iversen, E. (1957) 'The Egyptian origin of the Archaic Greek canon', *Mitteilungen des deutschen archaeologischen Instituts Abt. Kairo* 15: 134–47.

—— (1961) *The Myth of Egypt and Its Hieroglyphs in European Tradition.* Copenhagen: Gad.

Ivimy, J. (1974) *The Sphinx and the Megaliths.* London: Abacus.

Jacobsen, T. (1976) *The Treasures of Darkness: A History of Mesopotamian Religion.* New Haven and London: Yale University Press.

Jacobsen, T. W. (1976) '17,000 years of Greek prehistory', *Scientific American* 234. 6: 76–87.

Jacoby, F. (ed. and ann.) (1904) *Das Marmor Parium.* Berlin: Weidmann.

—— (1923–9) *Fragmente der griechischen Historiker.* Berlin: Weidmann.

Jahnkuhn, D. (1980) 'Iunit', in W. Helck and E. Otto, *Lexikon der Ägyptologie*, Wiesbaden: Harrassowitz. vol. III, col. 212.

Jairazbhoy, R. A. (1985) 'Egyptian civilization in Colchis on the Black Sea', in R. Rashidi and I. van Sertima, eds., *African Presence in Early Asia*, special issue of *Journal of African Civilizations*, pp. 58–63.

James, G. G. M. (1954) *Stolen Legacy, the Greeks Were Not The Authors of Greek Philosophy, But the People of North Africa, Commonly Called the Egyptians.* New York: Philosophical Library.

James, T. G. H. (1971) 'Aegean place-names in the mortuary temple of Amenophis III at Thebes', *Bulletin of the Institute of Classical Studies of the University of London* 18: 144–5.

—— (1973) 'Egypt: from the expulsion of the Hyksos to Amenophis I', in *Cambridge Ancient History*, 3rd edn., vol. II, pt. 1, pp. 289–309.

Jaspers, K. (1949) *Vom Ursprung und Ziel der Geschichte*. Munich: Piper Verlag.

Jeanmaire, H. (1951) *Dionysos*. Paris: Payot.

Jeffery, L. H. (1961) *The Local Scripts of Archaic Greece: A Study in the Origin of the Greek Alphabet and Its Development from the Eighth to the Fifth Centuries B.C.* Oxford: Clarendon Press.

—— (1976) *Archaic Greece: The City-States c. 700–500 BC*. London and New York: St. Martins.

—— (1982) 'Greek alphabetic writing', in *Cambridge Ancient History*, 2nd edn., vol. III, pt. 1, pp. 819–33.

Jensen, H. (1969) *Sign, Symbol and Script: An Account of Man's Efforts to Write*, 3rd rev. edn., G. Unwin, trans. New York: Putnam.

Jespersen, O. (1922) *Language: Its Nature, Development and Origin*. London: Allen & Unwin.

Jidejian, N. (1968) *Byblos Through the Ages*. Beirut: Dar el-Machreq.

—— (1969) *Tyre Through the Ages*. Beirut: Dar el-Machreq.

Joffe, A. H. (1980) *Sea Peoples in the Levant*. Undergraduate thesis, Cornell, Department of Near Eastern Studies.

Jones, A. H. (1975) *Bronze Age Civilization: The Philistines and the Danites*. Washington, DC: Public Affairs Press.

Jones, T. (1969) *The Sumerian Problem*. London, New York, Toronto and Sidney: Wiley.

Josephus. (1926) *Against Apion*, H. St. J. Thackeray, trans., in *The Life*, vol. 1 of *Josephus in Nine Volumes*. Cambridge, Mass.: Harvard University Press (Loeb); London: Heinemann.

—— (1930) *Antiquities of the Jews*, vols. 4–9 of *Josephus in Nine Volumes*. Cambridge, Mass: Harvard University Press (Loeb); London: Heinemann.

Junker, H. (1933) *Die Völker des antiken Orients: Die Ägypter*. Freiburg in Breisgau: Herder.

Kadish, B. (1971) 'Excavations of prehistoric remains at Aphrodisias, 1968 and 1969', *American Journal of Archaeology* 75: 121–40.

Kakosy, L. (1982) 'Mnevis', in W. Helck and E. Otto, *Lexikon der Ägyptologie*, vol. IV, cols. 165–7.

Kalcyk, H. and Heinrich, B. (1986) 'Hochwasserschutzbauten in Arkadien', *Antike Welt* 2 Sondernummer 'Antiker Wasserbau', pp. 3–14.

Kammenhuber, A. (1968) *Die Arier im Vorderen Orient*. Heidelberg: Indogermanische Bibliothek, 3rd series.

—— (1977) 'Die Arier im Vorderen Orient und die historischen Wohnsitze der Hurriter', *Orientalia* NS 46: 129–43.

Kanta, A. (1980) 'The Late Minoan III Period in Crete: a survey of sites, pottery and their distribution', *Studies in Mediterranean Archaeology* 58.

Kantor, H. J. (1947) 'The Aegean and the Orient in the second millennium BC', *American Journal of Archaeology* 51: 1–106.

—— (1956) 'Syro-Palestinian ivories', *Journal of Near Eastern Studies* 15: 153–74.

Kaplony, P. (1980) 'Ka', in W. Helck and E. Otto, *Lexikon der Ägyptologie*, vol. III, cols. 275–82.

Karageorghis, V. (1988) *Blacks in Ancient Cypriot Art*. Houston, Tex: Menil Foundation.

Karlgren, B. (1950) *The Book of Odes: Chinese Text Transcription and Translation*. Stockholm: Museum of Far Eastern Antiquities.

—— (1957) 'Grammata Serica Recensa', *The Museum of Far Eastern Antiquities Bulletin* (Stockholm) 29.

Katz, S. T. (1986) 'Hitler's "Jew": on microbes and Manicheanism', *Ninth World Congress of Jewish Studies*, Division B, vol. III, *History of the Jewish People (The Modern Times)*, Jerusalem: Magnes, pp. 165–81.

Katzenstein, H. J. (1973) *The History of Tyre: From the Beginning of the Second Millennium B.C.E. until the Fall of the Neo-Babylonian Empire in 538 B.C.E.* Jerusalem: The Schocken Institute for Jewish Research.

Kaufman, S. A. (1982) 'Reflections on the Assyrian-Aramaic Bilingual from Tell Fakhariyeh', *MAARAV* 3/2: 137–75.

Keightley, D. N. (1978) *Sources of Shang History: The Oracle Bone Inscriptions of Bronze Age China*. Berkeley: University of California Press.

—— (1983) 'The Late Shang state: when, where, what?' in D. N. Keightley, ed., *The Origins of Chinese Civilisation*. Berkeley: University of California Press, pp. 523–64.

Keimer, L. (1931) 'Pendeloques en formes d'insectes', *Annales de Service* 31: 145–82.

Keinast, B. (1981) 'Die Sprache von Ebla und das Altsemitische', in L. Cagni, ed., *La Lingua di Ebla*. Naples: Istituto Universitario Orientale, Seminario di Studi Asiatici, 14, pp. 83–98.

Kelly, P. M. and Sear, C. B. (1985) 'The climatic impact of explosive volcanic eruptions', in *Proceedings of the 3rd Conference on Climatic Variations Symposium on Contemporary Climate: 1850–2100* (American Meteorological Society), pp. 178–9.

Kemp, B. J. (1980) 'Egyptian radiocarbon dating: a reply to James Mellaart', *Antiquity* 54: 25–8.

Kemp, B. J. and Merrillees, R. S. (1980) *Minoan Pottery in Second Millennium Egypt*. Deutsches archäologisches Institut, Abteilung Kairo. Mainz am Rhein: Philipp von Zabern.

Kempinski, A. (1985) 'Some observations on the Hyksos (XVth) dynasty and its Canaanite origins', in Sarah Israelit-Groll, ed., *Pharaonic Egypt: The Bible and Christianity*. Jerusalem: Magnes, pp. 129–37.

Kenyon, K. M. (1973) 'Palestine in the Middle Bronze Age', in *Cambridge Ancient History*, 3rd edn., vol. II, pt. 1, pp. 17–116.

Keramopoullos, A. (1917) 'Θηβαικά', *Archaiologikon Deltion* 3: 1–503.

Kern, O. (1896) 'Bakis', *Pauly-Wissowa* II, cols. 2801–2.

—— (1926) *Die Religion der Griechen*. Berlin: Weidmann.

Keys, D. (1988) 'Cloud of volcanic dust blighted North Britain 3,000 years ago', *Independent*, 16 August.

Khattab, A. (1982) *Das Ägyptenbild in den deutschsprachigen Reisebeschreibungen der Zeit von 1285–1500*. Frankfort a. M.: Europäische Hochschulschriften, 1. Deutsche Sprache und Literatur.

Khramalkov, P. (1981) 'A critique of Professor Goedicke's Exodus theories', *Biblical Archaeology Review* 7. 5: 51–4.

Kilian, K. (1985) 'La caduta dei palazzi Micenei continentali: aspetti archeologici', in D. Musti, ed., *Le Origini dei Greci: Dori e Mondo Egeo*. Rome, pp. 73–95.

Killen, J. T. (1964) 'The wool industry of Crete in the Late Bronze Age', *Annual of the British School in Athens* 59: 1–15.

King, L. W. and Hall, H. R. (1907) *Egypt and Western Asia in the Light of Recent Discoveries*. London: Grolier Society.

Kingsley, P. (1990) 'The Greek origin of the sixth-century dating of Zoroaster', *Bulletin of the School of Oriental and African Studies* 53: 245–65.

Kinkel, G. (1877) *Epicorum Graecorum Fragmenta*. Leipzig: Teubner.

Kircher, A. (1652) *Oedipus Aegyptiacus*. Rome.

Kirk, G. S. (1970) *Myth, Its Meanings and Functions in Ancient and Other Cultures*. Berkeley and Cambridge: University of California Press.

—— (1974) *The Nature of Greek Myth*. London: Penguin.

—— (1985) *The Iliad: A Commentary, Volume 1, Books 1–4*. Cambridge: Cambridge University Press.

Kirk, G. S., Raven, J. E. and Schofield, M. (1983) *The Presocratic Philosophers: A Critical History with a Selection of Texts*, 2nd edn. Cambridge: Cambridge University Press.

Kitchen, K. A. (1965) 'Theban topographical lists old and new', *Orientalia* 34: 1–9.

—— (1966a) 'Aegean place names in a list of Amenophis III', *Bulletin of the American Schools of Oriental Research* 181: 23–4.

—— (1966b) *Ancient Orient and the Old Testament*. London: Tyndale Press.

—— (1967) 'Byblos, Egypt, and Mari in the early second millennium BC'. *Orientalia* 36: 39–54.

—— (1987) 'The basics of Egyptian chronology in relation to the Bronze Age', in P. Åström, *High, Middle or Low? Acts of an International Colloquium on Absolute Chronology Held at the University of Gothenburg 20–22 August 1987*, pt. 1, pp. 37–55.

—— (1989) 'Supplementary notes on the basics of Egyptian chronology', in P. Åström, *High, Middle or Low? Acts of an International Colloquium on Absolute Chronology Held at the University of Gothenburg 20–22 August 1987*, pt. 3, pp. 152–9.

Klausner, J. (1976) 'The first Hasmonean rulers: Jonathan and Simeon', in A. Schalit, ed., *World History of the Jewish People*, vol. VI, *The Hellenistic Age*. London: W. H. Allen, pp. 183–210.

Knapp, A. B. (1985) 'Production and exchange in the Aegean and East Mediterranean', in A. B. Knapp and T. Stech, *Prehistoric Production and Exchange: The Aegean and the East Mediterranean*, pp. 1–11.

—— (1986) 'Production, exchange and socio-political complexity on Bronze Age Cyprus', *Oxford Journal of Archaeology* 5: 43.

Knapp, A. B. and Stech, T. (1985) *Prehistoric Production and Exchange: The Aegean and the East Mediterranean*. Los Angeles: University of California Institute of Archaeology, Monograph 25.

Knauss, J. (1985) 'Antike Landgewinnung und Binnenschiffahrt im Kopais-Becken, Boötien, Mittelgriechenland', *Münstersche Beiträge zur antiken Handelsgeschichte* 7: 42–64.

—— (1986) 'Munich Copais Expedition, progress report on October 1985 and May 1986 surveys', *Teiresias* 17. *Appendix: Boetica*, pp. 3–7.

—— (1987a) *Die Melioration des Kopaisbeckens durch die Minyer im 2. jt. v. Chr. Kopais 2- Wasserbau und Siedlungsbedingungen im Altertum*. Institut für Wasserbau und Wassermengenwirtschaft und Versuchsanstalt für Wasserbau Oskar v. Miller-Institut in Obernach, Technische Universität München, No. 57.

—— (1987b) 'Munich Copais Expedition, progress report on October 1986 and May 1987 surveys', *Teiresias* 17. *Appendix: Boetica*, pp. 1–4.

—— (1987c) 'Der Damm im Takka See beim alten Tegea (Arkadien, Peloponnes)', *Athenische Mitteilungen* 102: 47–62.

—— (1987d) 'Deukalion, Lykorea, die große Flut am Parnaß und der Vulkanausbruch von Thera (im Jahr 1529 v. Chr.?)', *Antike Welt* 23–40.

Knauss, J., Heinrich, B. and Kalcyk, H. (1984) *Die Wasserbauten der Minyer in der Kopais – die älteste Flußregulierung Europas*. Institut für Wasserbau und Wassermengenwirtschaft und Versuchsanstalt für Wasserbau Oskar v. Miller-Institut in Obernach Technische Universität München, No. 50.

—— (1986) 'Der Damm bei Kaphyai und Orchomenos in Arkadian', *Archaeologischer Anzeiger* 583–611.

Knudtzon, J. A. (1915) *Die Amarna Tafeln*. Leipzig: Vorderasiatische Bibliothek.

Konsola, D. (1981) 'Προμυκηναϊκη Θήβα', Ph.D. dissertation, Athens University.

Korfmann, M. (1986) 'Beşik Tepe: new evidence for the Trojan sixth and seventh settlements', in Machteld Mellink, ed., *Troy and the Trojan War: A Symposium Held at Bryn Mawr College October 1984*. Bryn Mawr, Pa.: Bryn Mawr College, pp. 17–31.

Korres, G. S. (1984) 'The relations between Crete and Messenia in the Late Middle Helladic Period' in R. Hägg and N. Marinatos, eds., *The Minoan Thalassocracy: Myth and Reality: Proceedings of the 3rd International Symposium at the Swedish Institute in Athens 31 May–5 June 1982, Skrifter utgivna av Svenska Institutet i Athen*, 4, pp. 141–3.

Krauss, R. (1985) 'Sothis-und Monddaten, Studien zur astronomischen und technischen Chronologie Altägyptens', *Hildersheimer Ägyptologische Beiträge* 20.

Kretschmer, P. (1896) *Einleitung in die Geschichte der griechischen Sprache*. Göttingen: Vandenhoeck & Ruprecht.

—— (1924) 'Das nt-suffix', *Glotta* 13: 84–106.

—— (1927) 'Mythische Namen', *Glotta* 16: 74–78.

—— (1936) 'Nochmals die Hypachäer und Aleksandus', *Glotta* 25: 203–51.

Kroll, J. (1923) 'Kulturhistorisches aus astrologischen Texten', *Klio* 18: 213–25.

Krzyszkowska, O. H. (1983) 'Wealth and prosperity in Pre-Palatial Crete: The case of ivory', in O. Krzyszkowska and L. Nixon, eds., *Minoan Society: Proceedings of the Cambridge Colloquium 1981*. Bristol: Bristol Classical Press, pp. 163–70.

Kuhn, T. S. (1970) *The Structure of Scientific Revolutions*, 2nd edn. Chicago: University of Chicago Press.

—— (1977) 'Second thoughts on paradigms', in F. Suppe, ed., *The Structure of Scientific Theories*. Champaign: University of Illinois Press, pp. 459–82.

Kulke, H. (1976) 'Die Lapis-Lazuli-Lagerstätte Sare Sang (Badakhshan) Geologie Entstehung, Kulturgeschichte und Bergbau', *Afghanistan Journal* 3.1: 43–56.

Kuniholm, P. I. and Newton, M. W. (1989) 'A 677-year tree-ring chronology for the Middle Bronze Age', in K. Emre, M. Mellink, B. Hrouda and N. Özgüç, eds., *Anatolia and the Ancient Near East: Studies in Honor of Tahsin Özgüç*. Ankara: Türk Tarih Kurumu Basimevi.

Kupper, J.-R. (1973) 'Northern Mesopotamia and Syria', in *Cambridge Ancient History*, 3rd edn., vol. II, pt. 1, pp. 1–41.

Kurth, D. (1980) 'Manu', in W. Helck and E. Otto, *Lexikon der Ägyptologie*, vol. III, cols. 1185–6.

Labat, R. (1975) 'Elam and Western Persia, *c.* 1200–1000 BC', in *Cambridge Ancient History*, 3rd edn., vol. II, pt. 2, pp. 482–506.

Labib, P. (1936) *Die Herrschaft der Hyksos in Ägypten und ihr Sturz*. Glückstadt, Hamburg and New York: Augustin.

La Capra, D. (1987) *History, Politics and the Novel*. Ithaca, NY: Cornell University Press.

Lacau, P. (1904–06) *Sarcophages antérieur au Nouvel Empire*. 2 vols., in *Catalogue Générales Antiquités Égyptiennes du Musée du Caire*. Cairo: Imprimerie de l'Institut français d'archéologie.

Lacy, P. D. and Einarson, B. (1954) *Plutarch's Moralia VII*. Cambridge, Mass.: Harvard University Press (Loeb); London: Heinemann.

Laffineur, R. (1984) 'Mycenaeans at Thera', in R. Hägg and N. Marinatos, eds., *The Minoan Thalassocracy: Myth and Reality: Proceedings of the 3rd International Symposium at the Swedish Institute in Athens 31 May–5 June 1982*, *Skrifter Utgivna av Svenska Institutet i Athen*, 4, pp. 133–9.

—— (1987) 'Le cercle des tombes de Schliemann: cent ans après', in R. Laffineur, ed., *Thanatos: Les coutumes funéraires en Égée à l'âge du Bronze: Actes du Colloque de Liège (21–23 avril 1986)*. Université de l'État à Liège: Histoire de l'art et archéologie de la Grèce antique, pp. 117–25.

Lakatoš, I. (1970) 'Falsification and the methodology of scientific research programmes', in I. Lakatoš and A. Musgrave, eds., *Criticism and the Growth of Knowledge*. Cambridge: Cambridge University Press, pp. 106–17.

La Marche, V. C. and Hirschbeck, K. K. (1984) 'Frost rings in trees as records of major volcanic eruptions', *Nature* 307: 121–6.

Lambropoulou, A. (1988) 'Erechtheus, Boutes, Itys and Xouthos: notes on Egyptian presence in early Athens', *The Ancient World* 18: 77–86.

Lambrou-Phillipson, C. (1987) 'A model for the identification of enclave colonies', paper delivered at the 6th International Colloquium on Aegean Prehistory, Athens, 30 August–5 September 1987.

—— (1990) 'Cypriot and Levantine pottery from house AD center at Pseira, Crete', *Journal of Oriental and African Studies* [Athens] 2: 1–10.

Lane-Fox, R. (1980) *The Search for Alexander*. Boston and Toronto: Little Brown.

Lang, D. M. (1966) *The Georgians*. London: Thames & Hudson.

—— (1978) *Armenia: Cradle of Civilization*, 2nd edn. London: Allen & Unwin.

Lang, M. L. (1969) *The Palace of Nestor at Pylos in Western Messenia;* Vol. II, *The Frescoes*. Princeton: Princeton University Press for the University of Cincinnati.

Langdon, S. (1990) 'From monkey to man: the evolution of a geometric sculptural type', *American Journal of Archaeology* 94: 407–20.

Lange, K. (1954) *Sesostris: Ein ägyptischer König in Mythos, Geschichte und Kunst.* Munich: Hirmer.

Langham, I. (1981) *The Building of British Social Anthropology: W. H. R. Rivers and His Cambridge Disciples in the Development of Kinship Studies, 1898–1931.* Dordrecht, Boston and London: Reidel.

Lanzone, R. V. (1881–6) *Dizionario di mitologia egizia,* 4 vols. Turin: Fratelli Doyen. Reprint. Amsterdam: John Benjamins, 1974.

Laroche, E. (1958) 'Adana et les Danauiens', *Syria* 35: 252–83.

—— (1965) 'Sur le nom grec de l'ivoire', *Revue de philologie* 39: 56–60.

—— (1966) *Les noms des Hittites*. Paris: Études Linguistiques 4.

—— (1976–7) *Glossaire de la Langue Hourrite,* 2 pts. *Revue Hittite et Asianique* 34 and 35.

—— (1977?) 'Toponymes et frontières linguistiques en Asie Mineure', in T. Fahd *et al.*, eds., *La Toponymie Antique: Actes du Colloque de Strassbourg 12–14 juin 1975.* Leiden: Brill, pp. 205–13.

Larsen, M. T. (1976) *The Old Assyrian City State and Its Colonies, Mesopotamia,* vol. 4 of *Copenhagen Studies in Assyriology.* Copenhagen: Akademisk Forlag.

Lattimore, R. (1939) 'Herodotus and the names of the Egyptian gods', *Classical Philology* 34: 357–65.

Lauer, J. F. (1948) *Le Problème des Pyramides d'Égypte.* Paris: Payot.

—— (1960) *Observations sur les pyramides.* Cairo: Institut français d'archéologie orientale.

Lauffer, S. (1981) 'Wasserbauliche Anlagen des Altertums am Kopaissee', *Leichtweiss-Institut f. Wasserbau d. techn. Univ. Braunschweig Mitteilungen* 71: 237–64.

—— (1986) *Kopais: Untersuchungungen zur historischen Landeskunde Mittelgriechenlands,* vol. I. Frankfurt a. M., Bern and New York: Peter Lang.

Leach, E. (1986) 'Aryan invasions over four millennia', *Wenner-Gren Symposium no. 100, 'Symbolism Through Time' 12–21 Jan, Fez.*

Leclant, J. (1960) 'Astarté à cheval', *Syria* 37: 1–67.

Lee, H. D. P. (1955) *Plato: The Republic.* London: Penguin.

Legge, J. (1972) *The Chinese Classics: With a Translation, Critical and Exegetical Notes, Prolegomena, and Copious Indexes,* 5 vols. Taibei: Shizhe Chubanshe Reprint.

Lehmann, W. P. (1973) *Historical Linguistics: An Introduction.* New York: Holt, Rinehart & Winston.

Lejeune, M. (1958) *Mémoires de philologie mycénienne.* Paris: Centre National de Recherche Scientifique.

—— (1972) *Phonétique historique du mycénien et du grec ancien.* Paris: Klincksieck.

Lepsius, R. (1871) 'Des Sesostris-Herakles Körperlänge', *Zeitschrift für ägyptische Sprache und Altertumskunde* 9: 52–6.

Lesko, L. H. and Switalski-Lesko, B. (1982–90) *A Dictionary of Late Egyptian.* 5 vols. Berkeley: Scribe Publications.

Leslau, W. (1950) *Ethiopia Documents: Gurage.* New York: Viking Fund.

Levenson, J. D. (1985) *Sinai and Zion: An Entry into the Jewish Bible.* Minneapolis, Chicago and New York: Winston Press.

Levi, P. (1971) *Pausanias' Guide to Greece,* 2 vols. London: Penguin.

Levin, S. (1968) 'Indo-European penetration of the civilized Aegean world as seen in the 'horse' tablet of Knosos (Ca895)', *Atti e memorie del 1° congresso internazionale di micenilogica. Roma, 27 Settembre–3 Ottobre 1967,* pp. 1179–85.

—— (1971a) *The Indo-European and Semitic Languages.* Albany, NY: State University of New York Press.

—— (1971b) The etymology of νέκταρ exotic scents in early Greece', *Studi Micenei ed Egeo-Anatolici* 13: 31–50.

—— (1973) 'The accentual system of Hebrew, in comparison with the ancient Indo-European languages', *Fifth World Congress of Jewish Studies* 4: 71–7.

—— (1977) 'Something stolen': a Semitic participle and an Indo-European neuter substantive', in P. Hopper, ed., *Studies in Descriptive and Historical Linguistics: Festschrift for Winfred P. Lehmann.* Amsterdam: John Benjamins, pp. 317–39.

—— (1978) 'The perfumed goddess', *Bucknell Review* 24: 49–59.

—— (1979) 'Jocasta and Moses' Mother Jochabed', *TEIRESIAS-TEIPEΣIAΣ* suppl. 2: 49–61.

—— (1984) 'Indo-European descriptive adjectives with 'oxytone' accent and Semitic stative verbs', *General Linguistics* 24. 2: 83–110.

—— (1989) 'The etymology of the place-name Thisbe', paper given at the 6th International Boeotian Conference, Bradford, 26–30 June.

Levy, R. G. (1934) 'The Oriental origin of Herakles', *Journal of Hellenic Studies* 54: 40–53.

Lewthwaite, J. (1983) 'Why did civilization not emerge more often? a comparative development of Minoan Crete', in O. Krzyszkowska and L. Nixon, eds., *Minoan Society: Proceedings of the Cambridge Colloquium 1981*. Bristol: Bristol Classical Press, pp. 171–83.

Lewy, H. (1895) *Die semitischen Fremdwörter im Greichischen*. Berlin: Gaertner.

Lhote, H. (1959) *The Search for the Tassili Frescoes: The Story of the Prehistoric Rock-Paintings of the Sahara*, A. H. Brodrick, trans. London: Hutchinson.

Lichtheim, M. (1975) *Ancient Egyptian Literature*, 3 vols. Berkeley, Los Angeles and London: University of California Press.

Linforth, J. M. (1911–16) 'Epaphos and the Egyptian Apis', *University of California Publications in Classical Philology* 2: 81–92.

—— (1926) 'Greek gods and foreign gods in Herodotos', *University of California Publications in Classical Philology* 9: 1–25.

—— (1940) 'Greek and Egyptian gods (Herodotus II, 50, 52)', *Classical Philology* 35: 300–1.

Lipinski, E. (1978) 'Ditanu', *Studies in the Bible and the Ancient Near East, Separatum*, pp. 91–110.

—— (1981) 'Formes verbales dans les noms propres d'Ebla et système verbale Sémitique', in L. Cagni, ed., *La Lingua di Ebla: Atti del convegno internazionale (Napoli, 21–23 aprile 1980)*. Naples: Istituto Universitario Orientale, Seminario di Studi Asiatici, 14, pp. 191–210.

Littauer, M. A. and Crouwel, J. H. (1979) *Wheeled Vehicles and Ridden Animals in the Ancient Near East*. Leiden: Brill.

Liverani, M. (1987) 'The collapse of the Near Eastern regional system at the end of the Bronze Age: the case of Syria', in M. Rowlands, M. T. Larsen and K. Kristiansen, eds., *Centre and Periphery in the Ancient World*. Cambridge: Cambridge University Press, pp. 67–73.

Lloyd, A. B. (1970) 'The Egyptian labyrinth', *Journal of Egyptian Archaeology* 56: 81–100.

—— (1976) *Herodotos Book II*, vol. II, *Commentary 1–98*. Leiden: Brill.

—— (1978) 'Strabo and the Memphite tauromachy', in M. de Boer and I. A. Edridge, eds., *Hommages à Maarten J. Vermaseren: Recueil d'études offerts par les auteurs de la série 'Études préliminaires aux religions orientales dans l'empire romain à Maarten J. Vermaseren: à l'occasion de son soixantième anniversaire le 7 avril 1978*, 3 vols. Leiden: Brill, pp. 609–26.

—— (1982) 'Nationalist propaganda in Ptolemaic Egypt', *Historia* 31: 33–55.

—— (1983) 'The Late Period', in B. Trigger, B. J. Kemp, D. O'Connor and A. B. Lloyd, eds., *Ancient Egypt: A Social History*. Cambridge: Cambridge University Press, pp. 279–364.

—— (1988) *Herodotus Book II*, vol. III, *Commentary 99–182*. Leiden and New York: Brill.

Lochner-Hüttenbach, F. (1960) *Die Pelasger*. Vienna: Gerold.

Lorimer, H. L. (1950) *Homer and the Monuments*. London: Macmillan.

Loucas, I. and Loucas, E. (1987) 'La tombe des jumeaux divins Amphion et Zethos', in R. Laffineur, ed., *Thanatos: Les coutumes funéraires en Égée à l'âge du Bronze: Actes du Colloque de Liège (21–23 avril 1986)*. Université de l'État à Liège: Histoire de l'art et archéologie de la Grèce antique, pp. 95–106.

Lucas, A. and Harris, J. R. (1962) *Ancient Egyptian Materials and Industries*, 4th edn. London: Edward Arnold.

Luce, J. V. (1969) *Lost Atlantis: New Light on an Old Legend.* New York, St. Louis and San Francisco: McGraw-Hill.

—— (1978) 'The literary perspective: the sources and literary form of Plato's Atlantis', in E. S. Ramage, ed., *Atlantis: Fact or Fiction.* Bloomington: Indiana University Press, pp. 49–80.

Lucretius, *De Rerum Natura.*

Lung, G. E. (1912) *Memnon: Archäologische Studien zur Aithiopis.* Bonn: Ludwig.

Luria, S. (1926) 'Die ägyptische Bibel (Joseph und Moses Sagen)', *Zeitschrift für die alttestamentliche Gesellschaft* NF 3: 94–135.

Macalister, R. A. S. (1914) *The Philistines, Their History and Civilization.* London: British Academy.

McAlpin, D. W. (1974) 'Toward Proto-Elamite-Dravidian', *Language* 50.1: 89–101.

—— (1975) 'Elamite and Dravidian: the morphological evidence', *International Journal of Dravidian Linguistics* 3: 343–5.

McCann, A. M. (1970) 'Review of G. F. Bass, *Cape Gelidonya: A Bronze Age Shipwreck*', *American Journal of Archaeology* 74: 105–6.

Maccarrone, N. (1938) 'Contatti lessicali mediterranei, pt 1', *Archivio glottologico italiano* 30: 120–31.

—— (1939) 'Contatti lessicali mediterranei, pt 2', *Archivio glottologico italiano* 31: 102–13.

McCarter, K. (1975) *The Antiquity of the Greek Alphabet and the Early Phoenician Scripts.* Missoula, Mont.: Scholars Press for Harvard Semitic Museum.

McClain, E. G. (1976) *The Myth of Invariance: the Origin of the Gods, Mathematics and Music from the Rg Veda to Plato.* New York: Nicholas Hays.

—— (1978) *The Pythagorean Plato.* New York: Nicholas Hays.

McCoy, F. W. (1980) 'The Upper Thera (Minoan) ash in deep-sea sediments: distribution and comparison with other ash layers', in C. Doumas, ed., *Thera and the Aegean World: Papers Presented at the Second International Scientific Congress, Santorini, Greece, August 1978*, vol. II. London, pp. 57–78.

MacGillivray, J. A. (1984) 'Cycladic jars from Middle Minoan III Knossos', in R. Hägg and N. Marinatos, eds., *The Minoan Thalassocracy: Myth and Reality: Proceedings of the 3rd International Symposium at the Swedish Institute in Athens 31 May–5 June 1982, Skrifter utgivna av Svenska Institutet i Athen*, 4, pp. 153–7.

McGready, A. G. (1968) 'Egyptian words in the Greek vocabulary', *Glotta* 46: 247–54.

Machiavelli, N. (1964) *Discourses*, in A. Gilbert, *Macchiavelli; Chief Works and Others.* Durham, NC: Durham Press.

McKerrell, H. (1972) 'On the origins of British faience beads and some aspects of the Wessex-Mycenae relationship', *Proceedings of the Prehistoric Society* 38: 286–301.

McNeal, R.A. (1972) 'The Greeks in history and prehistory', *Antiquity* 46: 19–28.

Macqueen, J .G. (1975) *The Hittites and Their Contemporaries in Asia Minor.* London: Thames & Hudson.

Maddin, R.; Wheeler, T. S, and Muhly, J. D. (1977) 'Tin and the Ancient Near East: Old Questions and New Finds', *Expedition* 19: 2: 35–47.

Malaise, M. (1966) 'Sésostris', pharaon de légende et d'histoire', *Chronique d'Égypte* 41: 244–72.

Malek, J. (1982) 'The Original Version of the Royal Canon of Turin', *The Journal of Egyptian Archaeology* 68: 93–108.

Mallet, D. (1888) *Le Culte de Neïth à Saïs.* Paris: Leroux.

Mallory, J. P. (1989) *In Search of the Indo-Europeans: Language, Archaeology and Myth.* London: Thames & Hudson.

Malten, L. (1924) 'Khvr' Pauly Wissowa supplement. IV. Stuttgart, cols. 884–97.

Manetho. (1940) *Manetho: With an English Translation,* by W. G. Waddell. Cambridge, Mass.: Harvard University Press (Loeb); London: Heinemann.

Manning, S. W. (1988) 'Dating of the Santorini eruption', *Nature* 332. 31/3: 401.

—— (1989) 'The Eruption of Thera: Date and Implications', in C. Doumas, ed. *Thera and the Aegean World III: Papers to be presented at the Third International Congress at Santorini Greece. 3–9th September 1989.* Thera Foundation, pp. 91–101.

—— (1990) 'The Thera eruption: the Third Congress and the problem of the Date', *Archaeometry* 32: 91–100.

Marinatos, N. (1983) 'The West House at Akrotiri as a Cult Centre', *Athenische Mitteilungen* 98: 1–19.

—— (1984) *Art and religion in Thera: Reconstructing a Bronze Age Society.* Athens: Mathioulakis.

Marinatos, S. (1939) 'The volcanic destruction of Minoan Crete', *Antiquity* 13: 425–39.

—— (1946) 'Greniers de l'Helladique Ancien', *Bulletin de Correspondance Hellénique* 70: 337–50.

—— (1949) 'Les Légendes Royales de la Crète Minoenne', *Revue Archéologique* 1: 5–18.

—— (1958) 'Grammatōn didaskalia', *Minoica* 32: 226–31.

—— (1960) *Crete and Mycenae.* London: Thames & Hudson.

—— (1969) 'An African in Thera', *Analekta Archaiologika Athenon* 2. pp. 374–5.

—— (1973a) 'The First Mycenaeans in Greece', in R. A. Crossland and A. Birchall, eds., *Bronze Age Migrations in the Aegean,* pp. 107–13.

—— (1973b) 'Ethnic problems raised by recent discoveries on Thera', in R. A. Crossland and A. Birchall eds. *Bronze Age Migrations in the Aegean,* pp. 199–201.

—— (1976) *Excavations at Thera VII (1973 Season).* Athens: E en Athenais Archaiologike Hetaireia.

Marketou, T. (1989) 'Santorini Tephra from Rhodes and Kos: Some Chronological Remarks Based on Stratigraphy', pp. 101–23 in *Thera and the*

Aegean World III: Papers to be Presented at the Third International Congress at Santorini, Greece, 3–9th September 1989. Thera Foundation.

Marthari, M. (1980) 'Akrotiri Kerameiki MH paradosis sto strōma tis iphaisteikis katastrophis', *Archaiologike Ephemeris* 119: 182–211.

Masica, C. P. (1978) *Defining a Linguistic Area: South Asia*. Chicago: Chicago University Press.

Mason, M. (1986) 'Sphaira, Sphairoter: Problème d'étymologie Grecque', Bulletin de la Societé de linguistique. 81: 231–52.

Maspero, G. (1884) Histoire ancien des peuples d'l'orient, vol. I. Paris: Hachette.

—— (1886) 'Communication sur le nom donné en Égypte à l'île de Chypre vers le XVIe ou le XVIIe siècle avant notre ére', *Comptes Rendus des Séances de l'Academie des Inscriptions et Belles Lettres* 14: 361–2.

—— (1893) *Études de mythologie et d'archéologie égyptiennes*, Paris: Leroux.

—— (1901) 'La Geste de Sésostris', *Journal des Savants Octobre:* 593–609.

Masson, E. (1967) *Recherches sur les plus anciens emprunts sémitiques en grec*. Paris: Klinsieck.

Matthäus, H. (1983) 'Minoische Kriegegräber', in O. Krzyszkowska and L. Nixon, eds., *Minoan Society: Proceedings of the Cambridge Colloquium 1981*. Bristol: Bristol Classical Press, pp. 203–16.

Matthews, S. H. (1976) 'What's happening to our climate?', *National Geographic* 150: 676–87.

Matthiae, P. (1981) *Ebla: An Empire Rediscovered*. C. Holme, trans. Garden City, NY: Doubleday.

—— (1988) 'On the Economic Foundations of the Early Syrian Culture at Ebla', in H. Waetzold and H. Hauptmann, eds., *Wirtschaft und Gesellschaft von Ebla: Akten der Internationale Tagung, Heidelberg, 4.-7. November 1986, Heidelberger Studien zum alten Orient II*. Heidelberg: Heidelberger Orientverlag, pp. 75–80.

—— (1989) 'The Destruction of Ebla Royal Palace: Interconnections between Syria, Mesopotamia and Egypt in the Late EB IVA', in P. Äström, ed., *High, Middle or Low? Acts of an International Colloquium on Absolute Chronology Held at the University of Gothenburg 20th–22nd August 1987. pt III*, pp. 163–9.

Matz, F. (1928) *Die fruhkretischen Siegel*. Berlin and Leipzig: de Gruyter.

—— (1973a) 'The maturity of Minoan civilization', in *Cambridge Ancient History*, 3rd edn., vol. II, pt. 1, pp. 141–64.

—— (1973b) 'The zenith of Minoan civilisation', in *Cambridge Ancient History*, 3rd edn., vol. II, pt. 1, pp. 557–81.

Matzker, I. (1986) *Die letzten Könige der 12. Dynastie. Europäische Hochschulschriften 297*. Frankfurt a. M.: Peter Lang.

Maxwell-Hyslop, R. (1946) 'Daggers and swords in Western Asia: a study from prehistoric times to 600 BC', *Iraq* 8: 1–65.

Mayer, M. L. (1964) 'Note etimologiché III', *Acme* 17: 223–9.

—— (1967) 'Note etimologiché IV', *Acme*. 20: 287–91.

Mayrhofer, M. (1953) *Kurzegefaßtes etymologisches Wörterbuch des Altindischen*. Heidelberg: Winter.

—— (1974) *Die Arier im Vorderen Orient-ein Mythos? – Mit einem biographischen Supplement*. Vienna: Östereichische Akademie der Wissenschaften-philosophisch-historische Klasse-Sitzungberichte 294 Abhandlung 3.

Mee, C. (1982) *Rhodes in the Bronze Age: An Archaeological Survey*. Warminster: Aris & Phillips.

—— (1984) 'The Mycenaeans and Troy', in Lin Foxhall and John K. Davies, eds., *The Trojan War: Its Historicity and Context: Papers of the First Greenbank Colloquium, Liverpool 1981*. Bristol: Bristol Classical Press, pp. 45–56.

Mellaart, J. (1955) 'Some prehistoric sites in Northwestern Anatolia', *Istanbuler Mitteilungen* 6: 53–88.

—— (1957) 'Anatolian chronology in the Early and Middle Bronze Age', *Anatolian Studies* 7: 55–88.

—— (1958) 'The end of the Early Bronze Age in Anatolia and the Aegean', *American Journal of Archaeology* 62: 9–33.

—— (1959) 'The Dorak Treasure', *Illustrated London News*, 28 November, p. 754.

—— (1967) 'Anatolia *c*. 2300–1750 BC', in *Anatolia Before c. 4000 B.C. and c. 2300–1750 BC*. (fascicule) for *Cambridge Ancient History*, 3rd edn., vol. I, pp. 363–416.

—— (1978) *The Archaeology of Ancient Turkey*. Totowa, NJ: Rowman and Littlefield.

—— (1979) 'Egyptian and Near Eastern chronology: a dilemma?', *Antiquity* 53: 6–19.

—— (1982) 'Archaeological evidence for trade and trade routes between Syria and Mesopotamia and Anatolia during the Early Bronze Age and the Beginning of the Middle Bronze Age', *Studi Eblaiti* 5: 15–32.

—— (1984) 'Troy VIIA in Anatolian perspective', in Lin Foxhall and John K. Davies, eds., *The Trojan War: Its Historicity and Context: Papers of the First Greenbank Colloquium, Liverpool 1981*. Bristol: Bristol Classical Press, pp. 63–82.

Mellink, M. J. (1956) 'The royal tombs at Alaca Huyuk and the Aegean world', in S. S. Weinberg, ed., *The Aegean and the Near East: Studies Presented to Hetty Goldman*. Locust Valley, NY: Augustin, pp. 39–58.

—— (1967) 'Review of *Interconnections in the Bronze Age* by W. S. Smith', *American Journal of Archaeology* 71: 92–4.

—— (1976) 'Archaeology in Asia Minor', *American Journal of Archaeology* 80: 261–89.

—— (1977) 'Archaeology in Asia Minor', *American Journal of Archaeology* 81: 289–321.

—— (1979) 'Archaeology in Asia Minor', *American Journal of Archaeology* 83: 331–44.

—— (1983) 'The Hittites and the Aegean world: part 2, archaeological comments on Ahhiyawa-Achaians in Western Anatolia', *American Journal of Archaeology* 87: 138–41.

—— (1986a) 'Postscript', in M. Mellink, ed., *Troy and the Trojan War: A Sym-*

posium Held at Bryn Mawr College, October 1984. Bryn Mawr, Pa.: Bryn Mawr College, pp. 93–101.

—— (1986b) 'The Early Bronze Age in West Anatolia', in G. Cadogan, ed., *The End of the Early Bronze Age in the Aegean.* Leiden: Brill, pp. 141–52.

Mendenhall, G. E. (1962) 'The Hebrew conquest of Palestine', *Biblical Archaeology* 25: 66–87.

Mercer, S. (1949) *The Religion of Egypt.* London: Luzac.

Merkelbach, R. and West, M. L. (1983) 'Fragmenta Selecta', new improved edition in F. Solmsen, ed., *Hesiodi: Theogonia Opera et Dies, Scutum.* Oxford: Clarendon Press.

Merrillees, R. S. (1972) 'Aegean Bronze Age relations with Egypt', *American Journal of Archaeology* 76: 281–94.

—— (1974) *Trade and Transcendence in the Bronze Age Levant. Studies in Mediterranean Archaeology* 39. Göteborg: Paul Åströms Förlag.

—— (1977) 'The absolute chronology of the Bronze Age in Cyprus', *Report of the Department of Antiquities, Cyprus.* Nicosia, pp. 33–50.

—— (1982) 'Review of *Caphtor/Keftiu: A New Investigation* by John Strange', *Report of the Department of Antiquities, Cyprus.* Nicosia, pp. 244–53.

—— (1987) *Alashia Revisited.* Paris: J. Gabalda.

See also Kemp and Merrillees.

Meyer, E. (1884) *Geschichte des Altertums.* Stuttgart and Berlin: Cotta.

—— (1892) *Forschungen zur alten Geschichte,* 2 vols. Halle: Niemeyer.

—— (1904) 'Aegyptische Chronologie', in *Abhandlungen der Königlich Preußischen Akademie der Wissenschaft, Philosophisch-historische Classe I:* pp. 1–212.

—— (1907a) 'Das erste Auftreten der Arier in der Geschichte', *Sitzungberichte der Preußischen Akademie der Wissenschaften,* pp. 14–19.

—— (1907b) 'Nachträge zur ägyptischen Chronologie', in *Abhandlungen der Königlich Preußischen Akademie der Wissenschaft, Philosophisch-historische Classe* III: 1–67.

—— (1909) *Geschichte des Altertums,* 2nd edn. Stuttgart and Berlin: Cotta.

—— (1921) *Ursprung und Anfange des Christentums, II, Die Entwicklung des Judentums und Jesus von Nazareth.* Stuttgart and Berlin: Cotta.

—— (1925) 'Die Volkstämme Kleinasiens, das erste Auftreten der Indogermanen in der Geschichte und die Probleme ihrer Ausbreitung', *Sitzungberichte der Preußischen Akademie der Wissenschaften* 34: 244–60.

—— (1928–36) *Geschichte des Altertums,* 3rd edn., 4 vols. Stuttgart and Berlin: Cotta.

Michael, H. N. (1976) 'Radiocarbon dates from Akrotiri on Thera', *Temple University Aegean Symposium* 1: 7–9.

—— (1977) 'Radiocarbon dates from the site of Akrotiri, Thera', in C. Doumas, ed., *Thera and the Aegean World,* vol. 1, pp. 791–5.

Michael, H. N. and Betancourt, P. P. (1988a) 'The Thera eruption: continuing discussion of the dating, II, further arguments for an early date', *Archaeometry* 30: 169–75.

—— (1988b) 'The Thera eruption: continuing discussion of the dating, IV, addendum', *Archaeometry* 30: 180–1.

Michael, H. N. and Weinstein, G. A. (1977) 'New radiocarbon dates from Akrotiri, Thera', *Temple University Aegean Symposium* 2: 27–30.

Michailidou, A. (1987) *Knossos: A Complete Guide to the Palace of Minos.* Athens: Ekdotike Athenon.

Michalowski, K. (1968) 'The labyrinth enigma: archaeological suggestions', *Journal of Egyptian Archaeology* 54: 219–22.

Millard, A. R. (1973) 'Cypriot copper in Babylonia *c.* 1745 BC', *Journal of Cuneiform Studies* 25: 211–13.

—— (1976) 'The Canaanite linear alphabet and its passage to the Greeks', *Kadmos* 15: 130–44.

Millard, A. R. and Bordrueil, P. (1982) 'A statue with Assyrian and Aramaic inscriptions', *Biblical Archaeologist* 45. 3: 135–41.

See also under Abou-Assaf.

Mironov, N. D. (1933) 'Aryan vestiges in the Near East of the second millenary BC', *Acta Orientalia* 11: 140–217.

Mitford, W. (1784–1804) *The History of Greece,* 8 vols. London.

Monteagudo, L. (1985) 'Orientales e indoeuropeos en la Iberia prehistórica', in J. de Hoz, ed., *Actas del III coloquio sobre lenguas y culturas paleohispanicas (Lisboa, 5–8 Noviembre 1980).* Salamanca: Ediciones Universitad de Salamanca, pp. 15–135.

Montet, P. (1928–9) *Byblos et l'Égypte, quatres campagnes de fouilles à Gebeil, 1921–1922–1923–1924.* Bibliothèque archéologique et historique, 11. Haut-Commisariat de la République Française en Syrie et au Liban. Paris: Geuthner.

Moran, W. L. (1961) 'The Hebrew language in its Northwest Semitic background', in G. E. Wright, ed., *The Bible and the Ancient Near East: Essays in Honour of William Foxwell Albright.* Garden City, NY: Doubleday, pp. 54–72.

—— (1987) *Les Lettres d' el Amarna: correspondance diplomatique du pharaon. Littératures anciennes du Proche-Orient.* Paris: Éditions du Cerf.

Morenz, S. (1973) *Egyptian Religion,* A. E. Keep, trans. London: Methuen.

Morgan (Brown), L. (1978) 'The ship procession in the miniature fresco', in C. Doumas, ed., *Thera and the Aegean World: Papers Presented at the Second International Scientific Congress, Santorini, Greece, August 1978,* vol. I. London, pp. 629–44.

—— (1981) 'The West House paintings at Thera', *Bulletin of the Institute of Classical Studies* 28: 166.

—— (1983) 'Theme in the West House paintings at Thera', *Archaiologike Ephemeris* 122: 85–105.

—— (1988) *The Miniature Wall Paintings of Thera: A Study in Aegean Culture and Iconography.* Cambridge: Cambridge University Press.

Morpurgo-Davis, A. (1986) 'The linguistic evidence', in G. Cadogan, ed., *The End of the Early Bronze Age in the Aegean.* Leiden: Brill, pp. 93–123.

Moscati, S. (1968) *Fenici e Cartaginesi in Sardegna.* Milan: A. Mondadori.

—— (1985) 'I Fenici e il mondo Mediterraneo al tempo di Omero', *Rivista di Studi Fenici* 13: 179–87.

Moscati, S., Spitaler, A., Ullendorf, E. and v. Soden, W. (1969) *An Introduction to the Comparative Grammar of the Semitic Languages: Phonology and Morphology.* Wiesbaden: Harrassowitz.

Moule, A. C. and Yetts, P. (1957) *The Rulers of China: 221 B.C.–A.D. 1949: Chronological Tables by A. C. Moule: With an Introductory Section on the Earlier Rulers by Perceval Yetts.* London: Routledge & Kegan Paul.

Movers, F. C. (1841–50) *Die Phönizier,* 2 vols., 4 books. Bonn and Berlin: Weber.

Muhly, J. D. (1965) 'Review of *Hellenosemitica* by M. C. Astour', *Journal of the American Oriental Society* 85: 585–8.

—— (1970a) 'Homer and the Phoenicians: the relations between Greece and the Near East in the Late Bronze Age and Early Iron Ages', *Berytus* 19: 19–64.

—— (1970b) 'Review of *Interconnections in the Ancient Near East* by W. S. Smith', *Journal of the American Oriental Society* 90: 305–9.

—— (1973a) 'The Philistines and their pottery', paper presented to the Third International Colloquium on Aegean Prehistory, Sheffield, August.

—— (1973b) 'Copper and tin: the distribution of mineral resources and the nature of the metals trade in the Bronze Age', *Transactions of the Connecticut Academy of Arts and Sciences* 43: 155–535.

—— (1976) 'Supplement to "Copper and tin: the distribution of mineral resources and the nature of the metals trade in the Bronze Age"', *Transactions of the Connecticut Academy of Arts and Sciences* 46: 77–136.

—— (1979a) 'On the Shaft Graves at Mycenae', in M. A. Powell and R. M. Sack, eds., *Studies in Honor of Tom B. Jones.* Kevelaer: Butzon and Bercker/Neukirchen-Vluyn, pp. 311–23.

—— (1979b) 'Cypriote copper: some geological and metallurgical problems', *Acts of the International Archaeological Symposium, The Relations between Cyprus and Crete, ca. 2000–500 BC.* Nicosia: Department of Antiquities, pp. 87–100.

—— (1984) 'The role of the Sea Peoples in Cyprus during the L.C. III period', in V. Karageorghis, ed., *Cyprus at the Close of the Late Bronze Age.* Nicosia: A. G. Leventis Foundation, pp. 39–56.

—— (1985) 'Phoenicia and the Phoenicians', in A. Biran *et al.,* eds., *Biblical Archaeology Today: Proceedings of the International Congress on Biblical Archaeology, Jerusalem, April 1984.* Jerusalem: Israel Exploration Society, Israel Academy of Sciences and Humanities and the American Schools of Oriental Research, pp. 177–91.

Mulder, M. J. (1986) 'Die Bedeutung von Jachin und Boaz in 1 *Kön.* 7:21 (2 *Chr.* 3:17)', in *Tradition and Reinterpretation in Jewish and Early Christian Literature: Essays in Honour of Jürgen C. H. Lebram, Studia Post Biblica* 36. Leiden: Brill, pp. 19–25.

Müller, C. (1841–70) *Fragmenta Historicorum Graecorum.* Paris.

Müller, K. O. (1820–4) *Geschichten hellenischer Stämme und Städte,* vol. I, *Orchomenos und die Minyer,* vols. II and III, *Die Dorier.* Breslau: Max. Vols. II and III trans. H. Tufnell and G. C. Lewis as *The History and Antiquities of the Doric Race,* 2 vols. London, 1830.

—— (1825) *Prolegomena zu einer wissenschaftlichen Mythologie*, Göttingen. Trans. J. Leitch as *Introduction to a Scientific System of Mythology*, London, 1844.

Müller, W. M. (1898) 'Studien zur vorderasiatischen Geschichte', *Mitteilungen der vorderasiatischen Gesellschaft* 3: 1–108.

Muss-Arnolt, W. (1892) 'On Semitic words in Greek and Latin', *Transactions of the American Philological Association* 23: 35–157.

Mylonas, G. E. (1956) 'Seated and multiple Mycenaean figurines in the National Museum of Athens Greece', in S. S. Weinberg, ed., *The Aegean and the Near East: Studies Presented to Hetty Goldman on the Occasion of her Seventy-fifth Birthday*. Locust Valley, NY: Augustin, pp. 110–25.

—— (1962) 'The Luvian invasions of Greece', *Hesperia* 23: 188–301.

—— (1972–3) *'Ο Ταφικός Κύκλος Β' των Μυκηνῶν.* 2 vols. Athens: E en Athenais Archaiologike Etaireia.

Myres, J. L. (1923) 'Primitive man in geological time', in *Cambridge Ancient History*, 1st edn., vol. I, pp. 1–97.

Nagel, W. (1987) 'Indogermanen und Alter Orient Rückblick und Ausblick auf den Stand des Indogermanenproblems', *Mitteilungen der deutschen Orient-Gesellschaft zu Berlin* 119: 157–213.

Nagy, G. (1979) *The Best of the Achaeans: Concepts of the Hero in Archaic Greek Poetry*. Baltimore, Md. and London: The Johns Hopkins University Press.

Naveh, J. (1973) 'Some Semitic epigraphical considerations on the antiquity of the Greek alphabet', *American Journal of Archaeology* 77: 1–8.

—— (1982) *Early History of the Alphabet: An Introduction to West Semitic Epigraphy and Paleography*. Jerusalem: Magnes; Leiden: Brill.

Naville, E. (1894–1908) *The Temple of Deir el Bahari*, 6 vols. London: Offices of the Egypt Exploration Fund.

Needham, J. (1954–) *Science and Civilisation in China*, vol. III, *Mathematics and the Sciences of the Heavens and the Earth*. Cambridge: Cambridge University Press.

Needham, J. and Lu, G. D. (1985) *Transpacific Echoes and Resonances: Listening Once Again*. Singapore: World Scientific.

Negbi, O. (1976) *Canaanite Gods in Metal*. Tel Aviv: Tel Aviv University, Institute of Archaeology.

—— (1978) 'Cypriot imitations of Tel el-Yahudieh ware from Tomba tou Skourou', *American Journal of Archaeology* 82: 137–49.

—— (1982) 'Evidence for Early Phoenician communities on the Eastern Mediterranean islands', *Levant* 14: 179–82.

Neiman, D. (1965) 'Phoenician place names', *Journal of Near Eastern Studies* 24: 113–5.

Neugebauer, O. (1945) *Mathematical Cuneiform Texts*. New Haven, Conn.: American Oriental Society and the American Schools of Oriental Research.

—— (1950) 'The alleged Babylonian discovery of the precession of the equinoxes', *Journal of the American Oriental Society* 70.1: 1–8.

—— (1957) *The Exact Sciences in Antiquity*. Providence, RI: Brown University Press.

Neugebauer, O. and Parker, R. A. (1960–9) *Egyptian Astronomical Texts*, 4 vols. Providence, RI and London: Brown University Press.

Newberry, P. E. (1893) *Beni Hasan*, pts 1 and 2, *Archæological Survey of Egypt*, nos. 1 and 2. London: Kegan Paul.

—— (1906) 'To what race did the founders of Sais belong?', *Proceedings of the Society of Biblical Archaeology* 28: 71–3.

—— (1909) 'Two cults of the Old Kingdom', *Liverpool Annals of Archaeology and Anthropology* 1: 24–31.

Nibbi, A. (1975) *The Sea Peoples and Egypt*. Park Ridge, NJ: Noyes Press.

Niebuhr, B. (1847) *Vorträge über alte Geschichte an der Universität zu Bonn gehalten*, 3 vols. Berlin. Trans. L. Schmitz as *Lectures on Ancient History from the Earliest Times to the Taking of Alexandria by Octavius*, 3 vols. Philadelphia, 1852.

Niemeier, H. G. (1984) 'Die Phönizier und die Mittelmeerwelt im Zeitalten Homers', *Jahrbuch des Römisch-Germanischen Zentralmuseums* 31: 1–94.

Niemeier, W.-D. (1980) 'Die Katastrophe von Thera und die spätminoische Chronologie', *Jahrbuch des deutschen archäologischen Instituts* 95: 1–76.

—— (1982a) 'Mycenaean Knossos and the Age of Linear B', *Studi micenei ed egeo-anatolici* 23: 219–87.

—— (1982b) 'Das mykenische Knossos und das Alter von Linear B', *Beiträge zur ägäischen Bronzezeit*. Marburg: Kleine Schriften aus dem Vorgeschichtlichen Seminar Marburg 11, pp. 29–127.

—— (1983) 'The character of the Knossian palace society in the second half of the fifteenth century BC: Mycenaean or Minoan?', in O. Krzyszkowska and L. Nixon, eds., *Minoan Society: Proceedings of the Cambridge Colloquium 1981*. Bristol: Bristol Classical Press, pp. 217–36.

—— (1984) 'The End of the Minoan Thalassocracy', in R. Hägg and N. Marinatos, eds., *The Minoan Thalassocracy: Myth and Reality: Proceedings of the 3rd International Symposium at the Swedish Institute in Athens 31 May–5 June 1982*, *Skrifter utgivna av Svenska Institutet i Athen*, 4, pp. 206–15.

Nilsson, M. P. (1932) *The Mycenaean Origin of Greek Mythology*. Berkeley: University of California Press.

—— (1933) *Homer and Mycenae*. London: Methuen.

—— (1950) *The Minoan Mycenaean Religion*. Lund: Gleerup.

—— (1972) *The Mycenaean Origin of Greek Mythology*. Paperback edn. Berkeley: University of California Press.

Nivison, D. S. (1983) 'The dates of Western Chou', *Harvard Journal of Asian Studies* 43: 481–580.

Nixon, L. (1983) 'Changing views of Minoan society', in O. Krzyszkowska and L. Nixon, eds., *Minoan Society: Proceedings of the Cambridge Colloquium 1981*. Bristol: Bristol Classical Press, pp. 237–44.

Noegel, S. (1990) 'Ogygos of Boiotia and the biblical Og of Bashan: reflections on the same myth', undergraduate paper for Government 454, Cornell, Spring.

Nonnos (1940) *Dionysiaca*, 3 vols, W. H. D. Rouse, trans., notes by H. J. Rose and L. R. Lind. Cambridge, Mass.: Harvard University Press (Loeb); London: Heinemann.

Nougayrol, J. (1957) 'Nouveaux textes d'Ugarit en cuneiformes babyloniens', *Compte rendu de la Rencontre Assyriologique Internationale*, pp. 77–85.

Oates, J. (1979) *Babylon*. London: Thames & Hudson.

O'Connor, D. (1990) 'The Bronze Age evidence', paper given at the 42nd Annual Meeting of the American Research Center in Egypt, Berkeley, 26–29 April.

Olivier, J. P. (1971) 'Notes épigraphiques sur les tablettes en linéare B de la série Ug de Thèbes', *Archaiologika Analekta ex Athenon* 4: 269–72.

O'Mara, P. F. (1979) *The Palermo Stone and the Archaic Kings*. La Canada, Calif.: Paulette Publishing Co.

Onians, R. B. (1988) *The Origins of European Thought: About the Body, the Mind, the Soul, the World, Time and Fate*. Cambridge: Cambridge University Press.

Otto, E. (1938) 'Beitrage zur Geschichte der Stierkulte in Aegypten', in *Untersuchungen zur Geschichte und Altertumskunde Aegyptens XIII*. Reprint. Hildersheim: Olms, 1964.

—— (1966) *Osiris und Amun: Kult und heilige Statten*. Trans. K. Bosse Griffiths as *Ancient Egyptian Art: The Cult of Osiris and Amon*. London: Thames & Hudson.

—— (1975a) 'Ägypten im Selbstbewußtsein des Ägypters', in W. Helck and E. Otto, *Lexikon der Ägyptologie*, vol. I, cols. 76–8.

—— (1975b) 'Amun', in W. Helck and E. Otto, *Lexikon der Ägyptologie*, vol. I, cols. 245–6.

—— (1975c) 'Anuket', in W. Helck and E. Otto, *Lexikon der Ägyptologie*, vol. I, cols. 333–4.

Packard, D. W. (1974) *Minoan Linear A*. Berkeley and Los Angeles: University of California Press.

Page, D. L. (1970) *The Santorini Volcano and the Desolation of Minoan Crete*. London: Society for the Promotion of Hellenic Studies.

—— (1976) 'The miniature fresco from Akrotiri, Thera', *Praktika tes Akademias Athenon* 51: 136–52.

Palaima, T. G. (1988) 'The development of the Mycenaean writing system', in J.-P. Olivier and T. G. Palaima, eds., *Texts, Tablets and Scribes: Studies in Mycenaean Epigraphy and Economy*, *Minos* suppl. 10, Salamanca, 1988, pp. 321–8.

Pallottino, M. (1978) *The Etruscans*, rev. and enlarged edn., J. Cremona, trans., D. Ridgeway, ed. London: Penguin.

—— (1984) *Storia della Prima Italia*. Milan: Rusconi.

Palmer, L. R. (1956) 'Military arrangements for the defence of Pylos', *Minos* 4: 120–45.

—— (1958) 'Luvian and Linear A', *Transactions of the Philological Society* 56: 75–100.

—— (1965) *Mycenaeans and Minoans: Aegean Prehistory in the Light of the Linear B Tablets*, 2nd rev. edn. London: Faber.

—— (1969) *A New Guide to the Palace of Knossos*. London: Faber.

—— (1984a) 'The Mycenaean Palace and the *Damos*', in *Aux origines de l'Hellénisme: La Crète et La Grèce: Hommage à Henri van Effenterre*. Paris: Publications de la Sorbonne: Histoire Ancienne et Médiéval 15, pp. 151–9.

—— (1984b) 'The Linear B Palace at Knossos', in P. Åström, L. R. Palmer and L. Pomerance, eds., *Studies in Aegean Chronology*. Göteborg: Paul Åströms Förlag, pp. 26–119.

Pålsson-Hallager, B. (1983) 'Crete and Italy in the Late Bronze Age III Period', *American Journal of Archaeology* 89: 293–305.

Pang, K. D. (1985) 'Extraordinary floods in early Chinese history and their absolute dates', paper presented to the U.S.–China Bilateral Symposium on the Analysis of Extraordinary Flood Events, Nanking, October.

—— (1987) 'Extraordinary floods in early Chinese history and their absolute dates', *Journal of Hydrology* 96: 139–55.

Pang, K. D. and Chou, H. H. (1984) 'A correlation between Greenland ice core climatic horizons and ancient oriental meteriological records', *Eos* 65: 846.

—— (1985) 'Three very large volcanic eruptions in Antiquity and their effects on the climate of the ancient world', paper abstract, *Eos* 66: 816.

Pang, K. D., Espenak, F., Huang, Y. L., Chou, H. H. and Yau, K. C. (1988) 'The origin and extent of Chinese civilization', paper given to the 5th International Conference on Chinese Science, San Diego, 5–10 August.

Pang, K. D., Pieri D. and Chou, H. H. (1986) 'Climatic impacts of the 44–42 BC eruptions of Etna, reconstructed from ice core and historical records', *Eos* 67: 880.

Pang, K. D., Slavin, J. A. and Chou, H. H. (1987) 'Climatic anomalies of the late third century BC; correlations with volcanism, solar activity and planetary alignment', *Eos* 68: 1234.

Pang, K. D., Yau, K. C., Chou, H. H. and Wolff, R. (1988) 'Computer analysis of some Chinese sunrise eclipse records to determine the earth's past rotation rate'. *Vistas in Astronomy* 16: 109.

Pankenier, D. W. (1981–2) 'Astronomical dates in the Shang and Western Zhou', *Early China* 2: 2–37.

—— (1983) '*Mozi* and the dates of Xia, Shang and Zhou: a research note', *Early China* 9–10: 175–83.

Parke, H. W. (1967) *The Oracles of Zeus: Dōdōna, Olympia and Ammon*. Oxford: Oxford University Press.

—— (1977) *Festivals of the Athenians*. London: Thames & Hudson; Ithaca, NY: Cornell University Press.

Parker, R. A. (1950) *The Calendars of Ancient Egypt. Studies in Ancient Oriental Civilization* 26. Chicago: Oriental Institute.

—— (1957) 'The lunar dates of Thutmose III and Ramesses II', *Journal of Near Eastern Studies* 16: 39–43.

—— (1976) 'The Sothic dating of the Twelfth and Eighteenth Dynasties', in J. H. Johnson and E. F. Wente, eds., *Studies in Honor of George R. Hughes. Studies in Ancient Oriental Civilization* 39. Chicago: Oriental Institute.

Parker, R. A. and Neugebauer, O. (1960–4) *Egyptian Astronomical Texts*, 4 vols. London: Lund Humphries for Brown University Press.

Parmentier, L. (1913) *Recherches sur le traité d'Isis et d'Osiris de Plutarque*. Brussels: Académie Royale de Belgique.

Partridge, E. (1958) *Origins: A Short Etymological Dictionary of Modern English*. London: Routledge & Kegan Paul.

Pârvulescu, A. (1968) 'L'homérique KHP étude sémantique', *Helikon* 8: 277–310.

Pausanias, *Guide to Greece*, see Frazer and Levi.

Peake, H. and Fleure, H. J. (1927) *Priests and Kings: The Corridors of Time IV*. Oxford: Clarendon Press.

Pearson, K. and Connor, P. (1968) *The Dorak Affair*. New York: Atheneum.

Pelon, O. (1976) *Tholoi, tumuli et cercles funéraires: Recherches sur les monuments funéraires de plan circulaire dans l'Égée de l'âge du bronze*. Athens: École Française d'Athènes.

—— (1987) 'L'architecture funéraire de Grèce continentale à la transition du bronze moyen et du bronze récent', in R. Laffineur, ed., *Thanatos: Les coutumes funéraires en Égée à l'âge du Bronze: Actes du Colloque de Liège (21–23 avril 1986)*. Université de l'État à Liège: Histoire de l'Art et Archéologie de la Grèce antique, pp. 107–15.

Pendlebury, J. D. S. (1930a) *Aegyptiaca*. Cambridge: Cambridge University Press.

—— (1930b) 'Egypt and the Aegean in the Late Bronze Age', *Journal of Egyptian Archaeology* 16: 75–92.

—— (1963) *The Archaeology of Crete an Introduction*. New York: Biblo & Tannen.

Peradotto, J. and Myerowitz Levine, M. (1989) 'The Challenge of "Black Athena"', *Arethusa*, special issue.

Persson, A.W. (1932) 'Alkmenes Grav. En kunglig utgrävning un den Antiken', in *Gustavus Adolphus: Arkeologiska Studier tillagnade H. K. H. Kronprins Gustaf Adolf*. Lund: Gleerup, pp. 3–37.

—— (1942) *New Tombs at Dendra*. Lund: Gleerup.

Peruzzi, E. (1959–60) 'Le iscrizioni minoiche', *Atti dell' Accademia Toscana di Scienze e Lettere 'La Colombaria'* 24: 31–128.

Petrie, W. M. F. (1883) *The Pyramids and Temples of Gizeh*. London: Field & Tuer.

—— (1890) 'The Egyptian bases of Greek history', *Journal of Hellenic Studies* 11: 271–7.

—— (1891) *Ilahun, Kahun and Gurob, 1889–90*. London: David Nutt.

—— (1893) *The Great Pyramid*. London: Methuen.

—— (1894) *Tell el Amarna*. London: Methuen.

—— (1894–1905) *A History of Egypt*, 3 vols. London: Methuen, New York: Scribner.

—— (1903) *History of Egypt from the Earliest Kings to the XVIth Dynasty*, 5th ed. London: Methuen.

—— (1908) 'Historical references in Hermetic writings', *Transactions of the*

Third International Congress of the History of Religions, Oxford, 1: 196–225.

—— (1909) *Personal Religion in Egypt before Christianity*. London: Harpers Library of Living Thought.

—— (1923) *History of Egypt from the Earliest Kings to the XVIth Dynasty*, 10th edn. London: Methuen.

—— (1931) *70 Years of Archaeology*, London: Sampson Low.

—— (1952) *City of Shepherd Kings and Gaza V*. London: British School of Egyptian Archaeology 64.

Petrie, W. F. and Walker, J. H. (1909) *Memphis 1: British School of Archaeology in Egypt and Egyptian Research Account: Fourteenth Year*. London: London School of Archaeology in Egypt.

Pettinato, G. (1978) 'L'atlante geografico ne Vicino Oriente Antíco attestate ad Ebla ed ad Abu Salabikh', *Orientalia* 47: 50–73.

—— (1981) *Ebla: un impero inciso nell' argilla*. Milan: Mondadori. Trans. as *The Archives of Ebla: An Empire Inscribed in Clay, with an Afterword by Mitchell Dahood, S. J.* Garden City, NY: Doubleday.

—— (1985). *Semiramide*. Milan: Rusconi.

Pharaklas, N. (1967) 'Archaiotetes kai Mnemeia Boiotias', *Archaiologikon Deltion* 22.2: 225–57.

Phelps, R. (1963) ' "Before Hitler Came": The Thule Society and the Germanen Orden', *The Journal of Modern History* 35.3: 245–61.

Phillips, E. D. (1965) *The Royal Hordes: Nomad Peoples of the Steppes*. London: Thames & Hudson.

Philo of Byblos, *The Phoenician History*, see Baumgarten.

Picard, C. (1937) 'Homère et les religions de l'Égypte', *Revue archéologique*, series 6, 10: 110–13.

—— (1948) *Les Religions Préhelléniques*. Paris: Presses universitaires de France.

Pictet, A. (1858) 'Iren und Arier', in A. Kuhn and A. Schleicher, eds., *Beiträge zur vergleichende Sprachforschung, auf dem Gebiete der arischen, celtischen und slawischen Sprachen*, 8 vols. Berlin: Dümmler, I: 81–99.

Pierce, R. H. (1971) 'Egyptian loan words in Ancient Greek?', *Symbolae Osloenses* 46: 96–107.

Pini, I. (1968) *Beiträge zur minoischen Gräberkunde*. Wiesbaden: Harrassowitz.

—— (1984) 'Minoische Siegel außerhalb Kretas', in R. Hägg and N. Marinatos, eds., *The Minoan Thalassocracy: Myth and Reality: Proceedings of the 3rd International Symposium at the Swedish Institute in Athens 31 May–5 June 1982, Skrifter utgivna av Svenska Institutet i Athen*, 4, 123–30.

Pisani, V. (1950) 'gr. 'ἄρτος'. *Ricerci Linguistiche* I.141.

Plato (1914–2?) 12 vols. H. N. Fowler, trans.

—— *Kratylus*.

—— *Kritias*.

—— *Menexenus*.

—— *Phaedo*.

—— *Republic*.

—— *Timaeus*. (1929) R. G. Bury, trans.

See Lee, 1955.

Platon, N. (1956) 'La Cronologie Minoenne', in C. Zervos, ed., *L'Art de la Crète néolithique et minoenne*. Paris: Éditions Cahier d'Art, pp. 509–12.

Platon, N. and Stassinopouloutouloupa, E. (1964) 'Oriental seals from the palace of Cadmus: unique discoveries in Boeotian Thebes', *Illustrated London News*, 12 May, pp. 896–9.

Plutarch, *De Iside et Osiride*, trans. F. C. Babbit (1934–5) in *Plutarch's Moralia*, 16 vols. Cambridge, Mass.: Harvard University Press (Loeb); London: Heinemann, vol. V, pp. 7–191.

—— *De genio Socratis*, trans. P. de Lacy and B. Einarsen in *Plutarch's Moralia*, 16 vols. Cambridge, Mass.: Harvard University Press (Loeb); London: Heinemann, vol. VII, pp. 362–434.

Podzuweit, C. (1982) 'Die mykenische Welt und Troja', in *Südosteuropa zwischen 1600 und 1000 vor Chr.*, in B. Hänsel, ed., *Prähistorische Archäologie in Südosteuropa*, vol. I. Berlin, pp. 80–8.

Pois, R. A. (1986) *National Socialism and the Religion of Nature*. New York: St. Martin's.

Pokorny, J. (1959–69) *Indogermanisches etymologisches Wörterbuch*, 2 vols. Bern and Munich: Franke.

Pollinger Foster, K. (1979) *Aegean Faience of the Bronze Age*. New Haven and London: Yale University Press.

—— (1986) 'Review of *Art and Religion in Thera* by Nanno Marinatos', *American Journal of Archaeology* 90: 353–4.

—— (1987) 'Snakes and lions: a new reading of the West House frescoes from Thera', *Expedition* 30 (February): pp. 10–20.

Polomé, E. C. (1981) 'Can graphemic change cause phonemic change?', in Y. Arbeitman and A. R. Bomhard, eds., *Bono Homini Donum*. Amsterdam: John Benjamins, pp. 881–8.

Pomerance, L. (1970) 'The final collapse of Thera (Santorini)', *Studies in Mediterranean Archaeology* 26.

—— (1978) 'The improbability of a Theran collapse during the New Kingdom 1503–1447 BC', in C. Doumas, ed., *Thera and the Aegean World: Papers Presented at the Second International Scientific Congress, Santorini, Greece, August 1978*, vols. I–II. London, pp. 778–803.

—— (1984) 'A note on the carved stone ewers from the Khyan lid deposit', in *Studies in Aegean Chronology*, Göteborg: Paul Åströms Förlag, pp. 15–25.

Pope, M. (1981) 'The cult of the dead at Ugarit', in G. Young, ed., *Ugarit in Retrospect: 50 Years of Ugarit and Ugaritic*. Winona Lake, Ind.: Eisenbrauns, pp. 170–5.

—— (1973) *Job: A New Translation with Introduction and Commentary*, 3rd edn. Garden City, NY: Anchor.

Pope, M. and Raison, J. (1978) 'Linear A: changing perspectives', *Études minoennes* I: 5–64.

Popham, M. (1965) 'Some late Minoan pottery from Crete', *Annual of the British School at Athens* 60: 316–42.

Porada, E. (1950) 'Critical review of the corpus of Near Eastern seals in North

American collections', vol. I, ed. E. Porada, *Journal of Cuneiform Studies* 9: 155–62.

—— (1965) 'Cylinder seals from Thebes: a preliminary report', *American Journal of Archaeology* 69: 173.

—— (1966) 'Further notes on the cylinders from Thebes', *American Journal of Archaeology* 70: 194.

—— (1981) 'The cylinder seals found at Thebes in Boeotia', with contributions from Hans G. Güterbock and John A. Brinkman, *Archiv für Orientforschung* 28: 1–78.

—— (1982) 'Remarks on the Tôd Treasure in Egypt', in M. A. Dandamayev *et al.*, eds., *Societies and Languages of the Ancient Near East, Studies in Honour of I. M. Diakonoff*. Warminster: Aris & Phillips.

—— (1984) 'The cylinder seal from Tell el-Dab'a', *American Journal of Archaeology* 88: 485–8.

Portugali, Y. and Knapp, A. B. (1985) 'Cyprus and the Aegean: a spatial analysis of interaction in the 17th-14th centuries BC', in A. B. Knapp and T. Stech, eds., *Prehistoric Production and Exchange: The Aegean and East Mediterranean*. Los Angeles: University of California, Institute of Archaeology, Monograph 25, pp. 44–78.

Porzig, W. (1954a) 'Sprachgeographische Untersuchungen zu den griechischen Dialekten', *Indogermanische Forschungen* 61: 147–69.

—— (1954b) *Die Gliederung des indogermanischen Sprachgebiets*. Heidelberg: Winter.

Posener, G. (1940) *Princes et pays d'Asie et de Nubie*. Brussels: Fondation Égyptologique Reine Élisabeth.

—— (1956) *Littérature et politique dans l'Égypte de la XIIe Dynastie*. Paris: Bibliothèque de l'École des Hautes Études, fascicule 307.

—— (1957) 'Les Asiatiques en Égypte sous les XIIe et XIIIe dynasties', *Syria* 34: 145–63.

—— (1960) 'La divinité du pharaon', *Cahiers de la Societé Asiatique* 15.

—— (1966) 'Une réinterpretation tardive du nom du dieu Khonsu', *Zeitschrift für ägyptische Sprache* 93: 115–19.

—— (1971) 'Syria and Palestine *c.* 2160–1780 BC', in *Cambridge Ancient History*, 3rd edn., vol. 1, pt 2, pp. 532–58.

—— (1975) 'Ächtungstexte', in W. Helck and E. Otto, *Lexikon der Ägyptologie*, vol. I, cols. 67–8.

—— (1982) 'A new inscription of the XIIth Dynasty', *Society for the Study of Egyptian Antiquities* [Toronto] 12: 7–8.

Poursat, J.-C. (1977) *Les Ivoires mycéniens*. Athens: Bibliothèque des écoles françaises d'Athènes et de Rome.

—— (1984) 'Une Thalassocratie minoenne à Minoen Moyen II', in R. Hägg and N. Marinatos, eds., *The Minoan Thalassocracy: Myth and Reality: Proceedings of the 3rd International Symposium at the Swedish Institute in Athens 31 May–5 June 1982, Skrifter utgivna av Svenska Institutet i Athen*, 4, pp. 85–7.

Powell, B. (1977) 'The significance of the so-called "Horns of Consecration"', *Kadmos* 16: 70–81.

Power, E. (1929) 'The ancient gods and language of Cyprus revealed by the Accadian inscriptions of Amathus', *Biblica* 10: 129–69.

Prausnitz, M. W. (1985) 'On Early to Middle Iron Age pottery of Israel, Tyre and Cyprus', *Praktika tou Diethnous Kypriologikou Synedriou*, vol. I, *Archion Tema*, Nicosia, pp. 191–5.

Prellwitz, W. (1905) *Etymologisches Wörterbuch der griechischen Sprache*. Göttingen: Vandenhoeck & Ruprecht.

Prendi, F. (1982) 'The prehistory of Albania', in *Cambridge Ancient History*, 2nd edn., vol. III, pt 1, pp. 187–237.

Pritchard, J. B. (1955) *Ancient Near Eastern Texts*, 2nd edn. Princeton, NJ: Princeton University Press.

Pulak, C. (1988) 'The Bronze Age shipwreck at Ulu Burun, Turkey: 1985 campaign', *American Journal of Archaeology* 92: 1–37.

Purpura, G. (1981) 'Sulle vicende ed il luogo di rinveniemento del cosidetto Melqart di Selinunte', *Sicilia Archeologica* 14: 46–7; 87–90.

Quattordio, A. M. (1977) 'Per l'interpretazione di miceneo O-pa', *Studi e saggi linguistici* NS 17: 31–66.

—— (1979a) 'Denominativi in -εύω nomi comuni in -εύς', *Studi e saggi linguistici* NS 19: 109–65.

—— (1979b) 'HRA ed ΗΡΩΣ : un tentativo di esegesi etimologica', *Studi e saggi linguistici* NS 19: 167–98.

Raban, A. (1984) 'The Thera ships: another interpretation', *American Journal of Archaeology* 88: 11–19.

Rabin, C. (1974) 'The origin of the Hebrew word *pilageš*', *Journal of Jewish Studies* 25: 353–64.

Raison, J. and Brixhe, C. (1961) 'Compte rendu de *Minoica*', *Kratylos* 6: 127–36.

Raison, J. and Pope, M. (1971) *Index du linéaire A*. Rome: Edizione dell'Ateneo.

—— (1978) 'Le vocabulaire du linéaire A en translittération', *Études minoennes* I: 131–90.

See also Pope and Raison.

Ramage, E. S., ed. (1978) *Atlantis: Fact or Fiction?* Bloomington: Indiana University Press.

Ranke, O. (1935–52) *Die ägyptischen Personenamen*, 3 vols. Glückstadt: Augustin.

Rashidi, R. (1985) 'Africans in early Asian civilization, historical overview', in Rashidi, ed., *African Presence in Early Asia*, special issue of *Journal of African Civilizations*, pp. 15–52.

Rattenbury, R. M. (1933) 'Romance in the the Greek novel', in J. U. Powell, ed., *New Chapters in Greek Literature*, 3rd series. Oxford: Clarendon Press, pp. 211–57.

Rebuffat, R. (1966) 'Les Phéniciens à Rome', *Mélanges de l'École française de Rome* 78: 7–48.

Reisner, G. A. (1961) 'The Egyptian forts from Halfa to Semna', *Kush* 9: 11–24.

Reisner, G. A. and Reisner, M. B. (1933) 'Inscribed monuments from Gebel Barkal, II' *Zeitschrift für ägyptische Sprache und Altertumskunde* 69: 35–46.

Rendsburg, G. (1981) 'Orientation in Egypt and Palestine', *Biblical Archaeologist* 44: 198.

—— (1982) 'A new look at the Pentateuchal Hw'', *Biblica* 63: 351–69.

—— (1984) '*UT* 68 and the Tell Asmar seal', *Orientalia* 53: 448–52.

—— (1989) '*Black Athena:* an etymological response', in M. M. Levine, ed., *'The Challenge of "Black Athena"'*, *Arethusa* special issue: 67–82.

—— (1990) 'The internal consistency and historical reliability of the biblical genealogies', *Vetus Testamentum* 40: 185–206.

—— (forthcoming) 'Monophthongization of AW/AY > A, in Eblaite and in Northwest Semitic.'

Renfrew, C. (1972) *The Emergence of Civilisation: The Cyclades and the Aegean in the Third Millennium BC.* London: Methuen.

—— (1973) 'Problems in the general correlation of archaeological and linguistic strata in prehistoric Greece: the model of autochthonous origin', in R. A. Crossland and A. Birchall, eds., *Bronze Age Migrations in the Aegean: Archaeological and Linguistic Problems of Greek Prehistory.* London: Duckworth, pp. 265–79.

—— (1978) 'The Mycenaean sanctuary at Phylakopi', *Antiquity* 52: 7–15.

—— (1984) *Approaches to Social Archaeology.* Cambridge, Mass: Harvard University Press.

—— (1987) *Archaeology and Language: The Puzzle of Indo-European Origins.* London: Cape.

Renfrew, C., Rowlands, M. J. and Seagraves, B. A. (1982) *Theory and Explanation in Archaeology: The Southampton Conference.* New York and London: Academic Press.

Ridgeway, W. (1911) 'Achaeans', in *Encyclopaedia Britannica*, 10th ed., vol. I, pp. 141–2.

Riis, P. J. (1969) 'The first Greeks and their settlement at Sukas', *Ugaritica* 6: 1–72.

—— (1970) *Sūkās I: The North East Sanctuary and the First Settling of Greeks in Syria and Palestine.* Publications of the Carlsberg Expedition to Phoenicia. Copenhagen: Det Konglige Danske.

Risch, E. (1949) 'Altgriechische Dialektgeographie', *Museum Helveticum* 6: 19–28.

—— (1955) 'Die Gliederung der griechischen Dialekte in neuer Sicht', *Museum Helveticum* 12: 61–75.

Ritner, R. K. (1985) 'Anubis and the lunar disk', *Journal of Egyptian Archaeology* 71: 149–55.

Roberts, J. J. M. (1971) 'Erra scorched earth', *Journal of Cuneiform Studies* 24: 11–16.

Robertson, J. (1788) *The Parian Chronicle; or the Chronicle of the Arundelain Marbles: with a Dissertation Concerning Its Authenticity.* London: J. Walter.

Robertson Smith, W. (1894) *The Religion of the Semites: The Fundamental Institutions.* Cambridge.

Roesch, P. (1982) *Études Béotiennes.* Paris: Bocard.

Röllig, V. W. and Mansfeldt, J. (1970) 'Zwei Ostraka vom Tell Kāmid el Lōz und ein neuer Aspekt für die Entstehung des kanaanäischen Alphabets', *Die Welt des Orients* 3/2: 265–70.

Roscher, W. H. (1884–1937) *Ausführliches Lexikon der griechischen und römischen Mythologie*, 7 vols. Leipzig: Teubner.

Rosenthal, F. (1978) 'Review of *Recherches sur les plus anciens emprunts sémitiques en grec*, by E. Masson', *Journal of the American Oriental Society* 90: 338–9.

Rowlands, M., Larsen, M. T. and Kristiansen, K., eds. (1987) *Centre and Periphery in the Ancient World*. Cambridge: Cambridge University Press.

Rowley, H. H. (1950) *From Joseph to Joshua: Biblical Traditions in the Light of Archaeology*. London: Oxford University Press.

Ruijgh, C. H. (1967) *Études sur la grammaire et le vocabulaire du grec mycénien*. Amsterdam: Hakkert.

Rundle-Clark, R. T. (1959) *Myth and Symbol in Ancient Egypt*. London: Thames & Hudson.

Rusch, A. (1922) *Die entwicklung der Himmelsgottin Nut zu einen Totengottheit*. Leipzig: Hinrichs.

Saggs, H. W. F. (1962) *The Greatness That Was Babylon*. New York: Hawthorn Books.

Saint Martin, V. d. (1863) *Le Nord de l'Afrique dans l'antiquité grecque et romaine*. Paris.

Sakellarakis, E. and Sakellarakis, J. A. (1984) 'The Keftiu and the Minoan thalassocracy', in R. Hägg and N. Marinatos, eds., *The Minoan Thalassocracy: Myth and Reality: Proceedings of the 3rd International Symposium at the Swedish Institute in Athens 31 May–5 June 1982, Skrifter utgivna av Svenska Institutet i Athen*, 4, pp. 198–223.

Sakellarakis, J. A. (1981) *Herakleion Museum: Illustrated Guide to the Museum*. Athens: Ekdotike Athenon.

Sakellerakis, J. A. and Sapouna-Sakellaraki, E. (1981) 'Drama of Death in a Minoan temple', *National Geographic*, February, pp. 205–23.

Sakellariou, M. (1977) *Peuples Préhélleniques d'Origine Indo-européenne*. Athens: Ekdotike Athenon.

—— (1981) *Les Proto-Grecs*. Athens: Ekdotike Athenon.

—— (1986) 'Who were the immigrants?', in G. Cadogan, ed., *The End of the Early Bronze Age in the Aegean*. Leiden: Brill, pp. 125–37.

Saldit-Trappmann, R. (1970) *Tempel der ägyptischen Götter in Griechenland und an der Westküste Kleinasiens*. Leiden: Brill.

Salmon, M. H. (1982) *Philosophy and Archaeology*. New York and London: Academic Press.

Sandars, N. K. (1961) 'The first Aegean swords and their ancestry', *American Journal of Archaeology* 65: 17–28.

—— (1978) *The Sea Peoples: Warriors of the Ancient Mediterranean 1250–1150 BC*, London: Thames & Hudson.

Santillana, G. de (1963) 'On forgotten sources in the history of science', in A. C. Crombie, ed., *Scientific Change: Historical Studies in the Intellectual, So-*

cial and Technical Conditions for Scientific Discovery and Technical Invention, from Antiquity to the Present. New York: Basic Books, pp. 813–28.

Santillana, G. de and von Dechend, H. (1969) *Hamlet's Mill: an Essay in Myth and the Frame of Time.* Boston: Gambit.

Sasson, J. M. (1966a) 'Canaanite maritime involvement in the second millennium B.C.', *Journal of the American Oriental Society* 86: 126–38.

—— (1966b) 'A sketch of North Syrian economic relations in the Middle Bronze Age', *Journal of the Economic and Social History of the Orient.* 9: 161–81.

—— (1971) 'Mari notes', *Revue d'Assyriologie et d'Archéologie Orientale* 65: 172.

—— (1980) 'The 'Tower of Babel' as a clue to the redactional structuring of primeval history', in G. Rendsburg *et al.*, ed., *The Bible World: Essays in Honor of Cyrus H. Gordon.* New York: KTAV Publishing, pp. 211–20.

Sauneron, S. (1960) 'Le nouveau sphinx composite du Brooklyn Museum et le rôle du dieu Tou-tou-Tithoès', *Journal of Near Eastern Studies* 19: 269–87.

—— (1968) *Esna III, Textes*, in series *Esna* (1959–). Publications de l'Institut française à Caire.

Säve-Söderbergh, T. (1946) 'The Egyptian navy of the Eighteenth Egyptian Dynasty', *Uppsala Universitets Årsskrift* 6.

—— (1951) 'The Hyksos in Egypt', *Journal of Egyptian Archaeology* 37: 53–71.

Sayce, A. H. (1885) 'The season and the extent of the travels of Herodotos in Egypt', *Journal of Philology* 14: 258–86.

Sayeed, e. R. (1982) *La Déese Neïth de Saïs*, vol. I, *Importance et rayonnement de son culte*, vol. II, *Documentation.* Cairo: Bibliothèque d'Étude, vol. 86.1.

Scaliger, J. J. (1565) *Coniectanea in M. Terentium Varronem de lingua Latina.* Paris: Stephanus.

Schachermeyr, F. (1962a) 'Forschungsbericht über die Ausgrabungen und Neufunde zur ägäischen Frühzeit 1957–1960', *Jahrbuch des deutschen archäologischen Instituts* 77: 104–382.

—— (1962b) 'Luwier auf Kreta?', *Kadmos* 1: 27–39.

—— (1967) *Ägais und Orient: Die überseeischen Kulturbeziehungen von Kreta und Mykenai mit Ägypten, der Levante und Kleinasien unter besonderer Berücksichtigung des 2. Jahrtausend v. Chr.* Vienna: Abhandlungen der östereichichischen Akademie der Wissenschaften in Wien.

—— (1984) *Griechische Fruhgeschichte: ein Versuch frühe Geschichte wenigstens in Umrissen Verständlich zu machen.* Vienna: Österreichische Akademie.

Schachter, A. (1981) 'Cults of Boiotia, 1. Acheloos to Hera', *Bulletin of the Institute of Classical Studies Supplement.* 38.1.

—— (1986) 'Cults of Boiotia, 2. Herakles to Poseidon', *Bulletin of the Institute of Classical Studies Supplement* 38.2.

Schaeffer, C. F. A. (1933) 'Les fouilles de Minet el Beida et de Ras Shamra: quatrième campagne (printemps 1932); rapport sommaire', *Syria* 14: 93–127.

—— (1948) *Stratigraphie Comparée et Chronologie de l'Asie Occidentale.* Oxford: Oxford University Press.

—— (1971–) *Mission archéologique d'Alasia Dirigée par Claude F. A. Schaeffer*, vol. I. Paris: Mission archéologique d'Alasia.

Schenkel, W. (1984) *Die Bewasserungsrevolution im alten Ägypten*. Mainz: Philipp von Zabern; deutsches archäologisches Institut, Abteilung Kairo.

Schiering, W. (1984) 'The connections between the oldest settlement at Miletus and Crete', in R. Hägg and N. Marinatos, ed., *The Minoan Thalassocracy: Myth and Reality: Proceedings of the 3rd International Symposium at the Swedish Institute in Athens 31 May–5 June 1982, Skrifter utgivna av Svenska Institutet i Athen*, 4, pp. 186–9.

Schiffrin, H. Z. (1968) *Sun Yat-sen and the Origins of the Chinese Revolution*. Berkeley and Los Angeles: University of California Press.

Schliemann, H. (1878) *Mycenae: A Narrative of Research and Discoveries at Mycenae and Tiryns*. London: John Murray.

Schwabe, C. W., Adams, J. and Hodge, C. T. (1982) 'Egyptian beliefs about the bull's spine: an anatomical origin for the ankh', *Anthropological Linguistics* (Winter): 445–79.

Schwartz, B. I. (1975) 'The age of transcendence', in 'Wisdom, Revelation and Doubt', *Daedalus* special issue: 3–4.

—— (1985) *The World of Thought in Ancient China*. Cambridge, Mass.: Harvard University Press.

Schwartz, J. (1950) 'Le cycle de Petoubastis et les comentaires égyptiens de l'Exode', *Bulletin de l'Institut Français d'Archéologie Orientale* [Cairo] 49: 75–83.

Scoufopoulos, N. C. (1971) *Mycenaean Citadels. Studies in Mediterranean Archaeology* 22. Göteborg: Paul Åströms Förlag.

Scullard, H. H. (1967) *The Etruscan Cities and Rome*. Ithaca, NY: Cornell University Press.

Seaton, R. C. (trans.) (1912) *The Argonautica of Apollonios of Rhodes*. Cambridge, Mass.: Harvard University Press; London: Heinemann (Loeb).

Seeden, H. (1980) *The Standing Armed Figurines of the Levant*. Munich: Beck.

Segert, S. (1983) 'The last sign of the Ugaritic alphabet', *Ugarit-Forschungen* 15: 201–18.

Sergent, B. (1977) 'La liste de Kom el-Hetan et le Péloponnèse', *Minos* 16: 126–73.

Sethe, K. (1900) 'Sesostris', in *Untersuchungen zur alten Geschichte*, vol. II. Leipzig: Hinrichs, pp. 3–24.

—— (1904) 'Der Name Sesostris', *Zeitschrift für ägyptische Sprache und Altertumskunde* 41: 43–57.

—— (1905) 'Zur Königsfolge der 11th Dynastie', *Zeitschrift für ägyptische Sprache und Altertumskunde* 42: 131–4.

—— (1906–9) *Urkunden der 18 Dynastie, historisch-biographische Urkunden*, 4 vols. Leipzig: Hinrichs.

—— (1908) 'Verkehr mit Byblos und dem Libanon Gebiet', *Zeitschrift für ägyptische Sprache und Altertumskunde* 45: 7–36.

—— (1910a) 'Osiris und die Zeder von Byblos', *Zeitschrift für ägyptische Sprache und Altertumskunde* 47: 71–8.

—— (1910b) 'Neue Spuren der Hyksos im Inschriften der 18 Dynastie', *Zeitschrift für ägyptische Sprache und Altertumskunde* 48: 73–86.

—— (1917–18) 'Der Name der Phönizier bei Griechen und Ägyptern', in *Orientalische Studien, Fritz Hommel zum sechsigsten Geburtstag. am 31 Juli 1914: gewidmet von Freunden, Kollegen und Schülern*, 2 vols. Leipzig: Hinrichs, vol. I, pp. 305–32.

—— (1923) 'Die Vokalisation des Ägyptischen', *Zeitschrift der deutschen morgenländischen Gesellschaft* 77: 145–207.

—— (1925a) *Die Vokalisation des Ägyptischen.* Leipzig: Verlag der Deutschen Morgenlandische Gesellschaft, Brockhaus.

—— (1925b) 'Das Verhältnis zwischen Demotisch und Koptisch und seine Lehren für die Geschichte der ägyptischen Sprache', *Zeitschrift der deutschen morgenländischen Gesellschaft* 79: 290–316.

—— (1929) *Amun und die acht Urgötter von Hermopolis.* Berlin: de Gruyter.

—— (1937) *Übersetzung und Komentar zu den altägyptischen Pyramidtexten.* 6 vols. Glückstadt, Hamburg and New York: Augustin.

Settegast, M. (1987) *Plato Prehistorian: 10,000 to 5,000 BC in Myth and Archaeology.* Cambridge, Mass.: Rotenberg Press.

Seyrig, H. (1944–5) 'Héraklés-Nergal', *Syria* 24: 62–80.

Shaanxi Zhouyuan Kaogu Dui (1979) 'Shaanxi Qishan Fengchu Cun XiZhou Jianzhu jichi fagu jianbao', *Kaogu* 10: 27–37.

Shack, W. A. and Habte, M. M. (1974) *Gods and Heroes: Oral Tradition of the Gurage of Ethiopia.* Oxford: Oxford University Press.

Shanks, H. (1981) 'The Exodus and the crossing of the Red Sea, according to Hans Goedicke', *Biblical Archaeology Review* 7. 5: 42–50.

Shaughnessy, E. L. (1985–7) 'The "current" Bamboo Annals and the date of the Zhou conquest of Shang', *Early China* 11/12: 33–60.

Shaw, I. M. (1985) 'Egyptian chronology and the Irish oak calibration', *Journal of Near Eastern Studies* 44: 295–317.

Shaw, J. W. (1978) 'Evidence for the Minoan tripartite shrine', *American Journal of Archaeology* 82: 429–48.

—— (1980) 'Excavations at Kommos (Crete) during 1978', *Hesperia* 49: 207–50.

—— (1981) 'Excavations at Kommos (Crete) during 1980', *Hesperia* 50: 211–51.

—— (1987) 'The Early Helladic II corridor house: development and form', *American Journal of Archaeology* 91: 59–79.

Sheppard, J. T. (1911) 'The first scene of *The Suppliants* of Aeschylus, *Classical Quarterly* 5: 220–9.

Sherratt, E. S. (1982) 'Patterns of contact: manufacture and distribution of Mycenaean pottery, 1400–1100 BC', in J. G. P. Best and N. M. W. de Vries, éd., *Interaction and Acculturation in the Mediterranean: Proceedings of the Second Congress of Mediterranean Pre- and Protohistory, Amsterdam, 19–23 November 1980*, vol. II. Amsterdam: Grüner, pp. 179–96.

Sherratt, E. S. and Crouwel, J. H. (1987) 'Mycenaean pottery from Cilicia in Oxford', *Oxford Journal of Archaeology* 6: 341.

Shima, K. (1958) *Inkyo bokuji kenkyū*. Tokyo: Kyūko Shōin.

Shrimpton, G. (1987) 'Regional drought and the decline of Mycenae', *Échos du monde classique/Classical Views 31*. N.S. 6: 137–77.

Siegert, H. (1941–2) 'Zur Geschichte der Begriffe "Arische" und "arisch"', *Wörter und Sachen* 4: 73–99.

Silberman, N. A. (1989) *Between Past and Present: Archaeology, Ideology, and Nationalism in the Modern Middle East*. New York: Henry Holt.

Sima Qian (1959) *Shiji*, 10 vols. Peking: Zhonghua Shuju.

Simpson, W. K. (1953) 'New light on the god Reshef', *Journal of the American Oriental Society* 73: 86–9.

—— (1960) 'Reshep in Egypt', *Orientalia* 29: 63–74.

—— (1984a) 'Sesostris I, II, III and IV', in W. Helck and E. Otto, *Lexikon der Ägyptologie*, vol. V, cols 890–907.

—— (1984b) 'Sinuhe', in W. Helck and E. Otto, *Lexikon der Ägyptologie*, vol. V, cols 950–6.

Singer, I. (1983a) 'Western Anatolia in the 13th century B.C. according to the Hittite sources', *Anatolian Studies* 23: 205–17.

—— (1983b) 'Takuhlinu and Haya: two governors in the Ugarit letter from Tel Aphek', *Tel Aviv* 10: 3–25.

Smelik, K. A. D. and Hemelrijk, E. A. (1984) '"Who knows not what monsters demented Egypt worships?" Opinions on Egyptian animal worship in Antiquity as part of the ancient conception of Egypt', in H. Temporini & W. Haase, eds., *Aufstieg und Niedergang der römischen Welt: Geschichte und Kultur Roms im Spiegel der neueren Forschung* 17.4, *Religion (Heidentum: römische Götterkulte, orientalische Kulte in der römischen Welt [Forts.])*, ed. W. Haase, pp. 1852–2000.

Smith, E. B. (1968) *Egyptian Architecture as Cultural Expression*. Watkins Glen, NY: Century House.

Snodgrass, A. (1971) *The Dark Age of Greece: An Archaeological Survey of the Eleventh to the Eighth Centuries BC*. Edinburgh: Edinburgh University Press.

Snowden, F. M. S. (1970) *Blacks in Antiquity: Ethiopians in the Greco-Roman Experience*. Cambridge, Mass.: Harvard University Press.

—— (1983) *Before Color Prejudice: The Ancient View of the Blacks*. Cambridge, Mass.: Harvard University Press.

Soden, v. W. (1937) *Der Aufstieg des Assyrerreichs als geschichtliches Problem. Der Alte Orient* 37. Leipzig: Hinrichs.

Sourvinou-Inwood, C. (1973) 'The problem of the Dorians in tradition and archaeology', paper presented to the Third International Colloquium on Aegean Prehistory, Sheffield, August.

Speiser, E. A. (1930) *Mesopotamian Origins The Basic Population of the Near East*. Philadelphia: University of Pennsylvania Press.

—— (1933) 'Ethnic movements in the Near East in the second millennium BC: Hurrians and their connections with the Habiru and the Hyksos', *Annual of the American Schools of Oriental Research* 13: 13–54.

—— (1967) *Oriental and Biblical Studies: Collected Writings of E. A. Speiser*, ed.

J. J. Finkelstein and M. Greenberg. Philadelphia: University of Pennsylvania Press.

Spiegelberg, W. (1927) *The Credibility of Herodotus' Account of Egypt in the Light of the Egyptian Monuments*. Oxford: Blackwell.

Springborg, P. (1990) *Royal Persons: Patriarchal Monarchy and the Feminine Principle*. London: Unwin Hyman.

Spyropoulos, T. (1972a) 'Aigyptiakos Epoikismos en Boiotiai', *Archaiologika Analekta ex Athēnōn* 5: 16–27.

—— (1972b) 'Archaiotetes kai Mnemeia Boiotias-Phthiotas', *Archaiologikon Deltion* 27.2: 307–26.

—— (1973a) 'Eisagoge eis ten Meleten tou Kopaïkou Chorou', *Archaiologika Analekta ex Athenon* 6: 201–14.

—— (1973b) 'Archaiotetes kai Mnemeia Boiotias-Phthiotas', *Archaiologikon Deltion* 28.2: 247–73.

—— (1981) *Ampheion Ereuna kai meletai tou mnemeiou tou Ampheiou Thebon*. Sparta.

Stanley, D. J. and Sheng, H. (1986) 'Volcanic shards from Santorini (Upper Minoan ash) in the Nile Delta, Egypt', *Nature* 320. 24/4: 733–5.

Stech, T. (1985) 'Copper and society in Late Bronze Age Cyprus', in A. B. Knapp and T. Stech, eds., *Prehistoric Production and Exchange: The Aegean and East Mediterranean*. Los Angeles: University of California, Institute of Archaeology, Monograph 25, pp. 100–6.

Steinberg, R. (1981) *Modern Shadows on Ancient Greece: Aegean-Levantine Connections in the Late Bronze Age*. MA thesis, Cornell University.

Steiner, R. C. (1977) *The Case for Fricative-Laterals in Proto-Semitic*. New Haven, Conn.: American Oriental Society, vol. 59.

Steinhauser, W. (1937) *Glotta* 25: 229–38.

Steinkeller, P. (1986) 'Some observations on the Abu Salabikh–Ebla list of capital names (L. G. M.)', *Vicino Oriente* 6: 31–40.

Stella, L. A. (1951–2) 'Chi furono i Populi del Mare', *Rivista di antropologia* 39: 3–17.

Steuerwald, H. (1983) *Der Untergang von Atlantis—das Ende einer Legende*. Berlin: Kulturbuch Verlag.

Stevenson Smith, W. (1958) *The Art and Architecture of Ancient Egypt*. Harmondsworth and Baltimore: Penguin.

—— (1965) *Interconnections in the Ancient Near East: A Study of the Relationships between the Arts of Egypt, the Aegean and Western Asia*. New Haven and London: Yale University Press.

—— (1971) 'The Old Kingdom in Egypt and the beginning of the First Intermediate Period', in *Cambridge Ancient History*, 3rd edn., vol. I, pt 2A, pp. 145–208.

Stieglitz, R. R. (1976) 'The Eteocretan inscription from Psychro', *Kadmos* 15: 84–6.

—— (1978) 'Minoan mathematics or music', *Bulletin of the American Society of Papyrologists* 15: 127–32.

—— (1981a) 'The Letters of Kadmos: mythology, archaeology and Eteo-cretan', *Anatypo apo ton 1, 2 tomo ton pepragmenon tou 4 Diethnous Kretologikou Synedriou, Herakleion, 29 August–3 September 1976*, Athens.

—— (1981b) 'Labyrinth: Anatolian axe or Egyptian edifice', in L. Casson and M. Price, ed., *Coins, Culture and History in the Ancient World*. Detroit: Wayne State University Press, pp. 195–8.

—— (1982) 'Numerical structuralism and cosmogony in the ancient Near East,' *Journal of Social and Biological Structures* 5: 255–66.

Stock, H. (1949) *Die erste Zwischenzeit Ägyptens: Untergang der Pyramidenzeit Zwischen reiche von Abydos und Herakleopolis, Aufstieg Thebens*, Studia Aegyptiaca II. Rome: Pontificium Institutum Biblicum.

—— (1955) *Studien zur Geschichte und Archäologie der 13. bis 17. Dynastie Ägyptens: Unter besonderer Berücksichtigung der Skarabäen dieser Zwischenzeit. Ägyptologische Forschungen* 12. Glückstadt, Hamburg and New York: Augustin.

Stos-Gale, Z. A. (1984) 'Comment on Poursat "Une thalassocratie minoenne à Minoen Moyen II"', in R. Hägg and N. Marinatos, eds., *The Minoan Thalassocracy: Myth and Reality: Proceedings of the 3rd International Symposium at the Swedish Institute in Athens 31 May–5 June 1982, Skrifter utgivna av Svenska Institutet i Athen*, 4, p. 87.

Stos-Gale, Z. A. and Gale, N. H. (1982) 'The sources of Mycenaean silver and lead', *Journal of Field Archaeology* 9: 467–85.

—— (1984a) 'The Minoan thalassocracy and the Aegean metal trade', in R. Hägg and N. Marinatos, eds., *The Minoan Thalassocracy: Myth and Reality: Proceedings of the 3rd International Symposium at the Swedish Institute in Athens 31 May–5 June 1982. Skrifter utgivna av Svenska Institutet i Athen*, 4, pp. 59–63.

—— (1984b) 'The results of the examination of lead objects from Lithares', in Ch. Tzabella-Evjen, *Lithares*. Athens: Tameio Archaiologikon kai apallotrioseon, p. 217.

Strange, J. L. (1973) 'Biblical material on the origin of the Philistines', paper presented to the Third International Colloquium on Aegean Prehistory, Sheffield, August.

—— (1980) *Caphtor Keftiu: A New Investigation*. Leiden: Brill.

Stricker, B. H. (1949) 'The Corpus Hermeticum', *Mnemosyne* 4.2: 79–80.

Strøm, I. 'Aspects of Minoan foreign relations, LMI-LMII', in R. Hägg and N. Marinatos, eds., *The Minoan Thalassocracy: Myth and Reality: Proceedings of the 3rd International Symposium at the Swedish Institute in Athens 31 May–5 June 1982, Skrifter utgivna av Svenska Institutet i Athen*, 4, pp. 191–5.

Strommenger, E. (1964) *5,000 Years of Mesopotamian Art*, C. Haglund, trans. New York: Abrams.

Stubbings, F. H. (1959) *Mycenaean Pottery in the Levant*. Cambridge: Cambridge University Press.

—— (1973) 'The rise of Mycenaean civilization', in *Cambridge Ancient History*, 3rd edn., vol. II, pt. 1, pp. 627–58.

—— (1975) 'The expansion of Mycenaean civilization', in *Cambridge Ancient History*, 3rd edn., vol. II, pt. 2, pp. 165–87.

Stucchi, S. (1967) 'Il Giardino della Esperidi e le tappe della conoscenza greca della costa cirenaica', *Quaderni di archeologia della Libia 8* (Cirene e la Grecia): 19–73.

Suppe, F. (1977) *The Structure of Scientific Theories*, 2nd edn. Urbana, Chicago and London: University of Illinois Press.

Suret-Canale, J. (1974) *Sur le 'Mode de Production Asiatique'*, Paris: Centre des études et de récherches marxistes.

Symeonoglou, S. (1973) 'Kadmeia I: Mycenaean finds from Thebes, Greece', in *Studies in Mediterranean Archaeology* 35. Göteborg: Paul Åströms Förlag.

—— (1985) *The Topography of Thebes: From the Bronze Age to Modern Times.* Princeton: Princeton University Press.

Syncellus, Georgius (1719) *Chronographia.* Venice.

Szemerényi, O. (1960) *Studies in the Indo-European System of Numerals.* Heidelberg: Winter.

—— (1964) 'Structuralism and substratum: Indo-Europeans and Aryans in the Ancient Near East', *Lingua* 13: 1–29.

—— (1966a) 'Etyma Graeca I', *Sprache* 11: 1–24.

—— (1966b) 'The labiovelars in Mycenaean and historical Greek', *Studi miceni ed egeo-anatolici* 2: 29–52.

—— (1967) 'Iranica II'. *Sprache* 12: 190–226.

—— (1968a) 'The Development of *s* > *h* in Indo-European languages', *Sprache* 14: 161–3.

—— (1968b) 'Mycenaean: a milestone between Indo-European and historical Greek', *Atti e memorie del 1. Congresso Internazionale di Micenologia* 1: 715–25.

—— (1968c) 'Review of E. Masson, *Les plus anciens emprunts sémitiques en grec*', Indogermanische Forschungen 73: 192–7.

—— (1969) 'Etyma Graeca II', *Studia classica et orientalia, Antonio Pagliaro oblata*, III: 233–50.

—— (1970) 'Iranica III', in M. Boyce and I. Gershevitch, eds., *W. B. Henning memorial volume.* London: Asia Major Library, pp. 417–26.

—— (1971) 'Iranica IV', *Orbis* 19: 500–19.

—— (1971–81) 'Review of P. Chantraine, *Dictionnaire étymologique de la langue grecque*, Paris 1968–1980', *Gnomon* 43: 641–75; 49: 1–10; 53: 113–16.

—— (1972a) 'Etyma Graeca III', in *Mélanges de linguistique et de philologie grecques offerts à Pierre Chantraine*, Paris: Klincksieck, pp. 243–53.

—— (1972b) 'Review of G. Nagy, *Greek Dialects and the Transformation of an Indo-European Process*', Cambridge, Mass., 1970', *Kratylos* 14: 157–65.

—— (1974a) 'The origins of the Greek lexicon: ex oriente lux', *Journal of Hellenic Studies* 94: 144–57.

—— (1974b) 'Review J.-L. Perpillou, *Les substantifs grecs en -εύς*, Paris, 1972', *Kratylos* 18: 43–53.

—— (1975) 'Iranica V', *Monumentum H. S. Nyberg II. Acta Iranica* 5: 313–94.

—— (1978) 'Studies in the kinship terminology of Indo-European languages', *Acta Iranica* 16: 1–240.

—— (1979) 'Etyma Graeca IV', *Studi miceni ed egeo-anatolici* 20: 207–26.

—— (1980a) 'Semitic influence on the Iranian lexicon I', in Gary Rendsburg et al., eds., *The Bible World: Essays in Honor of Cyrus H. Gordon*. New York: KTAV Publishing, pp. 221–37.

—— (1986) 'Etyma Graeca V: Vocabula maritima tria', in *Festschrift Ernst Risch*. Berlin and New York: de Gruyter, pp. 425–50.

—— (1987) *Scripta Minora: Selected Essays in Indo-European, Greek and Latin*, ed. P. Considine and J. T. Hooker, 3 vols. Innsbruck: Innsbrucker Beiträger zur Sprachwissenschaft.

Sznycer, M. (1979) 'L'inscription phénicienne de Tekké près de Cnossos', *Kadmos* 18: 89–93.

Taylour, W. D. (1958) *Mycenaean Pottery in Italy*. Cambridge: Cambridge University Press.

—— (1964) *The Mycenaeans*. London: Thames & Hudson.

te Velde, H. (1970) 'The god Heka in Egyptian theology', *Jaarbericht van het Voorasiatisch-Egyptisch Genootshap. Ex Oriente Lux* 21: 175–86.

—— (1982) 'Mut', in W. Helck and E. Otto, *Lexikon der Ägyptologie*, vol. IV, cols. 246–8.

—— (1984) 'Schu', in W. Helck and E. Otto, *Lexikon der Ägyptologie*, vol. V, cols. 735–7.

Thapar, R. (1975) *The Past and Prejudice*. New Delhi: National Book Trust.

—— (1977) 'Ideology and the interpretation of early Indian history', in *Society and Change: Essays in Honour of Sachin Chaudhuri*. New Delhi, pp. 1–19.

Thieme, P. (1938) *Der Fremdling im Rgveda, eine Studie über die Bedeutung der Worte 'ari', 'arya', 'aryaman' und 'ārya'*. Leipzig: Brockhaus.

Thirlwall, C. (1835–44) *A History of Greece*, 8 vols. London: Longman.

Thissen, H.-J. (1980) 'Manetho', in W. Helck and E. Otto, *Lexikon der Ägyptologie*, vol. III, cols. 1179–81.

Thompson, L. A. (1989) *Romans and Blacks*. London: Routledge; Norman: University of Oklahoma Press.

Thomson, G. (1941) *Aeschylus and Athens – A Study in the Social Origin of Drama*. London: Lawrence and Wishart.

—— (1949) *Studies in Ancient Greek Society 1: The Prehistoric Aegean*. London: Lawrence and Wishart.

Thorpe-Scholes, K. (1978) 'Akrotiri: genesis, life and death', in C. Doumas, ed., *Thera and the Aegean World*, pp. 435–47.

Thucydides. (1954) *The Peloponnesian War*, R. Warner, trans. London: Penguin.

—— (1980) *Histories*. C. F. Smith, trans. 4 vols. Cambridge, Mass.: Harvard University Press (Loeb).

Traill, W. M. (1986) 'Schliemann's acquisition of the Helios Metope and his psychopathic tendencies', in Calder and Traill, *Myth, Scandal and History: The Heinrich Schliemann Controversy and the First Edition of the Mycenaean Diary*. Detroit: Wayne State University Press, pp. 48–67.

Treuil, R. (1983) *Le Néolithique et le Bronze Ancien Égéens les Problemes Stratigraphiques et Chronologiques*. Athens: École française d'Athènes.

Trigger, B. G. (1980) *Gordon Childe: Revolutions in Archaeology*. London: Thames & Hudson.

—— (1989) *A History of Archaeological Thought*. Cambridge: Cambridge University Press.

Trump, D. H. (1981) *The Prehistory of the Mediterranean*. Harmondsworth: Penguin.

Tsountas, C. and Manatt, J. (1897) *The Mycenaean Age*. Boston.

Tusa, V. (1973) 'La statuetta fenicia del Museo Nazionale di Palermo', *Studi Fenici* 1: 173–9.

Tylecoat, R. F. (1976) *A History of Metallurgy*. London: Metals Society.

Tynes, S. (1973) 'Many Africans came to the Soviet Union during Turkish rule', *The Afro-American* 16 (February).

Tzavella-Evjen, Ch. (1984) Λιθαρές. Athens: Tameio Archaiologikōn kai Apallotriōseōn.

—— (1989) '*Litharés* revisited', *Boeotia Antiqua* 1: 5–12.

Ullman, B. J. (1927) 'The origin and development of the alphabet', *American Journal of Archaeology* 31: 311–28.

Usener, H. (1907) 'Philologie und Geschichtswissenschaft', in *Vorträge und Aufsätze*, 2 vols. Leipzig, vol. II, p. 11.

Uy Ban Khoa Học Xã Hôi Việt Nam (1971) *Lịch Sử Việt Nam I*. Hanoi: Nhà Xuât Ban Khoa Học Xã Hôi.

Van Berchem, D. (1967) 'Sanctuaires d'Hercule – Melqart: Contribution à l'étude de l'expansion Phénicienne en Méditeranée', *Syria* 44: 73–109; 307–38.

Van den Brink, E. C. M. (1982) *Tombs and Burial Customs at Tell el-Dab'a*. Vienna: Beiträge zur Ägyptologie 4. Berichte des Österreichischen Archäologischen Institutes in Kairo.

Vandier, J. (1972) 'Le temple de Tôd', *Textes et langages de l'Égypte Pharaonique: Cent cinquante années de recherches 1822–1972: Hommage à Jean-François Champollion*. Cairo: Institut français d'archaeologie orientale.

Van Royen, R. A. and Isaac, B. H. (1979) *The Arrival of the Greeks: The Evidence from the Settlements*. Amsterdam: Grüner.

Van Seters, J. (1966) *The Hyksos: A New Investigation*. New Haven, Conn.: Yale University Press.

—— (1983) *In Search of History: Historiography in the Ancient World and the Origins of Biblical History*. New Haven, Conn., and London: Yale University Press.

Varoufakis, G. (1982) 'The origin of Mycenaean and Geometric iron on the Greek mainland and the Aegean islands', in J. D. Muhly, R. Maddin and V. Karageorghis, eds., *Early Metallurgy in Cyprus. Acta of the International Archaeological Symposium: Early Metallurgy in Cyprus 4000–500 BC, Larnaca, Cyprus, 1–6 June 1981*. Nicosia: Peirides Foundation, pp. 315–22.

Vaux, R. d. (1967) 'Les Hurrites de l'histoire et les Horites de la Bible', *Revue Biblique* 74: 481–503.

—— (1971) 'Palestine in the Early Bronze Age', in *Cambridge Ancient History*, 3rd edn., vol. I, pt. 2, pp. 208–37.

Vellacott, P., trans. (1972) *Euripides: Orestes and Other Plays*. London: Penguin.

Ventris, M. and Chadwick, J. (1973) *Documents in Mycenaean Greek*, 2nd edn. Cambridge: Cambridge University Press.

Vercoutter, J. (1953) *L'Égypte et le monde égéen préhéllenique*. Paris: Maisonneuve.

—— (1954) 'Essai sur les relations entre Égyptiens et PréHellénes', *L'Orient Ancien Illustré* 6: 37–51.

—— (1956) *L'Égypte et le monde égéen préhellénique: Étude critique des sources égyptiennes (du début de la XVIIIe à la fin de la XIXe Dynastie)*. Cairo: l'Institut français d'archéologie orientale.

—— (1975) 'Apis', in W. Helck and E. Otto, *Lexikon der Ägyptologie*, vol. I, cols. 338–50.

Vergote, J. (1959) 'Ou en est la vocalisation de l'Égyptien?', *Bulletin de l'Institut Français d'Archéologie Orientale* 58: 1–19.

—— (1962) 'Le roi Moiris-Mares', *Zeitschrift für ägyptische Sprache und Altertumskunde* 87: 66–76.

Vermeule, E. (1960) 'The fall of the Mycenaean Empire', *Archaeology* 13.1: 66–75.

—— (1964) *Greece in the Bronze Age*. Chicago: University of Chicago Press.

—— (1975) *The Art of the Shaft Graves of Mycenae: Lecture in Memory of Louise Taft Semple*. Cincinnati: University of Cincinnati Press.

—— (1979) *Aspects of Death in Early Greek Art and Poetry*. Berkeley and Los Angeles: University of California Press.

—— (1986) ' "Priam's castle blazing": a thousand years of Trojan memories', in M. J. Mellink, ed., *Troy and the Trojan War: A Symposium Held at Bryn Mawr College, October 1984*, pp. 77–92.

Vermeule, E. and Karageorghis, V. (1982) *Mycenaean Pictorial Vase Painting*. Cambridge, Mass., and London: Harvard University Press.

Vermeule, E. and Vermeule, C. (1970) 'Aegean gold hoard and the court of Egypt', *Curator* 13: 32–42.

Vian, F. (1960) 'Le mythe de Typhée et le problème de ses origines orientales', in *Éléments orientaux dans la religion grecque ancienne*. Paris, pp. 17–37.

—— (1963) *Les origines de Thèbes: Cadmos et les Spartes*. Paris: Études et Commentaires no. 48.

Vichos, Y. and Kyriakopoulou, V. (1989) Αὐτοψια στον υποβρύχιο αρχαιολογικό χώρα τόυ Δοκόυ, *Enalia* 3–4: 12–13. Summarised as 'The Dokos Project', *Enalia* 3–4: 20–1.

Vitaliano, D. B. (1978) 'Atlantis from a geologic point of view', in E. S. Ramage, ed., *Atlantis Fact or Fiction?* Bloomington: Indiana University Press.

Von der Mühll, P. (1952) *Kritisches Hypomnema zur Ilias*. Basel: Reinhardt.

Voss, J. H. (1827–34) *Mythologische Briefe*, 5 vols. Stuttgart: Metzler.

Voss, v. M. H. (1980) 'Horuskinder', in Helck & Otto, *Lexickon der Ägyptologie*, vol. III, cols. 52–3.

Vradii, V. P. (1914) *Negry batumskoy oblasti*. Batumi: G. Tavartkiladze.

Wace, A. J. B. (1924) 'Greece and Mycenae', in *Cambridge Ancient History*, 1st edn., vol. II, pp. 431–72.

—— (1964) *Mycenae: An Archaeological History and Guide*. New York: Biblio & Tannen.

Wace, A. J. P. and Blegan, C. W. (1939) 'Pottery as evidence for trade and colonisation in the Aegean Bronze Age', *Klio* 32: 138–9.

Wace, A. J. P. and Stubbings, F. H. (1962) *A Companion to Homer*. London: Macmillan.

Wachsmann, S. (1987) *Aegeans in the Theban Tombs*. Orientalia Lovaniensa Analecta 20. Leuven: Peeters.

Waddell, W. G. (1940) *Manetho*. Cambridge, Mass.: Harvard University Press (Loeb); London: Heinemann.

Wagler, P. R. (1894) 'Athiopis', *Pauly Wissowa I*, cols. 1103–6.

Wainwright, G. A. (1915) 'Alashia-Alasa; and Asy', *Klio* 14: 1–36.

—— (1931) 'The emblem of Min', *Journal of Egyptian Archaeology* 17: 185–95.

—— (1949) 'Pharaonic survivals, Lake Chad to the west coast', *Journal of Egyptian Archaeology* 35: 167–75.

Walberg, G. (1986) *Tradition and Innovation: Essays in Minoan Art*. Mainz am Rhein: Philipp von Zabern.

Walcot, P. (1966) *Hesiod and the Near East*. Cardiff: University of Wales Press.

Wallace, P. (1973) *Commentary on Strabo's Description of Boiotia*. Ph.D. dissertation, Indiana University.

—— (1979) 'The dikes in the Kopais', in J. M. Fossey and A. Schachter, eds., *The Proceedings of the Second International Conference on Boiotian Antiquities* (held in Montreal), pp. 7–9.

Wang Guowei (1941) 'Jinben Zhushujinian Shuzheng' [A running commentary on the new version of the Bamboo Annals], in *Haining Wangjingshan Xiansheng Yishu* [*The Literary Remains of Wang Guowei*] 48 *quan*. Shanghai: Commercial Press.

Ward, W. A. (1961) 'Egypt and the East Mediterranean in the early second millennium BC', *Orientalia* 30: 22–45, 129–55.

—— (1971) *Egypt and the East Mediterranean World 2200–1900 BC: Studies in Egyptian Foreign Relations During the First Intermediate Period*. Beirut: American University of Beirut.

—— (1978) *The Four Egyptian Homographic Roots B3*. Rome: Studia.

—— (1986) 'Review of Giveon, *Egyptian Scarabs from Western Asia*'. *Bibliotheca Orientalis* 43: 702–5.

—— (1987) 'Scarab typology and archaeological context', *American Journal of Archaeology* 91: 507–32.

Wardle, K. A. (1973) 'Northwest Greece in the Late Bronze Age: the archaeological background', paper presented to the Third International Colloquium on Aegean Prehistory, Sheffield, August.

Warmington, B. H. (1960) *Carthage*. London: Robert Hale.

Warren, P. M. (1965) 'The first Minoan stone vases and Early Minoan chronology', *Kretika Chronika* 19: 1–43.

—— (1967) 'Minoan stone vases as evidence for Minoan foreign connections in the Aegean Late Bronze Age', *Proceedings of the Prehistoric Society* 33: 37–48.

—— (1969) *Minoan Stone Vases*. Cambridge: Cambridge University Press.

—— (1973) 'Crete, 3000–1400 B.C.: immigration and the archaeological evidence', in R. A. Crossland and A. Birchall, eds., *Bronze Age Migrations*. London: Duckworth: 41–7.

—— (1979a) 'The stone vessels from the Bronze Age settlement at Akrotiri, Thera', *Archaiologike Ephemeris* 82–113.

—— (1979b) 'The miniature fresco from Akrotiri', *Journal of Hellenic Studies* 99: 116–29.

—— (1981) 'Minoan Crete and ecstatic religion: preliminary observations on the 1979 excavations at Knossos', in R. Hägg and N. Marinatos, eds., *Sanctuaries and Cults in the Aegean Bronze Age: Proceedings of the First International Symposium at the Swedish Institute in Athens, 12–13 May 1980*. Stockholm: Skrifter utgivna av svenska Institutet i Athen 4, p. 28.

—— (1984) 'Absolute dating of the Bronze Age eruption of Thera (Santorini)', *Nature* 308: 492–3.

—— (1985) 'Review of *Minoan Pottery in Second Millennium Egypt* (B. J. Kemp and R. S. Merrillees)', *Classical Review* 35: 14–51.

—— (1987) 'Absolute dating of the Aegean Late Bronze Age', *Archaeometry* 29: 205–10.

—— (1988) 'The Thera eruption: continuing the discussion on dating, III. Further arguments against an early date', *Archaeometry* 30: 176–8.

Watkins, C. (1986) 'The language of the Trojans', in M. J. Mellink, ed., *Troy and the Trojan War, A Symposium Held at Bryn Mawr College, October 1984*, pp. 45–62.

Watrous, L. V. (1987a) 'The rise of the state in Central Anatolia and Crete in Middle Bronze I: a comparative view', paper given to the annual meeting of the Society for Biblical Literature.

—— (1987b) 'The role of the Near East in the rise of the Cretan palaces', in R. Hägg and N. Marinatos, eds., *The Function of the Minoan Palaces: Proceedings of the Fourth International Symposium at the Swedish Institute in Athens, 10–16 June 1984*, pp. 65–70.

Webster, T. B. L. (1958) *From Mycenae to Homer*. London: Methuen.

Wegner, M. (1933) 'Stilentwickelung der thebanischen Beamtergräber', *Mitteilungen des deutschen Instituts für ägyptische Altertumskunde im Kairo*, pp. 38–164.

Weill, R. (1923) 'L'installation des Israélites en Palestine et la légende patriarcale', *Revue de l'histoire des religions* 87: 69–120; 88: 1–4.

Weinberg, S. S. (1954) 'The relative chronology of the Aegean in the Neolithic period and the Early Bronze Age', in R. W. Ehrich, ed., *Relative Chronologies in Old World Archaeology*. Chicago: University of Chicago Press, pp. 86–107.

—— (1965a) 'The relative chronology of the Aegean in the Neolithic period and the Early Bronze Age', in R. W. Ehrich, ed., *Relative Chronologies in Old World Archaeology*. Chicago: University of Chicago Press, pp. 285–320.

—— (1965b) 'The Stone Age in the Aegean', in *Cambridge Ancient History*, 3rd edn., vol. 1, pp. 557–618.

Weinstein, G. A. and Betancourt, P. P. (1977) 'Problems of interpretation of the Akrotoiri radiocarbon dates', in C. Doumas, ed., *Thera and the Aegean World*. London, pp. 805–14.

Weinstein, G. A. and Michael, H. N. (1978) 'Radiocarbon dates from Akrotiri, Thera', *Archaeometry* 20: 203–9.

Weinstein, J. (1973) *Foundation Deposits in Ancient Egypt*. Ph.D. dissertation, University of Pennsylvania.

—— (1974) 'A statuette of the princesse Sobeknofru at Tell Gezer', *Bulletin of the American Schools of Oriental Research* 213: 49–56.

—— (1980) 'Palestinian radiocarbon dating: a reply to James Mellaart', *Antiquity* 54: 21–4.

—— (1981) 'The Egyptian empire in Palestine, a reassessment', *Bulletin of the American Schools of Oriental Research* 241: 1–23.

—— (1989a) 'The gold scarab of Nefertiti from Ulu Burun: its implications for Egyptian history and Egyptian-Aegean relations', in G. F. Bass, C. Pulak, D. Collon, and J. Weinstein, 'The Bronze Age shipwreck at Ulu Burun: 1986 campaign', *American Journal of Archaeology* 93: 17–29.

—— (1989b) 'Review of *Chronologies du Proche Orient, Chronologies in the Near East, Relative Chronologies and Absolute Chronology 16,000–4000 BP*; ed. Oliver Aurenche, Jacques Evin and Francis Hours, Oxford 1987', *Radiocarbon* 31: 101–3.

Weisburd, S. (1985) 'Excavating words: a geological tool', *Science News* 127.6: 81–96.

Weise, O. (1883) 'Miscellen', *Beiträge zur Kunde der indogermanischen Sprachen*. 7: 167–71.

Wente, E. F. and Van Siclen, C. C. III (1976) 'A chronology of the New Kingdom', in *Studies in Honour of George R. Hughes (Studies in Ancient Oriental Civilization*, No. 39). Chicago: Oriental Institute, pp. 217–61.

West, M. L. (1971) *Early Greek Philosophy and the Orient*. Oxford, Clarendon Press.

—— (1988) *Hesiod: Theogony*. Oxford: Oxford University Press.

West, S. (1977) 'The Sesonchosis romance', *Erotica Antiqua: Acta of the International Conference on the Ancient Novel at the University College of North Wales Bangor, 12–17 July 1976*. University of Wales, pp. 47–8.

White, G. (1986) '1985 Excavations on Bates Island, Marsa Matruh', *Journal of the American Research Center in Egypt* 23: 51–84.

Whitelaw, T. M. (1983) 'The settlement at Fornou Korifi Myrtos and aspects of early Minoan social organisation', in O. Krzyszkowska and L. Nixon, eds., *Minoan Society: Proceedings of the Cambridge Colloquium 1981*. Bristol: Bristol Classical Press, pp. 323–45.

Wiener, M. A. (1984) 'Crete and the Cyclades in LMI: the tale of the conical cups', in R. Hägg and N. Marinatos, eds., *The Minoan Thalassocracy: Myth and Reality: Proceedings of the 3rd International Symposium at the Swedish Institute in Athens 31 May–5 June 1982, Skrifter utgivna av Svenska Institutet i Athen*, 4, pp. 17–26.

Wilamowitz-Moellendorff (1931–32) *Der Glaube der Hellenen.* 2 vols. Berlin: Weidmann.

Wildung, D. (1984) *Sesostris und Amenenmhet: Ägypten im Mittleren Reich.* Freibourg: Office du Livre; Munich: Hirmer Verlag.

Wilkie, N. C. (1987) 'Burial customs at Nichoria: the MME Tholos', in R. Laffineur, ed., *Thanatos: Les coutumes funéraires en Égée à l'âge du bronze: Actes du colloque de Liège (21–23 avril 1986).* Université de l'État à Liège, Histoire de l'art et archaeologie de la Grèce antique, pp. 127–35.

Willetts, R. (1962) *Cretan Cults and Festivals.* London: Routledge & Kegan Paul.

Williams, B. (1980, 1985) 'The lost pharaohs of Nubia', *Archaeology* 5.3: 12–19. Reprint. *Journal of African Civilizations* 4.2 (1985): 38–52.

—— (1986) *The A-group Royal Cemetery at Qustul. Cemetery L.* Chicago: Excavations, between Abu Simbel and the Sudan frontier, 5. Oriental Institute Nubian Expedition 5.

Williams, R. J. (1981) 'The sages of Ancient Egypt in the light of recent scholarship', *Journal of the American Oriental Society* 101.1: 1–19.

Wilson, J. A. (1969) 'Egyptian myths, tales, and mortuary texts', in *Ancient Near Eastern Texts: Relating to the Old Testament,* ed. J. B. Pritchard, 3rd edn. with Supplement. Princeton: Princeton University Press, pp. 3–59.

Winkler, J. J. (1985) *Auctor & Actor: A Narratological Reading of Apuleius's The Golden Ass.* Berkeley and Los Angeles: University of California Press.

Winlock, H. E. (1940) 'Neb-Ḥepet Rēʿ Mentu-Ḥotpe of the Eleventh Dynasty', *Journal of Egyptian Archaeology* 26: 116–19.

—— (1947) *The Rise and Fall of the Middle Kingdom in Thebes.* New York: Macmillan.

Winter, I. J. (1976) 'Phoenician and North Syrian ivory carving in historical context', *Iraq* 38: 1–22.

Wiseman, D. J. (1953) *The Alalakh Tablets.* London: British Institute of Archaeology at Ankara, Occasional Papers 2.

Wolf, W. (1926) *Die Bewaffnung des altägyptischen Heeres.* Leipzig: Teubner.

—— (1929) 'Der Stand der Hyksos Frage', *Zeitschrift der Deutschen Morgenländischen Gesellschaft* 83: 67–79.

Wood, M. (1987) *In Search of the Trojan War,* 2nd edn. London: BBC Publications.

Woodside, A. (1971) *Vietnam and the Chinese Model: A Comparative Study of Nguyên and Ch'ing Civil Government in the First Half of the Nineteenth Century.* Cambridge, Mass.: Harvard University Press.

Woolley, L. (1938) 'Excavations at Al Mina, Sueidia, 1 & 2', *Journal of Hellenic Studies* 58: 1–30; 133–70.

—— (1953) *A Forgotten Kingdom.* London: Penguin.

Wortham, J. D. (1971) *British Egyptology 1549–1906.* Newton Abbot: David & Charles.

Wright, J. C. (1987) 'Death and power at Mycenae', in R. Laffineur, ed., *Thanatos: Les coutumes funéraires en Égée à l'âge du bronze: Actes du colloque de*

Liège (21–23 avril 1986). Université de l'État à Liège, Histoire de l'art et archaeologie de la Grèce antique, pp. 170–84.

Wyatt, W. (1970) 'The Indo-Europeanization of Greece', in G. Cardona, H. M. Hoenigswald and A. Senn, eds., *Indo-European and Indo-Europeans: Papers Presented at the Third Indo-European Conference at the University of Pennsylvania.* Philadelphia: University of Pennsylvania Press, pp. 89–111.

—— (1972) 'Greek dialectology and Greek prehistory', *Acta of the Second Colloquium on Aegean Prehistory: The First Arrival of Indo-European Elements in Greece.* Athens: Ministry of Culture and Science, pp. 18–22.

Xanthoudides, S. (1924) *The Vaulted Tombs of the Mesara: An Account of Some Cemeteries of Southern Crete,* trans. J. P. Droop. Liverpool: Liverpool University Press; London: Hodder & Stoughton.

Yadin, Y. (1963) *The Art of Warfare in Biblical Lands,* 2 vols. M. Pearlman, trans. Jerusalem: International Publishing.

—— (1968) 'And Dan, why did he remain in the ships?' *Australian Journal of Biblical Archaeology* I.1: 9–23.

—— (1973) 'And Dan, why did he remain in the ships?' in J. Best, ed., *The Arrival of the Greeks.* Amsterdam: Hakkert, pp. 55–73.

—— (1982) 'New gleanings of Resheph from Ugarit', in *Biblical and Related Studies Presented to Samuel Iwry.* Winona Lake, Ind.: Eisenbrauns.

Yakar, J. (1985) 'Regional and local schools of metalwork in Early Bronze Age Anatolia, pt. 2', *Anatolian Studies* 35: 25–38.

Yannai, A. (1983) *Studies on Trade Between the Levant and the Aegean in the 14th to the 12th Centuries BC.* D.Phil., Oxford University.

Yokoyama, T. (1978) 'The tsunami caused by the prehistoric eruption of Thera', in C. Doumas, ed., *Thera and the Aegean World,* pp. 277–89.

Yoyotte, J. (1982) 'Le Panthéon égyptien de J.-F. Champollion', *Bulletin de la Société Française d'Égyptologie: Séance solonelle Consacrée à la commémoration du Cent-Cinquantenaire de la Mort de J.-F. Champollion* 95: 76–108.

Zaccagnini, C. (1987) 'Aspects of ceremonial exchange in the Near East in the Late 2nd Millennium BC', in M. Rowlands, M. T. Larsen and K. Kristiansen, ed., *Centre and Periphery in the Ancient World.* Cambridge: Cambridge University Press, pp. 57–65.

Zhao Zhiquan and Liu Zhongfu (1984) 'Excavation of the palace site of the Shang Dynasty at Shixianggou Yanshi in Henan, spring 1984', *Kaogu* 4: 322–35.

Zhongguo Shehuikexueyuan Kaogu Yanjiusuo Shiyuanshi (1983) 'Fanshexing huisu ceding niandai baogao 10 [10th report of radiocarbon dating]' *Kaogu* 190: 646–52.

Ziegler, K. and Sontheimer, W. (1979) *Der Kleine Pauly: Lexikon der Antike: Auf der Grundlage von Pauly's Realencyclopädie der clasischen Altertumswissenschaft,* 5 vols. Munich: Deutscher Taschenbuch.

Zimmer, H. (1879) 'Arisch', *Bezzenbergers Beiträge* 3: 137–51.

Zohary, D. and Hopf, M. (1988) *Domestication of Plants in the Old World.* Oxford: Clarendon Press.

INDEX